Managerial Accounting
Concepts for Planning, Control, Decision Making

Managerial Accounting

Concepts for Planning, Control, Decision Making

Ray H. Garrison, D.B.A., CPA

School of Accountancy
Brigham Young University

Fifth Edition

1988
Business Publications, Inc.
Plano, Texas 75075

Acquisitions editor: John R. Black
Developmental editor: Jennifer Owen Cole
Production editor: Karen Smith
Copy editor: Loretta Scholten
Copyediting coordinator: Jean Roberts
Production manager: Bette Ittersagen
Designer: Keith J. McPherson
Cover and part-opening photographs: David Bentley
Compositor: Arcata Graphics/Kingsport
Typeface: 10½/12 Times Roman
Printer: R. R. Donnelley & Sons Company

The Publishers gratefully acknowledge the cooperation of the Teleflex Communications Department for permitting the use of the crystalline image appearing on the cover. The image was created from a photograph appearing on the cover of the Teleflex Annual Report for 1984, and represents the strategically balanced structure of the company serving diverse markets with related technologies.

ISBN 0-256-05833-4

Library of Congress Catalog Card No. 87–71554

Printed in the United States of America

1 2 3 4 5 6 7 8 9 0 DO 5 4 3 2 1 0 9 8

To
The many colleagues who
have used prior editions of this book

Preface

This text is designed for a one-term course in managerial accounting for use by students who have already completed one or two terms of basic financial accounting. The emphasis of *Managerial Accounting* is on uses of accounting data internally by managers in directing the affairs of business and nonbusiness organizations.

As suggested by the subtitle to the book, managers need information to carry out three essential functions in an organization: (1) to plan operations; (2) to control activities; and (3) to make decisions. The purpose of *Managerial Accounting* is to show *what kinds* of information the manager needs, *where* this information can be obtained, and *how* this information is used in carrying out these three essential functions.

This edition of the book continues the tradition of a "top-down" focus in that it looks at accounting data through the eyes of those who must use the data in the management of an enterprise. Looking at accounting data from this perspective allows several things to be accomplished in the teaching and learning processes. First, it helps students to realize that accounting data are a *means* rather than an *end*. Second, it gives students a "management" orientation, thereby allowing instructors to develop concepts and ideas rather than simply to rely on procedures. And third, it permits instructors to portray the internal accountant in his or her true role—that of a key participant in all functions of management.

Although the emphasis of the book is on uses of accounting data, care has been taken not to sacrifice the student's need for basic technical understanding. To this end, topics are covered in enough depth to ensure full comprehension of basic concepts. The student is then able to proceed with confidence in applying these concepts to a wide variety of organizational problems as contained in homework assignments.

A paramount objective in the writing of *Managerial Accounting* and in its various revisions has been to make a clear and balanced presentation of relevant subject material. This focus on relevance continues in the current edition where greater recognition is given to the need for accounting data by organizations in the service industries. Accordingly, users will find more examples and more homework problems dealing with service industries than have been present in prior editions. Also, in recognition of the widespread application of management accounting concepts, users will find many examples and problems in the current edition that deal with not-for-profit, retail, and wholesale organizations as well as examples and problems that deal with manufacturing organizations. In short, the watchwords for this edition of *Managerial Accounting* have been *relevance* of subject matter, *balance* of topics, and a continued tradition of *clarity* in presentation.

New in This Edition

The revision just completed is more extensive in both breadth and depth than one might expect for a book going into its fifth edition. An extensive revision was needed, however, in response to several factors. These factors include the increased need for accounting information by companies in the service industries, as mentioned above; a major change in the federal tax laws; and a significant pronouncement by the Financial Accounting Standards Board (FASB) on the statement of cash flows. These and other factors have resulted in the following additions and changes in the current edition of *Managerial Accounting:*

1. The book is now divided into four parts rather than three, as shown in the contents. This new division provides for a more logical grouping of chapter material, and the new part headings are more descriptive of the overall structure and thrust of the book.
2. As in the prior edition, special attention has been given to writing new exercise and problem material. The majority of exercises and problems in the current edition are therefore either new or completely rewritten. Users will again find a wide range of problems in terms of level of difficulty.
3. A new feature in the book is the addition of a number of short cases to selected chapters. These short cases tend to be more rigorous and less structured than the problems, but they still focus on key concepts and ideas contained in the chapter material.
4. A new section has been added to Chapter 3 (''Systems Design: Job-Order Costing'') discussing the importance of identifying ''cost drivers'' in the incurrence and in the application of overhead costs. Discussion regarding the decreased importance of direct labor cost in many industries has also been added to this chapter.
5. Another new section has been added to Chapter 3 discussing the use of job-order costing methods in service organizations.
6. The computation of equivalent units in Chapter 4 (''Systems Design: Process Costing'') is now done by the so-called alternative method that has become popular in recent years. This method is preferred by many instructors because it involves only addition and it parallels the flow of units in a process costing system.
7. The change in the way in which the equivalent units figure is computed has made it possible to simplify the production report in Chapter 4.

The report now flows more logically from top to bottom and involves fewer computations.

8. In the portion of Chapter 7 dealing with segmented reporting, the fixed costs of a segment are now identified as *traceable* fixed costs rather than as direct fixed costs. This change in terminology helps to resolve the confusion that sometimes results from multiple uses of the term *direct*.

9. A new section has been added to Chapter 8 (''Profit Planning'') discussing the use of ''just-in-time'' (JIT) inventory systems. This new section is timely as evidenced by the growing interest in the JIT approach.

10. The discussion of flexible budgets in Chapter 10 (''Flexible Budgets and Overhead Analysis'') has been expanded to include a master flexible budget for the entire organization. This new master flexible budget contains data on sales, selling expenses, and administrative expenses as well as data on other costs.

11. A new section has been added to Chapter 11 (''Control of Decentralized Operations'') that discusses the use of net book value and gross cost in valuing plant and equipment in ROI computations. Also, a new section has been added that outlines the major criticisms of the ROI method. In addition, the material on transfer pricing in the chapter has been largely rewritten to improve clarity and flow.

12. Material has been added to Chapter 14 (''Capital Budgeting Decisions'') discussing the use of capital budgeting methods in nonprofit organizations.

13. The first half of Chapter 15 (''Further Aspects of Investment Decisions'') has been rewritten to include the new ACRS depreciation rules and other changes mandated by the *Tax Reform Act of 1986*.

14. The material in Chapter 16 (''Service Department Cost Allocations'') has been totally rewritten to shift the emphasis in the chapter away from companies in the manufacturing sector and toward companies in the service, not-for-profit, and administrative sectors.

15. Chapter 18 (''Statement of Cash Flows'') has also been rewritten to reflect the FASB's new requirements for the statement of cash flows. Material dealing with working capital has been included as an appendix to this chapter.

16. Many questions in the Workbook/Study Guide have been rewritten, and worked-out explanatory answers are now provided for the true/false and multiple choice questions as well as for the exercises.

In addition to the above, scores of small ''polishing'' changes have been made throughout the book in an effort to further improve flow, comprehension, and readability. In no case, however, has change been made simply for the sake of change (other than in the assignment material). Rather, the revision has been completed with a single thought in mind—to make the fifth edition of *Managerial Accounting* the most up-to-date and teachable book available in its field.

Using the Text and Its Supplements

As in the prior editions, flexibility in meeting the needs of courses varying in length, content, and student composition continues to be a prime concern in the organization and content of the book. Sufficient text material is available to permit the instructor to choose topics and depth of coverage as desired. Appendixes, parts of chapters, or even whole chapters can be omitted without adversely affecting the continuity of the course. An instructor's manual is available which gives a number of alternate assignment outlines and suggestions as to the problems to be assigned from various chapters.

The book contains over 780 questions, exercises, problems, and cases for in-class use or for homework assignment. In addition, both a study guide and a comprehensive test bank are available. The test bank contains over 1,000 objective questions and numerous short problems designed specifically for examinations. My appreciation is extended to professors Roland Minch, SUNY at Albany; Ronald B. Pawliczek, Boston College; and Eldred A. Johnson, Brigham Young University, who prepared the bulk of the test bank materials.

A computer package titled *Microcomputer Exercises for the IBM PC*, by James C. Stallman and James E. Parker, both of the University of Missouri, has been prepared to accompany the fifth edition of *Managerial Accounting*. The exercises in the package relate directly to problem material in the text and use the power of the computer (through both computations and graphics) to increase student understanding of key relationships and concepts.

Acknowledgments

Ideas and suggestions have been received from many faculty members who used the prior edition of *Managerial Accounting*. Each has my thanks, since the book is a better product as a result of their insightful comments.

The efforts of many people are needed to develop a book and to improve it from edition to edition. Some of the most important of these are the reviewers who point out areas of concern, cite areas of strength, and make recommendations for change. In this regard, the following professors spent considerable time providing in-depth reviews for the current edition of *Managerial Accounting:* June Y. Aono, University of Hawaii; Gyan Chandra, Miami University; Frank P. Daroca, University of Southern California; Thomas R. Hrubec, Northern Illinois University; Charles Konkol, University of Wisconsin–Milwaukee; Roland A. Minch, State University of New York–Albany; Richard J. Murdock, Ohio State University; Avi Rushinek, University of Miami; and Thomas J. O'Neil, American International College.

We also wish to recognize the following professors who, over the years, have provided reviews for prior editions of *Managerial Accounting*. We make this special recognition because their comments and suggestions, along with those of the current edition reviewers listed above, have aided materially in the development of this book. They are: John M. Alvis, University of Tennessee at Chattanooga; Stephen L. Buzby, Michigan State University; Lee Dexter, North Dakota State University; Jesse F. Dillard, Ohio State University; Clarence E. Fries, University of Arkansas; Stanford C. Gunn, State University of New York–Buffalo; James A. Hallam, Illinois State University; Richard Hodges, Western Michigan University; E. Dee Hubbard, Brigham Young University; Phillip A. Jones, Sr., University of Richmond; Edward H. Julius, California Lutheran University; Robert W. Koehler, Penn State University; Felix P. Kollaritsch, Ohio State University; Leslie R. Loschen, Eastern New Mexico University; Franklin Lowenthal, California State University–Hayward; Linda M. Marquis, Northern Kentucky University; Morton Nelson, Wilfrid Laurier College; Thomas J. O'Neil, American International College; Ray M. Powell, University of Notre Dame; Lloyd Seaton, Jr., University of Arkansas; Donald E. Stone, University of Massachusetts; Murat Neset Tanju, University of Albama–Birmingham; George D. Welch, Drake University; and Jeffrey L. Williams, President, Charter Arms Corporation.

Permission has been received from the Institute of Certified Management Accountants of the National Association of Accountants to use questions and/or unofficial answers from past Certificate in Management Accounting (CMA) examinations. Also, my appreciation is extended to the American Institute of Certified Public Accountants and to the Society of Management Accountants of Canada for permission to use (or to adapt) selected problems from their examinations. These problems bear the notations CMA, CPA, and SMA, respectively.

Ray H. Garrison

Contents in Brief

PART FOUR Selected Topics for Further Study

Contents

CHAPTER 3   Systems Design: Job-Order Costing   68

CHAPTER 4   Systems Design: Process Costing   128

CHAPTER 8 Profit Planning   320

CHAPTER 9 Control through Standard Costs   382

CHAPTER 14 Capital Budgeting Decisions   642

Managerial Accounting
Concepts for Planning, Control, Decision Making

CHAPTER 1

Managerial Accounting— A Perspective

LEARNING OBJECTIVES

After studying Chapter 1, you should be able to:

- Explain what an organization is, and describe the work done by management in organizations.

- Name the steps in the planning and control cycle, and explain how each step impacts on the work of management.

- Prepare an organization chart, and explain its purpose.

- Distinguish between "line" and "staff" responsibilities in an organization.

- Name the three groups into which organizations can be classified, and discuss the ways in which nearly all organizations are similar.

- Describe the three broad purposes for which the manager needs accounting information.

- Identify the major differences and similarities between financial and managerial accounting.

- Define or explain the key terms listed at the end of the chapter.

Managerial accounting is concerned with providing information to *managers*—that is, to those who are *inside* an organization and who are charged with directing and controlling its operations. Managerial accounting can be contrasted with **financial accounting,** which is concerned with providing information to stockholders, creditors, and others who are *outside* an organization.

Because it is manager oriented, any study of managerial accounting must be preceded by some understanding of the management process and of the organizations in which managers work. Accordingly, the purpose of this chapter is to examine briefly the work of the manager and to look at the characteristics, structure, and operation of the organizations in which this work is carried out. The chapter concludes by examining the major differences and similarities between financial and managerial accounting.

ORGANIZATIONS AND THEIR OBJECTIVES

An **organization** can be defined as a group of people united for some common purpose. A bank providing financial services is an organization, as is a university providing educational services and a manufacturing firm providing appliances or other products for consumers. An organization consists of *people,* not physical assets. Thus, a bank building is not an organization; rather, the organization consists of the people who work in the bank and who are bound together for the common purpose of providing financial services to a community.

The common purpose toward which an organization works is called its *objective.* Not all organizations have the same objective. For some organizations the objective is to produce a product and earn a profit. For other organizations the objective may be to render humanitarian service (the Red Cross), to provide aesthetic enrichment (a symphony orchestra), or to provide government services (a water department). To assist in our discussion, we will focus on a single organization, the Bestway Furniture Company, and look closely at this organization's objectives, structure, and management, and at how these factors influence its need for managerial accounting data.

Setting Objectives

The Bestway Furniture Company is a corporation, and its owners have placed their money in the organization with the thought in mind of earning a return, or profit, on their investment. Thus, the first objective of the company is to earn a profit on the funds committed to it. The profit objective is tempered by other objectives, however. The company is anxious to acquire and maintain a reputation of integrity, fairness, and dependability. It also wants to be a positive force in the social and ecological environment in which it carries out its activities.

The owners of the Bestway Furniture Company prefer not to be involved in the day-to-day operation of the company. Instead, they have outlined the broad objectives of the organization and have selected a president to oversee the implementation of these objectives. Although the president is charged with the central objective of earning a profit on the owners' invest- ment, he[1] must do so with a sensitivity for the other objectives that the organization desires to achieve.

Strategic Planning

The implementation of an organization's long-term objectives is known as *strategic planning*. In any organization, **strategic planning** occurs in two phases:

1. Deciding on the products to produce and/or the services to render.
2. Deciding on the marketing and/or manufacturing strategy to employ in getting the intended products or services to the proper audience.

The set of strategies emerging from strategic planning is often referred to as an organization's *policies*, and strategic planning itself is often referred to as *setting policy*.[2]

Phase 1: Product strategy In deciding on the products to produce or the services to render, there are several strategies that the president of the Bestway Furniture Company could follow. The company could specialize in office furniture, it could specialize in appliances, it could be a broad "supermarket" type of furniture outlet, or it could employ any one of a number of other product and/or service strategies.

After careful consideration of the various strategies available, the presi- dent has decided to sell only home furnishings, including appliances. For one reason or another, several other possible strategies were rejected. For example, the president has decided not to service appliances. He has also decided not to sell office furniture or to deal in institutional-type furnishings.

Phase 2: Marketing strategy Having decided to concentrate on home furnishings, the president of the Bestway Furniture Company is now faced with a second strategy decision. Some furniture dealers handle only the highest quality home furnishings, thereby striving to maintain the image of a "quality" dealer. The markups of these dealers are usually quite high, their volume is quite low, and their promotional efforts are directed toward a relatively small segment of the public. Other furniture dealers operate

---

[1] The English language lacks a generic singular pronoun signifying he *or* she. For this reason the masculine pronouns *he* and *his* are used to some extent in this book for purposes of succinctness and to avoid repetition in wording. As used, these pronouns are intended to refer to both females and males.

[2] For an expanded discussion of strategic planning, see Harold Koontz and Cyril J. O'Don- nell, *Management,* 7th ed. (New York: McGraw-Hill, 1980); and William H. Newman and E. Kirby Warren, *Process of Management,* 5th ed. (Englewood Cliffs, N.J.: Prentice-Hall, 1982).

"volume" outlets. They try to keep markups relatively low, with the thought that overall profits will be augmented by a larger number of units sold. Still other dealers may follow different strategies. The selection of a particular strategy is simply a matter of managerial judgment; some companies make a profit by following one strategy, while other companies are equally profitable following another. The Bestway Furniture Company has decided to operate "volume" outlets and to focus on maintaining a "discount" image.

Every organization must make similar strategy decisions. The set of strategies resulting from these decisions may not be written down, but they exist nonetheless and they are a central guiding force in the organization's activities and in its need for accounting information.

The Work of Management

The work of management centers on what is to be managed—the organization itself. Essentially, the manager carries out four broad functions in an organization:

1. Planning.
2. Organizing and directing.
3. Controlling.
4. Decision making.

These functions are carried on more or less simultaneously and often under considerable stress, urgency, and pressure. Rarely (if ever) will managers stop to examine which function they are engaged in at a particular moment. Perhaps they couldn't tell even if they tried, since a specific action might touch on all four.

Planning In **planning,** managers outline the steps to be taken in moving the organization toward its objectives. These plans will be both long and short term in nature. We saw the planning function in operation in the Bestway Furniture Company, as the president decided on a set of strategies to be followed. The president's next step will be to develop further, more specific plans, such as store locations, methods of financing customer purchases, hours of operation, and discount policies. As these plans are made, they will be communicated throughout the organization. When implemented, the plans will serve to coordinate, or meld together, the efforts of all parts of the organization toward the company's objectives.

Organizing and directing In **organizing,** managers decide how best to put together the organization's human and other resources in such a way as to most effectively carry out established plans. As a customer enters one of the Bestway Furniture Company's stores, the results of the managers' organizational efforts should be obvious in several ways. Certain persons will be performing specific functions, some directly with the customer and some not. Some persons will be overseeing the efforts of other persons.

The store's physical assets will be arranged in particular ways, and certain procedures will be followed if a sale is made. These and a host of other things, seen and unseen, will all exist to ensure that the customer is assisted in the best way possible and to ensure that the company moves toward its profit objectives. In short, the organization that is apparent in most companies doesn't simply happen; it is a result of the efforts of managers who must visualize and fit together the structure that is needed to get the job done, whatever the job may be.

In **directing,** managers oversee day-to-day activities and keep the organization functioning smoothly. Employees are assigned to tasks; disputes between departments or between employees are arbitrated; questions are answered; on-the-spot problems are solved; and numerous small routine and nonroutine decisions are made involving customers and/or procedures. In effect, directing is that part of the managers' work that deals largely with the routine and with the here and now.

Controlling   In carrying out the **control** function, managers take those steps necessary to ensure that each part of the organization is following the plan that was outlined for it at the planning stage. To do this, managers study the accounting and other reports coming to them and compare these reports against the plans set earlier. These comparisons may show where operations are not proceeding effectively or where certain persons need help in carrying out their assigned duties. The accounting and other reports coming to management are called **feedback.** The feedback that management receives may suggest the need to replan, to set new strategies, or to reshape the organizational structure. Feedback is a key to the effective management of any organization. As we shall see in chapters following, the generation of feedback to the manager is one of the central purposes of internal accounting.

Decision making   In **decision making,** managers attempt to make rational choices among alternatives. Decision making isn't a separate management function, per se; rather, it is an inseparable part of the *other* functions already discussed. Planning, organizing and directing, and controlling all require that decisions be made. For example, when first establishing its organizational strategies, the Bestway Furniture Company had to make a decision as to which of several available strategies would be followed. Such a decision is often called a *strategic decision* because of its long-term impact on the organization. In organizing and in directing day-to-day operations, as well as in controlling, managers must make scores of lesser decisions, all of which are important to the organization's overall well-being.

All decisions are based on *information.* In large part, the quality of management's decisions will be a reflection of the quality of the accounting and other information that it receives. Simply put, bad information will generally lead to bad decisions—thus the need for a course in managerial accounting in which we deal directly with the informational needs of management in carrying out decision-making responsibilities.

EXHIBIT 1–1
The planning and control cycle

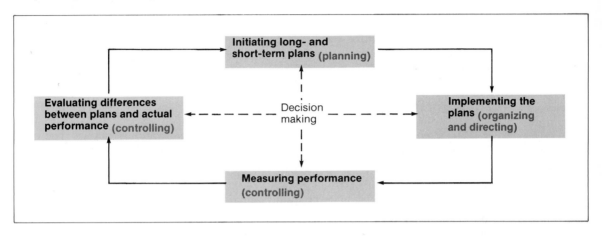

The Planning and Control Cycle

The work of management can be summarized very nicely in a model such as that shown in Exhibit 1–1. This model, which depicts the **planning and control cycle,** illustrates the smooth flow of management activities from planning through organizing, directing, and controlling, and then back to planning again. All of these activities turn on the hub of decision making.

ORGANIZATIONAL STRUCTURE

Just as organizations are made up of people, management accomplishes its objectives by working *through* people. The president of the Bestway Furniture Company could not possibly execute all of the company's strategies alone. He must rely on other people to carry a large share of the management load. This is done by the creation of an organizational structure that permits a *decentralization* of management responsibilities.

Decentralization

Decentralization means the delegation of decision-making authority throughout an organization by allowing managers at various operating levels to make key decisions relating to their area of responsibility. In effect, decentralization moves the decision-making point to the lowest managerial level possible for each decision that must be made.

All organizations are decentralized to some extent out of economic necessity. It would be impossible for top management to have the time or to be well-enough informed to make every one of the myriad decisions that arise daily. Thus, top management in virtually all organizations must delegate some decision-making authority to managers at lower levels. The greater the degree of this delegation, the greater is the amount of decentralization that exists. In some companies, top management delegates virtually all decisions to managers at lower levels; these companies are viewed as being strongly decentralized. In other companies, top management delegates only minor or routine decisions to managers at lower levels; these companies are viewed as being strongly centralized. Most companies fall somewhere between these extremes.

Under the presumption that the manager closest to a problem is the one best qualified to solve the problem, the president of the Bestway Furniture Company has delegated broad decision-making authority to the various operating levels within the organization. These levels are as follows: The company has three stores, each of which has a furnishings department and an appliances department. Each store has a store manager, as well as a separate manager over each department. In addition, the company has a purchasing department and an accounting department. As stated above, the managers of these stores and departments have broad decision-making authority over matters relating to their areas of responsibility. The organizational structure of the company is depicted in Exhibit 1–2.

The arrangement of boxes shown in Exhibit 1–2 is commonly called an **organization chart.** Each box depicts an area of management responsibility, and the lines between the boxes show the lines of authority between managers. The chart tells us, for example, that the managers of the stores are responsible to the vice president in charge of sales. In turn, the latter is responsible to the company president, who in turn is responsible to the board of directors. The purpose of an organization chart, then, is to show how responsibility has been divided between managers and to show formal lines of reporting and communication. If the manager of store 3 has a problem, she should not go directly to the company president but should take the problem to the sales manager, who is her immediate superior.

In very large organizations, *informal* relationships and channels of communication often develop. These informal lines of communication are spontaneous and come about through the personal and social contacts between managers. The informal structure that may exist in an organization is never depicted on a formal organization chart, but its existence is often very helpful in maintaining a smooth flow of activity. Generally, these informal channels are unstable and subject to frequent change.

Line and Staff Relationships

An organization chart also depicts *line* and *staff* positions in an organization. A **line** position is one that is *directly related* to the achievement of the basic objectives of an organization. A **staff** position, by contrast, is one that is only *indirectly related* to the achievement of these basic objectives. Staff positions are *supportive* in nature, in that they provide service or assistance to line positions or to other parts of the organization. Refer again to the organization chart in Exhibit 1–2. Since the basic objective of

Bestway obj → sell Fur @ profit.
line vs staff pos?

EXHIBIT 1–2

Organization chart, Bestway Furniture Company

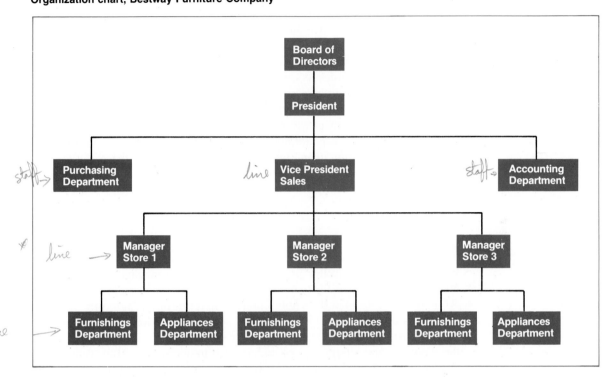

staff → Purchasing Department

line Vice President Sales

staff → Accounting Department

line → Manager Store 1 / Manager Store 2 / Manager Store 3

line → Furnishings Department / Appliances Department

line

the Bestway Furniture Company is to sell furnishings and appliances to the public, those managers whose areas of responsibility are directly related to the sales effort occupy line positions. These positions would include the managers of the separate departments in each store, the store managers, and the vice president in charge of sales.

By contrast, the manager of the purchasing department occupies a staff position, since the only function of the purchasing department is to support and serve the line (sales) departments by doing their purchasing for them. The company has found that better buys can be obtained by having one central unit purchase for the entire organization. Therefore, the purchasing department has been organized as a staff department to perform this service function. It cannot be called a line department, since it is involved only indirectly with the sales effort and since its role is *supportive* in nature. By this line of reasoning, the accounting department is also a staff department, since its purpose is to provide specialized accounting services to other departments.

The Bestway Furniture Company's organization chart shows only two staff departments. In a larger organization, there would be many more staff departments, including perhaps finance, engineering, medical services, cafeteria, personnel, advertising, and research and development.

The distinction we have drawn between line and staff is an important one, since the role of staff persons is basically advisory in nature, and thus they have no authority over line units. Because their role is advisory, in most organizations persons occupying staff positions do not formulate policy. Rather, policy setting and the making of key operating decisions are done by line managers, with staff persons either providing input or carrying out other duties as directed by top management.

Since accounting is in a staff position, where does it get the authority to set policy in accounting and financial reporting matters? The answer is simple. Top management *delegates* to the accounting department the right to prescribe uniform accounting procedures and the right to require reports and other information from line units. In carrying out these duties, the accounting department is not exercising line authority over other departments; it is simply acting for top management as its delegated voice.

The Controller

The manager in charge of the accounting department is known as the **controller.** The controller is a member of the top-management team and an active participant in the planning, control, and decision-making processes. Although the controller does not "control" in terms of line authority (remember, accounting is a staff function), as chief information officer he or she is in a position to exercise control in a very special way. This is through the reporting and interpreting of data needed in decision making. By supplying and interpreting relevant and timely data, the controller has a significant influence on decisions and thus plays a key part in directing an organization toward its objectives.

Because of the controller's position as a member of the top-management team, his or her time is generally kept free of technical and detailed activities. The controller oversees the work of others, directs the preparation of special reports and studies, and advises top management in special problem situations. The organization of a modern controller's office is shown in Exhibit 1–3.

Since the focus of this book is on managerial accounting, we are particularly interested in the work of the controller and the department he or she manages. The information that the accounting department generates is used throughout an organization in many different ways, as we shall see in chapters following.

Basic Similarities among Organizations

Organizations can be classified into three basic groups:

1. Profit-oriented business enterprises that are privately owned and operated as corporations, partnerships, and proprietorships.

EXHIBIT 1–3
Organization of the controller's office

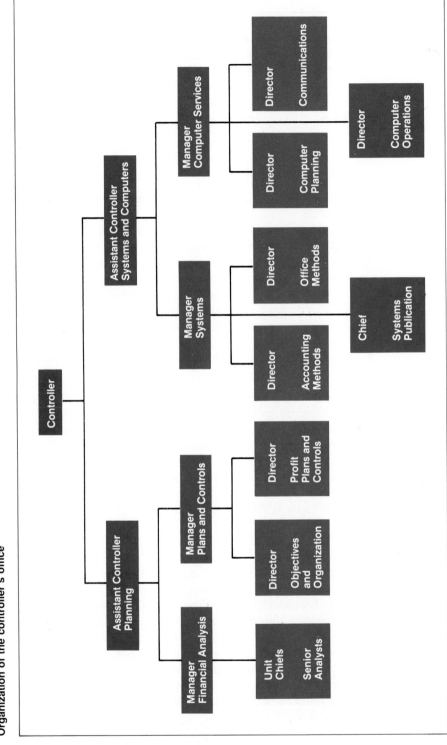

Source: W. Joseph Littlefield, "Developments in Financial Organizations: 1915–1965," *Financial Executive* 33, no. 9 (September 1965), p. 14, supplement. Reproduced by permission from the Financial Executive Institute, Inc.

non-profit

state-run

2. Service-oriented agencies and associations that are either publicly or privately controlled, such as the Red Cross, the YMCA, and the Salvation Army, and that are usually operated as nonprofit corporations.
3. Service-oriented agencies such as the Department of Defense, a state university, and a city water department that are created and controlled by government bodies.

Each of these groups contains thousands of organizations. Each organization may be unique in its own right, but nearly all organizations will share the following basic similarities:

1. Each will have an objective or group of objectives toward which it is working.
2. Each will have a set of strategies designed to assist in achieving the basic objective or objectives.
3. Each will have a manager or managers who plan, organize, direct, and control the organization's activities, and who make numerous decisions of both a long- and short-term nature.
4. Each will have an organizational structure that shows responsibility relationships between various managers and that shows line and staff relationships.
5. Each will have an insatiable need for information to assist in the execution of its strategies.

Because of these basic similarities, much of what we say in this book about managerial accounting and its uses will have almost universal application among organizations. To the extent that organizations differ, some of our topics will of necessity be narrower in their focus. It is our intent, however, to be concerned with the nature and uses of managerial accounting data in all types of organizations; for this reason, the reader will find chapter examples and problems relating to organizations that are service oriented as well as to those that are profit oriented.

THE MANAGER'S NEED FOR INFORMATION

Information is the "motor" that makes management go. In the absence of a steady flow of information, management would be powerless to do anything. Fortunately, a large part of management's information needs are satisfied within the structure of the organization itself. As suggested by the organization chart in Exhibit 1–2, there are channels of communication extending throughout an organization through which the various levels of management can communicate. Through these channels, policies and instructions are submitted to subordinates, problems are discussed, formal and informal contacts are made, reports and memos are transmitted, and so on. Without these channels of communication, it would be impossible for management to function effectively.

The management of an organization also depends on specialists to provide a large part of its information needs. Economists, marketing specialists, organizational behavior specialists, accountants, and others all provide information to management, and they advise on various phases of the organization's activities. Economists, for example, provide information on contemplated economic conditions; marketing specialists provide information essential to the effective promotion and distribution of goods and services; and organizational behavior specialists assist in the structure and functioning of the organization itself.

Accounting Information

The information provided by accounting is essentially financial in nature, helping the manager to do three things:

1. Plan effectively and focus attention on deviations from plans.
2. Direct day-to-day operations.
3. Arrive at the best solutions to the operating problems faced by the organization.

Plan effectively The plans of management are expressed formally as **budgets,** and the term *budgeting* is often applied to management planning generally. Budgets are usually prepared on an annual basis, and they express the desires and goals of management in specific, quantitative terms. For example, the Bestway Furniture Company plans sales by month a full year in advance. These plans are expressed as departmental budgets, which are communicated throughout the organization.

But planning is not enough. Once the budgets have been set, the president and other managers of the Bestway Furniture Company will need information inflows that indicate how well the plans are working out. Accounting assists in meeting this information need by supplying *performance reports* that help a manager focus on problems or opportunities that might otherwise go unnoticed. A **performance report** is a detailed report to management comparing budgeted data against actual data for a specific time period. If the performance report on a particular department indicates that problems exist, then the manager will need to find the cause of the problems and take corrective action. If the performance report indicates that things are going well, then the manager is free to do other work. In sum, performance reports are a form of feedback to managers, directing their attention toward those parts of the organization where managerial time can be used most effectively.

Direct operations Managers have a constant need for accounting information in the routine conduct of day-to-day operations. For example, as departmental managers in the Bestway Furniture Company price new items going onto the display floor, they will rely on information provided by accounting to ensure that cost-price relationships are in harmony with the marketing strategies adopted by the firm. The company's store managers will rely on other accounting information such as sales volumes and inventory levels as they attempt to prepare advertising programs. And the purchasing department manager will rely on still other accounting information in evaluating the costs of storage and handling. In these and a score of other ways, the work of the accountant and the manager is inextricably connected in the conduct of day-to-day operations.

Solve problems   Accounting information is often a key factor in analyzing alternative methods of solving a problem. The reason is that various alternatives usually have specific costs and benefits that can be measured and used as an input in deciding which alternative is best. Accounting is generally responsible for gathering available cost and benefit data and for communicating it in a usable form to the appropriate manager. For example, the Bestway Furniture Company may discover that competitors are making inroads on the company's business. In deciding among the alternatives of reducing prices, increasing advertising, or doing both in an attempt to maintain its market share, the company will rely heavily on cost-benefit data provided by accounting. It is important to note here that the needed information may not be in readily available form; in fact, accounting may find it necessary to do a large amount of special analytical work, including some forecasting, in order to prepare the needed data.

Information Must Be in Summary Form

An essential element of managerial accounting information is that it be in summary form. In your study of financial accounting, you learned that an accounting system handles an enormous amount of detail in recording the results of day-to-day transactions. The availability of this detail is vital to the effective management of an organization. However, a manager's *initial* need is not for detail but rather for *summaries* of detailed information that have been drawn from the accounting records. Using these summaries, the manager can see where problems exist and where time must be spent to improve the effectiveness of the organization.

Because of the great value of summarized data to the manager, the bulk of our time in this book is spent on learning the *kinds* of summarized data that the manager needs and on learning how these data are used in directing the affairs of an enterprise.

COMPARISON OF FINANCIAL AND MANAGERIAL ACCOUNTING

In our discussion of managerial accounting, we have noted that it differs in several ways from financial accounting. To assist the reader in making the transition from the study of financial accounting to the study of managerial accounting, it is desirable to summarize these differences, as well as to point out certain similarities between the two fields of study.

Differences between Financial and Managerial Accounting

In all, we can identify eight major differences between financial and managerial accounting:

Man. Acty vs Financial

1. Managerial accounting focuses on providing data for internal uses by the manager.
2. Managerial accounting places more emphasis on the future.
3. Managerial accounting is not governed by generally accepted accounting principles.
4. Managerial accounting emphasizes the relevance and flexibility of data.
5. Managerial accounting places less emphasis on precision and more emphasis on nonmonetary data.
6. Managerial accounting emphasizes the segments of an organization, rather than just looking at the organization as a whole.
7. Managerial accounting draws heavily from other disciplines.
8. Managerial accounting is not mandatory.

Internal uses by the manager   For internal purposes, the manager does not need the same kinds of information as are needed externally by stockholders and others. The manager must direct day-to-day operations, plan for the future, solve problems, and make numerous routine and nonroutine decisions, all of which require their own special information inputs. Much of the information needed by the manager for these purposes would be either confusing or valueless to stockholders and others because of the form in which the information is prepared and used.

Emphasis on the future   Since a large part of the overall responsibilities of the manager have to do with *planning*, the manager's information needs have a strong future orientation. Summaries of past costs and other historical data are useful in planning, but only to a point. The difficulty with summaries of the past is that the manager can't assume that the future will simply be a reflection of what has happened in the past. Changes are constantly taking place in economic conditions, customer needs and desires, competitive conditions, and so on. All of these changes demand that the manager's planning framework be built in large part on estimated data that may or may not be reflective of past experience.

By contrast, financial accounting records the *financial history* of an organization. Financial accounting has little to do with estimates and projections of the future. Rather, entries are made in the accounting records only after transactions have already occurred.

Generally accepted accounting principles   Financial accounting statements must be prepared in accordance with generally accepted accounting principles. The reason is that these statements are relied on by persons outside the organization. These outside persons must have some assurance that the information they are receiving has been prepared in accordance with some common set of ground rules; otherwise, great opportunity could exist for fraud or misrepresentation, and confidence in financial statements would be destroyed. The managers of a company, by contrast, are not governed by generally accepted accounting principles in the information that they receive. Managers can set their own ground rules on the form and content of information that is to be used internally. Whether these ground rules conform to generally accepted accounting principles is immaterial. For example, management might direct that for internal uses, financial statements be expressed on a cash basis, depreciation of plant and equipment be based on appraised value, and that fixed production costs be ignored in product costing, even though all of these procedures would be in violation of generally accepted accounting principles. In sum, when information is to be used internally, managers are free to reshape data as they desire in order to obtain information in its most useful form.

Relevance and flexibility of data Financial accounting data are expected to be objectively determined and to be verifiable. For internal uses, the manager is often more concerned about receiving information that is relevant and flexible than about receiving information that is completely objective or even verifiable. By relevant, we mean *pertinent to the problem at hand*. So long as information inflows are relevant to problems that must be solved, the manager may view objectivity and verification as matters of secondary importance. The manager must also have information that is flexible enough to be used in a variety of decision-making situations. For example, the cost information needed for pricing transfers of goods between sister divisions may be far different from the cost information needed for pricing sales to outside customers.

Less emphasis on precision When information is needed, speed is often more important than precision. The more rapidly information comes to a manager, the more rapidly problems are attended to and resolved. For this reason, a manager is often willing to trade off some accuracy for information that is immediately available. If a decision must be made, waiting a week for information that will be slightly more accurate may be considered less desirable than simply acting on the information that is already available. This means that the manager's need is often for good estimates and good approximations rather than for numbers that are accurate to the last penny. Managerial accounting recognizes this need and therefore tends to place less emphasis on precision than does financial accounting. In addition, managerial accounting places considerable weight on nonmonetary data. For example, factors such as time lost due to machine breakdowns, sales representatives' impressions concerning a new product, information on weather conditions, and even rumors could be helpful to the manager, even though some of this information might be difficult to quantify or express in a monetary form.

Segments of an organization Financial accounting is primarily concerned with the reporting of business activities for a company as a whole. By contrast, managerial accounting focuses less on the whole and more on the parts, or **segments,** of a company. These segments may be the product lines, the sales territories, the divisions, the departments, or any other way that a company can be broken down. In financial accounting, it is true that some companies do report some breakdown of revenues and costs, but this tends to be a secondary emphasis. In managerial accounting, segmented reporting is the primary emphasis.

Draws from other disciplines   Managerial accounting extends beyond the boundaries of the traditional accounting system and draws heavily from other disciplines, including economics, finance, statistics, operations research, and organizational behavior. These ''outside'' sources give managerial accounting a strong interdisciplinary flavor as well as a decidedly pragmatic orientation.

Not mandatory.   Financial accounting is mandatory; that is, it must be done. Financial records must be kept so that sufficient information will be available to satisfy the requirements of various outside parties. Often the financial records that are to be kept are specified by regulatory bodies, such as the Securities and Exchange Commission (SEC). Even if a company is not covered by SEC or other regulations, it must meet certain financial accounting requirements if it is to have its statements examined by professional outside accountants. In addition, *all* companies must keep adequate records to meet the requirements of taxing authorities. By contrast, managerial accounting is not mandatory. A company is completely free to do as much or as little as it wishes. There are no regulatory bodies or other outside agencies that specify what is to be done, or for that matter, whether anything is to be done at all. Since managerial accounting is completely optional, the important question is always ''Is the information useful?'' rather than ''Is the information required?''

Similarities between Financial and Managerial Accounting

Although many differences exist between financial and managerial accounting, they are similar in at least two ways. First, both rely on the accounting information system. It would be a total waste of money to have two *different* data-collecting systems existing side by side. For this reason, managerial accounting makes extensive use of routinely generated financial accounting data, although it both expands on and adds to these data, as discussed earlier. Second, both financial and managerial accounting rely heavily on the concept of *responsibility,* or *stewardship.* Financial accounting is concerned with stewardship over the company *as a whole;* managerial accounting is concerned with stewardship over its *parts,* and this concern extends to the last person in the organization who has any responsibility over cost. In effect, from a responsibility accounting point of view, financial accounting can be viewed as being the apex, with managerial accounting filling in the bulk of the pyramid underneath.

THE EXPANDING ROLE OF MANAGERIAL ACCOUNTING

Managerial accounting is in its infancy. Historically, it has played a secondary role to financial accounting, and in many organizations it still is little more than a by-product of the financial reporting process. However, events of the last three decades have spurred the development of managerial accounting, and it is becoming widely recognized as a field of expertise separate from financial accounting.

Increased Needs for Information

Among the events that have spurred the development of managerial accounting, we can note increased business competition that has become worldwide in its scope, a severe cost-price squeeze, rapidly developing technology in the form of greater automation and greater ability to gather and report information, and a strong move toward deregulation of service type industries. The changes brought about by these events have intensified the manager's need for information, and particularly for information relating to internal operations that can't be obtained from the traditional income statement and balance sheet. Consider the following:

Over the last three decades products have become obsolete at accelerating rates. Various scientific breakthroughs have resulted in the development of many new basic components, such as the transistor and the electronic "chip," which have literally revolutionized many industries and their products. Scientific researchers report that this "revolution" is only in its beginnings.

Dramatic changes have taken place in production methods over the last three decades. The term *automation* was coined in the early 1950s to describe a process that was new at the time. Today many products are produced virtually untouched by human hands. Oil refinery operations are controlled by massive computers; machine tools are electronically controlled; and there are even entire manufacturing plants where workers do little more than monitor instrument panels. In many settings, robots are becoming the new "steel collar" workers of industry. These robots can be programmed to "see" and "feel" small objects and can work in virtually any environment.

Modes of management and methods of decision making have been affected by the development of powerful new quantitative tools such as linear programming, probability analysis, and decision theory. These new tools, which have come from the mathematical and statistical sciences, are becoming indispensable in day-to-day decision making.

Whole new industries have emerged as a result of various technological breakthroughs. A few short years ago, petrochemicals and laser beams were little more than laboratory novelties, and space exploration was little more than a dream. Today the petrochemical industry stands as a powerful competitive force in the business environment, laser beams are used for everything from cutting steel to delicate eye surgery, and students work amazingly complex mathematical computations on tiny electronic calculators that are a direct outgrowth of aerospace exploration.

In many industries, costs are increasing rapidly and at the same time are changing in form. The move toward automation and toward the use of the computer to monitor various tasks is causing a shift away from labor costs, for example, with the result that labor costs are becoming less of a factor in total costs in both manufacturing and service activities. These labor costs are being replaced with less flexible costs such as depreciation.

Service industries are being deregulated with surprising speed. As companies in the transportation, financial services, and telecommunications industries break away from a highly regulated environment, managers are being forced to struggle with costing and pricing problems that did not exist previously.

The economic impact of these and other factors has been far-reaching. As managers have grappled with the effects of increased competition, escalating costs, and evolving technology, the role of managerial accounting has expanded manyfold from what was common in earlier years. Looking to the future, we can expect this role to expand even further. As many business writers have observed, the ability of an organization to survive in this time of rocketing change will be directly related to how quickly and how well it responds to new challenges. Certainly the role of managerial accounting in meeting these challenges will be very significant.[3]

The Certified Management Accountant (CMA)

Specific recognition is given to the management accountant as a trained professional in the National Association of Accountants' (NAA) *Certified Management Accountant (CMA)* program. The purpose and operation of the program are described in the following excerpts from a brochure issued by the NAA:

> A Certified Management Accountant is well prepared to be an active participant in management. The CMA program is founded upon the dynamic role the management accountant plays in the management process. The program recognizes all aspects of business, with the focus on the development and analysis of information used in decision making. A CMA has demonstrated the knowledge and professional skills to become an influential member of the management team.
>
> CMAs are found in all levels of management accounting and financial management. Those early in their careers hold staff and supervisory positions. CMAs further along in their careers hold positions of corporate controller, chief financial officer, and CPA firm partners.

To earn the CMA and become a Certified Management Accountant, the following four steps must be completed:

1. Apply for admission to the CMA program and register for the CMA examination.
2. Pass all five parts of the Certified Management Accountant examination within a three-year period.
3. Meet the accounting experience requirement before or within seven years of passing the examination.
4. Comply with the Standards of Ethical Conduct for Management Accountants.

---

[3] For an expanded discussion of the points covered in this section, see Robert S. Kaplan, "The Evolution of Management Accounting," *Accounting Review* 59, no. 3 (July 1984), pp. 390–418.

SUMMARY

Understanding organizations and the work of those who manage organizations helps us to understand managerial accounting and its functions. All organizations have basic objectives and a set of strategies for achieving those objectives. Both the setting of strategy, sometimes called strategic planning, and planning of a more short-term nature are basic functions of the manager. In addition to planning, the work of the manager centers on organizing and directing day-to-day operations, controlling, and decision making.

The managers of an organization choose an organizational structure that will permit a decentralization of responsibility by placing managers over specific departments and other units. The responsibility relationships between managers are shown by the organization chart. The organization chart also shows which organizational units are performing line functions and which are performing staff functions. Line functions relate to the specific objectives of the organization, whereas staff functions are supportive in nature, their purpose being to provide specialized services of some type.

A large part of the information needs of management is provided within the structure of the organization itself. Channels of communication exist between various levels of management through which information flows. Management also calls on various specialists to provide information, including the economist, the engineer, the operations research specialist, and the accountant. The information provided internally by the accountant is used by management in three ways: (1) to make plans and to monitor how well these plans are working out; (2) to direct day-to-day operations, including the setting of prices and the establishment of advertising policy; and (3) to solve problems confronting the organization.

Since managerial accounting is geared to the needs of the manager rather than to the needs of stockholders and others, it differs substantially from financial accounting. Among other things, managerial accounting is oriented more toward the future, it is not governed by generally accepted accounting principles, it places less emphasis on precision, it emphasizes segments of an organization (rather than the organization as a whole), it draws heavily on other disciplines, and it is not mandatory. The role of managerial accounting is expanding rapidly, and managerial accounting has become recognized as a field of professional study through which professional certification can be obtained.

KEY TERMS FOR REVIEW

At the end of each chapter, a list of key terms for review is given, along with the definition of each term. (These terms are set in boldface type where they first appear in the chapter.) Each term should be studied with care to be sure you understand its meaning, since these terms are used repeatedly in the chapters that follow. The list for Chapter 1 is:

Budget A detailed plan for the future, usually expressed in formal quantitative terms.

Control The process of instituting procedures and then obtaining feedback as needed to ensure that all parts of the organization are functioning effectively and moving toward overall company goals.

Controller The manager in charge of the accounting department in an organization.

Decentralization The delegation of decision-making authority throughout an organization by allowing managers at various operating levels to make key decisions relating to their area of responsibility.

Decision making The process of making rational choices among alternatives.

Directing The overseeing of day-to-day activities in order to keep an organization functioning smoothly.

Feedback Accounting and other reports that help managers monitor performance and focus on problems and/or opportunities that might otherwise go unnoticed.

Financial accounting The phase of accounting that is concerned with providing information to stockholders and others for use in evaluating operations and current financial condition.

Line A position in an organization that is directly related to the achievement of the organization's basic objectives.

Managerial accounting The phase of accounting that is concerned with providing information to managers for use in planning and controlling operations and for use in decision making.

Organization A group of people united for some common purpose.

Organization chart A visual diagram of a firm's organizational structure that depicts formal lines of reporting, communication, and responsibility between managers.

Organizing The process of putting together an organization's human and other resources in such a way as to most effectively carry out established plans.

Performance report A detailed report to management comparing budgeted data against actual data for a specific time period.

Planning The development of objectives in an organization and the preparation of various budgets to achieve these objectives.

Planning and control cycle The flow of management activities through the steps (in sequence) of planning, organizing and directing, controlling, and then back to planning again.

Segment Any part of an organization that can be evaluated independently of other parts and about which the manager seeks cost data. Examples would include a product line, a sales territory, a division, or a department.

Staff A position in an organization that is only indirectly related to the achievement of the organization's basic objectives. Such positions are supportive in nature, in that they provide service or assistance to line positions or to other staff positions.

Strategic planning The planning that leads to the implementation of an organization's objectives. Such planning occurs in two phases: (1) deciding on the products to produce and/or the services to render, and (2) deciding on the marketing and/or manufacturing methods to employ in getting the intended products or services to the proper audience.

QUESTIONS

1–1. Contrast financial and managerial accounting.

1–2. What objectives, other than earning a profit, might be important to the managers of a profit-oriented organization?

1–3. Assume that you are about to go into the retail grocery business. Describe some of the operating strategies that you might follow.

1–4. A labor union is an organization. Describe a labor union in terms of what might be its objectives, its strategies, its organizational structure, the work of its managers, and its need for information.

1–5. Some persons consider strategic planning to be the most important work that a manager does. In what ways might this be true? In what ways might this be false?

1–6. Assume that the central objective of a college basketball team is to win games. What strategies might the team follow to achieve this objective?

1–7. Managerial accounting isn't as important in the government as it is in private industry, since the government doesn't have to worry about earning a profit. Do you agree? Explain.

1–8. What function does *feedback* play in the work of the manager?

1–9. "Essentially, the job of a manager is to make decisions." Do you agree? Explain.

1–10. What is the relationship, if any, between information and decision making?

1–11. Choose an organization with which you are familiar. Prepare an organization chart depicting the structure of the organization you have chosen. (The organization you choose should be sufficiently complex to have at least one staff function.) Be prepared to place your organization chart on the board, if your instructor so directs.

1–12. One of the key responsibilities of an accounting department is to keep records for the entire organization. Why don't line managers keep their own records?

1–13. Managerial accounting information is sometimes described as a means to an end, whereas financial accounting information is described as an end in itself. In what sense is this true?

1–14. A student planning a career in management commented, "Look, I'm going to be a manager, so why don't we just leave the accounting to the accountants?" Do you agree? Explain.

1–15. Accountants are sometimes compared to journalists in that accountants don't just "report" information to the manager; they "editorialize" the information. What implications does this hold for the accountant "managing the news," so to speak?

1–16. Distinguish between line and staff positions in an organization.

1–17. "The term *controller* is a misnomer, because the controller doesn't 'control' anything." Do you agree? Explain.

1–18. A production superintendent once complained, "Accounting is a staff function. Those people have no right to come down here and tell us what to do." Do you agree? Why or why not?

1–19.   What are the major differences between financial and managerial accounting? In what ways are the two fields of study similar?

1–20.   "If an organization's managerial accounting system functions properly, it will provide management with all the information needed to operate with maximum effectiveness." Do you agree? Explain.

PROBLEMS

P1–1.   **Preparing an organization chart.**   Bristow University is a large private school located in the Midwest. The university is headed by a president, who has five vice presidents reporting to him. These vice presidents are responsible for, respectively, auxiliary services, admissions and records, academics, financial services (controller), and physical plant.

In addition, the university has managers over several areas who report to these vice presidents. These include managers over central purchasing, the university press, and the university bookstore, all of whom report to the vice president for auxiliary services; managers over computer services and over accounting and finance, who report to the vice president for financial services; and managers over grounds and custodial services and over plant and maintenance, who report to the vice president for physical plant.

The university has four colleges—business, humanities, fine arts, and engineering and quantitative methods—and a law school. Each of these units has a dean who is responsible to the academic vice president. There are several departments in each college.

1. Prepare an organization chart for Bristow University.
2. Which of the positions on your chart would be line positions? Why would they be line positions? Which would be staff positions? Why?
3. Which of the positions on your chart would have need for accounting information? Explain.

P1–2.   **Strategic planning.**   One element necessary to the life of an organization is strategic planning. Strategic planning establishes an organization's long-range goals or objectives and the means to achieve them. Even before a company can begin operations, its managers must develop the plan or plans necessary to determine its future. Among the questions that must be answered are the following: What products or services will the company provide? How will the company be financed and structured? Where will the company and its distributors be located? How will the company's products or services be marketed?

Line and staff management play specific roles in strategic planning. They have different responsibilities and functions in an organization. In addition, the activities of these two management groups must be coordinated.

Required: 1.   In the *formulation* of an organization's strategic plans, describe the contribution to be made by:
    a.   The line managers.
    b.   The staff groups or departments.
    In your answer, identify the types of decisions that these two groups of managers would probably make as they participate in the formulation of strategic plans.

2. In the *implementation* of an organization's strategic plans:
   a. State how the responsibilities of line management differ from those of staff management.
   b. Describe how line and staff responsibilities interrelate in the implementation of strategic planning.

(CMA, Adapted)

P1–3. **Line and staff positions.** Special Alloys Corporation is a specialized production firm that manufactures a variety of metal products for industrial use. Most of the revenues are generated by large contracts with companies that have government defense contracts. The company also develops and markets parts to the major automobile companies. The company employs many metallurgists and skilled technicians because most of its products are made from highly sophisticated alloys.

The company recently signed two large contracts; as a result, the work load of Wayne Washburn, the general manager, has become overwhelming. To relieve some of this overload, Mark Johnson was transferred from the research planning department to the general manager's office. Johnson, who had been a senior metallurgist and supervisor in the planning department, was given the title "assistant to the general manager."

Washburn assigned several responsibilities to Johnson in their first meeting. Johnson will oversee the testing of new alloys in the product planning department and be given the authority to make decisions as to the use of these alloys in product development; he will also be responsible for maintaining the production schedules for one of the new contracts. In addition to these duties, he will be required to meet with the supervisors of the production departments regularly to consult with them about production problems they may be experiencing. Washburn is expecting that he will be able to manage the company much more efficiently with Johnson's help.

Required:
1. Positions within organizations are often described as having *(a)* line authority or *(b)* staff authority. Describe what is meant by these two terms.
2. Of the responsibilities assigned to Mark Johnson as assistant to the general manager, which ones are considered line authority and which have staff authority?
3. Identify and discuss the conflicts Mark Johnson may experience in the production departments as a result of his new responsibilities.

(CMA, Adapted)

PART ONE

The Foundation: Cost Terms, Cost Behavior, and Systems Design

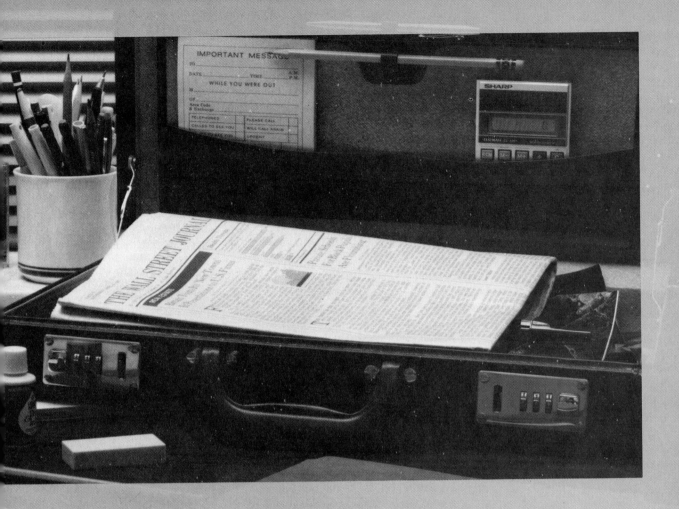

Cost Terms, Concepts, and Classifications

LEARNING OBJECTIVES

After studying Chapter 2, you should be able to:

■ Identify and give examples of each of the three basic cost elements involved in the manufacture of a product.

■ Distinguish between product costs and period costs and give examples of each.

■ Explain the difference between the financial statements of a manufacturing firm and those of a merchandising firm.

■ Prepare a schedule of cost of goods manufactured in good form.

■ Explain the flow of direct materials cost, direct labor cost, and manufacturing overhead cost from the point of incurrence to sale of the completed product.

■ Properly classify costs associated with idle time, overtime, and labor fringe benefits in an organization.

■ Identify and give examples of variable costs and fixed costs and explain the difference in their behavior.

■ Define or explain the key terms listed at the end of the chapter.

As explained in Chapter 1, the work of management centers on (1) planning, which includes setting objectives and outlining the means of attaining those objectives; and (2) control, which includes the steps taken or the means used to ensure that objectives are realized. In order to discharge planning and control responsibilities, the manager needs *information* about the organization. From an accounting point of view, the manager's information needs most often relate to the *costs* of the organization.

In financial accounting, the term *cost* is defined as the sacrifice made in order to obtain some good or service. The sacrifice may be measured in cash expended, property transferred, service performed, and so on. This definition is easily stated and widely accepted in financial accounting.

In managerial accounting, the term *cost* is used in many different ways. The reason is that there are many different types of costs, and these costs are classified differently according to the immediate needs of management. In this chapter, we look at some of these different types of costs and at some of the ways in which managers classify them for their own use internally.

GENERAL COST CLASSIFICATIONS

Costs are associated with all types of organizations—business, nonbusiness, service, retail, and manufacturing. Generally, the kinds of costs that are incurred and the way in which these costs are classified will depend on the type of organization involved. Cost accounting is as applicable to one type of organization as to another; for this reason, we shall consider the cost characteristics of a variety of organizations—manufacturing, merchandising, and service—in our discussion.

Manufacturing Costs

A manufacturing firm is more complex than most other types of organizations. The reason is that the manufacturing firm is broader in its activities, being involved in production as well as in marketing and administration. An understanding of the cost structure of a manufacturing firm therefore provides a broad, general understanding of costing that can be very helpful in understanding the cost structures of other types of organizations.

Manufacturing involves the conversion of raw materials into finished products through the efforts of factory workers and the use of production equipment. By contrast, **merchandising** is the marketing of products that are in a finished form and that have been acquired from a manufacturer or other outside source. The cost of a manufactured product is made up of three basic elements:

1. Direct materials.
2. Direct labor.
3. Manufacturing overhead.

Direct materials   A wide variety of materials can go into the manufacture of a product. These are generally termed **raw materials.** The term is somewhat misleading in that raw materials seems to imply basic, natural resources. Actually, raw materials are inclusive of any materials input into a product; and the finished product of one firm can become the raw materials of another firm. For example, the finished lumber products of a sawmill become the raw materials of a construction company.

Direct materials are those materials that become an integral part of a company's finished product and that can be conveniently traced into it. This would include, for example, the sheet steel in a file cabinet or the wood in a table. Some items of materials may become an integral part of the finished product but may be traceable into the product only at great cost and inconvenience. Such items might include the glue used to put a table together or the welding materials used to bond the sheet metal in a file cabinet. Glue and welding materials would be called **indirect materials** and would be included as part of manufacturing overhead.

Direct labor   The term **direct labor** is reserved for those labor costs that can be physically traced to the creation of products in a ''hands on'' sense, and that can be so traced without undue cost or inconvenience. The labor costs of assembly line workers, for example, would be direct labor costs, as would the labor costs of carpenters, bricklayers, and machine operators.

Labor costs that cannot be physically traced to the creation of products, or that can be traced only at great cost and inconvenience, are termed **indirect labor** and are treated as part of manufacturing overhead, along with indirect materials. Indirect labor includes the labor costs of janitors, supervisors, materials handlers, engineers, and night security guards. Although the efforts of these workers are essential to production, it would be either impractical or impossible to accurately relate their costs to specific units of product. Hence, such labor costs are treated as indirect labor.

Manufacturing overhead   Manufacturing overhead can be defined very simply as including all costs of manufacturing except direct materials and direct labor. Included in this classification one would expect to find such costs as indirect materials, indirect labor, heat and light, property taxes, insurance, depreciation on factory facilities, repairs, maintenance, and all other costs of operating the manufacturing division of a company. A company also incurs costs for heat and light, property taxes, insurance, depreciation, and so forth associated with the selling and administrative functions in an organization, but these costs would not be included as part of manufacturing overhead. Only those costs that are associated with *operating the factory* would be included in the manufacturing overhead category.

Manufacturing overhead is known by various names. Sometimes it is called manufacturing expense, factory expense, overhead, factory overhead, or factory burden. All of these terms are synonymous with ''manufacturing overhead.''

Conversion cost { Direct Labour + Manufacturing Overhead

Prime cost { Direct labour + Direct material

Manufacturing overhead combined with direct labor is known as **conversion cost.** This term stems from the fact that direct labor costs and overhead costs are incurred in the *conversion* of materials into finished products. Direct labor combined with direct materials is known as **prime cost.**

Nonmanufacturing Costs

2.

Expenses or {

Traditionally, the central focus of managerial accounting has been on manufacturing costs and activities. The reason is probably traceable to the complexity of manufacturing operations and to the need for carefully developed costs for pricing and other decisions. However, costing techniques are now coming into use in many nonmanufacturing areas, as firms attempt to get better control over their costs and to provide management with more usable cost data.

Generally, nonmanufacturing costs are subclassified into two categories:

1.   Marketing or selling costs.
2.   Administrative costs.

Marketing or selling costs include all costs necessary to secure customer orders and get the finished product or service into the hands of the customer. Since marketing costs relate to contacting customers and providing for their needs, these costs are often referred to as **order-getting and order-filling costs.** Examples of marketing costs include advertising, shipping, sales travel, sales commissions, sales salaries, and costs associated with finished goods warehouses. *All* organizations have marketing costs, regardless of whether the organizations are manufacturing, merchandising, or service in nature.

Administrative costs include all executive, organizational, and clerical costs that cannot logically be included under either production or marketing. Examples of such costs include executive compensation, general accounting, secretarial, public relations, and similar costs having to do with the overall, general administration of the organization *as a whole.* As with marketing costs, *all* organizations have administrative costs.

As stated earlier, managerial accounting concepts and techniques apply just as much to nonmanufacturing activities as they do to manufacturing activities, although in the past the central focus has been on the manufacturing environment. Service organizations in particular are making increased use of cost concepts in analyzing and costing their services. For example, banks now use cost analysis in determining the cost of offering such services as checking accounts, consumer loans, and credit cards; and insurance companies determine costs of servicing customers by geographic location, age, marital status, and occupation. Cost breakdowns of these types provide data for control over selling and administrative functions in the same way that manufacturing cost breakdowns provide data for control over manufacturing functions.

Period Costs

In addition to being placed in manufacturing and nonmanufacturing categories, costs can also be classified as either *period* costs or *product* costs.

Period costs are those costs that are matched against revenues on a time period basis. As such, period costs are not included as part of the cost of either purchased or manufactured goods. Sales commissions and office rent are good examples of the kind of costs we are talking about. Neither commissions nor office rent is included as part of the cost of purchased or manufactured goods. Rather, both items are treated as expenses and deducted from revenues in the time period in which they are incurred. Thus, they are said to be period costs.

As suggested above, *all selling and administrative expenses are considered to be period costs.* Therefore, advertising, executive salaries, sales commissions, public relations, and other nonmanufacturing costs discussed earlier would all be period costs, and they will appear on the income statement as expenses in the time period in which they are incurred.

Product Costs

Some costs are better matched against products than they are against periods of time. Costs of this type—called **product costs**—consist of the costs involved in the purchase or manufacture of goods. In the case of manufactured goods, these costs consist of direct materials, direct labor, and manufacturing overhead. Product costs are viewed as "attaching" to units of product as the goods are purchased or manufactured, and they remain attached until sale takes place. At the point of sale, the costs are released from inventory as expenses (typically called "cost of goods sold") and matched against sales revenue.

We must emphasize that unlike period costs, product costs are not necessarily treated as expenses in the time period in which they are incurred. Rather, as explained above, they are treated as expenses in the time period in which the related products *are sold*. This means that a product cost such as direct materials or direct labor might be incurred during one time period but not treated as an expense until a following period when sale of the completed product takes place.

Exhibit 2–1 contains a summary of the cost terms that we have introduced so far in our discussion.

COST CLASSIFICATIONS ON FINANCIAL STATEMENTS

In your prior accounting training, you learned that firms prepare periodic reports for creditors, stockholders, and others to show the financial condition of the firm and the firm's earnings performance over some specified interval. The reports you studied were probably those of merchandising firms, such as retail stores, which simply purchase goods from suppliers for resale to customers.

EXHIBIT 2–1
Summary of cost terms

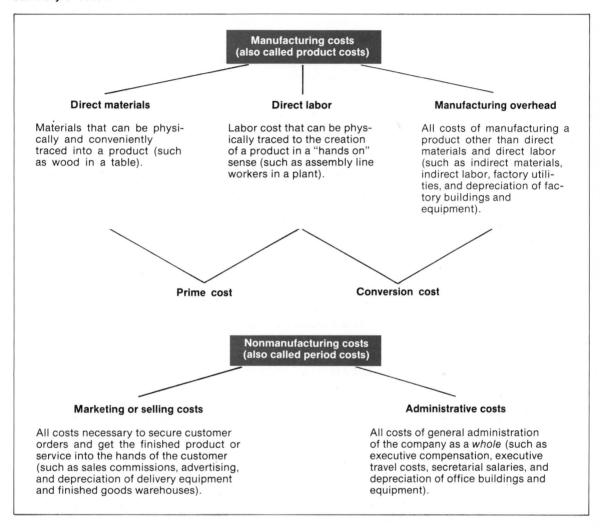

The financial statements prepared by a *manufacturing* firm are more complex than the statements prepared by a merchandising firm. As stated earlier, manufacturing firms are more complex organizations than merchandising firms because the manufacturing firm must produce its goods as well as market them. The production process gives rise to many costs that do not exist in a merchandising firm, and somehow these costs must be accounted for on the manufacturing firm's financial statements. In this section, we focus our attention on how this accounting is carried out from a cost classification point of view.

EXHIBIT 2–2

Comparative income statements: Merchandising and manufacturing companies

MERCHANDISING COMPANY

The cost of goods sold to customers comes from the purchased cost of these goods from an outside supplier.

Sales.		$1,000,000
Cost of goods sold:		
Beginning inventory	$100,000	
Add purchases	650,000	
Goods available for sale	750,000	
Ending inventory	150,000	600,000
Gross margin		400,000
Less operating expenses:		
Selling expense	100,000	
Administrative expense	200,000	300,000
Net income		$ 100,000

MANUFACTURING COMPANY

The cost of goods sold to customers comes from the manufacturing costs that have been incurred in the manufacture of the goods. These costs consist of direct materials, direct labor, and manufacturing overhead (see Exhibit 2–3).

Sales.		$1,500,000
Cost of goods sold:		
Beginning finished goods inventory	$125,000	
Add cost of goods manufactured	850,000	
Goods available for sale	975,000	
Ending finished goods inventory	175,000	800,000
Gross margin		700,000
Less operating expenses:		
Selling expense	250,000	
Administrative expense	300,000	550,000
Net income		$ 150,000

The Income Statement

Exhibit 2–2 compares the income statement of a merchandising company with the income statement of a manufacturing company.

Notice in the case of a merchandising company that the cost of goods sold simply consists of the purchase cost of the goods from a supplier. By contrast, the cost of goods sold in a manufacturing company consists of many different costs that have been incurred in the manufacturing process.

The income statement of a manufacturing company is supported by a schedule of **cost of goods manufactured,** as illustrated in Exhibit 2–3. This schedule shows the specific costs that have gone into the goods that have been manufactured during the period. Notice that it contains the three elements of cost—direct materials, direct labor, and manufacturing over-head—that we discussed earlier as being the costs that go into any produced item. Also notice at the bottom of the schedule that one must add the beginning work in process inventory to the production costs of a period and then deduct the ending work in process inventory in order to determine the cost of goods manufactured. **Work in process** means goods that are only partially completed at the beginning or at the end of a period.

EXHIBIT 2–3

Schedule of cost of goods manufactured

MANUFACTURING COMPANY
Schedule of Cost of Goods Manufactured
For the Year Ended May 31, 19xx

Direct materials:		
Beginning raw materials inventory	$ 20,000*	
Add: Purchases of raw materials.	165,000	
Raw materials available for use	185,000	
Deduct: Ending raw materials inventory	15,000	
Raw materials used in production		$170,000
Direct labor		300,000
Manufacturing overhead:		
Indirect materials	6,000	
Indirect labor	100,000	
Machine rental	50,000	
Utilities, factory	75,000	
Insurance, factory	21,000	
Depreciation, factory	90,000	
Property taxes, factory	8,000	
Total overhead costs		350,000
Total manufacturing costs		820,000
Add: Beginning work in process inventory		90,000
		910,000
Deduct: Ending work in process inventory		60,000
Cost of goods manufactured (see Exhibit 2–2) . . .		$850,000

* We assume in this example that the Raw Materials inventory account contains only direct materials, and that indirect materials are carried in a separate "Supplies" account. Using a "Supplies" account for indirect materials is a common practice among companies. In Chapter 3, we discuss the procedure to be followed if *both* direct and indirect materials are carried in a single account.

The Balance Sheet

The preparation of the balance sheet, or statement of financial position, is also more complex in a manufacturing company than in a merchandising company. A merchandising company has only one class of inventory—goods purchased from suppliers that are awaiting resale to customers. By contrast, manufacturing companies have three classes of inventory—goods purchased as raw materials to go into manufactured products (known as **raw materials**), goods only partially completed as to manufacturing at the end of a period (known as **work in process**), and goods completed as to manufacturing but not yet sold to customers (known as **finished goods**).

The current asset section of a manufacturing company's balance sheet is compared to the current asset section of a merchandising company's balance sheet in Exhibit 2–4. The inventory accounts shown in these current asset sections constitute the *only difference* between the balance sheets of the two types of companies.

EXHIBIT 2–4
Current asset data: Merchandising versus manufacturing companies

MERCHANDISING COMPANY

A single inventory account consisting of goods purchased from suppliers.

Current assets:		
Cash		$ 10,000
Accounts receivable		60,000
Merchandise inventory		150,000
Prepaid expenses		5,000
Total current assets		$225,000

MANUFACTURING COMPANY

Three inventory accounts consisting of materials to be used in production, goods partially manufactured, and goods completely manufactured.

Current assets:		
Cash		$ 15,000
Accounts receivable		100,000
Inventories:		
Raw materials	$ 15,000	
Work in process	60,000	
Finished goods	175,000	250,000
Prepaid expenses		10,000
Total current assets		$375,000

Product Costs—a Closer Look

Earlier in the chapter, we defined product costs as being the costs that are involved in either the purchase or the manufacture of goods. For manufactured goods, we stated that these costs consist of direct materials, direct labor, and manufacturing overhead. To understand product costs more fully, it will be helpful at this point to look briefly at the flow of costs in a manufacturing firm. By doing so, we will be able to see how product costs move through the various accounts and affect the balance sheet and the income statement in the course of the manufacture and sale of goods.

Exhibit 2–5 illustrates the flow of costs in a manufacturing firm. Notice that direct materials cost, direct labor cost, and manufacturing overhead cost are all added into Work in Process. Work in Process can be viewed most simply as the assembly line in a manufacturing plant, where workers are stationed and where products slowly take shape as they move from one end of the assembly line to the other. The direct materials, direct labor, and manufacturing overhead costs shown in Exhibit 2–5 as being added into Work in Process are the costs needed to complete these products as they move along this assembly line.

As goods are completed, notice from the exhibit that their cost is transferred from Work in Process into Finished Goods. Here the goods await sale to a customer. As goods are sold, their cost is then transferred from Finished Goods into Cost of Goods Sold. It is at this point that the various material, labor, and overhead costs that have been involved in the manufacture of the units being sold are treated as expenses in determining the net income or loss for the period.

EXHIBIT 2–5

Cost flows and classifications

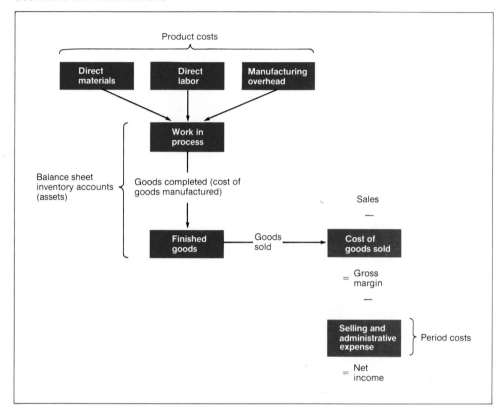

Product costs are often called **inventoriable costs.** The reason, of course, is that these costs go directly into inventory accounts as they are incurred (first into Work in Process and then into Finished Goods), rather than going into expense accounts. Thus, they are termed inventoriable costs. *This is a key concept in managerial accounting, since such costs can end up on the balance sheet as assets if goods are only partially completed or are unsold at the end of a period.* To illustrate this point, refer again to the data in Exhibit 2–5. The materials, labor, and overhead costs that are associated with the units in the Work in Process and Finished Goods inventory accounts at the end of a period will appear on the balance sheet at that time as part of the company's assets. As explained earlier, these costs will not become expenses until later when the goods are completed and sold.

As shown in Exhibit 2–5, selling and administrative expenses are not involved in the manufacture of a product. For this reason, they are not treated as product costs but as period costs and go directly into expense accounts as they are incurred.

EXHIBIT 2–6

An example of cost flows in a manufacturing company

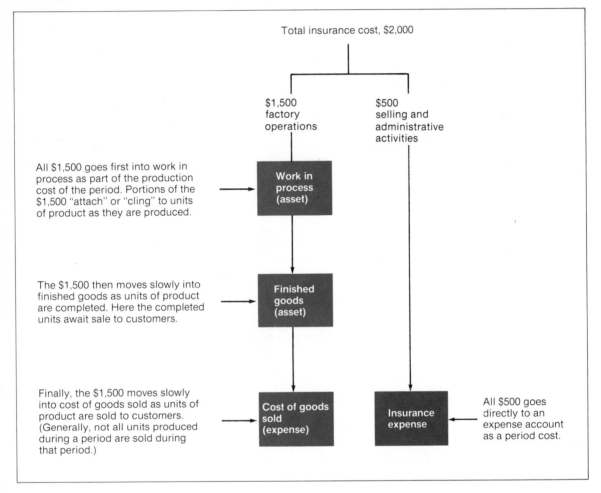

An example of cost flows   To provide a numerical example of cost flows in a manufacturing company, assume that a company's cost outlay for insurance is $2,000 annually, of which three fourths applies to operation of the factory and one fourth applies to selling and administrative activities. In this case, $1,500 (three fourths) of the $2,000 insurance cost would be a product (inventoriable) cost and would be added to the cost of the goods produced during the year. This concept is illustrated in Exhibit 2–6, where $1,500 of insurance cost is added into Work in Process. As shown in Exhibit 2–6, this portion of the year's insurance cost will not become an expense until the goods that are produced during the year are sold (sale may not take place until the following year). Until the goods are sold, the $1,500

EXHIBIT 2–7

A summary of product and period costs

Type of firm	Product costs	Period costs	Treatment
Merchandising firm	Cost of purchased inventory from suppliers		These costs are placed in an inventory account until the goods are sold. When sale takes place, the costs are then taken to expense as cost of goods sold.
Manufacturing firm	Direct materials Direct labor Manufacturing overhead (consists of all costs of production other than direct materials and direct labor)		These costs are placed in inventory accounts until the associated goods are completed and sold. When sale takes place, the costs are then taken (released) to expense as cost of goods sold.

Both merchandising and manufacturing firms		Selling expenses:
		    Salespeople's salaries
		    Depreciation on sales equipment
		    Insurance on sales equipment
		Administration expenses:
		    Secretarial salaries
		    Depreciation on office equipment
		    Insurance on office equipment
			These costs are taken directly to expense accounts. They are classified as operating expenses and deducted from gross margin.

[handwritten annotations: WIP → Finished Prod → when sold: Cost of goods]

[handwritten annotation: Product cost vs. Period cost — Summary of ...]

will remain as part of the asset inventory (either as part of Work in Process or as part of Finished Goods), along with the other costs of producing the goods.

By contrast, the $500 of insurance cost that applies to the company's selling and administrative activities will go into an expense account immediately as a charge against the period.

A summary of product and period costs   The chart in Exhibit 2–7 contains a summary of product and period costs in both manufacturing and merchandising firms. The reader should study this exhibit with care, noting particularly the treatment of each type of cost as shown in the extreme right column.

FURTHER CLASSIFICATION OF LABOR COSTS

Of all the costs of production, labor costs often present the most difficult problems of segregation and classification. Although firms vary considerably in their breakdown of labor costs, the following subdivisions represent the most common approach:

Direct labor	Indirect labor (part of manufacturing overhead)	Other labor costs
(Discussed earlier)	Janitors Supervisors Materials handlers Engineers Night security guards Maintenance workers	Idle time Overtime premium Labor fringe benefits

The costs listed under "Indirect labor" and under "Other labor costs" should not be viewed as being inclusive but rather as being representative of the kinds of costs that one might expect to find under these classifications. Certain of these costs require further comment.

Idle Time

Idle time represents the costs of direct labor workers who are unable to perform their assignments due to machine breakdowns, materials shortages, power failures, and the like. Although direct labor workers are involved, the costs of idle time are treated as part of manufacturing overhead cost rather than as part of direct labor cost. The reason is that managers feel that such costs should be spread over *all* the production of a period rather than just over the jobs that happen to be in process when breakdowns and the like occur.

To give an example of how the cost of idle time is computed, assume that a press operator earns $12 per hour. If the press operator is paid for a normal 40-hour workweek but is idle for 3 hours during a given week due to breakdowns, labor cost would be allocated as follows:

Direct labor ($12 × 37 hours)	$444
Manufacturing overhead (idle time: $12 × 3 hours)	36
Total cost for the week	$480

Overtime Premium

The overtime premium paid to *all* factory workers (direct labor as well as indirect labor) is usually considered to be part of manufacturing overhead and not assignable to any particular order or batch of production. At first glance this may seem strange, since overtime is always spent working on some particular order. Why not charge that order for the overtime cost? The reason is that production is usually scheduled on a random basis. If production is randomly scheduled, then it would be unfair to charge an overtime premium against a particular batch of goods simply because the batch *happened* to fall on the tail end of the daily scheduling sheet.

To illustrate, assume that two batches of goods, order A and order B, each take three hours to complete. The production run on order A is scheduled early in the day, but the production run on order B isn't scheduled until late in the afternoon. By the time the run on order B is completed, two hours of overtime have been logged in. The necessity to work overtime was a result of the fact that *total* production exceeded the regular time available. Order B was no more responsible for the overtime than was order A. Therefore, all production should share in the premium charge that resulted. This is a much more equitable way of handling overtime premium in that it doesn't penalize one run simply because it happens to fall late in the day.

Let us again assume that a press operator in a plant earns $12 per hour. He is paid time and a half for overtime (time in excess of 40 hours a week). During a given week he works 45 hours and has no idle time. His labor cost for the week would be allocated as follows:

Direct labor ($12 × 45 hours)	$540
Manufacturing overhead (overtime premium: $6 × 5 hours) . . .	30
Total cost for the week	$570

Observe from this computation that only the overtime premium of $6 per hour is charged to the overhead account—*not* the entire $18 earned for each hour of overtime work ($12 regular rate × 1.5 = $18).

Labor Fringe Benefits

The proper classification of labor fringe benefits is not so clearly defined in practice as is idle time or overtime premium. Labor fringe benefits are made up of employment-related costs paid by the employer and include the costs of insurance programs, retirement plans, various supplemental unemployment benefits, and hospitalization plans. Many firms treat all such costs as indirect labor by adding them in total to manufacturing overhead. Other firms treat that portion of fringe benefits that relates to direct labor as additional direct labor cost. This approach is conceptually superior since the fringe benefits provided to direct labor workers clearly represent an added cost of their services.

The cost to the employer for fringe benefits is substantial. A recent nationwide survey by the Chamber of Commerce shows that fringe benefits, on the average, cost 37 cents for every dollar of gross wages.

COSTS AND CONTROL

The cost classifications that are used to prepare financial statements may not be the same cost classifications that a manager uses to control operations and to plan for the future. For control purposes, costs are often classified as being variable or fixed, direct or indirect, and controllable or noncontrollable.

Variable and Fixed Costs

From a planning and control standpoint, perhaps the most useful way to classify costs is by behavior. **Cost behavior** means how a cost will react or respond to changes in the level of business activity. As the activity level rises and falls, a particular cost may rise and fall as well—or it may remain constant. For planning purposes, the manager must be able to anticipate which of these will happen, and if a cost can be expected to change, he or she must know by how much. To provide this information, costs are classified into two categories—variable and fixed.

Variable costs　**Variable costs** are costs that vary, in total, in direct proportion to changes in the level of activity. A good example of a variable cost is direct materials. The cost of direct materials used during a period will vary, in total, in direct proportion to the number of units that are produced. To illustrate this idea, assume that a company produces automobiles and that each auto produced requires one battery. As the output of autos increases and decreases, the number of batteries used will increase and decrease proportionately. If auto production goes up 10 percent, then the number of batteries used will go up 10 percent as well.

It is important to note that when we speak of a cost as being variable, we do so in terms of its *total dollar amount*—the total cost rises and falls as the activity level rises and falls. This idea is presented below, assuming that batteries cost $10 each:

Number of autos produced	Cost per battery	Total variable cost— batteries
1	$10	$　　10
10	10	100
100	10	1,000
1,000	10	10,000

One interesting aspect of variable cost behavior is that a variable cost is constant if expressed on a *per unit* basis. Observe from the tabulation above that the per unit cost of batteries remains constant at $10 even though the total amount of cost involved increases and decreases with activity.

There are many examples of variable costs. In a manufacturing firm, they would include direct materials, direct labor, and some items of manufacturing overhead (such as utilities, supplies, and lubricants). In a merchandising firm, they would include cost of goods sold, commissions to salespersons, and billing costs.

Fixed costs　**Fixed costs** are costs that remain constant in total, regardless of changes in the level of activity. That is, unlike variable costs, fixed costs are not affected by changes in activity from period to period. Consequently, as the activity level rises and falls, the fixed costs remain constant in total amount unless influenced by some outside force, such as price changes. Rent is a good example of a fixed cost. If the monthly rental cost of a machine is $5,000, then that amount of cost will be sustained regardless of the number of units that may be produced by the machine in a given month.

The presence of fixed costs in an organization can create difficulties if it becomes necessary to express the costs on a per unit basis. This is because if fixed costs are expressed on a per unit basis, they will react *inversely* with changes in activity. In a manufacturing company, for example, the average cost per unit of product will fall as production increases, since the fixed costs will be spread over more units. Conversely, as production declines, the average cost per unit will rise as the fixed costs are spread over fewer units. This idea is illustrated below, assuming again a monthly rental cost of $5,000 for a machine that is capable of producing up to 1,000 units of product each month.

Fixed costs causes difficulties when need to allocate it per unit.
P↑ = FC spread out more evenly
P↓ = FC/unit will rise

→ eg.
10 units → $500
1000 " → $5.

Monthly rental cost	Number of units produced	Average cost per unit
$5,000	10	$500
5,000	100	50
5,000	1,000	5

Note that if the company produces only 10 units each month, the rental cost will average $500 per unit. But if 1,000 units are produced each month, the average cost will drop to only $5 per unit. More will be said later on the problems created for both the accountant and the manager by this type of variation in unit costs.

Examples of fixed costs include depreciation, insurance, property taxes, rent, supervisory salaries, and advertising.

eg. of fixed costs

Summary of variable and fixed costs   Understanding the behavior of variable and fixed costs is one of the most difficult parts of this chapter. To assist in this understanding, a summary of both variable and fixed cost behavior is presented in Exhibit 2–8. Study this exhibit with care, along with the material in the preceding paragraphs, until you thoroughly understand the concepts involved.

Direct and Indirect Costs

Costs are often classified as being either direct or indirect. However, these terms have no meaning unless one first identifies some organizational segment to which the costs are to be related. The organizational segment might be a product line, a sales territory, a division, or some other subpart of a company. A **direct cost** is a cost that can be obviously and physically traced to the particular segment under consideration. For example, if the segment under consideration is a product line, then the materials and labor involved in the manufacture of the line would both be direct costs.

EXHIBIT 2–8
Summary of variable and fixed cost behavior

| | Behavior of the cost | |
Cost	In total	Per unit
Variable cost	Total variable cost increases and decreases in proportion to changes in the activity level.	Variable costs remain constant per unit.
Fixed cost	Total fixed cost is not affected by changes in the activity level (i.e., total fixed cost remains constant even if the activity level changes).	Fixed costs decrease per unit as the activity level rises and increase per unit as the activity level falls.

An **indirect cost** is a cost that must be allocated in order to be assigned to the segment under consideration. Manufacturing overhead, for example, would be an indirect cost of a product line. The reason is that manufacturing overhead is not directly identifiable with any particular product line but rather is incurred as a consequence of general, overall operating activities. Indirect costs are also known as *common costs*.

In sum, the following guidelines prevail in distinguishing between direct and indirect (common) costs:

1. If a cost can be obviously and physically traced to a unit of product or some other organizational segment, then it is a direct cost with respect to that segment.
2. If a cost must be allocated in order to be assigned to a unit of product or some other organizational segment, then it is an indirect (common) cost with respect to that segment.

Controllable and Noncontrollable Costs

As with direct and indirect costs, whether a cost is controllable or noncontrollable depends on the point of reference. *All* costs are controllable at some level or another in a company. Only at the lower levels of management can some costs be considered noncontrollable. Top management has the power to expand or contract facilities, hire, fire, set expenditure policies, and generally exercise control over any cost as it desires. At lower levels of management, however, authority may not exist to control the incurrence of some costs, and these costs will therefore be considered noncontrollable *so far as that level of management is concerned.*

A cost is considered to be a **controllable cost** at a particular level of management if that level has power to *authorize* the cost. For example, entertainment expense would be controllable by a sales manager if he or she had power to authorize the amount and type of entertainment for customers. On the other hand, depreciation of warehouse facilities would not be controllable by the sales manager, since he or she would have no power to authorize warehouse construction.

In some situations, there is a time dimension to controllability. Costs that are controllable over the long run may not be controllable over the short run. A good example is advertising. Once an advertising program has been set and a contract signed, management has no power to change the amount of spending. But when the contract expires, advertising costs can be renegotiated, and thus management can exercise control over the long run. Another example is plant acquisition. Management is free to build any size plant it desires, but once a plant has been built, management is largely powerless to change the attendant costs over the short run.

OTHER COST CONCEPTS

There are three other cost concepts with which we should be familiar as we start our study of managerial accounting. These concepts are differential costs, opportunity costs, and sunk costs.

Differential Costs

In making decisions, managers compare the alternatives before them. Each alternative will have certain costs associated with it that must be compared to the costs associated with the other alternatives available. Any cost that is present under one alternative but is absent in whole or in part under another alternative is known as a **differential cost.** Differential costs are also known as **incremental costs,** although technically an incremental cost should refer only to an increase in cost from one alternative to another; decreases in cost should be referred to as *decremental costs.* Differential cost is a broader term, encompassing both cost increases (incremental costs) and cost decreases (decremental costs) between alternatives.

The accountant's differential cost concept can be compared to the economist's marginal cost concept. In speaking of changes in cost and revenue, the economist employs the terms *marginal cost* and *marginal revenue.* The revenue that can be obtained from selling one more unit of product is called marginal revenue, and the cost involved in producing one more unit of product is called marginal cost. The economist's marginal concept is basically the same as the accountant's differential concept.

Differential costs can be either fixed or variable. To illustrate, assume that Cosmetics, Inc., is thinking about changing its marketing method from distribution through retailers to distribution by direct sale. Present costs and revenues are compared to projected costs and revenues below:

	Retailer distribution (present)	Direct sale distribution (proposed)	Differential costs and revenues
Revenues (V)	$700,000	$800,000	$100,000
Cost of goods sold (V)	350,000	400,000	50,000
Advertising (F)	80,000	45,000	(35,000)
Commissions (V)	–0–	40,000	40,000
Warehouse depreciation (F)	50,000	80,000	30,000
Other expenses (F)	60,000	60,000	–0–
Total	540,000	625,000	85,000
Net income	$160,000	$175,000	$ 15,000

V = variable; F = fixed.

The differential revenue is $100,000, and the differential costs total $85,000, leaving a positive differential net income of $15,000 under the proposed marketing plan. As noted earlier, those differential costs representing cost increases could have been referred to more specifically as incremental costs, and those representing cost decreases could have been referred to more specifically as decremental costs. The reader should be acquainted with all of these terms, since they are widely used in day-to-day business practice.

Opportunity Costs

An **opportunity cost** can be defined as the potential benefit that is lost or sacrificed when the selection of one course of action makes it necessary to give up a competing course of action. To illustrate, consider the following:

Example 1

Vicki has a part-time job that pays her $100 per week. She would like to spend a week at the beach during spring vacation from school, but she has no vacation time available. If she takes the trip anyway, the $100 in lost wages will be an opportunity cost of doing so.

Example 2

A firm is considering the investment of a large sum of money in land that is to be held for future expansion. Rather than being invested in land, the funds could be invested in high-grade securities. If the land is acquired, the opportunity cost will be the investment income that could have been realized if the securities had been purchased instead.

Example 3

Steve is employed with a company that pays him a salary of $20,000 per year. He is thinking about leaving the company in order to return to school. Since returning to school would require that he give up his $20,000 salary, the forgone salary would be an opportunity cost of seeking further education.

Opportunity cost is not usually entered on the books of an organization, but it is a cost that must be explicitly considered in every decision a manager makes. Virtually every alternative has some opportunity cost attached to it. In example 3 above, for instance, if Steve decides to stay at his job there still is an opportunity cost involved: it is the greater income that could be realized in future years as a result of returning to school.

In short, every alternative course of action facing a manager has a mixture of good and bad features. In rejecting a course of action, the good features must be given up along with the bad. The net good features of a rejected alternative become the opportunity costs of the alternative that is selected.

Sunk Costs

Sunk cost — when cost cannot be recovered.

A **sunk cost** is a cost *that has already been incurred* and that cannot be changed by any decision made now or in the future. Since sunk costs cannot be changed by any present or future decision, they are not differential costs, and therefore they should not be used in analyzing future courses of action.

To illustrate the notion of a sunk cost, assume that a firm has just paid $50,000 for a special-purpose machine. Since the cost outlay *has been made,* the $50,000 investment in the machine is a sunk cost. Even though by hindsight the purchase may have been unwise, no amount of regret can relieve the company of its decision, nor can any future decision cause the cost to be avoided. In short, the $50,000 is "out the window" from a decision point of view and will have to be reckoned with regardless of what future course of action the company may take. For this reason, such costs are said to be sunk.

SUMMARY

Although the term *cost* has a fairly distinctive meaning in financial accounting, it can be used in many different ways in managerial accounting. In this chapter, we have looked at some of the ways in which it is used by the manager in order to organize and classify data.

We have learned that costs can be classified as being either period costs or product costs. Period costs are incurred as a function of time rather than as a function of the purchase or the manufacture of goods. Product costs, by contrast, are those costs involved in the purchase of goods in a merchandising firm or the manufacture of goods in a manufacturing firm.

In a manufacturing situation, product costs consist of all costs associated with operating the factory; these would include direct materials, direct labor, and manufacturing overhead. These costs go first into Work in Process. As goods are completed, the costs come out of Work in Process and go into Finished Goods. As goods are shipped to customers, the costs come out of Finished Goods and go into Cost of Goods Sold. The costs of partially completed or unsold goods appear on the balance sheet of a manufacturing company as assets in the form of work in process inventory or in the form of finished goods inventory.

We have found that costs can also be classified as being either variable or fixed, direct or indirect, and controllable or noncontrollable. In addition, we defined differential costs, opportunity costs, and sunk costs. A differential cost is the difference in cost between two alternatives. An opportunity cost is the benefit that is forgone in rejecting some course of action, and a sunk cost is a cost that has already been incurred.

All of these cost terms and classifications are basic to managerial accounting. We shall use them repeatedly, as well as refine them further, in chapters ahead.

REVIEW PROBLEM ON COST TERMS

Many new cost terms have been introduced in this chapter. It will take you some time to learn what each term means and to learn how to properly classify costs in an organization. To assist in this learning process, consider the following example: Porter Company manufactures a number of furniture products, including tables. Selected costs associated with the manufacture of the tables and associated with the general operations of the company are given below:

1. Wood is used in the manufacture of the tables, at a cost of $100 per table.
2. The tables are assembled by workers, at a cost of $40 per table.
3. Workers assembling the tables are supervised by a factory supervisor who is paid $25,000 per year.
4. Electrical costs of $2 per labor-hour are incurred in the factory in the manufacture of the tables. (It requires four labor-hours to produce a table.)
5. The depreciation cost of the machines used in the manufacture of the tables totals $10,000 per year.
6. The salary of the president of Porter Company is $100,000 per year.
7. Porter Company spends $250,000 per year to advertise its products.
8. Salespersons are paid a commission of $30 for each table sold.
9. Instead of producing the tables, Porter Company could rent its factory space out at a rental income of $50,000 per year.

In the tabulation on the following page, these costs are classified according to various cost terms used in the chapter. *Carefully study the classification of each cost.* If you don't understand why a particular cost is classified the way it is, turn back and read the section of the chapter dealing with the cost term involved.

Solution to the review problem

	Variable cost	Fixed cost	Period (selling and administrative) cost	Product cost — Direct materials	Product cost — Direct labor	Product cost — Manufacturing overhead	To units of product — Direct	To units of product — Indirect	Sunk cost	Opportunity cost
1. Wood used in a table (at $100 per table)	X			X			X			
2. Labor cost to assemble a table (at $40 per table)	X-				X		X			
3. Salary of the factory supervisor (at $25,000 per year)		X				X		X		
4. Cost of electricity to produce tables (at $2 per labor-hour)	X					X		X		
5. Depreciation of machines used to produce tables (at $10,000 per year)		X				X		X	X*	
6. Salary of the company president (at $100,000 per year)		X	X							
7. Advertising expense (at $250,000 per year)		X	X							
8. Commissions paid to salespersons (at $30 per table sold)	X		X							
9. Rental income forgone on factory space										X†

*This is a sunk cost since the outlay for the equipment was made in some previous period.

†This is an opportunity cost since it represents the potential benefit that is lost or sacrificed as a result of using the factory space to produce tables. Notice that the cost is not classified as a fixed cost or in any other way. Such classifications are of no significance, since opportunity costs are not recorded on the books of an organization.

KEY TERMS FOR REVIEW

Administrative costs All executive, organizational, and clerical costs associated with the general management of an organization.

Common costs See Indirect cost.

Controllable costs A cost is controllable at a particular level of management if that level has power to authorize the cost.

Conversion cost The term used to describe direct labor cost combined with manufacturing overhead cost.

Cost behavior The way in which a cost will react or respond to changes in the level of business activity.

Cost of goods manufactured The materials, labor, and overhead costs that have gone into the products that have been produced during a period.

Differential cost Any cost that is present under one alternative but is absent in whole or in part under another alternative in a decision-making situation. Also see *Incremental cost.*

Direct cost A cost that can be obviously and physically traced to a unit of product or other organizational segment.

Direct labor Those factory labor costs that can be physically traced to the creation of products in a ''hands on'' sense.

Direct materials Those materials that become an integral part of a finished product and that can be conveniently traced into it.

Finished goods Goods that are completed as to manufacturing but not yet sold to customers.

Fixed cost A cost that remains constant, in total, regardless of changes in the level of activity. If a fixed cost is expressed on a per unit basis, it varies inversely with the level of activity.

Incremental cost An increase in cost between two alternatives. Also see *Differential cost.*

Indirect cost A cost that must be allocated in order to be assigned to a unit of product or some other organizational segment. An indirect cost is also known as a *common cost.*

Indirect labor The factory labor costs of janitors, supervisors, engineers, and others that cannot be traced directly to the creation of products in a ''hands on'' sense.

Indirect materials Small items of material such as glue and nails that may become an integral part of a finished product but that are traceable into the product only at great cost or inconvenience.

Inventoriable costs All costs that are involved in the purchase or manufacture of goods. In the case of manufactured goods, these costs consist of direct materials, direct labor, and manufacturing overhead costs used in the production process. Also see *Product costs.*

Manufacturing The conversion of raw materials into finished products through the efforts of factory workers and the use of production equipment.

Manufacturing overhead All costs associated with the manufacturing process except direct materials and direct labor.

Marketing or selling costs All costs necessary to secure customer orders and get the finished product or service into the hands of the customer. This term is synonymous with *order-getting and order-filling costs.*

Merchandising The sale of products that are in finished form and that have been acquired from a manufacturer or other outside source.

Opportunity cost The potential benefit that is lost or sacrificed when the selection of one course of action makes it necessary to give up a competing course of action.

Order-getting and order-filling costs All costs necessary to secure customer orders and get the finished product or service into the hands of the customer. This term is synonymous with *marketing or selling costs.*

Period costs All costs that are matched against revenues on a time period basis; such costs consist of selling (marketing) and administrative expenses.

Prime cost The term used to describe direct materials cost combined with direct labor cost.

Product costs All costs that are involved in the purchase of manufacture of goods. In the case of manufactured goods, these costs consist of direct materials, direct labor, and manufacturing overhead. Also see *Inventoriable costs.*

Raw materials Any materials going into a manufactured product.

Sunk cost Any cost that has already been incurred and that can't be changed by any decision made now or in the future.

Variable cost A cost that varies, in total, in direct proportion to changes in the level of activity. A variable cost is constant per unit.

Work in process Goods that are only partially completed as to manufacturing at the beginning or end of a period and that will need further work before being ready for sale to a customer.

QUESTIONS

2–1.   Distinguish between merchandising and manufacturing.

2–2.   What are the three major elements in the cost of a manufactured product?

2–3.   Distinguish between the following: *(a)* direct materials, *(b)* indirect materials, *(c)* direct labor, *(d)* indirect labor, and *(e)* manufacturing overhead.

2–4.   Explain the difference between a product cost and a period cost.

2–5.   Describe how the income statement of a manufacturing company differs from the income statement of a merchandising company.

2–6.   Of what value is the schedule of cost of goods manufactured? How does it tie into the income statement?

2–7.   Distinguish between prime cost and conversion cost. What is meant by conversion cost?

2–8.   Describe how the balance sheet of a manufacturing company differs from the balance sheet of a merchandising company so far as current assets are concerned.

2–9.   Why are product costs sometimes called inventoriable costs? Describe the flow of such costs in a manufacturing company from the point of incurrence until they finally become expenses on the income statement.

why costs get put in WIP ∴ on B/S.

Yes **2–10.**   Is it possible for costs such as salaries or depreciation to end up as assets on the balance sheet? Explain.

O/H, overhead, indirect, mfg overhead **2–11.**   Give at least three terms that may be substituted for the term *manufacturing overhead*.

direct labour — only when doing work **2–12.**   Mary Adams is employed by Acme Company. Last week she worked 34 hours
idle, set-up time etc →O/H. assembling one of the company's products and was idle 6 hours due to material shortages. Acme's employees are engaged at their workstations for a normal 40-hour week. Ms. Adams is paid $8 per hour. Allocate her earnings between direct labor cost and manufacturing overhead cost.

2–13.   John Olsen operates a stamping machine on the assembly line of the Drake Manufacturing Company. Last week Mr. Olsen worked 45 hours. His basic wage rate is $5 per hour, with time and a half for overtime (time worked in excess of 40 hours per week). How should last week's wage cost be allocated between direct labor cost and manufacturing overhead cost?

Δ in cost given Δ in activity → **2–14.**   What is meant by the term *cost behavior?*

False **2–15.**   "A variable cost is a cost that varies per unit of product, whereas a fixed cost is constant per unit of product." Do you agree? Explain.

in allocating the amount w respect to A in activity **2–16.**   How do fixed costs create difficulties in costing units of product?

2–17.   Why is manufacturing overhead considered an indirect cost of a unit of product?

2–18.   Under what conditions is a cost controllable at a particular level of management?

2–19.   Define the following terms: differential cost, opportunity cost, and sunk cost.

False **2–20.**   Only variable costs can be differential costs. Do you agree? Explain.

EXERCISES

E2–1.   The following cost and inventory data are taken from the books of Mason Company for the year 19x8:

Costs incurred:

Direct labor cost	$ 70,000
Purchases of raw materials	118,000
Indirect labor	30,000
Maintenance, factory equipment	6,000
Advertising expense	90,000
Insurance, factory equipment	800
Sales salaries	50,000
Rent, factory facilities	20,000
Indirect materials	4,200
Depreciation, office equipment	3,000
Depreciation, factory equipment	19,000

	January 1, 19x8	December 31, 19x8
Inventories:		
Raw materials	$ 7,000	$15,000
Work in process	10,000	5,000
Finished goods	20,000	35,000

Required: 1.   Prepare a schedule of cost of goods manufactured in good form.

2.   Prepare the cost of goods sold section of Mason Company's income statement for the year.

E2–2.   The Devon Motor Company produces automobiles. During April 19x5, the company purchased 8,000 batteries at a cost of $10 per battery. Devon withdrew 7,600 batteries from the storeroom during the month. Of these, 100 were used to replace batteries in autos being used by the company's traveling sales staff. The remaining 7,500 batteries withdrawn from the storeroom were placed in autos being produced by the company. Of the autos in production during April, 90 percent were completed and transferred from work in process to finished goods. Of the cars completed during the month, 30 percent were unsold at April 30.

There were no inventories of any type on April 1, 19x5.

Required: 1.   Determine the cost of batteries that would appear in each of the following accounts at April 30, 19x5:
  a.   Raw Materials.
  b.   Work in Process.
  c.   Finished Goods.
  d.   Cost of Goods Sold.
  e.   Selling Expense.
  2.   Specify whether each of the above accounts would appear on the balance sheet or on the income statement at April 30.

E2–3.   Following are a number of cost terms introduced in the chapter:

Variable cost	Product cost
Fixed cost	Sunk cost
Prime cost	Conversion cost
Opportunity cost	Period cost

Choose the term or terms above that most appropriately describe the cost identified in each of the following situations. A cost term can be used more than once.

  1.   Lake Company produces a tote bag that is very popular with college students. The cloth going into the manufacture of the tote bag would be called direct materials and classified as a _____ cost. In terms of cost behavior, the cloth could also be described as a _____ cost.
  2.   The direct labor cost required to produce the tote bags, combined with the manufacturing overhead cost involved, would be known as _____ cost.
  3.   The company could have taken the funds that it has invested in production equipment and invested them in interest-bearing securities instead. The interest forgone on the securities would be called _____ cost.
  4.   Taken together, the direct materials cost and the direct labor cost required to produce tote bags would be called _____ cost.
  5.   The company used to produce a smaller tote bag that was not very popular. Some three hundred of these smaller bags are stored in one of the company's warehouses. The amount invested in these bags would be called a _____ cost.
  6.   The tote bags are sold through agents who are paid a commission on each bag sold. These commissions would be classified by Lake Company as a _____ cost. In terms of cost behavior, commissions would be classified as a _____ cost.
  7.   Depreciation on the equipment used to produce tote bags would be classified by Lake Company as a _____ cost. However, deprecia-

tion on any equipment used by the company in selling and administrative activities would be classified as a _____ cost. In terms of cost behavior, depreciation would probably be classified as a _____ cost.

8. A _____ cost is also known as an inventoriable cost, since such costs go into the work in process inventory account and then into the finished goods inventory account before appearing on the income statement as part of cost of goods sold.

9. The salary of Lake Company's president would be classified as a _____ cost, since the salary will appear on the income statement as an expense in the time period in which it is incurred.

10. Costs can often be classified in several ways. For example, Lake Company pays $5,000 rent each month on its factory building. The rent would be part of manufacturing overhead. In terms of cost behavior, it would be classified as a _____ cost. The rent can also be classified as a _____ cost and as part of _____ cost.

E2–4.   Below are a number of costs that might be incurred in a manufacturing or service organization. Copy the list of costs down on your answer sheet, and then place an X in the appropriate column for each cost to indicate whether the cost involved would be variable or fixed.

		Cost behavior	
Cost		**Variable**	**Fixed**
1. Steering wheels used in automobile production . . .			
2. Straight-line depreciation of a building			
3. Product advertising			
4. Electrical costs of running machines			
5. Top-management salaries			
6. X-ray film in a hospital			
7. Commissions to salespersons			
8. Property taxes on a factory building			
9. Direct labor workers in a factory			
10. Rent on a doctor's office			

E2–5.   Several days ago you took your TV set into a shop to have some repair work done. When you later picked up the set, the bill showed a $75 charge for labor. This charge represented two hours of service time—$30 for the first hour and $45 for the second hour.

When questioned about the difference in hourly rates, the shop manager explained that work on your set was started at 4 o'clock in the afternoon. By the time work was completed two hours later at 6 o'clock, an hour of overtime had been put in by the repair technician. The manager further explained that the $45 charge for the second hour therefore contained an ''overtime premium'' since the company had to pay the repair technician time and a half for any work in excess of eight hours and also had to maintain its normal profit margin.

Required: 1. Do you agree with the shop's computation of the service charge on your job?
2. Assume that the shop pays its technicians $14 per hour. Prepare computations to show how the cost of the repair technician's time for the day (nine hours)

should be allocated between direct labor cost and general overhead cost on the shop's books.

3. Under what circumstances might the shop be justified in charging an overtime premium for repair work on your set?

E2–6. A product cost is also known as an inventoriable cost. Classify the following costs as being either product (inventoriable) costs or period (noninventoriable) costs in a manufacturing company:

1. Depreciation on salespersons' cars.
2. Rent on equipment used in the factory.
3. Lubricants used for maintenance of machines.
4. Salaries of finished goods warehouse personnel.
5. Soap and paper towels used by workers at the end of a shift.
6. Factory supervisors' salaries.
7. Heat, water, and power consumed in the factory.
8. Materials used in boxing units of finished product for shipment overseas. (Units are not normally boxed.)
9. Advertising outlays.
10. Workers' compensation insurance.
11. Depreciation on chairs and tables in the factory lunchroom.
12. The salary of the switchboard operator for the company.
13. Depreciation on a Lear Jet used by the company's executives.
14. Rent on rooms at a Florida resort for holding of the annual sales conference.
15. Attractively designed box for packaging breakfast cereal.

E2–7. Fred Austin is employed by White Company. He works on the company's assembly line and assembles a component part for one of the company's products. Fred is paid $12 per hour for regular time, and he is paid time and a half for all work in excess of 40 hours per week.

Required:

1. Assume that during a given week Fred is idle for two hours due to machine breakdowns and that he is idle for four more hours due to material shortages. No overtime is recorded for the week. Allocate Fred's wages for the week as between direct labor cost and manufacturing overhead cost.

2. Assume that during a following week Fred works a total of 50 hours. He has no idle time for the week. Allocate Fred's wages for the week as between direct labor cost and manufacturing overhead cost.

3. Fred's company provides an attractive package of fringe benefits for its employees. This package includes a retirement program and a health insurance program. So far as direct labor workers are concerned, explain two ways that the company could handle the costs of fringe benefits in its cost records.

E2–8. The following information has been taken from the cost records of Arbor Company for the month of March 19x7:

Insurance, factory equipment	$ 500
Insurance, office equipment	300
Direct labor cost	90,000
Purchases of raw materials	130,000
Indirect labor cost	29,000
Indirect materials cost	4,000
Depreciation, office equipment	2,000
Rent, factory facilities	17,000
Maintenance, factory equipment	3,000

Depreciation, factory equipment	6,500
Advertising expense	100,000
Raw materials inventory, March 1	20,000
Raw materials inventory, March 31.	10,000
Work in process inventory, March 1	30,000
Work in process inventory, March 31	40,000
Finished goods inventory, March 1	56,000
Finished goods inventory, March 31	41,000

Required: 1.   Prepare a schedule of cost of goods manufactured for March 19x7.
2.   Prepare the cost of goods sold section of the company's income statement for the month.

PROBLEMS

P2–9.   **Cost classification.**   Various costs associated with the operation of a factory are given below:
1.   Electricity used in operating machines.
2.   Rent on a factory building.
3.   Cloth used in drapery production.
4.   Production superintendent's salary.
5.   Cost of laborers assembling a product.
6.   Glue used in furniture production.
7.   Janitorial salaries.
8.   Peaches used in canning fruit.
9.   Lubricants needed for machines.
10.   Sugar used in soft drink production.
11.   Property taxes on the factory.
12.   Cost of workers painting a product.
13.   Depreciation of cafeteria equipment.
14.   Solder used in producing TV sets.
15.   Cabinets used in producing TV sets.

Required: Classify each cost as being either variable or fixed with respect to volume or level of activity. Also classify each cost as being either direct or indirect with respect to units of product. Prepare your answer sheet as shown below:

	Cost behavior		To units of product	
Cost item	**Variable**	**Fixed**	**Direct**	**Indirect**
Example: Factory insurance		X		X

If you are unsure whether a cost would be variable or fixed, consider how it would behave over fairly wide ranges of activity.

P2–10.   **Cost identification.**   Ridge Company acquired its factory building about 10 years ago. For several years the company has rented out a small annex attached to the rear of the building. Ridge Company has received a rental income of $30,000 per year on this space. The renter's lease will expire soon, and rather than renewing the lease, Ridge Company has decided to use the space itself to manufacture a new product.

Direct materials cost for the new product will total $80 per unit. In order to have a place to store finished units of product, the company will rent a small warehouse nearby. The rental cost will be $500 per month. In addition, the company must rent equipment for use in producing the new product; the rental cost will be $4,000 per month. Workers will be hired to manufacture the new product, with direct labor cost amounting to $60 per unit. The space in the annex will continue to be depreciated on a straight-line basis, as in prior years. This depreciation is $8,000 per year.

Advertising costs for the new product will total $50,000 per month. A supervisor will be hired to oversee production; her salary will be $1,500 per month. Electricity for operating machines will be $1.20 per unit. Costs of shipping the new product to customers will be $9 per unit.

In order to have funds to purchase materials, meet payrolls, and so forth, the company will have to liquidate some temporary investments. These investments are presently yielding a return of about $3,000 per year.

Required: Prepare an answer sheet with the following column headings:

Name of the cost	Variable cost	Fixed cost	Product cost			Period (selling and adminis- trative) cost	Oppor- tunity cost	Sunk cost
			Direct materials	Direct labor	Manufacturing overhead			

List the different costs associated with the new product decision down the extreme left column (under "Name of the cost"). Then place an X under each heading that helps to describe the type of cost involved. There may be X's under several column headings for a single cost. (For example, a cost may be a fixed cost, a period cost, and a sunk cost; you would place an X under each of these column headings opposite the cost.)

P2–11.   **Allocating labor costs.**   Mark Hansen is employed by Eastern Products, Inc., and works on the company's assembly line. Mark's basic wage rate is $10 per hour. The company's union contract states that employees are to be paid time and a half for any work in excess of 40 hours per week. Answer the following questions:

1.   Suppose that in a given week Mark works 46 hours. Compute Mark's total wages for the week. How much of this amount would be allocated to direct labor cost? To manufacturing overhead cost?

2.   Suppose in another week that Mark works 48 hours but is idle for 3 hours during the week due to machine breakdowns. Compute Mark's total wages for the week. How much of this amount would be allocated to direct labor cost? To manufacturing overhead cost?

3.   Eastern Products, Inc., has an attractive package of fringe benefits that costs the company $3 for each hour of employee time (either regular time or overtime). During a particular week, Mark works 50 hours but is idle for 2 hours due to material shortages. Compute Mark's total wages and fringe benefits for the week. If the company treats all fringe benefits as part of manufacturing overhead cost, how much of Mark's wages and fringe benefits for the week would be allocated to direct labor cost? To manufacturing overhead cost?

4. Refer to the data in (3) above. If the company treats that part of fringe benefits relating to direct labor as added direct labor cost, how much of Mark's wages and fringe benefits for the week will be allocated to direct labor cost? To manufacturing overhead cost?

P2–12. **Schedule of cost of goods manufactured; cost behavior.**   Various sales and cost data for Meriwell Company for 19x6 are given below:

Finished goods inventory, January 1	$ 20,000
Finished goods inventory, December 31	40,000
Depreciation, factory	27,000
Administrative expenses	110,000
Utilities, factory	8,000
Maintenance, factory	40,000
Indirect materials	11,000
Insurance, factory	4,000
Purchases of raw materials	75,000
Raw materials inventory, January 1	9,000
Raw materials inventory, December 31	6,000
Direct labor	120,000
Indirect labor	15,000
Work in process inventory, January 1	17,000
Work in process inventory, December 31	30,000
Sales	500,000
Selling expenses	80,000

Required: 1. Prepare a schedule of cost of goods manufactured for 19x6.
2. Prepare an income statement for 19x6.
3. Assume that the company produced the equivalent of 10,000 units of product during 19x6. What was the unit cost for direct materials? What was the unit cost for factory depreciation?
4. Assume that the company expects to produce 15,000 units of product during the coming year. What total cost and what per unit cost would you expect the company to incur for direct materials at this level of activity? For factory depreciation? (In preparing your answer, assume that direct materials is a variable cost and that depreciation is a fixed cost; also assume that depreciation is computed on a straight-line basis.)
5. As the manager responsible for production costs, explain to the president any difference in unit costs between (3) and (4) above.

P2–13. **Supply missing production and cost data.**   Supply the missing data in the cases below. Each case is independent of the others.

	Case			
	1	**2**	**3**	**4**
Direct materials	$ 4,500	$ 6,000	$ 5,000	$ 3,000
Direct labor	?	3,000	7,000	4,000
Manufacturing overhead	5,000	4,000	?	9,000
Total manufacturing costs	18,500	?	20,000	?
Beginning work in process inventory . .	2,500	?	3,000	?
Ending work in process inventory . . .	?	1,000	4,000	3,000
Cost of goods manufactured	$ 18,000	$ 14,000	$?	$?

Sales	$30,000	$21,000	$36,000	$40,000
Beginning finished goods inventory . .	1,000	2,500	?	2,000
Cost of goods manufactured	?	?	?	17,500
Goods available for sale	?	?	?	?
Ending finished goods inventory. . . .	?	1,500	4,000	3,500
Cost of goods sold	17,000	?	18,500	?
Gross margin.	13,000	?	17,500	?
Operating expenses	?	3,500	?	?
Net income.	$ 4,000	$?	$ 5,000	$ 9,000

P2–14.   **Cost identification.**   The Dorilane Company specializes in a set of wood patio furniture consisting of a table and four chairs. The set enjoys great popularity, and the company has ample orders to keep production going at its full capacity of 2,000 sets per month. Monthly cost data at full capacity follow:

Factory labor, direct	$118,000
Advertising	50,000
Factory supervision	40,000
Property taxes, factory building	3,500
Sales commissions	80,000
Insurance, factory	2,500
Depreciation, office equipment	4,000
Lease cost, factory equipment	12,000
Indirect materials, factory	6,000
Depreciation, factory building	10,000
General office supplies (billing)	3,000
General office salaries	60,000
Materials used (wood, bolts, etc.) . . .	94,000
Utilities, factory.	20,000

Required: 1.   Prepare an answer sheet with the column headings shown below. Enter each cost item on your answer sheet, placing the dollar amount under the appropriate headings. As examples, this has been done already for the first two items in the list above. Note that each cost item is classified two ways: first, as being either variable or fixed; and second, as being either a selling and administrative cost or a product cost. (If the item is a product cost, it should be classified as being either direct or indirect as shown.)

	Cost behavior		Selling or administrative cost	Product cost	
Cost item	Variable	Fixed		Direct	Indirect*
Factory labor, direct . .	$118,000			$118,000	
Advertising.		$50,000	$50,000		

* To units of product.

If you are uncertain whether a cost would be variable or fixed, consider how you would expect it to behave over fairly wide ranges of activity.

2.   Total the dollar amounts in each of the columns in (1) above. Compute the cost to produce one patio set.

3.   Assume that production drops to only 1,000 sets annually. Would you expect the cost per set to increase, decrease, or remain unchanged? Explain. No computations are necessary.

4.   Refer to the original data. The president's brother-in-law has considered making himself a patio set and has priced the necessary materials at a building supply

store. The brother-in-law has asked the president if he could purchase a patio set from the Dorilane Company "at cost," and the president has agreed to let him do so.

    a. Would you expect any disagreement between the two men over the price the brother-in-law should pay? Explain. What price does the president probably have in mind? The brother-in-law?

    b. Since the company is operating at full capacity, what cost term used in the chapter might be justification for the president to charge the full, regular price to the brother-in-law and still be selling at "cost"?

P2–15. **Classification of salary cost.** You have just been hired by the Ogden Company, which was organized on January 2 of the current year. The company manufactures and sells a single product. It is your responsibility to coordinate shipments of the product from the factory to distribution warehouses located in various parts of the United States so that goods will be available as orders are received from customers.

    The company is unsure how to classify your $30,000 annual salary in its cost records. The company's cost analyst says that your salary should be classified as a manufacturing (product) cost; the controller says that it should be classified as a selling expense; and the president says that it doesn't matter which way your salary cost is classified.

Required: 1. Which viewpoint is correct? Why?

        2. From the point of view of the reported net income for the year, is the president correct in his statement that it doesn't matter which way your salary cost is classified? Explain, using the data from Exhibit 2–5 and/or Exhibit 2–6 as needed.

P2–16. **Preparing manufacturing statements.** The Swift Company has just completed operations for March 19x5. The company's chief accountant resigned two weeks ago; accordingly, the company's assistant accountant (who is very inexperienced) has prepared the following income statement for the month's activities:

SWIFT COMPANY		
Income Statement		
For the Month Ended March 31, 19x5		
Sales		$450,000
Less operating expenses:		
Indirect labor cost	$ 12,000	
Utilities	15,000	
Direct labor cost	90,000	
Depreciation, factory equipment	21,000	
Raw materials purchased	159,000	
Depreciation, sales equipment	18,000	
Insurance expired during the month . . .	4,000	
Rent on facilities	50,000	
Selling and administrative salaries . . .	32,000	
Advertising	75,000	476,000
Net loss		$ (26,000)

    Since up until March the company had been earning a profit every month, the company's president is concerned as to the accuracy of the income statement above.

You have been asked to "check over" the statement and make corrections as needed. You have determined the following additional information:

a.   The Swift Company is a manufacturing firm.
b.   Some 60 percent of the utilities cost and 75 percent of the expired insurance apply to factory operations; the remaining amounts apply to selling and administrative activities.
c.   Inventory balances at the beginning and end of the month were:

	March 1	March 31
Raw materials	$ 8,000	$27,000
Work in process	16,000	21,000
Finished goods	40,000	60,000

d.   Only 80 percent of the rent on facilities applies to factory operations; the remainder applies to selling and administrative activities.

Required: 1.   Prepare a schedule of cost of goods manufactured in good form for March 19x5.
2.   Prepare a corrected income statement for the month.

P2–17.   Cost identification.   Sandi Meyers began dabbling in pottery several years ago as a hobby. The pottery work has been so enjoyable that she has decided to quit her job with an aerospace firm and manufacture pottery full time. The salary from Sandi's aerospace job is $1,500 per month.

Sandi will rent a small building near her home in order to have a place in which to manufacture the pottery. The rent will be $500 per month. She figures that the cost of clay and glaze will be about $2 for each finished piece of pottery. She will hire workers to produce the pottery at a labor rate of $3 per pot. In order to sell her products, Sandi feels that she must advertise heavily in the local area. An advertising agency states that it will handle all advertising for a fee of $400 per month. Sandi's brother will sell the pots; he will be paid a commission of $0.50 for each pot sold.

Sandi owns some pottery wheels and other items of equipment that were purchased several years ago. This equipment will be depreciated at a rate of $100 per month and used in the pottery manufacturing operation. In addition, other equipment needed to manufacture the pots will be rented at a cost of $600 per month.

Sandi has a room in her home that is presently being rented to a friend at a rental rate of $150 per month. She has asked the friend to move so that the room can be used as a sales office. The space in the room will continue to be depreciated at a straight-line rate of $250 per year, as in the past. A phone installed in the room for taking orders will cost $40 per month. In addition, a recording device will be attached to the phone for taking after-hours messages; the phone company will charge Sandi $0.60 for each message recorded.

For the time being, Sandi does not intend to draw any salary from the new company.

Required: Prepare an answer sheet with the following column headings:

Name of the cost	Variable cost	Fixed cost	Product cost			Period (selling and administrative) cost	Oppor-tunity cost	Differ-ential cost*	Sunk cost
			Direct materials	Direct labor	Manufacturing overhead				

* Between the alternatives of producing the pottery or staying with the aerospace firm.

List the different costs associated with the new company down the extreme left column (under "Name of the cost"). Then place an X under each heading that helps to describe the type of cost involved. There may be X's under several column headings for a single cost. (That is, a cost may be a fixed cost, a period cost, and a differential cost; you would place an X under each of these column headings opposite the cost.)

P2–18. **Schedule of cost of goods manufactured; cost behavior.**   Selected account balances for the year ended May 31, 19x1, are provided below for Superior Company:

Raw materials inventory, June 1, 19x0	$ 40,000
Raw materials inventory, May 31, 19x1	37,000
Purchases of raw materials	150,000
Insurance, factory	8,000
Work in process inventory, June 1, 19x0	?
Utilities, factory	45,000
Indirect labor	60,000
Finished goods inventory, June 1, 19x0	85,000
Direct labor	?
Indirect materials	7,000
Work in process inventory, May 31, 19x1	48,000
Rent, factory building	120,000
Finished goods inventory, May 31, 19x1	?
Maintenance, factory.	30,000

The goods available for sale for the year totaled $635,000; the total manufacturing costs were $563,000; and the cost of goods sold totaled $560,000 for the year.

Required: 1. Prepare a schedule of cost of goods manufactured in the form illustrated in Exhibit 2–3 in the text and the cost of goods sold section of an income statement.

2. Assume that the dollar amounts given above are for the equivalent of 40,000 units produced during the year. Compute the unit cost for direct materials. Compute the unit cost for rent on the factory building.

3. Assume that in 19x2 the company produces 50,000 units. What per unit and total cost would you expect to be incurred for direct materials? For rent on the factory building? (In preparing your answer, you may assume that direct materials is a variable cost and that rent is a fixed cost.)

4. As the manager in charge of production costs, explain to the president the reason for any difference in unit costs between (2) and (3) above.

P2–19.   **Cost classification.**   Listed below are a number of costs that might typically be found in a merchandising, manufacturing, or service company:
1. Property taxes, factory.
2. Boxes used for packaging detergent.
3. Salespersons' commissions.
4. Supervisor's salary, factory.
5. Depreciation, executive automobiles.
6. Workers assembling computers.

7. Packing supplies for out-of-state shipment.
8. Insurance, finished goods warehouses.
9. Lubricants for machines.
10. Advertising costs.
11. "Chips" used in producing calculators.
12. Shipping costs on merchandise sold.
13. Magazine subscriptions, factory lunchroom.
14. Thread in a garment factory.
15. Billing costs.
16. Executive life insurance.
17. Ink used in textbook production.
18. Fringe benefits, assembly line workers.
19. Yarn used in sweater production.
20. Receptionist, executive offices.

Required: Prepare an answer sheet with column headings as shown below. For each cost item, indicate whether it would be variable or fixed in behavior, and then whether it would be a selling cost, an administrative cost, or a manufacturing cost. If it is a manufacturing cost, indicate whether it would be direct or indirect to units of product. Three sample answers are provided for illustration. If you are unsure about whether a cost would be variable or fixed, consider whether it would fluctuate substantially over a fairly wide range of volume.

| | | | | Manufacturing (product) cost | |
Cost item	Variable or fixed	Selling cost	Administrative cost	Direct	Indirect
Direct labor	V			X	
Executive salaries . . .	F		X		
Factory rent	F				X

P2–20.   **Schedule of cost of goods manufactured; inventory computation.**   On January 2, 19x4, Roger Strong organized a company to manufacture and sell a device that he has designed for use as an attachment on small personal computers. Shortly after the end of the first quarter, Roger's accountant had a serious accident and therefore has been unable to prepare financial statements for the quarter. In order to have information on which to base a decision as to whether or not the company should be continued, Roger has prepared the following income statement for the first quarter's activities:

STRONG MANUFACTURING COMPANY
Income Statement
For the Quarter Ended March 31, 19x4

Sales		$700,000
Less operating expenses:		
Utilities	$ 30,000	
Advertising	100,000	
Direct labor cost	160,000	
Indirect labor cost	53,000	
Raw materials purchased	130,000	
Maintenance cost, factory	9,000	
Insurance	8,000	
Depreciation, factory equipment	30,000	
Rent on facilities	60,000	
Sales salaries	50,000	
Other factory overhead costs	35,000	
Administrative salaries	70,000	
Total operating expenses		735,000
Net loss		$ (35,000)

Roger is very disappointed in the results of the first quarter and feels that he should discontinue operations and sell his patents to another company. To add to his troubles, just after the quarter had ended, the company's finished goods warehouse was broken into by thieves who took all of the unsold units on hand. The company's insurance policy states that the company will be reimbursed for the "cost" of any finished units destroyed or stolen. Roger figures that this cost is $73.50 per unit, computed as follows:

$$\frac{\text{Total expenses for the quarter, } \$735,000}{\text{Units produced during the quarter, } 10,000} = \$73.50 \text{ per unit}$$

Since the company sold 8,000 of the 10,000 units produced during the quarter, Roger figures that the insurance company owes him $147,000 (10,000 units − 8,000 units = 2,000 units; 2,000 units × $73.50 = $147,000). The insurance company refuses to pay this amount; it has asked you to prepare corrected statements for the quarter and a corrected computation of its liability under the insurance policy. You have obtained the following additional information:

a.   Inventories at the beginning and end of the quarter were:

	January 2, 19x4	March 31, 19x4
Raw materials	–0–	$10,000
Work in process	–0–	30,000
Finished goods	–0–	?

b.   Ninety percent of the utilities cost and 80 percent of the rent on facilities relate to factory operations. The remaining amounts relate to selling and administrative activities.

Required: 1. What conceptual errors were made in preparing the income statement above?
2. Prepare a schedule of cost of goods manufactured for the quarter.

3.   Determine the cost of the 2,000 units in the finished goods inventory at March 31. Using this figure and other data from the problem as needed, prepare a corrected income statement for the quarter. (Note that the finished goods warehouse was broken into *after* the quarter had ended; thus, no loss for this theft should be shown on the income statement.) Based on these data, do you agree that Roger should discontinue operations?

4.   Do you agree that the insurance company owes Roger $147,000 as computed above? Explain your answer.

 P2–21 **Cost behavior; manufacturing statement; unit costs.**   Hickey Company, a manufacturing firm, produces a single product. The following information has been taken from the company's production, sales, and cost records for the year 19x6:

Production in units	30,000
Sales in units	? 26,000
Ending finished goods inventory in units	? 4,000
Sales in dollars	$650,000

Costs:

Advertising	$ 90,000
Direct labor	160,000
Indirect labor	60,000
Raw materials purchased	80,000
Building rent (production uses 80% of the space; administrative and sales offices use the rest)	50,000
Utilities, factory	35,000
Royalty paid for use of production patent, $1 per unit produced	? 30,000
Maintenance, factory	25,000
Rent for special production equipment, $6,000 per year plus $0.10 per unit produced	? 9,000
Selling and administrative salaries	100,000
Other factory overhead costs	11,000
Other selling and administrative expenses	20,000

	January 1, 19x6	December 31, 19x6
Inventories:		
Raw materials	$20,000	$10,000
Work in process	30,000	40,000
Finished goods	–0–	?60,000

The finished goods inventory is being carried at the average unit production cost for the year. The selling price of the product is $25 per unit.

Required: 1.   Prepare a schedule of cost of goods manufactured for the year.
2.   Compute the following:
   a.   The number of units in the finished goods inventory at December 31.
   b.   The cost of the units in the finished goods inventory at December 31.
3.   Prepare an income statement for the year.

CASES

 C2–22. **Inventory computations from incomplete data.**   Hector P. Wastrel, a careless employee, left some combustible materials near an open flame in Salter Company's plant. The resulting explosion and fire destroyed the entire plant and administrative offices. Justin Quick, the company's controller, and Constance Trueheart, the operations manager, were able to save only a few bits of information as they escaped from the roaring blaze.

"What a disaster," cried Justin. "And the worse part is that we have no records to use in filing an insurance claim."

"I know," replied Constance. "I was in the plant when the explosion occurred, and I managed to grab only this brief summary sheet that contains information on one or two of our costs. It says that our direct labor cost this year has totaled $180,000 and that we have purchased $290,000 in raw materials. But I'm afraid that doesn't help much; the rest of our records are just ashes."

"Well, not completely," said Justin. "I was working on the year-to-date income statement when the explosion knocked me out of my chair. I instinctively held onto the page I was working on, and from what I can make out our sales to date this year have totaled $1,200,000 and our gross margin rate has been 40 percent of sales. Also, I can see that our goods available for sale to customers has totaled $810,000 at cost."

"Maybe we're not so bad off after all," exclaimed Constance. "My sheet says that prime cost has totaled $410,000 so far this year and that manufacturing overhead is 70 percent of conversion cost. Now if we just had some information on our beginning inventories."

"Hey, look at this," cried Justin. "It's a copy of last year's annual report, and it shows what our inventories were when this year started (January 1, 19x3). Let's see, Raw Materials was $18,000, Work in Process was $65,000, and Finished Goods was $45,000."

"Super," yelled Constance. "Let's go to work."

In order to file an insurance claim, the company must determine the amount of cost in its inventories as of August 20, 19x3, the date of the fire. You may assume that all materials used in production during the year were direct materials.

Required: Determine the amount of cost in the Raw Materials, Work in Process, and Finished Goods inventory accounts as of the date of the fire. (Hint: One way to proceed would be to reconstruct the various schedules and statements that would have been affected by the company's inventory accounts during the period.)

CHAPTER 3

Systems Design: Job-Order Costing

LEARNING OBJECTIVES

After studying Chapter 3, you should be able to:

- Distinguish between process costing and job-order costing and identify companies that would use each costing method.

- Identify the documents used to control the flow of costs in a job-order costing system.

- Prepare journal entries to record the flow of direct materials cost, direct labor cost, and manufacturing overhead cost in a job-order costing system.

- Compute predetermined overhead rates and explain why estimated overhead costs (rather than actual overhead costs) are used in the costing process.

- Apply overhead cost to Work in Process by use of a predetermined overhead rate.

- Compute any balance of under- or overapplied overhead cost for a period and prepare the journal entry needed to close the balance into the appropriate accounts.

- Explain why multiple overhead rates are needed in many organizations.

- Describe the purpose of normalized overhead rates.

- Define or explain the key terms listed at the end of the chapter.

As discussed in Chapter 2, product costing is the process of assigning manufacturing costs to manufactured goods. An understanding of this process is vital to any manager, since the way in which a product is costed can have a substantial impact on reported net income, as well as on the current assets section of the balance sheet.

In this chapter and in Chapter 4, we look at product costing from the **absorption cost** approach. The approach is so named because it provides for the absorption of all manufacturing costs, fixed and variable, into units of product. It is also known as the **full cost** approach. Later, in Chapter 7, we will look at product costing from another point of view (called *direct costing*) and then discuss the strengths and weaknesses of the two approaches.

As we study product costing, we must keep clearly in mind that *the essential purpose of any costing system is to accumulate costs for managerial use.* A costing system is not an end in itself. Rather, it is a managerial tool in that it exists to provide the manager with the cost data needed to direct the affairs of an organization.

THE NEED FOR UNIT COST DATA

In studying product costing, we will focus initially on *unit cost of production,* an item of cost data that is generally regarded as being highly useful to managers.

Managers need unit cost data for a variety of reasons. First, unit costs are needed in order to cost inventories on financial statements. The units of product remaining on hand at the end of an operating period must have costs attached to them as the units are carried forward on the balance sheet to the next period.

Second, unit costs are needed for determination of a period's net income. The cost of each unit sold during a period must be placed on the income statement as a deduction from total sales revenue. If unit costs are incorrectly computed, then net income will be equally incorrect.

Finally, managers need unit cost data to assist them in a broad range of decision-making situations. Without unit cost data, managers would find it very difficult to set selling prices for factory output.[1] A knowledge of unit costs is also vital in a number of special decision areas, such as whether to add or drop product lines, whether to make or buy production components, whether to expand or contract operations, and whether to accept special orders at special prices. The particular unit costs that are relevant in this variety of decision-making situations will differ, so we need to learn not only how to derive unit costs but also how to differentiate between those costs that are relevant in a particular situation and those that are not. The matter of relevant costs is reserved until Chapter 13. For the moment, we

---

[1] We should note here that unit cost represents only one of many factors involved in pricing decisions. Pricing is discussed in depth in Chapter 12.

are concerned with gaining an understanding of the concept of unit cost in its broadest sense.

TYPES OF COSTING SYSTEMS

a) Process costing.
b) Job-order costing.

In computing unit costs, managers are faced with a difficult problem. Many costs (such as rent) are incurred uniformly from month to month whereas production may change frequently, with production going up in one month and then down in another. In addition to variations in the level of production, several different *types* of goods may be produced in a given period. Under these conditions, how is it possible to determine accurate unit costs? The answer is that the computation of unit costs must involve an *averaging* of some type. The way in which this averaging is carried out will depend heavily on the type of manufacturing process involved. Two costing systems have emerged in response to variations in the manufacturing process; these two systems are commonly known as *process costing* and *job-order costing*. Each has its own unique way of averaging costs and thus providing management with unit cost data.

Process Costing

where single homogeneous product, ie cement, brick etc -

A **process costing system** is employed in those situations where manufacturing involves a single, homogeneous product that is produced for long periods at a time. Examples of industries that use process costing include cement, flour, brick, and various utilities (e.g., natural gas, electricity). All of these industries are characterized by a basically homogeneous product that flows evenly through the production process on a continuous basis.

The basic approach to process costing is to accumulate costs in a particular operation or department for an entire period (month, quarter, year) and then to divide this total by the number of units produced during the period. The basic formula for process costing would be:

$$\frac{\text{Total costs of manufacturing}}{\text{Total units produced (gallons, pounds, bottles)}}$$
$$= \text{Unit cost (per gallon, pound, bottle)}$$

Since one unit of product (gallon, pound, bottle) is completely indistinguishable from any other unit of product, each unit bears the same average cost as any other unit produced during the period. This costing technique results in a broad, average unit cost figure that applies to many thousands of like units flowing in an almost endless stream off the assembly or processing line.

Job-Order Costing

A **job-order costing system** is used in those manufacturing situations where many *different* products, jobs, or batches of production are being

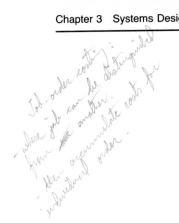

produced each period. Examples of industries that would typically use job-order costing include special-order printing, furniture manufacturing, ship-building, and equipment manufacturing.

Job-order costing is also used extensively in the service industries. Hospitals, law firms, movie studios, accounting firms, advertising agencies, and repair shops, for example, all use job-order costing to accumulate costs for accounting and billing purposes. Although the detailed example of job-order costing provided in the following section deals with a manufacturing firm, the reader should keep in mind that the same basic concepts and procedures are used by many service organizations. More is said on this point later in the chapter.

Because the output of firms involved in the industries mentioned above tends to be heterogeneous, managers need a costing system in which costs can be accumulated *by job (or by client or customer)* and in which distinct unit costs can be determined for each job completed. Job-order costing provides such a system. However, it is a more complex system than that required by process costing. Under job-order costing, rather than dividing total costs by many thousands of like units, one must somehow divide total costs by a few, basically unlike units. Thus, job-order costing involves certain problems of record keeping and cost assignment that are not found in a process costing system.

Summary of Costing Methods

To summarize this brief introduction to process and job-order costing, regardless of which system one is dealing with, the problem of determining unit costs involves a need for averaging of some type. The essential difference between the process and job-order methods is the way in which this averaging is carried out. In this chapter, we focus on the design of a job-order costing system. In the following chapter, we focus on process costing and also look more closely at the similarities and differences between the two costing methods.

JOB-ORDER COSTING—AN OVERVIEW

In the preceding chapter, the point was made that there are three broad categories of costs involved in the manufacture of any product:

1.   Direct materials.
2.   Direct labor.
3.   Manufacturing overhead.

As we study the design and operation of a job-order costing system, we will look at each of these costs to see how it is involved in the costing of a unit of product. In doing this, we will also look at the various documents involved in job-order costing and give special emphasis to a key document known as a job cost sheet.

Measuring Direct Materials Cost

The production process begins with the transfer of raw materials from the storeroom to the production line. The bulk of these raw materials will be traceable directly to the goods being produced and will therefore be termed *direct materials*. Other materials, generally termed *indirect materials*, will not be charged to a specific job but rather will be included within the general category of manufacturing overhead. As discussed in Chapter 2, indirect materials would include costs of glue, nails, and miscellaneous supplies.

Raw materials are drawn from the storeroom on presentation of a **materials requisition form.** A materials requisition form is shown in Exhibit 3–1.

As shown in the exhibit, the materials requisition form is a detailed source document that specifies the type and quantity of materials that are to be drawn from the storeroom and that identifies the job to which the materials are to be charged. Thus, the form serves as a means both for controlling the flow of materials into production and for making entries in the accounting records.

If the job being worked on involves a product that is frequently manufactured by a company, then any requisition of materials will typically be based on a **bill of materials** that has been prepared for the product. A bill of materials is simply a control sheet that shows the type and quantity of each item of material going into a completed unit.

EXHIBIT 3–1

Materials requisition form

Materials Requisition Number ___14873___   Date ___March 2, 19x2___
Job Number to Be Charged ___2B47___
Department ___Milling___

Description	Quantity	Unit Cost	Total Cost
M46 Housing	2	$123	$246
G7 Connector	8	52	416
			$662

Authorized
Signature ___Bill White___

The Job Cost Sheet

The cost of direct materials is entered on a job cost sheet similar to the one presented in Exhibit 3–2. A **job cost sheet** is a form prepared for each separate job initiated into production; it serves (1) as a means for accumulating materials, labor, and overhead costs chargeable to a job, and (2) as a means for computing unit costs. Normally, the job cost sheet is not prepared until the accounting department has received notification from the production department that a production order has been issued for a

EXHIBIT 3–2
Job cost sheet

JOB COST SHEET

Job Number   2B47   Date Initiated   March 2, 19x2
                                                Date Completed _____

Department   Milling   Units Completed _____
Item   Special order coupling
For Stock _____

Direct Materials		Direct Labor			Manufacturing Overhead		
Req. No.	Amount	Ticket	Hours	Amount	Hours	Rate	Amount
14873	$662						

Cost Summary		Units Shipped		
Direct Materials	$	Date	Number	Balance
Direct Labor	$			
Manufacturing Overhead	$			
Total Cost	$			
Unit Cost	$			

particular job. In turn, a production order is not issued until a definite agreement has been reached with the customer in terms of quantities, prices, and shipment dates.

As direct materials are issued, the accounting department makes entries directly on the job cost sheet, thereby charging the specific job noted on the sheet with the cost of materials used in production. When the job is completed, the total cost of materials used can be summarized in the cost summary section as one element involved in determining the total unit cost of the order.

Measuring Direct Labor Cost

Direct labor cost is accumulated and measured in much the same way as direct materials cost. Direct labor includes those labor charges that are directly traceable to the particular job in process. By contrast, those labor charges that cannot be traced directly to a particular job, or that can be traced only with the expenditure of great effort, are treated as part of manufacturing overhead. As discussed in Chapter 2, this latter category of labor costs is termed *indirect labor* and would include such tasks as maintenance, supervision, and cleanup.

Labor costs are generally accumulated by means of some type of work record prepared each day by each employee. These work records, often termed **time tickets,** constitute an hour-by-hour summary of the activities completed during the day by the employee. When working on a specific job, the employee enters the job number on the time ticket and notes the number of hours spent on the particular task involved. When not assigned to a particular job, the employee enters the type of indirect labor tasks to which he or she was assigned (such as cleanup and maintenance) and the number of hours spent on each separate task. An example of an employee time ticket is shown in Exhibit 3–3.

At the end of the day, the time tickets are gathered and the accounting department carefully analyzes each in terms of the number of hours assignable as direct labor to specific jobs and the number of hours assignable to manufacturing overhead as indirect labor. Those hours assignable as direct labor are entered on individual job cost sheets (such as the one shown in Exhibit 3–2), along with the appropriate charges involved. When all direct labor charges associated with a particular job have been accumulated on the job cost sheet, the total can be summarized in the cost summary section. The daily time tickets, in essence, constitute basic source documents used as a basis for labor cost entries into the accounting records.

Application of Manufacturing Overhead

Manufacturing overhead must be considered along with direct materials and direct labor in determining unit costs of production. However, the assign-

EXHIBIT 3–3

Employee time ticket

| Time Ticket No. 843 | | | Date | March 3, 19x2 | |
| Employee | Mary Holden | | Station | 4 | |

Started	Ended	Time Completed	Rate	Amount	Job Number
7:00	12:00	5.0	$9	$45	2B47
12:30	2:30	2.0	9	18	2B50
2:30	3:30	1.0	9	9	Maintenance
Totals		8.0		$72	

Supervisor R. W. Pace

ment of manufacturing overhead to units of product is often a difficult task. There are several reasons why this is so.

First, as explained in Chapter 2, manufacturing overhead is an *indirect* cost to units of product and therefore can't be traced directly to a particular product or job. Second, manufacturing overhead consists of many unlike items, involving both variable and fixed costs. It ranges from the grease used in machines to the annual salary of the production superintendent. Finally, firms with large seasonal variations in production often find that even though output is fluctuating, manufacturing overhead costs tend to remain relatively constant. The reason is that fixed costs generally constitute a large part of manufacturing overhead.

Given these problems, about the only acceptable way to assign overhead costs to units of product is to do so through an allocation process. This allocation of overhead costs to products is accomplished by having the manager select an *activity base* that is common to all products that the company manufactures or to all services that the company renders. Then by means of this base, an appropriate amount of overhead cost is assigned to each product or service. The trick, of course, is to choose the right base so that the overhead application will be equitable between jobs.

Historically, the most widely used activity bases have been direct labor-hours (DLH) and direct labor cost, with machine-hours (MH) and even units of product (where a company has only a single product) also used to some extent. Recent studies indicate, however, that direct labor is beginning to decrease in importance in some industries.[2] As a result, a shift away

---

[2] See Robert S. Kaplan, "Yesterday's Accounting and Today's Economy," *Harvard Business Review* 62 (July–August 1984), pp. 95–101; and Rick Hunt, Linda Garrett, and C. Mike Merz, "Direct Labor Cost Not Always Relevant at H-P," *Management Accounting* 66, no. 8 (February 1985), pp. 58–62.

from direct labor and toward other bases, such as machine-hours, is beginning to take place in the applying of overhead cost to products. The importance of this shift is discussed further in a following section titled, "What drives overhead cost?"

Once an activity base has been chosen, it is divided into the estimated total manufacturing overhead cost of the period in order to obtain a **predetermined overhead rate.** The rate is called "predetermined" because it is computed before the period begins and because it is based entirely on estimated data. After the predetermined overhead rate has been computed, it is then used to apply overhead cost to jobs. In sum, the formula for computing the predetermined overhead rate is:

$$\frac{\text{Estimated total manufacturing overhead costs}}{\text{Estimated total units in the base (MH, DLH, etc.)}} = \text{Predetermined overhead rate}$$

The need for estimated data   Actual overhead costs are rarely, if ever, used in overhead costing. The reason is that actual overhead costs are not available until *after* a period is over. This is too late so far as computing unit costs is concerned, since the manager must have unit cost data available at once in order to set prices on products and make other key marketing and operating decisions. The postponing of such decisions until year-end (in order to have actual overhead cost data available) would destroy an organization's ability to compete effectively. Therefore, in order to have timely data for decision making, most firms *estimate* total overhead costs at the beginning of a year, *estimate* the level of activity for the year, and develop a predetermined overhead rate based on these estimates. Such rates are widely used by both manufacturing and service organizations for costing purposes.

Using the predetermined overhead rate   The assigning of overhead cost to jobs (and thereby to units of product) is called **overhead application.** To illustrate the steps involved, assume that a firm has estimated its total manufacturing overhead costs for the year to be $320,000 and has estimated 40,000 total direct labor-hours for the year. Its predetermined overhead rate for the year would be $8 per direct labor-hour, as shown below:

$$\frac{\$320,000}{40,000 \text{ direct labor-hours}} = \$8 \text{ per direct labor-hour}$$

If a particular job required 27 direct labor-hours to complete, then $216 of overhead cost (27 hours × $8 = $216) would be applied to that job. This overhead application is shown on the job cost sheet in Exhibit 3–4.

Whether the overhead application in Exhibit 3–4 is made slowly as the job is worked on during the period, or in a single application at the time of completion, is a matter of choice and convenience to the company involved. If a job is not completed at year-end, however, overhead should

EXHIBIT 3–4
A completed job cost sheet

JOB COST SHEET

Job Number   2B47   Date Initiated   March 2, 19x2
                                     Date Completed   March 8, 19x2

Department   Milling
Item   Special order coupling   Units Completed   150
For Stock

Direct Materials		Direct Labor			Manufacturing Overhead		
Req. No.	Amount	Ticket	Hours	Amount	Hours	Rate	Amount
14873	$ 662	843	5	$ 45	27	$8/DLH	$216
14875	504	846	8	60			
14912	238	850	4	21			
	$1,404	851	10	54			
			27	$180			

Cost Summary		Units Shipped		
Direct Materials	$1,404	Date	Number	Balance
Direct Labor	$ 180	3/8/x2	—	150
Manufacturing Overhead	$ 216			
Total Cost	$1,800			
Unit Cost	$ 12*			

* $1,800 ÷ 150 units = $12 per unit.

be applied to the extent needed to properly value the work in process inventory.

Although estimates are involved in the computation of predetermined overhead rates, managers typically become very skilled at making these estimates. As a result, predetermined overhead rates are generally quite accurate, and any difference between the amount of overhead cost that is actually incurred during a period and the amount that is applied to products is usually quite small. This point is discussed further in a following section.

What Drives Overhead Cost?

We stated earlier that major shifts are taking place in the structure of costs in some industries. In the past, direct labor has typically accounted for up to 60 percent of the cost of many products with overhead cost making up only a portion of the remainder. With the advent of automation, however, sophisticated new machines are now taking over various functions that used to be performed by direct labor workers. Robots are appearing on the assembly line, and computer-integrated manufacturing (CIM), which requires almost no direct labor input, is being used to control the entire manufacturing process in some companies. As a result of these shifts toward automation, direct labor is becoming less of a factor in the cost of a number of products.

This decrease in the importance of direct labor is being accompanied by an increase in the importance of manufacturing overhead, since costly equipment must be depreciated, expensive software must be developed to control manufacturing operations, and so forth. Where processes are largely automated (sometimes referred to as ''capital intensive''), direct labor probably has little to do with the incurrence of overhead cost and therefore may not be appropriate as a base for computing overhead rates. Instead, a base should be used that acts as a *cost driver* in the incurrence of overhead cost. A **cost driver** is a measure of activity, such as machine-hours, beds occupied, computer time, flight-hours, or miles driven that is a *causal factor* in the incurrence of cost in an organization. In an automated setting, either machine-hours or computer time would typically act as a cost driver and therefore would be an appropriate base for computing overhead rates. If a base is used to compute overhead rates that does not ''drive'' overhead costs, then the result will be inaccurate rates and distorted product costs.

We must hasten to add that although direct labor is decreasing in importance in some industries, in other industries it continues to be a significant part of total product cost. In these latter industries, therefore, it remains a viable base for computing overhead rates and for applying overhead cost to products. The key point managers must recognize is that direct labor is not an appropriate allocation base in *every* situation and indeed has become totally irrelevant in some settings.

Computation of Unit Costs

With the application of manufacturing overhead to the job cost sheet, total costs of the job can be summarized in the cost summary section. (See Exhibit 3–4 for an example of a completed job cost sheet.) The cost of the individual units in the job can then be obtained by dividing the total costs by the number of units produced. The completed job cost sheet is then ready to be transferred to the finished goods inventory file, where it will serve as a basis for either costing unsold units in the ending inventory or charging expense for units sold.

A Summary of Document Flows

The sequence of events just discussed is summarized in Exhibit 3–5. A careful study of the flow of documents in this exhibit will provide an excellent visual review of the overall operation of a job-order costing system.

JOB-ORDER COSTING—THE FLOW OF COSTS

Having obtained a broad, conceptual perspective of the operation of a job-order costing system, we are now prepared to take a look at the flow of actual costs through the system itself. We shall consider a single month's activity for a hypothetical company, presenting all data in summary form. As a basis for discussion, let us assume that the Rand Company had two jobs in process during April, the first month of its fiscal year. Job A was started during March and had $30,000 in manufacturing costs (materials, labor, and overhead) already accumulated on April 1. Job B was started during April.

The Purchase and Issue of Materials

During April, the Rand Company purchased $60,000 in raw materials for use in production. The purchase is recorded in entry (1) below:

(1)		
Raw Materials	60,000	
Accounts Payable		60,000

As explained in Chapter 2, Raw Materials is an inventory account. Thus, any materials remaining in the account at the end of a period will appear on the balance sheet under an inventory classification.

Issue of direct materials   During the month, the Rand Company drew $50,000 in raw materials from the storeroom for use in production. Entry (2) records the issue of the materials to the production departments.

(2)		
Work in Process	50,000	
Raw Materials		50,000

The materials charged to Work in Process represent direct materials assignable to specific jobs on the production line. As these materials are entered into the Work in Process account, they are also recorded on the separate job cost sheets to which they relate. This point is illustrated in Exhibit 3–6.

EXHIBIT 3–5

The flow of documents in a job-order costing system

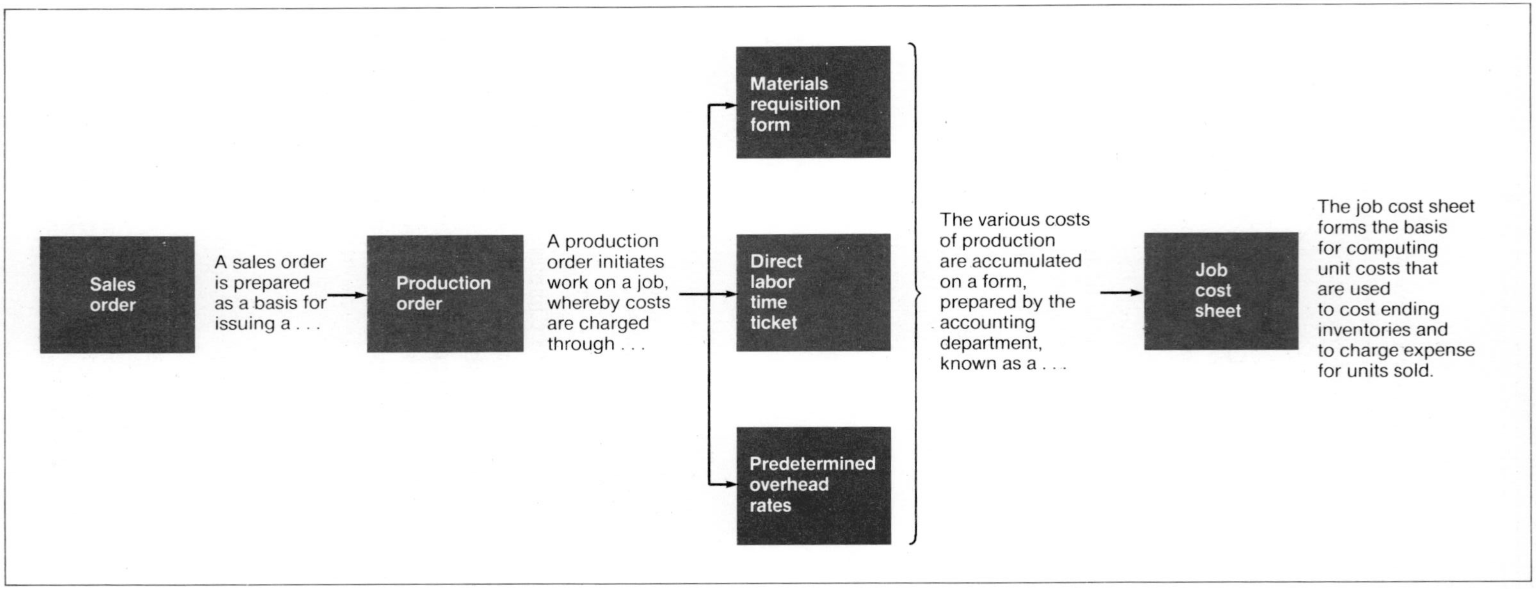

Sales order

A sales order is prepared as a basis for issuing a . . . .

Production order

A production order initiates work on a job, whereby costs are charged through . . .

Materials requisition form

Direct labor time ticket

Predetermined overhead rates

The various costs of production are accumulated on a form, prepared by the accounting department, known as a . . . .

Job cost sheet

The job cost sheet forms the basis for computing unit costs that are used to cost ending inventories and to charge expense for units sold.

EXHIBIT 3–6

Raw materials cost flows

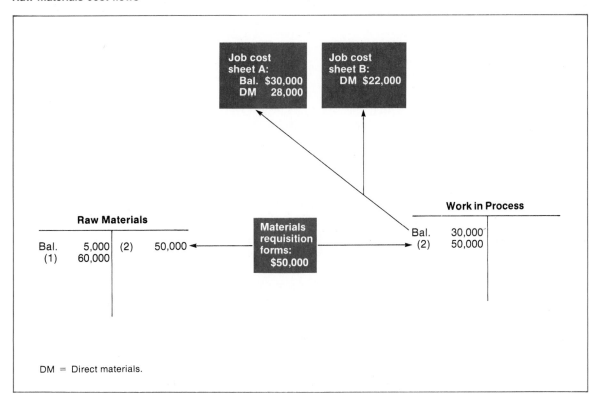

DM = Direct materials.

Notice from the job cost sheets that job A contains the $30,000 in manu-facturing cost which we mentioned was carried forward from last month. Also note that the Work in Process account contains the same $30,000 balance. The reason the $30,000 appears in both places is that the Work in Process account is a control account and the job cost sheets form a subsidiary ledger. Thus, the Work in Process account contains a summarized total of all costs appearing on the individual job cost sheets for all jobs in process at any given point in time. (Since the Rand Company had only job A in process at the beginning of April, job A's $30,000 balance on that date is equal to the balance in the Work in Process account.) Of the $50,000 in materials added to Work in Process during April, $28,000 was chargeable directly to job A and $22,000 was chargeable to job B, as shown in Exhibit 3–6.

Issue of both direct and indirect materials   In entry (2) above, we have assumed that all of the materials drawn from the Raw Materials inven-tory account were assignable to specific jobs as direct materials. If some of the materials drawn are not assignable to specific jobs, then they must be charged to Manufacturing Overhead as indirect materials. The entry to do this would be:

```
Work in Process (direct materials)  . . . . . . . . . . . . . . . XXX
Manufacturing Overhead (indirect materials)  . . . . . . . . . . XXX
    Raw Materials  . . . . . . . . . . . . . . . . . . . . . . .         XXX
```

Observe that the Manufacturing Overhead account is separate from Work in Process. The purpose of the Manufacturing Overhead account is to accumulate all manufacturing overhead costs as they are incurred during a period.

Labor Cost

As work is performed in various departments of the Rand Company from day to day, employee time tickets are generated, collected, and forwarded to the accounting department. There the tickets are costed according to the various rates paid to the employees, and the resulting costs are classified in terms of being either direct or indirect labor. This costing and classification for the month of April resulted in the following entry:

```
                                      (3)
Work in Process . . . . . . . . . . . . . . . . . . . . . . . .  60,000
Manufacturing Overhead  . . . . . . . . . . . . . . . . . . . .  15,000
    Salaries and Wages Payable  . . . . . . . . . . . . . . .            75,000
```

Only that portion of labor cost that represents direct labor is added to the Work in Process account. For the Rand Company, this amounted to $60,000 for April.

At the same time that direct labor costs are added to Work in Process they are also added to the individual job cost sheets, as shown in Exhibit 3–7. During April, $40,000 of direct labor cost was chargeable to job A and the remaining $20,000 was chargeable to job B.

The labor costs charged to Manufacturing Overhead represent the indirect labor costs of the period, such as supervision, janitorial work, and maintenance.

Manufacturing Overhead Costs

As we learned in Chapter 2, all costs of operating the factory other than direct materials and direct labor are classified as manufacturing overhead costs. These costs are entered directly into the Manufacturing Overhead account as they are incurred. To illustrate, assume that the Rand Company incurred the following general factory costs during the month of April:

EXHIBIT 3–7

Labor cost flows

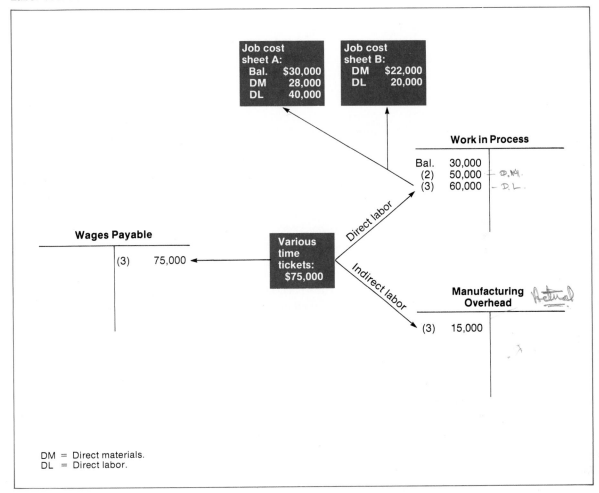

DM = Direct materials.
DL = Direct labor.

Utilities (heat, water, and power)	. . .	$21,000
Rent on equipment	. . . .	16,000
Miscellaneous factory costs	. . . . .	3,000
Total	. . . .	$40,000

The entry to record the incurrence of these costs would be:

(4)		
Manufacturing Overhead	40,000	
Accounts Payable		40,000

In addition, let us assume that during April the Rand Company recognized $13,000 in accrued property taxes and $9,000 in insurance expired on factory buildings and equipment. The entry to record these items would be:

```
                                  (5)
Manufacturing Overhead  . . . . . . . . . . . . . . . . . .   22,000
        Property Taxes Payable . . . . . . . . . . . . . . .              13,000
        Prepaid Insurance . . . . . . . . . . . . . . . . .                9,000
```

Let us further assume that the company recognized $18,000 in depreciation on factory equipment during April. The entry to record the accrual of depreciation would be:

```
                                  (6)
Manufacturing Overhead  . . . . . . . . . . . . . . . . . .   18,000
        Accumulated Depreciation . . . . . . . . . . . . . .              18,000
```

In short, *all* manufacturing overhead costs are recorded directly into the Manufacturing Overhead account as they are incurred day by day throughout a period. Notice from the entries above that the recording of *actual* manufacturing overhead costs has no effect on the Work in Process account.

The Application of Manufacturing Overhead

How is the Work in Process account charged for manufacturing overhead cost? The answer is, by means of the predetermined overhead rate. Recall from our discussion earlier in the chapter that for costing purposes a predetermined overhead rate is established at the beginning of each year. The rate is calculated by dividing the estimated manufacturing overhead cost for the year by the estimated activity (measured in machine-hours, direct labor-hours, or some other base). As the year progresses, overhead cost is then applied to each job by multiplying the number of hours it requires for completion by the predetermined overhead rate that has been set.

To illustrate the cost flows involved, assume that the Rand Company has used machine-hours in computing its predetermined overhead rate and that this rate is $6 per machine-hour. Also assume that during April, 10,000 machine-hours were worked on job A and 5,000 machine-hours were worked on job B (a total of 15,000 machine-hours). Thus, $90,000 in overhead cost (15,000 machine-hours $\times$ $6 = $90,000) would be applied to Work in Process. The entry to record the application would be:

```
                                  (7)
Work in Process . . . . . . . . . . . . . . . . . . . . . .   90,000
        Manufacturing Overhead  . . . . . . . . . . . . . .               90,000
```

EXHIBIT 3–8

The flow of costs in overhead application

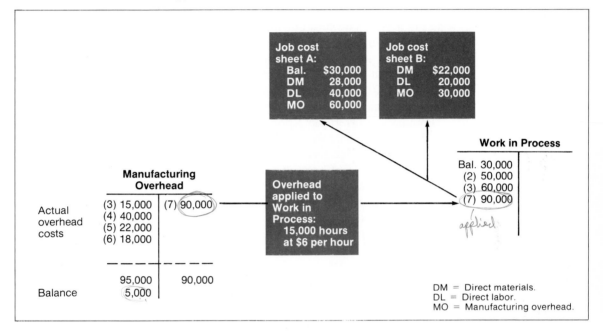

The flow of costs through the Manufacturing Overhead account is shown in T-account format in Exhibit 3–8.

The "actual overhead costs" in the Manufacturing Overhead account in Exhibit 3–8 are the costs that were added to the account in entries (2)–(6). Observe that the incurrence of these actual overhead costs [entries (2)–(6)] and the application of overhead to Work in Process [entry (7)] represent two separate and distinct processes.

The concept of a clearing account   The Manufacturing Overhead account operates as a clearing account. As we have noted, actual factory overhead costs are charged to it as they are incurred day by day throughout the year. At certain intervals during the year, usually when a job is completed, overhead cost is released from the Manufacturing Overhead account and is applied to the Work in Process account by means of the predetermined overhead rate. This sequence of events is illustrated below:

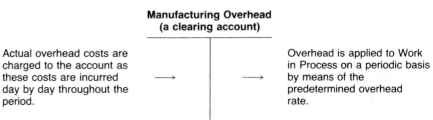

Manufacturing Overhead
(a clearing account)

| Actual overhead costs are charged to the account as these costs are incurred day by day throughout the period. | Overhead is applied to Work in Process on a periodic basis by means of the predetermined overhead rate. |

As we emphasized earlier, the predetermined overhead rate is based entirely on estimates of what overhead costs are *expected* to be, and it is established before the year begins. As a result, the overhead cost applied during a year may turn out to be more or less than the overhead cost that is actually incurred. For example, notice from Exhibit 3–8 that the Rand Company's actual overhead costs for the period are $5,000 greater than the overhead cost that has been applied to Work in Process, resulting in a $5,000 debit balance in the Manufacturing Overhead account. We will reserve discussion of what to do with this $5,000 balance until a later section, "Problems of Overhead Application."

For the moment, we can conclude by noting from Exhibit 3–8 that the cost of a completed job consists of the actual materials cost of the job, the actual labor cost of the job, and an *applied* amount of overhead cost to the job. The fact that it is applied overhead cost (not actual overhead cost) that goes into the Work in Process account and onto the job cost sheets is a subtle point that is easy to miss. Thus, this section of the chapter requires special study and consideration.

Nonmanufacturing Costs

In addition to incurring costs such as salaries, utilities, and insurance as part of the operation of the factory, manufacturing firms will also incur these same kinds of costs in relation to other parts of their operations. For example, there will be these types of costs arising from activities in the "front office" where secretaries, top management, and others work. There will be identical kinds of costs arising from the operation of the sales staff. *The costs of these nonfactory operations should not go into the Manufacturing Overhead account because the incurrence of these costs is not related to the manufacture of products.* Rather, these costs should be treated as expenses of the period, as explained in Chapter 2, and charged directly to the income statement. To illustrate, assume that the Rand Company incurred selling and administrative costs as follows during the month of April:

Top-management salaries . . .	$21,000
Other office salaries	9,000
Total salaries	$30,000

The entry to record these salaries would be:

(8)		
Salaries Expense	30,000	
Salaries and Wages Payable		30,000

Assume that depreciation on office equipment during the month of April was $7,000. The entry would be:

(9)

Depreciation Expense	7,000	
Accumulated Depreciation		7,000

Pay particular attention to the difference between this entry and entry (6) on page 84 where we recorded depreciation on factory equipment.

Finally, assume that advertising was $42,000 and that other selling and administrative expenses totaled $8,000 for the month. The entry to record these items would be:

(10)

Advertising Expense	42,000	
Other Selling and Administrative Expense	8,000	
Accounts Payable		50,000

Since the amounts in entries (8) through (10) all go directly into expense accounts, they will have no effect on the costing of the Rand Company's production for the month. The same will be true of all other selling and administrative expenses incurred during the month, including sales commissions, depreciation on sales equipment, rent on office facilities, insurance on office facilities, and related costs.

Cost of Goods Manufactured

When a job has been completed, the finished output is transferred from the production departments to the finished goods warehouse. By this time, the accounting department will have charged the job with direct materials and direct labor cost, and the job will have absorbed a portion of manufacturing overhead through the application process discussed earlier. A transfer of these costs must be made within the costing system that *parallels* the physical transfer of the goods to the finished goods warehouse. The transfer within the costing system will be to move the costs of the completed job out of the Work in Process account and into the Finished Goods account. The sum of all amounts transferred between these two accounts represents the cost of goods manufactured for the period. (This point was illustrated earlier in Exhibit 2–5 in Chapter 2. The reader may wish to go back to Exhibit 2–5 and refresh this point before reading on.)

In the case of the Rand Company, let us assume that job A was completed during April. The entry to transfer the cost of job A from Work in Process to Finished Goods would be:

(11)

Finished Goods	158,000	
Work in Process		158,000

The $158,000 represents the completed cost of job A, as shown on the job cost sheet in Exhibit 3–8. Since job A was the only job completed during April, the $158,000 also represents the cost of goods manufactured for the month.

Job B was not completed by month-end, so its cost will remain in the Work in Process account and carry over to the next month. If a balance sheet is prepared at the end of April, the cost accumulated thus far on job B will appear under the caption "Work in process inventory" in the assets section.

Cost of Goods Sold

As units of product in finished goods are shipped to fill customer orders, the unit cost appearing on the job cost sheets is used as a basis for transferring the cost of the sold items from the Finished Goods account into the Cost of Goods Sold account. If a complete job is shipped, as in the case where a job has been done to a customer's specifications, then it is a simple matter to transfer the entire cost appearing on the job cost sheet into the Cost of Goods Sold account. In most cases, however, only a portion of the units involved in a particular job will be sold. In these situations, the unit cost is particularly important in knowing how much product cost should be removed from Finished Goods and charged into Cost of Goods Sold.

For the Rand Company, we will assume that three fourths of the units in job A were shipped to customers by month-end. The total selling price of these units was $225,000. The entries needed to record the sale would be (all sales are on account):

(12)

Accounts Receivable	225,000	
Sales		225,000

(13)

Cost of Goods Sold	118,500	
Finished Goods		118,500
($158,000 total cost × ¾ = $118,500)		

With entry (13), the flow of costs through our job-order costing system is completed.

A Summary of Cost Flows

To pull the entire Rand Company example together, a summary of cost flows is presented in T-account form in Exhibit 3–9. The flows of costs through the exhibit are keyed to the numbers (1) through (13). These numbers relate to the numbers of the transactions appearing on the preceding pages.

EXHIBIT 3–9

A summary of cost flows—The Rand Company

Accounts Receivable

XX		
(12) 225,000		

Prepaid Insurance

XX	(5) 9,000

Raw Materials

Bal. 5,000	(2) 50,000
(1) 60,000	
Bal. 15,000	

Work in Process

Bal. 30,000	(11) 158,000
(2) 50,000	
(3) 60,000	
(7) 90,000	
Bal. 72,000	

Finished Goods

Bal. 10,000	(13) 118,500
(11) 158,000	
Bal. 49,500	

Accumulated Depreciation

	XX
	(6) 18,000
	(9) 7,000

Manufacturing Overhead

(3) 15,000	(7) 90,000
(4) 40,000	
(5) 22,000	
(6) 18,000	
Bal. 5,000	

Accounts Payable

	XX
	(1) 60,000
	(4) 40,000
	(10) 50,000

Salaries and Wages Payable

	XX
	(3) 75,000
	(8) 30,000

Property Taxes Payable

	XX
	(5) 13,000

Capital Stock

	XX

Retained Earnings

	XX

Sales

	(12) 225,000

Cost of Goods Sold

(13) 118,500	

Salaries Expense

(8) 30,000	

Depreciation Expense

(9) 7,000	

Advertising Expense

(10) 42,000	

Other Selling and Administrative Expense

(10) 8,000	

Note: XX = Normal balance in the account (for example, Accounts Receivable normally carries a debit balance).
Explanation of entries:
(1) Raw materials purchased.
(2) Raw materials issued into production.
(3) Factory labor costs incurred.
(4) Utilities and other factory costs incurred.
(5) Property taxes and insurance incurred on the factory.
(6) Depreciation recorded on factory assets.
(7) Overhead cost applied to Work in Process.
(8) Administrative salaries expense incurred.
(9) Depreciation recorded on office equipment.
(10) Advertising and other expense incurred.
(11) Cost of goods manufactured transferred into finished goods.
(12) Sale of job A recorded.
(13) Cost of goods sold recorded for job A.

Exhibit 3–10 presents a schedule of cost of goods manufactured and a schedule of cost of goods sold for the Rand Company. Note particularly from Exhibit 3–10 that the cost of goods manufactured for the month ($158,000) agrees with the amount transferred from Work in Process to Finished Goods for the month as recorded earlier in entry (11).

EXHIBIT 3–10

Schedules of cost of goods manufactured and cost of goods sold

Cost of Goods Manufactured

Direct materials:		
Raw materials inventory, April 1	$ 5,000	
Add: Purchases of raw materials	60,000	
Total raw materials available	65,000	
Deduct: Raw materials inventory, April 30	15,000	
Raw materials used in production		$ 50,000
Direct labor		60,000
Manufacturing overhead:		
Indirect labor	15,000	
Utilities	21,000	
Rent	16,000	
Miscellaneous factory costs	3,000	
Property taxes	13,000	
Insurance	9,000	
Depreciation	18,000	
Actual overhead costs	95,000	
Less underapplied overhead	5,000*	
Overhead applied to work in process		90,000
Total manufacturing costs		200,000
Add: Beginning work in process inventory		30,000
		230,000
Deduct: Ending work in process inventory		72,000
Cost of goods manufactured		$158,000

Cost of Goods Sold

Opening finished goods inventory	$ 10,000
Add: Cost of goods manufactured	158,000
Goods available for sale	168,000
Ending finished goods inventory	49,500
Cost of goods sold	118,500
Add: Underapplied overhead	5,000
Adjusted cost of goods sold	$123,500

*Note that underapplied overhead must be deducted from actual overhead costs and only the difference ($90,000) is added to direct materials and direct labor. The reason is that the schedule of cost of goods manufactured represents a summary of costs flowing through the Work in Process account during a period and therefore must exclude any overhead costs that were incurred but never applied to production. If a reverse situation had existed and overhead had been overapplied during the period, then the amount of overapplied overhead would have been added to actual overhead costs on the schedule. This would have brought the actual overhead costs up to the amount that had been applied to production.

Also note that the underapplied overhead deducted on the schedule of cost of goods manufactured is added to cost of goods sold. The reverse would be true if overhead had been overapplied.

PROBLEMS OF OVERHEAD APPLICATION

The Concept of Underapplied and Overapplied Overhead

Since the predetermined overhead rate is established before a period begins, and is based entirely on estimated data, there will generally be a difference between the amount of overhead cost that is applied to the Work in Process account and the actual overhead costs that materialize during the period. In the case of the Rand Company, for example, the predetermined overhead rate of $6 per hour resulted in $90,000 of overhead cost being applied to Work in Process, whereas actual overhead costs proved to be $95,000 for the month (see Exhibit 3–8). The difference between the overhead cost applied to Work in Process and the actual overhead costs of a period is termed either **underapplied** or **overapplied overhead.** For the Rand Company, overhead was underapplied because the applied cost ($90,000) was $5,000 less than the actual cost ($95,000). If the tables had been reversed and the company had applied $95,000 in overhead cost to Work in Process while incurring actual overhead costs of only $90,000, then a situation of overapplied overhead would have existed.

Since the amount of overhead applied to Work in Process is dependent on the predetermined overhead rate, any difference between applied overhead cost and actual overhead cost must be traceable to the estimates going into the overhead rate computation. To illustrate, refer again to the formula used in computing the predetermined overhead rate:

$$\frac{\text{Estimated total manufacturing overhead costs}}{\text{Estimated total units in the base (machine-hours, etc.)}}$$
$$= \text{Predetermined overhead rate}$$

If either the estimated cost or the estimated level of activity used in this formula differs from the actual cost or the actual level of activity for a period, then the predetermined overhead rate will prove to be inaccurate. The result will be either under- or overapplied overhead for the period. Assume, for example, that two companies have prepared the following estimated data for the year 19x1:

	Company A	Company B
Predetermined overhead rate based on	Machine-hours	Direct labor cost
Estimated manufacturing overhead for 19x1 . . .	$100,000 *(a)*	$120,000 *(a)*
Estimated machine-hours for 19x1	50,000 *(b)*	—
Estimated direct labor cost for 19x1	—	$ 80,000 *(b)*
Predetermined overhead rate, *(a) ÷ (b)*	$2 per machine-hour	150% of direct labor cost

Now assume that the *actual* overhead costs and the *actual* level of activity for 19x1 for each company are shown as follows:

	Company A	Company B
Actual manufacturing overhead costs	$99,000	$128,000
Actual machine-hours	48,000	—
Actual direct labor cost	—	88,000

For each company, notice that the actual cost and activity data differ from the estimates used in computing the predetermined overhead rate. The computation of the resulting under- or overapplied overhead for each company is given below:

	Company A	Company B
Actual manufacturing overhead costs	$99,000	$128,000
Manufacturing overhead cost applied to Work in Process during 19x1:		
48,000 *actual* machine-hours × $2	96,000	
$88,000 *actual* direct labor cost × 150%		132,000
Underapplied (overapplied) overhead	$ 3,000	$ (4,000)

For Company A, notice that the amount of overhead cost that has been applied to Work in Process ($96,000) is less than the actual overhead cost for the year ($99,000). Therefore, overhead is underapplied. Also notice that the original estimate of overhead in Company A ($100,000) is not directly involved in this computation. Its impact is felt only through the $2 predetermined overhead rate that is used.

For Company B, the amount of overhead cost that has been applied to Work in Process ($132,000) is greater than the actual overhead cost for the year ($128,000), and so a situation of overapplied overhead exists.

A summary of the concepts discussed in this section is presented in Exhibit 3–11.

Disposition of Under- or Overapplied Overhead Balances

What disposition should be made of any under- or overapplied balance remaining in the Manufacturing Overhead account at the end of a period? Generally, any balance in the account is treated in one of two ways:

1.   Closed out to Cost of Goods Sold.

EXHIBIT 3–11

Summary of overhead concepts

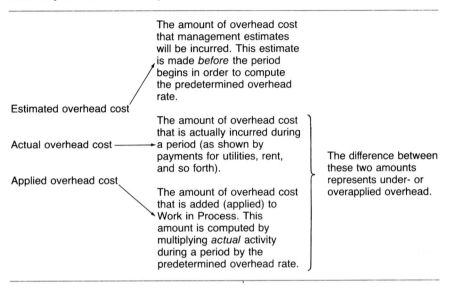

Estimated overhead cost

The amount of overhead cost that management estimates will be incurred. This estimate is made *before* the period begins in order to compute the predetermined overhead rate.

Actual overhead cost

The amount of overhead cost that is actually incurred during a period (as shown by payments for utilities, rent, and so forth).

Applied overhead cost

The amount of overhead cost that is added (applied) to Work in Process. This amount is computed by multiplying *actual* activity during a period by the predetermined overhead rate.

The difference between these two amounts represents under- or overapplied overhead.

2. Allocated between Work in Process, Finished Goods, and Cost of Goods Sold in proportion to the ending balances in these accounts.[3]

Closed out to cost of goods sold   Most firms close out any under- or overapplied overhead to Cost of Goods Sold, since this approach is simpler than allocation. Returning to the example of the Rand Company, the entry to close the underapplied overhead to Cost of Goods Sold would be (see Exhibit 3–9 for the $5,000 cost figure):

	(14)	
Cost of Goods Sold	5,000	
Manufacturing Overhead		5,000

With this entry, the cost of goods sold for the month increases to $123,500, as shown earlier:

Cost of goods sold (from Exhibit 3–9)	$118,500
Add underapplied overhead [entry (14) above] . . .	5,000
Adjusted cost of goods sold	$123,500

---

[3] Some firms prefer to make the allocation on a basis of the amount of *overhead cost* in the above accounts at the end of a period. This approach to allocation will yield more accurate results in those situations where the amount of overhead cost differs substantially between jobs. For purposes of consistency, when we allocate in this book it will always be on a basis of the ending balances in the above accounts.

EXHIBIT 3–12

THE RAND COMPANY
Income Statement
For the Month of April 19xx

Sales		$225,000
Less cost of goods sold ($118,500 + $5,000) . . .		123,500
Gross margin		101,500
Less selling and administrative expenses:		
Salaries expense	$30,000	
Depreciation expense	7,000	
Advertising expense	42,000	
Other expense	8,000	87,000
Net income		$ 14,500

An income statement for the Rand Company for April would therefore appear as shown in Exhibit 3–12.

Allocated between accounts Allocation of under- or overapplied overhead between Work in Process, Finished Goods, and Cost of Goods Sold is more accurate than closing the entire balance into Cost of Goods Sold. The reason is that allocation assigns overhead costs to where they would have gone in the first place had it not been for the errors in the estimates going into the predetermined overhead rate. Although allocation is more accurate than direct write-off, it is used less often in actual practice because of the time and difficulty involved in the allocation process. Most firms feel that the greater accuracy simply isn't worth the extra effort that allocation requires, particularly when the dollar amounts are small.

Had we chosen to allocate the underapplied overhead in the Rand Company example, the computations and entry would have been:

Work in process inventory, April 30	$ 72,000	30.0%
Finished goods inventory, April 30	49,500	20.6
Cost of goods sold	118,500	49.4
Total cost	$240,000	100.0%

Work in Process (30.0% × $5,000)	1,500	
Finished Goods (20.6% × $5,000)	1,030	
Cost of Goods Sold (49.4% × $5,000)	2,470	
Manufacturing Overhead		5,000

If overhead had been overapplied, the entry above would have been just the reverse, since a credit balance would have existed in the Manufacturing Overhead account.

A General Model of Product Cost Flows

The flow of costs in a product costing system can be presented in general model form, as shown in Exhibit 3–13. This model applies as much to a process costing system as it does to a job-order costing system. Visual inspection of the model can be very helpful in gaining a perspective as to

EXHIBIT 3–13

A general model of cost flows

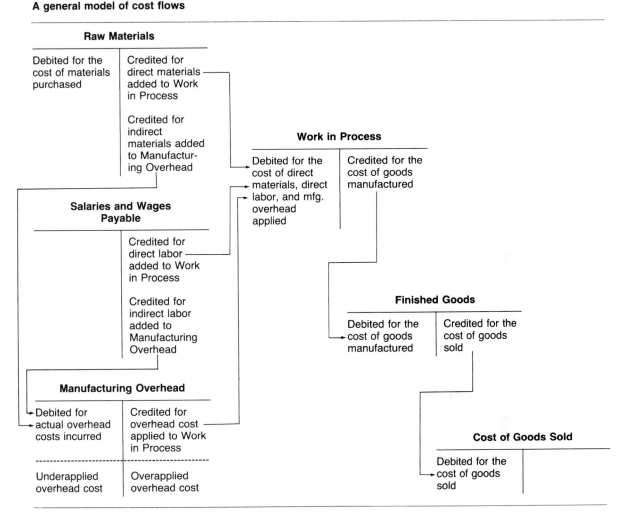

how costs enter a system, flow through it, and finally end up as cost of goods sold on the income statement.

Multiple Predetermined Overhead Rates

Our discussion in this chapter has assumed that a single overhead rate was being used throughout an entire factory operation. In small companies, and even in some medium-sized companies, a single overhead rate (called a **plantwide overhead rate**) is used and is entirely adequate as a means of allocating overhead costs to production jobs. But in larger companies, **multiple predetermined overhead rates** are common for the reason that a single rate may not be capable of equitably handling the overhead costs of all departments. One department may be labor intensive, for example, and rely almost solely on the efforts of workers in performing needed functions. Allocation of overhead costs in such a department could, perhaps, be done most equitably on a basis of labor-hours or labor cost. Another department in the same factory may be machine intensive, requiring little in the way of worker effort. Allocation of overhead costs in this department could, perhaps, be done most equitably on a basis of machine-hours.

In short, larger organizations often have many predetermined overhead rates—perhaps a different one for each department. As a unit of product moves along the production line, overhead is applied in each department, according to the various overhead rates that have been set. The accumulation of all of these overhead applications represents the total overhead cost of the job.

Job-Order Costing in Service Companies

We stated earlier in the chapter that job-order costing is used extensively in service organizations such as law firms, movie studios, hospitals, and repair shops, as well as in manufacturing firms. In a law firm, for example, each client represents a ''job,'' and the costs of that job are accumulated day by day on a job cost sheet as the client's case is handled by the firm. Paper supplies and similar inputs represent the direct materials for the job, the time expended by attorneys represents the direct labor, and the costs of secretaries, clerks, rent, depreciation, and so forth, represent the overhead.

In a movie studio, each picture produced by the studio is a ''job,'' and costs for direct materials (costumes, props, film, etc.) and direct labor (actors, directors, and extras) are carefully accounted for and charged to each picture's job cost sheet. A proportionate share of the studio's overhead costs, such as utilities, depreciation of equipment, salaries of maintenance workers, and so forth, is also charged to each picture. In a movie studio, overhead would typically be applied to jobs on a basis of camera time, or space and time occupied in a studio, rather than applied on a basis of actors' time or cost. On the other hand, in a law firm an attorney's time may be the most appropriate basis for recognizing overhead cost when determining the cost of a case and billing a client.

In sum, the reader should be aware that job-order costing is a versatile and widely used costing method, and that he or she may expect to encounter it in virtually any organization where the output differs between products, patients, clients, or customers.

SUMMARY

Unit cost of production is one of the most useful items of cost data to a manager. There are two methods in widespread use for determining unit costs; these two methods are known as job-order costing and process costing, respectively. Job-order costing is used in those manufacturing situations where products differ from each other, such as in furniture manufacture and shipbuilding. Process costing is used in those situations where units of product are homogeneous, such as in the manufacture of flour or cement. We have also noted that job-order costing is used extensively in the service industries.

Materials requisition forms and labor time tickets control the assignment of direct materials and direct labor cost to production. Indirect manufacturing costs are assigned to production through use of a predetermined overhead rate, which is developed by estimating the level of manufacturing overhead to be incurred during a period and by dividing this estimate by a base common to all the jobs to be worked on during the period. The most frequently used bases are machine-hours and direct labor-hours.

Since the predetermined overhead rate is based on estimates, the actual overhead cost incurred during a period may be somewhat more or somewhat less than the amount of overhead cost applied to production. Such a difference is referred to as under- or overapplied overhead. The under- or overapplied overhead of a period can be either (1) closed out to Cost of Goods Sold or (2) allocated between Work in Process, Finished Goods, and Cost of Goods Sold.

KEY TERMS FOR REVIEW

Absorption cost A costing method that includes all manufacturing costs—direct materials, direct labor, and both variable and fixed overhead—as part of the cost of a finished unit of product. This term is synonymous with *full cost*.

Bill of materials A control sheet that shows the type and quantity of each item of material going into a completed unit of product.

Cost driver Machine-hours, direct labor-hours, or a similar base that is a causal factor in the incurrence of overhead cost, or is closely correlated with its incurrence.

Full cost See *Absorption cost*.

Job cost sheet A form prepared for each job initiated into production that serves as a means for accumulating the materials, labor, and overhead costs chargeable to the job and as a means for computing unit costs.

Job-order costing system A costing system used in those manufacturing situations where many different products, jobs, or batches of production are being produced each period.

Materials requisition form A detailed source document that specifies the type and quantity of materials that are to be drawn from the storeroom and identifies the job to which the materials are to be charged.

Multiple predetermined overhead rates The setting of a different predetermined overhead rate in each department, rather than having a single predetermined overhead rate for the entire company.

Overapplied overhead A credit balance in the Manufacturing Overhead account that arises when the amount of overhead cost applied to Work in Process is greater than the amount of overhead cost actually incurred during a period.

Overhead application The charging of manufacturing overhead cost to the job cost sheets and to the Work in Process account.

Plantwide overhead rate A single predetermined overhead rate that is used in all departments of a company, rather than each department having its own separate predetermined overhead rate.

Predetermined overhead rate A rate used to charge overhead cost to jobs in production; the rate is established in advance for each period by use of estimates of manufacturing overhead cost and production activity for the period.

Process costing system A costing system used in those manufacturing situations where a single, homogeneous product (such as cement or flour) is produced for long periods of time.

Time ticket A detailed source document that is used to record an employee's hour-by-hour activities during a day.

Underapplied overhead A debit balance in the Manufacturing Overhead account that arises when the amount of overhead cost actually incurred is greater than the amount of overhead cost applied to Work in Process during a period.

APPENDIX: NORMALIZED OVERHEAD RATES

Many firms hesitate to set predetermined overhead rates on the basis of the expected production of a single period if that production is subject to wide variations. The reason is that as production levels fluctuate, the predetermined overhead rate also fluctuates, resulting in high per unit costs in periods when production is low and in low per unit costs in periods when production is high. This problem is traceable to the fact that fixed costs often make up a large part of manufacturing overhead, and, as explained in Chapter 2, these costs go on basically unchanged in total regardless of the level of activity. As a result, when production is low, the fixed overhead costs are spread over a small number of units, resulting in a high cost per unit. When production is high, these costs are spread over a large number of units, resulting in a lower cost per unit.

Fluctuating Overhead Rates

To illustrate the problems caused by fluctuating overhead rates, let us assume the following production, sales, and cost data for a manufacturing firm:

	Year 1	Year 2
Production and sales data:		
Production in units	10,000	6,000
Sales in units	8,000	8,000
Estimated manufacturing overhead cost:		
Variable overhead cost ($1 per unit)	$10,000	$ 6,000
Fixed overhead cost	24,000	24,000
Total estimated overhead cost	$34,000	$30,000

If the company sets its overhead rates on the basis of the expected production of each year, the rates will be:

$$\text{Year 1:} \quad \frac{\text{Estimated overhead cost, \$34,000}}{\text{Estimated production, 10,000 units}^*} = \$3.40 \text{ per unit}$$

$$\text{Year 2:} \quad \frac{\text{Estimated overhead cost, \$30,000}}{\text{Estimated production, 6,000 units}} = \$5 \text{ per unit}$$

 * Rather than setting the overhead rate on a basis of the number of units produced, the company could have set it on a basis of the number of direct labor-hours needed to produce the units; units of product are being used in this example simply for ease of illustration.

If we further assume that each unit of product requires $2 in direct materials cost and $3 in direct labor cost, then the total cost of a unit of product manufactured in each separate year will be:

	Year 1	Year 2
Direct materials	$2.00	$ 2.00
Direct labor	3.00	3.00
Manufacturing overhead	3.40	5.00
Total cost per unit	$8.40	$10.00

Notice the wide variation in unit costs between the two years. Looking at the overhead portion of the cost, we can see that the higher production level in year 1 has caused the overhead to be spread thinner, resulting in a lower cost per unit. Many managers feel that this type of variation in unit costs can lead to distorted financial statements and can cause confusion on the part of statement users. With unit costs jumping up and down, statements become difficult to interpret and can lead to faulty conclusions and unwise decisions.

This point can be seen clearly by preparing a partial income statement for each of the two years from the data above. (Recall from the original data that sales are planned at 8,000 units annually; we will assume a selling price of $10 per unit.)

	Year 1	Year 2	Total
Sales (8,000 units at $10 each)	$80,000	$80,000	$160,000
Cost of goods sold:			
Year 1 (8,000 units at $8.40 each)	67,200		
Year 2 (2,000 units at $8.40 each)		16,800	144,000
(6,000 units at $10 each)		60,000	
Total cost of goods sold	67,200	76,800	144,000
Gross margin	$12,800	$ 3,200	$ 16,000

Although sales are constant at 8,000 units in each year, the gross margin drops dramatically in year 2. The reason, of course, is that production dropped off in year 2, causing a jump in cost per unit and a drop in gross margin per unit. Yet an uninformed manager seeing these data might be misled into thinking that massive inefficiencies were developing or that a substantial jump in labor or raw materials prices had just taken place. An uninformed stockholder might be led to believe that difficulties were developing in the company that warranted the selling of his or her stock. In reality, we can see that none of these conclusions are correct; the variation in gross margin is simply a result of a temporary imbalance between production and sales.

The Concept of a Normalized Overhead Rate

The company in our illustration may have had good reasons for producing more than it sold in year 1. For example, the company may have been building inventories in anticipation of a strike or a supply interruption in year 2, in order to have goods on hand to meet customer needs. In short, the question isn't whether variations in the level of production are desirable—such variations are often unavoidable. The question is whether these variations should be permitted to influence unit costs—pushing costs up in times of low activity and pulling them down in times of high activity. Many managers would argue that the cost of a unit of product should be the same whether it is produced in year 1, year 2, or any other year, so long as long-run demand for the product is reasonably stable.

How can uniformity in unit cost be attained if a firm's production is fluctuating from year to year? The answer lies in **normalized overhead rates.** A normalized overhead rate is not based on the expected activity of a single period. Rather, a normalized overhead rate is based on an average activity level that spans many periods—past, present, and future. The approach is to determine what level of activity is *normal* over the long run, and then to set predetermined overhead rates on that figure. Such rates are said to be normalized in the sense that they smooth out the hills and valleys in activity that are largely beyond management's control.

An Illustration of Normalized Overhead Rates

To show how normalized overhead rates work, let us return to the data used earlier. On a normalized basis, overhead rates would be set on an average production figure of 8,000 units per year rather than on a basis of 10,000 units in year 1 and 6,000 units in year 2. The computations would be:

	Per unit
Fixed overhead cost	
($24,000 ÷ 8,000 units)	$3
Variable overhead cost	1
Total predetermined overhead rate . . .	$4

This overhead rate would be used to cost units of product in both years; therefore, the full cost of a unit produced in either year would be:

Direct materials (as before)	$2
Direct labor (as before)	3
Manufacturing overhead	4
Total cost per unit	$9

With stable unit costs, the erratic behavior that we observed earlier on the company's income statement will be eliminated, as shown below:

	Year 1	Year 2	Total
Sales (8,000 units at $10 each)	$80,000	$80,000	$160,000
Cost of goods sold (8,000 units at $9 each) . . .	72,000	72,000	144,000
Gross margin	$ 8,000	$ 8,000	$ 16,000

Notice that as a result of using normalized overhead rates, the gross margin pattern is even over the two-year period. By contrast, recall from our earlier income statement that when fluctuating overhead rates are used to cost production, the gross margin pattern is erratic, even though the same number of units is sold in each year. In years when production is high, income is also high; in years when production is low, income is also low.

In short, normalized overhead rates largely eliminate from inventories, from cost of goods sold, and from gross margin any unfavorable impact of having production out of balance with the long-run demand for a company's products.

KEY TERM FOR REVIEW (APPENDIX)

Normalized overhead rate An overhead rate that is based on the long-run avera (or "normal") level of activity in a company rather than based on the expecte activity of any given year.

QUESTIONS

3–1. State the purposes for which it is necessary or desirable to compute unit costs.

3–2. Distinguish between job-order costing and process costing.

3–3. What is the essential purpose of any costing system?

3–4. What is the purpose of the job cost sheet in a job-order costing system?

3–5. What is a predetermined overhead rate, and how is it computed?

3–6. Explain how a sales order, a production order, a materials requisition form, and a labor time ticket are involved in the production and costing of products.

3–7. Explain why some production costs must be assigned to products through an allocation process. Name several such costs. Would such costs be classified as *direct* or as *indirect* costs?

3–8. Why do firms use predetermined overhead rates rather than actual mamufacturing overhead costs in applying overhead to units of product?

3–9. What factors should be considered in selecting a base to be used in computing the predetermined overhead rate?

3–10. What is meant by the statement that overhead is ''absorbed'' into units of product? If a company fully absorbs its overhead costs, does this guarantee that a profit will be earned for the period?

3–11. What account is credited when overhead cost is applied to Work in Process? Would you expect the amount applied for a period to equal the actual overhead costs of the period? Why or why not?

3–12. What is underapplied overhead? Overapplied overhead? What disposition is made of these amounts at period end?

3–13. Enumerate several reasons why overhead might be underapplied in a given year.

3–14. What adjustment is made for underapplied overhead on the schedule of cost of goods manufactured, and why is this adjustment necessary? What adjustment is made on the schedule of cost of goods sold?

3–15. What adjustment is made for overapplied overhead on the schedule of cost of goods manufactured, and why is this adjustment necessary? What adjustment is made on the schedule of cost of goods sold?

3–16. Sigma Company applies overhead cost to jobs on a basis of direct labor cost. Job A, which was started and completed during the current period, shows charges of $5,000 for direct materials, $8,000 for direct labor, and $6,000 for overhead on its job cost sheet. Job B, which is still in process at year-end, shows charges of $2,500 for direct materials and $4,000 for direct labor. Should any overhead cost be added to job B at year-end? Explain.

3–17. A company assigns overhead cost to completed jobs on a basis of 125 percent of direct labor cost. The job cost sheet for job 313 shows that $10,000 in direct material has been used on the job and that $12,000 in direct labor cost has been incurred. If 1,000 units were produced in job 313, what is the cost per unit?

3–18. What is a ''plantwide'' overhead rate? Why are multiple overhead rates, rather than a plantwide rate, used in some companies?

3–19. If overhead rates are set on a basis of each period's activity, then unit costs will rise as the activity level rises, and vice versa. Do you agree? Explain.

3–20. What is the purpose of a normalized overhead rate? Are such rates more or less apt to lead to confusion on the part of statement users than using rates based on the activity of individual periods? Explain.

EXERCISES

E3–1. Which method of accumulating product costs, job-order costing or process costing, would be more appropriate in each of the following situations?

    a. A textbook publisher.
    b. An oil refinery.
    c. A manufacturer of powdered milk.
    d. A manufacturer of ready-mix cement.
    e. A custom home builder.
    f. A shop for customizing vans.
    g. A chemical manufacturer.
    h. An auto repair shop.
    i. A tire manufacturing plant.
    j. An advertising agency.

 E3–2. Harwood Company is a manufacturing firm that operates a job-order costing system. Overhead costs are charged to production on a basis of machine-hours. At the beginning of 19x6, management estimated that the company would incur $192,000 in manufacturing overhead costs for the year and work 80,000 machine-hours.

Required: 1. Compute the company's predetermined overhead rate for 19x6.
    2. Assume that during the year the company works only 75,000 machine-hours and incurs the following costs in the Manufacturing Overhead and Work in Process accounts:

	Manufacturing Overhead			Work in Process	
(Maintenance)	21,000	?	(Direct materials)	710,000	
(Indirect materials)	8,000		(Direct labor)	90,000	
(Indirect labor)	60,000		(Overhead)	?	
(Utilities)	32,000				
(Insurance)	18,000				
(Depreciation)	45,000				

Copy the data in the T-accounts above onto your answer sheet. Compute the amount of overhead cost that should be applied to Work in Process for the year, and make the entry in your T-accounts.

    3. Compute the amount of under- or overapplied overhead for the year, and show the balance in your Manufacturing Overhead T-account. Show the general journal entry that most companies would make to close out the balance in this account.

E3–3. Kingsport Manufacturing Company experiences a wide variation in demand for its product. Unit costs are computed on a quarterly basis by dividing each quarter's manufacturing costs (materials, labor, and overhead) by the quarter's production in units. The company's estimated costs, by quarter, for the coming year are given below:

	Quarter			
	First	Second	Third	Fourth
Direct materials	$ 72,000	$ 36,000	$ 18,000	$ 54,000
Direct labor	120,000	60,000	30,000	90,000
Manufacturing overhead	186,000	168,000	159,000	177,000
Total manufacturing costs	$378,000	$264,000	$207,000	$321,000
Number of units to be produced . . .	40,000	20,000	10,000	30,000
Estimated cost per unit	$9.45	$13.20	$20.70	$10.70

Management finds the variation in unit costs to be confusing and difficult to work with. It has been suggested that the problem lies with manufacturing overhead, since it is the largest element of cost. Accordingly, you have been asked to find a more equitable way of assigning manufacturing overhead cost to units of product. After some analysis, you have determined that the company's overhead costs are mostly fixed and therefore show little sensitivity to changes in the level of production.

Required: 1. The company uses a job-order costing system. How would you recommend that manufacturing overhead cost be assigned to production? Be specific, and show computations.
2. Recompute the company's unit costs in accordance with your recommendations in (1) above.

E3–4.   The Polaris Company uses a job-order costing system. The following data relate to the month of October 19x8, the first month of the company's fiscal year:

a.   Raw materials purchased on account, $150,000.
b.   Raw materials issued to production, $120,000 (90 percent direct, 10 percent indirect).
c.   Direct labor cost incurred, $140,000; indirect labor cost incurred, $60,000.
d.   Depreciation on factory equipment, $18,000.
e.   Other manufacturing overhead costs incurred during the month, $90,000 (credit Accounts Payable).
f.   The company applies manufacturing overhead cost to production on a basis of $9 per machine-hour. There were 21,000 machine-hours recorded for the month.
g.   Production orders costing $450,000 were completed during the month and transferred to Finished Goods.
h.   Production orders that had cost $400,000 to complete were shipped to customers during the month. These goods were invoiced at 50 percent above cost. The goods were sold on account.

Required: 1. Prepare journal entries to record the information given above.
2. Prepare T-accounts for Manufacturing Overhead and Work in Process. Post the relevant information above to each account. Compute the ending balance in each account, assuming that Work in Process has a beginning balance of $33,000.

E3–5.   Estimated cost and operating data for three companies for 19x1 are given below:

	Company		
	X	**Y**	**Z**
Direct labor-hours	80,000	45,000	60,000
Machine-hours	30,000	70,000	21,000
Direct labor cost	$400,000	$290,000	$300,000
Manufacturing overhead cost . . .	536,000	315,000	480,000

Predetermined overhead rates are computed on the following bases in the three companies:

Company	Overhead rate based on–
X	Direct labor-hours
Y	Machine-hours
Z	Direct labor cost

Required: 1. Compute the predetermined overhead rate to be used in each company during 19x1.

2. Assume that three jobs are worked on during 19x1 in Company X. Direct labor-hours by job are: job 418, 12,000 hours; job 419, 36,000 hours; job 420, 30,000 hours. How much overhead cost will the company apply to Work in Process for the year? If actual overhead costs total $530,000 for the year, will overhead be underapplied or overapplied?

E3–6. The following cost data relate to the manufacturing activities of the Black Company during 19x5:

Manufacturing overhead costs
incurred during the year:

Property taxes	$ 3,000
Utilities, factory	5,000
Indirect labor	10,000
Depreciation, factory	24,000
Insurance, factory	6,000
Total actual costs	$48,000

Other costs incurred
during the year:

Purchases of raw materials	$32,000
Direct labor cost	40,000

Inventories:

Raw materials, January 1	8,000
Raw materials, December 31	7,000
Work in process, January 1	6,000
Work in process, December 31	7,500

The company uses a predetermined overhead rate to charge overhead cost to production. The rate for 19x5 was $5 per machine-hour; a total of 10,000 machine-hours was recorded for the year.

Required: 1. Compute the amount of under- or overapplied overhead cost for 19x5.
2. Prepare a schedule of cost of goods manufactured for 19x5.

E3–7. White Company has two departments, cutting and finishing. The company uses a job-order costing system and computes a predetermined overhead rate in each department. The cutting department bases its rate on machine-hours, and the finishing department bases its rate on direct labor cost. At the beginning of 19x3, the company made the following estimates:

	Department	
	Cutting	Finishing
Direct labor-hours	6,000	30,000
Machine-hours	48,000	5,000
Manufacturing overhead cost . . .	$360,000	$486,000
Direct labor cost	50,000	270,000

Required:

1. Compute the predetermined overhead rate to be used in each department during 19x3.

2. Assume that the overhead rates that you computed in (1) are in effect. The job cost sheet for job 203, which was started and completed during the year, showed the following:

	Department	
	Cutting	Finishing
Direct labor-hours	6	20
Machine-hours	80	4
Materials requisitioned . . .	$500	$310
Direct labor cost.	70	150

Compute the total overhead cost of job 203.

3. Would you expect substantially different amounts of overhead cost to be assigned to some jobs if the company used a plantwide overhead rate based on direct labor cost, rather than using departmental rates? Explain. No computations are necessary.

E3–8. Dillon Products, Inc., manufactures various machine parts to customer specifications. The company uses a job-order cost system and applies overhead cost to jobs on a basis of machine-hours. For the year 19x1, it was estimated that the company would work 220,000 machine-hours and incur $1,870,000 in manufacturing overhead costs.

The company spent the entire month of April working on a very large order, which called for 16,000 custom made machine parts. Cost data relating to April follow:

a. Raw materials purchased on account, $135,000.

b. Raw materials requisitioned for production, $100,000 (90 percent direct materials and 10 percent indirect materials).

c. Labor cost incurred in the factory, $210,000 (80 percent direct labor and 20 percent indirect labor).

d. Depreciation recorded on factory equipment, $30,000.

e. Other manufacturing overhead costs incurred, $85,000 (credit Accounts Payable).

f. Manufacturing overhead cost was applied to production on a basis of 20,000 machine-hours worked during the month.

g. The completed job was moved into the finished goods warehouse on April 30 to await delivery to the customer. (In computing the dollar amount for this entry, remember that the cost of a completed job consists of direct materials, direct labor, and *applied* overhead.)

Required: 1. Prepare journal entries to record items *(a)* through *(f)* above (ignore item *[g]* for the moment).

2. Prepare T-accounts for Manufacturing Overhead and Work in Process. Post the relevant items from your jornal entries to these T-accounts.

3. Prepare a journal entry for item *(g)* above, and then compute the unit cost that will appear on the job cost sheet.

E3–9. The Tyler Company uses a job-order costing system. The table below provides selected data on the three jobs worked on during the company's first month of operations:

	Job Number		
	101	102	103
Units of product in the job	2,000	1,800	1,500
Direct labor-hours worked	1,200	1,000	900
Direct materials cost	$4,500	$3,700	$1,400
Direct labor cost	9,600	8,000	7,200

Actual overhead costs totaling $30,000 were incurred during the month. Manufacturing overhead cost is applied to production on a basis of direct labor-hours at a predetermined rate of $9 per hour. Jobs 101 and 102 were completed during the month; job 103 was not completed.

Required: 1. Compute the amount of manufacturing overhead cost that would have been charged to each job during the month.

2. Compute the unit cost of jobs 101 and 102.

3. Prepare a journal entry showing the transfer of the completed jobs into the finished goods warehouse.

4. What is the balance in the Work in Process account at the end of the month?

E3–10. The following information is taken from the end-of-year account balances of the Sevier Manufacturing Company:

Manufacturing Overhead			
(a)	100,000	(b)	90,000
Bal.	10,000		

Work in Process			
Bal.	40,000	(c)	250,000
	75,000		
	60,000		
(b)	90,000		
Bal.	15,000		

Finished Goods			
Bal.	35,000	(d)	240,000
(c)	250,000		
Bal.	45,000		

Cost of Goods Sold		
(d)	240,000	

Required: 1. Identify the dollar figures appearing by the letters *(a)*, *(b)*, and so forth.
          2. Assume that the company closes any balance in the Manufacturing Overhead account directly to Cost of Goods Sold. Prepare the necessary journal entry.
          3. Assume that the company allocates any balance in the Manufacturing Overhead account to the other accounts. Prepare the necessary journal entry, with supporting computations.

E3–11.   Leeds Company began operations on January 2, 19x1. The following activity was recorded in the company's Work in Process account for the first month of operations:

Work in Process

Direct materials	90,000	To finished goods	260,000
Direct labor	75,000		
Manufacturing overhead	120,000		

Leeds Company uses a job-order costing system and applies manufacturing overhead to Work in Process on a basis of direct labor cost. At the end of January, only one job was still in process. This job (job 12) had been charged with $6,500 in direct labor cost.

Required: 1. Compute the predetermined overhead rate that was in use during January.
          2. Complete the following job cost sheet for the partially completed job 12:

Job Cost Sheet—Job 12
As of January 31, 19x1

Direct materials	$?
Direct labor.	?
Manufacturing overhead	?
Total cost to January 31	$?

PROBLEMS

P3–12.   **Entries directly into T-accounts; income statement.**   Hudson Company's trial balance as of January 1, 19x8, is given below:

Cash	$ 7,000	
Accounts Receivable	18,000	
Raw Materials	9,000	
Work in Process	20,000	
Finished Goods.	32,000	
Prepaid Insurance	4,000	
Plant and Equipment	210,000	
Accumulated Depreciation		$ 53,000
Accounts Payable.		38,000
Capital Stock.		160,000
Retained Earnings		49,000
Totals	$300,000	$300,000

Hudson Company is a manufacturing firm and employs a job-order costing system. During 19x8, the following transactions took place:

a. Raw materials were purchased on account, $40,000.
b. Raw materials were requisitioned for use in production, $38,000 (85 percent direct and 15 percent indirect).
c. Factory utility costs incurred, $19,100.
d. Depreciation was recorded on plant and equipment, $36,000. Three fourths of the depreciation related to factory equipment, and the remainder related to selling and administrative equipment.
e. Advertising expense incurred, $48,000.
f. Costs for salaries and wages were incurred as follows:

Direct labor	$45,000
Indirect labor	10,000
Administrative salaries . . .	30,000

g. Insurance expired during the year, $3,000 (80 percent related to factory operations, and 20 percent related to selling and administrative activities).
h. Miscellaneous selling and administrative expenses incurred, $9,500.
i. Manufacturing overhead was applied to production. The company applies overhead on a basis of $8 per machine-hour; 7,500 machine-hours were recorded for the month.
j. Goods costing $140,000 to manufacture were transferred to the finished goods warehouse.
k. Goods that had cost $130,000 to manufacture were sold on account for $250,000.
l. Collections from customers during the year totaled $245,000.
m. Payments to suppliers on account during the year, $150,000; payments to employees for salaries and wages, $84,000.

Required:
1. Prepare a T-account for each account in the company's trial balance, and enter the opening balances shown above.
2. Record the transactions above directly into the T-accounts. Prepare new T-accounts as needed. Key your entries to the letters *(a)* through *(m)* above. Find the ending balance in each account.
3. Is manufacturing overhead underapplied or overapplied for the year? Make an entry in the T-accounts to close any balance in the Manufacturing Overhead account to Cost of Goods Sold.
4. Prepare an income statement for the year. (Do not prepare a schedule of cost of goods manufactured; all of the information needed for the income statement is available in the T-accounts.)

P3–13. **Straightforward journal entries; partial T-accounts; income statement.**   Slater Company manufactures products to customer specifications; a job-order cost system is used to accumulate costs in the company's plant. On July 1, 19x5, the start of Slater Company's fiscal year, inventory balances were as follows:

Raw materials	$25,000
Work in process	10,000
Finished goods	40,000

The company applies overhead cost to jobs on a basis of machine-hours of operating time. For the fiscal year starting July 1, 19x5, it was estimated that the plant would operate 45,000 machine-hours and incur $270,000 in manufacturing overhead cost. During the year, the following transactions were completed:

a.   Raw materials were purchased on account, $275,000.

b.   Raw materials were requisitioned for use in production, $280,000 (materials costing $220,000 were chargeable directly to jobs; the remaining materials were indirect).

c.   Costs for employee services were incurred as follows:

Direct labor	$180,000
Indirect labor	72,000
Sales commissions	63,000
Administrative salaries . . .	90,000

d.   Prepaid insurance expired during the year, $18,000 ($13,000 of this amount related to factory operations, and the remainder related to selling and administrative activities).

e.   Utility costs were incurred in the factory, $57,000.

f.   Advertising costs were incurred, $140,000.

g.   Depreciation was recorded on equipment, $100,000. (Some $88,000 of this amount was on equipment used in factory operations; the remaining $12,000 was on equipment used in selling and administrative activities.)

h.   Manufacturing overhead cost was applied to production, $___?___ . (The company recorded 50,000 machine-hours of operating time during the year.)

i.   Goods costing $675,000 to manufacture were transferred into the finished goods warehouse.

j.   Sales (all on account) to customers during the year totaled $1,250,000. These goods had cost $700,000 to manufacture.

Required:
1.   Prepare journal entries to record the transactions for the year.

2.   Prepare T-accounts for inventories, Manufacturing Overhead, and Cost of Goods Sold. Post relevant data from your journal entries to these T-accounts (don't forget to enter the opening balances in your inventory accounts). Compute an ending balance in each account.

3.   Is Manufacturing Overhead underapplied or overapplied for the year? Prepare a journal entry to close any balance in the Manufacturing Overhead account to Cost of Goods Sold.

4.   Prepare an income statement for the year. (Do not prepare a schedule of cost of goods manufactured; all of the information needed for the income statement is available in the journal entries and T-accounts you have prepared.)

P3–14.   **Entries directly into T-accounts; overhead balance allocation; income statement.**   A balance sheet for Supreme Company as of January 1, 19x1, is given below:

SUPREME COMPANY
Balance Sheet
January 1, 19x1

Assets

Current assets:
Cash		$ 15,000
Accounts receivable		40,000
Inventories:		
Raw materials	$ 25,000	
Work in process	30,000	
Finished goods	45,000	100,000
Prepaid insurance		5,000
Total current assets		160,000
Plant and equipment	500,000	
Less accumulated depreciation	210,000	290,000
Total assets		$450,000

Liabilities and Stockholders' Equity

Accounts payable		$ 75,000
Capital stock	$250,000	
Retained earnings	125,000	375,000
Total liabilities and stockholders' equity		$450,000

Supreme Company is a manufacturing firm and uses a job-order cost system. For 19x1, the company estimated that it would incur $80,000 in manufacturing overhead cost and $100,000 in direct labor cost. The following transactions were recorded for the year:

a. Raw materials were purchased on account, $80,000.
b. Raw materials were issued to production, $90,000; $5,000 of this amount was for indirect materials.
c. Payroll costs incurred and paid: direct labor, $120,000; indirect labor, $30,000; and selling and administrative salaries, $75,000.
d. Factory utilities costs incurred, $12,000.
e. Depreciation recorded for the year, $30,000 ($5,000 on selling and administrative assets; $25,000 on factory assets).
f. Insurance expired, $4,800 ($4,000 related to factory operations, and $800 related to selling and administrative activities).
g. Advertising expenses incurred, $40,000.
h. Other manufacturing overhead costs incurred, $17,000 (credit Accounts Payable).
i. Manufacturing overhead was applied to production. Overhead is applied on a basis of direct labor cost.
j. Goods costing $310,000 to manufacture were completed during the year.
k. Goods that had cost $300,000 to manufacture were sold on account for $450,000.
l. Collections on account from customers, $445,000.
m. Payments on account to suppliers, $150,000.

Required: 1. Prepare a T-account for each account on the company's balance sheet, and enter the opening balances above.
2. Make entries directly into the T-accounts for the transactions given above.

Create new T-accounts as needed. Determine an ending balance for each T-account.

3. Was manufacturing overhead underapplied or overapplied for the year? Assume that the company allocates any overhead balance between the Work in Process, Finished Goods, and Cost of Goods Sold accounts. Prepare a journal entry to show the allocation for 19x1. (Round allocation percentages to one decimal place.)

4. Prepare an income statement for the year. (Do not prepare a schedule of cost of goods manufactured; all of the information needed for the income statement is available in the T-accounts.)

P3–15. Straightforward journal entries; partial T-accounts; income statement. Almeda Products, Inc., uses a job-order cost system to accumulate costs in its manufacturing plant. The company's inventory balances on April 1, 19x2 (the start of its fiscal year), were as follows:

Raw materials	$32,000
Work in process	20,000
Finished goods	48,000

During the year, the following transactions were completed:

a. Raw materials were purchased on account, $170,000.

b. Raw materials were issued from the storeroom for use in production, $180,000 (80 percent direct and 20 percent indirect).

c. Employee salaries and wages were accrued as follows: direct labor, $200,000; indirect labor, $82,000; and selling and administrative salaries, $90,000.

d. Utility costs were incurred in the factory, $65,000.

e. Advertising costs were incurred, $100,000.

f. Prepaid insurance expired during the year, $20,000 (90 percent related to factory operations, and 10 percent related to selling and administrative activities).

g. Depreciation was recorded, $180,000 (85 percent related to factory assets, and 15 percent related to selling and administrative assets).

h. Overhead cost was applied to production at a rate of 175 percent of direct labor cost.

i. Goods costing $700,000 to complete were transferred to the finished goods warehouse.

j. Sales for the year (all on account) totaled $1,000,000. These goods had cost $720,000 to manufacture.

Required:
1. Prepare journal entries to record the transactions for the year.

2. Prepare T-accounts for Raw Materials, Work in Process, Finished Goods, Manufacturing Overhead, and Cost of Goods Sold. Post the appropriate parts of your journal entries to these T-accounts. Compute the ending balance in each account. (Don't forget to enter the opening balances in the inventory accounts.)

3. Is Manufacturing Overhead underapplied or overapplied for the year? Prepare a journal entry to close this balance to Cost of Goods Sold.

4. Prepare an income statement for the year. (Do not prepare a schedule of cost of goods manufactured; all of the information needed for the income statement is available in the journal entries and T-accounts you have prepared.)

P3–16. Computation of overhead rates; costing units of product. Morris Company manufactures products to customer specifications and employs a job-order costing system. Predetermined overhead rates are used to apply manufacturing overhead cost to jobs. The predetermined overhead rate in Department A is based on machine-hours, and the rate in Department B is based on direct labor cost. At the beginning of 19x5, the company's management made the following estimates:

	Department	
	A	B
Direct labor-hours	12,000	60,000
Machine-hours	70,000	8,000
Direct labor cost	$130,000	$420,000
Manufacturing overhead cost . . .	602,000	735,000

Job 205 was initiated into production on August 1 and completed on August 10. The company's cost records show the following information on the job:

	Department	
	A	B
Direct labor-hours	30	85
Machine-hours	110	20
Materials placed into production	$470	$332
Direct labor cost	290	680

Required:

1. Compute the predetermined overhead rate that should be used during the year in Department A. Compute the rate that should be used in Department B.
2. Compute the total overhead cost applied to job 205.
3. What would be the total cost of job 205? If the job contained 50 units, what would be the cost per unit?
4. At the end of 19x5, the records of Morris Company revealed the following *actual* cost and operating data for all jobs worked on during the year:

	Department	
	A	B
Direct labor-hours	10,000	62,000
Machine-hours	65,000	9,000
Direct labor cost	$108,000	$436,000
Manufacturing overhead cost . . .	570,000	750,000

What was the amount of under- or overapplied overhead in each department at the end of 19x5?

P3–17. **Schedule of cost of goods manufactured; pricing; work in process analysis.** The Pacific Manufacturing Company operates a job-order cost system and applies overhead cost to jobs on a basis of direct labor cost. In computing an overhead rate for 19x6, the company's estimates were: manufacturing overhead cost, $126,000; direct labor cost, $84,000. The company's inventory accounts at the beginning and end of the year were:

	January 1, 19x6	December 31, 19x6
Raw materials	$21,000	$16,000
Work in process.	44,000	40,000
Finished goods	68,000	60,000

The following actual costs were incurred during 19x6:

Purchase of raw materials	$133,000
Direct labor cost	80,000
Manufacturing overhead costs:	
Insurance, factory	7,000
Depreciation of equipment	18,000
Indirect labor	42,000
Property taxes	9,000
Maintenance	11,000
Rent, building	36,000

Required: 1. a. Compute the predetermined overhead rate for 19x6.
            b. Compute the amount of under- or overapplied overhead for the year.
         2. Prepare a schedule of cost of goods manufactured for the year.
         3. Compute the cost of goods sold for the year. (Do not include any under- or overapplied overhead in your cost of goods sold figure.) What options are available for disposing of under- or overapplied overhead?
         4. Job 137 was started and completed during the year. What price would have been charged to the customer if the job required $3,200 in materials and $4,200 in direct labor cost, and the company priced its jobs at 40 percent above cost to manufacture?
         5. Direct labor made up $10,000 of the $32,000 ending Work in Process inventory balance. Supply the information missing below:

Direct materials	$?
Direct labor	10,000
Manufacturing overhead	?
Work in process inventory	$32,000

P3–18.   **T-accounts; periodic inventory method; overhead balance allocation.**   Decker Furniture Company employs a job-order costing system. At the beginning of 19x1, the company's records showed inventory balances as follows:

Raw materials	$10,000
Work in process.	32,000
Finished goods	60,000

During the year, the following transactions were completed:

a. Raw materials were acquired from suppliers on account, $200,000.
b. Raw materials were requisitioned for use in production, $185,000 (80 percent direct and 20 percent indirect).
c. Costs for employee services were accrued:

Direct labor	$160,000
Indirect labor	70,000
Administrative salaries . . .	80,000

    d. Depreciation was recorded on equipment, of which $54,000 related to equipment used in the factory and $18,000 related to equipment used in selling and adminis- trative activities.

    e. Advertising expense was accrued, $150,000.

    f. Utility costs were accrued, $20,000 (80 percent related to factory operations, and the remainder related to selling and administrative activities).

    g. Rent was accrued on facilities, $70,000 (90 percent related to factory operations, and the remainder related to selling and administrative activities).

    h. Overhead was applied to jobs on a basis of 125 percent of direct labor cost.

    i. The ending balance for the year in the Work in Process inventory account was determined to be $30,000.

    j. Sales for the year (all on account) were $800,000. The ending balance for the year in the Finished Goods inventory account was determined to be $120,000.

Required: 1. Enter the above transactions directly into T-accounts.

    2. As stated in (1) above, the ending balance in Work in Process was $30,000. Direct labor constituted $8,000 of this balance. Complete the following schedule:

Direct materials	$?
Direct labor	8,000
Manufacturing overhead	?
Total work in process	$30,000

    3. Was manufacturing overhead underapplied or overapplied for the year? By how much?

    4. What two options does the company have for disposing of its under- or overap- plied overhead? Prepare a journal entry for *each* of these options showing disposition of the under- or overapplied overhead balance for the year.

P3–19. **Job cost sheets; overhead rates; journal entries.** Madsen Company employs a job-order costing system. Only three jobs—job 208, job 209, and job 210—were worked on during May and June 19x1. Job 208 was completed on June 20; the other two jobs were uncompleted on June 30. Job cost sheets on the three jobs are given below:

	Job 208 cost sheet		Job 209 cost sheet		Job 210 cost sheet	
	May costs	June costs	May costs	June costs	May costs	June costs
Direct materials	$ 9,500	—	$5,100	$6,000	—	$7,200
Direct labor	8,000	$4,000	3,000	7,500	—	8,500
Manufacturing overhead . .	11,200	?	4,200	?	—	?

The following additional information is available:

    a. Manufacturing overhead is assigned to jobs on a basis of direct labor cost.

    b. Balances in the inventory accounts at May 31 were:

Raw materials	$30,000
Work in process	?
Finished goods	50,000

Required: 1.   Prepare T-accounts for Raw Materials, Work in Process, Finished Goods, and Manufacturing Overhead. Enter the May 31 balances given above; in the case of Work in Process, compute the May 31 balance and enter it into the Work in Process T-account.

2.   Prepare journal entries for the *month of June* as follows:

   a.   Prepare an entry to record the issue of materials into production, and post the entry to appropriate T-accounts. (In the case of direct materials, it is not necessary to make a separate entry for each job.) Indirect materials used during June totaled $3,600.

   b.   Prepare an entry to record the incurrence of labor cost, and post the entry to appropriate T-accounts. (In the case of direct labor cost, it is not necessary to make a separate entry for each job.) Indirect labor cost totaled $7,000 for June.

   c.   Prepare an entry to record the incurrence of $19,400 in various actual manufacturing overhead costs for June. (Credit Accounts Payable.)

3.   What apparent predetermined overhead rate does the company use to assign overhead cost to jobs? Using this rate, prepare a journal entry to record the application of overhead cost to jobs for June (it is not necessary to make a separate entry for each job). Post this entry to appropriate T-accounts.

4.   As stated earlier, job 208 was completed during June. Prepare a journal entry to show the transfer of this job off of the production line and into the finished goods warehouse. Post the entry to appropriate T-accounts.

5.   Determine the balance at June 30 in the Work in Process inventory account. How much of this balance consists of costs traceable to job 209? To job 210?

P3–20.   **Job-order cost journal entries; complete T-accounts; income statement.**   Warner Company's trial balance as of January 1, 19x3, is given below:

Cash	$ 8,000	
Accounts Receivable	35,000	
Raw Materials	20,000	
Work in Process	19,000	
Finished Goods	40,000	
Prepaid Insurance	6,000	
Plant and Equipment	280,000	
Accumulated Depreciation.		$ 86,000
Accounts Payable		70,000
Salaries and Wages Payable . . .		4,000
Capital Stock		150,000
Retained Earnings		98,000
Totals	$408,000	$408,000

Warner Company manufactures custom-made products. A job-order costing system is used to accumulate and record costs in the company's plant. Manufacturing overhead costs are charged to production on a basis of machine-hours of activity. For 19x3, management estimated that the company would incur $315,000 in manufacturing overhead costs and operate at an activity level of 21,000 machine-hours. The following transactions occurred during 19x3:

   a.   Raw materials were purchased on account, $225,000.

   b.   Raw materials were issued to production, $230,000 (80 percent direct and 20 percent indirect).

   c.   Factory payrolls were accrued, $300,000 (70 percent direct labor and 30 percent indirect labor).

    d. Sales and administrative salaries were accrued, $85,000.

    e. Insurance expired during the year, $4,000 (75 percent related to factory opera-
tions, and 25 percent related to selling and administrative activities).

    f. Factory utility costs were incurred, $72,000.

    g. Advertising costs were incurred, $130,000.

    h. Depreciation was recorded for the year, $60,000 (90 percent related to factory
operations, and the remainder related to selling and administrative activities).

    i. Rental costs were incurred on factory equipment, $48,000.

    j. Shipping costs were incurred in transporting goods to customers, $20,000.

    k. Manufacturing overhead cost was applied to production, $_____. (The company
operated at an activity level of 20,000 machine-hours for the year.)

    l. Goods costing $690,000 to manufacture were transferred into the finished
goods warehouse.

    m. Sales for the year (all on account) totaled $1,000,000; these goods cost $700,000
to manufacture.

    n. Collections on account from customers during the year, $950,000.

    o. Cash payments made during the year: to creditors on account, $550,000; to
employees for salaries and wages, $380,000.

Required: 1. Prepare journal entries to record the year's transactions.

    2. Prepare a T-account for each account in the company's trial balance, and enter
the opening balances given above. Post your journal entries to the T-accounts.
Prepare new T-accounts as needed. Compute the ending balance in each account.

    3. Is manufacturing overhead underapplied or overapplied for the year? Prepare
the necessary journal entry to close the balance in Manufacturing Overhead to
Cost of Goods Sold.

    4. Prepare an income statement for the year. (Do not prepare a schedule of cost
of goods manufactured; all of the information needed for the income statement
is available in the T-accounts.)

P3–21. **Disposition of under- or overapplied overhead.** Whitney Furniture Company
uses a job-order costing system and applies manufacturing overhead cost to products
on a basis of machine-hours of activity. The following estimates were used in
preparing a predetermined overhead rate for 19x3:

Machine-hours	75,000
Manufacturing overhead cost	$900,000

    During 19x3, a glut of furniture on the market resulted in a curtailment of
production and a buildup of furniture in Whitney Furniture Company's warehouses.
The company's cost records revealed the following actual cost and operating data
for the year:

Machine-hours.	60,000
Manufacturing overhead cost . . .	$ 850,000
Inventories at year-end:	
Raw materials	30,000
Work in process	100,000
Finished goods	500,000
Cost of goods sold	1,400,000

Required: 1. Compute the company's predetermined overhead rate for 19x3.

    2. Compute the under- or overapplied overhead for 19x3.

    3. Assume that the company closes any under- or overapplied overhead directly
to Cost of Goods Sold. Prepare the appropriate journal entry.

4. Assume that the company allocates any under- or overapplied overhead to the appropriate accounts. Prepare the journal entry to show the allocation for 19x3.
5. How much higher or lower will net income be for 19x3 if the under- or overapplied overhead is allocated rather than closed directly to Cost of Goods Sold?

P3–22. **T-account analysis of cost flows.** Selected ledger accounts of Moore Company are given below for 19x8:

Raw Materials

Bal. 1/1	15,000	19x8 credits	?
19x8 debits	120,000		
Bal. 12/31	25,000		

Manufacturing Overhead

19x8 debits	230,000	19x8 credits	?

Work in Process

Bal. 1/1	20,000	19x8 credits	470,000
Direct materials	90,000		
Direct labor	150,000		
Overhead	240,000		
Bal. 12/31	?		

Factory Wages Payable

19x8 debits	185,000	Bal. 1/1	9,000
		19x8 credits	180,000
		Bal. 12/31	4,000

Finished Goods

Bal. 1/1	40,000	19x8 credits	?
19x8 debits	?		
Bal. 12/31	60,000		

Cost of Goods Sold

19x8 debits	?	

Required:
1. What was the cost of raw materials put into production during the year?
2. How much of the materials in (1) consisted of indirect materials?
3. How much of the factory labor cost for the year consisted of indirect labor?
4. What was the cost of goods manufactured for the year?
5. What was the cost of goods sold for the year (before considering under- or overapplied overhead)?
6. If overhead is applied to production on a basis of direct labor cost, what rate was in effect for 19x8?
7. Was manufacturing overhead under- or overapplied for 19x8? By how much?
8. Compute the ending balance in the Work in Process inventory account. Assume that this balance consists entirely of goods started during the year. If $8,000 of this balance is direct labor cost, how much of it is direct materials cost? Manufacturing overhead cost?

P3–23. **Schedule of cost of goods manufactured.** The Alberta Company manufactures a single product. The chief accountant has asked your help in preparing a schedule of cost of goods manufactured for the month ended June 30, 19x3. The following information is available:

a. Ten thousand units were sold at $20 per unit.
b. Twelve thousand units were produced. (One unit of raw materials is required for each finished unit.)
c. The finished goods inventory on June 1 was 3,000 units valued at $16 each.

d.   The raw materials inventory on June 1 was 1,000 units valued at $5 each.

e.   During June, two purchases of raw materials were made:

June 6 . . . . . .   8,000 units at $6 each
June 22 . . . . .   5,000 units at $5 each

f.   The company uses the first-in, first-out method of determining raw materials inventories.

g.   The work in process inventories were:

June 1 . . . . . .   2,000 units valued at $18,000
June 30 . . . . .   2,000 units valued at $21,000

h.   Depreciation is determined on a straight-line basis, at a rate of 10 percent per annum. Depreciable assets include:

Factory machinery . . . . . $240,000 original cost
Office equipment . . . . . .   6,000 original cost

i.   Overhead is applied to production on a basis of 70 percent of direct labor cost.

j.   Other information provided:

Direct labor $100,000
Indirect labor   45,000
Salespersons' salaries   10,500
Office salaries   16,000
Sales returns and allowances   5,000
Freight-out   2,500
Heat, light, and power   2,000
Factory rent   8,000
Interest expense   2,000
Miscellaneous factory overhead   10,000

Required: Prepare a schedule of cost of goods manufactured for the month in good form. Show supporting computations.

(SMA, Adapted)

P3–24.   **Plantwide and departmental overhead rates.**   "Blast it!" said David Wilson, president of Teledex Company. "We've just lost the bid on the Koopers job. It seems we're either too high to get the job or too low to make any money on half the jobs we bid."

Teledex Company manufactures products to customers' specifications and operates a job-order cost system. Manufacturing overhead cost is applied to jobs on a basis of direct labor cost. The following estimates were made at the beginning of 19x7, the current year:

	Department			**Total plant**
	Fabricating	**Machining**	**Assembly**	
Direct labor	$200,000	$100,000	$300,000	$600,000
Manufacturing overhead . . .	350,000	400,000	90,000	840,000

Jobs require varying amounts of work in the three departments. The Koopers job, for example, would have required manufacturing costs in the three departments as follows:

	Department			Total plant
	Fabricating	Machining	Assembly	
Direct materials	$3,000	$200	$1,400	$4,600
Direct labor	2,800	500	6,200	9,500
Manufacturing overhead.	?	?	?	?

The company uses a plantwide overhead rate to apply manufacturing overhead cost to jobs.

Required:

1. Assuming use of a plantwide overhead rate:
   - a. Compute the rate for the current year.
   - b. Determine the amount of manufacturing overhead cost that would have been applied to the Koopers job.
2. Suppose that instead of using a plantwide overhead rate, the company had used a separate predetermined overhead rate in each department. Under these conditions:
   - a. Compute the rate for each department for the current year.
   - b. Determine the amount of manufacturing overhead cost that would have been applied to the Koopers job.
3. Assume that it is customary in the industry to bid jobs at 150 percent of total manufacturing cost (direct materials, direct labor, and applied overhead). What was the company's bid price on the Koopers job? What would the bid price have been if departmental overhead rates had been used to apply overhead cost?
4. At the end of the current year, the company assembled the following *actual* cost data relating to all jobs worked on during the year:

	Department			Total plant
	Fabricating	Machining	Assembly	
Direct materials	$190,000	$ 16,000	$114,000	$320,000
Direct labor.	210,000	108,000	262,000	580,000
Manufacturing overhead	360,000	420,000	84,000	864,000

Compute the under- or overapplied overhead for the year *(a)* assuming that a plantwide overhead rate is used and *(b)* assuming that departmental overhead rates are used.

P3–25. **Comprehensive problem: journal entries; T-accounts; statements; pricing.** Rockwood Company is a manufacturer of custom-made equipment. The company uses a job-order costing system and applies manufacturing overhead cost to jobs on a basis of direct labor-hours. At the beginning of 19x5, the following estimates were made as a basis for computing a predetermined overhead rate for the year: manufacturing overhead cost, $360,000; and direct labor-hours, 18,000.

The following transactions took place during the year (all purchases and services were acquired on account):

a. Raw materials were purchased for use in production, $200,000.
b. Raw materials were requisitioned for use in production (all direct materials), $185,000.

    c. Utility bills were incurred, $70,000 (90 percent related to factory operations, and the remainder related to selling and administrative activities).

    d. Salary and wage costs were incurred:

Direct labor (19,500 hours)	$230,000
Indirect labor	90,000
Selling and administrative salaries . . .	110,000

    e. Maintenance costs were incurred in the factory, $51,000.

    f. Advertising costs were incurred, $136,000.

    g. Depreciation was recorded for the year, $95,000 (80 percent related to factory equipment and the remainder related to selling and administrative equipment).

    h. Rental cost incurred on buildings, $120,000 (85 percent related to factory operations and the remainder related to selling and administrative facilities).

    i. Manufacturing overhead cost was applied to jobs, ____?____ .

    j. Cost of goods manufactured for the year, $770,000.

    k. Sales for the year (all on account) totaled $1,200,000. These goods cost $800,000 to manufacture.

  The balances in the inventory accounts at the beginning of the year were:

Raw materials	$30,000
Work in process	21,000
Finished goods	60,000

Required:

1. Prepare journal entries to record the above data.
2. Post your entries to T-accounts. (Don't forget to enter the opening inventory balances above.) Determine the ending balances in the inventory accounts and in the Manufacturing Overhead account.
3. Prepare a schedule of cost of goods manufactured.
4. Prepare a journal entry to close any balance in the Manufacturing Overhead account to Cost of Goods Sold. Prepare a schedule of cost of goods sold.
5. Prepare an income statement for the year. Ignore income taxes.
6. Job 412 was one of the many jobs started and completed during the year. The job required $3,800 in materials and 350 hours of direct labor time at $12 per hour. If the job contained 640 units and the company billed at 60 percent above the cost to manufacture, what price per unit would have been charged to the customer?

P3–26. **Comprehensive problem: T-accounts; job-order cost flows; statements; pricing.** Top-Products, Inc., produces goods to customers' orders and uses a job-order costing system. A trial balance for the company as of January 1, 19x3, is given below:

Cash	$ 18,000	
Accounts Receivable	40,000	
Raw Material Inventory	25,000	
Work in Process Inventory	32,000	
Finished Goods Inventory	60,000	
Prepaid Insurance	5,000	
Plant and Equipment	400,000	
Accumulated Depreciation		$148,000
Accounts Payable		90,000
Salaries and Wages Payable		3,000
Capital Stock		250,000
Retained Earnings		89,000
Totals	$580,000	$580,000

The company applies manufacturing overhead cost to jobs on a basis of direct labor cost. The following estimates were made at the beginning of 19x3 for purposes of computing a predetermined overhead rate for the year: manufacturing overhead cost, $228,000; direct labor cost, $190,000. Summarized transactions of the company for 19x3 are given below:

a. Raw materials were purchased on account, $180,000.
b. Raw materials were requisitioned for use in production, $190,000 (all direct materials).
c. Utility costs were incurred in the factory, $57,000.
d. Salary and wage costs were incurred: direct labor, $200,000; indirect labor, $90,000; salaries of selling and administrative employees, $120,000.
e. Insurance expired during the year, $4,000 (75 percent related to factory operations, and 25 percent related to selling and administrative activities).
f. Property taxes were incurred on the factory building, $16,000.
g. Advertising costs were incurred, $150,000.
h. Depreciation was recorded for the year, $50,000 (80 percent related to factory assets, and the remainder related to selling and administrative assets).
i. Other costs were incurred (credit Accounts Payable): for factory overhead, $30,000; for miscellaneous selling and administrative expenses, $18,000.
j. Manufacturing overhead cost was applied to jobs, _____?_____ .
k. Cost of goods manufactured for the year, $635,000.
l. Sales for the year totaled $1,000,000 (all on account); the cost of goods sold was _____?_____ . (The ending balance in the Finished Goods inventory account was $45,000.)
m. Cash collections from customers during the year, $950,000.
n. Cash payments during the year: to employees, $412,000; on accounts payable, $478,000.

Required: 1. Enter the company's transactions for the year directly into T-accounts. (Don't forget to enter the opening balances into the T-accounts.) Key your entries to the letters (a) through (n) above. Create new T-accounts as needed. Find the ending balance in each account.
2. Prepare a schedule of cost of goods manufactured.
3. Prepare a journal entry to close any balance in the Manufacturing Overhead account to Cost of Goods Sold. Prepare a schedule of cost of goods sold.
4. Prepare an income statement for 19x3. Ignore income taxes.
5. Job 316 was one of the many jobs started and completed during the year. The job required $2,400 in materials and $3,000 in direct labor cost. If the job contained 300 units and the company billed the job at 140 percent of the cost to manufacture, what price per unit would have been charged to the customer?

CASES

C3–27. **Incomplete data; review of cost flows.**   In an attempt to conceal a theft of funds, Snake N. Grass, controller of Bucolic Products, Inc., placed a bomb in the company's record vault. The ensuing explosion left only fragments of the company's factory ledger, as shown below:

Raw Materials		
Bal. 6/1	8,000	

Manufacturing Overhead		
Actual costs for June	79,000	
		Overapplied overhead 6,100

Work in Process		
Bal. 6/1	7,200	

Accounts Payable		
		Bal. 6/30 16,000

Finished Goods		
Bal. 6/30	21,000	

Cost of Goods Sold		

In order to bring Mr. Grass to justice, the company must reconstruct its activities for the month of June. You have been assigned to perform the task of reconstruction. After interviewing selected employees and sifting through charred fragments, you have determined the following additional information:

a. According to the company's treasurer, the accounts payable are for raw material purchases only. The company's balance sheet, dated May 31, shows that Accounts Payable had a $20,000 balance at the beginning of June. The company's bank has provided photocopies of all checks that cleared the bank during June. These photocopies show that payments to suppliers during June totaled $119,000. (All materials used during the month were direct materials.)

b. The production superintendent states that manufacturing overhead cost is applied to jobs on a basis of direct labor-hours. However, he does not remember the rate currently being used by the company.

c. Cost sheets kept in the production superintendent's office show that only one job was in process on June 30, at the time of the explosion. The job had been charged with $6,600 in materials, and 500 direct labor-hours at $8 per hour had been worked on the job.

d. A log is kept in the finished goods warehouse showing all goods transferred in from the factory. This log shows that the cost of goods transferred into the finished goods warehouse from the factory during June totaled $280,000.

e. The company's May 31 balance sheet indicates that the finished goods inventory totaled $36,000 at the beginning of June.

f. A charred piece of the payroll ledger, found after sifting through piles of smoking debris, indicates that 11,500 direct labor-hours were recorded for the month of June. The company's employment department has verified that as a result of a firm union contract, there are no variations in pay rates among factory employees.

g. The production superintendent states that there was no under- or overapplied overhead in the Manufacturing Overhead account at May 31.

Required: Determine the following amounts:

1. Predetermined overhead rate being used by the company.
2. Raw materials purchased during June.
3. Work in process inventory, June 30.
4. Overhead applied to work in process during June.
5. Raw materials usage during June.
6. Raw materials inventory, June 30.
7. Cost of goods sold for June.

(Hint: A good way to proceed is to bring the fragmented T-accounts up to date through June 30 by posting whatever entries can be developed from the information given.)

C3–28.   Analysis of cost flows and inventories under job-order costing.   Targon, Inc., manufactures lawn equipment. A job-order costing system is used, since the products are manufactured in batches rather than on a continuous basis. The company started operations on January 2, 19x1. Operating activities during the first 11 months of the year (through November 30) resulted in the following balances in selected accounts:

Raw Materials			Manufacturing Overhead		
Bal.	36,000			2,260,000*	?
			Bal.	?	

Work in Process			Cost of Goods Sold		
Bal.	1,200,000		Bal.	14,200,000	

Finished Goods		
Bal.	2,785,000	

* This figure represents actual manufacturing overhead costs incurred through November 30, 19x1.

The following additional information is available on the company:

a.   The work in process inventory at November 30 consisted of two jobs:

Job no.	Units	Items	Total cost as of November 30
1105	50,000	Estate sprinklers	$ 700,000
1106	40,000	Economy sprinklers	500,000
			$1,200,000

b.   The finished goods inventory at November 30 consisted of five separate items in stock:

Items	Quantity and unit cost	Total cost
Estate sprinklers	5,000 units at $22 each	$ 110,000
Deluxe sprinklers	115,000 units at $17 each	1,955,000
Brass nozzles.	10,000 gross at $14 per gross	140,000
Rainmaker nozzles	5,000 gross at $16 per gross	80,000
Connectors	100,000 gross at $5 per gross	500,000
		$2,785,000

c. Manufacturing overhead cost is applied to jobs on a basis of direct labor-hours. For 19x1, management estimated that the company would work 400,000 direct labor-hours and incur $2,400,000 in manufacturing overhead cost.

d. A total of 367,000 direct labor-hours were worked during the first 11 months of the year (through November 30).

Items *(e)* through *(j)* below summarize the activity that took place in the company during December 19x1.

e. A total of $708,000 in raw materials was purchased during the month.

f. Raw materials were drawn from inventory and charged as follows:

Job No.	Quantity and items	Material charged
1105	See above	$210,000
1106	See above	6,000
1201	30,000 gross rainmaker nozzles	181,000
1202	10,000 deluxe sprinklers	92,000
1203	50,000 ring sprinklers	163,000
—	Indirect materials	20,000
		$672,000

g. The payroll during December was as follows:

Job No.	Hours	Total cost
1105	6,000	$ 62,000
1106	2,500	26,000
1201	18,000	182,000
1202	500	5,000
1203	5,000	52,000
Indirect labor	8,000	84,000
Sales and administration . . .	—	120,000
		$531,000

h. Other costs incurred in the factory during December were:

Depreciation	$62,500
Utilities	15,000
Insurance.	1,000
Property taxes	3,500
Maintenance	5,000
	$87,000

i. Jobs completed during December and the number of good units transferred to the finished goods warehouse were:

Job No.	Quantity	Items
1105	48,000 units	Estate sprinklers
1106	39,000 units	Economy sprinklers
1201	29,500 gross	Rainmaker nozzles
1203	49,000 units	Ring sprinklers

j. Finished products were shipped to customers during December as follows:

Items	Quantity
Estate sprinklers	16,000 units
Deluxe sprinklers	32,000 units
Economy sprinklers	20,000 units
Ring sprinklers	22,000 units
Brass nozzles.	5,000 gross
Rainmaker nozzles	10,000 gross
Connectors	26,000 gross

Required:

1. Determine the amount of under- or overapplied overhead for the year 19x1.
2. What is the appropriate accounting treatment for this under- or overapplied overhead balance? Explain your answer.
3. Determine the dollar balance in the Work in Process inventory account as of December 31, 19x1. Show all computations in good form.
4. For the estate sprinklers only, determine the dollar balance in the Finished Goods inventory account as of December 31, 19x1. Assume a FIFO flow of units. Show all computations in good form.

(CMA, Heavily Adapted)

CHAPTER 4

Systems Design: Process Costing

LEARNING OBJECTIVES

After studying Chapter 4, you should be able to:

- Enumerate the major similarities and differences between job-order and process costing.

- Prepare journal entries to record the flow of materials, labor, and overhead through a process costing system.

- Compute equivalent units of production by both the weighted-average and FIFO methods.

- Prepare a quantity schedule and explain its significance.

- Compute unit costs for a period under both the weighted-average and FIFO methods.

- Prepare a cost reconciliation for a period under both the weighted-average and FIFO methods.

- Combine the quantity schedule, the unit costs, and the cost reconciliation into a production report.

- Define or explain the key terms listed at the end of the chapter.

As explained in the preceding chapter, there are two basic costing systems in use: job-order costing and process costing. We have found that a job-order costing system is used in those situations where many different jobs or batches of production are worked on each period. Examples of · industries that would typically use job-order costing include furniture manufacture, special-order printing, shipbuilding, and many types of service organizations.

By contrast, **process costing** is used in those industries that produce basically homogeneous products such as bricks, flour, cement, screws, bolts, and pharmaceutical items. In addition, process costing is employed in assembly-type operations that manufacture typewriters, automobiles, and small appliances, as well as in utilities producing gas, water, and electricity. As suggested by the length of this list, process costing is in widespread use and warrants study by anyone involved in accounting, management, or systems work.

Our purpose in this chapter is to extend the discussion of product costing that was started in the preceding chapter in order to include a process costing system.

COMPARISON OF JOB-ORDER AND PROCESS COSTING

In some ways process costing is very similar to job-order costing, and in some ways it is very different. In the following two sections, we focus on these similarities and differences in order to provide a foundation for the detailed discussion of process costing that follows.

Similarities between Job-Order and Process Costing

It is important to recognize that much of what was learned in the preceding chapter about costing and about cost flows applies equally well to process costing in this chapter. That is, we are not throwing out all that we have learned about costing and starting from ''scratch'' with a whole new system. The similarities that exist between job-order and process costing can be summarized as follows:

1. The same basic purposes exist in both systems, which are: *(a)* to assign material, labor, and overhead costs to products; *(b)* to provide a mechanism for computing unit costs; and *(c)* to provide data essential for planning, control, and decision making.
2. Both systems maintain and use the same basic manufacturing accounts, including Manufacturing Overhead, Raw Materials, Work in Process, and Finished Goods.
3. Cost flows through the manufacturing accounts in (2) above move in basically the same way in both systems.

As can be seen from this comparison, much of the knowledge that we have already acquired about costing is applicable to a process costing system.

EXHIBIT 4–1

Differences between job-order and process costing

Job-order costing	Process costing
1. Many different jobs are worked on during each period, with each job having different production requirements.	1. A single product is produced either on a continuous basis or for long periods of time. All units of product are identical.
2. Cost are accumulated by individual job.	2. Costs are accumulated by department.
3. The *job cost sheet* is the key document controlling the accumulation of costs by a job.	✗3. The *department production report* is the key document showing the accumulation and disposition of costs by a department.
4. Unit costs are computed *by job* on the job cost sheet.	4. Unit costs are computed *by department* on the department production report.

Our task now is simply to refine and extend this knowledge to meet special process costing needs.

Differences between Job-Order and Process Costing

The differences between job-order and process costing arise from two factors. The first is that the flow of units in a process costing system is more or less continuous, and the second is that these units are indistinguishable from one another. Under process costing, it makes no sense to try to identify materials, labor, and overhead costs with a particular order from a customer (as we did with job-order costing), since each order is just one of many that are filled from a continuous flow of units from the production line. Under process costing, instead of accumulating costs by order, we accumulate costs *by department* and assign these costs equally to all units that pass through the department during a period.

A further difference between the two cost systems is that since we are department oriented rather than job oriented under process costing, the job cost sheet is of no value in a process costing system. In a process costing system, instead of using job cost sheets, a document known as a **production report** is prepared for each department. The production report serves several functions. It provides a summary of the number of units moving through a department during a period, and it also provides a computation of unit costs. In addition, it shows what costs were charged to a department during a period and what disposition was made of these costs. As these comments suggest, the department production report is a key document in a process costing system.

The major differences between job-order and process costing are summarized in Exhibit 4–1.

A PERSPECTIVE OF PROCESS COST FLOWS

Before presenting a detailed example of process costing, it will be helpful to gain a visual perspective of how manufacturing costs flow through a process costing system.

EXHIBIT 4–2

Sequential processing departments

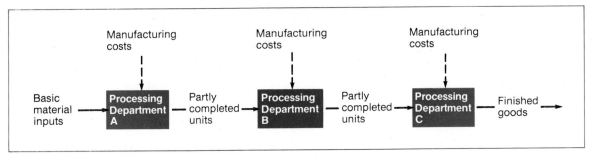

Processing Departments

A **processing department** is any location in the factory where work is performed on a product and where materials, labor, or overhead costs are added to the product. For example, a brick factory might have two processing departments—one for mixing and molding clay into brick form and one for firing the molded brick. There can be as many or as few processing departments as are needed to complete the manufacture of a product. Some products may go through several processing departments, while others may go through only one or two. Regardless of the number of departments involved, all processing departments have two essential features. First, the activity performed in the processing department must be performed uniformly on all of the units passing through it. Second, the output of the processing department must be homogeneous.

The processing departments involved in the manufacture of a product such as bricks would probably be organized in a *sequential* pattern. By **sequential processing,** we mean that units flow in sequence from one department to another. An example of processing departments arranged in a sequential pattern is given in Exhibit 4–2.

A different type of processing pattern, known as *parallel processing,* is required in the manufacture of some products. **Parallel processing** is used in those situations where, after a certain point, some units may go through different processing departments than others. For example, the petroleum industry may input crude oil into one processing department and then use the refined output for further processing into several end products. Each end product may undergo several steps of further processing after the initial refining, some of which may be shared with other end products and some of which may not. Exhibit 4–3 illustrates one type of parallel processing. The number of possible variations in parallel processing patterns is virtually limitless. The example given in Exhibit 4–3 is intended as just one sample of the many parallel patterns in use today.

EXHIBIT 4–3

Parallel processing departments

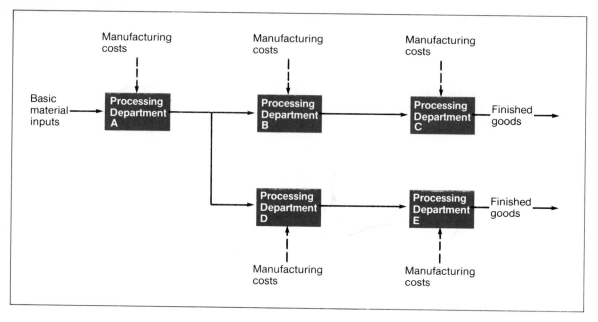

The Flow of Materials, Labor, and Overhead Costs

Cost accumulation is simpler in a process costing system than in a job-order costing system. The reason is that costs need to be identified only by processing department—not by separate job. Thus, in a process costing system, instead of having to trace costs to hundreds of different jobs, costs are traced to only a few processing departments. This means that costs can be accumulated for longer periods of time and that just one allocation is needed at the end of a period (week, month, and so forth) in order to assign the accumulated costs to the period's output.

A T-account model of materials, labor, and overhead cost flows in a process costing system is given in Exhibit 4–4. Several key points should be noted from this exhibit. First, note that a separate Work in Process account is maintained for *each processing department,* rather than having only a single Work in Process account for the entire company. Second, note that the completed production of the first processing department (Department A in the exhibit) is transferred into the Work in Process account of the second processing department (Department B), where it undergoes further work. After this further work, the completed units are then transferred into Finished Goods. (In Exhibit 4–4, we show only two processing departments; there may be several such departments in some companies.)

Finally, note that materials, labor, and overhead costs can be entered directly into *any* processing department—not just the first. Costs in Depart-

EXHIBIT 4–4
A T-account model of process costing flows

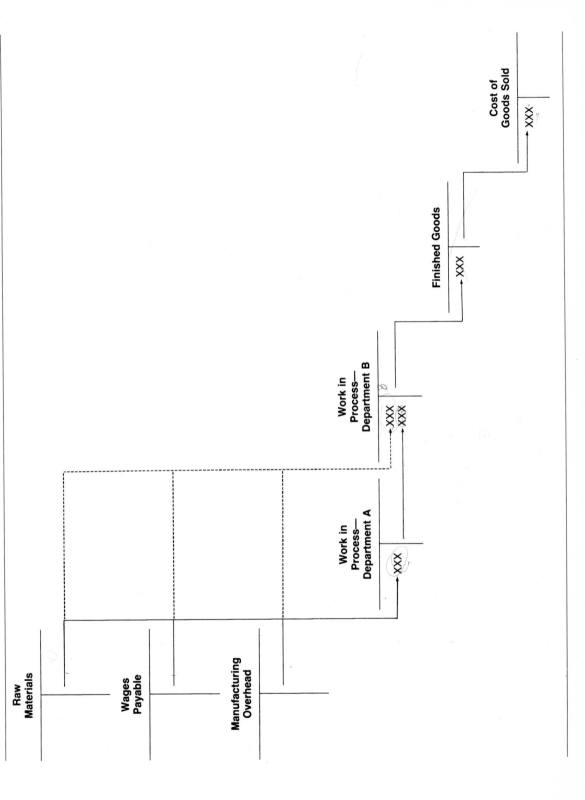

ment B's Work in Process account would therefore consist of the materials, labor, and overhead costs entered directly into the account plus the costs attached to partially completed units transferred in from Department A (called **transferred-in costs**).

Materials, Labor, and Overhead Cost Entries

To complete our discussion of cost flows in a process costing system, in the following sections we show journal entries relating to materials, labor, and overhead costs and also make brief, further comments relating to each of these cost categories.

Materials costs As in job-order costing, materials are drawn from the storeroom by use of a materials requisition form. Charging these materials to departments, rather than to jobs, generally reduces the amount of requisitioning needed, since large amounts of materials can be drawn and put into production at a time. As stated earlier, materials can be added in any processing department, although it is not unusual for materials to be added only in the first processing department, with subsequent departments adding only labor and overhead costs as the partially completed units move along toward completion.

Assuming that the first processing department in a company is Department A, the journal entry for placing materials into process would be:

Work in Process—Department A	XXX	
Raw Materials		XXX

If other materials are subsequently added in another processing department, the entry would be:

Work in Process—Department B	XXX	
Raw Materials		XXX

Labor costs Since it is not necessary to identify costs with specific jobs, a time clock is generally adequate for accumulating labor costs and for allocating them to the proper department in a process costing system. Assuming again that a company has two processing departments, A and B, the journal entry to record labor costs for a period would be:

Work in Process—Department A	XXX	
Work in Process—Department B	XXX	
Salaries and Wages Payable		XXX

[handwritten margin notes: "M. Overhead: Use actual rather than estimate applied", "Why only actual?", "Most use predetermined because prod. fluctuates"]

Overhead costs   The simplest method of handling overhead costs in a process costing system is to charge products with the actual overhead costs of the period rather than with applied overhead costs. Under this approach, no predetermined overhead rate is computed; overhead costs in each department are simply added directly to that department's Work in Process account either as the costs are incurred or at specified intervals. Since there is no "applied" overhead cost in the sense we talked about in Chapter 3, there is no under- or overapplied overhead balance remaining at the end of a period when this approach is used.

Why is it possible to use actual overhead costs in a process costing system when it is not possible under job-order costing? The answer lies in the nature of the work flowing through the two systems. Under job-order costing, jobs tend to be heterogeneous, requiring different inputs and different times to complete. Also, several jobs will be in process at a given time, each having different output requirements. Thus, the overhead cost chargeable to a job has to be estimated. Under process costing, homogeneous units flow continuously through a department, thus making it possible to charge units with the department's actual overhead costs as the costs are incurred. This approach works well, however, only if production is quite stable from period to period and only if overhead costs are incurred uniformly over the year.

If production levels fluctuate or if overhead costs are not incurred uniformly, then predetermined overhead rates should be used to charge overhead cost to products, the same as in job-order costing. When predetermined overhead rates are used, each department has its own separate rate with the rates being computed in the same way as was discussed in Chapter 3. Overhead cost is then applied to units of product as the units move through the various departments. Since predetermined overhead rates are widely used even in process costing situations, we will assume their use throughout the remainder of this chapter.

If a company has two processing departments, A and B, the journal entry to apply overhead cost to products would be:

Work in Process—Department A	XXX	
Work in Process—Department B	XXX	
Manufacturing Overhead.		XXX

As we stated in Chapter 2, direct labor cost combined with manufacturing overhead cost is often referred to as **conversion cost,** since these cost inputs are necessary to convert raw materials into finished products. The term *conversion cost* is widely used in process costing in the preparation of department production reports.

Completing the cost flows   Once processing has been completed in a department, the units are transferred to the next department for further processing, as illustrated earlier in the T-accounts in Exhibit 4–4. The entry

transfer from dept

to transfer partially completed units from Department A into Department B would be:

Work in Process—Department B XXX
    Work in Process—Department A   XXX

After processing has been completed in department B, the completed units are then transferred into the Finished Goods inventory account:

Finished Goods XXX
    Work in Process—Department B   XXX

Finally, when a customer's order is filled and units are sold, the cost of the units is transferred into Cost of Goods Sold:

Cost of Goods Sold XXX
    Finished Goods.   XXX

To summarize, we stated earlier that the cost flows between accounts are basically the same in a process costing system as they are in a job-order costing system. As shown by the entries above, the reader can see that this is indeed correct. The only differences are that in a process costing system *(a)* a separate Work in Process account is maintained for each department, and *(b)* each department can be charged directly for manufacturing costs in addition to those transferred in from the preceding department.

EQUIVALENT UNITS OF PRODUCTION

After materials, labor, and overhead costs have been accumulated in a department, the department's output must be determined so that unit costs can be computed. A department's output is always stated in terms of **equivalent units of production.** Equivalent units can be defined as the number of units that would have been produced during a period if all of a department's efforts had resulted in completed units of product. Equivalent units are computed by taking completed units and adjusting them for partially completed units in the work in process inventory.

The reasoning behind the computation of equivalent units is as follows: Completed units alone will not accurately measure output in a department, since part of the department's efforts during a period will have been expended on units that are only partially complete. To accurately measure output, these partially completed units must also be considered in the output computation. This is done by mathematically converting the partially completed units into fully completed *equivalent units* and then adjusting the output figure accordingly.

To illustrate, assume that a company has 500 units in its ending work in process inventory that are 60 percent complete. Five hundred units 60 percent complete would be equivalent to 300 fully completed units (500 × 60% = 300). Therefore, the ending inventory would be said to contain 300 *equivalent units*. These equivalent units would be added to the fully completed units in determining the period's output.

There are two ways of computing a department's equivalent units, depending on whether the company is accounting for its cost flows by the *weighted-average method* or by the *first-in, first out (FIFO) method*.

Weighted-Average Method

Under the **weighted-average method,** a department's equivalent units are computed just as described above: Equivalent units of production = Completed units + Equivalent units in the ending work in process inventory.

To provide an extended example, assume the following data:

The Regal Company manufactures a product that goes through two departments—mixing and firing. During 19x1, the following activity took place in the mixing department:

	Units	Percent completed	
		Materials	Conversion
Work in process, beginning	10,000	100	70
Units started into production during the year	150,000		
Units completed during the year and transferred to the firing department	140,000		
Work in process, ending	20,000	60	25

Since the work in process inventories are at different stages of completion in terms of the amount of materials and conversion cost that has been added, two equivalent unit figures will have to be computed—one for equivalent units in terms of materials and the other for equivalent units in terms of conversion. The equivalent units computations are given in Exhibit 4–5.

Note from the computations in Exhibit 4–5 that units in the beginning inventory are ignored and that an adjustment is made only for partially completed units in the ending inventory. This is a key point in the computation of equivalent units under the weighted-average method: *Units in the beginning inventory are always treated as if they were started and completed during the current period.* Thus, no adjustment is made for these units, regardless of how much work was done on them before the period started.

EXHIBIT 4–5

Equivalent units of production: Weighted-average method

	Materials	Conversion
Units transferred to firing	140,000	140,000
Work in process, ending:		
20,000 units × 60%	12,000	
20,000 units × 25%		5,000
Equivalent units of production	152,000	145,000

Although this procedure may seem illogical and inconsistent, it greatly simplifies the preparation of a department production report, as we shall see shortly.

FIFO Method

The computation of equivalent units under the **FIFO method** differs from the computation under the weighted-average method in two ways.

First, the "units transferred out" figure is divided into two parts. One part consists of the units from the beginning inventory that were completed and transferred out, and the other part consists of the units that were both *started* and *completed* during the current period.

Second, full consideration is given to the amount of work expended during the current period on units in the *beginning* work in process inventory as well as on units in the ending inventory. Thus, under the FIFO method, it is necessary to convert both inventories to an equivalent units basis. For the beginning inventory, the equivalent units represent the work done *to complete* the units; for the ending inventory, the equivalent units represent the work done to bring the units to a stage of partial completion at the end of the period (the same as with the weighted-average method).

In sum, the equivalent units figure under the FIFO method consists of three amounts:

1.   The work needed *to complete* the units in the beginning inventory.
2.   The work expended on the units *started* and *completed* during the period.
3.   The work expended on partially completed units in the ending inventory.

To illustrate, refer again to the Regal Company data. The mixing department completed and transferred 140,000 units to the firing department during the year. Since 10,000 of these units came from the beginning inventory, the mixing department must have started and completed 130,000 units during the year. The 10,000 units in the beginning inventory had all materials added in the prior year and were 70 percent complete as to conversion costs when the current year started. Thus, during the current year the mixing department would have added the other 30 percent of conversion cost (100%

EXHIBIT 4–6

Equivalent units of production: FIFO method

	Materials	Conversion
Work in process, beginning:		
10,000 units × 0%*	—	
10,000 units × 30%*		3,000
Units started and completed this year . . .	130,000[†]	130,000[†]
Work in process, ending:		
20,000 units × 60%[‡]	12,000	
20,000 units × 25%[‡]		5,000
Equivalent units of production	142,000	138,000

---

* Work needed *to complete* the units in the beginning inventory.
  [†] 140,000 units transferred out − 10,000 units in the beginning inventory = 130,000 units started and completed during the year.
  [‡] Work *completed* on the units in the ending inventory.

− 70% = 30%). Given these data, the equivalent units for the mixing department for the year would be computed as shown in Exhibit 4–6.

Comparison of the Weighted-Average and FIFO Methods

The reader should stop at this point and compare the data in Exhibit 4–6 with the data in Exhibit 4–5. Note that the major difference between the two exhibits is that the FIFO method separates the units in the beginning inventory from other units transferred out and converts the units in the beginning inventory to an equivalent units basis. A logical question to ask is, why the difference in the handling of the beginning inventory? The answer lies in what the two methods are trying to accomplish.

The purpose of the weighted-average method is to *simplify the computation of unit costs*. This is accomplished by treating units in the beginning inventory as if they were started and completed during the current period. By treating units in the beginning inventory in this way, the manager is relieved from having to distinguish between which units were on hand at the start of the year and which were not. Thus, he or she is able to treat all units equally when unit costs are computed. This greatly simplifies the costing process.

By contrast, the purpose of the FIFO method is to distinguish between (a) units in the beginning inventory and (b) units that were started during the period, so that separate unit costs can be computed for each. Under the FIFO method, units in the beginning inventory are assumed to be completed and transferred out first (thus, a "first-in, first-out" flow) and to carry their own unit costs. Units started during the year are assumed to be completed next and to carry their own unit costs. This is a more complex costing approach than the weighted-average method, although it can be argued that it is also more accurate.

EXHIBIT 4–7

A visual perspective of equivalent units

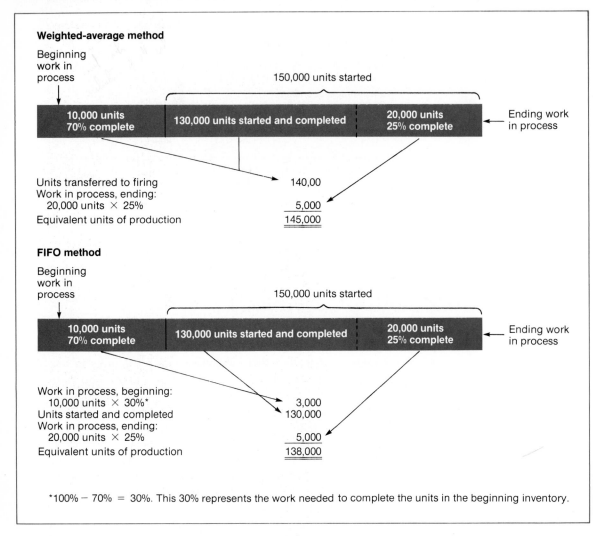

*100% − 70% = 30%. This 30% represents the work needed to complete the units in the beginning inventory.

A Visual Perspective of Equivalent Units

To assist in your understanding of equivalent units, Exhibit 4–7 contains a visual perspective of the computation of equivalent units (the data are for Regal Company's conversion costs). The exhibit also shows the relationship between equivalent units as computed by the weighted-average method and equivalent units as computed by the FIFO method. Study Exhibit 4–7 carefully before going on.

EXHIBIT 4–8

The production report in a process costing system

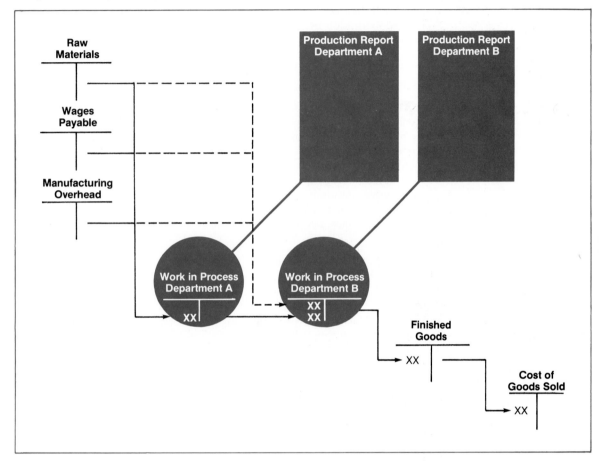

PRODUCTION REPORT—WEIGHTED-AVERAGE METHOD

To summarize all W.I.P. for a period.
a) units
b) costs

The purpose of the production report is to summarize for the manager all of the activity that takes place in a department's Work in Process account for a period. This activity includes the units that flow through the Work in Process account as well as the costs that flow through it. A separate production report is prepared for each department, as illustrated in Exhibit 4–8.

Earlier, when we outlined the differences between job-order costing and process costing, we stated that the production report takes the place of a job cost sheet in a process costing system. Thus, the production report is a key document for the manager and is vital to the proper operation of the system. There are three separate (though highly interrelated) parts to the production report:

1. A quantity schedule (which shows the flow of units through the department).
2. A computation of equivalent units and unit costs.
3. A reconciliation of all cost flows into and out of the department during the period.

We will use the following data to show a numerical example of a production report:

> The Stabler Chemical Company has two departments—mixing and cooking. Production activity begins in the mixing department; after mixing, the units are transferred to the cooking department. From cooking, the units are transferred to finished goods.
>
> All of the materials involved in mixing are added at the beginning of work in the mixing department. Labor and overhead costs in that department are incurred uniformly as work progresses. Overhead cost is applied at the rate of 150 percent of direct labor cost.
>
> Cost and other data for May 19x1 include the following for the mixing department:

Work in process, beginning:	
Units in process	20,000
Stage of completion*	30%
Cost in the beginning inventory:	
Materials cost	$ 8,000
Labor cost	3,600
Overhead cost	5,400
Total cost in process	$ 17,000
Units started into production during the month	180,000
Units completed and transferred to cooking	170,000
Costs added to production during the month:	
Materials cost	$ 63,000
Labor cost	88,000
Overhead cost applied	132,000
Work in process, ending:	
Units in process	30,000
Stage of completion*	40%

> *This refers to labor and overhead costs only, since all materials are added at the beginning of work in the mixing department.

In the following sections, we show how a production report is prepared when the weighted-average method is used to compute unit costs. Later in the chapter, we show how a production report is prepared when the FIFO method is used.

Step 1: Prepare a Quantity Schedule

The first section of a production report consists of a **quantity schedule,** which accounts for the physical flow of units through a department. The most widely used format for a quantity schedule shows the number of units worked on during a period and then shows the disposition of those units.

To illustrate, a quantity schedule for the Stabler Chemical Company is given below:

Units to be accounted for:	
Work in process, beginning (all materials,	
30% labor and overhead added last month)	20,000
Started into production	180,000
Total units to be accounted for	200,000
Units accounted for as follows:	
Transferred to cooking	170,000
Work in process, ending (all materials, 40%	
labor and overhead added this month)	30,000
Total units accounted for	200,000

The quantity schedule deals with *whole units,* not with equivalent units, although the stage of completion is always shown parenthetically. (The computation of equivalent units comes later.) The quantity schedule permits the manager to see at a glance how many units moved through the department during a period as well as to see the stage of completion of any in-process units. In addition to providing this information for the manager, the quantity schedule serves as an essential guide in preparing and tying together the remaining parts of a production report.

Step 2: Compute Equivalent Units and Unit Costs

Earlier in the chapter, we stated that in order to compute unit costs the manager must first compute the equivalent units for the period. The data for computing the equivalent units can be found on the quantity schedule. Notice from the quantity schedule that 170,000 units were completed and transferred to the cooking department during the month, and that another 30,000 units were still in process at the end of the month. The units in process were 100 percent complete as to materials, but they were only 40 percent complete as to labor and overhead.

Using these data and other data from the example, the computation of equivalent units and unit costs would be:

	Materials	Labor	Overhead	Total
Work in process, beginning	$ 8,000	$ 3,600	$ 5,400	$ 17,000
Cost added by the department	63,000	88,000	132,000	283,000
Total cost *(a)*	$71,000	$91,600	$137,400	$300,000
Equivalent units completed:				
Units transferred out	170,000	170,000	170,000	
Work in process, ending	30,000	12,000*	12,000*	
Total equivalent units *(b)*	200,000	182,000	182,000	
Unit cost, *(a)* ÷ *(b)*	$0.355	$0.503	$0.755	$1.613

* 30,000 units × 40% = 12,000 equivalent units.

As we stated earlier, the weighted-average method treats units in the beginning work in process inventory as if they were started and completed during the current period. Thus, the cost in the beginning work in process inventory has been added in with current period costs above in determining units costs for the month.

The units costs that we have computed will be used to apply cost to units that are transferred to the next department and will also be used to compute the cost in the ending work in process inventory. A total of all unit costs from both the mixing and cooking departments will represent the final manufactured cost of a unit of product.

Step 3: Prepare a Cost Reconciliation

The purpose of a **cost reconciliation** is to *(a)* show what costs have been charged to a department during a period and *(b)* show how these costs are accounted for. Typically, the costs charged to a department will consist of:

1. Cost in the beginning work in process inventory.
2. Materials, labor, and overhead cost added during the period.
3. Cost (if any) transferred in from the preceding department.

These costs are accounted for by showing:

1. Cost transferred out to the next department (or into Finished Goods).
2. Cost remaining in the ending work in process inventory.

Since this section of the production report is called a cost reconciliation, *the totals of these two groups of cost must always be in agreement.* The content of a cost reconciliation is shown graphically in Exhibit 4–9. Study this exhibit carefully before going on to the next section where we present a cost reconciliation for the Stabler Chemical Company.

Example of a cost reconciliation   The cost reconciliation depends heavily on the quantity schedule that was developed earlier. In fact, *the simplest way to prepare a cost reconciliation is to follow the quantity schedule line for line and show the cost associated with each group of units.* This is done in Exhibit 4–10, where we present a completed production report for the Stabler Chemical Company.

Note that the production report has the three sections that we mentioned earlier: (1) a quantity schedule; (2) a computation of equivalent units and unit costs; and (3) a cost reconciliation. As stated, *we follow the quantity schedule line for line in preparing the cost reconciliation.* For example, the quantity schedule shows that 20,000 units were in process at the start of the month and that an additional 180,000 units were started into production. Looking at the cost reconciliation part of the report, notice that the 20,000 units in process at the start of the month had $17,000 in cost attached to them and that the mixing department added another $283,000 in cost to

EXHIBIT 4–9

Graphic illustration of the cost reconciliation part of a production report

The costs charged to a department will consist of the beginning inventory plus costs added during the period.*	**Work in Process—Department A**		
	Bal. 1/1	X	XX Transferred out
	Materials added	XX	
	Labor added	XX	
	Overhead added	XX	
	Bal. 1/31	XX	

The costs charged to a department are accounted for by showing the amount transferred out plus the amount in the ending inventory.

* Departments that follow Department A (Department B and so forth) will also need to show the amount of cost transferred in from the preceding department.

production during the month. Thus, the mixing department has $300,000 in cost to be accounted for.

This cost is accounted for in two ways. As shown on the quantity schedule, 170,000 units were transferred to the cooking department during the month and another 30,000 units were still in process at the end of the month. Thus, part of the $300,000 "cost to be accounted for" goes with the 170,000 units to the cooking department, and part of it remains with the 30,000 units in the ending work in process inventory.

Each of the 170,000 units transferred to the cooking department is assigned $1.613 in cost, for a total of $274,254. The 30,000 units still in process at the end of the month are assigned cost according to their stage of completion. To determine the stage of completion, we refer to the equivalent units computation and bring the equivalent units figures down to the cost reconciliation part of the report. We then assign cost to these units, using the unit cost figures already computed.

After cost has been assigned to the ending work in process inventory, the total cost that we have accounted for ($300,000) agrees with the amount that we had to account for ($300,000). Thus, the cost reconciliation is complete.

PRODUCTION REPORT—FIFO METHOD

When the FIFO method is used to account for cost flows in a process costing system, the steps followed in preparing a production report are the same as those discussed above for the weighted-average method. Those steps are: (1) prepare a quantity schedule; (2) compute equivalent units

EXHIBIT 4–10
Production report—weighted-average method

Quantity schedule

	Units
Units to be accounted for:	
Work in process, beginning (all materials, 30% labor and overhead added last month)	20,000
Started into production	180,000
Total units to be accounted for	200,000
Units accounted for as follows:	
Transferred to cooking	170,000
Work in process, ending (all materials, 40% labor and overhead added this month)	30,000
Total units accounted for	200,000

Equivalent units and unit costs

	Materials	Labor	Overhead	Total
Work in process, beginning	$ 8,000	$ 3,600	$ 5,400	$ 17,000
Cost added by the department	63,000	88,000	132,000	283,000
Total cost *(a)*	$71,000	$91,600	$137,400	$300,000
Equivalent units:				
Units transferred out	170,000	170,000	170,000	
Work in process, ending	30,000	12,000*	12,000*	
Total equivalent units *(b)*	200,000	182,000	182,000	
Unit cost, *(a)* ÷ *(b)*	$0.355	$0.503	$0.755	$1.613

Cost reconciliation

	Equivalent units (EU)			Costs
Cost to be accounted for:				
Work in process, beginning				$ 17,000
Cost added by the department				283,000
Total cost to be accounted for				$300,000
Cost accounted for as follows:				
Transferred to cooking: 170,000 units × $1.613	—	—	—	$274,254[†]
Work in process, ending:				
Materials, at $0.355 per EU	30,000			10,650
Labor, at $0.503 per EU		12,000		6,036
Overhead, at $0.755 per EU			12,000	9,060
Total work in process, ending				25,746
Total cost accounted for				$300,000

* 40% × 30,000 units = 12,000 EU.
[†] Rounded upward to avoid a decimal discrepancy in the column totals.

and unit costs; and (3) prepare a cost reconciliation. However, since the FIFO method makes a distinction between units in the opening inventory and units started during the year, step three above is more complex when the FIFO method is used than it is when the weighted-average method is used. To see how a production report is prepared under the FIFO method, refer again to the data for the Stabler Chemical Company found on page 142. We will again follow these data step by step in the preparation of the report.

Step 1: Prepare a Quantity Schedule

There is only one difference between a quantity schedule prepared under the FIFO method and one prepared under the weighted-average method. This difference relates to units transferred out. As explained earlier in our discussion of equivalent units, the FIFO method divides units transferred out into two parts. One part consists of the units in the opening inventory, and the other part consists of the units started and completed during the current period. A quantity schedule showing this format for units transferred out is presented below for the Stabler Chemical Company.

Units to be accounted for:	
Work in process, beginning (all materials,	
30% labor and overhead added last month)	20,000
Started into production	180,000
Total units to be accounted for	200,000
Units accounted for as follows:	
Transferred to cooking:	
Units from the beginning inventory	20,000
Units started and completed this month.	150,000*
40% labor and overhead added this month)	30,000
Total units accounted for	200,000

* 170,000 units transferred − 20,000 units in the beginning inventory = 150,000 units started and completed this month.

As with the weighted-average method, once the quantity schedule has been prepared, it becomes a key factor in the preparation of the other two parts of the production report. We have seen that the information it contains is essential in computing equivalent units (and therefore unit costs) and in doing a cost reconciliation.

Step 2: Compute Equivalent Units and Unit Costs

The equivalent units for the month can easily be computed by referring to the data in the quantity schedule. We explained earlier that in computing equivalent units under the FIFO method, we must first show the amount of work required to complete the units in the beginning inventory. We then show the number of units started and completed during the period, and finally we show the amount of work completed on the units still in process at the end of the period. These equivalent unit computations are provided below for the Stabler Chemical Company.

In computing unit costs, we use only those costs that were incurred during the current period, and we ignore any costs in the beginning work in process inventory. The reason we ignore costs in the beginning inventory is that under the FIFO method, *unit costs are intended to relate only to work done during the current period.*

	Materials	Labor	Overhead	Total
Cost added by the department *(a)* . . .	$63,000	$88,000	$132,000	$283,000
Equivalent units completed:				
Work in process, beginning.	—	14,000*	14,000*	
Started and completed this month . .	150,000	150,000	150,000	
Work in process, ending	30,000	12,000†	12,000†	
Total equivalent units *(b)*.	180,000	176,000	176,000	
Unit cost, *(a)* ÷ *(b)*	$0.35	$0.50	$0.75	$1.60

* 100% − 30% = 70%; 70% × 20,000 units = 14,000 equivalent units.
† 40% × 30,000 units = 12,000 equivalent units.

The unit costs we have computed are used to add cost to units of product as they are transferred to the next department; in addition, they are used to show the amount of cost attached to partially completed units in the ending work in process inventory.

Step 3: Prepare a Cost Reconciliation

We learned earlier that the purpose of a cost reconciliation is *(a)* to show what costs have been charged to a department during a period and *(b)* to show how these costs are accounted for. We also learned that the best way to prepare a cost reconciliation is to follow the quantity schedule line for line and show the cost associated with each group of units.

The first part of the reconciliation (where we show the "cost to be accounted for") is the same under the FIFO method as it was under the weighted-average method. As before, the Stabler Chemical Company must account for a total of $300,000 in cost for the month. This $300,000 consists of $17,000 of cost associated with the beginning work in process inventory and an additional $283,000 of cost added during the month. These amounts are shown under the "Cost to be accounted for" part of the cost reconciliation in Exhibit 4–11.

The second part of the cost reconciliation (where we show how these costs are accounted for) is more complex under the FIFO method than it is under the weighted-average method. This is because we must again keep units in the beginning inventory separate from units started and completed during the month. For units in the beginning inventory, two cost elements are involved. The first element is the $17,000 of cost carried over from

EXHIBIT 4–11

Production report—FIFO method

Quantity schedule

	Units
Units to be accounted for:	
Work in process, beginning (all materials,	
30% labor and overhead added last month)	20,000
Started into production	180,000
Total units to be accounted for	200,000
Units accounted for as follows:	
Transferred to cooking:	
Units from the beginning inventory	20,000
Units started and completed this month	150,000*
Work in process, ending (all materials,	
40% labor and overhead added this month)	30,000
Total units accounted for	200,000

Equivalent units and unit costs

	Materials	Labor	Overhead	Total
Cost added by the department (a)	$63,000	$88,000	$132,000	$283,000
Equivalent units:				
Work in process, beginning	—	14,000[†]	14,000[†]	
Started and completed this month	150,000	150,000	150,000	
Work in process, ending	30,000	12,000[‡]	12,000[‡]	
Total equivalent units (b)	180,000	176,000	176,000	
Unit cost, (a) ÷ (b)	$0.35	$0.50	$0.75	$1.60

Cost reconciliation

	Equivalent units (EU)			Costs
Cost to be accounted for:				
Work in process, beginning				$ 17,000
Cost added by the department				283,000
Total cost to be accounted for				$300,000
Cost accounted for as follows:				
Transferred to cooking:				
Units from the beginning inventory:				
Cost in the beginning inventory				$ 17,000
Cost to complete these units:				
Materials, at $0.35 per EU	—			—
Labor, at $0.50 per EU		14,000		7,000
Overhead, at $0.75 per EU			14,000	10,500
Total cost				34,500
Units started and completed during				
the month: 150,000 units × $1.60	—	—	—	240,000
Total cost transferred				274,500
Work in process, ending:				
Materials, at $0.35 per EU	30,000			10,500
Labor, at $0.50 per EU		12,000		6,000
Overhead, at $0.75 per EU			12,000	9,000
Total work in process, ending				25,500
Total cost accounted for				$300,000

---

* 170,000 units transferred − 20,000 units in the beginning inventory = 150,000 units.
[†] 100% − 30% = 70%; 70% × 20,000 units = 14,000 EU.
[‡] 40% × 30,000 units = 12,000 EU.

the prior month. The second element is the cost needed to complete these units. As shown in Exhibit 4–11, this second element is computed by multiplying the unit cost figures for the month times the equivalent units completed for materials, labor, and overhead in the beginning inventory. (The equivalent units figures used in this computation are brought down from the "equivalent units" portion of the production report.)

For units started and completed during the month, we simply multiply the number of units started and completed (as shown on the quantity schedule) by the total unit cost to determine the amount transferred out. This would be $240,000 (150,000 units $\times$ $1.60 = $240,000) for the Stabler Chemical Company.

Finally, the amount of cost attached to the ending work in process inventory is computed by multiplying the unit cost figures for the month times the equivalent units for materials, labor, and overhead in the ending inventory. Once again, the equivalent units needed for this computation are brought down from the "equivalent units" portion of the production report.

A Comparison of Production Report Content

The production report is the most difficult part of this chapter, and it will require some effort on the reader's part to master the report's content and structure. To assist in this study, Exhibit 4–12 summarizes the major similarities and differences between production reports prepared under the weighted-average and FIFO methods.

EVALUATION OF THE WEIGHTED-AVERAGE AND FIFO METHODS

Although the weighted-average and FIFO methods seem to be very different, in most process costing situations they will produce unit costs that are nearly the same. Any major difference in unit costs between the two methods is likely to be traceable to erratic movements in raw materials prices. The reason is that conversion costs (labor and overhead) usually will not fluctuate widely from month to month due to the continuous nature of the flow of goods in process costing situations. In addition, inventory levels in most companies tend to remain quite stable, thereby adding to the general stability of unit costs. Raw materials prices can fluctuate considerably from period to period, however, which can result in a difference in unit costs between the two methods. This is because the weighted-average method will always be averaging the costs of one period in with those of the following period.

From the standpoint of cost control, the FIFO method is clearly superior to the weighted-average method. The reason is that current performance should be measured in relation to costs of the current period only, and the weighted-average method inherently mixes these costs in with costs of the prior period. Thus, under the weighted-average method, the manager's performance is influenced to some extent by what happened in a prior period. This problem does not arise under the FIFO method, since it makes a

EXHIBIT 4–12

A comparison of production report content

Weighted-average method	FIFO method
Quantity schedule	
1. The quantity schedule includes all units transferred out in a single figure.	1. The quantity schedule divides the units transferred out into two parts. One part consists of units in the beginning inventory, and the other part consists of units started and completed during the current period.
Equivalent units and unit costs	
1. Costs in the beginning inventory are added in with current period costs in unit cost computations.	1. Only current period costs are included in unit cost computations.
2. Units in the beginning inventory are treated as if they were started and completed during the current period.	2. Only work needed *to complete* units in the beginning inventory is included in the computation of equivalent units. Units started and completed during the current period is shown as a separate figure.
3. Unit costs will contain some element of cost from the prior period.	3. Unit costs will contain only elements of cost from the current period.
Cost reconciliation	
1. The "cost to be accounted for" section of the report is the same for both methods.	1. The "cost to be accounted for" section of the report is the same for both methods.
2. All units transferred out are treated the same, regardless of whether they were part of the beginning inventory or started and completed during the period.	2. Units transferred out are divided into two groups: *(a)* units in the beginning inventory and *(b)* units started and completed during the period.
3. Units in the ending inventory have cost applied to them in the same way under both methods.	3. Units in the ending inventory have cost applied to them in the same way under both methods.

clear distinction between costs in the beginning inventory and costs incurred during the current period.

On the other hand, some managers feel that the weighted-average method is simpler to apply than the FIFO method. Although this may have been true in the past when much accounting work was done by hand, due to the advent of the computer it is doubtful whether it is still true today. The computer can handle either method with ease. The FIFO method would require a more complex programming effort when a process costing system is first set up, but after that there should be little difference between the two methods so far as difficulty in operating the system is concerned.

SUMMARY

Process costing is used in those manufacturing situations where homogeneous products are produced on a continuous basis. A process costing system is similar to a job-order costing system in that (1) both systems have the same basic purpose of providing data for the manager, (2) both systems use the same manufacturing accounts, and (3) costs flow through the manufacturing accounts in basically the same way in both systems. A process costing system differs from a job-order system in that (1) a single product is involved, (2) costs are accumulated by department (rather than by job), (3) the department production report replaces the job cost sheet, and (4) unit costs are computed by department (rather than by job).

In order to compute unit costs in a department, the department's equivalent units must be determined. Equivalent units can be computed in two ways— by the weighted-average method and by the FIFO method. The weighted-average method treats partially completed units in the beginning work in process inventory as if they were started and completed during the current period. The FIFO method distinguishes between work completed in the prior period and work completed currently, so that equivalent units represent only work completed during the current period.

The activity in a department is summarized on a production report. There are three separate (though highly interrelated) parts to a production report. The first part is a quantity schedule, which shows the flow of units through a department during a period. The second part consists of a computation of equivalent units and unit costs, with unit costs being provided individually for materials, labor, and overhead as well as in total for the period. The third part consists of a cost reconciliation, which summarizes all cost flows through a department for a period.

Although the weighted-average and FIFO methods are somewhat different, in most process costing situations they will produce unit costs that are nearly the same, except perhaps for raw materials. From the viewpoint of cost control, the FIFO method is superior to the weighted-average method because of its focus on current period costs. Although the FIFO method seems more complex in its operation, this complexity is largely overcome today due to the widespread use of the computer.

KEY TERMS FOR REVIEW

Conversion cost Direct labor cost combined with manufacturing overhead cost.

Cost reconciliation The part of a production report that shows what costs a department has to account for during a period and how those costs are accounted for.

Equivalent units of production The number of units that would have been produced during a period if all of a department's efforts had resulted in completed units of product.

FIFO method A method of accounting for cost flows in a process costing system in which equivalent units and unit costs relate only to work done during the current period.

Parallel processing A method of arranging processing departments in which, after a certain point, some units may go through different processing departments than others.

Process costing A costing method used in those industries that produce homogeneous products on a continuous basis.

Processing department Any location in a factory where work is performed on a product and where materials, labor, or overhead costs are added to the product.

Production report A report that summarizes all activity in a department's Work in Process account during a period and that contains three sections: a quantity schedule, a computation of equivalent units and unit costs, and a cost reconciliation.

Quantity schedule The part of a production report that shows the flow of units through a department during a period.

Sequential processing A method of arranging processing departments in which all units flow in sequence from one department to another.

Transferred-in cost The amount of cost attached to units of product that have been received from a prior processing department.

Weighted-average method A method of accounting for cost flows in a process costing system in which units in the beginning work in process inventory are treated as if they were started and completed during the current period.

QUESTIONS

4–1. Under what conditions would it be appropriate to use a process costing system?

4–2. What similarities exist between job-order and process costing?

4–3. Costs are accumulated by job in a job-order costing system; how are costs accumulated in a process costing system?

4–4. What two essential features must characterize any processing department?

4–5. Distinguish between departments arranged in a sequential pattern and departments arranged in a parallel pattern.

4–6. Why is cost accumulation easier under a process costing system than it is under a job-order costing system?

4–7. How many Work in Process accounts are maintained in a company using process costing?

4–8. Assume that a company has two processing departments, mixing and firing. Prepare a journal entry to show a transfer of partially completed units from the mixing department to the firing department.

4–9. Assume again that a company has two processing departments, mixing and firing. Explain what costs might be added to the firing department's Work in Process account during a period.

4–10. What is meant by the term *equivalent units of production?*

4–11. Under the weighted-average method, what assumption is made relative to units in the beginning work in process inventory when equivalent units and unit costs are computed?

4–12. How does the computation of equivalent units under the FIFO method differ from the computation of equivalent units under the weighted-average method?

4–13. What is a quantity schedule, and what purpose does it serve?

4–14. On the cost reconciliation part of the production report, the weighted-average method treats all units transferred out in the same way. How does this differ from the FIFO method of handling units transferred out?

4–15. Under processing costing, it is often suggested that a product is like a rolling snowball as it moves from department to department. Why is this an apt comparison?

4–16. From the standpoint of cost control, why is the FIFO method superior to the weighted-average method?

EXERCISES

E4–1. The Superior Pulp Company processes wood pulp for various manufacturers of paper products. Data relating to tons of pulp processed during June 19x5 are provided below:

		Percent Completed	
	Tons of Pulp	Materials	Labor and Overhead
Work in process, June 1	20,000	90	80
Work in process, June 30	30,000	60	40
Started into processing during June . .	190,000	—	—

Required:
1. Compute the number of tons completed and transferred out during the month.
2. Prepare a quantity schedule for the month, assuming *(a)* that the company uses the weighted-average method and *(b)* that the company uses the FIFO method.

E4–2. Clonex Labs, Inc., uses a process costing system. The following data are available for one department for October 19x6:

		Percent Completed	
	Units	Materials	Conversion
Work in process, October 1	30,000	65	30
Work in process, October 31	15,000	80	40

The department started 175,000 units into production during the month and transferred 190,000 completed units to the next department.

Required:
1. Assuming that the company uses the weighted-average method of accounting for units and costs, compute the equivalent units of production for the month.
2. Repeat the computations in (1) above, assuming that the company uses the FIFO method of accounting for units and costs.

E4–3.   The Alaskan Fisheries, Inc., processes salmon for various distributors. Two departments are involved—department 1 and department 2. Data relating to pounds of salmon processed in department 1 during July 19x3 are presented below:

	Pounds of Salmon	Percent Completed*
Work in process, July 1	20,000	30
Started into processing during July . .	380,000	—
Work in process, July 31	25,000	60

*Labor and overhead only.

All materials are added at the beginning of processing in department 1. Labor and overhead costs are incurred uniformly throughout processing.

Required: 1.   Prepare a quantity schedule and a computation of equivalent units for the month, assuming that the company uses the weighted-average method of accounting for units.

2.   Repeat the computations in (1), assuming that the company uses the FIFO method of accounting for units.

E4–4.   Pureform, Inc., manufactures a product that passes through two departments. Data for a recent month for department A follow:

	Units	Materials	Labor	Overhead
Work in process, beginning	5,000	$ 4,500	$ 1,250	$ 1,875
Units started in process	45,000			
Units transferred out	42,000			
Work in process, ending	8,000			
Cost added during the month . . .	—	52,800	21,500	32,250

The beginning work in process inventory was 80 percent complete as to materials and 60 percent complete as to processing. The ending work in process inventory was 75 percent complete as to materials and 50 percent complete as to processing.

Required: 1.   Assume that the company uses the weighted-average method of accounting for units and costs. Prepare a computation of equivalent units and unit costs for the month.

2.   Repeat the computations in (1), assuming that the company uses the FIFO method of accounting for units and costs.

E4–5.   Malex Company uses a process costing system. The company's single product passes through two processes, cooking and molding. T-accounts showing the flow of costs through the two processes for a recent month follow:

Work in Process—Cooking

Bal. 4/1	8,000	Transferred out	160,000
Direct materials	42,000		
Direct labor	50,000		
Overhead	75,000		

Work in Process—Molding

Bal. 4/1	4,000	Transferred out 240,000
Transferred in	160,000	
Direct labor	36,000	
Overhead	45,000	

Required: Prepare journal entries showing the flow of costs through the two processes during April.

E4–6. Helox, Inc., manufactures a product that passes through two production processes. A quantity schedule for a recent month for process A follows:

Units to be accounted for:
Units in process, beginning (all materials, 40% labor
and overhead added last month) 5,000
Units started into production 180,000
Total units to be accounted for 185,000

Units accounted for as follows:
Units transferred to process B 175,000
Units in process, ending (all materials, 30% labor
and overhead added this month) 10,000
Total units accounted for 185,000

Costs in the beginning work in process inventory were: materials, $1,200; labor, $1,800; and overhead, $2,000. Costs added during the month were: materials, $54,000; labor, $140,800; and overhead, $211,200.

Required: Assuming that the company uses the weighted-average cost method, prepare a computation showing equivalent units and unit costs for the month.

E4–7. (This exercise should be assigned only if Exercise 4–6 is also assigned.) Refer to the data in Exercise 4–6 and to the unit costs that you have computed there.

Required: Complete the following cost reconciliation for process A:

	Equivalent Units (EU)	Costs
Cost to be accounted for:		
Work in process, beginning		$?
Added by the department during the month . . .		?
Total cost to be accounted for		$411,000
Cost accounted for as follows:		
Transferred to process B (?).	— — —	$?
Work in process, ending:		
Materials (?)	?	?
Labor (?)	?	?
Overhead (?)	?	?
Total work in process, ending		?
Total cost accounted for		$411,000

E4–8. Refer to the data in Exercise 4–6. Assume that the company uses the FIFO cost method.

Required: 1. Explain how the quantity schedule prepared under the FIFO method would differ from the quantity schedule shown in Exercise 4–6 (which has been prepared under the weighted-average method).

2. Prepare a computation of equivalent units and unit costs for the month.

E4–9. (This exercise should be assigned only if Exercise 4–8 is also assigned.) Refer to the data in Exercise 4–6 and to the unit costs you have computed in Exercise 4–8.

Required: Complete the following cost reconciliation for process A:

	Equivalent Units (EU)	Cost
Cost to be accounted for:		
Work in process, beginning		$ 5,000
Added by the department during the month		406,000
Total cost to be accounted for		$411,000
Cost accounted for as follows:		
Transferred to process B:		
Units from the beginning inventory:		
Cost in the beginning inventory		$?
Cost to complete these units:		
Materials (?)	?	?
Labor (?)	?	?
Overhead (?)	?	?
Total cost		?
Units started and completed during the month (?)	— — —	?
Total cost transferred		?
Work in process, ending:		
Materials (?)	?	?
Labor (?)	?	?
Overhead (?)	?	?
Total work in process, ending		?
Total cost accounted for		$411,000

PROBLEMS

P4–10. **Partial production report.** Martin Company uses a process costing system and manufactures a single product. Activity for June 19x6 has just been completed. An incomplete production report for department X for the month follows:

Production Report—Department X
For the Month Ended June 30, 19x6

Quantity schedule

	Units
Units to be accounted for:	
Work in process, June 1 (all materials, 75% labor and overhead added last month)	8,000
Started into production	45,000
Total units to be accounted for	53,000

Units accounted for as follows:

Transferred to department Y	48,000
Work in process, June 30 (all materials, 40% labor and overhead added this month)	5,000
Total units accounted for	53,000

Equivalent units and unit costs

	Materials	Labor	Overhead	Total
Work in process, June 1	$ 5,150	$ 660	$ 1,320	$ 7,130
Cost added during June	29,300	9,840	19,680	58,820
Total cost *(a)*	$34,450	$10,500	$21,000	$65,950
Equivalent units *(b)*	53,000	50,000	50,000	
Unit cost, *(a)* ÷ *(b)*.	$0.65	$0.21	$0.42	$1.28

Cost reconciliation

Cost to be accounted for:
        ?
Cost accounted for as follows:
        ?

Required: 1. By scrutinizing the incomplete production report, identify two ways in which you can tell whether the company is using the weighted-average method or the FIFO method.
  2. Prepare a schedule showing how the equivalent units were computed.
  3. Complete the "cost reconciliation" part of the production report.

P4–11. **Step-by-step production report; weighted-average method.** Builder Products, Inc., manufactures a caulking compound that goes through three processing stages prior to completion. Information on work in the first department, cooking, is given below for May 19x2:

Production data:

Units in process, May 1; 80% complete as to labor and overhead	10,000
Units started into production during May	100,000
Units completed and transferred out	95,000
Units in process, May 31; 60% complete as to materials and 20% complete as to labor and overhead	?

Cost data:

Work in process inventory, May 1:

Materials cost	$ 1,500
Labor cost	1,800
Overhead cost	5,400

Cost added during May:

Materials cost	154,500
Labor cost	22,700
Overhead cost	68,100

Materials are added at several stages during the cooking process, whereas labor and overhead costs are incurred uniformly. The company uses the weighted-average method.

Required: Prepare a production report for the cooking department. Use the following three steps in preparing your report:

1. Prepare a quantity schedule.
2. Compute the equivalent units and unit costs for the month.
3. Using the data from (1) and (2), prepare a cost reconciliation.

P4–12. **Partial production report.** Tumwater, Inc., manufactures a single product that moves through two departments, A and B. A partially completed production report for a recent month in department A follows:

Department A—Production Report
For the Month Ended March 31, 19x5

Quantity schedule

	Units
Units to be accounted for:	
Work in process, March 1 (all materials, ⅔	
labor and overhead added last month)	6,000
Started into production	40,000
Total units to be accounted for	46,000
Units accounted for as follows:	
Transferred to department B:	
Units from the beginning inventory	6,000
Units started and completed this month	36,000
Work in process, March 31 (all materials, ¼	
labor and overhead added this month	4,000
Total units accounted for.	46,000

Equivalent units and unit costs

	Materials	Labor	Overhead	Total
Cost added during March (a)	$60,000	$29,250	$48,750	$138,000
Equivalent units (b)	40,000	39,000	39,000	
Unit cost, (a) ÷ (b)	$1.50	$0.75	$1.25	$3.50

Cost reconciliation

Cost to be accounted for:
    ?

Cost accounted for as follows:
    ?

Required: 1. By scrutinizing the incomplete production report, identify two ways in which you can tell whether the company is using the weighted-average cost method or the FIFO cost method.
2. Prepare a schedule showing how the equivalent units were computed.
3. Assume that the cost in the work in process inventory totaled $27,000 at the beginning of the month (March 1). Complete the "cost reconciliation" part of the production report above.

P4–13. **Step-by-step production report; FIFO method.** Selzik Company manufactures a single product that goes through two processes, blending and packaging. The following activity was recorded in the blending department during July 19x4:

Production data:
Units in process, July 1; 30% complete
    as to conversion costs   10,000
Units started into production   170,000
Units completed and transferred to packaging . . .   ?
Units in process, July 31; 40% complete
    as to conversion costs   20,000
Cost data:
Work in process inventory, July 1:
    Materials cost . . . . $ 8,500
    Conversion cost . . . .   4,900 $ 13,400
Cost added during the month:
    Materials cost   139,400
    Conversion cost   244,200   383,600
    Total cost $397,000

All materials are added at the beginning of work in the blending department. Conversion costs are added uniformly during processing. The company uses the FIFO cost method.

Required: Prepare a production report for the blending department for the month of July. Use the following three steps as a guide in preparing your report:

1. Prepare a quantity schedule.
2. Compute equivalent units and unit costs for the month.
3. Using the data from (1) and (2), prepare a cost reconciliation.

P4–14.   **Basic production report; weighted-average method.**   (P4–15 uses these same data with the FIFO method.) Suncrest, Inc., manufactures a product that goes through several departments prior to completion. The following information is available on work in the mixing department during June 19x1:

	Units	Percent Completed	
		Materials	**Conversion**
Work in process, beginning	20,000	100	75
Started into production	180,000		
Completed and transferred out	160,000		
Work in process, ending	40,000	100	25

Cost in the beginning work in process inventory and cost added during June were as follows:

	Materials	Conversion
Work in process, beginning	$ 25,200	$ 24,800
Cost added during June	334,800	238,700

The company uses the weighted-average method to compute unit costs. The mixing department is the first department in the production process; after mixing has been completed, the units are transferred to the molding department.

Required: Prepare a production report for the mixing department for the month of June 19x1.

P4–15.   **Basic production report; FIFO method.**   Refer to the data in P4–14. Assume that the company uses the FIFO method to compute unit costs rather than the weighted-average method.

Required: Prepare a production report for the mixing department for the month of June 19x1.

P4–16.   **Straightforward production report; weighted-average method.**   Quality Adhesives, Inc., manufactures a high-quality rubber cement product. Three departments are involved—grinding, cooking, and mixing. Data on work in the grinding department is given below for June 19x8:

	Units	Percent Completed	Materials	Labor	Overhead
Work in process, June 1	15,000	60	$ 15,225	$ 900	$ 5,320
Pounds started into production . . .	105,000	—			
Pounds transferred to cooking . . .	?	—			
Work in process, June 30	9,000	20			
Cost added during June	—	—	110,775	10,380	68,000

The "percent completed" above relates to labor and overhead, since all materials are added at the beginning of work in the grinding department.

Required: Prepare a production report for the grinding department for the month.

P4–17.   **Straightforward production report; FIFO method.**   Hilox, Inc., produces an antacid product that goes through two departments. Cost and production data for the first department, blending, are given below for May 19x5:

Units:
  In process, May 1: 5,000 units (40% complete as to conversion).
  In process, May 31: 4,000 units (75% complete as to conversion).
  Started into production: 80,000 units.
  Completed and transferred out: 81,000 units.

Costs:
  In process, May 1: $7,600.
  Added to production during May:
    Material X: $60,000.
    Material Y: $25,500.
    Conversion: $36,900.

Material X is added at the beginning of work in the blending department. Material Y is also added in the blending department, but it is not added until units of product are 60 percent complete as to conversion. Conversion costs are incurred uniformly during work in the blending department. The company uses the FIFO cost method.

Required: Prepare a production report for the blending department for the month.

P4–18.   **Analysis of Work in Process T-account; FIFO method.**   Superior Brands, Inc., manufactures paint. The paint goes through three processes—cracking, mixing, and cooking. Activity in the cracking department during a recent month is summarized in the department's Work in Process account below:

Work in Process—Cracking Department

Inventory, April 1 (10,000 gals., 80% processed)	39,000	Completed and transferred to mixing (? gals.)	?
April costs added:			
Materials (140,000 gals.)	259,000		
Labor and overhead	312,000		
Inventory, April 30 (30,000 gals., 60% processed)	?		

The materials are entered into production at the beginning of work in the cracking department. Labor and overhead costs are incurred uniformly throughout the cracking process. The company uses the FIFO cost method.

Required: 1. Prepare a production report for the cracking department for the month.
2. In a process costing system, would you expect per unit materials cost or per unit labor and overhead cost to show the greater fluctuation from period to period? Why?

P4–19. **Analysis of Work in Process T-account; weighted-average method.**   Weston Products manufactures an industrial cleaning compound that goes through three processing departments: grinding, mixing, and cooking. Raw materials are introduced at the start of work in the grinding department, with conversion costs being incurred evenly throughout the grinding process. The Work in Process T-account for the grinding department for a recent month is given below:

Work in Process—Grinding Department

Inventory, May 1 (18,000 lbs, 1/3 processed)	21,800	Completed and transferred to mixing (? lbs.)	?
May costs added:			
Raw materials (167,000 lbs.)	133,400		
Labor and overhead	226,800		
Inventory, May 31 (15,000 lbs., 2/3 processed)	?		

The May 1 work in process inventory consists of $14,600 in materials cost and $7,200 in labor and overhead cost. The company uses the weighted-average method to account for units and costs.

Required: 1. Prepare a production report for the grinding department for the month.
2. What criticism can be made of the unit costs that you have computed on your production report?

P4–20. **Equivalent units; costing of inventories.**   You are employed by Spirit Company, a manufacturer of digital watches. The company's chief financial officer is trying to verify the accuracy of the December 31, 19x6, work in process and finished goods inventories prior to closing the books for the year. You have been asked to assist in this verification. The year-end balances shown on Spirit Company's books are as follows:

	Units	Costs
Work in process (50% complete as to labor and overhead)	300,000	$ 660,960
Finished goods	200,000	1,009,800

Materials are added to production at the beginning of the manufacturing process, and overhead is applied to each product at the rate of 60% of direct labor cost. There was no finished goods inventory on January 1, 19x6. A review of Spirit Company's inventory and cost records has disclosed the following information:

		Costs	
	Units	Materials	Labor
Work in process, January 1, 19x6 (80% complete as to labor and overhead)	200,000	$ 200,000	$ 315,000
Units started into production . . .	1,000,000		
Cost added during 19x6:			
Materials cost		1,300,000	
Labor cost			1,995,000
Units completed during 19x6 . . .	900,000		

The company uses the weighted-average cost method.

Required: 1.   Prepare a computation showing the equivalent units for 19x6 and unit costs for materials, labor, and overhead.

2.   Determine the amount of cost that should be assigned to the ending work in process and finished goods inventories.

3.   Prepare the necessary correcting journal entry to adjust the work in process and finished goods inventories to the correct balances as of December 31, 19x6.

(CPA, Adapted)

P4–21.   **Production report; journal entries; weighted-average method.**   Lubricants, Inc., produces a special kind of grease that is widely used by race car drivers. The grease is produced in two processes: refining and blending.

Raw oil products are introduced at the start of work in the refining department; labor and overhead costs are incurred evenly throughout the refining operation. The refined output is then transferred to the blending department.

The following incomplete Work in Process account is available for the refining department for March 19x2:

Work in Process—Refining Department

March 1 inventory (5,000 gal., ⅘ processed)	6,500	Completed and transferred to blending (? gal.)	?
March costs added:			
Raw oil materials (30,000 gal.)	12,500		
Direct labor	14,500		
Overhead	21,750		
March 31 inventory (6,000 gal., ⅔ processed)	?		

The March 1 work in process inventory consists of the following cost elements: raw materials, $1,500; direct labor, $2,000; and overhead, $3,000. The company accounts for units and costs by the weighted-average method.

Required: 1.   Prepare a production report for the refining department for the month.
2.   Assume the following cost and activity in the blending department during March: raw materials used, $4,000; direct labor cost incurred, $8,500; and overhead cost applied to production, $12,750. The blending department completed 25,000 units at a cost of $2.88 per unit. Prepare journal entries to show the flow of costs through the two departments during March.

P4–22.   Production report; journal entries; FIFO method.   ZAB, Inc., produces a very popular low-calorie soft drink. Two processes, blending and bottling, are used to produce the drink.

All materials are added at the start of work in the blending department; labor and overhead costs are incurred evenly during the blending operation. The blended liquid is then transferred to the bottling department, where it is put into bottles for distribution.

The following incomplete Work in Process account for the blending department is available for June 19x8:

Work in Process—Blending Department

June 1 inventory (10,000 gal.,		Completed and transferred to	
10% processed)	6,500	bottling (70,000 gal.)	?
June costs added:			
Materials (? gal.)	32,500		
Direct labor	64,800		
Overhead	97,200		
June 30 inventory (5,000 gal.,			
60% processed)	?		

The company uses the FIFO method to account for units and costs.

Required: 1.   Prepare a production report for the blending department for the month.
2.   Assume the following costs and activity in the bottling department for June: raw materials used, $16,000; direct labor cost incurred, $25,200; and overhead cost applied to production, $31,500. The bottling department completed production on 72,000 gallons of the soft drink during June at a cost of $3.60 per gallon. Prepare journal entries to show the flow of costs through the two departments during June.

CASES

C4–23.   Production report; second department; FIFO cost method.   "I think we goofed when we hired that new assistant controller," said Ruth Scarpino, president of Provost Industries. "Just look at this production report that he prepared for last month for the finishing department. I can't make heads or tails out of it."

Finishing department costs:
Work in process inventory, April 1, 450
   units, 60% complete as to conversion costs . . . . $ 8,190*
Cost transferred in during the month from
   the preceding department on 1,950 units   17,940
Materials cost added during the month (materials
   are added when processing is 50% complete
   in the finishing department)   6,210
Conversion costs incurred during the month   13,920
Total departmental costs $46,260

Finishing department costs assigned to:
Units completed and transferred to finished
   goods, 1,800 units at $25.70 per unit $46,260
Work in process inventory, April 30, 600
   units, 35% complete as to processing . . . .   –0–
Total departmental costs assigned $46,260

   * Consists of: cost transferred in, $4,050; materials cost, $1,980; and conversion cost, $2,160.

"He's struggling to learn our system," replied Frank Harrop, the operations manager. "The problem is that he's been away from process costing for a long time, and it's coming back slowly."

"It's not just the format of his report that I'm concerned about. Look at that $25.70 unit cost that he's come up with for April. Doesn't that seem high to you?" said Ms. Scarpino.

"Yes, it does seem high; but on the other hand, I know we had an increase in materials prices during April, and that may be the explanation," replied Mr. Harrop. "I'll get someone else to redo this report and then we may be able to see what's going on."

Provost Industries manufactures a ceramic product that goes through two processing departments—molding and finishing. The company uses the FIFO method to account for units and costs.

Required: 1. Prepare a revised production report for the finishing department.
           2. As stated above, the company experienced an increase in materials prices during April. Would the effects of this price increase tend to show up more under the weighted-average method or under the FIFO method? Why?

C4–24.   **Production report; second department; weighted-average method.**   Refer to the data for Provost Industries in the preceding case. Assume that the company uses the weighted-average method to account for units and costs.

Required: 1. Prepare a production report for the finishing department for the month.
           2. As stated in the case, the company experienced an increase in materials prices during April. Would you expect unit costs for April to be lower under the weighted-average method or under the FIFO method? Why?

CHAPTER 5

Cost Behavior: Analysis and Use

- Identify examples of variable costs and explain the effect of a change in activity on both total variable costs and per unit variable costs.

- Identify examples of fixed costs and explain the effect of a change in activity on both total fixed costs and fixed costs expressed on a per unit basis.

- Define the relevant range and explain its significance in cost behavior analysis.

- Distinguish between committed and discretionary fixed costs.

- Analyze a mixed cost by the high-low method, the scattergraph method, and the least squares method, and enumerate the strengths and weaknesses of each of these analytical approaches.

- Prepare an income statement using the contribution format.

- Define or explain the key terms listed at the end of the chapter.

I n our discussion of cost terms and concepts in Chapter 2, we stated that one way in which costs can be classified is by behavior. We defined cost behavior as meaning how a cost will react or change as changes take place in the level of business activity. An understanding of cost behavior is the key to many decisions in an organization in that by understanding how costs behave, a manager is better able to predict what costs will be under various operating circumstances. Experience has shown that attempts at decision making without a thorough understanding of the costs involved— and how these costs may change with the activity level—can lead to disaster. A decision to double production of a particular product line, for example, might result in the incurrence of far greater costs than could be generated in additional revenues. To avoid such problems, a manager must be able to accurately predict what costs will be at various activity levels. In this chapter, we shall find that the key to effective cost prediction lies in an understanding of cost behavior patterns.

TYPES OF COST BEHAVIOR PATTERNS

In our brief discussion of cost behavior in Chapter 2, we mentioned only variable and fixed costs. There is a third behavior pattern, generally known as a *mixed* or *semivariable* cost. All three cost behavior patterns— variable, fixed, and mixed—are found in most organizations. The relative proportion of each type of cost present in a firm is known as the firm's **cost structure.** For example, a firm might have many fixed costs but few variable costs or mixed costs. Alternatively, it might have many variable costs but few fixed or mixed costs. A firm's cost structure is very significant in that the decision-making process can be affected by the relative amount of fixed or variable cost that is present in the firm. We must reserve a detailed discussion of cost structure until the next chapter, however, and concentrate for the moment on gaining a full understanding of the behavior of each type of cost that a manager might encounter.

In the following sections, we briefly review the definition of variable costs and fixed costs and then discuss the behavior of these costs in greater depth than we were able to do in Chapter 2. After this review and discussion, we turn our attention to the identification and analysis of mixed costs. We conclude the chapter by introducing a new income statement format—called the contribution format—in which costs are organized by behavior rather than by the traditional functions of production, sales, and administration.

Variable Costs

We found in Chapter 2 that a variable cost is so named because its total dollar amount varies in direct proportion to changes in the activity level. If the activity level doubles, then one would expect the total dollar amount of the variable costs to also double. If the activity level increases by only 10 percent, then one would expect the total dollar amount of the variable costs to increase by 10 percent as well.

We also found in Chapter 2 that a variable cost remains constant if expressed on a *per unit* basis. To provide an example, assume that the Premier Motor Company produces trucks. There is one radiator to each truck, and the radiators cost $30 each. Thus, if we look at the cost of radiators on a *per truck* basis, the cost remains constant at $30 per truck. The $30 figure will not change, regardless of how many trucks are produced during a period, unless influenced by some outside factor.[1] The behavior of a variable cost, on both a per unit and a total basis, is illustrated in the following tabulation:

Number of trucks produced	Radiator cost per truck	Total radiator cost
250	$30	$ 7,500
500	30	15,000
750	30	22,500
1,000	30	30,000

The idea that a variable cost is constant per unit but varies in total with the activity level is crucial to an understanding of cost behavior patterns. We shall rely on this concept again and again in this chapter and in chapters ahead. Exhibit 5–1 contains a graphical illustration of variable cost behavior.

The activity base   For a cost to be variable, it must be variable *with something*. That "something" is its **activity base.** An activity base is a measure of effort that operates as a causal factor in the incurrence of variable cost. In Chapter 3 we mentioned that an activity base is sometimes referred to as a *cost driver.* Some of the most common activity bases are machine-hours, units produced, and units sold. Other activity bases (cost drivers) might include the number of miles driven by salespersons, the number of pounds of laundry processed by a hotel, the number of letters typed by a secretary, the number of hours of labor time logged, and the number of occupied beds in a hospital.

In order to plan and control variable costs, a manager must be well acquainted with the various activity bases within the firm. People sometimes get the notion that if a cost doesn't vary with production or with sales, then it is not really a variable cost. This, of course, is not correct. As suggested by the range of bases listed above, costs can be incurred as a function of many different activities within an organization. Whether a cost is variable depends on whether its incurrence is a function of the activity measure under consideration. For example, if a manager is analyzing the cost of service calls under a product warranty, the relevant activity measure

---

[1] Frequently, discounts are allowed on quantity purchases. The handling of such discounts in the cost records of a firm is discussed in Chapter 9.

EXHIBIT 5–1

Variable cost behavior

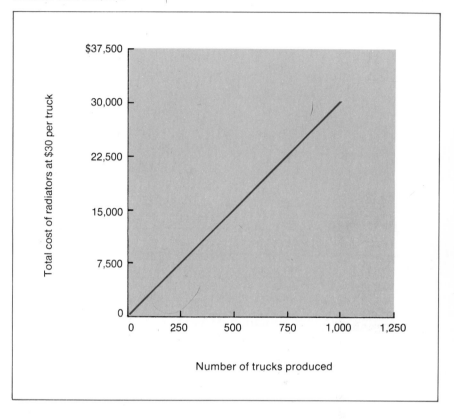

will be the number of service calls made. Those costs that vary in total with the number of service calls made will be variable costs.

Extent of variable costs   The number and type of variable costs present in an organization will depend in large part on the organization's structure and purpose. A highly capital-intensive organization such as a public utility will tend to have few variable costs. The bulk of its costs will be associated with its plant, and these costs will tend to be quite insensitive to changes in levels of service provided. A manufacturing firm, by contrast, will often have many variable costs; these costs will be associated both with the manufacture of its products and with their distribution to customers. A service organization or a merchandising firm will tend to fall between these two extremes.

A few of the more frequently encountered variable costs are shown in the tabulation in Exhibit 5–2. The costs listed under "Variable portion of manufacturing overhead" in the exhibit should not be viewed as being inclusive but rather as being representative of the kinds of variable costs found in this classification.

EXHIBIT 5–2
Examples of variable costs

Type of organization	Variable costs
Merchandising firm	Cost of goods (merchandise) sold

Manufacturing firm	Manufacturing costs:
	  Prime costs:
	    Direct materials
	    Direct labor
	  Variable portion of manufacturing overhead:
	    Indirect materials
	    Lubricants
	    Supplies
	    Utilities
	    Setup time
	    Indirect labor

Both merchandising and manufacturing firms	Selling and administrative costs:
	  Commissions to salespersons
	  Clerical costs, such as invoicing
	  Freight-out

Service organizations	Supplies, travel, clerical

True Variable versus Step-Variable Costs

Not all variable costs have exactly the same behavior pattern. Some variable costs behave in a *true variable* or *proportionately variable* pattern. Other variable costs behave in a *step-variable* pattern.

True variable costs   Direct materials would be a true or proportionately variable cost because the amount used during a period will vary in direct proportion to the level of production activity. Moreover, any amounts purchased but not used can be stored up and carried forward to the next period as inventory.

Step-variable costs   Indirect labor is also considered to be a variable cost, but it doesn't behave in quite the same way as direct materials. As an example, let us consider the labor cost of maintenance workers, which would be part of indirect labor.

Unlike direct materials, the time of maintenance workers is obtainable only in large chunks, rather than in exact quantities. Moreover, any maintenance time not utilized cannot be stored up as inventory and carried forward to the next period. Either the time is used effectively as it expires hour by hour, or it is gone forever. Furthermore, the utilization of indirect labor time can be quite flexible, whereas the utilization of direct materials is usually quite set. A maintenance crew, for example, can work at a fairly leisurely pace if pressures are light, but then the crew can intensify its efforts if pressures build up. For this reason, somewhat small changes in the level of production may have no effect on the number of maintenance people needed to properly carry on maintenance work.

EXHIBIT 5–3

True variable versus step-variable costs

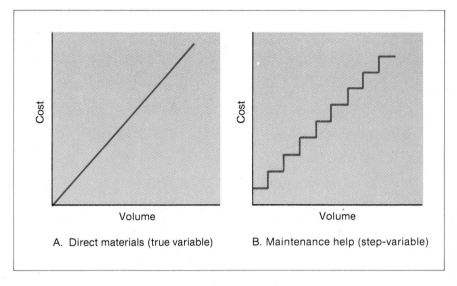

A. Direct materials (true variable)   B. Maintenance help (step-variable)

A cost (such as the labor cost of maintenance workers) that is obtainable only in large chunks and that increases or decreases only in response to fairly wide changes in the activity level is known as a **step-variable cost.** The behavior of a step-variable cost, contrasted with the behavior of a true variable cost, is illustrated in Exhibit 5–3.

Notice that the need for maintenance help changes only with fairly wide changes in volume and that when additional maintenance time is obtained, it comes in large, indivisible pieces. The strategy of management in dealing with step-variable costs must be to obtain the fullest use of services possible for each separate step. Great care must be taken in working with these kinds of costs to prevent "fat" from building up in an organization. There is a tendency to employ additional help more quickly than might be needed, and there is generally a reluctance to lay people off when volume declines.

The Linearity Assumption and the Relevant Range

In dealing with variable costs, we have assumed a strictly linear relationship between cost and volume, except in the case of step-variable costs. Economists correctly point out that many costs that the accountant classifies as variable actually behave in a *curvilinear* fashion. The behavior of a **curvilinear cost** is shown in Exhibit 5–4. Notice that a strictly linear relationship between cost and volume does not exist either at very high or at very low levels of activity.

Although the accountant recognizes that many costs are not linear in their relationship to volume at some points, he or she concentrates on their

EXHIBIT 5–4
Curvilinear costs and the relevant range

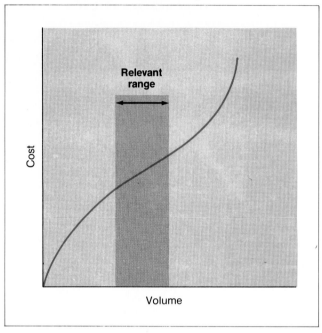

behavior within narrow bands of activity known as the **relevant range.**
The relevant range can be defined as that range of activity within which
assumptions relative to cost behavior are valid. Generally, the relationship
between variable cost and activity is stable enough within this range that
an assumption of strict linearity can be used with insignificant loss of accuracy. The concept of the relevant range is illustrated in Exhibit 5–4.

Fixed Costs

    In our discussion of cost behavior patterns in Chapter 2, we stated that
fixed costs remain constant in total dollar amount regardless of changes in
the level of activity. To continue the Premier Motor Company example, if
the company rents a factory building for $50,000 per year, the *total* amount
of rent paid will not change regardless of the number of trucks produced
in a year. This concept is shown graphically in Exhibit 5–5.
    Since fixed costs remain constant in total, the amount of cost computed
on a *per unit* basis will get progressively smaller as the number of units
produced becomes greater. If the Premier Motor Company produces only
250 trucks in a year, the $50,000 fixed rental cost would amount to $200
per truck. If 1,000 trucks are produced, the fixed rental cost would amount
to only $50 per truck. As we noted in Chapter 2, this aspect of fixed costs

EXHIBIT 5–5

Fixed cost behavior

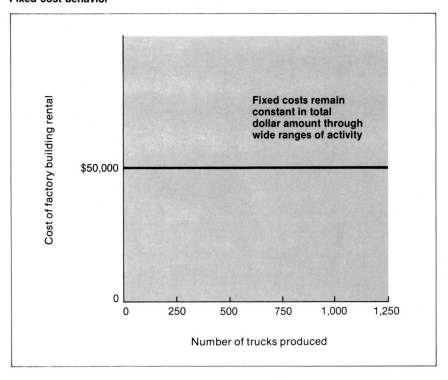

can be confusing to the manager, although it is necessary in some contexts to express fixed costs on an average per unit basis. We found in Chapter 3, for example, that for purposes of preparing financial statements the manager needs a broad unit cost figure containing both variable and fixed cost elements. For *internal* uses, however, the manager rarely expresses a fixed cost on a per unit basis because of the potential confusion involved. Experience has shown that for internal uses, fixed costs are most easily (and most safely) dealt with on a total basis rather than on a per unit basis.

The Trend toward Fixed Costs

The trend in many companies today is toward greater fixed costs relative to variable costs. There are at least two factors responsible for this trend. First, automation is becoming increasingly important in all types of organizations. Although automation has played a significant role in factory operations for well over a century, its role continues to increase. In addition, automation is rapidly becoming a significant factor in some traditionally service-oriented industries as well. Increased automation means increased investment in machinery and equipment, with the attendant fixed depreciation or lease charges.

Second, labor unions have been increasingly successful in stabilizing employment through labor contracts. Labor leaders have set guaranteed annual salaries or guaranteed minimum weeks of work high on their list of goals for the future. Although most people would agree that a stabilization of employment is desirable from a social point of view, guaranteed salaries and workweeks do reduce the response of direct labor costs to changes in production.

This shift away from variable costs toward fixed costs has been so significant in some firms that they have become largely "fixed cost" organizations. The textile industry, for example, can be cited as one in which most firms have moved heavily toward automation, with basically inflexible fixed costs replacing flexible, more responsive variable costs to a considerable extent. These shifts are very significant from a managerial accounting point of view in that planning in many ways becomes much more crucial when one is dealing with large amounts of fixed costs. The reason is that when dealing with fixed costs, the manager is much more "locked in" and generally has fewer options available in day-to-day decisions.

Types of Fixed Costs

Fixed costs are sometimes referred to as capacity costs, since they result from outlays made for plant facilities, equipment, and other items needed to provide the basic capacity for sustained operations. For planning purposes, fixed costs can be viewed as being either *committed* or *discretionary*.

Committed fixed costs   **Committed fixed costs** are those that relate to the investment in plant, equipment, and the basic organizational structure of a firm. Examples of such costs include depreciation of plant facilities (buildings and equipment), taxes on real estate, insurance, and salaries of top management and operating personnel.

The two key factors about committed fixed costs are that (1) they are long term in nature, and (2) they can't be reduced to zero even for short periods of time without seriously impairing either the profitability or the long-run goals of a firm. Even if operations are interrupted or cut back, the committed fixed costs will still continue unchanged. During a period of economic recession, for example, a firm can't discharge its key executives or sell off part of the plant. Facilities and the basic organizational structure must be kept intact at all times. In terms of long-run goals, the costs of any other course of action would be far greater than any short-run savings that might be realized.

Since committed fixed costs are basic to the long-run goals of a firm, their planning horizon usually encompasses many years. The commitments involved in these costs are made only after careful analysis of long-run sales forecasts and after relating these forecasts to future capacity needs. Careful control must be exercised by management in the planning stage to ensure that a firm's long-run needs are properly evaluated. Once a decision is made to build a certain size plant, a firm becomes locked into that decision for many years to come.

After a firm becomes committed to a basic plant and organization, how are the associated costs controlled from year to year? Control of committed fixed costs comes through *utilization*. The strategy of management must be to utilize the plant and organization as effectively as possible in bringing about desired goals.

Discretionary fixed costs   **Discretionary fixed costs** (often referred to as *managed* fixed costs) arise from *annual* decisions by management to spend in certain fixed cost areas. Examples of discretionary fixed costs would include advertising, research, and management development programs.

Basically, two key differences exist between discretionary fixed costs and committed fixed costs. First, the planning horizon for a discretionary fixed cost is fairly short term—usually a single year. By contrast, as we indicated earlier, committed fixed costs have a planning horizon that encompasses many years. Second, under dire circumstances it may be possible to cut certain discretionary fixed costs back for short periods of time with minimal damage to the long-run goals of the organization. For example, a firm that has been spending $50,000 annually on management development programs may be forced because of poor economic conditions to reduce its spending in that area during a given year. Although some unfavorable consequences might result from the cutback, it is doubtful that these consequences would be as great as those that would result if the company decided to economize during the year by disposing of a portion of its plant.

The key factor about discretionary fixed costs is that management is not locked into a decision regarding such costs for any more than a single budget period. Each year a fresh look can be taken at the expenditure level in the various discretionary fixed cost areas. A decision can then be made on whether to continue a particular expenditure, increase it, reduce it, or discontinue it altogether.

Top-management philosophy   In our discussion of fixed costs, we have drawn a sharp line between committed fixed costs and discretionary fixed costs. As a practical matter, the line between these two classes of costs should be viewed as being somewhat flexible. The reason is that whether a cost is committed or discretionary will depend in large part on the philosophy of top management.

Some management groups prefer to exercise discretion as often as possible on as many costs as possible. They prefer to review costs frequently and to adjust costs frequently, as conditions and needs warrant. Managers who are inclined in this direction tend to view fixed costs as being largely discretionary. Other management groups are slow to make adjustments in costs (especially adjustments downward) as conditions and needs change. They prefer to maintain the status quo and to leave programs and personnel largely undisturbed, even though changing conditions and needs might suggest the desirability of adjustments. Managers who are inclined in this direction tend to view virtually all fixed costs as being committed.

To cite an example, during recessionary periods when the level of home building is down, many construction companies lay off their workers and virtually disband operations for a period of time. Other construction companies continue large numbers of employees on the payroll, even though the workers have little or no work to do. In the first instance, management is viewing its fixed costs as being largely discretionary in nature. In the second instance, management is viewing its fixed costs as being largely committed. The philosophy of most management groups will fall somewhere between these two extremes.

Fixed Costs and the Relevant Range

The concept of the relevant range, which was introduced in our discussion of variable costs, also has application in dealing with fixed costs, particularly those of a discretionary nature. At the beginning of a period, programs are set and budgets established. The level of discretionary fixed costs will depend on the support needs of the programs that have been planned, which in turn will depend at least in part on the level of activity envisioned in the organization overall. At very high levels of activity, programs are usually broadened or expanded to include many things that might not be pursued at lower levels of activity. In addition, the support needs at high levels of activity are usually much greater than the support needs at lower levels of activity. For example, the advertising needs of a company striving to increase sales by 25 percent would probably be much greater than if no sales increase was planned. Thus, fixed costs often move upward in steps as the activity level increases. This concept is illustrated in Exhibit 5–6, which depicts fixed costs and the relevant range.

Although discretionary fixed costs are most susceptible to adjustment according to changing needs, the step pattern depicted in Exhibit 5–6 also has application to committed fixed costs. As a company expands its level of activity, it may outgrow its present plant, or the key management core may need to be expanded. The result, of course, will be increased committed fixed costs as a larger plant is built and as new key management positions are created.

One's first reaction to the step pattern depicted in Exhibit 5–6 is to say that discretionary and committed fixed costs are really just step-variable costs. To some extend this is true, since *all* costs vary in the long run. There are two major differences, however, between the step-variable costs depicted earlier in Exhibit 5–3 and the fixed costs depicted in Exhibit 5–6.

The first difference is that the step-variable costs can be adjusted very quickly as conditions change, whereas once fixed costs have been set, they often can't be changed easily, even if they are discretionary in nature. A step-variable cost such as maintenance labor, for example, can be adjusted upward or downward very quickly by the hiring and firing of maintenance

EXHIBIT 5–6

Fixed costs and the relevant range

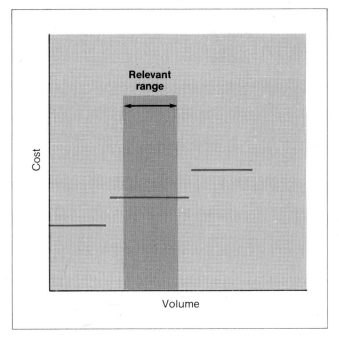

workers. By contrast, once a company has committed itself to a particular program, it becomes locked into the attendant fixed costs, at least for the budget period under consideration. Once an advertising contract has been signed, for example, the company is locked into the attendant costs for the contract period.

The second difference is that the *width of the steps* depicted for step-variable costs is much narrower than the width of the steps depicted for the fixed costs in Exhibit 5–6. The width of the steps relates to volume or level of activity. For step-variable costs, the width of a step may be 40 hours of activity or less if one is dealing, for example, with maintenance labor cost. For fixed costs, however, the width of a step may be *thousands* or even *tens of thousands* of hours of activity. In essence, the width of the steps for step-variable costs is generally so narrow that these costs can be treated essentially as variable costs. The width of the steps for fixed costs, on the other hand, is so wide that these costs must generally be treated as being entirely fixed within the relevant range.

Mixed Costs

A **mixed cost** is one that contains both variable and fixed cost elements. Mixed costs are also known as **semivariable costs.** At certain levels of

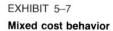

EXHIBIT 5–7

Mixed cost behavior

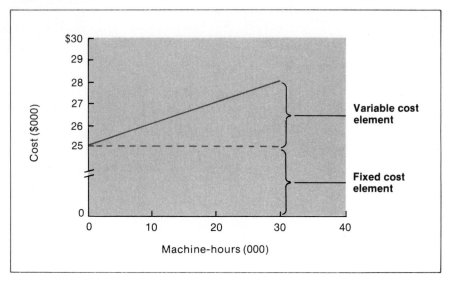

activity, mixed costs may display essentially the same characteristics as a fixed cost; at other levels of activity, they may display essentially the same characteristics as a variable cost.

To continue the Premier Motor Company example, assume that the company leases a large part of the machinery used in its operations. The lease agreement calls for a flat annual lease payment of $25,000, plus 10 cents for each hour that the machines are operated during the year. If during a particular year the machines are operated a cumulative total of 30,000 hours, then the lease cost of the machines will be $28,000, made up of $25,000 in fixed cost plus $3,000 in variable cost. The concept of a mixed cost is shown graphically in Exhibit 5–7.

Even if the machines leased by the Premier Motor Company aren't used a single hour during the year, the company will still have to pay the minimum $25,000 charge. This is why the cost line in Exhibit 5–7 intersects the vertical cost axis at the $25,000 point. For each hour that the machines are used, the *total* cost of leasing will increase by 10 cents. Therefore, the total cost line slopes upward as the variable cost element is added onto the fixed cost element.

THE ANALYSIS OF MIXED COSTS

The concept of a mixed cost is important, since mixed costs are common to a wide range of firms. Examples of mixed costs include electricity, heat, repairs, telephone, and maintenance.

The fixed portion of a mixed cost represents the basic, minimum charge for just having a service *ready and available* for use. The variable portion represents the charge made for *actual consumption* of the service. As one would expect, the variable element varies in proportion to the amount of the service that is consumed.

For planning purposes, how does management handle mixed costs? The ideal approach would be to take each invoice as it comes in and break it down into its fixed and variable elements. As a practical matter, even if it were possible to make this type of minute breakdown, the cost of doing so would probably be prohibitive. Analysis of mixed costs is normally done on an aggregate basis, concentrating on the past behavior of a cost at various levels of activity. If this analysis is done carefully, good approximations of the fixed and variable elements of a cost can be obtained with a minimum of effort.

We will examine three methods of breaking mixed costs down into their fixed and variable elements—the *high-low method*, the *scattergraph method*, and the *least squares method*.

The High-Low Method

The **high-low method** of analyzing mixed costs requires that the cost involved (for example, maintenance) be observed at both the high and low levels of activity within the relevant range. The difference in cost observed at the two extremes is divided by the change in activity in order to determine the amount of variable cost involved.

To illustrate, assume that maintenance costs for the Arco Company have been observed as follows within the relevant range of 5,000 to 8,000 direct labor-hours (DLH):

Month	Direct labor-hours	Maintenance cost incurred
January	5,500	$ 745
February	7,000	850
March	5,000	700
April	6,500	820
May	7,500	960
June	8,000	1,000
July	6,000	825

Since total maintenance cost increases as the activity level increases, it seems obvious that some variable cost element is present. To separate the variable cost element from the fixed cost element, we must relate the change in direct labor-hours between the high and low points to the change that we observe in cost:

	Direct labor-hours	Maintenance cost incurred
High point observed	8,000	$1,000
Low point observed	5,000	700
Change observed	3,000	$ 300

$$\text{Variable rate} = \frac{\text{Change in cost}}{\text{Change in activity}} = \frac{\$300}{3,000} = \$0.10 \text{ per direct labor-hour}$$

Having determined that the variable rate is 10 cents per direct labor-hour, we can now determine the amount of fixed cost present. This is done by taking total cost at *either* the high or the low point and deducting the variable cost element. In the computation below, total cost at the high point of activity is used in computing the fixed cost element:

$$\text{Fixed cost element} = \text{Total cost} - \text{Variable cost element}$$
$$= \$1,000 - (\$0.10 \times 8,000 \text{ labor-hours})$$
$$= \$200$$

Both the variable and fixed cost elements have now been isolated. The cost of maintenance within the relevant range analyzed can be expressed as being $200 plus 10 cents per direct labor-hour. This is sometimes referred to as a **cost formula.**

$$\left. \begin{array}{c} \text{Cost formula for maintenance—over} \\ \text{the relevant range of 5,000 to} \\ \text{8,000 direct labor-hours} \end{array} \right\} = \begin{array}{c} \$200 \text{ fixed cost} + \$0.10 \\ \text{per direct labor-hour} \end{array}$$

The data used in this illustration are shown graphically in Exhibit 5–8. Three things should be noted in relation to this exhibit:

1. Notice that cost is always plotted on the vertical axis and that it is represented by the letter *Y*. Cost is known as the **dependent variable** since the amount of cost incurred during a period will be dependent on the level of activity for the period. (That is, as the level of activity increases, total cost will also increase.)
2. Notice that activity (direct labor-hours in this case) is always plotted on the horizontal axis and that it is represented by the letter *X*. Activity is known as the **independent variable** since it controls the amount of cost that will be incurred during a period.
3. Notice that the relevant range is highlighted on the exhibit. In using a cost formula, the manager must remember that the formula will not be valid outside the relevant range from which the underlying data have been drawn.

The high-low method is very simple to apply, but it suffers from a major (and sometimes critical) defect in that it utilizes only two points in determin-

EXHIBIT 5–8

High-low method of cost analysis
Arco Company—maintenance cost

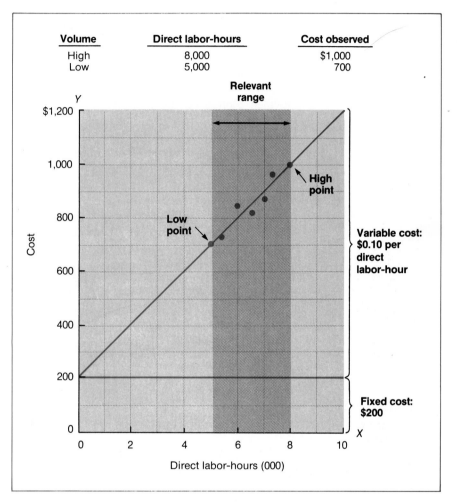

Volume	Direct labor-hours	Cost observed
High	8,000	$1,000
Low	5,000	700

Handwritten margin note: Hi-lo — only uses 2 pts. not always rep. average.

ing a cost formula. Generally, two points are not enough to produce accurate results in cost analysis work unless the points *happen* to fall in such a way as to represent a true average of all points of cost and activity. As one might suppose, only rarely will the two points in the high-low method happen to fall in just this way. For this reason, other methods of cost analysis that utilize a greater number of points will generally be more accurate than the high-low method in deriving a cost formula. If a manager chooses to use the high-low method, he or she should do so with a full awareness of the method's limitations.

The Scattergraph Method

In mixed cost analysis, the manager is trying to find the *average* rate of variability in a mixed cost. A more accurate way of doing this than the high-low method is to use the **scattergraph method,** which includes all points of observed cost data in the analysis through use of a graph. A graph much like the one that we used in Exhibit 5–8 is constructed, in which cost is shown on the vertical axis and the volume or rate of activity is shown on the horizontal axis. Costs observed at various levels of activity are then plotted on the graph, and a line is fitted to the plotted points. However, rather than just fitting the line to the high and low points, *all points* are considered in the placement of the line. This is done through simple visual inspection of the data, with the analyst taking care that the placement of the line is representative of all points, not just the high and low ones. Typically, the line is placed so that approximately equal numbers of points fall above and below it.

A graph of this type is known as a *scattergraph,* and the line fitted to the plotted points is known as a **regression line.** The regression line, in effect, is a line of averages, with the average variable cost per unit of activity represented by the slope of the line and the average fixed cost in total represented by the point where the regression line intersects the cost axis.

To illustrate how a scattergraph is prepared, assume that Western Company has recorded costs for water over the last eight months as follows:

Water consumed (000 gallons)	Total cost
12.	$260
15.	270
10.	230
9.	220
11.	250
13.	240
8.	220
14.	260

The observed costs for water at the various activity levels have been plotted on a graph in Exhibit 5–9, and a regression line has been fitted to the plotted data by visual inspection. Note that the regression line has been placed in such a way that approximately equal numbers of points fall above and below it.

Since the regression line strikes the cost axis at the $150 point, that amount represents the fixed cost element. The variable cost element would be $8 per 1,000 gallons of water consumed, computed as follows:

Total cost observed for 10,000 gallons of water consumed (a point falling on the regression line in Exhibit 5–9)	$230
Less fixed cost element	150
Variable cost element	$ 80

$80 ÷ 10,000 gallons = $0.008 per gallon, or $8 per thousand gallons.

EXHIBIT 5–9

**A completed scattergraph
Western Company—water cost**

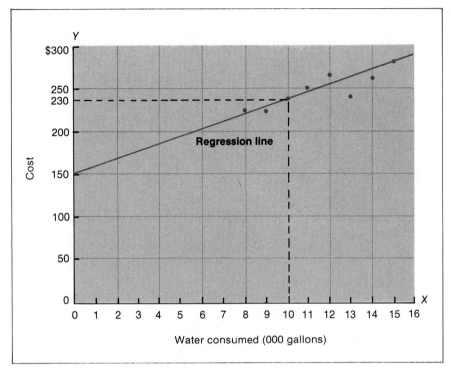

Thus, the cost formula for water would be $150 per month plus $8 per thousand gallons of water consumed.

A scattergraph can be an extremely useful tool in the hands of an experienced analyst. Quirks in cost behavior due to strikes, bad weather, breakdowns, and so on, become immediately apparent to the trained observer, who can make appropriate adjustment to the data in fitting the regression line. Many cost analysts would argue that a scattergraph should be the beginning point in all cost analyses, due to the benefits to be gained from having the data visually available in graph form.

The Least Squares Method

The **least squares method** is a more sophisticated approach to the scattergraph idea. Rather than fitting a regression line through the scattergraph data by simple visual inspection, the least squares method fits the line by statistical analysis.

The least squares method is based on computations that find their foundation in the equation for a straight line. A straight line can be expressed in equation form as:

$$Y = a + bX$$

with Y as the dependent variable; a as the fixed element; b as the degree of variability, or the slope of the line; and X as the independent variable. From this basic equation, and a given set of observations, n, two simultaneous linear equations can be developed that will fit a regression line to a linear array of data. The equations are:[2]

$$\Sigma XY = a\Sigma X + b\Sigma X^2 \tag{1}$$
$$\Sigma Y = na + b\Sigma X \tag{2}$$

where

X = activity measure (hours, etc.)
Y = total mixed cost observed
a = fixed cost
b = variable rate
n = number of observations

An example of least squares The application of the least squares method can best be seen through a detailed example. Let us assume that a company is anxious to break its power (electrical) costs down into basic variable and fixed cost elements. Over the past year, power costs (Y) have been observed as shown in the tabulation below. The number of hours of machine time logged (X) in incurring these costs is also shown in the tabulation.

Month	Machine-hours (000) (X)	Power costs (Y)	XY	X^2
January	9	$ 3,000	$ 27,000	81
February	8	2,500	20,000	64
March	9	2,900	26,100	81
April	10	2,900	29,000	100
May	12	3,600	43,200	144
June	13	3,400	44,200	169
July	11	3,200	35,200	121
August	11	3,300	36,300	121
September . . .	10	3,000	30,000	100
October	8	2,600	20,800	64
November . . .	7	2,300	16,100	49
December . . .	8	2,600	20,800	64
Totals	116	$35,300	$348,700	1,158

---

[2] The Appendix at the end of this chapter contains an alternative approach to the least squares method.

Substituting these amounts in the two linear equations given earlier, we have:

$$\Sigma XY = a\Sigma X + b\Sigma X^2 \qquad (1)$$
$$\Sigma Y = na + b\Sigma X \qquad (2)$$

$$\$348,700 = 116a + 1,158b \qquad (1)$$
$$\$35,300 = 12a + 116b \qquad (2)$$

In order to solve the equations, it will be necessary to eliminate one of the terms. The a term can be eliminated by multiplying equation (1) by 12, by multiplying equation (2) by 116, and then by subtracting equation (2) from equation (1). These steps are shown below:

Multiply equation (1) by 12:	$\$4,184,400 = 1,392a + 13,896b$
Multiply equation (2) by 116:	$\$4,094,800 = 1,392a + 13,456b$
Subtract (2) from (1):	$\$89,600 = \qquad\qquad 440b$
	$\$203.64 = b$

Therefore, the variable rate for power cost is $203.64 for each thousand machine-hours of operating time (or $0.20364 per hour). The fixed cost of power can be obtained by substituting the value for term b in either equation (1) or equation (2). We will use equation (2) since the numbers are smaller and easier to deal with:

$$\$35,300 = 12a + 116b \qquad (2)$$
$$\$35,300 = 12a + 116(\$203.64)$$
$$\$35,300 = 12a + \$23,622.24$$
$$\$11,677.76 = 12a$$
$$\$973.15 = a$$

The fixed cost for power is $973.15 per month. The cost formula for the mixed cost is therefore $973.15 per month plus $203.64 per thousand machine-hours worked.

Cost formula for power—over the relevant range of 7,000 to 13,000 machine-hours $=$ $973.15 fixed cost + $203.64 per thousand machine-hours ($0.20364 per hour)

In terms of the linear equation $Y = a + bX$, the cost formula can be expressed as:

$$Y = \$973.15 + \$203.64X$$

where activity (X) is expressed in thousands of machine-hours. We can show how the cost formula is used for planning purposes by assuming that 10,500 machine-hours will be worked during the coming month. Under this assumption, the expected power costs will be:

Variable costs:	
10.5 thousand machine-hours × $203.64 . .	$2,138.22
Fixed costs	973.15
Total expected power costs	$3,111.37

What does least squares mean?   The term *least squares* means that the sum of the squares of the deviations from the plotted points to the regression line *is smaller* than would be obtained from any other line fitted to the data. This idea can be illustrated as shown in Exhibit 5–10.

Notice from the exhibit that the deviations from the plotted points to the regression line are measured vertically on the graph. They are not measured perpendicular to the regression line. Least squares will have been attained when $\Sigma(Y - Y_1)^2$ is at the lowest possible figure. At the point of least squares, the best possible fit of a regression line to the plotted points will have been achieved in terms of slope and placement of the line.

The Use of Judgment in Cost Analysis

Although a cost formula has the appearance of exactness, the user should recognize that the breakdown of any mixed cost by any of the three techniques that we have discussed involves a substantial amount of estimating. The breakdowns represent *good approximations* of the fixed and variable cost elements involved; they should not be construed as being precise analyses. Managers must be ready to step in at any point in their analysis of a cost and adjust their computations for judgment factors that in their view are critical to a proper understanding of the mixed cost involved. However, the fact that computations are not exact and involve estimates and judgment factors does not prevent data from being useful and meaningful in decision making. The managers who wait to make a decision until they have perfect data available will rarely have an opportunity to demonstrate their decision-making ability.

Multiple Regression Analysis

In all of our computations involving mixed costs, we have assumed a single causative factor as the basis for the behavior of the variable element. That causative factor has been the volume or rate of some activity, such as direct labor-hours, machine-hours, production, or sales. This assumption is acceptable for many mixed costs, but in some situations there may be more than one causative factor involved in the behavior of the variable element. For example, in a shipping department the cost of freight-out might depend on both the number of units shipped and the weight of the units as dual causative factors. In a situation such as this, the equation for a simple regression would have to be expanded to include the additional variable:

$$Y = a + bX + cW$$

where c = the factor of variability and W = the weight of a unit. When dealing with an expanded equation such as this one, the simple regression analysis that we have been doing is no longer adequate. A **multiple regres-**

EXHIBIT 5–10

The concept of least squares

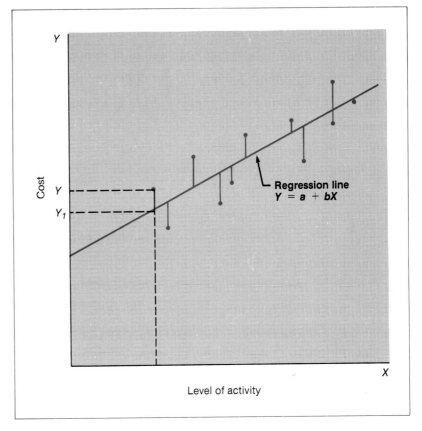

Level of activity

sion analysis is necessary. Although the added variable or variables will make the computations more complex, the principles involved are the same as in a simple regression such as we have been doing. Because of the complexity of the computations involved, multiple regression is generally done with the aid of a computer.

Engineering Approach to Cost Study

Some firms use the engineering approach to the study of cost behavior. Essentially, this approach involves a quantitative analysis of what cost behavior should be, based on the industrial engineer's evaluation of the production methods to be used, the materials specifications, labor needs, equipment needs, efficiency of production, power consumption, and so on. The engineering approach must be used in those situations where no past experience is available on activity and costs. In addition, it is often used in tandem with the methods we have discussed above in order to sharpen the accuracy of cost analysis. An NAA (National Association of Accountants) research report of actual business practices describes the use of the engineering approach as follows:

> The industrial engineering approach to determination of how costs should vary with volume proceeds by systematic study of materials, labor, services, and facilities needed at varying volumes. The aim is to find the best way to obtain the desired production. These studies generally make use of past experience, but it is used as a guide or as a check upon the results obtained by direct study of the production methods and facilities. Where no past experience is available, as with a new product, plant, or method, this approach can be applied to estimate the changes in cost that will accompany changes in volume.[3]

THE CONTRIBUTION FORMAT

Once the manager has separated costs into fixed and variable elements, what does he or she do with the data? To answer this question will require most of the remainder of this book, since virtually everything the manager does rests in some way on an understanding of cost behavior. One immediate and very significant application of the ideas we have developed, however, is found in a new format to the income statement known as the **contribution approach.** The unique thing about the contribution approach is that it provides the manager with an income statement geared directly to cost behavior.

Why a New Income Statement Format?

The **traditional approach** to the income statement, such as illustrated in Chapter 2 and such as you studied in financial accounting, is not organized in terms of cost behavior. Rather, it is organized in a "functional" format—emphasizing the functions of production, administration, and sales in the classification and presentation of cost data. No attempt is made to distinguish between the behavior of costs included under each functional heading. Under the heading "Administrative expense," for example, one can expect to find both variable and fixed costs lumped together.

Although an income statement prepared in the functional format may be useful for external reporting purposes, it has serious limitations so far as usefulness internally to the manager is concerned. Internally, the manager needs cost data organized in a format that will facilitate the carrying out of major responsibilities of planning, control, and decision making. As we

---

[3] National Association of Accountants, Research Report No. 16, "The Analysis of Cost-Volume-Profit Relationships" (New York, 1960), p. 17.

EXHIBIT 5–11

Comparison of the contribution income statement with the traditional income statement

Traditional approach (costs organized by function)			Contribution approach (costs organized by behavior)		
Sales		$12,000	Sales		$12,000
Less cost of goods sold		6,000*	Less variable expenses:		
Gross margin		6,000	Variable production	$2,000	
Less operating expenses:			Variable selling	600	
Selling	$3,100*		Variable administrative . . .	400	3,000
Administrative	1,900*	5,000	Contribution margin		9,000
Net income		$ 1,000	Less fixed expenses:		
			Fixed production	4,000	
			Fixed selling	2,500	
			Fixed administrative	1,500	8,000
			Net income		$ 1,000

*Contains both variable and fixed expenses. This is the income statement for a *manufacturing* firm; thus, when the income statement is placed in the contribution format, the "cost of goods sold" figure is divided between variable production costs and fixed production costs. If this were the income statement for a *merchandising* firm (which simply purchases completed goods from a supplier), then the "cost of goods sold" would *all* be variable.

shall see in chapters ahead, these responsibilities are discharged most effectively when cost data are available in a fixed and variable format. The contribution approach to the income statement has been developed in response to this need.

The Contribution Approach

Exhibit 5–11 presents a model of the contribution approach to the income statement, along with the traditional approach with which you are already familiar.

Notice that the contribution approach separates costs into fixed and variable categories, first deducting variable expenses from sales to obtain what is known as the *contribution margin*. The term **contribution margin** can be defined as the amount remaining from sales revenues after variable expenses have been deducted that can be used *to contribute* toward the covering of fixed expenses and then toward profits for the period.

The contribution approach to the income statement is widely used as an internal planning and decision-making tool. Its emphasis on costs by behavior facilitates cost-volume-profit analysis, such as we shall be doing in the following chapter. The approach is also very useful in appraisal of management performance, in segmented reporting of profit data, in budgeting, and in organizing data pertinent to all kinds of special decisions, such as product line analysis, pricing, use of scarce resources, and make or buy analyses. All of these topics are covered in later chapters.

SUMMARY

Managers analyze cost behavior to have a basis for predicting how costs will respond to changes in activity levels throughout the organization. We have looked at three types of cost behavior—variable, fixed, and mixed. In the case of mixed costs, we have studied three methods of breaking a mixed cost into its basic variable and fixed elements. The high-low method is the simplest of the three, having as its underlying assumption that the rate of variability is constant per unit of activity. When the rate of variability in a mixed cost is not constant, an average rate of variability must be computed. This can be done by either the scattergraph method or the least squares method. Both methods require the construction of a regression line, the slope of which represents the average rate of variability in the mixed cost being analyzed. The least squares method is the more accurate of the two in that it uses statistical analysis to fit a regression line to an array of data.

Managers use costs organized by behavior as a basis for many decisions. To facilitate this use, costs are often prepared in a contribution format. The unique thing about the contribution format is that it classifies costs on the income statement by cost behavior rather than by the functions of production, administration, and sales.

REVIEW PROBLEM ON COST BEHAVIOR

Consider the following costs of X Company over the relevant range of 5,000 to 20,000 units produced:

	Units produced			
	5,000	10,000	15,000	20,000
Total costs:				
Variable costs	$ 20,000	$?	$?	$?
Fixed costs	180,000	?	?	?
Total costs	$200,000	$?	$?	$?
Cost per unit:				
Variable cost	$?	$?	$?	$?
Fixed cost	?	?	?	?
Total cost per unit	$?	$?	$?	$?

Required: Compute the missing amounts.

Solution: The variable cost per unit of product can be computed as:

$$\$20,000 \div 5,000 \text{ units} = \$4 \text{ per unit}$$

Therefore, in accordance with the behavior of variable and fixed costs, the missing amounts are:

	Units produced			
	5,000	10,000	15,000	20,000
Total costs:				
Variable costs	$ 20,000	$ 40,000	$ 60,000	$ 80,000
Fixed costs	180,000	180,000	180,000	180,000
Total costs	$200,000	$220,000	$240,000	$260,000
Cost per unit:				
Variable cost	$ 4	$ 4	$ 4	$ 4
Fixed cost	36	18	12	9
Total cost per unit	$ 40	$ 22	$ 16	$ 13

Observe that the variable costs increase, in total, proportionately with increases in the number of units produced, but that these costs remain constant at $4 if expressed on a per unit basis. In contrast, the fixed costs by definition do not change in total with changes in the level of output. They remain constant at $180,000. With increases in production, however, the fixed costs decrease on a per unit basis, dropping from $36 per unit when 5,000 units are produced to only $9 per unit when 20,000 units are produced. *Because of this troublesome aspect of fixed costs, they are most easily (and most safely) dealt with on a total basis, rather than on a unit basis, in cost analysis work.*

KEY TERMS FOR REVIEW

Activity base A measure of effort, such as production, sales, or miles driven by salespersons, that operates as a causal factor in the incurrence of variable costs. An activity base is also known as a *cost driver.*

Committed fixed costs Those fixed costs that relate to the investment in plant, equipment, and the basic organizational structure of a firm.

Contribution approach An income statement format that is geared to cost behavior in that costs are separated into variable and fixed categories rather than being separated according to the functions of production, sales, and administration.

Contribution margin The amount remaining from sales revenues after variable expenses have been deducted.

Cost formula A quantitative expression of the fixed and variable elements of a cost. This expression is generally in the form of the linear equation $Y = a + bX$.

Cost structure The relative proportion of fixed, variable, and mixed costs found within an organization.

Curvilinear costs The economist's expression of the relationship between cost and activity in an organization.

Dependent variable A variable that reacts or responds to some controlling factor in a situation; total cost is the dependent variable, as represented by the letter Y, in the equation $Y = a + bX$.

Discretionary fixed costs Those fixed costs that arise from annual decisions by management to spend in certain fixed cost areas, such as advertising and research.

High-low method A method of separating a mixed cost into its fixed and variable elements by analyzing the change in activity and cost between the high and low points of a group of observed data.

Independent variable A variable that acts as the controlling factor in a situation; activity is the independent variable, as represented by the letter X, in the equation $Y = a + bX$.

Least squares method A method of separating a mixed cost into its fixed and variable elements; under this method, a regression line is fitted to an array of plotted points by statistical analysis.

Mixed cost A cost that contains both variable and fixed cost elements. Also see *Semivariable cost*.

Multiple regression analysis An analytical method required in those situations where more than one causative factor is involved in the behavior of the variable element of a mixed cost.

Regression line A line fitted to an array of plotted points. The slope of the line, denoted by the letter b in the linear equation $Y = a + bX$, represents the average variable cost per unit of activity; the point where the line intersects the cost axis, denoted by the letter a in the equation above, represents the average total fixed cost.

Relevant range That range of activity within which assumptions relative to variable and fixed cost behavior are valid.

Scattergraph method A method of separating a mixed cost into its fixed and variable elements; under this method, a regression line is fitted to an array of plotted points by simple, visual inspection.

Semivariable cost A cost that contains both variable and fixed cost elements. Also see *Mixed cost*.

Step-variable cost A cost (such as the cost of a maintenance worker) that is obtainable only in large pieces and that increases and decreases only in response to fairly wide changes in the activity level.

Traditional approach An income statement format in which costs are organized and presented according to the functions of production, administration, and sales.

APPENDIX: ALTERNATIVE APPROACH TO LEAST SQUARES

Some managers prefer an alternative approach to the least squares method that does not require use of the equations given in the chapter. Assume that a firm wishes to develop a cost formula for its maintenance expense. The company has determined that the variable portion of maintenance is incurred as a function of the number of machine-hours worked. Data on machine-hours and attendant maintenance expense for the first six months

EXHIBIT 5–12
Alternative approach to least squares analysis

| Month | Machine-hours (X) | Maintenance expense (Y) | Difference from average | | X'Y' | X'² |
			Machine-hours (X')	Maintenance expense (Y')		
January	400	$ 180	−100	−$20	+$ 2,000	10,000
February	575	215	+ 75	+ 15	+ 1,125	5,625
March	350	170	−150	− 30	+ 4,500	22,500
April	475	195	− 25	− 5	+ 125	625
May	550	210	+ 50	+ 10	+ 500	2,500
June	650	230	+150	+ 30	+ 4,500	22,500
Totals	3,000	$1,200	−0−	−0−	$12,750	63,750
Average	500 (X̄)	$ 200 (Ȳ)				

Variable rate: $\dfrac{\Sigma X'Y'}{\Sigma X'^2} = \dfrac{\$12,750}{63,750} = \$0.20$ per machine-hour

Total fixed cost: $\bar{Y} = a + b\bar{X}$
$\$200 = a + \$0.20(500 \text{ machine-hours})$
$a = \$200 - \$100$
$a = \$100$

of 19x1 are given in Exhibit 5–12. The exhibit also contains computations showing how a mixed cost can be broken down into its basic variable and fixed cost elements by the alternative approach.

As shown in the exhibit, the cost formula for maintenance expense is $100 fixed cost plus 20 cents per machine-hour. Or, it can be expressed in equation form as:

$$Y = \$100 + \$0.20X$$

There are six basic steps to computing a cost formula by this method. The reader should trace these six steps back through the computations in Exhibit 5–12.

Step 1:   Determine the average level of activity $(\bar{X})$ and the average amount of cost $(\bar{Y})$ for the period of time being analyzed. In Exhibit 5–12, machine-hours average 500 hours per month (3,000 machine-hours ÷ 6 months = 500 machine-hours) and power costs average $200 per month ($1,200 ÷ 6 months = $200).

Step 2:   Compute the difference between the actual activity for each month and the average activity computed in step 1, and enter this difference in a column labeled X'. Then compute the difference between the actual cost for each month and the average cost, and enter this difference in a second column labeled Y'. Use plus (+) and minus (−) notations to signify whether monthly amounts are greater or less than the average.

Step 3:   For each month, multiply the amount in the X' column times the amount in the Y' column and enter the result in a column labeled $X'Y'$. (In obtaining the data for the $X'Y'$ column, remember that algebraically a minus times a minus is a plus, but a minus times a plus is a minus.)

Step 4:   Square the X' amount for each month, and enter the result in a new column labeled X'^2.

Step 5:   Compute the variable rate by the formula:

$$\frac{\Sigma X'Y'}{\Sigma X'^2} = \text{Variable rate}$$

Step 6:   Compute the total fixed cost by substituting in the equation:

$$\overline{Y} = a + b\overline{X}$$

where $\overline{Y}$ = the average cost observed, a = the total fixed cost that you are seeking, b = the variable rate computed in step 5, and $\overline{X}$ = the average activity level observed.

QUESTIONS

5–1.   Distinguish between (a) a variable cost, (b) a fixed cost, and (c) a mixed cost.

5–2.   What effect does an increase in volume have on—
    a.   Unit fixed costs?
    b.   Unit variable costs?
    c.   Total fixed costs?
    d.   Total variable costs?

5–3.   Define the following terms: (a) cost behavior and (b) relevant range.

5–4.   What is meant by an "activity base" when dealing with variable costs? Give several examples of activity bases.

5–5.   Distinguish between (a) a variable cost, (b) a mixed cost, and (c) a step-variable cost. Chart the three costs on a graph, with activity plotted horizontally and cost plotted vertically.

5–6.   The accountant often assumes a strictly linear relationship between cost and volume. How can this practice be defended in light of the fact that many variable costs are curvilinear in form?

5–7.   Distinguish between discretionary fixed costs and committed fixed costs.

5–8.   Classify the following fixed costs as normally being either committed (C) or discretionary (D):
    a.   Depreciation on buildings.
    b.   Advertising.
    c.   Research.
    d.   Insurance.
    e.   The president's salary.
    f.   Management development and training.

5–9.   What factors are contributing to the trend toward increasing numbers of fixed costs, and why is this trend significant from a managerial accounting point of view?

5–10.   Does the concept of the relevant range have application to fixed costs? Explain.

5–11.   What is the major disadvantage of the high-low method? Under what conditions would this analytical method provide an accurate cost formula?

5–12.   What methods are available for separating a mixed cost into its fixed and variable elements? Which method is most accurate? Why?

5–13.   What is meant by a regression line? Give the general formula for a regression line. Which term represents the variable cost? The fixed cost?

5–14.   Once a regression line has been drawn, how does one determine the fixed cost element? The variable cost element?

5–15.   What is meant by the term *least squares?*

5–16.   What is the difference between single regression analysis and multiple regression analysis?

5–17.   What is the difference between the contribution approach to the income statement and the traditional approach to the income statement?

5–18.   What is meant by contribution margin? How is it computed?

EXERCISES

E5–1.   The Lakeshore Hotel's guest-days of occupancy and custodial supplies expense over the last seven months were:

Month	Guest-days of occupancy	Custodial supplies expense
March	4,000	$ 7,500
April	6,500	8,250
May	8,000	10,500
June	10,500	12,000
July	12,000	13,500
August	9,000	10,750
September	7,500	9,750

Required: 1.   Using the high-low method, determine the cost formula for custodial supplies expense.

2.   What amount of custodial supplies expense would you expect to be incurred at an occupancy level of 11,000 guest-days?

E5–2.   Refer to the data in Exercise 5–1.

Required: 1.   Prepare a scattergraph using the data from Exercise 5–1. Plot cost on the vertical axis and activity on the horizontal axis. Fit a regression line to your plotted points by visual inspection.

2.   What is the approximate monthly fixed cost? The approximate variable cost per guest-day?

3.   Scrutinize the points on your graph and explain why the high-low method would or would not yield an accurate cost formula in this situation.

E5–3.   The following data relating to units shipped and total shipping expense have been assembled by Archer Company:

Month	Units shipped	Total shipping expense
January	3	$18
February	6	23
March	4	17
April	5	20
May	7	23
June	8	27
July	2	12

Required:
1. Using the high-low method, determine the cost formula for shipping expense.
2. For the scattergraph method, do the following:
   - a. Prepare a scattergraph using the data given above. Plot cost on the vertical axis and activity on the horizontal axis. Fit a regression line to your plotted points by visual inspection.
   - b. Using the data from your scattergraph, determine the approximate variable cost per unit shipped and the approximate fixed cost per month.

E5–4. Refer to the data in Exercise 5–3.

Required:
1. Using the least squares method, determine the cost formula for shipping expense.
2. If you also completed Exercise 5–3, prepare a simple table comparing the variable and fixed cost elements of shipping expense as computed under the high-low method, the scattergraph method, and the least squares method.

E5–5. Parker Company manufactures and sells a single product. The company typically operates within a relevant range of 60,000 to 100,000 units produced and sold each year. A partially completed schedule of the company's total and per unit costs over this range is given below:

	Units produced and sold		
	60,000	80,000	100,000
Total costs:			
Variable costs	$150,000	?	?
Fixed costs	360,000	?	?
Total costs	$510,000	?	?
Cost per unit:			
Variable cost	?	?	?
Fixed cost	?	?	?
Total cost per unit	?	?	?

Required:
1. Complete the schedule of the company's total and unit costs above.
2. Assume that the company produces and sells 90,000 units during a year. The selling price is $7.50 per unit. Prepare an income statement in the contribution format for the year.

E5–6. St. Mark's Hospital contains 450 beds. The average occupancy rate is 80 percent per month. At this level of occupancy, the hospital's operating costs are $32 per occupied bed per day, assuming a 30-day month. This $32 figure contains both variable and fixed cost elements.

During June, the hospital's occupancy rate was only 60 percent. A total of $326,700 in operating cost was incurred during the month.

Required: 1.   Using the high-low method, determine:
        a.   The variable cost per occupied bed on a daily basis.
        b.   The total fixed operating costs per month.
     2.   Assume an occupancy rate of 70 percent. What amount of total operating cost would you expect the hospital to incur?

E5–7.   Oki Products, Ltd., has observed the following processing costs at various levels of activity over the last 15 months:

Month	Units produced	Processing cost
1.	4,500	$38,000
2.	11,000	52,000
3.	12,000	56,000
4.	5,500	40,000
5.	9,000	47,000
6.	10,500	52,000
7.	7,500	44,000
8.	5,000	41,000
9.	11,500	52,000
10.	6,000	43,000
11.	8,500	48,000
12.	10,000	50,000
13.	6,500	44,000
14.	9,500	48,000
15.	8,000	46,000

Required: 1.   Prepare a scattergraph by plotting the above data on a graph. Plot cost on the vertical axis and activity on the horizontal axis. Fit a line to your plotted points by visual inspection.
     2.   What is the approximate monthly fixed cost? The approximate variable cost per unit? Show computations.

E5–8.   Mercury Transit, Inc., operates a fleet of delivery trucks in a large city. The company has determined that if a truck is driven 105,000 miles during a year, the operating cost is 11.4 cents per mile. If a truck is driven only 70,000 miles during a year, the operating cost increases to 13.4 cents per mile.

Required: 1.   Using the high-low method, determine the variable and fixed cost elements of the annual cost of truck operation.
     2.   Express the variable and fixed costs in the form $Y = a + bX$.
     3.   If a truck is driven 80,000 miles during a year, what total cost would you expect to be incurred?

E5–9.   One of Fenwick Company's products goes through an etching process. The company has observed etching costs as follows over the last six quarters:

Quarter	Units	Total etching cost
1	4	$ 18
2	3	17
3	8	25
4	6	20
5	7	24
6	2	16
	30	$120

For planning purposes, Fenwick Company's management would like to know the amount of variable etching cost per unit and the total etching cost per quarter.

Required: 1. Using the least squares method, determine the variable and fixed elements of etching cost as desired by management.
2. Express the cost data in (1) above in the form $Y = a + bX$.
3. If the company processes 5 units next quarter, what would be the expected total etching cost?

E5–10.   The Alpine House, Inc., is a large retailer of winter sports equipment. An income statement for the company's Ski Department for the most recent quarter is presented below:

THE ALPINE HOUSE, INC.
Income Statement—Ski Department
For the Quarter Ended March 31, 19x5

Sales		$150,000
Less cost of goods sold		90,000
Gross margin		60,000
Less operating expenses:		
Selling expenses	$30,000	
Administrative expenses	10,000	40,000
Net income		$ 20,000

Skis sell, on the average, for $150 per pair. Variable selling expenses are $10 per pair of skis sold. The remaining selling expenses are fixed. The administrative expenses are 20 percent variable and 80 percent fixed. The company does not manufacture its own skis; it purchases them from a supplier for $90 per pair.

Required: 1. Prepare an income statement for the quarter, using the contribution approach.
2. For every pair of skis sold during the quarter, what was the contribution toward covering fixed expenses and toward earning profits?

PROBLEMS

P5–11.   **High-low method; contribution income statement.**   Vencil Company, a merchandising firm, is the sole distributor of a product that is increasing in popularity among consumers. The company's income statements for the three most recent months are given below:

VENCIL COMPANY
Income Statements
For the Three Months Ending September 30, 19x1

	July	August	September
Sales in units	4,000	4,500	5,000
Sales revenue	$400,000	$450,000	$500,000
Less cost of goods sold	240,000	270,000	300,000
Gross margin	160,000	180,000	200,000
Less operating expenses:			
Advertising expense	21,000	21,000	21,000
Shipping expense	34,000	36,000	38,000
Salaries and commissions . . .	78,000	84,000	90,000
Insurance expense	6,000	6,000	6,000
Depreciation expense	15,000	15,000	15,000
Total operating expenses . . .	154,000	162,000	170,000
Net income	$ 6,000	$ 18,000	$ 30,000

Required: 1. Identify each of the company's expenses (including cost of goods sold) as being variable, fixed, or mixed.

2. By use of the high-low method, separate each mixed expense into variable and fixed elements. State the cost formula for each mixed expense.

3. Redo the company's income statement at the 5,000-unit level of activity by placing the revenue and expense data in the contribution format.

P5–12. High-low method of cost analysis. Sawaya Company's management has noted that total factory overhead costs fluctuate considerably from year to year according to increases and decreases in the number of direct labor-hours worked in the factory. Total factory overhead costs at high and low levels of activity for recent years are given below:

	Level of activity	
	Low	**High**
Direct labor-hours	50,000	75,000
Total factory overhead costs . .	$142,500	$176,250

The factory overhead costs above consist of indirect materials, rent, and maintenance. The company has analyzed these costs at the 50,000-hour level of activity and has determined that at this activity level these costs exist in the following proportions:

Indirect materials (V)	$ 50,000
Rent (F)	60,000
Maintenance (M)	32,500
Total factory overhead costs . . .	$142,500

V = variable; F = fixed; M = mixed.

In order to have data available for planning, the company wants to break down the maintenance cost into its variable and fixed cost elements.

Required: 1. Determine how much of the $176,250 factory overhead cost at the high level of activity above consists of maintenance cost. (Hint: To do this, it may be helpful to first determine how much of the $176,250 consists of indirect materials and rent. Think about the behavior of variable and fixed costs within the relevant range!)

2. By means of the high-low method of cost analysis, determine the cost formula for maintenance.

3. Express the company's maintenance costs in the linear equation form $Y = a + bX$.

4. What *total* factory overhead costs would you expect the company to incur at an operating level of 70,000 direct labor-hours? Show computations.

P5–13. **Least squares method of cost analysis; graphing.**   Professor John Morton has just been appointed chairperson of the finance department at Westland University. In reviewing the department's cost records, Professor Morton has found the following total cost associated with Finance 101 over the last several terms:

Term	Number of sections offered	Total cost
Fall 19x1	4	$10,000
Winter 19x2.	6	14,000
Summer 19x2	2	7,000
Fall 19x2	5	13,000
Winter 19x3.	3	9,500

Professor Morton knows that there are some variable costs, such as amounts paid to graduate assistants, associated with the course. He would like to have the variable and fixed costs separated for planning purposes.

Required: 1. Using the least squares method, compute the variable cost per section and the total fixed cost per term for Finance 101.

2. Express the cost data derived in (1) above in the linear equation form $Y = a + bX$.

3. Assume that because of the small number of sections offered during the Winter Term 19x3, Professor Morton will have to offer eight sections of Finance 101 during the Fall Term. Compute the expected total cost for Finance 101. Can you see any problem with using the cost formula from (2) to derive this total cost figure?

4. Prepare a scattergraph, and fit a regression line to the plotted points using the cost formula expressed in (2) above.

P5–14. **Least squares analysis; contribution income statement.**   "Our managers need better information in order to plan more effectively and to get a better control over costs," said Alfredo Ruiz, president of Comptex, Inc., a merchandising firm. "One way to get better information is to use a contribution-type income statement internally. We need to have our costs separated into fixed and variable categories." Accordingly, the accounting department has made the following analysis:

Cost	Cost formula
Cost of goods sold	$40 per unit
Advertising	$70,000 per year
Sales commissions	8.5% of sales
Administrative salaries . . .	$160,000 per year
Clerical expense	?
Depreciation	$24,500 per year
Insurance	$18,000 per year

The accounting department believes that clerical expense is a mixed cost, containing both fixed and variable cost elements. A tabulation has been made of clerical expense and unit sales over the last several years, as follows:

Year	Units sold (000)	Clerical expense
19x1	10	$125,000
19x2	7	100,000
19x3	8	105,000
19x4	11	140,000
19x5	9	120,000
19x6	15	160,000

Mr. Ruiz would like a cost formula developed for clerical expenses so that a contribution-type income statement can be prepared for management's use.

Required:
1. Using the least squares method, derive a cost formula for clerical expense. (Since the "Units sold" above are in thousands of units, the variable rate you compute will also be in thousands of units. It can be left in this form, or you can convert your variable rate to a per unit basis by dividing it by 1,000.)
2. Assume that the company plans to sell 12,000 units during 19x7 at a selling price of $100 per unit. Prepare a budgeted income statement for the year, using the contribution format.

P5–15. High-low method of cost analysis. Nova Company's total overhead costs at various levels of activity are presented below:

Month	Machine-hours	Total overhead costs
April	70,000	$198,000
May	60,000	174,000
June	80,000	222,000
July	90,000	246,000

Assume that the total overhead costs above consist of utilities, supervisory salaries, and maintenance. The proportion of these costs at the 60,000 machine-hour level of activity is:

Utilities (V)	$ 48,000
Supervisory salaries (F) . . .	21,000
Maintenance (M)	105,000
Total overhead costs . . .	$174,000

Nova Company's management wants to break down the maintenance cost into its basic variable and fixed cost elements.

Required: 1. As shown above, overhead costs in July amounted to $246,000. Determine how much of this consisted of maintenance cost. (Hint: To do this, it may be helpful to first determine how much of the $246,000 consisted of utilities and supervisory salaries. Think about the behavior of variable and fixed costs within the relevant range!)

2. By means of the high-low method, determine the cost formula for maintenance.

3. Express the company's *total* overhead costs in the linear equation form $Y = a + bX$.

4. What *total* overhead costs would you expect to be incurred at an operating activity level of 75,000 machine-hours? Show computations.

P5–16. Identifying cost patterns. Below are a number of cost behavior patterns that might be found in a company's cost structure. The vertical axis on each graph represents cost, and the horizontal axis on each graph represents level of activity (volume).

Required: 1. For each of the following situations, identify the graph that illustrates the cost pattern involved. Any graph may be used more than once.

a. Cost of raw materials, where the cost decreases by 5 cents per unit for each of the first 100 units purchased, after which it remains constant at $2.50 per unit.

b. Electricity bill—a flat fixed charge, plus a variable cost after a certain number of kilowatt-hours are used.

c. City water bill, which is computed as follows:

First 1,000,000 gallons or less . . . $1,000 flat fee
Next 10,000 gallons . . . . 0.003 per gallon used
Next 10,000 gallons . . . . 0.006 per gallon used
Next 10,000 gallons . . . . 0.009 per gallon used
Etc. . . . . Etc.

d. Depreciation of equipment, where the amount is computed by the straight-line method. When the depreciation rate was established, it was anticipated that the obsolescence factor would be greater than the wear and tear factor.

e. Rent on a factory building donated by the city, where the agreement calls for a fixed fee payment unless 200,000 labor-hours are worked, in which case no rent need be paid.

f. Salaries of maintenance workers, where one maintenance worker is needed for every 1,000 hours of machine-hours or less (that is, 0 to 1,000 hours requires one maintenance worker, 1,001 to 2,000 hours requires two maintenance workers, etc.)

g. Cost of raw material used.

h. Rent on a factory building donated by the county, where the agreement calls for rent of $100,000 less $1 for each direct labor-hour worked in excess of 200,000 hours, but a minimum rental payment of $20,000 must be paid.

i. Use of a machine under a lease, where a minimum charge of $1,000 is paid for up to 400 hours of machine time. After 400 hours of machine time, an additional charge of $2 per hour is paid up to a maximum charge of $2,000 per period.

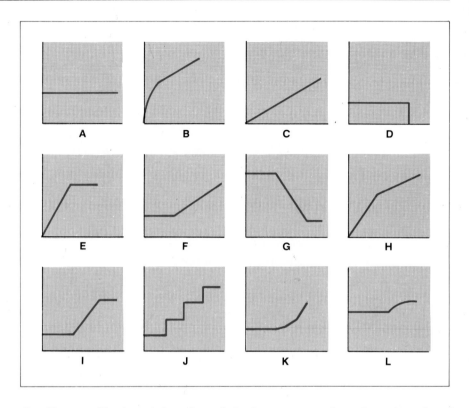

2. How would a knowledge of cost behavior patterns such as those above be of
    help to a manager in analyzing the cost structure of his firm?

(CPA, Adapted)

P5–17.   Contribution versus traditional income statement.   Marwick's Pianos, Inc., purchases pianos from a large manufacturer and sells them at the retail level. The
pianos cost, on the average, $750 each from the manufacturer. Marwick's Pianos,
Inc., sells the pianos at an average price of $1,250 each to its customers. The
selling and administrative costs that the company incurs in a typical month are
presented below:

Costs	Cost formula
Selling:	
Advertising	$700 per month
Sales salaries and commissions . . .	$950 per month, plus 8% of sales
Delivery of pianos to customers . . .	$30 per piano sold
Utilities	$350 per month
Depreciation of sales facilities	$800 per month
Administrative:	
Executive salaries	$2,500 per month
Insurance	$400 per month
Clerical	$1,000 per month, plus $20 per piano sold
Depreciation of office equipment . . .	$300 per month

During the month of August 19x2, Marwick's Pianos, Inc., sold and delivered 40 pianos.

Required: √1. Prepare an income statement for Marwick's Pianos, Inc., for the month of August 19x2. Use the traditional format, with costs organized by function.

√2. Redo (1), this time using the contribution format, with costs organized by behavior. Show costs and revenues on both a total and a per unit basis down through contribution margin.

3. Refer to the income statement prepared in (2). Why might it be misleading to show the fixed costs on a per unit basis?

P5–18. Scattergraph and least squares.   Molina Company has several autos that have been purchased for use by the sales staff. All expenses of operating these autos have been entered into an ''Automobile Expense'' account on the company's books. Along with this record of expenses, the company has also kept a careful record of the number of miles the autos have been driven each month.

The company's records of miles driven and total auto expenses over the past 10 months are given below:

Month	Total mileage (000)	Total cost
January	4	$3,000
February	8	3,700
March	7	3,300
April	12	4,000
May	6	3,300
June	11	3,900
July	14	4,200
August	10	3,600
September	13	4,100
October	15	4,400

Molina Company's president wants to know the cost of operating the fleet of cars, in terms of the fixed monthly cost and the variable cost per mile driven.

Required: 1. Prepare a scattergraph using the data given above. Place cost on the vertical axis and activity (miles driven) on the horizontal axis. Fit a regression line to the plotted points by simple visual inspection.

2. By analyzing the data on your scattergraph, compute the approximate fixed cost per month and the approximate variable rate per mile driven.

3. By use of the least squares method, determine the variable and fixed cost elements associated with the company's fleet of autos. (Since the ''Total mileage'' is in thousands of miles, the variable rate you compute will also be in thousands of miles. The rate can be left in this form, or you can convert it to a per mile basis by dividing the rate you get by 1,000.)

4. From the data in (3) above, express the cost formula for auto use in the linear equation form $Y = a + bX$.

P5–19. Least squares analysis; contribution income statement.   Milden Company has an exclusive franchise to purchase a product from the manufacturer and distribute it on the retail level. As an aid in planning, the company has decided to start using the contribution approach to the income statement internally. In order to have data to prepare such a statement, the company has analyzed its expenses and developed the following cost formulas:

Costs	Cost formula
Cost of goods sold	$35 per unit sold
Advertising expense	$210,000 per quarter
Sales commissions	6% of sales
Shipping expense	?
Administrative salaries	$145,000 per quarter
Insurance expense	$9,000 per quarter
Depreciation expense	$76,000 per quarter

Management has concluded that shipping expense is a mixed cost, containing both variable and fixed cost elements. Units sold and the related shipping expense over the last eight quarters are given below:

Quarter	Units sold (000)	Shipping expense
19x1:		
First	10	$119,000
Second	16	175,000
Third	18	190,000
Fourth	15	164,000
19x2:		
First	11	130,000
Second	17	185,000
Third	20	210,000
Fourth	13	147,000

Milden Company's president would like a cost formula derived for shipping expense so that a budgeted income statement using the contribution approach can be prepared for the next quarter.

Required: 1. Using the least squares method, derive a cost formula for shipping expense. (Since the "Units sold" above are in thousands of units, the variable rate you compute will also be in thousands of units. It can be left in this form, or you can convert your variable rate to a per unit basis by dividing it by 1,000.)

2. Assume that in the first quarter, 19x3, the company plans to sell 12,000 units at a selling price of $100 per unit. Prepare an income statement for the quarter, using the contribution format.

P5–20.   Mixed cost analysis by three methods.   Pleasant View Hospital has just hired a new chief administrator who is anxious to employ sound management and planning techniques in the business affairs of the hospital. Accordingly, she has directed her assistant to summarize the cost structure existing in the various departments so that data will be available for planning purposes.

The assistant is unsure how to classify the utilities costs in the radiology department since these costs do not exhibit either strictly variable or fixed cost behavior. Utilities costs are very high in this department due to a large CAT scanner that draws a large amount of power and is kept running at all times. The scanner can't be turned off due to the long warm-up period required for its use. When the scanner is used to scan a patient, it consumes an additional burst of power. The assistant has accumulated the following data on utilities costs and use of the scanner since the first of the year:

Month	Number of scans	Utilities cost
January	60	$2,200
February	70	2,600
March	90	2,900
April	120	3,300
May	100	3,000
June	130	3,600
July	150	4,000
August	140	3,600
September	110	3,100
October	80	2,500

The chief administrator has informed her assistant that the utilities cost is probably a mixed cost that will have to be broken down into its variable and fixed cost elements by use of a scattergraph. The assistant feels, however, that if an analysis of this type is necessary, then the high-low method should be used, since it is easier and quicker. The controller has suggested that statistical least squares is the best approach.

Required:

1. Using the high-low method, determine the cost formula for utilities. Express the formula in the form $Y = a + bX$. (The variable rate should be stated in terms of cost per scan.)

2. Prepare a scattergraph by plotting the above data on a graph. (The number of scans should be placed on the horizontal axis, and utilities cost should be placed on the vertical axis.) Fit a regression line to the plotted points by visual inspection, and determine the cost formula for utilities.

3. Using the least squares method, calculate the cost formula for utilities. Again express the formula in the form $Y = a + bX$. (Round the variable rate to two decimal places.)

4. Refer to the graph prepared in (2). Explain why in this case the high-low method would be the least accurate of the three methods in deriving a cost formula.

P5–21. **Manufacturing statements: High-low method of cost analysis.** Amfac Company manufactures a single product. The company keeps careful records of manufacturing activities from which the following information has been extracted:

	Level of activity	
	March—low	June—high
Equivalent number of units produced	6,000	9,000
Cost of goods manufactured	$168,000	$257,000
Work in process inventory, beginning	9,000	32,000
Work in process inventory, ending	15,000	21,000
Direct materials cost per unit	6	6
Direct labor cost per unit	10	10
Manufacturing overhead cost, total	?	?

The company's manufacturing overhead costs consist of both variable and fixed cost elements. In order to have data available for planning, management wants to determine how much of the overhead cost is variable with units produced and how much of it is fixed per month.

Required: 1. For both March and June, determine the amount of manufacturing overhead cost added to production. The company had no under- or overapplied overhead in either month. (Hint: A useful way to proceed might be to construct a schedule of cost of goods manufactured.)

2. By means of the high-low method of cost analysis, determine the cost formula for manufacturing overhead. Express the variable portion of the formula in terms of a variable rate per unit of product.

3. If 7,000 units are produced during a month, what would be the cost of goods manufactured? (Assume that work in process inventories do not change and that there is no under- or overapplied overhead for the month.)

P5–22. **Missing data; mixed cost analysis by three methods.** While arm wrestling at the office Christmas party, you accidently spilled the contents of a drink onto some papers on your desk. One of the papers contained an analysis of a mixed cost that the president had asked you to complete before leaving for the holidays. Unfortunately, the liquid from the drink obliterated much of your analysis, as shown below (the question marks indicate obliterated data):

Month	Units sold (X)	Total cost (Y)	?	?
January	3	$1,600	$ 4,800	9
February	5	?	?	?
March	?	3,200	25,600	?
April	9	3,700	33,300	81
May	7	?	?	?
June	?	?	18,000	36
July	?	?	9,600	?
Totals	?	$?	$126,000	?

(1) $\Sigma XY = a\Sigma X + b\Sigma?$
(2) $\Sigma Y = ?a + b\Sigma X$

(1) $126,000 = ?a + ?b$
(2) $?   = ?a + ?b$

(1) $126,000 = ?a + ?b$
(2) Multiply by 6: $?   = ?a + ?b$
    Subtract (2) from (1): $?   =   ?b$
                          $?   = b$

Therefore, the variable rate is ??? per unit sold. To compute the monthly fixed cost, substitute in equation (2):

$$\$ \ ? \ = ?a + ?b$$
$$\$ \ ? \ = ?a + \$12,600$$
$$\$ \ ? \ = ?a$$
$$\$1,000 = a$$

Therefore, the fixed cost is $1,000 per month.

Horrified at the accident, you realize that you will have to figure out the missing data before your train leaves in two hours. Working is particularly difficult with all of the merriment going on around you, but you are spurred on by the realization that the president is not an understanding person.

Before starting the reconstruction of the data, you remember that the total cost for May can be obtained by applying the cost formula (as derived by the least squares method) to the month's activity. (That is, fixed cost plus variable rate times units sold.)

Required: 1. Copy all of the information above onto a clean, dry piece of paper. Complete the least squares analysis by finding *all* items of missing data. (The president detests incomplete work.)
2. Since part (1) took only one hour to complete and you still have an hour before your train leaves, you decide to "check out" your work by doing a high-low analysis of the data. Complete the high-low analysis, and state the cost formula derived by this analytical method.
3. Surprised that the cost formula by the high-low method is so different from that derived by the least squares method, and still having 45 minutes before your train leaves, you decide to prepare a scattergraph as a final check on your work.
    a. Prepare a scattergraph, and fit a regression line to the plotted points by simple visual inspection.
    b. By analyzing the data on your scattergraph, compute the approximate fixed cost per month and the approximate variable rate per unit sold.
4. Look again at the graph prepared in (3). Explain why the cost formula derived by the high-low method is so different from the cost formula derived by the least squares method.

P5–23. Regression analysis; graphing.   The Ramon Company manufactures a wide range of products at several plant locations. The Franklin plant, which manufactures electrical components, has been experiencing difficulties with fluctuating monthly overhead costs. The fluctuations have made it difficult to estimate the level of overhead that will be incurred for any one month.

Management wants to be able to estimate overhead costs accurately in order to better plan its operational and financial needs. A trade association publication to which Ramon Company subscribes indicates that for companies manufacturing electrical components, overhead tends to vary with direct labor-hours.

One member of the accounting staff has proposed that the cost behavior pattern of the overhead costs be determined. Then overhead costs could be predicted from the budgeted direct labor-hours.

Another member of the accounting staff has suggested that a good starting place for determining the cost behavior pattern of overhead costs would be an analysis of historical data. The historical cost behavior pattern would provide a basis for estimating future overhead costs. The methods that have been proposed for determining the cost behavior pattern include the high-low method, the scattergraph method, simple linear regression, multiple regression, and exponential smoothing. Of these methods, Ramon Company has decided to employ the high-low method, the scattergraph method, and simple linear regression. Data on direct labor-hours and the respective overhead costs incurred have been collected for the past two years. The raw data are as follows:

	19x1		19x2	
Month	Direct labor- hours	Overhead costs	Direct labor- hours	Overhead costs
January	20,000	$84,000	21,000	$86,000
February	25,000	99,000	24,000	93,000
March	22,000	89,500	23,000	93,000
April	23,000	90,000	22,000	87,000
May	20,000	81,500	20,000	80,000
June	19,000	75,500	18,000	76,500
July	14,000	70,500	12,000	67,500
August	10,000	64,500	13,000	71,000
September	12,000	69,000	15,000	73,500
October	17,000	75,000	17,000	72,500
November	16,000	71,500	15,000	71,000
December	19,000	78,000	18,000	75,000

All equipment in the Franklin plant is leased under an arrangement calling for a flat fee up to 19,500 direct labor-hours of activity in the plant, after which lease charges are assessed on an hourly basis. Lease expense is a major item of overhead cost.

Required:

1. Using the high-low method, determine the cost formula for overhead in the Franklin plant.
2. Repeat (1) above, this time using the least squares method. Your assistant has computed the following amounts, which may be helpful in your analysis:

Equation method:

$$\Sigma X = 435,000$$
$$\Sigma Y = \$1,894,000$$
$$\Sigma XY = \$35,170,500,000$$
$$\Sigma X^2 = 8,275,000,000$$

Alternative method:

Twenty-four month average:

$$\overline{X} = 18,125$$
$$\overline{Y} = \$78,917$$
$$\Sigma X'Y' = \$841,750,000$$
$$\Sigma X'^2 = 390,625,000$$

3. Prepare a scattergraph, including on it all data for the two-year period. Fit a regression line to the plotted points by visual inspection. (Take care in how you fit your regression line; remember that it must reflect appropriate fixed and variable costs throughout the *entire* relevant range. In this part, however, it is not necessary to compute the fixed and variable cost elements.)
4. Assume that the Franklin plant works 22,500 direct labor-hours during a month. Compute the expected overhead cost for the month, using the cost formulas developed above with:
   a. The high-low method.
   b. The least squares method.

    c.   The scattergraph method [read the expected costs directly off the graph prepared in (3) above].

5.   Of the three proposed methods, which one should the Ramon Company use to estimate monthly overhead costs in the Franklin plant? Explain fully, indicating the reasons why the other methods are less desirable.

6.   Would the relevant range concept probably be more or less important in the Franklin plant than in most companies?

(CMA, Adapted)

The Central Theme: Planning and Control

CHAPTER 6

Cost-Volume-Profit Relationships

LEARNING OBJECTIVES

After studying Chapter 6, you should be able to:

- Explain how changes in activity affect contribution margin and net income.

- Compute the contribution margin ratio (C/M ratio) and use it to compute changes in contribution margin and net income.

- Compute and explain operating leverage.

- Show the effects on contribution margin of changes in variable costs, fixed costs, selling price, and volume.

- Compute the break-even point by both the equation method and the unit contribution method.

- Prepare a cost-volume-profit (CVP) graph and explain the significance of each of its components.

- Compute the margin of safety (M/S) and explain its significance.

- Explain the effects of shifts in the sales mix on contribution margin and the break-even point.

- Define or explain the key terms listed at the end of the chapter.

ost-volume-profit (CVP) analysis involves a study of the interrelationship between the following factors:

1. Prices of products.
2. Volume or level of activity.
3. Per unit variable costs.
4. Total fixed costs.
5. Mix of products sold.

CVP analysis is a key factor in many decisions, including choice of product lines, pricing of products, marketing strategy, and utilization of productive facilities. The concept is so pervasive in managerial accounting that it touches on virtually everything that a manager does. Because of its wide range of usefulness, CVP analysis is undoubtedly the best tool the manager has for discovering the untapped profit potential that may exist in an organization.

THE BASICS OF COST-VOLUME-PROFIT (CVP) ANALYSIS

Our study of CVP analysis begins where our study of cost behavior in the preceding chapter left off—with the contribution income statement. The contribution income statement has a number of interesting characteristics that can be helpful to the manager in trying to judge the impact on profits of changes in selling price, cost, or volume. To demonstrate these characteristics, we shall use the following income statement of the Norton Company, a small manufacturer of microwave ovens:

NORTON COMPANY
Contribution Income Statement
For the Month of June 19x1

	Total	Per unit
Sales (400 ovens)	$100,000	$250
Less variable expenses	60,000	150
Contribution margin	40,000	$100
Less fixed expenses	35,000	
Net income	$ 5,000	

For purposes of discussion, we shall assume that the Norton Company produces only one model of oven.

Notice that the company expresses its sales, variable expenses, and contribution margin on a per unit basis as well as in total. This is commonly done on those income statements prepared for management's use internally, since, as we shall see, it facilitates profitability analysis.

Contribution Margin

As explained in Chapter 5, contribution margin is the amount remaining from sales revenue after variable expenses have been deducted that can be used to contribute toward the covering of fixed expenses and then toward profits for the period. Notice the sequence here—contribution margin is used first to cover the fixed expenses, and then whatever remains after the fixed expenses are covered goes toward profits. If the contribution margin is not sufficient to cover the fixed expenses, then a loss occurs for the period. To illustrate, assume that by the middle of a particular month the Norton Company has been able to sell only one oven. At that point, the company's income statement will appear as follows:

	Total	Per unit
Sales (1 oven)	$ 250	$250
Less variable expenses	150	150
Contribution margin	100	$100
Less fixed expenses	35,000	
Net loss	$(34,900)	

For each additional oven that the company is able to sell during the month, $100 more in contribution margin will become available to help cover the fixed expenses. If a second oven is sold, for example, then the total contribution margin will increase by $100 (to a total of $200) and the company's loss will decrease by $100, to $34,800:

	Total	Per unit
Sales (2 ovens)	$ 500	$250
Less variable expenses	300	150
Contribution margin	200	$100
Less fixed expenses	35,000	
Net loss	$(34,800)	

If enough ovens can be sold to generate $35,000 in contribution margin, then all of the fixed costs will be covered and the company will have managed to at least *break even* for the month—that is, to show neither profit nor loss but just cover all of its costs. To reach this **break-even point,** the company will have to sell 350 ovens in a month, since each oven sold yields $100 in contribution margin:

	Total	Per unit
Sales (350 ovens)	$87,500	$250
Less variable expenses	52,500	150
Contribution margin	35,000	$100
Less fixed expenses	35,000	
Net income	$ 0	

Computation of the break-even point is discussed in detail later in the chapter; for the moment, we can note that it can be defined either as the point where total sales revenue equals total expenses, variable and fixed, or as the point where total contribution margin equals total fixed expenses.

Once the break-even point has been reached, net income will increase by the unit contribution margin for each additional unit sold. If 351 ovens are sold in a month, for example, then we can expect that the net income for the month will be $100, since the company will have sold 1 oven more than the number needed to break even:

	Total	Per unit
Sales (351 ovens)	$87,750	$250
Less variable expenses	52,650	150
Contribution margin	35,100	$100
Less fixed expenses	35,000	
Net income	$ 100	

If 352 ovens are sold (2 ovens above the break-even point), then we can expect that the net income for the month will be $200, and so forth. To know what the profits will be at various levels of activity, therefore, it is not necessary for a manager to prepare a whole series of income statements. The manager can simply take the number of units to be sold over the break-even point and multiply that number by the unit contribution margin. The result will represent the anticipated profits for the period. Or, if an increase in sales is planned and the manager wants to know what the impact of that increase will be on profits, he or she can simply multiply the increase in units sold by the unit contribution margin. The result will be the expected increase in profits. To illustrate, if the Norton Company is selling 400 ovens per month and plans to increase sales to 425 ovens per month, the impact on profits will be:

Increased number of ovens to be sold	25
Contribution margin per oven	×$100
Increase in net income	$2,500

As proof:

	Sales volume		Difference	
	400 Ovens	425 Ovens	25 ovens	Per unit
Sales	$100,000	$106,250	$6,250	$250
Less variable expenses	60,000	63,750	3,750	150
Contribution margin	40,000	42,500	2,500	$100
Less fixed expenses	35,000	35,000	–0–	
Net income	$ 5,000	$ 7,500	$2,500	

To summarize the series of examples in this section, we can say that the contribution margin first goes to cover an organization's fixed expenses, and that the potential loss represented by these fixed expenses is reduced successively by the unit contribution margin for each incremental unit sold up to the break-even point. Once the break-even point has been reached, then overall net income is increased by the unit contribution margin for each incremental unit sold from that point forward.

Contribution Margin Ratio (C/M Ratio)

In addition to being expressed on a per unit basis, revenues, variable expenses, and contribution margin for the Norton Company can also be expressed on a percentage basis:

	Total	Per unit	Percent
Sales (400 ovens)	$100,000	$250	100
Less variable expenses	60,000	150	60
Contribution margin	40,000	$100	40
Less fixed expenses	35,000		
Net income	$ 5,000		

The percentage of contribution margin to total sales is referred to either as the **contribution margin ratio** (C/M ratio) or as the **profit-volume ratio** (P/V ratio). This ratio is extremely useful in that it shows how contribution margin will be affected by a given dollar change in total sales. To illustrate, notice that the Norton Company has a C/M ratio of 40 percent. This means that for each dollar increase in sales, total contribution margin will increase by 40 cents ($1 sales × C/M ratio of 40 percent). Net income will also increase by 40 cents, assuming that there are no changes in fixed costs.

As this illustration suggests, *the impact on net income of any given dollar change in total sales can be computed in seconds by simply applying the C/M ratio to the dollar change.* If the Norton Company plans a $30,000 increase in sales during the coming month, for example, management can expect contribution margin to increase by $12,000 ($30,000 increased sales × C/M ratio of 40 percent). As we noted above, net income will increase by a like amount if the fixed costs do not change. As proof:

	Sales volume			
	Present	Expected	Increase	Percent
Sales	$100,000	$130,000	$30,000	100
Less variable expenses	60,000	78,000 *	18,000	60
Contribution margin	40,000	52,000	12,000	40
Less fixed expenses	35,000	35,000	–0–	
Net income	$ 5,000	$ 17,000	$12,000	

* $130,000 × 60% = $78,000.

Many managers find the C/M ratio easier to work with than the unit contribution margin figure, particularly where a company has multiple product lines. This is because an item in ratio form facilitates comparisons between products. Other things equal, the manager will search out those product lines that have the highest C/M ratios. The reason, of course, is that for a given dollar increase in sales these product lines will yield the greatest amount of contribution margin toward the covering of fixed costs and toward profits.

Cost Structure

We stated in the preceding chapter that *cost structure* refers to the relative proportion of fixed and variable costs in an organization. We also stated that an organization often has some latitude in trading off between fixed and variable costs. Such a trade-off is possible, for example, by automating facilities rather than using direct labor workers.

When the manager does have latitude in trading off between fixed and variable costs, which cost structure is best—high variable costs and low fixed costs, or the opposite? No categorical answer to this question is possible; we can simply note that there may be advantages either way, depending on the specific circumstances involved. To show what we mean by this statement, refer to the income statements given below for Company X and Company Y. Notice that the two companies have very different cost structures—Company X has high variable costs and low fixed costs, with the opposite true for Company Y.

	Company X		Company Y	
	Amount	Percent	Amount	Percent
Sales	$100,000	100	$100,000	100
Less variable expenses	60,000	60	30,000	30
Contribution margin	40,000	40	70,000	70
Less fixed expenses	30,000		60,000	
Net income	$ 10,000		$ 10,000	

The question as to which company has the best cost structure depends on many factors, including the long-run trend in sales, year-to-year fluctuations in the level of sales, and the attitude of the managers toward risk. If sales are expected to trend above $100,000 in the future, then Company Y probably has the best cost structure. The reason is that its C/M ratio is higher, and its profits will therefore increase more rapidly as sales increase. To illustrate, assume that each company experiences a 10 percent increase in sales. The new income statements will be:

	Company X		Company Y	
	Amount	Percent	Amount	Percent
Sales	$110,000	100	$110,000	100
Less variable expenses	66,000	60	33,000	30
Contribution margin	44,000	40	77,000	70
Less fixed expenses	30,000		60,000	
Net income	$ 14,000		$ 17,000	

As we would expect, for the same dollar increase in sales, Company Y has experienced a greater increase in net income due to its higher C/M ratio.

But what if $100,000 represents maximum sales for the two companies, and what if sales can be expected to drop well below $100,000 from time to time? Under these circumstances, Company X probably has the best cost structure. There are two reasons why this is so. First, due to its lower C/M ratio, Company X will not lose contribution margin as rapidly as Company Y when sales fall off. Thus, Company X's income will tend to show more stability. Second, Company X has lower fixed costs, which suggests that it will not incur losses as quickly as Company Y in periods of sharply declining sales.

If sales fluctuate above and below $100,000, it becomes more difficult to tell which company is in a better position.

To summarize, Company Y will experience wider movements in net income as changes take place in sales, with greater profits in good years and greater losses in bad years. Company X will enjoy somewhat greater stability in net income, but it will do so at the risk of losing substantial profits if sales trend upward in the long run.

Operating Leverage

To the scientist, leverage explains how one is able to move a large object with a small force. To the manager, leverage explains how one is able to achieve a large increase in profits (in percentage terms) with only a small increase in sales and/or assets. One type of leverage that the manager uses to do this is known as *operating leverage*.[1]

Operating leverage is a measure of the extent to which fixed costs are being used in an organization. It is greatest in companies that have a high proportion of fixed costs in relation to variable costs. Conversely, operating leverage is lowest in companies that have a low proportion of fixed costs in relation to variable costs. If a company has high operating leverage (that is, a high proportion of fixed costs in relation to variable costs), then

---

[1] There are two types of leverage—operating and financial. Financial leverage is discussed in Chapter 17.

profits will be very sensitive to changes in sales. Just a small percentage increase (or decrease) in sales can yield a large percentage increase (or decrease) in profits.

Operating leverage can be illustrated by returning to the data in the preceding section. Company Y has a higher proportion of fixed costs in relation to its variable costs than does Company X, although *total* costs are the same in the two companies at a $100,000 sales level. Observe that with a 10 percent increase in sales (from $100,000 to $110,000 in each company), net income in Company Y increases by 70 percent (from $10,000 to $17,000), whereas net income in Company X increases by only 40 percent (from $10,000 to $14,000). Thus, for a 10 percent increase in sales, Company Y experiences a much greater percentage increase in profits than does Company X. The reason is that Company Y has greater operating leverage as a result of the greater amount of fixed cost used in the production and sale of its product.

The **degree of operating leverage** existing in a company at a given level of sales can be measured by the following formula:

$$\frac{\text{Contribution margin}}{\text{Net income}} = \text{Degree of operating leverage}$$

The degree of operating leverage is a measure, at a given level of sales, of how a percentage change in sales volume will affect profits. To illustrate, the degree of operating leverage existing in Company X and Company Y at a $100,000 sales level would be:

$$\text{Company X: } \frac{\$40,000}{\$10,000} = 4$$

$$\text{Company Y: } \frac{\$70,000}{\$10,000} = 7$$

By interpretation, these figures tell us that *for a given percentage change in sales* we can expect a change four times as great in the net income of Company X and a change seven times as great in the net income of Company Y. Thus, if sales increase by 10 percent, then we can expect the net income in Company X to increase by four times this amount, or by 40 percent, and the net income in Company Y to increase by seven times this amount, or by 70 percent.

	(1) Percent increase in sales	(2) Degree of operating leverage	(3) Percent increase in net income (1) × (2)
Company X	10	4	40
Company Y	10	7	70

These computations explain why the 10 percent increase in sales mentioned earlier caused the net income of Company X to increase from $10,000 to $14,000 (an increase of 40 percent), and the net income of Company Y to increase from $10,000 to $17,000 (an increase of 70 percent).

The degree of operating leverage in a company is greatest at sales levels near the break-even point and decreases as sales and profits rise. This can be seen from the tabulation below, which shows the degree of operating leverage for Company X at various sales levels. (Data used earlier for Company X are shown in color.)

Sales	$80,000	$100,000	$150,000	$200,000
Less variable expenses	48,000	60,000	90,000	120,000
Contribution margin (a)	32,000	40,000	60,000	80,000
Less fixed expenses	30,000	30,000	30,000	30,000
Net income (b)	$ 2,000	$ 10,000	$ 30,000	$ 50,000
Degree of operating leverage, (a) ÷ (b)	16	4	2	1.6

Thus, a 10 percent increase in sales would increase profits by only 16 percent (10% × 1.6) if the company were operating at a $200,000 sales level, as compared to the 40 percent increase we computed earlier at the $100,000 sales level. The degree of operating leverage will continue to decrease the farther the company moves from its break-even point. At the break-even point, the degree of operating leverage will be infinitely large.

The operating leverage concept provides the manager with a tool that can signify quickly what impact various percentage changes in sales will have on profits, without the necessity of preparing detailed income statements. As shown by our examples, the effects of operating leverage can be dramatic. If a company is fairly near its break-even point, then even small increases in sales can yield large increases in profits. *This explains why management will often work very hard for only a nominal increase in sales volume.* If the degree of operating leverage is 5, then a 6 percent increase in sales would translate into a 30 percent increase in profits.

Some Applications of CVP Concepts

The concepts that we have developed on the preceding pages have many applications in planning and decision making. We will return now to the example of the Norton Company (a manufacturer of microwave ovens) to illustrate some of these applications. The Norton Company's basic cost and revenue data are:

	Per unit	Percent		
Sales price	$250	100	250	100
Less variable expenses	150	60	125	50
Contribution margin	$100	40	125	50

Recall that fixed expenses are $35,000 per month.

Change in fixed costs and sales volume   Assume that the Norton Company is currently selling 400 ovens per month (monthly sales of $100,000). The sales manager feels that a $10,000 increase in the monthly advertising budget would increase monthly sales by $30,000. Should the advertising budget be increased?

Solution:

Expected total contribution margin:	
$130,000 × 40% C/M ratio.	$52,000
Present total contribution margin:	
$100,000 × 40% C/M ratio.	40,000
Incremental contribution margin	12,000
Change in fixed costs:	
Less incremental advertising expense	10,000
Increased net income	$ 2,000

Yes, the advertising budget should be increased.

Since in this case only the fixed costs and the sales volume are changing, the solution can be presented in an even shorter format, as follows:

Alternative Solution:

Incremental contribution margin:	
$30,000 × 40% C/M ratio	$12,000
Less incremental advertising expense	10,000
Increased net income	$ 2,000

Notice that this approach does not depend on a knowledge of what sales were previously. Also notice that it is unnecessary under either approach to prepare an income statement. Both of the solutions above involve an **incremental analysis** in that they consider only those items of revenue, cost, and volume that will change if the new program is implemented. Although in each case a new income statement could have been prepared, most managers would prefer the incremental approach. The reason is that it is simpler and more direct, and it permits the decision maker to focus attention on the specific items involved in the decision.

Change in variable costs and sales volume   Refer to the original data. Assume again that the Norton Company is currently selling 400 ovens per month. Management is contemplating the use of less costly components in the manufacture of the ovens, which would reduce variable costs by $25 per oven. However, the sales manager predicts that the lower overall quality would reduce sales to only 350 ovens per month. Should the change be made?

Solution: The $25 decrease in variable costs will cause the contribution margin per unit to increase from $100 to $125.

Expected total contribution margin:	
350 ovens × $125	$43,750
Present total contribution margin:	
400 ovens × $100	40,000
Increase in total contribution margin	$ 3,750

Yes, the less costly components should be used in the manufacture of the ovens. Since the fixed costs will not change, net income will increase by the $3,750 increase in contribution margin shown above.

Change in fixed cost, sales price, and sales volume   Refer to the original data. Assume again that the Norton Company is currently selling 400 ovens per month. In order to increase sales, management would like to cut the selling price by $20 per oven and increase the advertising budget by $15,000 per month. Management feels that if these two steps are taken, unit sales will increase by 50 percent. Should the changes be made?

Solution: A decrease of $20 per oven in the selling price will cause the unit contribution margin to decrease from $100 to $80.

Expected total contribution margin:	
400 ovens × 150% × $80	$48,000
Present total contribution margin:	
400 ovens × $100	40,000
Incremental contribution margin	8,000
Change in fixed costs:	
Less incremental advertising expense	15,000
Reduction in net income.	$(7,000)

No, the changes should not be made. The same solution can be obtained by preparing comparative income statements:

	Present 400 ovens per month		Expected 600 ovens per month		
	Total	**Per unit**	**Total**	**Per unit**	**Difference**
Sales	$100,000	$250	$138,000	$230	$38,000
Less variable expenses	60,000	150	90,000	150	30,000
Contribution margin	40,000	$100	48,000	$ 80	8,000
Less fixed expenses	35,000		50,000*		15,000
Net income (loss).	$ 5,000		$ (2,000)		$(7,000)

* $35,000 + $15,000 = $50,000.

Notice that the answer is the same as that obtained by the incremental analysis above.

Change in variable cost, fixed cost, and sales volume   Refer to the original data. Assume again that the Norton Company is currently selling 400 ovens per month. The sales manager would like to place the sales staff on a commission basis of $15 per oven sold, rather than on flat salaries that now total $6,000 per month. The sales manager is confident that the change will increase monthly sales by 15 percent. Should the change be made?

Solution: Changing the sales staff from a salaried basis to a commission basis will affect both fixed and variable costs. Fixed costs will decrease by $6,000, from \$35,000 to \$29,000. Variable costs will increase by \$15, from \$150 to \$165, and the unit contribution margin will decrease from \$100 to \$85.

Expected total contribution margin:	
400 ovens × 115% × \$85	\$39,100
Present total contribution margin:	
400 ovens × \$100	40,000
Decrease in total contribution margin	(900)
Change in fixed costs:	
Add salaries avoided if a commission is paid	6,000
Increase in net income	\$ 5,100

Yes, the changes should be made. Again, the same answer can be obtained by preparing comparative income statements:

	Present 400 ovens per month		Expected 460 ovens per month		Difference: increase or (decrease) in net income
	Total	Per unit	Total	Per unit	
Sales	\$100,000	\$250	\$115,000*	\$250	\$ 15,000
Less variable expenses	60,000	150	75,900	165	(15,900)
Contribution margin	40,000	\$100	39,100	\$ 85	(900)
Less fixed expenses	35,000		29,000		6,000
Net income	\$ 5,000		\$ 10,100		\$ 5,100

*400 ovens × 115% = 460 ovens.
460 ovens × \$250 = \$115,000.

Change in regular sales price   Refer to the original data. Assume again that the Norton Company is currently selling 400 ovens per month. The company has an opportunity to make a bulk sale of 150 ovens to a wholesaler if an acceptable price can be worked out. This sale would not disturb regular sales currently being made. What price per oven should be quoted to the wholesaler if the Norton Company wants to increase its monthly profits by \$3,000?

Solution:

Variable cost per oven	\$150
Desired profit per oven:	
\$3,000 ÷ 150 ovens	20
Quoted price per oven	\$170

Notice that no element of fixed cost is included in the computation. This is because the Norton Company's regular business puts it beyond the break-even point, and the fixed costs are therefore covered. Thus, the quoted price on the special order only needs to be large enough to cover the variable costs involved with the order and to provide the desired \$3,000 contribution margin. As shown above, this is \$170 per unit, consisting of \$150 in variable costs and \$20 per unit in contribution margin.

If the Norton Company had been operating at a loss rather than at a profit, how would the price on the new ovens have been computed? A loss would have meant that a portion of the fixed costs was not being covered by regular sales. Therefore, it would have been necessary to quote a price on the 150 new ovens that was high enough to include part or all of these unrecovered fixed costs (as represented by the loss), in addition to the variable costs and the desired profit on the sale.

To illustrate this point, assume that the Norton Company is reporting a loss of $6,000 per month and that the company wants to turn this loss into a profit of $3,000 per month. Under these circumstances, the quoted price on the 150 new ovens would be computed as shown below.

Solution:

Variable cost per oven	$150
Present net loss:	
$6,000 ÷ 150 ovens	40
Desired profit:	
$3,000 ÷ 150 ovens	20
Quoted price per oven	$210

The $210 price we have computed represents a substantial discount from the $250 regular selling price per oven. Thus, both the wholesaler and the company would benefit from the bulk order.

Importance of the Contribution Margin

As stated in the introduction to the chapter, CVP analysis seeks the most profitable combination of variable costs, fixed costs, selling price, and sales volume. The examples that we have just provided show that the effect on the contribution margin is a major consideration in deciding on the most profitable combination of these factors. We have seen that profits can sometimes be improved by reducing the contribution margin if fixed costs can be reduced by a greater amount. More commonly, however, we have seen that the way to improve profits is to increase the total contribution margin figure. Sometimes this can be done by reducing the selling price and thereby increasing volume; sometimes it can be done by increasing the fixed costs (such as advertising) and thereby increasing volume; and sometimes it can be done by trading off variable and fixed costs with appropriate changes in volume. Many other combinations of factors are possible.

The size of the unit contribution margin figure (and the size of the C/M ratio) will have a heavy influence on what steps a company is willing to take to improve profits. For example, the greater the unit contribution margin for a product, the greater is the amount that a company will be willing to spend in order to increase sales of the product by a given percentage. This explains in part why companies with high unit contribution margins (such as auto manufacturers) advertise so heavily, while companies with low unit contribution margins (such as dishware manufacturers) tend to spend much less for advertising.

In short, the effect on the contribution margin holds the key to most cost-revenue decisions in a company.

BREAK-EVEN ANALYSIS

CVP analysis is sometimes referred to simply as break-even analysis. This is unfortunate, because break-even analysis is just one part of the entire CVP concept. However, it is often a key part, and it can give the manager many insights into the data with which he or she is working.

As a basis for discussion, we will continue with the example of the Norton Company. Recall that the selling price is $250 per oven, the variable expenses are $150 per oven, and the fixed costs total $35,000 per month.

Break-Even Computations

Earlier in the chapter, we stated that the break-even point can be defined equally well as the point where total sales revenue equals total expenses, variable and fixed, or as the point where total contribution margin equals total fixed expenses. As suggested by these two definitions of the break-even point, break-even analysis can be approached in two ways—first, by what is called the *equation method;* and second, by what is called the *unit contribution method.*

The equation method   The **equation method** centers on the contribution approach to the income statement illustrated earlier in the chapter. The format of this statement can be expressed in equation form as:

$$\text{Sales} = \text{Variable expenses} + \text{Fixed expenses} + \text{Profits}$$

At the break-even point, profits will be zero. Therefore, the break-even point can be computed by finding that point where sales just equal the total of the variable expenses plus the fixed expenses. For the Norton Company, this would be:

$$\text{Sales} = \text{Variable expenses} + \text{Fixed expenses} + \text{Profits}$$

$$\$250X = \$150X + \$35,000 + 0$$
$$\$100X = \$35,000$$
$$X = 350 \text{ ovens}$$

where:

$$X = \text{break-even point in ovens}$$
$$\$250 = \text{unit sales price}$$
$$\$150 = \text{unit variable expenses}$$
$$\$35,000 = \text{total fixed expenses}$$

After the break-even point in units sold has been computed, the break-even point in sales dollars can be computed by multiplying the break-even level of units by the sales price per unit:

$$350 \text{ ovens} \times \$250 = \$87,500$$

At times, the *dollar* relationship between variable expenses and sales may not be known. In these cases, if one knows the *percentage* relationship between variable expenses and sales, then the break-even point can still be computed, as follows:

$$\text{Sales} = \text{Variable expenses} + \text{Fixed expenses} + \text{Profits}$$

$$X = 0.60X + \$35,000 + 0$$
$$0.40X = \$35,000$$
$$X = \$87,500$$

where:

$$X = \text{break-even point in sales dollars}$$
$$0.60 = \text{variable expenses as a percentage of sales}$$
$$\$35,000 = \text{total fixed expenses}$$

Firms often have data available only in percentage form, and the approach we have just illustrated must then be used to find the break-even point. Notice that use of percentages in the equation yields a break-even point in sales dollars rather than in units sold. The break-even point in units sold would be:

$$\$87,500 \div \$250 = 350 \text{ ovens}$$

The unit contribution method   The **unit contribution method** is actually just a variation of the equation method already described. The approach centers on the idea discussed earlier that each unit sold provides a certain amount of contribution margin that goes toward the covering of fixed costs. To find how many units must be sold to break even, one must divide the total fixed costs by the contribution margin being generated by each unit sold:

$$\frac{\text{Fixed expenses}}{\text{Unit contribution margin}} = \text{Break-even point}$$

Each oven that the Norton Company sells generates a contribution margin of $100 ($250 selling price, less $150 variable expenses). Since the total fixed expenses are $35,000, the break-even point is:

$$\frac{\text{Fixed expenses}}{\text{Unit contribution margin}} = \frac{\$35,000}{\$100} = 350 \text{ ovens}$$

If only the percentage relationship between variable expenses, contribution margin, and sales is known, the computation becomes:

$$\frac{\text{Fixed expenses}}{\text{C/M ratio}} = \frac{\$35,000}{40\%} = \$87,500$$

This approach to break-even analysis is particularly useful in those situations where a company has multiple product lines and wishes to compute a single break-even point for the company as a whole. More is said on this point in a later section titled ''The concept of sales mix.''

CVP Relationships in Graphic Form

The cost data relating to the Norton Company's microwave ovens can be expressed in graphic form by preparing a **cost-volume-profit (CVP) graph.** A CVP graph can be very helpful in that it highlights CVP relationships over wide ranges of activity and gives managers a perspective that can be obtained in no other way. Such graphing is sometimes referred to as preparing a **break-even chart.** This is correct to the extent that the break-even point is clearly shown on the graph. The reader should be aware, however, that a graphing of CVP data highlights CVP relationships throughout the *entire* relevant range—not just at the break-even point.

Preparing the CVP graph   Preparing a CVP graph (sometimes called a *break-even chart*) involves three steps. These steps are keyed to the graph in Exhibit 6–1.

1. Draw a line parallel to the volume axis, to represent total fixed expenses. For the Norton Company, total fixed expenses are $35,000.
2. Choose some volume of sales, and plot the point representing total expenses (fixed and variable) at the activity level you have selected. In

EXHIBIT 6–1

Preparing the CVP graph

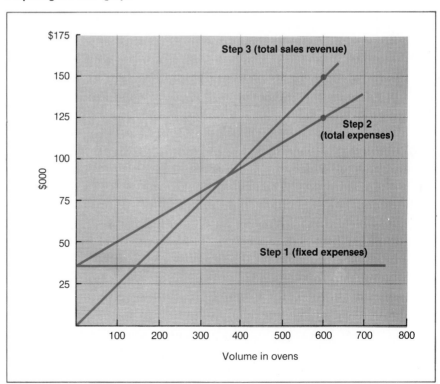

Exhibit 6–1, we have chosen a volume of 600 ovens. Total expenses at that activity level would be:

Fixed expenses . . . . $ 35,000
Variable expenses (600 ovens × $150) . . .   90,000
Total expenses $125,000

After the point has been plotted, draw a line through it back to the point where the fixed expenses line intersects the dollars axis.

3.   Again choose some volume of sales, and plot the point representing total sales dollars at the activity level you have selected. In Exhibit 6–1, we have again chosen a volume of 600 ovens. Sales at that activity level total $150,000 (600 ovens × $250). Draw a line through this point back to the origin.

The interpretation of the completed CVP graph is given in Exhibit 6–2. The anticipated profit or loss at any given level of sales is measured by

EXHIBIT 6–2
The completed CVP graph

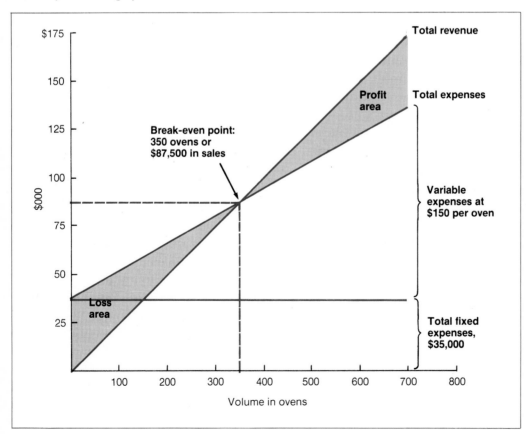

the vertical distance between the total revenue line (sales) and the total expenses line (variable expenses plus fixed expenses).

The break-even point is where the total revenue and total expenses lines cross. The break-even point of 350 ovens in Exhibit 6–2 agrees with the break-even point obtained for the Norton Company in earlier computations.

An alternative format   Some managers prefer an alternative format to the CVP graph, as illustrated in Exhibit 6–3.

Note that the total revenue and total expenses lines are the same as in Exhibit 6–2. However, the new format in Exhibit 6–3 places the fixed expenses above the variable expenses, thereby allowing the contribution margin to be depicted on the graph. Otherwise, the graphs in the two exhibits are the same.

The profitgraph   Another approach to the CVP graph is presented in Exhibit 6–4. This approach, called a **profitgraph,** is preferred by some

EXHIBIT 6–3

Alternative format to the CVP graph

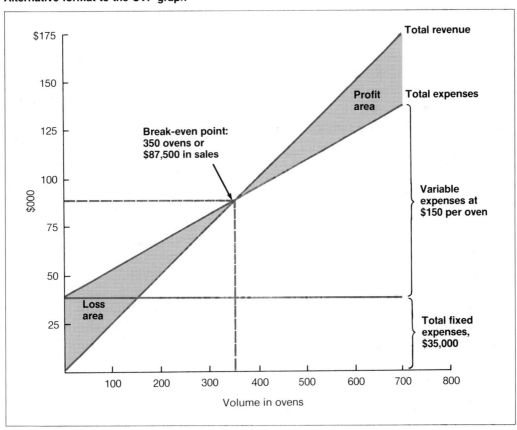

managers because it focuses more directly on how profits change with changes in volume. It has the added advantage of being easier to interpret than the more traditional approaches illustrated in Exhibits 6–2 and 6–3. It has the disadvantage, however, of not showing as clearly how costs are affected by changes in the level of sales.

The profitgraph is constructed in two steps. These steps are illustrated in Exhibit 6–4.

1.   Locate total fixed expenses on the vertical axis, assuming zero level of activity. This point will be in the "loss area," equal to the total fixed expenses expected for the period.

EXHIBIT 6–4

Preparing the profitgraph

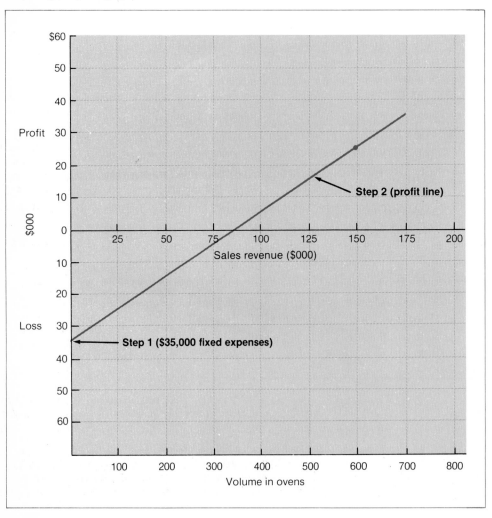

2. Plot a point representing expected profit or loss at any chosen level of sales. In Exhibit 6–4, we have chosen to plot the point representing expected profits at a sales volume of 600 ovens. At this activity level, expected profits are:

Sales (600 ovens × $250) $150,000
Less variable expenses
    (600 ovens × $150)   90,000
Contribution margin   60,000
Less fixed expenses   35,000
Net income . . . . $ 25,000

EXHIBIT 6–5

The completed profitgraph

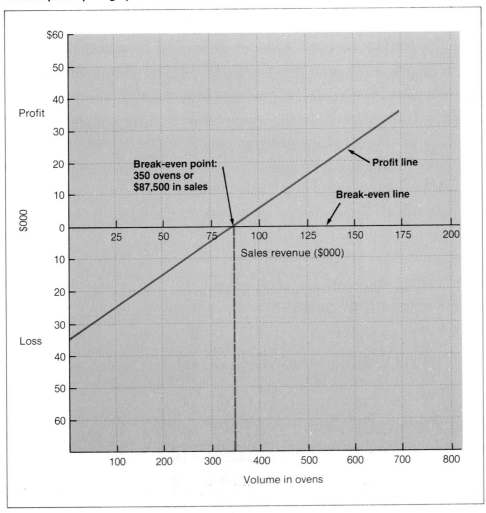

After this point is plotted, draw a line through it back to the point on the vertical axis representing total fixed expenses. The interpretation of the completed profitgraph is given in Exhibit 6–5. The break-even point is where the profit line crosses the break-even line.

The vertical distance between the two lines represents the expected profit or loss at any given level of sales volume. This vertical distance can be translated directly into dollars by referring to the profit and loss figures on the vertical axis.

Target Net Profit Analysis

CVP formulas can be used to determine the sales volume required to meet a target net profit figure. Suppose that the Norton Company would like to earn a target net profit of $40,000 per month. How many ovens would have to be sold?

The CVP equation   One approach to the solution would be to use the CVP equation. The target net profit requirement can be added into the basic equation data, and the solution will then show what level of sales is necessary to cover all expenses and yield the target net profit.

$$\text{Sales} = \text{Variable expenses} + \text{Fixed expenses} + \text{Profits}$$

$$\$250X = \$150X + \$35,000 + \$40,000$$
$$\$100X = \$75,000$$
$$X = 750 \text{ ovens}$$

where:

$$X = \text{number of ovens sold}$$
$$\$250 = \text{unit sales price}$$
$$\$150 = \text{unit variable expenses}$$
$$\$35,000 = \text{total fixed expenses}$$
$$\$40,000 = \text{target net profit}$$

Thus, the target net profit can be achieved by selling 750 ovens per month, which represents $187,500 in total sales ($250 × 750 ovens).

The unit contribution approach   A second approach would be to expand the unit contribution formula to include the target net profit requirement:

$$\frac{\$35,000 \text{ fixed expenses} + \$40,000 \text{ target net profit}}{\$100 \text{ contribution margin per oven}} = 750 \text{ ovens}$$

This approach is simpler and more direct than using the CVP equation. In addition, it shows clearly that once the fixed costs are covered, the unit contribution margin is fully available for meeting profit requirements.

The Margin of Safety (M/S)

The **margin of safety (M/S)** can be defined as the excess of budgeted (or actual) sales over the break-even volume of sales. It states the amount by which sales can drop before losses begin to be incurred in an organization. The formula for its calculation is:

Total sales − Break-even sales = Margin of safety (M/S)

Computations involving the M/S are presented in Exhibit 6–6. Notice that the two companies in the exhibit have equal sales and net income figures but that Alpha Company has an M/S of $40,000, whereas Beta Company has an M/S of only $20,000. The difference in the M/S can be traced to the fact that the two companies have very different cost structures. Beta Company has higher fixed costs and thus will incur losses more quickly than Alpha Company if sales drop off. As indicated by the M/S, if sales drop by only $20,000, Beta Company will be at its break-even point, whereas sales can drop by $40,000 before Alpha Company will be at its break-even point.

The M/S can also be expressed in percentage form. This percentage is obtained by dividing the M/S in dollar terms by total sales:

$$\frac{\text{M/S in dollars}}{\text{Total sales}} = \text{M/S percentage}$$

Exhibit 6–6 contains the M/S expressed in percentage form for both Alpha Company and Beta Company. The M/S can also be expressed in

EXHIBIT 6–6
Margin of safety (M/S)

	Alpha Company		Beta Company	
	Amount	**Percent**	**Amount**	**Percent**
Sales	$200,000	100	$200,000	100
Less variable expenses	150,000	75	100,000	50
Contribution margin	50,000	25	100,000	50
Less fixed expenses	40,000		90,000	
Net income	$ 10,000		$ 10,000	
Break-even point:				
$40,000 ÷ 25%	$160,000			
$90,000 ÷ 50%			$180,000	
M/S in dollars (total sales less break-even sales):				
$200,000 − $160,000	40,000			
$200,000 − $180,000			20,000	
M/S in percentage form (M/S in dollars divided by total sales):				
$40,000 ÷ $200,000	20%			
$20,000 ÷ $200,000			10%	

terms of units of product (if a company is a single-product firm) by dividing the M/S in dollars by the unit selling price.

If the M/S is low, as in Beta Company, what does management do to correct the problem? There is no universal answer to this question, other than to point out that management's efforts must be directed toward either reducing the break-even point or increasing the overall level of sales in the company. In short, the M/S is a tool designed to point out a problem (or the lack of one), the solution to which must be found by analyzing the company's cost structure and by applying the general CVP techniques that have been illustrated in this chapter.

STRUCTURING SALES COMMISSIONS

Some firms base salespersons' commissions on contribution margin generated rather than on sales generated. The reasoning goes like this: Since contribution margin represents the amount of sales revenue available to cover fixed expenses and profits, a firm's well-being will be maximized when contribution margin is maximized. By tying salespersons' commissions to contribution margin, the salespersons are automatically encouraged to concentrate on the element that is of most importance to the firm. There is no need to worry about what mix of products the salespersons sell, because they will *automatically* sell the mix of products that will maximize the base on which their commissions are to be paid. That is, if salespersons are aware that their commissions will depend on the amount of contribution margin that they are able to generate, then they will use all of the experience, skill, and expertise at their command to sell the mix of products that will maximize the contribution margin base. In effect, by maximizing their own well-being, they automatically maximize the well-being of the firm.

As a further step, some firms deduct from the total contribution margin generated by salespersons the amount of the traveling, entertainment, and other expenses that are incurred. This encourages the salespersons to be sensitive to their own costs in the process of making sales.

THE CONCEPT OF SALES MIX

The preceding sections have given us some insights into the principles involved in CVP analysis, as well as some selected examples of how these principles are used by the manager. Before concluding our discussion, it will be helpful to consider one additional application of the ideas that we have developed—the use of CVP concepts in analyzing sales mix.

The Definition of Sales Mix

The term **sales mix** means the relative combination in which a company's products are sold. Managers try to achieve the combination, or mix, that will yield the greatest amount of profits. Most companies have several products, and often these products are not equally profitable. Where this is true, profits will depend to some extent on the sales mix that the company is able to achieve. Profits will be greater if high-margin items make up a relatively large proportion of total sales than if sales consist mostly of low-margin items.

Changes in the sales mix can cause interesting (and sometimes confusing) variations in a company's profits. A shift in the sales mix from high-margin items to low-margin items can cause total profits to decrease even though total sales may increase. Conversely, a shift in the sales mix from low-margin items to high-margin items can cause the reverse effect—total profits may increase even though total sales decrease. Given the possibility of these types of variations in profits, one measure of the effectiveness of a company's sales force is the sales mix that it is able to generate. It is one thing to achieve a particular sales volume; it is quite a different thing to sell the most profitable mix of products.

Sales Mix and Break-Even Analysis

If a company is selling more than one product, break-even analysis is somewhat more complex than discussed earlier in the chapter. The reason is that different products will have different selling prices, different costs, and different contribution margins. Consequently, the break-even point will depend on the mix in which the various products are sold. To illustrate, assume that a company has two product lines—line A and line B. For 19x1, the company's sales, costs, and break-even point were as shown in Exhibit 6–7.

As shown in the exhibit, the break-even point is $60,000 in sales. This is computed by dividing the fixed costs by the company's *average* C/M ratio of 45 percent. But $60,000 in sales represents the break-even point

EXHIBIT 6–7

Multiple-product break-even analysis

	Line A		Line B		Total	
	Amount	**Percent**	**Amount**	**Percent**	**Amount**	**Percent**
Sales	$20,000	100	$80,000	100	$100,000	100
Less variable expenses	15,000	75	40,000	50	55,000	55
Contribution margin	$ 5,000	25	$40,000	50	45,000	45
Less fixed expenses					27,000	
Net income					$ 18,000	

Computation of the break-even point:

$$\frac{\text{Fixed expenses, } \$27,000}{\text{Average C/M ratio, } 45\%} = \$60,000$$

EXHIBIT 6–8

Multiple-product break-even analysis: A shift in sales mix (see Exhibit 6–7)

	Line A		Line B		Total	
	Amount	**Percent**	**Amount**	**Percent**	**Amount**	**Percent**
Sales	$80,000	100	$20,000	100	$100,000	100
Less variable expenses	60,000	75	10,000	50	70,000	70
Contribution margin	$20,000	25	$10,000	50	30,000	30
Less fixed expenses					27,000	
Net income					$ 3,000	

Computation of the break-even point:

$$\frac{\text{Fixed expenses, \$27,000}}{\text{Average C/M ratio, 30\%}} = \$90,000$$

for the company only so long as the sales mix does not change. *If the sales mix changes, then the break-even point will also change.* We can illustrate this by assuming that in 19x2, the following year, the sales mix shifts away from the more profitable line B (which has a 50 percent C/M ratio) toward the less profitable line A (which has only a 25 percent C/M ratio). Assume that sales in 19x2 are as shown in Exhibit 6–8.

Although sales have remained unchanged at $100,000, the sales mix is exactly the reverse of what it was in Exhibit 6–7, with the bulk of the sales now coming from line A rather than from line B. Notice that this shift in the sales mix has caused both the average C/M ratio and total profits to drop sharply from the prior year—the average C/M ratio has dropped from 45 percent in 19x1 to only 30 percent in 19x2, and net income has dropped from $18,000 to only $3,000. In addition, with the drop in the average C/M ratio, the company's break-even point is no longer $60,000 in sales. Since the company is now realizing less average contribution margin per dollar of sales, it takes more sales to cover the same amount of fixed costs. Thus, the break-even point has increased from $60,000 to $90,000 in sales per year.

In preparing a break-even analysis, some assumption must be made concerning the sales mix. Usually the assumption is that it will not change. However, if the manager knows that shifts in various factors (consumer tastes, market share, and so forth) are causing shifts in the sales mix, then these factors must be explicitly considered in any CVP computations. Otherwise, the manager may be making decisions on the basis of outmoded or faulty data.

Sales Mix and per Unit Contribution Margin

Sometimes the sales mix is measured in terms of the average per unit contribution margin. To illustrate, assume that a company has two prod-

EXHIBIT 6–9

Sales mix and per unit contribution margin analysis

	Contri-bution margin per unit	Total units sold		Total contribution margin	
		19x1	19x2	19x1	19x2
Product X.	$5	1,000	2,000	$ 5,000	$10,000
Product Y.	3	3,000	2,000	9,000	6,000
		4,000	4,000	$14,000	$16,000
Average per unit contribution margin ($14,000 ÷ 4,000 units) . . .				$3.50	
Average per unit contribution margin ($16,000 ÷ 4,000 units) . . .					$4

ucts—X and Y. During 19x1 and 19x2, sales of products X and Y were as shown in Exhibit 6–9.

Two things should be noted about the data in this exhibit. First, note that the sales mix in 19x1 was 1,000 units of product X and 3,000 units of product Y. This sales mix yielded $3.50 in average per unit contribution margin.

Second, note that the sales mix in 19x2 shifted to 2,000 units for both products, although *total* sales remained unchanged at 4,000 units. This sales mix yielded $4 in average per unit contribution margin, an increase of 50 cents per unit over the prior year.

What caused the increase in average per unit contribution margin between the two years? The answer is the shift in sales mix toward the more profitable product X. Although total volume (in units) did not change, total and per unit contribution margin changed simply because of the change in sales mix.

LIMITING ASSUMPTIONS IN CVP ANALYSIS

Several limiting assumptions must be made when using data for CVP analysis. These assumptions are:

1. The behavior of both revenues and costs is linear throughout the entire relevant range. The economists would differ from this view. They would say that changes in volume will trigger changes in both revenues and costs in such a way that relationships will not remain linear.
2. Costs can be accurately divided into variable and fixed elements.
3. The sales mix is constant.
4. Inventories do not change in break-even computations, e.g., the number of units produced equals the number of units sold (this assumption is considered further in Chapter 7).

5. Worker and machine productivity and efficiency do not change throughout the relevant range.

6. The value of a dollar received today is the same as the value of a dollar received in any future year (the time value of money is considered in Chapter 14).

SUMMARY

The analysis of CVP relationships is one of management's most significant responsibilities. Basically, it involves finding the most favorable combination of variable costs, fixed costs, selling price, sales volume, and mix of products sold. We have found that trade-offs are possible between types of costs, as well as between costs and selling price, and between selling price and sales volume. Sometimes these trade-offs are desirable, and sometimes they are not. CVP analysis provides the manager with a powerful tool for identifying those courses of action that will and will not improve profitability.

The concepts developed in this chapter represent a *way of thinking* rather than a mechanical set of procedures. That is, in order to put together the optimum combination of costs, selling price, and sales volume, the manager must be trained to think in terms of the unit contribution margin, the break-even point, the C/M ratio, the sales mix, and the other concepts developed in this chapter. These concepts are dynamic in that a change in one will trigger changes in others—changes that may not be obvious on the surface. Only by learning to *think* in CVP terms can the manager move with assurance toward the firm's profit objectives.

KEY TERMS FOR REVIEW

Break-even chart The relationship between revenues, costs, and level of activity in an organization presented in graphic form. Also see *Cost-volume-profit (CVP) graph.*

Break-even point The level of activity at which an organization neither earns a profit nor incurs a loss. The break-even point can also be defined as the point where total revenue equals total costs and as the point where total contribution margin equals total fixed costs.

Contribution margin ratio The contribution margin per unit expressed as a percentage of the selling price per unit. This term is synonymous with *profit-volume ratio.*

Cost-volume-profit (CVP) graph The relationship between revenues, costs, and level of activity in an organization, presented in graphic form. Also see *Break-even chart.*

Degree of operating leverage A measure, at a given level of sales, of how a percentage change in sales volume will affect profits. The degree of operating leverage is computed by dividing contribution margin by net income.

Equation method A method of computing the break-even point that relies on the equation: Sales = Variable expenses + Fixed expenses + Profits.

Incremental analysis An analytical approach that focuses only on those items of revenue, cost, and volume that will change as a result of a decision in an organization.

Margin of safety (M/S) The excess of budgeted (or actual) sales over the break-even volume of sales.

Operating leverage A measure of the extent to which fixed costs are being used in an organization. The greater the fixed costs, the greater is the operating leverage available and the greater is the sensitivity of net income to changes in sales.

Profitgraph An alternative form of the cost-volume-profit graph that focuses more directly on how profits change with changes in volume.

Profit-volume ratio See *Contribution margin ratio.*

Sales mix The relative combination in which a company's products are sold. Sales mix is computed by expressing the sales of each product as a percentage of total sales.

Unit contribution method A method of computing the break-even point in which the fixed costs are divided by the contribution margin per unit.

QUESTIONS

6–1. Cost-volume-profit (CVP) analysis is a study of the interaction of a number of factors. Name the factors involved.

6–2. What is meant by a product's contribution margin ratio (C/M ratio)? How is this ratio useful in the planning of business operations?

6–3. Able Company and Baker Company are competing firms. Each company sells a single product, widgets, in the same market at a price of $50 per widget. Variable costs are the same in each company—$35 per widget. Able Company has discovered a way to reduce its variable costs by $4 per unit and has decided to pass half of this cost savings on to its customers in the form of a lower price. Although Baker Company has not been able to reduce its variable costs, it must also lower its selling price in order to remain competitive with Able Company. If each company sells 10,000 units per year, what will be the effect of the changes on each company's profits?

6–4. Often the most direct route to a business decision is to make an incremental analysis based on the information available. What is meant by an "incremental analysis"?

6–5. Company A's cost structure includes costs that are mostly variable, whereas Company B's cost structure includes costs that are mostly fixed. In a time of increasing sales, which company will tend to realize the most rapid increase in profits? Explain.

6–6. What is meant by the term *operating leverage?*

6–7. A 10 percent decrease in the selling price of a product will have the same impact on net income as a 10 percent increase in the variable expenses. Do you agree? Why or why not?

6–8. "Changes in fixed costs are much more significant to a company than changes in variable costs." Do you agree? Explain.

6–9. What is meant by the term *break-even point?*

6–10. Name three approaches to break-even analysis. Briefly explain how each approach works.

6–11. Why is the term *break-even chart* a misnomer?

6–12. In response to a request from your immediate supervisor, you have prepared a CVP graph portraying the cost and revenue characteristics of your company's product and operations. Explain how the lines on the graph would change if *(a)* the selling price per unit decreased, *(b)* fixed costs increased throughout the entire range of activity portrayed on the graph, and *(c)* variable costs per unit increased.

6–13. Using the following notations, write out the correct formula for computing the break-even level of sales in units: S = sales in units, SP = selling price per unit, FC = total fixed costs, and VC = variable cost per unit. Is the formula you have derived the formula for the equation method or the formula for the unit contribution method?

6–14. Al's Auto Wash charges $2 to wash a car. The variable costs of washing a car are 15 percent of sales. Fixed costs total $1,020 monthly. How many cars must be washed each month for Al to break even?

6–15. What is meant by the margin of safety (M/S)?

6–16. Companies X and Y are in the same industry. Company X is highly automated, whereas Company Y relies primarily on labor in the manufacture of its products. If sales in the two companies are about the same, which would you expect to have the lowest M/S? Why?

6–17. What is meant by the term *sales mix?* CVP analysis includes some inherent, simplifying assumptions. What assumption is usually made concerning sales mix?

6–18. Explain how a shift in the sales mix could result in both a higher break-even point and a lower net income.

EXERCISES

E6–1. Lindon Company manufactures and sells a single product. The product sells for $40 per unit and has a C/M ratio of 30 percent. The company's fixed expenses are $180,000 per year.

Required: 1. What are the variable expenses per unit?
2. Using the equation method:
   a. What is the break-even point in units and in sales dollars?
   b. What sales level in units and in sales dollars is required to earn an annual profit of $60,000?
   c. Assume that by using less costly inputs, the company is able to reduce its variable expenses by $4 per unit. What is the company's new break-even point in units and in sales dollars?
3. Repeat (2) above, using the unit contribution method.

E6–2. Menlo Company manufactures and sells a single product. The company's sales and expenses for last quarter follow:

	Total	Per unit
Sales	$450,000	$30
Less variable expenses	180,000	12
Contribution margin	270,000	$18
Less fixed expenses	216,000	
Net income	$ 54,000	

Required: 1.   What is the quarterly break-even point in units sold and in sales dollars?
  2.   Without resorting to computations, what is the total contribution margin at the break-even point?
  3.   How many units would have to be sold each quarter to earn a target net income of $90,000? Use the unit contribution method. Prove your answer by preparing a contribution income statement at the target level of sales.
  4.   Refer to the original data. Compute the company's M/S in both dollar and percentage terms.
  5.   What is the company's C/M ratio? If sales increase by $50,000 per quarter, by how much would you expect quarterly net income to increase? (Do not prepare an income statement; use the C/M ratio to compute your answer.)

E6–3.   Bestway Toys, Inc., has developed a new board game. The company sold 15,000 games last year at a selling price of $20 per game. Fixed costs associated with the game total $182,000 per year, and variable costs are $6 per game.

Required: 1.   Prepare an income statement for last year, and compute the degree of operating leverage.
  2.   Management is confident that the company can sell 18,000 games next year (an increase of 3,000 games, or 20 percent, over last year). Compute:
    a.   The expected percentage increase in net income for next year.
    b.   The expected total dollar net income for next year. (Do not prepare an income statement; use the operating leverage concept to compute your answer.)

E6–4.   The Hartford Symphony Guild is planning its annual dinner-dance. The dinner-dance committee has assembled the following expected costs for the event:

Dinner (per person)	$ 18
Favors and program (per person) . . .	2
Orchestra	2,800
Rental of ballroom	900
Professional entertainment	
during intermission	1,000
Tickets and advertising	1,300

The committee members would like to charge $35 per person for the evening's activities.

Required: 1.   Compute the break-even point for the dinner-dance (in terms of the number of persons that must attend).
  2.   Assume that last year only 300 persons attended the dinner-dance. If the same number attend this year, what price per ticket must be charged in order to break even?

3. Refer to the original data ($35 ticket price per person). Prepare a cost-volume-profit graph for the dinner-dance. Number of persons should be placed on the horizontal *(X)* axis, and dollars should be placed on the vertical *(Y)* axis. (Note: Exercise 6–5 has further requirements for the data in this exercise.)

E6–5.   (This exercise is a continuation of Exercise 6–4.) Refer to the data in Exercise 6–4.

Required: 1. Prepare a profitgraph for the dinner-dance.
2. If the dinner-dance committee charges $40 per person rather than $35, will this cause the slope of the profit line to be steeper or flatter? Explain.

E6–6.   Miller Company's most recent income statement is shown below:

	Total	Per unit
Sales (20,000 units)	$300,000	$15.00
Less variable expenses	180,000	9.00
Contribution margin	120,000	$ 6.00
Less fixed expenses	70,000	
Net income	$ 50,000	

Required: Prepare a new income statement under each of the following conditions (consider each case independently):

1. The sales volume increases by 15 percent.
2. The selling price decreases by $1.50 per unit, and the sales volume increases by 25 percent.
3. The selling price increases by $1.50 per unit, fixed expenses increase by $20,000, and the sales volume decreases by 5 percent.
4. The selling price increases by 12 percent, variable expenses increase by 60 cents per unit, and the sales volume decreases by 10 percent.

E6–7.   Fill in the missing amounts in each of the eight case situations below. Each case is independent of the others. (Hint: One way to find the missing amounts would be to prepare a contribution income statement for each case, enter the known data, and then compute the missing items.)

a. Assume that only one product is being sold in each of the four following case situations:

Case	Units sold	Sales	Variable expenses	Contribution margin per unit	Fixed expenses	Net income (loss)
1.	15,000	$180,000	$120,000	$?	$ 50,000	$?
2.	?	100,000	?	10	32,000	8,000
3.	10,000	?	70,000	13	?	12,000
4.	6,000	300,000	?	?	100,000	(10,000)

b. Assume that more than one product is being sold in each of the four following case situations:

Case	Sales	Variable expenses	Average contribution margin (percent)	Fixed expenses	Net income (loss)
1	$500,000	$?	20	$?	$ 7,000
2	400,000	260,000	?	100,000	?
3	?	?	60	130,000	20,000
4	600,000	420,000	?	?	(5,000)

E6–8.   Dixon Company manufactures and sells recreational equipment. One of the company's products, a small camp stove, sells for $50 per unit. Variable expenses are $32 per stove, and fixed expenses associated with the stove total $108,000 per month.

Required: 1.   Compute the break-even point in number of stoves and in total sales dollars.

2.   If the variable expenses per stove increase as a percentage of the selling price, will it result in a higher or a lower break-even point? Why? (Assume that the fixed expenses remain unchanged.)

3.   At present, the company is selling 8,000 stoves per month. The sales manager is convinced that a 10 percent reduction in the selling price would result in a 25 percent increase in monthly sales of stoves. Prepare two contribution income statements, one under present operating conditions, and one as operations would appear after the proposed changes. Show both total and per unit data on your statements.

4.   Refer to the data in (3) above. How many stoves would have to be sold at the new selling price to yield a minimum net income of $35,000 per month?

E6–9.   Wiley Company sells two products, X and Y. Monthly sales and the contribution margin ratios for the two products follow:

	Product		
	X	Y	Total
Sales	$150,000	$250,000	$400,000
Contribution margin ratio . . .	80%	36%	?

Fixed expenses in Wiley Company total $183,750 per month.

Required: 1.   Prepare an income statement for the company as a whole. Use the format shown in Exhibit 6–7, and carry computations to one decimal place.

2.   Compute the break-even point for the company, based on the current sales mix.

PROBLEMS

P6–10.   **Basic CVP analysis; graphing.**   The Fashion Headwear Company operates a chain of hat shops around the country. The shops carry many styles of hats that are all sold at the same price. Sales personnel in the shops are paid a substantial commission on each hat sold (in addition to a small basic salary) in order to encourage them to be aggressive in their sales efforts.

The following cost and revenue data relate to Shop 48 and are typical of one of the company's many outlets:

	Per hat
Sales price	$ 30.00
Variable expenses:	
Invoice cost.	$ 13.50
Sales commission	4.50
Total variable expenses . . .	$ 18.00
	Annual
Fixed expenses:	
Advertising	$ 30,000
Rent	20,000
Salaries	100,000
Total fixed expenses	$150,000

Required:
1. Calculate the annual break-even point in dollar sales and in unit sales for Shop 48.
2. Prepare a CVP graph showing cost and revenue data for Shop 48 from a zero level of activity up to 20,000 hats sold each year. Clearly indicate the break-even point on the graph.
3. If 12,000 hats are sold in a year, what would be Shop 48's net income or loss?
4. The company is considering paying the store manager of Shop 48 an incentive commission of 75 cents per hat (in addition to the salespersons' commission). If this change is made, what will be the new break-even point in dollar sales and in unit sales?
5. Refer to the original data. As an alternative to (4) above, the company is considering paying the store manager 50 cents commission on each hat sold in excess of the break-even point. If this change is made, what will be the shop's net income or loss if 15,000 hats are sold?
6. Refer to the original data. The company is considering eliminating sales commissions entirely in its shops and increasing fixed salaries by $31,500 annually. If this change is made, what will be the new break-even point in dollar sales and in unit sales for Shop 48? Would you recommend that the change be made? Explain.

P6–11.   **Basics of CVP analysis.**   Harwood Company manufactures a product that sells for $20 per unit. Variable costs are $8 per unit, and fixed costs total $180,000 per year.

Required: Answer the following independent questions:

1. What is the product's C/M ratio?
2. Use the C/M ratio to determine the break-even point in sales dollars.
3. Due to an increase in demand, the company estimates that sales will increase by $75,000 during the next year. By how much should net income increase (or net loss decrease), assuming that fixed costs do not change?

4.   Assume that operating results for last year were:

Sales $400,000
Less variable expenses   160,000
Contribution margin   240,000
Less fixed expenses   180,000
Net income . . . . $ 60,000

    a.   Compute the degree of operating leverage at the current level of sales.

    b.   The president expects sales to increase by 20 percent next year. By what percentage should net income increase?

5.   Refer to the original data. Assume that the company sold 18,000 units last year. The sales manager is convinced that a 10 percent reduction in the selling price, combined with a $30,000 increase in advertising, would cause annual sales in units to increase by one third. Prepare two contribution income statements, one showing the results of last year's operations and one showing the results of operations if these changes are made. Would you recommend that the company do as the sales manager suggests?

6.   Refer to the original data. Assume again that the company sold 18,000 units last year. The president does not want to change the selling price. Instead, he wants to increase the sales commission by $1 per unit. He thinks that this move, combined with some increase in advertising, would increase annual sales by 25 percent. By how much could advertising be increased with profits remaining unchanged? Do not prepare an income statement; use the incremental analysis approach.

7.   Refer to the original data. Assume that due to a recession the company is selling only 14,000 units per year. An order has been received from a wholesale distributor who wants to purchase 4,000 units on a special price basis. What unit price would have to be quoted to the distributor if Harwood Company wants to earn an overall profit of $20,000 per year? (Present sales would not be disturbed by this special order.)

P6–12.   **Basics of CVP analysis; cost structure.**   Due to erratic sales, Mercer Company has been experiencing difficulty for some time. The company's income statement for the most recent month is given below:

Sales (19,500 units × $30) $585,000
Less variable expenses   409,500
Contribution margin   175,500
Less fixed expenses   180,000
Net loss . . . . $ (4,500)

Required: 1.   Compute the company's C/M ratio and its break-even point in both units and dollars.

    2.   The president is certain that a $16,000 increase in the monthly advertising budget, combined with an intensified effort by the sales staff, will result in an $80,000 increase in monthly sales. If the president is right, what will be the effect on the company's monthly net income or loss? (Use the incremental approach in preparing your answer.)

    3.   Refer to the original data. The sales manager is convinced that a 10 percent reduction in the selling price, combined with an increase of $60,000 in the monthly advertising budget, will cause unit sales to double. What will the new income statement look like if these changes are adopted?

4. Refer to the original data. The president's wife thinks that a fancy new package for Mercer Company's product would help sales. The new package would increase packaging costs by 75 cents per unit. Assuming no other changes in cost behavior, how many units would have to be sold each month to earn a profit of $9,750?

5. Refer to the original data. By automating certain operations, the company could reduce variable costs by $3 per unit. However, fixed costs would increase by $72,000 each month.

    a. Compute the new C/M ratio and the new break-even point in both units and dollars.

    b. Assume that the company expects to sell 26,000 units next month. Prepare two income statements, one assuming that operations are not automated and one assuming that they are. (Show data on a per unit and percentage basis, as well as in total, for each alternative.)

    c. Would you recommend that the company automate its operations? Explain.

6. Refer to the original data. A large distributor has offered to make a bulk purchase of 5,000 units each month on a special price basis. Variable selling expenses of $1 per unit could be avoided on this sale. What price per unit should Mercer Company quote to this distributor if Mercer desires to make an overall net income of $18,000 each month for the company as a whole? (Present sales would not be disturbed by this order.)

P6–13.   **Interpretive questions on the CVP graph.**   A CVP graph, as illustrated below, is a useful technique for showing relationships between costs, volume, and profits in an organization.

Required: 1. Identify the numbered components in the CVP graph.

    2. State the effect of each of the following actions on line 3, line 9, and the break-even point. For line 3 and line 9, state whether the action will cause the line to:

        Remain unchanged.
        Shift upward.
        Shift downward.
        Have a steeper slope (i.e., rotate upward).
        Have a flatter slope (i.e., rotate downward).
        Shift upward *and* have a steeper slope.
        Shift upward *and* have a flatter slope.
        Shift downward *and* have a steeper slope.
        Shift downward *and* have a flatter slope.

In the case of the break-even point, state whether the action will cause the break-even point to:

        Remain unchanged.
        Increase.
        Decrease.
        Probably change, but the direction is uncertain.

Treat each case independently.

    x. *Example.*   Fixed costs are reduced by $5,000 per period.

      Answer (see choices above):   Line 3:   Shift downward.
                               Line 9:   Remain unchanged.
                               Break-even point: Decrease.

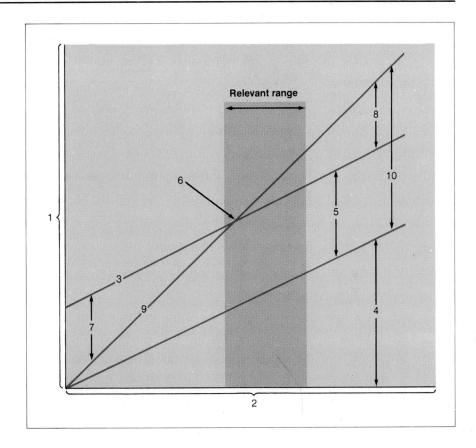

a. The unit selling price is increased from $18 to $20.

b. Unit variable costs are decreased from $12 to $10.

c. Fixed costs are increased by $3,000 per period.

d. Two thousand more units are sold during the period than were budgeted.

e. Due to paying salespersons a commission rather than a flat salary, fixed costs are reduced by $8,000 per period and unit variable costs are increased by $3.

f. Due to an increase in the cost of materials, both unit variable costs and the selling price are increased by $2.

g. Advertising costs are increased by $10,000 per period, resulting in a 10 percent increase in the number of units sold.

h. Due to automating an operation previously done by workers, fixed costs are increased by $12,000 per period and unit variable costs are reduced by $4.

P6–14. **Sales mix assumptions; break-even analysis.** Valtek Company has recently acquired an exclusive franchise to sell three products—A, B, and C—in its area. The company is anxious to establish a budgeting and planning program as an aid to management. To this end, budgeted sales by product and in total for the coming month have been set as shown below:

	Products							
	A		B		C		Total	
Percentage of total sales ..	20%		52%		28%		100%	
Sales	$150,000	100%	$390,000	100%	$210,000	100%	$750,000	100%
Less variable expenses . . .	108,000	72	78,000	20	84,000	40	270,000	36
Contribution margin	$ 42,000	28%	$312,000	80%	$126,000	60%	480,000	64%
Less fixed expenses							449,280	
Net income							$ 30,720	

$$\text{Break-even sales: } \frac{\text{Fixed expenses, \$449,280}}{\text{C/M ratio, 0.64}} = \$702,000$$

As shown by these data, net income is budgeted at $30,720 for the month, and break-even sales at $702,000.

Assume that actual sales for the month total $750,000 as planned. Actual sales by product are: A, $300,000; B, $180,000; and C, $270,000.

Required:
1. Prepare a contribution income statement for the month based on actual sales data. Present the income statement in the format shown above.
2. Compute the break-even sales for the month, based on your actual data.
3. Considering the fact that the company met its $750,000 sales budget for the month, the president is shocked at the results shown on your income statement in (1). Prepare a brief memo for the president explaining why both the operating results and the break-even sales are different from what was budgeted.

P6–15. **Various CVP questions: Break-even point; cost structure; target sales.** Northwood Company manufactures basketballs. The company has a standard ball that sells for $25. At present, the standard ball is manufactured in a small plant that relies heavily on direct labor workers. Thus, variable costs are high, totaling $15 per ball.

Last year the company sold 30,000 standard balls, with the following operating results:

Sales (30,000 standard balls)	$750,000
Less variable expenses	450,000
Contribution margin	300,000
Less fixed expenses	210,000
Net income	$ 90,000

Required:
1. Compute *(a)* the C/M ratio and the break-even point in balls, and *(b)* the degree of operating leverage at last year's level of sales.
2. Due to an increase in labor rates, the company estimates that variable costs will increase by $3 per ball next year. If this change takes place and the selling price per ball remains constant at $25, what will be the new C/M ratio and break-even point in balls?
3. Refer to the data in (2) above. If the expected change in variable costs takes place, how many balls will have to be sold next year to earn the same net income ($90,000) as last year?
4. Refer to the data in (2) above. The president feels that the company must raise the selling price on the standard balls. If Northwood Company wants to

maintain *the same C/M ratio as last year,* what selling price per ball must it charge next year to cover the increased labor costs?

5. Refer to the original data. The company is discussing the construction of a new, automated plant to manufacture the standard balls. The new plant would slash variable costs per ball by 40 percent, but it would cause fixed costs to double in amount per year. If the new plant is built, what would be the company's new C/M ratio and break-even point in balls?

6. Refer to the data in (5) above.

    a. If the new plant is built, how many balls will have to be sold next year to earn the same net income as last year?

    b. Assume the new plant is built and that next year the company manufactures and sells 30,000 balls (the same number as sold last year). Prepare a contribution income statement, and compute the degree of operating leverage.

    c. Explain why the operating leverage figure you have just computed is so much higher than the operating leverage figure computed in (1) above.

P6–16. **Graphing; incremental analysis; operating leverage.** Teri Hall has recently opened Sheer Elegance, Inc., a store specializing in fashionable stockings. Ms. Hall has just completed a course in managerial accounting at the state university, and she believes that she can apply certain aspects of the course to her business. She is particularly interested in adopting the cost-volume-profit approach to decision making. Thus, she has prepared the following analysis:

Sales price per pair of stockings	$2.00
Variable expense per pair of stockings	0.80
Contribution margin per pair of stockings . . .	$1.20

Fixed expenses per year:

Building rental	$12,000
Equipment depreciation	3,000
Selling.	30,000
Administrative	15,000
Total fixed expenses	$60,000

Required:

1. How many pairs of stockings must be sold to break even? What does this represent in total dollar sales?

2. Prepare a CVP graph for the store from a zero level of activity up to 90,000 pairs of stockings sold each year. Indicate the break-even point on the graph.

3. How many pairs of stockings must be sold in order to earn a $9,000 target net income for the first year?

4. Ms. Hall now has one full-time and one part-time salesperson working in the store. It will cost her an additional $8,000 per year to convert the part-time position to a full-time position. Ms. Hall believes that the change would bring in an additional $20,000 in sales each year. Should she convert the position? Use the incremental approach (do not prepare an income statement).

5. Refer to the original data. Actual operating results for the first year are as follows:

Sales.	$125,000
Less variable expenses	50,000
Contribution margin	75,000
Less fixed expenses	60,000
Net income	$ 15,000

a. What is the store's degree of operating leverage?

b. Ms. Hall is confident that with some effort she can increase sales by 20 percent next year. What would be the expected percentage increase in net income? Use the operating leverage concept to compute your answer.

P6–17. **Sales mix; commission structure; break-even point.** Larkin Shoes, Inc., manufactures several shoe lines, all of which are sold through the company's own retail outlets. Sales and expenses are accumulated by line for evaluation purposes.

The company has a line of jogging shoes that include two styles, the Regular and the Marathon. The Regular sells for $65 a pair, and the Marathon sells for $80 a pair. Variable expenses associated with each style are given below (in cost per pair of shoes):

	Regular	Marathon
Production expenses*	$18.20	$34.40
Sales commissions (12% of sales price) . . .	7.80	9.60

* Direct materials, direct labor, and variable overhead.

Monthly fixed expenses associated with the jogging shoes are:

Production	$215,000
Advertising	100,000
Insurance	3,000
Administrative salaries . . .	47,000

Salespersons are paid on a commission basis in order to encourage them to be aggressive in their sales efforts. Janet Rogers, the financial vice president, watches sales commissions carefully and has noted that they have risen steadily over the last year. For this reason, she was surprised to find that even though sales have increased, profits from the jogging shoes for the current month—July 19x2—are down substantially from July of the previous year. Sales of jogging shoes, in pairs, for July over the last two years are given below:

	Regular	Marathon	Total
July 19x1	9,000	3,000	12,000
July 19x2	4,000	8,000	12,000

Required: 1. Prepare an income statement for July 19x1 and an income statement for July 19x2. Use the contribution format, with the following headings:

	Regular		Marathon		Total	
	Amount	Percent	Amount	Percent	Amount	Percent
Sales . . .						
Etc. . . .						

2. Explain why net income is lower in July 19x2 than in July 19x1, even though the same *total* number of jogging shoes was sold in each month.

3. What can be done to the sales commissions to optimize the sales mix?

4. Using July 19x1's figures, what was the break-even point (in sales dollars) for jogging shoes for the month?

√ 5. Has July 19x2's break-even point for jogging shoes gone up or down from that of July 19x1? Explain your answer without calculating the break-even point for July 19x2.

P6–18.   **Sensitivity analysis of net income; changes in volume.**   Minden Company's marketing expert, Mr. Rand, believes that the firm can increase sales by 5,000 units for each $2 per unit reduction in selling price. The company's present selling price is $80 per unit, and variable expenses are $50 per unit. Fixed expenses are $600,000 per year. The present sales volume is 30,000 units.

Required: 1.   *a.*   What is the present yearly net income?
            b.   What is the present break-even point in units and in dollar sales?
        2.   *a.*   Assuming that Mr. Rand is correct, what is the *maximum* profit that the firm could generate yearly? At how many units and at what selling price per unit would the firm generate this profit?
            b.   What would be the break-even point in units and in dollar sales using the selling price you have determined above?

P6–19.   **The case of the elusive contribution margin.**   The Shirt Works sells a large variety of tee shirts and sweat shirts. Steve Hooper, the owner, is thinking of expanding his sales by hiring local high school students, on a commission basis, to sell sweat shirts bearing the name and mascot of the local high school.

These sweat shirts would have to be ordered from the manufacturer six weeks in advance, and they could not be returned because of the unique printing required. The sweat shirts would cost Mr. Hooper $8 each with a minimum order of 75 sweat shirts. Any additional sweat shirts would have to be ordered in increments of 75.

Since Mr. Hooper's plan would not require any additional facilities, the only costs associated with the project would be the costs of the sweat shirts and the costs of the sales commissions. The selling price of the sweat shirts would be $13.50 each. Mr. Hooper would pay the students a commission of $1.50 for each shirt sold.

Required: 1.   In order to make the project worthwhile, Mr. Hooper would require a $1,200 profit for the first three months of the venture. What level of sales in units and in dollars would be required to reach this target net income? Show all computations.
        2.   Assume that the venture is undertaken and an order is placed for 75 sweat shirts. What would be Mr. Hooper's break-even point in units and in sales dollars? Show computations, and explain the reasoning behind your answer.

P6–20.   **Sales mix; break-even analysis.**   Topper Sports, Inc., produces high-quality sports equipment. The company's racket division manufactures three tennis rackets—the Standard, the Deluxe, and the Pro—that are widely used in amateur play. Selected information on the rackets is given below:

	Standard	Deluxe	Pro
Selling price per racket	$40.00	$60.00	$90.00
Variable expenses per racket:			
Production	22.00	27.00	31.50
Selling (5% of selling price) . .	2.00	3.00	4.50

All sales are made through the company's own retail outlets. The cost records show that the following fixed costs are assignable to the racket division:

	Per month
Fixed production costs	$120,000
Advertising expense	100,000
Administrative salaries	50,000
Total	$270,000

Sales, in units, over the past two months have been:

	Standard	Deluxe	Pro	Total
April . . .	2,000	1,000	5,000	8,000
May . . .	8,000	1,000	3,000	12,000

Required: 1.   Using the contribution approach, prepare an income statement for April and an income statement for May, with the following headings:

	Total		Standard		Deluxe		Pro	
	Amount	Percent	Amount	Percent	Amount	Percent	Amount	Percent
Sales . . .								
Etc. . . .								

Place the fixed expenses only in the total column. Do not show percentages for the fixed expenses.

2.   Upon seeing the income statements in (1), the president stated, "I can't believe this! We sold 50 percent more rackets in May than in April, yet profits went down. It's obvious that costs are out of control in that division." What other explanation can you give for the drop in net income?

3.   Compute the racket division's break-even point in dollars for the month of April.

4.   Has May's break-even point in dollars gone up or down from April's break-even point? Explain without computing a break-even point for May.

5.   Assume that sales of the Standard racket increase by $20,000. What would be the effect on net income? What would be the effect if Pro racket sales increased by $20,000? Do not prepare income statements; use the incremental analysis approach in determining your answer.

P6–21.   **Changing levels of fixed and variable costs.**   Neptune Company produces toys and other items for use in beach and resort areas. A small, inflatable toy has come onto the market that the company is anxious to produce and sell. Enough capacity exists in the company's plant to produce 16,000 units of the toy each month. Variable costs to manufacture and sell one unit would be $1.25, and fixed costs associated with the toy would total $35,000 per month.

The company's marketing department predicts that demand for the new toy will exceed the 16,000 units that the company is able to produce. Additional manufacturing space can be rented from another company at a fixed cost of $1,000 per month. Variable costs in the rented facility would total $1.40 per unit, due to somewhat less efficient operations than in the main plant. The new toy will sell for $3 per unit.

Required: 1.   Compute the monthly break-even point for the new toy in units and in total dollar sales. Show all computations in good form.

2.   How many units must be sold each month in order to make a monthly profit of $12,000?

3.   If the sales manager receives a bonus of 10 cents for each unit sold in excess of the break-even point, how many units must be sold each month in order to earn a return of 25 percent on the monthly investment in fixed costs?

P6–22.   **Changes in cost structure.**   Morton Company's income statement for last month is given below:

Sales (15,000 units × $30)	$450,000
Less variable expenses	315,000
Contribution margin	135,000
Less fixed expenses	90,000
Net income	$ 45,000

The industry in which Morton Company operates is quite sensitive to cyclical movements in the economy. Thus, profits vary considerably from year to year according to general economic conditions. The company has a large amount of unused capacity and is studying ways of improving profits.

Required: 1.   New equipment has come onto the market that would allow Morton Company to automate a portion of its operations. Variable costs would be reduced by $9 per unit. However, fixed costs would increase to a total of $225,000 each month. Prepare two contribution-type income statements, one showing present operations and one showing how operations would appear if the new equipment is purchased. Show an amount column, a per unit column, and a percent column on each statement. Do not show percentages for the fixed costs.

2.   Refer to the income statements in (1) above. For both present operations and the proposed new operations, compute *(a)* the degree of operating leverage, *(b)* the break-even point in dollars, and *(c)* the margin of safety in both dollar and percentage terms.

3.   Refer again to the data in (1) above. As a manager, what factor would be paramount in your mind in deciding whether to purchase the new equipment? (You may assume that ample funds are available to make the purchase.)

4.   Refer to the original data. Rather than purchase new equipment, the president is thinking about changing the company's marketing method. Under the new method, sales would increase by 20 percent each month and net income would increase by one third. Fixed costs could be slashed to only $48,000 per month. Compute the break-even point for the company after the change in marketing method.

P6–23.   **Break-even analysis with step fixed costs.**   Wymont Hospital operates a general hospital that rents space and beds to separate departments such as pediatrics, maternity, and surgery. Wymont Hospital charges each separate department for common services to its patients such as meals and laundry and for administrative services such as billing and collections. Space and bed rentals are fixed for the year.

For the year ended June 30, 19x7, the pediatrics department at Wymont Hospital charged its patients an average of $65 per day, had a capacity of 60 beds, operated 24 hours per day for 365 days, and had total revenue of $1,138,800.

Expenses charged by the hospital to the pediatrics department for the year were as follows:

	Basis for allocation	
	Patient-days	Bed capacity
Dietary	$ 42,952	
Janitorial.		$ 12,800
Laundry	28,000	
Laboratory	47,800	
Pharmacy	33,800	
Repairs and maintenance	5,200	7,140
General administrative services . . .		131,760
Rent		275,320
Billings and collections.	87,000	
Other	18,048	25,980
	$262,800	$453,000

The only personnel directly employed by the pediatrics department are supervising nurses, nurses, and aides. The hospital has minimum personnel requirements based on total annual patient-days. Hospital requirements, beginning at the minimum expected level of operation, follow:

Annual patient-days	Aides	Nurses	Supervising nurses
10,000–14,000	21	11	4
14,001–17,000	22	12	4
17,001–23,725	22	13	4
23,726–25,550	25	14	5
25,551–27,375	26	14	5
27,376–29,200	29	16	6

These staffing levels represent full-time equivalents, and it should be assumed that the pediatrics department always employs only the minimum number of required full-time equivalent personnel.

Annual salaries for each class of employee are: supervising nurses, $18,000; nurses, $13,000; and aides, $5,000. Salary expense for the year ended June 30, 19x7, was $72,000, $169,000, and $110,000 for supervising nurses, nurses, and aides, respectively.

Required: 1.   Compute the following:

　　　　　a.   The number of patient-days in the pediatrics department for the year ended June 30, 19x7. (Each day a patient is in the hospital is known as a ''patient-day.'')

　　　　　b.   The variable cost per patient-day for the year ended June 30, 19x7.

　　　　　c.   The total fixed costs, including both allocated fixed costs and personnel costs, in the pediatrics department for each level of operation shown above (i.e., total fixed costs at the 10,000–14,000 patient-day level of operation, total fixed costs at the 14,001–17,000 patient-day level of operation, etc.).

2. Using the data computed in (1) and using any other data as needed, compute the *minimum* number of patient-days required for the pediatrics department to break even. You may assume that variable and fixed cost behavior and that revenue per patient-day will remain unchanged in the future.
3. Determine the minimum number of patient-days required for the pediatrics department to earn an annual profit of $80,000.

(CPA, Heavily Adapted)

P6–24.   Missing data; integration of CVP factors.   You were employed just this morning by Pyrrhic Company, a prominent and rapidly growing organization. As your initial assignment, you were asked to complete an analysis of one of the company's products for the Board of Directors meeting later in the day. After completing the analysis, you left your office for a few moments only to discover on returning that a broken sprinkler in the ceiling had destroyed most of your work. Only the following bits remained:

PYRRHIC COMPANY
Actual Income Statement
For the Month Ended June 30, 19x1

	Total	Per unit	Percent
Sales (? units)	$?	$?	100%
Less variable expenses . . .	?	?	?
Contribution margin	?	$?	? %
Less fixed expenses	?		
Net income	$?		

Break-even point:
   In units . . . .   ? units
   In dollars. $180,000

Margin of safety:
   In dollars. . . . . $?
   In percentage. 20%

Degree of operating leverage . . .   ?

The computations above are all based on actual results for June 19x1. The company's *projected* income statement for this product for July 19x1 follows:

PYRRHIC COMPANY
Projected Income Statement
For the Month Ended July 31, 19x1

	Total	Per unit	Percent
Sales (33,000 units)	$?	$?	? %
Less variable expenses . . .	?	?	?
Contribution margin	?	$?	? %
Less fixed expenses	?		
Net income	$40,500		

To add to your woes, the computer is down so no data are available from that source. You do remember that sales for July are projected to increase by 10 percent over sales for June. You also remember that June's net income was $27,000—the same amount as your annual salary from the company. Finally, you remember that the degree of operating leverage is highly useful to the manager as a predictive tool.

Total fixed expenses, the unit selling price, and the unit variable expenses are planned to be the same in July as they were in June.

The Board meets in just one hour.

Required:

1. For the June 19x1 data, do the following:
   a. Complete the June 19x1 income statement (all three columns).
   b. Compute the break-even point in units, and prove the break-even point in dollars. Use the unit contribution method.
   c. Compute the margin of safety in dollars, and prove the margin of safety percentage.
   d. Compute the degree of operating leverage as of June 30, 19x1.
2. For the July 19x1 data, do the following:
   a. Complete the July 19x1 projected income statement (all three columns).
   b. Compute the margin of safety in dollars and percent, and compute the degree of operating leverage. Why has the margin of safety gone up and the degree of operating leverage gone down?
3. Brimming with confidence after having completed (1) and (2) in less than one hour, you decide to give the Board some added data. You know that direct labor accounts for $1.80 of the company's per unit variable expenses. You have learned that direct labor costs may increase by one third next year. Assuming that this cost increase takes place and that selling price and other cost factors remain unchanged, how many units will the company have to sell in a month to earn a net income equal to 20 percent of sales?

CASES

C6–25. **Detailed income statement; CVP sensitivity analysis.**   The most recent income statement for Whitney Company appears below:

WHITNEY COMPANY
Income Statement
For the Year Ended December 31, 19x8

Sales (45,000 units at $10)			$450,000
Less cost of goods sold:			
Direct materials		$ 90,000	
Direct labor		78,300	
Manufacturing overhead		98,500	266,800
Gross margin			183,200
Less operating expenses:			
Selling expenses:			
Variable:			
Sales commissions	$27,000		
Shipping	5,400	32,400	
Fixed (advertising, salaries)		120,000	
Administrative:			
Variable (billing and other)		1,800	
Fixed (salaries and other)		48,000	202,200
Net loss			$ (19,000)

All variable expenses in the company vary in terms of units sold, except for sales commissions, which are based on sales dollars. Variable manufacturing overhead is 30 cents per unit. Whitney Company's plant has a capacity of 75,000 units per year.

The company has been operating at a loss for several years. Management is studying several possible courses of action to determine what should be done to make 19x9 profitable.

Required:

1. Redo Whitney Company's 19x8 income statement in the contribution format. Show both a total column and a per unit column on your statement. Leave enough space to the right of your numbers to enter the solution to both parts of (2).

2. The president is considering two proposals prepared by members of his staff:

   a. For next year, the vice president would like to reduce the unit selling price by 20 percent. She is certain that this would fill the plant to capacity.

   b. For next year, the sales manager would like to increase the unit selling price by 20 percent, increase the sales commission to 9 percent of sales, and increase advertising by $100,000. Based on marketing studies, he is confident that this would increase unit sales by one third.

   Prepare two contribution income statements, one showing what profits would be under the vice president's proposal and one showing what profits would be under the sales manager's proposal. On each statement, include both total and per unit columns (do not show per unit data for the fixed costs).

3. Refer to the original data. The president believes it would be a mistake to change the unit selling price. Instead, he wants to use less costly materials in manufacturing units of product, thereby reducing unit costs by 70 cents. How many units would have to be sold next year to earn a target profit of $30,200?

4. Refer to the original data. Whitney Company's board of directors believes that the company's problem lies in inadequate promotion. By how much can advertising be increased and still allow the company to earn a target return of 4.5 percent on sales of 60,000 units?

5. Refer to the original data. The company has been approached by an overseas distributor who wants to purchase 9,500 units on a special price basis. There would be no sales commission on these units. However, shipping costs would be increased by 50 percent, and variable administrative costs would be reduced by 25 percent. In addition, a $5,700 special insurance fee would have to be paid by Whitney Company to protect the goods in transit. What unit price would have to be quoted on the 9,500 units by Whitney Company to allow the company to earn a profit of $14,250 on total operations? Regular business would not be disturbed by this special order.

C6–26.   Cost structure; break even; target profits.   Pittman Company is a small but growing manufacturer of telecommunications equipment. The company has no sales force of its own; rather, it relies completely on independent sales agents to market its products. These agents are paid a commission of 15 percent of selling price for all items sold.

Barbara Cheney, Pittman's controller, has just prepared the company's budgeted income statement for next year. The statement follows:

PITTMAN COMPANY
Budgeted Income Statement
For the Year Ended December 31, 19x6

Sales		$16,000,000
Manufacturing costs:		
Variable	$7,200,000	
Fixed overhead	2,340,000	9,540,000
Gross margin		6,460,000
Selling and administrative costs:		
Commissions to agents	2,400,000	
Fixed marketing costs	120,000*	
Fixed administrative costs	1,800,000	4,320,000
Net operating income		2,140,000
Less fixed interest cost		540,000
Income before income taxes		1,600,000
Less income taxes (30%)		480,000
Net income		$ 1,120,000

* Primarily depreciation on storage facilities.

As Barbara handed the statement to Karl Vecci, Pittman's president, she commented, "I went ahead and used the agents' 15 percent commission rate in completing these statements, but we've just learned that they refuse to handle our products next year unless we increase the commission rate to 20 percent."

"That's the last straw," angrily replied Frank. "Those agents have been demanding more and more, and this time they've gone too far. How can they possibly defend a 20 percent commission rate?"

"They claim that after paying for advertising, travel, and the other costs of promotion, there's nothing left over for profit," replied Barbara.

"I say it's just plain robbery," retorted Karl. "And I also say it's time we dumped those guys and got our own sales force. Can you get your people to work up some cost figures for us to look at?"

"We've already worked them up," said Barbara. "Several companies we know about pay a 7.5 percent commission to their own salespeople, along with a small salary. Of course, we would have to handle all promotion costs, too. We figure our fixed costs would increase by $2,400,000 per year, but that would be more than offset by the $3,200,000 (20% × $16,000,000) that we would avoid on agents' commissions."

The breakdown of the $2,400,000 cost figure follows:

Salaries:	
Sales manager	$ 100,000
Salespersons	600,000
Travel and entertainment . . .	400,000
Advertising	1,300,000
Total	$2,400,000

"Super," replied Karl. "And I note that the $2,400,000 is just what we're paying the agents under the old 15 percent commission rate."

"It's even better than that," explained Barbara. "We can actually save $75,000 a year, because that's what we're having to pay the auditing firm now to check out the agents' reports. So our overall administrative costs would be less."

"Pull all of these numbers together and we'll show them to the executive committee tomorrow," said Karl. "With the approval of the committee, we can move on the matter immediately."

Required:

1. Compute Pittman Company's break-even point in sales dollars for 19x6, assuming:
   - *a.* That the agents' commission rate remains unchanged at 15 percent.
   - *b.* That the agents' commission rate is increased to 20 percent.
   - *c.* That the company employs its own sales force.
2. Assume that Pittman Company decides to continue selling through agents and pays the 20 percent commission rate. Determine the volume of sales that would be required to generate the same net income as contained in the budgeted income statement for 19x6.
3. Determine the volume of sales at which net income would be equal regardless of whether Pittman Company sells through agents (at a 20 percent commission rate) or employs its own sales force.
4. Compute the degree of operating leverage that the company would expect to have on December 31, 19x6, assuming:
   - *a.* That the agents' commission rate remains unchanged at 15 percent.
   - *b.* That the agents' commission rate is increased to 20 percent.
   - *c.* That the company employs its own sales force.

   Use income *before* income taxes in your operating leverage computation.
5. Based on the data in (1) through (4) above, make a recommendation as to whether the company should continue to use sales agents (at a 20 percent commission rate) or employ its own sales force. Give reasons for your answer.

(CMA, Heavily Adapted)

CHAPTER 7

Segmented Reporting and the Contribution Approach to Costing

LEARNING OBJECTIVES
After studying Chapter 7, you should be able to:

- Explain how costs are allocated to segments of an organization when the contribution approach is used.

- Differentiate between traceable fixed costs and common fixed costs.

- Compute the segment margin and explain how it differs from the contribution margin.

- Prepare a segmented income statement using the contribution approach.

- Explain how direct costing differs from absorption costing and compute the cost of a unit of product under each method.

- Describe how fixed overhead costs are deferred in inventory and released from inventory under absorption costing.

- Prepare income statements using both absorption costing and direct costing and reconcile the two net income figures.

- Define or explain the key terms listed at the end of the chapter.

O ne aspect of the accountant's work centers on the problem of assigning costs to various parts of an organization. Cost assignment is necessary to provide useful and relevant data for three purposes:

1.   For product costing and for pricing.
2.   For appraisal of managerial performance.
3.   For making special decisions.

In assigning costs for these purposes, the accountant can use either of two approaches. One approach, known as absorption costing, was discussed at length in Chapter 3. The other, generally called the contribution approach to costing, was introduced in the preceding chapter in conjunction with our discussion of cost-volume-profit (CVP) analysis. The purpose of this chapter is to study the contribution approach in greater depth. We have already seen how it can be used in making a variety of special decisions. We shall now see how it can be used in preparing segmented statements for management's use, and how the cost of a unit of product or the cost of a service is computed under this costing method.

SEGMENTED REPORTING

To operate effectively, managers must have a great deal more information available to them than the information provided by a single, companywide income statement. The reason is that such a statement usually provides only a summary of overall operations; as such, it typically does not contain enough detail to allow the manager to detect problems that may exist in the organization. For example, some product lines may be profitable while others may be unprofitable; some salespersons may be more effective than others; some sales territories may have a poor sales mix or may be overlooking sales opportunities; or some producing divisions may be ineffectively using their capacity and/or resources. To uncover problems such as these, the manager needs not just one but several income statements, and these statements must be designed to focus on the *segments* of the company. The preparation of income statements of this type is known as **segmented reporting.**

A **segment** can be defined as any part or activity of an organization about which a manager seeks cost or revenue data. Examples of segments would include sales territories, individual stores or other retail outlets, service centers, manufacturing divisions or plants, sales departments, and individual product lines. How does the manager prepare income statements that show the results of segment activities? As illustrated in the pages that follow, such statements are generally prepared using the contribution approach with which we are already familiar. Statements prepared in this format are indispensable to the manager in analyzing the parts of an organization as well as operations for the company as a whole.

Differing Levels of Segmented Statements

Segmented statements can be prepared for activity at many different levels in an organization and in differing formats. Exhibit 7–1 illustrates three levels of segmented statements, presented in a format that is widely used. Observe from this exhibit that the total company is first segmented in terms of divisions. Then one of these divisions, Division 2, is further segmented in terms of the product lines sold within the division. In turn, one of these product lines, the regular model, is further segmented in terms of the territories in which it is sold.

Notice that as we go from one segmented statement to another, we are looking at smaller and smaller pieces of the company. This is a widely used approach to segmented reporting. If management desired, Division 1 could also be segmented into smaller pieces in the same way as we have segmented Division 2, thereby providing a detailed look at all aspects and levels of the company's operations.

The benefits accruing to the manager from a series of statements such as those contained in Exhibit 7–1 are very great. By carefully examining trends and results in each segment, the manager will be able to gain considerable insight into the company as a whole, and perhaps will discover opportunities and courses of action that would otherwise have remained hidden from view.

Assigning Costs to Segments

Segmented statements for internal use are typically prepared in the contribution format, as stated earlier. The same costing guidelines are used in preparing these statements as are used in preparing contribution-type statements generally, with one exception. This lies in the handling of the fixed costs. Notice from Exhibit 7–1 that the fixed costs are divided into two parts on a segmented statement—one part labeled *traceable* and the other part labeled *common*. Only those fixed costs labeled traceable are charged to the various segments. If a fixed cost is not traceable directly to some segment, then it is treated as a common cost and kept separate from the segments themselves. Thus, under the contribution approach, a cost is never arbitrarily assigned to a segment of an organization.

In sum, two guidelines are followed in assigning costs to the various segments of a company under the contribution approach:

1. First, according to cost behavior patterns (that is, variable and fixed).
2. Second, according to whether the costs are *directly traceable* to the segments involved.

We will now consider various parts of Exhibit 7–1 in greater depth.

EXHIBIT 7–1

Segmented income statements

Segments defined as divisions

		Segments	
	Total company	Division 1	Division 2
Sales	$500,000	$300,000	$200,000
Less variable expenses:			
Variable cost of goods sold	180,000	120,000	60,000
Other variable expenses	50,000	30,000	20,000
Total variable expenses.	230,000	150,000	80,000
Contribution margin	270,000	150,000	120,000
Less traceable fixed expenses.	170,000	90,000	80,000*
Divisional segment margin	100,000	$ 60,000	$ 40,000
Less common fixed expenses	25,000		
Net income	$ 75,000		

Segments defined as product lines of Division 2

		Segments	
	Division 2	Deluxe model	Regular model
Sales	$200,000	$75,000	$125,000
Less variable expenses:			
Variable cost of goods sold	60,000	20,000	40,000
Other variable expenses	20,000	5,000	15,000
Total variable expenses.	80,000	25,000	55,000
Contribution margin	120,000	50,000	70,000
Less traceable fixed expenses.	70,000	30,000	40,000
Product line segment margin	50,000	$20,000	$ 30,000
Less common fixed expenses	10,000		
Divisional segment margin	$ 40,000		

Segments defined as sales territories for one product line of Division 2

		Segments	
	Regular model	Home sales	Foreign sales
Sales	$125,000	$100,000	$25,000
Less variable expenses:			
Variable cost of goods sold.	40,000	32,000	8,000
Other variable expenses	15,000	5,000	10,000
Total variable expenses	55,000	37,000	18,000
Contribution margin	70,000	63,000	7,000
Less traceable fixed expenses	25,000	15,000	10,000
Territorial segment margin	45,000	$ 48,000	$ (3,000)
Less common fixed expenses	15,000		
Product line segment margin	$ 30,000		

*Notice that this $80,000 in traceable fixed expense is divided into two parts—$70,000 traceable and $10,000 common—when Division 2 is broken down into product lines. The reasons for this are discussed in a later section, "Traceable costs can become common."

Sales and Contribution Margin

In order to prepare segmented statements, it is necessary to keep records of sales by individual segment, as well as in total for the organization. After deducting related variable expenses, a contribution margin figure can then be computed for each segment, as illustrated in Exhibit 7–1.

Recall from the prior chapter that the contribution margin is an extremely useful piece of data to the manager—particularly for determining the effect on net income of increases and decreases in sales volume. If sales volume goes up or down, the impact on net income can easily be computed by simply multiplying the unit contribution margin figure by the change in units sold or by multiplying the change in sales dollars by the C/M ratio. Segmented statements give the manager the ability to make such computations on a product-by-product, division-by-division, or territory-by-territory basis, thereby providing the information needed to shore up areas of weakness or to capitalize on areas of strength.

It is important to keep in mind that *the contribution margin is basically a short-run planning tool.* As such, it is especially valuable in decisions relating to temporary uses of capacity, to special orders, and to short-run product line promotion. Decisions relating to the short run usually involve only variable costs and revenues, which of course are the very elements involved in contribution margin. By carefully monitoring segment contribution margins and segment contribution margin ratios, the manager will be in a position to make those short-run decisions that will maximize the contribution of each segment to the overall profitability of the organization.

The Importance of Fixed Costs

The emphasis that we place on the usefulness of the contribution margin should not be taken as a suggestion that fixed costs are not important. *Fixed costs are very important in any organization.* What the contribution approach does imply is that *different costs are needed for different purposes.* For one purpose, variable costs and revenues alone may be adequate for a manager's needs; for another purpose, his or her needs may encompass the fixed costs as well.

The breaking apart of fixed and variable costs also emphasizes to management that the costs are controlled differently and that these differences must be kept clearly in mind for both short-run and long-run planning. Moreover, the grouping of fixed costs under the contribution approach highlights the fact that net income emerges only after the fixed costs have been covered. It also highlights the fact that after the fixed costs have been covered, net income will increase to the extent of the contribution margin generated on each additional unit sold. All of these concepts are useful to the manager *internally* for planning purposes.

Traceable and Common Fixed Costs

Traceable fixed costs can be defined as those fixed costs that can be identified with a particular segment and that arise because of the existence of the segment. **Common fixed costs** can be defined as those fixed costs that cannot be identified with any particular segment but rather arise because of overall operating activities. In order to be assigned to segments, a common fixed cost would have to be allocated on some highly arbitrary basis, such as sales dollars. Common costs are also known as *indirect costs*.

Examples of traceable fixed costs would include advertising outlays made in behalf of a particular segment, the salary of a segment manager (such as a product line supervisor), and depreciation of buildings and equipment acquired for use in a particular segment. Examples of common fixed costs would include corporate image advertising (from which many segments may benefit), salaries of top administrative officers, and depreciation of facilities shared by more than one segment.

Identifying Traceable Fixed Costs

The distinction that we have drawn between traceable and common fixed costs is crucial in segmented reporting, since traceable fixed costs are charged to the segments, whereas common fixed costs are not, as mentioned earlier. As the reader may suppose, in an actual situation it is sometimes hard to determine whether a cost should be classified as traceable or common. One widely used rule of thumb is to treat as traceable costs *only those costs that would disappear over time if the segment itself disappeared.* For example, if Division 1 in Exhibit 7–1 were discontinued, then it is unlikely that the division manager would be retained. Since she would disappear with her division, then her salary should be classified as a traceable fixed cost of the division. On the other hand, the president of the company undoubtedly would continue even if Division 1 were dropped. Therefore, his salary is common to both divisions. The same idea can be expressed in another way: *treat as traceable costs only those costs that are added as a result of the creation of a segment.*

There will always be some costs that fall between the traceable and common categories, and considerable care and good judgment will be required for their proper classification. The important point is to resist the temptation to allocate arbitrarily. From a managerial point of view, *any arbitrary allocation of common costs would simply destroy the value of the segment margin as a guide to long-run segment profitability.*

Traceable Costs Can Become Common

Fixed costs that are traceable on one segmented statement may become common if the company is divided into smaller segments. This is because there are limits to how finely a cost can be separated without resorting to arbitrary allocation. The more finely segments are defined, the more costs there are that become common.

This concept can be seen from the diagram below. Notice from the diagram that when segments are defined as divisions, Division 2 has $80,000 in traceable fixed expenses. Only $70,000 of this amount remains traceable, however, when we narrow our definition of a segment from divisions to that of the product lines within Division 2. Notice that the other $10,000 then becomes a common cost of these product lines.

	Total company	**Segments**	
		Division 1	**Division 2**
Contribution margin	$270,000	$150,000	$120,000
Less traceable fixed expenses	170,000	90,000	80,000

	Division 2	**Segments**	
		Deluxe model	**Regular model**
Contribution margin	$120,000	$50,000	$70,000
Less traceable fixed expenses	70,000	30,000	40,000
Product line segment margin	50,000	$20,000	$30,000
Less common fixed expenses	10,000		
Divisional segment margin	$ 40,000		

Why would $10,000 of traceable fixed costs become common costs when the division is divided into product lines? The $10,000 could be depreciation on Division 2's plant building. This depreciation would be a *traceable* cost when we are speaking of the division as a whole, but it would be *common* to the product lines produced within the building because both lines would share in the building's use. Any allocation of the depreciation between the two product lines would have to be on some arbitrary basis. To avoid this, we would treat the depreciation on the building as a common cost when Division 2 is segmented into product lines.

The $70,000 that remains a traceable fixed cost even after the division is segmented into product lines would consist of amounts that can be identified directly with the product lines on a nonarbitrary basis. This $70,000 might consist of advertising, for example, expended for product line promotion, of which $30,000 was expended for promotion of the deluxe model and $40,000 was expended for promotion of the regular model. Product line advertising would be a traceable fixed cost of the division as a whole, and it would still be a traceable cost when looking only at the product lines within the division, since it could be assigned to the lines without the necessity of making an arbitrary allocation.

Segment Margin

Observe from Exhibit 7–1 that the **segment margin** is obtained by deducting the traceable fixed costs of a segment from the segment's contribution margin. It represents the margin available after a segment has covered all of its own costs that can be applied toward the organization's common costs and then toward profits. *The segment margin is viewed as being the best gauge of the long-run profitability of a segment,* since only those costs that are assignable to the segment are used in its computation. If in the long run a segment can't cover its own costs, then that segment probably should not be retained (unless it is essential to sales in other segments). Notice from Exhibit 7–1, for example, that one sales territory (foreign) has a negative segment margin. This means that the segment is not covering its own costs and thus is not contributing to the overall profits of the company. In fact, it is detracting from profits in that its loss must be covered by other segments.[1]

From a decision-making point of view, the segment margin is most useful in those decisions relating to long-run needs and performance, such as capacity changes, long-run pricing policy, and segment return on investment. By contrast, as we noted earlier, the contribution margin is most useful in decisions relating to the short run, such as pricing of special orders and utilization of existing capacity through short-term promotional campaigns.

To emphasize these ideas, refer to the data in Exhibit 7–2. Here we have an income statement segmented by products. Notice that all three products are covering their own costs and thus have positive segment margins.

Which is the company's best product? The answer depends on your point of reference. In terms of *long-run performance,* product B is the company's best product. Note that it is generating a $15,000 segment margin each period, which by itself is adequate to cover all of the company's common fixed costs. Product B's segment margin ratio is also very high (30 percent), which indicates that its overall costs are low in relation to sales. Thus, as shown by its segment margin data, product B represents the company's best product in terms of long-run performance.

In terms of *short-run* promotional campaigns or *short-run* capacity utilization, however, management might prefer product A over product B. The reason is that product A has a higher contribution margin ratio. Note that product A's C/M ratio is 70 percent as compared to only 50 percent for product B. Thus, product A will generate a greater amount of contribution

---

[1] Retention or elimination of product lines and other segments is covered in depth in Chapter 13.

EXHIBIT 7–2

Income statement segmented by products

	Total company		Products					
			A		B		C	
Sales	$100,000	100%	$30,000	100%	$50,000	100%	$20,000	100%
Less variable expenses	46,000	46	9,000	30	25,000	50	12,000	60
Contribution margin	54,000	54	21,000	70	25,000	50	8,000	40
Less traceable fixed expenses	30,000	30	15,000	50	10,000	20	5,000	25
Product segment margin	24,000	24	$ 6,000	20%	$15,000	30%	$ 3,000	15%
Less common fixed expenses.	15,000	15						
Net income.	$ 9,000	9%						

(margin annotations: "Short run" pointing to Contribution margin; "long run" pointing to Product segment margin)

margin for a given increase in sales. As we learned in Chapter 6, the greater the amount of contribution margin that a company is able to generate, the more quickly it will cover its fixed costs or increase its profits.

Of course, in making short-run decisions of this type, management must consider other factors as well, such as available capacity, the degree of market saturation, and the amount of sales that can be generated per dollar of advertising. But other factors equal, in short-run promotional decisions or in capacity utilization decisions, management will focus on those products that will generate the greatest amount of contribution margin toward the covering of fixed costs.

To summarize, in evaluating the long-run performance of a segment, the manager will look at the segment margin and at the segment margin ratio. In short-run decision making, however (such as a two-week promotional campaign), the manager will look for the segments that will generate the greatest amount of contribution margin for the effort expended. Typically, this will be the segments that have the highest C/M ratios.

Breakdown of Traceable Fixed Costs

In preparing segmented income statements, some managers like to separate the traceable fixed costs into two classes—discretionary and committed. As discussed in Chapter 5, discretionary fixed costs are under the immediate control of the manager, whereas committed fixed costs are not. Therefore, a breakdown of the traceable fixed costs into these two classes *allows a company to make a distinction between the performance of the segment manager and the performance of the segment as a long-term investment.*

In some situations, this distinction in performance can be very important. A top-flight manager, for example, may be assigned to a division that has an antiquated plant or that is saddled with other committed fixed costs that are beyond the segment manager's control. Under these conditions, it would be unfair to judge the segment manager's performance simply on a basis of the overall margin generated by the segment. Rather, in these circumstances, the discretionary fixed costs should be separated from the committed fixed costs and deducted as a separate group from the segment's contribution margin. The amount remaining after deducting the discretionary fixed costs, sometimes called a ''segment performance margin,'' should then be used as a basis for evaluating the segment manager's performance. This would be a valid measure of performance, since the amount involved would represent the margin generated by the segment after deducting all costs controllable by the segment manager. The committed fixed costs would then be deducted from the ''segment performance margin'' to determine the overall segment margin for the period.

The traceable costs of a segment can be broken down in still other ways. However, the discussion above is adequate for our purposes. Any further discussion, as well as numerical examples, is reserved for more advanced texts.

Common Fixed Costs

Common fixed costs are not allocated to segments but simply deducted in total amount to arrive at the net income for the company as a whole.[2] (See Exhibits 7–1 and 7–2.) The managerial accountant contends that nothing is added to the overall usefulness of a segmented statement by allocating the common costs among segments. Rather, the accountant would argue that such allocations tend to *reduce* the usefulness of segmented statements. The reason is that arbitrary allocations draw attention away from those costs that are traceable to a segment and that should form a basis for appraising performance.

Moreover, it is argued that any attempt to allocate common fixed costs among segments may result in misleading data or may obscure important relationships between segment revenues and segment earnings. Backer and McFarland state the problem as follows:

> A characteristic of all arbitrary allocations is that they lack universality. Sooner or later circumstances arise in which allocation procedures break down and yield misleading or even absurd results.[3]

Backer and McFarland point out that arbitrary allocations of common fixed costs often result in a segment *appearing* to be unprofitable, whereas it may be contributing substantially above its own traceable costs toward the overall profitability of the firm. In such cases, the allocated costs may

---

[2] For external reporting purposes, the Financial Accounting Standards Board requires that all common costs be allocated among segments on a ''reasonable'' basis. FASB, *Statement of Financial Accounting Standards No. 14*, ''Financial Reporting for Segments of a Business Enterprise'' (Stamford, Conn., 1976), par. 10(d).

[3] Morton Backer and Walter B. McFarland, *External Reporting for Segments of a Business* (New York: National Association of Accountants, 1968), p. 23.

lead to the unwise elimination of a segment and to a *decrease* in profits for the company as a whole.

Varying Breakdowns of Total Sales

In order to obtain more detailed information, a company may show total sales broken down into several different segment arrangements. For example, a company may show total sales segmented in three different ways: (1) segmented according to divisions; (2) segmented according to product lines, without regard to the divisions in which the products are sold; and (3) segmented according to the sales territories in which the sales were made. In each case, the sum of the sales by segments would add up to total company sales; the variation in segment arrangements would simply give management the power to look at the total company from several different directions. This type of segmented reporting provides much the same perspective as looking at a beautiful landscape from several different views—from each view you see something you didn't see before.

After this type of segmentation of total sales has been made, many companies then go ahead and break each segment down more finely, such as we illustrated earlier in Exhibit 7–1 and such as is illustrated graphically in Exhibit 7–3. With the availability of the computer, the type of segmentation that we describe here is well within the reach of most companies today.

To illustrate how total sales can be divided into more than one segment arrangement, assume that Fairfield Company sells two products, X and Y, in two sales territories, the East and the West. Cost and revenue data on the products and the sales territories follow:

1. Selling price, variable expenses, and contribution margin per unit:

	Products	
	X	Y
Selling price per unit	$10	$6
Variable expense per unit	6	4
Contribution margin per unit	$ 4	$2

2. Sales in units during 19x1 were:

	Sales territory		Total sales
	East	West	
Product X sales	3,000	7,000	10,000
Product Y sales	6,000	9,000	15,000

EXHIBIT 7–3

Graphic presentation of segmented reporting—the Detroit Motor Company

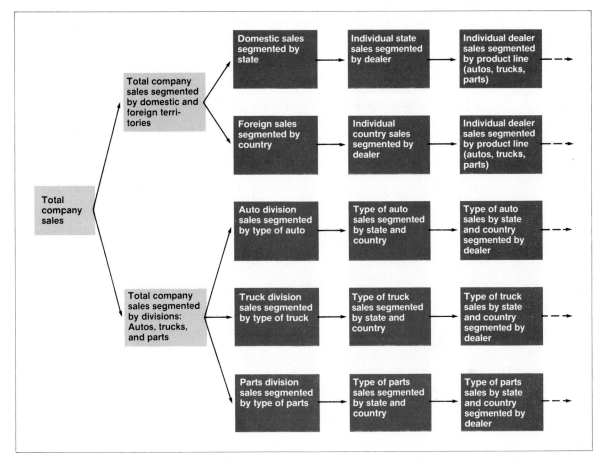

3.   Fixed costs incurred during 19x1 were:

	Products		Sales territory	
	X	**Y**	**East**	**West**
Fixed production costs	$8,000	$6,000	—	—
Fixed selling costs	—	—	$12,000	$10,000
Fixed administrative costs	2,000	1,500	2,200	2,300

In addition, the company had $9,000 in fixed general administrative costs during 19x1 that cannot be charged directly to any segment.

Exhibit 7–4 presents total sales for the company for 19x1, broken down first between products and then between sales territories. Notice from the

EXHIBIT 7–4

Total sales segmented by products and by sales territories

Total Sales Presented by Products

	Total company	Products X	Products Y
Sales	$190,000	$100,000	$90,000
Less variable expenses	120,000	60,000	60,000
Contribution margin	70,000	40,000	30,000
Less traceable fixed expenses:			
Production	14,000	8,000	6,000
Administration—products	3,500	2,000	1,500
Total traceable fixed expenses	17,500	10,000	7,500
Product segment margin	52,500	$ 30,000	$22,500
Less common fixed expenses:			
Selling—sales territories	22,000		
Administration—sales territories	4,500		
General administration	9,000		
Total common fixed expenses.	35,500		
Net income	$ 17,000		

Total Sales Presented by Sales Territories

	Total company	Sales territory East	Sales territory West
Sales	$190,000	$66,000*	$124,000*
Less variable expenses	120,000	42,000[†]	78,000[†]
Contribution margin	70,000	24,000	46,000
Less traceable fixed expenses:			
Selling—sales territories	22,000	12,000	10,000
Administration—sales territories	4,500	2,200	2,300
Total traceable fixed expenses	26,500	14,200	12,300
Territorial segment margin	43,500	$ 9,800	$ 33,700
Less common fixed expenses:			
Production	14,000		
Administration—products	3,500		
General administration	9,000		
Total common fixed expenses.	26,500		
Net income	$ 17,000		

	Total company	Sales territory East	Sales territory West
* Sales by sales territories:			
Product X sales at $10 per unit	$100,000	$30,000	$ 70,000
Product Y sales at $6 per unit	90,000	36,000	54,000
Total sales, as above	$190,000	$66,000	$124,000
[†] Variable expenses by sales territories:			
Product X variable expenses, at $6 per unit	$ 60,000	$18,000	$ 42,000
Product Y variable expenses, at $4 per unit	60,000	24,000	36,000
Total variable expenses, as above	$120,000	$42,000	$ 78,000

exhibit that although the products are about equally profitable, this equality does not carry over to the sales territories. The West is much more profitable than the East. Thus, the segmented statements point out to management those areas that may be in need of attention.

In summary, segmented reporting gives a company the ability to look at itself from many different directions. Some of the ways in which cost and profitability data can be generated include:

1. By division.
2. By company.
3. By store or other retail outlet.
4. By service center.
5. By product or product line.
6. By salesperson.
7. By sales territory.
8. By region of the country.
9. By domestic and foreign operations.

As we have noted, each of these segments can in turn be broken down into many parts. Indeed, the number of possible directions in which segments can be defined is limited only by one's imagination or by the needs of the firm.

INVENTORY VALUATION UNDER THE CONTRIBUTION APPROACH— DIRECT COSTING

As discussed in Chapter 3, absorption costing allocates a portion of fixed manufacturing overhead to each unit produced during a period, along with variable manufacturing costs. Since absorption costing mingles variable and fixed costs together, units of product costed by that method are not well suited for inclusion in a contribution-type income statement. This has led to an alternative costing method that focuses on cost behavior in computing unit costs. This alternative method is called *direct costing*. It harmonizes fully with the contribution approach and is widely used by manufacturing companies and other organizations in their preparation of contribution-type income statements.

Direct Costing

Under **direct costing,** only those costs of production that vary directly with activity are treated as product costs. This would include direct materials, direct labor, and the variable portion of manufacturing overhead. Fixed manufacturing overhead is not treated as a product cost under this method. Rather, fixed manufacturing overhead is treated as a period cost and, like selling and administrative expenses, it is charged off in its entirety against revenue each period. Consequently, the inventory cost of a unit of product under the direct costing method contains no element of fixed overhead cost.

Although it is widely used, the term *direct costing* is really a misnomer. More accurate terms for this costing method would be **variable** or **marginal costing,** since the method centers on the notion that only variable production costs should be added to the cost of goods produced. The term *direct costing* is so firmly embedded in the literature and in everyday usage, however, that it seems unlikely that any change in terminology will be made.

Absorption Costing  (accepted by GAAP).

As we learned in Chapter 3, **absorption costing** treats *all* costs of production as product costs, regardless of whether they are variable or fixed in nature. Thus, unlike direct costing, absorption costing allocates a portion of the fixed manufacturing overhead to each unit of product, along with the variable manufacturing costs. The cost of a unit of product under the absorption costing method therefore consists of direct materials, direct labor, and *both* variable and fixed overhead. Because absorption costing includes all costs of production as product costs, it is frequently referred to as the *full cost* method.

To complete this summary comparison of direct and absorption costing, we need to consider briefly the handling of selling and administrative expenses. These expenses are never treated as product costs, regardless of the costing method in use. Thus, under either direct or absorption costing, selling and administrative expenses are always treated as period costs and deducted from revenues as incurred.

Unit Cost Computations

To illustrate the computation of unit costs under both direct and absorption costing, assume the following data:

The Boley Company produces a single product. The cost characteristics of the product and of the manufacturing plant are given below:

Number of units produced each year	6,000
Variable costs per unit:	
Direct materials	$ 2
Direct labor	4
Variable manufacturing overhead	1
Variable selling and administrative expense	3
Fixed cost per year:	
Manufacturing overhead	30,000
Selling and administrative expense	10,000

Required: 1. Compute the cost of a unit of product under absorption costing.

2. Compute the cost of a unit of product under direct costing.

Solution:

Absorption Costing

Direct materials	$ 2
Direct labor	4
Variable overhead	1
Total variable production cost	7
Fixed overhead ($30,000 ÷ 6,000 units of product) . . .	5
Total cost per unit	$12

Direct Costing

Direct materials	$ 2
Direct labor	4
Variable overhead	1
Total cost per unit	$ 7

(The $30,000 fixed overhead will be charged off in total against income as a period expense along with the fixed selling and administrative expense.)

Under the absorption costing method, notice that *all* production costs, variable and fixed, have been added to the cost of units produced during the period. Thus, if the company sells a unit of product and absorption costing is being used, then $12 (consisting of $7 variable cost and $5 fixed cost) will be deducted on the income statement as cost of goods sold. Similarly, any unsold units will be carried as inventory on the balance sheet at $12 each.

Under the direct costing method, notice that only the variable production costs have been added to the cost of units produced during the period. Thus, if the company sells a unit of product, only $7 will be deducted as cost of goods sold, and unsold units will be carried in the balance sheet inventory account at only $7 each.

The Controversy over Fixed Overhead Cost

Probably no subject in all of managerial accounting has created as much controversy among accountants as has direct costing. The controversy isn't over whether costs should be separated as between variable and fixed in matters relating to planning and control. Rather, the controversy is over the theoretical justification for excluding fixed overhead costs from the cost of units produced and therefore from inventory.

Advocates of direct costing argue that fixed overhead costs relate to the *capacity* to produce rather than to the actual production of units of product in a given year. That is, they argue that costs for facilities and equipment, insurance, supervisory salaries, and the like, represent costs of being *ready* to produce and therefore will be incurred regardless of whether any actual production takes place during the year. For this reason, advocates of direct costing feel that such costs should be charged against the period rather than against the product.

Advocates of absorption costing argue, on the other hand, that so far as product costing is concerned, it makes no difference whether a manufacturing cost is variable or fixed. They argue that fixed overhead costs such as depreciation and insurance are just as essential to the production process as are the variable costs, and therefore cannot be ignored in costing units of product. They argue that to be fully costed, each unit of product must bear an equitable portion of *all* manufacturing costs.

Although this difference in the handling of fixed overhead might seem slight, it can have a substantial impact on both the clarity and the usefulness of statement data, as we shall see in the following sections.

Comparison of Absorption and Direct Costing

Income statements prepared under the absorption and direct costing approaches are shown in Exhibit 7–5. In preparing these statements, we use the data for the Boley Company presented earlier, along with other information about the company as given below:

Beginning inventory in units	–0–
Units produced	6,000
Units sold	5,000
Ending inventory in units.	1,000
Selling price per unit	$ 20
Selling and administrative expenses:	
Variable per unit	$ 3
Fixed per year	10,000

	Absorption costing	Direct costing
Cost of a unit of product:		
Direct materials.	$ 2	$ 2
Direct labor	4	4
Variable overhead	1	1
Fixed overhead ($30,000 ÷ 6,000 units)	5	—
Total cost per unit.	$12	$ 7

Several points can be made from the statements in Exhibit 7–5:

1.   Under the absorption costing method, it is possible to defer a portion of the fixed overhead costs of the current period to future periods through the inventory account (known as **fixed overhead cost deferred in inventory).** This deferral can be explained as follows: During the current period, Boley Company produced 6,000 units but sold only 5,000 units, thus leaving 1,000 units in the ending inventory. Under the absorption costing method, each unit produced was asssigned $5 in fixed overhead cost (see the unit cost computations above). Therefore, each of the 1,000 units going into inventory at the end of the period has $5 in fixed overhead cost attached to it, or a total of $5,000 for the 1,000 units involved. *This amount of fixed overhead cost of the current period has thereby been deferred in inventory to the next period, when, hopefully, these units will be taken out of inventory and sold.* The deferral of fixed overhead cost we are talking

EXHIBIT 7–5

Comparison of direct and absorption costing

Absorption Costing

Sales (5,000 units × $20)			$100,000
Cost of goods sold:			
Beginning inventory		$ –0–	
Cost of goods manufactured			
(6,000 units × $12)		72,000	
Goods available for sale		72,000	
Less ending inventory (1,000 units × $12)		12,000	60,000
Gross margin			40,000
Less selling and administrative expense			
($15,000 total variable plus $10,000 fixed)			25,000
Net income			$ 15,000

> Note the difference in ending inventories. Fixed overhead cost at $5 per unit is included under the absorption approach. This explains the difference in ending inventory and in net income (1,000 units × $5 = $5,000).

Direct Costing

Sales (5,000 units × $20)			$100,000
Less variable expenses:			
Variable cost of goods sold:			
Beginning inventory		$ –0–	
Variable manufacturing costs			
(6,000 units × $7)		42,000	
Goods available for sale		42,000	
Less ending inventory (1,000 units × $7)		7,000	
Variable cost of goods sold		35,000	
Variable selling and administrative expense			
(5,000 units × $3)		15,000	50,000
Contribution margin			50,000
Less fixed costs:			
Fixed overhead costs		30,000	
Fixed selling and administrative expenses		10,000	40,000
Net income			$ 10,000

about can be seen clearly by analyzing the $12,000 ending inventory figure under the absorption costing method:

Variable manufacturing costs: 1,000 units × $7 . . .	$ 7,000
Fixed overhead costs: 1,000 units × $5	5,000
Total inventory value	$12,000

In summary, of the $30,000 in fixed overhead cost incurred during the period, only $25,000 (5,000 units sold × $5) has been included in cost of goods sold. The remaining $5,000 (1,000 units *not* sold × $5) has been deferred in inventory to the next period.

2. Under the direct costing method, the entire $30,000 in fixed overhead cost has been treated as an expense of the current period (see the bottom portion of the direct costing income statement).

3. The ending inventory figure under the direct costing method is $5,000 lower than it is under the absorption costing method. The reason is that under direct costing, only the variable manufacturing costs have been added to units of product and therefore included in inventory:

Variable manufacturing costs: 1,000 units × $7 . . . . <u>$7,000</u>

The $5,000 difference in ending inventories explains the difference in net income reported between the two costing methods. Net income is $5,000 *higher* under absorption costing since, as explained above, $5,000 of fixed overhead cost has been deferred in inventory to the next period under that costing method.

4. The absorption costing income statement makes no distinction between fixed and variable costs; therefore, it is not well suited for CVP computations, which we have emphasized as being important to good planning and control. In order to generate data for CVP analysis, it would be necessary to spend considerable time reworking and reclassifying the absorption statement.

5. The direct costing approach to costing units of product blends very well with the contribution approach to the income statement, since both concepts are based on the idea of classifying costs by behavior. The direct costing data in Exhibit 7–5 could be used immediately in CVP computations.

The Definition of an Asset

Essentially, the difference between the absorption costing method and the direct costing method centers on the matter of timing. Advocates of direct costing say that fixed manufacturing costs should be released against revenues immediately in total, whereas advocates of absorption costing say that fixed manufacturing costs should be released against revenues bit by bit as units of product are sold. Any units of product not sold under absorption costing result in fixed costs being inventoried and carried forward *as assets* to the next period. The solution to the controversy as to which costing method is "right" should therefore rest in large part on whether fixed costs added to inventory fall within the definition of an asset as this concept is generally viewed in accounting theory.

What is an asset?   A cost is normally viewed as being an asset if it can be shown that it has revenue-producing powers, or if it can be shown that it will be beneficial in some way to operations in future periods. In short, a cost is an asset if it can be shown that it has *future service potential* that can be identified. For example, insurance prepayments are viewed as being assets, since they have future service potential. The prepayments acquire protection that can be used in future periods to guard against losses that might otherwise hinder operations. If fixed production costs added to inventory under absorption costing are indeed properly called assets, then they too must meet this test of service potential.

The absorption costing view   Advocates of absorption costing argue that fixed production costs added to inventory do, indeed, have future service potential. They take the position that if production exceeds sales, then a benefit to future periods is created in the form of an inventory that can be carried forward and sold, resulting in a future inflow of revenue. They argue that *all costs* involved in the creation of inventory should be carried forward as assets—not just the variable costs. The fixed costs of depreciation, taxes, insurance, supervisory salaries, and so on, are just as essential to the creation of units of product as are the variable costs. It would be just as impossible to create units of product in the absence of equipment as it would be to create them in the absence of raw materials or in the absence of workers to operate the machines. In sum, until the fixed production costs have been recognized and attached, units of product have not been fully costed. Both variable and fixed costs become inseparably attached as units are produced and *remain* inseparably attached regardless of whether the units are sold immediately or carried forward as inventory to generate revenue in future periods.

The direct costing view   Advocates of direct costing argue that a cost has service potential and is therefore an asset *only if its incurrence now will make it unnecessary to incur the same cost again in the future.* Service potential is therefore said to hinge on the matter of *future cost avoidance.* If the incurrence of a cost now will have no effect on whether or not the same cost will be incurred again in the future, then that cost is viewed as having no relevance to future events. It is argued that such a cost can in no way represent a future benefit or service.

For example, the prepayment of insurance is viewed as being an asset because the cash outlays made when the insurance is acquired make it unnecessary to sustain the same outlays again in the future periods for which insurance protection has been purchased. In short, by making insurance payments now, a company *avoids* having to make payments in the future. Since prepayments of insurance result in *future cost avoidance,* the prepayments qualify as assets.

This type of cost avoidance does not exist in the case of fixed production costs. The incurrence of fixed production costs in one year in no way reduces the necessity to incur the same costs again in the following year. Since the incurrence of fixed production costs does not result in *future cost avoidance,* the costs of one year can have no relevance to future events and therefore cannot possibly represent a future benefit or service. Direct costing advocates argue, therefore, that no part of the fixed production costs of one year should ever be carried forward as an asset to the following year. Such costs do not result in future cost avoidance—the key test for any asset.[4]

---

[4] For further discussion, see David Green, Jr., "A Moral to the Direct Costing Controversy," *Journal of Business* 33, no. 3 (July 1960), pp. 218–26; and Charles T. Horngren and George H. Sorter, "Direct Costing for External Reporting," *Accounting Review* 36, no. 1 (January 1961), pp. 88–93.

Extended Comparison of Income Data

Having gained some insights into the conceptual differences between absorption and direct costing, we are now prepared to take a more detailed look at the differences in the income data generated by these two approaches to cost allocation. Exhibit 7–6 presents data covering a span of three years. In the first year, production and sales are equal. In the second year, production exceeds sales. In the third year, the tables are reversed, with sales exceeding production.

Certain generalizations can be drawn from the data in Exhibit 7–6.

1.   When production and sales are equal, the same net income will be realized regardless of whether absorption or direct costing is being used (see year 1 in Exhibit 7–6). The reason is that when production and sales are equal, there is no chance for fixed overhead costs to be deferred in inventory or released from inventory under absorption costing.

2.   When production exceeds sales, the net income reported under absorption costing will generally be greater than the net income reported under direct costing (see year 2 in Exhibit 7–6). The reason is that when more is produced than is sold, part of the fixed overhead costs of the current period are deferred in inventory to the next period under absorption costing, as discussed earlier. In year 2, for example, $30,000 of fixed overhead cost (5,000 units $\times$ $6 per unit) has been deferred in inventory to year 3 under the absorption approach. Only that portion of the fixed overhead costs of year 2 under absorption costing that is associated with *units sold* is charged against income for that year.

Under direct costing, however, *all* of the fixed overhead costs of year 2 have been charged immediately against income as a period cost. As a result, the net income for year 2 under direct costing is $30,000 *lower* than it is under absorption costing. Exhibit 7–7 contains a reconciliation of the direct costing and absorption costing net income figures.

3.   When sales exceed production, the net income reported under the absorption costing approach will generally be less than the net income reported under the direct costing approach (see year 3 in Exhibit 7–6). The reason is that when more is sold than is produced, inventories are drawn down and fixed overhead costs that were previously deferred in inventory under absorption costing are released and charged against income (known as **fixed overhead cost released from inventory).** In year 3, for example, the $30,000 in fixed overhead cost deferred in inventory under the absorption approach from year 2 to year 3 is released from inventory through the sales process and charged against income. As a result, the cost of goods sold for year 3 contains not only all of the fixed overhead costs for year 3 (since all that was produced in year 3 was sold in year 3) but $30,000 of fixed overhead cost from year 2 as well.

EXHIBIT 7–6

Absorption costing versus direct costing—extended income data

Basic Data

Sales price per unit	$ 20
Variable manufacturing costs per unit (direct materials, direct labor,	
and variable overhead)	11
Fixed manufacturing overhead costs (total).	150,000
Cost of producing one unit of product:	
Under direct costing:	
Variable manufacturing costs.	$ 11
Under absorption costing:	
Variable manufacturing costs.	$ 11
Fixed overhead costs (based on a normal production volume of 25,000	
units per year—$150,000 ÷ 25,000).	6
Total absorption costs	$ 17

Selling and administrative expenses are assumed, for simplicity, to be all fixed at $30,000 per year.

	Year 1	Year 2	Year 3	Three years together
Opening inventory in units	–0–	–0–	5,000	–0–
Units produced during the year	25,000	25,000	25,000	75,000
Units sold during the year	25,000	20,000	30,000	75,000
Ending inventory in units	–0–	5,000	–0–	–0–

Direct Costing

	Year 1	Year 2	Year 3	Three years together
Sales	$500,000	$400,000	$600,000	$1,500,000
Less variable expenses.	275,000*	220,000*	330,000*	825,000
Contribution margin	225,000	180,000	270,000	675,000
Less fixed expenses:				
Manufacturing overhead	150,000	150,000	150,000	450,000
Selling and administrative expenses	30,000	30,000	30,000	90,000
Total fixed expenses	180,000	180,000	180,000	540,000
Net income	$ 45,000	$ –0–	$ 90,000	$ 135,000

Absorption Costing

	Year 1	Year 2	Year 3	Three years together
Sales	$500,000	$400,000	$600,000	$1,500,000
Opening inventory	–0–	–0–	85,000	–0–
Add cost of goods manufactured	425,000†	425,000	425,000	1,275,000
Goods available for sale	425,000	425,000	510,000	1,275,000
Less ending inventory	–0–	85,000‡	–0–	–0–
Cost of goods sold	425,000	340,000	510,000	1,275,000
Gross margin	75,000	60,000	90,000	225,000
Less selling and administrative expenses	30,000	30,000	30,000	90,000
Net income	$ 45,000	$ 30,000	$ 60,000	$ 135,000

* Year 1: 25,000 units sold × $11 = $275,000.
  Year 2: 20,000 units sold × $11 = $220,000.
  Year 3: 30,000 units sold × $11 = $330,000.
† 25,000 units produced × $17 = $425,000.
‡ 5,000 units in inventory × $17 = $85,000.

EXHIBIT 7–7

Reconciliation of direct costing and absorption costing—net income data from Exhibit 7–6

	Year 1	Year 2	Year 3
Direct costing net income	$45,000	$ –0–	$ 90,000
Add fixed overhead costs deferred in inventory under absorption costing (5,000 units × $6 per unit)	—	30,000	—
Deduct fixed overhead costs released from inventory under absorption costing (5,000 units × $6 per unit)	—	—	(30,000)
Absorption costing net income.	$45,000	$30,000	$ 60,000

By contrast, under direct costing only the fixed overhead costs of year 3 have been charged against year 3. The result is that net income under direct costing is $30,000 *higher* than it is under absorption costing. Exhibit 7–7 contains a reconciliation of the direct costing and absorption costing net income figures.

4.   Over an *extended* period of time, the net income figures reported under absorption costing and direct costing will tend to be the same. The reason is that over the long run sales can't exceed production, nor can production much exceed sales. The shorter the time period, the more the net income figures will tend to vary.

Sales Constant, Production Fluctuates

Exhibit 7–8 presents a reverse situation from that depicted in Exhibit 7–6. In Exhibit 7–6, we made production constant and allowed sales to fluctuate from period to period. In Exhibit 7–8, sales are constant and production fluctuates. Our purpose in Exhibit 7–8 is to observe the effect of changes in production on net income under both absorption and direct costing.

Direct costing   Net income is *not* affected by changes in production under direct costing. Notice from Exhibit 7–8 that net income is the same for all three years under the direct costing approach, although production exceeds sales in one year and is less than sales in another year. In short, the only thing that can affect net income under direct costing is a change in sales—a change in production has no impact when direct costing is in use.

Absorption costing   Net income *is* affected by changes in production when absorption costing is in use, however. As shown in Exhibit 7–8, net income under the absorption approach goes up in year 2, in response to the increase in production for that year, and then goes down in year 3, in response to the drop in production for that year. Note particularly that net income goes up and down between these two years *even though the same*

EXHIBIT 7–8

Sensitivity to changes in production and sales

Basic Data

Sales price per unit	$ 25
Variable manufacturing costs per unit	10
Fixed manufacturing overhead costs (total)	300,000
Selling and administrative expenses	
(all assumed, for simplicity, to be fixed)	210,000

	Year 1	Year 2	Year 3
Number of units produced	40,000	50,000	30,000
Number of units sold	40,000	40,000	40,000
Cost of producing one unit:			
Under direct costing (variable manufacturing costs only) . . .	$10.00	$10.00	$10.00
Under absorption costing:			
Variable manufacturing costs	$10.00	$10.00	$10.00
Fixed overhead costs ($300,000 total spread in each			
year over the number of units produced)	7.50	6.00	10.00
Total cost per unit	$17.50	$16.00	$20.00

Direct Costing

	Year 1	Year 2	Year 3
Sales (40,000 units)	$1,000,000	$1,000,000	$1,000,000
Less variable expenses (40,000 units)	400,000	400,000	400,000
Contribution margin	600,000	600,000	600,000
Less fixed expenses:			
Manufacturing overhead	300,000	300,000	300,000
Selling and administrative expenses	210,000	210,000	210,000
Total fixed expenses	510,000	510,000	510,000
Net income	$ 90,000	$ 90,000	$ 90,000

Absorption Costing

	Year 1	Year 2	Year 3
Sales (40,000 units)	$1,000,000	$1,000,000	$1,000,000
Opening inventory	–0–	–0–	160,000
Add cost of goods manufactured	700,000*	800,000*	600,000*
Goods available for sale	700,000	800,000	760,000
Less ending inventory	–0–	160,000†	–0–
Cost of goods sold (40,000 units)	700,000	640,000	760,000
Gross margin	300,000	360,000	240,000
Less selling and administrative expenses	210,000	210,000	210,000
Net income	$ 90,000	$ 150,000	$ 30,000

---

*Cost of goods manufactured:
   Year 1: 40,000 units × $17.50 = $700,000.
   Year 2: 50,000 units × $16.00 = $800,000.
   Year 3: 30,000 units × $20.00 = $600,000.
†Observe that 50,000 units are produced in year 2, but only 40,000 units are sold. The 10,000 units going into the ending inventory have the following costs attached to them:

Variable manufacturing costs: 10,000 units × $10	$100,000
Fixed manufacturing overhead costs: 10,000 units × $6 . . .	60,000
Total inventory cost	$160,000

number of units is sold in each year. The reason for this effect can be traced to the shifting of fixed overhead cost between periods under the absorption costing method.

Since this shifting of fixed overhead cost has already been discussed in preceding sections, at this point all we need to consider is how it affects the data in Exhibit 7–8. As shown in the exhibit, production exceeds sales in year 2, thereby causing 10,000 units to be carried forward as inventory to year 3. Each unit produced during year 2 has $6 in fixed overhead cost attached to it (see the unit cost computations at the top of Exhibit 7–8). Therefore, $60,000 (10,000 units × $6) of the fixed overhead costs of year 2 are not charged against that year but rather are added to the inventory account (along with the variable manufacturing costs). As a result, the net income of year 2 rises sharply, even though the same number of units is sold in year 2 as in the other years.

The reverse effect occurs in year 3. Since sales exceed production in year 3, that year is forced to cover all of its own fixed overhead costs as well as the fixed overhead costs carried forward in inventory from year 2. The result is a substantial drop in net income during year 3, although, as we have noted, the same number of units is sold in that year as in the other years.

Opponents of absorption costing argue that this shifting of fixed overhead cost between periods can be confusing to a manager and can cause him or her either to misinterpret data or to make faulty decisions. To avoid mistakes, the manager must be alert to any changes that may take place during a period in the level of inventory or in unit costs. By this means, he or she should be able to properly interpret any erratic movement in net income that may occur under the absorption costing method.

The reader may recall from Chapter 3 that one way to overcome problems such as those discussed above is to use *normalized* overhead rates. Even if normalized overhead rates are used, however, the same problems can arise if the under- or overapplied overhead that results from an imbalance between production and sales is taken to cost of goods sold. The only way to avoid the problems entirely is to use normalized overhead rates and to place any under- or overapplied overhead in a balance sheet clearing account of some type. However, this is rarely done in practice.

CVP Analysis and Absorption Costing

Absorption costing is widely regarded as a product costing method. Many firms use the absorption approach exclusively because of its focus on "full" costing of units of product. If the approach has a weakness, it is to be found in its inability to dovetail well with CVP analysis under certain conditions.

To illustrate, refer again to Exhibit 7–6. Let us compute the break-even point for the firm represented by the data in this exhibit. To obtain the break-even point, we divide total fixed costs by the contribution margin per unit:

Sales price per unit	$20
Variable costs per unit	11
Contribution margin per unit	$ 9
Fixed overhead costs	$150,000
Fixed selling and administrative costs . . .	30,000
Total fixed costs	$180,000

$$\frac{\text{Total fixed costs}}{\text{Contribution margin per unit}} = \frac{\$180,000}{\$9} = 20,000 \text{ units}$$

We have computed the break-even point to be 20,000 units sold. Notice from Exhibit 7–6 that in year 2 the firm sold exactly 20,000 units, the break-even volume. Under the contribution approach, using direct costing, the firm does break even in year 2, showing zero net income or loss. *Under absorption costing, however, the firm shows a positive net income of $30,000 for year 2.* How can this be so? How can absorption costing produce a positive net income when the firm sold exactly the break-even volume of units?

The answer lies in the fact that in year 2 under absorption costing, $30,000 in fixed overhead costs were deferred in inventory and did not appear as charges against income. By deferring these fixed overhead costs in inventory, the firm was able to show a profit even though it sold exactly the break-even volume of units. This leads us to a general observation about absorption costing. The only way that absorption costing data can be used in a break-even analysis is to assume that inventories will not change. Unfortunately, such an assumption often falls far short of reality.

Absorption costing runs into similar kinds of difficulty in other areas of CVP analysis and often requires considerable manipulation of data before figures are available that are usable for decision-making purposes.

External Reporting and Income Taxes

For external reporting on financial statements, a company is required to cost units of product by the absorption costing method. In like manner, the absorption costing method must be used in preparing tax returns. In short, the contribution approach is limited to *internal* use by the managers of a company.

The majority of accountants would agree that absorption costing *should* be used in external reporting. That is, most accountants feel that for *external reporting purposes,* units of product *should* contain a portion of fixed manufacturing overhead, along with variable manufacturing costs. The absorption costing argument that a unit of product is not fully costed until it reflects a portion of the fixed costs of production is difficult to refute, particularly as it applies to the preparing of information to be reported to stockholders and others.

The contribution approach finds its greatest application internally as an assist to the manager in those situations where the absorption costing data are not well suited for CVP analysis or are not well suited for a segment-type analysis, such as was covered earlier in the chapter. No particular problems are created by using *both* costing methods—the contribution method internally and the absorption method externally. As we demonstrated earlier in Exhibit 7–7, the adjustment from direct costing net income to absorption costing net income is a simple one and can be made in a few hours' time at year-end in order to produce an absorption costing net income figure for use on financial statements.

ADVANTAGES OF THE CONTRIBUTION APPROACH

As stated in the preceding section, many accountants feel that under the appropriate circumstances there are certain advantages to be gained from using the contribution approach (with direct costing) internally, even if the absorption approach is used externally for reporting purposes. These advantages have been summarized by the National Association of Accountants as follows:[5]

1. CVP relationship data wanted for profit planning purposes are readily obtained from the regular accounting statements. Hence management does not have to work with two separate sets of data to relate one to the other.
2. The profit for a period is not affected by changes in absorption of fixed expenses resulting from building or reducing inventory. Other things remaining equal (for example, selling prices, costs, sales mix), profits move in the same direction as sales when direct costing is in use.
3. Manufacturing cost and income statements in the direct cost form follow management's thinking more closely than does the absorption cost form for these statements. For this reason, management finds it easier to understand and to use direct cost reports.
4. The impact of fixed costs on profits is emphasized because the total amount of such cost for the period appears in the income statement.
5. Marginal income figures facilitate relative appraisal of products, territories, classes of customers, and other segments of the business without having the results obscured by allocation of joint (common) fixed costs.
6. Direct costing ties in with such effective plans for cost control as standard costs and flexible budgets.[6] In fact, the flexible budget is an aspect of direct costing, and many companies thus use direct costing methods for this purpose without recognizing them as such.

---

[5] National Association of Accountants, *Research Series No. 23,* "Direct Costing" (New York, 1953), p. 55.

[6] Standard costs and flexible budgets are covered in Chapters 9 and 10.

7.   Direct cost constitutes a concept of inventory cost that corresponds closely with the current out-of-pocket expenditure necessary to manufacture the goods.

SUMMARY

Cost allocation problems exist in every company. The contribution approach attempts to handle these problems by defining segments of an organization and by classifying costs as being either traceable or common to the segments. Only those costs that are traceable to the segments are allocated. Costs that are not traceable to the segments are treated as common costs and are not allocated.

The contribution approach also classifies costs by behavior. For this reason, those costs traceable to a segment are classified as between variable and fixed. Deducting total variable costs from sales yields a contribution margin, which is highly useful in short-run planning and decision making. The traceable fixed costs of a segment are then deducted from the contribution margin, yielding a segment margin. The segment margin is highly useful in long-run planning and decision making. Segments can be arranged in many ways—by sales territory, by division, by product line, by salesperson, and so on.

In costing units of product in a manufacturing firm, the contribution method with direct costing adds only the variable manufacturing costs to units of product. The fixed manufacturing costs are taken immediately to the income statement as expenses of the period.

Although the contribution approach cannot be used externally either for financial reporting or for tax purposes, it is often used internally by management. Its popularity internally can be traced in large part to the fact that it dovetails well with CVP concepts that are often indispensable in profit planning and decision making.

REVIEW PROBLEM ON ABSORPTION AND DIRECT COSTING

Dexter Company produces and sells a single product. Selected cost and operating data relating to the product for a recent year are given below:

Opening inventory in units.	–0–
Units produced during the year	10,000
Units sold during the year	8,000
Ending inventory in units	2,000
Selling price per unit . . . . $	50
Selling and administrative costs:	
Variable per unit	5
Fixed per year	70,000

Manufacturing costs:
Variable per unit:
Direct materials   11
Direct labor   6
Variable overhead   3
Fixed per year   100,000

Required: 1.   Assume that the company uses absorption costing.
      a.   Compute the manufactured cost of one unit of product.
      b.   Prepare an income statement for the year.
    2.   Assume that the company uses direct costing.
      a.   Compute the manufactured cost of one unit of product.
      b.   Prepare an income statement for the year.
    3.   Reconcile the direct costing and absorption costing net income figures.

Solution: 1.   *a.*   Under absorption costing, all manufacturing costs, variable and fixed, are added to the cost of a unit of product:

Direct materials $11
Direct labor   6
Variable overhead   3
Fixed overhead ($100,000 ÷ 10,000 units) . . .   10
Total cost per unit $30

      b.   The absorption costing income statement follows:

Sales (8,000 units × $50) $400,000
Cost of goods sold:
  Opening inventory . . . . $ –0–
  Add cost of goods manufactured
    (10,000 units × $30)   300,000
  Goods available for sale   300,000
  Less ending inventory (2,000 units × $30) . . .   60,000   240,000
Gross margin   160,000
Less selling and administrative expense 110,000*
Net income . . . . $ 50,000

    *Variable (8,000 units × $5) . . . $ 40,000
    Fixed per year   70,000
      Total $110,000

    2.   *a.*   Under direct costing, only the variable manufacturing costs are added to the cost of a unit of product:

Direct materials $11
Direct labor   6
Variable overhead   3
Total cost per unit $20

      b.   The direct costing income statement follows. Notice that the variable cost of goods sold is computed in a simpler, more direct manner than in the example provided earlier in Exhibit 7–5. On a direct costing income statement, either approach is acceptable.

Sales (8,000 units × $50)		$400,000
Less variable expenses:		
Variable cost of goods sold		
(8,000 units × $20)	$160,000	
Variable selling and administrative		
expense (8,000 units × $5)	40,000	200,000
Contribution margin		200,000
Less fixed expense:		
Fixed overhead cost for the year	100,000	
Fixed selling and administrative expense . . .	70,000	170,000
Net income		$ 30,000

3. The reconciliation of the direct and absorption costing net income figures follows:

Direct costing net income	$30,000
Add fixed overhead costs deferred in	
inventory under absorption costing	
(2,000 units × $10)	20,000
Absorption costing net income	$50,000

KEY TERMS FOR REVIEW

Absorption costing A costing method that includes all manufacturing costs—direct materials, direct labor, and both variable and fixed manufacturing overhead—in the cost of a unit of product. Absorption costing is also referred to as the *full cost* method.

Common fixed cost A cost that cannot be identified with any particular segment of an organization. Such costs, which are also known as *indirect costs*, exist to serve the combined needs of two or more segments.

Direct costing A costing method that includes only variable manufacturing costs—direct materials, direct labor, and variable overhead—in the cost of a unit of product. Also see *Marginal costing* or *Variable costing*.

Fixed overhead cost deferred in inventory The portion of the fixed overhead cost of a period that goes into inventory under the absorption costing method as a result of production exceeding sales.

Fixed overhead cost released from inventory The portion of the fixed overhead cost of a *prior* period that becomes an expense of the current period under the absorption costing method as a result of sales exceeding production.

Full cost See *Absorption costing*.

Marginal costing Another term for direct costing. See *Direct costing*.

Segment Any part or activity of an organization about which the manager seeks cost or revenue data.

Segment margin The amount remaining from the sales of a segment after the segment has covered all of its own costs, variable and fixed.

Segmented reporting An income statement or other report in an organization in which data are divided according to product lines, division, territories, or similar organizational segments.

Traceable fixed cost A cost that can be identified with a particular segment and that arises because of the existence of that segment.

Variable costing Another term for direct costing. See *Direct costing.*

QUESTIONS

7–1.   Define a segment of an organization. Give several examples of segments.

7–2.   How does the contribution approach attempt to assign costs to segments of an organization?

7–3.   Distinguish between a traceable cost and a common cost. Given several examples of each.

7–4.   How does the manager benefit from having the income statement in a segmented format?

7–5.   Explain how the segment margin differs from the contribution margin. Which concept is most useful to the manager? Why?

7–6.   Why aren't common costs allocated to segments under the contribution approach?

7–7.   How is it possible for a cost that is traceable under one segment arrangement to become a common cost under another segment arrangement?

7–8.   What is the basic difference between absorption costing and direct costing?

7–9.   Are selling and administrative expenses treated as product costs or as period costs under direct costing?

7–10.   Explain how fixed overhead costs are shifted from one period to another under absorption costing.

7–11.   What arguments can be advanced in favor of treating fixed overhead costs as product costs?

7–12.   What arguments can be advanced in favor of treating fixed overhead costs as period costs?

7–13.   If production and sales are equal, which method would you expect to show the highest net income, direct costing or absorption costing? Why?

7–14.   If production exceeds sales, which method would you expect to show the highest net income, direct costing or absorption costing? Why?

7–15.   If fixed overhead costs are released from inventory under absorption costing, what does this tell you about the level of production in relation to the level of sales?

7–16.   What special assumption must be made in order to compute a break-even point under absorption costing? *no change in inventory*

7–17.   Under absorption costing, how is it possible to increase net income without increasing sales? *increasing prod.*

7–18.   What limitations are there to the use of direct costing? *– not accepted by GAAP.*

EXERCISES

E7–1.   Royal Company produces and sells two products, X and Y. Revenue and cost information relating to the products follows:

	Products	
	X	Y
Selling price per unit	$ 6.00	$ 7.50
Variable expenses per unit	2.40	5.25
Traceable fixed expenses per year . . .	45,000	21,000

Common fixed expenses in the company total $33,000 annually. During 19x2, the company produced and sold 15,000 units of product X and 28,000 units of product Y.

Required: Prepare an income statement for 19x2 segmented by product lines. Show both "Amount" and "Percent" columns for the company as a whole and for each of the product lines.

E7–2. Raintree, Ltd., operates two divisions, A and B. A segmented income statement for the company's most recent year is given below:

			Segments			
	Total company		Division A		Division B	
Sales	$450,000	100%	$150,000	100%	$300,000	100%
Less variable expenses	225,000	50	45,000	30	180,000	60
Contribution margin	225,000	50	105,000	70	120,000	40
Less traceable fixed expenses . . .	126,000	28	78,000	52	48,000	16
Divisional segment margin	99,000	22	$ 27,000	18%	$ 72,000	24%
Less common fixed expenses. . . .	63,000	14				
Net income.	$ 36,000	8%				

Required: 1. By how much would the company's net income increase if Division B increased its sales by $75,000 per year? Assume no change in cost behavior patterns in the company.

2. Refer to the original data. Assume that sales in Division A increase by $50,000 next year and that sales in Division B remain unchanged. Assume no change in fixed costs in the divisions or in the company.

    a. Prepare a new segmented income statement for the company, using the format above. Show both amounts and percentages.

    b. Observe from the income statement you have prepared that the contribution margin ratio for Division A has remained unchanged at 70 percent (the same as in the data above) but that the segment margin ratio has changed. How do you explain the change in the segment margin ratio?

E7–3. Refer to the data in Exercise 7–2. Assume that Division B's sales by product line are:

	Division B		Segments			
			Product X		Product Y	
Sales	$300,000	100%	$200,000	100%	$100,000	100%
Less variable expenses	180,000	60	128,000	64	52,000	52
Contribution margin	120,000	40	72,000	36	48,000	48
Less traceable fixed expenses	33,000	11	12,000	6	21,000	21
Product line segment margin	87,000	29	$ 60,000	30%	$ 27,000	27%
Less common fixed expenses	15,000	5				
Divisional segment margin	$ 72,000	24%				

The company would like to initiate an intensive advertising campaign on one of the two products during the next month. The campaign would cost $5,000. Marketing studies indicate that such a campaign would increase sales of product X by $40,000 or increase sales of product Y by $35,000.

Required: 1. On which of the products would you recommend that the company focus its advertising campaign? Show computations to support your answer.

2. In Exercise 7–2, Division B shows $48,000 in traceable fixed expenses. What happened to the $48,000 in this exercise?

E7–4. Hartley Company manufactures two products, Meps and Zins. The Zins product is a relatively new line and is manufactured in a highly automated plant. Sal Monson, a very capable manager hired just a few months ago by Hartley Company, is serving as the manager of the Zins line. Cost and revenue data on the two products for last month follow:

	Products	
	Meps	Zins
Sales	$300,000	$200,000
Contribution margin ratio	60%	75%
Traceable fixed expenses:		
Committed	$ 30,000	$ 90,000
Discretionary	105,000	40,000

In addition to the costs given above, the company incurs $60,000 in common fixed expenses each month.

Required: 1. Prepare a segmented income statement for last month, showing both "Amount" and "Percent" columns for the company as a whole and for each product. Present the statement in enough detail to allow the company to evaluate the performance of the manager over each product.

2. From a standpoint of cost control, which segment manager seems to be doing the best job?

E7–5. Wingate Company has been experiencing losses for some time, as shown by its most recent monthly income statement below:

```
Sales. . . . . . . . . . .   $1,000,000
Less variable expenses . . .    390,000
Contribution margin  . . . .    610,000
Less fixed expenses  . . . .    625,000
Net income (loss)  . . . . .  $  (15,000)
```

In an effort to isolate the problem, the president has asked for an income statement segmented by division. Accordingly, the accounting department has developed the following information:

	Divisions		
	East	**Central**	**West**
Sales	$250,000	$400,000	$350,000
Variable expenses as a percentage of sales	52%	30%	40%
Traceable fixed expenses . . .	$160,000	$200,000	$175,000

Required: 1. Prepare an income statement segmented by divisions, as desired by the president. Show both ''Amount'' and ''Percent'' columns for the company as a whole and for each division.

2. As a result of a marketing study, the president believes that sales in the West Division could be increased by 20 percent if advertising in that division were increased by $15,000 each month. Would you recommend the increased advertising? Show computations.

E7–6.   Selected information on the operations of Diston Company for 19x8 is given below:

```
Opening inventory in units . . . . . . . .     –0–
Units produced during the year . . . . . .   25,000
Units sold during the year . . . . . . . .   20,000
Ending inventory in units. . . . . . . . .    5,000

Variable costs per unit:
  Direct materials. . . . . . . . . . . .     $4
  Direct labor  . . . . . . . . . . . .        7
  Variable overhead  . . . . . . . . . .       1
  Variable selling expenses . . . . . . .      2

Fixed costs per year:
  Manufacturing overhead . . . . . . . .   $200,000
  Selling and administrative expenses . . .   90,000
```

The company produces and sells a single product. Work in process inventories are nominal and can be ignored.

Required: 1. Assume that the company uses absorption costing. Compute the cost of one unit of product.

2. Assume that the company uses direct costing. Compute the cost of one unit of product.

E7–7.   Refer to the data in Exercise 7–6. An income statement prepared under the absorption costing method for 19x8 follows:

Sales (20,000 units × $30)		$600,000
Cost of goods sold:		
Opening inventory	$ –0–	
Cost of goods manufactured (25,000 units × $?) . . .	500,000	
Goods available for sale	500,000	
Less ending inventory (5,000 units × $?)	100,000	400,000
Gross margin		200,000
Less selling and administrative expenses:		
Variable selling	40,000	
Fixed selling and administrative	90,000	130,000
Net income		$ 70,000

Required: 1.   Determine how much of the $100,000 ending inventory above consists of fixed overhead cost deferred in inventory to the next period.

2.   Prepare an income statement for 19x8, using the direct costing method. How do you explain the difference in net income between the two costing methods?

E7–8.   Sierra Company produces and sells a single product. The following costs relate to its production and sale:

Variable costs per unit:	
Direct materials	$ 9
Direct labor	10
Manufacturing overhead	5
Selling and administrative expenses . . .	3
Fixed costs per year:	
Manufacturing overhead	$150,000
Selling and administrative expenses . . .	400,000

During last year, 25,000 units were produced and 22,000 units were sold. The Finished Goods inventory account at the end of the year shows a balance of $72,000 for the 3,000 unsold units.

Required: 1.   Is the company using absorption costing or direct costing to carry units in the Finished Goods inventory account? Show computations to support your answer.

2.   Assume that the company wishes to prepare financial statements for the year to issue to its stockholders.

   a.   Is the $72,000 figure for finished goods inventory the correct amount to use on these statements for external reporting purposes? Explain.

   b.   At what dollar amount *should* the 3,000 units be carried in the inventory account for external reporting purposes?

E7–9.   Whitman Company has just completed its first year of operations. The company's accountant has prepared an income statement for the year, as follows (absorption costing basis):

WHITMAN COMPANY
Income Statement
For the Year 19x1

Sales (35,000 units at $25)		$875,000
Less cost of goods sold:		
Opening inventory	$ –0–	
Cost of goods manufactured (40,000 units at $16) . .	640,000	
Goods available for sale	640,000	
Ending inventory (5,000 units at $16)	80,000	560,000
Gross margin		315,000
Less selling and administrative expenses		280,000
Net income		$ 35,000

The company's selling and administrative expenses consist of $210,000 per year in fixed expenses and $2 per unit sold in variable expenses. The $16 manufacturing cost per unit given above is computed as follows:

Direct materials	$ 5
Direct labor	6
Variable factory overhead	1
Fixed factory overhead ($160,000 ÷ 40,000 units) . .	4
Total cost per unit	$16

Required: 1. Redo the company's income statement in the contribution format, using direct costing.

2. Reconcile any difference between the net income figure on your direct costing income statement and the net income figure on the absorption costing income statement above.

E7–10. Lynch Company manufactures and sells a single product. The following costs were incurred during 19x1, the company's first year of operations:

Variable costs per unit:	
Production:	
Direct materials	$6
Direct labor	9
Variable manufacturing overhead . . .	3
Selling and administrative	4
Fixed costs per year:	
Manufacturing overhead	$300,000
Selling and administrative	190,000

During 19x1, the company produced 25,000 units and sold 20,000 units. The selling price of the company's product is $50 per unit.

Required: 1. Assume that the company uses the absorption costing method:

    a. Compute the cost of one unit of product.

    b. Prepare an income statement for 19x1.

2. Assume that the company uses the direct costing method:

    a. Compute the cost of one unit of product.

    b. Prepare an income statement for 19x1.

PROBLEMS

Problems 7–11 through 7–19 deal primarily with segmented reporting issues; problems 7–20 through 7–28 deal primarily with absorption versus direct costing issues.

P7–11. **Segmented reporting.** Vulcan Company's income statement for last month is given below:

VULCAN COMPANY
Income Statement
For the Month Ended June 30, 19x1

Sales	$750,000
Less variable expenses	336,000
Contribution margin	414,000
Less fixed expenses	378,000
Net income	$ 36,000

Management is disappointed with the company's performance and is wondering what can be done to improve profits. By examining sales and cost records, you have determined the following:

a. The company is divided into two sales territories—Northern and Southern. The Northern territory recorded $300,000 in sales and $156,000 in variable expenses during June; the remaining sales and variable expenses were recorded in the Southern territory. Fixed expenses of $120,000 and $108,000 are traceable to the Northern and Southern territories, respectively. The rest of the fixed expenses are common to the two territories.

b. The company sells two products—Paks and Tibs. Sales of Paks and Tibs totaled $50,000 and $250,000, respectively, in the Northern territory during June. Variable expenses are 22 percent of the selling price for Paks and 58 percent for Tibs. Cost records show that $30,000 of the Northern territory's fixed expenses are traceable to Paks and $40,000 to Tibs, with the remainder common to the two products.

Required: 1. Prepare segmented income statements such as illustrated in Exhibit 7–1, first showing the total company broken down between sales territories and then showing the Northern territory broken down by product line. Show both "Amount" and "Percent" columns for the company in total and for each segment.

2. Look at the statement you have prepared showing the total company segmented by sales territory. What points revealed by this statement should be brought to the attention of management?

3. Look at the statement you have prepared showing the Northern territory segmented by product line. What points revealed by this statement should be brought to the attention of management?

P7–12. **Basic segmented statement.** Diversified Products, Inc., has recently acquired a small publishing company that Diversified Products intends to operate as one of its subsidiaries. The newly acquired company has three books that it offers for sale—a cookbook, a travel guide, and a handy speller. Each book sells for $10. It costs $3 to print a cookbook, $4 to print a travel guide, and $2 to print a handy speller. Sales commissions are 10 percent of sales for any book.

The publishing company's income statement for the most recent month is given below:

| | Total company | | Product lines | | |
			Cookbook	Travel guide	Handy speller
Sales	$200,000	100.0%	$60,000	$100,000	$40,000
Less expenses:					
Printing costs	66,000	33.0	18,000	40,000	8,000
Sales commissions	20,000	10.0	6,000	10,000	4,000
Advertising	25,000	12.5	9,000	13,000	3,000
Salaries and wages	27,000	13.5	12,000	7,000	8,000
Equipment depreciation	20,000	10.0	6,000	10,000	4,000
Warehouse rent	10,000	5.0	3,000	5,000	2,000
General administration	27,000	13.5	9,000	9,000	9,000
Total expenses	195,000	97.5	63,000	94,000	38,000
Net income	$ 5,000	2.5%	$ (3,000)	$ 6,000	$ 2,000

The following additional information is available about the company:

a. The same equipment is used to print all three books, and the same warehouse is used to store the books awaiting sale. Therefore, these costs have been allocated to the product lines on a basis of sales dollars.

b. The general administration costs above relate to administration of the company as a whole; therefore, they have been allocated equally among the three product lines.

c. All other costs are traceable to the product lines.

The management of Diversified Products is anxious to improve the company's 2.5 percent margin on sales.

Required:

1. Prepare a new segmented income statement for the month, using the contribution approach. Show both an "Amount" and a "Percent" column for the company as a whole and for each product line.

2. After seeing the statement in the main body of the problem, management has decided to eliminate the cookbook, since it is not returning a profit, and to focus all available resources on promoting the travel guide.

   a. Based on the statement you have prepared, do you agree with the decision to eliminate the cookbook? Explain.

   b. Based on the statement you have prepared, do you agree with the decision to focus all available resources on promoting the travel guide? Explain. (You may assume that an ample market is available for all three product lines.)

3. What additional points would you bring to the attention of management that might help to improve profits?

P7–13.   **Restructuring a segmented statement.**   Losses have been incurred in Millard Company for some time. In an effort to isolate the problem and thereby improve the company's performance, management has requested that the monthly income statement be segmented by sales region. The company's first effort at preparing a segmented statement is given below. This statement is for May 19x5, the most recent month of activity.

	Sales regions		
	A	B	C
Sales	$450,000	$800,000	$ 750,000
Less regional expenses:			
Cost of goods sold	162,900	280,000	376,500
Advertising	108,000	200,000	210,000
Salaries	90,000	88,000	135,000
Utilities	13,500	12,000	15,000
Depreciation	27,000	28,000	30,000
Shipping expense	17,100	32,000	28,500
Total regional expenses	418,500	640,000	795,000
Regional income (loss) before			
corporate expenses	31,500	160,000	(45,000)
Less corporate expenses:			
Advertising (general)	18,000	32,000	30,000
General administrative expense . . .	50,000	50,000	50,000
Total corporate expenses	68,000	82,000	80,000
Net income (loss)	$ (36,500)	$ 78,000	$(125,000)

Cost of goods sold and shipping expense are both variable; other costs are all fixed.

Millard Company is a wholesale distributor of office products. It purchases various office products from the manufacturer and distributes them in the three regions given above. The three regions are about the same size, and each has its own manager and sales staff. The products that the company distributes vary widely in profitability.

Required: 1. List any disadvantages or weaknesses that you see to the statement format illustrated above.

2. Explain the basis being used to allocate the corporate expenses to the regions. Do you agree with these allocations? Explain.

3. Prepare a new segmented income statement for May 19x5, using the contribution approach. Show a "Total" column as well as data for each region. Include percentages on your statement for all columns.

4. Analyze the statement that you prepared in (3) above. What points that might help to improve the company's performance would you be particularly anxious to bring to the attention of management?

P7–14.   **Multiple segmented income statements.**   Kelvin Products, Inc.'s income statement segmented by divisions for last year is given below:

| | Total company | Divisions | |
		Plastics	Glass
Sales	$1,500,000	$900,000	$600,000
Less variable expenses	700,000	400,000	300,000
Contribution margin	800,000	500,000	300,000
Less traceable fixed expenses:			
Advertising	300,000	180,000	120,000
Depreciation.	140,000	92,000	48,000
Administration	220,000	118,000	102,000
Total	660,000	390,000	270,000
Divisional segment margin	140,000	$110,000	$ 30,000
Less common fixed expenses . . .	100,000		
Net income	$ 40,000		

Top management doesn't understand why the Glass Division has such a low segment margin when its sales are only one third less than sales in the Plastics Division. Accordingly, management has directed that the Glass Division be further segmented into product lines. The following information is available on the product lines in the Glass Division:

| | Product lines | | |
	X	Y	Z
Sales	$200,000	$300,000	$100,000
Traceable fixed expenses:			
Advertising	30,000	42,000	48,000
Depreciation	10,000	24,000	14,000
Administration	14,000	21,000	7,000
Variable expenses as a			
percentage of sales	65%	40%	50%

Analysis shows that $60,000 of the Glass Division's administration expenses are common to the product lines.

Required: 1. Prepare a segmented income statement for the Glass Division, with segments defined as product lines. Use the contribution approach and the format shown in Exhibit 7–1. Show both an "Amount" and a "Percent" column for the division in total and for each product line.

2. Management is very surprised by product line Z's poor showing and would like to have the product line segmented by market. The following information is available about the two markets in which product line Z is sold:

| | Markets | |
	Domestic	Foreign
Sales	$60,000	$40,000
Traceable fixed expenses:		
Advertising	18,000	30,000
Variable expenses as a		
percentage of sales . . .	50%	50%

All of product line Z's depreciation and administration expenses are common to the markets in which the product is sold. Prepare a segmented income statement for product line Z, with segments defined as markets. Again use the format in Exhibit 7–1 and show both "Amount" and "Percent" columns.

3. Refer to the statement prepared in (1) above. The sales manager wants to run a special promotional campaign on one of the products over the next month. A market study indicates that such a campaign would increase sales of product line X by $40,000 or sales of product line Y by $30,000. The campaign would cost $8,000. Show computations to determine which product line should be chosen.

P7–15. **Multiple segmented income statements.**   Hopwood Company divided its products into two divisions about a year ago. Since that time, one of the divisions has done well but the other division has shown steadily declining profits. The company's most recent monthly income statement is presented below:

	Total company	Divisions	
		Metal Products	**Wood Products**
Sales	$2,800,000	$1,600,000	$1,200,000
Less variable expenses:			
Production	891,000	420,000	471,000
Selling and other.	273,000	140,000	133,000
Total variable expenses. . . .	1,164,000	560,000	604,000
Contribution margin	1,636,000	1,040,000	596,000
Less traceable fixed expenses . . .	1,302,000	710,000	592,000
Divisional segment margin	334,000	$ 330,000	$ 4,000
Less common fixed expenses . . .	185,000		
Net income	$ 149,000		

In an attempt to isolate the problem in the Wood Products Division, management has decided to segment that division by product line. The following data are available on the three products that the division manufactures and sells:

	Total	Product lines		
		A	**B**	**C**
Sales	$1,200,000	$300,000	$500,000	$400,000
Variable costs as a percentage of sales:				
Production	—	35%	30%	54%
Selling and other	—	13	10	11
Traceable fixed expenses	$ 502,000	$120,000	$170,000	$212,000

Required: 1. Prepare a segmented income statement for the Wood Products Division, with segments defined by products. Use the contribution approach and the format shown in Exhibit 7–1. Show both an "Amount" and a "Percent" column for the division in total and for each product line.

2. The president now wants more information about product line C. This product is sold in two sales markets—the East and the West. Sales and other data about the two markets follow:

| | | Sales markets | |
	Total	East	West
Sales	$400,000	$150,000	$250,000
Variable expenses as a percentage of sales:			
Production.	—	54%	54.0%
Selling and other		20	5.6
Traceable fixed expenses	$160,000	$108,000	$ 52,000

Prepare a segmented income statement for product line C, with segments defined as markets. Again use the format in Exhibit 7–1 and show both "Amount" and "Percent" columns.

3. Scrutinize the statements you have prepared in (1) and (2). What points should be brought to the attention of management?

4. Assume that the president wants more information about the East sales market. Suggest ways in which this market might be further segmented.

P7–16.   **Segmented statements; product line analysis.** "At last, I can see some light at the end of the tunnel," said Steve Adams, president of Jelco Products. "Our losses have shrunk from over $75,000 a month at the beginning of the year to only $26,000 for August. If we can just isolate the remaining problems with products A and C, we'll be in the black by the first of next year."

The company's income statement for the latest month (August) is presented below (absorption costing basis):

JELCO PRODUCTS
Income Statement
For the Year 19x1

| | Total company | Products | | |
		A	B	C
Sales	$1,500,000	$600,000	$400,000	$500,000
Less cost of goods sold	922,000	372,000	220,000	330,000
Gross margin	578,000	228,000	180,000	170,000
Less operating expenses:				
Selling	424,000	162,000	112,000	150,000
Administrative.	180,000	72,000	48,000	60,000
Total operating expenses . . .	604,000	234,000	160,000	210,000
Net income (loss)	$ (26,000)	$ (6,000)	$ 20,000	$ (40,000)

"What recommendations did that business consultant make?" asked Mr. Adams. "We paid the guy $100 an hour; surely he found something wrong." "He says our problems are concealed by the way we make up our statements," replied Sally Warren, the executive vice president. "He left us some data on what he calls 'traceable' and 'common' costs that he says we should be isolating in our reports." The data to which Ms. Warren was referring are shown below:

	Total company	Products		
		A	B	C
Variable costs:[*]				
Production (materials, labor, and variable overhead)	—	18%	32%	20%
Selling	—	10	8	10
Traceable fixed costs:				
Production	$376,000	$180,000	$36,000	$160,000
Selling	282,000	102,000	80,000	100,000
Common fixed costs:				
Production	210,000	—	—	—
Administrative	180,000	—	—	—

[*] As a percentage of sales.

"I don't see anything wrong with our statements," said Mr. Adams. "Bill, our chief accountant, says that he has been using this format for over 30 years. He's also very careful to allocate all of our costs to the products."

"I'll admit that Bill always seems to be on top of things," replied Ms. Warren. "By the way, purchasing says that the X7 chips we use in products A and B are on back order and won't be available for several weeks. From the looks of August's income statement, we had better concentrate our remaining inventory of X7 chips on product B." (Two X7 chips are used in both product A and product B.)

The following additional information is available on the company:

a. Work in process and finished goods inventories are nominal and can be ignored.
b. Products A and B each sell for $250 per unit, and product C sells for $125 per unit. Strong market demand exists for all three products.

Required:
1. Prepare a new income statement for August, segmented by product and using the contribution approach. Show both "Amount" and "Percent" columns for the company in total and for each product.
2. Assume that Mr. Adams is considering the elimination of product C, due to the losses it is incurring. Based on the statement you prepared in (1), what points would you make for or against elimination of product C?
3. Do you agree with the company's decision to concentrate the remaining inventory of X7 chips on product B? Why or why not?
4. Product C is sold in both a vending and a home market, with sales and cost data as follows:

	Total	Markets	
		Vending	Home
Sales	$500,000	$50,000	$450,000
Variable costs:[*]			
Production	—	20%	20%
Selling	—	28	8
Traceable fixed costs:			
Selling	$ 75,000	$45,000	$ 30,000

[*] As a percentage of sales.

The remainder of product C's fixed selling costs and all of product C's fixed production costs are common to the markets in which product C is sold.

a. Prepare an income statement showing product C segmented by market. Use the contribution approach, and show both an "Amount" and a "Percent" column for the product in total and for each market.

b. What points revealed by this statement would you be particularly anxious to bring to the attention of management?

P7–17.   Analyzing segmented statements.   "Rats! We're still in the red," said Jana Andrews, executive vice president of the Ashland Company. "I know," said Steve Clark, the controller. "Just look at this income statement for March. At least placing it in a segmented format this month tells us where our problem is. We've got to forget about Districts A and B and zero in on District C." The statement to which Mr. Clark was referring is shown below:

	Total company	Districts A	B	C
Sales @ $20 per unit	$1,000,000	$300,000	$500,000	$200,000
Less cost of goods sold @ $9 per unit	450,000	135,000	225,000	90,000
Gross margin	550,000	165,000	275,000	110,000
Less operating expenses:				
Marketing expenses:				
Freight-out	51,250	11,250	25,000	15,000
Warehouse depreciation	80,000	24,000	40,000	16,000
Sales commissions	60,000	18,000	30,000	12,000
Sales salaries	30,000	12,000	10,000	8,000
District advertising	75,000	20,000	25,000	30,000
National advertising	115,000	34,500	57,500	23,000
Total marketing expenses	411,250	119,750	187,500	104,000
Administrative expenses:				
District management salaries	40,000	12,000	15,000	13,000
Central office administrative expenses	100,000	30,000	50,000	20,000
Total administrative expenses	140,000	42,000	65,000	33,000
Total operating expenses	551,250	161,750	252,500	137,000
Net income (loss)	$ (1,250)	$ 3,250	$ 22,500	$ (27,000)

* Allocated on a basis of sales dollars.

The company is a retail organization that sells a single product. The product is sold in three districts, as shown above. Additional information on the company follows:

a. The sales and administrative offices are centrally located, being about the same distance from each district.

b. Each district specifies on the sales order what freight method is to be used (by truck, rail, or air). All goods are shipped from a central warehouse. Freight is a variable cost, and it is traceable to the districts; differences in amounts above are reflective of the different freight methods used.

c. All salespersons are paid a base salary of $500 per month, plus a commission of 6 percent of sales. There are 24 salespersons in District A, 20 in District B, and 16 in District C.

d. Each district manager must arrange his or her own district advertising program. The national advertising is provided by the central office.

e. It costs the central office $5 to process an order from any of the districts. During March, District A had 3,000 orders, District B had 1,500 orders, and District C had 500 orders. Although the $5 per order processing cost is variable and is traceable directly to the districts, this cost for March has been included in the "Central office administrative expenses" above. The remainder of the "Central office administrative expenses" are fixed and relate to general administrative assistance provided to all parts of the organization.

f. Inventories are negligible and can be ignored.

Required:

1. Garth Hansen, the president, has asked that the company's income statement be redone using the contribution format, which he heard about in a recent industry convention. Prepare the income statement as requested by Mr. Hansen. Show both an "Amount" and a "Percent" column for the company in total and for each district. (Carry computations to one decimal place.)

2. Compute the contribution margin per order for each district. What problems does this computation suggest?

3. The manager of District B would like to spend an extra $25,000 next month in a special promotional campaign. If sales increase by $100,000 as a result, would the expenditure be justified?

4. Analyze the data in the statement you prepared in (1) above. What points should be brought to the attention of management?

P7–18. **Segmented reporting; expansion analysis.**   Meredith Company produces and sells three products (A, B, and C), which are sold in a local market and a regional market. At the end of the first quarter of the current year, the following absorption basis income statement has been prepared:

MEREDITH COMPANY
Income Statement
For the First Quarter

	Total company	Markets Local	Regional
Sales	$1,300,000	$1,000,000	$300,000
Cost of goods sold	1,010,000	777,000	233,000
Gross margin	290,000	223,000	67,000
Selling expenses	105,000	60,000	45,000
Administrative expenses . . .	52,000	40,000	12,000
Total expenses	157,000	100,000	57,000
Net income	$ 133,000	$ 123,000	$ 10,000

Management has expressed special concern with the regional market because of the extremely poor return on sales. This market was entered a year ago because of excess capacity. It was originally believed that the return on sales would improve with time, but after a year no noticeable improvement can be seen from the results in the above quarterly statement.

In attempting to decide whether to eliminate the regional market, the following information has been gathered:

	Product lines		
	A	**B**	**C**
Sales	$500,000	$400,000	$400,000
Variable manufacturing expenses as			
a percentage of sales	40%	35%	30%
Variable selling expenses as a			
percentage of sales.	3	2	2
Fixed manufacturing expenses traceable			
directly to the product lines	$190,000	$150,000	$210,000

Product	**Sales by markets**	
lines	**Local**	**Regional**
A	$ 400,000	$100,000
B	300,000	100,000
C	300,000	100,000
Total sales . . .	$1,000,000	$300,000

The administrative expenses shown on the income statement above are common to both the markets and the product lines. They have been allocated to the markets above on a basis of sales dollars. The selling expenses shown on the income statement above are all traceable to the markets, as shown. Inventory levels are nominal and can be ignored.

Required: 1. Prepare a segmented income statement for the quarter using the contribution approach, segmented into local and regional markets. Show an ''Amount'' and a ''Percent'' column for the company in total and for each market. (Carry percentages to one decimal place.)

2. Assuming that there are no alternative uses for the company's present capacity, would you recommend that the regional market be dropped? Why or why not?

3. Prepare another segmented income statement for the quarter, again using the contribution approach, but this time segmented by product line. (Do not allocate the fixed selling expenses to the product lines; treat these as common costs.) Show both an ''Amount'' column and a ''Percent'' column for the company in total and for each product line.

4. Assume that product lines B and C are both at full capacity. The company would like to add sufficient additional capacity to double the output of one of these product lines. Overall cost relationships for the added capacity would follow the same cost behavior patterns as with present capacity for each product line. The company's executive committee has decided to double the capacity of product C because of its higher C/M ratio. Explain why you do or do not agree with this decision.

(CMA, Adapted)

P7–19. Preparing various segmented reports; segment profitability analysis. ''We're clearly one of the industry leaders,'' declared Roxanne Richie, president of Hewtex, Inc., as she looked at the company's most recent monthly operating statement.

"Our 5.5 percent ratio of income to sales is well above the 4.25 percent industry average."

Hewtex, Inc., produces and distributes three product lines throughout the United States. To facilitate distribution, the country is divided into three sales regions—the East, the Midwest, and the West. The operating statement to which Ms. Richie was referring is shown below:

Sales	$500,000	100.0%
Less production and packaging expenses . .	336,500	67.3
Gross margin	163,500	32.7
Less operating expenses:		
Marketing. $88,000		
Administration. 48,000	136,000	27.2
Net income	$ 27,500	5.5%

"If we're going to maintain our profit position, we'll need to keep things moving smoothly," said Ms. Richie to the controller. "How's that new business school graduate doing that is supposed to be well trained in internal reporting?" "He's trying," replied the controller, "but I'm afraid they aren't too practical in those business schools. He wants us to break our operating statement down two or three different ways. I know he means well, but as you've pointed out, we're already one of the most profitable firms in the industry, so why go to a lot of unnecessary bookkeeping expense? Besides, we already know that line A is our best line and that the East is our best sales region. He's worked up a lot of figures showing what he calls traceable costs and common costs that he thinks we ought to be using in our statements." The data to which the controller was referring are shown below:

	Total sales	Production and packaging	Marketing	Adminis-tration
Sales and variable expenses:				
Line A	$250,000	55%	5%	—
Line B	100,000	47	5	—
Line C	150,000	35	5	—
Traceable fixed expenses:				
Line A		$10,000	$15,000	—
Line B		45,000	9,000	—
Line C		44,500	5,000	—
West Region		—	10,000	$ 9,500
Midwest Region		—	13,500	7,000
East Region		—	10,500	16,500
Common fixed expenses:				
General administration . . .		—	—	15,000

The percentage figures above are in terms of total sales. Corporate headquarters does some advertising directly for each product line on a national basis, which is supplemented by each sales region doing whatever additional advertising it deems necessary. The sales by region (which have been constant in terms of mix for some time) are shown below:

	Percentage of product line sales		
	Line A	Line B	Line C
West Region	15	50	60
Midwest Region . . .	25	20	30
East Region	60	30	10
	100	100	100

Required:

1. Prepare segmented income statements, as follows:

   a. For the company as a whole, broken down into product line segments. Use the contribution format. Show both amount and percent columns, with the percentages rounded to one decimal place.

   b. For the company as a whole, broken down into regional markets. Use the contribution format. Show both amount and percent columns, with the percentages rounded to one decimal place. (Do not allocate the traceable fixed expenses of the product lines to the regions; treat these as common costs.)

2. Refer to the statement you prepared in (1a) above.

   a. Analyze the statement and indicate the points you would be particularly anxious to bring to the attention of management.

   b. The company is about to launch a national promotional campaign for one of the product lines. Assuming that ample capacity exists and that none of the product lines has reached market saturation, which product line would you recommend to management? Explain the reason for your choice.

3. Refer to the statement you prepared in (1b) above. Analyze the statement and indicate the points you would be particularly anxious to bring to the attention of management.

P7–20. **Straightforward direct costing statements.**   Heaton Company was organized on January 1, 19x4. During its first two years of operations, the company reported net income as follows (absorption costing basis):

	19x4	19x5
Sales (@ $25)	$1,000,000	$1,250,000
Less cost of goods sold:		
Opening inventory	–0–	90,000
Add cost of goods manufactured (@ $18) . .	810,000	810,000
Goods available for sale	810,000	900,000
Less ending inventory (@ $18)	90,000	–0–
Cost of goods sold	720,000	900,000
Gross margin	280,000	350,000
Less selling and administrative expenses* . . .	210,000	230,000
Net income	$ 70,000	$ 120,000

* $2 per unit variable; $130,000 fixed per year.

The company's $18 unit cost is computed as follows:

Direct materials	$ 4
Direct labor	7
Variable manufacturing overhead	1
Fixed manufacturing overhead ($270,000 ÷ 45,000 units) . .	6
Total cost per unit	$18

Production and cost data for the two years are:

	19x4	19x5
Units produced	45,000	45,000
Units sold	40,000	50,000

Required:
1. Prepare an income statement for each year in the contribution format, using direct costing.
2. Reconcile the absorption costing and the direct costing net income figures for each year.

P7–21. **Straightforward comparison of costing methods.** High Country, Inc., produces and sells many recreational products. The company has just opened a new plant to produce a folding camp cot that will be marketed throughout the United States. The following cost and revenue data relate to May 19x8, the first month of the plant's operation:

Opening inventory	–0–
Units produced	10,000
Units sold	8,000
Sales price per unit . . . . $	75
Selling and administrative expenses:	
Variable per unit	6
Fixed (total)	200,000
Manufacturing costs:	
Direct materials cost per unit	20
Direct labor cost per unit	8
Variable overhead cost per unit	2
Fixed overhead (total)	100,000

Management is anxious to see how profitable the new camp cot will be and has asked that an income statement be prepared for the month.

Required:
1. Assume that the company uses absorption costing.
   a. Determine the cost to produce one unit of product.
   b. Prepare an income statement for the month.
2. Assume that the company uses the contribution approach with direct costing.
   a. Determine the cost to produce one unit of product.
   b. Prepare an income statement for the month.
3. Explain the reason for any difference in the ending inventory under the two costing methods and the impact of this difference on reported net income.

P7–22. **A comparison of costing methods.** Audio Products, Inc., has organized a new division to manufacture and sell CB radios. Monthly costs associated with the radios and with the plant in which the radios are manufactured are shown below:

Manufacturing costs:
   Variable cost per unit:

Direct materials	$	40
Direct labor		8
Variable overhead		2
Fixed overhead costs (total)		360,000

Selling and administrative costs:

Variable	12% of sales
Fixed (total)	470,000

During September 19x6, the first month of operations, the following activity was recorded:

Units produced	12,000
Units sold	10,000

The radios sell for $150 each.

Required:

1. Compute the cost of a single unit of product under:
   a. Absorption costing.
   b. Direct costing.
2. Prepare an income statement for the year, using absorption costing.
3. Prepare an income statement for the year, using direct costing.
4. Assume that the company must obtain additional financing in order to continue operations. As a member of top management, would you prefer to take the statement in (2) above or in (3) above with you as you meet with a group of prospective investors?
5. Reconcile the absorption costing and direct costing net income figures in (2) and (3) for the month.

P7–23.   Prepare and reconcile direct costing statements.   Denton Company was organized on July 1, 19x3. The company manufactures and sells a single product. Cost data for the product are given below:

Variable cost per unit:

Direct materials	$ 7
Direct labor	10
Variable manufacturing overhead . . .	5
Variable selling and administrative . . .	3
Total variable cost per unit	$25

Fixed cost per month:

Manufacturing overhead	$315,000
Selling and administrative	245,000
Total fixed cost per month	$560,000

The product sells for $60 per unit. Production and sales data for July and August follow:

	Units produced	Units sold
July	17,500	15,000
August	17,500	20,000

The company's accounting department has prepared income statements for both July and August. These statements, which have been prepared using absorption costing, are presented below:

	July 19x3	August 19x3
Sales	$900,000	$1,200,000
Less cost of goods sold:		
Opening inventory	–0–	100,000
Add cost of goods manufactured	700,000	700,000
Goods available for sale.	700,000	800,000
Less ending inventory.	100,000	–0–
Cost of goods sold	600,000	800,000
Gross margin	300,000	400,000
Less selling and administrative expense . .	290,000	305,000
Net income	$ 10,000	$ 95,000

Required: 1.   Determine the cost of a single unit of product under:
        a.   Absorption costing.
        b.   Direct costing.
    2.   Prepare income statements for July and August using the contribution approach, with direct costing.
    3.   Reconcile the direct costing and absorption costing net income figures.
    4.   The company's accounting department has determined the company's break-even point to be 16,000 units per month, computed as follows:

$$\frac{\text{Fixed costs per month}}{\text{Unit contribution margin}} \quad \frac{\$560,000}{\$35} = 16,000 \text{ units}$$

      "I'm confused," said the president. "The accounting people say that our break-even point is 16,000 units per month, but we sold only 15,000 units in July, and the income statement they prepared shows a $10,000 profit for that month. Either the income statement is wrong or the break-even point is wrong." Prepare a brief explanation for the president of what happened on the July income statement.

P7–24.   **Absorption and direct costing; production constant, sales fluctuate.**   Tami Tyler opened Tami's Creations, Inc., a small manufacturing company, at the beginning of the year. In order to get the company through its first quarter of operations, it has been necessary for Ms. Tyler to place a considerable strain on her own personal finances. An income statement for the first quarter is shown below. The statement was prepared by a friend who has just completed a course in managerial accounting at State University.

TAMI'S CREATIONS, INC.
Income Statement
For the Quarter Ended March 31, 19x1

Sales (28,000 units)		$1,120,000
Less variable expenses:		
Variable cost of goods sold*	$462,000	
Selling and administrative	168,000	630,000
Contribution margin		490,000
Less fixed expenses:		
Fixed manufacturing overhead	300,000	
Selling and administrative	200,000	500,000
Net loss		$ (10,000)

*Consists of direct materials, direct labor, and variable overhead.

Ms. Tyler is discouraged over the loss shown for the quarter, particularly since she had planned to use the statement as support for a bank loan. Another friend, a CPA, insists that the company should be using absorption costing rather than direct costing, and argues that if absorption costing had been used the company would probably have reported at least some profit for the quarter.

At this point, Ms. Tyler is manufacturing only one product, a swimming suit. Production and cost data relating to the suit for the first quarter follow:

Units produced	30,000
Units sold	28,000
Variable cost per unit:	
Direct materials	$ 3.50
Direct labor	12.00
Variable overhead	1.00
Variable selling and administrative . .	6.00

Required: 1. Complete the following:
    a. Compute the cost of a unit of product under absorption costing.
    b. Redo the company's income statement for the quarter, using absorption costing.
    c. Reconcile the direct costing and absorption costing net income (loss) figures.
  2. Was the CPA correct in suggesting that the company really earned a ''profit'' for the quarter? Explain.
  3. During the second quarter of operations, the company again produced 30,000 units but sold 32,000 units. (Assume no change in total fixed costs.)
    a. Prepare an income statement for the quarter, using direct costing.
    b. Prepare an income statement for the quarter, using absorption costing.
    c. Reconcile the direct costing and absorption costing net income figures.

P7–25. **Prepare and reconcile direct costing statements; sales constant, production varies.** ''This makes no sense at all,'' said Bill Sharp, president of Essex Company. ''We sold the same number of units this year as we did last year, yet our profits have more than doubled. Who made the goof—the computer or the people who operate it?'' The statements to which Mr. Sharp was referring are shown below (absorption costing basis):

	19x1	19x2
Sales (20,000 units each year)	$700,000	$700,000
Less cost of goods sold	460,000	400,000
Gross margin	240,000	300,000
Less selling and administrative expenses . . .	200,000	200,000
Net income	$ 40,000	$100,000

The company was organized on January 1, 19x1, so the statements above show the results of its first two years of operation. In the first year, the company produced and sold 20,000 units; in the second year, the company again sold 20,000 units, but it increased production in order to have a stock of units on hand, as shown below:

	19x1	19x2
Production in units	20,000	25,000
Sales in units	20,000	20,000
Variable production cost per unit . . .	$8	$8
Fixed overhead costs (total)	$300,000	$300,000

Essex Company produces a single product; fixed overhead costs are applied to the product on the basis of *each year's production*. (Thus, a new fixed overhead rate is computed each year, as in Exhibit 7–8.)

Required:
1. Compute the cost of a single unit of product for each year under:
   a. Absorption costing.
   b. Direct costing.
2. Prepare an income statement for each year, using the contribution approach with direct costing.
3. Reconcile the direct costing and absorption costing net income figures for each year.
4. Explain to the president why, under absorption costing, the net income for 19x2 was higher than the net income for 19x1, although the same number of units was sold in each year.

P7–26. **Prepare and interpret statements; changes in both sales and production.**   Starfax, Inc., was organized on January 2, 19x1. The company manufactures a small part that is widely used in various electronic products such as home computers. Operating results for the first three years of activity were as follows (absorption costing basis):

	19x1	19x2	19x3
Sales	$800,000	$640,000	$800,000
Cost of goods sold:			
Opening inventory.	–0–	–0–	200,000
Add cost of goods manufactured . .	580,000	600,000	560,000
Goods available for sale	580,000	600,000	760,000
Less ending inventory	–0–	200,000	140,000
Cost of goods sold	580,000	400,000	620,000
Gross margin.	220,000	240,000	180,000
Selling and administrative expenses . .	190,000	180,000	190,000
Net income (loss)	$ 30,000	$ 60,000	$ (10,000)

In the latter part of 19x2, a competitor went out of business and in the process dumped a large number of units on the market. As a result, Starfax's sales dropped by 20 percent during 19x2 even though production increased during that year. In order to work off the excessive inventories, Starfax cut back production during 19x3, as shown below:

	19x1	19x2	19x3
Production in units	50,000	60,000	40,000
Sales in units	50,000	40,000	50,000

Additional information about the company follows:

a. Variable manufacturing costs (direct materials, direct labor, and variable overhead) were $2 per unit in each year. Fixed manufacturing costs totaled $480,000 per year.

b. Fixed manufacturing costs are applied to units of product on the basis of each year's production. (That is, a new fixed overhead rate is computed each year, as in Exhibit 7–8.)

c. Variable selling and administrative expenses were $1 per unit sold in each year. Fixed selling and administrative expenses totaled $140,000 each year.

d. The company uses a FIFO inventory flow.

Required:

1. Prepare a new income statement for each year using the contribution approach, with direct costing.

2. Refer to the absorption costing income statements above.
   a. Compute the cost to produce one unit of product in each year under absorption costing. (Show how much of this cost is variable and how much is fixed.)
   b. Reconcile the direct costing and absorption costing net income figures for each year.

3. Refer again to the absorption costing income statements. Explain why net income was higher in 19x2 than it was in 19x1 under the absorption approach, in light of the fact that fewer units were sold in 19x2 than in 19x1.

4. Refer again to the absorption costing income statements. Explain why the company suffered a loss in 19x3 but reported a profit for 19x1, although the same number of units was sold in each year.

CASES

C7–27. **The case of the plummeting profits.** "These statements can't be right," said Ben Yoder, president of Rayco, Inc. "Our sales in the second quarter were up by 25 percent over the first quarter, yet these income statements show a precipitous drop in net income for the second quarter. Those accounting people have fouled something up." The statements to which Mr. Yoder was referring are shown below:

RAYCO, INC.
Income Statements
For the First Two Quarters

	First quarter		Second quarter	
Sales		$480,000		$600,000
Cost of goods sold:				
Beginning inventory	$ 80,000		$140,000	
Cost of goods manufactured . .	300,000		180,000	
Goods available for sale	380,000		320,000	
Ending inventory	140,000		20,000	
Cost of goods sold	240,000		300,000	
Add underapplied overhead . .	—	240,000	72,000	372,000
Gross margin		240,000		228,000
Less selling and administrative				
expenses		200,000		215,000
Net income		$ 40,000		$ 13,000

After studying the statements briefly, Mr. Yoder called in the controller to see if the mistake in the second quarter could be located before the figures were released to the press. The controller stated, "I'm sorry to say that those figures are correct, Ben. I agree that sales went up during the second quarter, but the problem is in production. You see, we budgeted to produce 15,000 units each quarter, but a strike on the west coast among some of our suppliers forced us to cut production in the second quarter back to only 9,000 units. That's what caused the sharp drop in net income."

Mr. Yoder was confused by the controller's explanation. He replied, "This doesn't make sense. I ask you to explain why net income dropped when sales went up and you talk about production! So what if we had to cut back production? We still were able to increase sales by 25 percent. If sales go up, then net income should go up. If your statements can't show a simple thing like that, then it's time for some changes in your area!"

Budgeted production and sales for the year, along with actual production and sales for the first two quarters, are given below:

	Quarters			
	First	Second	Third	Fourth
Budgeted sales (units)	12,000	15,000	15,000	18,000
Actual sales (units)	12,000	15,000	—	—
Budgeted production (units) . . .	15,000	15,000	15,000	15,000
Actual production (units)	15,000	9,000	—	—

Fixed manufacturing overhead amounts to $180,000 each quarter. Variable manufacturing costs are $8 per unit. The fixed overhead is applied to units of product at a rate of $12 per unit (based on the budgeted production shown above). Any under- or overapplied overhead is taken directly to cost of goods sold for the quarter. The company had 4,000 units in inventory to start the first quarter and uses the FIFO inventory method. Variable selling and administrative expenses are $5 per unit.

Required:

1. What characteristic of absorption costing caused the drop in net income for the second quarter and what could the controller have said to explain the problem more fully?
2. Prepare income statements for each quarter using the contribution approach, with direct costing.
3. Reconcile the absorption costing and the direct costing net income figures for each quarter.
4. Identify and discuss the advantages and disadvantages of using the direct costing method for internal reporting purposes.

C7–28.   **Absorption and direct costing; uneven production; break-even analysis.**   ''Now this doesn't make any sense at all,'' said Flora Fisher, financial vice president for Warner Company. ''Our sales have been steadily rising over the last several months, but profits have been going in the opposite direction. In September we finally hit $2,000,000 in sales, but the bottom line for that month drops off to a $100,000 loss. Why aren't profits more closely correlated with sales?''

The statements to which Ms. Fisher was referring are shown below:

WARNER COMPANY
Monthly Income Statements

	July	August	September
Sales (@ $25)	$1,750,000	$1,875,000	$2,000,000
Less cost of goods sold:			
Opening inventory	80,000	320,000	400,000
Cost applied to production:			
Variable manufacturing cost (@ $9) . . .	765,000	720,000	540,000
Fixed manufacturing overhead	595,000	560,000	420,000
Cost of goods manufactured	1,360,000	1,280,000	960,000
Goods available for sale	1,440,000	1,600,000	1,360,000
Less ending inventory	320,000	400,000	80,000
Cost of goods sold	1,120,000	1,200,000	1,280,000
Underapplied or (overapplied) fixed overhead cost	(35,000)	—	140,000
Adjusted cost of goods sold	1,085,000	1,200,000	1,420,000
Gross margin	665,000	675,000	580,000
Less selling and administrative expenses . . .	620,000	650,000	680,000
Net income (loss)	$ 45,000	$ 25,000	$ (100,000)

Hal Taylor, a recent graduate from State University who has just been hired by Warner Company, has stated to Ms. Fisher that the contribution approach, with direct costing, is a much better way to report profit data to management. ''The contribution approach is a particularly good method to use when production is not moving in the same direction as sales,'' said Taylor. Sales and production data for the last quarter follow:

	July	August	September
Production in units . . .	85,000	80,000	60,000
Sales in units	70,000	75,000	80,000

Additional information about the company's operations is given below:

a. Five thousand units were in inventory on July 1.

b. Fixed manufacturing overhead costs total $1,680,000 per quarter and are incurred evenly throughout the quarter. This fixed overhead cost is applied to units of product on the basis of a budgeted production volume of 80,000 units per month.

c. Variable selling and administrative expenses are $6 per unit sold. The remainder of the selling and administrative expenses on the statements above are fixed.

d. The company uses a FIFO inventory flow. Work in process inventories are nominal and can be ignored.

Required: 1. Prepare an income statement for each month, using the contribution approach with direct costing.

2. Compute the monthly break-even point under:
    a. Direct costing.
    b. Absorption costing.

3. Explain to Ms. Fisher why profits have moved erratically over the three-month period shown in the absorption costing statements above and why profits have not been more closely correlated with changes in sales volume.

4. Reconcile the direct costing and absorption costing net income (loss) figures for each month. Show all computations, and show how you derive each figure used in your reconciliation.

CHAPTER 8

Profit Planning

LEARNING OBJECTIVES

After studying Chapter 8, you should be able to:

- Define budgeting and explain the difference between planning and control.

- Enumerate the principal advantages of budgeting.

- Diagram and explain the master budget interrelationships.

- Prepare a sales budget, including a computation of expected cash receipts.

- Prepare a production budget.

- Prepare a direct materials purchases budget, including a computation of expected cash disbursements.

- Prepare a manufacturing overhead budget and a selling and administrative expense budget.

- Prepare a cash budget, along with a budgeted income statement and a budgeted balance sheet.

- Compute the economic order quantity and the reorder point.

- Define or explain the key terms listed at the end of the chapter.

In this chapter, we focus our attention on those steps taken by business organizations to achieve certain desired levels of profits—a process that is generally called *profit planning*. In our study, we shall see that profit planning is accomplished through the preparation of a number of budgets, which, when brought together, form an integrated business plan known as the *master budget*. We shall find that the data going into the preparation of the master budget focus heavily on the future, rather than on the past.

THE BASIC FRAMEWORK OF BUDGETING

Definition of Budgeting

A **budget** is a detailed plan outlining the acquisition and use of financial and other resources over some given time period. It represents a plan for the future expressed in formal quantitative terms. The act of preparing a budget is called *budgeting*. The use of budgets to control a firm's activities is known as *budgetary control*.

The **master budget** is a summary of all phases of a company's plans and goals for the future. It sets specific targets for sales, production, distribution, and financing activities, and it generally culminates in a projected statement of net income and a projected statement of cash position. In short, it represents a comprehensive expression of management's plans for the future and how these plans are to be accomplished.

Personal Budgets

Nearly everyone budgets to some extent, even though many of the people who prepare and use budgets do not recognize what they are doing as budgeting. For example, most people make estimates of the income to be realized over some future time period and plan expenditures for food, clothing, housing, and so on, accordingly. As a result of this planning, spending will usually be restricted by limiting it to some predetermined, allowable amount. In taking these steps, the individual clearly goes through a budget process in that he or she (1) makes an estimate of income, (2) plans expenditures, and (3) restricts spending in accordance with the plan. In other situations, individuals use estimates of income and expenditures to predict what their financial condition will be in the future. The budgets involved here may exist only in the mind of the individual, but they are budgets nonetheless in that they involve plans of how resources will be acquired and used over some specific time period.

The budgets of a business firm serve much the same functions as the budgets prepared informally by individuals. Business budgets tend to be more detailed and to involve more work in preparation (mostly because they are formal rather than informal), but they are similar to the budgets prepared by individuals in most other respects. Like personal budgets, they assist in planning and controlling expenditures; they also assist in predicting operating results and financial condition in future periods.

Difference between Planning and Control

The terms *planning* and *control* are often confused, and occasionally these terms are used in such a way as to suggest that they mean the same thing. Actually, planning and control are two quite distinct concepts. **Planning** involves the development of future objectives and the preparation of various budgets to achieve these objectives. **Control** involves the steps taken by management to ensure that the objectives set down at the planning stage are attained, and to ensure that all parts of the organization function in a manner consistent with organizational policies. To be completely effective, a good budgeting system must provide for *both* planning and control. Good planning without effective control is time wasted. On the other hand, unless plans are laid down in advance, there are no objectives toward which control can be directed.

Advantages of Budgeting

There is an old saying to the effect that "a man is usually down on what he isn't up on." Managers who have never tried budgeting or attempted to find out what benefits might be available through the budget process are usually quick to state that budgeting is a waste of time. These managers may argue that even though budgeting may work well in *some* situations, it would never work well in their companies because operations are too complex or because there are too many uncertainties involved. In reality, however, managers who argue this way usually will be deeply involved in planning (albeit on an informal basis). These managers will have clearly defined thoughts about what they want to accomplish and when they want it accomplished. The difficulty is that unless they have some way of communicating their thoughts and plans to others, the only way their companies will ever attain the desired objectives will be through accident. In short, even though companies may attain a certain degree of success without budgets, they never attain the heights that could have been reached had a coordinated system of budgets been in operation.

One of the great values of budgeting is that it requires managers to give planning top priority among their duties. Moreover, budgeting provides managers with a vehicle for communicating their plans in an orderly way throughout an entire organization. When budgets are in use, no one has any doubt about what the managers want to accomplish or how they want it done. Other benefits of budgeting are:

1. It provides managers with a way to *formalize* their planning efforts.
2. It provides definite goals and objectives that serve as *benchmarks* for evaluating subsequent performance.

3. It uncovers potential *bottlenecks* before they occur.
4. It *coordinates* the activities of the entire organization by *integrating* the plans and objectives of the various parts. By so doing, budgeting ensures that the plans and objectives of the parts are consistent with the broad goals of the entire organization.

Consider the following situation encountered by the author:

Company X is a mortgage banking firm. For years, the company operated with virtually no system of budgets whatever. Management contended that budgeting wasn't well suited to the firm's type of operation. Moreover, management pointed out that the firm was already profitable. Indeed, outwardly the company gave every appearance of being a well-managed, smoothly operating organization. A careful look within, however, disclosed that day-to-day operations were far from smooth, and often approached chaos. The average day was nothing more than an exercise in putting out one brush fire after another. The Cash account was always at crisis levels. At the end of a day, no one ever knew whether enough cash would be available the next day to cover required loan closings. Departments were uncoordinated, and it was not uncommon to find that one department was pursuing a course that conflicted with the course pursued by another department. Employee morale was low, and turnover was high. Employees complained bitterly that when a job was well done, nobody ever knew about it.

Company X was bought out by a new group of stockholders who required that the company establish an integrated budgeting system to control operations. Within one year's time, significant changes were evident. Brush fires were rare. Careful planning virtually eliminated the problems that had been experienced with cash, and departmental efforts were coordinated and directed toward predetermined overall company goals. Although the employees were wary of the new budgeting program initially, they became "converted" when they saw the positive effects that it brought about. The more efficient operations caused profits to jump dramatically. Communication increased throughout the organization. When a job was well done, everybody knew about it. As one employee stated, "For the first time, we know what the company expects of us."

Responsibility Accounting

Most of what we say in the remainder of this chapter and in Chapters 9, 10, and 11 following centers on the concept of *responsibility accounting*. The basic idea behind **responsibility accounting** is that each manager's performance should be judged by how well he or she manages those items directly under his or her control. To judge a manager's performance in this way, the costs (and revenues) of an organization must be carefully scrutinized and classified according to the various levels of management under whose control the costs rest. Each level of management is then charged with those costs under its care, and the managers at each level are held responsible for variations between budgeted goals and actual results. In effect, responsibility accounting *personalizes* the accounting system by looking at costs from a *personal control* standpoint, rather than from an *institutional* standpoint. This concept is central to any effective profit planning and control system.

We will look at responsibility accounting in more detail in Chapters 9, 10, and 11. For the moment, we can summarize the overall idea by noting that it rests on three basic premises. The first premise is that costs can be organized in terms of levels of management responsibility. The second premise is that the costs charged to a particular level are controllable at that level by its managers. And the third premise is that effective budget data can be generated as a basis for evaluating actual performance. This chapter on profit planning is concerned with the third of these premises, in that the purpose of the chapter is to show the steps involved in budget preparation.

Choosing a Budget Period

Budgets covering acquisition of land, buildings, and other items of capital equipment (often called **capital budgets**) generally have quite long time horizons and may extend 30 years or more into the future. The later years covered by such budgets may be quite indefinite, but at least management is kept planning ahead sufficiently to ensure that funds will be available when purchases of equipment become necessary. As time passes, capital equipment plans that were once somewhat indefinite come more sharply into focus, and the capital budget is updated accordingly. Without such long-term planning, an organization can suddenly come to the realization that substantial purchases of capital equipment are needed, but find that no funds are available to make the purchases.

Operating budgets are ordinarily set to cover a one-year period. The one-year period should correspond to whatever fiscal year the company is following, so that the budget figures can be compared with the actual results. Many companies divide their budget year into four quarters. The first quarter is then subdivided into months, and monthly budget figures are established. These near-term figures can usually be established with considerable accuracy. The last three quarters are carried in the budget at quarterly totals only. As the year progresses, the figures for the second quarter are broken down into monthly amounts, then the third quarter figures are broken down, and so forth. This approach has the advantage of requiring a constant review and reappraisal of budget data.

Continuous or perpetual budgets are becoming very popular. A continuous or perpetual budget is one that covers a 12-month period but which is constantly adding a new month on the end as the current month is completed. Advocates of continuous budgets state that this approach to budgeting is superior to other approaches in that it keeps management thinking and planning a full 12 months ahead. Thus, it stabilizes the planning horizon. Under other budget approaches, the planning horizon becomes shorter as the year progresses.

The Self-Imposed Budget

The success of any budget program will be determined in large part by the way in which the budget itself is developed. Generally, the most successful budget programs are those that permit managers with responsibility over cost control to prepare their own budget estimates, as illustrated in Exhibit 8–1. This approach to preparing budget data is particularly important if the budget is to be used in controlling a manager's activities after it has been developed. If a budget is forced on a manager from above, it will probably generate resentment and ill will rather than cooperation and increased productivity.

When managers prepare their own budget figures, the budgets that they prepare become *self-imposed* in nature. Certain distinct advantages arise from the **self-imposed budget** (also called a **participative budget**):

team-building

1. Individuals at all levels of the organization are recognized as members of the team, whose views and judgments are valued by top management.

man. in dept knows best

2. The person in direct contact with an activity is in the best position to make budget estimates. Therefore, budget estimates prepared by such persons tend to be more accurate and reliable.

because self-imposed ∴ want to fulfill it

3. A person is more apt to work at fulfilling a budget that he has set

EXHIBIT 8–1

The initial flow of budget data

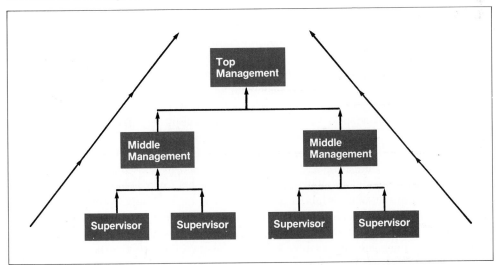

The initial flow of budget data is from lower levels of responsibility to higher levels of responsibility. Each person with responsibility for cost control will prepare his or her own budget estimates and submit them to the superior. These estimates are consolidated as they move upward in the organization.

himself than he is to work at fulfilling a budget imposed on him from above.

since they made budget only themselves to blame or credit.

4. A self-imposed budget contains its own unique system of control in that if people are not able to meet budget specifications, they have only themselves to blame. On the other hand, if a budget is imposed on them from above, they can always say that the budget was unreasonable or unrealistic to start with, and therefore was impossible to meet.

Once self-imposed budgets are prepared, are they subject to any kind of review? The answer is yes. Even though individual preparation of budget estimates is critical to a successful budgeting program, such budget estimates cannot necessarily be accepted without question by higher levels of management. If no system of checks and balances is present, the danger exists that self-imposed budgets will be too loose and allow too much freedom in activities. The result will be inefficiency and waste. Therefore, before budgets are accepted, they must be carefully reviewed by immediate superiors. If changes from the original budget seem desirable, the items in question are discussed and compromises are reached that are acceptable to all concerned.

In essence, all levels of an organization work together to produce the budget. Since top management is generally unfamiliar with detailed, day-to-day cost matters, it will rely on subordinates to provide detailed budget information. On the other hand, top management has a perspective on the company as a whole that is vital in making broad policy decisions in budget preparation. Each level of responsibility in an organization contributes in the way that it best can in a *cooperative* effort to develop an integrated budget document.

The Matter of Human Relations

Whether or not a budget program is accepted by lower management personnel will be reflective of (1) the degree to which top management accepts the budget program as a vital part of the company's activities, and (2) the way in which top management uses budgeted data.

If a budget program is to be successful, it must have the complete acceptance and support of the persons who occupy key management positions. If lower or middle management personnel sense that top management is lukewarm about budgeting, or if they sense that top management simply tolerates budgeting as a necessary evil, then their own attitudes will reflect a similar lack of enthusiasm. Budgeting is hard work, and if top management is not enthusiastic about and committed to the budget program, then it is unlikely that anyone else in the organization will be either.

In administering the budget program, it is particularly important that top management not use the budget as a "club" to pressure employees or as a way to find someone to "blame" for a particular problem. This type of negative emphasis will simply breed hostility, tension, and mistrust rather than greater cooperation and productivity. Unfortunately, research suggests that the budget is often used as a pressure device and that great emphasis is placed on "meeting the budget" under all circumstances.[1]

Rather than being used as a pressure device, the budget should be used as a positive instrument to assist in establishing goals, in measuring operating results, and in isolating areas that are in need of extra effort or attention. Any misgivings that employees have about a budget program can be overcome by meaningful involvement at all levels and by proper use of the program over a period of time. Administration of a budget program requires a great deal of insight and sensitivity on the part of management. The ultimate objective must be to develop the realization that the budget is designed to be a positive aid in achieving both individual and company goals.

Management must keep clearly in mind that the human dimension in budgeting is of key importance. It is easy for the manager to become preoccupied with the technical aspects of the budget program to the exclusion of the human aspects. Accountants are particularly open to criticism in this regard. Indeed, the study cited earlier found that use of budget data in a rigid and inflexible manner was the greatest single complaint of persons whose performance was being evaluated through the budget process.[2] In light of these facts, management should remember that the purposes of the budget are to motivate employees and to coordinate efforts. Preoccupation with the dollars and cents in the budget, or being rigid and inflexible in budget administration, can only lead to frustration of these purposes.

The Budget Committee

A standing **budget committee** will usually be responsible for overall policy matters relating to the budget program and for coordinating the preparation of the budget itself. This committee generally consists of the president; vice presidents in charge of various functions such as sales, production, and purchasing; and the controller. Difficulties and disputes between segments of the organization in matters relating to the budget are resolved by the budget committee. In addition, the budget committee approves the final budget and receives periodic reports on the progress of the company in attaining budgeted goals.

The Master Budget—a Network of Interrelationships

The master budget is a network consisting of many separate budgets that are interdependent. This network is illustrated in Exhibit 8–2.

The sales budget   A **sales budget** is a detailed schedule showing the expected sales for coming periods; typically, it is expressed in both dollars

---

[1] Paul J. Carruth, Thurrell O. McClendon, and Milton R. Ballard, "What Supervisors Don't Like about Budget Evaluations," *Management Accounting* 64, no. 8 (February 1983), p. 42.

[2] Ibid.

EXHIBIT 8-2

The master budget interrelationships

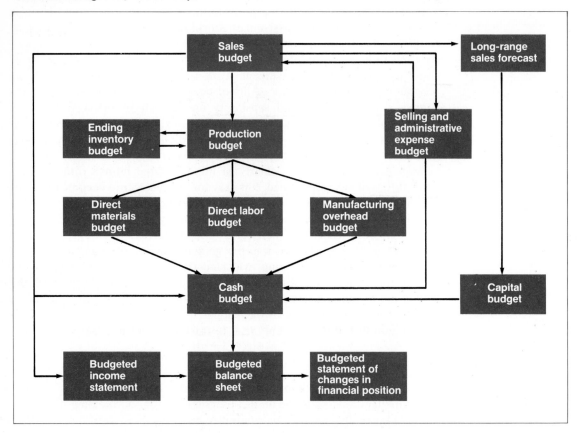

and units of product. Much time and effort is put into preparing an accurate sales budget since it is the key to the entire budgeting process. The reason it is the key is that all other parts of the master budget are dependent on the sales budget in some way, as illustrated in Exhibit 8–2. Thus, if the sales budget is sloppily done, then the rest of the budgeting process is largely a waste of time.

After the sales budget has been set, a decision can be made on the level of production that will be needed for the period to support sales, and the production budget can be set as well. The production budget then becomes a key factor in the determination of other budgets, including the direct materials budget, the direct labor budget, and the manufacturing overhead budget. These budgets, in turn, are needed to assist in formulating a cash budget for the budget period. In essence, the sales budget triggers a chain reaction that leads to the development of many other budget figures in an organization.

As shown in Exhibit 8–2, the selling and administrative expense budget is both dependent on and a determinant of the sales budget. This reciprocal relationship arises from the fact that sales will in part be determined by the funds available for advertising and sales promotion.

The cash budget Once the operating budgets (sales, production, and so on) have been established, the cash budget and other financial budgets can be prepared. A **cash budget** is a detailed plan showing how cash resources will be acquired and used over some specified time period. Observe from Exhibit 8–2 that all of the operating budgets, including the sales budget, have an impact of some type on the cash budget. In the case of the sales budget, the impact comes from the planned cash receipts to be received on sales. In the case of the other budgets, the impact comes from the planned cash expenditures within the budgets themselves.

Sales Forecasting—a Critical Step

The sales budget is prepared from the *sales forecast*. A **sales forecast** is broader than a sales budget, generally encompassing potential sales for the entire industry, as well as potential sales for the firm preparing the forecast. Factors that are considered in making a sales forecast include the following:

1. Past experience in terms of sales volume.
2. Prospective pricing policy.
3. Unfilled order backlogs.
4. Market research studies.
5. General economic conditions.
6. Industry economic conditions.
7. Movements of economic indicators such as gross national product, employment, prices, and personal income.
8. Advertising and product promotion.
9. Industry competition.
10. Market share.

Sales results from prior years are used as a starting point in preparing a sales forecast. Forecasters examine sales data in relation to various factors, including prices, competitive conditions, availability of supplies, and general economic conditions. Projections are then made into the future, based on those factors that the forecasters feel will be significant over the budget period. In-depth discussions generally characterize the gathering and interpretation of all data going into the sales forecast. These discussions, held at all levels of the organization, develop perspective and assist in assessing the significance and usefulness of data.

Statistical tools such as regression analysis, trend and cycle projection, and correlation analysis are widely used in sales forecasting. In addition, some firms have found it useful to build econometric models of their industry or of the nation to assist in forecasting problems. Such models hold great promise for improving the overall quality of budget data.

PREPARING THE MASTER BUDGET

To show how the separate budgets making up the master budget are developed and integrated, we focus now on Meredith Company. Meredith Company produces and sells a single product that we will call product A. Each year the company prepares the following budget documents:

1. A sales budget, including a computation of expected cash receipts.
2. A production budget (or merchandise purchases budget for a merchandising firm).
3. A direct materials budget, including a computation of expected cash payments for raw materials.
4. A direct labor budget.
5. A manufacturing overhead budget.
6. An ending finished goods inventory budget.
7. A selling and administrative expense budget.
8. A cash budget.
9. A budgeted income statement.
10. A budgeted balance sheet.

These budgets for the year 19x1 are illustrated in Schedules 1 through 10 following.

The Sales Budget

The sales budget is the starting point in preparing the master budget. As shown earlier in Exhibit 8–2, nearly all other items in the master budget, including production, purchases, inventories, and expenses, depend on it in some way.

The sales budget is constructed by multiplying the expected sales in units by the sales price. Schedule 1 on the following page contains the sales budget for Meredith Company for 19x1, by quarters. Notice from the schedule that the company plans to sell 100,000 units during the year, with sales peaking out in the third quarter.

Generally, the sales budget is accompanied by a computation of expected cash receipts for the forthcoming budget period. This computation is needed to assist in preparing the cash budget for the year. Expected cash receipts are composed of collections on sales made to customers in prior periods, plus collections on sales made in the current budget period. Schedule 1 below contains a computation of expected cash collections for Meredith Company.

The Production Budget

After the sales budget has been prepared, the production requirements for the forthcoming budget period can be determined and organized in the form of a **production budget.** Sufficient goods will have to be available to meet sales needs and provide for the desired ending inventory. A portion

Schedule 1

MEREDITH COMPANY
Sales Budget
For the Year Ended December 31, 19x1

	Quarters				
	1	**2**	**3**	**4**	**Year**
Expected sales in units.	10,000	30,000	40,000	20,000	100,000
Selling price per unit	× $20	× $20	× $20	× $20	× $20
Total sales	$200,000	$600,000	$800,000	$400,000	$2,000,000

Schedule of Expected Cash Collections

	1	**2**	**3**	**4**	**Year**
Accounts receivable, 12/31/x0	$ 90,000				$ 90,000
First quarter sales ($200,000)	140,000	$ 60,000			200,000
Second quarter sales ($600,000)		420,000	$180,000		600,000
Third quarter sales ($800,000)			560,000	$240,000	800,000
Fourth quarter sales ($400,000)				280,000	280,000
Total cash collections	$230,000	$480,000	$740,000	$520,000	$1,970,000

Note: Seventy percent of a quarter's sales is collected in the quarter of sale; the remaining 30 percent is collected in the quarter following.

of these goods will already exist in the form of a beginning inventory. The remainder will have to be produced. Therefore, production needs can be determined by adding budgeted sales (in units or in dollars) to the desired ending inventory (in units or in dollars), and deducting the beginning inventory (in units or in dollars) from this total. Schedule 2 below contains a production budget for Meredith Company.

Schedule 2

MEREDITH COMPANY
Production Budget
For the Year Ended December 31, 19x1
(in units)

	Quarters				
	1	**2**	**3**	**4**	**Year**
Expected sales (Schedule 1)	10,000	30,000	40,000	20,000	100,000
Add desired ending inventory of finished goods*	6,000	8,000	4,000	3,000	3,000[†]
Total needs	16,000	38,000	44,000	23,000	103,000
Less beginning inventory of finished goods‡	2,000	6,000	8,000	4,000	2,000
Units to be produced	14,000	32,000	36,000	19,000	101,000

*Twenty percent of the next quarter's sales.
†Estimated.
‡The same as the prior quarter's *ending* inventory.

Students are often surprised to learn that firms budget the level of their ending inventories. Budgeting of inventories is a common practice, however. If inventories are not carefully planned, the levels remaining at the end of a period may be excessive, causing an unnecessary tie-up of funds and an unneeded expense of carrying the unwanted goods. On the other hand, without proper planning, inventory levels may be too small, thereby requiring crash production efforts in following periods, and perhaps loss of sales due to inability to meet shipping schedules.

Inventory Purchases—Merchandising Firm

Meredith Company prepares a production budget since it is a *manufacturing* firm. If it were a *merchandising* firm, then instead of a production budget it would prepare a **merchandise purchases budget** showing the amount of goods to be purchased from its suppliers during the period. The merchandise purchases budget is in the same basic format as the production budget, except that it shows goods to be purchased rather than goods to be produced, as shown below:

Budgeted cost of goods sold (in units or in dollars)	XXXXX
Add desired ending merchandise inventory	XXXXX
Total needs.	XXXXX
Less beginning merchandise inventory	XXXXX
Required purchases (in units or in dollars)	XXXXX

The merchandising firm would prepare an inventory purchases budget such as this one for each item carried in stock. Some large retail organizations make such computations on a frequent basis (particularly at peak seasons) in order to ensure that adequate stocks are on hand to meet customer needs.

The Direct Materials Budget

Returning to the Meredith Company example, after production needs have been computed, a **direct materials budget** should be prepared to show the materials that will be required in the production process. Sufficient raw materials will have to be available to meet production needs, and to provide for the desired ending raw materials inventory for the budget period. Part of this raw materials requirement will already exist in the form of a beginning raw materials inventory. The remainder will have to be purchased from suppliers. In sum, the format for computing raw materials needs is:

Raw materials needed to meet the production schedule . . .	XXXXX
Add desired ending inventory of raw materials	XXXXX
Total raw materials needs	XXXXX
Less beginning inventory of raw materials	XXXXX
Raw materials to be purchased	XXXXX

Preparing a budget of this kind is one step in a company's overall **material requirements planning (MRP).** MRP is an operations research tool that employs the computer to assist the manager in overall materials and inventory planning. The objective of MRP is to ensure that the right materials are on hand, in the right quantities, and at the right time to support the production process. The detailed operation of MRP is covered in most operations research textbooks; for this reason, it will not be considered further here, other than to point out that the concepts we are discussing are an important part of the overall MRP technique.

Schedule 3 contains a direct materials purchases budget for Meredith Company. Notice that materials requirements are first determined in units (pounds, gallons, and so on) and then translated into dollars by multiplying by the appropriate unit cost.

The direct materials budget is usually accompanied by a computation of

Schedule 3

MEREDITH COMPANY
Direct Materials Budget
For the Year Ended December 31, 19x1

	Quarters				
	1	**2**	**3**	**4**	**Year**
Units to be produced (Schedule 2)	14,000	32,000	36,000	19,000	101,000
Raw material needs per unit (pounds)	× 5	× 5	× 5	× 5	× 5
Production needs (pounds)	70,000	160,000	180,000	95,000	505,000
Add desired ending inventory of raw materials˙ (pounds)	16,000	18,000	9,500	7,500	7,500
Total needs (pounds)	86,000	178,000	189,500	102,500	512,500
Less beginning inventory of raw materials (pounds)	7,000	16,000	18,000	9,500	7,000
Raw materials to be purchased (pounds)	79,000	162,000	171,500	93,000	505,500
Cost of raw materials to be purchased at $0.60 per pound	$47,400	$ 97,200	$102,900	$ 55,800	$303,300

˙Ten percent of the next quarter's production needs. For example, the second-quarter production needs are 160,000 pounds. Therefore, the desired ending inventory for the first quarter would be 10 percent × 160,000 pounds = 16,000 pounds. The ending inventory of 7,500 pounds for the fourth quarter is estimated.

Schedule of Expected Cash Disbursements

	1	2	3	4	Year
Accounts payable, 12/31/x0	$25,800				$ 25,800
First-quarter purchases ($47,400)	23,700	$ 23,700			47,400
Second-quarter purchases ($97,200)		48,600	$ 48,600		97,200
Third-quarter purchases ($102,900)			51,450	$ 51,450	102,900
Fourth-quarter purchases ($55,800)				27,900	27,900
Total cash disbursements	$49,500	$ 72,300	$100,050	$ 79,350	$301,200

Note: Fifty percent of a quarter's purchases is paid for in the quarter of purchase; the remaining 50 percent is paid for in the quarter following.

expected cash disbursements for raw materials. This computation is needed to assist in developing a cash budget. Disbursements for raw materials will consist of payments for prior periods, plus payments for purchases for the current budget period. Schedule 3 contains a computation of expected cash disbursements for Meredith Company.

The Direct Labor Budget

The **direct labor budget** is also developed from the production budget. Direct labor requirements must be computed so that the company will know whether sufficient labor time is available to meet production needs. By knowing in advance just what will be needed in the way of labor time throughout the budget year, the company can develop plans to adjust the labor force as the situation may require. Firms that neglect to budget run the risk of facing labor shortages or having to hire and fire at awkward times. Erratic labor policies lead to insecurity and inefficiency on the part of employees.

To compute direct labor requirements, the number of units of finished product to be produced each period (month, quarter, and so on) is multiplied by the number of direct labor-hours required to produce a single unit. Many different types of labor may be involved. If so, then computations should be by type of labor needed. The hours of direct labor time resulting from these computations can then be multiplied by the direct labor cost per hour to obtain budgeted total direct labor costs. Schedule 4 following contains such computations for Meredith Company.

The Manufacturing Overhead Budget

The **manufacturing overhead budget** should provide a schedule of all costs of production other than direct materials and direct labor. These costs should be broken down by cost behavior for budgeting purposes, and a

Schedule 4

MEREDITH COMPANY **Direct Labor Budget** **For the Year Ended December 31, 19x1**					
	Quarters				
	1	**2**	**3**	**4**	**Year**
Units to be produced (Schedule 2)	14,000	32,000	36,000	19,000	101,000
Direct labor time per unit (hours)	× 0.8	× 0.8	× 0.8	× 0.8	× 0.8
Total hours of direct labor time needed	11,200	25,600	28,800	15,200	80,800
Direct labor cost per hour	× $7.50	× $7.50	× $7.50	× $7.50	× $7.50
Total direct labor cost	$84,000	$192,000	$216,000	$114,000	$606,000

Schedule 5

MEREDITH COMPANY Manufacturing Overhead Budget For the Year Ended December 31, 19x1					
	Quarters				
	1	**2**	**3**	**4**	**Year**
Budgeted direct labor-hours	11,200	25,600	28,800	15,200	80,800
Variable overhead rate	× $2	× $2	× $2	× $2	× $2
Budgeted variable overhead	$22,400	$ 51,200	$ 57,600	$30,400	$161,600
Budgeted fixed overhead	60,600	60,600	60,600	60,600	242,400
Total budgeted overhead	83,000	111,800	118,200	91,000	404,000
Less depreciation	15,000	15,000	15,000	15,000	60,000
Cash disbursements for overhead	$68,000	$ 96,800	$103,200	$76,000	$344,000

predetermined overhead rate developed. This rate will be used to apply manufacturing overhead to units of product throughout the budget period.

A computation showing budgeted cash disbursements for manufacturing overhead should be made for use in developing the cash budget. The critical thing to remember in making this computation is that depreciation is a noncash charge. Therefore, any depreciation charges included in manufacturing overhead must be deducted from the total in computing expected cash payments.

We will assume that the variable overhead rate is $2 per direct labor-hour, and that fixed overhead costs are budgeted at $60,600 per quarter, of which $15,000 represents depreciation. All overhead costs involving cash disbursements are paid for in the quarter incurred. The manufacturing overhead budget, by quarters, and the expected cash disbursements, by quarters, are both shown in Schedule 5.

Ending Finished Goods Inventory Budget

After completing Schedules 1–5, sufficient data will have been generated to compute the cost of a unit of finished product. This computation is needed for two reasons: first, to know how much to charge as cost of goods sold on the budgeted income statement; and second, to know what amount to place on the balance sheet for unsold units. The dollar amount of the unsold units planned to be on hand is known as the **ending finished goods inventory budget.**

For Meredith Company, the cost of a unit of finished product is $13—consisting of $3 of direct materials, $6 of direct labor, and $4 of manufacturing overhead—and the ending finished goods inventory is budgeted to be $39,000. The computations behind these figures are shown in Schedule 6.

Schedule 6

MEREDITH COMPANY
Ending Finished Goods Inventory Budget
For the Year Ended December 31, 19x1

Item	Quantity	Cost	Total
Production cost per unit:			
Direct materials	5.0 pounds	$0.60 per pound	$ 3
Direct labor.	0.8 hours	7.50 per hour	6
Manufacturing overhead . . .	0.8 hours	5.00 per hour*	4
			$13

Budgeted finished goods inventory:
Ending finished goods inventory in units (Schedule 2)   3,000
Total production cost per unit (see above) . . . .   × $13
Ending finished goods inventory in dollars $39,000

*$404,000 ÷ 80,800 hours = $5.00.

The Selling and Administrative Expense Budget

The **selling and administrative expense budget** contains a listing of anticipated expenses for the budget period that will be incurred in areas other than manufacturing. The budget will be made up of many smaller, individual budgets submitted by various persons having responsibility for cost control in selling and administrative matters. If the number of expense items is very large, separate budgets may be needed for the selling and administrative functions.

Schedule 7 contains the selling and administrative expense budget for Meredith Company for 19x1.

The Cash Budget

The cash budget pulls together much of the data developed in the preceding steps, as illustrated earlier in Exhibit 8–2. The reader should restudy this exhibit before reading on.

The cash budget is composed of four major sections:

1.   The receipts section.
2.   The disbursements section.
3.   The cash excess or deficiency section.
4.   The financing section.

The receipts section consists of the opening cash balance added to whatever is expected in the way of cash receipts during the budget period. Generally, the major source of receipts will be from sales, as discussed earlier.

The disbursements section consists of all cash payments that are planned for the budget period. These payments will include raw materials purchases,

337

Schedule 7

MEREDITH COMPANY
Selling and Administrative Expense Budget
For the Year Ended December 31, 19x1

	Quarters				
	1	2	3	4	Year
Budgeted sales in units	10,000	30,000	40,000	20,000	100,000
Variable selling and administrative expense per unit*	× $1.80	× $1.80	× $1.80	× $1.80	× $1.80
Budgeted variable expense	$18,000	$ 54,000	$ 72,000	$ 36,000	$180,000
Fixed selling and administrative expense:					
Advertising	40,000	40,000	40,000	40,000	160,000
Executive salaries	35,000	35,000	35,000	35,000	140,000
Insurance	—	1,900	37,750	—	39,650
Property taxes	—	—	—	18,150	18,150
Total budgeted selling and administrative expenses	$93,000	$130,900	$184,750	$129,150	$537,800

*Commissions, clerical, and freight-out.

direct labor payments, manufacturing overhead costs, and so on, as contained in their respective budgets. In addition, other cash disbursements such as income taxes, capital equipment purchases, and dividend payments will also be included.

The cash excess or deficiency section consists of the difference between the cash receipts section totals and the cash disbursements section totals. If a deficiency exists, the company will need to arrange for borrowed funds from its bank. If an excess exists, funds borrowed in previous periods can be repaid or the idle funds can be placed in short-term investments.

The financing section provides a detailed account of the borrowings and repayments projected to take place during the budget period. It also includes a detail of interest payments that will be due on money borrowed. Banks are becoming increasingly insistent that firms in need of borrowed money give long advance notice of the amounts and times that funds will be needed. This permits the banks to plan and helps to assure that funds will be ready when needed. Moreover, careful planning of cash needs via the budgeting process avoids unpleasant surprises for companies as well. Few things are more disquieting to an organization than to run into unexpected difficulties in the Cash account. A well-coordinated budgeting program eliminates uncertainty as to what the cash situation will be two months, six months, or a year from now.

The cash budget should be broken down into time periods that are as short as feasible. Many firms budget cash on a weekly basis, and some larger firms go so far as to plan daily cash needs. The more common planning horizons are geared to monthly or quarterly figures. The cash

MEREDITH COMPANY
Cash Budget
For the Year Ended December 31, 19x1

	Schedule	1	2	3	4	Year
				Quarters		
Cash balance, beginning		$ 42,500	$ 40,000	$ 40,000	$ 40,500	$ 42,500
Add receipts:						
Collections from customers	1	230,000	480,000	740,000	520,000	1,970,000
Total cash available before current financing		272,500	520,000	780,000	560,500	2,012,500
Less disbursements:						
Direct materials	3	49,500	72,300	100,050	79,350	301,200
Direct labor	4	84,000	192,000	216,000	114,000	606,000
Manufacturing overhead	5	68,000	96,800	103,200	76,000	344,000
Selling and administrative	7	93,000	130,900	184,750	129,150	537,800
Income taxes	9	18,000	18,000	18,000	18,000	72,000
Equipment purchases		30,000	20,000	—	—	50,000
Dividends		10,000	10,000	10,000	10,000	40,000
Total disbursements		352,500	540,000	632,000	426,500	1,951,000
Excess (deficiency) of cash available over disbursements		(80,000)	(20,000)	148,000	134,000	61,500
Financing:						
Borrowings (at beginning)		120,000*	60,000	—	—	180,000
Repayments (at ending)		—	—	(100,000)†	(80,000)†	(180,000)
Interest (at 10% per annum)		—	—	(7,500)†	(6,500)†	(14,000)
Total financing		120,000	60,000	(107,500)	(86,500)	(14,000)
Cash balance, ending		$ 40,000	$ 40,000	$ 40,500	$ 47,500	$ 47,500

*The company requires a minimum cash balance of $40,000. Therefore, borrowing must be sufficient to cover the cash deficiency of $80,000 and to provide for the minimum cash balance of $40,000. All borrowings and all repayments of principal are in round $1,000 amounts.

†The interest payments relate only to the principal being repaid at the time it is repaid. For example, the interest in quarter 3 relates only to the interest due on the $100,000 principal being repaid from quarter 1 borrowing, as follows: $100,000 × 10% × ¾ = $7,500. The interest paid in quarter 4 is computed as follows:

$20,000 × 10% × 1 year		$2,000
$60,000 × 10% × ¾		4,500
Total interest paid		$6,500

budget for Meredith Company for 19x1 is shown on a quarterly basis in Schedule 8.[3]

The Budgeted Income Statement

A budgeted income statement can be prepared from the data developed in Schedules 1–8. *The budgeted income statement is one of the key schedules in the budget process.* It is the document that tells how profitable operations are anticipated to be in the forthcoming period. After it has been developed, it stands as a benchmark against which subsequent company performance can be measured.

Schedule 9 below contains a budgeted income statement for Meredith Company for 19x1.

The Budgeted Balance Sheet

The budgeted balance sheet is developed by beginning with the current balance sheet and adjusting it for the data contained in the other budgets. A budgeted balance sheet for Meredith Company for 19x1 is presented in Schedule 10. The company's beginning-of-year balance sheet, from which

Schedule 9

MEREDITH COMPANY Budgeted Income Statement For the Year Ended December 31, 19x1		
	Schedule	
Sales (100,000 units at $20)	1	$2,000,000
Less cost of goods sold (100,000 units at $13)	6	1,300,000
Gross margin		700,000
Less selling and administrative expense	7	537,800
Net operating income		162,200
Less interest expense	8	14,000
Income before taxes		148,200
Less income taxes	*	72,000
Net income		$ 76,200

*Estimated.

---

[3] Meredith Company has an open line of credit with its bank, which can be used as needed to bolster the cash position. Borrowings and repayments must be in round $1,000 amounts, and interest is 10 percent per annum. Interest is computed and paid on the principal as the principal is repaid. All borrowings take place at the beginning of a quarter, and all repayments are made at the end of a quarter.

the budgeted balance sheet in Schedule 10 has been derived in part, is presented below:

MEREDITH COMPANY
Balance Sheet
December 31, 19x0

Assets

Current assets:

Cash	$ 42,500	
Accounts receivable	90,000	
Raw materials inventory (700 pounds)	4,200	
Finished goods inventory (2,000 units)	26,000	
Total current assets		$162,700

Plant and equipment:

Land	80,000	
Buildings and equipment	700,000	
Accumulated depreciation	(292,000)	
Plant and equipment, net		488,000
Total assets		$650,700

Liabilities and Stockholders' Equity

Current liabilities:

Accounts payable (raw materials)		$ 25,800

Stockholders' equity:

Common stock, no par	$175,000	
Retained earnings	449,900	
Total stockholders' equity		624,900
Total liabilities and stockholders' equity		$650,700

JUST IN TIME (JIT) INVENTORY SYSTEMS

In the Meredith Company example we have just completed, inventories of raw materials, fabricated parts, and finished goods were planned for and carried in stock *just in case* something unexpected happened—such as a supply interruption, a production snag, or a flurry of orders—that required the inventory to act as a buffer. By contrast to the "just in case" approach, a new approach to inventory control—called a **just in time (JIT) inventory system**—is gaining widespread attention. Simply stated, the purpose of a JIT inventory system is to:

> Produce and deliver finished goods *just in time* to be sold, subassemblies *just in time* to be assembled into finished goods, fabricated parts *just in time* to go into subassemblies, and purchased materials *just in time* to be [manufactured] into fabricated parts.[4] (Emphasis supplied.)

---

[4] Richard J. Schonberger, *Japanese Manufacturing Techniques: Nine Hidden Lessons in Simplicity* (New York: The Free Press, a Division of Macmillan, Inc., 1982), p. 16. © 1982 by Richard J. Schonberger.

Schedule 10

MEREDITH COMPANY
Budgeted Balance Sheet
December 31, 19x1

Assets

Current assets:
Cash	$ 47,500	(a)
Accounts receivable	120,000	(b)
Raw materials inventory	4,500	(c)
Finished goods inventory	39,000	(d)

Total current assets $211,000

Plant and equipment:
Land	80,000	(e)
Buildings and equipment	750,000	(f)
Accumulated depreciation	(352,000)	(g)

Plant and equipment, net   478,000

Total assets $689,000

Liabilities and Stockholders' Equity

Current liabilities:

Accounts payable (raw materials) . . . . $ 27,900 (h)

Stockholders' equity:
Common stock, no par	$175,000	(i)
Retained earnings	486,100	(j)

Total stockholders' equity   661,100

Total liabilities and stockholders' equity $689,000

Explanation of December 31, 19x1, balance sheet figures:
a. The ending cash balance, as projected by the cash budget in Schedule 8.
b. Thirty percent of fourth-quarter sales, from Schedule 1 ($400,000 × 30% = $120,000).
c. From Schedule 3, the ending raw materials inventory will be 7,500 pounds. This material costs $0.60 per pound. Therefore, the ending inventory in dollars will be 7,500 pounds × $0.60 = $4,500.
d. From Schedule 6.
e. From the December 31, 19x0, balance sheet (no change).
f. The December 31, 19x0, balance sheet indicated a balance of $700,000. During 19x1, $50,000 additional equipment will be purchased (see Schedule 8), bringing the December 31, 19x1, balance to $750,000.
g. The December 31, 19x0, balance sheet indicated a balance of $292,000. During 19x1, $60,000 of depreciation will be taken (see Schedule 5), bringing the December 31, 19x1, balance to $352,000.
h. One half of the fourth-quarter raw materials purchases, from Schedule 3.
i. From the December 31, 19x0, balance sheet (no change).
j. December 31, 19x0, balance $449,900
   Add net income, from Schedule 9 76,200
                            526,100
   Deduct dividends paid, from Schedule 8 . . 40,000
   December 31, 19x1, balance $486,100

As this statement suggests, JIT is designed to reduce (or even to eliminate) inventories in a company. JIT accomplishes this feat through what is described as a "pull" approach to the manufacture of products.[5] The "pull" approach can be explained as follows: At the final assembly stage, a signal is sent to the preceding workstation as to the exact amount of parts and materials that will be needed *over the next few hours* for the assembly of products, and *only* that amount of parts and materials is provided. The same signal is sent back through each preceding workstation so that a smooth flow of parts and materials is maintained with no inventory buildup at any point. Thus, all workstations respond in turn to the "pull" exerted by the final assembly stage.

The "pull" approach described above can be contrasted to the "push" approach required by the "just-in-case" inventory system. In the "just-in-case" system, inventories of parts and materials are built up and "pushed" forward to the next workstation, resulting in a tie-up of funds and a stockpiling of parts that may not be used for days or even weeks.

Key Elements in a JIT System

Three key elements are involved in the successful operation of a JIT inventory system. First, a company must learn to rely on a few suppliers who are bound under long-term contracts. Since under a JIT system a company is highly vulnerable to any interruption in supply, undependable or marginal suppliers must be weeded out and all purchasing concentrated in those suppliers with proven records of dependability.

Second, the suppliers chosen must be willing to make frequent deliveries in small lots. Rather than deliver a week's (or a month's) parts and materials at one time, suppliers must be willing to make deliveries *several times a day* and in the exact quantities specified by the buyer. Obviously, this type of purchasing requires constant and direct communication between a company and its suppliers.

Third, a company must develop a system of **total quality control (TQC)** over its parts and materials. By TQC we mean that no defects can be allowed. The need for TQC is obvious: since one workstation provides only the parts and materials being requested (pulled) by the next workstation, one or two defective parts could close down the entire assembly line. To avoid this happening, a company must maintain TQC through a continuous monitoring of operations and through an early warning system that detects and eliminates all defective items.

---

[5] For excellent discussions of the characteristics and use of JIT inventory systems, see: Arjan T. Sadhwani, M. H. Sarhan, and Dayal Kiringoda, "Just-in-Time: An Inventory System Whose Time Has Come," *Management Accounting* 67, no. 6 (December 1985), pp. 36–44; and Ragnor Seglund and Santiago Ibarreche, "Just-in-Time: The Accounting Implications," *Management Accounting* 66, no. 2 (August 1984), pp. 43–45.

Benefits of a JIT System

Although the requirements for a JIT system may seem unduly stringent, many companies have employed JIT with great success. Following are some of the benefits cited as coming from a JIT system:

1. Inventories of all types can be reduced significantly with a corresponding release of investment funds that can be used elsewhere in the company.
2. Storage space being used for inventories can be made available for other, more productive uses.
3. Through TQC, waste can be reduced with ''zero defects'' resulting in some cases.
4. Machine setup time can be reduced by improving the flow of goods between workstations.

As a result of benefits such as those cited above, more companies are employing JIT systems each year. In time, the JIT approach probably will become the dominant method of inventory control in many industries.

ZERO-BASE BUDGETING

Zero-base budgeting has received considerable attention recently as a new approach to preparing budget data, particularly for use in not-for-profit, governmental, and service type organizations. The type of budget prepared under this approach—called a **zero-base budget**—is so named because managers are required to start at zero budget levels every year and justify all costs as if the programs involved were being initiated for the first time. By ''justify,'' we mean that no costs are viewed as being ongoing in nature; the manager must start at the ground level each year and present justification for all costs in the proposed budget, regardless of the type of cost involved. This is done in a series of ''decision packages'' in which the manager ranks all of the activities in the department according to relative importance, going from those that he or she considers essential to those that he or she considers of least importance. Presumably, this allows top management to evaluate each decision package independently and to pare back in those areas that appear less critical or that do not appear to be justified in terms of the cost involved.

This process differs from traditional budgeting, in which budgets are generally initiated on an incremental basis; that is, the manager starts with last year's budget and simply adds to it (or subtracts from it) according to anticipated needs. The manager doesn't have to start at the ground each year and justify ongoing costs (such as salaries) for existing programs.

In a broader sense, zero-base budgeting isn't really a new concept at all. Managers have always advocated in-depth reviews of departmental costs. The only difference is the frequency with which this review is carried out. Zero-base budgeting says that it should be done annually; critics of the zero-base idea say that this is too often and that such reviews should be made only every five years or so. These critics say that annual in-depth reviews are too time-consuming and too costly to be really feasible, and that in the long run such reviews probably cannot be justified in terms of the cost savings involved. In addition, it is argued that annual reviews soon become mechanical and that the whole purpose of the zero-base idea is then lost.

The question of frequency of zero-base reviews must be left to the judgment of the individual manager. In some situations, annual zero-base reviews may be justified; in other situations, they may not because of the time and cost involved. Whatever the time period chosen, however, most managers would agree that zero-base reviews can be helpful and should be an integral part of the overall budgeting process.

THE NEED FOR FURTHER BUDGETING MATERIAL

The material covered in this chapter represents no more than an introduction into the vast area of budgeting and profit planning. Our purpose has been to present an overview of the budgeting process and to show how the various operating budgets build on each other in guiding a firm toward its profit objectives. However, the matter of budgeting and profit planning is so critical to the intelligent management of a firm in today's business environment that we can't stop with simply an overview of the budgeting process. We need to look more closely at budgeting to see how it helps managers in the day-to-day conduct of business affairs. We will do this by studying standard costs and flexible budgets in the following two chapters and by introducing the concept of performance reporting. In Chapter 11, we will expand on these ideas by looking at budgeting and profit planning as tools for control of decentralized operations and as facilitating factors in judging managerial performance.

In sum, the materials in the following two chapters build on the budgeting and profit planning foundation that has been laid in this chapter by expanding on certain concepts that have been introduced and by refining others. The essential thing to keep in mind at this point is that the material covered in this chapter does not conclude our study of budgeting and profit planning, but rather just introduces the ideas.

KEY TERMS FOR REVIEW

Budget A detailed plan outlining the acquisition and use of financial and other resources over some given time period.

Budget committee A group of key management persons who are responsible for overall policy matters relating to the budget program and for coordinating the preparation of the budget itself.

Capital budget A budget covering the acquisition of land, buildings, and items of equipment; such a budget may have a time horizon extending 30 years or more into the future.

Cash budget A detailed plan showing how cash resources will be acquired and used over some specific time period.

Continuous or perpetual budget A budget that covers a 12-month period but is constantly adding a new month on the end as the current month is completed.

Control Those steps taken by management to ensure that the objectives set down at the planning stage are attained and to ensure that all parts of the organization function in a manner consistent with organizational policies.

Direct labor budget A detailed plan showing labor requirements over some specific time period.

Direct materials budget A detailed plan showing the amount of raw material that must be purchased during a period to meet both production and inventory needs.

Ending finished goods inventory budget A budget showing the dollar amount of cost expected to appear on the balance sheet for unsold units at the end of a period.

Just-in-time (JIT) inventory system A method of inventory control designed to reduce (or even eliminate) inventories in a company. Under this approach, all workstations respond to signals from the final assembly stage and provide only those parts and supplies needed to keep products moving smoothly with no inventory buildup at any point.

Manufacturing overhead budget A detailed plan showing the production costs, other than direct materials and direct labor, that will be incurred in attaining the output budgeted for a period.

Master budget A summary of all phases of a company's plans and goals for the future in which specific targets are set for sales, production, and financing activities and that generally culminates in a projected statement of net income and a projected statement of cash position.

Material requirements planning (MRP) An operations research tool that employs the computer to assist the manager in overall materials and inventory planning.

Merchandise purchases budget A budget used by a merchandising firm that shows the amount of goods that must be purchased from suppliers during the period.

Participative budget See *Self-imposed budget.*

Planning The development of objectives in an organization and the preparation of various budgets to achieve these objectives.

Production budget A detailed plan showing the number of units that must be produced during a period in order to meet both sales and inventory needs.

Responsibility accounting A system of accounting in which costs are assigned to various managerial levels according to where control of the costs is deemed to rest, with the managers then held responsible for differences between budgeted and actual results.

Sales budget A detailed schedule showing the expected sales for coming periods; these sales are typically expressed in both dollars and units.

Sales forecast A schedule of expected sales for an entire industry.

Self-imposed budget A method of budget preparation in which managers with responsibility over cost control prepare their own budget figures; these budget figures are reviewed by the managers' supervisors, and any questions are then resolved in face-to-face meetings.

Selling and administrative expense budget A detailed schedule of planned expenses that will be incurred in areas other than manufacturing during a budget period.

Total quality control (TQC) A monitoring and early warning system used under JIT that is designed to detect and eliminate all defective parts and materials.

Zero-base budget A method of budgeting in which managers are required to start at zero budget levels every year and to justify all costs as if the programs involved were being initiated for the first time.

APPENDIX: ECONOMIC ORDER QUANTITY AND THE REORDER POINT

As stated in the main body of the chapter, inventory planning and control are an essential part of a budgeting system. We have seen that inventory levels are not left to chance but rather are carefully planned for, in terms of both opening and closing balances. Major questions that we have left unanswered are, "How does the manager know what inventory level is 'right' for the firm?" and "Won't the level that is 'right' vary from organization to organization?" The purpose of this section is to examine the inventory control methods available to the manager for answering these questions.

Costs Associated with Inventory

Three groups of costs are associated with inventory. The first group, known as **inventory ordering costs,** consists of costs associated with the acquisition of inventory. Examples include:

1. Clerical costs.
2. Transportation costs.

The second group, known as **inventory carrying costs,** consists of costs that arise from having inventory in stock. Examples include:

1. Storage space costs.
2. Handling costs.
3. Property taxes.
4. Insurance.
5. Obsolescence losses.
6. Interest on capital invested in inventory.

The third group, known as **costs of not carrying sufficient inventory,** consists of costs that result from not having enough inventory in stock to meet customers' needs. Costs in this group are more difficult to identify than costs in the other two groups, but nevertheless they can include items that are very significant to a firm. Examples of costs in this group are:

1. Customer ill will.
2. Quantity discounts foregone.
3. Erratic production (expediting of goods, extra setup, etc.).
4. Inefficiency of production runs.
5. Added transportation charges.
6. Lost sales.

In a broad conceptual sense, the "right" level of inventory to carry is the level that will minimize the total of these three groups of costs. Such a minimization is difficult to achieve, however, since certain of the costs involved are in direct conflict with one another. Notice, for example, that as inventory levels increase, the costs of carrying inventory will also increase, but the costs of not carrying sufficient inventory will decrease. In working toward total cost minimization, therefore, the manager must balance off the three groups of costs against one another. The problem really has two dimensions—how much to order (or how much to produce in a production run) and how often to do it.

Computing the Economic Order Quantity

The "how much to order" is commonly referred to as the **economic order quantity.** It is the order size that will result in a minimization of the first two groups of costs above. We will consider two approaches to computing the economic order quantity—the tabular approach and the formula approach.

The tabular approach   Given a certain annual consumption of an item, a firm might place a few orders each year of a large quantity each, or it might place many orders of a small quantity each. Placing only a few orders would result in low inventory ordering costs but in high inventory carrying costs, since the average inventory level would be very large. On the other hand, placing many orders would result in high inventory ordering costs but in low inventory carrying costs, since in this case the average inventory level would be quite small. As stated above, the economic order quantity seeks the order size that will balance off these two groups of costs. To show how it is computed, assume that a manufacturer uses 3,000 subassemblies in the manufacturing process each year. The subassemblies are purchased from a supplier at a cost of $20 each. Other cost data are given below:

Inventory carrying costs, per unit, per year . . . $ 0.80
Cost of placing a purchase order 10.00

Exhibit 8–3 contains a tabulation of the total costs associated with various order sizes for the subassemblies. Notice that total annual cost is lowest

EXHIBIT 8–3

Tabulation of costs associated with various order sizes

		Order size in units								
Symbol*		**25**	**50**	**100**	**200**	**250**	**300**	**400**	**1,000**	**3,000**
O/2	Average inventory in units. . . .	12.5	25	50	100	125	150	200	500	1,500
Q/O	Number of purchase orders . . .	120	60	30	15	12	10	7.5	3	1
C(O/2)	Annual carrying cost at									
	$0.80 per unit	$ 10	$ 20	$ 40	$ 80	$100	$120	$160	$400	$1,200
P(Q/O)	Annual purchase order cost									
	at $10 per order	1,200	600	300	150	120	100	75	30	10
T	Total annual cost	$1,210	$620	$340	$230	$220	$220	$235	$430	$1,210

*Symbols:
O = Order size in units (see headings above).
Q = Annual quantity used in units (3,000 in this example).
C = Annual cost of carrying one unit in stock.
P = Cost of placing one order.
T = Total annual cost.

(and is equal) at the 250- and 300-unit order sizes. The economic order quantity will lie somewhere between these two points. We could locate it precisely by adding more columns to the tabulation, and we would in time zero in on 274 units as being the exact economic order quantity.

The cost relationships from this tabulation are shown graphically in Exhibit 8–4. Notice from the graph that total annual cost is minimized at that point where annual carrying costs and annual purchase order costs are equal. The same point identifies the economic order quantity, since the purpose of the computation is to find the point of exact trade-off between these two classes of costs.

Observe from the graph that total cost shows a tendency to flatten out between 200 and 400 units. Most firms look for this minimum cost range and choose an order size that falls within it, rather than choosing the exact economic order quantity. The primary reason is that suppliers will often ship goods only in round-lot sizes.

The formula approach   The economic order quantity can also be found by means of a formula. The formula is (derived by calculus):

$$O = \sqrt{\frac{2\,QP}{C}}$$

where:

O = order size in units
Q = annual quantity used in units
P = cost of placing one order
C = annual cost of carrying one unit in stock

EXHIBIT 8–4

Graphic solution to economic order size

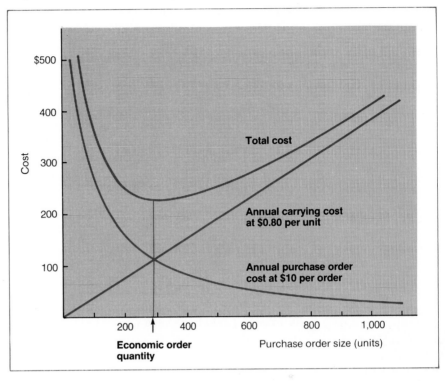

Substituting with the data used in our preceding example, we have:

Q = 3,000 subassemblies used per year
P = $10 cost to place one order
C = $0.80 cost to carry one subassembly in stock for one year

$$O = \sqrt{\frac{2(3,000)(\$10)}{\$0.80}} = \sqrt{\frac{\$60,000}{\$0.80}} = \sqrt{75,000}$$

O = 274 (the economic order quantity)

Although data can be obtained very quickly using the formula approach, it has the drawback of not providing as great a range of information as the methods discussed above.

Production Runs

The economic order quantity concept can also be applied to the problem of determining the **economic production-run size.** Deciding when to start and when to stop production runs is a problem that has plagued manufacturers for years. The problem can be solved quite easily by inserting the **setup**

cost for a new production run into the economic order quantity formula in place of the purchase order cost. The setup cost includes the labor and other costs involved in getting facilities ready for a run of a different production item.

To illustrate, assume that the Chittenden Company has determined that the following costs are associated with one of its product lines:

Q = 15,000 units produced each year
P = $150 setup costs to change a production run
C = $2 to carry one unit in stock for one year

What is the optimal production-run size for this product line? It can be determined by using the same formula as is used to compute the economic order quantity:

$$O = \sqrt{\frac{2(15,000)(\$150)}{\$2}} = \sqrt{\frac{\$4,500,000}{\$2}} = \sqrt{2,250,000}$$

O = 1,500 (economic production-run size in units)

The Chittenden Company will minimize its overall costs by producing in runs of 1,500 units each.

Reorder Point and Safety Stock

We stated earlier that the inventory problem has two dimensions—how much to order and how often to do it. The "how often to do it" involves what are commonly termed the *reorder point* and the *safety stock,* and seeks to find the optimal trade-off between the second two groups of inventory costs outlined earlier (the costs of carrying inventory and the costs of not carrying sufficient inventory). First, we will discuss the reorder point and the factors involved in its computation. Then, we will discuss the circumstances under which a safety stock must be maintained.

The **reorder point** tells the manager when to place an order or when to initiate production to replenish depleted stocks. It is dependent on three factors—the economic order quantity (or economic production-run size), the *lead time,* and the rate of usage during the lead time. The **lead time** can be defined as the interval between the time that an order is placed and the time that the order is finally received from the supplier or from the production line.

Constant usage during the lead time   If the rate of usage during the lead time is known with certainty, the reorder point can be determined by the following formula:

$$\text{Reorder point} = \text{Lead time} \times \text{Average daily or weekly usage}$$

To illustrate the formula's use, assume that a company's economic order quantity is 500 units, that the lead time is 3 weeks, and that the average weekly usage is 50 units.

$$\text{Reorder point} = 3 \text{ weeks} \times 50 \text{ units per week} = 150 \text{ units}$$

The reorder point would be 150 units. That is, the company will automatically place a new order for 500 units when inventory stocks drop to a level of 150 units, or three weeks' supply, left on hand.

Variable usage during the lead time   The previous example assumed that the 50 units per week usage rate was constant and was known with certainty. Although some firms enjoy the luxury of certainty, the more common situation is to find considerable variation in the rate of usage of inventory items from period to period. If usage varies from period to period, the firm that reorders in the way computed above may soon find itself out of stock. A sudden spurt in demand, a delay in delivery, or a snag in processing an order may cause inventory levels to be depleted before a new shipment arrives.

Companies that experience problems in demand, delivery, or processing of orders have found that they need some type of buffer to guard against stockouts. Such a buffer is usually called a **safety stock.** A safety stock serves as a kind of insurance against greater than usual demand and against problems in the ordering and delivery of goods. Its size is determined by deducting *average usage* from the *maximum usage* that can reasonably be expected during a period. For example, if the firm in the preceding example was faced with a situation of variable demand for its product, it would compute a safety stock as follows:

Maximum expected usage per week . . .	65 units
Average usage per week	50
Excess	15 units
Lead time	× 3 weeks
Safety stock	45 units

The reorder point is then determined by *adding the safety stock to the average usage during the lead time.* In formula form, the reorder point would be:

Reorder point
$$= (\text{Lead time} \times \text{Average daily or weekly usage}) + \text{Safety stock}$$

Computation of the reorder point by this approach is shown both numerically and graphically in Exhibit 8–5. As shown in the exhibit, the company will place a new order for 500 units when inventory stocks drop to a level of 195 units left on hand.

EXHIBIT 8–5

Determining the reorder point—variable usage

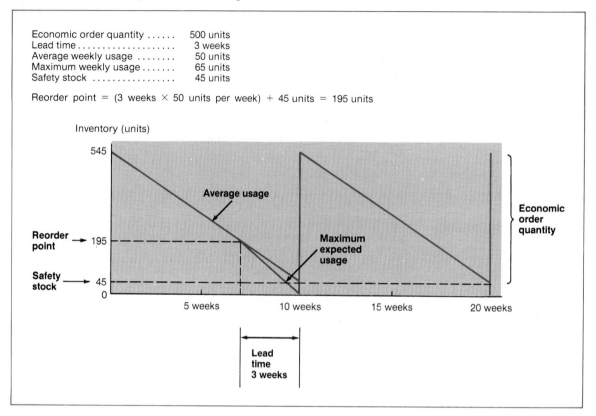

Economic order quantity . . . . . .   500 units
Lead time . . . .   3 weeks
Average weekly usage . . . .   50 units
Maximum weekly usage . . . .   65 units
Safety stock . . . .   45 units

Reorder point = (3 weeks × 50 units per week) + 45 units = 195 units

KEY TERMS FOR REVIEW (APPENDIX)

Costs of not carrying sufficient inventory Those costs that result from not having enough inventory in stock to meet customers' needs; such costs would include customer ill will, quantity discounts forgone, erratic production, added transportation charges, and lost sales.

Economic order quantity The order size for materials that will result in a minimization of the costs of ordering inventory and carrying inventory.

Economic production-run size The number of units produced in a production run that will result in a minimization of setup costs and the costs of carrying inventory.

Inventory carrying costs Those costs that result from having inventory in stock, such as rental of storage space, handling costs, property taxes, insurance, and interest on funds.

Inventory ordering costs Those costs associated with the acquisition of inventory, such as clerical costs and transportation costs.

Lead time The interval between the time that an order is placed and the time that the order is finally received from the supplier.

Reorder point The point in time when an order must be placed to replenish depleted stocks; it is determined by multiplying the lead time by the average daily or weekly usage.

Safety stock The difference between average usage of materials and maximum usage of materials that can reasonably be expected during the lead time.

Setup costs Labor and other costs involved in getting facilities ready for a run of a different production item.

QUESTIONS

8–1. What is a budget? What is budgetary control?

8–2. Discuss some of the major benefits to be gained from budgeting.

8–3. What is meant by the term *responsibility accounting?*

8–4. ''Budgeting is designed primarily for organizations that have few complexities and uncertainties in their day-to-day operations.'' Do you agree? Why or why not?

8–5. What is a master budget? Briefly describe its contents.

8–6. Which is a better basis for judging actual results, budgeted performance or past performance? Why?

8–7. Why is the sales forecast always the starting point in budgeting?

8–8. Is there any difference between a sales forecast and a sales budget? Explain.

8–9. ''As a practical matter, planning and control mean exactly the same thing.'' Do you agree? Explain.

8–10. Describe the flow of budget data in an organization. Who are the participants in the budgeting process, and how do they participate?

8–11. ''To a large extent, the success of a budget program hinges on education and good salesmanship.'' Do you agree? Explain.

8–12. What is a self-imposed budget? What are the major advantages of self-imposed budgets? What caution must be exercised in their use?

8–13. How can budgeting assist a firm in its employment policies?

8–14. ''The principal purpose of the cash budget is to see how much cash the company will have in the bank at the end of the year.'' Do you agree? Explain.

8–15. How does zero-base budgeting differ from traditional budgeting?

8–16. What three classes of costs are associated with a company's inventory policy? Which of these classes of costs is the most difficult to quantify?

8–17. List at least three costs associated with a company's inventory policy that do not appear as an expense on the income statement.

8–18. What trade-offs in costs are involved in computing the economic order quantity?

8–19.   "Managers are more interested in a minimum cost *range* than they are in a minimum cost point." Explain.

8–20.   Define *lead time* and *safety stock*.

EXERCISES

E8–1.   Atwood Products, Ltd., has budgeted sales for the next four months as follows:

	Sales in units
April	50,000
May	75,000
June	90,000
July	80,000

The company is now in the process of preparing a production budget for the second quarter. Past experience has shown that end-of-month inventory levels must equal 10 percent of the following month's sales. The inventory at the end of March was 5,000 units.

Required: Prepare a production budget for the second quarter; in your budget, show the number of units to be produced each month and for the quarter in total.

E8–2.   Three ounces of musk oil are required for each bottle of "Allure," a very popular perfume. The cost of the musk oil is $1.50 per ounce. Budgeted production of "Allure" is given below by quarters for 19x2 and for the first quarter of 19x3:

	19x2				19x3
	First	Second	Third	Fourth	First
Budgeted production, in bottles . . .	60,000	90,000	150,000	100,000	70,000

Musk oil has become so popular as a perfume base that it has become necessary to carry large inventories as a precaution against stockouts. For this reason, the inventory of musk oil at the end of a quarter must be equal to 20 percent of the following quarter's production needs. Some 36,000 ounces of musk oil will be on hand to start the first quarter, 19x2.

Required: Prepare a materials purchases budget for musk oil, by quarter and in total, for 19x2. At the bottom of your budget, show the dollar amount of purchases for each quarter and for the year in total.

E8–3.   A cash budget, by quarters, is given below (000 omitted). The company requires a minimum cash balance of $5,000 to start each quarter.

Cash Budget (handwritten)

	Quarters				
	1	**2**	**3**	**4**	**Year**
Cash balance, beginning	$ 9	$ 5 ?	$ 5 ?	$ 5 ?	$? 9
Add collections from customers . . .	76 ?	90 ?	125	100 ?	391
Total cash available	85	95 ?	130 ?	105 ?	400 ?
Less disbursements:					
Purchase of inventory	40	58	36 ?	32	166 ?
Operating expenses	36 ?	42	54	48 ?	180
Equipment purchases	10	8	8	10 ?	36
Dividends	2	2	2	2	8 ?
Total disbursements	88 ?	110	100 ?	92 ?	390 ?
Excess (deficiency) of cash available over disbursements . .	(3)	(15) ?	30	13 ?	10 ?
Financing:					
Borrowings	8 ?	20	(21)	(7)	?
Repayments (including interest)* . .	—	—	(4)(?)	(7)	(?)
Total financing	?	?	?	?	?
Cash balance, ending	5 $?	$5 ?	$ 5 ?	$6 ?	$6 ?

(handwritten margin notes: "Sales + credit sales that is collected"; "bank said carry we must carry"; "Assumptions interest 1) only worry about when payment 2) assume from beg of month to end of month payment 3) all int first")

* Interest will total $4,000 for the year.

Required: Fill in the missing amounts in the table above.

E8–4.   Silver Company makes a product that is very popular as a Mother's Day gift. Thus, peak sales occur in May of each year. The company's sales budget for the second quarter of 19x1, showing these peak sales, is given below:

	April	May	June	Total
Budgeted sales . . .	$300,000	$500,000	$200,000	$1,000,000

From past experience, the company has learned that 20 percent of a month's sales are collected in the month of sale, that another 70 percent is collected in the month following sale, and that the remaining 10 percent is collected in the second month following sale. Bad debts are negligible and can be ignored. February sales totaled $230,000, and March sales totaled $260,000.

Required: 1. Prepare a schedule of budgeted cash collections from sales, by month and in total, for the second quarter.
2. Assume that the company will prepare a budgeted balance sheet as of June 30. Compute the accounts receivable as of that date.

E8–5.   You have been asked to prepare a cash budget for December 19x8 for Ashton Company. The following information is available about the company's operations:

a.   The beginning cash balance on December 1 will be $40,000.
b.   Actual sales for October and November and expected sales for December are as follows:

	October	November	December
Cash sales	$ 65,000	$ 70,000	$ 83,000
Sales on account . . .	400,000	525,000	600,000

Sales on account are collected over a three-month period in the following ratio: 20 percent collected in the month of sale, 60 percent collected in the month following sale, and 18 percent collected in the second month following sale. The remaining 2 percent is uncollectible.

c. Purchases of inventory will total $280,000 for December. Thirty percent of a month's inventory purchases are paid during the month of purchase. The accounts payable remaining from November's inventory purchases total $161,000, all of which will be paid in December.

d. Selling and administrative expenses are budgeted at $430,000 for December. Of this amount, $50,000 is for depreciation.

e. Equipment costing $76,000 will be purchased for cash during December, and dividends totaling $9,000 will be paid during the month.

f. The company must maintain a minimum cash balance of $20,000. An open line of credit is available from the company's bank to bolster the cash position as needed.

Required: 1. Prepare a schedule of expected cash collections for the month of December.
2. Prepare a schedule of expected cash payments during December to suppliers for inventory purchases.
3. Prepare a cash budget for the month of December. Indicate in the financing section any borrowing that will be needed during the month.

E8–6. Greatday, Inc., makes a product that has peak sales in June of each year. The company has prepared a sales budget for the second quarter of 19x5, as shown below:

	April	May	June	Total
Budgeted sales . . .	$600,000	$750,000	$900,000	$2,250,000

The company is in the process of preparing a cash budget for the second quarter and must determine the expected cash collections by month. To this end, the following information has been assembled:

Collections on sales:
70% in month of sale
20% in month following sale
8% in second month following sale
2% uncollectible

The company gives a 2 percent cash discount for payments made by customers during the month of sale. The accounts receivable balance to start the quarter is $195,000, of which $45,000 represents uncollected February sales and $150,000 represents uncollected March sales.

Required: 1. What were the total sales for February? For March?
2. Prepare a schedule showing the budgeted cash collections from sales, by month and in total, for the second quarter.

E8–7. (Appendix)   Classify the following as either *(a)* costs of carrying inventory or *(b)* costs of not carrying sufficient inventory:

1. Airfreight on a rush order of a critical part needed in production.
2. Interest paid on investment funds.
3. State and local taxes on personal property.

4. Spoilage of perishable goods.
5. Excessive setup costs.
6. Customers lost through inability of the company to make prompt delivery.
7. Quantity discounts lost as a result of purchasing in small lots.
8. Fire insurance on inventory.
9. Loss sustained when a competitor comes out with a less expensive, more efficient product.
10. A general feeling of ill will among customers, due to broken delivery promises.

E8–8. (Appendix) Bedford Motor Company uses 3,125 units of Part S-10 each year. The cost of placing one order for Part S-10 is estimated to be about $10. Other costs associated with Part S-10 are:

	Annual cost per part
Insurance	$0.10
Property taxes	0.06
Interest on funds invested . . .	0.05
Other	0.04
Total cost	$0.25

Required: Compute the economic order quantity for Part S-10.

E8–9. (Appendix) Flint Company uses 9,000 units of part AK-4 each year. In order to get better control over its inventories, the company is anxious to determine the economic order quantity for this part.

Required:
1. The company has determined that the cost to place an order for the part is $30, and it has determined that the cost to carry one part in inventory for one year is $1.50. Compute the economic order quantity for the part.
2. Assume that the cost to place an order increases from $30 to $40 per order. What will be the effect on the economic order quantity? Show computations.
3. Assume that the cost to carry a part in inventory increases from $1.50 to $2.00 per part. (Ordering costs remain unchanged at $30 per order.) What will be the effect on the economic order quantity? Show computations.
4. In (2) and (3) above, why does an increase in cost cause the economic order quantity to go up in one case and to go down in the other?

E8–10. (Appendix) Selected information relating to an inventory item carried by the Santos Company is given below:

Economic order quantity	700 units
Maximum weekly usage	60 units
Lead time	4 weeks
Average weekly usage	50 units

Santos Company is trying to determine the proper safety stock to carry on this inventory item, and to determine the proper reorder point.

Required:
1. Assume that no safety stock is to be carried. What is the reorder point?
2. Assume that a full safety stock is to be carried.
   a. What would be the size of the safety stock in units?
   b. What would be the reorder point?

PROBLEMS

P8–11.   **Production and purchases budgets.**   Regal Products manufactures and distributes toys to retail outlets. One of the company's products, Supermix, requires 3 pounds of material A in the manufacture of each unit. The company is now planning raw material needs for the third quarter of 19x1, the quarter in which peak sales of Supermix occur. In order to keep production and sales moving smoothly, the company has the following inventory requirements:

a.   The finished goods inventory on hand at the end of each month must be equal to 3,000 units plus 20 percent of the next month's sales. The finished goods inventory on June 30 is budgeted to be 10,000 units.

b.   The raw materials inventory on hand at the end of each month must be equal to one half of the following month's production needs for raw materials. The raw materials inventory on June 30 is budgeted to be 54,000 pounds.

c.   The company maintains no work in process inventories.

A sales budget for Supermix for the last six months of 19x1 is given below:

	Budgeted sales in units
July	35,000
August	40,000
September	50,000
October	30,000
November	20,000
December	10,000

Required: 1.   Prepare a production budget for Supermix for the months July–October.

2.   Examine the production budget that you prepared in (1) above. Why will the company produce more units than it sells in July and August, and less units than it sells in September and October?

3.   Prepare a budget showing the quantity of material A to be purchased for July, August, and September 19x1, and for the quarter in total.

P8–12.   **Cash budget.**   Atlas Company is ready to begin its third quarter, in which peak sales occur. The company has requested a $40,000, 90-day loan from its bank to help meet cash requirements during the quarter. Since Atlas Company has experienced difficulty in paying off its loans in the past, the loan officer at the bank has asked the company to prepare a cash budget for the quarter. In response to this request, the following data have been assembled:

a.   On July 1, the beginning of the third quarter, the company will have a cash balance of $44,500.

b.   Actual sales for the last two months and budgeted sales for the third quarter follow:

May (actual)	$250,000
June (actual)	300,000
July (budgeted)	400,000
August (budgeted)	600,000
September (budgeted) . . .	320,000

Past experience shows that 25 percent of a month's sales are collected in the month of sale, 70 percent in the month following sale, and 3 percent in the second month following sale. The remainder is uncollectible.

c. Budgeted merchandise purchases and budgeted expenses for the third quarter are given below:

	July	August	September
Merchandise purchases . . .	$240,000	$350,000	$175,000
Salaries and wages	45,000	50,000	40,000
Advertising	130,000	145,000	80,000
Rent payments	9,000	9,000	9,000
Depreciation.	10,000	10,000	10,000

Merchandise purchases are paid in full during the month following purchase. Accounts payable for merchandise purchases on June 30, which will be paid during July, total $180,000.

d. Equipment costing $10,000 will be purchased for cash during July.

e. In preparing a cash budget, assume that the $40,000 loan will be made in July and repaid in September. Interest on the loan will total $1,200.

Required:
1. Prepare a schedule of budgeted cash collections for July, August, and September and for the quarter in total.
2. Prepare a cash budget, by month and in total, for the third quarter.
3. If the company needs a minimum cash balance of $20,000 to start each month, can the loan be repaid as planned? Explain.

P8–13. Production and direct materials budgets. A sales budget for the first six months of 19x3 is given below for a product manufactured by Bloor, Ltd.

Month	Budgeted sales (units)
January	6,000
February	10,000
March	15,000
April	9,000
May	7,000
June	6,500

The inventory of finished goods on hand at the end of each month must be equal to 30 percent of the budgeted sales for the next month. On January 1, there were 1,800 units of product on hand. Work in process inventories are nominal and can be ignored.

Each unit of product requires 5 yards of a material called Silven. The material is extremely expensive; therefore, Bloor has a policy of carrying only enough Silven in stock at the end of each month to meet 10 percent of the following month's production needs. You may assume that this requirement will be met on January 1 of the current year.

Required: Prepare a budget showing the quantity of Silven to be purchased each month for January, February, and March and in total for the three-month period. (Hint: Remember that a production budget must be prepared before a materials purchases budget can be prepared.)

P8–14. **Master budget preparation.** Minden Company's balance sheet as of April 30, 19x2, is given below:

MINDEN COMPANY
Balance Sheet
April 30, 19x2
Assets

Cash	$ 9,000
Accounts receivable, customers	54,000
Inventory	30,000
Plant and equipment, net of depreciation . . .	207,000
Total assets	$300,000

Liabilities and Stockholders Equity

Accounts payable, suppliers	$ 63,000
Note payable	14,500
Capital stock, no par	180,000
Retained earnings	42,500
Total liabilities and stockholders' equity . . .	$300,000

The company is in the process of preparing budget data for May 19x2. A number of budget items have already been prepared, as stated below:

a. Sales are budgeted at $200,000 for May. Of these sales, $60,000 will be for cash; the remainder will be credit sales. One half of a month's credit sales are collected in the month the sales are made, and the remainder is collected in the month following. All of the April 30 receivables will be collected in May.

b. Purchases of inventory are expected to total $120,000 during May. These purchases will all be on account. Forty percent of all purchases are paid for in the month of purchase; the remainder is paid in the following month. All of the April 30 accounts payable to suppliers will be paid during May.

c. The May 31 inventory balance is budgeted at $40,000.

d. Operating expenses for May are budgeted at $72,000, exclusive of depreciation. These expenses will be paid in cash. Depreciation is budgeted at $2,000 for the month.

e. The note payable on the April 30 balance sheet will be paid during May, with $100 in interest. (All of the interest relates to the month of May.)

f. New equipment costing $6,500 will be purchased for cash during May.

g. During May, the company will borrow $20,000 from its bank by giving a new note payable to the bank for that amount. The new note will be due in one year.

Required: 1. Prepare a cash budget for May 19x2. Support your budget with schedules showing budgeted cash receipts from sales and budgeted cash payments for inventory purchases.

2. Prepare a budgeted income statement for May 19x2. Use the traditional income statement format. Ignore income taxes.

3. Prepare a budgeted balance sheet as of May 31, 19x2.

P8–15. **Integration of the sales, production, and purchases budgets.** Milo Company manufactures a single product for which peak sales occur in August of each year.

The company is now preparing detailed budgets for the third quarter and has assembled the following information to assist in the budget preparation:

a.   The marketing department has estimated sales as follows for the remainder of the year (in units):

July	30,000	October	20,000
August	70,000	November	10,000
September	50,000	December	10,000

The selling price of the company's product is $12 per unit.

b.   All sales are on account. Based on past experience, sales are collected in the following pattern:

> 30 percent in the month of sale.
> 65 percent in the month following sale.
> 5 percent uncollectible.

Sales for June 19x6 totaled $300,000.

c.   The company maintains finished goods inventories equal to 15 percent of the following month's sales. This requirement will be met at the end of June.

d.   Each finished unit of product requires 4 feet of Gilden, a material that is sometimes hard to get. Therefore, the company requires that the inventory of Gilden on hand at the end of each month be equal to 50 percent of the following month's production needs. The inventory of Gilden on hand at the beginning and end of the quarter will be:

> June 30 . . . . . 72,000 feet
> September 30 . . . ? · feet

e.   The Gilden costs $0.80 per foot. One half of a month's purchases of Gilden is paid for in the month of purchase; the remainder is paid for in the following month. The accounts payable on July 1 for purchases of Gilden during June will be $76,000.

Required:

1.   Prepare a sales budget, by month and in total, for the third quarter. (Show your budget in both units and dollars.) Also prepare a schedule of expected cash collections, by month and in total, for the third quarter.
2.   Prepare a production budget for each of the months July–October.
3.   Prepare a materials purchases budget for Gilden, by month and in total, for the third quarter. Also prepare a schedule of expected cash payments for Gilden, by month and in total, for the third quarter.

P8–16.   **Planning bank financing by means of a cash budget.**   When the treasurer of Westex Products, Inc., approached the company's bank in late 19x1 seeking short-term financing, he was told that money was very tight and that any borrowing over the next year would have to be supported by a detailed statement of cash receipts and disbursements. The treasurer also was told that it would be very helpful to the bank if borrowers would indicate the quarters in which they would be needing funds, as well as the amounts that would be needed, and the quarters in which repayments could be made.

Since the treasurer is unsure as to the particular quarters in which the bank financing will be needed, he has assembled the following information to assist in preparing a detailed cash budget:

a. Budgeted sales and merchandise purchases for 19x2, as well as actual sales and purchases for the last quarter of 19x1, are:

	Sales	Merchandise purchases
19x1:		
Fourth quarter actual	$200,000	$126,000
19x2:		
First quarter estimated	300,000	186,000
Second quarter estimated	400,000	246,000
Third quarter estimated	500,000	305,000
Fourth quarter estimated	200,000	126,000

b. The company normally collects 65 percent of a quarter's sales before the quarter ends and another 33 percent in the following quarter. The remainder is uncollectable. This pattern of collections is now being experienced in the 19x1 fourth quarter actual data.

c. Eighty percent of a quarter's merchandise purchases are paid for within the quarter. The remainder is paid in the quarter following.

d. Operating expenses for 19x2 are budgeted quarterly at $50,000 plus 15 percent of sales. Of the fixed amount, $20,000 each quarter is depreciation.

e. The company will pay $10,000 in dividends each quarter.

f. Equipment purchases of $75,000 will be made in the second quarter, and purchases of $48,000 will be made in the third quarter. These purchases will be for cash.

g. The Cash account contained $10,000 at the end of 19x1. The treasurer feels that this represents a minimum balance that must be maintained.

h. Any borrowing will take place at the beginning of a quarter, and any repayments will be made at the end of a quarter at an annual interest rate of 10 percent. Interest is paid only when principal is repaid. All borrowings and all repayments of principal must be in round $1,000 amounts. Interest payments can be in any amount. (Compute interest on whole months, e.g., $1/12$, $2/12$.)

i. At present, the company has no loans outstanding.

Required: 1. Prepare the following by quarter and in total for 19x2:
    a. A schedule of budgeted cash collections on sales.
    b. A schedule of budgeted cash payments for merchandise purchases.

2. Compute the expected cash payments for operating expenses, by quarter and in total, for the year 19x2.

3. Prepare a cash budget for 19x2, by quarter and in total, for the year. Show clearly in your budget the quarter(s) in which borrowing will be necessary and the quarter(s) in which repayments can be made, as requested by the company's bank.

P8–17. Master budget preparation. Hillyard Company prepares its master budget on a quarterly basis. The following data have been assembled to assist in preparation of the master budget for the first quarter of 19x5:

a. As of December 31, 19x4 (the end of the prior quarter), the company's general ledger showed the following account balances:

Cash	$ 48,000
Accounts receivable	224,000
Inventory	60,000
Plant and equipment, net . . .	370,000
Accounts payable	$ 93,000
Capital stock	500,000
Retained earnings	109,000
	$702,000 $702,000

b. Actual sales for December and budgeted sales for the next four months are as follows:

December (actual) . . .	$280,000
January	400,000
February	600,000
March	300,000
April	200,000

c. Sales are 20 percent for cash and 80 percent on credit. All credit sale terms are n/30; therefore, accounts are collected in the month following sale. The accounts receivable at December 31 are a result of December credit sales.

 d. The company's gross profit rate is 40 percent of sales.

e. Monthly expenses are budgeted as follows: salaries and wages, $27,000 per month; advertising, $70,000 per month; freight-out, 5 percent of sales; depreciation, $14,000 per month; other expense, 3 percent of sales.

f. At the end of each month, inventory is to be on hand equal to 25 percent of the following month's sales needs, stated at cost.

g. One half of a month's inventory purchases is paid for in the month of purchase; the other half is paid for in the following month.

h. During February, the company will purchase a new copy machine for $1,700 cash. During March, other equipment will be purchased for cash at a cost of $84,500.

i. During January, the company will declare and pay $45,000 in cash dividends.

j. The company must maintain a minimum cash balance of $30,000. An open line of credit is available at a local bank for any borrowing that may be needed during the quarter. All borrowing is done at the beginning of a month, and all repayments are made at the end of a month. Borrowings and repayments of principal must be in multiples of $1,000. Interest is paid only at the time of payment of principal. The interest rate is 12 percent per annum. (Figure interest on whole months, e.g., $1/12$, $2/12$.)

Required: Using the data above, complete the following statements and schedules for the first quarter:

1. Schedule of expected cash collections:

	January	February	March	Quarter
Cash sales	$ 80,000			
Credit sales	224,000			
Total cash collections	$304,000			

2.   *a.*   Inventory purchases budget:

	January	February	March	Quarter
Budgeted cost of goods sold	$240,000*	$360,000		
Add: Desired ending inventory	90,000†			
Total needs	330,000			
Deduct: Beginning inventory	60,000			
Required purchases	$270,000			

* For January sales: $400,000 sales × 60% cost ratio = $240,000.
† $360,000 × 25% = $90,000.

b.   Schedule of cash disbursements for purchases:

	January	February	March	Quarter
December purchases	$ 93,000			$ 93,000
January purchases ($270,000)	135,000	$135,000		270,000
February purchases				
March purchases				
Total cash disbursements	$228,000			

3.   Schedule of cash disbursements for expenses:

	January	February	March	Quarter
Salaries and wages	$ 27,000	27,000	27,000	81,000
Advertising	70,000	70,000	70,000	210,000
Freight-out	20,000	30,000	15,000	65,000
Other expenses	12,000	12,000	18,000	39,000
Total cash disbursements	$129,000			

4.   Cash budget:

	January	February	March	Quarter
Cash balance, beginning	$ 48,000			
Add cash collections	304,000			
Total cash available	352,000			
Less disbursements:				
Purchases of inventory	228,000			
Operating expenses	129,000			
Purchases of equipment	—			
Cash dividends	45,000			
Total disbursements	402,000			
Excess (deficiency) of cash	(50,000)		$42,900	
Financing:				
Etc.				

5.   Prepare an income statement for the quarter ending March 31. (Use the functional format in preparing your income statement.)
6.   Prepare a balance sheet as of March 31.

P8–18. **Evaluating a company's budget procedures.**   Tom Emory and Jim Morris strolled back to their plant from the administrative offices of Ferguson & Son Mfg. Company. Tom was manager of the machine shop in the company's factory; Jim was manager of the equipment maintenance department.

The men had just attended the monthly performance evaluation meeting for plant department heads. These meetings had been held on the third Tuesday of each month since Robert Ferguson, Jr., the president's son, had become plant manager a year earlier.

As they were walking, Tom Emory spoke. "Boy, I hate those meetings! I never know whether my department's accounting reports will show good or bad performance. I'm beginning to expect the worst. If the accountants say I saved the company a dollar, I'm called 'Sir,' but if I spend even a little too much—boy, do I get in trouble. I don't know if I can hold on until I retire."

Tom had just been given the worst evaluation he had ever received in his long career with Ferguson & Son. He was the most respected of the experienced machinists in the company. He had been with Ferguson & Son for many years and was promoted to supervisor of the machine shop when the company expanded and moved to its present location. The president (Robert Ferguson, Sr.) had often stated that the company's success was due to the high quality of the work of machinists like Tom. As supervisor, Tom stressed the importance of craftsmanship and told his workers that he wanted no sloppy work coming from his department.

When Robert Ferguson, Jr., became the plant manager, he directed that monthly performance comparisons be made between actual and budgeted costs for each department. The departmental budgets were intended to encourage the supervisors to reduce inefficiencies and to seek cost reduction opportunities. The company controller was instructed to have his staff "tighten" the budget slightly whenever a department attained its budget in a given month; this was done to reinforce the plant supervisor's desire to reduce costs. The young plant manager often stressed the importance of continued progress toward attaining the budget; he also made it known that he kept a file of these performance reports for future reference when he succeeded his father.

Tom Emory's conversation with Jim Morris continued as follows:

Emory: I really don't understand. We've worked so hard to get up to budget, and the minute we make it they tighten the budget on us. We can't work any faster and still maintain quality. I think my men are ready to quit trying. Besides, those reports don't tell the whole story. We always seem to be interrupting the big jobs for all those small rush orders. All that setup and machine adjustment time is killing us. And quite frankly, Jim, you were no help. When our hydraulic press broke down last month, your people were nowhere to be found. We had to take it apart ourselves and got stuck with all that idle time.

Morris: I'm sorry about that, Tom, but you know my department has had trouble making budget, too. We were running well behind at the time of that problem, and if we'd spent a day on that old machine, we would never have made it up. Instead we made the scheduled inspections of the forklift trucks because we knew we could do those in less than the budgeted time.

Emory: Well, Jim, at least you have some options. I'm locked into what the scheduling department assigns to me and you know they're being harrassed by sales for those special orders. Incidentally, why didn't your report show all the supplies you guys wasted last month, when you were working in Bill's department?

Morris: We're not out of the woods on that deal yet. We charged the maximum we could to our other work and haven't even reported some of it yet.

Emory: Well, I'm glad you have a way of getting out of the pressure. The accountants seem to know everything that's happening in my department, sometimes even before I do. I thought all that budget and accounting stuff was supposed to help, but it just gets me into trouble. Its all a big pain. I'm trying to put out quality work; they're trying to save pennies.

Required:
1. Identify the problems which appear to exist in Ferguson & Son Mfg. Company's budgetary control system and explain how the problems are likely to reduce the effectiveness of the system.
2. Explain how Ferguson & Son Mfg. Company's budgetary control system could be revised to improve its effectiveness.

(CMA, Adapted)

P8–19. **Cash budget with supporting schedules.**   Garden Sales, Inc., is planning its cash needs for the second quarter of 19x2. The company usually has to borrow money during this quarter to support peak sales of lawn care equipment, which occur during May. The following information has been assembled to assist in preparing a cash budget for the quarter:

a. Budgeted monthly income statements for April–July 19x2 are:

	April	May	June	July
Sales.	$600,000	$900,000	$500,000	$400,000
Cost of goods sold	420,000	630,000	350,000	280,000
Gross margin	180,000	270,000	150,000	120,000
Less operating expenses:				
Selling expense	79,000	120,000	62,000	51,000
Administrative expense* . . .	45,000	52,000	41,000	38,000
Total expenses	124,000	172,000	103,000	89,000
Net income	$ 56,000	$ 98,000	$ 47,000	$ 31,000

* Includes $20,000 depreciation each month.

b. Sales are 20 percent for cash and 80 percent on account.
c. Sales on account are collected over a three-month period in the following ratio: 10 percent collected in the month of sale; 70 percent collected in the first month following the month of sale; and the remaining 20 percent collected in the second month following the month of sale. February's sales totaled $200,000, and March's sales totaled $300,000.
d. Inventory purchases are paid for within 15 days. Therefore, 50 percent of a month's inventory purchases are paid for in the month of purchase. The remaining 50 percent is paid in the following month. Accounts payable at March 31 for inventory purchases during March total $126,000.
e. At the end of each month, inventory must be on hand equal to 20 percent of the cost of the merchandise to be sold in the following month. The merchandise inventory at March 31 is $84,000.
f. Dividends of $49,000 will be declared and paid in April.

g. Equipment costing $16,000 will be purchased for cash in May.

h. The cash balance at March 31 is $52,000; the company must maintain a cash balance of at least $40,000 at all times.

i. The company can borrow from its bank as needed to bolster the cash account. Borrowings must be in multiples of $1,000. All borrowings take place at the beginning of a month, and all repayments are made at the end of a month. The interest rate is 12 percent per annum. Compute interest on whole months ($\frac{1}{12}$, $\frac{2}{12}$, and so forth).

Required: 1. Prepare a schedule of budgeted cash collections from sales for each of the months April, May, and June, and for the quarter in total.

2. Prepare the following for merchandise inventory:

   a. An inventory purchases budget for each of the months April, May, and June.

   b. A schedule of expected cash disbursements for inventory for each of the months April, May, and June, and for the quarter in total.

3. Prepare a cash budget for the third quarter of 19x2. Show figures by month as well as in total for the quarter. Show borrowings from the company's bank and repayments to the bank as needed to maintain the minimum cash balance.

P8–20. Master budget completion. Following is selected information relating to the operations of Shilow Company:

Current assets as of March 31, 19x4:

Cash	$ 8,000
Accounts receivable	20,000
Inventory	36,000
Plant and equipment, net	120,000
Accounts payable	21,750
Capital stock	150,000
Retained earnings	12,250

a. Gross profit is 25 percent of sales.

b. Actual and budgeted sales data:

March (actual) . . .	$50,000
April	60,000
May	72,000
June	90,000
July	48,000

c. Sales are 60 percent for cash and 40 percent on credit. Credit sale terms are n/30, and therefore accounts are collected in the month following sale. The accounts receivable at March 31 are a result of March credit sales.

d. At the end of each month, inventory is to be on hand equal to 80 percent of the following month's sales needs, stated at cost.

e. All inventory purchases are on terms of 2/15, n/30; therefore, half of a month's purchases are paid for in the month of purchase and half in the following month. All purchase discounts are taken and treated as "Other income" on the income statement. (Purchase discounts are not recorded until payment is made.) The accounts payable at March 31 are a result of March purchases of inventory.

f. Monthly expenses are as follows: salaries and wages, 12 percent of sales; rent, $2,500 per month; other expenses (excluding depreciation), 6 percent of sales. Assume that these expenses are paid monthly. Depreciation is $900 per month (includes depreciation on new assets).

g. Equipment costing $2,500 will be purchased for cash in April, and equipment costing $1,000 will be purchased for cash in May.

h. The company must maintain a minimum cash balance of $6,000. An open line of credit is available at a local bank. All borrowing is done at the beginning of a month, and all repayments are made at the end of a month; borrowing must be in multiples of $1,000. The interest rate is 12 percent per annum. Interest is paid only at the time of repayment of principal; figure interest on whole months ($\frac{1}{12}$, $\frac{2}{12}$, and so forth).

Required: Using the data above:

1. Complete the following schedule:

Schedule of Expected Cash Collections

	April	May	June	Total
Cash sales	$36,000			
Credit sales	20,000			
Total collections	$56,000			

2. Complete the following:

Inventory Purchases Budget

	April	May	June	Total
Budgeted cost of goods sold	$45,000*	$54,000		
Add: Desired ending inventory	43,200†			
Total needs	88,200			
Deduct: Opening inventory	36,000			
Required purchases	$52,200			

* For April sales: $60,000 sales × 75% cost ratio = $45,000.
† $54,000 × 80% = $43,200.

Schedule of Expected Cash Disbursements—Purchases

	April	May	June	Total
March purchases	$21,750			$21,750
April purchases	26,100	$26,100		52,200
May purchases				
June purchases				
Total purchases	47,850			
Less 2% discount	957			
Net disbursements	$46,893			

3. Complete the following:

Schedule of Expected Cash Disbursements—Expenses

	April	May	June	Total
Salaries and wages	$ 7,200			
Rent	2,500			
Other expenses	3,600			
Total disbursements	$13,300			

4.   Complete the following cash budget:

| | **Cash Budget** | | | |
	April	May	June	Quarter
Cash balance, beginning	$ 8,000			
Add cash collections	56,000	___	___	___
Total cash available	64,000	___	___	___
Less cash disbursements:				
For inventory	46,893			
For expenses	13,300			
For equipment.	2,500	___	___	___
Total cash disbursements . .	62,693	___	___	___
Excess (deficiency) of cash . . .	1,307			
Financing:				
Etc.				

5.   Prepare an income statement for the quarter ended June 30. (Use the functional format in preparing your income statement.)
6.   Prepare a balance sheet as of June 30.

P8–21.   Evaluating budget procedure.   RV Industries manufactures and sells recreation vehicles. The company has eight divisions strategically located to be near major markets. Each division has a sales force and two to four manufacturing plants. These divisions operate as autonomous profit centers responsible for purchasing, operations, and sales.

John Collins, the corporate controller, described the divisional performance measurement system as follows. ''We allow the divisions to control the entire operation from the purchase of raw materials to the sale of the product. We, at corporate headquarters, only get involved in strategic decisions, such as developing new product lines. Each division is responsible for meeting its market needs by providing the right products at a low cost on a timely basis. Frankly, the divisions need to focus on cost control, delivery, and services to customers in order to become more profitable.

''While we give the divisions considerable autonomy, we watch their monthly income statements very closely. Each month's actual performance is compared with the budget in considerable detail. If the actual sales or contribution margin is more than 4 or 5 percent below the budget, we jump on the division people immediately. I might add that we don't have much trouble getting their attention. All of the management people at the plant and division level can add appreciably to their annual salaries with bonuses if actual net income is considerably greater than budget.''

The budgeting process begins in August when, after consulting with their sales personnel, division sales managers estimate sales for the next calendar year. These estimates are sent to plant managers who use the sales forecasts to prepare production estimates. At the plants, production statistics, including raw material quantities, labor-hours, production schedules, and output quantities, are developed by operating personnel. Using the statistics prepared by the operating personnel, the plant accounting staff determines costs and prepares the plant's budgeted variable cost of goods sold and other plant expenses for each month of the coming calendar year.

In October, each division's accounting staff combines plant budgets with sales estimates and adds additional division expenses. ''After the divisional management is satisfied with the budget,'' said Collins, ''I visit each division to go over their budget and make sure it is in line with corporate strategy and projections. I really emphasize the sales forecasts because of the volatility in the demand for our product. For many years, we lost sales to our competitors because we didn't project high enough production and sales and we couldn't meet the market demand. More recently, we were caught with large excess inventory when the bottom dropped out of the market for recreational vehicles.

''I generally visit all eight divisions during the first two weeks in November. After that the division budgets are combined and reconciled by my staff, and they are ready for approval by the board of directors in early December. The board seldom questions the budget.

''One complaint we've had from plant and division management is that they are penalized for circumstances beyond their control. For example, they failed to predict the recent sales decline. As a result, they didn't make their budget and, of course, they received no bonuses. However, I point out that they are well rewarded when they exceed their budget. Furthermore, they provide most of the information for the budget, so it's their own fault if the budget is too optimistic.''

Required:

1. Identify and explain the biases the corporate management of RV Industries should expect in the communication of budget estimates by its division and plant personnel.
2. What sources of information can the top management of RV Industries use to monitor the budget estimates prepared by its divisions and plants?
3. What services could top management of RV Industries offer the divisions to help them in their budget development without appearing to interfere with the division budget decisions?
4. The top management of RV Industries is attempting to decide whether it should get more involved in the budget process. Identify and explain the variables management needs to consider in reaching its decision.

(CMA, Adapted)

P8–22. **Production budget; purchases budget; income statement.** Marvel Glue Company sells a number of products including a very popular adhesive called Formula 7. The company is in the process of preparing budgeted data on Formula 7 for the third quarter of 19x2. The following data are available on manufacture and sale of the product:

a. The selling price of Formula 7 is $5 per bottle. The company plans to sell 250,000 bottles during the third quarter.
b. Each bottle of Formula 7 contains 4 ounces of a material called Lactex and 2 ounces of a material called Mural.
c. The finished goods inventory of Formula 7 is planned to be reduced by 40 percent by the end of the third quarter. The inventory at the beginning of the quarter will be 90,000 bottles. Other inventory levels are planned as follows:

	Beginning of quarter	End of quarter
Lactex—ounces	60,000	74,000
Mural—ounces	115,000	82,000
Empty bottles	62,000	56,000

The inventory of Lactex is budgeted to increase during the quarter, since the material is sometimes hard to find.

d. Lactex costs $0.12 per ounce; Mural costs $0.65 per ounce; and empty bottles cost $0.10 each.

e. Only six minutes of labor time is required to process and fill one bottle of Formula 7. Direct labor cost is $9.50 per hour.

f. Variable manufacturing overhead costs are $0.07 per bottle. Fixed manufacturing overhead costs total $216,000 per quarter.

g. Variable selling and administrative expenses are 6 percent of sales. Fixed selling and administrative expenses total $140,000 per quarter.

Required:

1. Prepare a production budget for Formula 7 for the third quarter.

2. Prepare a raw materials purchases budget for Lactex, Mural, and empty bottles for the third quarter. Show the budgeted purchases in dollars as well as in ounces or bottles.

3. Compute the budgeted cost to manufacture one bottle of Formula 7. (Include only the variable manufacturing costs in your computations.)

4. Prepare a budgeted income statement for Formula 7 for the third quarter. Use the contribution approach, and show both per unit and total cost data.

P8–23.   **Cash budget for one month.**   Wallace Products, Ltd., is planning its cash needs for July 19x5. Since the company will be buying some new equipment during the month, the treasurer is sure that some borrowing will be needed, but he is uncertain how much. The following data have been assembled to assist the treasurer in preparing a cash budget for the month:

a. Equipment will be purchased during July for cash at a cost of $45,000.

b. Selling and administrative expenses will be:

Advertising	$110,000
Sales salaries.	50,000
Administrative salaries . . .	35,000
Freight-out	2,100

c. Sales are budgeted at $800,000 for July. Customers are allowed a 2½ percent cash discount on accounts paid within 10 days after the end of the month of sale. Only 50 percent of the payments made in the month following sale fall within the discount period. (All of the company's sales are on account.)

d. On June 30, the company will have the following accounts receivable outstanding:

Month	Sales	Accounts receivable at June 30	Percentage of sales uncollected at June 30	Percentage to be collected in July
March . . .	$430,000	$ 6,450	1½%	?
April	590,000	35,400	6	?
May	640,000	128,000	20	?
June. . . .	720,000	720,000	100	?

Bad debts are negligible. All March receivables shown above will have been collected by the end of July, and the collection pattern implicit in the schedule above will be the same in July as in previous months.

e.   Production costs are budgeted as follows for July:

Prime costs:		
Raw materials to be used in production . .		$342,000
Direct labor		95,000
Overhead costs:		
Indirect labor	$36,000	
Utilities	1,900	
Payroll benefits	14,800	
Depreciation.	28,000	
Property taxes	1,100	
Fire insurance	1,700	
Amortization of patents	3,500	
Scrapping of obsolete goods.	2,600	89,600
Total production costs.		$526,600

f.   The raw materials inventory is budgeted to increase by $18,000 during July; other inventories will not change.

g.   Half of the raw materials purchased each month is paid for in the month of purchase; the other half is paid for in the following month. Accounts payable at June 30 for raw materials purchases will be $172,000.

h.   All July payroll amounts will be paid for within the month of July.

i.   Utilities costs are paid for within the month.

j.   The $14,800 monthly charge above for "Payroll benefits" includes the following items:

Company pension plan, including 1/12 of a	
$9,600 special adjustment	
made in April	$7,000
Group insurance (payable semiannually,	
with the last payment having	
been made in January	900
Unemployment insurance (payable monthly) . . .	1,300
Vacation pay, which represents 1/12 of the	
annual cost (July's vacations	
will require $14,100)	5,600

k.   Property taxes are paid in June of each year.

l.   Fire insurance premiums are payable in January, in advance.

m.   The company has an open line of credit with the Royal Calgary Bank. All borrowing from the bank must be in round $1,000 amounts.

n.   The cash balance on June 30 will be $78,000; the company must maintain a cash balance of at least $75,000 at all times.

Required:
1.   Prepare a schedule showing expected cash collections for July 19x5.
2.   Compute *(a)* budgeted cash disbursements for raw materials purchases and *(b)* budgeted cash disbursements for overhead for July 19x5.
3.   Prepare a cash budget for July 19x5 in good form. Ignore income taxes.

P8–24.   **Integrated operating budgets.**   The West Division of Vader Corporation produces an intricate component part used in Vader's major product line. The division manager has recently been concerned about a lack of coordination between purchasing and production personnel and believes that a monthly budgeting system would be better than the present system.

     The manager of West Division has decided to develop budget information for the third quarter of the current year as a trial before the budget system is implemented for an entire fiscal year. In response to the manager's request for data that could be used to develop budget information, the controller of West Division accumulated the following data:

Sales

Sales through June 30, 19x7, the first six months of the current year, are 24,000 units. Actual sales in units for May and June and estimated unit sales for the next five months are detailed as follows:

May (actual)	4,000
June (actual)	4,000
July (estimated)	5,000
August (estimated)	6,000
September (estimated)	7,000
October (estimated)	7,500
November (estimated)	8,000

West Division expects to sell 65,000 units during the year ending December 31, 19x7.

Direct material

Data regarding the materials used in the component are shown in the following schedule. The desired monthly ending inventory for all direct materials is to have sufficient materials on hand to provide for 50 percent of the next month's production needs.

Direct material	Units of direct materials per finished component	Cost per unit	Inventory level 6/30/x7
No. 101	6 ounces	$2.40	35,000 ounces
No. 211	4 pounds	5.00	30,000 pounds

Direct labor

Each component must pass through three processes to be completed. Data regarding the direct labor are as follows:

Process	Direct labor-hours per finished component	Cost per direct labor-hour
Forming	0.80	$8.00
Assembly	2.00	5.50
Finishing	0.25	6.00

Factory overhead

West Division produced 27,000 components during the six-month period through June 30, 19x7. The actual variable overhead costs incurred during this six-month period are shown below. The controller of West Division believes that the variable overhead costs will be incurred at the same rate during the last six months of 19x7.

Supplies	$ 59,400
Electricity	27,000
Indirect labor	54,000
Other	8,100
Total variable overhead	$148,500

The fixed-overhead costs incurred during the first six months of 19x7 amounted to $93,500. Fixed-overhead costs are budgeted for the full year as follows:

Supervision	$ 60,000
Taxes	7,200
Depreciation	86,400
Other	32,400
Total fixed overhead	$186,000

Finished goods inventory

The desired monthly ending inventory in units of completed components is 80 percent of the next month's estimated sales. There are 4,000 finished units in inventory on June 30, 19x7.

Required:
1. Prepare a production budget for the West Division for the third quarter ending September 30, 19x7. Show computations by month and in total for the quarter.
2. Prepare a direct materials purchases budget in units and in dollars for each type of material for the third quarter ending September 30, 19x7. Again show computations by month and in total for the quarter.
3. Prepare a direct labor budget in hours and in dollars for the third quarter ending September 30, 19x7. This time it is *not* necessary to show monthly figures; show quarterly totals only.
4. Assume that the company plans to produce a total of 65,000 units for the year. Prepare a factory overhead budget for the six-month period ending December 31, 19x7. Again, it is *not* necessary to show monthly figures.

(CMA, Adapted)

P8–25. **Budgeted cash collections; purchases budget.** Hadley Company is a large retail firm whose sales are all on credit. Sales are billed twice monthly, on the 10th of the month for the last half of the prior month's sales and on the 20th of the month for the first half of the current month's sales. The terms of all sales are 2/10, net 30. Based on past experience, the collection pattern of accounts receivable is as follows:

Within the discount period	80%
On the 30th day	18
Uncollectible	2

Actual sales for May 19x1 and budgeted sales for the next four months are:

May (actual)	$500,000
June	600,000
July	700,000
August	900,000
September	400,000

Hadley Company's gross profit rate is 20 percent of sales.

The company purchases merchandise inventory each month as needed to meet the current month's sales demand and to maintain a desired monthly ending inventory of 25 percent of the next month's sales. All purchases are on credit with terms of net 30. Hadley Company pays for one half of a month's purchases in the month of purchase and the other half in the month following purchase.

All sales and purchases occur uniformly throughout the month.

Required: 1.   Determine the amount of cash that Hadley Company can plan to collect in September for sales made in August 19x1. Show all computations.

2.   Determine the amount of cash, in total, that Hadley Company can plan to collect from accounts receivable during July 19x1. Show all computations.

3.   Prepare a merchandise purchases budget for each of the months June, July, and August 19x1.

4.   Compute the budgeted cash payments for merchandise for August 19x1.

(CMA, Adapted)

P8–26.   Tabulation approach to EOQ.   (Appendix)   The Tolby Manufacturing Company uses 15,000 ingots of Klypton each year. The Klypton is purchased from a supplier in another state, according to the following price schedule:

Ingots	Per ingot
500	$30.00
1,000	29.90
1,500	29.85
2,000	29.80
2,500	29.75

The Tolby Manufacturing Company sends its own truck to the supplier's plant to pick up the ingots. The truck's capacity is 2,500 ingots per trip. The company has been getting a full load of ingots each trip, making six trips each year. The cost of making one round trip to the supplier's plant is $500. The paperwork associated with each trip is $30.

The supplier requires that all purchases be in round 500-ingot lots. The company's cost analyst estimates that the cost of storing one ingot for one year is $10.

Required: 1.   By use of the tabulation approach to EOQ, compute the volume in which the company should be purchasing its ingots. Treat the savings arising from quantity discounts as a reduction in total annual trucking and storing costs.

2.   Compute the annual cost savings that will be realized if the company purchases in the volume which you have determined in (1) above, as compared to its present purchase policy.

P8–27.   Economic order quantity and safety stock.   (Appendix).   Myron Metal Works, Inc., uses a small casting in one of its finished products. The castings are purchased from a foundry located in another state. In total, Myron Metal Works, Inc., purchases 24,000 castings per year at a cost of $8 per casting.

The castings are used evenly throughout the year in the production process on a 360-day-per-year basis. The company estimates that it costs $60 to place a single purchase order and about $2 to carry one casting in inventory for a year. The high carrying costs result from the need to keep the castings in carefully controlled temperature and humidity conditions, and from the high cost of insurance.

Delivery from the foundry generally takes 6 days, but it can take as much as 10 days. The days of delivery time and the percentage of their occurrence are shown in the following tabulation:

Delivery time (days)	Percentage of occurrence
6	75
7	10
8	5
9	5
10	5
	100

Required: 1. Compute the economic order quantity.
2. Assume that the company is willing to assume the risk of being out of stock 15 percent of the time. What would be the safety stock? The reorder point?
3. Assume that the company is willing to assume the risk of being out of stock only 5 percent of the time. What would be the safety stock? The reorder point?
4. Assume a 5 percent stockout risk as stated in (3) above. What would be the total cost of ordering and carrying inventory for one year?

P8–28. Economic order quantity and safety stock. (Appendix)   Pearl Manufacturing Company uses 100,000 units of material A each year. The material is used evenly throughout the year in the company's production process. A recent cost study indicates that it costs 60 cents to carry one unit of material A in stock for a year. The company estimates that the cost of placing an order for material A is $75.

On the average, it takes six days to receive an order from the supplier. Sometimes, orders do not arrive for 9 days, and at rare intervals (about 1 percent of the time) they do not arrive for 11 days. Each unit of material A costs the Pearl Manufacturing Company $4. The company works an average of 360 days per year. Round all figures to the nearest whole unit.

Required: 1. Compute the economic order quantity.
2. What size safety stock would you recommend for material A? Why?
3. What is the reorder point for material A in units?
4. Compute the *total cost* associated with ordering and carrying material A for a year.

P8–29. Integration of purchases budget, reorder point, and safety stock. (Appendix) The Press Company manufactures and sells industrial components. The Whitmore Plant is responsible for producing two components referred to as AD-5 and FX-3. Plastic, brass, and aluminum are used in the production of these two products.

Press Company has adopted a 13-period reporting cycle in all of its plants for budgeting purposes. Each period is four weeks long and has 20 working days. The projected inventory levels for AD-5 and FX-3 at the end of the current (seventh) period and the projected sales for these two products for the next three four-week periods are presented below.

| | Projected inventory level (in units) end of seventh period | Projected sales (in units) | | |
Component		Eighth period	Ninth period	Tenth period
AD-5	3,000	7,500	8,750	9,500
FX-3	2,800	7,000	4,500	4,000

Past experience has shown that adequate inventory levels for AD-5 and FX-3 can be maintained if 40 percent of the next period's projected sales are on hand at the end of a reporting period. Based on this experience and the projected sales, the Whitmore Plant has budgeted production of 8,000 units of AD-5 and 6,000 units of FX-3 in the eighth period. Production is assumed to be uniform for both products within each four-week period.

The raw material specifications for AD-5 and FX-3 are as follows:

	AD-5 (pounds)	FX-3 (pounds)
Plastic	2.0	1.0
Brass	0.5	—
Aluminum . . .	—	1.5

Data relating to the purchase of raw materials are presented below:

	Purchase price per pound	Standard purchase lot (pounds)	Reorder point (pounds)	Projected inventory status at the end of the seventh period (pounds)		Lead time in working days
				On hand	On order	
Plastic	$0.40	15,000	12,000	16,000	15,000	10
Brass	0.95	5,000	7,500	9,000	—	30
Aluminum . . .	0.55	10,000	10,000	14,000	10,000	20

The sales of AD-5 and FX-3 do not vary significantly from month to month. Consequently, the safety stock incorporated into the reorder point for each of the raw materials is adequate to compensate for variations in the sales of the finished products.

Raw material orders are placed the day the quantity on hand falls below the reorder point. Whitmore Plant's suppliers are very dependable so that the given lead times are reliable. The outstanding orders for plastic and aluminum are due to arrive on the tenth and fourth working days of the eighth period, respectively. Payments for all raw material orders are remitted in the month of delivery.

Required: Whitmore Plant is required to submit a report to corporate headquarters of Press Company summarizing the projected raw material activities before each period commences. The data for the eighth period report are being assembled. Determine the following items for plastic, brass, and aluminum for inclusion in the eighth period report:

1. Projected quantities (in pounds) of each raw material to be issued to production.
2. Projected quantities (in pounds) of each raw material ordered and the date (in terms of working days) the order is to be placed.
3. The projected inventory balance (in pounds) of each raw material at the end of the period.
4. The payments for purchases of each raw material.

(CMA, Adapted)

P8–30.   EOQ computations.   (Appendix)   SaPane Company is a regional distributor of automobile window glass. With the introduction of the new subcompact car models and the expected high level of consumer demand, management recognizes a need to determine the total inventory cost associated with maintaining an optimal supply of replacement windshields for the new subcompact cars introduced by each of the three major manufacturers. SaPane is expecting a daily demand for 36 windshields. The purchase price of each windshield is $50.

Other costs associated with ordering and maintaining an inventory of these windshields are as follows:

a. The historical ordering costs incurred in the purchase order department for placing and processing orders are shown below:

Year	Orders placed and processed	Total ordering costs
1985	20	$12,300
1986	55	12,475
1987	100	12,700

Management expects the ordering costs to increase 16 percent over the amounts and rates experienced during the last three years.

b. The windshield manufacturer charges SaPane a $75 shipping fee per order.

c. A clerk in the receiving department receives, inspects, and secures the windshields as they arrive from the manufacturer. This activity requires eight hours per order received. This clerk has no other responsibilities and is paid at the rate of $9 per hour. Related variable overhead costs in this department are applied at the rate of $2.50 per hour.

d. Additional warehouse space will have to be rented to store the new windshields. Space can be rented as needed in a public warehouse at an estimated cost of $2,500 per year plus $5.35 per windshield.

e. Breakage cost is estimated to be 6 percent of the cost per windshield.

f. Taxes and fire insurance on the inventory are $1.15 per windshield.

g. The desired rate of return on the investment in inventory is 21 percent of the purchase price.

Six working days are required from the time an order is placed with the manufacturer until it is received. SaPane uses a 300-day workyear when making economic order quantity computations.

Required: Calculate the following values for SaPane Company.

1. Value for ordering cost that should be used in the EOQ formula.
2. Value for storage cost that should be used in the EOQ formula.
3. Economic order quantity.
4. Minimum annual cost at the economic order quantity point.
5. Reorder point in units.

(CMA, Adapted)

CASE

C8–31.   **Master budget with supporting schedules.**   You have just been hired as a new management trainee by Earrings Unlimited, a distributor of earrings to various retail outlets located in shopping malls across the country. In the past, the company has done very little in the way of budgeting and at certain times of the year has experienced a shortage of cash.

Since you are well trained in budgeting, you have decided to prepare comprehensive budgets for the uncoming second quarter in order to show management the benefits that can be gained from an integrated budgeting program. To this end, you have worked with accounting and other areas to gather the information assembled below.

The company sells many styles of earrings, but all are sold for the same price—$10 per pair. Actual sales of earnings for the last three months and budgeted sales for the next six months follow (in pairs of earrings):

January (actual)	. . .	20,000	June	50,000
February (actual)	. . .	26,000	July	30,000
March (actual)	. . . .	40,000	August	28,000
April		65,000	September	25,000
May		100,000		

The concentration of sales before and during the month of May is due to Mother's Day. Sufficient inventory should be on hand at the end of each month to supply 40 percent of the earrings sold in the following month.

The company pays its suppliers $4 for a pair of earrings. One half of a month's purchases is paid for in the month of purchase; the other half is paid for in the following month. All sales are on credit, with no discount, and payable within 15 days. The company has found, however, that only 20 percent of a month's sales are collected in the month of sale. An additional 70 percent is collected in the following month, and the remaining 10 percent is collected in the second month following sale. Bad debts have been negligible.

The company's monthly operating expenses are given below:

Variable:	
Sales commissions	4% of sales
Fixed:	
Advertising	$200,000
Rent	18,000
Salaries	106,000
Utilities	7,000
Insurance expired	3,000
Depreciation	14,000

Insurance is paid on an annual basis, in November of each year.

The company plans to purchase $16,000 in new equipment during May and $40,000 in new equipment during June; both purchases will be for cash. The company declares dividends of $15,000 each quarter, payable in the first month of the following quarter.

A listing of the company's ledger accounts as of March 31 is given below:

Assets

Cash	$ 74,000
Accounts receivable ($26,000 February sales;	
$320,000 March sales)	346,000
Inventory	104,000
Prepaid insurance	21,000
Property and equipment, net.	950,000
Total assets	$1,495,000

Liabilities and Stockholders' Equity

Accounts payable	$ 100,000
Dividends payable	15,000
Capital stock	800,000
Retained earnings	580,000
Total liabilities and stockholders' equity	$1,495,000

Part of the use of the budgeting program will be to establish an ongoing line of credit at a local bank. Therefore, show borrowing as needed to maintain a minimum cash balance of $50,000. All borrowing will be done at the beginning of a month; any repayments will be made at the end of a month.

The interest rate will be 12 percent per annum. Interest will be computed and paid at the end of each quarter on all loans outstanding during the quarter. Compute interest on whole months ($1/12$, $2/12$, and so forth).

Required: Prepare a master budget for the three-month period ending June 30. Include the following detailed budgets:

1. *a.* A sales budget, by month and in total.
    b. A schedule of expected cash collections from sales, by month and in total.
    c. A merchandise purchases budget in units and in dollars. Show the budget by month and in total.
    d. A schedule of expected cash payments for merchandise purchases, by month and in total.
2. A cash budget. Show the budget by month and in total.
3. A budgeted income statement for the three-month period ending June 30. Use the contribution approach.
4. A budgeted balance sheet as of June 30.

CHAPTER 9

Control through Standard Costs

LEARNING OBJECTIVES

After studying Chapter 9, you should be able to:

■ Distinguish between ideal standards and practical standards.

■ Explain how direct materials standards and direct labor standards are set.

■ Enumerate the advantages and disadvantages of using standard costs.

■ Compute the direct materials price and quantity variances and explain their significance.

■ Compute the direct labor rate and efficiency variances and explain their significance.

■ Compute the variable overhead spending and efficiency variances.

■ Explain how the manager would determine whether a variance constituted an "exception" that would require his or her attention.

■ Prepare journal entries to record standard costs and variances.

■ Define or explain the key terms listed at the end of the chapter.

In attempting to control costs, managers have two types of decisions to make—decisions relating to prices paid and decisions relating to quantities used. To attain the objectives of their firms, managers are expected to pay the lowest possible prices that are consistent with the quality of output desired. In attaining these objectives, managers are also expected to consume the minimum quantity of whatever resources they have at their command, again consistent with the quality of output desired. Breakdowns in control over either price or quantity will lead to excessive costs and to deteriorating profit margins.

How do managers attempt to control price paid and quantity used? Managers could personally examine every transaction that takes place, but this obviously would be an inefficient use of management time. The answer to the control problem lies in *standard costs.*

STANDARD COSTS—MANAGEMENT BY EXCEPTION

A *standard* can be defined as a benchmark or ''norm'' for measuring performance. Standards are found in many facets of day-to-day life. Students who wish to enter a college or university are often required to perform at a certain level on a standard achievement exam as a condition for admittance; the autos we drive are built under exacting engineering standards; and the food we eat is prepared under standards of both cleanliness and nutritional content. Standards are also widely used in managerial accounting. Here the standards relate to the *cost* and *quantity* of inputs used in manufacturing goods or providing services.

Cost and quantity standards are set by managers for the three elements of cost input—materials, labor, and overhead—that we have discussed in preceding chapters. *Quantity standards* say how much of a cost element, such as labor time or raw materials, should be used in manufacturing a unit of product or in providing a unit of service. *Cost standards* say what the cost of the time or the materials should be. Actual quantities and actual costs of inputs are measured against these standards to see whether operations are proceeding within the limits that management has set. If either the quantity or the cost of inputs exceeds the bounds that management has set, attention is directed to the difference, thereby permitting the manager to focus his or her efforts where they will do the most good. This process is called **management by exception.**

Who Uses Standard Costs?

Manufacturing, service, food, and not-for-profit organizations all make use of standards (in terms of either costs or quantities) to some extent. Auto service centers, for example, often set specific labor time standards for the completion of certain work tasks, such as installing a carburetor or doing a valve job, and then measure actual performance against these standards. Fast-food outlets such as McDonald's have exacting standards as to the quantity of meat going into a sandwich, as well as standards for the cost of the meat. Hospitals have standard costs (for food, laundry, and other items) for each occupied bed per day, as well as standard time allowances for the performing of certain routine activities, such as laboratory tests. In short, the business student is likely to run into standard cost concepts in virtually any line of business that she or he may enter.

The broadest application of the standard cost idea is probably found in manufacturing firms, where standards relating to materials, labor, and overhead are developed in detail for each separate product line. These standards are then organized into a **standard cost card** that tells the manager what the final, manufactured cost should be for a single unit of product. In the following section, we provide a detailed example of the setting of standard costs and the preparation of a standard cost card.

SETTING STANDARD COSTS

The setting of standard costs is more an art than a science. It requires the combined thinking and expertise of all persons who have responsibility over prices and quantities of inputs. In a manufacturing setting, this would include the managerial accountant, the purchasing agent, the industrial engineer, production supervisors, and line managers.

The beginning point in setting standard costs is a rigorous look at past experience. The managerial accountant can be of great help in this task by preparing data on the cost characteristics of prior years' activities at various levels of operations. A standard for the future must be more than simply a projection of the past, however. Data must be adjusted and modified in terms of changing economic patterns, changing demand and supply characteristics, and changing technology. Past experience in certain costs may be distorted due to inefficiencies. To the extent that such inefficiencies can be identified, the data must be appropriately adjusted. The manager must realize that the past is of value only insofar as it helps to predict the future. In short, standards must be reflective of efficient *future* operations, not inefficient *past* operations.

Ideal versus Practical Standards

Should standards be attainable all of the time, should they be attainable only part of the time, or should they be so tight that they become, in effect, "the impossible dream"? Opinions among managers vary, but standards tend to fall into one of two categories—either ideal or practical.

Ideal standards are those that can be attained only under the best circumstances. They allow for no machine breakdowns or work interruptions, and they call for a level of effort that can be attained only by the most skilled and efficient employee working at peak effort 100 percent of the time. Some managers feel that such standards have a motivational value.

These managers argue that even though an employee knows he will never stay within the standard set, it is a constant reminder to him of the need for ever-increasing efficiency and effort. Few firms use ideal standards. Most managers are of the opinion that ideal standards tend to discourage even the most diligent workers. Moreover, when ideal standards are used, variances from standards have little meaning. The reason is that the variances contain elements of "normal" inefficiencies, not just the abnormal inefficiencies that managers would like to have isolated and brought to their attention.

Practical standards can be defined as standards that are "tight but attainable." They allow for normal machine downtime and employee rest periods, and are such that they can be attained through reasonable, though highly efficient, efforts by the average worker at a task. Variances from such a standard are very useful to management in that they represent deviations that fall outside of normal, recurring inefficiencies and signal a need for management attention. Furthermore, practical standards can serve multiple purposes. In addition to signaling abnormal deviations in costs, they can also be used in forecasting cash flows and in planning inventory. By contrast, ideal standards cannot be used in forecasting and planning; they do not allow for normal inefficiencies, and therefore they result in unrealistic planning and forecasting figures.

Throughout the remainder of this chapter, we will assume the use of practical rather than ideal standards.

Setting Direct Materials Standards

As stated earlier, managers prepare separate standards for the price and quantity of inputs. The **standard price per unit** for direct materials should reflect the final, delivered cost of the materials, net of any discounts taken. For example, the standard price of a pound of material A might be determined as follows:

Purchase price, top grade, in 500-pound quantities . . .	$3.60
Freight, by truck, from the supplier's plant	0.44
Receiving and handling	0.05
Less purchase discount	(0.09)
Standard price per pound	$4.00

Notice that the standard price reflects a particular grade of material (top grade), purchased in particular lot sizes (500 pounds), and delivered by a particular type of carrier (truck). Allowances have also been made for handling and discounts. If all proceeds according to plans, the net standard price of a pound of material A should therefore be $4.

The **standard quantity per unit** for direct materials should reflect the amount of material going into each unit of finished product, as well as an allowance for unavoidable waste, spoilage, and other normal inefficiencies. To illustrate, the standard quantity of material A going into a unit of product might be determined as follows:

Per bill of materials, in pounds 2.7
Allowance for waste and spoilage, in pounds 0.2
Allowance for rejects, in pounds 0.1
Standard quantity per unit of product, in pounds . . . 3.0

A **bill of materials** is simply a list that shows the type and quantity of each item of material going into a unit of finished product. It is a handy source for determining the basic material input per unit, but it must be adjusted for waste and other factors, as shown above, in determining the full standard quantity per unit of product. "Rejects" represents the direct material contained in units of product that are rejected at final inspection. The cost of this material must be added back to good units.

Once the price and quantity standards have been set, the standard cost of material A per unit of finished product can be computed as follows:

$$3.0 \text{ pounds} \times \$4 = \$12 \text{ per unit}$$

This $12 cost figure will appear as one item on the standard cost card of the product under consideration.

Setting Direct Labor Standards

Direct labor price and quantity standards are usually expressed in terms of labor rate and labor-hours. The **standard rate per hour** for direct labor would include not only wages earned but also an allowance for fringe benefits and other labor-related costs. The computation might be as follows:

Basic wage rate per hour. $10
Employment taxes at 10% of the basic rate . . .   1
Fringe benefits at 30% of the basic rate   3
Standard rate per direct labor-hour $14

Many companies prepare a single standard rate for all employees in a department, even though the actual wage rates may vary somewhat between employees due to seniority or other reasons. This simplifies the use of standard costs and also permits the manager to monitor the use of employees within departments. More is said on this point a little later. If all proceeds according to plans, the direct labor rate for our mythical company should average $14 per hour.

The standard direct labor time required to complete a unit of product (generally called the **standard hours per unit**) is perhaps the single most difficult standard to determine. One approach is to divide each operation performed on the product into elemental body movements (such as reaching, pushing, and turning over). Published tables of standard times for such movements are available. These times can be applied to the movements and then added together to determine the total standard time allowed per operation. Another approach is for an industrial engineer to do a time and motion study, actually clocking the time required for certain tasks. As stated earlier, the standard time developed must include allowances for coffee breaks, personal needs of employees, cleanup, and machine downtime. The resulting standard time might appear as follows:

Basic labor time per unit, in hours	1.9
Allowance for breaks and personal needs	0.1
Allowance for cleanup and machine downtime . . .	0.3
Allowance for rejects	0.2
Standard hours per unit of product	2.5

Once the rate and time standards have been set, the standard labor cost per unit of product can be computed as follows:

$$2.5 \text{ hours} \times \$14 = \$35 \text{ per unit}$$

This $35 cost figure will appear along with direct materials as one item on the standard cost card of the product under consideration.

Setting Variable Overhead Standards

As with direct labor, the price and quantity standards for variable overhead are generally expressed in terms of rate and hours. The rate represents *the variable portion of the predetermined overhead rate* discussed in Chapter 3; the hours represent whatever hours base is used to apply overhead to units of product (often machine-hours, computer time, or direct labor-hours, as we learned in Chapter 3). To illustrate, if the variable portion of the predetermined overhead rate was $3, and if overhead was applied to units of product on a basis of direct labor-hours, the standard variable overhead cost per unit of product in our example would be:

$$2.5 \text{ hours} \times \$3.00 = \$7.50 \text{ per unit}$$

A more detailed look at the setting of overhead standards is reserved until Chapter 10.

To summarize our example on the setting of standard costs, the completed standard cost card for one unit of product in our mythical company is presented in Exhibit 9–1. Observe that the **standard cost per unit** is computed by multiplying the standard quantity or hours by the standard price or rate.

EXHIBIT 9–1

Standard cost card—variable production cost

Inputs	(1) Standard quantity or hours	(2) Standard price or rate	(3) Standard cost (1) × (2)
Direct materials	3.0 pounds	$ 4.00	$12.00
Direct labor	2.5 hours	14.00	35.00
Variable overhead	2.5 hours	3.00	7.50
Total standard cost per unit . . .			$54.50

Are Standards the Same as Budgets?

yes
Standard — unit amt.
Budget — total amt.

Essentially, standards and budgets are the same thing. The only distinction between the two terms is that a standard is a *unit* amount, whereas a budget is a *total* amount. That is, the standard cost for materials in a unit of product may be $5. If 1,000 units of the product are to be produced during a period, then the budgeted cost of materials is $5,000. In effect, a standard may be viewed as being the *budgeted cost for one unit of product*.

Advantages of Standard Costs

A number of distinct advantages can be cited in favor of using standard costs in an organization.

1. As stated earlier, the use of standard costs makes possible the concept of management by exception. So long as costs remain within the standards set, no attention by management is needed. When costs fall outside the standards set, then the matter is brought to the attention of management at once as an "exception." Management by exception makes possible more productive use of management time.

2. Standard costs facilitate cash planning and inventory planning.

3. So long as standards are set on a "practical" basis, they promote economy and efficiency in that employees normally become very cost and time conscious. In addition, wage incentive systems can be tied to a system of standard costs once the standards have been set.

4. In income determination, a system of standard costs may be more economical and simpler to operate than a historical cost system. Standard cost cards can be kept for each product or operation, and costs for material, labor, and manufacturing overhead charged out according to the standards set. This greatly simplifies the bookkeeping process.

5. Standard costs can assist in the implementation of "responsibility accounting," in which responsibility over cost control is assigned, and the extent to which that responsibility has been discharged can be evaluated through performance reports.

Disadvantages of Standard Costs

Although the advantages of using standard costs are significant, we must recognize that certain difficulties can be encountered by the manager in applying the standard cost idea. Moreover, improper use of standard costs and the management by exception principle can lead to adverse behavioral problems in an organization. Managers cite the following as being either problems or potential problems in using standard costs:

1. Difficulty may be experienced in determining which variances are "material" or significant in amount. (Ways to overcome this problem are discussed later in the chapter.)

2. By focusing only on variances above a certain level (that is, on

variances that are considered to be material in amount), other useful information, such as trends, may not be noticed at an early stage.

3.   If management performance evaluation is tied to the exception principle, subordinates may be tempted to cover up negative exceptions or not report them at all. In addition, subordinates may not receive reinforcement for the positive things they do, such as controlling or reducing costs charged to their area of responsibility, but may only receive reprimands for those items that exceed the acceptable cost standards. Thus, subordinate morale may suffer because of the lack of positive reinforcement for work well done.

4.   The management by exception technique may also affect supervisory employees in an unsatisfactory manner. Supervisors may feel that they are not getting a complete review of operations because they are always just keying in on problems. In addition, supervisors may feel that they are constantly being critical of their subordinates, that is, always "running them down." This may have a negative impact on supervisory morale.[1]

These potential problems suggest that considerable care must be exercised by the manager in organizing and administering a standard cost system. It is particularly important that the manager focus on the positive, rather than on the negative, and that work that is well done be appropriately recognized.

A GENERAL MODEL FOR VARIANCE ANALYSIS

One reason for separating standards into two categories—price and quantity—is that control decisions relating to price paid and quantity used will generally fall at different points in time. In the case of raw materials, for example, control over price paid comes at the time of purchase. By contrast, control over quantity used does not come until the raw materials are used in production, which may be many weeks or months after the purchase date. In addition, control over price paid and quantity used will generally be the responsibility of two different managers and will therefore need to be assessed independently. As we have stressed earlier, no manager should be held responsible for a cost over which he or she has no control. It is important, therefore, that we separate price considerations from quantity considerations in our approach to the control of costs.

Price and Quantity Variances

The manager separates price considerations from quantity considerations in the control of costs through the use of a general model that distinguishes between these two cost elements and that provides a base for *variance* analysis. A **variance** is the difference between *standard* prices and quantities

---

[1] Institute of Management Accounting, *Certificate in Management Accounting Examination* (New York: National Association of Accountants, June 1979), p. 26.

EXHIBIT 9–2

A general model for variance analysis—variable production costs

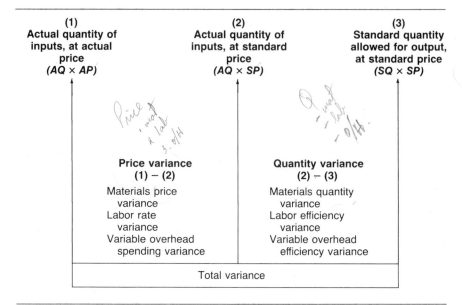

(1) **Actual quantity of** **inputs, at actual** **price** **(AQ × AP)**	(2) **Actual quantity of** **inputs, at standard** **price** **(AQ × SP)**	(3) **Standard quantity** **allowed for output,** **at standard price** **(SQ × SP)**
	Price variance **(1) − (2)** Materials price variance Labor rate variance Variable overhead spending variance	**Quantity variance** **(2) − (3)** Materials quantity variance Labor efficiency variance Variable overhead efficiency variance
	Total variance	

and *actual* prices and quantities. This model, which deals with variable costs, isolates price variances from quantity variances and shows how each of these variances is computed.[2] The model is presented in Exhibit 9–2.

Three things should be noted from Exhibit 9–2. First, note that a price variance and a quantity variance can be computed for all three variable cost elements—direct materials, direct labor, and variable manufacturing overhead—even though the variance is not called by the same name in all cases. For example, a price variance is called a *materials price variance* in the case of direct materials but a *labor rate variance* in the case of direct labor and an *overhead spending variance* in the case of variable manufacturing overhead.

Second, note that even though a price variance may be called by different names, it is computed in exactly the same way regardless of whether one is dealing with direct materials, direct labor, or variable manufacturing overhead. The same is true with the quantity variance.

Third, note that variance analysis is actually a matter of input-output analysis. The inputs represent the actual quantity of direct materials, direct labor, and variable manufacturing overhead used; the output represents the good production of the period, expressed in terms of the *standard quantity (or the standard hours) allowed* in its manufacture (see column 3 in Exhibit 9–2). By **standard quantity allowed** or **standard hours allowed,** we mean

---

[2] Variance analysis of fixed costs is reserved until Chapter 10.

the amount of direct materials, direct labor, or variable manufacturing over-head *that should have been used* to produce what was produced during the period. This might be more or less than what was *actually* used, depending on the efficiency or inefficiency of operations.

With this general model as a foundation, we will now examine the price and quantity variances in more detail.

USING STANDARD COSTS—DIRECT MATERIAL VARIANCES

To illustrate the computation and use of direct material variances, we will return to the standard cost data for direct materials contained in Exhibit 9–1. This exhibit shows the standard cost of direct materials per unit of product in our mythical company to be:

$$3.0 \text{ pounds} \times \$4 = \$12$$

We will assume that during June the company purchased 6,500 pounds of material at a cost of $3.80 per pound, including freight and handling costs, and net of the quantity discount. All of the material was used in the manufacture of 2,000 units of product. The computation of the price and quantity variances for the month is shown in Exhibit 9–3.[3]

EXHIBIT 9–3

Variance analysis—direct materials

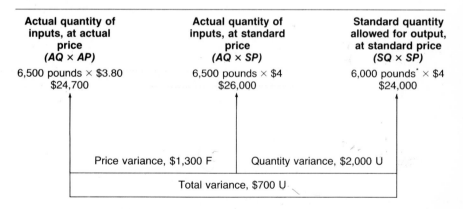

Actual quantity of inputs, at actual price (AQ × AP)	Actual quantity of inputs, at standard price (AQ × SP)	Standard quantity allowed for output, at standard price (SQ × SP)
6,500 pounds × $3.80 $24,700	6,500 pounds × $4 $26,000	6,000 pounds* × $4 $24,000

Price variance, $1,300 F   Quantity variance, $2,000 U

Total variance, $700 U

* 2,000 units × 3.0 pounds per unit = 6,000 pounds.
F = Favorable.
U = Unfavorable.

[3] Exhibit 9–3 shows the computation of the price and quantity variances when all materials purchased during a period are used in production and none remain in inventory at period-end. See the review problem at the end of the chapter for a computation of the price and quantity variances when only part of the materials purchased during a period is used in production during that period.

A variance is unfavorable if the actual price or quantity exceeds the standard price or quantity; a variance is favorable if the actual price or quantity is less than the standard.

Materials Price Variance—a Closer Look

A **materials price variance** measures the difference between what is paid for a given quantity of materials and what should have been paid according to the standard that has been set. From Exhibit 9–3, this difference can be expressed by the following formula:

$$(AQ \times AP) - (AQ \times SP) = \text{Materials price variance}$$

The formula can be factored into simpler form as:

$$AQ(AP - SP) = \text{Materials price variance}$$

Some managers prefer this simpler formula, since it permits variance computations to be made very quickly. Using the data from Exhibit 9–3 in this formula, we have:

$$6,500 \text{ pounds } (\$3.80 - \$4.00) = \$1,300 \text{ F}$$

Notice that the answer is the same as that yielded in Exhibit 9–3. If the company wanted to put these data into a performance report, the data would appear as follows:

MYTHICAL COMPANY
Performance Report—Purchasing Department

Item purchased	(1) Quantity purchased	(2) Actual price	(3) Standard price	(4) Difference in price (2) − (3)	(5) Total price variance (1) × (4)	Explanation
Material A	6,500 pounds	$3.80	$4.00	$0.20	$1,300 F	Second-grade materials purchased, rather than top grade

F = Favorable.
U = Unfavorable.

Isolation of variances   At what point should variances be isolated and brought to the attention of management? The answer is, the earlier the better. One of the basic reasons for utilizing standard costs is to facilitate cost control. Therefore, the sooner deviations from standard are brought to the attention of management, the sooner problems can be evaluated and corrected. If long periods are allowed to elapse before variances are computed, costs that could otherwise have been controlled may accumulate to the point of doing significant damage to profits. Most firms compute the materials price variance, for example, when materials *are purchased* rather than when the materials are placed into production. This permits earlier isolation of the variance, since materials may lay in the warehouse for many months before being used in production. Isolating the price variance when materials are purchased also permits the company to carry its raw materials in the inventory accounts at standard cost. This greatly simplifies the process of costing materials as they are later placed into production.[4]

Once a performance report has been prepared, what does management do with the price variance data? The variances should be viewed as "red flags," calling attention to the fact that an exception has occurred that will require some follow-up effort. Normally, the performance report itself will contain some explanation of the reason for the variance, as shown above.

Responsibility for the variance   Who is responsible for the materials price variance? Generally speaking, the purchasing agent has control over the price to be paid for goods and is therefore responsible for any price variances. Many factors control the price paid for goods, including size of lots purchased, delivery method used, quantity discounts available, rush orders, and the quality of materials purchased. To the extent that the purchasing agent can control these factors, he or she is responsible for seeing that they are kept in agreement with the factors anticipated when the standard costs were initially set. A deviation in any factor from what was intended in the initial setting of a standard cost can result in a price variance. For example, purchase of second-grade materials rather than top-grade materials would result in a favorable price variance, since the lower-grade materials would generally be less costly (but perhaps less suitable for production).

There may be times, however, when someone other than the purchasing agent is responsible for a materials price variance. Production may be scheduled in such a way, for example, that the purchasing agent is required to obtain delivery by airfreight, rather than by truck, or he or she may be forced to buy in uneconomical quantities. In these cases, the production manager would bear responsibility for the variances that develop.

A word of caution is in order. Variance analysis should not be used as an excuse to conduct witch hunts or as a means of beating line managers over the head. The emphasis must be on the control function in the sense of *supporting* the line managers and *assisting* them in meeting the goals that they have participated in setting for the company. In short, the emphasis must be positive rather than negative. Excessive dwelling on what has already happened, particularly in terms of trying to find someone to "blame," can often be destructive to the goals of an organization.

Materials Quantity Variance—a Closer Look

The **materials quantity variance** measures the difference between the quantity of materials used in production and the quantity that should have been used according to the standard that has been set. Although the variance

---

[4] See the Appendix at the end of the chapter for an illustration of journal entries in a standard cost system.

is concerned with the physical usage of materials, it is generally stated in dollar terms, as shown in Exhibit 9–3. The formula for the materials quantity variance is:

$$(AQ \times SP) - (SQ \times SP) = \text{Materials quantity variance}$$

Again, the formula can be factored into simpler terms:

$$SP(AQ - SQ) = \text{Materials quantity variance}$$

Using the data from Exhibit 9–3 in the formula, we have:

$$\$4(6{,}500 \text{ pounds} - 6{,}000 \text{ pounds}^*) = \$2{,}000 \text{ U}$$

* 2,000 units $\times$ 3.0 pounds per unit = 6,000 pounds.

The answer, of course, is the same as that yielded in Exhibit 9–3. The data would appear as follows if a formal performance report were prepared:

MYTHICAL COMPANY
Performance Report—Production Department

Type of materials	(1) Standard price	(2) Actual quantity	(3) Standard quantity allowed	(4) Difference in quantity (2) − (3)	(5) Total quantity variance (1) × (4)	Explanation
Material A . . .	$4	6,500 pounds	6,000 pounds	500 pounds	$2,000 U	Second-grade materials, unsuitable for production

F = Favorable.
U = Unfavorable.

The materials quantity variance is best isolated at the time that materials are placed into production.[5] Materials are drawn for the number of units to be produced, according to the standard bill of materials for each unit. Any additional materials are usually drawn on an excess materials requisition slip, which is different in color from the normal requisition slips. This procedure calls attention to the excessive usage of materials *while production is still in process* and permits opportunity for early control of any developing problem.

Excessive usage of materials can result from many factors, including faulty machines, inferior quality of materials, untrained workers, and poor supervision. Generally speaking, it is the responsibility of the production department to see that material usage is kept in line with standards. There may be times, however, when the *purchasing* department may be responsible

---

[5] If a company uses process costing, then it may be necessary in some situations to compute the materials quantity variance on a periodic basis as production is *completed*. This is because under process costing it is sometimes difficult to know in advance what the output will be for a period. We assume the use of a job-order costing system throughout this chapter (including all assignment materials).

for an unfavorable material quantity variance. If the purchasing department obtains materials of inferior quality in an effort to economize on price, the materials may prove to be unsuitable for use on the production line and may result in excessive waste. Thus, purchasing rather than production would be responsible for the quantity variance.

USING STANDARD COSTS—DIRECT LABOR VARIANCES

To illustrate the computation and use of direct labor variances, we will use the standard cost data for direct labor contained in Exhibit 9–1. This exhibit shows the standard cost of direct labor per unit of product in our mythical company to be:

$$2.5 \text{ hours} \times \$14 = \$35$$

We will assume that during June the company recorded 4,500 hours of direct labor time. The actual cost of this labor time was $64,350 (including employment taxes and fringe benefits), or an average of $14.30 per hour. Recall that the company produced 2,000 units of product during June. The computation of the labor rate and efficiency variances for the month is shown in Exhibit 9–4.

Notice that the column headings in Exhibit 9–4 are the same as those used in the prior two exhibits, except that in Exhibit 9–4 the terms *hours* and *rate* are used in place of the terms *quantity* and *price*.

Labor Rate Variance—a Closer Look

As explained earlier, the price variance for direct labor is commonly termed a **labor rate variance.** This variance measures any deviation from standard in the average hourly rate paid to direct labor workers. From Exhibit 9–4, the formula for the labor rate variance would be expressed as follows:

EXHIBIT 9–4

Variance analysis—direct labor

Actual hours of input, at the actual rate (AH × AR)	Actual hours of input, at the standard rate (AH × SR)	Standard hours allowed for output, at the standard rate (SH × SR)
4,500 hours × $14.30 $64,350	4,500 hours × $14 $63,000	5,000 hours* × $14 $70,000

Rate variance, $1,350 U   Efficiency variance, $7,000 F

Total variance, $5,650 F

* 2,000 units × 2.5 hours per unit = 5,000 hours.
F = Favorable.
U = Unfavorable.

$$(AH \times AR) - (AH \times SR) = \text{Labor rate variance}$$

The formula can be factored into simpler form as:

$$AH(AR - SR) = \text{Labor rate variance}$$

Using the data from Exhibit 9–4 in the formula, we have:

$$4{,}500 \text{ hours } (\$14.30 - \$14.00) = \$1{,}350 \text{ U}$$

In many firms, the rates paid workers are set by union contract; therefore, rate variances, in terms of amounts paid to workers, tend to be almost nonexistent. Rate variances can arise, though, through the way labor is used. Skilled workers with high hourly rates of pay can be given duties that require little skill and call for low hourly rates of pay. This type of misallocation of the work force will result in unfavorable labor rate variances, since the actual hourly rate of pay will exceed the standard rate authorized for the particular task being performed. A reverse situation exists when unskilled or untrained workers are assigned to jobs. The lower pay scale for these workers will result in favorable rate variances, although the workers may be highly inefficient in terms of output. Finally, unfavorable rate variances can arise from overtime work at premium rates if any portion of the overtime premium is added to the direct labor account.

Who is responsible for controlling the labor rate variance? Since rate variances generally arise as a result of how labor is used, those supervisors in charge of effective utilization of labor time bear responsibility for seeing that labor rate variances are kept under control.

Labor Efficiency Variance—a Closer Look

The quantity variance for direct labor, more commonly called the **labor efficiency variance,** measures the productivity of labor time. No variance is more closely watched by management, since increasing productivity of labor time is a vital key to reducing unit costs of production. From Exhibit 9–4, the formula for the labor efficiency variance would be expressed as follows:

$$(AH \times SR) - (SH \times SR) = \text{Labor efficiency variance}$$

Factored into simpler terms, the formula is:

$$SR(AH - SH) = \text{Labor efficiency variance}$$

Using the data from Exhibit 9–4 in the formula, we have:

$$\$14(4{,}500 \text{ hours} - 5{,}000 \text{ hours}^*) = \$7{,}000 \text{ F}$$

* 2,000 units × 2.5 hours per unit = 5,000 hours.

Causes of the labor efficiency variance include poorly trained workers; poor quality materials, requiring more labor time in processing; faulty equipment, causing breakdowns and work interruptions; and poor supervision of workers. The managers in charge of production would generally be responsible for control of the labor efficiency variance. However, the variance might be chargeable to purchasing if the acquisition of poor materials resulted in excessive labor processing time.

USING STANDARD COSTS—VARIABLE OVERHEAD VARIANCES

The variable portion of manufacturing overhead can be analyzed and controlled using the same basic variance formulas that are used in analyzing direct materials and direct labor. In order to lay a foundation for the following chapter, where we discuss overhead control at length, it will be helpful at this time to illustrate the analysis of variable overhead using these basic formulas. As a basis for discussion, we will again use the cost data found in Exhibit 9–1. The exhibit shows the standard variable overhead cost per unit of product in our mythical company to be:

$$2.5 \text{ hours} \times \$3.00 = \$7.50$$

We will assume that the total actual variable overhead cost for the month of June was $13,950. Recall from our earlier discussion that 4,500 hours of direct labor time were recorded during the month and that the company produced 2,000 units of product. Exhibit 9–5 contains an analysis of the variable overhead variances.

Notice the similarities between Exhibits 9–4 and 9–5. These similarities arise from the fact that direct labor-hours are being used as a base for allocating overhead to units of product; thus, the same hours figures appear in Exhibit 9–5 for variable overhead as in Exhibit 9–4 for direct labor. The main difference between the two exhibits is in the standard hourly rate being used, which is much lower for variable overhead.

EXHIBIT 9–5

Variance analysis—variable overhead

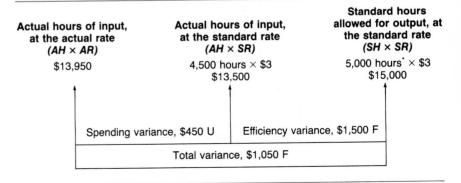

Actual hours of input, at the actual rate (AH × AR)	Actual hours of input, at the standard rate (AH × SR)	Standard hours allowed for output, at the standard rate (SH × SR)
$13,950	4,500 hours × $3 $13,500	5,000 hours* × $3 $15,000
	Spending variance, $450 U	Efficiency variance, $1,500 F
	Total variance, $1,050 F	

* 2,000 units × 2.5 hours per unit = 5,000 hours.
F = Favorable.
U = Unfavorable.

Overhead Variances—a Closer Look

As its name implies, the **variable overhead spending variance** measures deviations in amounts spent for overhead inputs such as lubricants and utilities. The formula for the variance can be expressed as:

$$(AH \times AR) - (AH \times SR) = \text{Variable overhead spending variance}$$

Or, factored into simpler terms:

$$AH(AR - SR) = \text{Variable overhead spending variance}$$

Using the data from Exhibit 9–5 in the formula, we have:

$$4{,}500 \text{ hours}(\$3.10^* - \$3.00) = \$450 \text{ U}$$
$$^* \$13{,}950 \div 4{,}500 \text{ hours} = \$3.10.$$

The **variable overhead efficiency variance** is a measure of the difference between the actual activity of a period and the standard activity allowed, multiplied by the variable part of the predetermined overhead rate. The formula for the variance can be expressed as:

$$(AH \times SR) - (SH \times SR) = \text{Variable overhead efficiency variance}$$

Or, factored into simpler terms:

$$SR(AH - SH) = \text{Variable overhead efficiency variance}$$

Again using the data from Exhibit 9–5, the computation of the variance would be:

$$\$3.00(4{,}500 \text{ hours} - 5{,}000 \text{ hours}^*) = \$1{,}500 \text{ F}$$
$$^* 2{,}000 \text{ units} \times 2.5 \text{ hours per unit} = 5{,}000 \text{ hours.}$$

We will reserve further discussion of the variable overhead spending and efficiency variances until Chapter 10, where overhead analysis is discussed in depth.

Before proceeding further, it will be helpful for the reader to pause at this point and go back and review the data contained in Exhibits 9–1 through 9–5. These exhibits and the accompanying text discussion represent a comprehensive, integrated illustration of standard setting and variance analysis.

GRAPHIC ANALYSIS OF THE PRICE AND QUANTITY VARIANCES

The way in which the price and quantity variances are computed can lead to a problem between the purchasing and production departments. The problem can best be seen by presenting these two variances in graphic form. To do this, we will assume that a company uses 4 pounds of material X in the manufacture of a unit of product. During a recent period, the company produced 950 units, using 4,000 pounds of material X in the process. Variances for the period are summarized below and then presented in graphic form in Exhibit 9–6.

Summary of data—material X

Standard price per pound $8.00
Actual price per pound 8.75
Standard quantity for production of 950 units of product
  (4 pounds per unit × 950 units) . . . . 3,800 pounds
Actual quantity used in production of 950 units of product . . . 4,000 pounds

Summary of variances—material X

$$AQ(AP - SP) = \text{Materials price variance}$$
$$4,000 \text{ pounds}(\$8.75 - \$8.00) = \$3,000 \text{ U}$$

$$SP(AQ - SQ) = \text{Materials quantity variance}$$
$$\$8(4,000 \text{ pounds} - 3,800 \text{ pounds}) = \$1,600 \text{ U}$$

EXHIBIT 9–6
Graphic analysis of price and quantity variances

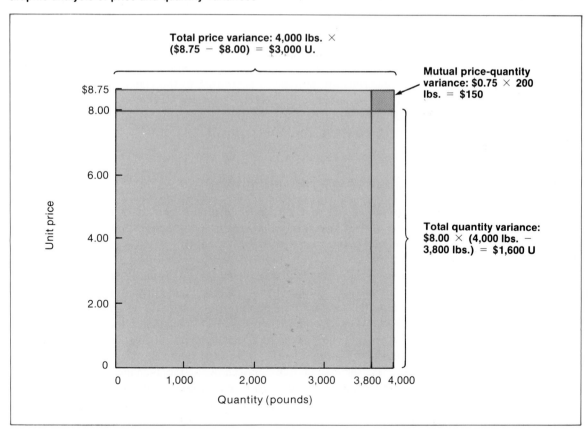

The problem referred to can arise from the upper right corner of the graph in Exhibit 9–6. This corner represents a **mutual price-quantity variance,** although we have shown it to be part of the price variance in our computations above. The purchasing agent may contend that it is unfair to charge her for the $150 mutual price-quantity variance represented in this corner, since it has arisen only because of the inefficient use of materials by the production department. If the production department had produced at standard and used only the 3,800 pounds of materials called for, then the extra 200 pounds of materials wouldn't have been purchased in the first place and the extra $150 of variance would not have arisen. The purchasing agent may argue, therefore, that the $150 mutual price-quantity variance should be charged to production, not to purchasing.

We should note that a dispute of this type is likely to arise only if the price and quantity variances are computed at the same time. The more typical situation is for the price variance to be computed at the time materials are purchased and for the quantity variance to be computed somewhat later, when the materials are used. Thus, when the two variances are computed at different times, it is unlikely that purchasing will ever raise any questions as to how efficiently the materials have been used.

It can be argued that even if the two variances are computed at the same time, the mutual price-quantity variance should still be included as part of the price variance. The reason is that purchasing is responsible for the acquisition of *any* materials needed in production and should ensure that the materials are purchased according to the standard prices that have been set. As we noted earlier, a price variance should be charged to production only if the variance arises from rush orders or similar problems caused by poor scheduling of production activities.

VARIANCE ANALYSIS AND MANAGEMENT BY EXCEPTION

Variance analysis and performance reports provide a vehicle for implementation of the concept of *management by exception.* Simply put, management by exception means that the manager's attention must be directed toward those parts of the organization where things are not proceeding according to plans. Since a manager's time is limited, every hour must be used as effectively as possible, and time and effort must not be wasted looking after those parts of the organization where things are going smoothly.

The budgets and standards discussed in this chapter and in the preceding chapter represent the "plans" of management. If all goes smoothly, then costs would be expected to fall within the budgets and standards that have been set. To the extent that this happens, the manager is free to spend time elsewhere, with the assurance that at least in the budgeted areas all is proceeding according to expectations. To the extent that actual costs and revenues do not conform to the budget, however, a signal comes to the manager that an "exception" has occurred. This exception comes in the form of a variance from the budget or standard that was originally set.

The major question at this point is, "Are *all* variances to be considered exceptions that will require the attention of management?" The answer is no. If every variance were considered an exception, then management would get little else done other than chasing down nickel-and-dime differences. Obviously, some criteria are needed to determine when a variance has occurred that can properly be called an exception. We consider some of these criteria below.

Criteria for Determining "Exceptions"

It is probably safe to say that only by the rarest of coincidences will actual costs and revenues ever conform exactly to the budgeted pattern. The reason is that even though budgets may be prepared with the greatest of care, it will never be possible to develop budgeted data that contain the precise allowances necessary for each of the multitude of variables that can affect actual costs and revenues. For this reason, one can expect that in every period virtually every budgeted figure will produce a variance of some type when compared to actual cost data. How do managers decide which of these variances are worthy of their attention? We can identify at least four criteria that are used in actual practice: materiality, consistency of occurrence, ability to control, and nature of the item.

Materiality   Ordinarily, management will be interested only in those variances that are material in amount. To separate the material variances from the immaterial variances, firms often set guidelines, such as stating that any variance that differs from the budget by 5 percent or more will be considered a material variance. Notice that we say "differs" from the budget, not "exceeds" the budget. We say "differs" because management will be just as interested in those variances that are *under* the budget as it is in those that exceed it. The reason is that a level of spending that is under the budget can be just as critical to profitability as a level of spending that exceeds the budget. For example, if advertising is budgeted to be $100,000 during a period and only $80,000 is spent, this favorable spending variance could be damaging to profits because of insufficient promotion of the firm's products.

Generally, a guideline such as a 5 percent deviation from budget will not be sufficient to judge whether a variance is material. The reason is that a 2 percent variance in some costs could be far more critical to profits than a 10 percent variance in other costs. Therefore, a firm will often supplement the percentage guideline with some minimum absolute dollar figure, stating that even if a variance doesn't exceed the percentage guideline, it will still be considered material if it exceeds the minimum dollar figure. To illustrate, a firm might state that any variance will be considered material if it differs from the budget by 5 percent or more, or by $1,000.

Consistency of occurrence   Even if a variance never exceeds the minimum stated percentage or the minimum dollar amount, many firms want it brought to the attention of management if it comes *close* to these limits period after period. The thinking here is that the budget or standard may be out of date, and that adjustment to more current levels might improve overall profit planning. Or, some laxness in cost control may be present, warranting an occasional check by the relevant supervisor.

Ability to control   Some costs are largely beyond the control of management. When such costs are present in a company, no follow-up action on management's part is necessary even though variances may occur that are material in amount. For example, utility rates and local tax rates are generally not controllable internally, and large variances resulting from rate increases will therefore require little or no follow-up effort on management's part. However, such variances are frequently presented on variance reports for information purposes.

Nature of the item   By their very nature, some costs are much more critical to long-run profitability than others. One such cost is advertising. As mentioned above, underutilization of the advertising budget can have an adverse impact on sales, with a resulting loss of revenue that greatly outweighs any saving in advertising dollars. Another such cost is maintenance. Although inadequate maintenance may produce short-run savings in costs, these savings will probably be more than offset by future breakdowns, repairs, and loss of revenue from reduced productivity and efficiency.

Because of the critical nature of such costs as advertising and maintenance, the guidelines for determining whether a variance is material are usually much more stringent for these costs than for other costs. That is, variances in these areas are generally watched more closely by management than variances in other, less critical, areas. It may be that management will want to see *any* variance in certain key areas such as advertising and promotion. In addition, the normal guidelines may be reduced by half in other key areas such as maintenance and certain critical component parts.

Statistical Analysis of Random Variances

The purpose of establishing criteria for separating material from immaterial variances is to isolate those variances that are *not* due to random causes, and that can and should be controlled by the company. The "5 percent of budget, or $1,000" approach described in the preceding section is a somewhat crude way of accomplishing this objective, although it is widely used. The approach is crude because it is based on rough guessing and on rules of thumb rather than on precise analysis.

A much more dependable way of separating random variances from variances that are controllable can be found in statistical analysis. This approach to segregating random variances has its basis in the idea that a budget or standard represents a *range* of acceptability, rather than a single point. Any variance falling within this range is considered to be due solely to

EXHIBIT 9–7

A statistical control chart

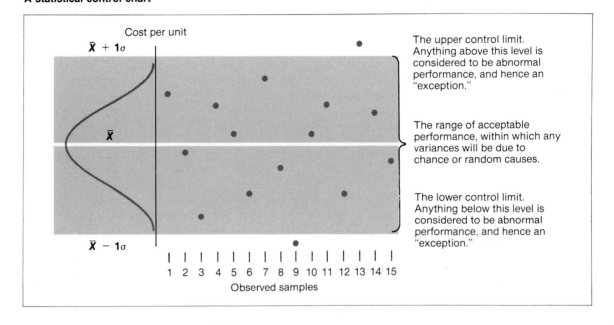

random causes that either are not within the ability of management to control or that would be impractical to control. One author puts the idea this way:

> Measured quality of manufactured product is always subject to a certain amount of variation as a result of chance. Some stable "system of chance causes" is inherent in any particular scheme of production and inspection. Variation within this stable pattern is inevitable. The reasons for variation outside this stable pattern [should] be discovered and corrected.[6]

How does a firm isolate the range within which variances from budget will be due to chance or random causes? This is done by means of statistical sampling of the population represented by the budgeted data. Random samples of the population are drawn, and the variances found in these samples are plotted on a *control chart* such as that illustrated in Exhibit 9–7. In effect, the upper and lower limits on the chart represent the normal distribution (bell-shaped curve), with the upper and lower limits generally being at least one standard deviation from the grand mean. Any variances falling within the upper and lower control limits will be due simply to chance occurrences and, therefore, either will not be within the ability of management to control or will not be large enough to warrant management time.

---

[6] Eugene L. Grant and Richard L. Leavenworth, *Statistical Quality Control*, 4th ed. (New York: McGraw-Hill, 1972), p. 3. Used with permission of McGraw-Hill Book Company.

Any variances falling outside these limits will not be due to random or chance causes and will be considered "exceptions" toward which management attention will need to be directed.

The value of a budgeting system is greatly increased if variances are analyzed by a statistical approach such as that described above, rather than by the "5 percent, or $1,000" approach described earlier. The reason, of course, is that the statistical approach eliminates guesswork and zeroes management in on those cost variations that are indeed within its ability to control.[7]

SUMMARY

A standard is a benchmark or "norm" for measuring performance. Standards are found in many facets of life, including in the business community. In business organizations, standards are set for both the cost and the quantity of inputs needed to manufacture goods or to provide services. Quantity standards say how much of a cost element, such as labor time or raw materials, should be used in manufacturing a unit of product or in providing a unit of service. Cost standards say what the cost of the time or the materials should be.

Generally, standards are set by the cooperative effort of many people in an organization, including the accountant, the industrial engineer, and various levels of management. Standards are normally "practical" in nature, meaning that they can be attained by reasonable, though highly efficient, efforts. Such standards are generally felt to have a favorable motivational impact on employees.

When standards are compared against actual performance, the difference is referred to as a variance. Variances are computed and reported to management on a regular basis for both the price and the quantity elements of materials, labor, and overhead. Specific formulas are available to assist in these computations.

Not all variances are considered to be "exceptions" that require management time or attention. Rather, parameters or limits are set within which variances are considered to be due to chance causes. If a variance falls outside the limits set by management, it is then considered to be an exception toward which management time and attention must be directed. Ordinarily, the accounting system will be organized in such a way as to bring exceptions to the attention of management as early in time as possible in order that control may be maintained and corrections made before significant damage is done to profits.

---

[7] For further discussion of this and other statistical uses in cost analysis, see Joel S. Demski, *Information Analysis,* 2nd ed. (Reading, Mass: Addison-Wesley Publishing, 1980), chap. 6.

REVIEW PROBLEM ON STANDARD COSTS

Xavier Company produces a single product. The standard costs for one unit of product are:

Direct material: 6 ounces at $0.50 per ounce . . . $ 3
Direct labor: 1.8 hours at $10 per hour   18
Variable overhead: 1.8 hours at $5 per hour   . . .   _9_
     Total standard variable cost per unit $30

During June, 2,000 units were produced. The costs associated with the month were:

Material purchased: 18,000 ounces at $0.60 . . . $10,800
Material used in production: 14,000 ounces   . . .   —
Direct labor: 4,000 hours at $9.75   39,000
Variable overhead costs incurred   20,800

Materials Variances

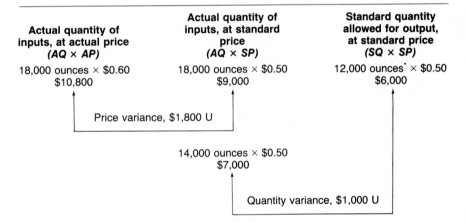

Actual quantity of inputs, at actual price (AQ × AP)	Actual quantity of inputs, at standard price (AQ × SP)	Standard quantity allowed for output, at standard price (SQ × SP)
18,000 ounces × $0.60 $10,800	18,000 ounces × $0.50 $9,000	12,000 ounces* × $0.50 $6,000

Price variance, $1,800 U

14,000 ounces × $0.50
$7,000

Quantity variance, $1,000 U

A total variance can't be computed in this situation, since the amount of materials purchased (18,000 ounces) differs from the amount of materials used in production (14,000 ounces).

* 2,000 units × 6 ounces = 12,000 ounces.

The same variances in shortcut format would be:

$$AQ(AP - SP) = \text{Materials price variance}$$
$$18,000 \text{ ounces}(\$0.60 - \$0.50) = \$1,800 \text{ U}$$

$$SP(AQ - SQ) = \text{Materials quantity variance}$$
$$\$0.50(14,000 \text{ ounces} - 12,000 \text{ ounces}) = \$1,000 \text{ U}$$

Notice that the price variance is computed on the entire amount of material purchased (18,000 ounces), whereas the quantity variance is computed only on the portion of this material used in production during the period (14,000 ounces). This is a common situation. The price variance is usually computed on whatever materials have been purchased. The quantity variance, however, is computed only on that portion of the purchased materials *actually used* during the period. In the example above, a quantity variance on the 4,000 ounces of materials that were purchased during the period but *not* used in production (18,000 ounces purchased − 14,000 ounces used = 4,000 ounces unused) will be computed in a future period when these materials are drawn out of inventory and used in the production process.

Labor Variances

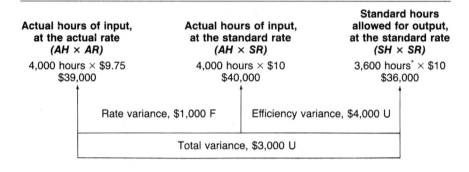

Actual hours of input, at the actual rate (AH × AR)	**Actual hours of input, at the standard rate (AH × SR)**	**Standard hours allowed for output, at the standard rate (SH × SR)**
4,000 hours × $9.75 $39,000	4,000 hours × $10 $40,000	3,600 hours* × $10 $36,000

Rate variance, $1,000 F   Efficiency variance, $4,000 U

Total variance, $3,000 U

* 2,000 units × 1.8 hours = 3,600 hours.

The same variances in shortcut format would be:

$$AH(AR - SR) = \text{Labor rate variance}$$
$$4{,}000 \text{ hours}(\$9.75 - \$10) = \$1{,}000 \text{ F}$$

$$SR(AH - SH) = \text{Labor efficiency variance}$$
$$\$10(4{,}000 \text{ hours} - 3{,}600 \text{ hours}) = \$4{,}000 \text{ U}$$

Variable Overhead Variances

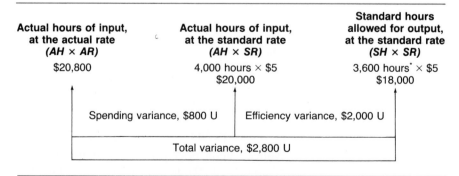

Actual hours of input, at the actual rate (AH × AR)	**Actual hours of input, at the standard rate (AH × SR)**	**Standard hours allowed for output, at the standard rate (SH × SR)**
$20,800	4,000 hours × $5 $20,000	3,600 hours* × $5 $18,000

Spending variance, $800 U   Efficiency variance, $2,000 U

Total variance, $2,800 U

* 2,000 units × 1.8 hours = 3,600 hours.

The same variances in shortcut format would be:

$$AH(AR - SR) = \text{Variable overhead spending variance}$$
$$4,000 \text{ hours}(\$5.20^* - \$5.00) = \$800 \text{ U}$$

* $20,800 ÷ 4,000 hours = $5.20.

$$SR(AH - SH) = \text{Variable overhead efficiency variance}$$
$$\$5(4,000 \text{ hours} - 3,600 \text{ hours}) = \$2,000 \text{ U}$$

KEY TERMS FOR REVIEW

Bill of materials A listing of the type and quantity of each item of material required in the manufacture of a unit of product.

Ideal standards Standards that allow for no machine breakdowns or other work interruptions and that require peak efficiency at all times.

Labor efficiency variance A measure of the difference between the actual hours required to complete a task and the standard hours allowed, multiplied by the standard hourly rate.

Labor rate variance A measure of the difference between the actual hourly labor rate and the standard rate allowed, multiplied by the number of hours worked during the period.

Management by exception A system of management in which standards are set for various operating activities, with actual results then compared against these standards and any differences that are deemed significant brought to the attention of management as "exceptions."

Materials price variance A measure of the difference between the actual unit price paid for an item and the standard price that should have been paid, multiplied by the quantity purchased.

Materials quantity variance A measure of the difference between the actual quantity of materials used in production and the standard quantity allowed, multiplied by the standard price per unit of materials.

Mutual price-quantity variance An overlapping of the price and quantity variances caused by deviations in both price and quantity from the standards that have been set.

Practical standards Standards that allow for normal machine downtime and other work interruptions and that can be attained through reasonable, though highly efficient, efforts by the average worker at a task.

Standard cost card A detailed listing of the standard amounts of materials, labor, and overhead that should go into a unit of product, multiplied by the standard price or rate that has been set.

Standard cost per unit The expected cost of a unit of product as shown on the standard cost card; it is computed by multiplying the standard quantity or hours by the standard price or rate.

Standard hours allowed The time that should have been taken to complete the period's output as computed by multiplying the number of units produced by the standard hours per unit.

Standard hours per unit The amount of labor time that should be required to complete a single unit of product, including allowances for breaks, machine downtime, cleanup, rejects, and other normal inefficiencies.

Standard price per unit The price that should be paid for a single unit of materials, including allowances for quality, quantity purchased, freight-in, receiving, and other such costs, net of any discounts allowed.

Standard quantity allowed The amount of materials that should have been used to complete the period's output as computed by multiplying the number of units produced by the standard quantity per unit.

Standard quantity per unit The amount of materials that should be required to complete a single unit of product, including allowances for normal waste, spoilage, rejects, and similar inefficiencies.

Standard rate per hour The labor rate that should be incurred per hour of labor time, including allowances for employment taxes, fringe benefits, and other such labor costs.

Variable overhead efficiency variance A measure of the difference between the actual activity (direct labor-hours, machine-hours, or some other base) of a period and the standard activity allowed, multiplied by the variable part of the predetermined overhead rate.

Variable overhead spending variance A measure of the difference between the actual variable overhead cost incurred during a period and the standard cost that should have been incurred, based on the actual activity of the period.

Variance The difference between standard prices and quantities and actual prices and quantities.

APPENDIX: GENERAL LEDGER ENTRIES TO RECORD VARIANCES

Although standard costs and variances can be computed and used by management without being formally entered into the accounting records, most organizations prefer to make formal entries for three reasons. First, entry into the accounting records encourages early recognition of variances. As mentioned in the main body of the chapter, the earlier that variances can be recognized, the greater is their value to management in the control of costs. Second, formal entry tends to give variances a greater emphasis than is generally possible through informal, out-of-record computations. This emphasis gives a clear signal of management's desire to keep costs within the limits that have been set. Third, formal use of standard costs simplifies the bookkeeping process. By using standard costs within the accounting system itself, management eliminates the need to keep track of troublesome variations in actual costs and quantities, thereby providing for a flow of costs that is smoother, simpler, and more easily accounted for.

Direct Materials Variances

To illustrate the general ledger entries needed to record standard cost variances, we will return to the data contained in the review problem at the end of the chapter. The entry to record the purchase of direct materials would be:

```
Raw Materials (18,000 ounces at $0.50) . . . . . . . . . .   9,000
Materials Price Variance (18,000 ounces at $0.10 U) . . . . . .   1,800
    Accounts Payable (18,000 ounces at $0.60) . . . . . . . .          10,800
```

Notice that the price variance is recognized when purchases are made, rather than when materials are actually used in production. This permits the price variance to be isolated early, and it also permits the materials to be carried in the inventory account at standard cost. As direct materials are later drawn from inventory and used in production, the quantity variance is isolated as follows:

```
Work in Process (12,000 ounces at $0.50) . . . . . . . . . .   6,000
Materials Quantity Variance (2,000 ounces U at $0.50) . . . . .   1,000
    Raw Materials (14,000 ounces at $0.50) . . . . . . . .           7,000
```

Thus, direct materials enter into the Work in Process account at standard cost, in terms of both price and quantity.

Notice that both the price variance and the quantity variance above are unfavorable, thereby showing up as debit (or additional cost) balances. If these variances had been favorable, they would have appeared as credit (or reduction in cost) balances, as in the case of the direct labor rate variance below.

Direct Labor Variances

Referring again to the cost data in the review problem at the end of the chapter, the general ledger entry to record the incurrence of direct labor cost would be:

```
Work in Process (3,600 hours at $10) . . . . . . . . . . . .  36,000
Labor Efficiency Variance (400 hours U at $10) . . . . . . . .   4,000
    Labor Rate Variance (4,000 hours at $0.25 F) . . . . . .           1,000
    Wages Payable (4,000 hours at $9.75) . . . . . . . . .          39,000
```

Thus, as with direct materials, direct labor costs enter into the Work in Process account at standard, both in terms of the rate and in terms of the hours allowed for the production of the period.

Variable Overhead Variances

Variable overhead variances generally are not recorded in the accounts separately but rather are determined as part of the general analysis of overhead, which is discussed in Chapter 10.

QUESTIONS

9–1.   What types of organizations make use of standard costs?

9–2.   What is a quantity standard? What is a price standard?

9–3.   What is the beginning point in setting a standard? Where should final responsibility for standard setting fall?

9–4.   Why must a standard for the future be more than simply a projection of the past?

9–5.   Distinguish between ideal and practical standards.

9–6.   If employees are unable to meet a standard, what effect would you expect this to have on their productivity?

9–7.   What is the difference between a standard and a budget?

9–8.   What is meant by the term *variance?*

9–9.   What is meant by the term *management by exception?*

9–10.   Why are variances generally segregated in terms of a price variance and a quantity variance?

9–11.   Who is generally responsible for the materials price variance? The materials quantity variance? The labor efficiency variance?

9–12.   The materials price variance can be computed at what two different points in time? Which point is better? Why?

9–13.   An examination of the cost records of the Chittenden Furniture Company indicates that the materials price variance is favorable but that the materials quantity variance is unfavorable by a substantial amount. What might this indicate?

9–14.   What dangers lie in using standards as punitive tools?

9–15.   "Our workers are all under labor contracts; therefore, our labor rate variance is bound to be zero." Discuss.

9–16.   What effect, if any, would you expect poor quality materials to have on direct labor variances?

9–17.   If variable manufacturing overhead is applied to production on a basis of direct labor-hours and the direct labor efficiency variance is unfavorable, will the variable overhead efficiency variance be favorable or unfavorable, or could it be either? Explain.

9–18.   What factors are considered by management in determining whether a variance is properly called an exception?

9–19.   What is a statistical control chart, and how is it used?

9–20.   (Appendix)   What advantages can be cited in favor of making formal journal entries in the accounting records for variances?

EXERCISES

E9–1.   Huron Company produces a commercial cleaning compound known as Zoom. The direct materials and direct labor standards for one unit of Zoom are given below:

	Standard quantity or hours	Standard price or rate	Standard cost
Direct materials . . .	4.6 pounds	$ 2.50 per pound	$11.50
Direct labor	0.2 hours	$12.00 per hour	2.40

During the most recent month, the following activity was recorded:

a. Twenty thousand pounds of material were purchased at a cost of $2.35 per pound.

b. All of the material purchased was used to produce 4,000 units of Zoom.

c. A total of 750 hours of direct labor time were recorded at a total labor cost of $10,425.

Required: 1. Compute the direct materials price and quantity variances for the month.

2. Compute the direct labor rate and efficiency variances for the month.

E9–2. Refer to the data in Exercise 9–1. Assume that instead of producing 4,000 units during the month, the company produced only 3,000 units, using 14,750 pounds of material in the production process. (The rest of the material purchased remained in inventory.)

Required: Compute the direct materials price and quantity variances for the month.

E9–3. As business organizations grow in size and complexity, cost control becomes more difficult. A system to provide information and assist in cost control is imperative for effective management. Management by exception is one technique that is often used to foster cost control.

Required: 1. Describe how a standard cost system helps to make management by exception possible.

2. Discuss the potential benefits of management by exception to an organization.

3. Identify and discuss the behavioral problems that might occur in an organization using standard costs and management by exception.

(CMA, Adapted)

E9–4. Dawson Toys, Ltd., produces a toy called the Maze. The company has recently established a standard cost system to help control costs and has established the following standards for the Maze toy:

Direct materials: 6 pieces per toy at $0.50 per piece.
Direct labor: 1.3 hours per toy at $8 per hour.

During the month of July 19x6, the company produced 3,000 Maze toys. Production data for the month on the toy follow:

Direct materials: 25,000 pieces were purchased for use in production at a cost of $0.48 per piece. Some 5,000 of these pieces were still in inventory at the end of the month.

Direct labor: 4,000 direct labor-hours were worked at a cost of $36,000.

Required: 1. Compute the following variances for the month:

a. Direct materials price and quantity variances.

b. Direct labor rate and efficiency variances.

2. Prepare a brief explanation of the significance and possible cause of each variance.

E9–5. Bronson Equipment, Inc., manufactures sporting equipment. One of the company's products, a football helmet, requires a special plastic in its manufacture. During the quarter ending June 30, the company manufactured 35,000 helmets, using 22,500 pounds of plastic in the process. The plastic cost the company $171,000.

According to the standard cost card, each helmet should require 0.6 pounds of plastic, at a cost of $8 per pound.

Required:

1. What cost for plastic should have been incurred in the manufacture of the 35,000 helmets? How much greater or less is this than the cost that was incurred?
2. Break down the difference computed in (1) in terms of a materials price variance and a materials quantity variance.

E9–6. Erie Company manufactures a small cassette player called the Jogging Mate. The company uses standards to control its costs. The labor standards that have been set for one Jogging Mate cassette player are as follows:

Standard hours	Standard rate per hour	Standard cost
18 minutes	$12	$3.60

During August, 5,750 hours of direct labor time were recorded in the manufacture of 20,000 units of the Jogging Mate. The direct labor cost totaled $73,600 for the month.

Required:

1. What direct labor cost should have been incurred in the manufacture of the 20,000 units of the Jogging Mate? By how much does this differ from the cost that was incurred?
2. Break down the difference in cost from (1) above in terms of a labor rate variance and a labor efficiency variance.
3. The budgeted variable overhead rate is $4 per direct labor-hour. During August, the company incurred $21,850 in variable overhead cost. Compute the variable overhead spending and efficiency variances for the month.

E9–7. Martin Company manufactures a powerful cleaning solvent. The main ingredient in the solvent is a raw material called Echol. Information on the purchase and use of Echol follows:

Purchase of Echol

Echol is purchased in 15-gallon containers at a cost of $115 per container. Discount terms of 2/10, n/30 are offered by the supplier, and Martin Company takes all discounts. Shipping costs, which Martin Company must pay, amount to $130 for an average shipment of 100 containers of Echol.

Use of Echol

The bill of materials calls for 7.6 quarts of Echol per bottle of cleaning solvent. About 5 percent of all Echol used is lost through spillage or evaporation (the 7.6 quarts above is the *actual* content per bottle). In addition, statistical analysis has shown that every 41st bottle is rejected at final inspection because of contamination.

Required:

1. Compute the standard price for purchase of one quart of Echol.
2. Compute the standard quantity of echol (in quarts) per salable bottle of cleaning solvent.
3. Using the data from (1) and (2), prepare a standard cost card showing the standard cost of Echol per bottle of cleaning solvent.

E9–8.   The auto repair shop of Quality Motor Company uses standards to control labor time and labor cost in the shop. The standard labor cost for a motor tune-up is given below:

Job	Standard hours	Standard rate	Standard cost
Motor tune-up. . . .	2.5	$9	$22.50

The record showing the time spent in the shop last week on motor tune-ups has been misplaced. However, the shop supervisor recalls that 50 tune-ups were completed during the week, and the controller recalls the following variance data relating to tune-ups:

Labor rate variance	$87 F
Total labor variance	93 U

Required: 1.   Determine the number of actual labor-hours spent on tune-ups last week.
2.   Determine the actual hourly rate of pay for tune-ups last week.

(Hint: A useful way to proceed would be to work from known to unknown data either by using the variance formulas or by using the columnar format shown in Exhibit 9–4.)

E9–9.   (Appendix)   Genola Fashions began production of a new product on June 1, 19x4. The company uses a standard cost system and has established the following standards for one unit of the new product:

	Standard quantity or hours	Standard price or rate	Standard cost
Direct materials . . .	2.5 yards	$14 per yard	$35.00
Direct labor	1.6 hours	8 per hour	12.80

During June, the following activity was recorded in relation to the new product:

a.   Purchasing acquired 10,000 yards of material at a cost of $13.80 per yard.
b.   Production used 8,000 yards of the material to manufacture 3,000 units of the new product.
c.   Production reported 5,000 hours of labor time worked directly on the new product; the cost of this labor time was $43,000.

Required: 1.   For materials:
a.   Compute the direct materials price and quantity variances.
b.   Prepare journal entries to record the purchase of materials and the use of materials in production.
2.   For direct labor:
a.   Compute the direct labor rate and efficiency variances.
b.   Prepare journal entries to record the incurrence of direct labor cost for the month.

3. Post the entries you have prepared to the T-accounts below:

Raw Materials			Accounts Payable	
	?	?		138,000
Bal.		?		

Materials Price Variance		Wages Payable	
			43,000

Materials Quantity Variance		Labor Rate Variance	

Work in Process—Product A		Labor Efficiency Variance	
Materials used ?			
Labor cost ?			

PROBLEMS

P9–10.   **Straightforward variance analysis.**   Becton Labs, Inc., produces various chemical compounds for industrial use. One compound, called Fludex, is prepared by means of an elaborate distilling process. The company has developed standard costs for one unit of Fludex, as follows:

	Standard quantity	Standard price or rate	Standard cost
Direct materials	2.5 ounces	$20.00 per ounce	$50.00
Direct labor	1.4 hours	12.50 per hour	17.50
Variable overhead . . .	1.4 hours	3.50 per hour	4.90
			$72.40

During November 19x5, the following activity was recorded by the company relative to production of Fludex:

$\sqrt{}$ *a.* Material purchased, 12,000 ounces at a cost of $225,000.

$\sqrt{}$ *b.* There was no beginning inventory of materials on hand to start the month; at the end of the month, 2,500 ounces of materials remained in the warehouse unused.

c. The company employs 35 lab technicians to work on the production of Fludex. During November, each worked an average of 160 hours at an average rate of $12 per hour.

d.   Variable overhead is assigned to Fludex on a basis of direct labor-hours. Variable overhead costs during November totaled $18,200.

e.   During November, 3,750 good units of Fludex were produced.

The company's management is anxious to determine the efficiency of the activities surrounding the production of Fludex.

Required: 1.   For materials used in the production of Fludex:
  a.   Compute the price and quantity variances.
  b.   The materials were purchased from a new supplier who is anxious to enter into a long-term purchase contract. Would you recommend that the company sign the contract? Explain.
2.   For direct labor employed in the production of Fludex:
  a.   Compute the rate and efficiency variances.
  b.   In the past, the 35 technicians employed in the production of Fludex consisted of 20 senior technicians and 15 assistants. During November, the company experimented with only 15 senior technicians and 20 assistants in order to save costs. Would you recommend that the new labor mix be continued? Explain.
3.   Compute the variable overhead spending and efficiency variances. What relationship can you see between this efficiency variance and the labor efficiency variance?

P9–11.   **Computations from incomplete data.**   Sharp Company manufactures a product for which the following standards have been set:

	Standard quantity or hours	Standard price or rate	Standard cost
Direct materials	3 feet	$5 per foot	$15
Direct labor	? hours	? per hour	?

During March, the company purchased direct materials at a cost of $55,650, all of which were used in the production of 3,200 units of product. In addition, 4,900 hours of direct labor time were worked on the product during the month. The cost of this labor time was $36,750. The following variances have been computed for the month:

Materials quantity variance . . . $4,500 U
Total labor variance . . . . . .   1,650 F
Labor efficiency variance . . . .   800 U

Required: 1.   For direct materials:
  a.   Compute the actual cost per foot for materials for the month.
  b.   Compute the materials price variance and a total variance for materials.
2.   For direct labor:
  a.   Compute the standard direct labor rate per hour.
  b.   Compute the standard hours allowed for the month's production.
  c.   Compute the standard hours allowed per unit of product.

(Hint: In completing the problem, it may be helpful to move from known to unknown data either by using the columnar format shown in Exhibits 9–3 and 9–4 or by using the variance formulas.)

P9–12. **Hospital; basic variance analysis.**   John Fleming, chief administrator for Valley View Hospital, is concerned about costs for tests in the hospital's lab. Charges for lab tests are consistently higher at Valley View than at other hospitals and have resulted in many complaints. Also, because of strict regulations on amounts reimbursed for lab tests, payments received from insurance companies and governmental units have not been high enough to provide an acceptable level of profit for the lab.

Mr. Fleming has asked you to evaluate costs in the hospital's lab for the past month. The following information is available:

a.   Basically, two types of tests are performed in the lab—blood tests and smears. During the past month, 1,800 blood tests and 2,400 smears were performed in the lab.

b.   Small glass plates are used in both types of tests. During the past month, the hospital purchased 12,000 plates at a cost of $28,200 (net of a 6 percent quantity discount). Some 1,500 of these plates were still on hand unused at the end of the month; there were no plates on hand at the beginning of the month.

c.   During the past month, 1,150 hours of labor time were recorded in the lab. The cost of this labor time was $13,800.

d.   Variable overhead last month in the lab for utilities and supplies totaled $7,820.

Valley View Hospital has never used standard costs. By searching industry literature, however, you have determined the following nationwide averages for hospital labs:

Plates: Two plates are required per lab test. These plates cost $2.50 each and are disposed of after the test is completed.

Labor: Each blood test should require 0.3 hours to complete, and each smear should require 0.15 hours to complete. The average cost of this lab time is $14 per hour.

Overhead: Overhead cost is based on direct labor-hours. The average rate for variable overhead is $6 per hour.

Mr. Fleming would like a complete analysis of the cost of plates, labor, and overhead in the lab for last month so that he can get to the root of the lab's cost problem.

Required: 1.   Compute a materials price variance for the plates purchased last month, and compute a materials quantity variance for the plates used last month.

2.   For labor cost in the lab:

a.   Compute a labor rate variance and a labor efficiency variance.

b.   In most hospitals, one half of the workers in the lab are senior technicians and one half are assistants. In an effort to reduce costs, Valley View Hospital employs only one fourth senior technicians and three fourths assistants. Would you recommend that this policy be continued? Explain.

3.   Compute the variable overhead spending and efficiency variances. Is there any relationship between the variable overhead efficiency variance and the labor efficiency variance? Explain.

P9–13. **Setting labor standards.**   The Mason Company is going to expand its punch press department. The company is about to purchase several new punch presses from Equipment Manufacturers, Inc. Equipment Manufacturers' engineers report that their mechanical studies indicate that for Mason's intended use, the output rate for one press should be 1,000 pieces per hour. The Mason Company has similar presses now in operation. At present, production from these presses averages 600 pieces per hour.

A detailed study of the Mason Company's experience shows that the average is derived from the following individual outputs:

Worker	Output per hour (pieces)
J. Smith	750
H. Brown	750
R. Jones.	600
J. Hardy	550
P. Clark	500
B. Randall	450
Total	3,600
Average	600

Mason's management also plans to institute a standard cost accounting system in the near future. The company's engineers are supporting a standard based on 1,000 pieces per hour; the accounting department is arguing for a standard of 750 pieces per hour; and the department supervisor is arguing for a standard of 600 pieces per hour.

Required: 1. What arguments would each proponent be likely to use to support his or her case?

2. Which alternative best reconciles the needs of cost control and motivation for improved performance? Explain the reasons for your choice.

(CMA, Adapted)

P9–14. **Basic variance analysis; the impact of variances on unit costs.** Landers Company manufactures a number of products. The standards relating to one of these products is shown below, along with actual cost data for May 19x6 (per unit):

	Standard cost	Actual cost
Direct materials:		
Standard: 3.6 feet at $1.50 per foot	$ 5.40	
Actual: 3.5 feet at $1.60 per foot.		$ 5.60
Direct labor:		
Standard: 1.8 hours at $9 per hour.	16.20	
Actual: 1.9 hours at $8.70 per hour		16.53
Variable overhead:		
Standard: 1.8 hours at $2.50 per hour	4.50	
Actual: 1.9 hours at $2.30 per hour		4.37
Total cost per unit	$26.10	$26.50
Excess of actual cost over standard cost		$0.40

Sam Davis, the production superintendent, was pleased when he saw the report above and commented: "This $0.40 excess cost is well within the 2 percent parameter management has set for acceptable variances. It's obvious that there's not much to worry about with this product.''

Actual production for the month was 6,000 units. Overhead is assigned to products on a basis of direct labor-hours.

Required: 1. Compute the following variances for the month of May:
       a. Materials price and quantity.
       b. Labor rate and efficiency.
       c. Variable overhead spending and efficiency.
    2. Show how much of the $0.40 excessive unit cost is traceable to each of the variances computed in (1) above.
    3. Scrutinize the data prepared in (1) and (2). Do you agree that there isn't "much to worry about" with the product? How much of the $0.40 excessive unit cost is traceable to the inefficient use of labor time?

P9–15. Basic variance analysis.   Miller Toy Company manufactures a plastic swimming pool at its Westwood Plant. The plant has been experiencing problems for some time as shown by its June 19x3 income statement below:

	Budgeted	Actual
Sales (15,000 pools)	$450,000	$450,000
Less variable expenses:		
Variable cost of goods sold˙ . . .	180,000	196,290
Variable selling expenses	20,000	20,000
Total variable expenses	200,000	216,290
Contribution margin.	250,000	233,710
Less fixed expenses:		
Manufacturing overhead.	130,000	130,000
Selling and administrative	84,000	84,000
Total fixed expenses	214,000	214,000
Net income	$ 36,000	$ 19,710

˙ Contains direct materials, direct labor, and variable overhead.

Janet Dunn, who has just been appointed general manager of the Westwood Plant, has been given instructions to "get things under control." Upon reviewing the plant's income statement, Ms. Dunn has concluded that the major problem lies in the variable cost of goods sold. She has been provided with the following standard cost per swimming pool:

	Standard quantity or hours	Standard price or rate	Standard cost
Direct materials	3.0 pounds	$2.00 per pound	$ 6.00
Direct labor.	0.8 hours	6.00 per hour	4.80
Variable overhead	0.8 hours˙	1.50 per hour	1.20
Total standard cost . . .			$12.00

˙ Based on direct labor-hours.

Ms. Dunn has determined that during the month of June the plant produced 15,000 pools and incurred the following costs:

√a. Purchased 60,000 pounds of materials at a cost of $1.95 per pound.

√b. Used 49,200 pounds of materials in production. (Finished goods and work in process inventories are nominal and can be ignored.)

√c. Worked 11,800 direct labor-hours at a cost of $7 per hour.

d. Incurred variable overhead cost totaling $18,290 for the month.

It is the company's policy to close all variances to cost of goods sold on a monthly basis.

Required: √1. Compute the following variances for the month:
  a. Direct materials price and quantity variance.
  b. Direct labor rate and efficiency variances.
  c. Variable overhead spending and efficiency variances.

√2. Summarize the variances that you computed in (1) above by showing the net overall favorable or unfavorable variance for the month. What impact did this figure have on the company's income statement? Show computations.

√3. Pick out the two most significant variances that you computed in (1) above. Explain to Ms. Dunn the possible causes of these variances.

P9–16. **Variance analysis with multiple lots.** Hillcrest Leisure Wear, Inc., manufactures men's clothing. The company has a single line of slacks that is produced in lots, with each lot representing an order from a customer. As a lot is completed, the customer's store label is attached to the slacks before shipment.

Hillcrest has a standard cost system and has established the following standards for a dozen slacks:

	Standard quantity or hours	Standard price or rate	Standard cost
Direct materials . . .	32 yards	$2.40 per yard	$76.80
Direct labor	6 hours	7.50 per hour	45.00

During October, Hillcrest worked on three orders for slacks. The company's job cost records for the month reveal the following:

Lot	Units in lot (dozens)	Materials used (yards)	Hours worked
48	1,500	48,300	8,900
49	950	30,140	6,130
50	2,100	67,250	10,270

The following additional information is available:

a. Hillcrest purchased 180,000 yards of material during the month at a cost of $424,800.

b. Direct labor cost incurred during October for production of slacks amounted to $192,280.

c. There was no work in process inventory on October 1. During October, lots 48 and 49 were completed, and all material was issued to lot 50, which was 80 percent completed as to labor.

Required:
1. Compute the materials price variance for the materials purchased during October.
2. Determine the materials quantity variance for October in both yards and dollars:
   a. For each lot worked on during the month.
   b. For the company as a whole.
3. Compute the labor rate variance for October.
4. Determine the labor efficiency variance for the month in both hours and dollars:
   a. For each lot worked on during the month.
   b. For the company as a whole.
5. In what situations might it be better to express variances in units (hours, yards, and so forth) rather than in dollars? In dollars rather than in units?

P9–17. **Missing data; variance analysis; standard cost card.**   Astro Company's Southland Plant manufactures a small computer table. A partial standard cost card on the table is given below:

	Standard quantity or hours	Standard price or rate	Standard cost
Direct materials	? board feet	$4 per board foot	$?
Direct labor	? hours	? per hour	?
Variable overhead . . .	? hours*	3 per hour	?
Total standard cost . .			$45

* Based on direct labor-hours.

The plant has just completed operations for the first quarter of 19x2. Retch P. Clod, the plant's production supervisor (who prides himself for "telling it like it is"), has summarized operations for the first quarter as follows in a memo to the plant manager:

"As usual, those incompetents at headquarters are trying to blame production for the excess cost on last quarter's output. Total cost for the 8,000 tables produced during the quarter came to $403,500. That's $50.4375 per table, or 12.1 percent over the standard cost of $45. A lot of the problem was those big spenders in purchasing. They paid $0.20 per board foot over standard for the 50,000 board feet of material that was purchased and used during the quarter. Twenty cents may not sound like much, but it was the cause of most of the $18,000 total variance (unfavorable) that the pencil pushers say we had with materials. To top that off, those wimps in personnel caved in to the union (again!) and agreed to a $0.50 per hour wage increase over standard. That really blew the budget!!

"But, like always, production saved the day. We managed to pare variable overhead back to only $2.75 per hour or a total of $49,500 for the quarter. That gave variable overhead a great, big $4,500 favorable spending variance! Can you believe, though, that the pencil pushers griped because the total variable overhead variance was a measly $1,500 unfavorable? It seems to me that instead of complaining, they should have given big, fat bonuses to me and the production crew for a job well done."

The plant had no inventory of materials on hand at either the beginning or end of the quarter.

Required:
1. Compute the following variances (show all computations):
   a. Materials price and quantity variances.
   b. Direct labor rate and efficiency variances.
   c. Variable overhead spending and efficiency variances.

2. Scrutinize the variances you prepared in (1). Do you agree that Retch and the production crew deserve "big, fat bonuses for a job well done"? Explain.

3. Complete the standard cost card shown at the beginning of the problem. Again, show all computations.

P9–18. Multiple products; standard cost card; variance analysis. Princeton Company produces two products, Lags and Zets, which pass through two operations. The company uses a standard cost system, with standard usage of materials and labor as follows for each product (on a per unit basis):

	Raw material		Standard labor time (hours)	
Product	X	Y	Operation 1	Operation 2
Lags	1.8 pounds	2.0 gallons	0.4 hours	1.6 hours
Zets	3.0 pounds	4.5 gallons	0.7 hours	1.8 hours

Information relating to materials purchased and materials used in production during May 19x5 follows:

Material	Purchases	Purchase cost	Standard price	Used in production*
X	14,000 pounds	$51,800	$3.50 per pound	8,500 pounds
Y	15,000 gallons	19,500	1.40 per gallon	13,000 gallons

* Materials purchased but not used in production remain in inventory and will be used in production in a following period.

The following additional information is available:

a. The company recognizes price variances at the time of purchase of material.

b. The standard labor rate is $10 per hour in operation 1 and $9.50 per hour in operation 2.

c. During May 19x5, 2,400 direct labor-hours were worked in operation 1 at a total labor cost of $27,000, and 5,700 direct labor-hours were worked in operation 2 at a total labor cost of $59,850.

d. Production during May 19x5 was: 1,500 Lags and 2,000 Zets.

Required:
1. Prepare a standard cost card for each product, showing the standard cost of direct materials and direct labor.

2. For materials, compute the following variances for May 19x5:
   a. The price variance for each type of material.
   b. The quantity variance for each type of material. Express the variance both in units (pounds or gallons) and in dollars.

3. For labor, compute the following variances for May 19x5:
   a. The labor rate variance for each operation.
   b. The labor efficiency variance for each operation. Express the variance both in hours and in dollars.

4. When might it be better to express variances in units (pounds, gallons, hours) rather than in dollars? In dollars rather than in units?

P9–19.   **Standards and variances from incomplete data.**   Highland Company produces a lightweight backpack that is very popular with college students. The following information is available on production of the backpack for March 19x1:

	Materials used	Direct labor	Variable overhead
Total standard cost allowed*	$16,800	$10,500	$4,200
Actual costs incurred	15,000	?	3,600
Materials price variance	?		
Materials quantity variance	1,200 U		
Labor rate variance		?	
Labor efficiency variance		?	
Overhead spending variance			?
Overhead efficiency variance. . . .			?

* For the month's production.

The following additional information is available for March's production:

Number of units produced	1,000
Actual direct labor-hours	1,500
Standard overhead rate per hour	$3.00
Standard price of one yard of materials	6.00
Difference between standard and actual cost per backpack produced during March . . .	0.15 F

Overhead is applied to production on a basis of direct labor-hours.

Required: 1.   What is the standard cost of a single backpack?
2.   What was the actual cost per backpack produced during March?
3.   How many yards of material are required at standard per backpack?
4.   What was the materials price variance for March?
5.   What is the standard direct labor rate per hour?
6.   What was the labor rate variance for March? The labor efficiency variance?
7.   What was the overhead spending variance for March? The overhead efficiency variance?
8.   Prepare a standard cost card for one backpack.

P9–20.   **Developing standard costs.**   Danson Company is a chemical manufacturer which supplies various products to industrial users. The company plans to introduce a new chemical solution, called Nysap, for which it needs to develop a standard product cost. The following information is available on the production of Nysap:

a.   Nysap is made by combining a chemical compound (nyclyn) and a solution (salex), and boiling the mixture. A 20 percent loss in volume occurs for both the salex and the nyclyn during boiling. After boiling, the mixture consists of 9.6 liters of salex and 12 kilograms of nyclyn.

b.   After the boiling process is complete, the solution is cooled slightly before 5 kilograms of protet are added. The addition of the protet does not affect the total liquid volume. The resulting solution is then bottled in 10-liter containers.

c.   The finished product is highly unstable, and one 10-liter batch out of six is rejected at final inspection. Rejected batches have no commercial value and are thrown out.

    d. It takes a worker 35 minutes to process one 10-liter batch of Nysap. Employees work an eight-hour day, including one hour per day for rest breaks and clean-up.

Required: 1. Determine the standard quantity for each of the raw materials needed to produce an acceptable 10-liter batch of Nysap.

    2. Determine the standard labor time to produce an acceptable 10-liter batch of Nysap.

    3. Assuming the following purchase prices and costs, prepare a standard cost card for materials and labor for one acceptable 10-liter batch of Nysap:

Salex.	$1.50 per liter
Nyclyn	2.80 per kilogram
Protet.	3.00 per kilogram
Direct labor cost . . .	9.00 per hour

(CMA, Adapted)

P9–21. **Preparation of a variance report.** Weaver Company produces and sells a single product. The company's most recent monthly income statement is given below:

WEAVER COMPANY
Income Statement
For the Month Ended June 30, 19x8

	Budget	Actual	Variance
Sales (500 units)	$30,000	$30,000	—
Less variable expenses:			
Variable production costs	10,500	11,710	$1,210 U
Other variable expenses	3,500	3,500	—
Total variable expenses	14,000	15,210	
Contribution margin.	16,000	14,790	
Less fixed expenses:			
Production	8,000	8,000	—
Selling and administrative	4,250	4,290	40 U
Total fixed expenses	12,250	12,290	
Net income	$ 3,750	$ 2,500	$1,250 U

Weaver Company uses a standard cost system for planning and control purposes. Management is unhappy with the system because great difficulty has been experienced in trying to interpret the cost variance reports coming from the accounting department. A typical cost variance report is shown below. This report relates to the $1,210 variance above in variable production costs:

Cost Variance Report—Variable Production Costs
For the Month of June 19x8

	Total	Per unit
Excess plastic used in production	$ 370	$0.74
Excess direct labor cost incurred	600	1.20
Excess variable overhead cost incurred . . .	240	0.48
Total excess cost incurred	$1,210	$2.42

During June, 500 units of this product were produced and sold. The per unit actual costs of production were:

Plastic: 3.8 pounds at $4.30 per pound	$16.34
Direct labor: 0.8 hours at $5.25 per hour	4.20
Variable overhead: 0.8 hours at $3.60 per hour . . .	2.88
Total actual cost per unit	$23.42

The standard cost of one unit of product is given below:

Plastic: 3.9 pounds at $4 per pound	$15.60
Direct labor: 0.6 hours at $5 per hour	3.00
Variable overhead: 0.6 hours at $4 per hour	2.40
Total standard cost per unit.	$21.00

Weaver Company has hired you, as an expert in cost analysis, to help management clarify the reports coming from accounting.

Required: 1.   What criticisms can be made of the cost variance reports presently being prepared by accounting?
2.   Compute the following variances for June 19x8:
   a.   Materials price and quantity.
   b.   Labor rate and efficiency.
   c.   Variable overhead spending and efficiency.
3.   Prepare a new cost variance report for management for the month of June. Show your variances on both a total and a per unit basis.

P9–22.   **Standard costs and variance analysis.**   Marvel Parts, Inc., manufactures auto accessories. One of the company's products is a set of seat covers that can be adjusted to fit nearly any small car. The company has a standard cost system in use for all of its products. According to the standards that have been set for the seat covers, the factory should work 2,850 hours each month in order to produce 1,900 sets of covers. The standard costs associated with this level of production activity are:

	Total	Per set of covers
Direct materials	$42,560	$22.40
Direct labor	17,100	9.00
Variable overhead (based on direct labor-hours)	6,840	3.60
		$35.00

During August 19x7, the factory worked only 2,800 direct labor-hours and produced 2,000 sets of covers. The following actual costs were recorded during the month:

	Total	Per set of covers
Direct materials (12,000 yards)	$45,600	$22.80
Direct labor	18,200	9.10
Variable overhead	7,000	3.50
		$35.40

At standard, each set of covers should require 5.6 yards of materials. All of the materials purchased during the month were used in production.

Required: Compute the following variances for August 19x7:

✓1.   The materials price and quantity variances.
✓2.   The labor rate and efficiency variances.
✓3.   The variable overhead spending and efficiency variances.

P9–23.   **Variances; unit costs; journal entries.**   (Appendix)   Trueform Products, Inc., produces a broad line of sports equipment and uses a standard cost system for control purposes. Last year the company produced 8,000 of its varsity footballs. The standard costs associated with this football, along with the actual costs incurred last year, are given below (per football):

	Standard cost	Actual cost
Direct materials:		
Standard: 3.7 feet at $5 per foot	$18.50	
Actual: 4.0 feet at $4.80 per foot		$19.20
Direct labor:		
Standard: 0.9 hours at $7.50 per hour . . .	6.75	
Actual: 0.8 hours at $8 per hour.		6.40
Variable overhead:		
Standard: 0.9 hours at $2.50 per hour . . .	2.25	
Actual: 0.8 hours at $2.75 per hour		2.20
Total cost per football	$27.50	$27.80

The president was elated when he saw that actual costs exceeded standard costs by only $0.30 per football. He stated, ''I was afraid that our unit costs might get out of hand when we gave out those raises last year in order to stimulate output. But it's obvious our costs are well under control.''

There was no inventory of materials on hand to start the year. During the year, 32,000 feet of materials were purchased and used in production.

Required: 1.   For direct materials:
  a.   Compute the price and quantity variances for the year.
  b.   Prepare journal entries to record all activity relating to direct materials for the year.
  2.   For direct labor:
  a.   Compute the rate and efficiency variances.
  b.   Prepare a journal entry to record the incurrence of direct labor cost for the year.
  3.   Compute the variable overhead spending and efficiency variances.
  4.   Was the president correct in his statement that ''our costs are well under control''? Explain.
  5.   State the possible causes of each variance that you have computed.

P9–24.   **Multiple products; journal entries.**   (Appendix)   Bestway Pharmaceutical Company produces two products, Milex and Silex, in Department 4. Materials and other inputs into each product are shown below:

	Per batch		Standard price or rate
	Milex	Silex	
Direct materials:			
Material A.	2 pounds	1 pound	$4 per pound
Material B.	—	3 pounds	3 per pound
Material C	1 gallon	1 gallon	5 per gallon
Direct labor	0.8 hours	1.5 hours	8 per hour
Variable overhead	0.8 hours	1.5 hours	3 per hour

During the month of March, the company produced 900 batches of Milex and 1,200 batches of Silex. The following additional information is available:

a. Materials purchased during the month:

	Amount (pounds)	Purchase cost
Material A	3,600	$14,940
Material B	3,800	10,830
Material C	—	—

b. Inventories on hand at the start of the month:

	Amount	Inventory cost
Material A	500 pounds	$ 2,000
Material B	400 pounds	1,200
Material C	2,500 gallons	12,500

c. Materials issued into production during the month:

	Amount	Cost
Material A	3,450 pounds	?
Material B	3,500 pounds	?
Material C	2,400 gallons	?

d. A total of 2,700 hours of direct labor time were recorded for the month; direct labor cost for the month was $20,250.

e. Variable overhead cost is allocated to production on a basis of direct labor-hours.

f. There was no work in process at the beginning or end of the month.

Required:
1. Determine the standard variable cost of one batch of each product.
2. For direct materials:
   a. Compute the price variance for each material purchased. Prepare a journal entry to record each purchase.
   b. Compute the quantity variance for the month for each material. Prepare journal entries to record the placing of materials into production.
3. For direct labor:
   a. Compute the rate and efficiency variances for the month.

b.   Prepare a journal entry to record the incurrence of direct labor cost for the month.

4.   State the possible causes of each variance that you have computed.

P9–25.   Variance analysis; incomplete data; journal entries.   (Appendix)   Maple Products, Ltd., manufactures a hockey stick that is used worldwide. The standard cost of one hockey stick is:

	Standard quantity or hours	Standard price or rate	Standard cost
Direct materials	? feet	$3.00 per foot	$?
Direct labor	2 hours	? per hour	?
Variable overhead	? hours	1.30 per hour	?
Total standard cost			$27.00

Last year, 8,000 hockey sticks were produced and sold. Selected cost data relating to last year's operations follow:

	Dr.	Cr.
Direct materials purchased (60,000 feet) . . .	$174,000	
Wages payable (? hours)		$79,200*
Work in process—direct materials	115,200	
Direct labor rate variance		3,300
Variable overhead efficiency variance	650	

*Relates to the actual direct labor cost for the year.

The following additional information is available for last year's operations:

a.   There were no materials on hand at the start of last year. Some of the materials purchased during the year were still on hand in the warehouse at the end of the year.

b.   The variable overhead rate is based on direct labor-hours. Total actual variable overhead cost for last year was $19,800.

c.   Actual direct materials usage for last year exceeded the standard by 0.2 feet per stick.

Required: 1.   For direct materials:
   a.   Compute the price and quantity variances for last year.
   b.   Prepare journal entries to record all activities relating to direct materials for last year.

2.   For direct labor:
   a.   Prove the rate variance given above, and compute the efficiency variance for last year.
   b.   Prepare a journal entry to record activity relating to direct labor for last year.

3.   Compute the variable overhead spending variance for last year, and prove the variable overhead efficiency variance given above.

4.   State the possible causes of each variance that you have computed.

5.   Prepare a completed standard cost card for one hockey stick.

CASE

C9–26.   **Unit costs, variances, and journal entries from incomplete data.**   (Appendix)
You are employed by Olster Company, which manufactures products for the senior
citizen market. As a rising young executive in the company, you are scheduled to
make a presentation in a few hours to your superior. This presentation relates to
last week's production of Maxitol, a popular health tonic that is manufactured by
Olster Company. Unfortunately, while studying ledger sheets and variance summaries by poolside in the company's fitness area, you were bumped and dropped the
papers into the pool. In desperation, you fished the papers from the water, but
you have discovered that only the following fragments are readable:

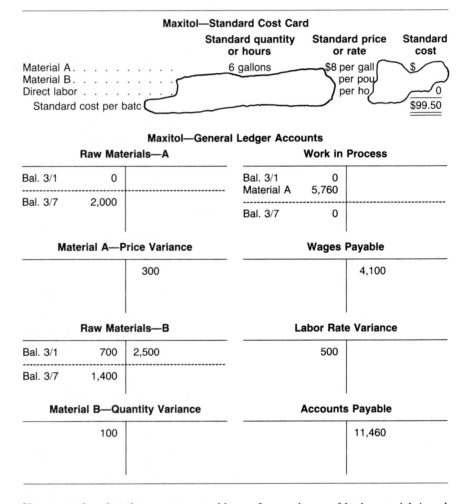

Maxitol—Standard Cost Card

	Standard quantity or hours	Standard price or rate	Standard cost
Material A	6 gallons	$8 per gall	$
Material B		per pou	
Direct labor		per ho	
Standard cost per batc			0
			$99.50

Maxitol—General Ledger Accounts

Raw Materials—A

Bal. 3/1	0	
Bal. 3/7	2,000	

Work in Process

Bal. 3/1	0	
Material A	5,760	
Bal. 3/7	0	

Material A—Price Variance

	300

Wages Payable

	4,100

Raw Materials—B

Bal. 3/1	700	2,500
Bal. 3/7	1,400	

Labor Rate Variance

500	

Material B—Quantity Variance

100	

Accounts Payable

	11,460

You remember that the accounts payable are for purchases of both material A and
material B. You also remember that only 10 direct labor workers are involved in
the production of Maxitol and that each worked 40 hours last week. The wages
payable above are for wages earned by these workers.

You realize that you must reconstruct all data relating to Maxitol very quickly in order to be ready for your presentation. As a start, you have called purchasing and found that 1,000 gallons of material A and 800 pounds of material B were purchased last week.

Required:

1. How many batches of Maxitol were produced last week? (This is a key figure; be sure it's right before going on.)
2. For material A:
   a. What was the cost of material A purchased last week?
   b. How many gallons were used in production last week?
   c. What was the quantity variance?
   d. Prepare journal entries to record all activity relating to material A for last week.
3. For material B:
   a. What is the standard cost per pound for material B?
   b. How many pounds of material B were used in production last week? How many pounds should have been used at standard?
   c. What is the standard quantity of material B per batch?
   d. What was the price variance for material B last week?
   e. Prepare journal entries to record all activity relating to material B for last week.
4. For direct labor:
   a. What is the standard rate per direct labor-hour?
   b. What are the standard hours per batch?
   c. What were the standard hours allowed for last week's production?
   d. What was the labor efficiency variance for last week?
   e. Prepare a journal entry to record all activity relating to direct labor for last week.
5. Complete the standard cost card shown above for one batch of Maxitol.

CHAPTER 10

Flexible Budgets and Overhead Analysis

LEARNING OBJECTIVES

After studying Chapter 10, you should be able to:

- Prepare a master flexible budget and an overhead flexible budget, and explain the advantages of the flexible budget approach over the static budget approach.

- Use the overhead flexible budget to prepare a variable overhead performance report containing (1) only a spending variance and (2) both a spending and an efficiency variance.

- Explain the cause of the spending and efficiency variances and how they are controlled.

- Explain the significance of the denominator activity figure in determining the standard cost of a unit of product.

- Properly apply overhead cost to units of product in a standard cost system.

- Compute and properly interpret the fixed overhead budget and volume variances.

- Define or explain the key terms listed at the end of the chapter.

In Chapter 8, we introduced the master budget and discussed how its preparation is the first step in the planning and control process. Then, in Chapter 9, we introduced standard costs and demonstrated how they can be used by service and manufacturing firms to plan and control material and labor inputs. In the present chapter we take these concepts one step further by showing how budgets can be prepared on a *flexible basis* for better planning and control. We also complete the study of overhead variances that we started in Chapter 9.

FLEXIBLE BUDGETS

The master budget that we studied in Chapter 8 was essentially a **static budget** in nature. A static budget has two characteristics:

1. It is geared toward only one level of activity.
2. Actual results are always compared against budgeted costs at this original budget activity level.

A **flexible budget** differs from a static budget on both of these points. First, it does not confine itself to only one level of activity, but rather is geared toward a *range* of activity. Second, actual results do not have to be compared against budgeted costs at the original budget activity level. Since the flexible budget covers a *range* of activity, if actual costs are incurred at a different activity level from what was originally planned, then the manager is able to construct a new budget, as needed, to compare against actual results. Hence, the term *flexible budget*. In sum, the characteristics of a flexible budget are:

1. It is geared toward *all* levels of activity within the relevant range, rather than toward only one level of activity.
2. It is *dynamic* in nature rather than static. A budget can be tailored for any level of activity within the relevant range, even after the period is over. That is, a manager can look at what activity level *was attained* during a period and then turn to the flexible budget to determine what costs *should have been* at that activity level.

Deficiencies of the Static Budget

To illustrate the difference between a static budget and a flexible budget, let us assume that in preparing its master budget for 19x1, Donner Company budgeted to produce and sell 25,000 units for the year. Let us further assume, however, that the company was not able to meet this goal; actual production and sales for the year totaled only 20,000 units. *If a static budget approach is used,* the company's overall performance for the year will appear as shown in Exhibit 10–1.

So far as performance evaluation is concerned, what's wrong with the income statement in Exhibit 10–1? The static budget approach used to prepare

EXHIBIT 10–1

DONNER COMPANY
Static Budget Income Statement
For the Year Ended March 31, 19x1

	Actual	Master budget	Variance
Number of units	20,000	25,000	5,000 U
Sales	$1,000,000	$1,250,000	$250,000 U
Less variable expenses:			
Direct materials	307,000	350,000	43,000 F
Direct labor	114,000	150,000	36,000 F
Variable overhead	71,000	75,000	4,000 F
Selling and administrative	20,000	25,000	5,000 F
Total variable expenses	512,000	600,000	88,000 F
Contribution margin	488,000	650,000	162,000 U
Less fixed expenses:			
Manufacturing overhead	308,000	300,000	8,000 U
Selling and administrative	150,000	150,000	—
Total fixed expenses	458,000	450,000	8,000 U
Net income	$ 30,000	$ 200,000	$170,000 U

the statement has a major deficiency in that it fails to distinguish between the *activity control* and the *cost control* dimensions of a manager's responsibility. Activity control is involved with seeing that sales and production goals are met. Cost control is involved with seeing that sales are made and that output is produced at the least possible cost, consistent with quality standards. These are different responsibilities, and they must be kept separate in attempting to assess how well a manager is doing his or her job.

Of these two responsibilities, the static budget does a good job of measuring only whether activity control is being maintained. Look again at the data in Exhibit 10–1. The data on the top line relate to sales activity for the year. These data properly reflect the fact that activity control was not maintained, and that the company failed to meet its budgeted sales by 5,000 units.

The remainder of the data in the statement deal with cost control. These data are of little value in that they are comparing apples to oranges. Note, for example, that all of the variances associated with the variable expenses are favorable. Does this mean that the company maintained good cost control over variable expenses for the year? Not necessarily. The reason the variances are favorable is that the master budget is based on an activity level of 25,000 units whereas the actual costs were incurred at an activity level substantially below this (only 20,000 units). From a cost control point of view, it is total nonsense to try to compare costs at one activity level with costs at a different activity level. Such comparisons will always make a manger look good so long as actual activity is less than budgeted activity.

How the Flexible Budget Works

The basic idea of the flexible budget approach is that through a study of cost behavior patterns, a budget can be prepared that is geared to a *range* of activity, rather than to a single level. The basic steps in preparing a flexible budget are:

1. Determine the relevant range over which activity is expected to fluctuate during the coming period.
2. Analyze costs that will be incurred over the relevant range in terms of determining cost behavior patterns (variable, fixed, mixed).
3. Separate costs by behavior, determining the formula for variable and mixed costs, as discussed in Chapter 5.
4. Using the formula for the variable portion of the costs, prepare a budget showing what costs will be incurred at various points throughout the relevant range.

To illustrate, let us assume that Donner Company's sales normally fluctuate between 15,000 and 30,000 units each year. A study of cost behavior patterns over this relevant range has revealed the following formulas for variable costs:

Cost	Variable cost formula (per unit)
Direct materials	$14
Direct labor	6
Variable overhead	3
Selling and administrative . . .	1

Based on these cost formulas, a master flexible budget for Donner Company would appear as shown in Exhibit 10–2.

Using the flexible budget   Once prepared, the master flexible budget has several uses. At the beginning of a period, it is used as a basis for determining expected revenues, costs, and net income at the budgeted activity level. In the case of Donner Company, for example, 25,000 units were budgeted to be sold during 19x1. By use of the flexible budget, the manager can easily determine expected revenues and expected costs for the year at this activity level.

At the end of a period, the manager can readily compare actual results against appropriate budget figures anywhere within the relevant range. Since the budget is *flexible,* it doesn't matter at what level these actual results occur. To illustrate, recall that Donner Company actually produced and sold only 20,000 units during 19x1. Under the flexible budget approach, the company's performance would appear as shown in Exhibit 10–3.

In contrast to the statement prepared earlier under the static budget approach (Exhibit 10–1), the statement in Exhibit 10–3 clearly distinguishes

EXHIBIT 10–2

DONNER COMPANY
Master Flexible Budget

	Budget formula (per unit)	Sales in units			
		15,000	20,000	25,000	30,000
Sales	$50	$750,000	$1,000,000	$1,250,000	$1,500,000
Less variable expenses:					
Direct materials	14	210,000	280,000	350,000	420,000
Direct labor	6	90,000	120,000	150,000	180,000
Variable overhead	3	45,000	60,000	75,000	90,000
Selling and administrative	1	15,000	20,000	25,000	30,000
Total variable expenses	24	360,000	480,000	600,000	720,000
Contribution margin	$26	390,000	520,000	650,000	780,000
Less fixed expenses:					
Manufacturing overhead		300,000	300,000	300,000	300,000
Selling and administrative		150,000	150,000	150,000	150,000
Total fixed expenses		450,000	450,000	450,000	450,000
Net income (loss).		$ (60,000)	$ 70,000	$ 200,000	$ 330,000

EXHIBIT 10–3

DONNER COMPANY
Flexible Budget Income Statement
For the Year Ended March 31, 19x1

Budgeted sales in units 25,000
Actual sales in units 20,000

	Actual 20,000 units	Budget based on 20,000 units	Variance
Sales	$1,000,000	$1,000,000	$ —
Less variable expenses:			
Direct materials	307,000	280,000	27,000 U
Direct labor	114,000	120,000	6,000 F
Variable overhead	71,000	60,000	11,000 U
Selling and administrative	20,000	20,000	—
Total variable expenses	512,000	480,000	32,000 U
Contribution margin	488,000	520,000	32,000 U
Less fixed expenses:			
Manufacturing overhead	308,000	300,000	8,000 U
Selling and administrative	150,000	150,000	—
Total fixed expenses	458,000	450,000	8,000 U
Net income	$ 30,000	$ 70,000	$40,000 U

between activity control and cost control. The sales data at the top of the statement indicate that the sales goal for the year was not met. The cost data within the statement tell how well costs were controlled for the 20,000 units that were sold during the year. Note that most of these variances are very different from the variances obtained earlier under the static budget approach. The reason is that by means of the flexible budget approach we are able to compare budgeted and actual costs *at the same activity level*.

What if actual sales had been some odd figure, such as 19,800 units, rather than 20,000 units? The manager would have used the flexible budget formulas to develop budget figures for the 19,800-unit level of activity to compare against actual results. Herein lies the strength and dynamic nature of the flexible budget approach. By simply applying the budget formulas, it is possible to develop a budget at any time for any activity level within the relevant range.

Reconciliation of Income Figures

To complete our discussion of the master flexible budget, we present below a reconciliation of net income figures from Exhibits 10–2 and 10–3.

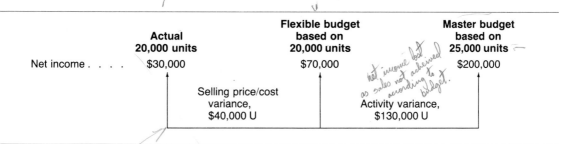

	Actual 20,000 units	Flexible budget based on 20,000 units	Master budget based on 25,000 units
Net income	$30,000	$70,000	$200,000
	Selling price/cost variance, $40,000 U	Activity variance, $130,000 U	

net income lost as sales not achieved according to budget.

The **activity variance** represents the net income lost through failure to achieve the budgeted sales in units for the period. This variance is also known as the *sales variance* or the *sales volume variance*. It is computed by multiplying the difference between budgeted sales and actual sales (in units) by the budgeted contribution margin per unit. For Donner Company, the computation would be:

$$(25,000 \text{ units} - 20,000 \text{ units}) \times \$26^* = \$130,000$$

$^*\$50 - \$24 = \$26$; see Exhibit 10–2.

In short, the company lost $130,000 in contribution margin (and net income) by failure to achieve the budgeted sales level in units for the year.

The **selling price/cost variance** measures the net income lost through failure to maintain control over selling price and over the various costs that a company may incur. The selling price element is computed by multiplying any difference between budgeted selling price and actual selling price per unit by the number of units sold. Since Donner Company maintained its selling price at $50 per unit during 19x1, it shows no variance for selling price in Exhibit 10–3. The cost element consists of the total amount of all cost variances on a company's income statement; for 19x1, this amounted to $40,000 for Donner Company (see Exhibit 10–3). Each period, the manager will analyze these individual cost variances in detail to determine their cause. We have already learned in Chapter 9 how direct materials and direct labor variances can be analyzed; we now focus our attention on a detailed analysis of overhead variances.

OVERHEAD FLEXIBLE BUDGET

There are four problems involved in overhead cost control. First, manufacturing overhead is usually made up of many separate costs. Second, these separate costs are often small in dollar amount, making it highly impractical to control them in the same way that direct materials and direct labor costs are controlled. Third, these small, separate costs are often the responsibility of different managers. Fourth, manufacturing overhead costs vary in behavior, some being variable, some fixed, and some mixed in nature.

Most of these problems can be overcome by using a flexible budget to plan and control overhead costs in much the same way that a flexible budget is used to plan and control operations for the company as a whole. The relationship between an *overhead* flexible budget and a *master* flexible budget is shown in Exhibit 10–4.

Note particularly from Exhibit 10–4 that the overhead flexible budget takes the variable and fixed overhead costs from the master flexible budget and shows these amounts in detailed format. *A similar approach can be used in preparing a separate flexible budget for selling and administrative expenses or for any other category of costs in an organization.*

The Measure of Activity

As shown in Exhibit 10–4, Donner Company's master flexible budget is based on units of product whereas the company's overhead flexible budget is based on machine-hours. If a company has only one product, then units can be used in the overhead flexible budget as well as in the master flexible budget. But most companies find it more practical to use some input measure, such as machine-hours or labor-hours, to plan and control overhead costs. This is especially true when more than one product is manufactured. At least three factors should be considered in selecting an activity base for an overhead flexible budget:

1.   The existence of a causal relationship between the activity base and overhead costs.
2.   The avoidance of dollars in the activity base itself.
3.   The selection of an activity base that is simple and easily understood.

Causal relationship   There should be a direct causal relationship between the activity base and a company's variable overhead costs. That is, the variable overhead costs should vary as a result of changes in the activity base. In a machine shop, for example, one would expect power usage and

EXHIBIT 10–4

Relationship between the master flexible budget and the overhead flexible budget

Master Flexible Budget

	Budget formula (per unit)	Sales in Units			
		15,000	20,000	25,000	30,000
Sales	$50	$750,000	$1,000,000	$1,250,000	$1,500,000
Less variable expenses:					
Direct materials	14	210,000	280,000	350,000	420,000
Direct labor	6	90,000	120,000	150,000	180,000
Variable overhead	3	45,000	60,000	75,000	90,000
Selling and administrative	1	15,000	20,000	25,000	30,000
Total variable expenses	24	360,000	480,000	600,000	720,000
Contribution margin	$26	390,000	520,000	650,000	780,000
Less fixed expenses:					
Manufacturing overhead		300,000	300,000	300,000	300,000
Selling and administrative		150,000	150,000	150,000	150,000
Total fixed expenses		450,000	450,000	450,000	450,000
Net income (loss)		$ (60,000)	$ 70,000	$ 200,000	$ 330,000

Overhead Flexible Budget

Overhead costs	Cost formula (per hour)	Machine-hours*			
		30,000	40,000	50,000	60,000
Variable costs:					
Indirect labor	$0.80	$ 24,000	$ 32,000	$ 40,000	$ 48,000
Lubricants	0.30	9,000	12,000	15,000	18,000
Power	0.40	12,000	16,000	20,000	24,000
Total variable costs	$1.50	45,000	60,000	75,000	90,000
Fixed costs:					
Depreciation		100,000	100,000	100,000	100,000
Supervisory salaries		160,000	160,000	160,000	160,000
Insurance		40,000	40,000	40,000	40,000
Total fixed costs		300,000	300,000	300,000	300,000
Total overhead costs		$345,000	$360,000	$375,000	$390,000

* Two machine-hours are required to complete one unit of product.

other variable overhead costs to vary in relationship to the number of machine-hours worked. Machine-hours would therefore be the proper base to use in the flexible budget. As explained in Chapter 3, an activity base is frequently referred to as a "cost driver," since it is the controlling factor in the incurrence of cost.

Other common activity bases (cost drivers) include direct labor-hours, miles driven by salespersons, contacts made by salespersons, number of invoices processed, number of occupied beds in a hospital, and number of X rays given. Any one of these could be used as the base for preparing a flexible budget in the proper situation.

Do not use dollars   Whenever possible, the activity base should be expressed in units rather than in dollars. If dollars are used, they should be standard dollars rather than actual dollars.

The problem with dollars is that they are subject to price-level changes, which can cause a distortion in the activity base if it is expressed in dollar terms. A similar problem arises when wage-rate changes take place if direct labor cost is being used as the activity base in a flexible budget. The change in wage rates will cause the activity base to change, even though a proportionate change may not take place in the overhead costs themselves. These types of fluctuations generally make dollars difficult to work with, and argue strongly for units rather than dollars in the activity base. The use of *standard* dollar costs rather than *actual* dollar costs overcomes the problem to some degree, but standard costs still have to be adjusted from time to time as changes in actual costs take place. On the other hand, *units* as a measure of activity (beds, hours, miles, and so on) are subject to few distorting influences and are less likely to cause problems in preparing and using a flexible budget.

Keep the base simple   The activity base should be simple and easily understood. A base that is not easily understood by the manager who works with it day by day will probably result in confusion and misunderstanding rather than serve as a positive means of cost control.

VARIABLE OVERHEAD PREFORMANCE REPORT

We stated earlier that the overhead flexible budget is used to plan and control overhead costs in much the same way that the master flexible budget is used to plan and control activities for the company as a whole. This similarity can be illustrated by continuing with the Donner Company example and showing how the overhead flexible budget is used to prepare overhead performance reports.

Recall that Donner Company budgeted to produce and sell 25,000 units during 19x1; this would be equivalent to 50,000 machine-hours of activity (since, as stated in Exhibit 10–4, two machine-hours are required to produce one unit of product). Also recall that the company actually produced and sold only 20,000 units during the year. Thus, the standard hours allowed for the year's output would be 40,000 machine-hours (20,000 units × 2 hours = 40,000 hours). We will assume that 42,000 machine-hours were actually required for the production of the 20,000 units. A summary of the year's activities follows:

Budgeted machine-hours	50,000
Actual machine-hours.	42,000
Standard machine-hours allowed	40,000
Actual variable overhead costs:	
Indirect labor	$36,000
Lubricants.	11,000
Power	24,000
Total actual costs	$71,000

In preparing a variable overhead performance report, what hour base should Donner Company use in computing budget allowances to compare against actual results? There are two possibilities. The company could use:

1.   The 42,000 machine-hours actually worked.
2.   The 40,000 standard machine-hours allowed for the year's output.

Which base the company chooses will depend on how much detailed variance information it wants. As we learned in the preceding chapter, variable overhead can be analyzed in terms of a *spending* variance and an *efficiency* variance. The two bases provide different variance output.

Spending Variance Alone

If Donner Company chooses alternative 1 and bases it performance report on the 42,000 machine-hours actually worked during the year, then the performance report will show only a spending variance for variable overhead. A performance report prepared in this way is shown in Exhibit 10–5.

The formula behind the spending variance was introduced in the preceding chapter. For review, that formula is:

$$(AH \times AR) - (AH \times SR) = \text{Variable overhead spending variance}$$

Or, in factored form:

$$AH(AR - SR) = \text{Variable overhead spending variance}$$

The report in Exhibit 10–5 is prepared around the first, or unfactored, format.

Interpreting the spending variance   The overhead spending variance is affected by two things. First, a spending variance may occur simply because of price increases over what is shown in the flexible budget. For Donner Company, this means that prices paid for overhead items may have gone up during the year, resulting in unfavorable spending variances. This portion of the overhead spending variance is just like the price variance for raw materials.

Second, the overhead spending variance is affected by waste or excessive usage of overhead materials. A first reaction is to say that waste or excessive usage of materials ought to show up as part of the efficiency variance. But this isn't true so far as overhead is concerned. Waste or excessive usage will show up as part of the spending variance. The reason is that the Manufacturing Overhead account is charged with *all* overhead costs incurred during a period, including those costs that arise as a result of waste. Since the spending variance represents any difference between the standard rate per hour and the actual costs incurred, waste will automatically show up as part of this variance, along with any excessive prices paid for variable overhead items.

In sum, the overhead spending variance contains both price and quantity (waste) elements. These two elements could be broken out and shown separately on the performance report, but this is rarely done in actual practice.

EXHIBIT 10–5

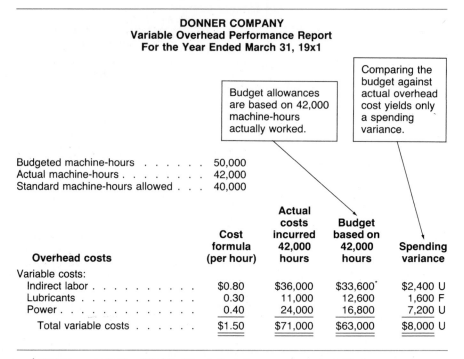

DONNER COMPANY
Variable Overhead Performance Report
For the Year Ended March 31, 19x1

Budget allowances are based on 42,000 machine-hours actually worked.

Comparing the budget against actual overhead cost yields only a spending variance.

Budgeted machine-hours   50,000
Actual machine-hours   42,000
Standard machine-hours allowed . . .   40,000

Overhead costs	Cost formula (per hour)	Actual costs incurred 42,000 hours	Budget based on 42,000 hours	Spending variance
Variable costs:				
Indirect labor	$0.80	$36,000	$33,600*	$2,400 U
Lubricants	0.30	11,000	12,600	1,600 F
Power	0.40	24,000	16,800	7,200 U
Total variable costs	$1.50	$71,000	$63,000	$8,000 U

*42,000 hours × $0.80 = $33,600. Other budget allowances are computed in the same way.

Usefulness of the spending variance   Most firms consider the overhead spending variance to be highly useful. Generally, the price element in this variance will be small, so the variance permits a focusing of attention on that thing over which the supervisor probably has the greatest control—usage of overhead in production. In many cases, firms will limit their overhead analysis to the spending variance alone, feeling that the information it yields is sufficient for overhead cost control.

Both Spending and Efficiency Variances

If Donner Company wants both a spending and an efficiency variance for overhead, then it should compute budget allowances for *both* the 40,000 machine-hour and the 42,000 machine-hour levels of activity. A performance report prepared in this way is shown in Exhibit 10–6.

Note from Exhibit 10–6 that the spending variance is the same as the spending variance shown in Exhibit 10–5. The performance report in Exhibit 10–6 has simply been expanded to include an efficiency variance as well. Together, the spending and efficiency variances make up the total variance, as explained in the preceding chapter. The reader should trace the total variance ($11,000) back into the overall performance report for the company in Exhibit 10–3.

EXHIBIT 10–6

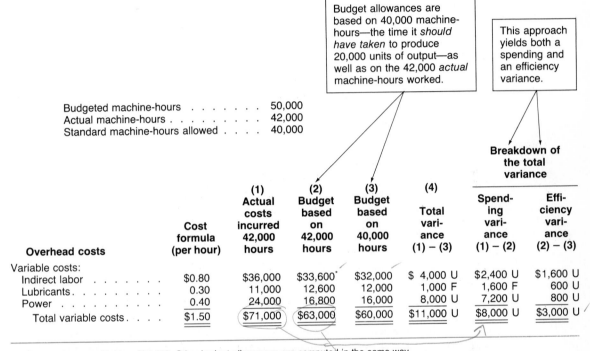

DONNER COMPANY
Variable Overhead Performance Report
For the Year Ended March 31, 19x1

Budget allowances are based on 40,000 machine-hours—the time it *should have taken* to produce 20,000 units of output—as well as on the 42,000 *actual* machine-hours worked.

This approach yields both a spending and an efficiency variance.

Budgeted machine-hours 50,000
Actual machine-hours 42,000
Standard machine-hours allowed 40,000

Breakdown of the total variance

Overhead costs	Cost formula (per hour)	(1) Actual costs incurred 42,000 hours	(2) Budget based on 42,000 hours	(3) Budget based on 40,000 hours	(4) Total variance (1) – (3)	Spending variance (1) – (2)	Efficiency variance (2) – (3)
Variable costs:							
Indirect labor	$0.80	$36,000	$33,600*	$32,000	$ 4,000 U	$2,400 U	$1,600 U
Lubricants.	0.30	11,000	12,600	12,000	1,000 F	1,600 F	600 U
Power	0.40	24,000	16,800	16,000	8,000 U	7,200 U	800 U
Total variable costs. . . .	$1.50	$71,000	$63,000	$60,000	$11,000 U	$8,000 U	$3,000 U

* 42,000 hours × $0.80 = $33,600. Other budget allowances are computed in the same way.

Interpreting the efficiency variance The term *overhead efficiency variance* is a misnomer, since this variance has nothing to do with efficiency in the use of overhead. What the variance really measures is how efficiently the *base* underlying the flexible budget is being utilized in production. Recall from the preceding chapter that the variable overhead efficiency variance is a function of the difference between the actual hours utilized in production and the hours that should have been taken to produce the period's output:

$$(AH \times SR) - (SH \times SR) = \text{Variable overhead efficiency variance}$$

Or, in factored form:

$$SR(AH - SH) = \text{Variable overhead efficiency variance}$$

If more hours are worked than are allowed at standard, then the overhead efficiency variance will be unfavorable to reflect this inefficiency. As a practical matter, however, the inefficiency is not in the use of overhead *but rather in the use of the base itself.*

This point can be illustrated by looking again at Exhibit 10–6. Two thousand more machine-hours were used during the period than should have been used to produce the period's output. Each of these hours required the incurrence of $1.50 of variable overhead cost, resulting in an unfavorable variance of $3,000 (2,000 hours $\times$ $1.50 = $3,000). Although this $3,000 variance is called an overhead efficiency variance, it could better be called a machine-hours efficiency variance, since it measures the efficiency of utilization of machine time. However, the term *overhead efficiency variance* is so firmly ingrained in day-to-day use that a change is unlikely. Even so, the user must be careful to interpret the variance with a clear understanding of what it really measures.

Control of the efficiency variance   Who is responsible for control of the overhead efficiency variance? Since the variance really measures efficiency in the utilization of the base underlying the flexible budget, whoever is responsible for control of this base is responsible for control of the variance. If the base is direct labor-hours, then the supervisor responsible for the use of labor time will be chargeable for any overhead efficiency variance.

FIXED COSTS AND THE FLEXIBLE BUDGET

Should the flexible budget contain fixed costs as well as variable costs? The term *flexible budget* implies variable costs only, since just the variable costs change with changes in activity. As a practical matter, however, most firms also include fixed overhead costs in their flexible budgets (as we have done for Donner Company). There are two reasons for doing so. First, to the extent that a fixed cost is controllable by a manager, it should be included in the evaluation of his or her performance. Such costs should be placed on the manager's performance report, along with the variable costs for which he or she is responsible. Second, fixed costs are needed in the overhead flexible budget for purposes of costing products and services. Recall from Chapter 3 that overhead costs are added to products and services by means of the predetermined overhead rate. *The overhead flexible budget provides the manager with the information needed to compute this rate.* In the remainder of this chapter, we discuss the use of the overhead flexible budget for this purpose; in the process, we also demonstrate the preparation and use of fixed overhead variances.

FIXED OVERHEAD ANALYSIS

The analysis of fixed overhead differs considerably from the analysis of variable overhead, simply because of the difference in the nature of the costs involved. To provide a background for our discussion, we will first review briefly the need for, and computation of, predetermined overhead rates. This review will be helpful since the predetermined overhead rate plays a role in fixed overhead analysis. We will then show how fixed overhead variances are computed and make certain observations as to their usefulness to the manager.

Flexible Budgets and Overhead Rates

Fixed costs come in large, indivisible pieces that by definition do not change with changes in the level of activity. As we learned in Chapter 3, this creates a problem in product costing, since a given level of fixed overhead cost spread over a small number of units will result in a higher cost per unit than if the same amount of cost is spread over a large number of units. Consider the data in the table below:

Month	(1) Fixed overhead cost	(2) Number of units produced	(3) Unit cost (1) ÷ (2)
January	$6,000	1,000	$6.00
February	6,000	1,500	4.00
March	6,000	800	7.50

Notice that the large number of units produced in February results in a low unit cost ($4), whereas the small number of units produced in March results in a high unit cost ($7.50). This problem arises only in connection with the fixed portion of overhead, since by definition the variable portion of overhead remains constant on a per unit basis, rising and falling in total proportionately with changes in the activity level. For product costing purposes, managers need to stabilize the fixed portion of unit cost so that a single unit cost figure can be used throughout the year without regard to month-by-month changes in activity levels. As we learned in Chapter 3, this stability can be accomplished through use of the predetermined overhead rate.

Denominator activity   The formula that we used in Chapter 3 to compute the predetermined overhead rate is given below, with one added feature. We have titled the estimated activity portion of the formula as being the **denominator activity:**

includes Variable and Fixed overhead.

$$\frac{\text{Estimated total manufacturing overhead costs}}{\text{Estimated total units in the base (MH, DLH, etc.)} \atop \text{(denominator activity)}} = \begin{array}{c}\text{Predetermined}\\\text{overhead rate}\end{array}$$

Recall from our discussion in Chapter 3 that once an estimated activity level (denominator activity) has been chosen, it remains unchanged throughout the year, even if actual activity later proves the estimate (denominator) to be somewhat in error. The reason for not changing the denominator, of course, is to maintain stability in the amount of overhead applied to each unit of product regardless of when it is produced during the year.

Computing the overhead rate   When we discussed predetermined overhead rates in Chapter 3, we did so without elaboration as to the source of the estimated data going into the formula. These data are normally derived from the overhead flexible budget. To illustrate, refer to Donner Company's overhead flexible budget in Exhibit 10–4. The company planned to produce 25,000 units during 19x1, which would require 50,000 machine-hours of time. The 50,000 machine-hours become the denominator activity in the predetermined overhead rate formula, and the overhead cost at this activity level from the overhead flexible budget becomes the estimated cost in the formula ($375,000 from Exhibit 10–4). In sum, the 19x1 predetermined overhead rate for Donner Company will be:

From O/H Flex Budget.

$$\frac{\$375,000}{50,000 \text{ MH}} = \$7.50 \text{ per machine-hour}$$

Or, the company can break its predetermined overhead rate down into variable and fixed elements rather than using a single combined figure:

$$\text{Variable element } \frac{\$75,000}{50,000 \text{ MH}} = \$1.50 \text{ per machine-hour}$$

$$\text{Fixed element } \frac{\$300,000}{50,000 \text{ MH}} = \$6 \text{ per machine-hour}$$

For every standard machine-hour of operation, work in process will be charged with $7.50 of overhead, of which $1.50 will be variable overhead and $6 will be fixed overhead. If a unit of product takes two machine-hours to complete, then its cost will include $3 variable overhead and $12 fixed overhead, as shown on the standard cost card below:

Standard Cost Card—per Unit

Direct materials (Exhibit 10–4)	$14
Direct labor (Exhibit 10–4)	6
Variable overhead (2 machine-hours at $1.50)	3
Fixed overhead (2 machine-hours at $6)	12
Total standard cost per unit	$35

In sum, the overhead flexible budget provides the manager with both the overhead cost figure and the denominator activity figure needed in computing the predetermined overhead rate; thus, the overhead flexible budget plays a key role in determining the amount of fixed and variable overhead cost that will be charged to units of product.

Overhead Application in a Standard Cost System

To understand the fixed overhead variances, it is necessary first to understand how overhead is applied to work in process in a standard cost system. In Chapter 3, recall that we applied overhead to work in process on a basis of actual hours of activity (multiplied by the predetermined overhead rate). This procedure was correct, since at the time we were dealing with an actual cost system. However, we are now dealing with a standard cost

EXHIBIT 10–7

Applied overhead costs: Actual cost system versus standard cost system

Actual cost system		Standard cost system	
Manufacturing Overhead		**Manufacturing Overhead**	
Actual overhead costs incurred.	Applied overhead costs: Actual hours × Predetermined overhead rate.	Actual overhead costs incurred.	Applied overhead costs: Standard hours allowed for output × Predetermined overhead rate.
Under- or overapplied overhead		Under- or overapplied overhead	

system; and when standards are in operation, overhead is applied to work in process on a basis of the *standard hours allowed for the output of the period* rather than on a basis of the actual number of hours worked. This point is illustrated in Exhibit 10–7.

The reason for using standard hours to apply overhead to production in a standard cost system is to assure that every unit of product moving along the production line bears the same amount of overhead cost, regardless of any time variations that may be involved in its manufacture.

The Fixed Overhead Variances

To illustrate the computation of fixed overhead variances, we will refer again to the overhead flexible budget data for Donner Company contained in Exhibit 10–4.

Denominator activity in machine-hours	50,000
Budgeted fixed overhead costs	$300,000
Fixed portion of the predetermined overhead rate (computed earlier)	$6

Let us assume that the following actual operating results were recorded for the year:

Actual machine-hours	42,000
Standard machine-hours allowed*	40,000
Actual fixed overhead costs:	
Depreciation	$100,000
Supervisory salaries.	172,000
Insurance	36,000
Total actual costs	$308,000

* For the actual production of the year.

From these data, two variances can be computed for fixed overhead—a *budget variance* and a *volume variance*. The variances are shown in Exhibit 10–8.

446

EXHIBIT 10–8

Computation of the fixed overhead variances

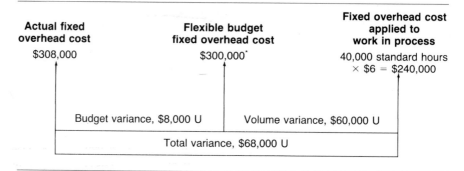

* As originally budgeted (see Exhibit 10–4). This figure can also be expressed as: 50,000 denominator hours × $6 = $300,000.

Notice from the exhibit that overhead has been applied to work in process on a basis of 40,000 standard hours allowed for the output of the year rather than on a basis of 42,000 actual hours worked. As stated earlier, this keeps unit costs from being affected by any efficiency variations.

The Budget Variance—a Closer Look

The **budget variance** represents the difference between actual fixed overhead costs incurred during the period and budgeted fixed overhead costs as contained in the flexible budget. The variance can also be presented in the following format:

Actual fixed overhead costs $308,000
Budgeted fixed overhead costs (from the
  flexible budget in Exhibit 10–4)   300,000
Budget variance . . . . $ 8,000 U

The reader should trace the $8,000 budget variance back into the company's overall performance report in Exhibit 10–3.

Although the budget variance is somewhat similar to the variable overhead spending variance, care must be exercised in how it is used. One must keep in mind that fixed costs are often beyond immediate managerial control. Therefore, rather than serving as a measure of managerial performance, in many cases the budget variance will be computed simply for information purposes in order to call management's attention to changes in price factors.

Fixed overhead costs and variances are often presented on the overhead performance report, along with the variable overhead costs. To show how this is done, an overhead performance report for Donner Company containing the fixed overhead budget variance is found in Exhibit 10–9. (The variable overhead cost data in the exhibit are taken from Exhibit 10–5.)

EXHIBIT 10–9

Fixed overhead costs on the overhead performance report

DONNER COMPANY
Overhead Performance Report
For the Year Ended March 31, 19x1

Budgeted machine-hours 50,000
Actual machine-hours. 42,000
Standard machine-hours allowed . . . 40,000

Overhead costs	Cost formula (per hour)	Actual costs 42,000 hours	Budget based on 42,000 hours	Spending or budget variance
Variable costs:				
Indirect labor.	$0.80	$ 36,000	$ 33,600	$ 2,400 U
Lubricants	0.30	11,000	12,600	1,600 F
Power	0.40	24,000	16,800	7,200 U
Total variable costs	$1.50	71,000	63,000	8,000 U
Fixed costs:				
Depreciation		100,000	100,000	—
Supervisory salaries		172,000	160,000	12,000 U
Insurance		36,000	40,000	4,000 F
Total fixed costs		308,000	300,000	8,000 U
Total overhead costs		$379,000	$363,000	$16,000 U

The Volume Variance—a Closer Look

The **volume variance** is a measure of utilization of plant facilities. It is computed by comparing the denominator activity figure with the standard hours allowed for the output of the period and multiplying any difference by the fixed portion of the predetermined overhead rate:

$$\begin{array}{c}\text{Fixed portion of}\\\text{the predetermined}\\\text{overhead}\end{array} \times \left(\begin{array}{c}\text{Denominator}\\\text{hours}\end{array} - \begin{array}{c}\text{Standard hours}\\\text{allowed}\end{array}\right) = \begin{array}{c}\text{Volume}\\\text{variance}\end{array}$$

Applying this formula to Donner Company, the volume variance would be:

$$\$6 \ (50{,}000 \ \text{MH} - 40{,}000 \ \text{MH}) = \$60{,}000 \ \text{unfavorable}$$

Note that this computation agrees with the volume variance as shown in Exhibit 10–8. At this point we should ask, "What caused a volume variance to arise in Donner Company, and what does the variance mean?" The cause of the variance can be explained as follows: If the company's activity level for the period had been 50,000 standard hours as planned, then work in process would have been charged with the full $300,000 in fixed costs contained in the overhead flexible budget:

$$50{,}000 \ \text{machine-hours} \times \$6 = \$300{,}000$$

But the activity level for the period (at standard) was only 40,000 machine-hours, *so even though the full $300,000 in fixed costs would have been incurred, less than this amount would have been charged to work in process:*

$$40,000 \text{ machine-hours} \times \$6 = \$240,000$$

The difference between these two figures is the volume variance:

$$\$300,000 - \$240,000 = \$60,000$$

As stated earlier, the volume variance is a measure of utilization of available plant facilities. An unfavorable variance, as above, means that the company operated at an activity level *below* that planned for the period; a favorable variance would mean that the company operated at an activity level *greater* than that planned for the period. It is important to note that the volume variance does not measure over- or underspending. A company normally would incur the same dollar amount of fixed overhead cost regardless of whether the period's activity was above or below the planned (denominator) level. In short, the volume variance is an activity-related variance in that it is explainable only by activity and is controllable only through activity.

To summarize:

1. If the denominator activity and the standard hours allowed for the output of the period are the same, then there is no volume variance.
2. If the denominator activity is greater than the standard hours allowed for the output of the period, then the volume variance is unfavorable, signifying an underutilization of available facilities.
3. If the denominator activity is less than the standard hours allowed for the output of the period, then the volume variance is favorable, signifying an overutilization of available facilities.

Graphic Analysis of Fixed Overhead Variances

Some insights into the budget and volume variances can be gained through graphic analysis. The needed graph is presented in Exhibit 10–10.

As shown in the graph, fixed overhead cost is applied to work in process at the predetermined rate of $6 for each standard hour of activity. (The applied-cost line is the upward-sloping line on the graph.) Since a denominator level of 50,000 machine-hours was used in computing the $6 rate, the applied-cost line crosses the budgeted-cost line at exactly the 50,000 machine-hour point. Thus, if the denominator hours and the standard hours allowed for output are the same, there can be no volume variance, since the applied-cost line and the budget-cost line will exactly meet on the graph. It is only when the standard hours differ from the denominator hours that a volume variance can arise.

In the case at hand, the standard hours allowed for output (40,000 machine-hours) are less than the denominator hours (50,000 hours); the result

EXHIBIT 10–10

Graphic analysis of fixed overhead variances

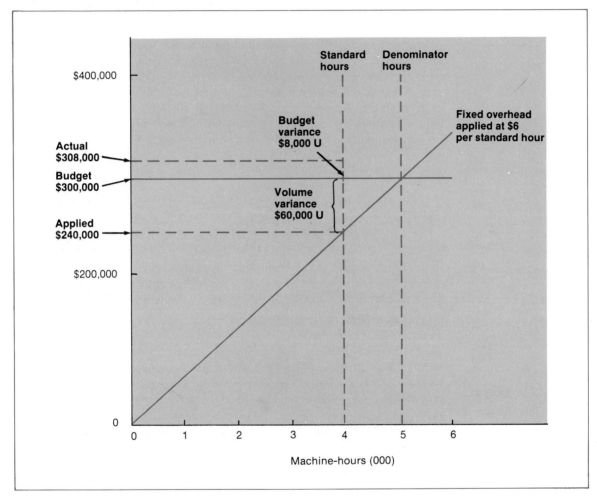

is an unfavorable volume variance, since less cost was applied to production than was originally budgeted. If the tables had been reversed and the standard hours allowed for output had exceeded the denominator hours, then the volume variance on the graph would have been favorable.

Cautions in Fixed Overhead Analysis

There can be no volume variance for variable overhead, since applied costs and budgeted costs are both dependent on activity and thus will always be moving together. The reason we get a volume variance for fixed overhead is that the incurrence of the fixed costs does not depend on activity; yet when applying the costs to work in process, we do so *as if* the costs were variable and depended on activity. This point can be seen from the graph in Exhibit 10–10. Notice from the graph that the fixed overhead costs are applied to work in process at a rate of $6 per hour *as if* they were indeed variable. Treating these costs as if they were variable is necessary for product costing purposes, but there are some real dangers here. The manager can easily become misled and start thinking of the fixed costs as if they were *in fact* variable.

The manager must keep clearly in mind that fixed overhead costs come in large, indivisible pieces. Any breakdown of such costs, though necessary for product costing purposes, is artificial in nature and has no significance in matters relating either to actual cost behavior or to cost control. This is why the volume variance, which arises as a result of treating fixed costs as if they were variable, is not a controllable variance from a spending point of view. The fixed overhead rate used to compute the variance is simply a derived figure needed for product costing purposes, but it has no significance in terms of cost control.

Because of these factors, some companies present the volume variance in physical units (hours) rather than in dollars. These companies feel that stating the variance in physical units gives management a clearer signal as to the cause of the variance and how it can be controlled.

PRESENTATION OF VARIANCES ON THE ABSORPTION COSTING INCOME STATEMENT

We have already shown in Exhibit 10–3 how variances are presented on the contribution income statement. To complete our discussion of standard costs and variance analysis, we will now show how variances are presented on income statements prepared under the absorption costing method.

The following variances have been computed for Donner company:

Direct materials (Exhibit 10–3)		$ 27,000 U
Direct labor (Exhibit 10–3)		6,000 F
Variable overhead (Exhibit 10–3):		
Spending variance (p. 440)	$8,000 U	
Efficiency variance (p. 441)	3,000 U	11,000 U
Fixed overhead:		
Budget variance (Exhibit 10–3 and p. 446)		8,000 U
Volume variance (p. 446)*		60,000 U
Total variances		$100,000 U

*Note that the volume variance does not appear on the contribution income statement in Exhibit 10–3, but that it is part of the $100,000 total variance on the absorption costing income statement in Exhibit 10–11. The reason it appears only on the absorption costing statement is that the volume variance represents the difference between the budgeted fixed overhead costs for a period and the amount applied to products. Under the contribution approach, there can be no volume variance since fixed overhead costs are not applied to products but rather are deducted in total on the income statement as period costs.

An absorption costing income statement for Donner Company containing the effects of these variances is presented in Exhibit 10–11. Note that the actual cost of goods sold exceeds the budgeted amount by $100,000, which

EXHIBIT 10–11

DONNER COMPANY
Absorption Costing Income Statement
For the Year Ended March 31, 19x1

20,000 units

	Actual	Budgeted	Variance
Sales	$1,000,000	$1,000,000	—
Less cost of goods sold (standard cost, $35 per unit)	800,000	700,000	$100,000 U
Gross margin	200,000	300,000	100,000 U
Less selling and administrative expense ($20,000 variable and $150,000 fixed)	170,000	170,000	—
Net income	$ 30,000	$ 130,000	$100,000 U

---

* The $35 standard cost is taken from Donner Company's standard cost card found on page 444.

agrees with the total of the variances summarized above. This type of presentation provides management with a clear picture of the impact of the variances on profits—a picture that could not be obtained by looking only at cost performance reports. In the case at hand, Donner Company's profits have been dramatically reduced by the variances that developed during the period.

REVIEW PROBLEM ON OVERHEAD ANALYSIS

(This problem provides a review of overhead flexible budgets, cost flows in a standard cost system, and the computation of overhead variances.)

An overhead flexible budget for Aspen Company is given below:

	Cost formula (per DLH)	Direct labor-hours		
Overhead costs		**4,000**	**6,000**	**8,000**
Variable costs:				
Supplies	$0.20	$ 800	$ 1,200	$ 1,600
Indirect labor	0.30	1,200	1,800	2,400
Total variable costs	$0.50	2,000	3,000	4,000
Fixed costs:				
Depreciation		4,000	4,000	4,000
Supervision		5,000	5,000	5,000
Total fixed costs		9,000	9,000	9,000
Total overhead costs		$11,000	$12,000	$13,000

Five hours of labor time are required per unit of product. The company has set denominator activity for the coming period at 6,000 hours (or 1,200 units). The computation of the predetermined overhead rate would be:

$$\text{Total} \frac{\$12,000}{6,000 \text{ DLH}} = \$2 \text{ per DLH}$$

$$\text{Variable element} \frac{\$3,000}{6,000 \text{ DLH}} = \$0.50 \text{ per DLH}$$

$$\text{Fixed element} \frac{\$9,000}{6,000 \text{ DLH}} = \$1.50 \text{ per DLH}$$

Assume the following actual results for the period:

Number of units produced	1,300
Actual direct labor-hours	6,800
Standard direct labor-hours allowed*	6,500
Actual variable overhead cost.	$4,200 ✓
Actual fixed overhead cost	9,400 ✓

*For 1,300 units of product.

Therefore, the company's manufacturing overhead account would appear as follows at the end of the period:

Manufacturing Overhead

Actual overhead costs	✓ 13,600*	13,000† ✓	Overhead costs applied
Underapplied overhead	600		

*$4,200 variable + $9,400 fixed = $13,600.
† 6,500 standard hours × $2 = $13,000.

Required: Analyze the $600 underapplied overhead in terms of:

1. A variable overhead spending variance. ✓
2. A variable overhead efficiency variance.
3. A fixed overhead budget variance.
4. A fixed overhead volume variance.

Variable Overhead Variances

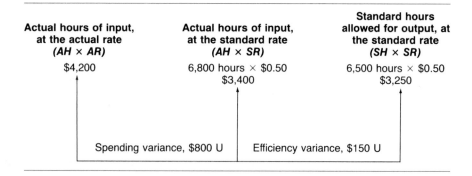

Actual hours of input, at the actual rate (AH × AR)	Actual hours of input, at the standard rate (AH × SR)	Standard hours allowed for output, at the standard rate (SH × SR)
$4,200	6,800 hours × $0.50 $3,400	6,500 hours × $0.50 $3,250

Spending variance, $800 U   Efficiency variance, $150 U

These same variances in the alternative format would be:

Variable overhead spending variance:

Actual variable overhead cost.		$4,200
Actual inputs at the standard rate:		
6,800 hours × $0.50		3,400
Spending variance		$ 800 U

Variable overhead efficiency variance:

$$SR(AH - SH) = \text{Efficiency variance}$$

$$\$0.50(6{,}800 \text{ hours} - 6{,}500 \text{ hours}) = \$150 \text{ U}$$

Fixed Overhead Variances

Actual fixed overhead cost	Flexible budget fixed overhead cost	Fixed overhead cost applied to work in process
$9,400	$9,000*	6,500 standard hours × $1.50 = $9,750
Budget variance, $400 U	Volume variance, $750 F	

Prod. more than budgeted

* Can be expressed as: 6,000 denominator hours × $1.50 = $9,000.

These same variances in the alternative format would be:

Fixed overhead budget variance:

Actual fixed overhead		$9,400
Budgeted fixed overhead		9,000
Budget variance.		$ 400 U

Fixed overhead volume variance:

$$\begin{array}{c} \text{Fixed portion of} \\ \text{the predetermined} \\ \text{overhead rate} \end{array} \times \left(\begin{array}{c} \text{Denominator} \\ \text{hours} \end{array} - \begin{array}{c} \text{Standard} \\ \text{hours} \end{array} \right) = \begin{array}{c} \text{Volume} \\ \text{variance} \end{array}$$

$$\$1.50 \ (6{,}000 \text{ hours} - 6{,}500 \text{ hours}) = \$750 \text{ F}$$

Summary of Variances

A summary of the four overhead variances is given below:

Variable overhead:	
Spending variance	$800 U
Efficiency variance	150 U
Fixed overhead:	
Budget variance	400 U
Volume variance	750 F
Underapplied overhead	$600

Notice that the $600 summary variance figure agrees with the underapplied balance in the company's Manufacturing Overhead account. This agreement stands as proof of the accuracy of our variance analysis. *Each period* the under- or overapplied overhead balance should be analyzed as we have done above. These variances will help the manager to see where his or her time and the time of the subordinates should be directed for better control of costs and operations.

KEY TERMS FOR REVIEW

Activity variance The net income lost through failure to achieve the budgeted sales in units for the period. This variance is computed by multiplying the difference between budgeted sales and actual sales by the budgeted contribution margin per unit.

Budget variance A measure of the difference between budgeted fixed overhead costs (as contained in the overhead flexible budget) and the actual fixed overhead costs incurred during a period.

Denominator activity The estimated activity figure used to compute the predetermined overhead rate.

Flexible budget A budget that is designed to cover a range of activity rather than a single point. It can be used to develop budgeted revenues and/or costs anywhere within that range to compare against actual results.

Selling price/cost variance A measure of the net income lost through failure to maintain control over selling price and over the various costs that a company may incur.

Static budget A budget designed to cover only one level of activity and in which actual costs are always compared against budgeted costs at this original activity level.

Volume variance A measure of the difference between the amount of fixed overhead cost contained in the overhead flexible budget and the amount of fixed overhead cost applied to work in process during a period.

QUESTIONS

10–1. What is a static budget?

10–2. What is a flexible budget, and how does it differ from a static budget? What is the main deficiency of the static budget?

10–3. What are the two prime responsibilities of the production manager? How do these two responsibilities differ?

10–4. What does the activity variance measure, and how is it computed?

10–5. Name three criteria that should be considered in choosing an activity base on which to construct an overhead flexible budget.

10–6. In comparing budgeted data with actual data in a performance report for variable manufacturing overhead, what variance(s) will be produced if the budgeted data are based on actual hours worked? On both actual hours worked and standard hours allowed?

10–7.   How does the variable manufacturing overhead spending variance differ from the materials price variance?

10–8.   Why is the term *overhead efficiency variance* a misnomer?

10–9.   "Fixed costs have no place in a flexible budget." Discuss.

10–10.   In what way is the overhead flexible budget involved in product costing?

10–11.   What costing problem is created by the fact that fixed overhead costs come in large, indivisible chunks?

10–12.   What is meant by the term *denominator level of activity?*

10–13.   Why do we apply overhead to work in process on a basis of standard hours allowed in Chapter 10, when we applied it on a basis of actual hours in Chapter 3? What is the difference in costing systems between the two chapters?

10–14.   In a standard cost system, what two variances can be computed for fixed overhead?

10–15.   What does the fixed overhead budget variance measure? Is the variance controllable by management? Explain.

10–16.   Under what circumstances would you expect the volume variance to be favorable? Unfavorable? Does the variance measure deviations in spending for fixed overhead items? Explain.

10–17.   How might the volume variance be measured, other than in dollars?

10–18.   What dangers are there in expressing fixed costs on a per unit basis?

10–19.   In Chapter 3, you became acquainted with the concept of under- or overapplied overhead. What four variances can be computed from the under- or overapplied overhead total?

10–20.   If factory overhead is overapplied for the month of August, would you expect the total of the overhead variances to be favorable or unfavorable? Why?

EXERCISES

E10–1.   An incomplete master flexible budget and an incomplete overhead flexible budget are given below:

Master Flexible Budget

	Budget formula (per unit)	Sales in units		
		30,000	40,000	50,000
Sales			$800,000	
Less variable expenses:				
Direct materials			160,000	
Direct labor			200,000	
Variable overhead			80,000	
Selling and administrative . . .			40,000	
Total variable expenses. . .				
Contribution margin				
Less fixed expenses:				
Manufacturing overhead . . .			160,000	
Selling and administrative . . .			90,000	
Total fixed expenses				
Net income (loss)				

Overhead Flexible Budget

Overhead costs	Cost formula (per hour)	Machine-hours*		
		15,000	20,000	25,000
Variable costs:				
Indirect materials				$ 15,000
Maintenance				60,000
Utilities				25,000
Total variable costs				
Fixed costs:				
Supervisory salaries				110,000
Rent				
Insurance				20,000
Total fixed costs				
Total overhead costs				

* One half hour of machine time is required to complete one unit of product.

Required: Provide the missing information in each budget.

E10–2.   Budget formulas for Palmer Company's costs are given below. These formulas cover a relevant range of 20,000 units to 40,000 units sold each year.

Cost	Budget formula
Direct materials	$6 per unit
Direct labor	9 per unit
Manufacturing overhead	2 per unit plus $450,000 per year
Selling expense	1 per unit plus $170,000 per year
Administrative expense	90,000 per year

The company's product sells for $50 per unit.

Required: 1. Prepare a master flexible budget in increments of 10,000 units.
       2. During 19x2, the company budgeted to sell 30,000 units but actually sold only 28,000 units for the year. Compute the company's activity variance.

E10–3.   The cost formulas for Emory Company's overhead costs are given below. These cost formulas cover a relevant range of 15,000 to 25,000 machine-hours each year.

Cost	Cost formula
Utilities	$0.30 per machine-hour
Indirect labor	52,000 plus $1.40 per machine-hour
Supplies	0.20 per machine-hour
Maintenance	18,000 plus $0.10 per machine-hour
Depreciation	90,000

Required: Prepare an overhead flexible budget in increments of 5,000 machine-hours. Include all costs on your budget.

E10–4. The variable portion of Murray Company's overhead flexible budget is given below:

Variable overhead costs	Cost formula (per hour)	Machine-hours		
		10,000	12,000	14,000
Supplies	$0.20	$ 2,000	$ 2,400	$ 2,800
Maintenance	0.80	8,000	9,600	11,200
Utilities	0.10	1,000	1,200	1,400
Rework time	0.40	4,000	4,800	5,600
Total variable costs . . .	$1.50	$15,000	$18,000	$21,000

During a recent period, the company recorded 11,500 machine-hours of activity. The variable overhead costs incurred were:

Supplies	$2,400
Maintenance	8,000
Utilities	1,100
Rework time	5,300

The budgeted activity for the period had been 12,000 machine-hours.

Required: 1. Prepare a variable overhead performance report for the period. Indicate whether variances are favorable (F) or unfavorable (U). Show only a spending variance on your report.
   2. Discuss the significance of the variances. Might some variances be the result of others? Explain.

E10–5. Operating at a normal activity level of 30,000 direct labor-hours, Lasser Company produces 10,000 units of product each period. The direct labor wage rate is $6 per hour. Two and one half yards of direct materials go into each unit of product; the material costs $8.60 per yard. The overhead flexible budget used to plan and control overhead costs is given below (in condensed form):

	Flexible Budget Data			
	Cost formula (per hour)	Direct labor-hours		
		20,000	30,000	40,000
Variable costs	$1.90	$ 38,000	$ 57,000	$ 76,000
Fixed costs		168,000	168,000	168,000
Total overhead costs . . .		$206,000	$225,000	$244,000

Required: 1. Using 30,000 direct labor-hours as the denominator activity, compute the predetermined overhead rate and break it down into variable and fixed elements.
   2. Complete the standard cost card below for one unit of product:

Direct materials, 2.5 yards at $8.60 . . .	$21.50
Direct labor, ?	
Variable overhead, ?	
Fixed overhead, ?	
Total standard cost per unit	$?

E10–6.   Marchant Company's overhead flexible budget (in condensed form) is given below:

Overhead costs	Cost formula (per hour)	Machine-hours 10,000	15,000	20,000
		Machine-hours		
Variable costs.	$2.40	$ 24,000	$ 36,000	$ 48,000
Fixed costs		90,000	90,000	90,000
Total overhead costs . . .		$114,000	$126,000	$138,000

The following information is available for 19x5:

a.   For 19x5, the company chose 15,000 machine-hours as the denominator activity level for computing the predetermined overhead rate.

b.   During 19x5, the company produced 7,250 units of product and worked 14,600 actual hours. The standard machine time is two hours per unit.

c.   Actual overhead costs incurred during 19x5 were: variable overhead, $34,800; and fixed overhead, $90,650.

Required: 1.   Compute the predetermined overhead rate used during 19x5. Divide it into fixed and variable elements.

2.   Compute the standard hours allowed for the output of 19x5.

3.   Compute the fixed overhead budget and volume variances for 19x5.

E10–7.   Selected operating information on four different companies for the year 19x6 is given below:

	A	B	C	D
	Company			
Full capacity direct labor-hours	10,000	18,000	20,000	15,000
Budgeted direct labor-hours*	9,000	17,000	20,000	14,000
Actual direct labor-hours.	9,000	17,800	19,000	14,500
Standard direct labor-hours allowed for actual production	9,500	16,000	20,000	13,000

* Denominator activity.

Required: In each case, state whether the company would have:

1.   No volume variance.

2.   A favorable volume variance.

3.   An unfavorable volume variance.

Also state in each case why you chose (1), (2), or (3).

E10–8.   Norwall Company's overhead flexible budget (in condensed form) is given below:

Overhead costs	Cost formula (per hour)	Machine-hours 50,000	60,000	70,000
		Machine-hours		
Variable costs.	$3	$150,000	$180,000	$210,000
Fixed costs		300,000	300,000	300,000
Total overhead costs . . .		$450,000	$480,000	$510,000

The following information is available:

a. For 19x3, a denominator activity figure of 60,000 machine-hours was chosen to compute the predetermined overhead rate.

b. At the 60,000 standard machine-hours level of activity, the company should produce 40,000 units of product.

c. During 19x3, the company's actual operating results were:

Number of units produced	42,000
Actual machine-hours	64,000
Actual variable overhead costs	$185,600
Actual fixed overhead costs	302,400

Required:

1. Compute the predetermined overhead rate for 19x3, and break it down into variable and fixed cost elements.
2. Compute the standard hours allowed for 19x3's production.
3. Compute the variable overhead spending and efficiency variances and the fixed overhead budget and volume variances for 19x3.

E10–9. Selected information relating to Yost Company's operations for 19x6 are given below:

Activity:

Denominator activity (machine-hours) . . .	45,000
Standard hours allowed per unit	3
Number of units produced	14,000

Costs:

Actual fixed overhead cost incurred	$267,000
Fixed overhead budget variance	3,000 F

The company applies overhead cost to products on a basis of machine-hours.

Required:

1. What were the standard hours allowed for 19x6 production?
2. What was the fixed portion of the predetermined overhead rate for 19x6?
3. What was the volume variance for 19x6?

E10–10. The standard cost card for the single product manufactured by Cutter, Inc., is given below:

Standard Cost Card—per Unit

Direct materials, 3 yards at $6	$18
Direct labor, 4 hours at $7.75	31
Variable overhead, 4 hours at $1.50	6
Fixed overhead, 4 hours at $5	20
Total standard cost per unit	$75

Overhead is applied to production on a basis of direct labor-hours. During 19x4, the company worked 37,000 hours and manufactured 9,500 units of product. Selected data relating to the company's operations for the year are shown below:

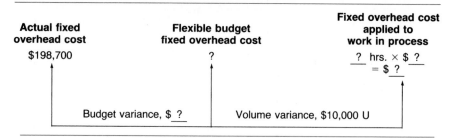

Actual fixed overhead cost	Flexible budget fixed overhead cost	Fixed overhead cost applied to work in process
$198,700	?	? hrs. × $? = $?

Budget variance, $?   Volume variance, $10,000 U

Required: 1.   What were the standard hours allowed for 19x4 production?
2.   What was the amount of fixed overhead cost contained in the flexible budget for the year?
3.   What was the fixed overhead budget variance for the year?
4.   What denominator activity level did the company use in setting the predetermined overhead rate for the year?

PROBLEMS

P10–11.   **Flexible budget income statement; net income variances.**   Hillman Company's master flexible budget is given below:

HILLMAN COMPANY
Master Flexible Budget

	Budget formula (per unit)	Sales in units 6,000	8,000	10,000
Sales	$50	$300,000	$400,000	$500,000
Less variable expenses:				
Direct materials	12	72,000	96,000	120,000
Direct labor	14	84,000	112,000	140,000
Variable overhead	3	18,000	24,000	30,000
Selling and administrative . . .	1	6,000	8,000	10,000
Total variable expenses. . .	30	180,000	240,000	300,000
Contribution margin	$20	120,000	160,000	200,000
Less fixed expenses:				
Manufacturing overhead . . .		75,000	75,000	75,000
Selling and administrative . . .		60,000	60,000	60,000
Total fixed expenses		135,000	135,000	135,000
Net income (loss)		$ (15,000)	$ 25,000	$ 65,000

For 19x2, the company's master budget called for 8,000 units to be produced and sold. Actual production and sales for the year was only 7,600 units. Actual costs for the year were:

Variable:
Direct materials . . . . $ 95,000
Direct labor   108,300
Variable overhead   20,100
Selling and administrative . . .   7,600

Fixed:

Manufacturing overhead	. . .	76,400
Selling and administrative	. . .	60,000

The company's selling price was $50 per unit during the year, as planned.

Required: 1. Prepare a flexible budget income statement for 19x2, showing the company's overall performance for the year.

2. If the company had produced and sold 8,000 units during the year as planned, net income would have been $25,000 (see the flexible budget above). Determine how much of the difference between the net income you computed in (1) and the expected $25,000 is due to (a) an activity variance and (b) a selling price/cost variance.

3. Suppose the president of Hillman Company wants more detailed information about the performance of individual managers. Can the cost variances on your income statement in (1) be broken down into more detailed figures? Explain (no computations are necessary).

P10–12. **Flexible budget income statement; all variances.** "This doesn't make any sense," declared Mike Hatch, president of Wheeler Company. "We missed our target profit figure last year by over $150,000, but yet most of our variances were favorable. I need someone to help me understand this statement." The statement to which Mr. Hatch was referring is shown below:

WHEELER COMPANY
Income Statement
For the Year Ended May 31, 19x5

	Budget formula (per unit)	Actual 40,000 units	Master budget 45,000 units	Variance
Sales.	$40	$1,600,000	$1,800,000	$200,000 U
Less variable expenses:				
Direct materials	8	357,000	360,000	3,000 F
Direct labor	6	253,000	270,000	17,000 F
Variable overhead	3	110,400	135,000	24,600 F
Selling and administrative . . .	1	40,000	45,000	5,000 F
Total variable expenses. . .	18	760,400	810,000	49,600 F
Contribution margin	$22	839,600	990,000	150,400 U
Less fixed expenses:				
Manufacturing overhead . . .		408,200	405,000	3,200 U
Selling and administrative . . .		345,000	345,000	—
Total fixed expenses		753,200	750,000	3,200 U
Net income		$ 86,400	$ 240,000	$153,600 U

As a new member of the management team, you have been asked to redo the statement and prepare an analysis to show how well the company is controlling costs. You have gathered the following information relative to last year's operations:

a. The company purchased 84,000 feet of material at a total cost of $357,000. All of this material was used in the production of 40,000 units of product during the year. (There was no change in either work in process or finished goods inventories.)

b. A total of 46,000 hours of direct labor time was recorded in the production of the 40,000 units of product.

c. Overhead cost is incurred and applied to products on a basis of direct labor-hours.

Required: 1. Prepare a flexible budget income statement for 19x5 so that the president can distinguish clearly between activity control and cost control for the year.

2. Prepare an analysis to show the president how much loss of income resulted from *(a)* an activity variance and *(b)* a selling price/cost variance.

3. The standard cost card for one unit of Wheeler Company's product follows:

	Standard quantity or hours	Standard price or rate	Standard cost
Direct materials	2 feet	$4.00 per foot	$ 8
Direct labor	1.2 hours	5.00 per hour	6
Variable overhead	1.2 hours	2.50 per hour	3
Fixed overhead	1.2 hours	7.50 per hour	9
Total standard cost . . .			$26

Given this standard cost card and other data provided in the problem, compute the following:

a. Direct materials price, quantity, and total variances.
b. Direct labor rate, efficiency, and total variances.
c. Variable overhead spending, efficiency, and total variances.
d. Fixed overhead budget variance.

4. Which of the variances computed in (3) are included in the company's selling price/cost variance?

P10–13. **Flexible budget income statement; all variances.**   Wyler Company produces and sells a high-quality ground cloth that is popular with backpackers. For 19x7, the company budgeted to produce and sell 50,000 ground cloths; at this activity level, net income should be $170,000 as shown in the company's master flexible budget below:

WYLER COMPANY
Master Flexible Budget

	Budget formula (per unit)	Sales in units 40,000	50,000	60,000
Sales	$35	$1,400,000	$1,750,000	$2,100,000
Less variable expenses:				
Direct materials	6	240,000	300,000	360,000
Direct labor	9	360,000	450,000	540,000
Variable overhead	3	120,000	150,000	180,000
Selling and administrative . . .	2	80,000	100,000	120,000
Total variable expenses . . .	20	800,000	1,000,000	1,200,000
Contribution margin	$15	600,000	750,000	900,000
Less fixed expenses:				
Manufacturing overhead . . .		420,000	420,000	420,000
Selling and administrative . . .		160,000	160,000	160,000
Total fixed expenses		580,000	580,000	580,000
Net income		$ 20,000	$ 170,000	$ 320,000

Due to labor problems, the company was able to produce and sell only 46,000 ground cloths during the year. Selected information on the year's activities follows:

a.   Costs incurred during the year:

	Variable	Fixed
Direct materials (190,000 yards) . . .	$323,000	
Direct labor (72,000 hours)	410,400	
Manufacturing overhead	136,800	$418,500
Selling and administrative	92,000	160,000

b.   All of the materials purchased were used in production during the year. Work in process and finished goods inventories are nominal in amount and can be ignored.

c.   As a result of foreign competition, the company had to reduce its selling price at one point during the year, resulting in an average selling price of $34.50 per unit for the year as a whole.

d.   Variable overhead is assigned to products on a basis of direct labor-hours.

Required: 1.   Prepare a flexible budget income statement for 19x7. Structure your statement so that Wyler Company's president can distinguish clearly between activity control and cost control.

2.   Upon seeing the income statement you prepared in (1), the president stated, "Wow, we sure missed our $170,000 target profit by a long ways. I would like to know how much of the difference is due to not meeting our sales goal and how much is due to problems with selling price and costs." Prepare this information for the president.

3.   The standard cost card for one ground cloth is given below:

	Standard quantity or hours	Standard price or rate	Standard cost
Direct materials	4 yards	$1.50 per yard	$ 6.00
Direct labor	1.5 hours	6.00 per hour	9.00
Variable overhead	1.5 hours	2.00 per hour	3.00
Fixed overhead	1.5 hours	5.60 per hour	8.40
Total standard cost . . .			$26.40

Compute the following variances for 19x7:

a.   Direct materials price, quantity, and total variances.
b.   Direct labor rate, efficiency, and total variances.
c.   Variable overhead spending, efficiency, and total variances.
d.   Fixed overhead budget variance.

4.   Using the information you have computed in (1) through (3), complete the following detailed reconciliation for 19x7:

Master budget net income $170,000
Variances for the year:
   (Show *all* appropriate variances.)
Actual net income . . . . $?

P10–14.   **Standard cost card; materials, labor, and all overhead variances.**   Flandro Company uses a standard cost system and sets predetermined overhead rates on a basis of direct labor-hours. The following data are taken from the company's overhead flexible budget for 19x1:

Denominator activity (direct labor-hours) . .   10,000
Variable overhead cost $25,000
Fixed overhead cost   59,000

A standard cost card showing the standard cost to produce one unit of the company's product is shown below:

Direct materials, 3 yards at $4.40 . . . . $13.20
Direct labor, 2 hours at $6 . . . .   12.00
Overhead, 140% of direct labor cost . . .   16.80
Standard cost per unit $42.00

During 19x1, the company produced 6,000 units of product and incurred the following costs:

Materials purchased, 24,000 yards at $4.80 . . . . $115,200
Materials used in production (in yards)   18,500
Direct labor cost incurred, 11,600 hours at $6.50 . . $ 75,400
Variable overhead cost incurred   29,580
Fixed overhead cost incurred   60,400

Required: 1.   Redo the standard cost card in a clearer, more usable format by detailing the variable and fixed overhead cost elements.
2.   Prepare an analysis of the variances for materials and labor for the year.
3.   Prepare an analysis of the variances for variable and fixed overhead for the year.
4.   What effect, if any, does the choice of a denominator activity level have on unit costs? Is the volume variance a controllable variance from a spending point of view? Explain.

P10–15.   **Basic overhead analysis.**   Baxter Company manufactures a single product and uses a standard cost system to help in the control of costs. Overhead is applied to production on a basis of machine-hours. According to the company's overhead flexible budget, the following overhead costs should be incurred at an activity level of 35,000 machine-hours (the denominator activity level chosen for 19x3):

Variable overhead costs . . . . . $ 87,500
Fixed overhead costs   210,000
Total overhead costs $297,500

During 19x3, the following operating results were recorded:

Activity:
    Actual machine-hours worked   30,000
    Standard machine-hours allowed for output . .   32,000
Cost:
    Actual variable overhead cost incurred . . . . $ 78,000
    Actual fixed overhead cost incurred   209,400

At the end of the year, the company's Manufacturing Overhead account contained the following data:

Manufacturing Overhead

Actual	287,400	272,000	Applied
	15,400		

Management would like to determine the cause of the $15,400 underapplied overhead before closing the amount to cost of goods sold.

Required: 1. Compute the predetermined overhead rate that would have been used during 19x3. Break the rate down into variable and fixed cost elements.
2. Show how the $272,000 "Applied" figure in the Manufacturing Overhead account was computed.
3. Analyze the $15,400 underapplied overhead figure in terms of the variable overhead spending and efficiency variances and the fixed overhead budget and volume variances.
4. Explain the meaning of each variance that you computed in (3) above, and indicate how each variance is controlled.

P10–16.   **Absorption costing statement; integration of materials, labor, and overhead variances.**   "Wonderful! Not only did our salespeople do a good job in meeting the sales budget this year, but our production people did a good job in controlling costs as well," said Kim Clark, president of Martell Company. "Our $18,000 cost variance is only 1.5 percent of the $1,200,000 standard cost of products sold during the year. That's well within the 3 percent parameter set by management for acceptable variances. It looks like everyone will be in line for a bonus this year." The company's income statement for the year is presented below:

	30,000 units		
	Actual	**Budgeted**	**Variance**
Sales	$1,680,000	$1,680,000	$ —
Less cost of goods sold (standard cost, $40 per unit)	1,218,000	1,200,000	18,000 U
Gross margin	462,000	480,000	18,000 U
Less operating expenses:			
Selling expenses	250,000	250,000	—
Administrative expenses	60,000	60,000	—
Total operating expenses	310,000	310,000	—
Net income	$ 152,000	$ 170,000	$18,000 U

The company produces and sells a single product. A standard cost card for the product follows:

Standard Cost Card—per Unit of Product	
Direct materials, 2 feet at $8.45	$16.90
Direct labor, 1.4 hours at $8	11.20
Variable overhead, 1.4 hours at $2.50	3.50
Fixed overhead, 1.4 hours at $6	8.40
Standard cost per unit	$40.00

The following additional information is available for the year just completed:

a. The company manufactured and sold 30,000 units of product during the year.
b. A total of 64,000 feet of material were purchased during the year at a cost of $8.55 per foot. All of this material was used to manufacture the 30,000 units. There were no beginning or ending inventories for the year.
c. The company worked 45,000 direct labor-hours during the year at a cost of $7.80 per hour.

d.   Overhead is applied to products on a basis of direct labor-hours. Data relating to overhead costs follows:

Denominator activity level (direct labor-hours)   35,000
Budgeted fixed overhead costs (from the overhead
    flexible budget) $210,000
Actual variable overhead costs incurred.   108,000
Actual fixed overhead costs incurred   211,800

e.   All variances are closed to cost of goods sold at the end of each year.

Required: 1.   Compute the direct materials price and quantity variances for the year.
            2.   Compute the direct labor rate and efficiency variances for the year.
            3.   For overhead, compute:
                 a.   The variable overhead spending and efficiency variances for the year.
                 b.   The fixed overhead budget and volume variances for the year.
            4.   Total the variances you have computed, and compare the net amount with the $18,000 variance on the income statement. Do you agree that bonuses should be given to everyone for good cost control during the year? Explain.

P10–17.   **Overhead flexible budget and overhead analysis.**   Harper Company assembles all of its products in the assembly department. Budgeted costs for the operation of this department during 19x2 have been set as follows:

Budgeted direct labor-hours . . . .   ?

Variable costs:
    Direct materials . . . . $ 900,000
    Direct labor   675,000
    Utilities   45,000
    Indirect labor   67,500
    Supplies   22,500
        Total variable costs   1,710,000

Fixed costs:
    Insurance.   8,000
    Supervisory salaries   90,000
    Depreciation   160,000
    Equipment rental   42,000
        Total fixed costs   300,000
Total budgeted costs $2,010,000

Since the assembly work is done mostly by hand, operating activity in this department is best measured by direct labor-hours. Direct labor cost is budgeted at $9 per hour. The cost formulas used to develop the budgeted costs above are valid over a relevant range of 60,000 to 90,000 direct labor-hours per year.

Required: 1.   Prepare an overhead flexible budget in good form for the assembly department. Make your budget in increments of 15,000 direct labor-hours. (The company does not include direct materials and direct labor costs in the overhead flexible budget.)
            2.   Assume that the company computes predetermined overhead rates by department. Compute the rate that will be used by the assembly department during 19x2 to apply overhead costs to production. Break this rate down into variable and fixed cost elements.
            3.   Suppose that during 19x2 the following actual activity and costs are recorded by the assembly department:

Actual direct labor-hours worked.	73,000
Standard direct labor-hours allowed	
for the output of the year	70,000
Actual variable overhead cost incurred	$124,100
Actual fixed overhead cost incurred	301,600

Complete the following:

a. A T-account for manufacturing overhead costs in the assembly department for 19x2 is given below. Determine the amount of applied overhead cost for the year, and compute the under- or overapplied overhead.

Manufacturing Overhead

Actual costs 425,700	

b. Analyze the under- or overapplied overhead figure in terms of the variable overhead spending and efficiency variances and the fixed overhead budget and volume variances.

P10–18. **Standard cost card and overhead analysis.**   Lane Company manufactures a single product that requires a large amount of labor time. Therefore, overhead cost is applied on a basis of direct labor-hours. The company's condensed overhead flexible budget is given below:

		Direct labor-hours		
Overhead costs	Cost formula (per hour)	45,000	60,000	75,000
Variable costs	$2	$ 90,000	$120,000	$150,000
Fixed costs	⸝	480,000	480,000	480,000
Total overhead costs . .		$570,000	$600,000	$630,000

The company's product requires 3 pounds of material that has a standard cost of $7 per pound and 1.5 hours of direct labor time that has a standard rate of $6 per hour.

During 19x1, the company planned to operate at a denominator activity level of 60,000 direct labor-hours and to produce 40,000 units of product. Actual activity and costs for the year were as follows:

Number of units produced	42,000
Actual direct labor-hours worked	65,000
Actual variable overhead costs incurred . . .	$123,500
Actual fixed overhead costs incurred	483,000

Required: 1. Compute the predetermined overhead rate that would have been used during 19x1. Break the rate down into variable and fixed elements.

2. Prepare a standard cost card for the company's product; show the details for all manufacturing costs on your standard cost card.

3. Do the following:
   a. Compute the standard hours allowed for 19x1 production.
   b. Complete the following Manufacturing Overhead T-account for the year:

Manufacturing Overhead

?	?
?	?

4. Determine the reason for any under- or overapplied overhead for the year by computing the variable overhead spending and efficiency variances and the fixed overhead budget and volume variances.
5. Suppose the company had chosen 65,000 direct labor-hours as the denominator activity rather than 60,000 hours. State which, if any, of the variances computed in (4) would have changed, and explain how the variance(s) would have changed. No computations are necessary.

P10–19. **Absorption costing statement; integration of materials, labor, and overhead variances.** "Wow! Just look at the size of that variance," said John Baker, president of Marvel, Inc. "We've got to do something to get costs back under control." The variance to which Mr. Baker was referring is shown in the company's most recent income statement below:

	12,500 units		
	Budgeted	**Actual**	**Variance**
Sales	$1,000,000	$1,000,000	$ —
Less cost of goods sold (standard			
cost, $60 per unit).	750,000	795,000	45,000*
Gross margin	250,000	205,000	(45,000)
Less operating expenses:			
Selling expenses	120,000	120,000	—
Administrative expenses	70,000	70,000	—
Total operating expenses.	190,000	190,000	—
Net income.	$ 60,000	$ 15,000	$(45,000)

*Consists of the following variances:

Direct materials	$ 4,000 U	
Direct labor	5,000 F	
Manufacturing overhead	46,000 U	
Total variance	$45,000 U	

The company produces and sells a single product. A standard cost card for the product follows:

Standard Cost Card—per Unit of Product

Direct materials: 3 pounds at $4 per pound	$12
Direct labor: 2.5 hours at $10 per hour	25
Variable manufacturing overhead: 2.5 hours at $2 per hour . . .	5
Fixed manufacturing overhead: 2.5 hours at $7.20 per hour* . . .	18
Total standard cost per unit	$60

*Based on a denominator activity of 37,500 hours.

The following additional information is available for the period:

a. The company purchased 40,000 pounds of materials during the period, at a cost of $3.85 per pound. All of the material was used to produce 12,500 units. There were no beginning or ending inventories.
b. The company worked 30,000 actual direct labor-hours during the period, at an average cost of $10.25 per hour.

c. The company incurred $62,000 in variable overhead cost during the period. Overhead is applied to products on a basis of direct labor-hours.

d. The company incurred $271,500 in fixed overhead costs during the period; budgeted fixed overhead costs were $270,000. A denominator activity of 37,500 hours is used to set overhead rates.

e. The company closes all variances to cost of goods sold each period, as shown in the income statement above.

Required:
1. Compute the direct materials price and quantity variances for the period.
2. Compute the direct labor rate and efficiency variances for the period.
3. Compute the variable overhead spending and efficiency variances and the fixed overhead budget and volume variances for the period.
4. Is the company's problem primarily one of poor control over costs? Explain.

P10–20. **Standard cost card; fixed overhead analysis; graphing.** In planning operations for 19x2, Southbrook Company chose a denominator activity figure of 40,000 direct labor-hours. According to the company's overhead flexible budget, the following overhead costs should be incurred at this activity level:

Variable overhead costs . . . . $ 72,000
Fixed overhead costs 360,000

The company produces a single product that requires 2.5 hours to complete. The direct labor rate is $6 per hour. Eight yards of material are needed to complete one unit of product; the material has a standard cost of $4.50 per yard. Overhead is applied to production on a basis of direct labor-hours.

Required:
1. Compute the predetermined overhead rate that the company will use during 19x2. Break the rate down into variable and fixed cost elements.
2. Prepare a standard cost card for one unit of product, using the following format:

Direct materials, 8 yards at $4.50 . $36
Direct labor,   ? . . . .   ?
Variable overhead, ? . . . .   ?
Fixed overhead,   ? . . . .   ?
Standard cost per unit . . . . . $?

3. Prepare a graph with cost on the vertical *(Y)* axis and direct labor-hours on the horizontal *(X)* axis. Plot a line on your graph from a zero level of activity to 60,000 direct labor-hours for each of the following costs:

a. Budgeted fixed overhead (in total).
b. Applied fixed overhead [applied at the hourly rate computed in (1) above].

4. Assume that during 19x2 actual activity is as follows:

Number of units produced   14,000
Actual direct labor-hours worked . . .   33,000
Actual fixed overhead cost incurred . . $361,800

a. Compute the fixed overhead budget and volume variances for the year.
b. Show the volume variance on the graph that you prepared in (3) above.

5. Disregard the data in (4). Assume instead that actual activity during 19x2 is as follows:

Number of units produced   20,000
Actual direct labor-hours worked   52,000
Actual fixed overhead cost incurred . . $361,800

a. Compute the fixed overhead budget and volume variances for the year.

b. Show the volume variance on the graph that you prepared in (3) above.

P10–21. **Selection of a denominator; overhead analysis.** Morton Company's condensed flexible budget is given below:

Overhead costs	Cost formula (per hour)	Direct labor-hours		
		20,000	30,000	40,000
Variable costs	$4.50	$ 90,000	$135,000	$180,000
Fixed costs		270,000	270,000	270,000
Total overhead costs . . .		$360,000	$405,000	$450,000

The company manufactures a single product that requires two direct labor-hours to complete. The direct labor wage rate is $5 per hour. Four feet of raw material is required for each unit of product; the standard cost of the material is $8.75 per foot.

Although long-run normal activity is 30,000 direct labor-hours each year, for the coming year (19x9) the company expects to operate at a 40,000-hour level of activity.

Required:

1. Assume that the company chooses 30,000 direct labor-hours as the denominator level of activity. Compute the predetermined overhead rate, breaking it down into variable and fixed cost elements.

2. Assume that the company chooses 40,000 direct labor-hours as the denominator level of activity. Repeat the computations in (1).

3. Complete two standard cost cards as outlined below. Each card should relate to a single unit of product.

Denominator Activity: 30,000 DLH

Direct materials, 4 feet at $8.75	$35.00
Direct labor, ?	?
Variable overhead, ?	?
Fixed overhead, ?	?
Standard cost per unit	$?

Denominator Activity: 40,000 DLH

Direct materials, 4 feet at $8.75	$35.00
Direct labor, ?	?
Variable overhead, ?	?
Fixed overhead, ?	?
Standard cost per unit	$?

4. Assume that the company produces 18,000 units and works 38,000 actual direct labor-hours during 19x6. Actual overhead costs for the year are:

Variable costs	$174,800
Fixed costs	271,600
Total overhead costs	$446,400

Do the following:

a. Compute the standard hours allowed for 19x6 production.

b.   Complete the Manufacturing Overhead account below. Assume that the company uses 30,000 direct labor-hours (long-run normal activity) as the denominator activity figure in computing predetermined overhead rates, as you have done in (1) above.

Manufacturing Overhead

Actual costs 446,400	?
?	?

c.   Determine the cause of the under- or overapplied overhead for the year by computing the variable overhead spending and efficiency variances and the fixed overhead budget and volume variances.

5.   Looking at the variances you have computed, what appears to be the major disadvantage of using long-run normal activity rather than expected actual activity as a denominator in computing the predetermined overhead rate? What advantages can you see to offset this disadvantage?

P10–22.   Standard cost card; overhead analysis; graphing.   Northwood company manufactures a product that has the following material and labor inputs:

Direct materials, 4 yards at $5
Direct labor, 2 hours at $7

The company uses an overhead flexible budget to plan and control overhead costs. Overhead rates are based on a normal activity level of 30,000 standard direct labor-hours each month. At this activity level, the overhead flexible budget shows monthly variable costs of $75,000 and monthly fixed costs of $180,000.

Required: 1.   Compute the predetermined overhead rate used by the company and divide it into variable and fixed cost elements. Prepare a standard cost card for one unit of product.

2.   Assume the following results for the month of June:

Standard hours allowed for the output of the month . .   28,000
Actual hours worked during the month.   29,000
Actual variable overhead cost . . . . $ 71,050
Actual fixed overhead cost   180,900

a.   Prepare a T-account for manufacturing overhead and enter the actual overhead costs shown above. Determine the amount of overhead cost that would have been applied to production during the month and enter this amount into the T-account. Compute the under- or overapplied overhead.

b.   Analyze the under- or overapplied overhead in terms of variable overhead spending and efficiency variances, and fixed overhead budget and volume variances.

c.   Prepare a graph showing the budgeted fixed overhead per month and showing applied fixed overhead from zero activity through 30,000 direct labor-hours of activity each month. Show where the volume variance for June would appear on the graph.

3.   Assume the following results for the month of July:

Standard hours allowed for the output of the month . .   34,000
Actual hours worked during the month.   32,000
Actual variable overhead cost . . . . $ 81,600
Actual fixed overhead cost   176,200

        a.   Again prepare a T-account for manufacturing overhead (do *not* carry over any figures in the account from the month of June), and enter the actual overhead costs shown above. Determine the amount of overhead that would have been applied to production during the month and enter this amount into the T-account. Again compute the under- or overapplied overhead.

        b.   Analyze the under- or overapplied overhead in terms of variable overhead spending and efficiency variances, and fixed overhead budget and volume variances.

        c.   Refer to the graph prepared in (2*c*) above. Show where the volume variance for the month of July would appear on the graph.

   4.   What effect, if any, does the choice of a denominator activity level have on unit costs? Is the volume variance controllable from a spending point of view? Explain.

P10–23.   **Comprehensive overhead analysis.** Pallas Company manufactures and sells a single product. Each unit requires 6 pounds of raw material, which has a standard cost of $3.75 per pound, and 2.5 hours of direct labor time, which has a standard rate of $4 per hour. Overhead costs are planned and controlled through an overhead flexible budget, which is shown in condensed form below:

	Cost formula (per hour)	Direct labor-hours		
		15,000	30,000	45,000
Variable costs	$3	$ 45,000	$ 90,000	$135,000
Fixed costs	=	360,000	360,000	360,000
Total overhead costs . . .		$405,000	$450,000	$495,000

Actual operating results for the most recent period are shown below:

Activity:
    Number of units produced   14,000
    Standard hours allowed for output . . . .   ?
    Actual direct labor-hours worked   36,000

Cost:
    Actual variable overhead cost $107,100
    Actual fixed overhead cost   362,500

Required: 1.   Assume that the company normally operates at an activity level of 30,000 standard direct labor-hours each period and that this figure is used as the denominator activity in computing predetermined overhead rates.

        a.   Compute the predetermined overhead rate, and break it down into fixed and variable cost elements.

        b.   Prepare a standard cost card, showing the standard cost to produce one unit of product.

   2.   Refer to the original data. Assume that the company decides to use 45,000 standard direct labor-hours as the denominator activity in computing predetermined overhead rates.

        a.   Under this assumption, compute the predetermined overhead rate and break it down into fixed and variable cost elements.

        b.   Prepare another standard cost card, showing the standard cost to produce one unit of product.

3. Refer to the computations you made in (1) above.
   a. Prepare a T-account for manufacturing overhead, and enter the actual overhead costs for the most recent period as shown in the original data to the problem. Determine the amount of overhead that would have been applied to production during the period, and enter this amount into the T-account.
   b. Compute the amount of under- or overapplied overhead for the period, and then analyze it in terms of the variable overhead spending and efficiency variances and the fixed overhead budget and volume variances.

4. Refer to the computations you made in (2) above.
   a. Prepare another T-account for manufacturing overhead, and again enter the actual overhead costs for the most recent period. Determine the amount of overhead that would have been applied to production during the period, and enter this amount into the T-account.
   b. Compute the amount of under- or overapplied overhead for the period, and then analyze it in terms of the variable overhead spending and efficiency variances and the fixed overhead budget and volume variances.

5. Firms are sometimes accused by competitors and others of selling products "below cost." What implications does this problem have for the "cost" of a unit of product so far as the setting of fixed overhead rates is concerned?

P10–24. Integrative problem; working backwards from variance data. You have recently graduated from State University and have accepted a position with Vitex, Inc., the manufacturer of a popular consumer product. During your first week on the job, the vice president has been favorably impressed with your work. She has been so impressed, in fact, that yesterday she called you into her office and asked you to attend the executive committee meeting this morning for the purpose of leading a discussion on the variances reported for last period. Anxious to favorably impress the executive committee, you took the variances and supporting data home with you last night to study.

On your way to work this morning, the papers were laying on the seat of your new, red convertible. As you were crossing a bridge on the highway, a sudden gust of wind caught the papers and blew them over the edge of the bridge and into the stream below. You managed to retrieve only one page, which contains the following information:

Standard Cost Card

Direct materials, 6 pounds at $3	$18.00
Direct labor, 0.8 hours at $5	4.00
Variable overhead, 0.8 hours at $3	2.40
Fixed overhead, 0.8 hours at $7	5.60
Standard cost per unit	$30.00

Variances reported

	Total standard cost*	Price or rate	Spending or budget	Quantity or efficiency	Volume
Direct materials . . .	$405,000	$6,900 F		$9,000 U	
Direct labor	90,000	4,850 U		7,000 U	
Variable overhead. .	54,000		$1,300 F	?† U	
Fixed overhead . . .	126,000		500 F		$14,000 U

* Applied to Work in Process during the period.
† Figure obliterated.

Overhead cost is assigned to production on a basis of direct labor-hours. All of the materials purchased during the period were used in production. Work in process inventories are nominal and can be ignored.

It is now 8:15 A.M. The executive committee meeting starts at 9:00 A.M., and you must have certain "backup" information ready in order to lead the discussion.

Required: 1. How many units were produced last period? (Think hard about this one!)
2. How many pounds of direct material were purchased and used in production?
3. What was the actual cost per pound of material?
4. How many actual direct labor-hours were worked during the period?
5. What was the actual rate paid per direct labor-hour?
6. How much actual variable overhead cost was incurred during the period?
7. What is the total fixed cost in the company's overhead flexible budget?
8. What were the denominator hours for last period?

P10–25.   **Preparing a revised performance report.**   Several years ago, Westmont Company developed a comprehensive budgeting system for profit planning and control purposes. The line supervisors have been very happy with the system and with the reports being prepared on their performance, but both middle and upper management have expressed considerable dissatisfaction with the information being generated by the system. A typical overhead performance report for a recent period is shown below:

WESTMONT COMPANY
Overhead Performance Report—Assembly Department
For the Quarter Ended March 31, 19x5

	Actual	Budget	Variance
Machine-hours	35,000	40,000	
Variable overhead:			
Indirect materials	$ 29,700	$ 32,000	$2,300 F
Rework time	7,900	8,000	100 F
Utilities	51,800	56,000	4,200 F
Machine setup	11,600	12,000	400 F
Total variable costs . . .	101,000	108,000	7,000 F
Fixed overhead:			
Maintenance	79,200	80,000	800 F
Inspection	60,000	60,000	—
Total fixed costs	139,200	140,000	800 F
Total overhead costs	$240,200	$248,000	$7,800 F

After receiving a copy of this overhead performance report, the supervisor of the assembly department stated, "These reports are super. It makes me feel really good to see how well things are going in my department. I can't understand why those people upstairs complain so much."

The "budget" data above are taken from the department's overhead flexible budget and represent the original planned level of activity for the quarter.

Required: 1.   The company's vice president is uneasy about the performance reports being prepared and would like you to evaluate their usefulness to the company.

                 2.   What changes, if any, would you recommend be made in the overhead performance report above in order to give better insight into how well the supervisor is doing his job?

                 3.   Prepare a new overhead performance report for the quarter, incorporating any changes you suggested in (2). (Include both the variable and the fixed costs in your report.)

P10–26.   **Overhead flexible budget and performance report.**   You have just been hired by FAB Company, the manufacturer of a revolutionary new garage door opening device. John Foster, the president, has asked that you review the company's costing system and ''do what you can to help us get better control of our overhead costs.'' You find that the company has never used a flexible budget, and you suggest that preparing such a budget would be an excellent first step in overhead planning and control.

After much effort and cost analysis, you are able to determine the following overhead cost formulas for the company's normal operating range of 20,000 to 30,000 machine-hours each month:

Cost	Cost formula
Utilities	$0.90 per machine-hour
Maintenance	1.60 per machine-hour plus $40,000 per month
Machine setup	0.30 per machine-hour
Indirect labor	0.70 per machine-hour plus $130,000 per month
Depreciation	70,000 per month

To show the president how the flexible budget concept works, you have gathered the following actual cost data for the most recent month (March 19x1), in which the company worked 26,000 machine-hours and produced 15,000 units:

Utilities	$ 24,200
Maintenance	78,100
Machine setup . . .	8,400
Indirect labor	149,600
Depreciation	71,500
Total costs	$331,800

The only variance in the fixed costs for the month was with depreciation, which was increased as a result of a purchase of new equipment.

The company had originally planned to work 30,000 machine-hours during March.

Required: 1.   Prepare an overhead flexible budget for the company in increments of 5,000 hours.

2. Prepare an overhead performance report for the company for March 19x1. (Use the format illustrated in Exhibit 10–9.)
3. What additional information would you need to have in order to compute an overhead efficiency variance for the company?
4. Explain to the president how the overhead flexible budget can be used for product costing purposes as well as for cost control purposes.

P10–27.   **Spending and efficiency variances; evaluating a performance report.**   Frank Western, supervisor of the machining department for Freemont Company, was visibly upset after being reprimanded for his department's poor performance over the prior month. The department's performance report is given below:

FREEMONT COMPANY
Overhead Performance Report—Machining Department

	Cost formula (per hour)	Actual	Budget	Variance
Machine-hours		38,000	35,000	
Variable overhead:				
Utilities	$0.40	$ 15,700	$ 14,000	$ 1,700 U
Indirect labor	2.30	86,500	80,500	6,000 U
Supplies	0.60	26,000	21,000	5,000 U
Maintenance	1.20	44,900	42,000	2,900 U
Total variable costs . . .	$4.50	173,100	157,500	15,600 U
Fixed overhead:				
Supervision		38,000	38,000	—
Maintenance		92,400	92,000	400 U
Depreciation		80,000	80,000	—
Total fixed costs		210,400	210,000	400 U
Total overhead costs		$383,500	$367,500	$16,000 U

"I just can't understand all the red ink," said Western to Sarah Mason, supervisor of another department. "When the boss called me in, I thought he was going to give me a pat on the back, because I know for a fact that my department worked more efficiently last month than it has ever worked before. Instead, he tore me apart. I thought for a minute that it might be over the supplies that were stolen out of our warehouse last month. But they only amounted to a couple of thousand dollars, and just look at this report. *Everything* is unfavorable, and I don't even know why."

The master budget for the machining department had called for production of 14,000 units last month, which is equal to a budgeted activity level of 35,000 machine-hours (at a standard time of 2.5 hours per unit). Actual production in the machining department for the month was 16,000 units.

Required: 1. Evaluate the overhead performance report given above, and explain why the variances are all unfavorable.
2. Prepare a new overhead performance report that will help Mr. Western's superiors assess efficiency and cost control in the machining department. (Hint: Exhibit

10–6 may be helpful in structuring your report; the report you prepare should include both variable and fixed costs.)

3. Would the supplies stolen out of the warehouse be included as part of the variable overhead spending or efficiency variance for the month? Explain.

P10–28. **Detailed performance report.** The cost formulas for variable overhead costs in a machining operation are given below:

Variable overhead cost	Cost formula (per machine-hour)
Power	$0.30
Setup time	0.20
Polishing wheels	0.16
Maintenance.	0.18
Total	$0.84

During the month of August, the machining operation was scheduled to work 11,250 machine-hours and to produce 4,500 units of product. The standard machine time per unit of product is 2.5 hours. A strike near the end of the month forced a curtailment of production. Actual results for the month were:

Actual machine-hours worked 9,250
Actual number of units produced 3,600

Actual costs for the month were:

	Total actual costs	Per machine-hour
Power	$2,405	$0.26
Setup time	2,035	0.22
Polishing wheels	1,110	0.12
Maintenance.	925	0.10
Total cost	$6,475	$0.70

Required: Prepare an overhead performance report for the machining operation for the month of August. Use column headings in your report as shown below:

Overhead item	Cost formula	Actual costs in-curred 9,250 hours	Budget based on ? hours	Budget based on ? hours	Total variance	Breakdown of the total variance	
						Spend-ing variance	Effi-ciency variance

P10–29. **Comprehensive problem: Flexible budget; performance reports.** Gant Products, Inc., has recently introduced budgeting as an intergral part of its corporate planning process. The company's first effort at constructing an overhead flexible budget is shown below.

Percentage of capacity	80%	100%
Direct labor-hours	4,800	6,000
Maintenance	$1,480	$ 1,600
Supplies	1,920	2,400
Utilities	1,940	2,300
Supervision	3,000	3,000
Machine setup	960	1,200
Total overhead cost	$9,300	$10,500

The budgets above are for costs over a relevant range of 80 percent to 100 percent of capacity on a monthly basis. The managers who will be working under these budgets have control over both fixed and variable costs.

Required: 1. Redo the company's overhead flexible budget, presenting it in better format. Show the budget at 80 percent, 90 percent, and 100 percent levels of capacity. (Use the high-low method to separate fixed and variable costs.)

2. Express the budget prepared in (1) above in cost formula form, using a single cost formula to express all overhead costs.

3. The company operated at 95 percent of capacity during April in terms of actual hours of direct labor time recorded in the factory. Five thousand six hundred standard direct labor-hours were allowed for the output of the month. Actual overhead costs incurred were:

Maintenance	$ 2,083
Supplies	3,420
Utilities	2,666
Supervision	3,000
Machine setup	855
Total costs	$12,024

There were no variances in the fixed costs. Prepare an overhead performance report for the month of April. Structure your report so that it shows only a spending variance for overhead. You may assume that the master budget for April called for an activity level during the month of 6,000 direct labor-hours.

4. Upon receiving the performance report you have prepared, the production manager commented, "I have two observations to make. First, I think there's an error on your report. You show an unfavorable spending variance for supplies, yet I know that we paid exactly the budgeted price for all the supplies we used last month. Pat Stevens, the purchasing agent, made a comment to me that our supplies prices haven't changed in over a year. Second, I wish you would modify your report to include an efficiency variance for overhead. The reason is that waste has been a problem in the factory for years, and the efficiency variance would help us get overhead waste under control."

a. Explain the probable cause of the unfavorable spending variance for supplies.

b. Compute an efficiency variance for *total* variable overhead, and explain to the production manager why it would or would not contain elements of overhead waste.

CASES

C10–30. **Incomplete data.**   Each of the cases below is independent. You may assume that
each company uses a standard cost system and that each company's overhead flexible
budget is based on standard machine-hours.

Item	Company A	Company B
1. Denominator activity in hours	?	40,000
2. Standard hours allowed for units produced . . .	32,000	?
3. Actual hours worked	30,000	?
4. Flexible budget variable overhead per machine-hour	$?	$ 2.80
5. Flexible budget fixed overhead (total)	?	?
6. Actual variable overhead cost incurred	54,000	117,000
7. Actual fixed overhead cost incurred	209,400	302,100
8. Variable overhead cost applied to production*	?	117,600
9. Fixed overhead cost applied to production*	192,000	?
10. Variable overhead spending variance	?	?
11. Variable overhead efficiency variance	3,500 F	8,400 U
12. Fixed overhead budget variance	?	2,100 U
13. Fixed overhead volume variance	18,000 U	?
14. Variable portion of the predetermined overhead rate	?	?
15. Fixed portion of the predetermined overhead rate	?	?
16. Underapplied or (overapplied) overhead	?	?

* Based on standard hours allowed for units produced.

Required: Compute the unknown amounts. (Hint: One way to proceed would be to use
the columnar format for variance analysis found in Exhibit 9–5 for variable overhead
and in Exhibit 10–8 for fixed overhead.)

C10–31. **Preparing a performance report.**   Boyne University offers an extensive continuing education program in many cities throughout the state. For the convenience of
its faculty and administrative staff and to save costs, the university employs a
supervisor to operate a motor pool. The motor pool operated with 20 vehicles
until February, when an additional automobile was acquired. The motor pool fur-
nishes gasoline, oil, and other supplies for its automobiles. A mechanic does routine
maintenance and minor repairs. Major repairs are done at a nearby commercial
garage.

Each year, the supervisor prepares an operating budget, which informs the university administration of the funds needed for operating the motor pool. Depreciation
(straight line) on the automobiles is recorded in the budget in order to determine
the cost per mile of operating the vehicles.

The schedule below presents the operating budget for the current year, which
has been approved by the university. The schedule also shows actual operating
costs for March of the current year, compared to one twelfth of the annual operating
budget.

UNIVERSITY MOTOR POOL
Budget Report for March

	Annual operating budget	Monthly budget[*]	March actual	(Over) under budget
Gasoline	$ 42,000	$ 3,500	$ 4,300	$(800)
Oil, minor repairs, parts	3,600	300	380	(80)
Outside repairs	2,700	225	50	175
Insurance	6,000	500	525	(25)
Salaries and benefits	30,000	2,500	2,500	—
Depreciation of vehicles	26,400	2,200	2,310	(110)
Total costs	$110,700	$ 9,225	$10,065	$(840)
Total miles	600,000	50,000	63,000	
Cost per mile	$ 0.1845	$0.1845	$0.1598	
Number of automobiles in use	20	20	21	

[*] Annual operating budget ÷ 12 months.

The annual operating budget was constructed upon the following assumptions:

a.   Twenty automobiles in the motor pool.
b.   Thirty thousand miles driven per year per automobile.
c.   Fifteen miles per gallon per automobile.
d. $1.05 per gallon of gasoline.
e. $0.006 cost per mile for oil, minor repairs, and parts.
f. $135 cost per automobile per year for outside repairs.
g. $300 cost per automobile per year for insurance.

The supervisor of the motor pool is unhappy with the monthly report comparing budget and actual costs for March, claiming it presents an unfair picture of performance. A previous employer used flexible budgeting to compare actual costs to budgeted amounts.

Required: 1.   Prepare a new performance report for the month of March, showing budgeted costs, actual costs, and variances. In preparing your report, use flexible budgeting techniques to compute the "monthly budget" figures.
2.   What are the deficiencies in the performance report presented above? How does the report which you prepared in (1) overcome these deficiencies?

(CMA, Adapted)

CHAPTER 11

Control of Decentralized Operations

LEARNING OBJECTIVES

After studying Chapter 11, you should be able to:

- Explain how a pyramiding system of reports is used to communicate information between various levels of responsibility in an organization.

- Enumerate the benefits to be gained by decentralization in an organization.

- Differentiate between cost centers, profit centers, and investment centers, and explain how performance is measured in each.

- Compute return on investment (ROI) by means of the ROI formula and show how changes in sales, expenses, and assets affect an organization's ROI.

- Compute the residual income and enumerate the strengths and weaknesses of this method of measuring managerial performance.

- Use the transfer pricing formula to compute an appropriate transfer price between segments of an organization under conditions of (1) full capacity and (2) idle capacity.

- Define or explain the key terms listed at the end of the chapter.

In this chapter, we expand our knowledge of performance reports by looking more closely at responsibility accounting. This concept was first introduced in Chapter 8 and has been the "why" behind most of our work with budgets and performance reports in preceding chapters. We shall now use the responsibility accounting concept to show how the reports developed in these chapters fit together into an integrated reporting system. In the process, we will extend the technique of performance reporting to the company as a whole and demonstrate methods of evaluating the performance of top management.

RESPONSIBILITY ACCOUNTING

Responsibility accounting centers on the idea that an organization is simply a group of individuals working toward common goals. The more each individual can be assisted in the performance of his or her tasks, the better chance the organization has of reaching the goals it has set. As we have seen in preceding chapters, responsibility accounting recognizes each person in an organization who has any control over cost or revenue to be a *separate responsibility center* whose stewardship must be defined, measured, and reported upward in the organization. One author expresses the idea this way:

> In effect, the system personalizes the accounting statements by saying, "Joe, this is what you originally budgeted and this is how you performed for the period with actual operations as compared against your budget." By definition it [responsibility accounting] is a system of accounting which is tailored to an organization so that costs are accumulated and reported by levels of responsibility within the organization. Each supervisory area in the organization is charged *only* with the cost for which it is responsible and over which it has control.[1]

Although the idea behind responsibility accounting is not new, the implementation of the idea on a widespread basis is quite recent and has come about in response to the manager's need for better and more efficient ways to control operations.

The Functioning of the System

In order to broaden our perspective of how a responsibility accounting system functions, we will consider selected data relating to Potter Company. Potter Company is part of the Western Division of General Products, Inc., a broadly diversified firm with interests in many product areas. A partial organization chart for Potter Company is shown in Exhibit 11–1. The data on this chart form the basis for exhibits found on the following pages.

---

[1] John A. Higgins, "Responsibility Accounting," *Arthur Andersen Chronicle,* April 1952, p. 94.

EXHIBIT 11–1

Organization chart—Potter Company

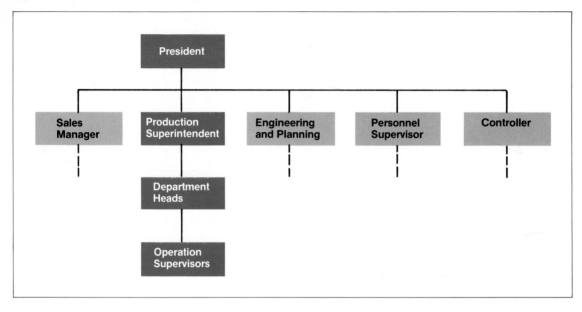

Although the concepts underlying responsibility accounting apply equally well to all parts of an organization, we will concentrate our discussion on the shaded area of Potter Company's organization chart. It depicts the line of responsibility for the production activities of the firm. This line of responsibility begins with the operation supervisors and moves upward in the organization, with each successive level having greater overall responsibility than the level that preceded it. To see how this concept of an upward-flowing, broadening line of responsibility can be integrated into the accounting statements, refer to Exhibit 11–2.

Exhibit 11–2 provides us with a bird's-eye view of the structuring of reports in a responsibility accounting system. Notice that the performance reports *start at the bottom and build upward,* with each manager receiving information on his own performance as well as on the performance of each manager under him in the chain of responsibility. We will now start at the bottom of this chain and follow it upward to show how the reports are used by the various levels of management.

The Flow of Information

The responsibility accounting system depicted in Exhibit 11–2 is structured around four levels of responsibility. The number of levels of responsibility will vary from company to company, according to organizational structure and needs.

EXHIBIT 11–2

POTTER COMPANY
An Overview of Responsibility Accounting

President's report:

The president's performance report summarizes all company data. Since variances are given, the president can trace the variances downward through the company as needed to determine where his and his subordinates' time can best be spent.

Responsibility center:	Budget	Actual	Variance
Sales manager	X	X	X
Production superintendent	$26,000	$29,000	$3,000 U
Engineering and planning	X	X	X
Personnel supervisor	X	X	X
Controller	X	X	X
	$54,000	$61,000	$7,000 U

Production superintendent:

The performance of each department head is summarized for the production superintendent. The totals on the superintendent's performance report are then passed upward to the next level of responsibility.

Responsibility center:	Budget	Actual	Variance
Cutting department	X	X	X
Machining department	X	X	X
Finishing department	$11,000	$12,500	$1,500 U
Packaging department	X	X	X
	$26,000	$29,000	$3,000 U

Finishing department head:

The performance report of each supervisor is summarized on the performance report of the department head. The department totals are then summarized upward to the production superintendent.

Responsibility center:	Budget	Actual	Variance
Sanding operation	X	X	X
Wiring operation	$ 5,000	$ 5,800	$ 800 U
Assembly operation	X	X	X
	$11,000	$12,500	$1,500 U

Wiring operation supervisor:

The supervisor of each operation receives a performance report on his or her center of responsibility. The totals on these reports are then communicated upward to the next higher level of responsibility.

Variable costs:	Budget	Actual	Variance
Direct materials	X	X	X
Direct labor	X	X	X
Manufacturing overhead	X	X	X
	$ 5,000	$ 5,800	$ 800 U

Fourth level of responsibility   The fourth, or lowest, level of responsibility is that of the wiring operation supervisor. The performance report prepared for the supervisor will be similar to the performance reports discussed in the two preceding chapters. This report will show budgeted data, actual data, and variances in terms of materials, labor, and overhead. This information will be communicated upward to the department head, along with detailed variance analyses.

Third level of responsibility   The third level of responsibility is that of the finishing department head who oversees the work of the wiring operation supervisor as well as the work of the other supervisors in this department. Notice from Exhibit 11–2 that the department head will receive summarized data from each of the operations within the department. If the department head desires to know the reasons behind the variances reported in these summaries (such as the $800 variance in the wiring operation), he or she can look at the detailed, individual performance reports prepared on the separate operations.

Second level of responsibility   The second level of responsibility is that of the production superintendent who has responsibility for all producing department activities. Notice from Exhibit 11–2 that the summarized totals from the performance report of the finishing department head are reported upward to the production superintendent, along with summarized totals from the performance reports of other departments. In addition to the summarized totals, the production superintendent will undoubtedly also require that detailed copies of the performance reports themselves be furnished to him, as well as detailed copies of the performance reports from all separate operations within the departments. The availability of these reports will permit the production superintendent to go right to the heart of any problem in cost control. This, of course, is the implementation of the management by exception principle discussed in earlier chapters. By having variances from budget highlighted on each performance report, the production superintendent is able to see where his or her time and the time of the department heads and supervisors can best be spent.

First level of responsibility   The president of a company has ultimate responsibility for all costs and revenues. On his or her performance report, therefore, the activities of all phases of the business must be summarized for review.

The president may require that copies of the detailed performance reports from *all* levels of responsibility be supplied to him. On the other hand, he may concern himself only with broad results, leaving the more detailed data for the scrutiny of the managers of the lower responsibility centers, such as the production superintendent. Thus, the system provides a great deal of flexibility and can be expanded or contracted in terms of data provided to suit the needs and interests of the particular manager involved.

In the absence of a responsibility accounting system, managers are left with little more than a "seat-of-the-pants" feel for what is going on in their own areas of responsibility, as well as those of their subordinates. In today's highly competitive business environment, a seat-of-the-pants feel for how well costs are being controlled is rarely sufficient to sustain profitable operations.

Expanding the Responsibility Accounting Idea

We have indicated earlier that Potter Company is a part of the Western Division of General Products, Inc. Exhibit 11–3 on the following page shows more clearly just how Potter Company fits into the structure of the General Products, Inc., organization.

This exhibit illustrates a further expansion of the responsibility accounting idea. Notice from the exhibit that contribution income statements are used to report company-level performance to the divisional manager and to report divisional performance to corporate headquarters.

On a corporate headquarters level, all data are summarized into various segment arrangements for an overall performance evaluation of the entire corporate structure (see Exhibit 11–3). Since variances from budgeted sales and costs are shown on the contribution income statements, managers at the various levels of responsibility can see clearly where profit objectives are not being met. An illustration of a contribution income statement with variances has already been provided in Exhibit 10–3 in the preceding chapter. (The reader may wish to refer back to Exhibit 10–3 on page 434 before going on.) Income statements such as the one in Exhibit 10–3 are prepared at both the company and division levels and then consolidated on a corporate level.

The Benefits of Decentralization

Managers have found that a responsibility accounting system functions most effectively in an organization that is *decentralized*. A **decentralized organization** is one in which decision making is not confined to a few top executives but rather is spread throughout the organization, with managers at various levels making key operating decisions relating to their sphere of responsibility. Decentralization must be viewed in terms of degree, since all organizations are decentralized to some extent out of economic necessity. At one extreme, a strongly decentralized organization is one in which there are few, if any, constraints on the freedom of a manager to make a decision, even at the lowest levels. At the other extreme, a strongly centralized organization is one in which little freedom exists to make a decision other than at top levels of management. Although most firms today fall somewhere between these two extremes, there is a pronounced tendency toward the decentralized end of the spectrum.

EXHIBIT 11–3

General Products, Inc., organization—an expansion of the responsibility accounting concept

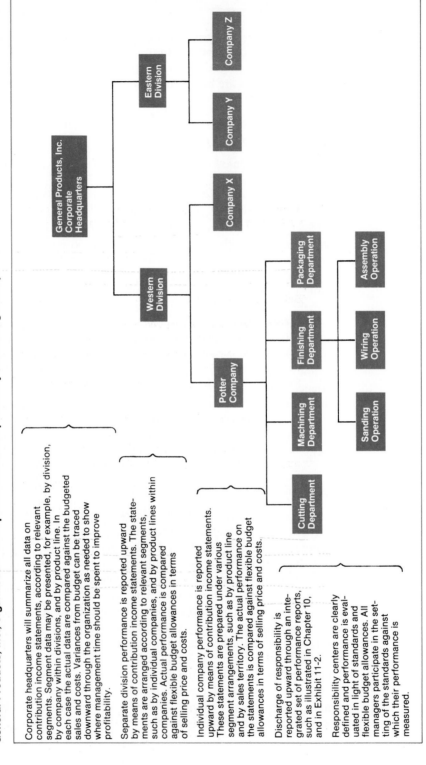

Corporate headquarters will summarize all data on contribution income statements, according to relevant segments. Segment data may be presented, for example, by division, by company within divisions, and by product line. In each case the actual data are compared against the budgeted sales and costs. Variances from budget can be traced downward through the organization as needed to show where management time should be spent to improve profitability.

Separate division performance is reported upward by means of contribution income statements. The statements are arranged according to relevant segments, such as by individual companies, and by product lines within companies. Actual performance is compared against flexible budget allowances in terms of selling price and costs.

Individual company performance is reported upward by means of contribution income statements. These statements are prepared under various segment arrangements, such as by product line and by sales territory. The actual performance on the statements is compared against flexible budget allowances in terms of selling price and costs.

Discharge of responsibility is reported upward through an integrated set of performance reports, such as illustrated in Chapter 10, and in Exhibit 11–2.

Responsibility centers are clearly defined and performance is evaluated in light of standards and flexible budget allowances. All managers participate in the setting of the standards against which their performance is measured.

Many benefits are felt to accrue from decentralization. These benefits include the following:

1. By spreading the burden of decision making among many levels of management, top management is relieved of much day-to-day problem solving and is left free to concentrate on long-range planning and on coordination of efforts.

2. Allowing managers greater decision-making control over their segments provides excellent training as these managers rise in the organization. In the absence of such training, managers may be ill-prepared to function in a decision-making capacity as they are given greater responsibility.

3. Added responsibility and decision-making authority often result in increased job satisfaction and provide greater incentive for the manager to put forth his or her best efforts.

4. Decisions are best made at that level in an organization where a problem arises. Members of top management are often in a poor position to make decisions in matters relating to the everyday operation of a given segment, since they are not intimately acquainted with the problems or local conditions that may exist.

5. Decentralization provides a more effective basis for measuring a manager's performance, since it typically leads to the creation of profit and investment centers. Profit and investment centers and the measurement of management performance are discussed in the following section.

Investment, Profit, and Cost Centers

In a decentralized organization, the responsibility accounting system is structured around a number of centers, such as are depicted in Exhibit 11–4 for General Products, Inc. These consist of investment centers, profit centers, and cost centers, each of which defines a particular area of responsibility in an organization.[2]

Responsibility center   A **responsibility center** is any point within an organization where control over the incurrence of cost, the generating of revenue, or the use of investment funds is found. Such a point could be an individual, an operation, a department, a company, a division, or the entire organization itself.

Cost center   A **cost center** is any responsibility center that has control over the incurrence of cost. A cost center has no control over either the generating of revenue or the use of investment funds.

---

[2] Some organizations also identify "revenue centers," which are responsible for sales activities only (products are shipped directly from the plant or from a warehouse as orders are submitted). An example of such a revenue center would be a Sears catalog outlet. Other companies would consider this to be just another type of profit center, since costs of some kind (salaries, rent, utilities) are usually present.

EXHIBIT 11–4

Investment, profit, and cost centers—General Products, Inc.

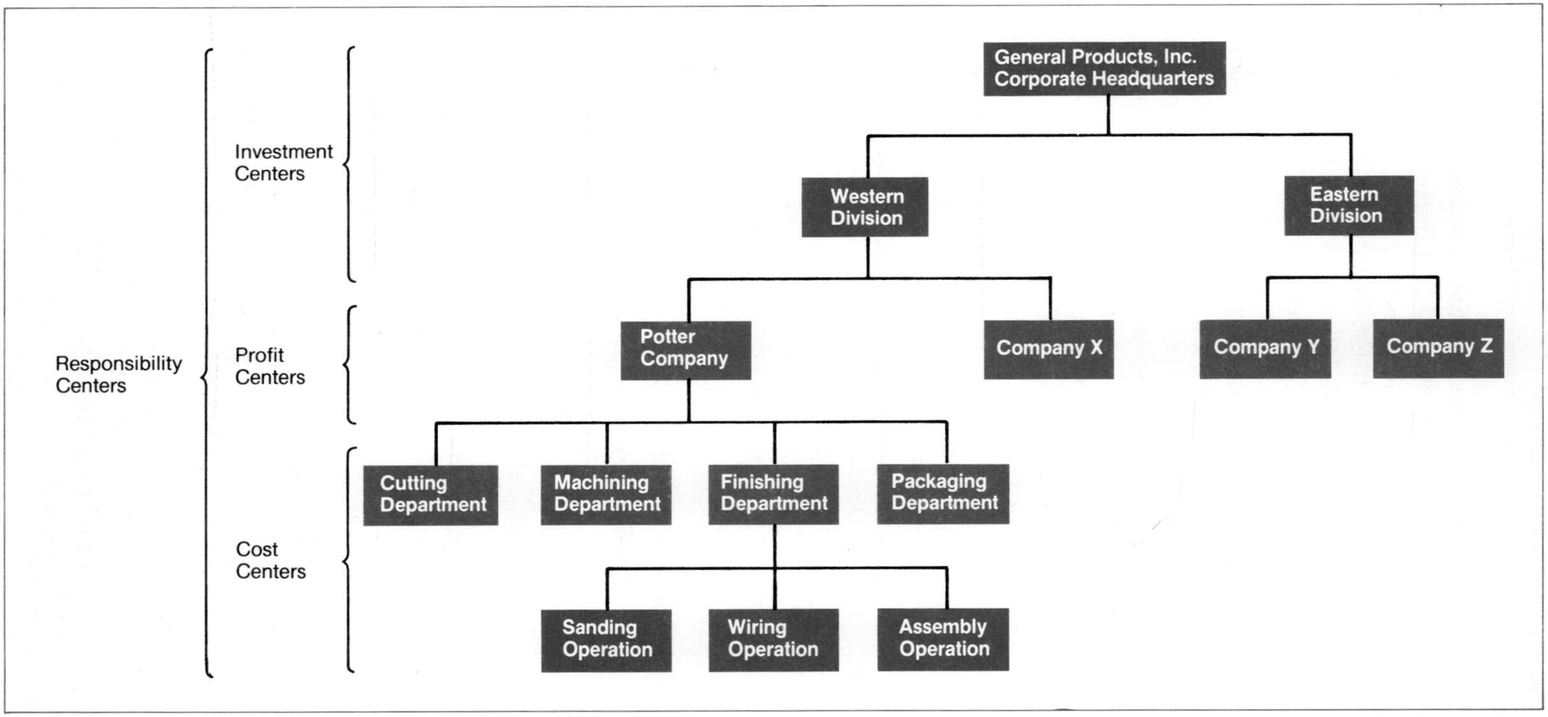

Profit center By contrast to a cost center, a **profit center** has control over both cost and revenue. Potter Company, for example, would be a profit center in the General Products, Inc., organization, since it would be concerned with marketing its goods as well as producing them. Like a cost center, however, a profit center generally does not have control over how investment funds are used.

Investment center An **investment center** is any responsibility center within an organization that has control over cost and revenue and also over the use of investment funds. The corporate headquarters of General Products, Inc., would clearly be an example of an investment center. Corporate officers have ultimate responsibility for seeing that production and marketing goals are met. In addition, they have responsibility for seeing that adequate facilities are available to carry out the production and marketing functions, and for seeing that adequate working capital is available for operating needs. Whenever a segment of an organization has control over investment in such areas as physical plant and equipment, receivables, inventory, and entry into new markets, then it is termed an *investment center*. Potter Company itself could be an investment center if it were given control over investment funds for some of these purposes. In the more usual situation, however, Potter Company would be a profit center within the larger organization, with most (or all) investment decisions being made at the divisional or central headquarters levels.

The reader should be cautioned that in everyday business practice the distinction between a profit center and an investment center is sometimes blurred, and the term *profit center* is often used to refer to either one. Thus, a company may refer to one of its segments as being a profit center when in fact the manager has full control over investment decisions in the segment. For purposes of our discussion, we will continue to maintain a distinction between the two, as made above.

Measuring Management Performance

These concepts of responsibility accounting are very important, since they assist in defining a manager's sphere of responsibility and also in determining how performance will be evaluated.

Cost centers are evaluated by means of performance reports, in terms of meeting cost standards that have been set. Profit centers are evaluated by means of contribution income statements, in terms of meeting sales and cost objectives. Investment centers are also evaluated by means of contribution income statements, but normally in terms of the *rate of return* that they are able to generate on *invested funds.* In the following section, we discuss rate of return as a tool for measuring managerial performance in an investment center.

RATE OF RETURN FOR MEASURING MANAGERIAL PERFORMANCE

The development of concepts such as investment centers, profit centers, and cost centers is largely a result of the rapid growth of decentralization in corporate structures. As mentioned earlier, in a decentralized organization managers are given a great deal of autonomy in directing the affairs in their particular areas of responsibility. So great is this autonomy that the various profit and investment centers are often viewed as being virtually independent businesses, with their managers having about the same control over decisions as if they were in fact running their own independent firms. With this autonomy, fierce competition often develops among managers, with each striving to make his or her operation the ''best'' in the company.

Competition is particularly keen when it comes to passing out funds for expansion of product lines, or for introduction of new product lines. How do top managers in corporate headquarters go about deciding who gets new investment funds as they become available, and how do these managers decide which investment centers are most profitably using the funds that have already been entrusted to their care? One of the most popular ways of making these judgments is to measure the rate of return that investment center managers are able to generate on their assets. This can be done through the *return on investment (ROI)* formula.

The ROI Formula

To understand the concepts behind the ROI formula, refer to the funds flow model illustrated in Exhibit 11–5. As shown in the exhibit, when a company is first organized, cash is obtained through the sale of capital stock (CS) and the issue of bonds and other long-term liabilities (LTL). Portions of this cash are used to acquire various fixed assets (FA) and other assets (OA), and a portion is used in day-to-day operations.

In the ''Operations'' part of the model, note that as a dollar leaves the central pool of cash, it is invested in inventory (I). The inventory is then sold, and an account receivable (AR) is created, which is subsequently collected from the customer. Upon collection from the customer, the dollar that was started through the system is returned to the central pool of cash from which it began its journey. This dollar will bring back with it whatever additional pennies the customer has been willing to pay above the cost of the goods that he or she purchased. Thus, the seller's profitability will at least in part be measured by the number of these additional pennies, which we will call the **margin** earned. ─> the profit after cost is recovered.

But a moment's reflection will indicate that a firm's profitability is also dependent on another factor. Realizing that a dollar going through the system will bring back a certain number of additional pennies with it, we will be anxious to send that dollar through the system as many times during the period as we possibly can. The number of trips a dollar makes through the system during a period is known as the **turnover.** Thus, we can see that a

# of trip the $ makes

EXHIBIT 11–5

The funds flow model

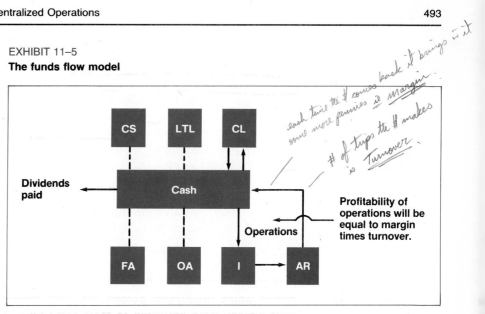

CS = capital stock; LTL = long-term liabilities; CL = current liabilities; FA = fixed assets; OA = other assets; I = inventory; and AR = accounts receivable.

firm's profitability or **return on investment (ROI)** will be a product of the margin (number of pennies brought back by a dollar in one trip through the system) multiplied by the turnover (number of times a dollar makes the trip through the system during the period). This line of reasoning gives rise to the ROI formula:

$$\text{Margin} \times \text{Turnover} = \text{Profitability, or ROI}$$

Factors Underlying Rate of Return

Armed with a conceptual perspective of the ROI formula, we can now examine the detailed factors making up the margin and turnover elements:

$$\text{Margin} \times \text{Turnover} = \text{ROI}$$

$$\text{Margin} = \frac{\text{Net operating income}}{\text{Sales}} \qquad \text{Turnover} = \frac{\text{Sales}}{\text{Average operating assets}}$$

Therefore,

$$\frac{\text{Net operating income}}{\text{Sales}} \times \frac{\text{Sales}}{\text{Average operating assets}} = \text{ROI}$$

In the past, managers have tended to focus only on the margin earned and have ignored the turnover of assets. To some degree at least, the margin earned can be a valuable measure of a manager's performance. Standing alone, however, it overlooks one very crucial area of a manager's responsibility—the control of investment in operating assets. Excessive funds tied up in operating assets can be just as much of a drag on profitability as excessive operating expenses. One of the real advantages of the ROI formula is that it forces the manager to control his or her investment in operating assets as well as to control expenses, the gross profit rate, and sales volume.

Du Pont was the first major corporation to recognize the importance of looking at both margin *and* turnover in assessing the performance of a manager. To it must go the credit for pioneering the ROI concept. Monsanto Company and other major corporations have followed Du Pont's lead, and the ROI formula is now recognized as one of the best single measures of a manager's performance when that manager has control of an investment center. The ROI formula blends together many aspects of the manager's responsibilities into a single figure that can be compared against the return of competing investment centers, as well as against that of other firms in the industry.

Net Operating Income and Operating Assets Defined

The reader may have noted that *net operating income,* rather than net income, was used in the ROI formula in computing the margin percentage. **Net operating income** is income before interest and taxes. In business jargon, it is sometimes referred to as EBIT (earnings before interest and taxes). The reader should become familiar with these terms. The reason for using net operating income in the formula is that the income figure used should be consistent with the base to which it is applied. Notice that the base in the turnover part of the formula consists of *operating assets.* Thus, to be consistent we use net operating income in computing the margin figure.

Operating assets would include cash, accounts receivable, inventory, plant and equipment, and all other assets held for productive use in the organization. Examples of assets that would not be included in the operating assets category (that is, examples of *non*operating assets) would include land being held for future use, or a factory building being rented to someone else. The operating assets base used in the formula is typically computed as the average between the beginning and the end of the year.

Plant and Equipment: Net Book Value or Gross Cost?

A major consideration in ROI computations is the dollar amount of plant and equipment that should be included in the operating assets base. To illustrate the problem involved, assume that a company reports the following amounts for plant and equipment on its balance sheet:

Plant and equipment	$3,000,000
Less accumulated depreciation . . .	900,000
Net book value	$2,100,000

What dollar amount of plant and equipment should the company include with its operating assets in computing ROI? One widely used approach is to include only the plant and equipment's *net book value*—that is, the plant's original cost less accumulated depreciation ($2,100,000 in the example above). A second approach is to ignore depreciation and include the plant's entire *gross cost* in the operating assets base ($3,000,000 in the example above). Both of these approaches are used in actual practice, even though they will obviously yield very different operating asset and ROI figures.

The following arguments can be raised for and against including only a plant's net book value as part of operating assets:

Arguments for net book value:

1. It is consistent with how plant and equipment items are reported on the balance sheet (that is, cost less accumulated depreciation to date).
2. It is consistent with the computation of net operating income, which includes depreciation as an operating expense.

Arguments against net book value:

1. It allows ROI to increase over time as assets get older and therefore have increasingly smaller net book values.
2. It discourages the replacement of old, worn-out equipment in that the purchase of new equipment can have a dramatic, adverse effect on ROI.

The following arguments can be raised for and against including a plant's entire gross cost as part of operating assets:

Arguments for gross cost:

1. It eliminates both age of equipment and method of depreciation as factors in ROI computations.
2. It allows the manager to replace old, worn-out equipment with a minimum adverse impact on ROI.

Arguments against gross cost:

1. It is not consistent with either the income statement or the balance sheet in that it ignores depreciation.
2. It involves double counting in that the original cost of an asset plus any recovery of that original cost (through the depreciation process) are both included in the operating assets base.

Managers generally view consistency as the most important of the considerations above. As a result, a majority of companies use the net book value approach in ROI computations.[3] In this book, we will also use the net book value approach unless a specific exercise or problem directs otherwise.

---

[3] For an excellent study of net book value and gross cost, and for additional discussion, see James S. Reese and William R. Cool, "Measuring Investment Center Performance," *Harvard Business Review*, May–June 1978, p. 28.

CONTROLLING THE RATE OF RETURN

When being measured by the ROI formula, a manager can improve profitability in three ways:

1. By increasing sales.
2. By reducing expenses.
3. By reducing assets.

To illustrate how the rate of return can be controlled by each of these three actions, let us assume the following data for an investment center:

Net operating income.	$ 10,000
Sales	100,000
Average operating assets	50,000

The rate of return generated by the investment center would be:

$$\frac{\text{Net operating income}}{\text{Sales}} \times \frac{\text{Sales}}{\text{Average operating assets}} = \text{ROI}$$

$$\frac{\$10,000}{\$100,000} \times \frac{\$100,000}{\$50,000} = \text{ROI}$$

$$10\% \quad \times \quad 2 \quad = 20\%$$

As we stated earlier, in order to improve the ROI figure the manager must (1) increase sales, (2) reduce expenses, or (3) reduce the operating assets.

Approach 1: Increase sales   Assume that the manager in our example is able to increase sales from $100,000 to $110,000. Assume further that either because of good cost control or because most costs in the company are fixed, the net operating income increases even more rapidly, going from $10,000 to $12,000 per period. The operating assets remain constant.

$$\frac{\$12,000}{\$110,000} \times \frac{\$110,000}{\$50,000} = \text{ROI}$$

$$10.91\% \times \quad 2.2 \quad = 24\% \text{ (as compared to 20\% above)}$$

Approach 2: Reduce expenses   Assume that the manager is able to reduce expenses by $1,000, so that net operating income increases from $10,000 to $11,000. Both sales and operating assets remain constant.

$$\frac{\$11,000}{\$100,000} \times \frac{\$100,000}{\$50,000} = \text{ROI}$$

$$11\% \quad \times \quad 2 \quad = 22\% \text{ (as compared to 20\% above)}$$

Approach 3: Reduce assets   Assume that the manager is able to reduce operating assets from $50,000 to $40,000. Sales and net operating income remain unchanged.

$$\frac{\$10,000}{\$100,000} \times \frac{\$100,000}{\$40,000} = \text{ROI}$$

$$10\% \quad \times \quad 2.5 \quad = 25\% \text{ (as compared to 20\% above)}$$

A clear understanding of these three approaches to improving the ROI figure is critical to the effective management of an investment center. We will now look at each approach in more detail.

Increase Sales

In first looking at the ROI formula, one is inclined to think that the sales figure is neutral, since it appears as the denominator in the margin computation and as the numerator in the turnover computation. We *could* cancel out the sales figure, but we don't do so for two reasons. First, this would tend to draw attention away from the fact that the rate of return is a function of *two* variables, margin and turnover. And second, it would tend to conceal the fact that a change in sales can affect *either* the margin or the turnover in an organization. To explain, a change in sales can affect the *margin* if expenses increase or decrease at a different rate than sales. For example, a company may be able to keep a tight control on its costs as its sales go up, thereby allowing the net operating income to increase more rapidly than sales and thus allowing the margin percentage to rise. Or, a company may have many fixed expenses that will remain constant as sales go up, thereby again allowing a rapid increase in the net operating income and causing the margin percentage to rise. Either (or both) of these factors could have been responsible for the increase in the margin percentage from 10 percent to 10.91 percent illustrated in approach 1 above.

Further, a change in sales can affect the *turnover* if sales either increase or decrease without a proportionate increase or decrease in the operating assets. In the first approach above, for example, sales increased from $100,000 to $110,000, but the operating assets remained unchanged. As a result, the turnover increased from 2 to 2.2 for the period.

In sum, because a change in sales can affect either the margin or the turnover in a company, such changes are particularly significant to the manager in his or her attempts to control the ROI figure.

Reduce Expenses

Often the easiest route to increased profitability and to a stronger ROI figure is to simply cut the "fat" out of an organization through a concerted effort to control expenses. When profit margins begin to be squeezed, this is generally the first line of attack by a manager. The discretionary fixed costs usually come under scrutiny first, and various programs are either curtailed or eliminated in an effort to cut costs. Firms under extreme pressures to reduce expenses have gone so far as to eliminate coffee breaks, under the reasoning that nothing could more emphatically impress the staff with the need to be cost conscious.

One of the most common ways to reduce variable expenses is to use less costly inputs of materials. Another way is to automate processes as much as possible, particularly where large volumes of units are involved.

Reduce Operating Assets

Managers have always been sensitive to the need to control sales, operating expenses, and operating margins. They have not always been equally sensitive, however, to the need to control investment in operating assets. Firms that have adopted the ROI approach to measuring managerial performance report that one of the first reactions on the part of investment center managers is to trim down their investment in operating assets. The reason, of course, is that these managers soon realize that an excessive investment in operating assets will reduce the asset turnover and hurt the rate of return. As these managers pare down their investment in operating assets, funds are released that can be used elsewhere in the organization. Consider the following actual situation:

X Company, a firm located in a western state, is a manufacturer of high-quality cast-iron pipe. A few years ago a large conglomerate acquired a controlling interest in the stock of X Company, and X Company became an investment center of the larger organization. The parent company measured the performance of the investment center managers by the ROI formula. X Company managers quickly found that their performance was below that of other investment centers within the organization. Because of their mediocre performance, X Company managers realized that they were in a poor position to compete for new investment funds. As one step in an effort to improve the rate of return, the company took a hard look at its investment in operating assets. As a result, it was able to reduce inventory alone by nearly 40 percent. This resulted in several million dollars becoming available for productive use elsewhere in the company. Within two years' time, the rate of return being generated by X Company improved dramatically. The controller of X Company, speaking at a management development conference, stated that the company had always been profitable in terms of net income to sales, so there really had been no incentive to watch the investment in operating assets prior to being put under the ROI microscope.

What approaches are open to an investment center manager in attempts to control the investment in operating assets? One approach is to pare out obsolete and redundant inventory. The computer has been extremely helpful in this regard, making perpetual inventory methods more feasible as well as facilitating the use of statistical methods of inventory control, such as those discussed in Chapter 8. Another approach is to devise various methods of speeding up the collection of receivables. For example, many firms now employ the lockbox technique by which customers in distant states remit directly to local post office boxes. The funds are received and deposited by a local banking institution in behalf of the payee firm. This can greatly speed up the collection process, thereby reducing the total investment required to carry accounts receivable. (The released funds are typically used to pay amounts due to short-term creditors.) As the level of investment in receivables is reduced, the asset turnover is increased.

The Problem of Allocated Expenses and Assets

In decentralized organizations such as General Products, Inc., it is common practice to allocate to the separate divisions the expenses incurred in operating corporate headquarters. When such allocations are made, a very thorny question arises as to whether these allocated expenses should be considered in the divisions' rate of return computations.

It can be argued on the one hand that allocated expenses should be included in rate of return computations, since they represent the value of services rendered to the divisions by central headquarters. On the other hand, it can be argued that they should not be included, since the divisional managers have no control over the incurrence of the expenses and since the "services" involved are often of questionable value, or are hard to pin down.

At the very least, *arbitrary* allocations should be avoided in rate of return computations. If arbitrary allocations are made, great danger exists of creating a bias for or against a particular division. Expense allocations should be limited to the cost of those *actual* services provided by central headquarters that the divisions would *otherwise* have had to provide for themselves. The amount of expense allocated to a division should not exceed the cost that the division would have incurred if it had provided the service for itself.

These same guidelines apply to asset allocations from central corporate headquarters to the separate divisions. Assets relating to overall corporate operations should not be included as part of the divisional operating assets in divisional ROI computations, unless there are clear and traceable benefits to the divisions from the assets involved. As before, any type of arbitrary allocations (such as allocations on the basis of sales dollars) should be avoided.

Criticisms of ROI

Although ROI is widely used in evaluating performance, it is far from being a perfect tool. The method is subject to the following criticisms:

1. ROI tends to emphasize short-run performance rather than long-run profitability. In an attempt to protect the current ROI, a manager may be motivated to reject otherwise profitable investment opportunities. (This point is discussed further in the following section.)
2. ROI is not consistent with the cash flow models used for capital expenditure analysis. (Cash flow models are discussed in Chapters 14 and 15.)
3. ROI may not be fully controllable by the division manager due to the presence of committed costs. This inability to control the ROI can make it difficult to distinguish between the performance of the manager and the performance of the division as an investment.

In an effort to overcome these problems, some companies use multiple criteria in evaluating performance rather than relying on ROI as a single measure. Other criteria used include the following:

Growth in market share.
Increases in productivity.
Dollar profits.
Receivables turnover.
Inventory turnover.
Product innovation.
Ability to expand into new and profitable areas.

It is felt that the use of multiple performance measures such as those above provide a more comprehensive picture of a manager's performance than can be obtained by relying on ROI alone.

The Concept of Residual Income

In our discussion, we have assumed that the purpose of an investment center should be to maximize the rate of return that it is able to generate on operating assets. There is another approach to measuring performance in an investment center that focuses on a concept known as *residual income*. **Residual income** is the net operating income that an investment center is able to earn *above* some minimum rate of return on its operating assets. When residual income is used to measure performance, the purpose is to maximize the total amount of residual income, *not* to maximize the overall ROI figure.

Consider the following data for two comparable divisions:

	Performance measured by—	
	Rate of return (Division A)	Residual income (Division B)
Average operating assets.	$100,000 *(a)*	$100,000
Net operating income	$ 20,000 *(b)*	$ 20,000
ROI, *(b)* ÷ *(a)*	20%	
Minimum required rate of return is assumed to be 15% (15% × $100,000) . . .		15,000
Residual income		$ 5,000

Notice that Division B has a positive residual income of $5,000. The performance of the manager of Division B is assessed according to how large or how small this residual income figure is from year to year. The larger the residual income figure, the better is the performance rating received by the division's manager.

Motivation and Residual Income

Many companies view residual income as being a better measure of performance than rate of return. They argue that the residual income approach encourages managers to make profitable investments that would be rejected by managers being measured by the ROI formula. To illustrate, assume that each of the divisions above is presented with an opportunity to make an investment of $25,000 in a new project that would generate a return of 18 percent on invested assets. The manager of Division A would probably reject this opportunity. Note from the tabulation above that his division is already earning a return of 20 percent on its assets. If he takes on a new project that provides a return of only 18 percent, then his overall ROI will be reduced, as shown below:

	Present	New project	Overall
Average operating assets *(a)* . . .	$100,000	$25,000	$125,000
Net operating income *(b)*	$ 20,000	$ 4,500*	$ 24,500
ROI, *(b)* ÷ *(a)*	20%	18%	19.6%

* $25,000 × 18% = $4,500.

Since the performance of the manager of this division is being measured according to the *maximum* rate of return that he is able to generate on invested assets, he will be unenthused about any investment opportunity that reduces his current ROI figure. He will tend to think and act along these lines, even though the opportunity he rejects might have benefited the company *as a whole*.

On the other hand, the manager of Division B will be very anxious to accept the new investment opportunity. The reason is that she isn't concerned about maximizing her rate of return. She is concerned about maximizing her residual income. Any project that provides a return greater than the minimum required 15 percent will be attractive, since it will add to the *total amount* of the residual income figure. Under these circumstances, the new investment opportunity with its 18 percent return will clearly be attractive, as shown below:

	Present	New project	Overall
Average operating assets	$100,000	$25,000	$125,000
Net operating income	$ 20,000	$ 4,500*	$ 24,500
Minimum required rate of return is again assumed to be 15% . .	15,000	3,750†	18,750
Residual income	$ 5,000	$ 750	$ 5,750

* $25,000 × 18% = $4,500.
† $25,000 × 15% = $3,750.

Thus, by accepting the new investment project, the manager of Division B will increase her division's overall residual income figure and thereby show an improved performance as a manager. The fact that her division's overall ROI might be lower as a result of accepting the project is immaterial, since performance is being evaluated by residual income, not ROI. The well-being of both the manager and the company as a whole will be maximized by accepting all investment opportunities down to the 15 percent cutoff rate.

Divisional Comparison and Residual Income

The residual income approach has one major disadvantage. It can't be used to compare the performance of divisions of different sizes, since by its very nature it creates a bias in favor of larger divisions. That is, one would expect larger divisions to have more residual income than smaller divisions, not necessarily because they are better managed but simply because of the bigger numbers involved.

As an example, consider the following residual income computations for Division A and Division B:

	Divisions	
	A	B
Average operating assets *(a)*	$1,000,000	$250,000
Net operating income	$ 120,000	$ 40,000
Minimum required return: 10% × *(a)* . . .	100,000	25,000
Residual income	$ 20,000	$ 15,000

Observe that Division A has slightly more residual income than Division B, but that Division A has $1,000,000 in operating assets as compared to only $250,000 in operating assets for Division B. Thus, Division A's greater residual income is probably more a result of its size than the quality of its management. In fact, it appears that the smaller division is better managed, since it has been able to generate nearly as much residual income with only one fourth as much in operating assets to work with.

TRANSFER PRICING

Special problems arise in applying the rate of return or residual income approaches to performance evaluation whenever segments of a company do business with each other. The problems revolve around the question of what transfer price to charge between the segments. A **transfer price** can be defined as the price charged when one segment of a company provides goods or services to another segment of the company.

The Need for Transfer Prices

Assume that a vertically integrated firm has three divisions. The three divisions are:

Mining Division.

Processing Division.

Manufacturing Division.

The Mining Division mines raw materials that are transferred to the Processing Division. After processing, the Processing Division transfers the processed materials to the Manufacturing Division. The Manufacturing Division then includes the processed materials as part of its finished product.

In this example, we have two transfers of goods between divisions within the same company. What price should control these transfers? Should the price be set so as to include some ''profit'' element to the selling division? Should it be set so as to include only the accumulated costs to that point? Or should it be set at yet another figure? The choice of a transfer price can be complicated by the fact that each division may be supplying portions of its output to outside customers, as well as to sister divisions. Another complication is that the price charged by one division becomes a cost to the other division, and the higher this cost, the lower will be the purchasing division's rate of return. Thus, the purchasing division would like the transfer price to be low, whereas the selling division would like it to be high, perhaps even charging the same ''market'' price internally as it charges to outside customers.

As the reader may guess, the problem of what transfer price to set between segments of a company has no easy solution and often leads to protracted and heated disputes between investment center managers. Yet some transfer price *must* be set if data are to be available for performance evaluation of the various parts or divisions of a company. In practice, three general approaches are used in setting transfer prices:

1.   Set transfer prices at cost using:
     a.   Variable cost.
     b.   Full (absorption) cost.
2.   Set transfer prices at the market price.
3.   Set transfer prices at a negotiated market price.

In the following sections, we consider each of these approaches to the transfer pricing problem.

Transfer Prices at Cost

Many firms make transfers between divisions on a basis of the accumulated cost of the goods being transferred, thus ignoring any profit element to the selling division. A transfer price computed in this way might be based only on the variable costs involved, or fixed costs might also be considered and the transfer price thus based on full (absorption) costs accumulated to the point of transfer. Although the cost approach to setting transfer prices is relatively simple to apply, it has some major defects. These defects can be brought out by the following illustration:

> Assume that a multidivisional company has a Relay Division that manufactures an electrical relay widely used as a component part by various governmental contractors. The relay requires $12 in variable costs to manufacture and sells for $20. Each relay requires one direct labor-hour to complete, and the division has a capacity of 50,000 relays per year.
>
> The company also has a Motor Division. This division has developed a new motor requiring an electrical relay, but this relay is different from the one presently being manufactured by the Relay Division. In order to acquire the needed relay, the Motor Division has two alternatives:
>
> 1. The new relay can be purchased from an outside supplier at a price of $15 per relay, based on an order of 50,000 relays per year.
> 2. The new relay can be manufactured by the company's Relay Division. This would require that the Relay Division give up its present busines, since manufacture of the new relay would require all of its capacity. One direct labor-hour would be required to produce each relay (the same time as that required by the old relay). Variable manufacturing costs would total $10 per relay.
>
> In addition to the relay, each motor would require $25 in other variable cost inputs. The motors would sell for $60 each.

Should the Relay Division give up its present relay business and start producing the new relays for the Motor Division, or should it continue its present business and let the Motor Division purchase the new relays from the outside supplier? Let us assume first that the Motor Division decides to purchase the new relays from the outside supplier at $15 each, thereby permitting the Relay Division to continue to produce and sell the old relay. Partial income statements are given at the top of Exhibit 11–6 to show the effects of this decision on each division and on the company as a whole. Notice from the exhibit (alternative 1) that each division will have a positive contribution margin, and that the company as a whole will have a contribution margin of $1,400,000 for the year if this alternative is accepted.

Let us assume second that the Motor Division purchases the new relays internally from the Relay Division at a transfer price of $10 per relay (the Relay Division's variable costs per unit). This would require that the Relay Division give up its present outside business. On the surface this would seem to be a good decision, since the variable costs to the Relay Division would be only $10 for the new relay as compared to $12 for the old relay, and since the Motor Division would otherwise have to purchase the new relays from the outside supplier at $15 each. But this illusion quickly vanishes when we look at the data at the bottom of Exhibit 11–6 (alternative 2). Notice that this alternative would reduce the contribution margin for the company as a whole by $150,000 per year.

EXHIBIT 11–6

Effects of pricing transfers between divisions at cost

Alternative 1: The Motor Division purchases the new relays from the outside supplier at $15 each; the Relay Division continues to produce and sell the old relays.

	50,000 units per year		
	Relay Division	Motor Division	Total company
Sales (at $20 per old relay and $60 per motor, respectively)	$1,000,000	$3,000,000	$4,000,000
Less variable expenses (at $12 per old relay and $40* per motor, respectively) . . .	600,000	2,000,000	2,600,000
Contribution margin	$ 400,000	$1,000,000	$1,400,000

Alternative 2: The Motor Division purchases the new relays from the Relay Division at an internal transfer price of $10 per relay (the Relay Division's variable cost of producing the new relay). This requires that the Relay Division give up its present outside business.

	Relay Division	Motor Division	Total company
Sales (at $10 per new relay and $60 per motor, respectively)	$ 500,000	$3,000,000	$3,000,000‡
Less variable expenses (at $10 per new relay and $35† per motor, respectively) . . .	500,000	1,750,000	1,750,000‡
Contribution margin	$ –0–	$1,250,000	$1,250,000
Decrease in contribution margin for the company as a whole if alternative 2 is accepted			$ 150,000

* $15 outside supplier's cost per new relay + Other variable costs of $25 per motor = $40 per motor.
† $10 internal transfer price per new relay + Other variable costs of $25 per motor = $35 per motor.
‡ The $500,000 in intracompany sales has been eliminated.

Herein lies one of the defects of the cost approach to setting transfer prices: Cost-based transfer prices can lead to dysfunctional decisions in a company because this approach has no built-in mechanism for telling the manager when transfers should or should not be made between divisions. In the case at hand, transfers should *not* be made; the Relay Division should go on selling the old relay to the governmental contractors, and the Motor Division should buy the new relay from the outside supplier. Although this is obvious after seeing the income statement data in Exhibit 11–6, such matters can be obscured when dealing with multiproduct divisions. Thus, as a result of using cost as a transfer price, profits for the company as a whole may be adversely affected and the manager may never know about it.

Exhibit 11–6 also illustrates another defect associated with cost-based transfer prices: The only division that will show any profits is the one that makes the final sale to an outside party. Other divisions, such as the Relay Division in the bottom portion of Exhibit 11–6, will show no profits for their efforts; thus, evaluation by the ROI formula or by the residual income approach will not be possible.

Another serious criticism of cost-based transfer prices lies in their general inability to provide incentive for control of costs. If the costs of one division are simply passed on to the next, then there is little incentive for anyone to control costs. The final selling division is simply burdened with the accumulated waste and inefficiency of intermediate processors and will be penalized with a rate of return that is deficient in comparison to that of competitors. Experience has shown that unless costs are subject to some type of competitive pressures at transfer points, waste and inefficiency almost invariably develop.

Despite these shortcomings, cost-based transfer prices are in fairly common use. Advocates argue that they are easily understood and highly convenient to use. If transfer prices are to be based on cost, then the costs should be standard costs rather than actual costs. This will at least avoid the passing on of inefficiency from one division to another.

A General Formula for Computing Transfer Prices

A general formula exists that can be used by the manager as a starting point in computing the appropriate transfer price between divisions or segments in a multidivisional company.[4] The formula is that *the transfer price should be equal to the unit variable costs of the good being transferred, plus the contribution margin per unit that is lost to the selling division as a result of giving up outside sales.* The formula can be expressed as:

Transfer price = Variable costs per unit + Lost contribution margin per unit on outside sales

Applying this formula to the data in the preceding section, the proper transfer price for the Relay Division to charge for the new relay would be:

Transfer price = $10 (the variable costs of the new relay) + $8 (the contribution margin per unit lost to the Relay Division as a result of giving up outside relay sales: $20 selling price − $12 variable costs = $8 lost contribution margin on the old relays)

Transfer price = $18 per unit

Upon seeing this transfer price, it becomes immediately obvious to management that no transfers should be made between the two divisions, since the Motor Division can buy its relays from an outside supplier at only $15 each. Thus, the transfer price enables management to reach the correct decision and to avoid any adverse effect on profits.

---

[4] For background discussion, see Ralph L. Benke, Jr., and James Don Edwards, ''Transfer Pricing: Techniques and Uses,'' *Management Accounting* 61, no. 12 (June 1980), pp. 44–46.

Two additional points should be noted before going on. First, *the price set by the transfer pricing formula always represents a lower limit for a transfer price since the selling division must receive at least the amount shown by the formula in order to be as well off as if it only sold to outside customers.* Under certain conditions (discussed later), the price can be more than the amount shown by the formula, but it can't be less or the selling division and the company as a whole will suffer. Second, the transfer price computed by using the formula is a price based on competitive market conditions. The remainder of our discussion will focus on the setting of market-based transfer prices.

Transfers at Market Price: General Considerations

Reasons:

① Some form of competitive **market price** (that is, the price charged for an item on the open market) is generally regarded as the best approach to the transfer pricing problem. The reason is that the use of market prices dovetails well with the profit center concept and makes profit-based performance evaluation feasible at many levels of an organization. By using market prices to control transfers, *all* divisions or segments are able to show profits for their efforts—not just the final division in the chain of transfers. The

② market price approach also helps the manager to decide when transfers should be made, as we saw earlier, and tends to lead to the best decisions involving transfer questions that may arise on a day-to-day basis.

The market price approach is designed for use in highly decentralized organizations. By this we mean that it is used in those organizations where divisional managers have enough autonomy in decision making so that the various divisions can be viewed as being-virtually independent businesses with independent profit responsibility. The idea in using market prices to control transfers is to create the competitive market conditions that would exist if the various divisions were *indeed* separate firms and engaged in arm's-length, open-market bargaining. To the extent that the resulting transfer prices reflect actual market conditions, divisional operating results provide an excellent basis for evaluating managerial performance.

The National Association of Accountants describes other advantages and the overall operation of the market price approach as follows:

> Internal procurement is expected where the company's products and services are superior or equal in design, quality, performance, and price, and when acceptable delivery schedules can be met. So long as these conditions are met, the receiving unit suffers no loss and the supplier unit's profit accrues to the company. Often the receiving division gains advantages such as better control over quality, assurance of continued supply, and prompt delivery.[5]

---

[5] National Association of Accountants, *Research Series No. 30,* ''Accounting for Intra-Company Transfers'' (New York: National Association of Accountants, June 1956), pp. 13–14.

In addition to the formula given earlier, there are certain guidelines that should be followed when using market prices to control transfers between divisions. These guidelines are:

1. The buying division must purchase internally so long as the selling division meets all bona fide outside prices and wants to sell internally.
2. If the selling division does not meet all bona fide outside prices, then the buying division is free to purchase outside.
3. The selling division must be free to reject internal business if it prefers to sell outside.[6]
4. An impartial board must be established to help settle disagreements between divisions over transfer prices.

Transfers at Market Price: Well-Defined Intermediate Market

Not all companies or divisions face the same market conditions. Sometimes the only customer a division has for its output is a sister division. In other situations, an **intermediate market** may exist for part or all of a division's output. By intermediate market, we mean that a market exists in which an item can be sold *immediately* and *in its present form* to outside customers, if desired, rather than being transferred to another division for use in its manufacturing process. Thus, if an intermediate market exists, a division will have a choice between selling its products to outside customers on the intermediate market or selling them to other divisions within the company. In this section, we consider transfer pricing in those situations where intermediate markets are strong and well defined.

Let us assume that Division A of International Company has a product that can be sold either to Division B or to outside customers in an intermediate market. The cost and revenue structures of the two divisions are given below:

Division A		Division B	
Intermediate selling price if sold outside	$25	Final market price outside	$100
Variable costs	15	Transfer price from Division A (or outside purchase price)	25
		Variable costs added in Division B	40

What transfer price should control transfers between the two divisions? In this case, the answer is easy; the transfer price should be $25—the price that Division A can get by selling in the intermediate market and the price that Division B would otherwise have to pay to purchase the desired

---

[6] Ibid., p. 14. Outside products may provide the selling division with a greater return (as in the case of the Relay Division in our earlier example).

EXHIBIT 11–7

Transfers at market price: Well-defined intermediate market

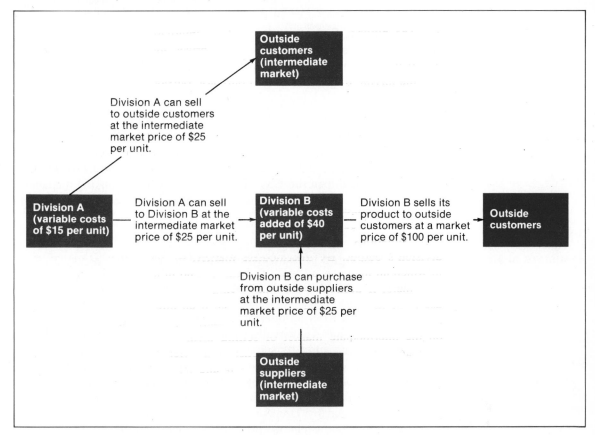

goods from an outside supplier in the intermediate market. This price can also be obtained by applying the formula developed earlier:

$$\text{Transfer price} = \text{Variable costs per unit} + \text{Lost contribution margin per unit on outside sales}$$

$$\text{Transfer price} = \$15 + (\$25 - \$15 = \$10)$$
$$\text{Transfer price} = \$25$$

The choices facing the two divisions are shown graphically in Exhibit 11–7.

So long as Division A receives a transfer price of $25 per unit from Division B, it will be willing to sell all of its output internally. In selling to Division B, Division A will be just as well off as if it had sold its product outside at the $25 price. In like manner, so long as the price charged by outside suppliers is not less than $25 per unit, Division B will be willing to pay that price to Division A. The $25 per unit intermediate market price, therefore, serves as an acceptable transfer price between the two divisions. The results of transfers at this price can be summarized as follows:

| | Divisions | | Total |
	A	B	company
Sales price per unit	$25	$100	$100
Variable costs added per unit . . .	15	40	55
Transfer cost per unit	—	25	—
Contribution margin per unit. . . .	$10	$ 35	$ 45

The contribution margin realized for the entire company is $45 per unit. By using the $25 intermediate market price to control intracompany transfers, the firm is able to show that a portion of this margin accrues from the efforts of Division A and that a portion accrues from the efforts of Division B. These data will then serve as an excellent basis for evaluating managerial performance in the divisions, using the rate of return or residual income approaches.

Transfers at Market Price: Price Changes in the Intermediate Market

In the preceding section, we assumed that there was complete price agreement in the intermediate market, and therefore that Division B could purchase the needed goods from an outside supplier at the same $25 price as being charged by Division A. In reality, complete price agreement often doesn't exist, or it may be upset by some suppliers deciding to cut their prices for various reasons. Returning to the example in the preceding section, let us assume that an outside supplier has offered to supply the goods to Division B for only $20 per unit, rather than at the normal $25 intermediate market price being charged by Division A. Should Division B accept this offer, or should Division A cut its price to $20 in order to get Division B's business? The answer will depend on whether Division A (the selling division) is operating at full or at partial capacity.

Selling division at full capacity   If Division A (the selling division) is operating at capacity, then it will have to give up outside sales in order to sell to Division B. Under these circumstances, the transfer price will be computed in the same way as we computed it earlier:

Transfer price = Variable costs per unit + Lost contribution margin per unit on outside sales

Transfer price = $15 + ($25 outside selling price − $15 variable costs = $10 lost contribution margin per unit)

Transfer price = $25

Recall that the price set by the formula always represents a *lower limit* for a transfer price, since the selling division must receive at least the amount shown by the formula in order to be as well off as if it sold only to outside customers. Therefore, Division A should not cut its price to $20 in order to sell to Division B. If Division A cuts its price, it will lose $5 per unit in contribution margin, and both it and the company as a whole will be worse off.

In short, whenever the selling division must give up outside sales in order to sell internally, it has an opportunity cost that must be considered in setting the transfer price. As shown by the formula, this opportunity cost is the contribution margin that will be lost as a result of giving up outside sales. Unless the transfer price can be set high enough to cover this opportunity cost, along with the variable costs associated with the sale, then no transfers should be made.

Selling division with idle capacity   If the selling division has idle capacity, then a different situation exists. Under these conditions, the selling division's opportunity cost *may* be zero (depending on what alternative uses it has for its idle capacity). Even if the opportunity cost is zero, many managers would argue that the transfer price should still be based on prevailing market prices, to the extent that these prices can be determined accurately and fairly. Other managers would argue that idle capacity combined with an opportunity cost of zero, or near zero, calls for a negotiation of the transfer price downward from prevailing market rates, so that both the buyer and the seller can profit from the intracompany business.

Under idle capacity conditions, so long as the selling division can receive a price greater than its variable costs (at least in the short run), all parties will benefit by keeping business inside the company rather than having the buying division go outside. The accuracy of this statement can be shown by returning to the example in the preceding section. Assume again that an outside supplier offers to sell the needed goods to Division B at $20 per unit. In this case, however, we will assume that Division A has enough idle capacity to supply all of Division B's needs, with no prospects for additional outside sales at the current $25 intermediate market price. Using our formula, the transfer price between Divisions A and B would be:

Transfer price = Variable costs per unit + Lost contribution margin per unit on outside sales

Transfer price = $15 + –0–
Transfer price = $15

As stated before, the $15 figure represents a lower limit for a transfer price. Actually, the transfer price can be anywhere between this figure and the $20 price being quoted to Division B from the outside. In this situation, therefore, we have a transfer price *range* in which to operate, as shown below:

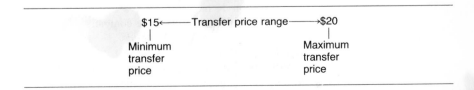

If Division A (the selling division) is hesitant to reduce its price, should it be required to at least meet the $20 figure to supply Division B's needs? The answer is no. The guidelines given earlier indicate that the selling division is not required to sell internally. Rather than accept a $20 price for its goods, Division A may prefer to let its capacity remain idle and search for other, more profitable products.

If Division A decides not to reduce its price to $20 to meet outside competition, should Division B be forced to continue to pay $25 and to buy internally? The answer again is no. The guidelines given earlier state that if the selling division is not willing to meet all bona fide outside prices, then the buying division is free to go outside to get the best price it can. However, if the selling division has idle capacity and the buying division purchases from an outside supplier, then **suboptimization**[7] will result for the selling division, possibly for the buying division, and certainly for the company as a whole. In our example, if Division A refuses to meet the $20 price, then *both it and the company as a whole will lose $5 per unit in potential contribution margin ($20 − $15 = $5).* In short, where idle capacity exists, every effort should be made to negotiate a price acceptable to both the buyer and the seller that will keep business within the company as a whole.

Transfers at Negotiated Market Price

There are some situations where a transfer price below the intermediate market price can be justified. For example, selling and administrative expenses may be less when intracompany sales are involved, or the volume of units may be large enough to justify quantity discounts. In addition, we have already seen that a price below the prevailing market price may be justified when the selling division has idle capacity. Situations such as these can probably be served best by some type of **negotiated market price.** A negotiated market price is one agreed upon between the buying and selling divisions that reflects unusual or mitigating circumstances.

Possibly the widest use of negotiated market prices is in those situations where no intermediate market prices are available. For example, one division may require an item that is not available from any outside source and therefore must be produced internally. Under these circumstances, the buying division must negotiate with another division in the company and agree to a transfer price that is attractive enough to the other division to cause it to take on the new business. To provide an example of how a transfer price would be set in such a situation, consider the following data:

> Division X has developed a new product that requires a custom-made fitting. Another division in the company, Division Y, has both the experience

---

[7] By *suboptimization,* we mean that overall profitability will be less than an organization is capable of earning.

and the equipment necessary to produce the fitting. Division X has approached Division Y for a quoted unit price based on the production of 5,000 fittings per year.

Division Y has determined that the fitting would require variable costs of $8 per unit. However, in order to have time to produce the fitting, Division Y would have to reduce production of a different product, product A, by 3,500 units per year. Product A sells for $45 per unit and has variable costs of $25 per unit. What transfer price should Division Y quote to Division X for the new fittings? Employing our formula, we get:

$$\text{Transfer price} = \text{Variable costs per unit} + \text{Lost contribution margin per unit on outside sales}$$

The lost contribution margin per unit would be:

Selling price of product A	$	45
Variable costs of product A		25
Contribution margin of product A . . .		20
Unit sales of product A given up . . .		× 3,500
Total lost contribution margin. . . .		$70,000

$$\frac{\$70,000 \text{ lost contribution margin on product A}}{5,000 \text{ fittings to be manufactured for Division X}} = \frac{\$14 \text{ lost contribution}}{\text{margin per fitting}}$$

Transfer price = $8 variable costs + $14 lost contribution margin
Transfer price = $22 per fitting

Thus, the transfer price quoted by Division Y should not be less than $22 per fitting. Division Y might quote a higher price if it wants to increase its overall profits (at the expense of Division X), but it should not quote less than $22, or the profits of the company as a whole will suffer. If Division X is not happy with the $22 price, it can get a quote from an outside manufacturer for the fitting.

If Division Y in our example has idle capacity, then the appropriate transfer price is less clear. The lower limit for a transfer price would be the $8 variable costs, as discussed earlier. However, no division wants to simply recover its costs, so the actual transfer price would undoubtedly be greater than $8, according to what could be negotiated between the two divisional managers. In situations such as this, the selling division will often add some "target" markup figure to its costs in quoting a transfer price to the buying division.

Divisional Autonomy and Suboptimization

A question often arises as to how much autonomy should be granted to divisions in setting their own transfer prices and in making decisions concerning whether to sell internally or to sell outside. Should the divisional heads have complete authority to make these decisions, or should top corporate management step in if it appears that a decision is about to be made that would result in suboptimization? For example, if idle capacity exists in the selling division and divisional managers are unable to agree on a transfer price, should top corporate management step in and *force* settlement of the dispute?

Efforts should always be made, of course, to bring disputing managers together. But the almost unanimous feeling among top corporate executives is that divisional heads should not be forced into an agreement over a transfer price. That is, if a particular divisional head flatly refuses to change his or her position in a dispute, *then this decision should be respected* even if it results in suboptimization. This is simply the price that is paid for the concept of divisional autonomy. If top corporate management steps in and forces the decisions in difficult situations, then the concepts that we have been developing in this chapter largely evaporate and the company simply becomes a centralized operation with decentralization of only minor decisions and responsibilities. In short, if a division is to be viewed as an autonomous unit with independent profit responsibility, then it must have control over its own destiny—even to the extent of having the right to make bad decisions.

We should note, however, that if a division consistently makes bad decisions, the results will soon have an impact on its rate of return and the divisional manager may find himself having to defend the division's performance. Even so, his right to get himself into an embarrassing situation must be respected if the divisional concept is to operate successfully. The overwhelming experience of multidivisional companies is that divisional autonomy and independent profit responsibility lead to much greater success and profitability than do closely controlled, centrally administered operations. Part of the price of this success and profitability is an occasional situation of suboptimization due to pettiness, bickering, or just plain managerial stubbornness.

SUMMARY

Responsibility accounting centers on the notion that any point within an organization having control over cost or revenue is a responsibility center. The way in which the various responsibility centers discharge their control over cost or revenue is communicated upward in an organization, from lower levels of responsibility to higher levels of responsibility, through a system of integrated performance reports.

Those responsibility centers having control over cost are known as cost centers; those having control over both cost and revenue are known as profit centers; and those having control over cost, revenue, and investment funds are known as investment centers. The ROI formula is widely regarded as a method of evaluating performance in an investment center because it summarizes into one figure many aspects of an investment center manager's responsibilities. As an alternative to the ROI formula, some companies use residual income as a measure of investment center performance. These companies argue that the residual income approach encourages profitable investment in many situations where the ROI approach might discourage investment.

Transfer pricing relates to the price to be charged in a transfer of goods or an exchange of services between two units (such as divisions) within an organization. A transfer price can be based on the cost of the goods being transferred, on the intermediate market price of the goods being transferred, or on a price negotiated between the buying and selling divisions. The predominant feeling is that the best transfer price is some version of market price—either intermediate or negotiated—to the extent that such a price exists or can be determined for the good or service involved. The use of market price or negotiated market price in transfers between units facilitates performance evaluation by permitting both the buyer and the seller to be treated as independent, autonomous units.

REVIEW PROBLEM ON TRANSFER PRICING

Situation A

Collyer Products, Inc., has a Valve Division that manufactures and sells a standard valve as follows:

Capacity in units	100,000
Selling price to outside customers on the intermediate market	$30
Variable costs per unit	16
Fixed costs per unit (based on capacity)	9

The company has a Pump Division that could use this valve in the manufacture of one of its pumps. The Pump Division is currently purchasing 10,000 valves per year from an overseas supplier at a cost of $29 per valve.

Required: 1. Assume that the Valve Division has ample idle capacity to handle all of the Pump Division's needs. What should be the transfer price between the two divisions?

2. Assume that the Valve Division is selling all that it can produce to outside customers on the intermediate market. What should be the transfer price between the two divisions? At this price, will any transfers be made?

3. Assume again that the Valve Division is selling all that it can produce to outside customers on the intermediate market. Also assume that $3 in variable expenses can be avoided on intracompany sales, due to reduced selling costs. What should be the transfer price between the two divisions?

Solution—Situation A: 1. Since the Valve Division has idle capacity, it is not necessary to give up any outside sales in order to take on the Pump Division's business. Therefore, applying the transfer pricing formula, we get:

Transfer price = Variable costs per unit + Lost contribution margin per
                                              unit on outside sales

Transfer price = $16 + $ –0–
Transfer price = $16

However, a transfer price of $16 represents a minimum price to
cover the Valve Division's variable costs. The actual transfer price
would undoubtedly fall somewhere between this amount and the $29
that the Pump Division is currently paying for its valves. Thus, we
have a transfer price range in this case of from $16 to $29 per unit,
depending on negotiations between the two divisions.

2. Since the Valve Division is selling all that it can produce on the interme-
    diate market, it would have to give up some of these outside sales in
    order to take on the Pump Division's business. Applying the transfer
    pricing formula, we get:

Transfer price = Variable costs per unit + Lost contribution margin per
                                              unit on outside sales

Transfer price = $16 + $14*
Transfer price = $30

  * $30 selling price – $16 variable costs = $14 contribution margin per unit.

Since the Pump Division can purchase valves from an outside supplier
at only $29 per unit, no transfers will be made between the two divisions.

3. Applying the transfer pricing formula, we get:

Transfer price = Variable costs per unit + Lost contribution margin per
                                              unit on outside sales

Transfer price = $13* + $14
Transfer price = $27

  * $16 variable expenses – $3 variable expenses avoided = $13.

In this case, we again have a transfer price range; it is between $27
(the lower limit) and $29 (the Pump Division's outside price) per unit.

Situation B

Refer to the original data in situation A above. Assume that the Pump
Division needs 20,000 special valves per year that are to be supplied by
the Valve Division. The Valve Division's variable costs to manufacture
and ship the special valve would be $20 per unit. To produce these special
valves, the Valve Division would have to give up one half of its production
of the regular valves (that is, cut its production of the regular valves from
100,000 units per year to 50,000 units per year). You can assume that the
Valve Division is selling all of the regular valves that it can produce to
outside customers on the intermediate market.

Required: If the Valve Division decides to produce the special valves for the Pump Division, what transfer price should it charge per valve?

Solution—Situation B: In order to produce the 20,000 special valves, the Valve Division will have to give up sales of 50,000 regular valves to outside customers. The lost contribution margin on the 50,000 regular valves will be:

$$50,000 \text{ valves} \times \$14 \text{ per unit} = \$700,000$$

Spreading this lost contribution margin over the 20,000 special valves, we get:

$$\frac{\$700,000 \text{ lost contribution margin}}{20,000 \text{ special valves}} = \$35 \text{ per unit}$$

Using this amount in the transfer pricing formula, we get the following transfer price per unit on the special valves:

Transfer price = Variable costs per unit + Lost contribution margin per unit on outside sales

Transfer price = $20 + $35
Transfer price = $55

Thus, the Valve Division must charge a transfer price of $55 per unit on the special valves in order to be as well off as if it just continued to manufacture and sell the regular valves on the intermediate market. If the Valve Division wishes to increase its profits, it could charge more than $55 per valve, but it must charge at least $55 in order to maintain its present level of profits.

KEY TERMS FOR REVIEW

Cost center A responsibility center that has control over the incurrence of cost but has no control over the generation of revenue or the use of investment funds.

Decentralization The delegation of decision-making authority throughout an organization by allowing managers at various operating levels to make key decisions relating to their areas of responsibility.

Decentralized organization An organization in which decision making is not confined to a few top executives but rather is spread throughout the organization.

Intermediate market A market in which an item can be sold immediately and in its present form to outside customers rather than just being transferred to another division for use in its manufacturing process.

Investment center A responsibility center that has control over the incurrence of cost and over the generating of revenue and that also has control over the use of investment funds.

Margin A percentage figure computed by dividing net operating income by sales.

Market price The price being charged for an item on the open (intermediate) market.

Negotiated market price A transfer price agreed upon between buying and selling divisions that reflects unusual or mitigating circumstances.

Net operating income The income of an organization before interest and income taxes have been deducted.

Operating assets Cash, accounts receivable, inventory, plant and equipment, and all other assets held for productive use in an organization.

Profit center A responsibility center that has control over the incurrence of cost and the generating of revenue but has no control over the use of investment funds.

Residual income The net operating income that an investment center is able to earn above some minimum rate of return on its operating assets.

Responsibility center Any point in an organization that has control over the incurrence of cost, the generating of revenue, or the use of investment funds.

Return on investment (ROI) A measure of profitability in an organization that is computed by multiplying the margin by the turnover.

Suboptimization An overall level of profitability that is less than an organization is capable of earning.

Transfer price The price charged when one division or segment provides goods or services to another division or segment of an organization.

Turnover An operating ratio computed by dividing sales by the average operating assets.

QUESTIONS

11–1. Describe the general flow of information in a responsibility accounting system.

11–2. What is meant by the term *responsibility center?* Could a responsibility center be a person as well as a department, and so on? Does the concept of a responsibility center apply to nonmanufacturing as well as to manufacturing activities?

11–3. What is meant by the term *decentralization?*

11–4. What benefits are felt to result from decentralization in an organization?

11–5. Distinguish between a cost center, a profit center, and an investment center.

11–6. How is performance in a cost center generally measured? Performance in a profit center? Performance in an investment center?

11–7. What is meant by the terms *margin* and *turnover?*

11–8. In what way is the ROI formula a more exacting measure of performance than the ratio of net income to sales?

11–9. When the ROI formula is being used to measure performance, what three approaches to improving the overall profitability are open to the manager?

11–10. The sales figure could be canceled out in the ROI formula, leaving simply net operating income over operating assets. Since this abbreviated formula would yield the same ROI figure, why leave sales in?

11–11. A student once commented to the author, ''It simply is not possible for a decrease in operating assets to result in an increase in profitability. The way to increase profits is to *increase* the operating assets.'' Discuss.

11–12. X Company has high fixed expenses and is currently operating somewhat above the break-even point. From this point on, will percentage increases in net income tend to be greater than, about equal to, or less than percentage increases in total sales? Why? (Ignore income taxes.)

11–13. What is meant by residual income?

11–14. In what way can ROI lead to dysfunctional decisions on the part of the investment center manager? How does the residual income approach overcome this problem?

11–15. Division A has operating assets of $100,000, and Division B has operating assets of $1,000,000. Can residual income be used to compare performance in the two divisions? Explain.

11–16. What is meant by the term *transfer price,* and why are transfer pricing systems needed?

11–17. Why are cost-based transfer prices in widespread use? What are the disadvantages of cost-based transfer prices?

11–18. If a market price for a product can be determined, why is it generally considered to be the best transfer price?

11–19. Under what circumstances might a negotiated market price be a better approach to pricing transfers between divisions than the actual market price?

11–20. In what ways can suboptimization result if divisional managers are given full autonomy in setting, accepting, and rejecting transfer prices?

EXERCISES

E11–1. Selected operating data for two divisions of Regal Company are given below:

	Divisions	
	Southern	Northern
Sales	$4,000,000	$7,000,000
Average operating assets	2,000,000	2,000,000
Net operating income	360,000	420,000
Property, plant, and equipment (net) . .	950,000	800,000

Required:
1. Compute the rate of return for each division, using the ROI formula.
2. So far as you can tell from the data, which divisional manager seems to be doing the better job? Why?

E11–2. Provide the missing data in the following tabulation:

	Divisions		
	A	B	C
Sales	$?	$11,500,000	$?
Net operating income	?	920,000	210,000
Average operating assets	800,000	?	?
Margin	4%	?	7%
Turnover	5	?	?
Return on investment (ROI) . . .	?	20%	14%

E11–3. Holiday Products, Inc., has two divisions, A and B. Selected data on the two divisions follow:

	Divisions	
	A	**B**
Sales	$3,000,000	$9,000,000
Net operating income . . .	210,000	720,000
Average operating assets . .	1,000,000	4,000,000

Required: 1. Compute the return on investment (ROI) for each division. Where necessary, carry computations to two decimal places.

2. Assume that the company evaluates performance by use of residual income and that the minimum required return for any division is 15 percent. Compute the residual income for each division.

3. Is Division B's greater amount of residual income an indication that it is better managed? Explain.

E11–4. Sako Company's Audio Division produces a speaker that is widely used by manufacturers of various audio products. Sales and cost data on the speaker follow:

Selling price per unit on the intermediate market . .	$60
Variable costs per unit	42
Fixed costs per unit (based on capacity)	8
Capacity in units	25,000

Sako Company has just organized a Hi-Fi Division that could use this speaker in one of its products. The Hi-Fi Division will need 5,000 speakers per year. It has received a quote of $60 per speaker from another manufacturer, less a 5 percent quantity discount.

Required: 1. Assume that the Audio Division is now selling only 20,000 speakers per year to outside customers on the intermediate market. If it begins to sell to the Hi-Fi Division and if each division is to be treated as an independent investment center, what transfer price would you recommend? Why?

2. Assume that the Audio Division is selling all of the speakers it can produce to outside customers on the intermediate market. Would this change the recommended transfer price? Explain.

E11–5. Listed below are three charges found on the monthly report of a division that manufactures and sells products primarily to outside customers. Divisional performance is evaluated by the use of ROI. You are to state which, if any, of the following charges are consistent with the responsibility accounting concept. Support each answer with a brief explanation.

1. A charge (at 10 percent of division sales) for the cost of operating general corporate headquarters.

2. A charge for goods purchased from another division. The charge is based on the competitive market price for the goods.
3. A charge for the use of the corporate computer facility. The charge is determined by taking actual annual computer department costs and allocating an amount to each division based on the ratio of its use to total corporate use.

(CMA, Adapted)

E11–6.   Supply the missing data in the tabulation below:

	Company		
	A	B	C
Sales	$9,000,000	$7,000,000	$4,500,000
Net operating income	?	280,000	?
Average operating assets	3,000,000	?	1,800,000
Return on investment (ROI)	18%	14%	?
Minimum required rate of return:			
Percentage	16%	?	15%
Dollar amount	?	320,000	?
Residual income	?	?	90,000

E11–7.   Division A manufactures electronic circuit boards. The boards can be sold either to Division B or to outside customers. During 19x5, the following activity occurred in Division A:

Selling price per circuit board	$125
Production cost per circuit board . . .	90
Number of circuit boards:	
Produced during the year	20,000
Sold to outside customers	16,000
Sold to Division B	4,000

Sales to Division B were at the same price as sales to outside customers. The circuit boards purchased by Division B were used in an electronic calculator manufactured by that division (one board per calculator). Division B incurred $100 in additional cost per calculator and then sold the calculators for $300 each.

Required: 1. Prepare income statements for 19x5 for Division A, Division B, and the company as a whole.

2. Assume that Division A's manufacturing capacity is 20,000 circuit boards. In 19x6, Division B wants to purchase 5,000 circuit boards from Division A, rather than only 4,000 as in 19x5. (Circuit boards of this type are not available from outside sources.) Should Division A sell the 1,000 additional circuit boards to Division B or continue to sell them to outside customers? Explain why this would or would not make any difference from the point of view of the company as a whole.

E11–8.   In each of the cases below, assume that Division X has a product that can be sold either to outside customers on an intermediate market or to Division Y for use in its production process.

	Case	
	A	**B**
Division X:		
Capacity in units	200,000	200,000
Number of units being sold on		
the intermediate market	200,000	160,000
Selling price per unit on the		
intermediate market.	$90	$75
Variable costs per unit	70	60
Fixed costs per unit (based on capacity) . .	13	8
Division Y:		
Number of units needed for production . .	40,000	40,000
Purchase price per unit now being paid		
to an outside supplier	$86	$74

Required: 1.   Refer to the data in case A above. Assume in this case that $3 per unit in variable costs can be avoided on intracompany sales.

    a.   Using the transfer pricing formula, determine the transfer price that Division X should charge for any sales to Division Y.

    b.   Will any transfers be made between the two divisions? Explain.

  2.   Refer to the data in case B above. Within what range should the transfer price be set for any sales between the two divisions? (Use the transfer pricing formula as needed.)

E11–9.   Selected sales and operating data for three companies are given below:

	Company		
	A	**B**	**C**
Sales	$12,000,000	$14,000,000	$25,000,000
Average operating assets	3,000,000	7,000,000	5,000,000
Net operating income	600,000	560,000	800,000
Stockholders' equity	1,500,000	2,900,000	3,000,000
Minimum required rate of return . .	14%	10%	16%

Required: 1.   Compute the return on investment (ROI) for each company.

  2.   Compute the residual income for each company.

  3.   Assume that each company is presented with an investment opportunity that would yield a 15 percent rate of return.

    a.   If performance is being measured by ROI, which company or companies will probably accept the opportunity? Reject? Why?

    b.   If performance is being measured by residual income, which company or companies will probably accept the opportunity? Reject? Why?

PROBLEMS

P11–10.   **ROI; comparison of industry performance.**   Comparative data on three companies in the same industry are given below:

	Company		
	A	**B**	**C**
Sales	$600,000	$500,000	$?
Net operating income	84,000	70,000	?
Average operating assets . . .	300,000	?	1,000,000
Margin	?	?	3.5%
Turnover	?	?	2
Return on investment (ROI) . .	?	7%	?

Required: 1.   What advantages can you see in breaking down the ROI computation into two separate elements, margin and turnover?
   2.   Fill in the missing information above, and comment on the relative performance of the three companies in as much detail as the data permit. Make *specific recommendations* on steps to be taken to improve the return on investment, where needed.

(Adapted from National Association of Accountants,
Research Report No. 35, p. 34)

P11–11.   **The appropriate transfer price; well-defined intermediate market.**   Hrubec Products, Inc., operates a Pulp Division that manufactures wood pulp for use in the production of various paper goods. Revenue and costs associated with a ton of pulp follow:

Selling price		$70
Less expenses:		
Variable	$42	
Fixed (based on a capacity of		
50,000 tons per year)	18	60
Net income		$10

Hrubec Products has just acquired a small company that manufactures paper cartons. This company will be treated as a division of Hrubec with full profit responsibility. The newly formed Carton Division is currently purchasing 5,000 tons of pulp per year from a supplier at a cost of $70 per ton, less a 10 percent quantity discount. Hrubec's president is anxious for the Carton Division to begin purchasing its pulp from the Pulp Division, if an acceptable transfer price can be worked out.

Required: For (1)–(4) below, assume that the Pulp Division can sell all of its pulp to outside customers at the normal $70 price.

   1.   If the Carton Division purchases 5,000 tons of pulp per year from the Pulp Division, what price should control the transfers? Why?
   2.   Refer to your computations in (1). What is the lower limit and the upper limit for a transfer price? Is an upper limit relevant in this situation?

3.   If the Pulp Division meets the price that the Carton Division is currently paying to its supplier and sells 5,000 tons of pulp to the Carton Division each year, what will be the effect on the profits of the Pulp Division, the Carton Division, and the company as a whole?

4.   If the intermediate market price for pulp is $70 per ton, is there any reason why the Pulp Division should sell to the Carton Division for less than $70? Explain.

For (5)–(8) below, assume that the Pulp Division is currently selling only 40,000 tons of pulp each year to outside customers at the stated $70 price.

5.   If the Carton Division purchases 5,000 tons of pulp from the Pulp Division each year, what price should control the transfers. Why?

6.   Suppose that the Carton Division's outside supplier drops its price (net of the quantity discount) to only $59 per ton. Should the Pulp Division meet this price? Explain. If the Pulp Division does *not* meet the $59 price, what will be the effect on the profits of the company as a whole?

7.   Refer to (6) above. If the Pulp Division refuses to meet the $59 price, should the Carton Division be required to purchase from the Pulp Division at a higher price, for the good of the company as a whole?

8.   Refer to (6) above. Assume that due to inflexible management policies, the Carton Division is required to purchase 5,000 tons of pulp each year from the Pulp Division at $70 per ton. What will be the effect on the profits of the company as a whole?

P11–12.   **Basic transfer pricing computations.**   Alpha and Beta are divisions within the same company. Assume the following information relative to the two divisions:

	Case			
	1	**2**	**3**	**4**
Alpha Division:				
Capacity in units	80,000	400,000	150,000	300,000
Number of units now being sold to outside customers on the intermediate market. . . .	80,000	400,000	100,000	300,000
Selling price per unit on the intermediate market.	$30	$90	$75	$50
Variable costs per unit	18	65	40	26
Fixed costs per unit (based on capacity)	6	15	20	9
Beta Division:				
Number of units needed annually . .	5,000	30,000	20,000	120,000
Purchase price now being paid to an outside supplier	$27	$89	$75*	—

*Before any quantity discount.

In cases 1–3, assume that Alpha Division's product can be sold either to Beta Division or to outside customers on an intermediate market.

Required: 1.   Refer to case 1 above. Alpha Division can avoid $2 per unit in commissions on any sales to Beta Division. Use the transfer pricing formula to determine what transfer price should be charged on any sales between the two divisions. Will any sales be made?

    2.   Refer to case 2 above. A study indicates that Alpha Division can avoid $5 per unit in shipping costs on any sales to Beta Division.

        a.   Again use the transfer pricing formula to compute an appropriate transfer price. Would you expect any disagreement between the two divisional managers over what the transfer price should be? Explain.

        b.   Assume that Alpha Division offers to sell 30,000 units to Beta Division at $88 per unit and that Beta Division refuses this price. What will be the loss in potential profits to the company as a whole?

    3.   Refer to case 3 above. Assume that Beta Division is now receiving an 8 percent quantity discount from the outside supplier.

        a.   Within what range should the transfer price be set for any sales between the two divisions?

        b.   Assume that Beta Division offers to purchase 20,000 units from Alpha Division at $60 per unit. If Alpha Division accepts this price, would you expect its ROI to increase, decrease, or remain unchanged? Why?

    4.   Refer to case 4 above. Assume that Beta Division wants Alpha Division to provide it with 120,000 units of a *different* product from the one that Alpha Division is now producing. The new product would require $21 per unit in variable costs and would require that Alpha Division cut back production of its present product by 45,000 units annually. Use the transfer pricing formula to determine the minimum transfer price per unit that Alpha Division should charge Beta Division for the new product.

P11–13.   **ROI and residual income.** Billings Products, Inc., is a decentralized organization with five autonomous divisions. The divisions are evaluated on the basis of the return that they are able to generate on invested assets, with year-end bonuses given to the divisional managers who have the highest ROI figures. Operating results for the company's Office Products Division for the most recent year are given below:

Sales	$10,000,000
Less variable expenses	6,000,000
Contribution margin	4,000,000
Less fixed expenses	3,200,000
Net operating income	$ 800,000
Divisional operating assets	$ 4,000,000

The company had an overall ROI of 15 percent last year (considering all divisions). The Office Products Division has an opportunity to add a new product line that would require an additional investment in operating assets of $1,000,000. The cost and revenue characteristics of the new product line per year would be:

Sales	$2,000,000
Variable expenses	60% of sales
Fixed expenses	$640,000

Required: 1. *a.*   Compute the Office Products Division's ROI for the most recent year; also compute the ROI as it will appear if the new product line is added.

        b.   As manager of the Office Products Division, would you accept or reject the new product line? Explain.

    2.   As the president of Billings Products, Inc., would you want the Office Products Division to accept or reject the new product line? Explain.

    3.   Suppose that the company views a return of 12 percent on invested assets as

being the minimum that any division should earn, and that performance is evaluated by the residual income approach.

 a. Compute the Office Products Division's residual income for the most recent year; also compute the residual income as it will appear if the new product line is added.

 b. Under these circumstances, as manager of the Office Products Division, would you accept or reject the new product line? Explain.

P11–14. **ROI and residual income.** Lawton Industries has manufactured prefabricated houses for over 20 years. The houses are constructed in sections to be assembled on customers' lots.

Lawton expanded into the precut housing market several years ago when it acquired Presser Company, one of its suppliers. In this market, various types of lumber are precut into the appropriate lengths, banded into packages, and shipped to customers' lots for assembly. Lawton decided to maintain Presser's separate identity and therefore established the Presser Division as an investment center of Lawton.

Lawton uses return on investment (ROI) as a performance measure. Management bonuses are based in part on ROI. All investments in operating assets are expected to earn a minimum return of 15 percent before income taxes.

Presser's ROI has ranged from 19 to 22 percent since it was acquired by Lawton. During the past year, Presser had an investment opportunity that had an estimated ROI of 18 percent. Presser's management decided against the investment because it believed the investment would decrease the division's overall ROI.

Last year's (19x5) income statement for Presser Division is given below. The division's operating assets employed were $15,500,000 at the end of the year, which represents a 24 percent increase over the 19x4 year-end balance. (Several purchases of new equipment were made during the year.)

PRESSER DIVISION
Divisional Income Statement
For the Year Ended December 31, 19x5

Sales		$35,000,000
Cost of goods sold		24,600,000
Gross margin		10,400,000
Less operating expenses:		
Selling expenses	$5,700,000	
Administrative expenses . . .	1,900,000	7,600,000
Net operating income		$ 2,800,000

Required: 1. Calculate the following performance measures for 19x5 for Presser Division:
 a. Return on investment (ROI).
 b. Residual income.

2. Would the management of Presser Division have been more likely to accept the investment opportunity it had in 19x5 if residual income were used as a performance measure instead of ROI? Explain.

3. The Presser Division is a separate investment center within Lawton Industries. Identify the items Presser Division must be free to control if it is to be evaluated fairly by either the ROI or residual income performance measures.

(CMA, Heavily Adapted)

P11–15. **Basic transfer pricing computations.**   Unless indicated otherwise, assume that each of the following situations is independent:

1. Given the following data for a product manufactured by East Division:

   Selling price on the intermediate market . . . $80
   Variable costs per unit   60
   Fixed costs per unit (based on capacity). . .   9
   Capacity in units   100,000

   East Division is selling all it can produce to outside customers on the intermediate market. Another division in the company, West Division, is currently purchasing 30,000 units of an identical product from an outside supplier at a price of $80 per unit, less a 6.25 percent quantity discount. If East Division begins selling to West Division, $12 per unit in sales commissions and shipping costs can be avoided. From the standpoint of the company as a whole, any sales made by East Division to West Division should be priced at what amount per unit?

2. Refer to the data in (1) above. Assume that East Division offers to sell 30,000 units to West Division each year at a price of $72 per unit. If West Division accepts this offer, what will be the effect on the profits in the company as a whole?

3. Petrovich Company has two divisions, A and B. Division A manufactures a product, called product X, which has the following cost and revenue characteristics:

   Selling price on the intermediate market . . . $45
   Variable costs per unit   27
   Fixed costs per unit (based on capacity). . .   6
   Capacity in units   75,000

   Division A is operating at capacity, producing 75,000 units of product X each period and selling the units to outside customers. Division B would like Division A to start producing 9,000 units of a new product—called product Y—for it each period. This would require that Division A cut back production of product X by 20 percent, to only 60,000 units each period. Division A has estimated the following cost per unit for the new product Y:

   Selling price to Division B . . . . $?
   Variable costs per unit   50
   Fixed costs per unit   10

   Division A would use existing personnel and equipment to manufacture product Y. What transfer price per unit should Division A charge to Division B for product Y?

P11–16. **ROI analysis.**   The income statement for Huerra Company for last year is given below:

	Total	Unit
Sales	$4,000,000	$80.00
Less variable expenses.	2,800,000	56.00
Contribution margin	1,200,000	24.00
Less fixed expenses	840,000	16.80
Net operating income	360,000	7.20
Less income taxes (30%)	108,000	2.16
Net income	$ 252,000	$ 5.04

The company had average operating assets of $2,000,000 during the year.

Required: 1.   Compute the company's return on investment for the period, using the ROI formula.

For each of the following questions, indicate whether the margin and turnover will increase, decrease, or remain unchanged as a result of the events described, and then compute the new ROI figure. Consider each question separately, starting in each case from the data used to compute the original ROI in (1) above.

2.   By using the computer to control inventory purchases, the company is able to reduce the average level of inventory by $400,000. (The released funds are used to pay off short-term creditors.)

3.   The company is able to achieve a cost savings of $32,000 per year by using less costly raw material inputs.

4.   The company issues bonds and uses the proceeds to purchase $500,000 in machinery and equipment. Interest on the bonds is $60,000 per year. Sales remain unchanged. The new, more efficient equipment reduces production costs by $20,000 per year.

5.   As a result of a more intense effort by salespeople, sales are increased by 20 percent; operating assets remain unchanged.

6.   Obsolete items of inventory carried on the records at a cost of $40,000 are scrapped and written off as a loss, since they are unsalable.

7.   The company uses $200,000 of cash (received on accounts receivable) to repurchase and retire some of its common stock.

P11–17.   **Choosing an appropriate transfer price.**   Whirlwind Products, Inc., has just acquired a small company that produces condenser units for refrigerators and similar products. The company will operate as a division of Whirlwind under the name of the Condenser Division. Selected data regarding the condenser units is given below:

Selling price per unit.	$50
Cost per unit:	
Direct materials	$18
Direct labor.	10
Variable overhead.	2
Fixed overhead	5*
Total cost per unit	$35

*Based on 60,000 units capacity.

Whirlwind Products, Inc., also has a Refrigerator Division that is currently purchasing 20,000 condenser units each year from an outside supplier. The Refrigerator Division is paying $48 per condenser, which represents the normal $50 price less a 4 percent quantity discount due to the large number of units being purchased. Whirlwind's president is anxious for the Refrigerator Division to begin purchasing its condenser units from the Condenser Division, but she is unsure what transfer price should control any sales.

Required: 1.   Assume that the Condenser Division has enough idle capacity to supply all of the Refrigerator Division's needs. Explain why each of the following transfer prices would or would not be an appropriate price to charge the Refrigerator Division on the intracompany sales.
   a. $50.
   b. $48.
   c. $39.

        d. $35.

        e. $30.

2. Assume that the Condenser Division is currently selling to outside customers all the condenser units that it can produce. Under these circumstances, explain why each of the transfer prices given in (1a) through (1e) above would or would not be an appropriate price to charge the Refrigerator Division on the intracompany sales.

P11–18.   **Negotiated transfer price.** Ditka Industries has several independent divisions. The company's Tube Division manufactures a picture tube used in television sets. The Tube Division's income statement for last year, in which 8,000 tubes were sold, is given below:

	Total	Unit
Sales	$1,360,000	$170.00
Less cost of goods sold	840,000	105.00
Gross margin	520,000	65.00
Less selling and administrative expenses . .	390,000	48.75
Divisional net income	$ 130,000	$ 16.25

As shown above, it costs the Tube Division $105 to produce a single tube. This figure consists of the following costs:

Direct materials	$ 38	
Direct labor	27	
Manufacturing overhead (75% fixed) . .	40	
Total cost per tube	$105	

The Tube Division has fixed selling and administrative expenses of $350,000 per year.

Ditka Industries has just formed a new division, called the TV Division, that will produce a television set that requires a high-resolution picture tube. The Tube Division has been asked to manufacture 2,500 of these tubes each year and sell them to the TV Division. As one step in determining the price that should be charged to the TV Division, the Tube Division has estimated the following cost for each of the new high-resolution tubes:

Direct materials	$ 60	
Direct labor	49	
Manufacturing overhead (⅔ fixed) . .	54	
Total cost per tube	$163	

In order to manufacture the new tubes, the Tube Division would have to reduce production of its regular tubes by 3,000 units per year. There would be no variable selling and administrative expenses on the intracompany business, and total fixed overhead costs would not change.

Required: 1. Determine the price that the Tube Division should charge the TV Division for each of the new high-resolution tubes.

      2. Assume that the TV Division has found an outside supplier that will provide the new tubes for only $200 each. If the Tube Division meets this price, what will be the effect on the profits of the company as a whole?

P11–19.   **Cost-volume profit analysis; ROI; transfer pricing.**   The Valve Division of Bendix, Inc., produces a small valve that is used by various companies as a component part in the manufacture of their products. Bendix, Inc., operates its divisions as autonomous units, giving its divisional managers great discretion in pricing and other decisions. Each division is expected to generate a return of at least 14 percent on its assets. The Valve Division has average operating assets as follows:

Cash	$ 9,000
Accounts receivable	81,000
Inventory	250,000
Plant and equipment (net)	360,000
Total assets	$700,000

The valves are sold for $5 each. Variable costs are $3 per valve, and fixed costs total $462,000 per year. The division has a capacity of 300,000 valves each year.

Required:
1.   How many valves must the Valve Division sell each year in order to generate the desired rate of return on its assets?
     a.   What is the margin earned at this level of sales?
     b.   What is the turnover of assets at this level of sales?
2.   Assume that the Valve Division's current ROI is just equal to the minimum required 14 percent. In order to increase the division's ROI, the divisional manager wants to increase the selling price per valve by 4 percent. Market studies indicate that an increase in the selling price would cause sales to drop by 20,000 units each year. However, operating assets could be reduced by $50,000 due to decreased needs for accounts receivable and inventory. Compute the margin, turnover, and ROI if these changes are made.
3.   Refer to the original data. Assume again that the Valve Division's current ROI is just equal to the minimum required 14 percent. Rather than increase the selling price, the sales manager wants to reduce the selling price per valve by 4 percent. Market studies indicate that this would fill the plant to capacity. In order to carry the greater level of sales, however, operating assets would increase by $50,000. Compute the margin, turnover, and ROI if these changes are made.
4.   Refer to the original data. Assume that the normal volume of sales is 280,000 valves each year at a price of $5 per valve. Another division of the company is currently purchasing 20,000 valves each year from an overseas supplier, at a price of $4.25 per valve. The manager of the Valve Division has adamantly refused to meet this price, pointing out that it would result in a loss for his division:

Selling price per valve		$ 4.25
Cost per valve:		
Variable	$3.00	
Fixed ($462,000 ÷ 300,000 valves) . .	1.54	4.54
Net loss per valve		$(0.29)

The manager of the Valve Division also points out that the normal $5 selling price barely allows his division the required 14 percent rate of return. "If we take on some business at only $4.25 per unit, then our ROI is obviously going to suffer," he reasons, "and maintaining that ROI figure is the key to my future. Besides, taking on these extra units would require us to increase our operating assets by at least $50,000 due to the larger inventories and receivables we would be carrying.'' Would you recommend that the Valve Division sell to the other division at $4.25? Show ROI computations to support your answer.

P11–20. **Negotiated transfer price.**   Zobel Machine Products, Inc., has a Castings Division, which does casting work of various types. The company also has a Machine Tool Division, which has asked the Castings Division to provide it with 20,000 special castings each year on a continuing basis. The special casting would require $12 per unit in variable production costs.

In order to have time and space to produce the new casting, the Castings Division would have to cut back production of another casting—the HS7—that it is currently producing. The company now produces and sells 100,000 units of the HS7 each year. Production and sales of this casting would drop by 25 percent if the new casting were produced.

The HS7 sells for $40 per unit and requires $18 per unit in variable production costs. Boxing and shipping costs of the HS7 are $6 per unit. Boxing and shipping costs for the new special casting would be only $1 per unit, thereby saving the company $5 per unit in cost. Some $240,000 in fixed production costs in the Castings Division are now being covered by the HS7 casting; 25 percent of these costs would have to be covered by the new casting if it were produced and sold to the Machine Tool Division. However, total fixed costs in the Castings Division would not change.

Required: What transfer price per casting should the Castings Division charge the Machine Tool Division for the special casting? Show all computations in good form.

P11–21. **Impact of transfer pricing on marketing decisions.**   Stavos Company's Cabinet Division manufactures a standard cabinet for television sets. The cost per cabinet is:

Variable cost per cabinet	$ 70
Fixed cost per cabinet	30*
Total cost per cabinet	$100

*Based on a capacity of 10,000 cabinets per year.

Part of the Cabinet Division's output is sold to outside manufacturers of television sets, and part is sold to Stavos Company's Quark Division, which produces a TV set under its own name. The Cabinet Division charges $140 per cabinet for all sales.

The costs, revenue, and net income associated with the Quark Division's TV set is given below:

Selling price per TV set		$480
Less variable cost per TV set:		
Cost of the cabinet	$140	
Variable cost of electronic parts . .	210	
Total variable cost		350
Contribution margin		130
Less fixed costs per TV set		80*
Net income per TV set.		$ 50

*Based on a capacity of 3,000 sets per year.

The Quark Division has an order from an overseas source for 1,000 TV sets. The overseas source wants to pay only $340 per set.

Required: 1.   Assume that the Quark Division has enough idle capacity to fill the 1,000-set order. Is the division likely to accept the $340 price, or to reject it? Explain.
  2.   Assume that both the Cabinet Division and the Quark Division have idle capacity. Under these conditions, would the Quark Division's actions benefit or be a disadvantage to the company as a whole? Explain.
  3.   Assume that the Quark Division has idle capacity, but that the Cabinet Division is operating at capacity and could sell all of its cabinets to outside manufacturers. Compute the dollar advantage or disadvantage of the Quark Division accepting the 1,000 set order at the $340 unit price.
  4.   What kind of transfer pricing information is needed by the Quark Division in making decisions such as these?

P11–22.   **Critique of a performance evaluation program.**   The Motor Works Division of Roland Industries is located in Fort Wayne, Indiana. A major expansion of the division's only plant was completed in April 19x4. The expansion consisted of an addition to the existing building, additional new equipment, and the replacement of obsolete and fully depreciated equipment that was no longer efficient or cost effective.

Donald Futak became the Division Manager of the Motor Works Division effective May 1, 19x4. Futak had a brief meeting with John Poskey, vice president of operations for Roland Industries, when he assumed the division manager position. Poskey told Futak that the company employed return on investment (ROI) for measuring performance of divisions and division managers. Futak asked whether any other performance measures were ever used in place of or in conjunction with ROI. Poskey replied, "Roland's top management prefers to use a single performance measure. There is no conflict when there is only one measure. Motor Works should do well this year now that it has expanded and replaced all of that old equipment. You should have no problem exceeding the division's historical rate. I'll check back with you at the end of each quarter to see how you are doing."

Poskey called Futak after the first quarter results were complete because the Motor Works' ROI was considerably below the historical rate for the division. Futak told Poskey at that time that he did not believe that ROI was a valid performance measure for the Motor Works Division. Poskey indicated that he would get back to Futak. Futak did receive perfunctory memorandums after the second and third quarters, but there was no further discussion on the use of ROI. Now Futak has received the memorandum reproduced below.

May 24, 19x5

To: Donald Futak, Manager—Motor Works Division

From: John Poskey, Vice President of Operations

Subject: Division Performance

   The operating results for the fourth quarter and for our fiscal year ended on April 30 are now complete. Your fourth quarter return on investment was only 9 percent, resulting in a return for the year of slightly under 11 percent. I recall discussing your low return after the first quarter and reminding

---

you after the second and third quarters that this level of return is not considered adequate for the Motor Works Division.

The return on investment at Motor Works has ranged from 15 percent to 18 percent for the past five years. An 11 percent return may be acceptable at some of Roland's other divisions, but not at a proven winner like Motor Works—especially in light of your recently improved facility.

I would like to meet with you at your office on Monday, June 3, to discuss ways to restore Motor Works' return on investment to its former level. Please let me know if this date is acceptable to you.

Futak is looking forward to meeting with Poskey. He knows the division's ROI is below the historical rate, but the dollar profits for the year are greater than prior years. He plans to explain to Poskey why he believes return on investment is not an appropriate performance measure for the Motor Works Division. He also plans to recommend that ROI be replaced with three measures—dollar profit, receivables turnover, and inventory turnover. These three measures would constitute a set of multiple criteria that would be used to evaluate performance.

Required: 1. On the basis of the relationship between John Poskey and Donald Futak as well as the memorandum from Poskey, identify apparent weaknesses in the performance evaluation process of Roland Industries. Do not include in your answer any discussion on the use of return on investment (ROI) as a performance measure.

2. From the information presented, identify a possible explanation of why Motor Works Division's ROI declined in the fiscal year ended April 30, 19x5.

3. Identify criteria that should be used in selecting performance measures to evaluate operating managers.

(CMA, Adapted)

P11–23. **Transfer pricing; divisional performance; behavioral problems.** Wexpro Company is a decentralized organization containing six divisions. The Brake Division has asked the Electrical Division (which is operating at capacity) to supply it with a large quantity of electrical fitting 1726. The Electrical Division sells this fitting to its regular customers for $7.50 each. The Brake Division, which is operating at 50 percent of capacity, wants to pay $5 each for the fittings. The Brake Division will put the fittings into a brake unit that it is manufacturing and will sell on essentially a cost basis to a large commercial airplane manufacturer.

The Electrical Division has a variable cost of producing fitting 1726 of $4.25. The cost of the brake unit being built by the Brake Division follows:

Purchased parts (from outside vendors) . . .	$22.50
Electrical fitting 1726	5.00
Other variable costs	14.00
Fixed overhead and administration	8.00
Total cost per brake unit	$49.50

Although the $5 price for electrical fitting 1726 represents a substantial discount from the regular $7.50 price, the manager of the Brake Division believes that the price concession is necessary if his division is to get the airplane manufacturer job.

The company uses ROI and dollar profits in the measurement of division and division-manager performance.

Required: 1. Assume that you are the division controller of the Electrical Division. Would you recommend that the Electrical Division supply fitting 1726 to the Brake Division as requested? Why or why not? (Ignore any tax issues.)

2. Would it be to the short-run economic advantage of the Wexpro Company for the Electrical Division to supply the Brake Division with the fittings at $5 each? Explain your answer. (Ignore any tax issues.)

3. Discuss the organizational and manager behavior difficulties, if any, inherent in this situation. As the Wexpro Company controller, what would you advise the Wexpro Company president to do in this situation?

(CMA, Adapted)

P11–24. **Transfer pricing with and without idle capacity.** Division A manufactures an electrical switching unit that can be sold either to outside customers or to Division B. Selected operating data on the two divisions are given below:

Division A:

Unit selling price to outside customers . . $	80
Variable production cost per unit	52
Variable selling and administrative	
expense per unit.	9
Fixed production cost in total	300,000*

Division B:

Outside purchase price per unit (before	
any quantity discount)	80

* Capacity 25,000 units per year.

Division B now purchases the electrical unit from an outside supplier at the regular $80 intermediate price less a 5 percent quantity discount. Since the relay manufactured by Division A is of the same quality and type used by Division B, consideration is being given to buying internally rather than from the outside supplier. As the company's president stated, ''It's just plain smart to buy and sell within the corporate family.''

A study has determined that the variable selling and administrative expenses of Division A would be cut by one third for any sales to Division B. Top management wants to treat each division as an autonomous unit with independent profit responsibility.

Required: 1. Assume that Division A is currently selling only 20,000 units per year to outside customers and that Division B needs 5,000 units per year.

   a. What is the lowest transfer price that can be justified between the two divisions? Explain.

   b. What is the highest transfer price that can be justified between the two divisions? Explain.

   c. Assume that Division B finds an outside supplier that will sell the electrical unit for only $65 per unit. Should Division A be required to meet this price? Explain.

   d. Refer to the original data. Assume that Division A decides to raise its price to $85 per unit. If Division B is forced to pay this price and to start purchasing from Division A, will this result in greater or less total corporate profits? How much per unit?

√e. Under the circumstances posed in (d) above, should Division B be forced to purchase from Division A? Explain.

2. Assume that Division A can sell all that it produces to outside customers. Repeat (a) through (e) above.

CASES

C11–25. **Negotiated transfer price.** Flores Products, Inc., is made up of several autonomous divisions. Each division's performance is evaluated on the basis of total dollar profits and return on division investment. Bonuses are given to divisional managers on a basis of improvements in these performance measures from year to year.

The company's Edger Division manufactures and sells a lawn edger. The division's budgeted income statement for the coming year, based on an expected sales volume of 18,000 edgers, is given below.

EDGER DIVISION
Budgeted Income Statement
For the Year 19x8

	Total	Per unit
Sales revenue	$5,400,000	$300
Less cost of goods sold	3,312,000	184
Gross margin	2,088,000	116
Less operating expenses:		
Variable selling	216,000	12
Fixed selling	432,000	24
Fixed administrative	630,000	35
Total operating expenses	1,278,000	71
Net income	$ 810,000	$ 45

The division's $184 per unit cost of goods sold consists of the following items:

Motor	$ 60
Other material and parts	39
Direct labor	50
Variable overhead.	7
Fixed overhead	28
Total cost per edger	$184

Edger Division's manager is searching for ways to improve the division's profits and ROI. A market research study just completed indicates that a 5 percent reduction in the selling price per edger would increase sales volume (in units) by 20 percent. _21,600 units_ The Edger Division has ample production capacity to manage this increased volume with no increase in fixed costs.

The manager of the Edger Division is also studying the possibility of purchasing the motors used in the edgers from the company's Motor Division. At present, the Edger Division is using a motor that it purchases from an outside supplier at a cost of $60. The Edger Division has offered to pay the Motor Division $54 per motor, which represents the current price less a 10 percent discount. The manager of the Edger Division believes that this discount is justified since the motor needed by the Edger Division is somewhat different in design from the motor normally produced by the Motor Division and would require $3 less per motor in raw materials. Also, there would be no variable selling expenses associated with the intracompany sales. The manager of the Edger Division has specified, however, that all motors must come from a single supplier.

The Motor Division has a capacity to produce 80,000 motors per year. The division's budgeted income statement for the coming year is shown below. This statement is based on an expected sales volume of 70,000 motors without considering the Edger Division's proposal.

MOTOR DIVISION
Budgeted Income Statement
For the Year 19x8

	Total	Per unit
Sales revenue	$6,300,000	$90
Less cost of goods sold	3,570,000	51
Gross margin	2,730,000	39
Less operating expenses:		
Variable selling	420,000	6
Fixed selling	770,000	11
Fixed administrative	980,000	14
Total operating expenses	2,170,000	31
Net income	$ 560,000	$ 8

The division's $51 per unit cost of goods sold consists of the following items:

Direct materials	$21
Direct labor	10
Variable overhead	3
Fixed overhead	17
Total cost per motor	$51

Required:
1. Should the Edger Division institute the 5 percent price reduction on its edgers even if it can't purchase the motors internally for $54 each? Support your answer with appropriate computations.
2. Assume that the Edger Division decides to institute the 5 percent price reduction and thus will need 21,600 motors next year. If you were the manager of the Motor Division, would you be willing to supply these motors for $54 each? Support your answer with appropriate computations.
3. As the manager of the Motor Division, what is the minimum transfer price per motor that you could charge the Edger Division? Show computations.
4. Assume again that the Edger Division will need 21,600 motors next year. Considering the company as a whole, would it be in the best interest of Flores Products, Inc., for the Motor Division to supply the motors to the Edger Division at $54 each? Support your answer with appropriate computations.

(Written by the Author, Based on a Problem Appearing on the CMA Examination.)

C11–26.   **Negotiated transfer price.**   PortCo Products is a divisionalized furniture manufacturer. The divisions are autonomous segments, with each division being responsible for its own sales, costs of operations, working capital management, and equipment acquisition. Each division serves a different market in the furniture industry. Because the markets and products of the divisions are so different, there have never been any transfers between divisions.

The Commercial Division manufactures equipment and furniture that is purchased by the restaurant industry. The division plans to introduce a new line of counter and chair units that feature a cushioned seat for the counter chairs. John Kline, the division manager, has discussed the manufacture of the cushioned seat with Russ Fiegel of the Office Division. They both believe that a cushioned seat currently made by the Office Division for use on its deluxe office stool could be modified for use on the new counter chair. Consequently, Kline has asked Fiegel for a price for 100-unit lots of the cushioned seat. The following conversation took place about the price to be charged for the cushioned seats.

Fiegel: John, we can make the necessary modifications to the cushioned seat easily. The raw materials used in your seat are slightly different and should cost about 10 percent more than those used in our deluxe office stool. However, the labor time should be the same because the seat fabrication operation is basically the same. I would price the seat at our regular rate—full cost plus 30 percent markup.

Kline: That's higher than I expected, Russ. I was thinking that a good price would be your variable manufacturing costs. After all, your capacity costs will be incurred regardless of this job.

Fiegel: John, I'm at capacity. By making the cushion seats for you, I'll have to cut my production of deluxe office stools. Of course, I can increase my production of economy office stools. The labor time freed by not having to fabricate the frame or assemble the deluxe stool can be shifted to the frame fabrication and assembly of the economy office stool. Fortunately, I can switch my labor force between these two models of stools without any loss of efficiency. As you know, overtime is not a feasible alternative in our community. I'd like to sell it to you at variable cost, but I have excess demand for both products. I don't mind changing my product mix to the economy model if I get a good return on the seats I make for you. Here are my standard costs for the two stools and a schedule of my manufacturing overhead. [See the following page.]

Kline: I guess I see your point, Russ, but I don't want to price myself out of the market. Maybe we should talk to corporate to see if they can give us any guidance.

OFFICE DIVISION
Standard Costs and Prices

	Deluxe office stool		Economy office stool
Raw materials:			
Framing	$ 8.15		$ 9.76
Cushioned seat:			
Padding	2.40		—
Vinyl	4.00		—
Molded seat (purchased)	—		6.00
Direct labor:			
Frame fabrication (0.5 × $7.50/DLH) . .	3.75	(0.5 × $7.50/DLH)	3.75
Cushion fabrication			
(0.5 × $7.50/DLH)	3.75		—
Assembly* (0.5 × $7.50/DLH)	3.75	(0.3 × $7.50/DLH)	2.25
Manufacturing:			
Overhead (1.5 DLH × $12.80/DLH) . .	19.20	(0.8 DLH × $12.80/DLH)	10.24
Total standard cost	$45.00		$32.00
Selling price (30% markup)	$58.50		$41.60

* Attaching seats to frames and attaching rubber feet.

OFFICE DIVISION
Manufacturing Overhead Budget

Overhead item	Nature	Amount
Supplies	Variable—at current market prices	$ 420,000
Indirect labor	Variable	375,000
Supervision	Nonvariable	250,000
Power	Use varies with activity; rates are fixed	180,000
Heat and light	Nonvariable—same regardless of production	140,000
Property taxes and	Nonvariable—any change in amounts or rates	
insurance	is independent of production	200,000
Depreciation	Fixed dollar total	1,700,000
Employee benefits	20% of supervision, direct and indirect labor	575,000
Total overhead		$3,840,000
Capacity in DLH		300,000
Overhead rate/DLH		$12.80

Required:

1. Assume that you are the corporate controller. What transfer price would you recommend for a 100-unit lot of seats? Show all computations.

2. Which alternative transfer pricing system—full cost, variable manufacturing cost, or variable cost plus lost contribution margin—would be best as the underlying concept for an intracompany transfer pricing policy? Explain your answer.

(CMA, Adapted)

PART THREE

The Capstone:
Using Cost Data in
Decision Making

CHAPTER 12

Pricing of Products and Services

LEARNING OBJECTIVES

After studying Chapter 12, you should be able to:

- Explain how the price of a product or service is obtained by using the economist's total revenue and total cost concepts and marginal revenue and marginal cost concepts.

- Define price elasticity and explain how it impacts on the pricing decision.

- Compute the target selling price for a product by use of cost-plus pricing under either the absorption or the contribution approach.

- Derive the markup percentage needed to achieve a target ROI for a product.

- Compute the target selling price for a service by use of time and material pricing.

- Make special pricing decisions under the contribution approach, using the range of flexibility concept.

- Define or explain the key terms listed at the end of the chapter.

Many firms have no pricing problems at all. They make a product that is in competition with other, similar products for which a market price already exists. Customers will not pay more than this price, and there is no reason for any firm to charge less. Under these circumstances, no price calculations are necessary. Any firm entering the market simply charges the price that the market directs it to accept. To a large extent, farm products follow this type of pattern. In these situations, the question isn't what price to charge; the question is simply how much to produce.

In this chapter, we are concerned with the more common situation in which a firm is faced with the problem of setting its own prices, as well as deciding how much to produce. The pricing decision is considered by many to be the single most important decision that a manager has to make. The reason is that the pricing of products isn't just a marketing decision or a financial decision; rather, it is a decision touching on *all* aspects of a firm's activities, and as such it affects the entire enterprise. Since the prices charged for a firm's products largely determine the quantities customers are willing to purchase, the setting of prices dictates the inflows of revenues into a firm. If these revenues consistently fail to cover all the costs of the firm, then in the long run the firm cannot survive. This is true regardless of how carefully costs may be controlled or how innovative the managers of the firm may be in the discharge of their other responsibilities.

Cost is a key factor in the pricing decision. As we have already seen, however, *cost* is a somewhat fluid concept that is sometimes hard to pin down. Our purpose in this chapter is to look at some of the cost concepts developed in earlier chapters and to see how these concepts can be applied in the pricing decision. This chapter is not intended to be a comprehensive guide to pricing; rather, its purpose is to integrate those cost concepts with which we are already familiar into a general pricing framework.

THE ECONOMIC FRAMEWORK FOR PRICING

A large part of microeconomic theory (theory of the firm) is devoted to the matter of pricing. In order to establish a framework for the pricing decision, it will be helpful to review certain concepts of microeconomic theory. This review will also assist us in showing the relationship between the models involved in microeconomic theory and the concept of incremental analysis discussed in preceding chapters.

Total Revenue and Total Cost Curves

Microeconomic theory states that the best price for a product is the price that maximizes the difference between total revenue and total costs. The economist illustrates this concept by constructing a model such as that shown in Exhibit 12–1.

This model is based on a number of assumptions. The economist assumes, first, that it is not possible to sell an unlimited number of units at the

EXHIBIT 12–1

Total revenue and total cost curves

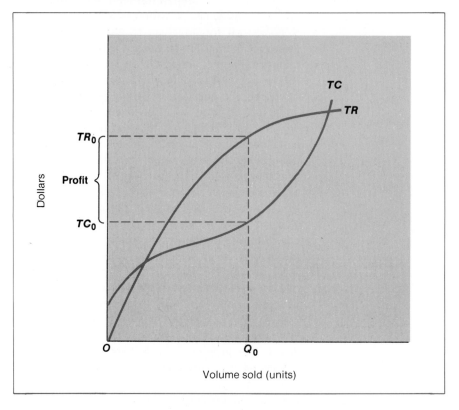

Volume sold (units)

same price. If an unlimited number of units could be sold at the same price, then the total revenue *(TR)* curve would appear as a straight line, beginning at the origin of the graph. Since the economist assumes that at some point price reductions will be necessary to sell more units, the *TR* curve is shown increasing at a decreasing rate as quantity sold increases. That is, as price is reduced to stimulate more sales, total revenue will continue to increase for each unit sold, but the *rate* of this increase will begin to decline. As price is reduced more and more, the increase in total revenue will continue to decline, as depicted by the flattening tendency in the *TR* curve in Exhibit 12–1.

The total cost *(TC)* curve in Exhibit 12–1 assumes that the cost of producing additional units of product is not constant, but rather increases as attempts are made to squeeze more and more production out of a given set of productive facilities. So long as the rate of this increase is less than the rate of increase in total revenue, the company can profit by producing and selling more units of product. At some point, however, the rate of increase in total cost will become equal to the rate of increase in total revenue—that is, at some point the two lines will become parallel to each other. At this point, the increase to total cost from producing and selling one more unit of product is exactly equal to the increase to total revenue from that unit of product, and its production and sale yield zero increase in total profits in the firm. This point is shown in the graph in Exhibit 12–1 as quantity Q_0, representing the optimum volume of production and sales for the firm.

At Q_0 volume of units, the difference between total revenue and total cost is maximized. If we move to the right of Q_0 volume, then total cost is increasing more rapidly than total revenue, and therefore total profits would be decreased. If we move to the left of Q_0 volume, then total revenue is increasing more rapidly than total cost, and the company can profit by further expanding output up to Q_0 level of activity. In sum, Q_0 represents the optimum volume of sales for the firm, and the correct price to charge is the price that will allow the firm to sell this volume of units.

Marginal Revenue and Marginal Cost Curves

These same concepts can be shown in terms of marginal revenue and marginal cost. **Marginal revenue** can be defined as the addition to total revenue resulting from the sale of one additional unit of product. **Marginal cost** can be defined as the addition to total cost resulting from the production and sale of one additional unit of product. The economist expresses these concepts in model form as shown in Exhibit 12–2.

The marginal revenue *(MR)* and marginal cost *(MC)* curves in Exhibit 12–2 have their basis in the economist's assumption that the total revenue and total cost curves behave in the way depicted earlier in Exhibit 12–1. That is, the marginal revenue and marginal cost curves are derived by measuring the rate of *change* in total revenue and total cost at various levels of activity, and by plotting this change in graph form. Since the total revenue curve in Exhibit 12–1 depicts a declining rate of increase in total revenue, the marginal revenue curve in Exhibit 12–2 slopes downward to the right. And since the total cost curve in Exhibit 12–1 depicts total cost as first increasing at a decreasing rate, then flattening out somewhat, and then increasing at an increasing rate, the marginal cost curve in Exhibit 12–2 slopes downward initially, bottoms out, and then slopes upward to the right. As discussed in Chapter 2, the economist's marginal concept is basically the same as the accountant's incremental concept.

The optimum price to charge is determined by the intersection of the marginal revenue and the marginal cost curves. The intersection of these two curves occurs at volume Q_0. This is the same volume as shown earlier in Exhibit 12–1, depicting the point of maximum difference between total revenues and total costs. At volume Q_0, price P_0 should be charged for each unit sold.

EXHIBIT 12–2

Marginal revenue and marginal cost curves

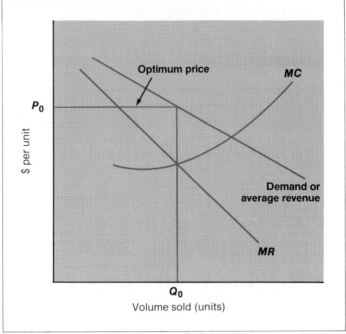

Elasticity of Demand

A product's price elasticity is a key concept in any pricing decision. **Price elasticity** measures the degree to which volume of sales is affected by a change in price per unit. Demand for a product is price inelastic if a change in price has little or no effect on the volume of units sold. Demand is price elastic if a change in price has a substantial effect on the volume of units sold. Salt is a good example of a product that tends to be price inelastic. Raising or lowering the price of salt would probably have little or no effect on the amount of salt sold in a given year.

Whether demand for a product tends to be price elastic or price inelastic can be a crucial factor in a decision relating to a change in price. The problem is that measuring the degree of price elasticity is an extremely difficult thing to do. It's one thing to observe generally that a given product tends to be price elastic, and it's another thing to determine the exact *degree* of that elasticity—that is, to determine what change in volume of sales will take place as a result of specific changes in price. Yet this is exactly the kind of information that managers need in their pricing decisions, and the kind of information that they attempt to obtain by carefully planned marketing research programs.

Pricing decisions are further complicated by the fact that cross-elasticity often exists in the demand for certain products. *Cross-elasticity* measures the degree to which demand for one product is affected by a change in the price of a substitute product. For example, as the price of galvanized pipe goes up, consumers may switch to plastic pipe. One of the problems in measuring cross-elasticity is trying to identify the substitutes for a particular product, and the willingness of consumers to accept those substitutes in place of the product itself. Although problems of this type are often difficult to quantify, the concept of cross-elasticity of demand is an important concept and cannot be disregarded in the pricing decision.

Limitations of the General Models

Although the models in Exhibits 12–1 and 12–2 do a good job of showing the general outlines of the incremental profit approach to pricing, they must be viewed as being only broad, conceptual guides in pricing decisions. There are several reasons why. First, the cost and revenue data available to managers are generally sufficient to provide only rough approximations of the shape of the various cost and revenue curves depicted in the models. As our methods of measurement are improved and refined in years to come, this situation may change, but at present managers usually have only a general idea of the shape of the demand curve that they are facing.

Second, the models are directly applicable only in conditions of **monopoly** (no directly competing product in the market) and **monopolistic competition** (many sellers of similar products, with no one seller having a large enough share of the market for other sellers to be able to discern the effect of its pricing decision on their sales). The models are not applicable between these two extremes, where the market is characterized by situations of **oligopoly** (a few large sellers competing directly with one another). The reason is that the models make no allowance for retaliatory pricing decisions by competing firms, and retaliatory pricing is a prime characteristic of oligopolistic industries.

A third limitation of the general models arises from the fact that price is just one element in the marketing of a product. Many other factors must also be considered that can have a significant impact on the number of units of a product that can be sold at a given price. Among these factors are promotional strategy, product design, intensity of selling effort, and the selection of distribution channels.

A final limitation of the general models is that even if business firms had a precise knowledge of the shape of their demand curves, we cannot automatically assume that they would price in such a way as to maximize profits. The reason is that this might bring accusations from the public of "profiteering" and "charging all that the traffic will bear." Rather than attempting to maximize profits, many firms seek only to earn a "satisfactory" profit for the company. They think in terms of a reasonable return on the investment that has been made in the company, and they strive to set prices in such a way as to earn that return. The concept of a satisfactory profit underlies the actions of a great many business firms today.

Although the limitations discussed above preclude the *direct* use of the economic pricing models in pricing decisions, these models are nonetheless highly useful in providing the general framework within which the price setter must work. They state the pricing problem in *conceptual* terms, and as such they constitute the starting point in any pricing decision.

PRICING STANDARD PRODUCTS

Not all pricing decisions are approached in the same way. Some pricing decisions relate to the pricing of standard products that are sold to customers in the routine day-to-day conduct of business activities. Other pricing decisions relate to special orders of standard or near-standard products, and still others relate to the pricing of special products that have been taken on in an effort to fill out unused productive capacity. In this section, we consider the pricing of standard products. The pricing of special orders of various types is reserved to a later section.

Cost-Plus Pricing Formulas

In pricing standard products, the key concept is to recognize that selling prices must be sufficient in the long run to cover *all* costs of production, administration, and sales, both fixed and variable, as well as to provide for a reasonable return on the stockholders' investment, if a firm is to survive and grow. This point is often missed by some pricing enthusiasts who seem to imply in their writings that any price above variable or incremental costs is an acceptable price for any product under any circumstances.[1]

In setting normal long-run prices on standard products, *all costs* are relevant to the pricing decision and must be explicitly considered by the price setter if long-run profit goals are to be met. This means that a portion of the fixed costs (even if the fixed costs are sunk) must be considered along with the variable costs, and that the costs of administration and sales must be weighted in along with the costs of production as prices are set.

The most common approach to the pricing of standard products is to employ some type of **cost-plus pricing** formula.[2] The approach is to compute a "cost" base and then to add to this base some predetermined **markup** to arrive at a target selling price. The "cost" in cost-plus pricing is defined according to the method being used to cost units of product. In Chapters 3 and 7, we found that units of product can be costed in two different ways—

---

[1] For a discussion of the circumstances under which variable or incremental costs are useful as a pricing guide, see the section "Special pricing decisions."

[2] For a study documenting the use of cost-plus pricing, see Lawrence A. Gordon, Robert Cooper, Haim Falk, and Danny Miller, *The Pricing Decision* (New York: National Association of Accountants, 1981), p. 23.

by the absorption approach or by the contribution approach (with direct costing). We consider both costing methods below, and the approach that each takes to cost-plus pricing of standard products.

The Absorption Approach

Under the absorption approach to cost-plus pricing, the cost base is defined as the cost to manufacture one unit of product. Selling and administrative costs are not included in this cost base, but rather are provided for through the markup that is added on to arrive at the target selling price. Thus, the markup must be high enough to cover these costs as well as to provide the company with a "satisfactory" profit margin.

To illustrate, let us assume that the Ritter Company is in the process of setting a selling price on one of its standard products, which has just undergone some slight modifications in design. The accounting department has accumulated the following cost data on the redesigned product:

	Per unit	Total
Direct materials	$6	
Direct labor	4	
Variable overhead	3	
Fixed overhead (based on 10,000 units)	7	$70,000
Variable selling and administrative expenses	2	
Fixed selling and administrative expenses		
(based on 10,000 units)	1	10,000

The first step is to compute the cost to manufacture one unit of product. For the Ritter Company, this amounts to $20 per unit, computed as follows:

Direct materials	$ 6
Direct labor	4
Overhead ($3 variable plus $7 fixed, or 250%	
of direct labor cost)	10
Total absorption cost to manufacture one unit	$20

Let us assume that in order to obtain its target selling price, the Ritter Company has a general policy of adding a markup equal to 50 percent of the cost to manufacture. A price quotation sheet for the company prepared under this assumption is presented in Exhibit 12–3.

As shown in Exhibit 12–3, even though this pricing approach is termed cost-plus, part of the costs involved are buried in the *plus*, or markup, part of the formula. The buried costs are those associated with the selling and administrative activities. Some firms break these costs out separately and add them to the cost base along with the cost to manufacture, and then apply a markup to this base that represents the expected profit on the

EXHIBIT 12–3

Price quotation sheet—absorption basis

Direct materials	$ 6
Direct labor	4
Overhead at 250% of direct labor cost	10
Total cost to manufacture	20
Markup to cover selling and administrative expenses and desired profit—50% of cost to manufacture	10
Target selling price	$30

goods being sold.[3] Other firms, however, such as Ritter Company in our example, prefer not to include the selling and administrative expenses in the cost base. This is because of the problems involved in trying to allocate the common selling and administrative expenses among the various products of the firm. For example, the salary of the company's president is a cost that is common to all products. It would be difficult to allocate the president's salary to these products in any meaningful way. Therefore, firms often provide for such costs in final, target selling prices by simply expanding the markup over cost to manufacture to include them as well as the desired profit, as we have done in Exhibit 12–3. This means, of course, that the markup must be structured with great care in order to ensure that it is sufficient to cover all that it is supposed to cover. More will be said on this point a little later.

If the Ritter Company produces and sells 10,000 units of its product at a selling price of $30 per unit, the income statement will appear as shown in Exhibit 12–4.

EXHIBIT 12–4

RITTER COMPANY
Income Statement
Absorption Basis

Sales (10,000 units at $30)	$300,000
Cost of goods sold (10,000 units at $20)	200,000
Gross margin	100,000
Selling and administrative expenses (10,000 units at $2 variable and $1 fixed)	30,000
Net income	$ 70,000

-----

[3] For a study showing the various bases used in cost-plus pricing, see V. Govindarajan and Robert N. Anthony, "How Firms Use Cost Data in Pricing Decisions," *Management Accounting* 65, no. 1 (July 1983), pp. 30–36.

The Contribution Approach

The contribution approach to cost-plus pricing differs from the absorption approach in that it emphasizes costs by behavior rather than by function. Thus, under the contribution approach the cost base consists of the variable expenses associated with a product. Included are the variable selling and administrative expenses, as well as the variable manufacturing expenses. Since no element of fixed cost is included in the base, the markup that is added must be adequate to cover the fixed costs, as well as to provide the desired profit per unit.

To illustrate, refer again to the cost data for the Ritter Company. The base to use in cost-plus pricing under the contribution approach would be $15, computed as follows:

Direct materials	$ 6
Direct labor	4
Variable overhead	3
Variable selling and administrative expenses	2
Total variable expenses	$15

Let us assume the Ritter Company has found that a markup of 100 percent of variable expenses is adequate to cover its fixed expenses and to provide the desired profit per unit. A price quotation sheet prepared under this assumption is shown in Exhibit 12–5.

Notice again that even though this pricing method is termed *cost*-plus pricing, a portion of the costs are buried in the *plus,* or markup, part of the formula. In this case, however, the buried costs are the fixed costs rather than the selling and administrative costs. Again, the reason for not including the fixed costs in the base can be traced to the time and difficulty that would be involved in any attempt to allocate. As a practical matter, there is no way to equitably allocate many common fixed costs, as discussed in Chapter 7. Any attempt to do so may result in less usable cost data for pricing, rather than more usable data. In addition, users of the contribution approach to pricing argue that keeping the cost base free of any element of fixed costs facilitates pricing in special and unusual situations. This point

EXHIBIT 12–5

Price quotation sheet—contribution basis

Direct materials	$ 6
Direct labor	4
Variable overhead	3
Variable selling and administrative expenses	2
Total variable expenses	15
Markup to cover fixed expenses and desired profit—	
100% of variable expenses	15
Target selling price	$30

EXHIBIT 12–6

RITTER COMPANY
Income Statement
Contribution Basis

Sales (10,000 units at $30).		$300,000
Less variable expenses (10,000 units at $15)		150,000
Contribution margin		150,000
Less fixed expenses:		
Production	$70,000	
Selling and administrative	10,000	80,000
Net income		$ 70,000

is discussed further in a following section dealing with special pricing problems.

Compare the contribution approach to cost-plus pricing in Exhibit 12–5 with the absorption approach in Exhibit 12–3. Although both approaches are employing the cost-plus concept, notice the difference in the way in which they handle the cost data and structure the price quotation sheet. Also notice that the Ritter Company can attain the *same* $30 target selling price by using either costing method.

In order to conclude the Ritter Company example, let us again assume that the company produces and sells 10,000 units of product at a selling price of $30 per unit. The company's income statement as it would appear under the contribution approach is shown in Exhibit 12–6.

Determining the Markup Percentage

By far the most crucial element in the cost-plus pricing formulas is the percentage markup added to the cost base. We have found that under both the absorption and the contribution approaches some elements of cost are buried in the markup figure. This means that the markup must be sufficient to cover these buried costs, as well as to provide a satisfactory return on assets employed, if long-run profit goals are to be met. How does the manager determine the "right" markup percentage to use in setting target selling prices? The markup chosen is a function of a number of variables, one of which is the company's desired return on investment (ROI).

Markup formulas   ROI is widely used by firms as a basis for determining the appropriate markup to add to products. The approach is to set a target ROI figure and then to structure the markup so that this target figure is achieved. A formula exists that can be used to determine the appropriate markup percentage, given the ROI figure that management wishes to obtain for the organization. Assuming use of the absorption approach to costing, the formula is:

$$\text{Markup percentage} = \frac{\dfrac{\text{Desired return on}}{\text{assets employed} } + \dfrac{\text{Selling and adminis-}}{\text{istrative expenses}} }{\text{Volume in units} \times \text{Unit cost to manufacture}} \qquad (1)$$

If the contribution approach to costing is used, the formula becomes:

$$\text{Markup percentage} = \frac{\dfrac{\text{Desired return on}}{\text{assets employed}} + \text{Fixed costs}}{\text{Volume in units} \times \text{Unit variable expenses}} \qquad (2)$$

Using the formulas   To show how the basic formula in (1) above is applied, assume Hart Company has determined that an investment of $2,000,000 is necessary to produce and market 50,000 units of product X each year. The $2,000,000 investment would cover purchase of equipment and provide funds needed to carry inventories and accounts receivable. In all, the company's accounting department estimates that the following costs and activity will be associated with the manufacture and sale of product X:

Number of units sold annually	50,000
Required investment in assets	$2,000,000
Cost to manufacture one unit	30
Selling and administrative expenses	700,000

If Hart Company desires a 25 percent ROI, then the required markup for the product will be [using formula (1) above]:

$$\text{Markup percentage} = \frac{\dfrac{\text{Desired return on}}{\text{assets employed}} + \dfrac{\text{Selling and adminis-}}{\text{trative expenses}}}{\text{Volume in units} \times \text{Unit cost to manufacture}}$$

$$\text{Markup percentage} = \frac{(25\% \times \$2,000,000) + \$700,000}{50,000 \text{ units} \times \$30}$$

$$= \frac{\$1,200,000}{\$1,500,000} = 80\%$$

Using this markup percentage, the selling price of a unit of product X would be set at $54:

Cost to manufacture	$30
Add markup—80% × $30	24
Target selling price.	$54

As proof that the $54 selling price for product X will permit Hart Company to achieve a 25 percent ROI, the company's income statement and a computation of its project ROI are presented in Exhibit 12–7.

As a concluding note, in our example we have focused on formula (1) given earlier. Formula (2) is applied in the same way, except that it is used when the manager prefers to base markups on variable costs and to use the contribution approach in preparing statements.

EXHIBIT 12–7

Income statement and ROI analysis—Hart Company

HART COMPANY
Budgeted Income Statement

Sales (50,000 units × $54)	$2,700,000
Less cost of goods sold (50,000 units × $30)	1,500,000
Gross margin	1,200,000
Less selling and administrative expenses	700,000
Net operating income	$ 500,000

Projected ROI (based on $2,000,000 in assets employed):

$$\frac{\text{Net operating income}}{\text{Sales}} \times \frac{\text{Sales}}{\text{Average operating assets}} = \text{ROI}$$

$$\frac{\$500,000}{\$2,700,000} \times \frac{\$2,700,000}{\$2,000,000} = \text{ROI}$$

$$18.52\%^* \times 1.35 = 25\%$$

* Rounded.

Adjusting Prices to Market Conditions

Although the cost-plus approach that we have been discussing can be of great assistance to the manager in determining target selling prices, care must be taken not to apply the cost-plus formulas too rigidly. The reason is that they tend to ignore the relationship between price and volume, and if applied too rigidly might result in less profits, rather than more profits, for the firm. For example, in the preceding illustration the competitive situation might be such for product X that a selling price of $54 would result in far less than 50,000 units being sold each year. On the other hand, at a $54 selling price, demand might be so great that the company would be swamped with orders.

In order to make cost-plus pricing formulas workable, companies usually do three things. First, they rarely price a product exactly at the target price suggested by the cost-plus formula. The costs used in the formula serve as a basis for establishing prices at their *lower limit*—the actual final selling price may be much higher than this minimum target figure. Many people have the mistaken notion that price is purely a function of cost, when in reality cost serves in large part simply to define the lower limit that can be set. Noncost factors, such as competitive position, promotional strategy, packaging, and ability to achieve long-term product differentiation, may permit a manager to set a price significantly higher than the minimum target figure provided by use of the cost formulas. The mark of real executives in pricing can be found in their ability to sense the market situation and to know when price adjustments can and should be made. If such executives sense that their competitive position is strong, they will adjust the prices upward; if they sense a strengthening of opposing competitive forces, then they will either shade the prices downward or attempt to further differentiate the product.

Second, the price setter must recognize that even if a particular margin has been obtainable for the last 20 or 30 years, this is no assurance that it will continue to be obtainable. For example, the neighborhood grocery stores suddenly discovered in the 1940s that the margins they had been obtaining for many decades were no longer obtainable because of the development of large chain supermarkets. In turn, the chain supermarkets discovered in the 1970s that the margins they had enjoyed for nearly three decades were being undercut by the self-service discount food outlets. In order to achieve target ROI figures, managers are often required to trade off some margin in order to achieve a higher turnover of assets, as we pointed out in our ROI discussion in Chapter 11. This means that markups must sometimes be reduced in the hope of stimulating the overall volume of sales.

Third, companies will not use the same markup for all product lines, but rather will vary the markup according to custom, need, or general industry practice. For example, one product line may carry a markup of 20 percent, whereas another may carry a markup of 60 percent. This is typical of clothing and department stores, where the percentage markup varies by department and occasionally even by item. Jewelry generally has a high markup, whereas stockings carry a relatively low markup.

Why Use Cost Data in Pricing?

If pricing executives end up setting prices according to how they sense the market, then an obvious question at this point is, ''Why bother using cost data in the pricing decision?'' Several reasons can be advanced in favor of computing target selling prices by means of the cost-plus formulas even if the resulting prices are later modified. First, in making pricing decisions, the manager is faced with a myriad of uncertainties. Cost-plus target prices represent a *starting point,* a way of perhaps removing some of the uncertainties and shedding some light on others. By this means, the manager may be able to feel his or her way more easily through the thicket and come up with a price that will be acceptable given the constraints at hand.

Second, cost might be viewed as a floor of protection, guarding the price setter from pricing too low and incurring losses. Although this line of reasoning is appealing and reassuring, the protection offered by the cost floor is more illusory than real. For one thing, we have already noted that neither the absorption approach nor the contribution approach includes all costs in the cost base. For another thing, unit cost depends on volume. This is because many costs are fixed, and unit cost will therefore depend on the number of units produced and sold. Even though selling prices may be set above total costs, losses may still be incurred if the volume of sales is less than estimated, thereby forcing per unit costs upward to the point that they exceed the selling price.

Third, formula-based target selling prices may give the price setter some insights into competitors' costs, or help him to predict what a competitive price will be. For example, if a company is operating in an industry where 30 percent markups over cost to manufacture are common, then the company may be able to assume that this same pattern will hold for new products, and thereby either predict competitors' prices or price in such a way as to gain quick acceptance of a new product line. On the other hand, by following standard markups over cost, a company may be able to largely *neutralize* the pricing issue and concentrate on competing in other ways, such as in delivery or in credit terms.

Finally, many firms have such a wide range of products that they simply don't have the time to do a detailed cost-volume-profit analysis on every item in every product line. Cost-plus pricing formulas provide a quick and direct way to reach at least a tentative price that can be further refined as time and circumstances permit.

TIME AND MATERIAL PRICING

Instead of computing prices by means of a cost-plus formula, some companies use an alternative approach called **time and material pricing.** Under this method, two pricing rates are established—one based on direct labor time and the other based on direct material used. In each case, the rate is constructed so that it includes an allowance for selling and administrative expenses, for other direct costs, and for a desired profit. This pricing method is widely used in television and appliance repair shops, in automobile repair shops, in printing shops, and in similar types of service organizations. In addition, it is used by various kinds of professionals, including accountants, attorneys, physicians, and consultants.

Time Component

The time component is typically expressed as a rate per direct labor-hour. The rate is computed by adding together three elements: (1) the direct costs of the employee, including salary and fringe benefits; (2) a pro rata allowance for selling and administrative expenses of the organization; and (3) an allowance for a desired profit per hour of employee time. In some organizations (such as a repair shop), the same hourly rate will be charged regardless of which employee is assigned to complete a job; in other organizations, the rate may vary by employee. For example, in an accounting firm, the rate charged for a new assistant accountant's time will generally be less than the rate charged for an experienced senior accountant or for a partner.

Material Component

The material component is determined by adding a *material loading charge* to the invoice price of any materials used on the job. The **material loading charge** is designed to cover the costs of ordering, handling, and carrying materials in stock, plus a profit margin on the materials themselves. Typically, a material loading charge will fall somewhere between 30 percent and 50 percent of the invoice cost of the materials.

An Example of Time and Material Pricing

To provide a numerical example of time and material pricing, assume the following data:

The Quality Auto Shop uses time and material pricing for all of its repair work. The shop's time and material rates have been computed as follows:

Computing the time rate

The shop pays its mechanics an average of $8 per hour and incurs another $3 per hour for fringe benefits. The shop manager estimates that the following additional shop costs and selling and administrative expenses are incurred each year:

Shop supervision (including costs of supervisory fringe benefits) . .	$ 40,000
Supplies	16,000
Depreciation	70,000
Miscellaneous selling and administrative expenses.	90,000
Total	$216,000

The mechanics employed by the shop work a total of 24,000 hours per year. The manager feels that a reasonable profit for the shop can be computed on a basis of $5 per hour of mechanic's time. Using these data, the charge to customers for each hour of service time on a repair job would be:

Mechanics' pay per hour, including fringes ($8 + $3) . . .	$11
Pro rata share of shop and other costs	9*
Desired profit per hour of mechanic time	5
Total charging rate per hour for service.	$25

* $216,000 ÷ 24,000 hours = $9 per hour.

Computing the material loading charge

For materials, the shop incurs the following costs each year in ordering, handling, and storing parts:

Parts employees—wages and fringe benefits . .	$30,000
Utilities	16,000
Property taxes	4,800
Insurance	1,200
Rent	8,000
Total	$60,000

The invoice cost of parts used in the shop totals $240,000 per year. If the company desires a profit margin equal to 15 percent of the invoice cost of parts used, then the material loading charge would be computed as follows:

Charge for ordering, handling, and storing parts ($60,000 ÷ $240,000)	25% of invoice cost
Desired profit margin on parts	15% of invoice cost
Material loading charge	40% of invoice cost

Thus, the amount charged for parts on a job will consist of the invoice cost of the parts plus a material loading charge equal to 40 percent of this cost.

Billing a job

To complete our example, a repair job in the shop that required 2½ hours of labor time and $60 in parts would be priced as follows:

Labor time: 2½ hours × $25		$ 62.50
Materials used:		
Invoice cost	$60.00	
Material loading charge (40% × $60) . . .	24.00	84.00
Total price of the job		$146.50

Rather than using labor-hours as a basis for computing a time rate, a machine shop, a printing shop, or a similar organization might use machine-hours. Some organizations might charge a different rate per machine-hour, depending on the type of machine used.

PRICING NEW PRODUCTS

New products easily present the most challenging pricing problems, for the reason that the uncertainties involved are so great. If a new product is unlike anything currently on the market, then demand will be uncertain. If the new product is similar to products already being sold, then uncertainty will exist as to the degree of substitution that will develop between the new product and the already available products. Uncertainty will also exist over ultimate marketing costs, and so forth. In order to reduce the level of these uncertainties, a firm will often resort to some type of experimental or test marketing.

Test Marketing of Products

Many firms have used **test marketing** with great success in order to gain data relative to the pricing decision. The approach is to introduce the new product in selected areas only, generally at different prices in different areas. By this means, a company can gather data on the competition that the product will encounter, on the relationship between volume and price, and on the contribution to profits that can be expected at various selling prices and volumes of sales. A price can then be selected that will result in the greatest overall contribution to profits, or that seems best in relation to the company's long-run objectives.

Of course, test marketing is not the same thing as the full-scale production and marketing of a product, but it can provide highly useful information that can help to ensure that the full-scale effort will be successful. An added benefit can be found in the fact that through test marketing it may be possible to keep any errors in pricing on a small scale, rather than nationwide.

Pricing Strategies

Two basic pricing strategies are available to the price setter in pricing new products. These pricing strategies are known as **skimming pricing** and **penetration pricing.**

Skimming pricing involves setting a high initial price for a new product, with a progressive lowering of the price as time passes and as the market broadens and matures. The purpose of skimming pricing is to maximize short-run profits. In effect, it represents a direct application of the economist's pricing models discussed earlier in the chapter.

Penetration pricing involves setting low initial prices in order to gain quick acceptance in a broad portion of the market. It calls for the sacrifice of some short-run profits in order to achieve a better long-run market position. Whether a firm adopts the skimming strategy or the penetration strategy will depend on what it is trying to accomplish and on which approach appears to offer the greatest chance for success.

For example, many new products have a certain novelty appeal that causes demand to be quite price inelastic. In these cases, high initial prices are often set and maintained until competitors develop competing products and begin price cutting. As sales volume becomes more sensitive to sales price, prices are slowly reduced until the point is reached where a penetration price is possible that permits access to a mass market. A good example of this type of skimming strategy can be found in the marketing of electronic calculators. Prices of hand-sized calculators started at about $300 in the early 1970s and dropped to less than $25 in about three years' time, finally permitting access to a market so wide that it included the purchasing of calculators for use in weekly grocery shopping. Television sets, stereo sets, automobiles, electronic ovens, and some drug products all went through a similar skimming pricing period before prices were eventually lowered to a mass market penetration level.

One strong argument in favor of skimming pricing is that it offers some protection against unexpected costs in the production and marketing of a product. If a new product is priced on a penetration basis and costs are unexpectedly high, then the company may be forced to raise prices later— not an easy thing to do when you are trying to gain wide market acceptance of a new product. On the other hand, if a new product is priced initially on a skimming level, the company has a layer of protection that can be used to absorb any unexpected costs or cost increases. Even if this later causes price reductions to be less than expected, the company will still be in the more favorable position of reducing prices rather than raising them.

Skimming pricing is most effective in those markets where entry is relatively difficult because of the technology or investment required. The easier that market entry becomes, the smaller is the likelihood that skimming can be carried off very effectively, or at least for a very long period of time. For example, skimming pricing was possible for many years in the computer industry because of technological barriers to entry. By contrast, it is doubtful whether skimming pricing was ever much of a factor in the marketing of household cleaning products.

Target Costs and Product Pricing

Our discussion thus far has presumed that a product has already been developed, has been costed, and that it is ready to be marketed as soon as a price is set. In many cases, the sequence of events is just the reverse. That is, the company will already *know* what price should be charged, and the problem will be to *develop* a product that can be marketed profitably at the desired price. Even in this situation, where the normal sequence of events is reversed, cost is still a crucial factor. The company's approach will be to set **target costs** that can be used as guides in developing a product that can be sold within the desired price range.

This approach is used widely in the household appliance industry, where a company will determine in advance the price range in which it wants a particular product model to sell and then will set about to develop the model. Component parts will be designed and then costed item by item to see whether the total cost is compatible with the target cost already set. If not, the parts will be redesigned and recosted, and features will be changed or eliminated until the expected costs fall within the desired targets. Prototypes will then be developed, and again costs will be carefully analyzed to be sure that the desired targets are being met. In these types of situations, the accountant can be of great help to management by continually pointing out the relationships between cost and volume, by segregating relevant costs where needed, and by assisting in the organization and interpretation of cost data.

To provide a numerical example of how to compute a target cost figure, assume the following situation:

Handy Appliance Company wants to produce a hand mixer that will sell for $29. In order to produce 25,000 mixers a year, an investment of $625,000 would be required. The company desires a 15 percent ROI. Selling and administrative costs associated with the mixer would total $200,000 per year. Given these data, the target cost to manufacture one mixer would be:

Projected sales (25,000 mixers × $29)		$725,000
Less required markup:		
Selling and administrative expenses	$200,000	
Desired ROI (15% × $625,000)	93,750	
Total markup		293,750
Target cost to manufacture 25,000 mixers		$431,250

Target cost to manufacture one mixer: $431,250 ÷ 25,000 = $17.25

Thus, the company should produce the new mixer only if it can be manufactured at a target cost of $17.25 or less per unit.

SPECIAL PRICING DECISIONS

When faced with a pricing decision, which pricing method should the manager use—the absorption approach illustrated in Exhibit 12–3 or the contribution approach illustrated in Exhibit 12–5? If all pricing decisions were related to the pricing of *standard* products, the answer would be that it really wouldn't matter which method was used.[4] We have already seen that the same target selling price for a standard product can be obtained using either method. The choice would probably depend on which method was otherwise being used to cost units of product. If the absorption method was otherwise in use, then it would be simpler to go ahead and use it as a basis for pricing decisions as well; the opposite would be the case if contribution costing was otherwise in use.

But not all pricing decisions relate to standard products; many pricing decisions relate to special or unusual situations. For example, a company may get a large order for a product but be asked to quote a special, one-time-only price. Or a special order may come in from a foreign customer who wants a special price on a standard item on a continuing basis because his or her order represents business that the company otherwise wouldn't have. A company may have substantial idle capacity and be faced with the problem of pricing special products that are not a part of the regular line and that are being produced on a limited basis. Finally, a company may be in a competitive bidding situation and forced to bid on many unlike jobs, some of which will be on a more or less continuing basis and others will be one-time-only affairs.

All of these situations present *special* pricing problems of one kind or another. Some managers believe that special problems such as these can be handled more easily by the contribution approach than by the absorption approach to pricing.[5] The reasons are twofold. First, advocates of the contribution approach argue that it provides the price setter with more detailed information than does the absorption approach, and that the information it provides is structured in a way that parallels the way in which the price setter is used to thinking—in terms of cost-volume-profit relationships. And second, it is argued that the contribution approach provides the price setter with a flexible framework that is immediately adaptable to *any* pricing problem, without the necessity of doing a lot of supplementary analytical work.

---

[4] The Govindarajan and Anthony study cited earlier found that 83 percent of the 504 companies in the study used some form of full cost (either absorption cost or absorption cost plus selling and administrative expenses) as a basis for normal, long-run pricing. The remaining 17 percent used only variable costs as a basis for pricing decisions. Ibid., p. 31.

[5] See Thomas M. Bruegelmann, Gaile Haessly, Claire P. Wolfangel, and Michael Schiff, "How Variable Costing Is Used in Pricing Decisions," *Management Accounting* 66, no. 10 (April 1985), pp. 58–65.

Pricing a Special Order

In order to illustrate the adaptability of the contribution approach to special pricing situations, and to show how the data it presents guides the price setter in decisions, let us assume the following price quotation sheets for the Helms Company:

Absorption method		Contribution method	
Direct materials	$ 6	Direct materials	$ 6
Direct labor	7	Direct labor	7
Overhead at 100% of direct		Variable overhead	2
labor	7	Variable selling and	
Total cost to manufacture	20	administrative	1
Markup—20%	4	Total variable expenses	16
Target selling price	$24	Markup—50%	8
		Target selling price	$24

These price quotation sheets relate to a vacuum pump that the Helms Company manufactures and markets through jobbers. The company has never been able to sell all of the pumps that it can produce, and for this reason it is constantly on the lookout for new business. Let us assume that the Helms Company has just been approached by a foreign distributor who wants to purchase 10,000 pumps at a price of $19 per pump. Should the company accept the offer?

The absorption method   The price quotation sheet prepared above by the absorption method is of little help in making the decision. If the Helms Company tries to relate the $20 "cost to manufacture" to the proposed $19 price, then the offer is clearly not attractive:

Sales (10,000 units at $19)	$190,000
Less absorption cost to manufacture (10,000 units at $20) . .	200,000
Net loss from the order	$ (10,000)

On the other hand, since there is idle capacity in the plant, management may be tempted to accept the offer. The dilemma is that no one really *knows* from looking at the price quotation sheet which course of action is best. The pricing system doesn't provide the essential keys that are needed to move in an intelligent way. As a result, whatever decision is made will be made either on a "seat of the pants" basis or only after much effort has been expended in trying to dig into the cost records for additional information.

The contribution method   By contrast, the price quotation sheet prepared by the contribution method provides the company with exactly the framework that it needs in making the decision. Since this price quotation sheet is organized by cost behavior, it dovetails precisely with cost-volume-profit concepts, and it enables the decision maker to reach his or her decisions without having to do all kinds of adding digging and analytical work in the cost records.

Consider the Helms Company data. Since the company has idle capacity (for which there is apparently no other use), fixed overhead costs are irrelevant to the decision over whether to accept the foreign distributor's offer. Any amount received over unit variable costs (and any *incremental* fixed costs[6]) will increase overall profitability; therefore, rather than relating the proposed purchase price to the $20 "cost to manufacture," the company should relate it to the unit variable costs involved. This is easy to do if the regular price quotation sheet on a product is organized by cost behavior, such as shown above under the contribution method. In the case of the Helms Company, the unit variable costs are $16. Assuming that the unit variable costs associated with the special order will be the same as those associated with regular business, the analysis would be:

Sales (10,000 units at $19)	$190,000
Less variable expenses (10,000 units at $16)	160,000
Contribution margin promised by the order (and also increased net income, if the fixed costs don't change)	$ 30,000

In sum, by using the price quotation sheet prepared by the contribution method, the Helms Company will be able to see a clear-cut, short-run advantage to accepting the foreign distributor's offer. Before any final decision can be made, however, the Helms Company will have to weigh long-run considerations very carefully, particularly the impact that accepting this offer might have on future efforts to secure a position in foreign markets. Accepting the $19 price might seriously undermine future negotiations with foreign dealers and cause disruptions in the long-run profitability of the firm. The Helms Company may feel that it would be better to forego the short-run $30,000 increase in contribution margin in order to protect its future long-run market position.

The essential point of our discussion is that the contribution approach to pricing contains a ready-made framework within which the price setter can operate in special pricing situations. By organizing costs in a way that is compatible with cost-volume-profit concepts, this approach to structuring price quotation sheets assists the manager in isolating those costs that are relevant in special pricing decisions and guides the manager in those decisions from a cost point of view.

The Variable Pricing Model

The contribution approach to pricing can be presented in general model form, as shown in Exhibit 12–8.

The contribution approach provides a **ceiling** and a **floor** between which the price setter operates. The ceiling represents the price that the manager would *like* to obtain, and indeed *must* obtain on the bulk of the sales over the long run. But under certain conditions, the model shows that the manager can move within the **range of flexibility** as far down as the floor of variable

---

[6] That is, any added fixed costs that are incurred solely as a result of added sales.

EXHIBIT 12–8
The contribution approach to pricing: A general model

Variable costs:
Direct materials . . . . $ XX
Direct labor   XX
Variable overhead   XX
Variable selling and administrative . .   XX
Total variable costs . . . .   XXX Floor ⎫
Markup (to cover the fixed costs   ⎬ Range of
    and desired profit)   XX   ⎰ flexibility
Target selling price . . . . $XXX Ceiling ⎭

costs in quoting a price to a prospective customer. What are the conditions under which a price based on variable costs alone might be appropriate? We can note three:

1. When idle capacity exists, as in the case of the Helms Company.
2. When operating under distress conditions.
3. When faced with sharp competition on particular orders under a competitive bidding situation.

When any of these conditions exist, it may be possible to increase overall profitability by pricing *some* jobs, products, or orders at *any amount* above variable costs, even if this amount is substantially less than the normal markup.

We will now examine each of the three special conditions listed above more closely to see how each relates to the range of flexibility depicted in Exhibit 12–8.

Idle capacity   There is no need to be concerned about the range of flexibility depicted in Exhibit 12–8 so long as a company can sell all that it can produce at regular prices. That is, no company is going to sell at less than regular prices if regular prices are obtainable.

However, a different situation exists if a company has idle capacity that can't be used to expand regular sales at regular prices. Under these conditions, any use to which the idle capacity can be put that increases revenues more than variable costs (and any *incremental* fixed costs) will increase overall net income.

The use might come in the form of a special order for a regular product from a customer that the company does not usually supply (such as a foreign market). Or the use might come in the form of a slight modification of a regular product to be sold under a new customer's own brand name. Alternatively, the use might come in the form of a special order for a product that the company does not usually produce. In any of these situations, so long as the price received on the extra business exceeds the variable costs (and any *incremental* fixed costs) involved, overall net income will be increased by utilizing the idle capacity.

The Helms Company is a good example of the sort of situation we are talking about. The company has idle capacity, and there is no prospect of using the idle capacity for regular business. Under these conditions, nothing will be lost by quoting a price to the foreign distributor that is below full cost, or even relaxing the price down very close to the floor of variable costs, if necessary.

Distress conditions   Occasionally a company is forced to operate under distress conditions when the market for its product has been adversely affected in some way. For example, demand may virtually dry up overnight, forcing the company to drop its prices sharply downward. Under these conditions, any contribution that can be obtained to help cover fixed costs may be preferable to ceasing operations altogether. If operations cease, then *no* contribution will be available to apply toward fixed costs.

Competitive bidding   The pricing model illustrated in Exhibit 12–8 is particularly useful in competitive bidding situations. Competition is often hot and fierce in situations where bidding is involved, so companies can't afford to be inflexible in their pricing. Unfortunately, many companies refuse to cut prices in the face of stiff competition, adamantly stating that they price only on a "full cost" basis and don't want the business unless they can get a "decent price" for the work. There are several problems associated with taking this kind of position on pricing. First, it involves faulty logic. The so-called decent price is obtained by adding some markup onto "full cost." But cost is dependent on *volume* of sales, which in turn is dependent on selling price.

Second, as discussed in Chapter 11, there are *two* determinants of profitability—margin and turnover. The "decent price" attitude ignores the turnover factor and focuses entirely on the margin factor. Yet many companies have demonstrated that a more modest margin combined with a faster turnover of assets can be highly effective from a profitability point of view. One way to increase turnover, of course, is to be flexible in bidding by shading prices in situations where competition is keen.

Finally, in situations where fixed costs are high, a company can't *afford* to be inflexible in its pricing policies. Once an investment in plant and other fixed productive facilities has been made, a company's strategy must be to generate every dollar of contribution that it can to assist in the covering of these costs. Even if a company is forced to operate at an accounting loss, this might be preferable to having no contribution at all toward recovery of investment.

CRITICISMS OF THE CONTRIBUTION APPROACH TO PRICING

Not all managers are enthusiastic about the contribution approach to pricing. Some argue that the contribution approach, with its reliance on variable costs, can lead to setting prices too low and to eventual bankruptcy. These managers argue that the absorption approach to pricing is superior to the contribution approach since it includes an element of fixed overhead cost in the pricing base, whereas the contribution approach includes only the variable costs. Including an element of fixed overhead cost in the pricing base is said to make the absorption approach safer in terms of long-run pricing. Managers who argue in this way feel that if variable costs alone are used in pricing, the price setter may be misled into accepting *any* price over variable costs on a long-run basis for any product.

This argument can be criticized on several points. We should note first that the absorption approach to pricing excludes as many costs from the pricing base as does the contribution approach. It just excludes *different* costs. For example, the absorption approach doesn't consider selling and administrative costs in its base, since the base typically consists of ''costs to manufacture.'' By contrast, the contribution approach does include variable selling and administrative expenses along with variable production expenses in developing a base for pricing.

Whether or not *any* pricing mechanism results in intelligent pricing decisions will depend in large part on the ability of the price setter to use the available data. As a practical matter, this means that pricing decisions must be restricted to managers who are qualified to make them. This point has been made very well in an NAA study of actual pricing practices:

> No instance of unprofitable pricing attributable to direct costing was reported, but on the contrary, opinion was frequently expressed to the effect that direct costing had contributed to better pricing decisions. However, companies restrict product cost and margin data to individuals qualified to interpret such data and responsible for pricing policy decisions.[7]

On the other hand, no matter how expert a decision maker may be, the decisions will be faulty if the cost information with which he or she is working is irrelevant, unclear, or inadequate. Firms that have adopted the contribution approach to pricing have found that the old pricing system often led to incorrect pricing decisions because of faulty data:

> Instances were cited in which management had unknowingly continued selling products below out-of-pocket cost or had decided to withdraw from the market when a substantial portion of the period costs would have been recovered. . . .
> In one interview . . . when direct costing was introduced, analysis demonstrated that contracts which would have contributed to period costs had often been refused at times when the company had a large amount of idle capacity.[8]

PRICE DISCRIMINATION

In structuring a pricing policy, firms must take care to keep their actions within the requirements of the various laws that deal with price setting and with price discimination. The most widely known of these is the **Robinson-Patman Act** of 1936. The act forbids quoting different prices to compet-

---

[7] National Association of Accountants, *Research Report No. 37,* ''Current Applications of Direct costing'' (New York, January 1961), p. 55.

[8] Ibid.

ing customers unless the difference in price can be traced directly to "differences in the cost of manufacture, sale, or delivery resulting from the differing methods or quantites in which commodities are to such purchasers sold or delivered." Both the Federal Trade Commission and the courts have consistently held that "cost" is to be interpreted as full cost and not just incremental or variable costs. This means that in the case of *competing* customers for the *same* goods, price differences cannot be defended on the basis of covering incremental costs alone. Note, though, that we are talking about *competing* customers for the *same* goods. We are not talking about a competitive bidding situation, nor are we talking about a situation in which idle capacity might be used to produce for a noncompeting market or for some purpose other than production of regular products.

In addition to the Robinson-Patman Act, all states have laws prohibiting the sale of goods or services below "cost." Cost is normally either specified as full cost or is so interpreted by the regulating agencies. Although these state laws might appear to greatly restrict the flexibility of management in pricing decisions, they are often interpreted to apply to a company's products *as a whole,* rather than to individual products. For example, a store may be able to sell bread below cost (often called a "loss leader") so long as it sells its products *as a whole* over cost. These laws do suggest, however, that firms should keep careful records of their costs and of the way their prices are structured in order to be able to answer questions of regulatory bodies.

An international law relating to pricing exists in the form of the Anti-Dumping Law of 1932. This law prohibits the sale of products below cost in international markets. Again, "cost" is interpreted as full cost, including fully allocated fixed costs. The law is designed to protect a domestic manufacturer in its home market in those instances where it is in direct competition with a foreign supplier.

SUMMARY

The general pricing models of the economist contain the basic framework for pricing decisions. Since these models are conceptual in nature, and since the specific information required for their direct application is rarely available, firms normally rely on pricing formulas to implement the ideas that the models contain. Pricing decisions can be divided into three broad groups:

1. Pricing standard products.
2. Pricing new products.
3. Pricing special orders.

The pricing of standard and new products is generally carried out through cost-plus pricing formulas. Such formulas require a cost base, to which a markup is added to derive a target selling price. Cost-plus pricing can be carried out equally well using either the absorption approach or the contribution approach.

Service-type organizations, such as repair shops and professional firms, use a pricing method known as time and material pricing. Under this approach, two pricing rates are established—one rate for time spent on a job, such as labor time or machine time, and another rate for materials used. In each case, the rate is structured so as to include a profit element as well as the direct costs of the time and material involved.

The pricing of special orders is somewhat different from the pricing of regular products or services in that in some situations full costs may not be applicable in setting prices. Circumstances may exist in which the price setter may be justified in pricing simply on a basis of variable or incremental costs. In these special pricing situations, price setters often find the contribution approach, with its emphasis on cost behavior, more useful than the absorption approach, which may require considerable reworking of data in order to generate the information needed for a pricing decision.

KEY TERMS FOR REVIEW

Ceiling A term used in relation to the range of flexibility that denotes the price that is obtained by adding a normal markup to the cost base in cost-plus pricing.

Cost-plus pricing A pricing method in which some predetermined markup is added to a cost base in determining a target selling price.

Floor A term used in relation to the range of flexibility that denotes the variable costs associated with a product.

Marginal cost A term used in economics that means the addition to total cost resulting from the production and sale of one additional unit of product.

Marginal revenue A term used in economics that means the addition to total revenue resulting from the sale of one additional unit of product.

Markup The amount added to a cost base in determining the target selling price in cost-plus pricing.

Material loading charge An amount added to the invoice cost of materials that is designed to cover (1) the costs of ordering, handling, and carrying the materials in stock and (2) a profit margin on the materials themselves.

Monopolistic competition A term used in economics that denotes a situation in which there are many sellers of similar products, with no one seller having a large enough share of the market for other sellers to be able to discern the effect of its pricing decisions on their sales.

Monopoly A term used in economics that denotes the absence of a directly competing product in the market.

Oligopoly A term used in economics that denotes a situation in which a few large sellers of a product are competing directly with one another.

Penetration pricing The setting of a low initial price for a product in order to gain quick acceptance in a broad portion of the market.

Price elasticity A term used in economics that means the degree to which volume of sales is affected by a change in price per unit.

Range of flexibility The range between the "floor" of variable costs and the "ceiling" of a normal target selling price in which a manager has to operate in special pricing decisions.

Robinson-Patman Act A federal law that prohibits discrimination in pricing between competing customers for a good or service.

Skimming pricing The setting of a high initial price for a product, with a progressive lowering of the price as time passes and as the market broadens and matures.

Target cost A maximum amount of production cost, which is used as a guide in developing a product that can be sold within a desired price range.

Test marketing The introduction of a product in selected areas in order to gain data on customer acceptance, volume of activity at various prices, and so forth.

Time and material pricing A pricing method, often used in service-type organizations, in which two pricing rates are established—one based on labor time and the other based on materials used.

QUESTIONS

12–1.   Why does the economist depict a slowing down of the rate of increase in total revenue as more and more units are sold?

12–2.   As depicted by the total revenue and total cost curves, what is the optimum point of production and what is the optimum price to be charged for a product?

12–3.   According to the marginal revenue and marginal cost curves, what is the optimum point of production and what is the optimum price to charge for a product?

12–4.   What is meant by price elasticity? Contrast a product that is price inelastic with a product that is price elastic.

12–5.   Identify four limitations of the economic pricing models.

12–6.   What costs are relevant in long-run pricing decisions?

12–7.   What is meant by the term *cost-plus pricing?* Distinguish between the absorption and contribution approaches to cost-plus pricing.

12–8.   In what sense is the term *cost-plus pricing* a misnomer?

12–9.   "Full cost can be viewed as a floor of protection. If a firm always sets its prices above full cost, it will never have to worry about operating at a loss." Discuss.

12–10.   In cost-plus pricing, what elements must be covered by the "markup" when the cost base consists of the cost to manufacture a product? What elements must be covered when the cost base consists of a product's variable expenses?

12–11.   What is time and material pricing? What type of organization would use time and material pricing?

12–12.   What is a material loading charge?

12–13.   Distinguish between skimming pricing and penetration pricing. Which strategy would you probably use if you were introducing a new product that was highly price inelastic? Why?

12–14.   What are *target costs,* and how do they enter into the pricing decision?

12–15.   What problem is sometimes encountered in trying to price special orders under absorption costing?

12–16.   Identify those circumstances under which the manager might be justified in pricing at any amount above variable costs.

12–17.   In what ways does the Robinson-Patman Act influence pricing decisions?

EXERCISES

E12–1.   Ortega Company must determine a target selling price for one of its products. Cost data relating to the product are given below:

	Per unit	Total
Direct materials	$ 8	
Direct labor	12	
Variable overhead	3	
Fixed overhead	7	$350,000
Variable selling and administrative expense	2	
Fixed selling and administrative expense	4	200,000

The costs above are based on an anticipated volume of 50,000 units produced and sold each period. The company uses cost-plus pricing, and it has a policy of obtaining target selling prices by adding a markup of 50 percent of cost to manufacture or by adding a markup of 80 percent of variable costs.

Required: 1.   Assuming that the company uses absorption costing, compute the target selling price for one unit of product.

2.   Assuming that the company uses the contribution approach to costing, compute the target selling price for one unit of product.

E12–2.   Martin Company is considering the introduction of a new product. In order to determine an estimated selling price, the company has gathered the following information:

Number of units to be produced and sold each year.	14,000
Unit cost to manufacture	$ 25
Projected annual selling and administrative expenses	50,000
Estimated investment required by the company	750,000
Desired ROI	12%

The company uses cost-plus pricing and the absorption costing method.

Required: 1.   Compute the markup the company will have to use in order to achieve the desired ROI.

2.   Compute the target selling price per unit.

E12–3.   Martice, Ltd., is ready to introduce a new product on the market and is trying to determine what price to charge. The new product has required a $2,000,000 investment in equipment and working capital. The company wants a 15 percent ROI on all products. The following cost information is available on the new product:

	Per unit	Annual total
Variable production costs (direct materials, direct labor, and variable overhead)	$32	
Fixed overhead costs	—	$400,000
Variable selling and administrative expenses . . .	8	
Fixed selling and administrative expenses	—	200,000

The company uses cost-plus pricing and the contribution approach to costing.

Required: 1. Assume that the company expects to sell 75,000 units each year. What percentage markup on variable costs would be required to achieve the target ROI? Using this markup, what would be the selling price per unit?
  2. Repeat the computations in (1) above, assuming that the company expects to sell 45,000 units each year.

E12–4.   The Reliable TV Repair Shop employs five technicians and incurs the following costs in its repair operations:

Repair technicians:		
Wage rate per hour	$	12
Fringe benefits per hour		3
Selling, administrative, and other costs of the repairs operation per year . . .		90,000
Materials:		
Costs of ordering, handling, and storing parts		20% of invoice cost

Each technician works a 40-hour week, 50 weeks a year. The company desires a profit of $6 per hour of technician time and a profit on materials equal to 40 percent of invoice cost.

Required: 1. Assume that the company uses time and material pricing. Compute the time rate and the material loading charge that should be used to bill jobs.
  2. One of the company's repair technicians has just completed a repair job that required 2.5 hours of time and $80 in parts (invoice cost). Compute the amount that should be billed for the job.

E12–5.   Westridge Electronics has a highly automated plant in which radio/cassette players are manufactured. The company has always used the absorption approach for product costing and for pricing. A price quotation sheet for the radio/cassette player is given below:

Direct materials	$ 80
Direct labor	27
Overhead ($8 variable + $35 fixed) . . .	43
Total cost to manufacture	150
Markup—40%	60
Target selling price	$210

The company incurs $5 in variable selling costs per unit and $300,000 per year in fixed selling and administrative costs. It produces and sells 8,000 radio/cassette players each year. Management is considering the use of the contribution approach internally and wants to see what a price quotation sheet would look like if this costing method were used rather than the absorption method.

Required: 1.   The accounting department has determined that the company would have to use a markup of 75 percent if the contribution approach were used in determining target selling prices. Prepare a price quotation sheet for a radio/cassette player using the contribution approach.
2.   Identify the ceiling and the floor on the price quotation sheet that you have prepared and explain their significance to the manager.
3.   Assume that the company has idle capacity and would like to run a 10-day special on radio/cassette players for $148 each. Does it appear that this price would add to the company's overall profits? Explain.

E12–6.   To a large extent, the selling price that must be obtained on a product will be dependent on the number of units that can be sold. Consider the following data on a new product:

Variable production cost per unit. . . . . $	12
Variable selling and administrative expenses per unit . .	3
Fixed production cost (total).	480,000
Fixed selling and administrative expenses (total)	500,000
Desired markup	75%

The company uses the absorption method for product costing and for pricing.

Required: 1.   What would be the target selling price per unit if the company can produce and sell *(a)* 30,000 units each period and *(b)* 60,000 units each period?
2.   If the company charges the prices that you computed in (1) above, will it be assured that no losses will be sustained? Explain.

E12–7.   Shimada Products is anxious to enter the electronic calculator market. Management believes that in order to be competitive, the electronic calculator that the company produces can't be priced at more than $15. Shimada requires a minimum return of 12 percent on all investments. An investment of $500,000 would be required in order to acquire the equipment needed to produce 30,000 calculators each year. Selling and administrative expenses would total $120,000 per year.

Required: Compute the target cost to manufacture one calculator.

E12–8.   Delsey Products, Inc., wants to produce and sell a small, portable vacuum cleaner. Projected costs and other information about the vacuum cleaner are given below:

Annual sales in units.	12,000
Manufacturing costs:	
Variable per unit:	
Direct materials . . . . $	30
Direct labor	8
Variable overhead	5
Fixed in total	90,000
Selling and administrative expenses:	
Variable per unit	2
Fixed in total	210,000

As a first approximation to a selling price, the company normally uses a markup of 60 percent of variable costs, which represents the markup typically used in the industry.

Required: 1.   Compute the target selling price for the new product, using the contribution approach.
2.   Assume that the company will not add a new product unless it promises a return on investment of at least 16 percent. The new vacuum clearner would require an investment in equipment and other assets of $825,000. What markup percentage would be required on the new product to provide the desired ROI? (Assume that the company uses the contribution approach to pricing.)

PROBLEMS

P12–9.   **Percentage markups and price quotation sheets.**   Dover Company produces and markets a number of consumer products, including a food blender. Cost and revenue data on the blender for 19x8, the most recent year, are given below:

	25,000 units sold	
	Total	Per unit
Sales	$1,200,000	$48.00
Cost of goods sold	750,000	30.00*
Gross margin.	450,000	18.00
Selling and administrative expenses . .	310,000	12.40
Net income	$ 140,000	$ 5.60

* Contains $9 per unit in direct materials, $6 per unit in direct labor, and $3 per unit in variable overhead.

Fixed overhead costs comprise $300,000 of the cost of goods sold, and $260,000 of the selling and administrative expenses are fixed.

Required: 1.   Using the data from the income statement above, do the following:
  a.   Compute the percentage markup on cost being used by the company (that is, the gross margin as a percentage of the cost of goods sold).
  b.   Prepare a model price quotation sheet for a single unit of product using the absorption approach.
2.   Recast the income statement for 19x8 in the contribution format, and then do the following:
  a.   Compute the percentage markup based on variable cost (that is, the contribution margin as a percentage of variable costs).
  b.   Prepare a model price quotation sheet for a single unit of product using the contribution approach.
3.   Assume that the company has sufficient capacity to produce 40,000 blenders each year. Savemore, a regional discount chain, is willing to purchase 6,000

blenders each year at a price of $27.50 per blender. The blenders would be imprinted with the Savemore name and would not affect regular sales.

   a. Using the model quotation sheet prepared in (1) above, should the offer be accepted? Explain.

   b. Explain how the model price quotation sheet prepared in (2) above can be helpful to the manager in making special pricing decisions. Using this sheet as a guide, should the offer be accepted? Show computations.

P12–10.   **Computation of markup percentages.**   Damon Foods, Inc., has just developed a new yogurt. The company's accounting department has determined the following costs for a case of the new product (based on 15,000 cases produced per year):

	Total cost per case	Total annual cost
Direct materials	$19.40	
Direct labor	8.10	
Variable overhead	3.50	
Fixed overhead—direct	9.00	$135,000
Variable selling	1.00	
Fixed selling and administrative . . .	12.34	185,000

In order to produce the new yogurt, it has been necessary for the company to make an investment of $400,000 in new equipment. The company's board of directors has stated that management should earn a minimum 16 percent return on all invested funds. The company uses cost-plus pricing.

Required: 1. Assume that the company uses absorption costing, and do the following:

     a. Compute the markup percentage needed for the company to achieve the required 16 percent return on invested funds.

     b. Using the markup percentage computed in (1*a*) above, compute the target selling price for a case of yogurt.

   2. Assume that the company uses the contribution approach, and do the following:

     a. Compute the markup percentage needed for the company to achieve the required 16 percent return on invested funds.

     b. Using the markup percentage computed in (2*a*) above, compute the target selling price for a case of yogurt.

   3. Look at the formula used to compute the markup percentage in (1) above. If management wants to reduce the markup percentage in order to be more competitive and yet earn a 16 percent ROI, what lines of attack does the formula suggest that management can follow?

P12–11.   **Time and material pricing.**   City Appliance, Inc., operates an appliance service business with a fleet of trucks dispatched by radio in response to calls from customers. The company's profit margin has dropped steadily over the last two years, and management is concerned that pricing rates for time and material may be out of date. According to industry trade magazines, the company should be earning $8.50 per hour of repair service time, and a profit of 10 percent of the invoice cost of parts use. The company maintains a large parts inventory in order to give prompt repair service to customers.

    Costs associated with repair work and with the parts inventory over the past year are provided below:

	Repairs	Parts
Repair service manager—salary	$ 25,000	$ —
Parts manager—salary	—	20,000
Repair technicians—wages	180,000	—
Office assistant—salary.	9,000	3,000
Depreciation—trucks and equipment	15,400	—
Depreciation—buildings and fixtures	6,000	17,500
Retirement benefits (15% of salaries and wages)	32,100	3,450
Health insurance (5% of salaries and wages)	10,700	1,150
Utilities	2,600	12,000
Truck operating costs	36,000	—
Property taxes	900	3,400
Liability and fire insurance	1,500	1,900
Supplies	800	600
Invoice cost of parts used.	—	210,000
Total costs	$320,000	$273,000

The company employs 10 repair technicians who work a 40-hour week, 50 weeks per year. During the past year, the company has billed repair service time at $20 per hour and has added a material loading charge of 35 percent to parts.

Required: 1.   Using the data above, compute the following:

   a.   The rate that should be charged per hour of repair service time. Your rate should contain three cost elements, as discussed in the body of the chapter.

   b.   The material loading charge that should be used in billing jobs. The material loading charge should be expressed as a percentage of the invoice cost of parts and should contain two elements, as discussed in the body of the chapter.

   2.   Are the time and material rates that the company has been using adequate to cover its costs and yield the desired profit margin? Explain. (No computations are necessary.)

   3.   Assume that the company adopts the rates that you have computed in (1) above. What should be the total price charged on a repair job that requires 1½ hours of service time and $108 in parts?

P12–12.   **Integrative problem: Markup percentages; price quotation sheets; special order.** Micron Industries wants to introduce a high-quality, low-cost turntable to go with its other stereo products. After careful study, the company has determined that the new turntable would entail the following costs (based on 20,000 turntables produced and sold each year):

	Per turntable	Total
Direct materials	$60	
Direct labor.	33	
Variable overhead.	10	
Fixed overhead	32	$640,000
Variable selling expense	5	
Fixed selling expense	25	500,000

Production and sale of the new turnable would require an investment of $3,000,000 in order to purchase new equipment, carry inventories, and provide for other working capital needs. The company requires a 16 percent return on investment for all new products.

Required:
1. Assume that the company uses the absorption costing method.
   a. Compute the markup percentage needed to achieve the company's required 16 percent ROI.
   b. Using the markup percentage you have computed, prepare a price quotation sheet for a single turntable.
2. Assume that the company uses the contribution approach to costing.
   a. Compute the markup percentage needed to achieve the company's required 16 percent ROI.
   b. Using the markup percentage you have computed, prepare a price quotation sheet for a single turntable.
3. Assume that the company purchases the necessary equipment and starts to produce and sell the new turntable. Although the company is able to produce and sell only 20,000 turntables a year at the price you computed in (1) and (2) above, it has a capacity to produce 30,000 units per year. A large retail outlet has offered to make a bulk purchase of 6,000 turntables at a price of $130 per unit.
   a. Using the model price quotation sheet prepared in (1) above, should the offer be accepted? Explain.
   b. Explain how the model price quotation sheet prepared in (2) above can be helpful to the manager in making special pricing decisions. Using this sheet as a guide, should the offer be accepted? Explain.

P12–13. **Distress pricing.** Rico's Toys, Inc., manufactures and sells a broad line of games and toys. In 19x1, hula hoops became very popular with the 8- to 12-year-old set. In order to supply what appeared to be a large and quite permanent demand for a new toy, the company acquired new equipment at a cost of $360,000. The equipment was estimated to be capable of producing 80,000 hula hoops per year and to have a five-year useful life.

In 19x1, production began. The hula hoops were priced as follows (per unit):

Direct materials	$0.61
Direct labor	0.09
Overhead (10% variable)	1.00
Total cost to manufacture	1.70
Markup: 40%	0.68
Target selling price	$2.38

The selling and administrative expenses relating to the hula hoops were:

Advertising and other fixed costs (per year)	$12,000
Shipping cost (per hula hoop)	$0.05

In 19x1 and 19x2, the company produced and sold 80,000 hula hoops each year. In 19x3, it suddenly became apparent that hula hoops were more of a fad than a permanent market. Almost overnight, the selling price dropped to $1.45 per unit.

The marketing manager has recommended that the company drop the hula hoop line and scrap the special equipment. "There is no reason to go on producing," he said. "At a selling price of $1.45 per unit, we would be losing $0.25 on every unit that we produce, and that doesn't even consider shipping costs."

Required: 1.   Redo the price quotation sheet above by placing it in the contribution format. (The appropriate markup would be 180 percent.)

2.   Assume that because of the reduced demand for hula hoops the company can expect to sell only 45,000 units per year even at the lower price. Do you agree with the marketing manager's recommendation to stop production and scrap the special equipment? Show computations to support your answer.

P12–14.   Time and material pricing.   Midland Motors, Inc., is an automobile dealership that provides a service department for its customers. As part of this service department, the company maintains a large parts inventory in order to have parts on hand when needed for repair work. Although the service department always operates at capacity, it has never been very profitable, and management is concerned that the pricing rates in use may be too low ($25 per hour for mechanics' labor, plus a 35 percent material loading charge on parts).

An analysis of the costs incurred by the service department over the past year has revealed the following:

a.   The department employs one service manager over repair work who is paid $24,000 per year and one parts manager who is paid $21,000 per year. In addition, an office assistant is employed who is paid $10,000 per year. The assistant's time is divided 60 percent to repair work and 40 percent to parts work.

b.   Five mechanics are employed for repair work who work 40 hours per week, 50 weeks per year. Their combined wages totaled $90,000 for the past year.

c.   Retirement and vacation benefits equal 12 percent of salaries and wages; health insurance costs equal 5 percent of salaries and wages; and employment taxes equal 10 percent of salaries and wages. (The company treats all of these items as employee fringe benefits.)

d.   Insurance costs allocable to repair work totaled $8,900 for the past year, and insurance costs allocable to parts totaled $4,750.

e.   Property taxes for the year on building, equipment, and inventories were allocable between repairs and parts as follows: repairs, $2,500; and parts, $3,000.

f.   Costs for utilities incurred during the past year: repairs, $10,000; and parts, $2,500.

g.   The repairs area incurred costs for cleaning supplies totaling $1,200 for the year.

h.   Depreciation on building and equipment for the year totaled $68,000, of which $50,000 was allocable to repair work and $18,000 was allocable to parts.

i.   The company has a target profit of $5 per hour of mechanics' work in the repair area and 15 percent of the invoice cost of parts in the parts area. Parts costing $200,000 were used in repair work during the year.

Required: 1.   Compute the rate that should be charged per hour of mechanics' time, and the material loading charge that should be used (as a percentage of the invoice cost of parts). Your time rate should contain three cost elments, as discussed in the body of the chapter. Your material loading charge should contain two cost elements.

2.   What should be the total price charged on a job that requires 3½ hours of mechanics' time and $60 in parts?

P12–15.   **Competitive bidding.**   Argon Products, Inc., manufactures radios and other electronic equipment. Due to heavy competition in the electronics industry, the company has a substantial amount of idle capacity. For this reason, management was very pleased when Argon was invited to bid on the design and manufacture of 6,000 2-meter radios for the U.S. Army. Argon has estimated the following costs relating to the 6,000 radios:

	Total	Per radio
Direct materials	$ 690,000	$115
Direct labor.	210,000	35
Variable overhead	120,000	20
Fixed overhead˙. . .⎸.	600,000	100
Design and cost study	54,000	9
Shipping cost	36,000	6
Total cost . . . . `.` . .	$1,710,000	$285

˙ Allocated on a basis of machine-hours.

Based on these data, the company has prepared a bid of $378 per radio. The price quotation sheet used to compute the bid is given below:

Direct materials	$115
Direct labor	35
Manufacturing overhead	120
Total cost to manufacture	270
Markup—40%	108
Bid price per radio	$378

Just as the company was preparing to mail its bid, it received word from the U.S. Army that due to budget constraints, no bid over $290 would be considered. Because of exacting specifications required by the Army, the design of the radio can't be changed. Upon hearing the $290 bid figure, the president of Argon stated, "Our cost is $285 per radio. At a bid price of $290, we wouldn't make enough profit to justify our time. Tear up the bid and forget it."

Required: What would you advise Argon Products to do? Prepare computations to support your recommendations.

P12–16.   **Distress pricing.**   Tanner Industries operates a number of smelters in the western United States, all of which are administered from the company's central headquarters. The following data relate to the company's copper smelter:

Number of ingots produced per year . . .	50,000
Cost of ore per ingot	$21
Direct labor cost per ingot	6
Shipping cost per ingot	2

Manufacturing overhead is applied to the ingots on a basis of 300 percent of direct labor cost. One sixth of the overhead cost is variable. The ingots sell for $60 each.

In the past several months, the market has been flooded with ingots from other countries. As a result, the selling price per ingot has dropped by one third. If it wants to retain its customers, Tanner will have to meet the current price. After making a few computations, Tanner's president stated, "We'll have to close the copper smelter. At the current price, we would lose $7 on every ingot that we produced and sold. We may be able to reopen the smelter in a year or two if the market recovers and if we can cut production costs somehow.''

Required: 1. How did the president compute the $7 per ingot loss?
2. Prepare a price quotation sheet in the contribution format for one ingot. (The appropriate markup would be 87.5 percent.) Do you agree with the president's decision to close the copper smelter? Explain, and show computations to support your answer.

P12–17. **Integrative problem: Standard costs; markup computations; pricing decisions.** Wilderness Products, Inc., has designed a self-inflating sleeping pad for use by backpackers and campers. The following information is available on the new product:

a. An investment of $1,350,000 will be necessary to carry inventories and accounts receivable and to purchase some new equipment needed in the manufacturing process. The company requires a 24 percent return on investment for new product lines.

b. A standard cost card has been prepared for the sleeping pad, as shown below:

	Standard quantity or hours	Standard price or rate	Standard cost
Direct materials	4.0 yards	$ 2.70 per yard	$10.80
Direct labor	2.4 hours	8.00 per hour	19.20
Overhead (⅕ variable)	2.4 hours	12.50 per hour	30.00
Total standard cost per pad . .			$60.00

c. The only variable selling or administrative expenses on the pads will be $9 per pad sales commission. Fixed selling and administrative expenses will be (per year):

Salaries	$ 82,000
Warehouse rent	50,000
Advertising and other . . .	600,000
Total	$732,000

d. Since the company manufactures many products, it is felt that no more than 38,400 hours of direct labor time per year can be devoted to production of the new sleeping pads.
e. Overhead costs are allocated to products on a basis of direct labor-hours.

Required: 1. Assume that the company uses absorption costing.
   a. Compute the markup that the company needs on the pads in order to achieve a 24 percent ROI.
   b. Using the markup you have computed, prepare a price quotation sheet for a single sleeping pad.
   c. Assume that the company is able to sell all of the pads that it can produce. Prepare an income statement for the first year of activity, and compute the company's ROI for the year on the pads, using the ROI formula from Chapter 11.
2. Assume that the company uses the contribution approach.
   a. Compute the markup that the company needs on the pads in order to achieve a 24 percent ROI.

    b. Using the markup you have computed, prepare a price quotation sheet for a single sleeping pad.

    c. Prepare an income statement for the first year of activity.

3. After marketing the sleeping pads for several years, assume that the company is experiencing a falloff in demand due to an economic recession. A large retail outlet will make a bulk purchase of pads if its label is sewn in and if an acceptable price can be worked out. Identify the range within which this price should fall.

P12–18. **High-low analysis; special order.** Integrated Circuits, Inc. (ICI), is currently operating at 50 percent of capacity, producing 50,000 units annually of a patented electronic component. ICI has received an offer from a company in Yokohama, Japan, to purchase 30,000 components at $7 per unit, FOB ICI's plant. ICI has not previously sold components in Japan. Budgeted production costs for 50,000 and 80,000 units of output follow:

Units	50,000	80,000
Costs:		
Direct materials	$ 75,000	$120,000
Direct labor.	200,000	320,000
Factory overhead	125,000	140,000
Total costs	$400,000	$580,000
Cost per unit	$8.00	$7.25

      The sales manager thinks that the order should be accepted, even if this results in a loss of $1 per unit, because the sale may build up future markets. The production manager does not wish to have the order accepted, primarily because the order would show a loss of 25 cents per unit when computed on the new average unit cost.

Required: 1. In terms of direct materials, direct labor, variable overhead, and fixed overhead, show the breakdown of the unit costs at the 50,000 and 80,000 unit levels of activity.

    2. Assume that the normal target selling price is $10 per unit. Using the contribution approach, prepare a price quotation sheet for one unit of product. (The appropriate markup would be 66⅔ percent.) Indicate the ceiling, the floor, and the range of flexibility on your sheet.

    3. On the basis of the information given in the problem and the information that you have computed above, should the order be accepted or rejected? Show computations to support your answer.

    4. In addition to revenue and costs, what additional factors should be considered before making a final decision?

(CPA, Adapted)

P12–19. **Integrative problem: Missing data; markup computations; ROI; pricing.** South Seas Products, Inc., has designed a new surfboard to replace its old surfboard line. Because of the unique design of the new surfboard, the company anticipates that it will be able to sell all of the boards that it can produce. On this basis, the following budgeted income statement for the first year of activity is available:

Sales (? boards at ? per board)	$	?
Less cost of goods sold (? boards at ? per board) . .		1,600,000
Gross margin		?
Less selling and administrative expenses		1,130,000
Net income	$	?

Additional information on the new surfboard is given below:

a.   An investment of $1,500,000 will be necessary to carry inventories and accounts receivable and to purchase some new equipment needed in the manufacturing process. The company requires an 18 percent return on investment for all products.

b.   A partially completed standard cost card for the new surfboard follows:

	Standard quantity or hours	Standard price or rate	Standard cost
Direct materials	6 feet	$4.50 per foot	$27
Direct labor	2 hours	? per hour	?
Overhead (⅓ variable)	?	? per hour	?
Total standard cost per surfboard			$?

c.   The company will employ 20 workers in the manufacture of the new surfboards. Each will work a 40-hour week, 50 weeks a year.

d.   Other information relating to production and costs follows:

Variable overhead cost (per board)	$	5
Variable selling cost (per board)		10
Fixed overhead cost (total)		?
Fixed selling and administrative cost (total)		?
Number of boards produced and sold (per year) . . .		?

e.   Overhead costs are allocated to production on a basis of direct labor-hours.

Required: 1.   Complete the standard cost card for a single surfboard.

2.   Assume that the company uses absorption costing.

    a.   Compute the markup that the company needs on the surfboards in order to achieve an 18 percent ROI.

    b.   Using the markup you have computed, prepare a price quotation sheet for a single surfboard.

    c.   Assume, as stated, that the company is able to sell all of the surfboards that it can produce. Complete the income statement for the first year of activity, and then compute the company's ROI for the year, using the ROI formula from Chapter 11.

3.   Assume that the company uses the contribution approach.

    a.   Compute the markup that the company needs on the surfboards in order to achieve an 18 percent ROI.

    b.   Using the markup you have computed, prepare a price quotation sheet for a single surfboard.

    c.   Prepare an income statement for the first year of activity.

P12–20.   **Special order; capacity utilization.**   Tiffany Company manufacturers several different styles of jewelry cases. Management estimates that during the third quarter of 19x6 the company will be operating at 80 percent of normal capacity. Because the company desires a higher utilization of plant capacity, it will consider a special order.

Tiffany has received special-order inquiries from two companies. The first inquiry is from JCP, Inc., which would like to market a jewelry case similar to one of Tiffany's cases. The JCP jewelry case would be marketed under JCP's own label. JCP, Inc., has offered Tiffany $5.75 per jewelry case for 20,000 cases to be shipped by October 1, 19x6. Cost data are given below for the Tiffany jewelry case that is similar to the jewelry case desired by JCP:

Regular selling price per unit	$9.00

Costs per unit:	
Raw materials	$2.50
Direct labor, 0.5 hours at $6	3.00
Overhead, 0.25 machine-hours at $4	1.00
Total costs per unit	$6.50

According to the specifications provided by JCP, Inc., the special order case requires less expensive raw materials. Consequently, the raw materials will only cost $2.25 per case. Management has estimated that the remaining costs, labor time, and machine time will be the same as those for the Tiffany jewelry case.

The second special order, submitted by the Krage Company, was for 7,500 jewelry cases at $7.50 per case. These jewelry cases would be marketed under the Krage label and would have to be shipped by October 1, 19x6. The Krage jewelry case is different from any jewelry case in the Tiffany line. The estimated costs per unit of this case are as follows:

Raw materials	$3.25
Direct labor, 0.5 hours at $6	3.00
Overhead, 0.5 machine-hours at $4	2.00
Total costs per unit	$8.25

In addition, Tiffany will incur $1,500 in additional setup costs and will have to purchase a $2,500 special device to manufacture these cases. The device will be discarded once the special order has been completed.

The Tiffany manufacturing capabilities are limited to the total machine-hours available. The plant capacity under normal operations is 90,000 machine-hours per year, or 7,500 machine-hours per month. The budgeted fixed overhead for 19x6 amounts to $216,000. All manufacturing overhead costs (fixed and variable) are applied to production on the basis of machine-hours, at $4 per hour.

During the third quarter, Tiffany will be able to use all of its excess capacity to work on special orders. Management does not expect any repeat sales to be generated from either special order. Company practice precludes Tiffany from subcontracting any portion of an order when special orders are not expected to generate repeat sales.

Required: Should Tiffany Company accept either special order? Justify your answer, and show your calculations. (Hint: It may be helpful to distinguish between fixed and variable overhead.)

(CMA, Adapted)

CASE

C12–21.   **Pricing a bid; opportunity cost.**   Wardl Industries is a manufacturer of standard and custom-designed bottling equipment. Early in December 19x3 Lyan Company asked Wardl to quote a price for a custom-designed bottling machine to be delivered on April 1, 19x4. Lyan intends to make a decision on the purchase of such a machine by January 1 so Wardl would have the entire first quarter of 19x4 to build the equipment.

Wardl's standard pricing policy for custom-designed equipment is 50 percent markup on cost to manufacture. Lyan's specifications for the equipment have been reviewed by Wardl's engineering and cost accounting departments, and they have made the following estimates for raw materials and direct labor.

Raw materials	$256,000
Direct labor (11,000 DLH @ $15) . .	165,000

Manufacturing overhead is applied on the basis of direct labor-hours. Wardl normally plans to run its plant 15,000 direct labor-hours per month and assigns overhead on the basis of 180,000 direct labor-hours per year. The overhead application rate for 19x4 of $9/DLH is based on the following budgeted manufacturing overhead costs for 19x4.

Variable manufacturing overhead	$ 972,000
Fixed manufacturing overhead	648,000
Total manufacturing overhead	$1,620,000

The Wardl production schedule calls for 12,000 direct labor-hours per month during the first quarter. If Wardl is awarded the contract for the Lyan equipment, production of one of its standard products would have to be reduced. This is necessary because production levels can only be increased to 15,000 direct labor-hours each month on short notice. Furthermore, Wardl's employees are unwilling to work overtime.

Sales of the standard product equal to the reduced production would be lost, but there would be no permanent loss of future sales or customers. The standard product whose production schedule would be reduced has a unit sales price of $12,000 and the following cost structure.

Raw materials	$2,500
Direct labor (250 DLH @ $15) . .	3,750
Overhead (250 DLH @ $9) . . .	2,250
Total cost	$8,500

Required: 1.   Calculate the bid that Wardl would submit on the bottling machine if it follows its standard pricing policy for special-purpose equipment.
          2.   Calculate the minimum bid that Wardl would be willing to submit on the bottling machine if Wardl wanted its profits for the first quarter of 19x4 to be the same as if it just continued to sell its standard products. Show all computations in good form.

(CMA, Adapted)

Relevant Costs for Decision Making

LEARNING OBJECTIVES

After studying Chapter 13, you should be able to:

■ State a general rule for distinguishing between relevant and irrelevant costs in a decision-making situation.

■ Identify sunk costs and explain why they are not relevant in decision making.

■ Prepare an analysis showing whether a product line or other organizational segment should be dropped or retained.

■ Explain what is meant by a "make or buy" decision and prepare a well-organized make or buy analysis.

■ Make appropriate computations to determine the most profitable utilization of scarce resources in an organization.

■ Prepare an analysis showing whether joint products should be sold at the split-off point or processed further.

■ Construct a graph that shows the optimal solution to a linear programming problem.

■ Define or explain the key terms listed at the end of the chapter.

Decision making is one of the basic functions of a manager. Managers are constantly faced with problems of deciding what products to sell, what production methods to use, whether to make or buy component parts, what prices to charge, what channels of distribution to use, whether to accept special orders at special prices, and so forth. At best, decision making is a·difficult and complex task. The difficulty of this task is usually increased by the existence of not just one or two but numerous courses of action that might be taken in any given situation facing a firm.

In decision making, *cost* is always a key factor. The costs of one alternative must be compared against the costs of other alternatives as one step in the decision-making process. The problem is that some costs associated with an alternative may not be *relevant* to the decision to be made. A **relevant cost** can be defined as a cost that is *applicable to a particular decision* in the sense that it will have a bearing on which alternative the manager selects.

To be successful in decision making, managers must have tools at their disposal to assist them in distinguishing between relevant and irrelevant costs so that the latter can be eliminated from the decision framework. The purpose of this chapter is to acquire these tools and to show their application in a wide range of decision-making situations.

COST CONCEPTS FOR DECISION MAKING

Three cost terms discussed in Chapter 2 are particularly applicable to this chapter. These terms are differential costs, opportunity costs, and sunk costs. The reader may find it helpful to turn back to Chapter 2 and refresh his or her memory of these terms before reading on.

Identifying Relevant Costs

What costs are relevant in decision making? The answer is easy. Any cost that is *avoidable* is relevant for decision purposes. An **avoidable cost** can be defined as a cost that can be eliminated (in whole or in part) as a result of choosing one alternative over another in a decision-making situation. *All* costs are considered to be avoidable, *except*:

1. Sunk costs.
2. Future costs that *do not differ* between the alternatives at hand.

As we learned in Chapter 2, a **sunk cost** is a cost that has already been incurred and that cannot be avoided regardless of which course of action a manager may decide to take. As such, sunk costs have no relevance to future events and must be ignored in decision making. Similarly, if a cost will be incurred regardless of which course of action a manager may take, then the cost cannot possibly be of any help in deciding which course of action is best. Such a cost is not avoidable, and hence it is not relevant to the manager's decision.

The term *avoidable cost* is synonymous with the term *differential cost* that we introduced in Chapter 2, and the terms are frequently used interchangeably. To identify the costs that are avoidable (differential) in a particular decision situation, the manager's approach to cost analysis should include the following steps:

1. Assemble *all* of the costs associated with *each* alternative being considered.
2. Eliminate those costs that are sunk.
3. Eliminate those costs that do not differ between alternatives.
4. Make a decision based on the remaining costs. These costs will be the **differential** or **avoidable costs,** and hence the costs relevant to the decision to be made.

Different Costs for Different Purposes

We need to recognize from the outset of our discussion that costs which are relevant in one decision situation are not necessarily relevant in another. Simply put, this means (as we've stated before) that *the manager needs different costs for different purposes*. For one purpose, a particular group of costs may be relevant; for another purpose, an entirely different group of costs may be relevant. Thus, in *each* decision situation the manager must examine the data at hand and then take the steps necessary to isolate the relevant costs. Otherwise, he or she runs the risk of being misled by irrelevant data.

The concept of "different costs for different purposes" is basic to managerial accounting; we shall see its application frequently in the pages that follow.

SUNK COSTS ARE NOT RELEVANT COSTS

One of the most difficult conceptual lessons that managers have to learn is that sunk costs are never relevant in decisions. The tendency to want to include sunk costs within the decision framework is especially strong in the case of book value of old equipment. We focus on book value of old equipment below, and then we consider other kinds of sunk costs in other parts of the chapter. We shall see that regardless of the kind of sunk cost involved, the conclusion is always the same—sunk costs are not avoidable, and therefore they must be eliminated from the manager's decision framework.

Book Value of Old Equipment

Assume the following data:

Old machine		Proposed new machine	
Original cost	$10,000	List price new	$12,000
Remaining book value	8,000	Expected life.	4 years
Remaining life	4 years	Disposal value in four years . .	–0–
Disposal value now	$ 3,000	Annual variable expenses	
Disposal value in four years . .	–0–	to operate	$15,500
Annual variable expenses		Annual revenue from sales . .	50,000
to operate	20,000		
Annual revenue from sales . .	50,000		

Should the old machine be disposed of and the new machine purchased? Some managers would say no, since disposal of the old machine would result in a "loss" of $5,000:

Old machine	
Remaining book value	$8,000
Disposal value now	3,000
Loss if disposed of now	$5,000

Given this potential loss if the old machine is sold, there is a general inclination for the manager to reason, "We've already made an investment in the old machine, so now we have no choice but to use it until our investment has been fully recovered." The manager will tend to think this way even though the new machine is clearly more efficient than the old machine. Although it may be appealing to think that an error of the past can be corrected by simply *using* the item involved, this, unfortunately, is not correct. The investment that has been made in the old machine is a sunk cost. The portion of this investment that remains on the company's books (the book value of $8,000) should not be considered in a decision about whether to buy the new machine. We can prove this assertion by the following analysis:[1]

---

[1] The computations involved in this example are taken one step further in Chapters 14 and 15 where we discuss the time value of money and the use of present value in decision making.

	Total costs and revenues— four years		
	Keep old machine	Differential costs	Purchase new machine
Sales	$200,000	–0–	$200,000
Variable expenses	(80,000)	$ 18,000	(62,000)
Cost (depreciation) of the new machine	–0–	(12,000)	(12,000)
Depreciation of the old machine or book value write-off	(8,000)	–0–	(8,000)*
Disposal value of the old machine	–0–	3,000	3,000*
Total net income over the four years . . .	$112,000	$ 9,000	$121,000

* For external reporting purposes, the $8,000 remaining book value of the old machine and the $3,000 disposal value would be netted together and deducted as a single $5,000 "loss" figure.

Looking at all four years together, notice that the firm will be $9,000 better off by purchasing the new machine. Also notice that the $8,000 book value of the old machine had *no effect* on the outcome of the analysis. Since this book value is a sunk cost, it must be absorbed by the firm regardless of whether the old machine is kept and used or whether it is sold. If the old machine is kept and used, then the $8,000 book value is deducted in the form of depreciation. If the old machine is sold, then the $8,000 book value is deducted in the form of a lump-sum write-off. Either way, the company bears the same $8,000 deduction.

Focusing on relevant costs   What costs in the example above are relevant in the decision concerning the new machine? Following the steps outlined earlier, we should eliminate (1) the sunk costs and (2) the future costs that do not differ between the alternatives at hand.

1. The sunk costs:
    a. The remaining book value of the old machine ($8,000).
2. The future costs that do not differ:
    a. The annual sales revenue ($50,000).
    b. The annual variable expenses (to the extent of $15,500).

The costs that remain will form the basis for a decision. The analysis is:

	Differential costs— four years
Reduction in variable expense promised by the new machine ($4,500* per year × 4 years)	$ 18,000
Cost of the new machine	(12,000)
Disposal value of the old machine	3,000
Net advantage of the new machine	$ 9,000

* $20,000 − $15,500 = $4,500.

Note that the items above are the same as those in the middle column of the earlier analysis and represent those costs and revenues that are differential as between the two alternatives.

Depreciation and relevant costs Since the book value of old equipment is not a relevant cost in decision making, there is a tendency to assume that depreciation of *any* kind is irrelevant in the decision-making process. This is not a correct assumption. Depreciation is irrelevant in decisions only if it relates to a sunk cost. Notice from the comparative income statements in the preceding section that the $12,000 depreciation on the new machine appears in the middle column as a relevant item in trying to assess the desirability of the new machine's purchase. By contrast, depreciation on the old machine does not appear as a relevant cost. The difference is that the investment in the new machine has *not yet been made,* and therefore it does not represent depreciation of a sunk cost.

FUTURE COSTS THAT DO NOT DIFFER ARE NOT RELEVANT COSTS

Any future cost that does not differ between the alternatives in a decision situation is not a relevant cost so far as that decision is concerned. As stated earlier, if a company is going to sustain the same cost regardless of what decision it makes, then that cost can in no way tell the company which decision is best. The only way a future cost can help in the decision-making process is by being different as between the alternatives under consideration.

An Example of Irrelevant Future Costs

To illustrate the irrelevance of future costs that do not differ, let us assume that a firm is contemplating the purchase of a new laborsaving machine. The machine will cost $30,000 and have a 10-year useful life. The company's sales and cost structure on an annual basis with and without the new machine are shown below:

	Present costs	Expected costs with the new machine
Units produced and sold	5,000	5,000
Sales price per unit	$ 40	$ 40
Direct materials cost per unit	14	14
Direct labor cost per unit	8	5
Variable overhead cost per unit	2	2
Fixed costs, other	62,000	62,000
Fixed costs, new machine	—	3,000

The new machine promises a saving of $3 per unit in direct labor costs but will increase fixed costs by $3,000 per period. All other costs, as well as the total number of units produced and sold, will remain the same. Following the steps outlined earlier, the analysis is:

1.   Eliminate the sunk costs. (No sunk costs are identified in this example.)
2.   Eliminate the future costs (and revenues) that do not differ:
     a.   The sales price per unit does not differ.
     b.   The direct materials cost per unit does not differ.
     c.   The variable overhead cost per unit does not differ.
     d.   The total "fixed costs, other" do not differ.

This leaves just the per unit labor costs and the fixed costs associated with the new machine as being differential costs:

Savings in direct labor costs (5,000 units at a cost saving of $3 per unit)	$15,000
Less increase in fixed costs	3,000
Net annual cost savings promised by the new machine . .	$12,000

The accuracy of this solution can be proved by looking at *all* items of cost data (both those that are relevant and those that are not) under the two alternatives for a period and then comparing the net income results. This is done in Exhibit 13–1. Notice from the exhibit that we obtain the same $12,000 net advantage in favor of buying the new machine as we obtained above when we focused only on relevant costs. Thus, we can see that future costs that do not differ between alternatives are indeed irrelevant in the decision-making process and can be safely eliminated from the manager's decision framework.

Why Isolate Relevant Costs?

In the preceding example, we used two different approaches to show that the purchase of the new machine was desirable. First, we considered only the relevant costs; and second, we considered all costs, both those that were relevant and those that were not. We obtained the same answer under both approaches. When students see that the same answer can be obtained under either approach, they often ask, "Why bother to isolate relevant costs when total costs will do the job just as well?" The isolation of relevant costs is desirable for at least two reasons.

First, only rarely will enough information be availabe to prepare a detailed income statement such as we have done in the preceding examples. Since normally only limited data are available, the decision maker *must* know how to recognize which costs are relevant and which are not. Assume, for example, that you are called upon to make a decision relating to a matter in a *single operation* of a multidepartmental, multiproduct firm. Under these circumstances, it would be virtually impossible to prepare an income statement of any type. You would have to rely on your ability to recognize which costs were relevant and which were not in order to assemble the data necessary to make a decision.

Second, the use of irrelevant costs mingled with relevant costs may con-

EXHIBIT 13–1

Differential cost analysis

	5,000 units produced and sold		
	Present method	Differential costs	New machine
Sales	$200,000	–0–	$200,000
Variable expenses:			
Direct materials.	70,000	–0–	70,000
Direct labor	40,000	$15,000	25,000
Variable overhead	10,000	–0–	10,000
Total variable expenses	120,000		105,000
Contribution margin	80,000		95,000
Less fixed expenses:			
Other	62,000	–0–	62,000
New machine	–0–	(3,000)	3,000
Total fixed expenses	62,000		65,000
Net income	$ 18,000	$12,000	$ 30,000

fuse the picture and draw the decision maker's attention away from the matters that are really critical to the problem at hand. Furthermore, the danger always exists that an irrelevant piece of data may be used improperly, resulting in an incorrect decision. The best approach is to isolate the relevant items and to focus all attention directly on them and on their impact on the decision to be made.

Relevant cost analysis, combined with the contribution approach to the income statement, provides a powerful tool for making decisions in special, nonroutine situations. We will investigate various uses of this tool in the remaining sections of this chapter.

ADDING AND DROPPING PRODUCT LINES

The decisions relating to when to drop old product lines and when to add new product lines are among the stickiest that a manager has to make. In such decisions, many factors must be considered that are both qualitative and quantitative in nature. Ultimately, however, any final decision to drop an old product line or to add a new product line is going to hinge primarily on the impact the decision will have on net income. In order to assess this impact, it is necessary to make a careful analysis of the costs involved.

An Illustration of Cost Analysis

As a basis for discussion, let us consider the product lines of the Discount Drug Company. The company has three major product lines—drugs, cosmetics, and housewares. Sales and cost information for the preceding month for each separate product line and for the store in total is given in Exhibit 13–2.

EXHIBIT 13–2

Discount Drug Company product lines

	Total	Product lines		
		Drugs	Cosmetics	Housewares
Sales	$250,000	$125,000	$75,000	$50,000
Less variable expenses	105,000	50,000	25,000	30,000
Contribution margin.	145,000	75,000	50,000	20,000
Less fixed expenses:				
Salaries	50,000	29,500	12,500	8,000
Advertising	15,000	1,000	7,500	6,500
Utilities	2,000	500	500	1,000
Depreciation—fixtures.	5,000	1,000	2,000	2,000
Rent	20,000	10,000	6,000	4,000
Insurance	3,000	2,000	500	500
General administrative	30,000	15,000	9,000	6,000
Total fixed expenses	125,000	59,000	38,000	28,000
Net income (loss)	$ 20,000	$ 16,000	$12,000	$ (8,000)

What can be done to improve the company's overall performance? One product line—housewares—shows a net loss for the month. Perhaps dropping this line would cause profits in the company as a whole to improve. In deciding whether the line should be dropped, management will need to reason as follows:

If the housewares line is dropped, then the company will lose $20,000 per month in contribution margin that is now available to help cover the fixed costs. By dropping the line, however, it may be possible to avoid certain of these fixed costs. It may be possible, for example, to discharge certain employees, or it may be possible to reduce advertising costs. If by dropping the housewares line the company is able to avoid more in fixed costs than it loses in contribution margin, then it will be better off if the line is eliminated, since overall net income should improve. On the other hand, if the company is not able to avoid as much in fixed costs as it loses in contribution margin, then the housewares line should be retained. In short, in order to identify the differential costs in decisions of this type, the manager must ask, "What costs can I avoid to offset my loss of revenue (or loss of contribution margin) if I drop this product line?"

As we have seen from our earlier discussion, not all costs are avoidable. Some of the costs associated with a product line may be sunk costs, for example; other costs may be allocated common costs that will not differ in total regardless of whether the product line is dropped or retained. To show how the manager should proceed in a product line analysis, suppose that the management of the Discount Drug Company has analyzed the costs being charged to the three product lines and has determined the following:

1. The salaries represent salaries paid to employees working directly in each product line area. All of the employees working in housewares can be discharged if the line is dropped.

2. The advertising represents direct advertising of each product line and is avoidable if the line is dropped.

3. The utilities represent utilities costs for the entire company. The amount charged to each product line represents an allocation based on space occupied.

4. The depreciation represents depreciation on fixtures used for display of the various product lines. Although the fixtures are nearly new, they are custom-built and will have little resale value if the housewares line is dropped.

5. The rent represents rent on the entire building housing the company; it is allocated to the product lines on a basis of sales dollars. The monthly rent of $20,000 is fixed under a long-term lease agreement.

6. The insurance represents insurance carried on inventories maintained within each of the three product line areas.

7. The general administrative expense represents the costs of accounting, purchasing, and general management, which are allocated to the product lines on a basis of sales dollars. Total administrative costs will not change if the housewares line is dropped.

With this information, management can identify those costs that are avoidable and those costs that are not avoidable if the product line is dropped:

	Total cost	Not avoidable*	Avoidable
Salaries.	$ 8,000		$ 8,000
Advertising	6,500		6,500
Utilities	1,000	$ 1,000	
Depreciation—fixtures	2,000	2,000	
Rent	4,000	4,000	
Insurance	500		500
General administrative	6,000	6,000	
Total fixed expenses	$28,000	$13,000	$15,000

* These costs represent either (1) sunk costs or (2) costs that will not change regardless of whether the housewares line is retained or discontinued.

To determine how dropping the line will affect the overall profits of the company, we can compare the contribution margin that will be lost against the costs that can be avoided if the line is dropped.

Contribution margin lost if the housewares line is discontinued (see Exhibit 13–2)	$(20,000)
Less fixed costs that can be avoided if the housewares line is discontinued (see above)	15,000
Decrease in overall company net income	$ (5,000)

In this case, the fixed costs that can be avoided by dropping the product line are less than the contribution margin that will be lost. Therefore, the housewares line should not be discontinued unless a more profitable use can be found for the floor and counter space that it is occupying.

A Comparative Format

Some managers prefer to approach decisions of this type by preparing comparative income statements showing the effects on the company as a whole of either keeping or dropping the product line in question. A comparative analysis of this type for the Discount Drug Company is shown in Exhibit 13–3.

As shown by column 3 in the exhibit, overall company net income will decrease by $5,000 each period if the housewares line is dropped. This is the same answer, of course, as we obtained in our earlier analysis.

Beware of Allocated Fixed Costs

Our conclusion that the housewares line should not be dropped seems to conflict with the data shown in Exhibit 13–2. Recall from the exhibit that the housewares line is showing a loss rather than a proft. Why keep a line that is showing a loss? The explanation for this apparent inconsistency lies at least in part with the common fixed costs that are being allocated to the product lines. As we observed in Chapter 7, one of the great dangers in allocating common fixed costs is that such allocations can make a product

EXHIBIT 13–3

A comparative format for product line analysis

	Keep housewares	Drop housewares	Difference: Net income increase or (decrease)
Sales.	$50,000	–0–	$(50,000)
Less variable expenses	30,000	–0–	30,000
Contribution margin	20,000	–0–	(20,000)
Less fixed expenses:			
Salaries.	8,000	–0–	8,000
Advertising	6,500	–0–	6,500
Utilities	1,000	$ 1,000	–0–
Depreciation—fixtures	2,000	2,000	–0–
Rent	4,000	4,000	–0–
Insurance	500	–0–	500
General administrative	6,000	6,000	–0–
Total fixed expenses	28,000	13,000	15,000
Net income (loss)	$ (8,000)	$(13,000)	$ (5,000)

line (or other segment of a business) *look* less profitable than it really is. Consider the following example:

> A bakery distributed its products through route salesmen, each of whom loaded a truck with an assortment of products in the morning and spent the day calling on customers in an assigned territory. Believing that some items were more profitable than others, management asked for an analysis of product costs and sales. The accountants to whom the task was assigned allocated all manufacturing and marketing costs to products to obtain a net profit for each product. The resulting figures indicated that some of the products were being sold at a loss, and management discontinued these products. However, when this change was put into effect, the company's overall profit declined. It was then seen that, by dropping some products, sales revenues had been reduced without commensurate reduction in costs because the joint manufacturing costs and route sales costs had to be continued in order to make and sell remaining products.[2]

The same thing has happened in the Discount Drug Company as happened in the bakery company. That is, by allocating the common fixed costs among all product lines, the Discount Drug Company has made the housewares line *look* as if it were unprofitable, whereas, in fact, dropping the line would result in a decrease in overall company net income. This point can be seen clearly if we recast the data in Exhibit 13–2 and eliminate the allocation of the common fixed costs. This recasting of data is shown in Exhibit 13–4 on the following page.

Exhibit 13–4 gives us a much different perspective of the housewares line than does Exhibit 13–2. As shown in Exhibit 13–4, the housewares line is covering all of its own direct fixed costs and is generating a $3,000 segment margin toward covering the common fixed costs of the company. Unless another product line can be found that will generate a greater segment margin than this, then, as we have noted, the company will be better off to keep the housewares line. By keeping the line, the company will get at least some contribution toward the common fixed costs of the organization from the space it is occupying.

Finally, we should note that even in those situations where the contribution of a particular product line is small in comparison with other products, managers will often retain the line instead of replacing it, if the line is necessary to the sale of other products or if it serves as a "magnet" to attract customers. Bread, for example, is not an especially profitable line in food stores, but customers expect it to be available, and many would undoubtedly shift their buying elsewhere if a particular store decided to stop carrying it.

---

[2] Walter B. McFarland, *Concepts for Management Accounting* (New York: National Association of Accountants, 1966), p. 46.

EXHIBIT 13–4

Discount Drug Company product lines—recast in contribution format (from Exhibit 13–2)

		Product lines		
	Total	Drugs	Cosmetics	Housewares
Sales	$250,000	$125,000	$75,000	$50,000
Less variable expenses	105,000	50,000	25,000	30,000
Contribution margin	145,000	75,000	50,000	20,000
Less traceable fixed expenses:				
Salaries	50,000	29,500	12,500	8,000
Advertising	15,000	1,000	7,500	6,500
Depreciation—fixtures	5,000	1,000	2,000	2,000
Insurance	3,000	2,000	500	500
Total.	73,000	33,500	22,500	17,000
Product line segment margin . .	72,000	$ 41,500	$27,500	$ 3,000*
Less common fixed expenses:				
Utilities.	2,000			
Rent.	20,000			
General administrative	30,000			
Total.	52,000			
Net income	$ 20,000			

* If the housewares line is dropped, this $3,000 in segment margin will be lost to the company. In addition, we have seen that the $2,000 depreciation on the fixtures is a sunk cost that cannot be avoided. The sum of these two figures ($3,000 + $2,000 = $5,000) represents another way of obtaining the $5,000 figure that we found earlier would be the decrease in the company's overall profits if the housewares line were discontinued.

THE MAKE OR BUY DECISION

Many steps are involved in getting a finished product into the hands of a consumer. First, raw materials must be obtained through mining, drilling, growing crops, raising animals, and so forth. Second, these raw materials must be processed to remove impurities or to extract the desirable and usable materials from the bulk of materials available. Third, the usable materials must be fabricated into desired form to serve as basic inputs for manufactured products. Fourth, the actual manufacturing of the finished product must take place, with several products perhaps coming from the same basic raw material input (as, for example, several different items of clothing coming from the same basic cloth input). And finally, the finished product must be distributed to the ultimate consumer.

When a company is involved in more than one of these steps, it is said to be **vertically integrated.** Vertical integration is very common. Some firms go so far as to control *all* of the activities relating to their products, from the mining of raw materials or the raising of crops right up to the final distribution of finished goods. Other firms are content to integrate on a less grand scale, and perhaps they will produce only certain fabricated parts that go into their finished products.

A decision to produce a fabricated part internally, rather than to buy the part externally from a supplier, is often called a **make or buy decision.** Actually, any decision relating to vertical integration is a make or buy decision, since the company is deciding whether to meet its own needs internally rather than to buy externally.

The Advantages of Integration

Certain advantages arise from integration. The integrated firm is less dependent on its suppliers and may be able to ensure a smoother flow of parts and materials for production than the nonintegrated firm. For example, a strike against a major parts supplier might cause the operations of a nonintegrated firm to be interrupted for many months, whereas the integrated firm that is producing its own parts might be able to continue operations. Also, many firms feel that they can control quality better by producing their own parts and materials, rather than by relying on the quality control standards of outside suppliers. In addition, the integrated firm realizes profits from the parts and materials that it is ''making'' rather than ''buying,'' as well as profits from its regular operations.

The advantages of integration are counterbalanced by a number of hazards. A firm that produces all of its own parts runs the risk of destroying long-run relationships with suppliers, which may prove harmful and disruptive to the firm. Once relationships with suppliers have been severed, they are often difficult to reestablish. If product demand becomes heavy, a firm may not have sufficient capacity to continue producing all of its own parts internally, but then it may experience great difficulty in its efforts to secure assistance from a severed supplier. In addition, changing technology often makes continued production of one's own parts more costly than purchasing them from the outside, but this change in cost may not be obvious to the firm. In sum, these factors suggest that although certain advantages may accrue to the integrated firm, the make or buy decision should be weighed very carefully before any move is undertaken that may prove to be costly in the long run.

An Example of Make or Buy

How does a firm approach the make or buy decision? Basically, the matters that must be considered fall into two broad categories—qualitative and quantitative. Qualitative matters deal with issues such as those raised in the preceding section. Quantitative matters deal with cost—what is the cost of producing as compared to the cost of buying? Several kinds of costs may be involved here, including opportunity costs.

To provide an illustration, assume that Bonner Company is now producing a small subassembly that is used in the production of one of the company's main product lines. Bonner Company's accounting department reports the following ''costs'' of producing the subassembly internally:

	Per unit	8,000 units
Direct materials	$ 6	$ 48,000
Direct labor	4	32,000
Variable overhead	1	8,000
Supervisor's salary	3	24,000
Depreciation of special equipment . . .	2	16,000
Allocated general overhead	5	40,000
Total cost.	$21	$168,000

Bonner Company has just received an offer from an outside supplier who will provide 8,000 subassemblies a year at a firm price of $19 each. Should Bonner Company stop producing the subassemblies internally and start purchasing them from the outside supplier? To make this decision, the manager must again focus on the differential costs. As we have seen, the differential costs can be obtained by eliminating from the cost data those costs that are not avoidable; that is, by eliminating (1) the sunk costs and (2) the future costs that will continue regardless of whether the subassemblies are produced internally or purchased outside. The costs that remain after making these eliminations will be the costs that are avoidable to the company by purchasing outside. If these costs are less than the outside purchase price, then the company should continue to manufacture its own subassemblies and reject the outside supplier's offer. That is, the company should purchase outside only if the outside purchase price is less than the costs that can be avoided internally as a result of stopping production of the subassemblies.

Looking at the data above, notice first that depreciation of special equipment is one of the "costs" of producing the subassemblies internally. Since this equipment has already been purchased, this represents a sunk cost. Also notice that the company is allocating a portion of its general overhead costs to the subassemblies. Since these costs are common to all items produced in the factory, they will continue unchanged even if the subassemblies are purchased from the outside. These allocated costs, therefore, are not differential costs (since they will not differ between the make or buy alternatives), and they must be eliminated from the manager's decision framework along with the sunk costs.

The variable costs of producing the subassemblies (materials, labor, and variable overhead) are differential costs, since they can be avoided by buying the subassemblies from the outside supplier. If the supervisor can be discharged and his or her salary avoided by buying the subassemblies, then it too will be a differential cost and relevant to the decision. Assuming that both the variable costs and the supervisor's salary can be avoided by buying from the outside supplier, then the analysis takes the form shown in Exhibit 13–5.

EXHIBIT 13–5

Make or buy analysis

	Production "cost" per unit	Per unit differential costs		Total differential costs—8,000 units	
		Make	Buy	Make	Buy
Direct materials	$ 6	$ 6		$48,000	
Direct labor	4	4		32,000	
Variable overhead	1	1		8,000	
Supervisor's salary	3	3		24,000	
Depreciation of special equipment	2	—		—	
Allocation of general overhead	5	—		—	
Outside purchase price			$19		$152,000
Total cost	$21	$14	$19	$112,000	$152,000
Difference in favor of continuing to make		$5		$40,000	

Since it costs $5 less per unit to continue to make the subassemblies, Bonner Company should reject the outside supplier's offer. There is one additional factor that the company may wish to consider before coming to a final decision, however. This factor is the opportunity cost of the space now being used to produce the subassemblies.

The Matter of Opportunity Cost

If the space now being used to produce the subassemblies *would otherwise be idle*, then Bonner Company should continue to produce its own subassemblies and the supplier's offer should be rejected, as we stated above. Idle space that has no alternative use has an opportunity cost of zero.

But what if the space now being used to produce subassemblies would not sit idle, but rather could be used for some other purpose? In this case, the space would have an opportunity cost that would have to be considered in assessing the desirability of the supplier's offer. What would this opportunity cost be? It would be the segment margin that could be derived from the best alternative use of the space.

To illustrate, assume that the space now being used to produce subassemblies could be used to produce a new product line that would generate a segment margin of $60,000 per year. Under these conditions, Bonner Company would be better off to accept the supplier's offer and to use the available space to produce the new product line:

	Make	Buy
Differential cost per unit (see prior example)	$ 14	$ 19
Number of units needed annually	× 8,000	× 8,000
Total annual cost	112,000	152,000
Opportunity cost—segment margin forgone on a potential new product line	60,000	
Total cost	$172,000	$152,000
Difference in favor of purchasing from the outside supplier		$20,000

Perhaps we should again emphasize that opportunity costs are not recorded in the accounts of an organization. They do not represent actual dollar outlays. Rather, they represent those economic benefits that are *forgone* as a result of pursuing some course of action. The opportunity costs of Bonner Company are sufficiently large in this case to make continued production of the subassemblies very costly from an economic point of view.

UTILIZATION OF SCARCE RESOURCES

Firms are often faced with the problem of deciding how scarce resources are going to be utilized. A department store, for example, has a limited amount of floor space and therefore cannot stock every product line that may be available. A manufacturing firm has a limited number of machine-hours and a limited number of direct labor-hours at its disposal. When capacity becomes pressed, the firm must decide which orders it will accept and which orders it will reject. In making these decisions, the contribution approach is necessary, since the firm will want to select the course of action that will maximize its *total* contribution margin.

Contribution in Relation to Scarce Resources

To maximize total contribution margin, a firm may not necessarily want to promote those products that have the highest *individual* contribution margins. Rather, total contribution margin will be maximized by promoting those products or accepting those orders that promise the highest contribution margin *in relation to the scarce resources of the firm*. This concept can be demonstrated by assuming that a firm has two product lines, A and B. Cost and revenue characteristics of the two product lines are given below:

	Product lines	
	A	B
Sales price per unit	$25	$30
Variable cost per unit	10	18
Contribution margin per unit	$15	$12
C/M ratio	60%	40%

Product line A appears to be much more profitable than product line B. It has a $15 per unit contribution margin as compared to only $12 per unit for product line B, and it has a 60 percent C/M ratio as compared to only 40 percent for product line B.

But now let us add one more piece of information—it takes two machine-hours to produce one unit of A and only one machine-hour to produce one unit of B. The firm has only 18,000 machine-hours of capacity available in the plant per period. If demand becomes strong, which orders should the firm accept, those for product line A or those for product line B? The firm should accept orders for product line B. Even though product line A has the highest *per unit* contribution margin, product line B provides the highest contribution margin in relation to the scarce resource of the firm, which in this case is machine-hours available.

	Product lines	
	A	B
Contribution margin per unit (above) *(a)*	$15.00	$12
Machine-hours required to produce one unit *(b)*	2 hours	1 hour
Contribution margin per machine-hour, *(a) ÷ (b)*	$ 7.50	$12
Total contribution margin promised:		
Total machine-hours available	18,000	18,000
Contribution margin per machine-hour	× $7.50	× $12
Total contribution margin	$135,000	$216,000

This example shows clearly that looking at unit contribution margins alone is not enough; the contribution margin promised by a product line must be viewed in relation to whatever resource constraints a firm may be working under.

One of the most common resource constraints is advertising dollars available. Firms typically concentrate their efforts on those product lines that promise the greatest contribution margin per dollar of advertising expended. Another common resource constraint is floor space. Various discount retail outlets and discount food chains have utilized the concept of maximum contribution margin per square foot by concentrating on those product lines that have a rapid turnover, thereby generating large amounts of contribution in small amounts of space available.

The Problem of Multiple Constraints

What does a firm do if it is operating under *several* scarce resource constraints? For example, a firm may have limited raw materials available, limited direct labor-hours available, limited floor space, and limited advertising dollars to spend on product promotion. How would it proceed to find the right combination of products to produce under such a variety of constraints? The proper combination or "mix" of products can be found by use of a quantitative method known as *linear programming*. Linear programming, a very powerful analytical tool, is illustrated in the Appendix to this chapter.

JOINT PRODUCT COSTS AND THE CONTRIBUTION APPROACH

The manufacturing processes of some firms are such that several end products are produced from a single raw material input. The meat-packing industry, for example, inputs a pig into the manufacturing process and comes out with a great variety of end products—bacon, ham, spare ribs, pork roasts, and so on. Firms that produce several end products from a common input (e.g., a pig) are faced with the problem of deciding how the cost of that input is going to be divided among the end products (bacon, ham, pork roasts, and so on) that result. Before we address ourselves to this problem, it will be helpful to define three terms—joint products, joint product costs, and split-off point.

Two or more products that are produced from a common input are known as **joint products.** The term **joint product costs** is used to describe those manufacturing costs that are incurred in producing joint products up to the split-off point. The **split-off point** is that point in the manufacturing process at which the joint products (bacon, ham, spare ribs, and so on) can be recognized as individual units of output. At that point, some of the joint products will be in final form, ready to be marketed to the consumer. Others will still need further processing on their own before they are in marketable form. These concepts are presented graphically in Exhibit 13–6.

The Pitfalls of Allocation

Joint product costs are really common costs incurred to simultaneously produce a variety of end products. Traditional cost accounting books contain various approaches to allocating these common costs among the different products at the split-off point. The most usual approach is to allocate the joint product costs according to the relative sales value of the end products.

Although allocation of joint product costs is needed for some purposes, such as balance sheet inventory valuation, allocations of this kind should be used with great caution *internally* in the decision-making process. Unless a manager proceeds with care, he or she may be led into incorrect decisions as a result of relying on allocated common costs. Consider the following situation, which occurred in a firm several years ago:

A company located on the Gulf of Mexico is a producer of soap products. Its six main soap product lines are produced from common inputs. Joint product costs up to the split-off point constitute the bulk of the production costs for all six product lines. These joint product costs are allocated to the six product lines on the basis of the relative sales value of each line at the split-off point.

The company has a waste product that results from the production of the

EXHIBIT 13–6
Joint products

Keep processing if incremental costs less than incremental revenue of further processing.

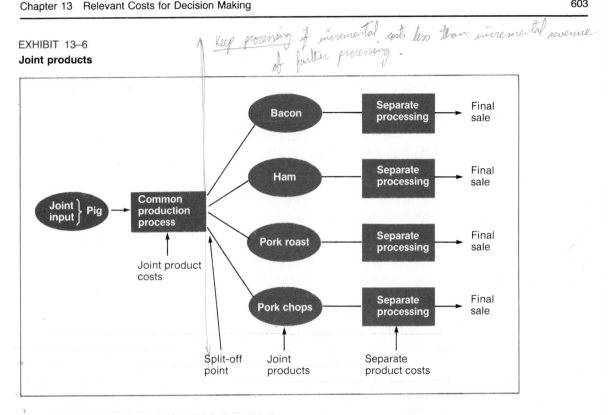

six main product lines. Until a few years ago, the company loaded the waste onto barges and dumped it into the Gulf of Mexico, since the waste was thought to have no commercial value. The dumping was stopped, however, when the company's research division discovered that with some further processing the waste could be made commercially salable as a fertilizer ingredient. The further processing was initiated at a cost of $175,000 per year. The waste was then sold to fertilizer manufacturers at a total price of $300,000 per year.

The accountants responsible for allocating manufacturing costs included the sales value of the waste product along with the sales value of the six main product lines in their allocation of the joint product costs at the split-off point. This allocation resulted in the waste product being allocated $150,000 in joint product cost. This $150,000 allocation, when added to the further processing costs of $175,000 for the waste, caused the waste product to show a net loss:

Sales value of the waste product after further processing	$300,000
Less costs assignable to the waste product	325,000
Net loss	$ (25,000)

When presented with this analysis, the company's management decided that further processing of the waste was not desirable after all. The company went back to dumping the waste in the Gulf.

Sell or Process Further Decisions

Joint product costs are irrelevant in decisions regarding what to do with a product from the split-off point forward. The reason is that by the time one arrives at the split-off point, the joint product costs have already been incurred, and therefore are sunk costs. In the case of the soap company example above, the $150,000 in allocated joint product costs should not have been permitted to influence what was done with the waste product from the split-off point forward. The analysis should have been:

	Dump in Gulf	Process further
Sales value	–0–	$300,000
Additional processing costs	–0–	175,000
Contribution margin	–0–	$125,000
Advantage of processing further		$125,000

Decisions of this type are known as **sell or process further decisions.** As a general guide, it will always be profitable to continue processing a joint product after the split-off point *so long as the incremental revenue from such processing exceeds the incremental processing costs.* Joint product costs that have already been incurred up to the split-off point are sunk costs, and are always irrelevant in decisions concerning what to do from the split-off point forward.

To provide a detailed example of a sell or process further decision, assume that three products are derived from a single raw material input. Cost and revenue data relating to the products are presented in Exhibit 13–7, along with an analysis of which products should be sold at the split-

EXHIBIT 13–7
Sell or process further decision

	Products		
	A	B	C
Sales value at the split-off point	$120,000	$150,000	$60,000
Sales value after further processing	160,000	240,000	90,000
Allocated joint product costs	80,000	100,000	40,000
Cost of further processing	50,000	60,000	10,000
Analysis of sell or process further:			
Sales value after further processing	$160,000	$240,000	$90,000
Sales value at the split-off point	120,000	150,000	60,000
Incremental revenue from further processing	40,000	90,000	30,000
Cost of further processing	50,000	60,000	10,000
Profit (loss) from further processing	$ (10,000)	$ 30,000	$20,000

off point and which should be processed further. As shown in the exhibit, products B and C should both be processed further; product A should be sold at the split-off point.

SUMMARY

The accountant is responsible for seeing that relevant, timely data are available to guide management in its decisions, particularly those decisions relating to special, nonroutine situations. Reliance by management on irrelevant data can lead to incorrect decisions, reduced profitability, and inability to meet stated objectives. *All* costs are relevant in decision making, *except:*

1. Sunk costs.
2. Future costs that will not differ between the alternatives under consideration.

The concept of cost relevance has wide application. In this chapter, we have observed its use in equipment replacement decisions, in make or buy decisions, in discontinuance of product line decisions, in joint product decisions, and in decisions relating to the effective use of scarce resources. This list does not include all of the possible applications of the relevant cost concept. Indeed, *any* decision involving costs hinges on the proper identification and use of those costs that are relevant, if the decision is to be made properly. For this reason, we shall continue to focus on the concept of cost relevance in the following two chapters, where we consider long-run investment decisions.

KEY TERMS FOR REVIEW

Avoidable cost Any cost that can be eliminated (in whole or in part) as a result of choosing one alternative over another in a decision-making situation. This term is synonymous with *relevant cost* and *differential cost.*

Differential cost Any cost that is present under one alternative in a decision-making situation but is absent in whole or in part under another alternative. This term is synonymous with *avoidable cost* and *relevant cost.*

Joint product costs Those manufacturing costs that are incurred up to the split-off point in producing joint products.

Joint products Two or more items that are produced from a common input.

Make or buy decision A decision as to whether an item should be produced internally or purchased from an outside supplier.

Relevant cost A cost that is applicable to a particular decision in the sense that it will have a bearing on which alternative the manager selects. This term is synonymous with *avoidable cost* and *differential cost.*

Sell or process further decision A decision as to whether a joint product should be sold at the split-off point or processed further and sold at a later time in a different form.

Split-off point That point in the manufacturing process where some or all of the joint products can be recognized as individual units of output.

Sunk cost Any cost that has already been incurred and that cannot be changed by any decision made now or in the future.

Vertical integration The involvement by a company in more than one of the steps from extracting or otherwise securing basic raw materials to the manufacture and distribution of a finished product.

APPENDIX: LINEAR PROGRAMMING

Linear programming is a mathematical tool designed to assist management in making decisions in situations where constraining or limiting factors are present. The limiting factors might include, for example, a scarcity of raw materials needed in the production of a firm's products, or a plant with inadequate machine time to produce all of the products being demanded by a firm's customers. Linear programming is designed to assist the manager in putting together the "right mix" of products in situations such as these, so that the scarce resources of the firm (e.g., raw materials, machine time) can be utilized in a way that will maximize profits.

A Graphic Approach to Linear Programming

To demonstrate a linear programming analysis, let us assume the following data:

A firm produces two products, X and Y. The contribution margin per unit of X is $8, and the contribution margin per unit of Y is $10. The firm has 36 hours of production time available each period. It takes six hours of production time to produce one unit of X and nine hours of production time to produce one unit of Y.

The firm has only 24 pounds of raw material available for use in production each period. It takes six pounds of raw material to produce one unit of X and three pounds to produce one unit of Y.

Management estimates that no more than three units of Y can be sold each period. The firm is interested in maximizing contribution margin. What combination of X and Y should be produced and sold?

There are four basic steps in a linear programming analysis:

1. Determine the *objective function,* and express it in algebraic terms.
2. Determine the *constraints* under which the firm must operate, and express each constraint in algebraic terms.
3. Determine the *feasible production area* on a graph. This area will be bounded by the constraint equations derived in (2) above, after the constraint equations have been expressed on the graph in linear form.
4. Determine from the feasible production area the *product mix* that will maximize (or minimize) the objective function.

We shall now examine each of these steps in order by relating them to the data in the example above.

1. Determine the objective function, and express it in algebraic terms.

The **objective function** represents the goal that management is trying to achieve. This goal might be to maximize total contribution margin, as in our example; alternatively, it might be to minimize total cost.

Looking at the data in our example, for each unit of X that is sold, $8 in contribution margin will be realized. For each unit of Y that is sold, $10 in contribution margin will be realized. Therefore, the total contribution margin for the firm can be expressed by the following **objective function equation:**

$$Z = \$8X + \$10Y \tag{1}$$

where Z = the total contribution margin that will be realized with an optimal mix of X and Y, X = the number of units of product X that should be produced and sold to yield the optimal mix, and Y = the number of units of product Y that should be produced and sold to yield the optimal mix.

2. Determine the constraints under which the firm must operate, and express each constraint in algebraic terms.

A **constraint** is simply some limitation under which the company must operate, such as limited production time available or a limited amount of raw materials on hand. From the data in our example, we can identify three constraints. First, only 36 hours of production time are available. Since it requires six hours to produce one unit of X and nine hours to produce one unit of Y, this constraint can be expressed in algebraic terms in the form of a **constraint equation,** as follows:

$$6X + 9Y \leq 36 \tag{2}$$

Notice the inequality sign ($\leq$) in the equation. This signifies that the total production of both products X and Y taken together cannot *exceed* the 36 hours available, but that this production *could* require *less* than the 36 hours available.

The second constraint deals with raw material usage. Only 24 pounds are available each period. It takes six pounds of raw material to produce one unit of X and three pounds to produce one unit of Y. This constraint can be expressed in the following algebraic terms:

$$6X + 3Y \leq 24 \tag{3}$$

The third constraint deals with market acceptance of product Y. The market can absorb only three units of Y each period. This constraint can be expressed as follows:

$$Y \leq 3 \tag{4}$$

3. Determine the feasible production area on a graph.

A graph containing the constraint equations [equations (2)–(4) above] is presented in Exhibit 13–8. In placing these three equations on the graph, we have asked the questions "How much product X could be produced if all resources were allocated to it and none were allocated to product Y?" and "How much product Y could be produced if all resources were allocated to it and none were allocated to product X?" For example, consider equation (2), dealing with production capacity. A total of 36 hours of production time is available. If all 36 hours are allocated to product X, six units can be produced each period (since it takes 6 hours to produce one unit of X, and 36 hours are available). On the other hand, if all 36 hours are allocated to product Y, then four units of Y can be produced each period (since it takes 9 hours to produce one unit of Y, and 36 hours are available).

If all production capacity is allocated to product X	If all production capacity is allocated to product Y
$6X + 0 \leq 36$	$0 + 9Y \leq 36$
$X = 6$	$Y = 4$

Therefore, the line on the graph in Exhibit 13–8 expressing the production constraint equation [equation (2)] extends from the six-unit point on the X axis to the four-unit point on the Y axis. Of course, production could fall *anywhere* on this constraint line; the points on the axes (6, 4) simply represent the *extremes* that would be possible.

The equation associated with the raw materials constraint [equation (3)] has been placed on the graph through a similar line of reasoning. Since 24 pounds of raw material are available, the firm could produce either four units of X or eight units of Y if all of the raw material was allocated to one or the other (since it takes 6 pounds to produce a unit of X and 3 pounds to produce a unit of Y). Therefore, the line expressing the equation extends from the four-unit point on the X axis to the eight-unit point on the Y axis. Again, production could fall *anywhere* on this constraint line; the points on the axes (4, 8) simply represent the *extremes* that would be possible.

Since the third constraint equation [equation (4)] concerns only product Y, the line expressing the equation on the graph does not touch the X axis at all. It extends from the three-unit point on the Y axis and runs horizontal to the X axis, thereby signifying that regardless of the number of units of X that are produced, there can never be more than three units of Y produced.

Having now plotted on the graph the lines representing the three constraint equations, we have isolated the **feasible production area.** This area has been shaded on the graph. Notice that the feasible production area is formed by the lines of the constraint equations. Each line has served to limit the

EXHIBIT 13–8

A linear programming graphic solution

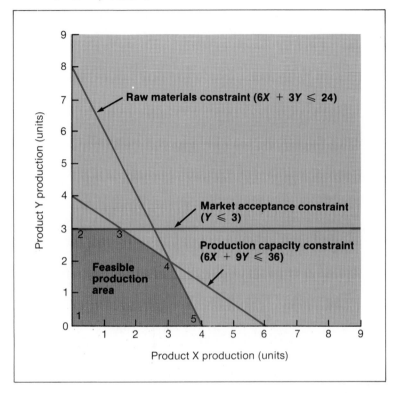

size of the area to some extent. The reason, of course, is that these lines represent *constraints* under which the firm must operate, and thereby serve to *limit* the range of choices available. The firm could operate *anywhere* within the feasible production area. One point within this area, however, represents an optimal mix of products X and Y that will result in a maximization of the objective function (contribution margin). Our task now is to find precisely where that point lies.

4. Determine from the feasible production area the product mix that will maximize the objective function.

The **optimal product mix** will always fall on a *corner* of the feasible production area. If we scan the graph in Exhibit 13–8, we can see that the feasible production area has five corners. The five corners will yield the following product mixes between X and Y (starting at the origin and going clockwise around the feasible production area):

	Units produced	
Corner	X	Y
1	0	0
2	0	3
3	1½	3
4	3	2
5	4	0

Which production mix is optimal? To answer this question, we will need to calculate the total contribution margin promised at each corner. We can do this by referring to the unit contribution margin data given in the objective function equation:

$$Z = \$8X + \$10Y \tag{1}$$

This equation tells us that each unit of X promises $8 of contribution margin and that each unit of Y promises $10 of contribution margin. Relating these figures to the production mixes at the five corners, we find that the following total contribution margins are possible:

X		Y		Total contribution margin
$8(0)	+	$10(0)	=	$ 0
8(0)	+	10(3)	=	30
8(1½)	+	10(3)	=	42
8(3)	+	10(2)	=	44
8(4)	+	10(0)	=	32

The firm should produce three units of X and two units of Y. This production mix will yield a maximum contribution margin of $44. Given the constraints under which the firm must operate, it is not possible to obtain a greater toal contribution margin than this amount. Any production mix different from three units of X and two units of Y will result in *less* total contribution margin.

Why Always on a Corner?

It was stated earlier that we will always find the optimal product mix on a *corner* of the feasible production area. Why does the optimal mix always fall on a corner? Look again at the objective function equation [equation (1)]. This equation expresses a straight line with a $-\frac{4}{5}$ slope. Place a ruler on the graph in Exhibit 13–8 extending from the 8 point on the Y axis to the 10 point on the X axis (a $-\frac{4}{5}$ slope). Now bring your ruler down toward the origin of the graph, taking care to keep it parallel to the line from which you started. Note that the first point which your ruler touches is the corner of the feasible production area showing a production mix of three units of X and two units of Y. Your ruler touches this point first because it is the farthest point from the origin in relation to the objective function line. Therefore, that point must yield the greatest total contribution margin for the firm. Any point closer to the origin would result in less total contribution margin.[3]

Direction of the Constraint

Exhibit 13–8 shows the direction of all the constraints to be *inward* toward the origin of the graph. The direction of the constraint will always be inward, so long as the constraint equation is stated in terms of less than or equal to ($\leq$).

The direction of the constraint will be *outward,* away from the origin of the graph, whenever the constraint equation is stated in terms of greater than or equal to ($\geq$). To illustrate, assume the following constraint:

X weighs 4 ounces, and Y weighs 9 ounces. X and Y must be mixed in such a way that their total weight is at least 72 ounces

Constraint equation: $4X + 9Y \geq 72$ ounces

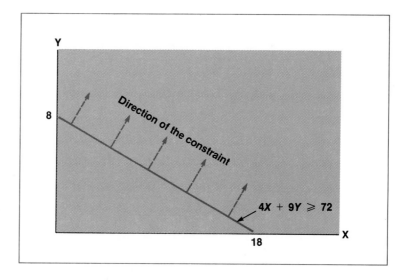

---

[3] The objective function line could coincide with one of the lines bounding the feasible production area. In this case, a number of different product combinations would be possible, each resulting in the same total contribution margin. However, our statement that the solution will always be found on a corner is still true even under these conditions, since the product mix at the corners of the line would yield the same total contribution margin as any point on the line.

Since the direction of this constraint line is upward rather than downward, the feasible production area will be found *above* it rather than below it. Constraints expressed in terms of *greater than or equal to,* as illustrated above, can be found in any linear programming problem but are most common in *minimization* problems.

The Simplex Method

In our examples, we have dealt with only two products, X and Y. When more than two products are involved in a linear programming problem, the graphic method is no longer adequate to provide a solution. In these cases, a more powerful version of linear programming is needed. This more powerful version is commonly called the **simplex method.**

The simplex method is much more complex in its operation than is the graphic method; however, the principles underlying the two methods are the same. Generally, linear programming simplex solutions are carried out on the digital computer. The mechanics of the simplex method are covered in most advanced managerial accounting texts.

Applications of Linear Programming

Linear programming has been applied to an extremely wide range of problems in many different fields. Decision makers have found that it is by far the best tool available for combining labor, materials, and equipment to the best advantage of a firm. Although the use of linear programming has been most extensive in the industrial, agricultural, and military sectors, it has also been applied to problems in economics, engineering, and the sciences. Problems to which linear programming has been successfully applied include gasoline blending, production scheduling to optimize the use of total facilities, livestock feed blending to obtain a desired nutritional mix at the least cost, the routing of boxcars to desired points at the least cost, the selection of sites for electrical transformers, forestry maintenance, and the choice of flight paths for space satellites.

KEY TERMS FOR REVIEW (APPENDIX)

Constraint A limitation under which a company must operate, such as limited machine time available or limited materials available.

Constraint equation An algebraic expression of one of the limitations (constraints) under which a company must operate.

Feasible production area The area on a linear programming graph, bounded by the constraint equations, within which production can take place.

Linear programming A mathematical tool designed to assist the manager in making decisions in situations where constraining or limiting factors are present.

Objective function A statement of the goal that management is trying to achieve. This goal might be, for example, to maximize total contribution margin or to minimize total cost.

Objective function equation An algebraic expression of the goal that management is trying to achieve in a linear programming analysis.

Optimal product mix The product mix that allows the firm to achieve the objective expressed in the objective function equation.

Simplex method A linear programming method that is designed to handle three or more variables in the objective function equation (for example, the optimal production mix of three or more products).

QUESTIONS

13–1.   What is a "relevant cost"?

13–2.   Define the following terms: incremental cost, opportunity cost, and sunk cost.

13–3.   Are variable costs always relevant costs? Explain.

13–4.   The book value of a machine (as shown on the balance sheet) is an asset to a company, but this same book value is irrelevant in decision making. Explain why this is so.

13–5.   "Sunk costs are easy to spot—they're simply the fixed costs associated with a decision." Do you agree? Explain.

13–6.   "Sometimes depreciation on equipment is a relevant cost in a decision, and sometimes it isn't." Do you agree? Explain.

13–7.   "My neighbor offered me $25 for the use of my boat over the weekend, but I decided that renting it out is just too risky." What cost term would you use to describe the $25? Explain.

13–8.   "Variable costs and differential costs mean the same thing." Do you agree? Explain.

13–9.   "All future costs are relevant in decision making." Do you agree? Why?

13–10. Prentice Company is considering dropping one of its product lines. What costs of the product line would be relevant to this decision? Irrelevant?

13–11. Why is the term *avoidable cost* used in connection with product line and make or buy decisions?

13–12. "If a product line is generating a loss, then that's pretty good evidence that the product line should be discontinued." Do you agree? Explain.

13–13. What is the danger in allocating common fixed costs among product lines or other segments of an organization?

13–14. What is meant by the term *make or buy?*

13–15. How does opportunity cost enter into the make or buy decision?

13–16. Give four examples of limiting or scarce factors that might be present in an organization.

13–17. How will the relating of product line contribution margins to scarce resources help a company ensure that profits will be maximized?

13–18. Define the following terms: joint products, joint product costs, and split-off point.

13–19. From a decision-making point of view, what pitfalls are there in allocating common costs among joint products?

13–20. What guideline can be used in determining whether a joint product should be sold at the split-off point or processed further?

13–21. Airlines often offer reduced rates during certain times of the week to members of a businessperson's family if they accompany him or her on trips. How does the concept of relevant costs enter into the decision to offer reduced rates of this type?

13–22. Schloss Company has decided to use linear programming as a planning tool. The company can't decide whether to use contribution margin per unit or gross profit per unit in its linear programming computations. Which would you suggest? Why?

13–23. Define *objective function* and *constraint* as these concepts relate to linear programming.

13–24. Sever Company produces two products. Product A has a contribution margin per unit of $10. Product B has a contribution margin per unit of $8. Explain why a linear programming analysis might suggest that the company produce more of product B than product A. (Ample market exists for either product.)

13–25. What is meant by the term *feasible production area?*

EXERCISES

E13–1. Listed below are a number of "costs" incurred by Rialdo Company:

		Case 1		Case 2	
	Item	**Relevant**	**Not relevant**	**Relevant**	**Not relevant**
a.	Sales revenue				
b.	Direct materials				
c.	Direct labor				
d.	Variable production overhead				
e.	Depreciation—machine A				
f.	Depreciation—machine B				
g.	Fixed production overhead (general)				
h.	Variable selling expense				
i.	Fixed selling expense				
j.	General administrative salaries				
k.	Book value—machine A				
l.	Market value—machine A (current resale)				
m.	Market value—machine B (cost)				
n.	Rate of return available from outside investments				

Required: Copy the information above onto your answer sheet, and place an "X" in the appropriate column to indicate whether each item is relevant or not relevant in the following situations (requirement 1 relates to Case 1 above, and requirement 2 relates to Case 2):

1. Rialdo Company wants to purchase machine B to replace machine A (machine A will be sold). Both machines have the same capacity and a remaining life of five years. Machine B will reduce direct materials costs by 20 percent, due to less waste. Other production costs will not change.

2. Rialdo Company wants to purchase machine B to increase production and sales. Machine A will continue to be used.

E13–2.   The costs associated with the acquisition and annual operation of a truck are given below:

Insurance	$1,600
Licenses	250
Taxes (vehicle)	150
Garage rent for parking (per truck) . . .	1,200
Depreciation ($9,000 ÷ 5 years)	1,800*
Gasoline, oil, tires, and repairs	0.07 per mile

Based on obsolescence rather than on wear and tear.

Required:

1. Assume that Hollings Company has purchased one truck, and that the truck has been driven 50,000 miles during the first year. Compute the average cost per mile of owning and operating the truck.

2. At the beginning of the second year, Hollings Company is unsure whether to use the truck or leave it parked in the garage and have all hauling done commercially. (The state requires the payment of vehicle taxes even if the vehicle isn't used.) What costs above are relevant to this decision?

3. Assume that the company decides to use the truck during the second year. Near year-end an order is received from a customer over 1,000 miles away. What costs above are relevant in a decision between using the truck to make the delivery and having the delivery done commercially?

4. Occasionally the company could use two trucks at the same time. For this reason, some thought is being given to purchasing a second truck. The total miles driven would be the same as if only one truck were owned. What costs above are relevant to a decision over whether to purchase the second truck?

E13–3.   Waukee Railroad is considering the purchase of a powerful, high-speed teletype machine to replace a standard teletype machine that is now in use. Selected information on the two machines is given below:

	Standard teletype	High-speed teletype
Original cost new	$20,000	$30,000
Accumulated depreciation to date . . .	6,000	—
Current salvage value	9,000	—
Estimated cost per year to operate . . .	15,000	7,000
Remaining years of useful life	5 years	5 years

Required: Prepare a computation covering the five-year period that will show the net advantage or disadvantage of purchasing the high-speed teletype machine. Ignore income taxes, and use only relevant costs in your analysis.

E13–4. Swanson Company has been experiencing losses on product line 6 for several years. The most recent quarterly income statement on product line 6 is given below:

SWANSON COMPANY
Income Statement—Product Line 6
For the Quarter Ended March 31, 19x7

Sales.		$850,000
Less variable expenses:		
Variable manufacturing expenses	$330,000	
Sales commissions	42,000	
Freight-out	18,000	
Total variable expenses		390,000
Contribution margin		460,000
Less fixed expenses:		
Advertising	270,000	
Depreciation of equipment (no resale value) . .	80,000	
General factory overhead	105,000*	
Salary of line manager	32,000	
Insurance on inventories	8,000	
Purchasing department expenses	45,000†	
Total fixed expenses		540,000
Net loss		$ (80,000)

* Allocated on a basis of machine-hours.
† Allocated on a basis of sales dollars.

The discontinuance of product line 6 would not effect sales of other product lines.

Required: Would you recommend that product line 6 be discontinued? Support your answer with appropriate computations.

E13–5. Troy Engines, Ltd., manufactures a variety of engines for use in heavy equipment. The company has always produced all of the necessary parts for its engines, including all of the carburetors. An outside supplier has offered to produce and sell one type of carburetor to Troy Engines, Ltd., for a cost of $35 per unit. In order to evaluate this offer, Troy Engines, Ltd., has gathered the following information relating to its own cost of producing the carburetor internally:

	Per unit	15,000 units per year
Direct materials	$14	$210,000
Direct labor	10	150,000
Variable manufacturing overhead	3	45,000
Fixed manufacturing overhead, traceable . .	6*	90,000
Fixed manufacturing overhead, allocated . .	9	135,000
Total cost	$42	$630,000

* One-third supervisory salaries; two-thirds depreciation of special equipment (no resale value).

Required: 1. Assuming that the company has no alternative use for the facilities that are now being used to produce the carburetors, should the outside supplier's offer be accepted? Show all computations.

2. Assuming that a new product that will generate a segment margin of $150,000 per year could be produced if the carburetors were purchased, should the offer be accepted? Show all computations.

E13–6. Barlow Company manufactures three products: A, B, and C. The selling price, variable costs, and contribution margin for one unit of each product follow:

	Products		
	A	**B**	**C**
Selling price	$180	$270	$240
Less variable expenses:			
Direct materials	24	72	32
Direct labor	97	86	140
Variable overhead	5	4	8
Total variable expenses . . .	126	162	180
Contribution margin	$ 54	$108	$ 60
Contribution margin ratio	30%	40%	25%

The same raw material is used in all three products. Barlow Company has only 5,000 pounds of material on hand and will not be able to obtain any more material for several weeks due to a strike in its supplier's plant. Management is trying to decide which product(s) to concentrate on next week in filling its backlog of orders. The material costs $8 per pound.

Required: 1. Compute the amount of contribution margin that will be obtained per pound of material used in each product.
2. Which orders would you recommend that the company work on next week— the orders for product A, product B, or product C? Show computations.

E13–7. Dorsey Company manufactures three products from a common input in a joint processing operation. Joint processing costs up to the split-off point total $350,000 per quarter. The company allocates these costs to the joint products on the basis of their total sales value at the split-off point. Unit selling prices and total output at the split-off point are as follows:

Product	Selling price	Quarterly output
A	$16 per pound	15,000 pounds
B	8 per pound	20,000 pounds
C	25 per gallon	4,000 gallons

Each product can be processed further after the split-off point. Additional processing requires no special facilities. The additional processing costs (per quarter) and unit selling prices after further processing are given below:

Product	Additional processing costs	Selling price
A	$63,000	$20 per pound
B	80,000	13 per pound
C	36,000	32 per gallon

Required:　1. Which product or products should be sold at the split-off point, and which product or products should be processed further? Show computations.

　　　　　2. What general statement can be made with respect to joint costs and the decision to process further?

E13–8.　Hasbro Products manufactures 30,000 units of part S-6 each year for use on its production line. At this level of activity, the cost per unit for part S-6 is as follows:

Direct materials	$ 3.60
Direct labor	10.00
Variable overhead	2.40
Fixed overhead	9.00
Total cost per part	$25.00

An outside supplier has offered to sell 30,000 units of part S-6 each year to Hasbro Products for $21 per part. If Hasbro Products accepts this offer, the facilities now being used to manufacture part S-6 could be rented to another company at an annual rental of $80,000. However, Hasbro has determined that two thirds of the fixed overhead being applied to part S-6 would continue even if part S-6 were purchased from the outside supplier.

Required:　Prepare computations to show the net dollar advantage or disadvantage of accepting the outside supplier's offer.

E13–9.　Bill has just returned from a duck hunting trip. He has brought home eight ducks. Bill's wife detests cleaning ducks, and to discourage him from further duck hunting, she has presented him with the following cost estimate per duck:

Camper and equipment:	
Cost, $12,000; usable for eight seasons; 10 hunting trips per season	$150
Travel expense (pickup truck):	
100 miles at $0.12 per mile (gas, oil, and tires—$0.07 per mile; depreciation and insurance—$0.05 per mile)	12
Shotgun shells (two boxes)	20
Boat:	
Cost, $320; usable for eight seasons; 10 hunting trips per season	4
Fine paid for speeding on the way to the river	25
Hunting license:	
Cost, $30 for the season; 10 hunting trips per season	3
Money lost playing poker:	
Loss, $18 (Bill plays poker every weekend)	18
A fifth of Old Grandad:	
Cost, $8 (used to ward off the cold)	8
Total cost	$240
Cost per duck ($240 ÷ 8 ducks)	$ 30

Required:　1. Assuming that the duck hunting trip Bill has just completed is typical, what costs are relevant to a decision as to whether Bill should go duck hunting again this season?

　　　　　2. Discuss the wife's computation of the cost per duck.

E13–10. The Regal Cycle Company manufactures three types of bicycles—a dirt bike, a 10-speed bike, and a touring bike. Data on sales and expenses for the past six months follow:

	Total	Dirt bikes	10-speed bikes	Touring bikes
Sales	$300,000	$90,000	$150,000	$60,000
Less variable manufacturing and selling expenses	120,000	27,000	60,000	33,000
Contribution margin	180,000	63,000	90,000	27,000
Less fixed expenses:				
Advertising, traceable	30,000	10,000	14,000	6,000
Depreciation of special equipment	23,000	6,000	9,000	8,000 _sunk_
Salary of line supervisor	35,000	12,000	13,000	10,000
Common, but allocated˙	60,000	18,000	30,000	12,000
Total fixed expenses	148,000	46,000	66,000	36,000
Net income (loss).	$ 32,000	$17,000	$ 24,000	$ (9,000)

˙ Allocated on a basis of sales dollars.

Management is concerned about the continued losses shown by the touring bikes and wants a recommendation as to whether or not the line should be discontinued. The special equipment used to produce touring bikes has no resale value.

Required: 1. Should production and sale of the touring bikes be discontinued? Show computations to support your answer.
2. Recast the above data in a format that would be more usable to management in assessing the long-run profitability of the various product lines.

E13–11. (Appendix)   Greenup Company produces two high-quality fertilizer products—Nitro-X and Nitro-Y. Each fertilizer product is produced in batches, with one batch of Nitro-X yielding a contribution margin of $70 and one batch of Nitro-Y yielding a contribution margin of $80. The company wants to maximize contribution margin. Either product can be sold in unlimited quantities.

Two raw materials go into the production of both Nitro-X and Nitro-Y, although not in the same proportions, as shown in the table below. In addition, Nitro-X uses a third raw material.

	Material A (pounds)	Material B (pounds)	Material C (pounds)
Nitro-X usage per batch	40	30	15
Nitro-Y usage per batch	30	60	—
Total raw material available each day	6,000	9,000	1,500

Required: 1. Prepare equations to express the objective function and the constraints under which the company must operate.
2. Determine how many batches of Nitro-X and Nitro-Y should be produced each day. Use the linear programming graphic method, with Nitro-X on the horizontal *(X)* axis and Nitro-Y on the vertical *(Y)* axis.

PROBLEMS

P13–12.   **Dropping a flight; analysis of operating policy.**   Profits have been decreasing for several years at Pegasus Airlines. In an effort to improve the company's performance, consideration is being given to dropping several flights that appear to be unprofitable.

A typical income statement for one such flight (flight 482) is given below (per flight):

Ticket revenue (175 seats × 40% occupancy × $200 ticket price)	$14,000	100.0%
Less variable expenses ($15 per person)	1,050	7.5
Contribution margin	12,950	92.5%
Less flight expenses:		
Salaries, flight crew	1,800	
Flight promotion	750	
Depreciation of aircraft	1,400*	
Fuel for aircraft	6,800	
Liability insurance	4,200	
Salaries, flight assistants	500	
Hanger parking fee for aircraft at destination	150	
Baggage loading and flight preparation	1,700	
Overnight costs for flight crew and assistants at destination	300	
Total flight costs	17,600	
Net loss	$ (4,650)	

  * Based on obsolescence.

The following additional information is available about flight 482:

a.   Members of the flight crew are paid fixed annual salaries, whereas the flight assistants are paid by the flight.

b.   One third of the liability insurance is a special charge assessed against flight 482 because in the opinion of the insurance company, the destination of the flight is in a "high-risk" area.

c.   The hanger parking fee is a standard fee charged for aircraft at all airports.

d.   The baggage loading and flight preparation expense is an allocation of ground crews' salaries and depreciation of ground equipment.

e.   If flight 482 is dropped, Pegasus Airlines has no authorization at present to replace it with another flight.

Required: 1.   Using the data available, prepare an analysis showing what impact dropping flight 482 would have on the airline's profits.

2.   The airline's scheduling officer has been criticized because only about 50 percent of the seats on Pegasus' flights are being filled compared to an average of 60 percent for the industry. The scheduling officer has explained that Pegasus' average seat occupancy could be improved considerably by eliminating about 10 percent of the flights, but that doing so would reduce profits. Explain how this could happen.

P13–13.   **Relevant cost analysis; book value.**   Murl Plastics, Inc., purchased a new machine one year ago at a cost of $60,000. Although the machine operates well, the president of Murl Plastics is wondering if the company should replace it with a new electronically operated machine that has just come on the market. The new machine would slash annual operating costs by two thirds, as shown in the comparative data below:

	Present machine	Proposed new machine
Purchase cost new	$60,000	$90,000
Estimated useful life new	6 years	5 years
Annual cost to operate	$42,000	$14,000
Annual straight-line depreciation . . .	10,000	18,000
Remaining book value	50,000	—
Salvage value now	10,000	—
Salvage value in 5 years	–0–	–0–

In trying to decide whether to purchase the new machine, the president has prepared the following analysis:

Book value of the old machine	$50,000
Less salvage value	10,000
Net loss from disposal	$40,000

"Even though the new machine looks good," said the president, "we can't get rid of that old machine if it means taking a huge loss on it. We'll have to use the old machine for at least a few more years."

Sales in the company are expected to be $200,000 per year, and selling and administrative expenses are expected to be $126,000 per year, regardless of which machine is used.

Required: 1. Prepare a summary income statement covering the next five years, assuming:
   a. That the new machine is not purchased.
   b. That the new machine is purchased.
2. Determine the desirability of purchasing the new machine, using only relevant costs in your analysis.

P13–14.   **Sell or process further decision.**   (Prepared from a situation suggested by Professor John W. Hardy.) Lone Star Meat Packers is a major processor of beef and other meat products. The company has a large amount of T-bone steak on hand, and it is trying to decide whether to sell the T-bone steaks as they are initially cut or to process them further into filet mignon and the New York cut.

If the T-bone steaks are sold as initially cut, the company figures that a one-pound T-bone steak would yield the following profit:

Selling price ($2.25 per pound)	$2.25
Less joint product cost	1.80
Profit per pound	$0.45

Instead of being sold as initially cut, the T-bone steaks could be further processed into filet mignon and New York cut steaks. Cutting one side of a T-bone steak provides the filet mignon, and cutting the other side provides the New York cut. One 16-ounce T-bone steak thus cut will yield one 6-ounce filet mignon and one 8-ounce New York cut; the remaining ounces are waste. The cost of processing the T-bone steaks into these cuts is $0.25 per pound. The filet mignon can be sold for $4 per pound, and the New York cut can be sold for $2.80 per pound.

Required: 1. Determine the profit per pound from further processing the T-bone steaks.
2. Would you recommend that the T-bone steaks be sold as initially cut or processed further? Why?

P13–15.   **Relevant cost potpourri.**   Unless otherwise indicated, each of the following parts is independent. In all cases, show computations to support your answer.

1. A merchandising company has two departments, A and B. A recent monthly income statement for the company follows:

	Total	Department A	Department B
Sales.	$4,000,000	$3,000,000	$1,000,000
Less variable expenses	1,300,000	900,000	400,000
Contribution margin	2,700,000	2,100,000	600,000
Less fixed expenses	2,200,000	1,400,000	800,000
Net income (loss)	$ 500,000	$ 700,000	$ (200,000)

A study indicates that $340,000 of the fixed expenses being charged to department B are sunk costs and allocated costs that will continue even if B is dropped. In addition, the elimination of department B will result in a 10 percent decrease in the sales of department A. If department B is dropped, what will be the effect on the income of the company as a whole?

2. For many years Futura Company has purchased the starters that it installs in its standard line of farm tractors. Due to a reduction in output of certain of its products, the company has idle capacity that could be used to produce the starters. The chief engineer has recommended against this move, however, pointing out that the cost to produce the starters would be greater than the current $8.40 per unit purchase price:

	Per unit	Total
Direct materials	$3.10	
Direct labor	2.70	
Supervision	1.50	$60,000
Depreciation	1.00	40,000
Variable overhead	0.60	
Rent	0.30	12,000
Total cost	$9.20	

A supervisor would have to be hired to oversee production of the starters. However, the company has sufficient idle tools and machinery that no new equipment would have to be purchased. The rent charge above is based on space utilized in the plant. The total rent on the plant is $80,000 per period. Prepare computations to show the dollar advantage or disadvantage per period of making the starters.

3. Wexpro, Inc., produces several products from processing of 1 ton of clypton, a rare mineral. Material and processing costs total $60,000 per ton, one fourth of which is allocable to product X. Seven thousand units of product X are produced from each ton of clypton. The units can either be sold at the split-

off point for $9 each, or processed further at a total cost of $9,500 and then sold for $12 each. Should product X be processed further or sold at the split-off point?

4.   Delta Company produces a single product. The cost of producing and selling a single unit of this product at the company's normal activity level of 60,000 units per year is:

Direct materials	$5.10
Direct labor	3.80
Variable overhead	1.00
Fixed overhead	4.20
Variable selling and administrative expense . .	1.50
Fixed selling and administrative expense . . .	2.40

The normal selling price is $21 per unit. The company's capacity is 75,000 units per year. An order has been received from a mail-order house for 15,000 units at a special price of $14 per unit. This order would not disturb regular sales. If the order is accepted, by how much will annual profits be increased or decreased? (The order will not change the company's total fixed costs.)

5.   Refer to the data in (4) above. Assume the company has 1,000 units of this product left over from last year that are vastly inferior to the current model. The units must be sold through regular channels at reduced prices. What unit cost figure is relevant for establishing a minimum selling price for these units? Explain.

P13–16.   **Make or buy analysis.**   "In my opinion, we ought to stop making our own drums and accept that outside supplier's offer," said Frank Avaroni, president of Trent Oil Refinery. "At a price of $18 per drum, we would be paying $5 less than it costs us to manufacture the drums in our own plant. Since we use 60,000 drums a year, that would be an annual cost savings of $300,000." Trent Oil's present cost to manufacture one drum is given below (based on 60,000 drums per year):

Direct materials	$10.35 — A
Direct labor	6.00 — A
Variable overhead	1.50 — A
Fixed overhead ($2.80 general company overhead, $1.60 depreciation, and $0.75 supervision)	0.75 — A
	5.15
Total cost per drum	$23.00

A decision about whether to make or buy the drums is especially important at this time since the equipment being used to make the drums is completely worn out and must be replaced. The choices facing the company are:

Alternative 1:   Purchase new equipment and continue to make the drums. The equipment would cost $810,000, it would have a six-year useful life, and no salvage value. The company uses straight-line depreciation.

Alternative 2:   Purchase the drums from an outside supplier at $18 per drum under a six-year contract.

The new equipment would be more efficient than the equipment that Trent Oil has been using and, according to the manufacturer, would reduce direct labor and variable overhead costs by 30 percent. Supervision cost ($45,000 per year) and direct materials cost per drum would not be affected by the new equipment. The new equipment's capacity would be 90,000 drums per year. The company has no other use for the space now being used to produce the drums.

Required: 1. In order to assist the president in making a decision, prepare an analysis showing what the total cost and the cost per drum would be under each of the two alternatives given above. Assume that 60,000 drums are needed each year. Which course of action would you recommend to the president?

2. Would your recommendation in (1) above be the same if the company's needs were *(a)* 75,000 drums per year or *(b)* 90,000 drums per year? Show computations to support your answer, with costs presented on both a total and a per unit basis.

3. What other factors would you recommend that the company consider before making a decision?

P13–17. Discontinuance of a department. Sales have never been good in Department C of Stacey's Department Store. For this reason, management is considering the elimination of the department. A summarized income statement for the store, by departments, for the most recent month is given below:

STACEY'S DEPARTMENT STORE
Income Statement
For the Month Ended June 30, 19x6

	Total	Department A	B	C
Sales	$1,000,000	$500,000	$320,000	$180,000
Less variable expenses	574,300	338,000	166,000	70,300
Contribution margin	425,700	162,000	154,000	109,700
Less fixed expenses:				
Salaries	49,000	18,000	16,000	15,000
Utilities	6,200	2,600	2,000	1,600
Direct advertising	89,000	32,000	27,000	30,000
General advertising*	25,000	12,500	8,000	4,500
Rent on building	38,000	16,000	12,000	10,000
Employment taxes†	4,900	1,800	1,600	1,500
Depreciation of fixtures	36,000	12,000	15,000	9,000
Insurance and property taxes on inventory and fixtures	7,900	2,300	4,000	1,600
General office expenses	54,000	18,000	18,000	18,000
Service department expenses	81,000	27,000	27,000	27,000
Total fixed expenses	391,000	142,200	130,600	118,200
Net income (loss)	$ 34,700	$ 19,800	$ 23,400	$ (8,500)

* Allocated on a basis of sales dollars.
† Based on salaries paid directly in each department.

The following additional information is available:

a. If Department C is eliminated, the utilities bill will be reduced by $700 per month.

b. All departments are housed in the same building. The store leases the entire building at a fixed annual rental rate.

c. One of the employees in Department C is Fred Jones, who has been with the company for many years. Mr. Jones will be transferred to another department if Department C is eliminated. His salary is $1,000 per month.

d. The fixtures in Department C would be transferred to the other departments if Department C is eliminated. One fourth of the insurance and property taxes in Department C relates to the fixtures in the department.

e. The company has two service departments—purchasing and warehouse. If Department C is eliminated, one employee in the warehouse can be discharged. This employee's combined salary and other employment costs is $900 per month. General office expenses will not change.

Required:

1. Assume that the store has no alternative use for the space now being occupied by Department C. Prepare computations to show whether or not the department should be eliminated. (You may assume that eliminating Department C would have no effect on sales in the other departments.)

2. Assume that due to an extreme shortage of store facilities, the space being occupied by Department C could be subleased at a rental rate of $48,000 per month. Would you advise the company to eliminate Department C and sublease the space? Show computations to support your answer.

P13–18. **Utilization of scarce resources; product mix.**   The Walton Toy Company manufactures a line of dolls and a doll dress sewing kit. Demand for the dolls is increasing, and management requests assistance from you in determining an economical sales and production mix for the coming year. The company's sales department provides the following information:

Product	Estimated demand next year (units)	Selling price per unit
Debbie	50,000	$13.50
Trish	42,000	5.50
Sarah.	35,000	21.00
Mike	40,000	10.00
Sewing kit	325,000	8.00

The standard costs for direct materials and direct labor per unit are as follows:

Product	Direct materials	Direct labor
Debbie	$4.30	$3.20
Trish	1.10	2.00
Sarah.	6.44	5.60
Mike	2.00	4.00
Sewing kit	3.20	1.60

The following additional information is available:

a. The company's plant has a capacity of 130,000 direct labor-hours per year on a single-shift basis. The company's present employees and equipment can produce all five products.

b. The direct labor rate is $8 per hour; this rate is expected to remain unchanged during the coming year.

c. Fixed costs total $520,000 per year. Variable overhead costs are equal to 25 percent of direct labor costs.

d. All of the company's nonmanufacturing costs are fixed.

e. The company's present inventory of finished products is nominal and can be ignored.

Required: 1. Determine the contribution margin for a unit of each product.

2. Determine the contribution margin that will be realized per direct labor-hour expended on each product.

3. Prepare a schedule showing the total direct labor-hours that will be required to produce the units estimated to be sold during the coming year.

4. Examine the data that you have computed in (1)–(3). Indicate the product and the number of units to be increased or decreased so that total production time is equal to the 130,000 production hours available.

5. Assume that the company does not want to reduce sales of any product. Identify the ways in which the company could obtain the additional output and any problems that might be encountered.

(CPA, Heavily Adapted)

P13–19.   **Selected relevant cost questions.**   Andretti Company has a single product called a Dak. The company normally produces and sells 60,000 Daks each year at a selling price of $32 per unit. The company's unit costs at this level of activity are given below:

Direct materials.	$10.00	
Direct labor	4.50	
Variable overhead	2.30	
Fixed overhead.	5.00	($300,000)
Variable selling expense	1.20	
Fixed selling expense	3.50	($210,000)
Total cost per unit	$26.50	

A number of questions relating to the production and sale of Daks are given below. Each question is independent.

Required: 1. Assume that Andretti Company has sufficient capacity to produce 90,000 Daks each year. The company could increase its sales by 25 percent above the present 60,000 units each year if it were willing to increase the fixed selling expenses by $80,000. Would the increased fixed expenses be justified?

2. Assume again that Andretti Company has sufficient capacity to produce 90,000 Daks each year. A customer in a foreign market wants to purchase 20,000 Daks. Import duties on the Daks would be $1.70 per unit, and costs for permits and licenses would be $9,000. The only selling costs that would be associated

with the order would be $3.20 per unit shipping cost. You have been asked by the president to compute the per unit break-even price on this order.

3. The company has 1,000 Daks on hand that have some irregularities and are therefore considered to be "seconds." Due to the irregularities, it will be impossible to sell these units at the regular price. If the company wishes to sell them through regular distribution channels, what unit cost figure is relevant for setting a minimum selling price?

4. Due to a strike in its supplier's plant, Andretti Company is unable to purchase more material for the production of Daks. The strike is expected to last for two months. Andretti Company has enough material on hand to continue to operate at 30 percent of normal levels for the two-month period. As an alternative, Andretti could close its plant down entirely for the two months. If the plant were closed, fixed overhead costs would continue at 60 percent of their normal level during the two-month period; the fixed selling costs would be reduced by 20 percent while the plant was closed. What would be the dollar advantage or disadvantage of closing the plant for the two-month period?

5. An outside manufacturer has offered to produce Daks for Andretti Company and to ship them directly to Andretti's customers. If Andretti Company accepts this offer, the facilities that it uses to produce Daks would be idle; however, fixed overhead costs would be reduced by 75 percent of their present level. Since the outside manufacturer would pay for all the costs of shipping, the variable selling costs would be only two thirds of their present amount. Compute the unit cost figure that is relevant for comparison against whatever quoted price is received from the outside manufacturer.

P13–20. **Discontinuance of a store.**   Superior Markets, Inc., operates three stores in a large metropolitan area. A segmented income statement for the company for the last quarter is given below:

SUPERIOR MARKETS, INC.
Income Statement
For the Quarter Ended September 30, 19x8

	Total	North store	South store	East store
Sales	$3,000,000	$720,000	$1,200,000	$1,080,000
Cost of goods sold	1,657,200	403,200	660,000	594,000
Gross margin	1,342,800	316,800	540,000	486,000
Operating expenses:				
Selling expenses	817,000	231,400	315,000	270,600
Administrative expenses . .	383,000	106,000	150,900	126,100
Total expenses	1,200,000	337,400	465,900	396,700
Net income (loss)	$ 142,800	$ (20,600)	$ 74,100	$ 89,300

The North Store has consistently shown losses over the past two years. For this reason, management is giving consideration to closing the store. The company has retained you to make a recommendation as to whether the store should be closed or kept open. The following additional information is available for your use:

a. The breakdown of the selling and administrative expenses is as follows:

	Total	North store	South store	East store
Selling expenses:				
Sales salaries	$239,000	$ 70,000	$ 89,000	$ 80,000
Direct advertising	187,000	51,000	72,000	64,000
General advertising*	45,000	10,800	18,000	16,200
Store rent	300,000	85,000	120,000	95,000
Depreciation of store fixtures . .	16,000	4,600	6,000	5,400
Delivery salaries	21,000	7,000	7,000	7,000
Depreciation of delivery				
equipment	9,000	3,000	3,000	3,000
Total selling expenses. . . .	$817,000	$231,400	$315,000	$270,600
Administrative expenses:				
Store management salaries . .	$ 70,000	$ 21,000	$ 30,000	$ 19,000
General office salaries*	50,000	12,000	20,000	18,000
Insurance on fixtures and				
inventory	25,000	7,500	9,000	8,500
Utilities	106,000	31,000	40,000	35,000
Employment taxes	57,000	16,500	21,900	18,600
General office—other*	75,000	18,000	30,000	27,000
Total administrative				
expenses	$383,000	$106,000	$150,900	$126,100

*Allocated on a basis of sales dollars.

b. The lease on the building housing the North Store can be broken with no penalty.

c. The fixtures being used in the North Store would be transferred to the other two stores if the North Store were closed.

d. The general manager of the North Store would be retained and transferred to another position in the company if the North Store were closed. Her salary is $9,000 per quarter. All other employees in the store would be discharged.

e. The company has one delivery crew that serves all three stores. One delivery person could be discharged if the North Store were closed. This person's salary is $4,000 per quarter.

f. The company's employment taxes are 15 percent of salaries.

g. One third of the insurance in the North Store is on the store's fixtures.

h. The "General office salaries" and "General office—other" relate to the overall management of Superior Markets, Inc. If the North Store were closed, one person in the general office could be discharged because of the decrease in overall workload. This person's salary is $6,000 per quarter.

Required: 1. Prepare a schedule showing the change in revenues and expenses and the impact on the company's overall net income that would result if the North Store were closed.

2. Assuming that the store space can't be subleased, what recommendation would you make to the management of Superior Markets, Inc.?

3. Assume that if the North Store were closed, at least one fourth of its sales would transfer to the East Store, due to strong customer loyalty to Superior Markets. The East Store has ample capacity to handle the increased sales. You may assume that the increased sales in the East Store would yield the same gross margin rate as present sales in that store. What effect would these

factors have on your recommendation concerning the North Store? Show all computations to support your answer.

P13–21. **Pricing a bid.** Martin Instruments produces thermostats for industrial use. The company prices its thermostats by adding a markup of 60 percent to variable costs (so that the selling price is equal to 160 percent of variable costs). This pricing policy has worked very well over the years.

Martin Instruments has received an invitation to bid on a government order for 8,000 specially designed thermostats. The company has made the following cost estimates:

Direct materials	$ 73,000
Direct labor	48,000
Variable overhead	9,000
Allocated fixed overhead	20,000
Tools, dies, and other special production costs . . .	32,000
Shipping costs	4,000
Special administrative costs	6,000
Total costs	$192,000
Cost per thermostat ($192,000 ÷ 8,000)	$ 24

Martin Instruments is now operating at capacity. If the company takes on the government order, it will have to forgo regular sales of $240,000.

Required:

1. In terms of contribution margin sacrificed, what is the opportunity cost of accepting the government order?
2. What is the lowest price that Martin Instruments can bid on the government order without sacrificing current profits?

P13–22. **Shutdown versus continue-to-operate decision.** (Note to the student: This type of decision is similar to that of dropping a product line, and the portion of the text dealing with the latter topic should be referred to, if needed.)

Birch Company normally produces and sells 30,000 units of RG-6 each month. RG-6 is a small electrical relay used in the automotive industry as a component part in various products. The selling price is $22 per unit, variable expenses are $14 per unit, fixed overhead costs total $150,000 per month, and fixed selling costs total $30,000 per month.

Employment-contract strikes in the companies that purchase the bulk of the RG-6 units have caused Birch Company's sales to temporarily drop to only 8,000 units per month. Birch Company estimates that the strikes will last for about two months, after which time sales of RG-6 should return to normal. Due to the current low level of sales, however, Birch Company is thinking about closing down its own plant during the two months that the strikes are on. If Birch Company does close down its plant, it is estimated that fixed overhead costs can be reduced to only $105,000 per month and that fixed selling costs can be reduced by 10 percent. Start-up costs at the end of the shutdown period would total $8,000. Since Birch Company normally produces strictly for customer orders, no inventories are on hand.

Required:

1. Assuming that the strikes continue for two months, as estimated, would you recommend that Birch Company close its own plant? Show computations in good form.
2. At what level of sales (in units) for the two-month period would Birch Company be indifferent as between closing the plant or keeping it open? Show computa-

tions. (Hint: This is a type of break-even analysis, except that the fixed cost portion of your break-even computation should include only those fixed costs that are relevant [i.e., avoidable] over the two-month period.)

P13–23.   **Accept or reject special orders.**   Polaski Company manufactures and sells a single product called a Ret. Operating at capacity, the company can produce and sell 30,000 Rets per year. Costs associated with this level of production and sales are given below:

	Unit	Total
Direct materials.	$15	$ 450,000
Direct labor	8	240,000
Variable overhead	3	90,000
Fixed overhead.	9	270,000
Variable selling expense . . .	4	120,000
Fixed selling expense	6	180,000
Total cost	$45	$1,350,000

The Rets normally sell for $50 per unit.

Required: 1.   Assume that due to a recession, Polaski Company expects to sell only 25,000 Rets through regular channels next year. A large retail chain has offered to purchase 5,000 Rets if Polaski is willing to accept a 16 percent discount off the regular price. There would be no sales commissions on this order; thus, variable selling expenses would be slashed by 75 percent. However, Polaski Company would have to purchase a special machine in order to engrave the retail chain's name on the 5,000 units. This machine would cost $10,000. Polaski Company has no assurance that the retail chain will purchase additional units any time in the future. Determine the impact on profits next year if this special order is accepted.

2.   Refer to the original data. Assume again that Polaski Company expects to sell only 25,000 Rets through regular channels next year. The U.S. Army would like to make a one-time-only purchase of 5,000 Rets. The Army would pay a fixed fee of $1.80 per Ret, and in addition it would reimburse Polaski Company for all costs of production (variable and fixed) associated with the units. Since the Army would pick up the Rets with its own trucks, there would be no variable selling expenses of any type associated with this order. If Polaski Company accepts the order, by how much will profits be increased or decreased for the year?

3.   Assume the same situation as that described in (2) above, except that the company expects to sell 30,000 Rets through regular channels next year. Thus, accepting the U.S. Army's order would require giving up regular sales of 5,000 Rets. If the Army's order is accepted, by how much will profits be increased or decreased from what they would be if the 5,000 Rets were sold through regular channels?

P13–24.   **Make or buy decision.**   Silven Industries, which manufactures and sells a highly successful line of summer lotions and insect repellents, has decided to diversify in order to stabilize sales throughout the year. A natural area for the company to consider is the production of winter lotions and creams to prevent dry and chapped skin.

After considerable research, a winter products line has been developed. However, because of the conservative nature of the company management, Silven's president has decided to introduce only one of the new products for this coming winter. If the product is a success, further expansion in future years will be initiated.

The product selected (called Chap-Off) is a lip balm that will be sold in a lipstick-type tube. The product will be sold to wholesalers in boxes of 24 tubes for $8 per box. Because of available capacity, no additional fixed overhead costs will be incurred to produce the product. However, a $90,000 charge for fixed overhead will be absorbed by the product to allocate a fair share of the company's present fixed overhead costs to the new product.

Using the estimated sales and production of 100,000 boxes of Chap-Off as the expected volume, the accounting department has developed the following costs per box:

Direct material	$3.60
Direct labor	2.00
Manufacturing overhead	1.40
Total cost	$7.00

The costs above include costs for producing both the lip balm and the tube into which the lip balm is to be placed. As an alternative to making the tubes, Silven has approached a cosmetics manufacturer to discuss the possibility of purchasing the tubes for Chap-Off. The purchase price of the empty tubes from the cosmetics manufacturer would be $1.35 per box of 24 tubes. If Silven Industries accepts the purchase proposal, it is predicted that direct labor and variable overhead costs per box of Chap-Off would be reduced by 10 percent, and that direct materials costs would be reduced by 25 percent.

Required: 1.   Should Silven Industries make or buy the tubes? Show calculations to support your answer.
2.   What would be the maximum purchase price acceptable to Silven Industries? Support your answer with an appropriate explanation.
3.   Instead of sales of 100,000 boxes, revised estimates show sales volume at 120,000 boxes. At this new volume, additional equipment at an annual rental of $40,000 must be acquired to manufacture the tubes. Assuming that the outside supplier will not accept an order for less than 100,000 boxes, should Silven Industries make or buy the tubes? Show computations to support your answer.
4.   Refer to the data in (3). Assume that the outside supplier will accept an order of any size for the tubes at $1.35 per box. How, if at all, would this change your answer? Show computations.
5.   What nonquantifiable factors should Silven Industries consider in determining whether they should make or buy the tubes?

(CMA, Heavily Adapted)

P13–25.   **Sell or process further decision.**   The Scottie Sweater Company is a large producer of sweaters under the "Scottie" label. The company buys raw wool on the market and processes it into wool yarn from which the sweaters are woven. One spindle of wool yarn is required to produce one sweater. The costs and revenues associated with the sweaters are given below:

		Per sweater
Selling price		$30.00
Cost to manufacture:		
Raw materials:		
Buttons, thread, lining . . .	$ 2.00	
Wool yarn	16.00	
Total raw materials . . .	18.00	
Direct labor	5.80	
Manufacturing overhead . .	8.70	32.50
Manufacturing profit (loss) . . .		$ (2.50)

Originally, all of the wool yarn was used to produce sweaters, but in recent years a market has developed for the wool yarn itself. The yarn is purchased by other companies for use in production of wool blankets and other wool products. Since the development of the market for the wool yarn, a continuing dispute has existed in the Scottie Sweater Company as to whether the yarn should be sold simply as yarn or processed into sweaters. Current cost and revenue data on the yarn is given below:

		Per spindle of yarn
Selling price		$20.00
Cost to manufacture:		
Raw materials (raw wool) . . .	$7.00	
Direct labor	3.60	
Manufacturing overhead . . .	5.40	16.00
Manufacturing profit		$ 4.00

The market for sweaters is temporarily depressed, due to unusually warm weather in the western states where the sweaters are sold. This has made it necessary for the company to discount the selling price of the sweaters to $30 from the normal $40 price. Since the market for wool yarn has remained strong, the dispute has again surfaced over whether the yarn should be sold outright rather than processed into sweaters. The sales manager thinks that the production of sweaters should be discontinued; she is upset about having to sell sweaters at a $2.50 loss, when the yarn could be sold for a $4 profit. However, the production superintendent is equally upset at the suggestion that he close down a large portion of the factory. He argues that the company is in the sweater business, not the yarn business, and that the company should focus on its area of strength.

Due to the nature of the production process, virtually all of the overhead costs are fixed. Overhead is assigned to products on a basis of 150 percent of direct labor cost.

Required:
1. Would you recommend that the wool yarn be sold outright, or processed into sweaters? Show computations in good form to support your answer.
2. What is the lowest price that the company should accept for a sweater? Show computations in good form to support your answer.

P13–26. **Optimal use of scarce resources.** Mileu Company manufactures and sells three products. The three products are manufactured in a factory consisting of four departments. Both labor and machine time are applied to the products as they pass through each applicable department. The nature of the machine processing and labor skills required in each department is such that neither machines nor labor can be switched from one department to another.

Mileu's management is attempting to plan its production schedule for the next several months. The planning is complicated by the fact that there are labor shortages in the community, and some machines will be down several months for repairs.

The following information regarding available machine and labor time by department and the machine-hours and direct labor-hours required per unit of product has been accumulated to aid in the decision. These data should be valid for at least the next six months.

	Department			
	1	2	3	4
Available monthly capacity:				
Normal machine capacity— machine-hours	3,500	3,500	3,000	3,500
Capacity of machine being repaired—machine-hours	(500)	(400)	(300)	(200)
Net available machine capacity— machine-hours	3,000	3,100	2,700	3,300
Labor capacity in direct labor-hours . .	4,000	4,500	3,500	3,000
Available labor in direct labor-hours . .	3,700	4,500	2,750	2,600

Labor and Machine Specifications per Unit of Product

		Department			
Product	Labor and machine time	1	2	3	4
401	Direct labor-hours	2	3	3	1
	Machine-hours	1	1	2	2
403	Direct labor-hours	1	2	—	2
	Machine-hours	1	1	—	2
405	Direct labor-hours	2	2	2	1
	Machine-hours	2	2	1	1

The sales department believes that the monthly demand for the next six months will be as follows:

Product	Monthly sales volume in units
401	500
403	400
405	1,000

Inventory levels are at satisfactory levels and need not be increased or decreased during the next six months. The unit price and cost data that will be valid for the next six months are presented below.

	Product		
	401	**403**	**405**
Unit costs:			
Direct material	$ 7	$ 13	$ 17
Direct labor:			
Department 1	12	6	12
Department 2	21	14	14
Department 3	24	—	16
Department 4	9	18	9
Variable overhead	27	20	25
Fixed overhead	15	10	32
Variable selling	3	2	4
Unit selling price	$196	$123	$167

Required:

1. Calculate the monthly requirement for machine-hours and direct labor-hours for the production of products 401, 403, and 405 to determine whether the monthly sales demand for the three products can be met by the factory.

2. What monthly production schedule should Mileu Company select in order to maximize its dollar profits? Explain how you selected this production schedule, and present a schedule of the contribution to profit that would be generated by your production schedule.

3. Identify the alternatives Mileu Company might consider so it can supply its customers with all the product they demand.

(CMA, Adapted)

P13–27. Straightforward maximization problem. (Appendix) The Hart Company can product two different products, A and B. The company has four manufacturing operations—cutting, sanding, assembly, and packing. Product B goes through all four operations. Product A goes through all operations except assembly. The manufacturing requirements in terms of hours per unit are given below for A and B for each of the company's operations:

	Products	
	A	**B**
Cutting operation	2	3
Sanding operation	3	1
Assembly operation	—	4
Packing operation	1	1

Each operation is limited in terms of number of hours available. The available hours by operation are: cutting, 30 hours; sanding, 15 hours; assembly, 24 hours; and packing, 8 hours.

Each unit of product A which is sold yields $3 in contribution margin, and each unit of product B which is sold yields $4 in contribution margin. The company wishes to maximize contribution margin.

Required:

1. Prepare equations to express the objective function and each of the constraints.

2. Determine the optimum mix of products A and B, using the graphic method of linear programming.

P13–28. Product mix to exhaust remaining stock of materials. (Appendix) Elton Company manufactures a line of carpeting that includes a commercial carpeting and a residential carpeting. Two grades of fiber—heavy duty and regular—are used in manufacturing both types of carpeting. The mix of the two grades of fiber differs in each type of carpeting, with the commercal grade using a greater amount of heavy-duty fiber.

In two months, Elton will introduce a new line of carpeting to replace the current line. The present fiber in stock will not be used in the new line. Management wants to exhaust the present stock of regular and heavy-duty fiber during the last month of production.

Data regarding the current line of commercial and residential carpeting are presented below:

	Commercial	Residential
Selling price per roll of carpet	$1,000	$800
Production specifications per roll of carpet:		
Heavy-duty fiber	80 pounds	40 pounds
Regular fiber	20 pounds	40 pounds
Direct labor-hours	15 hours	15 hours
Standard cost per roll of carpet:		
Heavy-duty fiber ($3/pound)	$240	$120
Regular fiber ($2/pound)	40	80
Direct labor ($10/DLH)	150	150
Variable manufacturing overhead (60% of direct labor cost)	90	90
Fixed manufacturing overhead (120% of direct labor cost)	180	180
Total standard cost per roll of carpet	$700	$620

Elton has 42,000 pounds of heavy-duty fiber and 24,000 pounds of regular fiber in stock.

A maximum of 10,500 direct labor-hours are available during the month. The labor force can work on either type of carpeting.

The demand for the present line of carpeting is such that all of the quantities produced can be sold.

Required: 1. A member of Elton Company's cost accounting staff has stated that linear programming should be used to determine how many rolls of commercial and residential carpeting to manufacture during the last month of production. Explain why linear programming should be used in this situation.

2. Prepare the objective function equation and the constraint equations needed for a linear programming solution to the problem. Use the letter C to denote rolls of commercial carpeting and the letter R to denote rolls of residual carpeting.

3. Using the equations from (2) above, prepare a linear programming graphic solution to the problem, showing how many rolls of commercial carpeting and how many rolls of residential carpeting should be produced. (Place commercial carpeting on the horizontal axis and residential carpeting on the vertical axis.)

4. Assume that any scrap fiber can be sold for 25 cents per pound. How much revenue would be realized from sale of the scrap? Show computations.

(CMA, Adapted)

P13–29.   **Linear programming—multiple departments.** (Appendix) Markov Company manufactures two industrial products—X–10, which sells for $90 a unit, and Y–12, which sells for $85 a unit. Each product is processed through both of the company's manufacturing departments. The limited availability of labor, material, and equipment capacity has restricted the ability of the firm to meet the demand for its products. The production department believes that linear programming can be used to routinize the production schedule for the two products.

The following data are available to the production department:

	Amount required per unit	
	X–10	**Y–12**
Direct material: Weekly supply limited to 1,800 pounds at $12 per pound	4 pounds	2 pounds
Direct labor:		
Department 1—weekly supply limited to 10 people at 40 hours each at an hourly rate of $6	⅔ hour	1 hour
Department 2—weekly supply limited to 15 people at 40 hours each at an hourly rate of $8	1¼ hours	1 hour
Machine time:		
Department 1—weekly capacity limited to 250 hours	½ hour	½ hour
Department 2—weekly capacity limited to 300 hours	0 hours	1 hour

The overhead costs for Markov Company are accumulated on a plantwide basis. Overhead is assigned to products on the basis of the number of direct labor-hours required to manufacture them. This base is appropriate for overhead assignment because most of the variable overhead costs vary as a function of labor time. The estimated overhead cost per direct labor-hour is:

Variable overhead cost.	$ 6
Fixed overhead cost	6
Total overhead cost per direct labor-hour . .	$12

The company wants to produce the mix of the two products that will allow it to maximize total contribution margin.

The production department formulated the following equations for the linear programming statement of the problem:

X = number of units of X–10 to be produced
Y = number of units of Y–12 to be produced

Objective function equation to minimize costs:

$$\text{Minimize:}\quad Z = \$85X + \$62Y$$

Constraint equations:

$$\text{Material:}\quad 4X + 2Y \leqslant 1{,}800 \text{ pounds}$$
$$\text{Department 1 labor:}\quad \tfrac{2}{3}X + \ Y \leqslant 400 \text{ hours}$$
$$\text{Department 2 labor:}\quad 1\tfrac{1}{4}X + \ Y \leqslant 600 \text{ hours}$$

Required: 1.   The linear programming equations as prepared by the company's production department contain a number of errors and omissions. Examine these equations, and explain what errors and omissions have been made.

2.   Prepare the proper equations for the linear programming statement of the company's problem.

3.   Using the equations that you prepared in (2) above, prepare a linear programming graphical solution to determine how many units of X–10 and Y–12 should be produced each week. (Place product X–10 on the horizontal axis and product Y–12 on the vertical axis.)

(CMA, Adapted)

P13–30.   **Cost minimization.**   (Appendix)   (Prepared from a situation described by Naylor and Byrne, *Linear Programming* [Wadsworth Publishing Company, p. 45.]) Recycled Metals, Inc., has received an order from a customer who wants to purchase a minimum of 2,500 pounds of scrap metal. The customer requires that the scrap metal contain at least 1,200 pounds of high-quality aluminum that can be melted down and used in fabrication. The customer also requires that the scrap delivered to him contain no more than 480 pounds of unfit metal. By "unfit" the customer means metal that contains so many impurities that it can't be melted down and used at all.

Recycled Metals, Inc., can purchase aluminum scrap metal from either of two suppliers. The scrap being sold by the two suppliers contains the following proportions of high-quality aluminum and unfit scrap:

	Supplier	
	A	**B**
High-quality aluminum	80%	30%
Unfit scrap	20	15

Either supplier has unlimited quantities of scrap metal available. Supplier A charges 25 cents per pound, and supplier B charges 12 cents per pound. Recycled Metals, Inc., would like to minimize the total cost it will have to pay to acquire the needed scrap metal to fill the customer's order.

Required: 1.   Prepare equations to express the objective function and the constraints under which Recycled Metals, Inc., must make its purchase.

2.   Determine the amount of scrap metal which should be purchased from each supplier, by using the linear programming graphic method.

CASES

C13–31.   **Plant closing decision.**   GianAuto Corporation manufactures automobiles, vans, and trucks. Among the various GianAuto plants around the United States is the Denver Cover Plant. Coverings made primarily of vinyl and upholstery fabric are sewn at the Denver Cover Plant and used to cover interior seating and other surfaces of GianAuto products.

Ted Vosilo is the plant manager for Denver Cover. The Denver Cover Plant was the first GianAuto plant in the region. As other area plants were opened, Vosilo, in recognition of his management ability, was given responsibility for managing them. Vosilo functions as a regional manager although the budget for him and his staff is charged to the Denver Cover Plant.

Vosilo has just received a report indicating that GianAuto could purchase the entire annual output of Denver Cover from outside suppliers for $30 million. Vosilo was astonished at the low outside price because the budget for Denver Cover's operating costs for the coming year was set at $52 million. Vosilo believes that GianAuto will have to close down operations at Denver Cover in order to realize the $22 million in annual cost savings.

The budget for Denver Cover's operating costs for the coming year is presented below. Additional facts regarding the plant's operations are as follows.

a.   Due to Denver Cover's commitment to use high-quality fabrics in all its products, the purchasing department was instructed to place blanket purchase orders with major suppliers to ensure the receipt of sufficient materials for the coming year. If these orders are canceled as a consequence of the plant closing, termination charges would amount to 20 percent of the cost of direct materials.

b.   Approximately 800 plant employees will lose their jobs if the plant is closed. This includes all of the direct laborers and supervisors as well as the plumbers, electricians, and other skilled workers classified as indirect plant workers. Some would be able to find new jobs while many others would have difficulty. All employees would have difficulty matching Denver Cover's base pay of $9.40 per hour that is the highest in the area. A clause in Denver Cover's contract with the union may help some employees; the company must provide employment assistance to its former employees for 12 months after a plant closing. The estimated cost to administer this service would be $1.5 million for the year.

c.   Some employees would probably elect early retirement because GianAuto has an excellent pension plan. In fact, $3 million of the 19x6 pension expense would continue whether Denver cover is open or not.

d.   Vosilo and his staff would not be affected by the closing of Denver Cover. They would still be responsible for administering three other area plants.

e.   Denver Cover considers equipment depreciation to be a variable cost and uses the units-of-production method to depreciate its equipment; Denver cover is the only GianAuto plant to use this depreciation method. However, Denver Cover uses the customary straight-line method to depreciate its building.

DENVER COVER PLANT
Budget for Operating Costs
For the Year Ending December 31, 19x6

Materials		$14,000,000
Labor:		
Direct	$13,100,000	
Supervision	900,000	
Indirect plant	4,000,000	18,000,000
Overhead:		
Depreciation—equipment	3,200,000	
Depreciation—building	7,000,000	
Pension expense	5,000,000	
Plant manager and staff	800,000	
Corporate allocation	4,000,000	20,000,000
Total budgeted costs		$52,000,000

Required: 1.   Without regard to costs, identify the advantages to GianAuto Corporation of continuing to obtain covers from its own Denver Cover Plant.

2.   GianAuto Corporation plans to prepare a dollar analysis that will be used in deciding whether or not to close the Denver Cover Plant. Management has asked you to identify:

   a.   The recurring annual budgeted costs that are relevant to the decision regarding closing the plant (show the dollar amounts).

   b.   The recurring annual budgeted costs that are *not* relevant to the decision regarding closing the plant, and explain why they are not relevant (again show the dollar amounts).

   c.   Any nonrecurring costs that would arise due to the closing of the plant, and explain how they would affect the decision (again show any dollar amounts).

3.   Looking at the data you have prepared in (2), should the plant be closed? Show computations, and explain your answer.

4.   Identify any revenues or costs not specifically mentioned in the problem that GianAuto should consider before making a decision.

(CMA, Adapted)

C13–32.   **Product line decisions.**   Olat Corporation produces three gauges. These gauges measure density, permeability, and thickness and are known as D-gauges, P-gauges, and T-gauges, respectively. For many years the company has been profitable and has operated at capacity. However, in the last two years prices on all gauges were reduced and selling expenses increased to meet competition and keep the plant operating at full capacity. Third quarter results, as shown below, are representative of recent experiences.

OLAT CORPORATION
Income Statement
For the Third Quarter, 19x3

	Total	Product lines		
		D-gauge	P-gauge	T-gauge
Sales	$3,400,000	$900,000	$1,600,000	$ 900,000
Less cost of goods sold	2,768,000	770,000	1,048,000	950,000
Gross margin	632,000	130,000	552,000	(50,000)
Less selling and administrative expenses	690,000	185,000	370,000	135,000
Income before income taxes . . .	$ (58,000)	$ (55,000)	$ 182,000	$(185,000)

Carl Burke, president, is very concerned about the results of the pricing, selling, and production policies. After reviewing the third-quarter results, he announced that he would ask his management staff to consider a course of action that includes the following three suggestions.

1.   Discontinue the T-gauge line immediately. T-gauges would not be returned to the line of products unless the problems with the gauge can be identified and resolved.

2.   Increase quarterly sales promotion by $100,000 on the P-gauge product line in order to increase sales volume 15 percent.

3. Cut production on the D-gauge line by 50 percent, a quantity sufficient to meet the demand of customers who purchase P-gauges. In addition, the traceable advertising and promotion for this line would be cut to $20,000 each quarter.

George Sperry, controller, suggested that a more careful study of the financial relationships be made to determine the possible effect on the company's operating results as a consequence of the president's proposed course of action. The president agreed and JoAnn Brower, assistant controller, was given the assignment to prepare an analysis. In order to prepare the analysis, she gathered the following information.

a. All three gauges are manufactured with common equipment and facilities.
b. The quarterly general selling and administrative expense of $170,000 is allocated to the three gauge lines in proportion to their dollar sales volume.
c. Special selling expenses (primarily advertising, promotion, and shipping) are incurred for each gauge as follows:

	Quarterly advertising and promotion	Shipping expense
D-gauge	$100,000	$ 4 per unit
P-gauge	210,000	10 per unit
T-gauge	40,000	10 per unit

d. The unit manufacturing costs for the three products are as follows.

	Product lines		
	D-gauge	P-gauge	T-gauge
Raw material.	$17	$ 31	$ 50
Direct labor	20	40	60
Variable manufacturing overhead	30	45	60
Fixed manufacturing overhead	10	15	20
	$77	$131	$190

e. The unit sales prices for the three products are as follows.

D-gauge . . . . . $ 90
P-gauge 200
T-gauge 180

f. The company is manufacturing at capacity and is selling all the gauges it produces.

Required: 1. JoAnn Brower has suggested that the Olat Corporation's product line income statement as presented for the third quarter of 19x3 is not suitable for analyzing proposals and making decisions such as the ones suggested by the president.
a. Explain why the product line income statement as presented is not suitable for analysis and decision making.
b. Describe an alternative income statement format that would be more suitable for analysis and decision making, and explain why it is better.
2. Use the operating data presented for Olat Corporation and assume that the president's proposed course of action had been implemented at the *beginning*

of the third quarter of 19x3. Then evaluate the president's proposed course of action by specifically responding to the following points.

    a. Are each of the three suggestions cost effective? Your discussion should be supported by a differential analysis that shows the net impact on income before taxes for each of the three suggestions.

    b. Was the president correct in eliminating the T-gauge line? Explain your answer.

    c. Was the president correct in promoting the P-gauge line rather than the D-gauge line? Explain your answer.

    d. Does the proposed course of action make effective use of Olat's capacity? Explain your answer.

3. Are there any nonquantitative factors that Olat Corporation should explore before it considers dropping the T-gauge line? Explain your answer.

(CMA, Adapted)

Capital Budgeting Decisions

LEARNING OBJECTIVES

After studying Chapter 14, you should be able to:

■ Explain the concept of present value and make present value computations with and without the present value tables.

■ Determine the acceptability of an investment project, using the net present value method.

■ Enumerate the typical cash inflows and cash outflows that might be associated with an investment project and explain how they would be used in a present value analysis.

■ Determine the acceptability of an investment project, using the time-adjusted rate of return method (with interpolation, if needed).

■ Explain how the cost of capital is used as a screening tool.

■ Prepare a net present value analysis of two competing investment projects, using either the incremental-cost approach or the total-cost approach.

■ Prepare a net present value analysis where a least-cost decision is involved.

■ Define or explain the key terms listed at the end of the chapter.

The term **capital budgeting** is used to describe actions relating to the planning and financing of capital outlays for such purposes as the purchase of new equipment, the introduction of new product lines, and the modernization of plant facilities. As such, capital budgeting decisions are a key factor in the long-run profitability of a firm. This is particularly true in situations where a firm has only limited investment funds available but has almost unlimited investment opportunities to choose from. The long-run profitability of the firm will depend on the skill of the manager in choosing those uses for limited funds that will provide the greatest return. This selection process is complicated by the fact that most investment opportunities are long term in nature, and the future is often distant and hard to predict.

To make wise investment decisions, managers need tools that will guide them in comparing the relative advantages and disadvantages of various investment alternatives. We are concerned in this chapter with gaining understanding and skill in the use of such tools.

CAPITAL BUDGETING—AN INVESTMENT CONCEPT

Capital budgeting is an *investment* concept, since it involves a commitment of funds now in order to receive some desired return in the future. When speaking of investments, one is inclined to think of a commitment of funds to corporate stocks and bonds. This is just one type of investment, however. The commitment of funds by a business to inventory, equipment, and related uses is *also* an investment in that the commitment is made with the expectation of receiving some return in the future from the funds committed.

Typical Capital Budgeting Decisions

What types of business decisions require capital budgeting analysis? Virtually any decision that involves an outlay now in order to obtain some return (increase in revenue or reduction in costs) in the future. Typical capital budgeting decisions encountered by the manager are:

1. Cost reduction decisions. Should new equipment be purchased in order to reduce costs?
2. Plant expansion decisions. Should a new plant, warehouse, or other facility be acquired in order to increase capacity and sales?
3. Equipment selection decisions. Would machine A, machine B, or machine C do the job best?
4. Lease or buy decisions. Should new plant facilities be leased or purchased?
5. Equipment replacement decisions. Should old equipment be replaced now or later?

Capital budgeting decisions tend to fall into two broad categories—*screening decisions* and *preference decisions*. **Screening decisions** are those relating to whether a proposed project meets some preset standard of acceptance. For example, a firm may have a policy of accepting cost reduction projects only if they promise a return of, say, 20 percent before taxes.

Preference decisions, by contrast, relate to selecting from among several *competing* courses of action. To illustrate, a firm may be considering five different machines to replace an existing machine on the assembly line. The choice as to which of the five machines to purchase is a *preference* decision.

In this chapter, we discuss ways of making screening decisions. The matter of preference decisions is reserved until the following chapter.

Characteristics of Business Investments

Business investments have two key characteristics that must be recognized as we begin our study of capital budgeting methods. These characteristics are (1) that most business investments involve *depreciable assets* and (2) that the returns on most business investments extend over long periods of time.

Depreciable assets   Although most business investments involve depreciable assets, some involve assets such as land that are not depreciable. In those situations where assets are not depreciable, the original sum invested in the assets will still exist at the time the project terminates. For example, if a firm purchases land for $5,000 and rents it out at $750 a year for 10 years, at the end of the 10-year term the land will still be intact and should be salable for at least its purchase price. The computation of the rate of return on such an investment is fairly simple. Since the asset (the land) will still be intact at the end of the 10-year period, each year's $750 inflow is a return *on* the original $5,000 investment. The rate of return is therefore a straight 15 percent ($750 ÷ $5,000).

A far more common kind of business investment involves assets that are depreciable in nature. An important characteristic of depreciable assets is that they generally have little or no resale value at the end of their useful lives. Thus, any returns provided by such assets must be sufficient to do two things:

1.   Provide a return *on* the original investment.
2.   Return the total amount *of* the original investment itself.

To illustrate, assume that the $5,000 investment in the preceding section was made in equipment rather than in land. Also assume that the equipment will reduce the firm's operating costs by $750 each year for 10 years. Is the return on the equipment a straight 15 percent, the same as it was on the land? The answer is no. The return being promised by the equipment is much less than the return being promised by the land. The reason is that part of the yearly $750 inflow from the equipment *must go to recoup the original $5,000 investment itself, since the equipment will be worthless at the end of its 10-year life.* Only what remains *after* recovery of this investment can be viewed as a return *on* the investment over the 10-year period.

The time value of money   As stated earlier, another characteristic of business investments is that they promise returns that are likely to extend over fairly long periods of time. Therefore, in approaching capital budgeting decisions, it is necessary to employ techniques that recognize the time value of money. Any business leader would rather receive a dollar today than a year from now. The same concept applies in choosing between investment projects. Those that promise returns earlier in time are preferable to those that promise returns later in time.

The capital budgeting techniques that recognize these two characteristics most fully are those involving *discounted cash flows*. We shall spend the remainder of this chapter illustrating the use of discounted cash flow methods in making capital budgeting decisions. Before discussing these methods, however, it will be helpful to consider the concept of *present value* and the techniques involved in *discounting*.

THE CONCEPT OF PRESENT VALUE

The point was made above that a business leader would rather receive a dollar today than a year from now. There are two reasons why this is true. First, a dollar received today is more valuable than a dollar received a year from now. The dollar received today can be invested immediately, and by the end of a year it will have earned some return, making the total amount in hand at the end of the year *greater* than the investment started with. The person receiving the dollar a year from now will simply have a dollar in hand at that time.

Second, the future involves uncertainty. The longer people have to wait to receive a dollar, the more uncertain it becomes that they will ever get the dollar that they seek. As time passes, conditions change. The changes may be such as to make future payments of the dollar impossible.

Since money has a time value, the manager needs a method of determining whether a cash outlay made now in an investment project can be justified in terms of expected receipts from the project in future years. That is, the manager must have a means of expressing future receipts in present dollar terms so that the future receipts can be compared *on an equivalent basis* with whatever investment is required in the project under consideration. The theory of interest provides managers with the means of making such a comparison.

The Theory of Interest

If a bank pays $105 one year from now in return for a deposit of $100 now, we would say that the bank is paying interest at an annual rate of 5 percent. The relationships involved in this notion can be expressed in mathematical terms by means of the following equation:

$$F_1 = P(1 + r) \tag{1}$$

where F_1 = the amount to be received in one year, P = the present outlay to be made, and r = the rate of interest involved.

If the present outlay is $100 deposited in a bank savings account that is to earn interest at 5 percent, then P = $100 and r = 0.05. Under these conditions, F_1 = $105, the amount to be received in one year.

The $100 present outlay can be called the **present value** of the $105 amount to be received in one year. It is also known as the *discounted value* of the future $105 receipt. The $100 figure represents the value in present terms of a receipt of $105 to be received a year from now by an investor who requires a return of 5 percent on his money.

Compounding of interest   What if the investor wants to leave his or her money in the bank for a second year? In that case, by the end of the second year the original $100 deposit will have grown to $110.25:

Original deposit	$100.00
Interest for the first year:	
$100 × 0.05	5.00
Amount at the end of the first year.	105.00
Interest for the second year:	
$105 × 0.05	5.25
Amount at the end of the second year	$110.25

Notice that the interest for the second year is $5.25, as compared to only $5 for the first year. The reason for the greater interest earned during the second year is that during the second year, interest is being paid *on interest*. That is, the $5 interest earned during the first year has been left in the account and has been added to the original $100 deposit in computing interest for the second year. This technique is known as **compounding of interest.** The compounding we have done is annual compounding. Interest can be compounded on a semiannual, quarterly, or even more frequent basis. Many savings institutions are now compounding interest on a daily basis. Of course, the more frequently compounding is done, the more rapidly the invested balance will grow.

How is the concept of compounding of interest expressed in equation form? It is expressed by taking equation (1) and adjusting it to state the number of years, n, that a sum is going to be left deposited in the bank:

$$F_n = P(1 + r)^n \tag{2}$$

where n = years.

If n = 2 years, then our computation of the value of F in two years will be:

$$F_2 = \$100(1 + 0.05)^2$$
$$F_2 = \$110.25$$

Present value and future value   Exhibit 14–1 shows the relationship between present value and future value as expressed in the theory of interest

EXHIBIT 14–1

The relationship between present value and future value

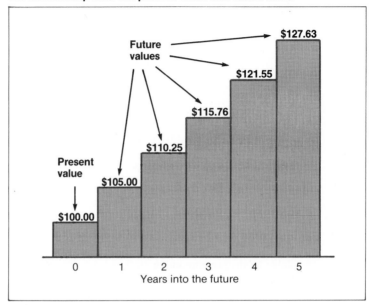

equations. As shown in the exhibit, if $100 is deposited in a bank at 5 percent interest, it will grow to $127.63 by the end of five years if interest is compounded annually.

Computation of Present Value

An investment can be viewed in two ways. It can be viewed either in terms of its future value or in terms of its present value. We have seen from our computations above that if we know the present value of a sum (such as our $100 deposit), it is a relatively simple task to compute the sum's future value in n years by using equation (2). But what if the tables are reversed, and we know the *future* value of some amount but we do not know its present value?

For example, assume that you are to receive $200 two years from now. You know that the future value of this sum is $200, since this is the amount that you will be receiving in two years. But what is the sum's present value—what is it worth *right now?* The present value of any sum to be received in the future can be computed by turning equation (2) around and solving for P:

$$P = \frac{F_n}{(1 + r)^n} \qquad\qquad (3)$$

In our example, F = $200 (the amount to be received in the future), r = 0.05 (the rate of interest), and n = 2 (the number of years in the future that the amount is to be received).

$$P = \frac{\$200}{(1 + 0.05)^2}$$

$$P = \frac{\$200}{1.1025}$$

$$P = \$181.40$$

As shown by the computation above, the present value of a $200 amount to be received two years from now is $181.40 if an interest return of 5 percent is required. In effect, we are saying that $181.40 received *right now* is equivalent to $200 received two years from now if the investor requires a 5 percent return on his or her money. The $181.40 and the $200 are just two ways of looking at the same item.

The process of finding the present value of a future cash flow, which we have just completed, is called **discounting.** We have *discounted* the $200 to its present value of $181.40. The 5 percent interest figure that we have used to find this present value is called the **discount rate.** Discounting of future sums to their present value is a common practice in business. A knowledge of the present value of a sum to be received in the future can be very useful to the manager, particularly in making capital budgeting decisions. However, we need to find a simpler way of computing present value than using equation (3) every time we need to discount a future sum. The computations involved in using this equation are complex and time-consuming.

Fortunately, tables are available in which most of the mathematical work involved in the discounting process has been done. Table 14–3 in Appendix B shows the discounted present value of $1 to be received at various periods in the future at various interest rates. The table indicates that the present value of $1 to be received two periods from now at 5 percent is 0.907. Since in our example we want to know the present value of $200 rather than just $1, we need to multiply the factor in the table by $200:

$$\$200 \times 0.907 = \$181.40$$

The answer we obtain is the same answer as we obtained earlier using the formula in equation (3).

Present Value of a Series of Cash Flows

Although some investments involve a single sum to be received (or paid) at a single point in the future, other investments involve a *series* of cash flows. A series (or stream) of cash flows is known as an **annuity.** To provide an example, assume that a firm has just purchased some government bonds in order to temporarily invest funds that are being held for future

EXHIBIT 14–2
Present value of a series of cash receipts

Year	Factor at 12 percent (Table 14–3)	Interest received	Present value
1	0.893	$15,000	$13,395
2	0.797	15,000	11,955
3	0.712	15,000	10,680
4	0.636	15,000	9,540
5	0.567	15,000	8,505
			$54,075

plant expansion. The bonds will yield interest of $15,000 each year and will be held for five years. What is the present value of the stream of interest receipts from the bonds? As shown in Exhibit 14–2, the present value of this stream is $54,075 if we assume a discount rate of 12 percent compounded annually. The discount factors used in this exhibit were taken from Table 14–3 in Appendix B.

Two points are important in connection with Exhibit 14–2. First, notice that the farther we go forward in time, the smaller is the present value of the $15,000 interest receipt. The present value of $15,000 received a year from now is $13,395, as compared to only $8,505 for the $15,000 interest payment to be received five years from now. This point simply underscores the fact that money has a time value.

The second point is that even though the computations involved in Exhibit 14–2 are accurate, they have involved unnecessary work. The same present value of $54,075 could have been obtained more easily by referring to Table 14–4 in Appendix B. Table 14–4 contains the present value of $1 to be received each year over a *series* of years at various interest rates. Table 14–4 has been derived by simply adding together the factors from Table 14–3. To illustrate, we used the following factors from Table 14–3 in the computations in Exhibit 14–2:

Year	Table 14–3 factors at 12 percent
1	0.893
2	0.797
3	0.712
4	0.636
5	0.567
	3.605

The sum of the five factors above is 3.605. Notice from Table 14–4 that the factor for $1 to be received each year for five years at 12 percent is also 3.605. If we use this factor and multiply it by the $15,000 annual cash inflow, then we get the same $54,075 present value that we obtained earlier in Exhibit 14–2:

$$\$15,000 \times 3.605 = \$54,075$$

Therefore, when computing the present value of a series (or stream) of cash flows, Table 14–4 should be used.

To summarize, the present value tables in Appendix B should be used as follows:

> Table 14–3: This table should be used to find the present value of a single cash flow (such as a single payment or receipt) occurring in the future.
>
> Table 14–4: This table should be used to find the present value of a series (or stream) of cash flows occurring in the future.

The use of both of these tables is illustrated in various exhibits on the following pages. *When a present value factor appears in an exhibit, the reader should take the time to trace it back into either Table 14–3 or Table 14–4 in order to get acquainted with the tables and how they work.* (Exercise 14–1 at the end of the chapter is designed for those readers who would like some practice in present value analysis before attempting other homework exercises and problems. A solution to Exercise 14–1 is provided immediately following the exercise itself.)

DISCOUNTED CASH FLOWS—THE NET PRESENT VALUE METHOD

Earlier in the chapter, the point was made that business investments have two distinguishing characteristics. The first is that they often involve depreciable assets, and the return that the assets provide must be sufficient to recoup the original investment itself as well as to provide a satisfactory yield on the investment. The second is that business investments are generally long term in nature, often spanning a decade or more. This characteristic lays heavy stress on the necessity to recognize the time value of money in business investment decisions.

If a capital budgeting method is to be fully useful to management, it must be capable of giving full recognition to *both* of the characteristics mentioned above. Although several methods of making capital budgeting decisions are in use, the ones that do the best job are those involving discounted cash flows. The discounted cash flow methods give full recognition to the time value of money and at the same time provide for full recovery of any investment in depreciable assets. No other capital budgeting method is capable of performing *both* of these functions.

There are two approaches to making capital budgeting decisions by means of discounted cash flow. One is known as the *net present value method,* and the other is known as the *time-adjusted rate of return method* (sometimes called the *internal rate of return method*). The net present value method is discussed below; the time-adjusted rate of return method is discussed in a following section.

The Net Present Value Method Illustrated

Under the net present value method, the present value of all cash inflows is compared against the present value of all cash outflows that are associated with an investment project. The difference between the present value of these cash flows, called the **net present value,** determines whether or not the project is an acceptable investment. To illustrate, let us assume the following data:

Example A

The Harper Company is contemplating the purchase of a machine capable of performing certain operations that are now performed manually. The machine will cost $5,000 new, and it will last for five years. At the end of the five-year period, the machine will have a zero scrap value. Use of the machine will reduce labor costs by $1,800 per year. The Harper Company requires a minimum return of 20 percent before taxes on all investment projects.

Should the machine be purchased? To answer this question, it will be necessary first to isolate the cash inflows and cash outflows associated with the proposed project. In order to keep the example free of unnecessary complications, we have assumed only one cash inflow and one cash outflow. The cash inflow is the $1,800 annual reduction in labor costs. The cash outflow is the $5,000 initial investment in the machine.

The investment decision: The Harper Company must determine whether a cash investment now of $5,000 can be justified if it will result in an $1,800 reduction in cost each year over the next five years, assuming that the company can get a 20 percent return on its money invested elsewhere.

To determine whether the investment is desirable, it will be necessary to discount the stream of annual $1,800 cost reductions to present value and to compare this discounted present value with the cost of the new machine. Since the Harper Company requires a minimum return of 20 percent on all investment projects, we will use this rate in the discounting process. Exhibit 14–3 on the following page gives a net present value analysis of the desirability of purchasing the machine.

According to the analysis, the Harper Company should purchase the new machine. The present value of the cost savings is $5,384, as compared to a present value of only $5,000 for the investment required (cost of the machine). Deducting the present value of the investment required from the present value of the cost savings gives a *net present value* of $384. Whenever the *net present value* is zero or greater, as in our example, an investment project is acceptable. Whenever the *net present value* is negative (the present value of the cash outflows exceeds the present value of the cash inflows), an investment project is not acceptable.

EXHIBIT 14–3

Net present value analysis of a proposed project

Initial cost			$5,000	
Life of the project (years)			5	
Annual cost savings			$1,800	
Salvage value.			–0–	
Required rate of return			20%	

Item	Year(s) having cash flows	Amount of cash flow	20 percent factor	Present value of cash flows
Annual cost savings	1–5	$ 1,800	2.991*	$ 5,384
Initial investment	Now	(5,000)	1.000	(5,000)
Net present value				$ 384

* From Table 14–4 in Appendix B.

A full interpretation of the solution would be as follows: The new machine promises slightly more than the required 20 percent rate of return. This is evident from the positive net present value of $384. The Harper Company could spend up to $5,384 for the new machine and still obtain the 20 percent rate of return it desires. The net present value of $384, therefore, shows the amount of "cushion" or "margin of error" that the company has in estimating the cost of the new machine. Alternatively, it also shows the amount of error that can exist in the present value of the cost savings, with the project remaining acceptable. That is, if the present value of the cost savings were only $5,000 rather than $5,384, the project would still promise the required 20 percent rate of return.

Emphasis on Cash Flows

In organizing data for making capital budgeting decisions, the reader may have noticed that our emphasis has been on cash flows and not on accounting net income. The reason is that accounting net income is based on accrual concepts that ignore the timing of cash flows into and out of an organization. As we stated earlier in the chapter, from a capital budgeting standpoint the timing of cash flows is important, since a dollar received today is more valuable than a dollar received in the future. Therefore, even though the accounting net income figure is useful for many things, it must be ignored in those capital budgeting computations that involve discounted cash flow analysis. Instead of determining accounting net income, the manager must concentrate on identifying the specific cash flows associated with various investment projects and on determining when these cash flows will take place.

In considering an investment project, what kinds of cash flows should the manager look for? Although the specific cash flows will vary from project to project, certain types of cash flows tend to recur and should be looked for, as explained in the following paragraphs.

Typical cash outflows   Usually a cash outflow in the form of an initial investment in equipment or other assets will be present. This investment is often computed on an incremental basis, in that any salvage realized from the sale of old equipment is deducted from the cost of the new equipment, leaving only the net difference as a cash outflow for capital budgeting purposes. In addition to this type of investment, some projects require that a firm expand its working capital in order to service the greater volume of business that will be generated. **Working capital** means the amount carried in cash, accounts receivable, and inventory (in excess of current liabilities) that is available to meet day-to-day operating needs. When a firm takes on a new project, the balances in these accounts will often increase. For example, the opening of a new store outlet would require added cash to operate sales registers, increased accounts receivable to carry new customers, and more inventory to stock the shelves. Any such incremental working capital needs should be treated as part of the initial investment in a project. Also, many projects require periodic outlays for repairs and maintenance and for additional operating costs. These should all be treated as cash outflows for capital budgeting purposes.

Typical cash inflows   On the cash inflow side, a project will normally either increase revenues or reduce costs. Either way, the amount involved should be treated as a cash inflow for capital budgeting purposes. (In regard to this point, notice that so far as cash flows are concerned, a *reduction in costs is equivalent to an increase in revenues*.) Cash inflows are also frequently realized from salvage of equipment when a project is terminated. In addition, upon termination of a project, any working capital that is released for use elsewhere should be treated as a cash inflow. Working capital is released, for example, when a company sells off its inventory, collects its receivables, and uses the resulting funds elsewhere in another investment project.

In summary, the following types of cash flows are common in business investment projects:

Cash outflows:

Initial investment (including installation costs).

Increased working capital needs.

Repairs and maintenance.

Incremental operating costs.

Cash inflows:

Incremental revenues.

Reduction in costs.

Salvage value.

Release of working capital.

Recovery of the Original Investment

When first introduced to present value analysis, students are often surprised by the fact that depreciation is not deducted in computing the profitability of a project. There are two reasons for not deducting depreciation.

First, depreciation is an accounting concept not involving a current cash outflow.[1] As discussed in the preceding section, discounted cash flow methods of making capital budgeting decisions focus on *flows of cash*. Although depreciation is a vital concept in computing accounting net income for financial statement purposes, it is not relevant in an analytical framework that focuses on flows of cash.

A second reason for not deducting depreciation is that discounted cash flow methods *automatically* provide for return of the original investment, thereby making a deduction for depreciation unnecessary. To demonstrate this point, let us assume the following data:

Example B

The Carver Hospital is considering the purchase of an attachment for its X-ray machine that will cost $3,170. The attachment will be usable for four years, after which time it will have no salvage value. It is estimated that the attachment will increase net cash inflows by $1,000 per year in the X-ray department. The hospital's board of directors has instructed that no investments are to be made unless they promise an annual return of at least 10 percent.

A present value analysis of the desirability of purchasing the attachment is presented in Exhibit 14–4. Notice that the attachment promises exactly

EXHIBIT 14–4

Net present value analysis of X-ray attachment

Initial cost				$3,170
Life of the project (years)				4
Annual net cash inflow				$1,000
Salvage value				–0–
Required rate of return				10%

Item	Year(s) having cash flows	Amount of cash flow	10 percent factor	Present value of cash flows
Annual net cash inflow	1–4	$ 1,000	3.170*	$ 3,170
Initial investment	Now	(3,170)	1.000	(3,170)
Net present value				$ –0–

*From Table 14–4 in Appendix B.

---

[1] Although depreciation itself does not involve a cash outflow, it does have an effect on cash outflows for income taxes. We shall take a look at this effect in the following chapter, when we discuss the impact of income taxes on management planning.

EXHIBIT 14–5

The Carver Hospital—breakdown of annual cash inflows

Year	(1) Investment outstanding during the year	(2) Cash inflow	(3) Return on investment (1) × 10%	(4) Recovery of investment during the year (2) – (3)	(5) Unrecovered investment at the end of the year (1) – (4)
1	$3,170	$1,000	$317	$ 683	$2,487
2	2,487	1,000	249	751	1,736
3	1,736	1,000	173	827	909
4	909	1,000	91	909	–0–
Total investment recovered . . .				$3,170	

a 10 percent return on the original investment, since the net present value is zero at a 10 percent discount rate.

Each annual $1,000 cash inflow arising from use of the attachment is made up of two parts. One part represents a recovery of a portion of the original $3,170 paid for the attachment, and the other part represents a return *on* this investment. The breakdown of each year's $1,000 cash inflow between recovery *of* investment and return *on* investment is shown in Exhibit 14–5.

The first year's $1,000 cash inflow consists of a $317 interest return (10 percent) *on* the $3,170 original investment, plus a $683 return *of* that investment. Since the amount of the unrecovered investment decreases over the four years, the dollar amount of the interest return also decreases. By the end of the fourth year, all $3,170 of the original investment has been recovered.

Limiting Assumptions

In working with discounted cash flows, at least two limiting assumptions are usually made. The first is that all cash flows occur at the end of a period. This is somewhat unrealistic in that cash flows typically occur somewhat uniformly *throughout* a period. The purpose of this assumption is just to simplify computations.

The second assumption is that all cash flows generated by an investment project are immediately reinvested in another project. It is further assumed that the second project will yield a rate of return at least as large as the discount rate used in the first project. Unless these conditions are met, the return computed for the first project will not be accurate. To illustrate, we used a discount rate of 10 percent for the Carver Hospital in Exhibit 14–4. Unless the funds released each period are immediately reinvested in another project yielding at least a 10 percent return, the return computed for the X-ray attachment will be overstated.

Choosing a Discount Rate

In using the net present value method, it is necessary to choose some rate of return for discounting cash flows to present value. In example A we used a rate of return of 20 percent before taxes, and in example B we used a rate of return of 10 percent. These rates were chosen somewhat arbitrarily simply for the sake of illustration.

As a practical matter, firms put much time and study into the choice of a discount rate. The rate generally viewed as being most appropriate is a firm's **cost of capital.** A firm's cost of capital is not simply the interest rate that it must pay for long-term debt. Rather, cost of capital is a broad concept, involving a blending of the costs of *all* sources of investment funds, both debt and equity. The mechanics involved in cost of capital computations are covered in finance texts and will not be considered here. The cost of capital is known by various names. It is sometimes called the **hurdle rate,** the **cutoff rate,** or the **required rate of return.**

Most finance people would agree that a before-tax cost of capital of 16 percent to 20 percent would be typical for an average industrial corporation. The appropriate after-tax figure would depend on the corporation's tax circumstances, but it would probably average around 8 to 10 percent.

An Extended Example of the Net Present Value Method

In order to conclude our discussion of the net present value method, we present below an extended example of how it is used in analyzing an investment proposal. This example will also help to tie together (and to reinforce) many of the ideas we have developed thus far.

Example C

Under a special licensing arrangement, the Swinyard Company has an opportunity to market a new product in the western United States for a five-year period. The product would be purchased from the manufacturer, with Swinyard Company responsible for all costs of promotion and distribution. The licensing arrangement could be renewed at the end of the five-year period at the option of the manufacturer. After careful study, Swinyard Company has estimated that the following costs and revenues would be associated with the new product:

Cost of equipment needed	$ 60,000
Working capital needed	100,000
Salvage value of the equipment in five years	10,000
Overhaul of the equipment in four years	5,000
Annual revenues and costs:	
Sales revenues	200,000
Cost of goods sold	125,000
Out-of-pocket operating costs (for salaries,	
advertising, and other direct costs)	35,000

At the end of the five-year period, the working capital would be released for investment elsewhere if the manufacturer decided not to renew the licensing

EXHIBIT 14–6

The net present value method—an extended example

Sales revenues				$200,000
Less cost of goods sold				125,000
Gross margin				75,000
Less out-of-pocket costs for salaries, advertising, etc.				35,000
Annual net cash inflows				$ 40,000

Item	Year(s) having cash flows	Amount of cash flows	20 percent factor	Present value of cash flows
Purchase of equipment. . . .	Now	$ (60,000)	1.000	$ (60,000)
Working capital needed . . .	Now	(100,000)	1.000	(100,000)
Overhaul of equipment	4	(5,000)	0.482*	(2,410)
Annual net cash inflows from sales of the product line . .	1–5	40,000	2.991†	119,640
Salvage value of the equipment	5	10,000	0.402*	4,020
Working capital released . . .	5	100,000	0.402*	40,200
Net present value				$ 1,450

* From Table 14–3 in Appendix B.
† From Table 14–4 in Appendix B.

arrangement. The Swinyard Company's cost of capital is 20 percent. Would you recommend that the new product be introduced? Ignore income taxes.

As shown in the data on the preceding page, Example 6 involves a variety of cash inflows and cash outflows. The solution is given in Exhibit 14–6.

Notice particularly how the working capital is handled in the exhibit. Also notice how the sales revenues, cost of goods sold, and out-of-pocket costs are handled. **Out-of-pocket costs** are actual cash outlays made during the period for salaries, advertising, and other operating expenses. Depreciation would not be an out-of-pocket cost, since it involves no current cash outlay.

Since the overall net present value is positive, the new product should be added, assuming that there is no better use for the investment funds involved.

DISCOUNTED CASH FLOWS—THE TIME-ADJUSTED RATE OF RETURN METHOD

The **time-adjusted rate of return** (or **internal rate of return**) can be defined as the true interest yield promised by an investment project over its useful life. It can be computed by finding the discount rate that will equate the present value of the investment (cash outflows) required by a project with the present value of the returns (cash inflows) that the project promises. In other words, the time-adjusted rate of return is that discount rate that will cause the net present value of a project to be equal to zero.

The Time-Adjusted Rate of Return Method Illustrated

Finding a project's time-adjusted rate of return can be very helpful to a manager in making capital budgeting decisions. To illustrate, let us assume the following data:

Example D

The Glendale School District is considering the purchase of a large tractor-pulled lawn mower. If the large mower is purchased, it will replace the hiring of persons to mow with small, individual gas mowers. The large mower will cost $16,950 and will have a life of 10 years. It will have only a negligible scrap value, which can be ignored. It will provide a savings of $3,000 per year in mowing costs because of the labor it will replace.

To compute the time-adjusted rate of return promised by the new mower, it will be necessary to find the discount rate that will cause the net present value of the project to be zero. How do we proceed to do this? The simplest and most direct approach is to divide the investment in the project by the expected annual cash inflow. This computation will yield a factor from which the time-adjusted rate of return can be determined. The formula is:

$$\frac{\text{Investment in the project}}{\text{Annual cash inflow}} = \text{Factor of the time-adjusted rate of return}$$

The factor derived from the formula is then located in the present value tables to see what rate of return it represents. We will now perform these computations for the Glendale School District's proposed project. Using the formula, we get:

$$\frac{\$16,950}{\$3,000} = 5.650$$

Thus, the discount factor that will equate a series of $3,000 cash inflows with a present investment of $16,950 is 5.650. Now we need to find this factor in Table 14–4 in Appendix B to see what rate of return it represents. If we refer to Table 14–4 and scan along the 10-period line, we find that a factor of 5.650 represents a 12 percent rate of return. Therefore, the time-adjusted rate of return promised by the mower project is 12 percent. We can prove this by computing the project's net present value, using a 12 percent discount rate. This computation is made in Exhibit 14–7.

Notice from Exhibit 14–7 that using a 12 percent discount rate equates the present value of the annual cash inflows with the present value of the investment required in the project, leaving a zero net present value. The 12 percent rate therefore represents the time-adjusted rate of return promised by the project.

EXHIBIT 14–7

Evaluation of the mower purchase using a 12 percent discount rate

Initial cost.	$16,950
Life of the project (years)	10
Annual cost savings	$ 3,000
Salvage value	–0–

Item	Year(s) having cash flows	Amount of cash flow	12 percent factor	Present value of cash flows
Annual cost savings	1–10	$ 3,000	5.650*	$ 16,950
Initial investment	Now	(16,950)	1.000	(16,950)
Net present value				$ –0–

*From Table 14–4 in Appendix B.

The Problem of Uneven Cash Flows

The technique just demonstrated works very well if a project's cash flows are even. But what if they are not? For example, what if a project will have some salvage value at the end of its life in addition to the annual cash inflows? Under these circumstances, a trial-and-error process is necessary to find the rate of return that will equate the cash inflows with the cash outflows. The trial-and-error process can be carried out by hand, or it can be carried out by means of computer software programs that perform the necessary computations in seconds. In short, simply because cash flows are erratic or uneven will not in any way prevent a manager from determining a project's time-adjusted rate of return.

The Process of Interpolation

Interpolation is the process of finding odd rates of return that do not appear in published interest tables. It is an important concept, since published interest tables are usually printed in terms of whole percentages (10 percent, 12 percent, and so forth), whereas projects often have rates of return that involve fractional amounts. To illustrate the process of interpolation, assume the following data:

Investment required	$6,000
Annual cost savings	1,500
Life of the project	10 years

What is the time-adjusted rate of return promised by this project? We can proceed as before and find that the relevant factor is 4.000:

$$\frac{\text{Investment required}}{\text{Annual cost savings}} = \frac{\$6,000}{\$1,500} = 4.000$$

Looking at Table 14–4 in Appendix B and scanning along the 10-period line, we find that a factor of 4.000 represents a rate of return somewhere between 20 and 22 percent. To find the rate we are after, we will need to interpolate, as follows:

	Present value factors	
20% factor	4.192	4.192
True factor	4.000	
22% factor		3.923
Difference	0.192	0.269

$$\text{Time-adjusted rate of return} = 20\% + \left(\frac{0.192}{0.269} \times 2\%\right)$$

$$\text{Time-adjusted rate of return} = 21.4\%$$

Using the Time-Adjusted Rate of Return

Once the time-adjusted rate of return has been computed, what does the manager do with the information? The time-adjusted rate of return is compared against whatever rate of return (usually the cost of capital) the organization requires on its investment projects. If the time-adjusted rate of return is *equal* to or *greater* than the cost of capital, then the project is acceptable. If it is *less* than the cost of capital, then the project is rejected. A project is not a profitable undertaking if it can't provide a rate of return at least as great as the cost of the funds invested in it.

In the case of the Glendale School District example used earlier, let us assume that the district has set a minimum required rate of return of 10 percent on all projects. Since the large mower promises a rate of return of 12 percent, it clears this hurdle and would therefore be an acceptable investment.

THE COST OF CAPITAL AS A SCREENING TOOL

As we have seen in preceding examples, the cost of capital operates as a *screening* tool, helping the manager to screen out undesirable investment projects. This screening is accomplished in different ways, depending on whether the company is using the time-adjusted rate of return method or the net present value method in its capital budgeting analysis.

When the time-adjusted rate of return method is being used, the cost of capital takes the form of a **hurdle rate** that a project must clear for acceptance. If the time-adjusted rate of return on a project is not great enough to clear the cost of capital hurdle, then the project is rejected. We saw the application of this idea in the Glendale School District example, where the hurdle rate was set at 10 percent.

When the net present value method is being used, the cost of capital

EXHIBIT 14–8

Capital budgeting screening decisions

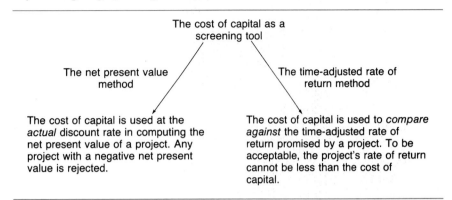

The cost of capital as a
screening tool

The net present value
method

The time-adjusted rate of
return method

The cost of capital is used at the
actual discount rate in computing the
net present value of a project. Any
project with a negative net present
value is rejected.

The cost of capital is used to *compare
against* the time-adjusted rate of
return promised by a project. To be
acceptable, the project's rate of return
cannot be less than the cost of
capital.

becomes the *actual discount rate* used to compute the net present value of
a proposed project. Any project yielding a negative net present value is
screened out and rejected.

The operation of the cost of capital as a screening tool is summarized
in Exhibit 14–8.

COMPARISON OF THE NET PRESENT VALUE AND THE TIME-ADJUSTED RATE OF RETURN METHODS

The net present value method has a number of advantages over the time-
adjusted rate of return method of making capital budgeting decisions.

First, the net present value method is simpler to use. As explained earlier,
the time-adjusted rate of return method often requires a trial-and-error process
to find the exact rate of return that will equate a project's cash inflows and
outflows. No such trial-and-error process is necessary when working with
the net present value method.

Second, using the net present value method makes it easier to adjust
for risk. The point was made earlier in the chapter that the longer one has
to wait for a cash inflow, the greater is the risk that the cash inflow will
never materialize. To show the greater risk connected with cash flows that
are projected to occur many years in the future, firms often discount such
amounts at higher discount rates than the discount rates used for flows that
are projected to occur earlier in time. For example, a firm might anticipate
that a project will provide cash inflows of $10,000 per year for 15 years.
If the firm's cost of capital is 18 percent before taxes, then it might discount
the first five years' inflows at this rate. The discount rate might then be
raised to, say, 20 percent for the next five years and then to, say, 25
percent for the last five years. This successive raising of the discount rate
would show the greater risk connected with the cash flows that are projected
to be received far into the future.

No such selective adjustment of discount rates is possible under the time-adjusted rate of return method. About the only way to adjust for risk is to raise the hurdle rate that the rate of return for a project must clear for acceptance. This is a somewhat crude approach to the risk problem in that it attaches the same degree of increased risk to *all* of the cash flows associated with a project—those that occur earlier in time as well as those that occur later in time.

Third, the net present value method provides more usable information than does the time-adjusted rate of return method. The dollar net present value figure generated by the net present value method is viewed as being particularly useful for decision-making purposes. This point is considered further in the following chapter.

CAPITAL BUDGETING AND NONPROFIT ORGANIZATIONS

The capital budgeting concepts that we have been studying have equal application to all types of organizations, regardless of whether they are profit or nonprofit in nature. Note, for example, the different types of organizations used in the examples in this chapter. These organizations include a hospital, a company working under a licensing agreement, a school district, a company operating a ferryboat service, and a manufacturing company. The diversity of these examples shows the range and power of the capital budgeting model.

The only real problem in the use of capital budgeting by nonprofit organizations is determining the proper discount rate to use in the analysis of data. Some nonprofit organizations use the rate of interest paid on special bond issues (such as an issue for street improvements or an issue to build a school) as their discount rate; others use the rate of interest that could be earned by placing money in an endowment fund rather than spending it on capital improvements; and still others use discount rates that are set somewhat arbitrarily by governing boards.

The greatest danger lies in using a discount rate that is too low. Most government agencies, for example, at one time used the interest rate on government bonds as their discount rate. It is now recognized that this rate is too low and has resulted in the acceptance of many projects that should not have been undertaken.[2] To resolve this problem, the Office of Management and Budget has specified that federal government units must use a discount rate of at least 10 percent on all projects.[3] For nonprofit units such as schools and hospitals, it is generally recommended that the discount rate should "approximate the average rate of return on private

---

[2] See *Federal Capital Budgeting: A Collection of Haphazard Practices,* GAO, P.O. Box 6015, Gaithersburg, MD, PAD-81-19, February 26, 1981.

[3] Office of Management and Budget Circular No. A-94, March 1972. The U.S. Postal Service is exempted from the 10 percent rate as are all water resource projects and all lease or buy decisions.

sector investments.''[4] Since this rate would include the experience of thousands of companies, it undoubtedly would provide more satisfactory results as a discount rate than simply using the interest rate on a special bond issue or the interest return on an endowment fund.

EXPANDING THE NET PRESENT VALUE APPROACH

So far we have confined all of our examples to the consideration of a single investment alternative. We will now expand the net present value approach to include two alternatives. In addition, we will integrate the concept of relevant costs into discounted cash flow analysis.

There are two ways that the net present value method can be used to compare competing investment projects. One is the *total-cost approach,* and the other is the *incremental-cost approach.* Each approach is illustrated below.

The Total-Cost Approach

The total-cost approach is the most flexible and the most widely used method of making a net present value analysis of competing projects. To illustrate the mechanics of the approach, let us assume the following data:

Example E

The Harper Ferry Company provides a ferry service across the Mississippi River. One of its ferryboats is in poor condition. This ferry can be renovated at an immediate cost of $20,000. Further repairs and an overhaul of the motor will be needed five years from now at a cost of $8,000. In all, the ferry will be usable for 10 years if this work is done. At the end of 10 years, the ferry will have to be scrapped at a salvage value of approximately $5,000. The scrap value of the ferry right now is $7,000. It will cost $16,000 each year to operate the ferry, and revenues will total $25,000 annually.

As an alternative, the Harper Ferry Company can purchase a new ferryboat at a cost of $36,000. The new ferry will have a life of 10 years, but it will require some repairs at the end of 5 years. It is estimated that these repairs will amount to $2,500. At the end of 10 years, it is estimated that the ferry will have a scrap value of $5,000. It will cost $12,000 each year to operate the ferry, and revenues will total $25,000 annually.

The Harper Ferry Company requires a return of at least 18 percent before taxes on all investment projects.

Should the company purchase the new ferry or renovate the old ferry? The solution is given in Exhibit 14–9 on the following page.

Two points should be noted from the exhibit. First, observe that *all* cash inflows and *all* cash outflows are included in the solution under each alternative. No effort has been made to isolate those cash flows that are

---

[4] Robert N. Anthony and David W. Young, *Management Control in Nonprofit Organizations,* 3rd ed. (Homewood, Ill: Richard D. Irwin, 1984), p. 325.

EXHIBIT 14–9

The total-cost approach to project selection

	New ferry	Old ferry
Annual revenues	$25,000	$25,000
Annual cash operating costs . . .	12,000	16,000
Net annual cash inflows	$13,000	$ 9,000

Item	Year(s) having cash flows	Amount of cash flows	18 percent factor*	Present value of cash flows
Buy the new ferry:				
Initial investment	Now	$(36,000)	1.000	$(36,000)
Repairs in five years	5	(2,500)	0.437	(1,093)
Net annual cash inflows	1–10	13,000	4.494	58,422
Salvage of the old ferry	Now	7,000	1.000	7,000
Salvage of the new ferry	10	5,000	0.191	955
Net present value				29,284
Keep the old ferry:				
Initial repairs	Now	$(20,000)	1.000	(20,000)
Repairs in five years	5	(8,000)	0.437	(3,496)
Net annual cash inflows	1–10	9,000	4.494	40,446
Salvage of the old ferry	10	5,000	0.191	955
Net present value				17,905
Net present value in favor of buying the new ferry				$ 11,379

* All factors are from Tables 14–3 and 14–4 in Appendix B.

relevant to the decision and those that are not relevant. The inclusion of all cash flows associated with each alternative gives the approach its name—the *total-cost* approach.

Second, notice that a net present value figure is computed for each of the two alternatives. This is a distinct advantage of the total-cost approach in that an unlimited number of alternatives can be compared side by side to determine the most profitable course of action. For example, another alternative for the Harper Ferry Company would be to get out of the ferry business entirely. If management desired, the net present value of this alternative could be computed to compare with the alternatives shown in Exhibit 14–9. Still other alternatives might be open to the company. Once management has determined the net present value of each alternative that it wishes to consider, it can select the course of action that will be most profitable. In the case at hand, given only the two alternatives, the data indicate that the most profitable course is to purchase the new ferry.[5]

---

[5] The alternative with the highest net present value is not always the best choice, although it is the best choice in this case. For further discussion, see the section titled ''Preference decisions—the ranking of investment projects'' in Chapter 15.

EXHIBIT 14–10

The incremental-cost approach to project selection

Items	Year(s) having cash flows	Amount of cash flows	18 percent factor*	Present value of cash flows
Incremental investment required to purchase the new ferry	Now	$(16,000)	1.000	$(16,000)
Repairs in five years avoided	5	5,500	0.437	2,403
Increased net annual cash inflows	1–10	4,000	4.494	17,976
Salvage of the old ferry	Now	7,000	1.000	7,000
Difference in salvage value in 10 years	10	–0–	—	–0–
Net present value in favor of buying the new ferry				$ 11,379

* All factors are from Tables 14–3 and 14–4 in Appendix B.

The Incremental-Cost Approach

When only two alternatives are being considered, the incremental-cost approach offers a simpler and more direct route to a decision. Unlike the total-cost approach, it focuses only on differential costs.[6] The procedure is to include in the discounted cash flow analysis only those costs and revenues that *differ* between the two alternatives being considered. To illustrate, refer again to the data in Example E relating to the Harper Ferry Company. The solution using only differential costs is presented in Exhibit 14–10.

Two things should be noted from the data in this exhibit. First, notice that the net present value of $11,379 shown in Exhibit 14–10 agrees with the net present value shown under the total-cost approach in Exhibit 14–9. This agreement should be expected, since the two approaches are just different roads to the same destination.

Second, notice that the costs used in Exhibit 14–10 are just mathematical differences between the costs shown for the two alternatives in the prior exhibit. For example, the $16,000 incremental investment required to purchase the new ferry in Exhibit 14–10 is the difference between the $36,000 cost of the new ferry and the $20,000 cost required to renovate the old ferry from Exhibit 14–9. The other figures in Exhibit 14–10 have been computed in the same way.

Least-Cost Decisions

Revenues are not directly involved in some decisions. For example, a company that makes no charge for delivery service may need to replace an old delivery truck, or a company may be trying to decide whether to

---

[6] Technically, the incremental-cost approach is misnamed, since it focuses on differential costs (that is, on both cost increases and decreases) rather than just on incremental costs. As used here, the term *incremental costs* should be interpreted broadly to include both cost increases and cost decreases.

lease or to buy its fleet of executive cars. In situations such as these, where no revenues are involved, the most desirable alternative will be the one that promises the *least total cost*. Hence, these are known as least-cost decisions. To illustrate a least-cost decision, assume the following data:

Example F

The Val-Tek Company is considering the replacement of an old threading machine that is used in the manufacture of a number of products. A new threading machine is available on the market that could substantially reduce annual operating costs. Selected data relating to the old and the new machines are presented below:

	Old machine	New machine
Purchase cost new.	$20,000	$25,000
Salvage value now	3,000	—
Annual cash operating costs.	15,000	9,000
Overhaul needed immediately	4,000	—
Salvage value in six years	–0–	5,000
Remaining life	6 years	6 years

The Val-Tek Company's cost of capital is 10 percent.

An analysis of the alternatives, using the total-cost approach, is provided in Exhibit 14–11.

EXHIBIT 14–11

The total-cost approach (least-cost decision)

Items	Year(s) having cash flows	Amount of cash flows	10 percent factor*	Present value of cash flows
Buy the new machine:				
Initial investment	Now	$(25,000)	1.000	$(25,000)†
Salvage of the old machine	Now	3,000	1.000	3,000†
Annual cash operating costs	1–6	(9,000)	4.355	(39,195)
Salvage of the new machine	6	5,000	0.564	2,820
Present value of net cash outflows . . .				(58,375)
Keep the old machine:				
Overhaul needed now	Now	$ (4,000)	1.000	(4,000)
Annual cash operating costs	1–6	(15,000)	4.355	(65,325)
Present value of net cash outflows . . .				(69,325)
Net present value in favor of buying the new machine				$ 10,950

* All factors are from Tables 14–3 and 14–4 in Appendix B.
† These two items could be netted into a single $22,000 incremental cost figure ($25,000 − $3,000 = $22,000).

EXHIBIT 14–12

The incremental-cost approach (least-cost decision)

Items	Year(s) having cash flows	Amount of cash flows	10 percent factor*	Present value of cash flows
Incremental investment required to purchase the new machine	Now	$(21,000)	1.000	$(21,000)†
Salvage of the old machine . . .	Now	3,000	1.000	3,000†
Savings in annual cash operating costs	1–6	6,000	4.355	26,130
Difference in salvage value in six years	6	5,000	0.564	2,820
Net present value in favor of buying the new machine				$ 10,950

* All factors are from Tables 14–3 and 14–4 in Appendix B.
† These two items could be netted into a single $18,000 incremental-cost figure ($21,000 − $3,000 = $18,000).

As shown in the exhibit, the new machine promises the lowest present value of total costs. An analysis of the two alternatives using the incremental-cost approach is presented in Exhibit 14–12. As before, the data going into this exhibit represent the differences between the alternatives as shown under the total-cost approach.

POSTAUDIT OF INVESTMENT PROJECTS

Postaudit of an investment project means a follow-up after the project has been approved to see whether or not expected results are actually realized. This is a key part of the capital budgeting process in that it provides management with an opportunity, over time, to see how realistic the proposals are that are being submitted and approved. It also provides an opportunity to reinforce successful projects as needed, to strengthen or perhaps salvage projects that are encountering difficulty, to terminate unsuccessful projects before losses become too great, and to improve the overall quality of future investment proposals.

In performing a postaudit, the same technique should be used as was used in the original approval process. That is, if a project was approved on a basis of a net present value analysis, then the same procedure should be used in performing the postaudit. However, the data going into the analysis should be *actual data* as observed in the actual operation of the project, rather than estimated data. This affords management with an opportunity to make a side-by-side comparison to see how well the project has worked out. It also helps assure that estimated data received on future proposals will be carefully prepared, since the persons submitting the data will know that their estimates will be given careful scrutiny in the postaudit process. Actual results that are far out of line with original estimates should be carefully reviewed by management, and corrective action taken as necessary. In accordance with the management by exception principle, those managers responsible for the original estimates should be required to provide a full explanation of any major differences between estimated and actual results.

SUMMARY

Decisions relating to the planning and financing of capital outlays are known as capital budgeting decisions. Such decisions are of key importance to the long-run profitability of a firm, since large amounts of money are usually involved and since whatever decisions are made may "lock in" a firm for many years.

A decision to make a particular investment hinges basically on whether the future returns promised by the investment can be justified in terms of the present cost outlay that must be made. A valid comparison between the future returns and the present cost outlay is difficult because of the difference in timing involved. This timing problem is overcome through use of the concept of present value and through employment of the technique of discounting. The future sums are discounted to their present value so that they can be compared on a valid basis with current cost outlays. The discount rate used may be the firm's cost of capital, or it may be some arbitrary rate of return that the firm requires on all investment projects.

There are two ways of using discounted cash flow in making capital budgeting decisions. One is the net present value method, and the other is the time-adjusted rate of return method. The net present value method simply involves the choosing of a discount rate, then the discounting of all cash flows to present value, as described in the preceding paragraph. If the present value of the cash inflows exceeds the present value of the cash outflows, then the net present value is positive and the project is acceptable. The opposite is true if the net present value is negative. The time-adjusted rate of return method finds the discount rate that equates the cash inflows and the cash outflows, leaving a zero net present value.

After an investment proposal has been approved, a postaudit should be performed to see whether expected results are actually being realized. This is a key part of the capital budgeting process, since it tends to strengthen the quality of the estimates going into investment proposals and affords management with an early opportunity to recognize any developing problems.

KEY TERMS FOR REVIEW

Annuity A series, or stream, of cash flows of equal amounts.

Capital budgeting Actions relating to the planning and financing of capital outlays for such purposes as the purchase of new equipment, the introduction of new product lines, and the modernization of plant facilities.

Compound interest The process of paying interest on interest in an investment.

Cost of capital The overall cost to an organization of obtaining investment funds, including the cost of both debt sources and equity sources.

Cutoff rate The minimum rate of return that an investment project must yield in order to be acceptable.

Discount rate The rate of return that is used to find the present value of a future cash flow.

Discounting The process of finding the present value of a future cash flow.

Hurdle rate The minimum rate of return that an investment project must yield in order to be acceptable.

Internal rate of return The discount rate that will cause the net present value of an investment project to be equal to zero; thus, the internal rate of return represents the true interest return promised by a project over its useful life. This term is synonymous with *time-adjusted rate of return*.

Interpolation The process of finding odd rates of return (such as 12.6 percent or 9.4 percent) that do not appear in published interest tables.

Net present value The difference between the present value of the cash inflows and the cash outflows associated with an investment project.

Out-of-pocket costs The actual cash outlays made during a period for salaries, advertising, repairs, and similar costs.

Postaudit The follow-up after a project has been approved and implemented to determine whether expected results are actually realized.

Preference decision A decision as to which of several competing acceptable investment proposals is best.

Present value The estimated value now of an amount that will be received in some future period.

Required rate of return The minimum rate of return that an investment project must yield in order to be acceptable.

Screening decision A decision as to whether a proposed investment meets some preset standard of acceptance.

Time-adjusted rate of return The discount rate that will cause the net present value of an investment project to be equal to zero; thus, the time-adjusted rate of return represents the true interest return promised by a project over its useful life. This term is synonymous with *internal rate of return.*

Working capital The excess of current assets over current liabilities.

APPENDIX A: INFLATION AND CAPITAL BUDGETING

Students frequently raise the question "What about inflation—doesn't it have an impact in a capital budgeting analysis?" The answer is a qualified yes in that inflation does have an impact on the *numbers* that are used in a capital budgeting analysis, but it does not have an impact on the *results* that are obtained. To show what we mean by this statement, assume the following data:

Example G

Martin Company wants to purchase a new machine that costs $36,000. The machine would provide annual cost savings of $20,000, and it would have a three-year life with no salvage value. For each of the next three years, the company expects a 10 percent inflation rate in cost items associated with its activities. If the company's cost of capital is 16 percent, should the new machine be purchased?

Two solutions to this example are provided in Exhibit 14–13. In the first solution (solution A), inflation is ignored and the net present value of the proposed investment is computed in the same way as we have been computing it throughout the chapter. In the second solution (solution B), inflation is given full consideration.

Adjustments for Inflation

Several points should be noted about solution B. First, note that the annual cost savings are adjusted for the effects of inflation by multiplying each year's savings by a price-index number that reflects a 10 percent inflation rate. (Observe from the footnotes to the exhibit how the index number is computed for each year.)

Second, note that the cost of capital must also be adjusted for the effects of inflation. This is done by adding together three cost elements: the cost of capital itself, the inflation rate, and a combined factor that allows for the reinvestment of inflation-generated earnings. A frequent error in adjusting data for inflation is to omit any adjustment at all to the cost of capital; or, if an adjustment is made, to simply add together the cost of capital and the inflation rate. Both of these procedures are incorrect and will yield erroneous results.[7]

---

[7] The proper way to adjust the discount rate for inflationary effects is widely misunderstood. If the manager omits any adjustment to the cost of capital, or just adds together the cost of capital and the inflation rate, then the result will be to overstate the net present value of an investment project.

EXHIBIT 14–13

Capital budgeting and inflation

Solution A: Inflation not considered

Items	Year(s) having cash flows	Amount of cash flows	16 percent factor	Present value of cash flows
Initial investment	Now	$(36,000)	1.000	$(36,000)
Annual cost savings	1–3	20,000	2.246	44,920
Net present value				$ 8,920

Solution B: Inflation considered

Items	Year(s) having cash flows	Amount of cash flows	Price index number	Price-adjusted cash flows	27.6† percent factor	Present value of cash flows
Initial investment . . .	Now	$(36,000)	—	$(36,000)	1.0000	$(36,000)
Annual cost savings . .	1	20,000	1.10	22,000	0.7837‡	17,241
	2	20,000	1.21˙	24,200	0.6142‡	14,864
	3	20,000	1.331˙	26,620	0.4814‡	12,815
Net present value . . .						$ 8,920

˙ Computation of the price-index numbers, assuming a 10 percent inflation rate each year: year 2, $(1.10)^2 = 1.21$; year 3, $(1.10)^3 = 1.331$.

† The inflation-adjusted cost of capital consists of three elements:

The basic cost of capital	16.0%
The inflation factor	10.0
The combined effect (16% × 10% = 1.6%) . . .	1.6
Inflation-adjusted cost of capital	27.6%

‡ Discount factors are computed using the formula $1/(1 + r)^n$ where r = discount factor and n = number of years. For year 1, the computations are: $1/1.276 = 0.7837$; for year 2: $1/(1.276)^2 = 0.6142$; for year 3: $1/(1.276)^3 = 0.4814$. Computations have been carried to four decimal places to avoid a rounding error.

Finally, note that the net present value obtained in solution B is *identical* to that obtained in solution A. It sometimes surprises students to learn that the same net present value will be obtained regardless of whether or not the data are adjusted for the effects of inflation. But if the reader will stop and reflect for a moment, this is a logical result. The reason is that, in adjusting the data for the effects of inflation, we adjust *both* the cash flows and the discount rate, and thus the inflationary effects cancel themselves out. As a result, the net present value is the same as if no adjustments had been made.

How Practical Are Adjustments for Inflation?

In actual practice, not all companies make adjustments for inflation when doing a capital budgeting analysis. The reasons are obvious—the computations are very complex, and the same net present value can be obtained by using unadjusted data. The one advantage that is sometimes cited in favor of using inflation-adjusted data is that it may be of more value in the postaudit process. It is argued that using inflation-adjusted data in the original capital budgeting analysis allows the manager to later compare like items in the postaudit, because *both* the estimated data and the actual data will contain the effects of inflation. If unadjusted data are used in the original capital budgeting analysis, then it is argued that the manager is forced to compare *unlike* items in the postaudit. Thus, the manager may be mislead in his or her evaluation of how the investment turned out.

Unfortunately, this "advantage" is more illusory than real. For one thing, if inflation-adjusted data are used in the original capital budgeting analysis, then these data and the actual data will be comparable only if the *same rate* of inflation is present in both. The likelihood of having the same rate present in both is small, since inflation is very difficult to predict. Economists rarely agree on the expected rate for the next year, let alone several years into the future. In addition, the use of inflation-adjusted data may conceal sloppy estimates of cash flows by enabling the manager to hide behind the excuse that inflation rates turned out to be different than expected, thus throwing his or her estimates off.

To overcome these problems, a better approach is to use unadjusted data (because of its simplicity) in the original capital budgeting analysis, and then *in the postaudit* to adjust the actual data in order to remove the effects of any inflation that may have taken place. This approach will then allow for a comparison of like items, since neither the original data nor the actual data will contain any inflationary elements. It will also preclude the manager from hiding behind the excuse that his or her estimates were thrown off because the rate of inflation was different than expected.

Summary

Although it is possible to make adjustments for inflation in a capital budgeting analysis, it is a very difficult and complex process. Moreover, if the adjustments are properly done, the same net present value will be obtained as if no adjustments had been made. A simpler and more effective approach is to use unadjusted data in capital budgeting computations, as we have done in the chapter, and then to make adjustments to the actual data in the postaudit (when the actual rate of inflation is known), if it is thought that such adjustments are warranted.

APPENDIX B: FUTURE VALUE AND PRESENT VALUE TABLES

TABLE 14–1
Future value of $1; $F_n = P(1 + r)^n$

Periods	4%	6%	8%	10%	12%	14%	20%
1	1.040	1.060	1.080	1.100	1.120	1.140	1.200
2	1.082	1.124	1.166	1.210	1.254	1.300	1.440
3	1.125	1.191	1.260	1.331	1.405	1.482	1.728
4	1.170	1.263	1.361	1.464	1.574	1.689	2.074
5	1.217	1.338	1.469	1.611	1.762	1.925	2.488
6	1.265	1.419	1.587	1.772	1.974	2.195	2.986
7	1.316	1.504	1.714	1.949	2.211	2.502	3.583
8	1.369	1.594	1.851	2.144	2.476	2.853	4.300
9	1.423	1.690	1.999	2.359	2.773	3.252	5.160
10	1.480	1.791	2.159	2.594	3.106	3.707	6.192
11	1.540	1.898	2.332	2.853	3.479	4.226	7.430
12	1.601	2.012	2.518	3.139	3.896	4.818	8.916
13	1.665	2.133	2.720	3.452	4.364	5.492	10.699
14	1.732	2.261	2.937	3.798	4.887	6.261	12.839
15	1.801	2.397	3.172	4.177	5.474	7.138	15.407
20	2.191	3.207	4.661	6.728	9.646	13.743	38.338
30	3.243	5.744	10.063	17.450	29.960	50.950	237.380
40	4.801	10.286	21.725	45.260	93.051	188.880	1469.800

TABLE 14–2
Future value of an annuity of $1 in arrears; $F_n = \dfrac{(1 + r)^n - 1}{r}$

Periods	4%	6%	8%	10%	12%	14%	20%
1	1.000	1.000	1.000	1.000	1.000	1.000	1.000
2	2.040	2.060	2.080	2.100	2.120	2.140	2.220
3	3.122	3.184	3.246	3.310	3.374	3.440	3.640
4	4.247	4.375	4.506	4.641	4.779	4.921	5.368
5	5.416	5.637	5.867	6.105	6.353	6.610	7.442
6	6.633	6.975	7.336	7.716	8.115	8.536	9.930
7	7.898	8.394	8.923	9.487	10.089	10.730	12.916
8	9.214	9.898	10.637	11.436	12.300	13.233	16.499
9	10.583	11.491	12.488	13.580	14.776	16.085	20.799
10	12.006	13.181	14.487	15.938	17.549	19.337	25.959
11	13.486	14.972	16.646	18.531	20.655	23.045	32.150
12	15.026	16.870	18.977	21.385	24.133	27.271	39.580
13	16.627	18.882	21.495	24.523	28.029	32.089	48.497
14	18.292	21.015	24.215	27.976	32.393	37.581	59.196
15	20.024	23.276	27.152	31.773	37.280	43.842	72.035
20	29.778	36.778	45.762	57.276	75.052	91.025	186.690
30	56.085	79.058	113.283	164.496	241.330	356.790	1181.900
40	95.026	154.762	259.057	442.597	767.090	1342.000	7343.900

TABLE 14-3
Present value of \$1; $P = \dfrac{F_n}{(1 + r)^n}$

Periods	4%	5%	6%	8%	10%	12%	14%	16%	18%	20%	22%	24%	26%	28%	30%	40%
1	0.962	0.952	0.943	0.926	0.909	0.893	0.877	0.862	0.847	0.833	0.820	0.806	0.794	0.781	0.769	0.714
2	0.925	0.907	0.890	0.857	0.826	0.797	0.769	0.743	0.718	0.694	0.672	0.650	0.630	0.610	0.592	0.510
3	0.889	0.864	0.840	0.794	0.751	0.712	0.675	0.641	0.609	0.579	0.551	0.524	0.500	0.477	0.455	0.364
4	0.855	0.823	0.792	0.735	0.683	0.636	0.592	0.552	0.516	0.482	0.451	0.423	0.397	0.373	0.350	0.260
5	0.822	0.784	0.747	0.681	0.621	0.567	0.519	0.476	0.437	0.402	0.370	0.341	0.315	0.291	0.269	0.186
6	0.790	0.746	0.705	0.630	0.564	0.507	0.456	0.410	0.370	0.335	0.303	0.275	0.250	0.227	0.207	0.133
7	0.760	0.711	0.665	0.583	0.513	0.452	0.400	0.354	0.314	0.279	0.249	0.222	0.198	0.178	0.159	0.095
8	0.731	0.677	0.627	0.540	0.467	0.404	0.351	0.305	0.266	0.233	0.204	0.179	0.157	0.139	0.123	0.068
9	0.703	0.645	0.592	0.500	0.424	0.361	0.308	0.263	0.225	0.194	0.167	0.144	0.125	0.108	0.094	0.048
10	0.676	0.614	0.558	0.463	0.386	0.322	0.270	0.227	0.191	0.162	0.137	0.116	0.099	0.085	0.073	0.035
11	0.650	0.585	0.527	0.429	0.350	0.287	0.237	0.195	0.162	0.135	0.112	0.094	0.079	0.066	0.056	0.025
12	0.625	0.557	0.497	0.397	0.319	0.257	0.208	0.168	0.137	0.112	0.092	0.076	0.062	0.052	0.043	0.018
13	0.601	0.530	0.469	0.368	0.290	0.229	0.182	0.145	0.116	0.093	0.075	0.061	0.050	0.040	0.033	0.013
14	0.577	0.505	0.442	0.340	0.263	0.205	0.160	0.125	0.099	0.078	0.062	0.049	0.039	0.032	0.025	0.009
15	0.555	0.481	0.417	0.315	0.239	0.183	0.140	0.108	0.084	0.065	0.051	0.040	0.031	0.025	0.020	0.006
16	0.534	0.458	0.394	0.292	0.218	0.163	0.123	0.093	0.071	0.054	0.042	0.032	0.025	0.019	0.015	0.005
17	0.513	0.436	0.371	0.270	0.198	0.146	0.108	0.080	0.060	0.045	0.034	0.026	0.020	0.015	0.012	0.003
18	0.494	0.416	0.350	0.250	0.180	0.130	0.095	0.069	0.051	0.038	0.028	0.021	0.016	0.012	0.009	0.002
19	0.475	0.396	0.331	0.232	0.164	0.116	0.083	0.060	0.043	0.031	0.023	0.017	0.012	0.009	0.007	0.002
20	0.456	0.377	0.312	0.215	0.149	0.104	0.073	0.051	0.037	0.026	0.019	0.014	0.010	0.007	0.005	0.001
21	0.439	0.359	0.294	0.199	0.135	0.093	0.064	0.044	0.031	0.022	0.015	0.011	0.008	0.006	0.004	0.001
22	0.422	0.342	0.278	0.184	0.123	0.083	0.056	0.038	0.026	0.018	0.013	0.009	0.006	0.004	0.003	0.001
23	0.406	0.326	0.262	0.170	0.112	0.074	0.049	0.033	0.022	0.015	0.010	0.007	0.005	0.003	0.002	
24	0.390	0.310	0.247	0.158	0.102	0.066	0.043	0.028	0.019	0.013	0.008	0.006	0.004	0.003	0.002	
25	0.375	0.295	0.233	0.146	0.092	0.059	0.038	0.024	0.016	0.010	0.007	0.005	0.003	0.002	0.001	
26	0.361	0.281	0.220	0.135	0.084	0.053	0.033	0.021	0.014	0.009	0.006	0.004	0.002	0.002	0.001	
27	0.347	0.268	0.207	0.125	0.076	0.047	0.029	0.018	0.011	0.007	0.005	0.003	0.002	0.001	0.001	
28	0.333	0.255	0.196	0.116	0.069	0.042	0.026	0.016	0.010	0.006	0.004	0.002	0.002	0.001	0.001	
29	0.321	0.243	0.185	0.107	0.063	0.037	0.022	0.014	0.008	0.005	0.003	0.002	0.001	0.001	0.001	
30	0.308	0.231	0.174	0.099	0.057	0.033	0.020	0.012	0.007	0.004	0.003	0.002	0.001	0.001	0.001	
40	0.208	0.142	0.097	0.046	0.022	0.011	0.005	0.003	0.001	0.001						

TABLE 14-4

Present value of an annuity of $1 in arrears; $P_n = \dfrac{1}{r}\left[1 - \dfrac{1}{(1+r)^n}\right]$

annuitur — *every year payments* (handwritten note)

Periods	4%	5%	6%	8%	10%	12%	14%	16%	18%	20%	22%	24%	26%	28%	30%	40%
1	0.962	0.952	0.943	0.926	0.909	0.893	0.877	0.862	0.847	0.833	0.820	0.806	0.794	0.781	0.769	0.714
2	1.886	1.859	1.833	1.783	1.736	1.690	1.647	1.605	1.566	1.528	1.492	1.457	1.424	1.392	1.361	1.224
3	2.775	2.723	2.673	2.577	2.487	2.402	2.322	2.246	2.174	2.106	2.042	1.981	1.923	1.868	1.816	1.589
4	3.630	3.546	3.465	3.312	3.170	3.037	2.914	2.798	2.690	2.589	2.494	2.404	2.320	2.241	2.166	1.879
5	4.452	4.330	4.212	3.993	3.791	3.605	3.433	3.274	3.127	2.991	2.864	2.745	2.635	2.532	2.436	2.035
6	5.242	5.076	4.917	4.623	4.355	4.111	3.889	3.685	3.498	3.326	3.167	3.020	2.885	2.759	2.643	2.168
7	6.002	5.786	5.582	5.206	4.868	4.564	4.288	4.039	3.812	3.605	3.416	3.242	3.083	2.937	2.802	2.263
8	6.733	6.463	6.210	5.747	5.335	4.968	4.639	4.344	4.078	3.837	3.619	3.421	3.241	3.076	2.925	2.331
9	7.435	7.108	6.802	6.247	5.759	5.328	4.946	4.607	4.303	4.031	3.786	3.566	3.366	3.184	3.019	2.379
10	8.111	7.722	7.360	6.710	6.145	5.650	5.216	4.833	4.494	4.192	3.923	3.682	3.465	3.269	3.092	2.414
11	8.760	8.306	7.887	7.139	6.495	5.988	5.453	5.029	4.656	4.327	4.035	3.776	3.544	3.335	3.147	2.438
12	9.385	8.863	8.384	7.536	6.814	6.194	5.660	5.197	4.793	4.439	4.127	3.851	3.606	3.387	3.190	2.456
13	9.986	9.394	8.853	7.904	7.103	6.424	5.842	5.342	4.910	4.533	4.203	3.912	3.656	3.427	3.223	2.468
14	10.563	9.899	9.295	8.244	7.367	6.628	6.002	5.468	5.008	4.611	4.265	3.962	3.695	3.459	3.249	2.477
15	11.118	10.380	9.712	8.559	7.606	6.811	6.142	5.575	5.092	4.675	4.315	4.001	3.726	3.483	3.268	2.484
16	11.652	10.838	10.106	8.851	7.824	6.974	6.265	5.669	5.162	4.730	4.357	4.033	3.751	3.503	3.283	2.489
17	12.166	11.274	10.477	9.122	8.022	7.120	6.373	5.749	5.222	4.775	4.391	4.059	3.771	3.518	3.295	2.492
18	12.659	11.690	10.828	9.372	8.201	7.250	6.467	5.818	5.273	4.812	4.419	4.080	3.786	3.529	3.304	2.494
19	13.134	12.085	11.158	9.604	8.365	7.366	6.550	5.877	5.316	4.844	4.442	4.097	3.799	3.539	3.311	2.496
20	13.590	12.462	11.470	9.818	8.514	7.469	6.623	5.929	5.353	4.870	4.460	4.110	3.808	3.546	3.316	2.497
21	14.029	12.821	11.764	10.017	8.649	7.562	6.687	5.973	5.384	4.891	4.476	4.121	3.816	3.551	3.320	2.498
22	14.451	13.163	12.042	10.201	8.772	7.645	6.743	6.011	5.410	4.909	4.488	4.130	3.822	3.556	3.323	2.498
23	14.857	13.489	12.303	10.371	8.883	7.718	6.792	6.044	5.432	4.925	4.499	4.137	3.827	3.559	3.325	2.499
24	15.247	13.799	12.550	10.529	8.985	7.784	6.835	6.073	5.451	4.937	4.507	4.143	3.831	3.562	3.327	2.499
25	15.622	14.094	12.783	10.675	9.077	7.843	6.873	6.097	5.467	4.948	4.514	4.147	3.834	3.564	3.329	2.499
26	15.983	14.375	13.003	10.810	9.161	7.896	6.906	6.118	5.480	4.956	4.520	4.151	3.837	3.566	3.330	2.500
27	16.330	14.643	13.211	10.935	9.237	7.943	6.935	6.136	5.492	4.964	4.525	4.154	3.839	3.567	3.331	2.500
28	16.663	14.898	13.406	11.051	9.307	7.984	6.961	6.152	5.502	4.970	4.528	4.157	3.840	3.568	3.331	2.500
29	16.984	15.141	13.591	11.158	9.370	8.022	6.983	6.166	5.510	4.975	4.531	4.159	3.841	3.569	3.332	2.500
30	17.292	15.373	13.765	11.258	9.427	8.055	7.003	6.177	5.517	4.979	4.534	4.160	3.842	3.569	3.332	2.500
40	19.793	17.159	15.046	11.925	9.779	8.244	7.105	6.234	5.548	4.997	4.544	4.166	3.846	3.571	3.333	2.500

QUESTIONS

14–1.   What is meant by the term *capital budgeting?*

14–2.   Distinguish between capital budgeting screening decisions and capital budgeting preference decisions.

14–3.   What is meant by the term *time value of money?*

14–4.   What is meant by the term *discounting,* and why is it important to the business manager?

14–5.   Why can't accounting net income figures be used in the net present value and time-adjusted rate of return methods of making capital budgeting decisions?

14–6.   Why are discounted cash flow methods of making capital budgeting decisions superior to other methods?

14–7.   What is net present value? Can it ever be negative? Explain.

14–8.   One real shortcoming of discounted cash flow methods is that they ignore depreciation. Do you agree? Why or why not?

14–9.   Identify two limiting assumptions associated with discounted cash flow methods of making capital budgeting decisions.

14–10.   If a firm has to pay interest of 14 percent on long-term debt, then its cost of capital is 14 percent. Do you agree? Explain.

14–11.   What is meant by an investment project's time-adjusted rate of return? How is the time-adjusted rate of return computed?

14–12.   Explain how the cost of capital serves as a screening tool when dealing with *(a)* the net present value method and *(b)* the time-adjusted rate of return method.

14–13.   Companies that invest in underdeveloped countries usually require a higher rate of return on their investment than they do when their investment is made in countries that are better developed and that have more stable political and economic conditions. Some people say that the higher rate of return required in the underdeveloped countries is evidence of exploitation. What other explanation can you offer?

14–14.   Riskier investment proposals should be discounted at lower rates of return. Do you agree? Why or why not?

14–15.   As the discount rate increases, the present value of a given future sum also increases. Do you agree? Explain.

14–16.   Refer to Exhibit 14–6 in the text. Is the return promised by this investment proposal exactly 20 percent, slightly more than 20 percent, or slightly less than 20 percent? Explain.

14–17.   If an investment project has a zero net present value, then it should be rejected since it will provide no return on funds invested. Do you agree? Why?

14–18.   A machine costs $12,000. It will provide a cost savings of $3,000 per year. If the company requires a 16 percent rate of return, how many years will the machine have to be used to provide the desired 16 percent return?

EXERCISES

(Ignore income taxes in all exercises.)

E14–1.   (The solution to this exercise is given below.) Each of the following situations is independent. Work out your own solution to each situation, and then check it against the solution provided.

1. John has just reached age 58. In 12 years, he plans to retire. Upon retiring, he would like to take an extended vacation, which he expects will cost at least $4,000. What lump-sum amount must he invest now in order to have the needed $4,000 at the end of 12 years if the desired rate of return is:

    a. Eight percent?

    b. Twelve percent?

2. The Morgans would like to send their daughter to an expensive music camp at the end of each of the next five years. The camp costs $1,000 each year. What lump-sum amount would have to be invested now in order to have the $1,000 at the end of each year if the desired rate of return is:

    a. Eight percent?

    b. Twelve percent?

3. You have just received an inheritance from your father's estate. You can invest the money and either receive a $20,000 lump-sum amount at the end of 10 years or receive $1,400 at the end of each year for the next 10 years. If the minimum desired rate or return is 12 percent, which alternative would you prefer?

Solution to Exercise 14–1:

1. a. The amount that must be invested now would be the present value of the $4,000, using a discount rate of 8 percent. From Table 14–3 in Appendix B, the factor for a discount rate of 8 percent for 12 periods is 0.397. Multiplying this discount factor times the $4,000 needed in 12 years will give the amount of the present investment required: $4,000 × 0.397 = $1,588.

    b. We will proceed as we did in *(a)* above, but this time we will use a discount rate of 12 percent. From Table 14–3 in Appendix B, the factor for a discount rate of 12 percent for 12 periods is 0.257. Multiplying this discount factor times the $4,000 needed in 12 years will give the amount of the present investment required: $4,000 × 0.257 = $1,028.

    Notice that as the discount rate (desired rate of return) increases, the present value decreases.

2. This part differs from (1) above in that we are now dealing with an annuity rather than with a single future sum. The amount that must be invested now will be the present value of the $1,000 needed at the end of each year for five years. Since we are dealing with an annuity, or a series of cash flows, we must refer to Table 14–4 in Appendix B for the appropriate discount factor.

    a. From Table 14–4 in Appendix B, the discount factor for 8 percent for five periods is 3.993. Therefore, the amount that must be invested now in order to have $1,000 available at the end of each year for five years is: $1,000 × 3.993 = $3,993.

    b. From Table 14–4 in Appendix B, the discount factor for 12 percent for five periods is 3.605. Therefore, the amount that must be invested now in order to have $1,000 available at the end of each year for five years is: $1,000 × 3.605 = $3,605.

    Again notice that as the discount rate (desired rate of return) increases, the present value decreases. This is logical, since at a higher rate of return we would expect to have to invest less than would have to be invested if a lower rate of return were being earned.

3. For this part we will need to refer to both Tables 14–3 and 14–4 in Appendix B. From Table 14–3, we will need to find the discount factor for 12 percent

for 10 periods, then apply it to the $20,000 lump sum to be received in 10 years. From Table 14–4, we will need to find the discount factor for 12 percent for 10 periods, then apply it to the series of $1,400 payments to be received over the 10-year period. Whichever alternative has the highest present value is the one that should be selected.

$$\$20,000 \times 0.322 = \$6,440.$$
$$\$1,400 \times 5.650 = \$7,910.$$

Thus, you would prefer to receive the $1,400 per year for 10 years, rather than the $20,000 lump sum.

E14–2. Consider each of the following situations independently:

1. In three years, when he is discharged from the Air Force, Steve wants to buy a power boat that will cost $8,000. What lump-sum amount must he invest now in order to have the $8,000 at the end of three years if he can invest money at:
   a. Ten percent?
   b. Fourteen percent?
2. Annual cash inflows that will arise from two competing investment projects are given below.

	Investment	
Year	A	B
1	$ 3,000	$12,000
2	6,000	9,000
3	9,000	6,000
4	12,000	3,000
	$30,000	$30,000

Each investment project will require the same investment outlay. You can invest money at an 18 percent rate of return. Compute the present value of the cash flows for each investment.

3. Julie has just retired. Her company's retirement program has two options as to how retirement benefits can be received. Under the first option, Julie would receive a lump sum of $150,000 immediately as her full retirement benefit. Under the second option, she would receive $14,000 each year for 20 years plus a lump-sum payment of $60,000 at the end of the 20-year period. If she can invest money at 12 percent, which option would you recommend that she accept? (Use present value analysis.)

E14–3. Each of the following parts is independent.

1. The Atlantic Medical Clinic can purchase a new computer system that will save $7,000 annually in billing costs. The computer system will last for eight years and have only a nominal salvage value, which can be ignored. What is the maximum purchase price that the Atlantic Medical Clinic would be willing to pay for the new computer system if the clinic's required rate of return is:
   a. Sixteen percent?
   b. Twenty percent?

2. The Caldwell Herald newspaper reported the following story:

    Frank Ormsby of Caldwell is the state's newest millionaire. By choosing the six winning numbers on last week's state lottery, Mr. Ormsby has won the week's grand prize totaling $1.6 million. The State Lottery Commission has indicated that Mr. Ormsby will receive his prize in 20 annual installments of $80,000 each.

    a. If Mr. Ormsby can invest money at a 12 percent rate of return, what is the present value of his winnings?
    b. Is it correct to say that Mr. Ormsby is the "state's newest millionaire"? Explain your answer.

3. Fraser Company will need a new warehouse in five years. The warehouse will cost $500,000 to build. What lump-sum amount should the company invest now in order to have the $500,000 available at the end of the five-year period? Assume that the company can invest money at:
    a. Ten percent.
    b. Fourteen percent.

E14–4. Complete the following cases:
1. Preston Company requires a minimum return of 14 percent on all investments. The company can purchase a new machine at a cost of $84,900. The new machine would generate cash inflows of $15,000 per year and have a 12-year useful life with no salvage value. Compute the machine's net present value. (Use the format shown in Exhibit 14–3.) Is the machine an acceptable investment? Explain.
2. The Walton Daily News is investigating the purchase of a new auxiliary press that has a projected life of 18 years. It is estimated that the new press will save $30,000 per year in cash operating costs. If the new press costs $217,500, what is its time-adjusted rate of return? Is the press an acceptable investment if the company's cost of capital is 16 percent? Explain.
3. Refer to the data above for the Walton Daily News. How much would the annual cash inflows (costs savings) have to be in order for the new press to provide the required 16 percent rate of return? (Round your answer to the nearest whole dollar.)

E14–5. Kathy Myers frequently purchases stocks and bonds, but she is uncertain how to determine the rate of return that she is earning. For example, on January 2, 19x1, she paid $13,000 for 200 shares of the common stock of Malti Company. She received a $420 cash dividend on the stock each year for three years. At the end of three years, she sold the stock for $16,000. Kathy would like to earn a return of at least 14 percent on all of her investments. She is not sure whether the Malti Company stock provided a 14 percent return and would like some help with the necessary computations.

Required: By use of the net present value method, determine whether or not the Malti Company stock provided a 14 percent return. Use the general format illustrated in Exhibit 14–3, and round all computations to the nearest whole dollar.

E14–6. Henrie's Drapery Service is investigating the purchase of a new machine for cleaning and blocking drapes. The machine would cost $130,400, including invoice cost, freight, and installation. Henrie's has estimated that the new machine would increase the company's cash inflows, net of expenses, by $25,000 per year. The machine would have a 10-year useful life and no salvage value.

Required:
1. Compute the machine's time-adjusted rate of return. (Do not round your computations.)
2. Compute the machine's net present value. Use a discount rate of 14 percent, and use the format shown in Exhibit 14–7. Why do you have a zero net present value? If the company's cost of capital is 10 percent, is this an acceptable investment? Explain.
3. Suppose that the new machine would increase the company's annual cash inflows, net of expenses, by only $22,500 per year. Under these conditions, compute the time-adjusted rate of return. Interpolate as needed, and round your final answer to the nearest tenth of a percent.

E14–7. Wendell's Donut Shoppe is investigating the purchase of a new donut-making machine. The new machine would permit the company to reduce the amount of part-time help needed, at a cost savings of $3,800 per year. In addition, the new machine would allow the company to produce one new style of donut, resulting in the sale of at least 1,000 dozen more donuts each year. The company realizes a contribution margin of $1.20 per dozen donuts sold. The new machine would cost $18,600 and have a six-year useful life.

Required:
1. What would be the total annual cash inflows associated with the new machine for capital budgeting purposes?
2. Compute the time-adjusted rate of return promised by the new machine. Interpolate, and round your final answer to the nearest tenth of a percent.
3. In addition to the data given above, assume that the machine will have a $9,125 salvage value at the end of six years. Under these conditions, compute the time-adjusted rate of return to the nearest *whole* percent. (Hint: You may find it helpful to use the net present value approach; find the discount rate that will cause the net present value to be closest to zero. Use the format shown in Exhibit 14–6.)

E14–8. Labeau Products has $35,000 to invest. The company is trying to decide between two alternative uses for the funds. The alternatives are:

	Invest in project X	Invest in project Y
Investment required	$35,000	$ 35,000
Annual cash inflows	9,000	—
Single cash inflow at the end of 10 years.	—	150,000
Life of the project	10 years	10 years

The company's cost of capital is 18 percent.

Required: Which alternative would you recommend that the company accept? (Use the net present value method and the format shown in Exhibit 14–6. Prepare a separate computation for each alternative.)

E14–9. Perot Industries has $100,000 to invest. The company is trying to decide between two alternative uses of the funds. The alternatives are:

	Project	
	A	**B**
Cost of equipment required	$100,000	—
Working capital investment required	—	$100,000
Annual cash inflows	21,000	16,000
Salvage value of equipment in six years . . .	8,000	—
Life of the project	6 years	6 years

The working capital needed for project B will be released at the end of six years for investment elsewhere. Perot Industries' cost of capital is 14 percent.

Required: Which investment alternative (if either) would you recommend that the company accept? Show all computations using the net present value format. (Prepare a separate computation for each project.)

E14–10. Solve the three following present value exercises.

1. The Cambro Foundation, a nonprofit organization, is planning to invest $104,950 in a project that will last for three years. The project will provide cash inflows as follows:

Year 1 . . . . . $30,000
Year 2   40,000
Year 3 . . . . .   ?

Assuming that the project will yield exactly a 12 percent rate of return, what is the expected cash inflow for year 3?

2. The Alpine Resort Hotel has just invested in a project that is expected to provide cost savings as follows over the next four years (the expected life of the project):

Year 1 . . . $5,000   Year 3 . . . $10,000
Year 2 . . .   8,000   Year 4 . . .   13,000

If the project has a $4,090 positive net present value when using a 16 percent discount rate, what was the amount of the original investment?

3. The Matchless Dating Service has made an investment in video and recording equipment that cost $106,700. The equipment is expected to generate cash inflows of $20,000 per year. How many years will the equipment have to be used in order to provide the company with a 10 percent rate of return on its investment?

PROBLEMS

P14–11. **Basic net present value analysis.**   The Sweetwater Candy Company would like to buy a new machine that would automatically "dip" chocolates as they are formed in the production process. The "dipping" operation is currently done largely by hand. The machine the company is considering costs $120,000. The manufacturer estimates that the machine would be usable for 12 years but would require the replacement of several key parts at the end of the sixth year. These parts would cost $9,000, including installation. After 12 years, the machine could be sold for about $7,500.

The company estimates that the cost to operate the machine will be only $7,000 per year. The present method of dipping chocolates costs $30,000 per year. In addition to reducing costs, the new machine will increase production by 6,000 boxes of chocolates per year. The company realizes a contribution margin of $1.50 per box. A 20 percent rate of return is required on all investments.

Required (ignore income taxes):

1. What are the net annual cash inflows that will be provided by the new dipping machine?
2. Compute the new machine's net present value. Use the incremental cost approach, and round all dollar amounts to the nearest whole dollar.

P14–12.   **Basic net present value analysis.**   Dayton Mines, Inc., is contemplating the purchase of equipment to exploit a mineral deposit that is located on land to which the company has mineral rights. An engineering and cost analysis has been made, and it is expected that the following cash flows would be associated with opening and operating a mine in the area:

Cost of new equipment and timbers	$275,000
Working capital required	100,000
Net annual cash receipts	120,000*
Cost to construct new roads in three years . . .	40,000
Salvage value of equipment in four years . . .	65,000

*Receipts from sales of ore, less out-of-pocket costs for salaries, utilities, insurance, and so forth.

It is estimated that the mineral deposit would be exhausted after four years of mining. At that point, the working capital would be released for reinvestment elsewhere. The company's cost of capital is 20 percent.

Required (ignore income taxes):

Determine the net present value of the proposed mining project. Should the project be undertaken? Explain.

P14–13.   **Time-adjusted rate of return; sensitivity analysis.**   Big Piney Lumber Company is investigating the purchase of a new laser saw that has just come onto the market. It would cost $300,000 but would save $40,000 per year in operating costs (primarily through less waste and reduced labor costs). If the new saw were purchased, present equipment could be sold to another mill for $65,000. The manufacturer estimates that the laser saw would have a service life of 12 years.

Required (ignore income taxes):

1. What would be the net initial (incremental) cost of the new saw for capital budgeting purposes?
2. Using the investment cost figure computed in (1) above, compute the time-adjusted rate of return on the new saw. Interpolate, and round your answer to the nearest tenth of a percent.
3. Since laser saws have just come onto the market, Big Piney's management is unsure about the estimated 12-year life. Compute what the time-adjusted rate of return would be if the useful life of the new saw were (a) 9 years and (b) 15 years, instead of 12 years. Again interpolate, and round your answer to the nearest tenth of a percent.
4. Refer to the original data. Technology in the laser saw industry is moving so rapidly that management may not want to keep the new saw for more than six years. If the new saw were disposed of at the end of six years, it would have a salvage value of $107,800.

    a. Again using the investment figure computed in (1) above, compute the time-adjusted rate of return to the nearest *whole* percent. (Hint: A useful way to proceed is to find the discount rate that will cause the net present value to be equal to, or near, zero.)

    b. If the company's cost of capital is 10 percent, would you recommend purchase? Explain.

P14–14. **Basic net present value analysis.** "I'm not sure we should lay out $380,000 for that new electronic welding machine," said Jim Alder, president of the Superior Equipment Company. "That's a lot of money, and it would cost us another $3,000 every month just to maintain the thing. In addition, the manufacturer admits that it would cost $45,000 more at the end of seven years to replace worn out parts."

"I admit it's a lot of money," said Franci Rogers, the controller. "But you know the turnover problem we've had with the welding crew. This machine would replace six welders at a cost savings of $108,000 per year. And we would save another $6,500 per year in reduced material waste. When you figure that the electronic welder would last for 12 years, that adds up to a pile of savings. I'm sure the return would be greater than our 16 percent cost of capital."

"I'm still not convinced," countered Mr. Alder. "We can only get $12,000 scrap value out of our old welding equipment if we sell it now, and all that new machine will be worth in 12 years is $20,000 for parts. But have your people work up the figures and we'll talk about them at the executive committee meeting tomorrow."

Required (ignore income taxes):

1. Compute the net annual cost savings promised by the new welding machine.
2. Using the data from (1) above and other data from the problem, compute the new machine's net present value. (Use the incremental-cost approach.) Would you recommend purchase? Explain.

P14–15. **Opening a small business; net present value.** In eight years, Kent Duncan will retire. He has $150,000 to invest, and he is exploring the possibility of opening a self-service auto wash. The auto wash could be managed in the free time he has available from his regular occupation, and it could be closed easily when he retires. After careful study, Mr. Duncan has determined the following:

    a. A building in which an auto wash could be installed is available under an eight-year lease at a cost of $1,700 per month.

    b. Purchase and installation costs of equipment would total $150,000. In eight years the equipment could be sold for about 10 percent of its original cost.

    c. An investment of an additional $2,000 would be required to cover working capital needs for cleaning supplies, change funds, and so forth. After eight years, this working capital would be released for investment elsewhere.

    d. Both an auto wash and a vacuum service would be offered, with a wash costing $1.50 and the vacuum costing 25 cents per use.

    e. The only variable costs associated with the operation would be 23 cents per wash for water and 10 cents per use of the vacuum for electricity.

    f. In addition to rent, monthly costs of operation would be: cleaning, $450; insurance, $75; and maintenance, $500.

    g. Gross receipts from the auto wash would be about $1,350 per week. According to the experience of other auto washes, 70 percent of the customers using the wash would also use the vacuum.

Mr. Duncan will not open the auto wash unless it provides at least a 10 percent return, since this is the amount that could be earned by simply placing the $150,000 in high-grade securities.

Required (ignore income taxes):

1. Assuming that the auto wash will be open 52 weeks a year, compute the expected net annual cash receipts (gross cash receipts less cash disbursements) from its operation. (Do not include the cost of the equipment, the working capital, or the salvage value in these computations.)
2. Would you advise Mr. Duncan to open the car wash? Show computations using the net present value method of investment analysis. Round all dollar figures to the nearest whole dollar.

P14–16. **Time-adjusted rate of return; sensitivity analysis.** ''In my opinion, a tanning salon would be a natural addition to our spa and very popular with our customers,'' said Stacey Winder, manager of the Lifeline Spa. ''Our figures show that we could remodel the building next door to our spa and install all of the necessary equipment for $330,000. I have contacted tanning salons in other areas, and I am told that the tanning beds will be usable for about nine years. I am also told that a four-bed salon such as we are planning would generate a cash inflow of about $80,000 per year after all expenses.''

''It does sound very appealing,'' replied Kevin Leblanc, the spa's accountant. ''Let me push the numbers around a bit and see what kind of a return the salon would generate.''

Required (ignore income taxes):

1. Compute the time-adjusted rate of return promised by the tanning salon. Interpolate to the nearest tenth of a percent.
2. Assume that Ms. Winder will not open the salon unless it promises a return of at least 14 percent. Compute the amount of annual cash inflow that would provide this return on the $330,000 investment.
3. Although nine years is the average life of tanning salon equipment, Ms. Winder has found that this life can vary substantially. Compute the time-adjusted rate of return if the life were *(a)* 6 years, and *(b)* 12 years, rather than 9 years. Interpolate to the nearest tenth of a percent. Is there any information provided by these computations that you would be particularly anxious to show Ms. Winder?
4. Ms. Winder has also found that although $80,000 is an average cash inflow from a four-bed salon, some salons vary as much as 20 percent from this figure. Compute the time-adjusted rate of return if the annual cash inflows were *(a)* 20 percent less, and *(b)* 20 percent greater, than $80,000. Interpolate to the nearest tenth of a percent.
5. Assume that the $330,000 investment is made and that the salon is opened as planned. Because of concerns about the effects of excessive tanning, however, the salon is not able to attract as many customers as planned. Cash inflows are only $50,000 per year, and after eight years the salon equipment is sold to a competitor for $135,440. Compute the time-adjusted rate of return (to the nearest *whole* percent) earned on the investment over the eight-year period. (Hint: A useful way to proceed is to find the discount rate that will cause the net present value to be equal to, or near, zero.)

P14–17. **Replacement decision.** Redwing Freightlines, Inc., has a small truck that it uses for intracity deliveries. The truck is in bad repair and must be either overhauled or replaced with a new truck. The company has assembled the following information:

	Present truck	New truck
Purchase cost new.	$21,000	$30,000
Remaining book value	11,500	—
Overhaul needed now	7,000	—
Annual cash operating costs	10,000	6,500
Salvage value—now	9,000	—
Salvage value—eight years from now. . .	1,000	4,000

If the company keeps and overhauls its present delivery truck, then the truck will be usable for eight more years. If a new truck is purchased, it will be used for eight years, after which it will be traded in on another truck. The new truck would be diesel-operated, resulting in a substantial reduction in annual operating costs, as shown above.

The company computes depreciation on a straight-line basis. All investment projects are evaluated on a basis of a 16 percent before-tax rate of return.

Required (ignore income taxes):

1. Should Redwing Freightlines, Inc., keep the old truck or purchase the new one? Use the total-cost approach to net present value in making your decision. Round to the nearest whole dollar.
2. Redo (1) above, this time using the incremental-cost approach.

P14–18.   **Net present value analysis of securities.**   In late 19x1, Linda Clark received $175,000 from her mother's estate. She placed the funds into the hands of a broker, who purchased the following securities on Linda's behalf:

a. Common stock was purchased at a cost of $95,000. The stock paid no dividends, but it was sold for $160,000 at the end of three years.

b. Preferred stock was purchased at its par value of $30,000. The stock paid a 6 percent dividend (based on par value) each year for three years. At the end of three years, the stock was sold for $27,000.

c. Bonds were purchased at a cost of $50,000. The bonds paid $3,000 in interest every six months. After three years, the bonds were sold for $52,700. (Note: In discounting a cash flow that occurs semiannually, the procedure is to halve the discount rate and double the number of periods. Use the same procedure in discounting the proceeds from the sale.)

The securities were all sold at the end of three years so that Linda would have funds available to open a new business venture. The broker stated that the investments had earned more than a 16 percent return, and he gave Linda the following computation to support his statement:

Common stock:	
Gain on sale ($160,000 − $95,000)	$65,000
Preferred stock:	
Dividends paid (6% × $30,000 × 3 years) . . .	5,400
Loss on sale ($27,000 − $30,000)	(3,000)
Bonds:	
Interest paid ($3,000 × 6 periods)	18,000
Gain on sale ($52,700 − $50,000)	2,700
Net gain on all investments	$88,100

$$\frac{\$88,100 \div 3\ \text{years}}{\$175,000} = 16.8\%$$

1. Using a 16 percent discount rate, compute the net present value of *each* of the three investments. On which investment(s) did Linda earn a 16 percent rate of return? (Round computations to the nearest whole dollar.)
2. Considering all three investments together, did Linda earn a 16 percent rate of return? Explain.
3. Linda wants to use the $239,700 proceeds ($160,000 + $27,000 + 52,700 = $239,700) from sale of the securities to open a retail store under a 12-year franchise contract. What net annual cash inflow must the store generate in order for Linda to earn a 14 percent return over the 12-year period? (Round computations to the nearest whole dollar.)

P14–19.   Net present value analysis; postaudit of a project.   Saxon Products, Inc., is investigating the purchase of a robot for use on the company's assembly line. Selected data relating to the robot are provided below:

Cost of the robot	$375,000
Installation costs	18,000
Annual savings in labor costs	?
Annual increase in power and	
maintenance costs.	17,500
Salvage value in 10 years	5,000
Useful life	10 years

A number of workers can be discharged if the robot is purchased, resulting in a reduction of 15,000 hours in labor time worked annually. The labor rate is $8 per hour. The company's cost of capital is 20 percent.

1. Determine the net annual cost savings if the robot is purchased. (Do not include intallation costs and salvage value in this computation.)
2. Compute the net present value of the proposed investment in the robot. Would you recommend that the robot be purchased? Explain.
3. Assume that the robot is purchased. At the end of the first year, the cost analyst who prepared the data above tells you that some items haven't worked out as planned. The installation costs were $20,000, due to unforeseen problems; the maintenance and power costs are $500 more per year than the amount planned; and the company has been able to reduce labor time by only 13,500 hours per year, rather than 15,000 hours as planned. Assuming that all the other items of cost data were accurate, did the company make a wise investment? Show computations, using the net present value format as in (2) above. (Hint: It might be helpful to place yourself back at the beginning of the first year, with the new data.)
4. If labor costs increase to $9 per hour, will this make the new robot more or less desirable? Explain. No computations are necessary.

P14–20.   Lease or buy decision.   The Riteway Ad Agency provides cars for its sales staff. In the past, the company has always purchased its cars outright from a dealer and then sold the cars after three years' use. The company's present fleet of cars is three years old and will be sold very shortly. In order to provide a replacement fleet, the company is considering two alternatives:

Alternative 1.   The company can purchase the cars outright, as in the past, and sell the cars after three years' use. Twenty cars will be needed, which can be purchased at a discounted price of $8,500 each. If this alternative is accepted, the following costs will be incurred on the fleet as a whole:

Annual cost of servicing,
taxes, and licensing $3,000
Repairs, first year 1,500
Repairs, second year 4,000
Repairs, third year 6,000

At the end of three years, the fleet could be sold for about one half of the original purchase price.

Alternative 2. The company can lease the cars under a three-year lease contract. The lease cost would be $55,000 per year (the first payment due in year 1). As part of this lease cost, the owner would provide all servicing and repairs, license the cars, and pay all taxes. Riteway would be required to make a $10,000 security deposit at the beginning of the lease period, which would be refunded when the cars were returned to the owner at the end of the lease contract.

Required (ignore income taxes):

1. Assume that the Riteway Ad Agency has an 18 percent cost of capital. Use the total-cost approach to determine the present value of the cash flows associated with each alternative. (Round all dollar amounts to the nearest whole dollar.) Which alternative should the company accept?
2. Using the data in (1) and other data as needed, explain why it is often less costly for a company to lease equipment and facilities rather than to buy them.

P14–21. **Equipment replacement decision.** Birney Products, Ltd., purchased a new glazing machine a year ago at a cost of $35,000. The machine will last the company 10 more years, after which it is expected to have a salvage value of about $2,000. Birney Products has just been approached by a sales representative selling a highly innovative computer-aided machine that costs $90,000. The computer-aided machine could increase the company's output by about 10 percent, while at the same time reduce per unit costs. Birney's engineering department has prepared the following comparative cost and revenue data (per year):

	Present machine	Computer-aided machine
Revenues from sales	$200,000	$220,000
Less expenses:		
Materials and supplies.	114,000	109,000
Maintenance of machine	9,000	21,000
—Depreciation of machine	3,000	8,400
Labor	60,000	52,000
Total expenses	186,000	190,400
Net income	$ 14,000	$ 29,600

The computer-aided machine would have a service life of 10 years, after which it would have a salvage value of $6,000. The machine now being used has a book value of $32,000, but it can be sold for only $10,000 due to the presence of the computer-aided machine on the market.

Birney Products' management is doubtful that the new machine would provide a return as great as the company's 16 percent cost of capital, due to the machine's high cost and the low resale value of the machine currently being used.

Required (ignore income taxes):

1. Use the total-cost approach to discounted cash flow analysis to determine whether the company should purchase the new machine.
2. Repeat the computations in (1), this time using the incremental-cost approach.

P14–22.   **Rental property decision.**   Raul Martinas, professor of languages at Eastern University, owns a small office building adjacent to the university campus. He acquired the property 10 years ago at a total cost of $530,000—$50,000 for the land and $480,000 for the building. He has just received an offer from a realty company that wants to purchase the property; however, the property has been a good source of income over the years, so Professor Martinas is unsure whether he should keep it or sell it. His alternatives are:

Keep the property.   Professor Martinas' accountant has kept careful records of the income realized from the property over the past 10 years. These records indicate the following annual revenues and expenses:

Rental receipts		$140,000
Less building expenses:		
Utilities	$25,000	
Depreciation of building	16,000	
Property taxes and insurance . . .	18,000	
Repairs and maintenance	9,000	
Custodial help and supplies . . .	40,000	108,000
Net income		$ 32,000

Professor Martinas makes a $12,000 mortgage payment each year on the property. The mortgage will be paid off in eight more years. He has been depreciating the building by the straight-line method, assuming a salvage value of $80,000 for the building which he still thinks is an appropriate figure. He feels sure that the building can be rented for another 15 years. He also feels sure that 15 years from now the land will be worth three times what he paid for it.

Sell the property.   A realty company has offered to purchase the property by paying $175,000 immediately and $26,500 per year for the next 15 years. Control of the property would go to the realty company immediately. In order to sell the property, Professor Martinas would need to pay the mortgage off, which could be done by making a lump-sum payment of $90,000.

Required (ignore income taxes):

Assume that Professor Martinas requires a 12 percent rate of return. Would you recommend he keep or sell the property? Show computations using discounted cash flow and the total-cost approach.

P14–23.   **Accept or reject a new product line.**   Matheson Electronics has just developed a new electronic device which, when mounted on an automobile, will tell the driver how many miles the automobile is going per gallon of gasoline. The device can be mounted on any model or make of automobile in a few minutes' time, and with negligible cost.

The company is anxious to begin production of the new device. To this end, marketing and cost studies have been made to determine probable costs and market potential. These studies have provided the following information.

a.   New equipment would have to be acquired in order to produce the device. The equipment would cost $315,000 and have a 12-year useful life. After 12 years, it would have a salvage value of about $15,000.

b.   Sales in units over the next 12 years are projected to be as follows:

Year	Sales in units
1.	6,000
2.	12,000
3.	15,000
4–12	18,000

c. Production and sales of the device would require working capital of $60,000 in order to finance accounts receivable, inventories, and day-to-day cash needs. This working capital would be released at the end of the project's life.

d. The devices would sell for $35 each; variable costs for production, administration, and sales would be $15 per unit.

e. Fixed costs for salaries, maintenance, property taxes, insurance, and straight-line depreciation on the equipment would total $135,000 per year. (Depreciation is based on cost less salvage value.)

f. In order to gain rapid entry into the market, the company would have to advertise heavily. The advertising program would be:

Year	Amount of yearly advertising
1–2 . . .	$180,000
3	150,000
4–12 . . .	120,000

g. Matheson Electronics' Board of Directors has specified that all new product lines must promise a return of at least 14 percent in order to be acceptable.

Required (ignore income taxes):

1. Compute the net cash inflow (cash receipts less yearly cash operating expenses) anticipated from sale of the device for each year over the next 12 years.

2. Using the data computed from (1) above and other data provided in the problem, determine the net present value of the proposed investment. Would you recommend that Matheson accept the device as a new product line?

P14–24.   **Expansion decision; net present value; postaudit of a project.**   Romano's Pizzas, Inc., operates pizza shops in several states. One of the company's most profitable shops is located adjacent to the campus of a large university. A small bakery next to the shop has just gone out of business, and Romano's Pizzas has an opportunity to lease the vacated space for $18,000 per year under a 15-year lease. Romano's management is considering two ways in which the available space might be used.

Alternative 1.   The pizza shop in this location is currently selling 40,000 pizzas per year. Management is confident that sales could be increased by 75 percent by taking out the wall between the pizza shop and the vacant space and expanding the pizza outlet. Costs for remodeling and for new equipment would be $550,000. Management estimates that 20 percent of the new sales would be small pizzas, 50 percent would be medium pizzas, and 30 percent would be large pizzas. Selling prices and costs for ingredients for the three sizes of pizzas follow (per pizza):

	Selling price	Cost of ingredients
Small	$ 6.70	$1.30
Medium	8.90	2.40
Large	11.00	3.10

An additional $7,500 of working capital would be needed to carry the larger volume of business. This working capital would be released at the end of the lease term. The equipment would have a salvage value of $30,000 in 15 years, when the lease ended.

Alternative 2.   Romano's sales manager feels that the company needs to diversify its operations. He has suggested that an opening be cut in the wall between the pizza shop and the vacant space and that video games be placed in the space, along with a small snack bar. Costs for remodeling and for the snack bar facilities would cost $290,000. The games would be leased from a large distributor of such equipment. The distributor has stated that, based on the use of game centers elsewhere, Romano's could expect about 26,000 people to use the center each year and to spend an average of $5 each on the machines. In addition, it is estimated that the snack bar would provide a net cash inflow of $15,000 per year. An investment of $4,000 in working capital would be needed to provide change funds and to provide inventory for the snack bar. This working capital investment would be released at the end of the lease term. The snack bar equipment would have a salvage value of about $12,000 in 15 years.

Romano's management is unsure which alternative to select and has asked you to help in making the decision. You have gathered the following information relating to added costs that would be incurred each year under the two alternatives:

	Expand the pizza shop	Install the game center
Rent—building space	$18,000	$18,000
Rent—video games	—	30,000
Salaries.	54,000	17,000
Utilities	13,200	5,400
Insurance and other	7,800	9,600

Required (ignore income taxes):

1. Compute the expected net *annual* cash inflow from each alternative (cash receipts from sales and games less related cash expenses). Do *not* include present sales from the pizza shop in this computation.

2. Assume that the company's cost of capital is 16 percent. Compute the net present value of each alternative. (Use the total-cost approach, and round all dollar amounts to the nearest whole dollar.) Which alternative would you recommend?

3. Assume that the company decides to accept alternative 2. At the end of the first year, the company finds that only 21,000 people used the game center during the year (each person spent $5 on games). Also the snack bar provided a net cash inflow of only $13,000. In light of this information, does it appear that the game center will provide the company's 16 percent required rate of return? Show computations to support your answer. (Hint: It might be useful to go back to the beginning of the first year under alternative 2, with the new information.)

4. The sales manager has suggested that an advertising program be initiated to draw another 5,000 people into the game center each year. Assuming that another 5,000 people can be attracted into the center and that the snack bar receipts increase to the level originally estimated, how much can be spent on

advertising each year and still allow the game center to provide a 16 percent rate of return?

P14–25.   **Equipment acquisition; uneven cash flows.**   Kingsley Products, Ltd., is using a single model 400 shaping machine in the manufacture of one of its products. The company is expecting to have a large increase in demand for the product and is anxious to expand its productive capacity. Two possibilities are under consideration:

> *Alternative 1.*   Purchase another model 400 shaping machine to operate along with the currently owned model 400 machine.

> *Alternative 2.*   Purchase a model 800 shaping machine and use the currently owned model 400 machine as standby equipment. The model 800 machine is a high-speed unit with double the capacity of the model 400 machine.

The following additional information is available on the two alternatives:

a.   Both the model 400 machine and the model 800 machine have a 10-year life from the time they are first used in production. The scrap value of both machines is nominal and can be ignored. Straight-line depreciation is used.

b.   The cost of a new model 800 machine is $300,000.

c.   The model 400 machine now in use cost $160,000 three years ago. Its present book value is $112,000, and its present market value is $90,000.

d.   A new model 400 machine costs $170,000 now. If the company decides not to buy the model 800 machine, then the currently owned model 400 machine will have to be replaced in seven years at a cost of $200,000. The replacement machine will have a market value of about $140,000 when it is three years old.

e.   Production over the next 10 years is expected to be:

Year	Production in units
1.	40,000
2.	60,000
3.	80,000
4–10	90,000

f.   The two models of machines are not equally efficient in output. Comparative variable costs per unit are:

	Model 400	Model 800
Materials per unit	$0.25	$0.40
Direct labor per unit	0.49	0.16
Supplies and lubricants per unit . . .	0.06	0.04
Total variable cost per unit	$0.80	$0.60

g.   The model 400 machine is less costly to maintain than the model 800 machine. Annual repairs and maintenance on a single model 400 machine are $2,500.

h.   Repairs and maintenance on a model 800 machine, with a model 400 machine used as standby, would total $3,800 per year.

i.   No other factory costs will change as a result of the decision between the two machines.

j.   Kingsley Products requires a before-tax rate of return of 20 percent on all investments.

Required (ignore income taxes):

1. Which alternative should the company choose? Show computations using discounted cash flow.
2. Suppose that the cost of labor increases by 10 percent. Would this make the model 800 machine more or less desirable? Explain. No computations are needed.
3. Suppose that the cost of materials doubles. Would this make the model 800 machine more or less desirable? Explain. No computations are needed.

CASES

C14–26 **Lease or buy decision.** Top-Quality Stores, Inc., owns a nationwide chain of supermarkets. The company is going to open another store soon, and a suitable building site has been located in an attractive and rapidly growing area. In discussing how the company can acquire the desired building and other facilities needed to open the new store, Sam Watkins, the company's vice president in charge of sales, stated, "I know most of our competitors are starting to lease facilities, rather than buy, but I just can't see the economics of it. Our development people tell me that we can buy the building site, put a building on it, and get all the store fixtures we need for just $850,000. They also say that property taxes, insurance, and repairs would run $20,000 a year. When you figure that we plan to keep a site for 18 years, that's a total cost of $1,210,000. But then when you realize that the property will be worth at least a half million in 18 years, that's a net cost to us of only $710,000. What would it cost to lease the property?"

"I understand that Beneficial Insurance Company is willing to purchase the building site, construct a building and install fixtures to our specifications, and then lease the facility to us for 18 years at an annual lease payment of $120,000," replied Lisa Coleman, the company's executive vice president.

"That's just my point," said Sam. "At $120,000 a year, it would cost us a cool $2,160,000 over the 18 years. That's three times what it would cost to buy, and what would we have left at the end? Nothing! The building would belong to the insurance company!"

"You're overlooking a few things," replied Lisa. "For one thing, the treasurer's office says that we could only afford to put $350,000 down if we buy the property, and then we would have to pay the other $500,000 off over four years at $175,000 a year. So there would be some interest involved on the purchase side that you haven't figured in."

"But that little bit of interest is nothing compared to over 2 million bucks for leasing," said Sam. "Also, if we lease I understand we would have to put up an $8,000 security deposit that we wouldn't get back until the end. And besides that, we would still have to pay all the yearly repairs and maintenance costs just like we owned the property. No wonder those insurance companies are so rich, if they can swing deals like this."

"Well, I'll admit that I don't have all the figures sorted out yet," replied Lisa. "But I do have the operating cost breakdown for the building, which includes $7,500 annually for property taxes, $8,000 for insurance, and $4,500 for repairs and maintenance. If we lease, Beneficial will handle its own insurance costs and of course the owner will have to pay the property taxes. I'll put all this together and see if leasing makes any sense with our 16 percent cost of capital. The president wants a presentation and recommendation in the executive committee meeting tomorrow. Let's see, development said the first lease payment would be due now and the remaining ones due in years 1–17. Development also said that this store should generate a net cash inflow of $300,000 per year, which is exactly 20 percent more than the average for our stores.''

Required (ignore income taxes):

1. By means of discounted cash flow, determine whether Top-Quality Stores, Inc., should lease or buy the new facility. Assume that you will be making your presentation before the company's executive committee, and remember that the president detests sloppy, disorganized reports.
2. What reply will you make in the meeting if Sam Watkins brings up the issue of the building's future sale value?

P14–27.   **Equipment financing decision.**   Middle University is a state supported, tax-exempt institution. The university has decided to replace the computer that is being used for Middleton's financial and administrative applications. The current computer is over eight years old and can no longer serve the university's needs adequately.

Donald Abel, vice president of finance, prepared the analysis of the proposed computer that was submitted to Middleton's Board of Regents. The analysis indicated that the new computer would provide the university with annual cost savings of $400,000, excluding the computer's maintenance and insurance. The proposed computer would cost $1,000,000 and have an economic life of five years. The vendor has assured Abel that the computer could be sold for $70,000 after five years. The annual maintenance and insurance costs are estimated to be $50,000.

Abel and the Board of Regents are convinced that the proposed computer is justified. The new computer will provide substantial cost savings. Furthermore, it will meet the university's needs and provide other benefits that cannot be quantified. How to finance the computer acquisition is the only decision left to be made on this project.

Abel has narrowed the financing decision down to two alternatives. The first financing alternative available to Abel is to borrow the money from a commercial bank to purchase the computer. Commerce Bank would give Middleton a five-year $1,000,000 loan at an annual interest rate of 14 percent. The bank would require the interest to be paid annually at the end of each year with the principal amount due at maturity.

The second financing alternative Abel is considering is a proposal from DataBit, a computer leasing company. DataBit would lease the proposed computer to Middleton under a five-year operating lease arrangement. The lease arrangement would call for rental payments at the beginning of each year starting with $340,000 at the beginning of the first year and decreasing by $40,000 in each of the subsequent four years.

Regardless of its decision to borrow or lease, Middleton would be responsible for paying the maintenance and insurance on the new computer. Abel believes that the university's opportunity investment rate is 12 percent.

Required (ignore income taxes):

1. By use of discounted cash flow, prepare an analysis that will show which computer financing arrangement—borrowing from Commerce Bank or leasing from DataBit—will be better for Middleton University. Be prepared to defend your analysis in class.
2. Identify factors other than the cost of financing that Middleton University should consider when making the lease-versus-borrow decision.

(CMA, Adapted)

CHAPTER 15

Further Aspects of Investment Decisions

LEARNING OBJECTIVES

After studying Chapter 15, you should be able to:

- Compute the after-tax cost of a tax-deductible cash expense and the after-tax benefit from a taxable cash receipt.

- Explain how depreciation deductions are computed under the Accelerated Cost Recovery System (ACRS).

- Compute the tax savings arising from the depreciation tax shield, using both the ACRS tables and the optional straight-line method.

- Compute the after-tax net present value of an investment proposal.

- Determine the profitability index for an investment proposal.

- Rank investment projects in order of preference under both the time-adjusted rate of return and net present value methods.

- Determine the payback period for an investment, using the payback formula.

- Determine the simple rate of return for an investment, using the simple rate of return formula.

- Define or explain the key terms listed at the end of the chapter.

e continue our discussion of capital budgeting in this chapter by focusing on three new topics. First, we focus on income taxes and their impact on the capital budgeting decision. Second, we focus on methods of ranking competing capital investment projects according to their relative desirability. And third, we focus on methods of making capital budgeting decisions, other than discounted cash flow.

INCOME TAXES AND CAPITAL BUDGETING

In our discussion of capital budgeting in the preceding chapter, the matter of income taxes was omitted for two reasons. First, many organizations have no taxes to pay. Such organizations include schools, hospitals, and governmental units on local, state, and national levels. These organizations will always use capital budgeting techniques on a before-tax basis, as illustrated in the preceding chapter. Second, the topic of capital budgeting is somewhat complex, and it is best absorbed in small doses. Now that we have laid a solid groundwork in the concepts of present value and discounting, we can explore the effects of income taxes on capital budgeting decisions with little difficulty.

The Concept of After-Tax Cost

If someone were to ask you how much the rent is on your apartment, you would probably answer with the dollar amount that you pay out each month. If someone were to ask a business executive how much the rent is on a factory building, he or she might answer by stating a lesser figure than the dollar amount being paid out each month. The reason is that rent is a tax-deductible expense to a business firm, and expenses such as rent are often looked at on an *after-tax* basis rather than on a before-tax basis. The true cost of a tax-deductible item is not the dollars paid out; rather, it is the amount of net cash outflow that results *after* taking into consideration any reduction in income taxes that the payment will bring about. An expenditure net of its tax effect is known as **after-tax cost.**

After-tax cost is not a difficult concept. To illustrate the ideas behind it, assume that two firms, A and B, normally have sales of $850,000 each month and cash expenses of $700,000 each month. Firm A is considering an advertising program that will cost $60,000 each month. The tax rate is 30 percent.[1] What will be the after-tax cost to Firm A of the contemplated $60,000 monthly advertising expenditure? The computations needed to compute the after-tax cost figure are shown in Exhibit 15–1.

---

[1] Under current tax law, the first $50,000 of corporate income is taxed at a 15 percent rate, the next $25,000 is taxed at a 25 percent rate, and any amount over $75,000 is taxed at a 34 percent rate. An additional 5 percent tax is levied on taxable income between $100,000 and $335,000. As a result of this additional tax, corporations with taxable income in excess of $335,000 effectively pay tax at a flat rate of 34 percent. For ease of computations, in this book we use an average corporate tax rate of 30 percent.

EXHIBIT 15–1

The computation of after-tax cost

	Firm A	Firm B
Sales	$850,000	$850,000
Less expenses:		
Salaries, insurance, and other	700,000	700,000
New advertising program	60,000	—
Total expenses	760,000	700,000
Income before taxes	90,000	150,000
Income taxes (30%)	27,000	45,000
Net income	$ 63,000	$105,000
After-tax cost of the new advertising program ($105,000 − $63,000)		$42,000

As shown in the exhibit, the after-tax cost of the advertising program would be only $42,000 per month. This figure must be correct, since it measures the difference in net income between the two companies and since their income statements are identical except for the $60,000 in advertising paid by Firm A. In effect, a $60,000 monthly advertising expenditure would *really* cost Firm A only $42,000 *after taxes*.

A formula can be developed from these data that will give the after-tax cost of *any* tax-deductible cash expense.[2] The formula is:

$$(1 - \text{Tax rate}) \times \text{Cash expense} = \text{After-tax cost (net cash outflow)} \qquad (1)$$

We can prove the accuracy of this formula by applying it to Firm A's $60,000 advertising expenditure:

$$(1 - 0.30) \times \$60,000 = \$42,000 \text{ after-tax cost of the advertising program}$$

The concept of after-tax cost is very useful to the manager, since it measures the *actual* amount of cash that will be leaving a company as a result of an expenditure decision. As we now integrate income taxes into capital budgeting decisions, it will be necessary to place all cash expense items on an after-tax basis by applying the formula above.

The same reasoning applies to revenues and other *taxable* cash receipts. When a cash receipt occurs, the amount of cash inflow realized by an organization will be the amount that remains after taxes have been paid. The **after-tax benefit,** or net cash inflow, realized from a particular cash receipt can be obtained by applying a simple variation of the cash expenditure formula used above:

$$(1 - \text{Tax rate}) \times \text{Cash receipt} = \text{After-tax benefit (net cash inflow)} \qquad (2)$$

---

[2] This formula assumes that a company is operating at a profit; if it is operating at a loss, then the after-tax cost of an item is simply the amount paid, since no tax benefits will be realized.

We emphasize the term *taxable cash receipts* in our discussion because not all cash inflows are taxable. For example, the release of working capital at the termination of an investment project would not be a taxable cash inflow since it simply represents a return of original investment.

The Concept of Depreciation Tax Shield

The point was made in the preceding chapter that depreciation deductions in and of themselves do not involve cash flows. For this reason, depreciation deductions were ignored in Chapter 14 in all discounted cash flow computations.

Even though depreciation deductions do not involve cash flows, they do have an impact on the amount of income taxes that a firm will pay, and income taxes *do* involve cash flows. Therefore, as we now integrate income taxes into capital budgeting decisions, it will be necessary to consider depreciation deductions to the extent that they affect tax payments.

A cash flow comparison   To illustrate the effect of depreciation deductions on tax payments, let us compare two firms, X and Y. Both firms have annual sales of $500,000 and cash operating expenses of $310,000. In addition, Firm X has a depreciable asset on which the depreciation deduction is $90,000 per year. The tax rate is 30 percent. A cash flow comparison of the two firms is given at the bottom of Exhibit 15–2.

Notice from the exhibit that Firm X's net cash inflow exceeds Firm Y's by $27,000. Also notice that in order to obtain Firm X's net cash inflow,

EXHIBIT 15–2

The impact of depreciation deductions on tax payments—a comparison of cash flows

Income Statements	Firm X	Firm Y
Sales	$500,000	$500,000
Expenses:		
Cash operating expenses	310,000	310,000
Depreciation expense	90,000	—
Total	400,000	310,000
Net income before taxes	100,000	190,000
Income taxes (30%)	30,000	57,000
Net income	$ 70,000	$133,000

Cash Flow Comparison		
Cash inflow from operations:		
Net income, as above	$ 70,000	$133,000
Add: Noncash deduction for depreciation	90,000	—
Net cash inflow	$160,000	$133,000
Greater amount of cash available to Firm X	$27,000	

it is necessary to add the $90,000 depreciation deduction back to the company's net income. This step is necessary since depreciation is a noncash deduction on the income statement.

Exhibit 15–2 presents an interesting paradox. Notice that even though Firm X's net cash inflow is $27,000 *greater* than Firm Y's, its net income is much *lower* than Firm Y's (only $70,000, as compared to Firm Y's $133,000). The explanation for this paradox lies in the concept of the *depreciation tax shield*.

The depreciation tax shield   Firm X's greater net cash inflow comes about as a result of the *shield* against tax payments that is provided by depreciation deductions. Although depreciation deductions involve no outflows of cash, they are fully deductible in arriving at taxable income. In effect, depreciation deductions *shield* revenues from taxation and thereby *lower* the amount of taxes that a company must pay.

In the case of Firm X, the $90,000 depreciation deduction taken involved no outflow of cash to the firm. Yet this depreciation was fully deductible on the company's income statement and thereby *shielded* $90,000 in revenues from taxation. Were it not for the depreciation deduction, the company's income taxes would have been $27,000 higher, since the entire $90,000 in shielded revenues would have been taxable at the regular tax rate of 30 percent (30 percent $\times$ $90,000 = $27,000). In effect, the depreciation tax shield *has reduced Firm X's taxes by $27,000,* permitting these funds to be retained within the company rather than going to the tax collector. Viewed another way, we can say that Firm X has realized a $27,000 *cash inflow* (through reduced tax payments) as a result of its $90,000 depreciation deduction.

Because depreciation deductions shield revenues from taxation, they are generally referred to as a **depreciation tax shield.** The reduction in tax payments made possible by the depreciation tax shield will always be equal to the amount of the depreciation deduction taken, multiplied by the tax rate. The formula is:

Tax rate $\times$ Depreciation deduction
$$= \text{Tax savings from the depreciation tax shield} \qquad (3)$$

We can prove this formula by applying it to the $90,000 depreciation deduction taken by Firm X in our example:

$0.30 \times \$90,000 = \$27,000$ reduction in tax payments (shown as ''Greater amount of cash available to Firm X'' in Exhibit 15–2)

As we now integrate income taxes into capital budgeting computations, it will be necessary to consider the impact of depreciation deductions on tax payments by showing the tax savings provided by the depreciation tax shield.

EXHIBIT 15–3

Tax adjustments required in a capital budgeting analysis

Item	Treatment
Cash expense*	Multiply by (1 − Tax rate) to get after-tax cost.
Cash receipt*	Multiply by (1 − Tax rate) to get after-tax cash inflow.
Depreciation deduction	Multiply by the tax rate to get the tax savings from the depreciation tax shield.

* Where cash receipts and cash expenses recur *each year,* the expenses should be deducted from the receipts and only the difference should be multiplied by (1 − Tax rate). See the example at the top of Exhibit 15–7.

The concepts that we have introduced in this section and in the preceding section are not complex and can be mastered fairly quickly. To assist you in your study, a summary of these concepts is given in Exhibit 15–3.

Accelerated Cost Recovery System (ACRS)

Historically, depreciation has been closely tied to the useful life of an asset, with year-by-year depreciation deductions typically computed by the straight-line method, the sum-of-the-years'-digits method, or the double-declining-balance method. Also, in computing depreciation deductions, companies have generally given recognition to an asset's expected salvage value by deducting the salvage value from the asset's cost and depreciating only the remainder. Although these concepts can still be used for computing depreciation deductions on financial statements, sweeping changes were made in 1981, and then modified somewhat in 1986, in the way that depreciation deductions are computed for tax purposes.

As enacted by Congress in 1981, the new approach, called the **Accelerated Cost Recovery System (ACRS),** abandoned the concept of useful life and accelerated depreciation deductions by placing all depreciable assets into one of five property classes. These property classes made it possible to depreciate assets over extremely short periods of time. ACRS provided for so much acceleration, in fact, that the cost of most assets was recovered in 3 to 5 years even though the assets may have had useful lives of 20 years or more. To correct what appeared to be excessive acceleration, Congress modified the Accelerated Cost Recovery System in two ways under the Tax Reform Act of 1986.

First, the number of property classes was increased from five to eight, thereby lengthening the recovery period for many assets. Second, in order

EXHIBIT 15–4

ACRS property classes

ACRS property class and depreciation method	Useful life (ADR midpoint life[*]) of assets included in this class	Examples of assets included in this class
3-year property 200% declining balance	4 years or less	Most small tools are included; the law specifically *excludes* autos and light trucks from this property class.
5-year property 200% declining balance	More than 4 years to less than 10 years	Autos and light trucks, computers, typewriters, copiers, duplicating equipment, heavy general-purpose trucks, and research and experimentation equipment are included.
7-year property 200% declining balance	10 years or more to less than 16 years	Office furniture and fixtures, and most items of machinery and equipment used in production are included.
10-year property 200% declining balance	16 years or more to less than 20 years	Various machinery and equipment, such as that used in petroleum distilling and refining and in the milling of grain, are included.
15-year property 150% declining balance	20 years or more to less than 25 years	Sewage treatment plants, telephone and electrical distribution facilities, and land improvements are included.
20-year property 150% declining balance	25 years or more	Service stations and other real property with an ADR midpoint life of less than 27.5 years are included.
27.5-year property Straight-line	Not applicable	All residential rental property is included.
31.5-year property Straight-line	Not applicable	All nonresidential real property is included.

[*] The term *ADR midpoint life* means the "useful life" of an asset in a business sense; the appropriate ADR midpoint lives for assets are designated in the tax *Regulations*.

to have some correlation between an asset's useful life and the length of time over which it is depreciated, Congress directed that an asset's useful life serve as the basis for placing it in the appropriate ACRS property class. The various property classes under the new ACRS rules are presented in Exhibit 15–4.

Several key points should be noted about the data in Exhibit 15–4. First, the exhibit contains a piece of tax jargon called the *ADR (Asset Depreciation Range) midpoint life*. The term **ADR midpoint life** simply means the "useful life" of an asset in a business sense, and it should be interpreted as "useful life" wherever it appears throughout the remainder of this chapter. Second, each ACRS property class has a prescribed life. This is the life that must be used to depreciate any asset within that property class, regardless of the asset's actual useful life. Thus, an asset with a useful life (ADR midpoint life) of, say, 12 years, would be in the 7-year property class and therefore would be depreciated over 7 years rather than over 12 years. (Remember, the only function of an asset's useful life is to place it in the correct ACRS property class.) Although the prescribed lives for the various property classes are less generous now than they were under the old ACRS rules, they still permit assets to be depreciated over quite short time periods. Office equipment, for example, typically has a useful life of 10 years or more, but it is in the ACRS 7-year property class. Therefore, the ACRS rules permit office equipment to be depreciated over a period equal to about 70 percent of its actual useful life. Similarly, an office building generally has a useful life of about 40 years, but it is depreciated over a 31.5-year period under ACRS.

Finally, note from Exhibit 15–4 that the ACRS property classes utilize various depreciation methods and rates. To simplify depreciation computations, preset tables are available that show allowable depreciation deductions, based on a percentage of the asset's original cost, by year for each of the ACRS property classes. These tables are presented in Exhibit 15–5.[3] The percentage figures used in the tables are based on the declining-balance method of depreciation. A 200 percent rate was used to develop the figures dealing with the 3-, 5-, 7-, and 10-year property classes; and a 150 percent rate was used to develop the figures dealing with the 15- and 20-year property classes. In all cases, the tables automatically switch to straight-line depreciation at the point where depreciation deductions would be greater under that method. The tables in Exhibit 15–5 are effective for assets placed into service after December 31, 1986, and apply to both new and used property.

Factors in the implementation of ACRS   When computing depreciation deductions under the ACRS approach, taxpayers are permitted to take only a half year's depreciation in the first year and the last year of an asset's life.[4] This is known as the **half-year convention;** in effect, it adds a full year onto the recovery period for an asset, as shown in the tables in Exhibit 15–5. Note from the exhibit, for example, that assets in the three-

---

[3] For ease of computations, percentage figures in the tables have been rounded to three decimal places (e.g., 33.3 percent for three-year property would be 0.333 in decimal form). Tables prepared by the Internal Revenue Service carry these computations to either four or five decimal places, depending on the property class (no official tables were provided by Congress in the Tax Reform Act). In preparing tax returns and other data for the Internal Revenue Service, the IRS tables should be used.

[4] An exception to this general rule is made when more than 40 percent of the assets acquired during a year are placed into service during the last quarter of the year. Under these circumstances, organizations are required to follow a *midquarter convention*. For further discussion of the midquarter convention, consult any standard tax book.

EXHIBIT 15–5

ACRS depreciation tables by property class

| | Property class | | | | | |
Year	3-year	5-year	7-year	10-year	15-year	20-year
1	33.3%	20.0%	14.3%	10.0%	5.0%	3.8%
2	44.5	32.0	24.5	18.0	9.5	7.2
3	14.8*	19.2	17.5	14.4	8.6	6.7
4	7.4	11.5*	12.5	11.5	7.7	6.2
5		11.5	8.9*	9.2	6.9	5.7
6		5.8	8.9	7.4	6.2	5.3
7			8.9	6.6*	5.9*	4.9
8			4.5	6.6	5.9	4.5*
9				6.5	5.9	4.5
10				6.5	5.9	4.5
11				3.3	5.9	4.5
12					5.9	4.5
13					5.9	4.5
14					5.9	4.5
15					5.9	4.5
16					3.0	4.4
17						4.4
18						4.4
19						4.4
20						4.4
21						2.2
Total	100.0%	100.0%	100.0%	100.0%	100.0%	100.0%

* Denotes the year of changeover to straight-line depreciation.

year property class are depreciated over *four* years with only a half year's depreciation being allowed in the first and fourth years. In like manner, assets in the five-year property class are depreciated over *six* years, with the same pattern holding true for all other property classes.

Another factor in the implementation of ACRS is that under the ACRS rules, salvage value is not considered in computing depreciation deductions. Thus, depreciation deductions are computed on a basis of the full, original cost of an asset without any offset for the asset's expected salvage value. This is actually a benefit to an organization, since it allows the entire cost of an asset to be written off as depreciation expense. However, since the entire cost of an asset is written off, any salvage value realized from sale of the asset at the end of its useful life is fully taxable as income.

Using the ACRS tables   To illustrate how the tables in Exhibit 15–5 are used to compute depreciation deductions, assume that Wendover Company purchased a piece of new equipment on January 2, 1987. Cost and other data relating to the equipment follow:

Cost of the equipment	$200,000
Salvage value	3,000
Useful (ADR midpoint) life	14 years

Since the equipment has a useful (ADR midpoint) life of 14 years, it will be in the ACRS 7-year property class (see Exhibit 15–4). Under ACRS, salvage value is ignored in computing depreciation deductions; therefore, Wendover Company's depreciation deductions for tax purposes will be computed on the equipment's full $200,000 original cost, as follows:

Year	Equipment cost	ACRS percentage*	Depreciation deduction
1.	$200,000	14.3%	$ 28,600
2.	200,000	24.5	49,000
3.	200,000	17.5	35,000
4.	200,000	12.5	25,000
5.	200,000	8.9	17,800
6.	200,000	8.9	17,800
7.	200,000	8.9	17,800
8.	200,000	4.5	9,000
		100.0%	$200,000

* From the table for seven-year property in Exhibit 15–5.

Note that eight years are involved in the depreciation process, as discussed earlier, since the tables provide for only a half year's depreciation in the first and last years.

Optional straight-line method   ACRS allows flexibility to the extent that a company can elect to compute depreciation deductions by the **optional straight-line method** if it desires. Under the optional straight-line method, a company is permitted to ignore the ACRS tables and to spread its depreciation deductions somewhat evenly over the years. In addition, if a company elects this method, it has a choice between depreciating an asset over its ACRS property class life or over its actual useful (ADR midpoint) life.[5] In either case, the company must observe the half-year convention in computing depreciation deductions.

To provide an example, assume that Emerson Company purchases duplicating equipment at a cost of $10,000 on April 1, 1988. The equipment has a $600 salvage value, and it has a useful (ADR midpoint) life of eight years. Thus, according to the data in Exhibit 15–4, it is in the ACRS five-year property class. If the company elects to use the optional straight-line method and to depreciate the equipment over the shorter five-year period, it can deduct $1,000 depreciation in 1988:

$$\$10,000 \div 5 \text{ years} = \$2,000 \text{ per year; } \$2,000 \times \tfrac{1}{2} = \$1,000$$

---

[5] Use of an asset's actual useful (ADR midpoint) life as the depreciation period is known as the "alternate depreciation method" in the Tax Reform Act of 1986. Rules governing use of this alternative method are very complex, and the reader should refer to the *Act* for further discussion.

For 1989–92 (the next four years) the company can deduct $2,000 depreciation each year, and in 1993 it can deduct the final $1,000 amount, as shown below:

Year	Depreciation deduction
1988 (half year's depreciation)	$1,000
1989	2,000
1990	2,000
1991	2,000
1992	2,000
1993 (half year's depreciation)	1,000

As mentioned above, the half-year convention must be observed when using the optional straight-line method, the same as with the ACRS tables. Also notice that in accordance with the ACRS rules, the asset's salvage value was not considered in computing the depreciation deductions. Finally, note that since the optional straight-line method was used, the company could have elected to depreciate the equipment over its longer, actual useful life of eight years if it had desired to do so. *For the sake of consistency, whenever the optional straight-line method is used in this book we will always assume that the asset is depreciated over its shorter, ACRS property class life as we have done above.*

The option of being able to use the straight-line method in lieu of the percentages in the ACRS tables is of particular value to new firms and to firms experiencing economic difficulties. The reason, of course, is that such firms often have little or no income and thus may prefer to stretch out depreciation deductions rather than to accelerate them.

The Choice of a Depreciation Method

As stated earlier, companies can still use any depreciation method they want (including sum-of-the-years' digits) on financial statements, even though they must use the ACRS rules for tax purposes. If a company uses a different depreciation method on its financial statements than it does for tax purposes, which method should be used in a capital budgeting analysis? Since capital budgeting is concerned with *actual cash flows,* the answer is that the same depreciation method should be used for capital budgeting purposes as is being used for tax purposes. Under the new law, this will be either the ACRS tables or the ACRS optional straight-line method.

For tax purposes, most firms will choose the ACRS tables, since this highly accelerated approach to depreciation will be more advantageous than the optional straight-line method from a present value of tax savings point of view. To illustrate, refer to the data in Exhibit 15–6. This exhibit compares the two depreciation methods in terms of the present value of the tax savings that they provide on a hypothetical asset costing $300,000.

As shown by Exhibit 15–6, the ACRS table approach (which is based

EXHIBIT 15–6

Tax shield effects of depreciation

Cost of the asset	$300,000
Useful (ADR midpoint) life	9 years
Property class life	5 years
Salvage value.	–0–
Cost of capital.	14% after taxes
Income tax rate	30%

Straight-line depreciation, with half-year convention:

Year*	Depreciation deduction	Tax shield: Income tax savings at 30 percent	14 percent factor	Present value of tax savings
1	$30,000	$ 9,000	0.877	$ 7,893
2	60,000	18,000	0.769	13,842
3	60,000	18,000	0.675	12,150
4	60,000	18,000	0.592	10,656
5	60,000	18,000	0.519	9,342
6	30,000	9,000	0.456	4,104
				$57,987

ACRS tables, five-year property class:

Year	Cost	ACRS percentage				
1	$300,000	20.0%	$60,000	$18,000	0.877	$15,786
2	300,000	32.0	96,000	28,800	0.769	22,147
3	300,000	19.2	57,600	17,280	0.675	11,664
4	300,000	11.5	34,500	10,350	0.592	6,127
5	300,000	11.5	34,500	10,350	0.519	5,372
6	300,000	5.8	17,400	5,220	0.456	2,380
						$63,476

*Under the optional straight-line method, the company could have chosen to depreciate the asset over its nine-year useful (ADR midpoint) life, but this would have reduced the present value of the tax savings even further under the straight-line method as compared to the ACRS tables.

on declining-balance depreciation) provides a larger present value of tax savings than does the optional straight-line method. This example goes far to explain why firms often prefer the accelerated method of depreciation over the straight-line method for tax purposes. Since the accelerated method provides more of its tax shield early in the life of an asset, the present value of the resulting tax savings will always be greater than the present value of the tax savings under the straight-line method.

Example of Income Taxes and Capital Budgeting

Armed with an understanding of the new ACRS depreciation rules, and with an understanding of the concepts of after-tax cost, after-tax revenue, and depreciation tax shield, we are now prepared to examine a comprehensive example of income taxes and capital budgeting. Assume the following data:

Holland Company owns the mineral rights to land on which there is a deposit of ore. The company is uncertain as to whether it should purchase equipment and open a mine on the property. After careful study, the following data have been assembled by the company:

Cost of equipment needed	$300,000
Working capital needed	75,000
Estimated annual cash receipts from sales of ore	250,000
Estimated annual cash expenses for salaries, insurance, utilities, and other cash expenses of mining the ore	170,000
Cost of road repairs needed in six years	40,000
Salvage value of the equipment in ten years	100,000
Useful (ADR midpoint) life of the equipment	15 years

The ore in the mine would be exhausted after 10 years of mining activity, at which time the mine would be closed. The equipment would then be sold for its salvage value above. Holland Company uses the ACRS tables in computing depreciation deductions. The company's after-tax cost of capital is 12 percent, and its tax rate is 30 percent.

Should Holland Company purchase the equipment and open a mine on the property? The solution to the problem is given in Exhibit 15–7. The reader should go through this solution item by item and note the following points:

Cost of new equipment.   The initial investment of $300,000 in the new equipment is included in full, with no reductions for taxes. The tax effects of this investment are considered in the depreciation deductions.

Working capital.   Observe that the working capital needed for the project is included in full, with no reductions for taxes. This represents an *investment*, not an expense, so no tax adjustment is needed. (Only revenues and expenses are adjusted for the effects of taxes.) Also observe that no tax adjustment is needed when the working capital is released at the end of the project's life. The release of working capital would not be a taxable cash inflow, since it merely represents a return of investment funds back to the company.

Net annual cash receipts.   The net annual cash receipts from sales of ore are adjusted for the effects of income taxes, as discussed earlier in the chapter. Note at the top of Exhibit 15–7 that the annual cash expenses are deducted from the annual cash receipts to obtain a net cash receipts figure. This just simplifies computations. (Many of the exercises and problems that follow already provide a net annual cash receipts figure, thereby eliminating the need to make this computation.)

Road repairs.   Since the road repairs occur just once (in the sixth year), they are treated separately from other expenses. Road repairs would be a tax-deductible cash expense, and therefore they are adjusted for the effects of income taxes, as discussed earlier in the chapter.

EXHIBIT 15–7
Example of income taxes and capital budgeting

	Per year
Cash receipts from sales of ore	$250,000
Less payments for salaries, insurance, utilities, and other cash expenses	170,000
Net cash receipts	$ 80,000

Items and computations	Year(s)	(1) Amount	(2) Tax effect*	After-tax cash flows (1) × (2)	12 percent factor	Present value of cash flows
Cost of new equipment	Now	$(300,000)	—	$(300,000)	1.000	$(300,000)
Working capital needed	Now	(75,000)	—	(75,000)	1.000	(75,000)
Net annual cash receipts (above)	1–10	80,000	1 − 0.30	56,000	5.650	316,400
Road repairs	6	(40,000)	1 − 0.30	(28,000)	0.507	(14,196)

Depreciation deductions:

Year	Cost	ACRS percentage	Depreciation deduction	Year(s)	(1) Amount	(2) Tax effect*	After-tax cash flows (1) × (2)	12 percent factor	Present value of cash flows
1	$300,000	14.3%	$42,900	1	42,900	0.30	12,870	0.893	11,493
2	300,000	24.5	73,500	2	73,500	0.30	22,050	0.797	17,574
3	300,000	17.5	52,500	3	52,500	0.30	15,750	0.712	11,214
4	300,000	12.5	37,500	4	37,500	0.30	11,250	0.636	7,155
5	300,000	8.9	26,700	5	26,700	0.30	8,010	0.567	4,542
6	300,000	8.9	26,700	6	26,700	0.30	8,010	0.507	4,061
7	300,000	8.9	26,700	7	26,700	0.30	8,010	0.452	3,621
8	300,000	4.5	13,500	8	13,500	0.30	4,050	0.404	1,636

	Year(s)	(1) Amount	(2) Tax effect*	After-tax cash flows (1) × (2)	12 percent factor	Present value of cash flows
Salvage value of equipment . . .	10	100,000	1 − 0.30	70,000	0.322	22,540
Release of working capital . . .	10	75,000	—	75,000	0.322	24,150
Net present value						$ 35,190

*Taxable cash receipts and tax-deductible cash expenses are multiplied by (1 − Tax rate) to get the after-tax cash flow. Depreciation deductions are multiplied by the tax rate itself to get the cash flow figure (i.e., tax savings from the depreciation tax shield).

Depreciation deductions. Since the equipment has a 15-year useful (ADR midpoint) life, it is in the ACRS 7-year property class. The tax savings provided by depreciation deductions under the ACRS rules are included in the present value computations in the same way as was illustrated earlier in the chapter (see Exhibit 15–6). Note that depreciation deductions are kept separate from cash expenses. These are unlike items, and they should be treated separately in a capital budgeting analysis.

Salvage value of equipment. Since under the ACRS rules a company does not consider salvage value in computing depreciation deductions, book value will be zero at the end of the life of an asset. Thus, any salvage value received is fully taxable as income to the company. The after-tax benefit is determined by multiplying the salvage value by (1 − Tax rate), as discussed earlier.

Since the net present value of the proposed mining project is positive, the equipment should be purchased and the mine opened. The reader should study Exhibit 15–7 until all of its points are thoroughly understood. *Exhibit 15–7 is a key exhibit in the chapter!*

The Total-Cost Approach and Income Taxes

As stated in the preceding chapter, the total-cost approach is used to compare two or more competing investment proposals. To provide an example of this approach when income taxes are involved, assume the following data:

The *Daily Globe* has an auxiliary press that was purchased two years ago. The newspaper is thinking about replacing this old press with a newer, faster model. The alternatives are:

Buy a new press. A new press could be purchased for $150,000. It would have a useful life of eight years, after which time it would be salable for $10,000. The old press could be sold now for $40,000. (The book value of the old press is $63,000.) If the new press is purchased, it would be depreciated using the ACRS tables and would be in the five-year property class. The new press would cost $60,000 each year to operate.

Keep the old press. The old press was purchased two years ago at a cost of $90,000. The press is in the ACRS five-year property class and is being depreciated by the optional straight-line method. The old press will last for eight more years, but it will need an overhaul in five years that will cost $20,000. Cash operating costs of the old press are $85,000 each year. The old press will have a salvage value of $5,000 at the end of eight more years.

The tax rate is 30 percent. The *Daily Globe* requires an after-tax return of 10 percent on all investments in equipment.

Should the *Daily Globe* keep its old press or buy the new press? The solution using the total-cost approach is presented in Exhibit 15–8. Most

EXHIBIT 15-8

Income taxes and capital budgeting: Total-cost approach

Items and computations	Year(s)	(1) Amount	(2) Tax effect	After-tax cash flows (1) × (2)	10 percent factor	Present value of cash flows
Buy the new press:						
Cost of the new press	Now	$(150,000)	—	$(150,000)	1.000	$(150,000)
Annual cash operating costs	1–8	(60,000)	1 − 0.30	(42,000)	5.335	(224,070)

Depreciation deductions:

Year	Cost	ACRS percentage	Depreciation deduction
1	$150,000	20.0%	$30,000
2	150,000	32.0	48,000
3	150,000	19.2	28,800
4	150,000	11.5	17,250
5	150,000	11.5	17,250
6	150,000	5.8	8,700

Items and computations	Year(s)	(1) Amount	(2) Tax effect	After-tax cash flows (1) × (2)	10 percent factor	Present value of cash flows
(Year 1)	1	30,000	0.30	9,000	0.909	8,181
(Year 2)	2	48,000	0.30	14,400	0.826	11,894
(Year 3)	3	28,800	0.30	8,640	0.751	6,489
(Year 4)	4	17,250	0.30	5,175	0.683	3,535
(Year 5)	5	17,250	0.30	5,175	0.621	3,214
(Year 6)	6	8,700	0.30	2,610	0.564	1,472
Cash flow from sale of the old press:						
Cash received from the sale	Now	40,000	—	40,000	1.000	40,000
Tax savings from the loss on sale:						
Present book value $63,000						
Sale price (above) 40,000						
Loss on the sale $23,000	1	23,000	0.30	6,900	0.909	6,272
Salvage value of the new press	8	10,000	1 − 0.30	7,000	0.467	3,269
Present value of cash flows						$(289,744)
Keep the old press:						
Annual cash operating costs	1–8	$(85,000)	1 − 0.30	$(59,500)	5.335	$(317,433)
Overhaul needed	5	(20,000)	1 − 0.30	(14,000)	0.621	(8,694)

Depreciation deductions:

Year	Cost	Depreciation deduction
1	$ 90,000	$18,000*
2	90,000	18,000
3	90,000	18,000
4	90,000	9,000

Items and computations	Year(s)	(1) Amount	(2) Tax effect	After-tax cash flows (1) × (2)	10 percent factor	Present value of cash flows
(Year 1)	1	18,000	0.30	5,400	0.909	4,909
(Year 2)	2	18,000	0.30	5,400	0.826	4,460
(Year 3)	3	18,000	0.30	5,400	0.751	4,055
(Year 4)	4	9,000	0.30	2,700	0.683	1,844
Salvage value of the old press	8	5,000	1 − 0.30	3,500	0.467	1,635
Present value of cash flows						$(309,224)
Net present value in favor of purchasing the new press						$ 19,480

*$90,000 ÷ 5 years = $18,000 per year. Two years' depreciation has already been taken on the old press.

of the items in this exhibit have already been discussed in connection with Exhibit 15–7. Only a couple of points need elaboration:

Annual cash operating costs. Since there are no revenues identified with the project, we simply place the cash operating costs on an after-tax basis and discount them as we did in Chapter 14.

Sale of the old press. The computation of the cash inflow from sale of the old press is somewhat more involved than the other items in Exhibit 15–8. Note that *two* cash inflows are connected with this sale. The first is a $40,000 cash inflow in the form of the sale price. The second is a $6,900 cash inflow in the form of a reduction in income taxes, resulting from the tax shield provided by the loss sustained on the sale. This tax shield functions in the same way as the tax shield provided by depreciation deductions. That is, the $23,000 loss shown in the exhibit on sale of the old press (the difference between the sale price of $40,000 and the book value of $63,000) is fully deductible from income in the year the loss is sustained. This loss shields income from taxation, thereby causing a reduction in the income taxes that would otherwise be payable. The tax savings resulting from the loss tax shield are computed by multiplying the loss by the tax rate (the same procedure as for depreciation deductions): $23,000 \times 0.30 =$ $6,900.

A second solution to this problem is presented in Exhibit 15–9, where the incremental-cost approach is used. Notice both from this exhibit and from Exhibit 15–8 that the net present value is $19,480 in favor of buying the new press.

PREFERENCE DECISIONS—THE RANKING OF INVESTMENT PROJECTS

In the preceding chapter, we indicated that there are two types of decisions that must be made relative to investment opportunities. These are screening decisions and preference decisions. Screening decisions have to do with whether or not some proposed investment is acceptable to a firm. We discussed ways of making screening decisions in the preceding chapter, where we studied the use of the cost of capital as a screening tool. Screening decisions are very important in that many investment proposals come to the attention of management, and those that are not worthwhile must be screened out.

Preference decisions come *after* screening decisions and attempt to answer the following question: "How do the remaining investment proposals, all of which have been screened and provide an acceptable rate of return, rank in terms of preference? That is, which one(s) would be *best* for the firm to accept?" Preference decisions are much more difficult to make than screening decisions. The reason is that investment funds are usually limited, and this often requires that some (perhaps many) otherwise very profitable investment opportunities be forgone.

EXHIBIT 15–9

Income taxes and capital budgeting: Incremental-cost approach

Items and computations	Year(s)	(1) Amount	(2) Tax effect	After-tax cash flows (1) × (2)	10 percent factor	Present value of cash flows
Cost of the new press	Now	$(150,000)	—	$(150,000)	1.000	$(150,000)
Savings in annual cash operating costs	1–8	25,000	1 − 0.30	17,500	5.335	93,363
Overhaul avoided	5	20,000	1 − 0.30	14,000	0.621	8,694

Difference in depreciation:

Depreciation deduction

Year	New press	Old press	Difference
1	$30,000	$18,000	$12,000
2	48,000	18,000	30,000
3	28,800	18,000	10,800
4	17,250	9,000	8,250
5	17,250	—	17,250
6	8,700	—	8,700

Year	Year(s)	(1) Amount	(2) Tax effect	After-tax cash flows (1) × (2)	10 percent factor	Present value of cash flows
1		12,000	0.30	3,600	0.909	3,272
2		30,000	0.30	9,000	0.826	7,434
3		10,800	0.30	3,240	0.751	2,433
4		8,250	0.30	2,475	0.683	1,690
5		17,250	0.30	5,175	0.621	3,214
6		8,700	0.30	2,610	0.564	1,472

Cash flow from sale of the old press:

	Year(s)	(1) Amount	(2) Tax effect	After-tax cash flows	10 percent factor	Present value
Cash received from the sale	Now	40,000	—	40,000	1.000	40,000
Tax savings from the loss on sale (see Exhibit 15–8)	1	23,000	0.30	6,900	0.909	6,272

Difference in salvage value in eight years:

Salvage from the new press		$10,000				
Salvage from the old press		5,000				
Difference	8	$ 5,000	1 − 0.30	3,500	0.467	1,635

Net present value in favor of purchasing the new press . . . . $ 19,480

Note: The figures in this exhibit are derived from the *differences* between the two alternatives given in Exhibit 15–8.

Preference decisions are sometimes called *ranking* decisions, or *rationing* decisions, because they attempt to ration limited investment funds among many competing investment opportunities. The choice may be simply between two competing alternatives, or many alternatives may be involved that must be ranked according to their overall desirability. Either the time-adjusted rate of return method or the net present value method can be used in making preference decisions.

Time-Adjusted Rate of Return Method

When using the time-adjusted rate of return method to rank competing investment projects, the preference rule is: *The higher the time-adjusted rate of return, the more desirable the project.* If one investment project promises a time-adjusted rate of return of 18 percent, then it is preferable over another project that promises a time-adjusted rate of return of only 15 percent.

Ranking projects according to time-adjusted rate of return is a widely used means of making preference decisions. The reasons are probably two-fold. First, no additional computations are needed beyond those already performed in making the initial screening decisions. The rates of return themselves are used to rank acceptable projects. Second, the ranking data are easily understood by management. Rates of return are very similar to interest rates, which the manager works with every day.

Net Present Value Method

If the net present value method is being used to rank competing investment projects, the net present value of one project cannot be compared directly to the net present value of another project unless the investments in the projects are of equal size. For example, assume that a company is considering two competing investments, as shown below:

	Investment A	Investment B
Investment required	$(50,000)	$(5,000)
Present value of cash inflows	51,000	6,000
Net present value	$ 1,000	$ 1,000

Each project has a net present value of $1,000, but the projects are not equally desirable. A project requiring an investment of only $5,000 that produces cash inflows with a present value of $6,000 is much more desirable than a project requiring an investment of $50,000 that produces cash inflows with a present value of only $51,000. In order to compare the two projects on a valid basis, it is necessary in each case to divide the present value of the cash inflows by the investment required. The ratio that this computation yields is called the **profitability index.** The formula for the profitability index is:

$$\frac{\text{Present value of cash inflows}}{\text{Investment required}} = \text{Profitability index (PI)}$$

The profitability indexes for the two investments above would be:

	Investment A	Investment B
Present value of cash inflows	$51,000 *(a)*	$6,000 *(a)*
Investment required	$50,000 *(b)*	$5,000 *(b)*
Profitability index *(a)* ÷ *(b)*	1.02	1.20

The preference rule to follow when using the profitability index to rank competing investment projects is: *The higher the profitability index, the more desirable the project.* Applying this rule to the two investments above, investment B should be chosen over investment A.

In computing the "Investment required" in a project, the amount of cash outlay should be reduced by any salvage recovered from the sale of old equipment. Also, the "Investment required" includes any working capital that the project may need, as explained in the preceding chapter. Finally, we should note that the "Present value of cash inflows" figure used in the PI formula is often a "net" amount. For example, if a project has small *out*flows (such as for repairs or for an overhaul) that occur after the project starts, then the present value of these small outflows should be deducted from the present value of the project's inflows and the resulting net figure used in the PI computation.

Comparing the Preference Rules

The profitability index is conceptually superior to the time-adjusted rate of return as a method of making preference decisions. This is because the profitability index will always give the correct signal as to the relative desirability of alternatives, even if the alternatives have different lives and different patterns of earnings. By contrast, if lives are unequal, the time-adjusted rate of return method can lead the manager to make incorrect decisions.

Assume the following situation:

Parker Company is considering two investment proposals, only one of which can be accepted. Project A requires an investment of $5,000 and will provide a single cash inflow of $6,000 in one year. Therefore, it promises a time-adjusted rate of return of 20 percent. Project B also requires an investment of $5,000. It will provide cash inflows of $1,360 each year for six years. Its time-adjusted rate of return is 16 percent. Which project should be accepted?

Although project A promises a time-adjusted rate of return of 20 percent, as compared to only 16 percent for project B, project A is not necessarily preferable over project B. It is preferable *only* if the funds released at the end of the year under project A can be reinvested at a high rate of return in some *other* project for the five remaining years. Otherwise, project B, which promises a return of 16 percent over the *entire* six years, is more desirable.

Let us assume that the company in the example above has a cost of capital of 12 percent. The net present value method, with the profitability index, would rank the two proposals as follows:

	Project A	Project B
Present value of cash inflows:		
$6,000 received at the end of one year at 12% (factor of 0.893)	$5,358 *(a)*	
$1,360 received at the end of each year for six years at 12% (factor of 4.111)		$5,591 *(a)*
Investment required	$5,000 *(b)*	$5,000 *(b)*
Profitability index, *(a) ÷ (b)*	1.07	1.12

The profitability index indicates that project B is more desirable than project A. This is in fact the case if the funds released from project A at the end of one year can be reinvested at only 12 percent (the cost of capital). Although the computations will not be shown here, in order for project A to be more desirable than project B, the funds released from project A would have to be reinvested at a rate of return *greater* than 14 percent for the remaining five years.

In short, the time-adjusted rate of return method of ranking tends to favor short-term, high-yield projects, whereas the net present value method of ranking (using the profitability index) tends to favor longer-term projects.

OTHER APPROACHES TO CAPITAL BUDGETING DECISIONS

The discounted cash flow methods of making capital budgeting decisions are relatively new. They were first introduced on a widespread basis in the 1950s, although their appearance in business literature predates this period by many years. Discounted cash flow methods have gained widespread acceptance as accurate and dependable decision-making tools. Other methods of making capital budgeting decisions are also available, however, and are preferred by some managers.

The Payback Method

The payback method centers on a span of time known as the *payback period*. The **payback period** can be defined as the length of time that it takes for an investment project to recoup its own initial cost out of the cash receipts that it generates. In business jargon, this period is sometimes spoken of as "the time that it takes for an investment to pay for itself." The basic premise of the payback method is that the more quickly the cost of an investment can be recovered, the more desirable is the investment.

The payback period is expressed in years. The formula used in computing the payback period is:

$$\text{Payback period} = \frac{\text{Investment required}}{\text{Net annual cash inflow}^*} \qquad (4)$$

* If new equipment is replacing old equipment, this becomes incremental net annual cash inflow.

To illustrate the mechanics involved in payback computations, assume the following data:

> York Company needs a new milling machine. The company is considering two machines, machine A and machine B. Machine A costs $15,000 and will reduce annual operating costs by $5,000. Machine B costs only $12,000 but will also reduce annual operating costs by $5,000.

Required: Which machine should be purchased? Make your calculations by the payback method.

$$\text{Machine A payback period} = \frac{\$15,000}{\$5,000} = 3.0 \text{ years}$$

$$\text{Machine B payback period} = \frac{\$12,000}{\$5,000} = 2.4 \text{ years}$$

According to the payback calculations, York Company should purchase machine B, since it has a shorter payback period than machine A.

Evaluation of the Payback Method

The payback method is not a measure of how profitable one investment project is compared to another. Rather, it is a measure of *time* in the sense that it tells the manager how many years will be required to recover the investment in one project as compared to another. This is a major defect in the approach, since a shorter payback period is not always an accurate guide as to whether one investment is more desirable than another. To illustrate this point, consider again the two machines used in the example above. Since machine B has a shorter payback period than machine A, it *appears* that machine B is more desirable than machine A. But if we add one more piece of data, this illusion quickly disappears. Machine A has a projected 10-year life, and machine B has a projected 5-year life. It would take two purchases of machine B to provide the same length of service as would be provided by a single purchase of machine A. Under these circumstances, machine A would be a much better investment than machine B, even though machine B has a shorter payback period. Unfortunately, the payback method has no inherent mechanism for highlighting differences in useful life between investments for the decision maker. Such differences can be very subtle, and relying on payback alone can cause the manager to make incorrect decisions.

A further criticism of the payback method is that it does not consider the time value of money. A cash inflow to be received several years in the future is weighed equally with a cash inflow to be received right now. To illustrate, assume that for an investment of $8,000 you can purchase either of the two following streams of cash inflows:

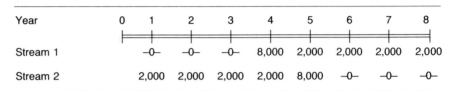

Year	0	1	2	3	4	5	6	7	8
Stream 1		–0–	–0–	–0–	8,000	2,000	2,000	2,000	2,000
Stream 2		2,000	2,000	2,000	2,000	8,000	–0–	–0–	–0–

Which stream of cash inflows would you prefer to receive in return for your $8,000 investment? Each stream has a payback period of 4.0 years. Therefore, if payback alone were relied on in making the decision, you would be forced to say that the streams are equally desirable. However, from the point of view of the time value of money, stream 2 is much more desirable than stream 1.

On the other hand, under certain conditions the payback method can be very useful to the manager. For one thing, it can help the manager to identify the "ballpark" in weeding out investment proposals. That is, it can be used as a screening tool to help answer the question "Should I consider this proposal further?" If a proposal doesn't provide a payback within some specified period, then there may be no need to consider it further. In addition, the payback period is often of great importance to new firms that are "cash poor." When a firm is cash poor, a project with a short payback period but a low rate of return might be preferred over another project with a high rate of return but a long payback period. The reason is that the company may simply need a faster return of its cash investment.

An Extended Example of Payback

As shown in the formula given earlier, the payback period is computed by dividing the investment in a project by the net annual cash inflows that the project will generate. If new equipment is replacing old equipment, then any salvage to be received on disposal of the old equipment should be deducted from the cost of the new equipment, and only the *incremental* investment should be used in the payback computation. In addition, any depreciation deducted in arriving at the net income promised by an investment project must be added back to obtain the project's expected net annual cash inflow. To illustrate, assume the following data:

Goodtime Fun Centers, Inc., operates many outlets in the eastern states. Some of the vending machines in one of its outlets provide very little revenue, so the company is considering the removal of the machines and the installation of equipment to dispense soft ice cream. The equipment would cost $80,000 and have an eight-year useful life. Incremental annual revenues and costs associated with the sale of ice cream would be:

Sales	$150,000
Less cost of ingredients	90,000
Contribution margin	60,000
Less fixed expenses:	
Salaries	27,000
Maintenance	3,000
Depreciation	10,000
Total fixed expenses	40,000
Net income	$ 20,000

The vending machines can be sold for a $5,000 scrap value. The company will not purchase equipment unless it has a payback of three years or less. Should the equipment to dispense ice cream be purchased? (Ignore income taxes.)

An analysis as to whether the proposed equipment meets the company's payback requirements is given in Exhibit 15–10. Several things should be noted from the data in this exhibit. First, notice that depreciation is added back to net income to obtain the net annual cash inflow promised by the new equipment. As stated in the preceding chapter, depreciation does not represent a present cash outlay; thus, it must be added back to net income in order to adjust net income to a cash basis. Second, notice in the payback computation that the salvage value from the old machines has been deducted from the cost of the new equipment, and that only the incremental investment has been used in computing the payback period.

Since the proposed equipment has a payback period of less than three years, the company's payback requirement has been met and the new equipment should be purchased.

EXHIBIT 15–10

Computation of the payback period

Step 1: *Compute the net annual cash inflow.* Since the net annual cash inflow is not given, it must be computed before the payback period can be determined:

Net income (given above)	$20,000
Add: Noncash deduction for depreciation . . .	10,000
Net annual cash inflow	$30,000

Step 2: *Compute the payback period.* Using the net annual cash inflow figure from above, the payback period can be determined as follows:

$$\frac{\text{Cost of the new equipment} - \text{Salvage from the old machines}}{\text{Net annual cash inflow}} = \text{Payback period}$$

$$\frac{\$80,000 - \$5,000}{\$30,000} = 2.5 \text{ years}$$

Payback and Uneven Cash Flows

When the cash flows associated with an investment project are erratic or uneven, the simple payback formula that we outlined earlier is no longer usable, and the computations involved in deriving the payback period can be fairly complex. Consider the following data:

Year	Investment	Cash inflow
1	$4,000	$1,000
2		–0–
3		2,000
4	2,000	1,000
5		500
6		3,000
7		2,000
8		2,000

What is the payback period on this investment? The answer is 5.5 years, but to obtain this figure it is necessary to balance off the cash inflows against the investment outflows on a year-by-year basis. The steps involved in this process are shown in Exhibit 15–11. By the middle of the sixth year, sufficient cash inflows will have been realized to recover the entire investment of $6,000 ($4,000 + $2,000).

The Simple Rate of Return Method

The **simple rate of return** method is another capital budgeting technique that does not involve discounted cash flows. The method is also known as the accounting rate of return, the unadjusted rate of return, and the financial statement method. It derives its popularity from the belief that it parallels conventional financial statements in its handling of investment data.

Unlike the other capital budgeting methods that we have discussed, the simple rate of return method does not focus on cash flows. Rather, it focuses on accounting net income. The approach is to estimate the revenues that

EXHIBIT 15–11

Payback and uneven cash flows

Year	(1) Beginning unrecovered investment	(2) Additional investment	(3) Total unrecovered investment (1) + (2)	(4) Cash inflow	(5) Ending unrecovered investment (3) – (4)
1	$4,000		$4,000	$1,000	$3,000
2	3,000		3,000	–0–	3,000
3	3,000		3,000	2,000	1,000
4	1,000	$2,000	3,000	1,000	2,000
5	2,000		2,000	500	1,500
6	1,500		1,500	3,000	–0–
7	–0–		–0–	2,000	–0–
8	–0–		–0–	2,000	–0–

will be generated by a proposed investment and then to deduct from these revenues all of the projected operating expenses associated with the project. This net income figure is then related to the initial investment in the project, as shown in the following formula:

$$\text{Simple rate of return} = \cfrac{\begin{array}{c}\text{Incremental} \\ \text{revenues}\end{array} - \begin{array}{c}\text{Incremental expenses,} \\ \text{including depreciation}\end{array} = \text{Net income}}{\text{Initial investment}^*} \quad (5)$$

*The investment should be reduced by any salvage from the sale of the old equipment.

Or, if a cost reduction project is involved, the formula becomes:

$$\text{Simple rate of return} = \cfrac{\text{Cost savings} - \begin{array}{c}\text{Depreciation on} \\ \text{new equipment}\end{array}}{\text{Initial investment}^*} \quad (6)$$

*The investment should be reduced by any salvage from the sale of old equipment.

Example 1

Brigham Tea, Inc., is a processor of a nontannic acid tea product. The company is contemplating the purchase of equipment for an additional processing line. The additional processing line would increase revenues by $90,000 per year. Incremental cash operating expenses would be $40,000 per year. The equipment would cost $180,000 and have a nine-year life. No salvage value is projected.

Required: 1.   Compute the simple rate of return. (Ignore income taxes.)
            2.   Compute the time-adjusted rate of return, and compare it to the simple rate of return. (Ignore income taxes.)

Solution: 1.   By applying the formula for the simple rate of return found in equation (5), we can compute the simple rate of return to be 16.7 percent:

Simple rate of return

$$= \cfrac{\left[\begin{array}{c}\$90,000 \\ \text{incremental} \\ \text{revenues}\end{array}\right] - \left[\begin{array}{c}\$40,000 \text{ cash operating expenses} \\ + \$20,000 \text{ depreciation}\end{array}\right] = \begin{array}{c}\$30,000 \\ \text{net income}\end{array}}{\$180,000 \text{ initial investment}}$$

Simple rate of return $= 16.7\%$

2.   The rate computed in (1) above, however, is far below the time-adjusted rate of return of approximately 24 percent:

$$\text{Time-adjusted rate of return} = \cfrac{\$180,000}{\$50,000^*} = \text{Factor of } 3.600$$

$$\text{Time-adjusted rate of return} = \begin{array}{l}\text{Approximately 24\% from Table 14–4} \\ \text{(in Chapter 14), scanning} \\ \text{across the nine-year line}\end{array}$$

*$30,000 net income + $20,000 depreciation = $50,000; or, the annual cash inflow can be computed as: $90,000 increased revenues − $40,000 cash expenses = $50,000.

Example 2

Midwest Farms, Inc., hires people on a part-time basis to sort eggs. The cost of this hand sorting process is $30,000 per year. The company is investigating the purchase of an egg sorting machine that would cost $90,000 and have a 15-year useful life. The machine would have only a nominal salvage value, and it would cost only $10,000 per year to operate and maintain. The egg sorting equipment currently being used could be sold now for a scrap value of $2,500.

Required: Compute the simple rate of return on the new egg sorting machine.

Solution: A cost reduction project is involved in this situation. By applying the formula for the simple rate of return found in equation (6), we can compute the simple rate of return as follows:

$$\text{Simple rate of return} = \frac{\$20,000^* \text{ cost savings} - \$6,000^\dagger \text{ depreciation on the new equipment}}{\$90,000 - \$2,500}$$

$$= 16.0\%$$

* 30,000 − $10,000 = $20,000 cost savings.
† 90,000 ÷ 15 years = $6,000 depreciation.

Criticisms of the Simple Rate of Return

The most damaging criticism of the simple rate of return method is that it does not consider the time value of money. A dollar received 10 years from now is viewed as being just as valuable as a dollar received today. Thus, the manager can be misled in attempting to choose between competing courses of action if the alternatives being considered have different cash flow patterns. For example, assume that project A has a high simple rate of return but yields the bulk of its cash flows many years from now. Another project, B, has a somewhat lower simple rate of return but yields the bulk of its cash flows over the next few years. The manager would probably choose project A over project B because of its higher simple rate of return; however, project B might in fact be a much better investment if the time value of money were considered.

A further criticism of the simple rate of retun method is that it often proves to be misleading in its basic approach. The method is supposed to parallel conventional financial statements in its handling of data. Yet studies show that this parallelism is rarely present.[6] The problem is that conventional accounting practice tends to write costs off to expense very quickly. As a result, the net income and asset structure actually reflected on financial statements may differ substantially from comparable items in rate of return computations, where costs tend to be expensed less quickly. This disparity

---

[6] See National Association of Accountants, Research Report No. 35, ''Return on Capital as a Guide to Managerial Decisions'' (New York, December 1959), p. 64.

in the handling of data is especially pronounced in those situations where rate of return computations are carried out by nonaccounting personnel.

The Choice of an Investment Base

In our examples, we have defined the investment base for simple rate of return computations to be the entire initial investment in the project under consideration [see formula (5)]. Actual practice varies between using the entire initial investment, as we have done, and using only the *average* investment over the life of a project. As a practical matter, which approach one chooses to follow is unimportant so long as consistency is maintained between projects and between years. If the average investment is used rather than the entire initial investment, then the resulting rate of return will be approximately doubled.

SUMMARY

Unless a company is a tax-exempt organization, such as a school or a governmental unit, income taxes should be considered in making capital budgeting computations. When income taxes are a factor in a company, tax-deductible cash expenditures must be placed on an after-tax basis by multiplying the expenditure by (1 − Tax rate). Only the after-tax amount is used in determining the desirability of an investment proposal. Similarly, taxable cash inflows must be placed on an after-tax basis by multiplying the cash inflow by the same formula.

Although depreciation deductions do not involve a present outflow of cash, they are valid expenses for tax purposes and as such affect income tax payments. Depreciation deductions shield income from taxation, resulting in decreased taxes being paid. This shielding of income from taxation is commonly called a depreciation tax shield. The savings in income taxes arising from the depreciation tax shield are computed by multiplying the depreciation deduction by the tax rate itself. Since accelerated methods of depreciation provide the bulk of their tax shield early in the life of an asset, they are superior to the straight-line method of depreciation, from a present value of tax savings point of view.

Preference decisions relate to ranking two or more investment proposals according to their relative desirability. This ranking can be performed using either the time-adjusted rate of return or the profitability index. The profitability index, which is the ratio of the present value of a proposal's cash inflows to the investment required, is generally regarded as the best way of making preference decisions when discounted cash flow is being used.

Instead of using discounted cash flow, some companies prefer to use either payback or the simple rate of return in evaluating investment proposals. Payback is determined by dividing a project's cost by the annual cash inflows that it will generate in order to find out how quickly the original investment can be recovered. The simple rate of return is determined by dividing a project's accounting net income either by the initial investment in the project or by the average investment over the life of the project. Both payback and the simple rate of return can be useful to the manager, so long as they are used with a full understanding of their limitations.

KEY TERMS FOR REVIEW

Accelerated Cost Recovery System (ACRS) A method of depreciation required for income tax purposes that places a depreciable asset into one of eight, preset property classes according to the asset's useful (ADR midpoint) life.

ADR midpoint life A term used in tax law that means the "useful life" of an asset in a business sense.

After-tax benefit The amount of net cash inflow realized by an organization from a taxable cash receipt after income tax effects have been considered. The amount is determined by multiplying the cash receipt by (1 − Tax rate).

After-tax cost The amount of net cash outflow resulting from a tax-deductible cash expense after income tax effects have been considered. The amount is determined by multiplying the cash expense by (1 − Tax rate).

Depreciation tax shield A reduction in the amount of income subject to tax that results from the presence of depreciation deductions on the income statement. The reduction in tax is computed by multiplying the depreciation deduction by the tax rate.

Half-year convention A requirement under the Accelerated Cost Recovery System that permits a company to take only a half year's depreciation in the first and last years of an asset's depreciation period.

Optional straight-line method A method of computing depreciation deductions under ACRS that can be used by an organization in lieu of the ACRS tables.

Payback period The length of time that it takes for an investment project to recoup its own initial cost out of the cash receipts that it generates.

Profitability index The ratio of the present value of a project's cash inflows to the investment required.

Simple rate of return The rate of return promised by an investment project when the time value of money is not considered; it is computed by dividing a project's annual net income by the initial investment required.

APPENDIX: INCOME TAX EFFECTS ON PAYBACK AND SIMPLE RATE OF RETURN

As with the discounted cash flow methods of capital budgeting, many managers prefer to deal with the payback and the simple rate of return methods on a before-tax basis rather than on an after-tax basis. For this reason, the discussion of payback and simple rate of return in the chapter did not deal with income tax issues. Other managers do include tax considerations in payback and simple rate of return computations, however, so it is desirable at this point to extend our discussion of these methods to include tax matters.

We will use a single example to demonstrate the tax effects on both payback and simple rate of return. Assume the following data:

Quick-Stop, Inc., operates several convenience-food outlets throughout the West. The company would like to open a new outlet that would require an investment of $280,000 in depreciable equipment. The equipment would be in the ACRS seven-year property class. The company would depreciate the equipment by the optional straight-line method.[7] Quick-Stop, Inc., estimates that the new outlet would generate the following yearly revenues and expenses:

Sales	$800,000
Less cost of merchandise	490,000
Contribution margin	310,000
Less fixed expenses:	
Selling expenses	160,000
Rent	52,000
Depreciation	40,000*
Other cash expenses	8,000
Total fixed expenses	260,000
Income before taxes	50,000
Less income taxes (30%)	15,000
Net income	$ 35,000

*$280,000 ÷ 7 years = $40,000.

The company requires a payback of 3.0 years or less for a project to be acceptable. The company's cost of capital is 15 percent.

In the following two sections, we compute both the payback and the simple rate of return on this project.

Payback and Tax Effects

The formula for computing the payback period when taxes are considered is the same as was used earlier in the chapter. The only thing we have to remember is that the cash flow figures used in the formula must be on an after-tax basis. By review, the payback formula is:

$$\text{Payback period} = \frac{\text{Investment required}}{\text{Net annual cash inflow}} \qquad (4)$$

The payback period for Quick-Stop, Inc.'s new outlet would be:

$$\text{Payback period} = \frac{\$280,000}{\$75,000^*}$$

$$= 3.7 \text{ years}$$

*$35,000 net income + $40,000 depreciation = $75,000 net annual cash inflow.

---

[7] For simplicity in computations, we will ignore the half-year convention in this example. In your problems, however, you should always observe the half-year convention unless the problem directs you to do otherwise.

Since the payback period of 3.7 years is greater than the maximum 3.0 years allowed, the company should not open the outlet. Perhaps another location can be found that will generate a larger amount of revenue for the investment required and thus reduce the payback period.

Simple Rate of Return and Tax Effects

When taxes are considered, the same formulas are used for the simple rate of return as were used earlier, except that income taxes are deducted along with other expenses in computing net income. The revised formulas are:

$$\frac{\text{Simple rate}}{\text{of return}} = \frac{\text{Incremental} \quad - \text{ including depreciation} = \text{Net income}}{\text{revenues} \quad \text{and income taxes}}{\text{Initial investment}} \tag{5a}$$

Or, if the project is a cost reduction project, the formula becomes:

$$\frac{\text{Simple rate}}{\text{of return}} = \frac{\text{Cost} \quad - \text{equipment and incremental}}{\text{savings} \quad \text{income taxes}}{\text{Initial investment}} \tag{6a}$$

In all simple rate of return computations, if a project involves the replacement of old equipment, then the salvage value of this old equipment (adjusted for tax effects) should be deducted from the cost of the new equipment in computing the "Initial investment" figure.

For Quick-Stop, Inc.'s new outlet, the simple rate of return would be [from formula (5a) above]:

$$\text{Simple rate of return} = \frac{\$35,000}{\$280,000}$$

$$= 12.5\%$$

Since the project's 12.5 percent simple rate of return is less than the company's 15 percent of capital, the new outlet should not be opened.

QUESTIONS

15–1.   Some organizations will always use capital budgeting techniques on a before-tax basis rather than on an after-tax basis. Name several such organizations.

15–2.   What is meant by after-tax cost, and how is the concept used in capital budgeting decisions?

15–3.   What is a depreciation tax shield, and how does it affect capital budgeting decisions?

15–4. The three most widely used depreciation methods are straight line, sum-of-the-years' digits, and double-declining balance, with the depreciation period based on the asset's actual useful life. Explain why a company might use one or more of these methods, instead of the Accelerated Cost Recovery System, for computing depreciation expense in its published financial statements.

15–5. Why are accelerated methods of depreciation superior to the straight-line method of depreciation from an income tax point of view?

15–6. Ludlow Company is considering the introduction of a new product line. Would an increase in the income tax rate tend to make the new investment more or less attractive? Explain.

15–7. Assume that an old piece of equipment is sold at a loss. From a capital budgeting point of view, what two cash inflows will be associated with the sale?

15–8. Assume that a new piece of equipment costs $40,000 and that the tax rate is 30 percent. Should the new piece of equipment be shown in the capital budgeting analysis as a cash outflow of $40,000, or should it be shown as a cash outflow of $28,000 [$40,000 × (1 − 0.30)]? Explain.

15–9. Assume that a company has cash operating expenses of $15,000 and a depreciation expense of $10,000. Can these two items be added together and treated as one in a capital budgeting analysis, or should they be kept separate? Explain.

15–10. Distinguish between capital budgeting screening decisions and capital budgeting preference decisions. Why are preference decisions more difficult to make than screening decisions?

15–11. Why are preference decisions sometimes called *rationing* decisions?

15–12. How is the profitability index computed, and what does it measure?

15–13. What is the preference rule for ranking investment projects under the net present value method?

15–14. Can an investment with a profitability index of less than 1.00 be an acceptable investment? Explain.

15–15. What is the preference rule for ranking investment projects under time-adjusted rate of return?

15–16. What is meant by the term *payback period?* How is the payback period determined?

15–17. Sharp Company is considering the purchase of certain new equipment in order to sell a new product line. Expected yearly net income from the new product line is given below. From these data, compute the net annual cash inflow that would be used to determine the payback period on the new equipment.

Sales.		$150,000
Less cost of goods sold		45,000
Gross margin		105,000
Less operating expenses:		
Advertising	$35,000	
Salaries and wages	50,000	
Depreciation	12,000	97,000
Net income		$ 8,000

15–18. In what ways can the payback method be useful to the manager?

15–19. What is the formula for computing the simple rate of return?

15–20. What is the major criticism of the payback and simple rate of return methods of making capital budgeting decisions?

EXERCISES

E15–1. *a.* Neal Company would like to initiate a management development program for its executives. The program would cost $100,000 per year to operate. What would be the after-tax cost of the program if the company's income tax rate is 30 percent?

b. Smerk's Department Store has rearranged the merchandise display cases on the first floor of its building, placing fast turnover items near the front door. This rearrangement has caused the company's contribution margin (and taxable income) to increase by $40,000 per month. If the company's income tax rate is 25 percent, what is the after-tax benefit from this rearrangement of facilities?

c. Perfect Press, Inc., has just purchased a new binding machine at a cost of $210,000. The machine has a 12-year useful (ADR midpoint) life and a $14,000 salvage value. Using the optional straight-line method, determine the yearly tax savings from the depreciation tax shield. Assume that the income tax rate is 30 percent.

d. Repeat *(c)* above, this time using the ACRS tables in Exhibit 15–5.

E15–2.   Morgan Industries has an opportunity to penetrate a new market by making some modifications to one of its existing products. These modifications would require the purchase of various tools and small items of equipment that would cost $80,000 and have a four-year useful (ADR midpoint) life. The equipment would have a $7,500 salvage value and would be depreciated using the ACRS tables.

The modified product would generate before-tax net cash receipts of $35,000 per year. It is estimated that the equipment would require repairs in the third year that would cost $14,000. The company's tax rate is 30 percent, and its after-tax cost of capital is 12 percent.

Required: 1. Compute the net present value of the proposed investment in tools and equipment.

2. Would you recommend that the tools and equipment be purchased? Explain.

E15–3.   Various assets used by organizations are listed below.

Assets	Useful (ADR midpoint) life
a. A pickup truck used by a construction company.	5 years
b. An office building used by an advertising agency	50 years
c. Power lines used in distribution of electricity	22 years
d. Small tools used on the assembly line of an auto plant	? years
e. Petroleum distilling equipment	16 years
f. An apartment house rented to college students	180 years*
g. A computer used by an airline to schedule flights	? years
h. A desk in the office of an attorney	10 years
i. Shrubbery and trees planted around a new medical clinic	? years

  * We're just kidding; it's really 45 years.

Required: Indicate the ACRS property class into which each of the assets above should be placed for depreciation purposes. Is it possible to depreciate an asset over its actual useful (ADR midpoint) life rather than over the period specified by its property class? Explain.

E15–4.   A company is considering two investment projects. Relevant cost and cash inflow information on the two projects is given below:

	Project A	Project B
Investment in passenger buses	$70,000	
Investment in working capital		$70,000
Net annual cash inflows	13,500	13,500
Life of the project	8 years*	8 years

* Useful (ADR midpoint) life of the buses.

The buses will have a $5,000 salvage value in eight years, and they will be depreciated by the optional straight-line method. At the end of eight years, the working capital will be released for use elsewhere. The company requires an after-tax return of 10 percent on all investments. The tax rate is 30 percent. (Be sure you place the buses in the correct property class for depreciation purposes.)

Required: Compute the net present value of each investment project. (Round all dollar amounts to the nearest whole dollar.)

E15–5.   (This exercise should be assigned only if Exercise 15–4 is also assigned.) Refer to the data in Exercise 15–4.

Required: 1.   Compute the profitability index for each investment project.
2.   Is an investment project with a profitability index of less than 1.0 an acceptable investment? Explain.

E15–6.   The Midtown Cafeteria employs five people to operate several items of antiquated dishwashing equipment. The cost of wages for these people and for maintenance of the equipment is $85,000 per year. Management is considering the purchase of a single, highly automated dishwashing machine that would cost $160,000 and have a useful (ADR midpoint) life of 12 years. This machine would require the services of only three people to operate at a cost of $48,000 per year. A maintenance contract on the machine would cost an additional $2,000 per year. New water jets would be needed on the machine in six years at a total cost of $15,000.

The old equipment is fully depreciated and has no resale value. The new machine will have a salvage value of $9,000 at the end of its 12-year useful life. The Midtown Cafeteria uses the ACRS tables for depreciation purposes. Management requires a 14 percent after-tax return on all equipment purchases. The company's tax rate is 30 percent.

Required: 1.   Determine the before-tax net annual cost savings that the new dishwashing machine will provide.
2.   Using the data from (1) and other data from the exercise, compute the new dishwashing machine's net present value. (Round all dollar amounts to the nearest whole dollar.) Would you recommend that it be purchased?

E15–7.   Information on four investment proposals is given below:

	Investment proposal			
	A	**B**	**C**	**D**
Investment required	$ (90,000)	$(100,000)	$ (70,000)	$(120,000)
Present value of cash inflows . . .	126,000	90,000	105,000	160,000
Net present value	$ 36,000	$ (10,000)	$ 35,000	$ 40,000
Life of the project	5 years	7 years	6 years	6 years

Required: 1.   Compute the profitability index for each investment proposal.
2.   Rank the proposals in terms of preference.

E15–8.   Nick's Novelties, Inc., is considering the purchase of electronic pinball machines to place in amusement houses. The machines would cost a total of $300,000, have an eight-year useful life, and have a total salvage value of $20,000. Based on experience with other equipment, the company estimates that annual revenues and expenses associated with the machines would be as follows:

Revenues from use		$200,000
Less operating expenses:		
Commissions to amusement houses	$100,000	
Insurance	7,000	
Depreciation.	35,000	
Maintenance	18,000	160,000
Net income		$ 40,000

Required (ignore income taxes):   1.   Assume that Nick's Novelties, Inc., will not purchase new equipment unless it provides a payback period of four years or less. Would you recommend purchase of the pinball machines?
2.   Compute the simple rate of return promised by the pinball machines (compute the investment at initial cost). If the company's before-tax cost of capital is 12 percent, would you recommend that the pinball machines be purchased?

E15–9.   A piece of labor-saving equipment has just come onto the market that Meriweather Company could use to reduce costs in one of its plants. Relevant data relating to the equipment follow:

Purchase cost of the equipment	$432,000
Annual cost savings that will be	
provided by the equipment	90,000
Life of the equipment.	12 years
Cost of capital	14%

Required (ignore income taxes):   1.   Compute the payback period for the equipment. If the company requires a payback period of four years or less, would you recommend purchase of the equipment? Explain.
2.   Compute the simple rate of return on the equipment. Use straight-line depreciation based on the equipment's useful life. Would you recommend that the equipment be purchased? Explain.

E15–10.   (Appendix)   Thor Pavocek has dreamed for years of opening a weight-lifting club. He has determined that the necessary equipment, including steam rooms and a whirlpool, would cost $270,000. The equipment would have a useful (ADR mid-point) life of 15 years and a 10 percent salvage value. The equipment would be depreciated by the optional straight-line method over the 15-year actual useful life, rather than over the property class life, as permitted by the ACRS rules.

From information provided by Thor, you have prepared the following statement of annual revenues and expenses:

Membership fees		$185,000
Less operating expenses:		
Salaries for trainers	$90,000	
Rent of facilities	10,800	
Insurance	3,000	
Depreciation of equipment	18,000	
Utilities	7,200	129,000
Income before taxes		56,000
Less income taxes (25%)		14,000
Net income		$ 42,000

(For simplicity in computations in this exercise, the half-year convention has been ignored in computing straight-line depreciation.)

Required: 1. Thor is interested in knowing "if I can get my investment back in five years or less." Compute the payback period on the equipment.

2. Thor could invest his $270,000 in a Jacobean lily plantation that the promoters say will yield a "sure" 14 percent return after taxes. Compute the simple rate of return promised by the weight-lifting club and advise Thor as to which investment he should make.

PROBLEMS

P15–11. **Basic net present value analysis.** The Diamond Freight Company has been offered a seven-year contract to haul munitions for the government. Since this contract would represent new business, the company would have to purchase several new heavy-duty trucks at a cost of $350,000 if the contract were accepted. Other data relating to the contract follow:

Net annual cash receipts (before	
taxes) from the contract	$105,000
Cost of replacing the motors in	
the trucks in four years	45,000
Salvage value of the trucks at	
termination of the contract	18,000

With the motors being replaced after four years, the trucks will have a useful (ADR midpoint) life of seven years. In order to raise money to assist in the purchase of the new trucks, the company will sell several old, fully depreciated trucks for a total selling price of $16,000. The company uses the ACRS tables to compute depreciation and requires a 16 percent after-tax return on all equipment purchases. The tax rate is 30 percent.

Required: Compute the net present value of this investment opportunity. Round all dollar amounts to the nearest whole dollar. Would you recommend that the contract be accepted?

P15–12.   **Straightforward net present value analysis.**   The Four-Seasons Timber Company estimates that the following costs would be associated with the cutting and sale of timber on land to which it has cutting rights:

Investment in equipment needed for cutting and removing the timber	$400,000
Working capital investment needed	75,000
Annual cash receipts from sale of timber, net of related cash operating costs (before taxes)	88,000
Cost of reseeding the land	60,000

The timber would be exhausted after 10 years of cutting and sales; all reseeding would be done in the 10th year. The equipment would have a useful (ADR midpoint) life of 15 years, but it would be sold for an estimated 20 percent of its original cost when cutting was completed. The company uses the ACRS tables in computing depreciation deductions. The tax rate is 30 percent, and Four-Seasons' after-tax cost of capital is 12 percent. The working capital would be released for use elsewhere at the completion of the project.

Since the timber is difficult to get to and of marginal quality, management is uncertain as to whether it should proceed with the project.

Required: 1.   Compute the net present value of this investment project. Round all dollar amounts to the nearest whole dollar.
2.   Would you recommend that the investment project be undertaken?

P15–13.   **Simple rate of return; payback.**   Paul Swanson has an opportunity to acquire a franchise from The Yogurt Place, Inc., to dispense frozen yogurt products under The Yogurt Place name. Mr. Swanson has assembled the following information relating to the franchise:

a.   A suitable location in a large shopping mall can be rented for $3,500 per month.
b.   Remodeling and necessary equipment would cost $270,000. The equipment would have an estimated 15-year life and an estimated $18,000 salvage value. Straight-line depreciation would be used, and salvage value would be considered in computing depreciation deductions.
c.   Based on similar outlets elsewhere, Mr. Swanson estimates that sales would total $300,000 per year. Ingredients would cost 20 percent of sales.
d.   Operating costs would include $70,000 per year for salaries, $3,500 per year for insurance, and $27,000 per year for utilities. In addition, Mr. Swanson would have to pay a commission to The Yogurt Place, Inc., of 12.5 percent of sales.

Rather than obtain the franchise, Mr. Swanson could invest his funds in long-term government bonds that would yield a 12 percent annual return.

Required (ignore income taxes):   1.   Prepare an income statement that shows the expected net income each year from the franchise outlet. Use the contribution format.
2.   Compute the simple rate of return promised by the outlet. Based on this return, should it be opened?
3.   Compute the payback period on the outlet. If Mr. Swanson wants a payback of four years or less, should the outlet be opened?

P15–14.   Various depreciation methods; net present value.   Fencik Laboratories has been offered an eight-year contract to provide materials relating to the government's space exploration program. Management has determined that the following costs and revenues would be associated with the contract:

Cost of special equipment	$600,000
Working capital needed.	115,000
Annual revenues from the contract	450,000
Annual out-of-pocket costs for materials,	
salaries, and so forth	280,000
Salvage value of the equipment in eight years	9,000

Although the equipment would have a useful (ADR midpoint) life of nine years, it would have little salvage value remaining at the end of the contract period, as shown above. Fencik's after-tax cost of capital is 14 percent; its tax rate is 30 percent. At the end of the contract period, the working capital will be released for use elsewhere.

Required: 1.   Assume that Fencik Laboratories uses the ACRS optional straight-line depreciation method. Determine the net present value of the proposed contract. (Round all dollar amounts to the nearest whole dollar.)

2.   Assume that Fencik Laboratories uses the ACRS tables to compute depreciation deductions. Determine the net present value of the proposed contract. (Round all dollar amounts to the nearest whole dollar.) How do you explain the difference in rate of return between (1) and (2)?

P15–15.   Preference ranking of investment projects.   The management of Revco Products is exploring five different investment opportunities. Information on the five projects under study is given below:

	Project number				
	1	2	3	4	5
Investment required	$(270,000)	$(450,000)	$(400,000)	$(360,000)	$(480,000)
Present value of cash inflows					
at a 10% discount rate	336,140	522,970	379,760	433,400	567,270
Net present value	$ 66,140	$ 72,970	$ (20,240)	$ 73,400	$ 87,270
Life of the project	6 years	3 years	5 years	12 years	6 years
Time-adjusted rate of return	18%	19%	8%	14%	16%

The company's cost of capital is 10 percent; thus, a 10 percent discount rate has been used in the present value computation above. Limited funds are available for investment, so the company can't accept all of the projects listed above.

Required: 1.   Compute the profitability index for each investment project.

2.   Rank the five projects according to preference, in terms of:

  a.   Net present value.

  b.   Profitability index.

  c.   Time-adjusted rate of return.

3.   Which ranking do you prefer? Why?

P15–16.   Various depreciation methods; profitability index.   The computer and related equipment in Tervort Industries' computer center is not adequate for the company's needs. Although the computer is fully depreciated, it is in good operating condition and will be donated to a local school system. Management is considering two other computers as a replacement, only one of which can be purchased. Cost and other data on the two computers are given below:

	Computer A	Computer B
Cost of the computer	$225,000	$300,000
Annual savings in cash operating costs	70,000	88,500
Cost of parts replacement and a major		
adjustment needed in four years	9,000	10,500
Salvage value	16,000	20,000
Useful (ADR midpoint) life	7 years	7 years
Depreciation method to be used	SL*	†

   * Straight-line depreciation over the minimum time period allowed for tax purposes.
   † ACRS tables.

Tervort Industries' after-tax cost of capital is 12 percent. The tax rate is 30 percent. Round all dollar amounts to the nearest whole dollar.

Required:

1. Compute the net present value of each investment alternative. Based on these data, which computer should be purchased?
2. Compute the profitability index for each investment alternative. Based on these data, which computer should be purchased?

P15–17.   Simple rate of return; payback.   Sharkey's Fun Center contains a number of electronic games as well as a miniature golf course and various rides located outside the building. Paul Sharkey, the owner, would like to construct a water slide on one portion of his property. Mr. Sharkey has gathered the following information about the slide:

a. Water slide equipment could be purchased and installed at a cost of $330,000. According to the manufacturer, the slide would be usable for 12 years after which it would have little or no salvage value.
b. Mr. Sharkey would use straight-line depreciation on the slide equipment.
c. In order to make room for the water slide, several rides would be dismantled and sold. These rides are full depreciated, but they could be sold for $60,000 to an amusement park in a nearby city.
d. Mr. Sharkey has concluded that about 50,000 more people would use the water slide each year than have been using the rides. The admission price would be $3.60 per person.
e. Based on experience at other water slides, Mr. Sharkey estimates that incremental operating expenses each year for the slide would be: salaries, $85,000; insurance, $4,200; utilities, $13,000; and maintenance, $9,800.
f. The before-tax cost of capital for Sharkey's Fun Center is 14 percent.

Required (ignore income taxes):

1. Prepare an income statement showing the expected net income each year from the water slide.
2. Compute the simple rate of return expected from the water slide. Based on this computation, should the water slide be constructed?
3. Compute the payback period for the water slide. If Mr. Sharkey requires a payback period of five years or less, should the water slide be constructed?

P15–18.   Simple rate of return; payback; time-adjusted rate of return.   The Elberta Fruit Farm has always hired transient workers to pick its annual cherry crop. Francie Wright, the farm manager, has just received information on a cherry picking machine that is being purchased by many fruit farms. The machine is a motorized device that shakes the cherry tree, causing the cherries to fall onto plastic tarps that funnel the cherries into bins. Ms. Wright has gathered the following information in order to decide whether a cherry picker would be a profitable investment for the Elberta Fruit Farm:

a.   At present, the farm is paying an average of $40,000 per year to transient workers to pick the cherries.

b.   The cherry picker would cost $94,500, and it would have an estimated 12-year useful life. The farm uses straight-line depreciation on all assets and considers salvage value in computing depreciation deductions. The estimated salvage value of the cherry picker is $4,500.

c.   Annual out-of-pocket costs associated with the cherry picker would be: cost of an operator and an assistant, $14,000; insurance, $200; fuel, $1,800; and a maintenance contract, $3,000.

d.   The Elberta Fruit Farm now earns a return of 16 percent before taxes on its investment in orchard properties. Ms. Wright feels that the farm would have to earn an equivalent return on the cherry picker in order to justify the purchase.

Required (ignore income taxes):

1.   Determine the annual savings in cash operating costs that would be realized if the cherry picker were purchased.

2.   Compute the simple rate of return expected from the cherry picker. (Hint: Note that this is a cost reduction project.) Based on the simple rate of return, should the cherry picker be purchased?

3.   Compute the payback period on the cherry picker. The Elberta Fruit Farm will not purchase equipment unless it has a payback period of five years or less. Should the cherry picker be purchased?

4.   Compute (to the nearest whole percent) the time-adjusted rate of return promised by the cherry picker. Based on this computation, does it appear that the simple rate of return would normally be an accurate guide in investment decisions?

P15–19.   Preference ranking of investment projects.   Oxford Company has limited funds available for investment and must ration the funds among five competing projects. Selected information on the five projects follows:

Project	Investment required	Net present value	Life of the project (years)	Time-adjusted rate of return (percent)
A	$160,000	$44,323	7	18
B	135,000	42,000	12	16
C	100,000	35,035	7	20
D	175,000	38,136	3	22
E	150,000	(8,696)	6	8

Oxford Company's cost of capital is 10 percent. (The net present value above has been computed using a 10 percent discount rate.) The company wants your assistance in determining which project to accept first, which to accept second, and so forth.

Required: 1. Compute the profitability index for each project.
2. Rank the five projects in order of preference, in terms of:
   a. Net present value.
   b. Profitability index.
   c. Time-adjusted rate of return.
3. Which ranking do you prefer? Why?

P15–20. **Optional straight-line method versus ACRS tables; net present value.** Walter Miller, manufacturing vice president of Atlantic Industries, has been anxious for some time to purchase a piece of high-pressure equipment for use in the company's coal liquefaction research project. The equipment would cost $720,000 and would have an eight-year useful (ADR midpoint) life. It would have a salvage value equal to about 5 percent of its original cost.

An analysis that Mr. Miller has just received from his staff indicates that the equipment will not provide the 16 percent after-tax return required by Atlantic Industries. In making this analysis, Mr. Miller's staff estimated that the equipment would save the company $200,000 per year in its research program as a result of speeding up several key processes. The only significant maintenance work required on the equipment would be the installation of new pressure seals five years from now at a cost of $80,000. Also in the analysis, Mr. Miller's staff depreciated the equipment by the optional straight-line method and used the equipment's eight-year life as the depreciation period, as permitted by the ACRS rules and as instructed by Mr. Miller. The company's tax rate is 30 percent.

The controller of Atlantic Industries has told Mr. Miller that he should instruct his staff to use the shorter five-year property class life and to use the ACRS tables to depreciate the equipment for capital budgeting purposes. Somewhat irritated by this suggestion, Mr. Miller replied, "You accountants and your fancy bookkeeping methods! What difference does it make what depreciation method we use—we have the same investment, the same cost savings, and the same total depreciation either way. That equipment just doesn't measure up to our rate of return requirements. How you make the bookkeeping entries for depreciation won't change that fact."

Required: 1. Compute the net present value of the equipment, using the optional straight-line method for computing depreciation. Depreciate the equipment over its eight-year useful life, as instructed by Mr. Miller.
2. Compute the net present value of the equipment, using the ACRS tables and the five-year property class life for computing depreciation, as suggested by the controller.
3. Explain to Mr. Miller how the depreciation method used can affect the rate of return generated by an investment project.

P15–21. **Net present value analysis.** The Island Travel Service (ITS) operates out of Kuna, Hawaii. ITS has an opportunity to purchase several small charter boats that were recently repossessed by a local bank. Although the boats cost $700,000 new and are only three years old, they can be purchased by ITS for the "bargain basement" price of $430,000, payable $250,000 down and $60,000 each year for three years, without interest.

After some study, ITS's manager, Biff Coletti, has determined that the boats could be operated an average of 250 days per year. Records kept by the previous owner (now in the hands of the bank) indicate that the boats carried an average of 100 tourists per day. Mr. Coletti is confident that this could be increased to at least 140 tourists per day by dropping the tour price from \$18 to \$10 per person. The local bank has estimated the following annual expenses associated with the boats:

Salaries for a manager and	
for boat operators	\$160,000
Insurance	9,000
Fuel	72,000
Bank payments*	60,000
Promotion.	18,000
Maintenance	4,200
Rent for docking space	10,000
Fees and maritime taxes	6,800
Depreciation.	27,333†
Total expenses	\$367,333

* For the first three years only.
† \$430,000 cost − \$20,000 estimated salvage value = \$410,000 depreciable cost; \$410,000 ÷ 15 years = \$27,333 per year.

In order to cover possible damage from docking, ITS would have to make an immediate deposit of \$1,800 to the harbor authorities; this deposit would be refundable at the end of the boats' 15-year remaining useful life. In nine years, the boat hulls would require major scraping and resealing at a cost of \$35,000.

If the boats are purchased, ITS will use the ACRS tables to compute depreciation for tax purposes. ITS's after-tax cost of capital is 10 percent, and the tax rate is 30 percent.

Required: 1. Compute the net cash receipts (before income taxes) each year from operating the boats.
2. By use of the net present value method, determine whether the boats should be purchased. (Round all dollar amounts to the nearest whole dollar.)

P15–22.   Comprehensive problem; simple rate of return; payback.   Westwood Furniture Company is considering the purchase of two different items of equipment, as described below:

Machine A.   A compacting machine has just come onto the market that would permit Westwood Furniture Company to compress sawdust into various shelving products. At present the sawdust is disposed of as a waste product. The following information is available on the machine:

    a. The machine would cost \$420,000 and would have a 10 percent salvage value at the end of its 12-year useful life. The company uses straight-line depreciation and considers salvage value in computing depreciation deductions.

    b. The shelving products manufactured from use of the machine would generate revenues of \$300,000 per year. Variable manufacturing costs would be 20 percent of sales.

    c. Fixed expenses associated with the new shelving products would be (per year): advertising, \$40,000; salaries, \$110,000; utilities, \$5,200; and insurance, \$800.

Machine B.   A second machine has come onto the market that would allow Westwood Furniture Company to automate a sanding process that is now done largely by hand. The following information is available:

a. The new sanding machine would cost $234,000 and would have little or no salvage value at the end of its 13-year useful life. The company would use straight-line depreciation on the new machine.

b. Several old pieces of sanding equipment that are fully depreciated would be disposed of at a scrap value of $9,000.

c. The new sanding machine would provide substantial annual savings in cash operating costs. It would require an operator at an annual salary of $16,350 and $5,400 in annual maintenance costs. The current, hand-operated sanding procedure costs the company $78,000 per year in total.

Westwood Furniture Company requires a return of 15 percent on all equipment purchases. Also, the company will not purchase equipment unless the equipment has a payback of 4.0 years or less.

Required (ignore income taxes):

1. For machine A:
    a. Prepare an income statement showing the expected net income each year from the new shelving products. Use the contribution format.
    b. Compute the simple rate of return.
    c. Compute the payback period.
2. For machine B:
    a. Compute the simple rate of return.
    b. Compute the payback period.
3. Which machine, if either, should the company purchase?

P15–23.   **Uneven cash flows; net present value.**   "All of the engineering studies say that tar sand is excellent for use in road construction," said Holly Edwards, chief engineer for Dieter Mining Company. "With road construction projected to be at peak levels over the next 10 years, now is the time for us to extract and sell the tar sand off of tract 370 in the southern part of the state."

"I'm not so sure," replied Tom Collins, the vice president. "Prices are really soft for tar sand. The best we can hope to get is $7 a ton, and the accounting people say it will cost us at least $3 a ton for utilities, supplies, and selling expenses. That doesn't leave much in the way of contribution margin."

"I know we won't get much per ton," replied Holly, "but our studies show that we have 1,735,000 tons of tar sand in the area. I figure we can extract 90,000, 145,000, and 240,000 tons the first three years, respectively, and then the remainder evenly over the next seven years. Even at only $7 a ton, that'll bring a lot of cash flow into the company."

"But you're forgetting that we have other costs, too," said Tom. "Fixed costs for salaries, insurance, and so forth directly associated with the tar sand project would be $450,000 a year. Besides that, we would have to pay out an additional $250,000 at the end of the project for filling and leveling of the land. You know how tough those environmental people can get if things don't look right. And all of this doesn't even consider the $800,000 cost of special equipment that we would need or the $75,000 we would have to put up for working capital to carry inventories and accounts receivable. I'm uneasy about the whole idea."

"You've got to look at the big picture, Tom. You'll get the working capital back in 10 years when the project is completed. In addition, we can depreciate that equipment and save a bundle in taxes at our 30 percent tax rate. Besides that, since the equipment would have a 12-year useful (ADR midpoint) life it would still have some use left when the project was completed. I'm sure we could sell it to someone for at least 5 percent of its original cost."

"All of that sounds fine, Holly, but I'll still bet the project won't provide the 18 percent after-tax return we require on high-risk investments. Let's give all this to accounting and have them do a present value analysis for us."

Required: 1. Compute the before-tax net cash receipts each year from the extraction and sale of the tar sand. (Do not include the cost of filling and leveling the land in this computation.)

2. Using the data from (1) and other data from the problem as needed, prepare a net present value analysis to determine whether the company should purchase the equipment and extract the tar sand. (Round all dollar amounts to the nearest whole dollar.) You may assume that for the company *as a whole*, there will be a positive taxable income in every year, so that a tax benefit would be realized from any operating losses associated with the tar sand project.

P15–24. **Equipment replacement; incremental cost approach; net present value.**   "That new RAM 8000 is the most sophisticated piece of duplicating equipment available," said Monte Salazar, purchasing agent for Blinko's Copy Service. "The copier it would replace is putting out 5,600,000 pages a year, but the RAM would increase that output by 20 percent."

"I agree it's a powerful machine," replied Angie Carlson, the operations manager. "But we can only get $110,000 out of the copier it would replace and that copier cost us $260,000 just two years ago. I don't think we can justify taking a huge loss on our old equipment every time something new hits the market. Besides, do you realize that the RAM 8000 costs $375,000?"

"Yes, and it's worth every dollar," said Monte. "To prove it, let's have accounting work up an analysis to see if the RAM 8000 meets the 14 percent after-tax rate of return that we require on new equipment."

In response to Monte's request, accounting has gathered the following information:

a. Both the old copier and the RAM 8000 are in the ACRS five-year property class (duplicating equipment).

b. The old copier is being depreciated by the optional straight-line method. Two years' depreciation has been taken; thus, the copier's book value is $182,000. Depreciation over the next four years will be: years 1–3, $52,000 per year; year 4, $26,000.

c. The RAM 8000 would be depreciated using the ACRS tables. The manufacturer estimates that it would have a $15,000 salvage value at the end of its eight-year useful (ADR midpoint) life. The old copier will be worth nothing in eight years.

d. Blinko's Copy Service pays 1.5 cents per page for paper; the company's customers pay an average of 9 cents per page for copy work.

e. In order to keep the RAM 8000 operating at peak efficiency, the company would purchase a maintenance contract that would cost $4,000 more per year than its present maintenance contract.

f. The RAM 8000 would need to have the drum and photo plates replaced in five years; the cost would be $30,000.

g. Blinko's Copy Service has a tax rate of 30 percent.

Required: 1.   Compute the incremental net annual cash receipts (before taxes) expected from the RAM 8000. (Do not include the cost of the drum and photo plates in this computation.)

2.   Use discounted cash flow to determine whether the RAM 8000 will provide the company's required rate of return. Use the incremental-cost approach. (Round all dollar amounts to the nearest whole dollar.)

P15–25.   **A comparison of investment alternatives; total-cost approach.**   Julia Vanfleet is professor of mathematics at a western university. She has received a $225,000 inheritance from her father's estate, and she is anxious to invest it between now and the time she retires in 12 years. Professor Vanfleet's position with the university pays a salary of $60,000 per year. Since the state in which the university is located is experiencing extreme budgetary problems, this salary is expected to remain unchanged in the foreseeable future. Professor Vanfleet is considering two alternatives for investing her inheritance.

Alternative 1.   Municipal bonds can be purchased that mature in 12 years and that bear interest at 8 percent. This interest would be tax-free and paid semiannually. (In discounting a cash flow that occurs semiannually, the procedure is to halve the interest rate and double the number of periods. Use the same procedure for discounting the principal returned when the bonds reach maturity.) This alternative would permit Professor Vanfleet to stay with the university.

Alternative 2.   A small retail business is available for sale that can be purchased for $225,000. The following information relates to this alternative:

a.   Of the purchase price, $80,000 would be for fixtures and other depreciable items. The remainder would be for the company's working capital (inventory, accounts receivable, and cash). The fixtures and other depreciable items would have a remaining useful life of at least 12 years and would be in the ACRS 7-year property class. At the end of 12 years these depreciable items would have a negligible salvage value; however, the working capital would be recovered (either through sale or liquidation of the business) for reinvestment elsewhere.

b.   The store building would be leased. At the end of 12 years, if Professor Vanfleet could not find someone to buy out the business it would be necessary to pay $2,000 to the owner of the building in order to break the lease.

c.   The ACRS tables would be used for depreciation purposes.

d.   Store records indicate that sales have averaged $850,000 per year and out-of-pocket costs (including rent on the building) have averaged $760,000 per year (*not* including income taxes).

e.   Since Professor Vanfleet would operate the store herself, it would be necessary for her to leave the university if this alternative were selected.

Professor Vanfleet's tax rate is 20 percent, and she wants an after-tax return of at least 8 percent on her investment.

Required: Advise Professor Vanfleet as to which alternative should be selected. Use the total-cost approach to discounted cash flow in your analysis. (Round all dollar amounts to the nearest whole dollar.)

P15–26.   Comparison of total-cost and incremental-cost approaches.   Reliable Waste Systems provides a solid waste collection service in a large metropolitan area. The company is considering the purchase of several new trucks to replace an equal number of old trucks now in use. The new trucks would cost $650,000, but they would require only one operator per truck (compared to two operators for the trucks now being used), as well as provide other cost savings. A comparison of total annual cash operating costs between the old trucks that would be replaced and the new trucks is provided below:

	Old trucks	New trucks
Salaries—operators	$170,000	$ 85,000
Fuel	14,000	9,000
Insurance.	6,000	11,000
Maintenance	10,000	5,000
Total annual cash operating costs	$200,000	$110,000

If the new trucks are purchased, the old trucks will be sold to a company in a nearby city for $85,000. These trucks have a current book value of $120,000 and have been used for four years. They are in the ACRS five-year property class; the optional straight-line method is being used to depreciate these trucks for tax purposes.

If the new trucks are not purchased, the old trucks will be used for seven more years and then sold for an estimated $15,000 scrap value. However, in order to keep the old trucks operating, extensive repairs will be needed in one year that will cost $170,000. These repairs will be expensed for tax purposes in the year incurred.

The new trucks would have a useful (ADR midpoint) life of seven years and would be depreciated using the ACRS tables. They would have an estimated $60,000 salvage value at the end of their useful life. The company's tax rate is 30 percent, and its after-tax cost of capital is 12 percent.

Required: 1.   By use of the total-cost approach to discounted cash flow, determine whether the new trucks should be purchased. (Round all dollar amounts to the nearest whole dollar.)

2.   Repeat the computations in (1), this time using the incremental-cost approach to discounted cash flow.

P15–27.   Fast-food operation; effects of write-offs.   B. Moss and R. Grassley have formed a corporation to franchise a quick food system for shopping malls. They have just completed experiments with the prototype machine that will serve as the basis for the operation, and they feel certain that the food it prepares will be well received by the public. However, because the system is new and has not yet been tried publicly, they have decided to conduct a pilot operation in a nearby mall. If it proves successful, they will aggressively market franchises for the system throughout the nation.

The income statements which follow represent their best estimates of income from the pilot mall operation for the next four years.

	Year ending December 31			
	19x5	19x6	19x7	19x8
Sales	$140,000	$160,000	$190,000	$220,000
Less:				
Cost of goods sold	70,000	80,000	95,000	110,000
Wages	14,000	20,000	30,000	40,000
Supplies.	3,000	3,300	3,400	4,200
Personal property taxes	1,000	1,200	1,600	1,800
Annual rental charge	12,000	12,000	12,000	12,000
Depreciation	10,000	10,000	10,000	10,000
Development costs	20,000	20,000	20,000	20,000
Total expenses	130,000	146,500	172,000	198,000
Net income before taxes.	10,000	13,500	18,000	22,000
Income taxes at 30%	3,000	4,050	5,400	6,600
Net income after taxes	$ 7,000	$ 9,450	$ 12,600	$ 15,400

At the end of the four-year period, Moss and Grassley intend to sell the pilot operation and concentrate their efforts on the sale and supervision of franchises for the system. Based on the projected income stream, they believe that the pilot operation can be sold for $130,000 at the end of the four-year period; the income tax liability from the sale will be $15,000.

The following additional information is available on the pilot operation:

a. The shopping mall requires tenants to sign a 10-year lease. Three years' rental is payable at the beginning of the lease period, with annual payments due for each of the next seven years (starting with the first year). The advance payment will apply to the last three years under the lease.

b. The cost of building an operational machine for the pilot operation will be $110,000. The machine will have a salvage value of $10,000 at the end of its 10-year life. Straight-line depreciation will be used for statement purposes, and the ACRS tables will be used for tax purposes. Since the machine has a 10-year useful life, it is in the ACRS 7-year property class.

c. An earlier prototype machine cost $200,000 to develop and build in 19x3. It is not usable for commercial purposes. However, since it was the early basis for the system, it is being amortized against revenues at $20,000 per year. The same amount is deductible for tax purposes. (The prototype machine does not qualify for ACRS treatment.)

Required: 1. Compute the before-tax net cash inflow from operations for each year.

2. Moss and Grassley want to employ discounted cash flow techniques to determine whether the pilot mall operation is a sound investment. Compute the net present value of the contemplated investment, using a minimum required rate of return of 16 percent after taxes.

(CMA, Heavily Adapted)

P15–28. **Simple rate of return; payback.** (Appendix) Top-Tone Health Centers is planning to open a new center in a western city. After careful study, Top-Tone's management has determined the following information relating to the new center:

a. Equipment needed to stock the center would cost $360,000. The equipment would be in the ACRS 5-year property class, but it would be depreciated by the optional straight-line method over its 12-year useful life, as allowed by the ACRS rules. (For purposes of this problem, ignore the half-year convention in computing depreciation deductions.) The equipment would have negligible salvage value at the end of its useful life.

b.   Membership dues from patrons would total $250,000 per year.

c.   Out-of-pocket costs for operating the center each year would be:

Advertising	$ 15,000
Salaries	100,000
Rent	18,000
Insurance.	7,000
Utilities	20,000

d.   Top-Tone's tax rate is 30 percent; its after-tax cost of capital is 14 percent; and it requires a payback period of four years or less on all new centers.

Required: 1.   Prepare an income statement showing the net income (after taxes) expected each year from the new center.

2.   Compute the simple rate of return promised by the new center. Should the new center be opened?

3.   Compute the payback period on the new center. Based on this figure, should the new center be opened?

P15–29.   **Payback; simple rate of return; discounted cash flow.**   (Appendix)   Sal's Soda Shop is investigating the purchase of a new soft ice cream dispensing machine that is capable of dispensing several flavors at one time. The machine costs $70,000. It would have a useful (ADR midpoint) life of eight years and a $6,000 scrap value. If the machine is purchased, Sal will use the straight-line method to depreciate it for tax purposes. The following operating results are expected from the new machine:

Increase in annual revenues		$60,000
Increase in expenses:		
Cash operating expenses	$38,000	
Depreciation	14,000*	52,000
Net income before taxes		8,000
Less income taxes (25%)		2,000
Net income		$ 6,000

* For simplicity in computations, ignore the half-year convention in answering parts (1) and (2) below.

An old, fully depreciated dispensing machine will be disposed of if the new machine is purchased. This old machine will have a negligible scrap value. Sal requires a 12 percent after-tax rate of return on all equipment purchases, and the shop has a 25 percent tax rate.

Required: 1.   What is the payback period on the new machine? If Sal has a required payback of three years or less, should the new machine be purchased?

2.   What is the simple rate of return on the new machine? Is it an acceptable investment?

3.   Sal is uneasy about the results obtained in (1) and (2) above, and he wants some further analysis done. Complete the following:

a.   Compute the net annual cash inflow (before taxes) promised by the new machine.

b.   Using the data from (a) and other data from the problem as needed, determine the net present value of the new machine. (Round all computations to the nearest whole dollar.) Will the machine provide the 12 percent after-tax return required by Sal?

P15–30.   **Simple rate of return; payback; sale of old equipment.**   (Appendix)   In the past, Marcroft Products had relied heavily on direct labor to manufacture its products. The small amount of equipment the company has used is fully depreciated, and management is considering the purchase of new, highly efficient equipment that would increase output and also reduce labor costs. The actual income statement for last year (19x1) with the old production method and the expected income statement for next year (19x2) with the new equipment follow:

	19x1 actual	19x2 expected
Sales revenue	$400,000	$450,000
Less variable production costs	235,000	180,000
Contribution margin	165,000	270,000
Less fixed expenses:		
Advertising	30,000	30,000
Salaries	85,000	85,000
Depreciation	—	25,000
Other	10,000	10,000
Total fixed expenses	125,000	150,000
Income before taxes	40,000	120,000
Less income taxes (30%)	12,000	36,000
Net income	$ 28,000	$ 84,000

The new equipment would cost $300,000 and have a negligible salvage value at the end of its 12-year useful (ADR midpoint) life. The company would depreciate the equipment by the optional straight-line method over its 12-year useful life, as permitted by the ACRS rules. (For purposes of this problem, ignore the half-year convention in computing depreciation deductions.)

The old equipment can be sold now for $12,000; although it is fully depreciated, it is still in good working order and could be used almost indefinitely. Marcroft Products' after-tax cost of capital is 14 percent. A payback period of four years or less is typically used by companies in Marcroft Products' industry.

Required: 1.   Compute the simple rate of return promised by the new equipment. Should it be purchased?
2.   Compute the payback period on the new equipment. Using this figure as a guide, should the new equipment be purchased?

CASES

C15–31.   **Make or buy decision; discounted cash flow.**   Lamb Company manufactures several lines of products, including all of the component parts that go into these products. One unique part, a valve stem, requires specialized tools in its manufacture that need to be replaced. Management has decided that the only alternative to replacing these tools is to acquire the valve stem from an outside source. A supplier is willing to provide the valve stem at a unit sales price of $20 if at least 70,000 units are ordered each year.

Lamb Company's average production of valve stems over the past three years has been 80,000 units each year. Expectations are that this volume will remain constant over the next four years. Cost records indicate that unit manufacturing costs for the valve stem over the last several years have been as follows:

Direct materials	$ 3.60
Direct labor	3.90
Variable overhead	1.50
Fixed overhead*	9.00
Total unit cost	$18.00

*Depreciation of tools (that must now be replaced) accounts for one third of the fixed overhead. The balance is for other fixed overhead costs of the factory that require cash expenditures.

If the specialized tools are purchased, they will cost $2,500,000 and will have a disposal value of $100,000 at the end of their four-year useful (ADR midpoint) life. Straight-line depreciation would be used for book purposes, but the ACRS tables would be used for tax purposes. Lamb Company has a 30 percent tax rate, and management requires a 12 percent after-tax return on investment.

The sales representative for the manufacturer of the specialized tools has stated, "The new tools will allow direct labor and variable overhead to be reduced by $1.60 per unit." Data from another company using identical tools and experiencing similar operating conditions, except that annual production generally averages 100,000 units, confirms the direct labor and variable overhead cost savings. However, the other company indicates that it experienced an increase in raw material cost due to the higher quality of material that had to be used with the new tools. The other company indicates that its costs have been as follows:

Direct materials	$ 4.50
Direct labor	3.00
Variable overhead	0.80
Fixed overhead	10.80
Total unit cost	$19.10

Referring to the figures above, Eric Madsen, Lamb's production manager, stated, "These numbers look great until you consider the difference in volume. Even with the reduction in labor and variable overhead cost, I'll bet our total unit cost figure would increase to over $20 with the new tools."

Although the old tools being used by Lamb Company are now fully depreciated, they have a salvage of $45,000. These tools will be sold if the new tools are purchased; however, if the new tools are not purchased, then the old tools will be retained as standby equipment. Lamb Company's accounting department has confirmed that total fixed overhead costs, other than depreciation, will not change regardless of the decision made concerning the valve stems. However, accounting has estimated that working capital needs will increase by $60,000 if the new tools are purchased due to the higher quality of material required in the manufacture of the valve stems. This working capital would be released at the end of the tools' useful life.

Required: 1. Prepare a discounted cash flow analysis that will help Lamb Company's management decide whether the new tools should be purchased. Use the incremental-cost approach, and round all dollar amounts to the nearest whole dollar.

2. Identify additional factors that Lamb Company's management should consider before a decision is made about whether to manufacture or buy the valve stems.

(CMA, Heavily Adapted)

C15–32. Replacement of riding horses; incremental cost approach; net present value.   The High-Step Riding Stables, Inc., operates a number of exclusive riding stables in the western United States. The company's Northmount Stable is not doing well even though it was provided with 60 new riding horses just two years ago. Evan Black, marketing vice president, wants to sell these horses and purchase 60 Appaloosa riding horses to use in their place. He feels certain that these beautiful animals would enhance the image of the stable and greatly increase revenues. In fact, he has asked the company's accounting department to develop a projected income statement for the coming year assuming use of both the present horses and the Appaloosa horses.

	Present horses	Appaloosa horses
Revenues from patrons	$235,000	$271,000
Less operating expenses:		
Salaries, manager and handlers	70,000	70,000
Feed	14,000	14,000
Insurance on the horses	6,000	10,500
Depreciation, stables and equipment	108,000	108,000
Depreciation, horses*	10,000	28,500
Total operating expenses	208,000	231,000
Income before income taxes	27,000	40,000
Less income taxes (30%)	8,100	12,000
Net income	$ 18,900	$ 28,000

* Present horses: $90,000 cost ÷ 9 years = $10,000. Appaloosa horses: $210,000 cost − (60 horses × $175 sale value = $10,500) = $199,500; $199,500 ÷ 7 years = $28,500.

Shauna Brosnan, operations vice president, is less enthused about the purchase. She stated, ''I agree that the Appaloosas are beautiful, but look at what they would cost us. There are many other ways we could use that $210,000 in the company, and according to my computations all of these other ways would yield a return well over our 10 percent after-tax cost of capital.''

''That's the best part of this whole deal,'' replied Evan. ''The Appaloosas would provide a fantastic rate of return. Just look at these figures I've worked up:''

$$\frac{\text{Net income}}{\underset{\text{investment}}{\text{Initial}} - \underset{\text{old horses}}{\text{Sale of the}}} = \text{Simple rate of return}$$

$$\frac{\$28,000}{\$210,000 - \$55,000} = 18.1\%$$

''Do you have any investments that will beat 18 percent?''

''No, I'll admit I don't,'' replied Shauna, ''and your figures are impressive; but I'm still uneasy about the whole thing. Give me time to look at these figures a little more closely, and then I'll get back with you later.''

After some effort, Shauna has accumulated the following additional information:

    a.   Both the horses currently owned and the Appaloosa horses are in the ACRS five-year property class. For tax purposes, the company is using the optional straight-line method to compute depreciation on the 60 horses now owned by Northmount Stable.

    b.   If the Appaloosa horses are purchased, they will be depreciated by use of the ACRS tables. These horses have a remaining useful (ADR midpoint) life of seven years.

    c.   The 60 horses now owned by Northmount Stable will have no resale value at the end of their useful life to the stable.

    d.   The Appaloosa horses would be registered; in order to maintain this registration, the company would have to pay a renewal fee of $80 per horse four years from now.

Required: 1.   By use of net present value analysis, determine whether the Appaloosa horses should be purchased. Use the incremental-cost approach, and round all dollar amounts to the nearest whole dollar.

           2.   Shauna Brosnan wants to know the amount of incremental net cash receipts (before taxes) that would have to be generated from the Appaloosa horses each year in order for the investment to provide exactly a 10 percent after-tax rate of return. Compute this figure for Shauna (to the nearest whole dollar).

PART FOUR

Selected Topics for Further Study

CHAPTER 16

Service Department Cost Allocations

LEARNING OBJECTIVES

After studying Chapter 16, you should be able to:

- Explain what is meant by a service department, and explain why it is necessary to allocate service department costs to operating departments.

- Allocate service department costs to other departments, using (1) the step method and (2) the direct method.

- Explain why variable service department costs should be allocated separately from fixed service department costs, and give the allocation guidelines for each type of cost.

- Explain why fixed service department costs should always be allocated in lump-sum amounts.

- Prepare an allocation schedule involving several service departments and several operating departments.

- Define or explain the key terms listed at the end of the chapter.

A s stated in Chapter 1, most organizations have one or more service
departments that carry on critical auxiliary services for the entire
organization. In this chapter, we look more closely at service departments
and consider how their costs are allocated to the units they serve for planning,
costing, and other purposes.

THE NEED FOR COST ALLOCATION

Departments within an organization can be divided into two broad classes:
(1) operating departments and (2) service departments. **Operating departments** include those departments or units where the central purposes of
the organization are carried out. Examples of such departments or units
would include the surgery department in a hospital; the undergraduate and
graduate programs in a university; various flight groups in an airline; and
producing departments such as milling, assembly, and painting in a manufacturing firm.

Service departments, by contrast, do not engage directly in operating
activities. Rather, they provide services or assistance that facilitate the activities of the operating departments. Examples of such services include cafeteria, internal auditing, personnel, X ray, cost accounting, and purchasing.
Although service departments do not engage directly in the operating activities of an organization, the costs that they incur are generally viewed as
being part of the cost of the final product or service, the same as are materials,
labor, and overhead in a manufacturing firm or medications in a hospital.

Equity in Allocation

The major question that we must consider in this chapter is: How does
the manager determine how much of a service department's cost is to be
allocated to each of the units that it serves? This is an important question,
since the amount of service department cost allocated to a particular unit
can have a major impact on the cost of the goods or services that the unit
is providing. As we shall see, many factors must be considered if allocations
are to be equitable between departments or other units that receive services
during a period.

GUIDELINES FOR COST ALLOCATION

There are several basic guidelines to follow in service department cost
allocation. These guidelines relate to (1) selecting the proper allocation
base, (2) allocating the costs of interdepartmental services, (3) allocating
costs by behavior, (4) avoiding certain allocation pitfalls, and (5) deciding
whether to allocate budgeted or actual costs. These topics are covered in
order in the following five sections.

Selecting Allocation Bases

Costs of service departments are allocated to other departments by means of some type of *allocation base*. An **allocation base** is a measure of activity; this activity may be stated in labor-hours, number of employees, square footage of floor space, or in many other ways. Managers try to select allocation bases that reflect as accurately as possible the benefits that are being received by the various departments within the company from the services involved. A number of such bases may be selected according to the nature of the services. Examples of allocation bases that are frequently used are presented in Exhibit 16–1.

Once allocation bases have been chosen, they tend to remain unchanged for long periods of time. The selection of an allocation base represents a *major policy decision* that is normally reviewed only at very infrequent intervals or when it appears that some major inequity exists.

As we stated earlier, the way in which service department costs are allocated to other departments can have a major impact on their performance or on the cost of the goods or services they are providing, so the selection of an allocation base is no minor decision. The criteria for making selections may include: (1) direct, traceable benefits from the service involved, as

EXHIBIT 16–1

Bases used in allocating service department costs

Service department	Base frequently used
Laundry	Pounds of laundry; number of items processed
Airport ground services	Number of flights
Cafeteria	Number of employees
Medical facilities	Periodic analysis of cases handled; number of employees; hours worked
Materials handling	Hours of service; volume handled
Custodial services (building and grounds)	Measure of square footage occupied
Engineering	Periodic analysis of services rendered; direct labor-hours
Production planning and control	Periodic analysis of services rendered; direct labor-hours
Cost accounting	Labor-hours; clients or patients serviced
Power	Measured usage (in kwh); capacity of machines
Personnel and employment	Number of employees; turnover of labor; periodic analysis of time spent
Receiving, shipping, and stores	Units handled; number of requisition and issue slips; square or cubic footage occupied
Factory administration	Total labor-hours
Maintenance	Machine-hours; total labor-hours (in order of preference)

measured, for example, by the number of service orders handled; and (2) the extent to which space or equipment is made available to a department, as measured, for example, by the number of square feet occupied in a building. In addition to these criteria, the manager must take care to assure that allocations are clear and straightforward, since complex allocation computations run the risk of yielding negative returns. That is, if allocation computations become too complex, the cost of the computations may exceed any benefits that they are trying to bring about. Allocation formulas should be simple and easily understood by all involved, particularly by the managers to whom the costs are being allocated.

Interdepartmental Services

Many service departments provide services for each other, as well as for operating departments. The cafeteria, for example, provides food for all employees, including those assigned to other service departments. In turn, the cafeteria may receive services from other service departments, such as from custodial services or from personnel. Services provided between service departments are known as **interdepartmental** or **reciprocal services.**

There are two approaches to handling the costs of services between departments. The first, called the **step method,** provides for allocation of a service department's costs to other service departments, as well as to operating departments, in a sequential manner. The second, called the **direct method,** ignores the costs of services between departments and allocates all service department costs directly to operating departments.

In the following two sections, we provide examples of both the step method and the direct method of making interdepartmental cost allocations.

Step method   In allocating by the step method, some sequence of allocation must be chosen. The sequence typically begins with the department that provides the greatest amount of service to other departments. After its costs have been allocated, the process continues, step by step, ending with the department providing the least amount of services to other service departments. This step procedure is illustrated graphically in Exhibit 16–2.

To provide a numerical example of the step method, assume that Mountain View Hospital has two service departments and two operating departments as shown below.

	Service departments		Operating departments		
	Hospital administration	Custodial services	Laboratory	Daily patient care	Total
Departmental costs before allocation	$360,000	$90,000	$261,000	$689,000	$1,400,000
Labor-hours	—	6,000	18,000	30,000	54,000
Proportion of labor	—	$1/9$	$3/9$	$5/9$	$9/9$
Space occupied–square feet . . .	10,000	—	5,000	45,000	60,000
Proportion of space	$2/12$	—	$1/12$	$9/12$	$12/12$

EXHIBIT 16–2
Graphic illustration—step method

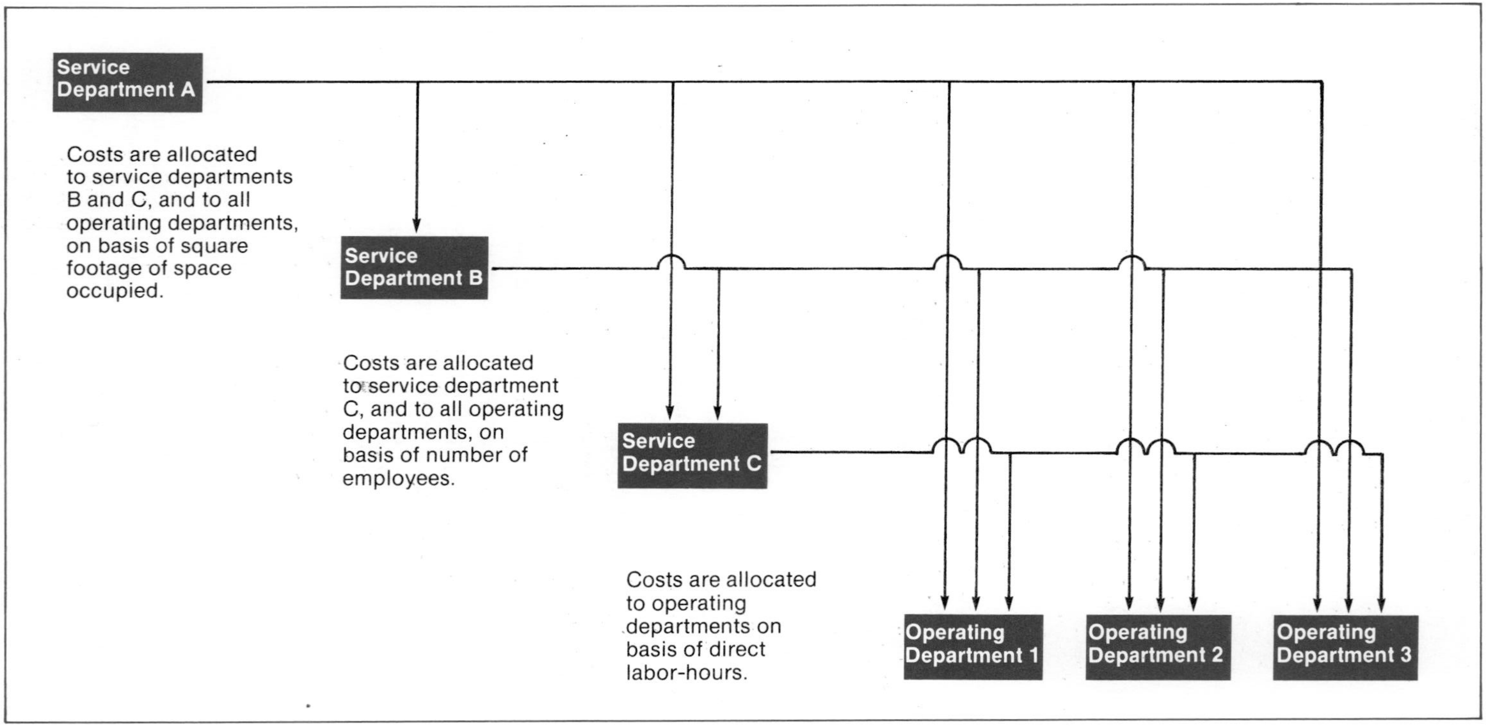

Service Department A

Costs are allocated to service departments B and C, and to all operating departments, on basis of square footage of space occupied.

Service Department B

Costs are allocated to service department C, and to all operating departments, on basis of number of employees.

Service Department C

Costs are allocated to operating departments on basis of direct labor-hours.

Operating Department 1

Operating Department 2

Operating Department 3

EXHIBIT 16–3

Step method of allocation

| | Service Departments | | Operating departments | | |
	Hospital administration	Custodial services	Laboratory	Daily patient care	Total
Departmental costs before allocation	$ 360,000	$ 90,000	$261,000	$ 689,000	$1,400,000
Allocation:					
Hospital administration costs (1/9, 3/9, 5/9)	(360,000)	40,000	120,000	200,000	
Custodial services costs (1/10, 9/10)*		(130,000)	13,000	117,000	
Total costs after allocation . . .	$ –0–	$ –0–	$394,000	$1,006,000	$1,400,000

* This allocation is based on the space occupied by the two operating departments, which is: 5,000 square feet + 45,000 square feet = 50,000 square feet.

The costs of hospital administration are allocated first on a basis of labor-hours in other departments. The costs of custodial services are then allocated on a basis of square footage of space occupied. Allocations of these service department costs by the step method are shown in Exhibit 16–3.

Several things should be noted from the data in this exhibit. First, note that the costs of hospital administration are borne by another service department (custodial services) as well as by the operating departments. Also note that those hospital administration costs that have been allocated to custodial services *are included with custodial services costs,* and that the total ($90,000 + $40,000 = $130,000) is allocated only to subsequent departments. That is, no part of custodial services' costs are reallocated back to hospital administration, even though custodial services may have provided services to hospital administration during the period. This is a key idea associated with the step method: After the allocation of a service department's costs has been completed, costs of other service departments are not reallocated back to it.

Finally, note from Exhibit 16–3 that after the allocations have been made, all of the departmental costs are contained in the two operating departments. These costs will form the basis for preparing overhead rates as well as for determining the overall profitability of the operating departments in the hospital.

Direct method   The direct method is much simpler than the step method in that services between departments are ignored, and all allocations are made directly to operating departments. Exhibit 16–4 on the following page illustrates the direct method, using the data provided earlier.

Although simpler than the step method, the direct method is less accurate, since it ignores interdepartmental services. This can be a major defect in that overhead rates can be affected if the resulting errors in allocation are significant. In turn, incorrect overhead rates can lead to distorted product

EXHIBIT 16–4

Direct method of allocation

	Service departments		Operating departments		
	Hospital administration	Custodial services	Laboratory	Daily patient care	Total
Departmental costs before allocation	$ 360,000	$ 90,000	$261,000	$689,000	$1,400,000
Allocation:					
Hospital administration costs (⅜, ⅝)*	(360,000)		135,000	225,000	
Custodial services costs (¹⁄₁₀, ⁹⁄₁₀)†		(90,000)	9,000	81,000	
Total costs after allocation . . .	$ –0–	$ –0–	$405,000	$995,000	$1,400,000

* This allocation is based only on the labor-hours in the two operating departments, which are: 18,000 hours + 30,000 hours = 48,000 hours.
† As in Exhibit 16–3, this allocation is based on the space occupied by the two operating departments.

and service costs and to ineffective pricing. Even so, many organizations use the direct method because of its ease of application.

Finally, for both the step and direct methods, it is important to note that although most service departments are simply cost centers and thus generate no revenues, a few, such as the cafeteria, may charge employees or other outside parties for the services they perform. If a service department (such as the cafeteria) generates revenues, these revenues should be offset against the department's costs, and only the net amount of cost remaining after this offset should be allocated to other departments within the organization. In this manner, the other departments will not be required to bear costs for which the service department has already been reimbursed.

Allocating Costs by Behavior

Whenever possible, service department costs should be separated into fixed and variable classifications and allocated separately. This approach is necessary to avoid possible inequities in allocation, as well as to provide more useful data for planning and control of departmental operations.

Variable costs   Variable costs represent direct costs of providing services and will generally vary in total in proportion to fluctuations in the level of service consumed. Food cost in a cafeteria would be a variable cost, for example, and one would expect this cost to vary proportionately with the number of persons using the cafeteria over a given period of time.

As a general rule, variable costs should be charged to consuming departments according to whatever activity base controls the incurrence of the cost involved. If, for example, the variable costs of a service department such as maintenance are incurred according to the number of machine-hours worked in the producing departments, then variable maintenance costs should be allocated to the producing departments on a machine-hours basis. By this means, the departments directly responsible for the incurrence of servicing costs are required to bear them in proportion to their actual usage of the service involved.

Technically, the assigning of variable servicing costs to consuming departments can more accurately be termed *charges* than allocations, since the service department is actually charging the consuming departments at some fixed rate per unit of service provided. In effect, the service department is saying, "I'll charge you *X* dollars for every unit of my service that you consume. You can consume as much or as little as you desire; the total charge you bear will vary proportionately."

Fixed costs The fixed costs of service departments represent the cost of having long-run service capacity available. As such, these costs are most equitably allocated to consuming departments on a basis of *predetermined lump-sum amounts*. By "predetermined lump-sum amounts" we mean that the amount charged to each consuming department is determined in advance and, once determined, does not change from period to period. Typically, the lump-sum amount charged to a department is based either on the department's peak-period or long-run average servicing needs. The logic behind lump-sum allocations of this type is as follows:

When a service department is first established, some basic capacity is built into it according to the observed needs of the other departments that it will service. This basic capacity may reflect the peak-period needs of the other departments, or it may reflect their long-run average or "normal" servicing needs. Depending on how much servicing capacity is provided for, it will be necessary to make a commitment of resources to the servicing unit, which will be reflected in its fixed costs. It is generally felt that these fixed costs should be borne by the consuming departments whose servicing needs have made the creation of the service department necessary, and that the costs should be borne in proportion to the individual servicing needs that have been provided for. That is, if available capacity in the service department has been provided to meet the peak-period needs of consuming departments, then the fixed costs of the service department should be allocated in predetermined lump-sum amounts to consuming departments on this basis. If available capacity has been provided only to meet "normal" or long-run average needs, then the fixed costs should be allocated on this basis.

Once set, allocations should not vary from period to period, since they represent each consuming department's "fair share" of having a certain level of service capacity available and on line. The fact that a consuming department does not need a peak level or even a "normal" level of servicing every period is immaterial; if it requires such servicing at certain times, then the capacity to deliver it must be available. It is the responsibility of the consuming departments to bear the cost of that availability.

To illustrate this idea, assume that Novak Company has just organized a maintenance department to service all machines in the cutting, assembly, and finishing departments. In determining the capacity that should be built into the newly organized maintenance department, the company recognized that the various producing departments would have the following peak-period needs for maintenance:

Department	Peak-period maintenance needs in terms of number of hours of maintenance work required	Percent of total hours
Cutting.	900	30
Assembly	1,800	60
Finishing	300	10
	3,000	100

Therefore, in allocating the maintenance department fixed costs to the producing departments, 30 percent should be allocated to the cutting department, 60 percent to the assembly department, and 10 percent to the finishing department. These lump-sum allocations *will not change* from period to period unless there is some shift in servicing needs due to structural changes in the organization.

Pitfalls in Allocating Fixed Costs

Rather than allocate fixed costs in predetermined lump-sum amounts, some firms allocate them by use of a *variable* allocation base. What's wrong with this practice? The answer is that it can create serious inequities between departments. The inequities will arise from the fact that the fixed costs allocated to one department will be heavily influenced by what happens in *other* departments or segments of the organization.

To illustrate, assume that Kolby Products has an auto service center that provides maintenance work on the fleet of autos used in the company's two sales territories. The auto service center costs are all fixed. Contrary to good practice, the company allocates these fixed costs to the sales territories on the basis of miles driven (a variable base). Selected cost data for the last two years are given below:

	Year 1	Year 2
Auto service center costs (all fixed) . . .	$ 120,000 *(a)*	$ 120,000 *(a)*
Sales territory A—miles driven	1,500,000	1,500,000
Sales territory B—miles driven	1,500,000	900,000
Total miles driven.	3,000,000 *(b)*	2,400,000 *(b)*
Allocation rate per mile, *(a) ÷ (b)*	$0.04	$0.05

Notice that sales territory A maintained an activity level of 1,500,000 miles driven in both years. On the other hand, sales territory B allowed its activity to drop off from 1,500,000 miles in year 1 to only 900,000 miles in year 2. The auto service center costs that would have been allocated to the two sales territories over the two-year span are as follows:

Year 1:
Sales territory A: 1,500,000 miles at $0.04 . . $ 60,000
Sales territory B: 1,500,000 miles at $0.04 . .   60,000
Total cost allocated $120,000

Year 2:
Sales territory A: 1,500,000 miles at $0.05 . . $ 75,000
Sales territory B: 900,000 miles at $0.05 . . .   45,000
Total cost allocated $120,000

In year 1, the two sales territories share the service department costs equally. In year 2, however, the bulk of the service department costs are allocated to sales territory A. This is not because of any increase in activity in sales territory A; rather, it is because of the *decrease* in effort in sales territory B, which did not maintain its activity level during year 2. Even though sales territory A maintained the same level of activity in both years, the use of a variable allocation base has caused it to be penalized with a heavier cost allocation in year 2 because of what has happened in *another* territory of the company.

This kind of inequity is almost inevitable when a variable allocation base is used to allocate fixed costs. The manager of sales territory A undoubtedly will be upset about the inequity forced on his territory, but he will feel powerless to do anything about it. The result will be a loss of confidence in the system and the accumulation of a considerable backlog of ill feeling.

Should Actual or Budgeted Costs Be Allocated?

Should a service department allocate its *actual* costs to operating departments, or should it allocate its *budgeted* costs? The answer is that budgeted costs should be allocated. What's wrong with allocating actual costs? Allocating actual costs burdens the operating departments with the inefficiencies of the service department managers. If actual costs are allocated, then any lack of cost control on the part of the service department manager is simply buried in a routine allocation to other departments.

Any variance over budgeted costs should be retained in the service department and closed out at year-end against the company's revenues or against cost of goods sold, along with other variances. Operating department managers rarely complain about being allocated a portion of service department costs, but they complain bitterly if they are forced to absorb service department inefficiencies.

EFFECT OF ALLOCATIONS ON OPERATING DEPARTMENTS

Once allocations have been completed, what do the operating departments do with the allocated service department costs? Since the amounts allocated are presumed to represent each department's "fair share" of the cost of services provided for it, the allocations are included in performance evaluations of the operating departments and also included in determining their individual profitability.

In addition, if the operating departments are responsible for developing overhead rates for costing of products or billing of services, then the allocated costs are combined with the other costs of the operating departments, and the total is used as a basis for rate computations. This rate development process is illustrated in Exhibit 16–5. Observe from the exhibit that the term *allocated* is used to describe the movement of service department costs to operating departments, whereas the term *applied* is used to describe the attaching of these costs (along with operating department costs) to products and services.

Typically, the flexible budget serves as the means for combining allocated service department costs with operating department costs and for computing overhead rates. An example of the combining of these costs on a flexible budget is presented in Exhibit 16–6. Note from the exhibit that both variable

EXHIBIT 16–5

Effect of allocations on products and services

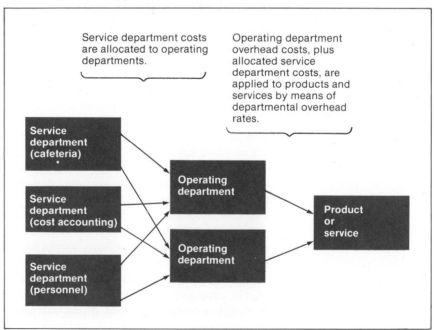

EXHIBIT 16–6

Flexible budget containing allocated service department costs

SUPERIOR COMPANY
Flexible Budget—Milling Department

Budgeted direct labor-hours   50,000

Overhead costs	Cost formula (per hour)	Direct labor-hours		
		40,000	50,000	60,000
Variable costs:				
Indirect labor	$1.45	$ 58,000	$ 72,500	$ 87,000
Indirect material	0.90	36,000	45,000	54,000
Utilities	0.10	4,000	5,000	6,000
Allocation—cafeteria	0.15	6,000	7,500	9,000
Total variable costs	$2.60	104,000	130,000	156,000
Fixed costs:				
Depreciation		85,000	85,000	85,000
Supervisory salaries		110,000	110,000	110,000
Property taxes		9,000	9,000	9,000
Allocation—cafeteria		21,000	21,000	21,000
Allocation—personnel department .		45,000	45,000	45,000
Total fixed costs		270,000	270,000	270,000
Total overhead costs		$374,000	$400,000	$426,000

$$\text{Predetermined overhead rate} = \frac{\$400,000}{50,000 \text{ DLH}} = \$8 \text{ per direct labor-hour}$$

and fixed service department costs have been allocated to Superior Company's milling department and are included on the latter's flexible budget. Since allocated service department costs become an integral part of the flexible budget, they are automatically included in overhead rate computations, as shown at the bottom of the exhibit. If this had been the flexible budget of an operating department in a service company, rather than a manufacturing company, then the overhead rate computation would have been for purposes of developing an appropriate billing rate for services.

A SUMMARY OF COST ALLOCATION GUIDELINES

To summarize the material covered in preceding sections, we can note five key points to remember about allocating service department costs:

1. If possible, the distinction between variable and fixed costs in service departments should be maintained.
2. Variable costs should be allocated at the budgeted rate, according to whatever activity measure (miles driven, direct labor-hours, number of employees) controls the incurrence of the cost involved.
    a. If the allocations are being made at the beginning of the year,

they should be based on the budgeted activity level planned for the consuming departments. The allocation formula would be:

$$\text{Budgeted rate} \times \text{Budgeted activity} = \text{Cost allocated}$$

b. If the allocations are being made at the end of the year, they should be based on the actual activity level that has occurred during the year. The allocation formula would be:

$$\text{Budgeted rate} \times \text{Actual activity} = \text{Cost allocated}$$

Allocations made at the beginning of the year would be to provide data for computing overhead rates for costing of products and billing of services in the operating departments. Allocations made at the end of the year would be to provide data for comparing actual performance against planned performance.

3. Fixed costs represent the costs of having service capacity available. Where feasible, these costs should be allocated in predetermined lump-sum amounts. The lump-sum amount going to each department should be in proportion to the servicing needs that gave rise to the investment in the service department in the first place. (This might be either peak-period needs for servicing or long-run average needs.) Budgeted fixed costs, rather than actual fixed costs, should always be allocated.

4. If it is not feasible to maintain a distinction between variable and fixed costs in a service department, then the costs of the department should be allocated to consuming departments according to the base that appears to provide the best measure of benefits received.

5. Where possible, reciprocal services between departments should be recognized.

IMPLEMENTING THE ALLOCATION GUIDELINES

We will now show the implementation of these guidelines by the use of specific examples. We will focus first on the allocation of costs for a single department, and then develop a more extended example where multiple departments are involved.

Basic Allocation Techniques

For purposes of illustration, assume that Seaboard Airlines is divided into a Freight Division and a Passenger Division. The company has a single aircraft maintenance department that provides servicing to both divisions. Variable servicing costs are budgeted at $10 per flight-hour. The fixed costs of the department are budgeted at $750,000 per year. Peak-period flight-hours per year and budgeted flight-hours for the coming year are shown below:

	Flight-hours	
	Peak-period	Budgeted
Freight Division	12,000	9,000
Passenger Division	18,000	15,000
Total flight-hours	30,000	24,000

Given these data, the amount of cost that would be allocated to each division from the aircraft maintenance department at the beginning of the coming year would be:

	Divisions	
	Freight	Passenger
Variable cost allocation:		
$10 × 9,000 flight-hours	$ 90,000	
$10 × 15,000 flight-hours		$150,000
Fixed cost allocation:		
40%* × $750,000	300,000	
60%* × $750,000		450,000
Total cost allocated	$390,000	$600,000

*These allocations are based on peak-period flight-hours in each division:

    Freight Division: 12,000 flight-hours ÷ 30,000 flight-hours = 40%.
    Passenger Division: 18,000 flight-hours ÷ 30,000 flight-hours = 60%.

As explained earlier, these allocations would be placed on the flexible budgets of the respective divisions and included in the computation of divisional overhead rates.

At the end of the year, Seaboard Airlines' management may want to make a second allocation, this time based on actual activity, in order to compare actual performance for the year against planned performance. To illustrate, assume that year-end records show that actual costs in the aircraft maintenance department for the year were: variable costs, $290,000; and fixed costs, $780,000. We will assume that one division logged more flight-hours during the year than planned and the other one logged less flight-hours than planned.

	Flight-hours	
	Budgeted (see above)	Actual
Freight Division	9,000	8,000
Passenger Division	15,000	17,000
Total flight-hours	24,000	25,000

The amount of actual service department cost chargeable to each division for the year would be as follows:

	Divisions	
	Freight	**Passenger**
Variable cost allocation:		
$10 × 8,000 flight-hours	$ 80,000	
$10 × 17,000 flight-hours		$170,000
Fixed cost allocation:		
40% × $750,000	300,000	
60% × $750,000		450,000
Total cost allocated	$380,000	$620,000

Notice that the variable cost is allocated according to the budgeted rate ($10 per hour) times the *actual activity* for the year, and that the fixed cost is allocated according to the original budgeted amount. As stated in the guidelines given earlier, allocations are always based on budgeted rates and amounts in order to avoid the passing on of inefficiency from one department to another. Thus, a portion of the actual costs of the aircraft maintenance department for the year will not be allocated, as shown below:

	Variable	**Fixed**
Total actual costs incurred	$290,000	$780,000
Costs allocated (above)	250,000*	750,000
Spending variance—not allocated . .	$ 40,000	$ 30,000

* $10 per flight-hour × 25,000 actual flight-hours = $250,000.

These variances will be closed out against the company's overall revenues for the year, along with any other variances that may occur.

An Extended Example

The Proctor Company has three service departments, building maintenance, cafeteria, and inspection. The company also has two operating departments, shaping and assembly. The service departments provide services to each other, as well as to the operating departments. Types of costs in the service departments and bases for allocation are:

Department	Type of cost	Base for allocation
Building maintenance . . .	Fixed costs	Square footage occupied
Cafeteria	Variable costs	Number of employees
	Fixed costs	10% to inspection, 40% to shaping, and 50% to assembly
Inspection	Variable costs	Direct labor-hours
	Fixed costs	70% to shaping and 30% to assembly

The Proctor Company allocates service department costs by the step method in the following order:

1.   Building maintenance.
2.   Cafeteria.
3.   Inspection.

Assume the following budgeted cost and operating data for 19x1:

Department	Variable cost	Fixed cost
Building maintenance	—	$130,000
Cafeteria	$200 per employee	250,000
Inspection	$0.06 per direct labor-hour	548,000

Department	Number of employees	Direct labor-hours	Square footage of space occupied (square feet)
Building maintenance	6*	—	3,000
Cafeteria	9*	—	4,000
Inspection	30	—	1,000
Shaping	190	300,000	8,000
Assembly	250	500,000	13,000
Total	485	800,000	29,000

* Although there are employees in both of these service departments, under the step method costs are only allocated *forward*—never backward. For this reason, the costs of the cafeteria will be allocated *forward* on the basis of the number of employees in the inspection, shaping, and assembly departments.

Using these data, cost allocations to the operating departments would be as shown in Exhibit 16–7 on the following page. To save space, we have placed the operating departments' flexible budget overhead costs in the exhibit and computed the predetermined overhead rates there.

No Distinction Made between Fixed and Variable Costs

As stated in the guidelines given earlier, in some cases it may not be feasible to maintain a distinction between fixed and variable service department costs. We noted that in such cases the costs should be allocated to operating departments according to the base that appears to provide the best measure of benefits received. An example of such an allocation was given earlier in Exhibit 16–3, where we first illustrated the step method. The reader may wish to turn back and review this example before reading on.

EXHIBIT 16–7

THE PROCTOR COMPANY
Beginning-of-Year Cost Allocations for Purposes of
Preparing Predetermined Overhead Rates

	Building maintenance	Cafeteria	Inspection	Shaping	Assembly
Variable costs to be allocated	–0–	$ 94,000	$ 42,000	—	—
Cafeteria allocation at $200 per employee:					
30 employees × $200.	—	(6,000)	6,000	—	—
190 employees × $200.	—	(38,000)	—	$ 38,000	—
250 employees × $200.	—	(50,000)	—	—	$ 50,000
Inspection allocation at $0.06 per direct labor-hour:					
300,000 DLH × $0.06	—	—	(18,000)	18,000	—
500,000 DLH × $0.06	—	—	(30,000)	—	30,000
Total.	–0–	–0–	–0–	56,000	80,000
Fixed costs to be allocated	$130,000	250,000	548,000		
Building maintenance allocation at $5 per square foot:*					
4,000 square feet × $5	(20,000)	20,000	—	—	—
1,000 square feet × $5	(5,000)	—	5,000	—	—
8,000 square feet × $5	(40,000)	—	—	40,000	—
13,000 square feet × $5	(65,000)	—	—	—	65,000
Cafeteria allocation:†					
10% × $270,000	—	(27,000)	27,000	—	—
40% × $270,000	—	(108,000)	—	108,000	—
50% × $270,000	—	(135,000)	—	—	135,000
Inspection allocation:‡					
70% × $580,000	—	—	(406,000)	406,000	—
30% × $580,000	—	—	(174,000)	—	174,000
Total.	–0–	–0–	–0–	554,000	374,000
Total allocated costs	$ –0–	$ –0–	$ –0–	610,000	454,000
Other flexible budget costs at the planned activity level				1,340,000	1,846,000
Total overhead costs				$1,950,000	$2,300,000 (a)
Budgeted direct labor-hours				300,000	500,000 (b)
Predetermined overhead rate, (a) ÷ (b)				$6.50	$4.60

---

* Square footage of space . . . . 29,000 square feet
Less building maintenance space . . . . 3,000 square feet
Net space for allocation . . . . 26,000 square feet

$$\frac{\text{Building maintenance fixed costs, \$130,000}}{\text{Net space for allocation, 26,000 square feet}} = \text{\$5 per square foot}$$

† Cafeteria fixed costs $250,000
Allocated from building maintenance 20,000
Total cost to be allocated $270,000
Allocation percentages are given in the problem.

‡ Inspection fixed costs $548,000
Allocated from building maintenance 5,000
Allocated from cafeteria 27,000
Total cost to be allocated $580,000
Allocation percentages are given in the problem.

Should All Costs Be Allocated?

As a general rule, any service department costs that are incurred as a result of specific services provided to operating departments should be allocated back to these departments and used to compute overhead rates and to measure profitability. The only time when this general rule is not followed is in those situations where, in the view of management, allocation would result in an undesirable behavioral response from operating departments. There are some servicing costs, for example, that are clearly beneficial to operating departments but which these departments may not utilize as fully as they should, particularly in times of cost economizing. Systems design is a good example of such a cost. Utilization of systems design services may be very beneficial to operating departments in terms of improving overall efficiency, reducing waste, and assuring adherence to departmental policies. But if a department knows that it will be charged for the systems design services it uses, it may be less inclined to take advantage of the benefits involved, especially if the department is feeling some pressure to trim costs. In short, the departmental manager may opt for the near-term benefit of avoiding a direct charge, in lieu of the long-term benefit of reduced waste and greater efficiency.

To avoid discouraging use of a service that is helpful to the entire organization, some firms do not charge for the service at all. These managers feel that by making such services a "free" commodity, departments will be more inclined to take full advantage of their benefits.

Other firms take a somewhat different approach. They agree that charging according to usage may discourage utilization of such services as systems design, but they argue that such services should not be free. Instead of providing free services, these firms take what is sometimes called a **retainer fee approach.** Each department is charged a flat amount each year, regardless of how much or how little of the service it utilizes. The thought is that if a department knows that it is going to be charged a certain amount for systems design services, *regardless of usage,* then it will probably utilize the services at least to that extent.

Beware of Sales Dollars as an Allocation Base

Over the years, sales dollars (or total revenues) have been a favorite allocation base for service department costs. One reason is that sales dollars are simple, straightforward, and easy to work with. Another reason is that people tend to view sales dollars as being a measure of well-being, or "ability to pay," and, hence, as being a measure of how extensively costs can be absorbed from other parts of the organization.

Unfortunately, sales dollars often constitute a very poor allocation base, for the reason that sales dollars vary from period to period, whereas the costs being allocated are often largely *fixed* in nature. As discussed earlier, if a variable base is used to allocate fixed costs, inequities can result between departments since the costs being allocated to one department will depend in large part on what happens in *other* departments. For example, a letup in sales effort in one department will shift allocated costs off that department and onto other, more productive departments. In effect, the departments putting forth the best sales efforts are penalized in the form of higher allocations, simply because of inefficiencies elsewhere that are beyond their control. The result is often bitterness and resentment on the part of the managers of the better departments.

Consider the following situation encountered by the author:

A large men's clothing store has one service department and three sales departments—suits, shoes, and accessories. The service department's costs total $60,000 per period and are allocated to the three sales departments according to sales dollars. A recent period showed the following allocation:

	Department			Total
	Suits	Shoes	Accessories	
Sales by department.	$260,000	$40,000	$100,000	$400,000
Percentage of total sales	65%	10%	25%	100%
Allocation of service department costs, based on percentage of total sales	$ 39,000	$ 6,000	$ 15,000	$ 60,000

In a following period, the manager of the suit department launched a very successful program to expand sales by $100,000 in his department. Sales in the other two departments remained unchanged. Total service department costs also remained unchanged, but the allocation of these costs changed substantially, as shown below:

	Department			Total
	Suits	Shoes	Accessories	
Sales by department	$360,000	$40,000	$100,000	$500,000
Percentage of total sales	72%	8%	20%	100%
Allocation of service department costs, based on percentage of total sales	$ 43,200	$ 4,800	$ 12,000	$ 60,000
Increase (or decrease) from prior allocation	4,200	(1,200)	(3,000)	—

The manager of the suit department complained that as a result of his successful effort to expand sales in his department, he was being forced to carry a larger share of the service department costs. On the other hand, the managers of the departments that showed no improvement in sales were being relieved of a portion of the costs that they had been carrying. Yet there had been no change in the amount of services provided for any department.

The manager of the suit department viewed the increased service department cost allocation to his department as a penalty for his outstanding performance, and he wondered whether his efforts had really been worthwhile after all in the eyes of top management.

Sales dollars should be used as an allocation base only in those cases where there is a direct causal relationship between sales dollars and the service department costs being allocated. In those situations where service department costs are fixed in nature, they should be allocated according to the guidelines discussed earlier in the chapter.

SUMMARY

Service departments are organized to provide some needed service in a single, centralized place, rather than to have all units within the organization provide the service for themselves. Although service departments do not engage directly in production or other operating activities, the costs that they incur are vital to the overall success of an organization and therefore are properly included as part of the cost of its products and services.

Service department costs are charged to operating departments by an allocation process. In turn, the operating departments include the allocated costs within their flexible budgets, from which overhead rates are computed for purposes of costing of products or billing of services.

In order to avoid inequity in allocations, variable and fixed service department costs should be allocated separately. The variable costs should be allocated according to whatever activity measure controls their incurrence. The fixed costs should be allocated in predetermined lump-sum amounts according to either the peak-period or the long-run average servicing needs of the consuming departments. Budgeted costs, rather than actual costs, should always be allocated, in order to avoid the passing on of inefficiency between departments. Any variances between budgeted and actual service department costs should be kept within the service departments for analysis purposes, then written off against revenues or against cost of goods sold, along with other variances.

KEY TERMS FOR REVIEW

Allocation base Any measure of activity (such as labor-hours, number of employees, or square footage of space) that is used to charge service department costs to other departments.

Direct method The allocation of all of a service department's costs directly to operating departments without recognizing services provided to other service departments.

Interdepartmental services Services provided between service departments. Also see *Reciprocal services*.

Operating department A department or similar unit in an organization within which the central purposes of the organization are carried out.

Reciprocal services Services provided between service departments. Also see *Interdepartmental services.*

Retainer fee approach A method of allocating service department costs in which other departments are charged a flat amount each period regardless of usage of the service involved.

Service department A department that provides support or assistance to operating departments and that does not engage directly in production or in other operating activities of an organization.

Step method The allocation of a service department's costs to other service departments as well as to operating departments in a sequential manner. The sequence starts with the service department that provides the greatest amount of service to other departments.

QUESTIONS

16–1.   What is the difference between a service department and an operating department? Give several examples of service departments.

16–2.   In what way are service department costs similar to such costs as lubricants, utilities, and factory supervision?

16–3.   "Products and services can be costed equally well with or without allocations of service department costs." Do you agree? Why or why not?

16–4.   How do service department costs enter into the final cost of products and services?

16–5.   What criteria are relevant to the selection of allocation bases for service department costs?

16–6.   What are interdepartmental service costs? How are such costs allocated to other departments under the step method?

16–7.   How are service department costs allocated to other departments under the direct method?

16–8.   If a service department generates revenues of some type, how do these revenues enter into the allocation of the department's costs to other departments?

16–9.   What guidelines should govern the allocation of fixed service department costs to other departments? The allocation of variable service department costs?

16–10.   "A variable base should never be used in allocating fixed service department costs to operating departments." Explain.

16–11.   Why might it be desirable not to allocate some service department costs to operating departments?

16–12.   What is the purpose of the retainer fee approach to cost allocation?

EXERCISES

E16–1.   The Ferre Publishing Company has three service departments and two operating departments. Selected data from a recent period on the five departments follow:

	Service departments			Operating departments		
	A	B	C	1	2	Total
Overhead costs	$140,000	$105,000	$48,000	$275,000	$430,000	$998,000
Number of employees . . .	60	35	140	315	210	760
Square feet of space occupied	15,000	10,000	20,000	40,000	100,000	185,000
Hours of press time	—	—	—	30,000	60,000	90,000

The company allocates service department costs by the step method in the following order: A (number of employees), B (space occupied), and C (hours of press time). The company makes no distinction between variable and fixed service department costs.

Required: Using the step method, make the necessary allocations of service department costs.

E16–2. Refer to the data for the Ferre Publishing Company in Exercise 16–1. Assume that the company allocates service department costs by the direct method, rather than by the step method.

Required: Assuming that the company uses the direct method, how much overhead cost would be chargeable to each operating department? Show computations in good form.

E16–3. Hannibal Steel Company has a transport services department that provides trucks to haul ore from the company's mine to its two steel mills—the Northern Plant and the Southern Plant. The transport services department has sufficient capacity to handle peak-period needs of 140,000 tons per year for the Northern Plant and 60,000 tons per year for the Southern Plant. At this level of activity, budgeted costs for the transport services department total $350,000 per year, consisting of $0.25 per ton variable cost and $300,000 fixed cost.

During 19x8, the coming year, 120,000 tons of ore are budgeted to be hauled for the Northern Plant and 60,000 tons of ore for the Southern Plant.

Required: Compute the amount of transport services cost that should be allocated to each plant at the beginning of 19x8, for purposes of computing predetermined overhead rates. (The company allocates variable and fixed costs separately.)

E16–4. Refer to the data in Exercise 16–3. Assume that it is now the end of 19x8. During the year, the transport services department actually hauled the following amounts of ore for the two plants: Northern Plant, 130,000 tons; Southern Plant, 50,000 tons. The transport services department incurred $364,000 in cost during the year, of which $54,000 was variable cost and $310,000 was fixed cost.

Management wants end-of-year service department cost allocations in order to compare actual performance against planned performance.

Required:
1. Determine how much of the $54,000 in variable cost should be allocated to each plant.
2. Determine how much of the $310,000 in fixed cost should be allocated to each plant.
3. Will any of the $364,000 in transport services cost not be allocated to the plants? Explain.

E16–5. Westlake Hospital has a radiology department that provides X-ray services to the hospital's three operating departments. The variable costs of the radiology department are allocated on a basis of the number of X rays provided for each department. Budgeted and actual data relating to the cost of X rays taken during 19x3 are given below:

	Variable costs—19x3	
	Budgeted	**Actual**
Radiology department	$18 per X ray	$20 per X ray

The budgeted and actual number of X rays provided for each operating department during 19x3 follows:

	Pediatrics	**OB care**	**General hospital**
Budgeted number of X rays	7,000	4,500	12,000
Actual number of X rays taken . . .	6,000	3,000	15,000

Required: Determine the amount of radiology department variable cost that should be allocated to each of the three operating departments at the end of 19x3, for purposes of comparing actual performance against planned performance.

E16–6. Refer to Westlake Hospital in Exercise 16–5. In addition to the radiology department, the hospital also has a janitorial services department that provides services to all other departments in the hospital. The fixed costs of the two service departments are allocated on the following bases:

Department	**Basis for allocation**
Janitorial services . . .	Square footage of space occupied:
	Radiology department . . 6,000 square feet
	Pediatrics . . . . 30,000 square feet
	OB care . . . . 24,000 square feet
	General hospital . . . . 90,000 square feet
Radiology	Long-run average X-ray needs per year:
	Pediatrics . . . . 9,000 X rays
	OB care . . . . 6,000 X rays
	General hospital . . . . 15,000 X rays

Budgeted and actual fixed costs in the two service departments for 19x3 follow:

	Janitorial services	**Radiology**
Budgeted fixed costs	$375,000	$590,000
Actual fixed costs	381,000	600,000

Required: 1. Show the allocation of the fixed costs of the two service departments at the beginning of 19x3 for purposes of computing overhead rates in the operating departments. The hospital uses the step method of allocation.

2. Show the allocation of the fixed costs of the two service departments at the

end of 19x3 for purposes of comparing actual performance against planned performance.

E16–7. Konig Products allocates its fixed administrative expenses to its three divisions on a basis of sales dollars. During 19x1, the fixed administrative expenses totaled $2,000,000. These expenses were allocated as follows:

	Divisions			
	A	**B**	**C**	**Total**
Total sales—19x1	$16,000,000	$15,000,000	$9,000,000	$40,000,000
Percentage of total sales . .	40%	37.5%	22.5%	100%
Allocation (based on the above percentages) . . .	$ 800,000	$ 750,000	$ 450,000	$ 2,000,000

During 19x2, the following year, Division B increased its sales by two thirds. The sales levels in the other two divisions remained unchanged. As a result of Division B's sales increase, the company's 19x2 sales data appeared as follows:

	Divisions			
	A	**B**	**C**	**Total**
Total sales—19x2	$16,000,000	$25,000,000	$9,000,000	$50,000,000
Percentage of total sales . .	32%	50%	18%	100%

Fixed administrative expenses in the company remained unchanged at $2,000,000 during 19x2.

Required: 1. Using sales dollars as an allocation base, show the allocation of the fixed administrative expenses between the three divisions for 19x2.
2. Compare your allocation from (1) above to the allocation for 19x1. As the manager of Division B, how would you feel about the allocation that has been charged to you for 19x2?
3. Comment on the usefulness of sales dollars as an allocation base.

PROBLEMS

P16–8. **Various allocation methods.** Sharp Motor Company has an Auto Division and a Truck Division. The company has a cafeteria that serves the employees of both divisions. The costs of operating the cafeteria are budgeted at $40,000 per month plus $3 per meal served. The cafeteria has a capacity to serve 80,000 meals per month—based on peak needs of 52,000 meals per month in the Auto Division and 28,000 meals per month in the Truck Division. The company pays all the cost of the meals.

For June, the Auto Division has estimated that it will need 35,000 meals served, and the Truck Division has estimated that it will need 20,000 meals served.

Required: 1. At the beginning of June, how much cafeteria cost should be allocated to each division for flexible budget planning purposes?
2. Assume that it is now the end of June. Cost records in the cafeteria show that

actual fixed costs for the month totaled $42,000 and that actual meal costs totaled $128,000. Due to unexpected layoffs of employees during the month, only 20,000 meals were served to the Auto Division. Another 20,000 meals were served to the Truck Division, as planned. How much of the actual cafeteria costs for the month should be allocated to each division? (Management uses these end-of-month allocations to compare actual performance with planned performance.)

3. Refer to the data in (2) above. Assume that the company follows the practice of allocating *all* cafeteria costs to the divisions in proportion to the number of meals served to each division during the month. On this basis, how much cost would be allocated to each division for June?

4. What criticisms can you make of the allocation method used in (3) above?

5. If managers of operating departments know that fixed service department costs are going to be allocated on a basis of long-run average usage of the service involved, what will be their probable strategy as they report their estimate of this usage to the company's budget committee? As a member of top management, what would you do to neutralize any such strategies?

P16–9.   **Cost allocation: Step method versus direct method.**   The Ashley Company has budgeted costs in its various departments as follows for the coming year:

Factory administration	$270,000
Custodial services	68,760
Personnel	28,840
Maintenance	45,200
Machining—overhead	376,300
Assembly—overhead	175,900
Total cost	$965,000

The company allocates service department costs to other departments, in the order listed below. Bases for allocation are to be chosen from the following:

	Number of employees	Total labor-hours	Square feet of space occupied	Direct labor-hours	Machine-hours
Factory administration . . .	12	—	5,000	—	—
Custodial services	4	3,000	2,000	—	—
Personnel	5	5,000	3,000	—	—
Maintenance	25	22,000	10,000	—	—
Machining	40	30,000	70,000	20,000	70,000
Assembly	60	90,000	20,000	80,000	10,000
	146	150,000	110,000	100,000	80,000

Machining and assembly are operating departments; the other departments all act in a service capacity. The company does not make a distinction between fixed and variable service department costs; allocations are made to using departments according to the base that appears to provide the best measure of benefits received (as discussed in the text).

Required: 1. Allocate service department costs to using departments by the step method. Then compute predetermined overhead rates in the operating departments, using a machine-hours basis in machining and a direct labor-hours basis in assembly.
2. Repeat (1) above, this time using the direct method. Again compute predetermined overhead rates in machining and assembly.
3. Assume that the company doesn't want to bother with allocating service department costs but simply wants to compute a single plantwide overhead rate based on total overhead costs (both service department and operating department) divided by total direct labor-hours. Compute the appropriate overhead rate.
4. Suppose that the company wants to bid on a job during the year that will require machine and labor time as follows:

	Machine-hours	Direct labor-hours
Machining department	190	25
Assembly department.	10	75
Total hours	200	100

Using the overhead rates computed in (1), (2), and (3) above, compute the amount of overhead cost that would be assigned to the job if the overhead rates were developed using the step method, the direct method, and the plantwide method.

P16–10.   **End-of-month cost allocations.**   Reese Company has a power services department that provides electrical power for other departments within the company. The power services department's budget for June 19x2 is $40,800. Of this amount, $30,000 is considered to be a fixed cost.

Power consumption in the company is measured by kilowatt-hours (kwh) used. The monthly power requirements of the company's other four departments are as follows (in kwh):

	Service departments		Operating departments		
	A	B	X	Y	Total
Long-run average usage . . .	28,000	60,000	120,000	192,000	400,000
Budgeted for June	24,000	48,000	120,000	168,000	360,000
Actual use during June . . .	16,000	50,000	89,000	145,000	300,000

The power services department incurred $40,200 in costs during June 19x2, of which $8,400 was variable and $31,800 was fixed. The department allocates variable and fixed costs separately.

Required: 1. Assume that management makes an allocation of power costs at the end of each month in order to compare actual performance against budgeted performance. How much of the power services department's actual costs for June 19x2 would be allocated to each department?
2. Will any portion of the month's power costs not be allocated to the four departments? Explain.

P16–11. **Beginning- and end-of-year allocations.** Bennett Products, Inc., has a maintenance department that services the equipment in the company's forming department
and assembly department. The cost of this servicing is allocated to the departments
on a basis of machine-hours of activity. Cost and other data relating to the maintenance department and to the other two departments for 19x5 are presented below.

Data for the maintenance department:

	19x5	
	Budget	**Actual**
Variable costs for lubricants	$ 96,000*	$110,000
Fixed costs for salaries and other . .	150,000	153,000

* Budgeted at $0.40 per machine-hour.

Data for the forming and assembly departments:

	Machine-hours of activity		
	Peak-period needs	19x5	
		Budget	**Actual**
Forming department	210,000	160,000	190,000
Assembly department	90,000	80,000	70,000
Total machine-hours	300,000	240,000	260,000

The company allocates variable and fixed costs separately.

Required: 1.   Assume that it is the beginning of 19x5. An allocation of maintenance department cost must be made to the operating departments to assist in computing
predetermined overhead rates. How much of the budgeted maintenance department cost above would be allocated to each department?

2.   Assume that it is now the end of 19x5. Management would like data to assist
in comparing actual performance against planned performance in the maintenance department and in the other departments.

a.   How much of the actual maintenance department costs above would be
allocated to the forming department and to the assembly department? Show
all computations.

b.   Is there any portion of the actual maintenance department costs that would
not be allocated to the other departments? If all costs would be allocated,
explain why; if a portion would not be allocated, compute the amount
and explain why it would not be allocated.

P16–12. **Equity in allocations; computer center.** "These allocations don't make any sense
at all," said Bob Cosic, manager of National Airlines' Freight Division. "We
used the computer less during the second quarter than we did during the first quarter,
yet we were allocated more cost. Is that fair? In fact, we picked up the lion's
share of the computer's cost during the second quarter, even though we're a lot
smaller than the Domestic Passenger Division."

National Airlines established a new computer center in the latter part of 19x1 to service its three operating divisions. The company allocates the cost of the center to the divisions on a basis of the number of pages of printout for invoices, tickets, and so forth, provided each quarter. Allocations for the first two quarters of 19x2, to which Mr. Cosic was referring, are given below.

| | | Divisions | | |
| | | | Passenger | |
	Total	Freight	Domestic	Overseas
First quarter actual results:				
Pages of printout	300,000	90,000	180,000	30,000
Percentage of total.	100%	30%	60%	10%
Computer cost allocated	$172,000	$51,600	$103,200	$17,200
Second quarter actual results:				
Pages of printout	200,000	80,000	70,000	50,000
Percentage of total.	100%	40%	35%	25%
Computer cost allocated	$168,000	$67,200	$ 58,800	$42,000

"Now don't get upset, Bob," replied Colleen Rogers, the controller. "Those allocations are fair. As you can see, your division received the largest share of the computer's output during the second quarter and therefore it has been allocated the largest share of cost. Although use of the computer center was off somewhat during the second quarter, keep in mind that most of the center's costs are fixed and therefore continue regardless of how much the computer is used. Also, remember that we built enough capacity into the computer center to handle the divisions' peak-period needs, and that cost has to be absorbed by someone. The fairest way to handle it is to charge according to usage from quarter to quarter. When you use the computer more, you get charged more; it's as simple as that."

"That's just the point," replied Cosic. "I didn't use the computer more, I used it less. So why am I charged more?"

The computer center has enough capacity to handle 400,000 pages of printout each quarter. This represents expected peak-period needs of 120,000 pages in the Freight Division, 200,000 pages in the Domestic Passenger Division, and 80,000 pages in the Overseas Passenger Division. However, management does not expect these levels of activity to be reached for two or three years, and even then they will be reached only in the third or fourth quarter when traffic is highest in the airline industry.

Required:
1. Is there any merit to Mr. Cosic's complaint? Explain.
2. By use of the high-low method, determine the cost formula for the computer center in terms of a variable rate per page and total fixed cost each quarter.
3. Reallocate the computer center costs for the first and second quarters in accordance with the cost allocation principles discussed in the chapter. Allocate the variable and fixed costs separately.

P16–13.   Step method; beginning- and end-of-year allocations.   Bonneville Castings, Inc., has two producing departments, department A and department B, and three service departments. The service departments and the bases on which their costs are allocated to using departments are listed below:

Department	Cost	Allocation base
Building and grounds	Fixed	Square footage occupied
Medical services	Variable	Number of employees
	Fixed	Employee needs at full capacity
Equipment maintenance . . .	Variable	Machine-hours
	Fixed	40% to department A
		60% to department B

Service department costs are allocated to using departments by the step method in the order shown above. The company has developed the cost and operating data given in the following table for purposes of preparing overhead rates in the two producing departments:

	Building and grounds	Medical services	Equipment maintenance	Department A	Department B	Total
Variable costs	–0–	$22,200	$16,900	$146,000	$320,000	$ 505,100
Fixed costs	$88,200	60,000	24,000	420,000	490,000	1,082,200
Total	$88,200	$82,200	$40,900	$566,000	$810,000	$1,587,300
Budgeted employees	6	4	30	450	630	1,120
Employee needs at capacity . .	8	4	45	570	885	1,512
Square footage of space occupied	600	500	1,400	12,000	15,500	30,000
Budgeted machine-hours . . .	—	—	—	70,000	105,000	175,000

Required:
1. Show the allocation of service department costs to using departments, for purposes of preparing overhead rates in departments A and B.
2. Assuming that overhead rates are set on a basis of machine-hours, compute the overhead rate for each producing department.
3. Assume the following *actual* data for the year for the medical services department:

Actual variable costs	$23,800
Actual employees for the year:	
Building and grounds	6
Medical services	4
Equipment maintenance.	32
Department A	460
Department B	625
	1,127

Compute the amount of end-of-year medical services variable cost that should be allocated to each department. (Management uses these end-of-year allocations to compare actual performance against planned performance.)

P16–14.   Cost allocation in a hospital; step method.   Woodbury Hospital has three service departments and three operating departments. Estimated cost and operating data for all departments in the hospital for the forthcoming quarter are presented in the table below.

| | Service departments | | | Operating departments | | | |
	Housekeeping services	Food services	Admin. services	Labor-atory	Radiology	General hospital	Total
Variable costs	$ —	$193,860	$158,840	$243,600	$304,800	$ 74,500	$ 975,600
Fixed costs.	87,000	107,200	90,180	162,300	215,700	401,300	1,063,680
Total costs	$87,000	$301,060	$249,020	$405,900	$520,500	$475,800	$2,039,280
Meals served	—	—	800	2,000	1,000	68,000	71,800
Peak-period needs—meals . .	—	—	800	2,400	1,600	95,200	100,000
Square feet of space	5,000	13,000	6,500	10,000	7,500	108,000	150,000
Files processed	—	—	—	14,000	7,000	25,000	46,000
Long run average—files processed . .	—	—	—	18,000	12,000	30,000	60,000

The costs of the service departments are allocated by the step method, using the bases and in the order shown in the following table:

Service department	Costs incurred	Base for allocation
Housekeeping services. . .	Fixed	Square feet of space
Food services.	Variable	Meals served
	Fixed	Peak-period needs—meals
Administrative services . . .	Variable	Files processed
	Fixed	Long-run average—files processed

All billing in the hospital is done through the laboratory, radiology, or general hospital. The hospital's administrator wants the costs of the three service departments allocated to these three billing centers.

Required: Prepare the cost allocation desired by the hospital administrator. (Use the step method.) Include under each billing center the direct costs of the center, as well as the costs allocated from the service departments.

P16–15.   **Direct method; plantwide overhead rates versus departmental overhead rates.**   Hobart Products manufactures a complete line of fiberglass attache cases and suitcases. Hobart has three manufacturing departments—molding, component, and assembly—and two service departments—power and maintenance.

The sides of the cases are manufactured in the molding department. The frames, hinges, locks, and so forth, are manufactured in the component department. The cases are completed in the assembly department. Varying amounts of materials, time, and effort are required for each of the various cases. The power department and maintenance department provide services to the manufacturing departments.

Hobart has always used a plantwide overhead rate. Direct labor-hours are used to assign the overhead to products. The overhead rate is computed by dividing the company's total estimated overhead cost by the total estimated direct labor-hours to be worked in the three manufacturing departments.

Whit Portlock, manager of cost accounting, has recommended that the company use departmental overhead rates rather than a single, plantwide rate. Planned operating costs and expected levels of activity for the coming year have been developed by Mr. Portlock and are presented below.

	Service departments	
	Power	**Maintenance**
Departmental activity measures:		
Maximum capacity	100,000 kwh	Adjustable*
Estimated usage in the coming year	80,000 kwh	12,500 hours*
Departmental costs:		
Materials and supplies	$ 500,000	$ 25,000
Variable labor	140,000	–0–
Fixed overhead	1,200,000	375,000
Total service department costs	$1,840,000	$400,000

*Hours of maintenance time.

	Manufacturing departments		
	Molding	**Component**	**Assembly**
Departmental activity measures:			
Direct labor-hours	50,000	200,000	150,000
Machine-hours	87,500	12,500	–0–
Departmental costs:			
Raw materials	$1,630,000	$3,000,000	$ 125,000
Direct labor	350,000	2,000,000	1,300,000
Variable overhead	210,500	1,000,000	1,650,000
Fixed overhead	1,750,000	620,000	749,500
Total departmental costs	$3,940,500	$6,620,000	$3,824,500
Use of service departments:			
Maintenance:			
Estimated usage in hours of maintenance time for the coming year	9,000	2,500	1,000
Long-run average usage in hours of maintenance time	10,500	3,000	1,500
Power:			
Estimated usage in kilowatt-hours for the coming year	36,000	32,000	12,000
Peak-period needs in kilowatt-hours	50,000	35,000	15,000

Required: 1. Assume that the company will use a single, plantwide overhead rate for the coming year, the same as in the past. Under these conditions, compute the plantwide rate that should be used.

2. Assume that Whit Portlock has been asked to develop departmental overhead rates for the three manufacturing departments for comparison with the plantwide rate. In order to develop these rates, do the following:

   a. By use of the direct method, allocate the service department costs to the manufacturing departments. In each case, allocate the variable and fixed costs separately.

 b. Compute overhead rates for the three manufacturing departments for the coming year. In computing the rates, use a machine-hours basis in the molding department and a direct labor-hours basis in the other two departments.

 3. Should Hobart Products use a single, plantwide rate or departmental rates to assign overhead costs to products? Explain your answer.

(CMA, Heavily Adapted)

P16–16. Cost allocation in a resort; step method.   The Bayview Resort has three operating units—the convention center, food services, and guest lodging—through which all billing is done. These three operating units are supported by three service units—general administration, cost accounting, and laundry. The costs of the service units are allocated by the step method, using the bases and in the order shown below:

General administration:
   Fixed costs—allocated 10% to cost accounting, 4% to the laundry, 30% to the convention center, 16% to food services, and 40% to guest lodging.
Cost accounting:
   Variable costs—allocated on a basis of the number of items processed each period.
   Fixed costs—allocated on a basis of peak-period needs for items processed.
Laundry:
   Variable costs—allocated on a basis of the number of pounds of laundry processed each period.
   Fixed costs—allocated on a basis of peak-period needs for pounds of laundry processed.

Cost and operating data for all units in the resort for a recent quarter are given in the table following:

	Service departments			Operating departments			
	General adminis- tration	Cost ac- counting	Laundry	Conven- tion center	Food services	Guest lodging	Total
Variable costs	$ –0–	$ 70,000	$143,000	$ –0–	$ 52,000	$ 24,000	$ 289,000
Fixed costs	200,000	110,000	65,900	95,000	375,000	486,000	1,331,900
Total overhead costs	$200,000	$180,000	$208,900	$95,000	$427,000	$510,000	$1,620,900
Pounds of laundry processed	—	—	—	20,000	15,000	210,000	245,000
Peak-period needs— pounds of laundry processed	—	—	—	30,000	18,000	252,000	300,000
Number of items processed . .	1,000	—	800	1,200	3,000	9,000	15,000
Peak-period needs—number of items processed	1,500	—	1,400	2,600	4,000	12,000	21,500

Since all billing is done through the convention center, food services, and guest lodging, the resort's general manager wants the costs of the three service units allocated to these three billing centers.

Required: Prepare the cost allocation desired by the resort's general manager. Include under each billing center the direct costs of the center, as well as the costs allocated from the service units.

CASES

C16–17.   **Step method versus direct method.**   "This is really an odd situation," said Jim Carter, general manager of Highland Publishing Company. "We get most of the jobs we bid on that require a lot of press time in the printing department, yet profits on those jobs are never as high as they ought to be. On the other hand, we lose most of the jobs we bid on that require a lot of time in the binding department. I would be inclined to think that the problem is with our overhead rates, but we're already computing separate overhead rates for each department like the trade journals advise. So what else would be wrong?"

Highland Publishing Company is a large organization that offers a variety of printing and binding work. The printing and binding departments are supported by three service departments. The costs of these service departments are allocated to other departments in the order listed below. (For each service department, use the allocation base that provides the best measure of service provided, as discussed in the chapter.)

	Total labor-hours	Square feet of space occupied	Number of employees	Machine-hours	Direct labor-hours
Personnel	20,000	4,000	10	—	—
Custodial services . .	30,000	6,000	15	—	—
Maintenance	50,000	20,000	25	—	—
Printing	90,000	80,000	40	150,000	60,000
Binding	260,000	40,000	120	30,000	175,000
	450,000	150,000	210	180,000	235,000

Budgeted overhead costs in each department for the current year are shown below (no distinction is made between variable and fixed costs):

Personnel	$ 360,000
Custodial services	141,000
Maintenance	201,000
Printing.	525,000
Binding.	373,500
Total budgeted costs . .	$1,600,500

Because of its simplicity, the company has always used the direct method to allocate service department costs to the two operating departments.

Required: 1.   By use of the step method, allocate the service department costs to the other departments. Then compute predetermined overhead rates for the current year, using a machine-hours basis in the printing department and a direct labor-hours basis in the binding department.

2.   Repeat (1) above, this time using the direct method. Again compute predetermined overhead rates in the printing and binding departments.

3.   Assume that during the current year the company bids on a job that requires machine and labor time as follows:

	Machine-hours	Direct labor-hours
Printing department . .	270	15
Binding department . .	60	90
Total hours	330	105

    a.   Determine the amount of overhead cost that would be assigned to the job if the company used the overhead rates developed in (1) above. Then determine the amount of overhead cost that would be assigned to the job if the company used the overhead rates developed in (2) above.

    b.   Explain to Mr. Carter, the general manager, why the step method would provide a better basis for computing predetermined overhead rates than the direct method.

C16–18.   **Determining allocation base: credit services.** Columbia Company is a regional office supply chain with 26 independent stores. Each store has been responsible for its own credit and collections. The assistant manager in each store is assigned the responsibility for credit activities, including the collection of delinquent accounts, because the stores do not need a full-time employee assigned to credit activities. The company has experienced a sharp rise in uncollectibles during the last two years. Corporate management has decided to establish a collections department in the home office to be responsible for the collection function company-wide. The home office of Columbia Company will hire the necessary full-time personnel. The size of this department will be based on the historical credit activity of all the stores.

The new centralized collections department was discussed at a recent management meeting. Management is having a difficult time deciding what method to use in charging the costs of the new department to the stores, since the type of service involved is somewhat unique. The controller favors using a predetermined or standard rate for charging the costs to the stores. The predetermined rate would be based on budgeted costs. The vice president of sales has a strong preference for an actual cost charging system.

In addition to these two methods of charging costs, possible bases for allocating collection charges to the stores was also discussed. The controller has identified the following four measures of services (allocation bases) that could be used:

    a.   Total dollar sales.
    b.   Average number of past-due accounts.
    c.   Number of uncollectible accounts written off.
    d.   One twenty-sixth of the cost to each of the stores.

The executive vice president has stated that he would like the accounting department to prepare a detailed analysis of the two charging methods and the four service measures (allocation bases).

Required: 1.   Evaluate the two proposed methods—(1) predetermined (standard) rate and (2) actual cost—which could be used to charge the individual stores with the costs of the new collections department. Evaluate each method in terms of *(a)* practicality of application and ease of use, and *(b)* cost control.

        2.   For each of the four measures of services (allocation bases) identified by the company's controller:

        a.   Discuss whether the service measure (allocation base) is appropriate to use in this situation.

        b.   Identify the behavioral problems, if any, that could arise as a consequence of adopting the service measure (allocation base).

(CMA, Adapted)

CHAPTER 17

"How Well Am I Doing?"— Financial Statement Analysis

LEARNING OBJECTIVES

After studying Chapter 17, you should be able to:

■ Explain the need for and limitations of financial statement analysis.

■ Prepare financial statements in comparative form and explain how such statements are used.

■ Place the balance sheet and the income statement in common-size form and properly interpret the results.

■ State what ratios are used to measure the well-being of the common stockholder and give the formula for each ratio.

■ Tell what is meant by the term *financial leverage* and explain how financial leverage is measured.

■ Enumerate the ratios used to analyze working capital and the well-being of creditors and give the formula for each ratio.

■ Define or explain the key terms listed at the end of the chapter.

N o matter how carefully prepared, all financial statements are essentially historical documents. They tell what *has happened* during a particular year or series of years. The most valuable information to most users of financial statements, however, concerns what probably *will happen* in the future. The purpose of financial statement analysis is to assist statement users in *predicting the future* by means of comparison, evaluation, and trend analysis.

THE IMPORTANCE OF STATEMENT ANALYSIS

Virtually all users of financial data have concerns that can be resolved to some degree by the predictive ability of statement analysis. The stockholders are concerned, for example, about such matters as whether they should hold or sell their shares of stock, whether the present management group should remain or be replaced, and whether the company should have their approval to sell a new offering of senior debt. The creditors are concerned about such matters as whether income will be sufficient to cover the interest due on their bonds or notes, and whether prospects are good for their obligations to be paid at maturity. The managers are concerned about such matters as dividend policy, the availability of funds to finance future expansion, and the probable future success of operations under their leadership.

The thing about the future that statement users are most interested in predicting is profits. It is profits, of course, that provide the basis for an increase in the value of the stockholder's stock and that encourage the creditor to risk his or her money in an organization. And it is largely profits that make future expansion possible. The dilemma is that profits are uncertain. For this reason, one must have various analytical tools to assist in interpreting the key relationships and trends that serve as a basis for judgments of potential future success. Without financial statement analysis, the story that key relationships and trends have to tell may remain buried in a sea of statement detail.

In this chapter, we consider some of the more important ratios and other analytical tools that analysts use in attempting to predict the future course of events in business organizations.

Importance of Comparisons

Financial statements are not only historical documents but they are also essentially static documents. They speak only of the events of a single period of time. However, statement users are concerned about more than just the present; they are also concerned about the *trend of events* over time. For this reason, financial statement analysis directed toward a single period is of limited usefulness. The results of financial statement analysis for a particular period are of value only when viewed in *comparison* with the results of other periods and, in some cases, with the results of other firms. It is only through comparison that one can gain insight into trends and make intelligent judgments as to their significance.

Unfortunately, comparisons between firms within an industry are often made difficult by differences in accounting methods in use. For example, if one firm values its inventories by LIFO and another firm values its inventories by average cost, then direct dollar-for-dollar comparisons between the two firms may not be possible. In such cases, comparisons can still be made, but they must focus on data in a broader, more relative sense. Although the analytical work required here may be tougher, it is often necessary if the manager is to have any data available for comparison purposes.

The Need to Look beyond Ratios

There is a tendency for the inexperienced analyst to assume that ratios are sufficient in themselves as a basis for judgments about the future. Nothing could be further from the truth. The experienced analyst realizes that the best-prepared ratio analysis must be regarded as tentative in nature and never as conclusive in itself. Ratios should not be viewed as an end, but rather they should be viewed as a *starting point*, as indicators of what to pursue in greater depth. They raise many questions, but they rarely answer any questions by themselves.

In addition to looking at ratios, the analyst must look at other sources of data in order to make judgments about the future of an organization. The analyst must look, for example, at industry trends, at technological changes that are anticipated or that are in process, at changes in consumer tastes, at regional and national changes in economic factors, and at changes that are taking place within the firm itself. A recent change in a key management position, for example, might rightly serve as a basis for much optimism about the future, even though the past performance of the firm (as shown by its ratios) may have been very mediocre.

STATEMENTS IN COMPARATIVE AND COMMON-SIZE FORM

As stated above, few figures appearing on financial statements have much significance standing by themselves. It is the relationship of one figure to another and the amount and direction of change from one point in time to another that are important in financial statement analysis. How does the analyst key in on significant relationships? How does the analyst dig out the important trends and changes in a company? Three analytical techniques are in wide-spread use:

1. Dollar and percentage changes on statements.
2. Common-size statements.
3. Ratios.

All three techniques are discussed in following sections.

Dollar and Percentage Changes on Statements

A good beginning place in financial statement analysis is to put statements in comparative form. This consists of little more than putting two or more years' data side by side. Statements cast in comparative form will underscore movements and trends and may give the analyst valuable clues as to what to expect in the way of financial and operating performance in the future.

An example of financial statements placed in comparative form is given in Exhibits 17–1 and 17–2. These are the statements of Brickey Electronics,

EXHIBIT 17–1

BRICKEY ELECTRONICS
Comparative Balance Sheets
December 31, 19x2, and 19x1
(dollars in thousands)

	19x2	19x1	Increase (decrease) Amount	Increase (decrease) Per-cent
Assets				
Current assets:				
Cash	$ 1,000	$ 2,270	$(1,270)	(55.9)
Accounts receivable, net	6,000	4,000	2,000	50.0
Inventory	8,000	10,000	(2,000)	(20.0)
Prepaid expenses	500	200	300	150.0
Total current assets	15,500	16,470	(970)	(5.9)
Property and equipment:				
Land	4,000	4,000	–0–	–0–
Buildings and equipment, net	12,000	8,500	3,500	41.2
Total property and equipment	16,000	12,500	3,500	28.0
Total assets	$31,500	$28,970	$ 2,530	8.7
Liabilities and Stockholders' Equity				
Current liabilities:				
Accounts payable	$ 5,800	$ 4,000	$ 1,800	45.0
Accrued payables	900	400	500	125.0
Notes payable, short term	300	600	(300)	(50.0)
Total current liabilities	7,000	5,000	2,000	40.0
Long-term liabilities:				
Bonds payable, 8%	7,500	8,000	(500)	(6.3)
Total liabilities	14,500	13,000	1,500	11.5
Stockholders' equity:				
Preferred stock, $100 par, 6%,				
$100 liquidation value	2,000	2,000	–0–	–0–
Common stock, $12 par	6,000	6,000	–0–	–0–
Additional paid-in capital	1,000	1,000	–0–	–0–
Total paid-in capital	9,000	9,000	–0–	–0–
Retained earnings	8,000	6,970	1,030	14.8
Total stockholders' equity	17,000	15,970	1,030	6.4
Total liabilities and stockholders' equity	$31,500	$28,970	$ 2,530	8.7

EXHIBIT 17–2

BRICKEY ELECTRONICS
Comparative Income Statements and Reconciliation
of Retained Earnings
For the Years Ended December 31, 19x2, and 19x1
(dollars in thousands)

	19x2	19x1	Increase (decrease) Amount	Increase (decrease) Percent
Sales	$52,000	$48,000	$4,000	8.3
Cost of goods sold	36,000	31,500	4,500	14.3
Gross margin	16,000	16,500	(500)	(3.0)
Operating expenses:				
Selling expenses	7,000	6,500	500	7.7
Administrative expenses	5,860	6,100	(240)	(3.9)
Total operating expenses	12,860	12,600	260	2.1
Net operating income	3,140	3,900	(760)	(19.5)
Interest expense	640	700	(60)	(8.6)
Net income before taxes	2,500	3,200	(700)	(21.9)
Less income taxes (30%)	750	960	(210)	(21.9)
Net income	1,750	2,240	$ (490)	(21.9)
Dividends to preferred stockholders,				
$6 per share (see Exhibit 17–1)	120	120		
Net income remaining for common				
stockholders	1,630	2,120		
Dividends to common stockholders				
($1.20 per share)	600	600		
Net income added to retained				
earnings	1,030	1,520		
Retained earnings, beginning of year	6,970	5,450		
Retained earnings, end of year	$ 8,000	$ 6,970		

a hypothetical firm. The data on these statements are used as a basis for discussion throughout the remainder of the chapter.

Horizontal analysis   Comparison of two or more years' financial data is known as **horizontal analysis.** Horizontal analysis is greatly facilitated by showing changes between years in both dollar *and* percentage form, as has been done in Exhibits 17–1 and 17–2. Showing changes in dollar form helps the analyst to zero in on key factors that have affected profitability or financial position. For example, observe in Exhibit 17–2 that sales for 19x2 were up $4 million over 19x1, but that this increase in sales was more than negated by a $4.5 million increase in cost of goods sold.

Showing changes between years in percentage form helps the analyst to gain *perspective* and to gain a feel for the *significance* of the changes that are taking place. One would have a different perspective of a $1 million increase in sales if the prior year's sales were $2 million than he would if the prior year's sales were $20 million. In the first situation, the increase would be 50 percent—undoubtedly a significant increase for any firm. In the second situation, the increase would be only 5 percent—perhaps a reflection of just normal growth.

Trend percentages   Horizontal analysis of financial statements can also be carried out by computing *trend percentages.* **Trend percentages** state several years' financial data in terms of a base year. The base year equals 100 percent, with all other years stated as some percentage of this base. To illustrate, assume that Martin Company has reported the following sales and income data for the past five years:

	19x5	19x4	19x3	19x2	19x1
Sales	$725,000	$700,000	$650,000	$575,000	$500,000
Net income. . . .	99,000	97,500	93,750	86,250	75,000

By simply looking at these data, one can see that both sales and net income have increased over the five-year period reported. But how rapidly have sales been increasing, and have the increases in net income kept pace with the increases in sales? By looking at the raw data alone, it is difficult to answer these questions. The increases in sales and the increases in net income can be put into proper perspective by stating them in terms of trend percentages, with 19x1 as the base year. These percentages are given below:

	19x5	19x4	19x3	19x2	19x1
Sales	145%	140%	130%	115%*	100%
Net income . . .	132	130	125	115	100

*For 19x2: $575,000 ÷ $500,000 = 115%; for 19x3: $650,000 ÷ $500,000 = 130%; and so forth.

Notice that the growth in sales dropped off somewhat between 19x3 and 19x4, and then dropped off even more between 19x4 and 19x5. Also notice that the growth in net income has not kept pace with the growth in sales. In 19x5, sales are 1.45 times greater than in 19x1, the base year; however, in 19x5, net income is only 1.32 times greater than in 19x1.

Common-Size Statements

Key changes and trends can also be highlighted by the use of *common-size statements.* A **common-size statement** is one that shows the separate items appearing on it in percentage form rather than in dollar form. Each item is stated as a percentage of some total of which that item is a part. The preparation of common-size statements is known as **vertical analysis.**

The balance sheet   One application of the vertical analysis idea is to state the separate assets of a company as percentages of total assets. A

EXHIBIT 17–3

BRICKEY ELECTRONICS
Common-Size Comparative Balance Sheets
December 31, 19x2, and 19x1
(dollars in thousands)

	19x2	19x1	Common-size percentages 19x2	Common-size percentages 19x1
Assets				
Current assets:				
Cash	$ 1,000	$ 2,270	3.2	7.8
Accounts receivable, net	6,000	4,000	19.0	13.8
Inventory	8,000	10,000	25.4	34.5
Prepaid expenses	500	200	1.6	0.7
Total current assets	15,500	16,470	49.2	56.9
Property and equipment:				
Land	4,000	4,000	12.7	13.8
Buildings and equipment, net	12,000	8,500	38.1	29.3
Total property and equipment	16,000	12,500	50.8	43.1
Total assets	$31,500	$28,970	100.0	100.0
Liabilities and Stockholders' Equity				
Current liabilities:				
Accounts payable	$ 5,800	$ 4,000	18.4	13.8
Accrued payables	900	400	2.8	1.4
Notes payable, short term	300	600	1.0	2.1
Total current liabilities	7,000	5,000	22.2	17.3
Long-term liabilities:				
Bonds payable, 8%	7,500	8,000	23.8	27.6
Total liabilities	14,500	13,000	46.0	44.9
Stockholders' equity:				
Preferred stock, $100 par, 6%,				
$100 liquidation value	2,000	2,000	6.4	6.9
Common stock, $12 par	6,000	6,000	19.0	20.7
Additional paid-in capital	1,000	1,000	3.2	3.5
Total paid-in capital	9,000	9,000	28.6	31.1
Retained earnings	8,000	6,970	25.4	24.0
Total stockholders' equity	17,000	15,970	54.0	55.1
Total liabilities and stockholders' equity	$31,500	$28,970	100.0	100.0

---

common-size statement of this type is shown in Exhibit 17–3 for Brickey Electronics.

Notice from Exhibit 17–3 that placing all assets in common-size form clearly shows the relative importance of the current assets as compared to the noncurrent assets. It also shows that significant changes have taken place in the *composition* of the current assets over the last year. Notice, for example, that the receivables have increased in relative importance and that both cash and inventory have declined in relative importance. Judging from the sharp increase in receivables, the deterioration in the cash position may be a result of inability to collect from customers.

EXHIBIT 17–4

BRICKEY ELECTRONICS
Common-Size Comparative Income Statements
For the Years Ended December 31, 19x2, and 19x1
(dollars in thousands)

			Common-size percentages	
	19x2	19x1	19x2	19x1
Sales	$52,000	$48,000	100.0	100.0
Cost of goods sold	36,000	31,500	69.2	65.7
Gross margin	16,000	16,500	30.8	34.3
Operating expenses:				
Selling expenses.	7,000	6,500	13.5	13.5
Administrative expenses	5,860	6,100	11.2	12.7
Total operating expenses	12,860	12,600	24.7	26.2
Net operating income.	3,140	3,900	6.0	8.1
Interest expense	640	700	1.2	1.5
Net income before taxes	2,500	3,200	4.8	6.6
Income taxes (30%)	750	960	1.4	2.0
Net income	$ 1,750	$ 2,240	3.4	4.6

The income statement   Another application of the vertical analysis idea is to place all items on the income statement in percentage form in terms of total sales. A common-size statement of this type is shown in Exhibit 17–4.

By placing all items on the income statement in common size in terms of sales, it is possible to see at a glance how each dollar of sales is distributed between the various costs, expenses, and profits. For example, notice from Exhibit 17–4 that 69.2 cents out of every dollar of sales was needed to cover cost of goods sold in 19x2, as compared to only 65.7 cents in the prior year; also notice that only 3.4 cents out of every dollar of sales remained for profits in 19x2—down from 4.6 cents in the prior year.

Common-size statements are also very helpful in pointing out efficiencies and inefficiencies that might otherwise go unnoticed. To illustrate, in 19x2, Brickey Electronics' selling expenses increased by $500,000 over 19x1. A glance at the common-size income statement shows, however, that on a relative basis selling expenses were no higher in 19x2 than in 19x1. In each year, they represented 13.5 percent of sales.

RATIO ANALYSIS—THE COMMON STOCKHOLDER

The common stockholder has only a residual claim on the profits and assets of a corporation. It is only after all creditor and preferred stockholder claims have been satisfied that the common stockholder can step forward and receive cash dividends or a distribution of assets in liquidation. Therefore, a measure of the common stockholder's well-being provides some perspective of the depth of protection available to others associated with a firm.

Earnings per Share

An investor buys and retains a share of stock with the thought in mind of a return coming in the future in the form of either dividends or capital gains. Since earnings form the basis for dividend payments, as well as the basis for any future increases in the value of shares, investors are always interested in a company's reported *earnings per share*. Probably no single statistic is more widely quoted or relied on in investor actions than earnings per share, although it has some inherent dangers, as discussed below.

The computation of **earnings per share** is made by dividing net income remaining for common stockholders by the number of common shares outstanding. "Net income remaining for common stockholders" is equal to the net income of a company, reduced by the dividends due to the preferred stockholders.

$$\frac{\text{Net income} - \text{Preferred dividends}}{\text{Common shares outstanding}} = \text{Earnings per share}$$

Using the data in Exhibits 17–1 and 17–2, we see that the earnings per share for Brickey Electronics for 19x2 would be:

$$\frac{\$1{,}750{,}000 - \$120{,}000}{500{,}000 \text{ shares}^*} = \$3.26 \tag{1}$$

* \$6,000,000 ÷ \$12 = 500,000 shares.

Two problems can arise in connection with the computation of earnings per share. The first arises whenever an extraordinary gain or loss appears as part of net income. The second arises whenever a company has convertible securities on its balance sheet. These problems are discussed in the following two sections.

Extraordinary Items and Earnings per Share

If a company has extraordinary gains or losses appearing as part of net income, *two* earnings per share figures must be computed—one showing the earnings per share resulting from *normal* operations and one showing the earnings per share impact of the *extraordinary* items. This approach to computing earnings per share accomplishes three things. First, it helps statement users to recognize extraordinary items for what they are—unusual events that probably will not recur. Second, it eliminates the distorting influence of the extraordinary items from the basic earnings per share figure. And third, it helps statement users to properly assess the *trend* of *normal* earnings per share over time. Since one would not expect the extraordinary or unusual items to be repeated year after year, they should be given less weight in judging earnings performance than is given to profits resulting from normal operations.

In addition to reporting extraordinary items separately, the accountant also reports them *net of their tax effect*. By "net of their tax effect," we mean that whatever impact the unusual item has on income taxes is *deducted from* the unusual item on the income statement. Only the net, after-tax gain or loss is used in earnings per share computations.

To illustrate these ideas, let us assume that Amata Company has suffered a fire loss of $6,000, and that management is wondering how the loss should be reported on the company's income statement. The correct and incorrect approaches to reporting the loss are shown in Exhibit 17–5.

As shown under the "correct approach" in the exhibit, the $6,000 loss is reduced to only $4,200 after tax effects are taken into consideration. The reasoning behind this computation is as follows: The fire loss is fully deductible for tax purposes. Therefore, this deduction will reduce the firm's taxable income by $6,000. If taxable income is $6,000 lower, then income taxes will be $1,800 *less* (30% × $6,000) than they *otherwise* would have been. In other words, the fire loss of $6,000 saves the company $1,800 in taxes that otherwise would have been paid. The $1,800 savings in taxes is

EXHIBIT 17–5

Reporting extraordinary items net of their tax effects

Incorrect approach

Sales		$100,000
Cost of goods sold		60,000
Gross margin		40,000
Operating expenses:		
Selling expenses	$18,000	
Administrative expenses . . .	12,000	
Fire loss	6,000	36,000
Net income before taxes		4,000
Income taxes (30%)		1,200
Net income		$ 2,800

Extraordinary gains and losses should not be included with normal items of revenue and expense. This distorts a firm's normal income-producing ability.

Correct approach

Sales		$100,000
Cost of goods sold		60,000
Gross margin		40,000
Operating expenses:		
Selling expenses	$18,000	
Administrative expenses . . .	12,000	30,000
Net operating income		10,000
Income taxes (30%)		3,000
Net income before extra-		
ordinary item		7,000
Extraordinary item:		
Fire loss, net of tax		4,200
Net income		$ 2,800

Reporting the extraordinary item separately and net of its tax effect leaves the normal items of revenue and expense unaffected.

Original loss	$6,000
Less reduction in taxes	
at a 30% rate	1,800
Loss, net of tax	$4,200

deducted from the loss that caused it, leaving a net loss of only $4,200. This same $4,200 figure could have been obtained by multiplying the original loss by the formula (1 − Tax rate). [$6,000 × (1 − 0.30) = $4,200]. *Any* before-tax item can be put on an after-tax basis by use of this formula.

This same procedure is used in reporting extraordinary gains. The only difference is that extraordinary gains *increase* taxes; thus, any tax resulting from a gain must be deducted from it, with only the net gain reported on the income statement.

To continue our illustration, assume that the company in Exhibit 17–5 has 2,000 shares of common stock outstanding. Earnings per share would be reported as follows:

Earnings per share on common stock:
On net income before extraordinary item ($7,000 ÷ 2,000 shares)* . . $ 3.50
On extraordinary item, net of tax ($4,200 ÷ 2,000 shares) . . . . . .   (2.10)
Net earnings per share . . . . $ 1.40

    * Sometimes called the *primary* earnings per share.

In sum, computation of earnings per share as we have done above is necessary to avoid misunderstanding of a company's normal income-producing ability. Reporting *only* the flat $1.40 per share figure would be misleading and perhaps cause investors to regard the company less favorably than they should.

Fully Diluted Earnings per Share

A problem sometimes arises in trying to determine the number of common shares to use in computing earnings per share. Until recent years, the distinction between common stock, preferred stock, and debt was quite clear. The distinction between these securities has now become somewhat diffused, however, due to a growing tendency to issue convertible securities of various types. Rather than simply issuing common stock, firms today often issue preferred stock or bonds that carry a **conversion feature** allowing the purchaser to convert holdings into common stock at some future time.

When convertible securities are present in the financial structure of a firm, the question arises as to whether these securities should be retained in their unconverted form or treated as common stock in computing earnings per share. The American Institute of Certified Public Accountants has taken the position that convertible securities should be treated *both* in their present and prospective forms. This requires the presentation of *two* earnings per share figures for firms that have convertible securities outstanding, one showing earnings per share assuming no conversion into common stock and the other showing full conversion into common stock. The latter figure is known as the **fully diluted earnings per share.**

To illustrate the computation of a company's fully diluted earnings per share, let us assume that the preferred stock of Brickey Electronics in Exhibit 17–1 is convertible into common on the basis of five shares of common for each share of preferred. Since 20,000 shares of preferred are outstanding, conversion would require issuing an additional 100,000 shares of common stock. Earnings per share on a fully diluted basis would be:

$$\frac{\text{Net income}}{(500,000 \text{ shares outstanding} + 100,000 \text{ converted shares})}$$

$$= \frac{\$1,750,000}{600,000 \text{ shares}} = \$2.92 \qquad (2)$$

In comparing equation (2) with equation (1), we can note that the earnings per share figure has dropped by 34 cents. Although the impact of full dilution is relatively small in this case, it can be very significant in situations where large amounts of convertible securities are present.

Price-Earnings Ratio

The relationship between the market price of a share of stock and the stock's current earnings per share is often quoted in terms of a **price-earnings ratio.** If we assume that the current market price for Brickey Electronics' stock is $40 per share, the company's price-earnings ratio would be computed as follows:

$$\frac{\text{Market price per share}}{\text{Earnings per share}} = \text{Price-earnings ratio}$$

$$\frac{\$40}{\$3.26 \text{ [see equation (1)]}} = 12.3 \qquad (3)$$

The price-earnings ratio is 12.3; that is, the stock is selling for about 12.3 times its current earnings per share.

The price-earnings ratio is widely used by investors as a general guideline in gauging stock values. Investors increase or decrease the price-earnings ratio that they are willing to accept for a share of stock according to how they view its *future prospects*. Companies with ample opportunities for growth generally have high price-earnings ratios, with the opposite being true for companies with limited growth opportunities. If investors decided that Brickey Electronics had greater than average growth prospects, then undoubtedly the price of the company's stock would begin to rise. If the price increased to, say, $52 per share, then the price-earnings ratio would rise to 16 ($52 price ÷ $3.26 EPS = 16.0 P-E ratio).

Dividend Payout and Yield Ratios

Investors hold shares of one stock in preference to shares of another stock because they anticipate that the first stock will provide them with a more attractive return. The return sought isn't always dividends. Many investors prefer not to receive dividends. Instead, they prefer to have the company retain all earnings and reinvest them internally in order to support growth. The stocks of companies that adopt this approach, loosely termed *growth stocks,* often enjoy rapid upward movement in market price. Other investors prefer to have a dependable, current source of income through regular dividend payments and prefer not to gamble on the fortunes of stock prices to provide a return on their investment. Such investors seek out stocks with consistent dividend records and payout ratios.

The dividend payout ratio   The **dividend payout ratio** gauges the portion of current earnings being paid out in dividends. Investors who seek growth in market price would like this ratio to be small, whereas investors who seek dividends prefer it to be large. This ratio is computed by relating dividends per share to earnings per share for common stock:

$$\frac{\text{Dividends per share}}{\text{Market price per share}} = \text{Dividend yield ratio}$$

For Brickey Electronics, the dividend payout ratio for 19x2 was:

$$\frac{\$1.20 \text{ (see Exhibit 17–2)}}{\$3.26 \text{ [see equation (1)]}} = 36.8\% \qquad\qquad (4)$$

There is no such thing as a "right" payout ratio, even though it should be noted that the ratio tends to be somewhat the same for the bulk of firms within a particular industry. Industries with ample opportunities for growth at high rates of return on assets tend to have low payout ratios, and the reverse tends to be true for industries with limited reinvestment opportunities.

The dividend yield ratio   The **dividend yield ratio** is obtained by dividing the current dividends per share by the current market price per share:

$$\frac{\text{Dividends per share}}{\text{Market price per share}} = \text{Dividend yield ratio}$$

If we continue the assumption of a market price of $40 per share for Brickey Electronics' stock, the dividend yield is:

$$\frac{\$1.20}{\$40} = 3.0\% \qquad\qquad (5)$$

In making this computation, note that we used the current market price of the stock rather than the price the investor paid for the stock initially (which might be above or below the current market price). By using current market price, we recognize the opportunity cost[1] of the investment in terms of its yield. That is, this is the yield that would be lost or sacrificed if the investor sold the stock for $40 and bought a new security in its place.

---

[1] Opportunity cost is the potential benefit that is lost or sacrificed when the selection of one course of action makes it necessary to give up a competing course of action.

Return on Total Assets

Managers have two basic responsibilities in managing a firm—*financing* responsibilities and *operating* responsibilities. Financing responsibilities relate to how one *obtains* the funds needed to provide for the assets in an organization. Operating responsibilities relate to how one *uses* the assets once they have been obtained. Proper discharge of both responsibilities is vital to a well-managed firm. However, care must be taken not to confuse or mix the two in assessing the performance of a manager. That is, whether funds have been obtained partly from creditors and partly from stockholders or entirely from stockholders should not be allowed to influence one's assessment of *how well* the assets have been employed since being received by the firm.

The **return on total assets** is a measure of how well assets have been employed; that is, it is a measure of operating performance. The formula is:

$$\frac{\text{Net income} + [\text{Interest expense} \times (1 - \text{Tax rate})]}{\text{Average total assets}} = \text{Return on total assets}$$

By adding interest expense back to net income, we derive a figure that shows earnings before any distributions have been made to either creditors or stockholders. Thus, we eliminate the matter of how the assets were financed from influencing the measurement of how well the assets have been employed. Notice that before being added back to net income, the interest expense must be placed on an after-tax basis by multiplying the interest figure by the formula $(1 - \text{Tax rate})$.

The return on total assets for Brickey Electronics for 19x2 would be (from Exhibits 17–1 and 17–2):

Net income	$ 1,750,000
Add back interest expense: $640,000 × (1 − 0.30) . .	448,000
Total	$ 2,198,000 *(a)*
Assets, beginning of year	$28,970,000
Assets, end of year	31,500,000
Total	$60,470,000
Average total assets: $60,470,000 ÷ 2	$30,235,000 *(b)*
Return on total assets, *(a)* ÷ *(b)*	7.3% (6)

Brickey Electronics has earned a return of 7.3 percent on average assets employed over the last year.

Return on Common Stockholders' Equity

One of the primary reasons for operating a corporation is to generate income for the benefit of the common stockholders. One measure of a company's success in this regard is the rate of **return on common stockholders' equity** that it is able to generate. The formula is:

$$\frac{\text{Net income} - \text{Preferred dividends}}{\begin{array}{c}\text{Average common stockholders' equity (Average}\\ \text{total stockholders' equity} - \text{Preferred stock)}\end{array}}$$

$$= \text{Return on common stockholders' equity}$$

For Brickey Electronics, the return on common stockholders' equity is 11.4 percent for 19x2, as shown below:

Net income.	$ 1,750,000	
Deduct preferred dividends	120,000	
Net income remaining for common stockholders . . .	$ 1,630,000	(a)
Average stockholders' equity	$16,485,000*	
Deduct preferred stock.	2,000,000	
Average common stockholders' equity	$14,485,000	(b)
Return on common stockholders' equity, (a) ÷ (b) . .	11.3%	(7)

*$15,970,000 + $17,000,000 = $32,970,000; $32,970,000 ÷ 2 = $16,485,000.

Compare the return on common stockholders' equity above (11.3 percent) with the return on total assets computed in the preceding section (7.3 percent). Why is the return on common stockholders' equity so much higher? The answer lies in the principle of *financial leverage* (sometimes called "trading on the equity").

The concept of financial leverage   **Financial leverage** (often called "leverage" for short) involves the financing of assets in a company with funds that have been acquired from creditors or from preferred stockholders at a fixed rate of return. If the assets in which the funds are invested are able to earn a rate of return *greater* than the fixed rate of return required by the suppliers of the funds, then financial leverage is **positive** and the common stockholders benefit.

For example, assume that a firm is able to earn an after-tax return of 12 percent on its assets. If that firm can borrow from creditors at a 10 percent interest rate in order to expand its assets, then the common stockholders can benefit from positive leverage. The borrowed funds invested in the business will earn an after-tax return of 12 percent, but the after-tax interest cost of the borrowed funds will be only 7 percent [10% interest rate × (1 − 0.30) = 7%]. The difference will go to the common stockholders.

We can see this concept in operation in the case of Brickey Electronics. Notice from Exhibit 17–1 that the company's bonds payable bear a fixed interest rate of 8 percent. The after-tax interest cost of these bonds is only 5.6 percent [8% interest rate × (1 − 0.30) = 5.6%]. The company's assets (which would contain the proceeds from the original sale of these bonds) are generating an after-tax return of 7.3 percent, as we computed earlier. Since this return on assets is greater than the after-tax interest cost of the bonds, leverage is positive, and the difference accrues to the benefit of the common stockholders. This explains in part why the return on common stockholders' equity (11.3 percent) is greater than the return on total assets (7.3 percent).

Sources of financial leverage   Financial leverage can be obtained from several sources. One source is long-term debt, such as bonds payable or notes payable. Two additional sources are current liabilities and preferred stock. Current liabilities are always a source of positive leverage in that funds are provided for use in a company with no interest return required by the short-term creditors involved. For example, when a company acquires inventory from a supplier on account, the inventory is available for use in the business, yet the supplier requires no interest return on the amount owed to him.

Preferred stock can also be a source of positive leverage so long as the dividend payable to the preferred stockholders is less than the rate of return being earned on the total assets employed. In the case of Brickey Electronics, positive leverage is being realized on the preferred stock. Notice from Exhibit 17–1 that the preferred dividend rate is only 6 percent, whereas the assets in the company are earning at a rate of 7.3 percent, as computed earlier. Again, the difference goes to the common stockholders, thereby helping to bolster their return to the 11.3 percent computed above.

Unfortunately, leverage is a two-edged sword. If assets are unable to earn a high enough rate to cover the interest costs of debt, or to cover the preferred dividend due to the preferred stockholders, *then the common stockholder suffers.* The reason is that part of the earnings from the assets that the common stockholder has provided to the company will have to go to make up the deficiency to the long-term creditors or to the preferred stockholders, and the common stockholder will be left with a smaller return than would otherwise have been earned. Under these circumstances, financial leverage is said to be **negative.**

The impact of income taxes   Long-term debt and preferred stock are not equally efficient in generating positive leverage. The reason is that interest on long-term debt is tax deductible, whereas preferred dividends are not. This makes long-term debt a much more effective source of positive leverage than preferred stock.

To illustrate this point, assume that a company is considering three ways of financing a $100,000 expansion of its assets:

1. $100,000 from an issue of common stock.
2. $50,000 from an issue of commn stock, and $50,000 from an issue of preferred stock bearing a dividend rate of 8 percent.
3. $50,000 from an issue of common stock, and $50,000 from an issue of bonds bearing an interest rate of 8 percent.

Assuming that the company can earn an additional $15,000 each year before interest and taxes as a result of the expansion, the operating results under each of the three alternatives are shown in Exhibit 17–6.

If the entire $100,000 is raised from an issue of common stock, then the return to the common stockholders will be only 10.5 percent, as shown under alternative 1 in the exhibit. If half of the funds are raised from an issue of preferred stock, then the return to the common stockholders increases to 13 percent, due to the positive effects of leverage. However, if half of

EXHIBIT 17–6

Leverage from preferred stock and long-term debt

	Alternatives: $100,000 issue of securities		
	Alternative 1: $100,000 common stock	Alternative 2: $50,000 common stock; $50,000 preferred stock	Alternative 3: $50,000 common stock; $50,000 bonds
Earnings before interest and taxes	$ 15,000	$15,000	$15,000
Deduct interest expense (8% × $50,000).	—	—	4,000
Net income before taxes	15,000	15,000	11,000
Deduct income taxes (30%)	4,500	4,500	3,300
Net income.	10,500	10,500	7,700
Deduct preferred dividends (8% × $50,000)	—	4,000	—
Net income remaining for common (a)	$ 10,500	$ 6,500	$ 7,700
Common stockholders' equity (b)	$100,000	$50,000	$50,000
Return on common stockholders' equity, (a) ÷ (b) . .	10.5%	13.0%	15.4%

the funds are raised from an issue of bonds, then the return to the common stockholders jumps to 15.4 percent, as shown under alternative 3. Thus, long-term debt is much more efficient in generating positive leverage than is preferred stock. The reason is that the interest expense on long-term debt is tax deductible, whereas the dividends on preferred stock are not.

The desirability of leverage   The leverage principle amply illustrates that having some debt in the capital structure can substantially benefit the common stockholder. For this reason, most companies today try to keep a certain level of debt within the organization—a level at least equal to that which is considered to be "normal" within the industry. Occasionally one comes across a company that boasts of having no debt outstanding. Although there may be good reasons for a company to have no debt, in view of the benefits that can be gained from positive leverage the possibility always exists that such a company is shortchanging its stockholders. As a practical matter, many companies, such as commercial banks and other financial institutions, rely heavily on leverage to provide an attractive return on their common shares.

Book Value per Share

Another statistic frequently used in attempting to assess the well-being of the common stockholder is book value per share. The **book value per share** measures the amount that would be distributed to holders of each share of common stock if all assets were sold at their balance sheet carrying amounts and if all creditors were paid off. Thus, book value per share is based entirely on historical costs. The formula for computing it is:

$$\frac{\text{Common stockholders' equity (Total stockholders' equity } - \text{ Preferred stock)}}{\text{Number of common shares outstanding}} = \text{Book value per share}$$

The book value of Brickey Electronics' common stock is:

$$\frac{\$17,000,000 - \$2,000,000}{500,000 \text{ shares}} = \$30 \qquad (8)$$

If this book value is compared with the $40 market value that we have assumed in connection with the Brickey Electronics stock, then the stock appears to be somewhat overpriced. It is not necessarily true, however, that a market value in excess of book value is an indication of overpricing. As we discussed earlier, market prices are geared toward future earnings and dividends. Book value, by contrast, purports to reflect nothing about the future earnings potential of a firm. As a practical matter, it is actually geared to the *past* in that it reflects the balance sheet carrying value of already completed transactions.

Of what use, then, is book value? Unfortunately, the answer must be that it is of limited use so far as being a dynamic tool of analysis is concerned. It probably finds its greatest application in situations where large amounts of liquid assets are being held in anticipation of liquidation. Occasionally some use is also made of book value per share in attempting to set a price on the shares of closely held corporations.

RATIO ANALYSIS—THE SHORT-TERM CREDITOR

Although the short-term creditor is always well advised to keep an eye on the fortunes of the common stockholder, as expressed in the ratios of the preceding section, the short-term creditor's focus of attention is normally channeled in another direction. The short-term creditor is concerned with the near-term prospects of having obligations paid on time. As such, he or she is much more interested in cash flows and in working capital management than in how much accounting net income a company is reporting.

Working Capital

The excess of current assets over current liabilities is known as **working capital.** The working capital for Brickey Electronics is given below:

	19x2	19x1	
Current assets	$15,500,000	$16,470,000	
Current liabilities	7,000,000	5,000,000	
Working capital	$ 8,500,000	$11,470,000	(9)

The amount of working capital available to a firm is of considerable interest to short-term creditors, *since it represents assets financed from long-*

term capital sources that do not require near-term repayment. Therefore, the greater the working capital, the greater is the cushion of protection available to short-term creditors and the greater is the assurance that short-term debts will be paid when due.

Although it is always comforting to short-term creditors to see a large working capital balance, their joy becomes full only after they have been satisfied that the working capital is turning over at an acceptable rate of speed, and that their obligations could be paid even under stringent operating conditions. The reason is that a large working capital balance standing by itself is no assurance that debts will be paid when due. Rather than being a sign of strength, a large working capital balance may simply mean that stagnant or obsolete inventory is building up. Therefore, to put the working capital figure into proper perspective, it must be supplemented with other analytical work. The following four ratios (the current ratio, the acid-test ratio, the accounts receivable turnover, and the inventory turnover) should all be used in connection with an analysis of working capital.

Current Ratio

The elements involved in the computation of working capital are frequently expressed in ratio form. A company's current assets divided by its current liabilities is known as the **current ratio:**

$$\frac{\text{Current assets}}{\text{Current liabilities}} = \text{Current ratio}$$

For Brickey Electronics, the current ratio for 19x1 and 19x2 would be:

19x2	**19x1**	
$\dfrac{\$15,500,000}{\$7,000,000} = 2.21 \text{ to } 1$	$\dfrac{\$16,470,000}{\$5,000,000} = 3.29 \text{ to } 1$	(10)

Although widely regarded as a measure of short-term debt-paying ability, the current ratio must be interpreted with a great deal of care. A *declining* ratio, as above, might be a sign of a deteriorating financial condition. On the other hand, it might be the result of a paring out of obsolete inventories or other stagnant assets. An *improving* ratio might be the result of an unwise stockpiling of inventory, or it might point up an improving financial situation. In short, the current ratio is useful, but tricky to interpret. To avoid a blunder, the analyst must take a hard look at the individual items of assets and liabilities involved.

The general rule of thumb calls for a current ratio of 2 to 1. This rule, of course, is subject to many exceptions, depending on the industry and the firm involved. Some industries can operate quite successfully on a current ratio of slightly over 1 to 1. The adequacy of a current ratio depends heavily on the *composition* of the assets involved. For example, although Company X and Company Y below both have current ratios of 2 to 1, one could hardly say that they are in comparable financial condition. Company Y most certainly will have difficulty in meeting its obligations as they come due.

	Company X	Company Y
Current assets:		
Cash	$ 25,000	$ 2,000
Accounts receivable . . .	60,000	8,000
Inventory.	85,000	160,000
Prepaid expenses	5,000	5,000
Total current assets . .	$175,000	$175,000
Current liabilities	$ 87,500	$ 87,500
Current ratio	2 to 1	2 to 1

Acid-Test Ratio

A much more rigorous test of a company's ability to meet its short-term debts can be found in the **acid-test,** or **quick, ratio.** Merchandise inventory and prepaid expenses are excluded from the total of current assets, leaving only the more liquid (or "quick") assets to be divided by current liabilities.

$$\frac{\text{Cash} + \text{Marketable securities} + \text{Current receivables}^*}{\text{Current liabilities}} = \text{Acid-test ratio}$$

* This would include both accounts receivable and any short-term notes receivable.

The acid-test ratio is designed to measure how well a company can meet its obligations without having to liquidate or depend too heavily on its inventory. Since inventory is not an immediate source of cash and may not even be salable in times of economic stress, it is generally felt that to be properly protected each dollar of liabilities should be backed by at least $1 of quick assets. Thus, an acid-test ratio of 1 to 1 is broadly viewed as being adequate in many firms.

The acid-test ratios for Brickey Electronics for 19x1 and 19x2 are given below:

	19x2	19x1	
Cash	$1,000,000	$2,270,000	
Accounts receivable . . .	6,000,000	4,000,000	
Total quick assets	$7,000,000	$6,270,000	
Current liabilities	$7,000,000	$5,000,000	
Acid-test ratio	1 to 1	1.25 to 1	(11)

Although Brickey Electronics has an acid-test ratio for 19x2 that is within the acceptable range, an analyst might be concerned about several disquieting trends revealed in the company's balance sheet. Notice that short-term debts are rising, while the cash position seems to be deteriorating. Perhaps the weakened cash position is a result of the greatly expanded volume of accounts receivable. One wonders why the accounts receivable have been allowed to increase so rapidly in so brief a time.

In short, as with the current ratio, to be used intelligently the acid-test ratio must be interpreted with one eye on its basic components.

Accounts Receivable Turnover

The **accounts receivable turnover** is a measure of how many times a company's accounts receivable have been turned into cash during the year. It is frequently used in conjunction with an analysis of working capital, since a smooth flow from accounts receivable into cash is an important indicator of the "quality" of a company's working capital and is critical to its ability to operate. The accounts receivable turnover is computed by dividing sales on account by the average accounts receivable balance for the year.

$$\frac{\text{Sales on account}}{\text{Average accounts receivable balance}} = \text{Accounts receivable turnover}$$

The accounts receivable turnover for Brickey Electronics for 19x2 is:

$$\frac{\text{Sales on account}}{\text{Average accounts receivable balance}} = \frac{\$52,000,000}{\$5,000,000^*} = 10.4 \text{ times} \qquad (12)$$

* $4,000,000 + \$6,000,000 = \$10,000,000; \$10,000,000 \div 2 = \$5,000,000$ average.

The turnover figure can then be divided into 365 to determine the average number of days being taken to collect an account (known as the **average collection period**).

$$\frac{365 \text{ days}}{\text{Accounts receivable turnover}} = \frac{365}{10.4 \text{ times}} = 35 \text{ days} \qquad (13)$$

Whether the average of 35 days taken to collect an account is good or bad depends on the credit terms Brickey Electronics is offering its customers. If the credit terms are 30 days, then a 35-day average collection period would be viewed as being very good. Most customers will tend to withhold payment for as long as the credit terms will allow and may even go over a few days. This factor, added to the ever-present few slow accounts, can cause the average collection period to exceed normal credit terms by a week to 10 days and should not be a matter for too much alarm.

On the other hand, if the company's credit terms are 10 days, then a 35-day average collection period may be a cause for some concern. The long collection period may be a result of the presence of many old accounts of doubtful collectibility, or it may be a result of poor day-to-day credit management. The firm may be making sales with inadequate credit checks on the companies to which the sales are being made, or perhaps no follow-ups are being made on slow accounts.

Inventory Turnover

The **inventory turnover** ratio measures how many times a company's inventory has been sold during the year. It is computed by dividing the cost of goods sold by the average level of inventory on hand:

$$\frac{\text{Cost of goods sold}}{\text{Average inventory balance}} = \text{Inventory turnover}$$

The average inventory figure is usually computed by taking the average of the beginning and ending inventory figures. Since Brickey Electronics has a beginning inventory figure of $10,000,000 and an ending inventory figure of $8,000,000, its average inventory for the year would be $9,000,000. The company's inventory turnover for 19x2 would be:

$$\frac{\text{Cost of goods sold}}{\text{Average inventory balance}} = \frac{\$36,000,000}{\$9,000,000} = 4 \text{ times} \qquad (14)$$

The number of days being taken to sell the entire inventory one time (called the **average sale period**) can be computed by dividing 365 by the inventory turnover figure:

$$\frac{365 \text{ days}}{\text{Inventory turnover}} = \frac{365}{4 \text{ times}} = 91\tfrac{1}{4} \text{ days} \qquad (15)$$

Grocery stores tend to turn their inventory over very quickly, perhaps as often as every 12 to 15 days. On the other hand, jewelry stores tend to turn their inventory over very slowly, perhaps only a couple of times each year.

If a firm has a turnover that is much slower than the average for its industry, then there may be obsolete goods on hand, or inventory stocks may be needlessly high. Excessive inventories simply tie up funds that could be used elsewhere in operations. Managers sometimes argue that they must buy in very large quantities in order to take advantage of the best discounts being offered. But these discounts must be carefully weighed against the added costs of insurance, taxes, financing, and risks of obsolescence and deterioration that result from carrying added inventories.

An inventory turnover that is substantially faster than the average is usually an indication that inventory levels are inadequate.

RATIO ANALYSIS—THE LONG-TERM CREDITOR

The position of long-term creditors differs from that of short-term creditors in that they are concerned with both the near-term *and* the long-term ability of a firm to meet its commitments. They are concerned with the near term since whatever interest they may be entitled to is normally paid on a current basis. They are concerned with the long term from the point of view of the eventual retirement of their holdings.

Since the long-term creditor is usually faced with somewhat greater risks than the short-term creditor, firms are often required to make various restrictive covenants for the long-term creditor's protection. Examples of such restrictive covenants would include the maintenance of minimum working capital levels and restrictions on payment of dividends to common stockholders. Although these restrictive covenants are in widespread use, they must be viewed as being a poor second to *prospective earnings* from the point of view of assessing protection and safety. Creditors do not want to go to court to collect their claims; they would much prefer staking the safety of their claims for interest and eventual repayment of principal on an orderly and consistent flow of funds from operations.

Times Interest Earned

The most common measure of the ability of a firm's operations to provide protection to the long-term creditor is the **times interest earned** ratio. It is computed by dividing earnings *before* interest expense and income taxes by the yearly interest charges that must be met:

$$\frac{\text{Earnings before interest expense and income taxes}^*}{\text{Interest expense}} = \text{Times interest earned}$$

* This amount is the same as *net operating income* on many financial statements.

For Brickey Electronics, the times interest earned ratio for 19x2 would be:

$$\frac{\$3,140,000}{\$640,000} = 4.9 \text{ times} \tag{16}$$

Earnings before income taxes must be used in the computation since interest expense deductions come *before* income taxes are computed. Income taxes are secondary to interest payments in that the latter have first claim on earnings. Only those earnings remaining after all interest charges have been provided for are subject to income taxes.

Various rules of thumb exist to gauge the adequacy of a firm's times interest earned ratio. Generally, earnings are viewed as adequate to protect long-term creditors if the times interest earned ratio is 2 or more. Before making a final judgment, however, it would be necessary to look at a firm's long-run *trend* of earnings, then decide how vulnerable the firm is to cyclical changes in the economy.

Debt-to-Equity Ratio

Although long-term creditors look primarily to prospective earnings and budgeted cash flows in attempting to gauge the risk of their position, they cannot ignore the importance of keeping a reasonable balance between the portion of assets being provided by creditors and the portion of assets being provided by the stockholders of a firm. This balance is measured by the **debt-to-equity ratio:**

$$\frac{\text{Total liabilities}}{\text{Stockholders' equity}} = \text{Debt-to-equity ratio}$$

	19x2	19x1	
Total liabilities	$14,500,000	$13,000,000 *(a)*	
Stockholders' equity	17,000,000	15,970,000 *(b)*	
Debt-to-equity ratio, *(a) ÷ (b)* . .	0.85 to 1	0.81 to 1	(17)

The debt-to-equity ratio indicates the amount of assets being provided by creditors for each dollar of assets being provided by the owners of a company. In 19x1, creditors of Brickey Electronics were providing 81 cents of assets for each $1 of assets being provided by stockholders; the figure increased only slightly to 85 cents by 19x2.

It should come as no surprise that creditors would like the debt-to-equity ratio to be relatively low. The lower the ratio, the larger is the amount of assets being provided by the owners of a company and the greater is the buffer of protection to creditors. By contrast, common stockholders would like the ratio to be relatively high, since through leverage common stockholders can benefit from the assets being provided by creditors.

In most industries, norms have developed over the years that serve as guides to firms in their decisions as to the "right" amount of debt to include in the capital structure. Different industries face different risks. For this reason, the level of debt that is appropriate for firms in one industry is not necessarily a guide to the level of debt that is appropriate for firms in a different industry.

SUMMARY OF RATIOS AND SOURCES OF COMPARATIVE RATIO DATA

As an aid to the reader, Exhibit 17–7 contains a summary of the ratios discussed in this chapter. Included in the exhibit are the formula for each ratio and a summary comment on each ratio's significance to the manager.

EXHIBIT 17–7
Summary of ratios

Ratio	Formula	Significance
Earnings per share (of common stock)	(Net income − Preferred dividends) ÷ Number of common shares outstanding	Tends to have an effect on the market price per share, as reflected in the price-earnings ratio
Fully diluted earnings per share	Net income ÷ (Number of common shares outstanding + Common stock equivalent of convertible securities)	Shows the potential effect on earnings per share of converting convertible securities into common stock
Price-earnings ratio	Market price per share ÷ Earnings per share	An index of whether a stock is relatively cheap or relatively expensive

EXHIBIT 17–7 *(concluded)*

Ratio	Formula	Significance
Dividend payout ratio	Dividends per share ÷ Earnings per share	An index showing whether a company pays out most of its earnings in dividends or reinvests the earnings internally
Dividend yield ratio	Dividends per share ÷ Market price per share	Shows the dividend return being provided by a stock, which can be compared to the return being provided by other stocks
Return on total assets	Net income + [Interest expense × (1 − Tax rate)] ÷ Average total assets	Measure of how well assets have been employed by management
Return on common stockholders' equity	(Net income − Preferred dividends) ÷ Average common stockholders' equity	When compared to the return on total assets, measures the extent to which financial leverage is being employed for or against the common stockholders
Book value per share	Common stockholders' equity ÷ Number of common shares outstanding	Measures the amount that would be distributed to holders of each share of common stock if all assets were sold at their balance sheet carrying amounts and if all creditors were paid off
Working capital	Current assets − Current liabilities	Represents current assets financed from long-term capital sources that do not require near-term repayment
Current ratio	Current assets ÷ Current liabilities	Test of short-term debt-paying ability
Acid-test (quick) ratio	(Cash + Marketable securities + Current receivables) ÷ Current liabilities	Test of short-term debt-paying ability without having to rely on inventory
Accounts receivable turnover	Sales on account ÷ Average accounts receivable balance	Measure of how many times a company's accounts receivable have been turned into cash during the year
Average collection period (age of receivables)	365 days ÷ Accounts receivable turnover	Measure of the average number of days taken to collect an account receivable
Inventory turnover	Cost of goods sold ÷ Average inventory balance	Measure of how many times a company's inventory has been sold during the year
Average sale period (turnover in days)	365 days ÷ Inventory turnover	Measure of the average number of days taken to sell the inventory one time
Times interest earned	Earnings before interest expense and income taxes ÷ Interest expense	Measure of the likelihood that creditors will continue to receive their interest payments
Debt-to-equity ratio	Total liabilities ÷ Stockholders' equity	Measure of the amount of assets being provided by creditors for each dollar of assets being provided by the stockholders

EXHIBIT 17–8

Published sources of financial ratios

Source	Content
Almanac of Business and Industrial Financial Ratios. Prentice-Hall. Published annually.	An exhaustive source that contains common-size income statements and financial ratios by industry and by size of companies within each industry.
Annual Statement Studies. Robert Morris Associates. Published annually.	A widely used publication that contains common-size statements and financial ratios on individual companies. The companies are arranged by industry.
Business Week. "The Top 1,000." McGraw-Hill. Published annually in March or April.	A special issue of *Business Week* that provides numerous financial ratios on the 1,000 largest companies in the United States.
Dow Jones-Irwin Business and Investment Almanac. Dow Jones-Irwin. Published annually.	This source contains mostly industry financial ratios and common-size income statements. Some information is given on very large companies.
Key Business Ratios. Dun & Bradstreet. Published annually.	Fourteen commonly used financial ratios are computed for major industry groupings. This source contains data on over 800 lines of business.
Standard & Poor's Industry Survey. Standard & Poor's. Published annually.	Various statistics, including some financial ratios, are provided by industry and on leading companies within each industry grouping.

Exhibit 17–8 contains a listing of published sources that provide comparative ratio data organized by industry. These sources are used extensively by managers, investors, and analysts in doing comparative analyses and in attempting to assess the well-being of companies.

SUMMARY

The data contained in financial statements represent a quantitative summary of a firm's operations and activities. If a manager is skillful at taking these statements apart, he or she can learn much about a company's strengths, its weaknesses, its developing problems, its operating efficiency, its profitability, and so forth.

Many analytical techniques are available to assist managers in taking financial statements apart and in assessing the direction and importance of trends and changes. In this chapter, we have discussed three such analytical techniques—dollar and percentage changes in statements, common-size statements, and ratio analysis. In the following chapter, we continue our discussion of statement analysis by focusing on a new topic—the statement of cash flows—and on its usefulness in assessing how well an organization is doing.

KEY TERMS FOR REVIEW

(Note: Definitions and formulas for all financial ratios are given in Exhibit 17–7. These definitions and formulas are not repeated here.)

Common-size statements A statement that shows the items appearing on it in percentage form rather than in dollar form. On the income statement, the percentages are based on total sales; on the balance sheet, the percentages are based on total assets or total equities.

Conversion feature The ability to exchange either bonds or preferred stock for common stock at some future time.

Financial leverage The financing of assets in a company with funds that have been acquired from creditors or from preferred stockholders at a fixed rate of return.

Horizontal analysis A comparison of two or more years' financial statements.

Negative financial leverage A situation in which the fixed return to a company's creditors and preferred stockholders is greater than the return on total assets. In this situation, the return to common stockholders' equity will be *less* than the return on total assets.

Positive financial leverage A situation in which the fixed return to a company's creditors and preferred stockholders is less than the return on total assets. In this situation, the return on common stockholders' equity will be *greater* than the return on total assets.

Trend percentages The expression of several years' financial data in percentage form in terms of a base year.

Vertical analysis The presentation of financial statements in common-size form.

QUESTIONS

17–1. What three analytical techniques are used in financial statement analysis?

17–2. Distinguish between horizontal and vertical analysis of financial statement data.

17–3. What is the basic objective in looking at trends in financial ratios and other data? Rather than looking at trends, to what other standard of comparison might a statement user turn?

17–4. In financial analysis, why does the analyst compute financial ratios rather than simply studying raw financial data? What dangers are there in the use of ratios?

17–5. What pitfalls are involved in computing earnings per share? How can these pitfalls be avoided?

17–6. What is meant by reporting an extraordinary item on the income statement net of its tax effect? Give an example of both an extraordinary gain and an extraordinary loss net of its tax effect. Assume a tax rate of 30 percent.

17–7. Assume that two companies in the same industry have equal earnings. Why might these companies have different price-earnings ratios? If a company has a price-earnings ratio of 20 and reports earnings per share for the current year of $4, at what price would you expect to find the stock selling on the market?

17–8. Armcor, Inc., is in a rapidly growing technological industry. Would you expect the company to have a high or a low dividend payout ratio?

17–9. Distinguish between a manager's *financing* and *operating* responsibilities. Which of these responsibilities is the return on total assets ratio designed to measure?

17–10. What is meant by the dividend yield on a common stock investment? In computing dividend yield, why do you use current market value rather than original purchase price?

17–11. What is meant by the term *financial leverage?*

17–12. The president of a medium-sized plastics company was recently quoted in a business journal as stating, "We haven't had a dollar of interest-paying debt in over 10 years. Not many companies can say that." As a stockholder in this firm, how would you feel about its policy of not taking on interest-paying debt?

17–13. Why is it more difficult to obtain positive financial leverage from preferred stock than from long-term debt?

17–14. If a stock's market value exceeds its book value, then the stock is overpriced. Do you agree? Explain.

17–15. Weaver Company experiences a great deal of seasonal variation in its business activities. The company's high point in business activity is in June; its low point is in January. During which month would you expect the current ratio to be highest? At what point would you advise the company to end its fiscal year? Why?

17–16. A company seeking a line of credit at a bank was turned down. Among other things, the bank stated that the company's 2 to 1 current ratio was not adequate. Give reasons why a 2 to 1 current ratio might not be adequate.

17–17. If you were a long-term creditor of a firm, would you be more interested in the firm's long-term or short-term debt-paying ability? Why?

17–18. A young college student once complained to the author, "The reason that corporations are such big spenders is that Uncle Sam always picks up part of the tab." What did he mean by this statement?

EXERCISES

E17–1. Comparative income statements are given below for Dearborn Sales, Ltd.:

DEARBORN SALES, LTD.
Income Statements
For the Years Ended June 30, 19x5, and 19x4

	19x5	19x4
Sales	$8,000,000	$6,000,000
Less cost of goods sold	4,984,000	3,516,000
Gross margin	3,016,000	2,484,000
Less operating expenses:		
Selling expenses	1,480,000	1,092,000
Administrative expenses	712,000	618,000
Total expenses	2,192,000	1,710,000
Net operating income	824,000	774,000
Less interest expense	96,000	84,000
Net income before taxes	$ 728,000	$ 690,000

Members of the company's Board of Directors are surprised to see that net income increased by only $38,000 when sales increased by two million dollars.

Required: 1. Express each year's income statement in common-size percentages. Carry computations to one decimal place.
2. Comment briefly on the changes between the two years.

E17–2.   Noble Company's current assets, current liabilities, and sales have been reported as follows over the last five years:

	19x5	19x4	19x3	19x2	19x1
Sales	$2,250,000	$2,160,000	$2,070,000	$1,980,000	$1,800,000
Cash	$ 30,000	$ 40,000	$ 48,000	$ 65,000	$ 50,000
Accounts receivable . .	570,000	510,000	405,000	345,000	300,000
Inventory	750,000	720,000	690,000	660,000	600,000
Total	$1,350,000	$1,270,000	$1,143,000	$1,070,000	$ 950,000
Current liabilities . . .	$ 640,000	$ 580,000	$ 520,000	$ 440,000	$ 400,000

Required: 1. Express the asset, liability, and sales data in trend percentages. (Show percentages for each item.) Use 19x1 as the base year, and carry computations to one decimal place.
2. Comment on the results of your analysis.

E17–3.   The financial statements for Castile Products, Inc., are given below:

CASTILE PRODUCTS, INC.
Balance Sheet
December 31, 19x4

Assets

Current assets:

Cash	$ 6,500
Accounts receivable, net.	35,000
Merchandise inventory	70,000
Prepaid expenses	3,500
Total current assets	115,000
Property and equipment, net	185,000
Total assets	$300,000

Liabilities and Stockholders' Equity

Liabilities:

Current liabilities		$ 50,000
Bonds payable, 10%		80,000
Total liabilities		130,000

Stockholders' equity:

Common stock, $5 par value	$ 30,000	
Retained earnings	140,000	
Total stockholders' equity		170,000
Total liabilities and equity		$300,000

CASTILE PRODUCTS, INC.
Income Statement
For the Year Ended December 31, 19x4

Sales	$420,000
Less cost of goods sold	292,500
Gross margin	127,500
Less operating expenses	89,500
Net operating income	38,000
Interest expense	8,000
Net income before taxes.	30,000
Income taxes (30%)	9,000
Net income	$ 21,000

Account balances on January 1, 19x4, were: accounts receivable, $25,000; and inventory, $60,000. All sales were on account.

Required: Compute financial ratios as follows:

1. Current ratio. (Industry average: 2.5 to 1.)
2. Acid-test ratio. (Industry average: 1.3 to 1.)
3. Debt-to-equity ratio.
4. Accounts receivable turnover in days. (Terms: 2/10; n/30.)
5. Inventory turnover in days. (Industry average: 64 days.)
6. Times interest earned.
7. Book value per share. (Market price: $42.)

E17–4. Refer to the financial statements for Castile Products, Inc., in Exercise 17–3. In addition to the data in these statements, assume that Castile Products, Inc., paid dividends of $2.10 per share during the year ended December 31, 19x4. Also assume that the company's common stock had a market price of $42 on December 31.

Required: Compute the following:

1. Earnings per share.
2. Dividend payout ratio.
3. Dividend yield ratio.
4. Price-earnings ratio. (Industry average: 10.)

E17–5. Refer to the financial statements for Castile Products, Inc., in Exercise 17–3. Assets at the beginning of the year totaled $280,000, and the stockholders' equity totaled $161,600.

Required: Compute the following:

1. Return on total assets.
2. Return on common stockholders equity.
3. Was financial leverage positive or negative for the year? Explain.

E17–6. Russo Products had a current ratio of 2.5 to 1 on June 30 of the current year. On that date, the company's assets were:

Cash.		$ 90,000
Accounts receivable	$300,000	
Less allowance for doubtful accounts . .	40,000	260,000
Inventory		490,000
Prepaid expenses		10,000
Plant and equipment, net		800,000
Total assets.		$1,650,000

Required: 1.   What was the company's working capital on June 30?
             2.   What was the company's acid-test ratio on June 30?
             3.   The company paid an account payable of $40,000 immediately after June 30.
                a.   What effect did this transaction have on working capital? Show computations.
                b.   What effect did this transaction have on the current ratio? Show computations.

E17–7.   Austin Company reported income as follows for the past year:

AUSTIN COMPANY
Income Statement
For the Year Ended September 30, 19x6

Sales	$600,000
Less cost of goods sold	350,000
Gross margin	250,000
Less operating expenses	190,000
Net income before taxes	60,000
Less income taxes (30%)	18,000
Net income	$ 42,000

A $30,000 loss resulting from flood-damaged merchandise is included in the operating expenses above.

Required: 1.   Redo the company's income statement by showing the loss net of tax.
             2.   Assume that the company has 20,000 shares of common stock outstanding. Compute the earnings per share as it should appear in the company's annual report to its stockholders.

E17–8.   Selected financial data from the June 30, 19x8, year-end statements of Safford Company are given below:

Total assets	$3,600,000
Long-term debt (12% interest rate)	500,000
Preferred stock, $100 par, 8%	900,000
Total stockholders' equity	2,400,000
Interest paid on long-term debt	60,000
Net income	280,000

Total assets at the beginning of the year were $3,000,000; total stockholders' equity was $2,200,000. There has been no change in the preferred stock during the year. The company's tax rate is 30 percent.

Required: 1.   Compute the return on total assets.
             2.   Compute the return on common stockholders' equity.
             3.   Is leverage positive or negative? Explain.

PROBLEMS

P17–9.   **Ratio analysis and common-size statements.**   Paul Sabin organized Sabin Electronics about 10 years ago in order to produce and sell several electronic devices on which he had secured patents. Although the company has been fairly profitable over the years, it is now experiencing a severe cash shortage. For this reason, it is requesting a $500,000 long-term loan from Gulfport State Bank, $100,000 of which will be used to bolster the Cash account and $400,000 of which will be used to modernize certain key items of equipment. The company's financial statements for the two most recent years follow:

SABIN ELECTRONICS
Comparative Balance Sheets

	This year	Last year
Assets		
Current assets:		
Cash	$ 70,000	$ 150,000
Marketable securities	—	18,000
Accounts receivable, net	480,000	300,000
Inventory	950,000	600,000
Prepaid expenses	20,000	22,000
Total current assets	1,520,000	1,090,000
Plant and equipment, net	1,480,000	1,370,000
Total assets	$3,000,000	$2,460,000
Liabilities and Stockholders' Equity		
Liabilities:		
Current liabilities	$ 800,000	$ 430,000
Bonds payable, 12%	600,000	600,000
Total liabilities	1,400,000	1,030,000
Stockholders' equity:		
Preferred stock, $25 par, 8%	250,000	250,000
Common stock, $10 par	500,000	500,000
Retained earnings	850,000	680,000
Total stockholders' equity	1,600,000	1,430,000
Total liabilities and equity	$3,000,000	$2,460,000

SABIN ELECTRONICS
Comparative Income Statements

	This year	Last year
Sales	$5,000,000	$4,350,000
Less cost of goods sold	3,875,000	3,450,000
Gross margin	1,125,000	900,000
Less operating expenses	653,000	548,000
Net operating income	472,000	352,000
Less interest expense	72,000	72,000
Net income before taxes	400,000	280,000
Less income taxes (30%)	120,000	84,000
Net income	280,000	196,000
Dividends paid:		
Preferred dividends	20,000	20,000
Common dividends	90,000	75,000
Total dividends paid	110,000	95,000
Net income retained	170,000	101,000
Retained earnings, beginning of year . . .	680,000	579,000
Retained earnings, end of year	$ 850,000	$ 680,000

During the past year the company introduced several new product lines and raised the selling prices on a number of old product lines, in order to improve its profit margin. The company also hired a new sales manager, who has expanded sales into several new territories. Sales terms are 2/10, n/30. All sales are on account. Assume that the following ratios are typical of firms in the electronics industry:

Current ratio	2.5 to 1
Acid-test ratio	1.3 to 1
Average age of receivables	18 days
Inventory turnover in days	60 days
Debt-to-equity ratio	0.90 to 1
Times interest earned	6.0 times
Return on total assets	13%
Price-earnings ratio	12

Required: 1. To assist the Gulfport State Bank in making a decision about the loan, compute the following ratios for both this year and last year:
    a. The current ratio.
    b. The acid-test ratio.
    c. The average age of receivables. (The accounts receivable at the beginning of last year totaled $250,000.)
    d. The inventory turnover in days. (The inventory at the beginning of last year totaled $500,000.)
    e. The debt-to-equity ratio.
    f. The number of times interest was earned.
  2. For both this year and last year:
    a. Present the balance sheet in common-size format.
    b. Present the income statement in common-size format down through net income.
  3. Comment on the results of your analysis in (1) and (2) above, and make a recommendation as to whether or not the loan should be approved.

P17–10. Investor ratios; recommendation on stock purchase.   Refer to the financial statements and other data in Problem 17–9. Assume that you are an account executive for a large brokerage house, and that one of your clients has asked for a recommendation about the possible purchase of Sabin Electronics' stock. You are not acquainted with the stock, and for this reason wish to do certain analytical work before making a recommendation.

Required: 1. You decide first to assess the well-being of the common stockholders. For both this year and last year, compute:
    a. The earnings per share.
    b. The fully diluted earnings per share. The preferred stock is convertible into common stock at the rate of two shares of common for each share of preferred. The bonds are not convertible.
    c. The dividend yield ratio for common. The company's stock is currently selling for $40 per share; last year it sold for $36 per share.
    d. The dividend payout ratio for common.
    e. The price-earnings ratio. How do investors regard Sabin Electronics as compared to other firms in the industry? Explain.
    f. The book value per share of common. Does the difference between market value and book value suggest that the stock is overpriced? Explain.

2. You decide next to assess the rate of return which the company is generating. Compute the following for both this year and last year:
   a. The return on total assets. (Total assets at the beginning of last year were $2,300,000.)
   b. The return on common equity. (Stockholders' equity at the beginning of last year was $1,329,000.)
   c. Is the company's financial leverage positive or negative? Explain.
3. Would you recommend that your client purchase shares of Sabin Electronics' stock? Explain.

P17–11. **Effect of various transactions on working capital, current ratio, and acid-test ratio.** Denna Company's working capital accounts at December 31, 19x6, are given below:

Cash	$ 50,000
Marketable securities	30,000
Accounts receivable (net)	200,000
Inventory	210,000
Prepaid expenses	10,000
Accounts payable	150,000
Notes due within one year	30,000
Accrued liabilities	20,000

During 19x7, Denna Company completed the following transactions:

x. Paid a cash dividend previously declared, $12,000.
a. Issued additional shares of capital stock for cash, $100,000.
b. Sold inventory costing $50,000 for $80,000, on account.
c. Wrote off uncollectible accounts in the amount of $10,000.
d. Declared a cash dividend, $15,000.
e. Paid accounts payable, $50,000.
f. Borrowed cash on a short-term note with the bank, $35,000.
g. Sold inventory costing $15,000 for $10,000 cash.
h. Purchased inventory on account, $60,000.
i. Paid off all short-term notes due, $30,000.
j. Purchased equipment for cash, $15,000.
k. Sold marketable securities costing $18,000 for cash, $15,000.
l. Collected cash on accounts receivable, $80,000.

Required:
1. Compute the following amounts and ratios as of December 31, 19x6:
   a. Working capital.
   b. Current ratio.
   c. Acid-test ratio.
2. For 19x7, indicate the effect of each of the transactions given above on working capital, the current ratio, and the acid-test ratio. Give the effect in terms of increase, decrease, or none. Item *(x)* is given below as an example of the format to use:

	The effect on		
Transaction	Working capital	Current ratio	Acid-test ratio
(x)	None	Increase	Increase

P17–12.   **Common-size statements; trend analysis; selected ratios.**   Comparative financial statements for the last three years are shown below for Palomar Company:

PALOMAR COMPANY
Comparative Income Statements
For the Years Ended May 31, 19x5, 19x4, and 19x3
(in thousands)

	19x5	19x4	19x3
Sales	$15,000	$12,000	$10,000
Less cost of goods sold	9,600	7,260	6,000
Gross margin	5,400	4,740	4,000
Less operating expenses	4,000	3,540	3,000
Net income before taxes	1,400	1,200	1,000
Less income taxes (30%)	420	360	300
Net income	$ 980	$ 840	$ 700

PALOMAR COMPANY
Comparative Balance Sheets
May 31, 19x5, 19x4, and 19x3
(in thousands)

	19x5	19x4	19x3
Assets			
Current assets:			
Cash	$ 80	$ 100	$ 90
Accounts receivable, net	720	500	400
Inventory	1,800	900	750
Total current assets	2,600	1,500	1,240
Plant and equipment, net	3,400	3,000	2,760
Total assets	$6,000	$4,500	$4,000
Liabilities and Stockholders' Equity			
Liabilities:			
Current liabilities	$1,250	$ 700	$ 500
Long-term debt	750	300	300
Total liabilities	2,000	1,000	800
Stockholders' equity:			
Common stock	1,000	1,000	1,000
Retained earnings	3,000	2,500	2,200
Total stockholders' equity	4,000	3,500	3,200
Total liabilities and stockholders' equity	$6,000	$4,500	$4,000

At the end of 19x4, Mr. John Pushard became president of Palomar Company. Mr. Pushard had become president after serving for many years as a district sales manager and then as vice president, sales. He knew that 19x5 (his first year as president) had been the best year in the company's history as a result of a 25 percent increase in sales and an extensive cost-cutting effort that he initiated. For this reason, he was staggered when he received the statements above and noticed the sharp drop in cash and the dramatic increase in current liabilities. He muttered to himself, "With $15,000,000 coming in from sales, how could our Cash account show a balance of only $80,000? These statements must be goofy."

Required: 1.   Prepare the income statement and the balance sheet in common-size form for all three years. (Round computations to one decimal place.)

2.   Prepare trend percentages covering the three years for both the income statements and the balance sheets. (Round computations to one decimal place, e.g., 115.6 percent.)

3.   For all three years, compute the following:

   a.   The working capital.
   b.   The current ratio. (Industry average: 2.5 to 1.)
   c.   The acid-test ratio. (Industry average: 1.0 to 1.)
   d.   The accounts receivable turnover in days. (Industry average: 13.0 days.) All sales are on account. The accounts receivable balance at the beginning of 19x3 was $360,000.
   e.   The inventory turnover in days. (Industry average: 40.0 days). The inventory balance at the beginning of 19x3 was $650,000.

4.   Comment on the results of your analytical work above. What strengths, weaknesses, or developing problems do you see in the company?

P17–13.   **Comprehensive problem on ratio analysis.**   You have just been hired as a loan officer at Slippery Rock State Bank. Your supervisor has given you a file containing a request from Lydex Company for a $50,000, five-year loan. Financial statement data on the company for the last two years are given below:

LYDEX COMPANY
Comparative Balance Sheets

	This year	Last year
Assets		
Current assets:		
Cash.	$ 16,000	$ 21,000
Marketable securities.	–0–	5,000
Accounts receivable, net	45,000	30,000
Inventory	65,000	40,000
Prepaid expenses	4,000	3,000
Total current assets	130,000	99,000
Plant and equipment, net	155,000	149,000
Total assets	$285,000	$248,000
Liabilities and Stockholders' Equity		
Liabilities:		
Current liabilities.	$ 65,000	$ 46,000
Note payable, 10%.	60,000	50,000
Total liabilities	125,000	96,000
Stockholders' equity:		
Preferred stock, 8%, $30 par value	30,000	30,000
Common stock, $20 par value	100,000	100,000
Retained earnings	30,000	22,000
Total stockholders' equity	160,000	152,000
Total liabilities and stockholders' equity	$285,000	$248,000

LYDEX COMPANY
Comparative Income Statements

	This year	Last year
Sales (all on account)	$262,500	$208,000
Less cost of goods sold	210,000	165,000
Gross margin	52,500	43,000
Less operating expenses	26,500	26,000
Net operating income	26,000	17,000
Less interest expense	6,000	5,000
Net income before taxes	20,000	12,000
Less income taxes (30%)	6,000	3,600
Net income	14,000	8,400
Dividends paid:		
Preferred dividends	2,400	2,400
Common dividends	3,600	1,800
Total dividends paid	6,000	4,200
Net income retained	8,000	4,200
Retained earnings, beginning of year	22,000	17,800
Retained earnings, end of year	$ 30,000	$ 22,000

H. P. McGuire, who just a year ago was appointed president of Lydex Company, argues that although the company has had a "spotty" record in the past, it has "turned the corner," as evidenced by a 25 percent jump in sales and by a greatly improved earnings picture between last year and this year. McGuire also points out that investors generally have recognized the improving situation at Lydex, as shown by the increase in market value of the company's common stock, which is currently selling for $18 per share (up from $10 per share last year). McGuire feels that with his leadership and with the modernized equipment that the $50,000 loan will permit the company to buy, profits will be even stronger in the future. McGuire has a reputation in the industry for being a good manager who runs a "tight" ship.

Not wanting to botch your first assignment, you decide to generate all the information that you can about the company. You determine that the following ratios are typical of firms in Lydex Company's industry:

Current ratio	2.3 to 1
Acid-test ratio	1.2 to 1
Average age of receivables	42 days
Inventory turnover	66 days
Return on assets	6.0%
Debt-to-equity ratio	0.65 to 1
Times interest earned	6.5
Price-earnings ratio	10

Required: 1. You decide first to assess the rate of return which the company is generating. Compute the following for both this year and last year:

     a. The return on total assets. (Total assets at the beginning of last year were $216,000.)

      b. The return on common equity. (Stockholders' equity at the beginning of last year totaled $150,800.)

      c. Is the company's leverage positive or negative? Explain.

  2. You decide next to assess the well-being of the common stockholders. For both this year and last year, compute:

      a. The earnings per share.

      b. The fully diluted earnings per share. The preferred stock is convertible into common at the rate of three shares of common for each share of preferred.

      c. The dividend yield ratio for common.

      d. The dividend payout ratio for common.

      e. The price-earnings ratio. How do investors regard Lydex Company as compared to other firms in the industry? Explain.

      f. The book value per share of common. Does the difference between market value per share and book value per share suggest that the stock at its current price is a bargain? Explain.

  3. You decide, finally, to assess creditor ratios to determine both short-term and long-term debt paying ability. For both this year and last year, compute:

      a. Working capital.

      b. The current ratio.

      c. The acid-test ratio.

      d. The average age of receivables. (The accounts receivable at the beginning of last year totaled $26,000.)

      e. The inventory turnover. (The inventory at the beginning of last year totaled $32,000.)

      f. The debt-to-equity ratio.

      g. The number of times interest was earned.

  4. Evaluate the data computed in (1) to (3) above, and using any additional data provided in the problem, make a recommendation to your supervisor as to whether the loan should be approved.

P17–14. **Common-size financial statements.** Refer to the financial statement data for Lydex Company, given in Problem 17–13.

Required: For both this year and last year:

  1. Present the balance sheet in common-size format.

  2. Present the income statement in common-size format down through net income.

  3. Comment on the results of your analysis.

P17–15. **Determining the effect of transactions on various financial ratios.** In the right-hand column below, certain financial ratios are listed. To the left of each ratio is a business transaction or event relating to the operating activities of Delta Company.

Business transaction or event	Ratio
1. The company declared a cash dividend.	Current ratio
2. Sold inventory on account at cost.	Acid-test ratio
3. The company issued bonds with an interest rate of 8%. The company's return on assets is 10%.	Return on common stockholders' equity

Business transaction or event	Ratio
4. The company's net income decreased by 10% between last year and this year. Long-term debt remained unchanged.	Times interest earned
5. A previously declared cash dividend was paid.	Current ratio
6. The market price of the company's common stock dropped from 24½ to 20. The dividend paid per share remained unchanged.	Dividend payout ratio
7. Obsolete inventory totaling $100,000 was written off as a loss.	Inventory turnover ratio
8. Sold inventory for cash at a profit.	Debt-to-equity ratio
9. Changed customer credit terms from 2/10, n/30 to 2/15, n/30 to comply with a change in industry practice.	Accounts receivable turnover ratio
10. Issued a common stock dividend on common stock.	Book value per share
11. The market price of the company's common stock increased from 24½ to 30.	Book value per share
12. The company paid $40,000 on accounts payable.	Working capital
13. Issued a common stock dividend to common stockholders.	Earnings per share
14. Paid accounts payable.	Debt-to-equity ratio
15. Purchased inventory on open account.	Acid-test ratio
16. Wrote off an uncollectible account against the Allowance for Bad Debts.	Current ratio
17. The market price of the company's common stock increased from 24½ to 30. Earnings per share remained unchanged.	Price-earnings ratio
18. The market price of the company's common stock increased from 24½ to 30. The dividend paid per share remained unchanged.	Dividend yield ratio

Required: Indicate the effect that each business transaction or event would have on the ratio listed opposite to it. State the effect in terms of increase, decrease, or no effect on the ratio involved, and give the reason for your choice of answer. In all cases, assume that the current assets exceed the current liabilities both before and after the event or transaction. Use the following format for your answers:

Effect on ratio	Reason for increase, decrease, or no effect
1.	
Etc.	

P17–16.   **Effect of leverage on the return on common equity.**   Several investors are in the process of organizing a new company. The investors believe that $1,000,000 will be needed to finance the new company's operations, and they are considering three methods of raising this amount of money.

Method A: All $1,000,000 can be obtained through issue of common stock.

Method B: $500,000 can be obtained through issue of common stock and the other $500,000 can be obtained through issue of $100 par value, 8 percent preferred stock.

Method C: $500,000 can be obtained through issue of common stock, and the other $500,000 can be obtained through issue of bonds carrying an interest rate of 8 percent.

The investors organizing the new company are confident that it can earn $170,000 each year before interest and taxes. The tax rate will be 30 percent.

Required:
1. Assuming that the investors are correct in their earnings estimate, compute the net income that would go to the common stockholders under each of the three financing methods listed above.
2. Using the income data computed in (1) above, compute the return on common equity under each of the three methods.
3. Why do methods B and C provide a greater return on common equity than does method A? Why does method C provide a greater return on common equity than method B?

P17–17. **Interpretation of completed ratios.**   Paul Ward is interested in the stock of Pecunious Products, Inc. Before purchasing the stock, Mr. Ward would like to learn as much as possible about the company. However, all he has to go on is the current year's (19x3) annual report, which contains no comparative data other than the summary of ratios given below:

	19x3	19x2	19x1
Sales trend	128.0	115.0	100.0
Current ratio	2.5:1	2.3:1	2.2: 1
Acid-test ratio	0.8:1	0.9:1	1.1: 1
Accounts receivable turnover . . .	9.4 times	10.6 times	12.5 times
Inventory turnover	6.5 times	7.2 times	8.0 times
Dividend yield	7.1%	6.5%	5.8%
Dividend payout ratio	40%	50%	60%
Return on total assets	12.5%	11.0%	9.5%
Return on common equity	14.0%	10.0%	7.8%
Dividends paid per share* . . .	$1.50	$1.50	$1.50

* There have been no issues or retirements of stock over the three-year period.

Mr. Ward would like answers to a number of questions about the trend of events in Pecunious Products, Inc., over the last three years. His questions are:

a. Is it becoming easier for the company to pay its bills as they come due?
b. Are customers paying their accounts at least as fast now as they were in 19x1?
c. Is the total of the accounts receivable increasing, decreasing, or remaining constant?
d. Is the level of inventory increasing, decreasing, or remaining constant?
e. Is the market price of the company's stock going up or down?
f. Is the amount of the earnings per share increasing or decreasing?
g. Is the price-earnings ratio going up or down?
h. Is the company employing leverage to the advantage of the common stockholders?

Required: Answer each of Mr. Ward's questions, using the data given above. In each case, explain how you arrived at your answer.

P17–18.   **Comprehensive problem—Part 1: Investor ratios.**   (Problems 17–19 and 17–20 delve more deeply into the data presented below. Each problem is independent.) Empire Labs, Inc., was organized several years ago to produce and market several new "miracle drugs." The company is small but growing, and you are considering the purchase of some of its common stock as an investment. The following data on the company are available for the past two years:

EMPIRE LABS, INC.
Comparative Income Statements
For the Years Ended December 31, 19x2, and 19x1

	19x2	19x1
Sales	$20,000,000	$15,000,000
Less cost of goods sold	13,000,000	9,000,000
Gross margin	7,000,000	6,000,000
Less operating expenses	5,260,000	4,560,000
Net operating income	1,740,000	1,440,000
Less interest expense	240,000	240,000
Net income before taxes	1,500,000	1,200,000
Less income taxes (30%)	450,000	360,000
Net income	$ 1,050,000	$ 840,000

EMPIRE LABS, INC.
Statements of Changes in Retained Earnings
For the Years Ended December 31, 19x2, and 19x1

	19x2	19x1
Retained earnings, January 1	$2,400,000	$1,960,000
Add net income (above)	1,050,000	840,000
Total	3,450,000	2,800,000
Deduct cash dividends paid:		
Preferred dividends	120,000	120,000
Common dividends	360,000	280,000
Total dividends paid	480,000	400,000
Retained earnings, December 31	$2,970,000	$2,400,000

EMPIRE LABS, INC.
Comparative Balance Sheets
December 31, 19x2, and 19x1

	19x2	19x1
Assets		
Current assets:		
Cash	$ 200,000	$ 400,000
Accounts receivable, net	1,500,000	800,000
Inventory	3,000,000	1,200,000
Prepaid expenses	100,000	100,000
Total current assets	4,800,000	2,500,000
Plant and equipment, net	5,170,000	5,400,000
Total assets	$9,970,000	$7,900,000
Liabilities and Stockholders' Equity		
Liabilities:		
Current liabilities	$2,500,000	$1,000,000
Bonds payable,12%	2,000,000	2,000,000
Total liabilities	4,500,000	3,000,000
Stockholders' equity:		
Preferred stock, 8%, $10 par	1,500,000	1,500,000
Common stock, $5 par	1,000,000	1,000,000
Retained earnings	2,970,000	2,400,000
Total stockholders' equity	5,470,000	4,900,000
Total Liabilities and stockholders' equity	$9,970,000	$7,900,000

After some research, you have determined that the following ratios are typical of firms in the pharmaceutical industry:

Dividend yield ratio	3%
Dividend payout ratio	40%
Price-earnings ratio	16
Return on total assets	13.5%
Return on common equity	20%

The company's common stock is currently selling for $60 per share. During 19x1, the stock sold for $45 per share.

Required: 1. In analyzing the company, you decide first to compute the earnings per share and related ratios. For both 19x1 and 19x2, compute:
   a. The earnings per share.
   b. The fully diluted earnings per share. Assume that each share of the preferred stock is convertible into two shares of common stock. The bonds are not convertible.
   c. The dividend yield ratio.
   d. The dividend payout ratio.
   e. The price-earnings ratio.
   f. The book value per share of common stock.

2. You decide next to determine the rate of return which the company is generating. For both 19x1 and 19x2, compute:
   a. The return on total assets. (Total assets were $6,500,000 on January 1, 19x1.)
   b. The return on common stockholders' equity. (Common stockholders' equity was $2,900,000 on January 1, 19x1.)
   c. Is financial leverage positive or negative? Explain.

3. Based on your work in (1) and (2), does the company's common stock seem to be an attractive investment? Explain.

P17–19. **Comprehensive problem—Part 2: Creditor ratios.**   Refer to the data in Problem 17–18. Although Empire Labs, Inc., has been very profitable since it was organized several years ago, the company is beginning to experience some difficulty in paying its bills as they come due. Management has approached Security National Bank requesting a two-year, $500,000 loan to bolster the cash account.

Security National Bank has assigned you to evaluate the loan request. You have gathered the following data relating to firms in the pharmaceutical industry:

Current ratio	2.4 to 1
Acid-test ratio	1.2 to 1
Average age of receivables	16 days
Inventory turnover in days	40 days
Times interest earned	7 times
Debt-to-equity ratio	0.70 to 1

The following additional information is available on Empire Labs, Inc.:

a. All sales are on account.
b. On January 1, 19x1, the accounts receivable balance was $600,000 and the inventory balance was $1,000,000.

Required: 1. Compute the following amounts and ratios for both 19x1 and 19x2:
   a. The working capital.
   b. The current ratio.

    c. The acid-test ratio.
    d. The accounts receivable turnover in days.
    e. The inventory turnover in days.
    f. The times interest earned.
    g. The debt-to-equity ratio.
  2. Comment on the results of your analysis in (1) above.
  3. Would you recommend that the loan be approved? Explain.

P17–20. **Comprehensive problem—Part 3: Common-size statements.** Refer to the data in Problem 17–18. The president of Empire Labs, Inc., is very concerned. Sales increased by $5 million in 19x2, yet the company's net income increased by only a small amount. Also, the company's operating expenses went up in 19x2, even though a major effort was launched during the year to cut costs.

Required: 1. For both 19x1 and 19x2, prepare the income statement and the balance sheet in common-size form. (Round computations to one decimal place.)
     2. From your work in (1), explain to the president why the increase in profits was so small in 19x2. Were any benefits realized from the company's cost-cutting efforts? Explain.

P17–21. **Interpretation of ratios.** Thorpe Company is a wholesale distributor of professional equipment and supplies. The company's sales have averaged about $900,000 annually for the three-year period 19x3–x5. The firm's total assets at the end of 19x5 amounted to $850,000.

    The president of Thorpe Company has asked the controller to prepare a report summarizing the financial aspects of the company's operations for the past three years. This report will be presented to the board of directors at their next meeting.

    In addition to comparative financial statements, the controller has decided to present a number of relevant financial ratios that can assist in the identification and interpretation of trends. At the request of the controller, the accounting staff has calculated the following ratios for the three-year period 19x3–x5:

	19x3	19x4	19x5
Current ratio	2.00	2.13	2.18
Acid-test ratio	1.20	1.10	0.97
Accounts receivable turnover	9.72	8.57	7.13
Percent of total debt to total assets	44%	41%	38%
Ratio of sales to fixed assets (sales divided by fixed assets)	1.75	1.88	1.99
Sales as a percent of 19x3 sales (trend analysis)	100%	103%	106%
Gross margin percentage	40.0%	38.6%	38.5%
Net income to sales	7.8%	7.8%	8.0%
Return on total assets	8.5%	8.6%	8.7%
Return on common stockholders' equity	15.1%	14.6%	14.1%
Inventory turnover	5.25	4.80	3.80
Percent of long-term debt to total assets	25%	22%	19%

    In the preparation of his report, the controller has decided first to examine the financial ratios independently of any other data to determine if the ratios themselves reveal any significant trends over the three-year period.

Required: Answer the following questions. Indicate in each case which ratio(s) you used in arriving at your conclusion.

1. The current ratio is increasing while the acid-test ratio is decreasing. Using the ratios provided, identify and explain the contributing factor(s) for this apparently divergent trend.

2. In terms of the ratios provided, what conclusion(s) can be drawn regarding the company's use of financial leverage during the 19x3–x5 period?

3. Using the ratios provided, what conclusion(s) can be drawn regarding the company's net investment in plant and equipment?

(CMA, Adapted)

P17–22. **Incomplete statements; analysis of ratios.** Incomplete financial statements for Pepper Industries are given below:

PEPPER INDUSTRIES
Balance Sheet
March 31, 19x8

Current assets:		
Cash	$	?
Accounts receivable, net		?
Inventory		?
Total current assets		?
Plant and equipment		?
Total assets	$	?
Liabilities:		
Current liabilities.	$	320,000
Bonds payable, 10%		?
Total liabilities		?
Stockholders' equity:		
Common stock, $5 par value		?
Retained earnings		?
Total stockholders' equity		?
Total liabilities and stockholders' equity . .	$	?

PEPPER INDUSTRIES
Income Statement
For the Year Ended March 31, 19x8

Sales	$4,200,000
Less cost of goods sold	?
Gross margin	?
Less operating expenses	?
Net operating income	?
Less interest expense	80,000
Net income before taxes	?
Less income taxes (30%)	?
Net income	$?

The following additional information is available about the company:

a. All sales during the year were on account.

b. There were no issues or retirements of common stock during the year.

c. The interest expense on the income statement relates to the bonds payable; the amount of bonds outstanding did not change during the year.

d. Selected balances at the *beginning* of the current fiscal year (April 1, 19x7) were:

Accounts receivable	$ 270,000
Inventory	360,000
Total assets	1,800,000

e. Selected financial ratios computed from the statements above for the current year are:

Earnings per share	$2.30
Debt-to-equity ratio	0.875 to 1
Accounts receivable turnover . .	14.0 times
Current ratio	2.75 to 1
Return on total assets	18.0%
Times interest earned	6.75 times
Acid-test ratio	1.25 to 1
Inventory turnover	6.5 times

Required: Compute the missing amounts on the company's financial statements. (Hint: What's the difference between the acid-test ratio and the current ratio?)

CHAPTER 18

"How Well Am I Doing?"– Statement of Cash Flows

LEARNING OBJECTIVES

After studying Chapter 18, you should be able to:

- Describe the purpose of a statement of cash flows.

- State the general rules for determining whether transactions should be classified as operating activities, investing activities, or financing activities.

- Explain what is meant by a direct exchange transaction and explain how such a transaction is reported to statement users.

- Compute the cash provided by operations, using the indirect method.

- Prepare working papers to gather data for a statement of cash flows.

- Prepare a statement of cash flows in good form.

- Adjust the income statement to a cash basis, using the direct method.

- Define or explain the key terms listed at the end of the chapter.

Three major statements are prepared annually by most companies—an income statement, a balance sheet, and a statement of cash flows. The statement of cash flows is less well known than the income statement or the balance sheet, but many view it as being equal in importance. This importance is underscored by the fact that the Financial Accounting Standards Board (FASB) requires that a statement of cash flows be provided whenever a balance sheet and an income statement are made available to users of financial data. In this chapter, our focus is on the development of the statement of cash flows and on its use as a tool for assessing the well-being of a company.

PURPOSE AND USE OF THE STATEMENT

The purpose of the **statement of cash flows** is to highlight the major activities that have provided cash and that have used cash during a period, and to show the resulting effect on the overall cash balance. The statement is a powerful analytical tool that can be used by managers, investors, and creditors in the following ways:

1. To determine the amount of cash provided by operations during a period and to reconcile this amount with net income.
2. To assess an organization's ability to meet its obligations as they come due and to assess its ability to pay cash dividends.
3. To determine the amount of investment in new plant, equipment, and other noncurrent assets during a period.
4. To determine the type and extent of financing required to expand the investment in long-term assets or to bolster operations.
5. To assess an organization's ability to generate a positive cash flow in future periods.

For the statement of cash flows to be useful to managers and others in gathering information such as that above, it is important that companies employ a common definition of cash and organize the statement in a consistent manner. Questions relating to the definition of cash and to the organization of the statement are considered in the following two sections.

Definition of cash

In preparing a statement of cash flows for inclusion in an annual report, the FASB has stated that the term *cash* must be broadly defined to include both cash and cash equivalents.[1] **Cash equivalents** consist of short-term, highly liquid investments such as treasury bills, commercial paper, and money market funds. Investments of this type are considered to be "equiva-

---

[1] Financial Accounting Standards Board, *Statement of Cash Flows*, Proposed Statement of Financial Accounting Standards, Exposure Draft No. 023 (Stamford, Conn., July 31, 1986), p. 2.

lent'' to cash in what they are made solely for the purpose of generating a return on cash that is temporarily idle. Because short-term investments are just temporary uses of cash and therefore part of a company's overall cash management program, they are included with cash in preparing a statement of cash flows.

In the past, some companies have used the term *funds* in lieu of the term *cash* in describing the contents of a statement of cash flows. Since the term *funds* often means different things to different people, the FASB has stated that its use should be discontinued and that more descriptive terms, such as *cash,* or *cash and cash equivalents,* should be used in its place.

ORGANIZATION OF THE STATEMENT

For many years, companies have had wide latitude in organizing the content of a statement of cash flows. One popular format has been to divide the statement into two sections—one titled ''Sources of cash'' and the other titled ''Uses of cash''—and to classify all cash flows under one of these two heads. Generally, this format has provided a separate figure for the amount of cash generated by operations, but it has provided little else in the way of organized data; as a result, investors and creditors have had difficulty in comparing one company with another.

To provide greater comparability of data, the FASB now requires that the statement of cash flows be divided into three sections. The first section must contain all cash flows relating to *operating activities* for a period; the next section must contain all cash flows relating to *investing activities;* and the final section must contain all cash flows relating to *financing activities.* Below we discuss the guidelines to be followed in classifying a company's cash flows under these three heads.

Operating Activities

As a general rule, any transactions that enter into the determination of net income are classified as **operating activities.** These transactions can result in either cash inflows or cash outflows.

Cash inflows come from the sale of goods or the providing of services; interest received from *all* sources; dividends received on stock held as an investment; and cash received from miscellaneous sources, such as rental income.

In reading this list of cash inflows, the reader may wonder why dividends received on stock held as an investment is treated as an *operating* item when the stock itself obviously represents an *investment* item. The reasons are twofold: first, the dividends enter into the determination of income; and second, investing activities are narrowly defined to include only the *principal amount* of stock purchased or sold. Thus, the income from an investment item such as stock is classified as part of operating activities even though the stock itself is classified under a different heading.

Cash outflows that are classified as operating activities consist of payments made for items *that appear as expenses on the income statement*. These would include payments to suppliers for inventory; payments to employees for services; payments to other entities for insurance, utilities, rent, and so forth; and payments to governmental agencies for taxes. In addition, payments to banks and other lenders for interest are included as part of operating activities even though the loans themselves are part of a company's financing activities. The reasons for this apparent inconsistency are the same as those given above for dividends: interest enters into the determination of income, and financing activities are narrowly defined to include only the principal amount borrowed or repaid.

The cash inflows and outflows discussed above are summarized in Exhibit 18–1 on the following page.

Investing Activities

Generally speaking, any transactions that are involved in the acquisition or disposition of noncurrent assets are classified as **investing activities.** These transactions include acquiring or selling property, plant, and equipment; acquiring or selling securities held for long-term investment, such as bonds and stocks of other companies; and the lending of money to another entity (such as to a subsidiary) and the subsequent collection of the loan.

In the preceding section we stated that any transactions that enter into the determination of income are treated as operating activities. This general rule is not followed in the case of gains or losses on sales of noncurrent assets. Such gains or losses are included as *investing activities* along with the assets to which they relate. The reason for this apparent violation of our general rule is that statement users can see the effects of a decision to sell an asset more clearly if these effects are reported *in one place* instead of being separated and reported in different places on the statement of cash flows.

Exhibit 18–1 provides a tabular summary of the cash inflows and outflows discussed above.

Financing Activities

As a general rule, any transactions (other than the payment of interest) involving borrowing from creditors, and any transactions (except stock dividends and stock splits) involving the owners of a company, are classified as **financing activities.**

On the cash inflow side, amounts obtained from creditors come from borrowing on either a short-term or a long-term basis through the issuance of notes, bonds, mortgages, and similar forms of debt. Amounts obtained from owners come from the sale of capital stock (preferred or common).

For those transactions involving creditors, note that accounts payable is

EXHIBIT 18–1

A summary of operating, investing, and financing activities

Operating activities

General rule: Any transactions that enter into the determination of net income are classified as operating activities. These transactions include:

Cash receipts from:
Sale of goods or providing of services
Interest (from all sources)
Dividends (on stock of other companies)
Miscellaneous income, such as from rentals

Cash payments to:
Suppliers for purchases of inventory
Employees for services
Other entities for insurance, utilities, rent, and so forth
Creditors for interest on debt
Governmental agencies for taxes

Investing activities

General rule: Any transactions that are involved in the acquisition or disposition of noncurrent assets are classified as investing activities. These transactions
include:

Cash provided by:
Sale of property, plant, and equipment
Sale of securities, such as bonds and stocks of other companies, that are not cash
equivalents
Collection of a loan made to another company

Cash used to:
Purchase property, plant, and equipment
Purchase securities, such as bonds and stocks of other companies, that are not
cash equivalents
Lend money to another company, such as to a subsidiary

Financing activities

General rule: Any transactions (other than the payment of interest) involving borrowing
from creditors, and any transactions (except stock dividends and stock
splits) involving the owners of a company, are classified as financing activities. These transactions include:

Cash provided by:
Borrowing from short-term or long-term creditors through notes, bonds, mortgages,
and similar forms of debt
Sale of capital stock to owners

Cash used to:
Retire notes, bonds, mortgages and similar forms of short-term and long-term debt
Repurchase capital stock from owners
Pay cash dividends to owners

not included among the forms of debt representing financing activities. This
is because accounts payable is used to obtain *goods and services* rather
than to obtain cash. Also, the goods and services obtained (such as inventory,
utilities, and supplies) relate to a company's day-to-day operating activities
rather than to its financing activities. For those transactions involving the
owners of a company, note that stock dividends and stock splits are not
included as financing activities. This is because neither stock dividends

nor stock splits involve the use of cash and therefore do not appear on a statement of cash flows.

On the cash outflow side, financing activities include the repayment of amounts borrowed from short-term and long-term creditors, the repurchase of stock held by the owners of a company, and the payment of cash dividends to owners. The payment of cash dividends is classified as a financing item, rather than as an operating item, because dividends do not enter into the determination of income. In repaying creditors for amounts borrowed, if a gain or a loss is involved (such as retiring bonds for less than their carrying value), then the gain or loss should be classified as a financing item along with the debt to which it relates.

A tabular summary of the cash inflows and outflows discussed above is presented in Exhibit 18–1.

DIRECT EXCHANGE TRANSACTIONS

Companies sometimes acquire assets or dispose of liabilities through **direct exchange transactions.** Examples of direct exchange transactions include the issue of capital stock in exchange for property and equipment, the conversion of long-term debt or preferred stock into common stock, and the acquisition of property and equipment under a long-term lease agreement.

Such exchanges have a common identifying characteristic in that they affect only noncurrent balance sheet accounts and have no effect on cash. Even though direct exchange transactions have no effect on cash, they must still be considered when the statement of cash flows is prepared. This is because these exchanges involve significant financing and investing activities, the existence of which must be made known to statement users. However, rather than being reported as part of a statement of cash flows, direct exchanges are reported in a separate, accompanying schedule. To illustrate how this is done, assume the following situation:

Delsey company acquired a building and paid for it in full by issuing 5,000 shares of its own common stock, which had a par value of $100 per share. Since the stock was selling for $120 per share at the time the building was acquired, the exchange was recorded as follows:

Building (5,000 shares × $120).	600,000	
Common stock, $100 par (5,000 shares × $100)		500,000
Paid-In Capital in Excess of Par (5,000 shares × $20) . .		100,000

This transaction had no effect on cash, but it did involve both an investing activity (the acquisition of a building) and a financing activity (the issue of common stock) through a direct exchange. To report this exchange to statement users, Delsey Company should provide the following information in a separate schedule:

Schedule of noncash investing and financing activities:
Common stock issued for property and equipment $600,000

OTHER FACTORS IN PREPARING THE STATEMENT OF CASH FLOWS

We must consider two other factors before we can illustrate the preparation of a statement of cash flows. These two factors are (1) whether amounts on the statement should be presented gross or net, and (2) whether operating activities should be presented by use of the direct method or the indirect method.

Cash Flows: Gross or Net?

For both *financing* and *investing* activities, items on the statement of cash flows should be presented in gross amounts rather than in net amounts. To illustrate, assume that a company purchases $500,000 in property during a year and sells other property for $300,000. Instead of showing a $200,000 net investment in property for the year, the company must show the gross amounts of both the purchases and the sales. In like manner, if a company receives $800,000 from the issue of bonds and then pays out $600,000 to retire other bonds, the receipts and the payments should be shown in their gross amounts, rather than being netted against each other.

The gross method of reporting does not extend to *operating* activities, where it is often necessary to net items against each other. For example, if $400,000 is added to accounts receivable as a result of sales during a year, and if $300,000 of receivables is collected, then only the $100,000 net difference would be used in determining the cash flow from operating activities for the year.

Operating Activities: Direct or Indirect Reporting?

The net result of the cash inflows and outflows arising from operating activities is often referred to as the **cash provided by operations.** It is possible to compute this figure by using either the *direct method* or the *indirect method*.

Under the **direct method,** the income statement is reconstructed on a cash basis from top to bottom. In place of sales, we have cash collected from customers; in place of cost of goods sold, we have payments to suppliers for inventory; and in place of operating expenses, we have payments to employees for services, payments for insurance, and so forth. The net result between the cash receipts and the cash payments represents the cash provided by operations for the period.

Under the **indirect method,** the cash provided by operations is computed by starting with net income (as reported on the income statement) and adjusting the net income figure to a cash basis. That is, rather than making *direct* adjustments to sales, cost of goods sold, and other income statement items in order to compute the cash provided by operations, these adjustments are made *indirectly* through the net income figure. Thus the term, *indirect method.* The indirect method has an advantage over the direct method in that it shows the reasons for any differences between net income and cash provided by operations. The indirect method is also known as the **reconciliation method.**

In preparing a statement of cash flows, should the manager use the direct method or the indirect method? If the statement is being prepared *for use within the company,* the choice between the two methods is simply a matter of individual preference. If the statement is being prepared *for external reporting purposes,* a choice may not be available. The reason is that at the time this chapter went to press, the FASB had an exposure draft in circulation which, if approved, will require that *both* methods be used. The direct method will be used in preparing the operating activities section of the statement,[2] and the indirect method will be presented in a separate, accompanying schedule. Thus, it is important for the manager to have an understanding of both methods of reporting, regardless of whether we are talking about internal or external use.

We have already noted that the direct and indirect methods are very different in their approach. We will be most effective in our study, therefore, if we discuss the two methods separately. Since many people find the indirect method to be the easiest of the two methods to apply, we will discuss it first. The indirect method also lends itself readily to working papers, so we will use it as a base for illustrating the use of working papers in preparing a statement of cash flows. After laying this foundation, we will then turn our attention to the direct method and show how the income statement can be adjusted to a cash basis for external reporting purposes.

THE INDIRECT METHOD OF DETERMINING CASH PROVIDED BY OPERATIONS

The items for which adjustments must be made to determine the cash provided by operations can be grouped into four broad categories, as follows:

1. Depreciation, depletion, and amortization.
2. Changes in current asset accounts affecting revenue or expense.
3. Changes in current liability accounts affecting revenue or expense.
4. Changes in the Deferred Income Taxes account.

A simple model is available that starts with net income and shows the adjustments that must be made for each of the items listed above in computing a cash flow figure under the indirect method. This model is presented in Exhibit 18–2. The various parts of the model are discussed in the following sections.

---

[2] The exposure draft would require that cash receipts be broken down between dividends, interest, and "other" receipts, and it would require that cash payments be broken down between taxes, interest, and "other" payments. In the view of the author, these breakdowns are too limited to be of much value to statement users.

EXHIBIT 18–2

General model: Indirect method of determining cash provided by operations

	Add (+) or deduct (−) to adjust net income
Net income	$XXX
Adjustments needed to convert net income to a cash basis:	
Depreciation, depletion, and amortization expense	+
Add (deduct) changes in current asset accounts affecting revenue or expense:*	
Increase in the account	−
Decrease in the account	+
Add (deduct) changes in current liability accounts affecting revenue or expense:†	
Increase in the account	+
Decrease in the account	−
Add (deduct) changes in the Deferred Income Taxes account:	
Increase in the account	+
Decrease in the account	−
Cash provided by operations	$XXX

* Examples include accounts receivable, accrued receivables, inventory, and prepaid expenses.
† Examples include accounts payable, accrued liabilities, and deferred revenue.

Depreciation, Depletion, and Amortization

As shown in Exhibit 18–2, depreciation and related items are added back to net income in computing the cash provided by operations. The mechanics of this process sometimes leads people to the hasty conclusion that depreciation is a source of cash to an organization. We must state emphatically that depreciation is not a source of cash. We add it back to net income for the reason that it requires no cash outlay during a period, yet it is deducted as an expense in arriving at net income. Thus, by adding it back, we are able to cancel out its effect and leave as part of net income only those items of revenue and expense that *do* affect the amount of cash provided during a period.

Besides depreciation, other deductions that reduce net income without involving an outflow of cash include depletion of natural resources and amortization of goodwill, patents, and similar items. Like depreciation, these items are added back to net income under the indirect method in computing the amount of cash provided by operations.

Changes in Current Asset and Current Liability Accounts

In adjusting the net income figure to a cash basis, the model in Exhibit 18–2 shows that certain additions and deductions must be made for changes in the current asset and current liability accounts. An explanation is provided in Exhibit 18–3 as to what the changes in these accounts mean and why

EXHIBIT 18–3

Explanation of adjustments for changes in current asset and current liability accounts (see Exhibit 18–2)

	Change in the account	This change means that . . .	Therefore, to adjust to a cash basis under the indirect method, we must . . .
Accounts receivable and accrued receivables	Increase	Sales (revenues) have been reported for which no cash has been collected.	Deduct the amount from net income to show that cash-basis sales are less than reported sales (revenues).
	Decrease	Cash has been collected for which no sale (revenue) has been reported for the current period.	Add the amount to net income to show that cash-basis sales are greater than reported sales (revenues).
Inventory	Increase	Goods have been purchased that are not included in cost of goods sold (COGS).	Deduct the amount from net income to show that cash-basis COGS is greater than reported COGS.
	Decrease	Goods have been included in cost of goods sold that were purchased in a prior period.	Add the amount to net income to show that cash-basis COGS is less than reported COGS.
Prepaid expenses	Increase	More cash has been paid out for services than has been reported as expense.	Deduct the amount from net income to show that cash-basis expenses are greater than reported expenses.
	Decrease	More has been reported as expense for services than has been paid out in cash.	Add the amount to net income to show that cash-basis expenses are less than reported expenses.
Accounts payable and accrued liabilities	Increase	More has been reported as expense for goods and services than has been paid out in cash.	Add the amount to net income to show that cash-basis expenses for goods and services are less than reported expenses.
	Decrease	More cash has been paid out for goods and services than has been reported as expense.	Deduct the amount from net income to show that cash-basis expenses for goods and services are greater than reported expenses.
Deferred revenue	Increase	More cash has been received than has been reported as revenue	Add the amount to net income to show that cash-basis revenue is greater than reported revenue.
	Decrease	More has been reported as revenue than has been received in cash.	Deduct the amount from net income to show that cash-basis revenue is less than reported revenue.

the adjustments are needed. This exhibit should be studied with care, and the "Add" and "Deduct" signal in the last column should be traced back into Exhibit 18–2.

Changes in the Deferred Income Taxes Account

Deferred income taxes represent amounts deducted currently on the income statement as income tax expense but not remitted to the Internal Revenue Service until a later time (perhaps several years later). Such taxes are generally carried as a long-term liability on the balance sheet. In adjusting the net income figure to a cash basis, changes in the Deferred Income Taxes account follow the same rules as for current liabilities. An increase in the account means that more expense has been shown on the income statement for taxes than has been paid out in cash. Therefore, in accordance with the rules already discussed (in Exhibit 18–3), we must add the increase back to net income to show that cash-basis expenses are less than reported expenses. The opposite will be true for a decrease in the Deferred Income Taxes account—the decrease must be deducted from net income to show that the amount of cash paid out was greater than reported expenses.

AN EXAMPLE OF THE STATEMENT OF CASH FLOWS

To pull together the ideas developed in preceding sections, we turn now to the financial statements of Imperial Company presented in Exhibits 18–4, 18–5, and 18–6 and prepare a statement of cash flows. The numbers in these exhibits have been simplified for ease of computation and discussion.

Four Basic Steps to the Statement of Cash Flows

There are four basic steps to follow in preparing a statement of cash flows. These steps are:

1. Find the change that took place in the Cash account during the year.
2. Determine the *cash provided by operations* by analyzing the changes in the appropriate balance sheet accounts and by following the model given in Exhibit 18–2 (or by following the model given for the direct method later in the chapter).
3. Analyze each additional balance sheet account and determine whether the change in the account was the result of an investing activity or a financing activity.
4. Summarize the cash flows obtained in steps 2 and 3 into operating, investing, and financing activities. The net result of the cash flows for these three activities will equal the change in cash obtained in step 1.

For step 1, we can determine from Imperial Company's balance sheet in Exhibit 18–4 that the Cash account has decreased by $2,100 during 19x2. By following the remaining steps above, we can prepare a statement of cash flows and find the reasons for this decrease.

EXHIBIT 18–4

IMPERIAL COMPANY
Balance Sheets
December 31, 19x2, and 19x1

	19x2	19x1
Assets		
Current assets:		
Cash	$ 900	$ 3,000
Accounts receivable	7,000	5,500
Inventory	8,000	10,000
Prepaid expenses	600	500
Total current assets	16,500	19,000
Long-term investments	2,000	5,000
Plant and equipment	80,000	60,000
Less accumulated depreciation	8,000	4,000
Net plant and equipment	72,000	56,000
Total assets	$90,500	$80,000
Liabilities and Stockholders' Equity		
Current liabilities:		
Accounts payable	$ 5,000	$ 8,000
Accrued liabilities	1,000	—
Total current liabilities	6,000	8,000
Bonds payable	24,000	10,000
Stockholders' equity:		
Common stock	20,000	25,000
Retained earnings	40,500	37,000
Total stockholders' equity	60,500	62,000
Total liabilities and stockholders' equity	$90,500	$80,000

EXHIBIT 18–5

IMPERIAL COMPANY
Income Statement
For the Year Ended December 31, 19x2

Sales		$70,000
Less cost of goods sold		40,000
Gross margin		30,000
Less operating expenses:		
Selling expenses	$ 9,000	
Administrative expenses	10,500	
Depreciation expense	4,000	
Total operating expenses		23,500
Net income		$ 6,500

EXHIBIT 18–6

IMPERIAL COMPANY
Statement of Retained Earnings
For the Year Ended December 31, 19x2

Retained earnings, December 31, 19x1	$37,000
Add: Net income	6,500
	43,500
Deduct: Dividends paid	3,000
Retained earnings, December 31, 19x2	$40,500

Cash Provided by Operations

Imperial Company's income statement shows that net income was $6,500 for 19x2. Starting with this figure and using the model presented in Exhibit 18–2 as a guide, an analysis of the cash provided by operations for 19x2 is given below.

Operating activities

Net income	$ 6,500
Adjustments needed to convert net income to a cash basis:	
Depreciation expense for the year	4,000
Add (deduct) changes in current assets:	
Increase in accounts receivable	(1,500)
Decrease in inventory	2,000
Increase in prepaid expenses	(100)
Add (deduct) changes in current liabilities:	
Decrease in accounts payable	(3,000)
Increase in accrued liabilities	1,000
Cash provided by operations	$ 8,900

The $4,000 depreciation expense figure used above is taken from Imperial Company's income statement. Note that this amount also agrees with the change in the Accumulated Depreciation account on the company's balance sheet in Exhibit 18–4.

Looking further at the balance sheet, the company has three current asset accounts in addition to Cash—Accounts Receivable, Inventory, and Prepaid Expenses. Adjustments have been made above for changes in these accounts (and for changes in the current liabilities) according to the guidelines given in Exhibit 18–3. These adjustments are summarized as follows: Accounts Receivable has increased by $1,500; since an increase in Accounts Receivable represents sales for which no cash has been received, the $1,500 is deducted from net income above in determining the cash provided by operations. Inventory has decreased by $2,000; as discussed in Exhibit 18–3, this decrease means that items have been included in Cost of Goods Sold that were purchased in a prior year. Since no cash was disbursed this year for these items, the $2,000 is added back to net income. Finally, Prepaid Expenses have increased by $100; this $100 represents payments for services (such as rent) that are not included as expenses on the income statement. The $100 is therefore deducted from the net income figure above to show that cash-basis expenses are greater than reported expenses.

Imperial Company has two current liability accounts—Accounts Payable and Accrued Liabilities. Accounts Payable has decreased by $3,000; this decrease means that the company made payment for goods and services that were acquired in a preceding year. Since the cash payment was made this year, we must deduct the $3,000 from net income to show that cash-basis expenses for goods and services are greater than reported expenses. Finally, the Accrued Liabilities account has increased by $1,000; this $1,000 represents items such as salaries that have been recorded as an expense but for which no cash payment has been made. Therefore, the $1,000 is added back to net income to show that cash expenses are less than reported expenses.

Changes in Other Balance Sheet Accounts

Having analyzed the current asset and current liability accounts and determined the cash provided by operations, we must now analyze each remaining balance sheet account and determine whether the change in the account was caused by an investing activity or a financing activity. So far as the end result is concerned, it makes no difference which of the remaining accounts we analyze first, nor does it matter in which order we proceed. This is simply a matter of choice. Since the Retained Earnings account usually contains a number of significant changes, managers often start with it.

Retained earnings From the balance sheet in Exhibit 18–4, we can see that Retained Earnings has increased by $3,500 during 19x2. To determine the cause of this change, we need to look at another exhibit—Exhibit 18–6—that contains an analysis of the Retained Earnings account. We can see from this exhibit that the $3,500 increase in Retained Earnings is a net result of $6,500 in net income for the year and $3,000 in dividends paid during the year. The net income figure has already been used in our computation of the cash provided by operations; the $3,000 dividends paid would be classified as a financing activity, as discussed earlier in Exhibit 18–1.

Financing activities
Cash was provided by:

Cash was used to:
    Pay dividends to owners $3,000

Long-term investments Imperial Company's balance sheet in Exhibit 18–4 shows that long-term investments decreased by $3,000 during 19x2. Long-term investments generally consist of securities (stocks and bonds) of other companies that are being held for some reason. If the amount of these investments decreases during a period, the most likely conclusion is that they were sold. From the guidelines given in Exhibit 18–1, any transaction involving the disposition of a noncurrent asset would be an investing activity.

Investing activities

Cash was provided by:
    Sale of long-term investments $3,000

Cash was used to:

Plant and equipment The Plant and Equipment account has increased by $20,000 during 19x2, as shown by the balance sheet in Exhibit 18–4. Since there is nothing on Imperial Company's statements to indicate that there were any sales of plant and equipment during 19x2, we can assume that this $20,000 represents the company's gross purchases for the year. (Remember, we can't "net" sales and purchases of assets off against each other; all amounts must be shown "gross" on the statement of cash flows.) The guidelines in Exhibit 18–1 indicate that a purchase of plant and equipment would be an investing activity.

Investing activities

Cash was provided by:
    Sale of long-term investments . . . . $ 3,000

Cash was used to:
    Purchase plant and equipment . . .   20,000

Accumulated depreciation Imperial Company's Accumulated Depreciation account has increased by $4,000 during 19x2, as shown in Exhibit 18–4. This change was accounted for earlier in our computation of the cash provided by operations.

Bonds payable Moving down Imperial Company's balance sheet in Exhibit 18–4, we find that Bonds Payable increased $14,000 during 19x2. Since we see no evidence of any bonds having been retired during the year, we can assume that the $14,000 represents the gross amount of bonds issued. The guidelines in Exhibit 18–1 show that an issue of long-term debt is a financing activity.

Financing activities

Cash was provided by:
    Issue of bonds $14,000

Cash was used to:
    Pay dividends to owners   3,000

Common stock Imperial Company's Common Stock account decreased by $5,000 during 19x2. Since we see no evidence of any stock having been issued during the year, we can assume that the $5,000 represents the company's only stock transaction. The most likely explanation for a $5,000 decrease in the Common Stock account is a repurchase of stock from the owners. Such a repurchase would be a financing activity, as shown in Exhibit 18–1.

Financing activities

Cash was provided by:
    Issue of bonds $14,000

Cash was used to:
    Pay dividends to owners   3,000
    Repurchase common stock   5,000

EXHIBIT 18–7

IMPERIAL COMPANY
Statement of Cash Flows
For the Year Ended December 31, 19x2

Operating activities

Net income	$ 6,500
Adjustments needed to convert net income to a cash basis:	
Depreciation expense for the year	4,000
Add (deduct) changes in current assets:	
Increase in accounts receivable	(1,500)
Decrease in inventory	2,000
Increase in prepaid expenses	(100)
Add (deduct) changes in current liabilities:	
Decrease in accounts payable	(3,000)
Increase in accrued liabilities	1,000
Cash provided by operations	8,900

Investing activities

Cash was provided by:		
Sale of long-term investments	$ 3,000	
Cash was used to:		
Purchase plant and equipment	(20,000)	
Net cash used for investing activities		(17,000)

Financing activities

Cash was provided by:		
Issue of bonds	14,000	
Cash was used to:		
Pay dividends to owners	(3,000)	
Repurchase common stock	(5,000)	
Net cash provided by financing activities		6,000
Net decrease in cash		$(2,100)

The Completed Statement of Cash Flows

We can now organize the results of our analytical work into statement form. Using the data we have developed, a complete statement of cash flows for Imperial Company is presented in Exhibit 18–7.

We noted at the beginning of this example that Imperial Company's Cash account had decreased by $2,100 during the year. We have now isolated the reasons for this decrease, as shown in the company's statement of cash flows.

The Statement of Cash Flows as a Planning Tool

The statement of cash flows is highly regarded as a management planning tool. Although it deals with historical costs, any lack of forward planning, coordination, or balance in working toward long-run objectives becomes quickly evident in the story it has to tell. For example, a company may

EXHIBIT 18–8

UNIVERSAL COMPANY
Balance Sheets
December 31, 19x5, and 19x4

	19x5	19x4
Assets		
Current assets:		
Cash	$ 11,000	$ 3,000
Marketable securities	5,000	7,000
Accounts receivable	72,000	81,000
Inventory	103,000	93,000
Prepaid expenses	2,000	6,000
Total current assets	193,000	190,000
Investment in Company Y	77,000	85,000
Plant and equipment (note 1)	340,000	300,000
Less accumulated depreciation	110,000	180,000
Net plant and equipment	230,000	120,000
Total assets	$500,000	$395,000
Liabilities and Stockholders' Equity		
Current liabilities:		
Accounts payable	$105,000	$ 90,000
Accrued liabilities	4,000	6,000
Total current liabilities	109,000	96,000
Deferred income taxes	15,000	21,000
Long-term notes payable	78,000	28,000
Total liabilities	202,000	145,000
Stockholders' equity:		
Common stock	175,000	140,000
Retained earnings	123,000	110,000
Total stockholders' equity	298,000	250,000
Total liabilities and stockholders' equity	$500,000	$395,000

Note 1:   Equipment that had cost $160,000 new, and on which there was accumulated depreciation of $90,000, was sold during the year for its book value of $70,000.

have as its stated objective to double plant capacity in five years using only cash provided by operations. If the company at the same time is paying dividends equal to half of its earnings and is retiring large amounts of long-term debt, the discrepancy between long-run plans and current actions will be brought to light very quickly by the information contained in the statement of cash flows.

Some of the more significant ways in which managers use the statement for planning purposes include:

1.   To coordinate dividend policy with other actions of the company.
2.   To plan the financing of new product lines, additional plant and equipment, or acquisitions of other companies.
3.   To find ways of strengthening a weak cash position and thereby strengthening credit lines.

4. To check the feasibility and implementation of plans set by top management.

A WORKING PAPER APPROACH TO THE STATEMENT OF CASH FLOWS

The procedure relied on to this point of simply developing a statement of cash flows through logic has allowed us to concentrate our efforts on learning basic concepts, with a minimum of time expended on mechanics. For some companies, this simple logic procedure is completely adequate as a means of developing a statement of cash flows.

For other companies, however, the balance sheet is so complex that working papers are needed to help organize the changes in the various accounts into statement form. A number of working paper approaches to the statement of cash flows are available. The one we have chosen to illustrate relies on the use of T-accounts to assist in the analysis and organization of data. In order to illustrate the T-account approach to working paper preparation, we will use the financial statements of Universal Company found in Exhibits 18–8 and 18–9.

The T-Account Approach

Note from Universal Company's balance sheet (Exhibit 18–8) that cash and cash equivalents (marketable securities) have increased from $10,000 ($3,000 + $7,000) in 19x4 to $16,000 ($11,000 + $5,000) in 19x5—an increase of $6,000. To determine the reasons for this change we will again prepare a statement of cash flows. As before, our basic analytical approach

EXHIBIT 18–9

UNIVERSAL COMPANY
Income Statement and
Reconciliation of Retained Earnings
For the Year Ended December 31, 19x5

Sales		$450,000
Less cost of goods sold		280,000
Gross margin		170,000
Less operating expenses (note 2)		80,000
Income before taxes		90,000
Less income taxes (30%)		27,000
Net income		63,000
Retained earnings, January 1, 19x5		110,000
Total		173,000
Less dividends distributed:		
Cash dividends	$40,000	
Stock dividends, common	10,000	50,000
Retained earnings, December 31, 19x5		$123,000

Note 2: Operating expenses contain $20,000 of depreciation expense.

will be to analyze the changes in the various balance sheet accounts. The only function the T-accounts will serve will be to assist us in the mechanical process of organizing our information as it develops.

In Exhibit 18–10 on page 848, we have prepared T-accounts and entered into these T-accounts the beginning and ending balances for every account on Universal Company's balance sheet, except for Cash and Marketable Securities. The exhibit also contains a T-account titled "Cash," which we will use to accumulate the cash "Provided" and the cash "Used" as these amounts develop through our analysis of the other accounts.

The procedure is to make entries directly in the T-accounts to explain the actions that have caused the changes in the various account balances. To the extent that these changes have affected cash, appropriate entries are made in the T-account representing Cash.

Retained earnings   As we stated earlier in the chapter, the Retained Earnings account is generally the most useful starting point in developing a statement of cash flows. A detail of the change in Universal Company's Retained Earnings account is presented in Exhibit 18–9. We can note from the exhibit that net income of $63,000 was added to Retained Earnings during 19x5 and that dividends of $50,000 were charged against Retained Earnings. The dividends consisted of $40,000 in cash dividends and $10,000 in stock dividends.

Exhibit 18–11 on page 849 contains a second set of T-accounts for Universal Company in which entries have been made to show the effect of the year's activities on the company's Cash account. These entries for Retained Earnings are as follows: Entry (1) shows the increase in Retained Earnings that resulted from the net income reported for 19x5 and the corresponding increase that would have taken place in the Cash account:

(1)		
Cash—Provided	63,000	
Retained Earnings		63,000

Entry (2) records the payment of cash dividends on common stock and the corresponding drain on Cash:

(2)		
Retained Earnings	40,000	
Cash—Used		40,000

Entry (3) records the distribution of a stock dividend to common stockholders. A stock dividend has no effect on Cash. It simply capitalizes a portion of Retained Earnings and results in no outflow of assets:

```
                                        (3)
Retained Earnings . . . . . . . . . . . . . . . . . . . . .   10,000
        Common Stock  . . . . . . . . . . . . . . . . . . . .           10,000
```

The reader should trace all three of these entries into the T-accounts in Exhibit 18–11.

Observe from Exhibit 18–11 that these three entries fully explain the change that has taken place in the Retained Earnings account during 19x5. We can now proceed through the remainder of the accounts in the exhibit, analyzing the change between the beginning and ending balances in each account, and recording the appropriate entries in the T-accounts.

Current asset accounts   The use of T-accounts greatly simplifies the computation of cash provided by operations. This is because the T-accounts automatically show the correct adjustment to make for the changes in the current asset and current liability accounts in order to adjust the net income figure to a cash basis. To demonstrate, Universal Company's Accounts Receivable has decreased by $9,000; the entry to record this change would be:

```
                                        (4)
Cash—Provided . . . . . . . . . . . . . . . . . . . . . .   9,000
        Accounts Receivable  . . . . . . . . . . . . . . . .         9,000
```

The Inventory account has increased by $10,000; the entry to record this change would be:

```
                                        (5)
Inventory . . . . . . . . . . . . . . . . . . . . . . . . .   10,000
        Cash—Used . . . . . . . . . . . . . . . . . . . . .           10,000
```

Finally, the Prepaid Expenses account has decreased by $4,000; the entry to record this change would be:

```
                                        (6)
Cash—Provided . . . . . . . . . . . . . . . . . . . . . .   4,000
        Prepaid Expenses . . . . . . . . . . . . . . . . . .         4,000
```

As before, the reader should trace all three of these entries into the T-accounts in Exhibit 18–11. Note that by posting the change to the appropriate account (e.g., Accounts Receivable has been credited for $9,000 to

EXHIBIT 18–10
T-accounts showing changes in account balances—Universal Company

Cash

Provided	Used

Accounts Receivable

Bal. 81,000	
Bal. 72,000	

Inventory

Bal. 93,000	
Bal. 103,000	

Prepaid Expenses

Bal. 6,000	
Bal. 2,000	

Investment in Company Y

Bal. 85,000	
Bal. 77,000	

Plant and Equipment

Bal. 300,000	
Bal. 340,000	

Accumulated Depreciation

	Bal. 180,000
	Bal. 110,000

Accounts payable

	Bal. 90,000
	Bal. 105,000

Accrued Liabilities

	Bal. 6,000
	Bal. 4,000

Deferred Income Taxes

	Bal. 21,000
	Bal. 15,000

Long-Term Notes Payable

	Bal. 28,000
	Bal. 78,000

Common Stock

	Bal. 140,000
	Bal. 175,000

Retained Earnings

	Bal. 110,000
	Bal. 123,000

EXHIBIT 18–11
T-accounts after posting of account changes—Universal Company

Cash

	Provided		Used	
(1)	63,000 Net income	(5)	10,000 Increase in inventory	
(4)	9,000 Decrease in accounts receivable	(12)	2,000 Decrease in accrued liabilities	
(6)	4,000 Decrease in prepaid expenses	(13)	6,000 Decrease in deferred income taxes	
(10)	20,000 Depreciation expense			
(11)	15,000 Increase in accounts payable			
	93,000 Cash provided by operations			
(7)	8,000 Sale of Company Y investment	(2)	40,000 Payment of cash dividends	
(8)	70,000 Sale of equipment	(9)	200,000 Purchase of plant and equipment	
(14)	50,000 Issue of long-term notes			
(15)	25,000 Sale of common stock			

Accounts Receivable

Bal.	81,000	(4)	9,000
Bal.	72,000		

Inventory

Bal.	93,000		
(5)	10,000		
Bal.	103,000		

Prepaid Expenses

Bal.	6,000	(6)	4,000
Bal.	2,000		

Investment in Company Y

Bal.	85,000	(7)	8,000
Bal.	77,000		

Plant and Equipment

Bal.	300,000	(8)	160,000
(9)	200,000		
Bal.	340,000		

Accumulated Depreciation

(8)	90,000	Bal.	180,000
		(10)	20,000
		Bal.	110,000

Accounts payable

		Bal.	90,000
		(11)	15,000
		Bal.	105,000

Accrued Liabilities

(12)	2,000	Bal.	6,000
		Bal.	4,000

Deferred Income Taxes

(13)	6,000	Bal.	21,000
		Bal.	15,000

Long-Term Notes Payable

		Bal.	28,000
		(14)	50,000
		Bal.	78,000

Common Stock

		Bal.	140,000
		(3)	10,000
		(15)	25,000
		Bal.	175,000

Retained Earnings

(2)	40,000	Bal.	110,000
(3)	10,000	(1)	63,000
		Bal.	123,000

show the decrease in the account), we *automatically* show the correct adjustment to cash as an offsetting entry. *Thus, the model given in Exhibit 18–2 for computing the cash provided by operations is not needed when working papers are prepared, since the adjustments shown in the model are made within the working papers themselves.*

Observe that in arranging the data on the working papers we have placed all operating items near the top of the Cash T-account, clustered around the net income figure. Then we have placed all investing and financing items in the lower portion of the Cash T-account. This helps us to assemble our data in an orderly manner.

Investment in Company Y   The next account on Universal Company's balance sheet is its investment in Company Y. This investment has decreased by $8,000 during 19x5. Since we see no evidence to the contrary, we will assume that this decrease represents a sale of a portion of the investment. The entry to record the sale would be:

(7)		
Cash—Provided	8,000	
Investment in Company Y		8,000

Plant and equipment   The next account to be analyzed is Plant and Equipment. The T-accounts in Exhibit 18–11 show that this account has increased by $40,000 during 19x5. The increase could simply represent $40,000 in plant and equipment purchases. On the other hand, there may have been retirements or sales during the year that are concealed in this net change.

From the footnote to the balance sheet, we find that certain items of equipment were, indeed, sold during 19x5 at a sale price of $70,000. The entry to record this sale and its effect on Cash would be:

(8)		
Cash—Provided.	70,000	
Accumulated Depreciation	90,000	
Plant and Equipment.		160,000

How much did the company expend on plant and equipment purchases during the year? Overall, we know that the Plant and Equipment account increased by $40,000. Since this $40,000 increase is what remains *after* the $160,000 retirement of equipment recorded above, then purchases during the year must have amounted to $200,000 ($40,000 + $160,000 = $200,000). Entry (9) records these purchases in the T-accounts:

(9)

Plant and Equipment	200,000	
Cash—Used		200,000

Accumulated depreciation The note on Universal Company's income statement indicates that depreciation expense totaled $20,000 for the year. The entry to record this depreciation in the T-accounts would be:

(10)

Cash—Provided	20,000	
Accumulated Depreciation		20,000

This entry, along with entry (8) above, explains the change in the Accumulated Depreciation account for the year.

Current liabilities The T-accounts in Exhibit 18–11 show that Universal Company has two current liability accounts—Accounts Payable and Accrued Liabilities. Accounts Payable has increased by $15,000 during 19x5. The entry in the T-accounts to show this increase would be:

(11)

Cash—Provided	15,000	
Accounts Payable		15,000

The Accrued Liabilities account has decreased by $2,000; the entry to record this change would be:

(12)

Accrued Liabilities	2,000	
Cash—Used		2,000

Since both of these changes are used to adjust net income to a cash basis, their cash effect is included in the upper portion of the Cash T-account along with the other operating items.

Deferred income taxes Universal Company's Deferred Income Taxes account has decreased by $6,000 during 19x5, which means that the company has paid some taxes during the year that were reported as expense in a preceding year. The entry to record this transaction in the T-accounts would be:

```
                                    (13)
Deferred Income Taxes . . . . . . . . . . . . . . . . . . . . .  6,000
         Cash—Used . . . . . . . . . . . . . . . . . . . . . .          6,000
```

Since deferred taxes are a factor in the amount of tax expense reported for a period, the cash effect of the entry has been included with the other operating items in Exhibit 18–11.

Long-term notes payable Universal Company's financial statements give no indication of any long-term notes having been retired during the year. Therefore, we must assume that the $50,000 increase in the Long-Term Notes Payable account represents the gross amount of borrowing for the year. The entry to record this borrowing would be:

```
                                    (14)
Cash—Provided . . . . . . . . . . . . . . . . . . . . . . . .  50,000
         Long-Term Notes Payable . . . . . . . . . . . . . .           50,000
```

Common stock Universal's Common Stock account has increased by $35,000 during 19x5. We have already accounted for $10,000 of this increase in entry (3) above where we recorded a stock dividend paid in common stock. Since we have no information to the contrary, we must assume that the remaining $25,000 represents a sale of common stock to owners. The entry to record this sale would be:

```
                                    (15)
Cash—Provided . . . . . . . . . . . . . . . . . . . . . . . .  25,000
         Common Stock . . . . . . . . . . . . . . . . . . . .          25,000
```

With entry (15), our analysis of changes in Universal Company's balance sheet accounts is complete.

Preparing the Statement of Cash Flows from the Completed T-Accounts

The Cash T-account in Exhibit 18–11 now contains the entries for those transactions that have affected Universal Company's cash position during the year. Our only remaining task is to organize these data into a formal statement of cash flows. This statement is easy to prepare, since the data relating to operating activities are grouped in the upper portion of the Cash T-account and the data relating to investing and financing activities are grouped in the lower portion of the account. Following the guidelines given earlier (Exhibit 18–1), these data have been organized into a formal statement of cash flows in Exhibit 18–12. As an exercise, the reader should review

EXHIBIT 18–12

UNIVERSAL COMPANY
Statement of Cash Flows
For the Year Ended December 31, 19x5

Operating activities

Net income	$ 63,000
Adjustments needed to convert net income to a cash basis:	
Depreciation expense for the year	20,000
Add (deduct) changes in current assets:	
Decrease in accounts receivable.	9,000
Decrease in prepaid expenses.	4,000
Increase in inventory	(10,000)
Add (deduct) changes in current liabilities:	
Increase in accounts payable	15,000
Decrease in accrued liabilities	(2,000)
Deduct the decrease in deferred income taxes	(6,000)
Cash provided by operations	93,000

Investing activities

Cash was provided by:		
Sale of Company Y stock	$ 8,000	
Sale of equipment	70,000	
Cash was used to:		
Purchase plant and equipment.	(200,000)	
Net cash used for investing activities		(122,000)

Financing activities

Cash was provided by:		
Issue of long-term notes	50,000	
Sale of common stock	25,000	
Cash was used to:		
Pay dividends to owners	(40,000)	
Net cash provided by financing activities		35,000
Net increase in cash and cash equivalents		$ 6,000

the contents of this statement and explain in his or her own words why cash increased by $6,000 during 19x5.

THE DIRECT METHOD OF DETERMINING CASH PROVIDED BY OPERATIONS

As stated earlier in the chapter, to compute the cash provided by operations under the direct method we must reconstruct the income statement on a cash basis from top to bottom. A model is presented in Exhibit 18–13 that shows the adjustments that must be made to sales, expenses, and so forth to adjust each to a cash basis. To illustrate the computations involved, we have included in the exhibit the data just used for Universal Company.

Note that Universal Company's cash provided by operations figure ($93,000) agrees with the amount computed above by the indirect method. We would expect the two amounts to agree, since the direct and indirect

EXHIBIT 18–13

General model: Direct method of determining cash provided by operations

Revenue or expense item	Add (+) or deduct (−) to adjust to a cash basis	Illustration— Universal Company	
Sales revenue (as reported).		$450,000	
Adjustments to a cash basis:			
1. Increase in accounts receivable	−		
2. Decrease in accounts receivable	+	+9,000	
Sales revenue adjusted to a cash basis			$459,000
Cost of goods sold (as reported).		280,000	
Adjustments to a cash basis:			
3. Increase in inventory	+	+10,000	
4. Decrease in inventory	−		
5. Increase in accounts payable	−	−15,000	
6. Decrease in accounts payable	+		
Cost of goods sold adjusted to a cash basis.			275,000
Operating expenses (as reported)		80,000	
Adjustments to a cash basis:			
7. Increase in prepaid expenses.	+		
8. Decrease in prepaid expenses	−	−4,000	
9. Increase in accrued liabilities	−		
10. Decrease in accrued liabilities	+	+2,000	
11. Period's depreciation, depletion, and amortization	−	−20,000	
Operating expenses adjusted to a cash basis			58,000
Income tax expense (as reported)		27,000	
Adjustments to a cash basis:			
12. Increase in accrued taxes payable	−		
13. Decrease in accrued taxes payable	+		
14. Increase in deferred income taxes.	−		
15. Decrease in deferred income taxes	+	+6,000	
Income tax expense adjusted to a cash basis			33,000
Cash provided by operations			$ 93,000

methods are just different roads to the same destination. The "Operating activities" section of Universal Company's statement of cash flows—prepared under the direct method—is presented below. (The investing and financing sections of the statement will be the same as shown for the indirect method in Exhibit 18–12.)

Operating activities

Cash received from customers		$459,000
Less cash disbursements for:		
Cost of merchandise purchased	$275,000	
Operating expenses	58,000	
Income taxes	33,000	
Total cash disbursements		366,000
Cash provided by operations		$ 93,000

Similarities and Differences in the Handling of Data

Although we arrive at the same destination under either the direct or the indirect methods, not all data are handled in the same way in the adjustment process. Stop for a moment, flip back to the general model for the indirect method on page 836, and compare the adjustments made in that model to the adjustments made for the direct method in Exhibit 18–13. The adjustments for accounts that affect revenue are the same in the two models. In either case, we deduct increases in the accounts and we add decreases in the accounts, in order to adjust our figures to a cash basis. The adjustments for accounts that affect expenses, however, are handled in *opposite* ways in the two models. This is because under the indirect method we are making our adjustments to *net income,* whereas under the direct method we are making our adjustments to the *expense accounts* themselves.

To illustrate this difference, note the handling of prepaid expenses and depreciation in the two models. Under the indirect method (Exhibit 18–2), an increase in the Prepaid Expenses account is *deducted* from net income in computing the amount of cash provided by operations. Under the direct method (Exhibit 18–13), an increase in Prepaid Expenses is *added* to operating expenses. The reason for the difference can be explained as follows: An increase in Prepaid Expenses means that more cash has been paid out for items such as insurance than has been included as expense for the period. Therefore, to adjust net income to a cash basis we must either deduct this increase from net income (indirect method) or we must add this increase to operating expenses (direct method). Either way, we will end up with the same figure for cash provided by operations. In like manner, depreciation is added to net income under the indirect method to cancel out its effect (Exhibit 18–2), whereas it is deducted from operating expenses under the direct method to cancel out its effect (Exhibit 18–13). These same differences in the handling of data are true for all other expense items in the two models.

Comparison of the Direct and Indirect Methods

Historically, *when a choice between the direct and indirect methods has been available,* few companies have chosen the direct method. We can cite three reasons why. First, it is argued that the direct method is more difficult to use than the indirect method because it involves a complete restructuring of the income statement. Moreover, this restructuring can't be integrated readily into working papers. Second, since the direct method adjusts all figures on the income statement to a cash basis, there is concern it may imply that the cash basis of reporting is a better measure of performance than the accrual basis. Third, although the direct method shows the amount of cash provided by operations, it does not tell statement users *why* the cash provided differs from net income. Statement users are left on their own to reconcile the two figures (which may pose an almost impossible task for some users). The indirect method, by contrast, *starts* with the net income figure and shows why the cash provided by operations figure is different.

On the other hand, managers who argue in favor of the direct method state that by restructuring the income statement to a cash basis, statement users can see clearly how cash is generated by operations without having the picture blurred by irrelevant, noncash items such as depreciation. These managers argue that including depreciation on the statement of cash flows confuses and may even mislead statements users. This confusion is avoided under the direct method, it is argued, since the direct method deals only with actual cash receipts and cash payments.

SUMMARY

The statement of cash flows is one of the three major statements prepared by business firms. Its purpose is analytical in that it attempts to explain how cash has been provided and used during a period. As such, the statement of cash flows is highly regarded as a tool for assessing the well-being of a firm and for assessing how well its management is performing.

The statement of cash flows is organized in terms of operating, investing, and financing activities. Operating activities encompass those transactions involved in the determination of net income, investing activities encompass those transactions involved in the acquisition or disposition of noncurrent assets, and financing activities encompass those transactions involved with owners and involved with borrowing from creditors. As this list of transactions suggests, to determine the reason for any change in the Cash account, we must analyze changes in all other balance sheet accounts.

The net result of cash flows arising from operating activities is often referred to as the cash provided by operations. This figure can be computed by either the direct method or the indirect method. Under the direct method, the income statement is reconstructed on a cash basis. Under the indirect method, adjustments for sales, cost of goods sold, and other income statement items are made indirectly through the net income figure.

KEY TERMS FOR REVIEW

Cash equivalents Short-term, highly liquid investments such as treasury bills, commercial paper, and money market funds that are made solely for the purpose of generating a return on funds that are temporarily idle.

Cash provided by operations The net result of the cash inflows and outflows that arise from operating activities.

Direct exchange transactions Transactions involving only noncurrent accounts, such as the issue of capital stock in exchange for property or equipment, the conversion of long-term debt into common stock, and the acquisition of property under a long-term lease agreement.

Direct method A method of computing the cash provided by operations in which the income statement is reconstructed on a cash basis.

Financing activities A section on the statement of cash flows that includes all transactions (other than payment of interest) involving borrowing from creditors and all transactions (except stock dividends and stock splits) involving the owners of a company.

Indirect method A method of computing the cash provided by operations that starts with net income (as reported on the income statement) and adjusts the net income figure to a cash basis. It is also known as the *reconciliation method.*

Investing activities A section on the statement of cash flows that includes any transactions that are involved in the acquisition or disposition of noncurrent assets.

Operating activities A section on the statement of cash flows that includes any transactions that enter into the determination of income.

Reconciliation method See *Indirect method.*

Statement of cash flows A statement designed to highlight the major activities that have provided cash and that have used cash during a period, and that shows the resulting effect on the overall cash balance.

APPENDIX: STATEMENT OF WORKING CAPITAL

Another statement is often prepared for management's use that focuses on changes in working capital rather than on changes in cash. (As defined in the preceding chapter, working capital represents the excess of current assets over current liabilities.) This statement, called a **statement of working capital,** shows those transactions that have caused working capital to increase during a period, those transactions that have caused it to decrease, and the net change in the working capital position. The format of the statement is similar to the statement of cash flows in that it is organized around operating, investing, and financing activities. Its preparation differs from the statement of cash flows, however, in that to find the reasons for a change in working capital we analyze only the changes in *noncurrent* balance sheet accounts. This makes the preparation of a statement of working capital much simpler than the preparation of a statement of cash flows.

Changes in Working Capital

Increases and decreases in a company's working capital position occur as a result of operating, investing, and financing activities, the same as for cash. We can summarize the major ways in which working capital is affected by these activities as follows:

858   Part Four   Selected Topics for Further Study

Operating activities

Working capital is provided by:
  Profitable operations

Working capital is used by:
  Unprofitable operations

Investing activities

Working capital is provided by:
  Sale of property, plant, and equipment
  Sale of other noncurrent assets
  Collection of a loan made to another company

Working capital is used to:
  Purchase property, plant, and equipment
  Purchase other noncurrent assets
  Lend money to another company, such as to a subsidiary

Financing activities

Working capital is provided by:
  Sale of stock to owners
  Borrowing from long-term creditors

Working capital is used to:
  Repurchase stock from owners
  Retire borrowing from long-term creditors
  Declare cash dividends to owners

The transactions summarized above differ in only two ways from the transactions discussed earlier in connection with cash. Both of these differences relate to financing activities. First, note that only borrowing from *long-term* creditors provides working capital. This is because short-term borrowing increases current assets and current liabilities by the same amount, thus leaving working capital unchanged (see the following section, "No effect on working capital"). Second, note that working capital is used when dividends are *declared* rather than when they are paid. This is because the declaration of a dividend increases current liabilities and thus reduces working capital. The later payment of the dividend so declared will have no effect on the working capital balance, as explained in the following section.

In short, the transactions that have an effect on working capital (causing it to either increase or decrease) have a common identifying characteristic: *They involve a change in a noncurrent balance sheet account that also affects a current asset or a current liability in some way.* Refer again to the list of transactions above. Run your finger down the list and note that each transaction involves a change in a noncurrent balance sheet account (asset, liability, or equity) that has an offsetting effect on either a current asset or a current liability account.

No Effect on Working Capital

There are certain transactions that do not appear on the statement of working capital because they have no effect on the working capital balance. These are transactions affecting only current asset and current liability accounts. For example, the collection of an account receivable will have no effect on the total amount of working capital in an organization. This is because the amount involved is simply transferred from one current asset account (Accounts Receivable) into another current asset account (Cash), with total working capital left unchanged.

Likewise, the payment of a current liability (such as dividends payable) has no effect on working capital, since both current assets and current liabilities are reduced by an equal amount. In short, if a transaction affects *only* current asset or current liability accounts, it will not change the total amount of working capital available and therefore will not be a factor in determining why working capital has increased or decreased during a period.

Three Basic Steps to Preparing a Statement of Working Capital

Three basic steps are involved in the preparation of a statement of working capital. These steps are:

1. Find the change that has taken place in working capital during the year.
2. Analyze each *noncurrent* balance sheet account to determine whether the change in the account provided or used working capital.
3. Organize the data obtained in step 2 into operating, investing, and financing activities. The net difference between the activities that have provided working capital and the activities that have used working capital should equal the change in working capital obtained in step 1.

To illustrate the implementation of these steps, we will return to the financial statements of Universal Company in Exhibits 18–8 and 18–9 and prepare a statement of working capital for the year.

Schedule of Changes in Working Capital Accounts

As stated, the starting point in our statement is to find the change that has taken place in the working capital balance during the year. This change is determined by preparing a **schedule of changes in working capital accounts,** which shows the effect of increases and decreases in current asset and current liability accounts on working capital during a period. A schedule of this type for Universal Company is presented in Exhibit 18–14.

The data in the schedule show that working capital has decreased by $10,000 during the year. By analyzing the noncurrent balance sheet accounts, we will be able to determine the reasons for this decrease.

Working Papers for Changes in Noncurrent Balance Sheet Accounts

Working papers are presented in Exhibit 18–15 that show the effect on working capital of changes in Universal Company's noncurrent accounts for the year. In preparing these working papers, our basic procedure has been the same as for a statement of cash flows. We have entered the beginning

EXHIBIT 18–14

UNIVERSAL COMPANY
Schedule of Changes in Working Capital Accounts
For the Year Ended December 31, 19x5

	19x5	19x4	Working capital increase (decrease)
Current assets:			
Cash	$ 11,000	$ 3,000	$ 8,000
Marketable securities	5,000	7,000	(2,000)
Accounts receivable	72,000	81,000	(9,000)
Inventory	103,000	93,000	10,000
Prepaid expenses	2,000	6,000	(4,000)
Total current assets	193,000	190,000	3,000
Current liabilities:			
Accounts payable	105,000	90,000	(15,000)
Accrued liabilities	4,000	6,000	2,000
Total current liabilities	109,000	96,000	(13,000)
Working capital	$ 84,000	$ 94,000	$(10,000)

and ending balance in each account, and then we have posted entries to the accounts to show the reasons for any change that has taken place. As we have posted these entries to the T-accounts, we have shown the effect on working capital as an offsetting entry. For example, entry (1) in the Retained Earnings account shows the recording of the company's net income for the year as follows:

(1)
Working Capital—Provided 63,000
　　Retained Earnings 63,000

Entry (2) shows cash dividends declared and paid:

(2)
Retained Earnings 40,000
　　Working Capital—Used 40,000

Entry (3) shows the stock dividend that was declared and issued:

(3)
Retained Earnings 10,000
　　Common Stock 10,000

EXHIBIT 18–15

Working papers for a statement of working capital—Universal Company

	Working Capital		
	Provided	**Used**	
Net income	(1) 63,000		
Depreciation expense	(7) 20,000		
		(8) 6,000	Decrease in deferred income taxes
Working capital from operations	77,000		
Sale of Company Y investment	(4) 8,000	(2) 40,000	Payment of cash dividends
Sale of equipment	(5) 70,000	(6) 200,000	Purchase of plant and equipment
Issue of long-term notes	(9) 50,000		
Sale of common stock	(10) 25,000		

Investment in Company Y

Bal.	85,000	
		(4) 8,000
Bal.	77,000	

Plant and Equipment

Bal.	300,000	
(6)	200,000	(5) 160,000
Bal.	340,000	

Accumulated Depreciation

		Bal. 180,000
(5)	90,000	(7) 20,000
		Bal. 110,000

Deferred Income Taxes

		Bal. 21,000
(8)	6,000	
		Bal. 15,000

Long-Term Notes Payable

		Bal. 28,000
		(9) 50,000
		Bal. 78,000

Common Stock

		Bal. 140,000
		(3) 10,000
		(10) 25,000
		Bal. 175,000

Retained Earnings

		Bal. 110,000
(2)	40,000	(1) 63,000
(3)	10,000	
		Bal. 123,000

Explanation of entries:

(1) Net income for the year.
(2) Declaration and payment of a cash dividend.
(3) Declaration and issue of a stock dividend.
(4) Sale of a long-term investment.
(5) Sale of equipment.
(6) Purchase of plant and equipment.
(7) Recording depreciation expense for the year.
(8) Decrease in deferred income taxes.
(9) Issue of long-term notes payable.
(10) Sale of common stock.

The remainder of the entries in the working papers follow this same pattern. Note that we have fewer entries than with cash, since we analyze only the changes in the noncurrent balance sheet accounts when preparing a statement of working capital.

The Completed Statement of Working Capital

Utilizing the data from the working papers in Exhibit 18–15, a completed statement of working capital is presented in Exhibit 18–16. Note that the format of the statement is similar to that of the statement of cash flows. Typically, the schedule of changes in working capital accounts (prepared earlier in Exhibit 18–14) is provided along with the statement of working capital so that the manager can see what specific working capital items have increased and decreased during the year.

EXHIBIT 18–16

UNIVERSAL COMPANY
Statement of Working Capital
For the Year Ended December 31, 19x5

Operating activities

Net income		$ 63,000
Add (deduct) expenses not requiring the use of working capital:		
Depreciation expense for the year		20,000
Decrease in deferred income taxes*		(6,000)
Working capital provided by operations		77,000

Investing activities

Working capital was provided by:		
Sale of Company Y investment	$ 8,000	
Sale of equipment	70,000	
Working capital was used to:		
Purchase plant and equipment.	(200,000)	
Net working capital used for investing activities. . . .		(122,000)

Financing activities

Working capital was provided by:		
Issue of long-term notes	50,000	
Sale of common stock	25,000	
Working capital was used to:		
Declare and pay cash dividends to owners	(40,000)	
Net working capital provided by financing activities . .		35,000
Net decrease in working capital		$ (10,000)

* Typically, the balance in the Deferred Income Taxes account increases over time as a company expands its investment in plant and equipment. The year-to-year increases shown in the account are added to net income on the statement of working capital since (like depreciation) they represent expenses for which no immediate cash outlay is made. To be consistent in application, in years for which there is a net payment of deferred taxes (such as for Universal Company above), we treat the payment as a negative item in computing the working capital provided by operations.

Although no longer included in annual reports, the statement of working capital is still of considerable use to managers in the discharge of their planning and control responsibilities. For example, bondholders and other long-term creditors frequently require that working capital be kept at a certain minimum level as a means of protection to them. If working capital falls below the minimum level, the debt can be declared in default and the company can face major problems. Thus, the statement of working capital can be a vital tool to the manager in planning and maintaining an adequate working capital balance.

In short, both the statement of cash flows and the statement of working capital have their uses, and well trained managers must be acquainted with both in order to properly direct the affairs of an organization.

KEY TERMS FOR REVIEW (APPENDIX)

Schedule of changes in working capital accounts A schedule that shows the effect of increases and decreases in current asset and current liability accounts on working capital for a period.

Statement of working capital A statement showing transactions that have caused working capital to increase during a period, transactions that have caused it to decrease, and the net change in the working capital position.

QUESTIONS

18–1. What is the purpose of a statement of cash flows?

18–2. What are *cash equivalents,* and why are they included with cash on a statement of cash flows?

18–3. What are the three major sections on a statement of cash flows, and what are the general rules that determine the transactions that should be included in each section?

18–4. Why is interest paid on amounts borrowed from banks and other lenders considered to be an operating activity when the amounts borrowed are financing activities?

18–5. If a piece of equipment is sold at a gain, will the gain be classified among operating activities or among investing activities on the statement of cash flows? Why?

18–6. Why aren't transactions involving accounts payable considered to be financing activities?

18–7. Give an example of a direct exchange, and explain how such exchanges are handled when preparing a statement of cash flows.

18–8. Assume that a company repays a $300,000 loan from its bank and then later in the same year borrows $500,000. What amount(s) would appear on the statement of cash flows?

18–9. How do the direct and the indirect methods differ in their approach to computing the cash provided by operations figure?

18–10.   In determining the cash provided by operations figure under the indirect method, why is it necessary to add depreciation back to net income? What other income statement items are similar to depreciation and must be handled in the same way?

18–11.   A business executive once stated, "Depreciation is one of our biggest sources of cash." Do you agree that depreciation is a source of cash? Explain.

18–12.   If the balance in Accounts Receivable increases during a period, how will this increase be handled under the indirect method in computing the cash provided by operations?

18–13.   If the balance in Accounts Payable decreases during a period, how will this decrease be handled under the direct method in computing the cash provided by operations?

18–14.   During the current year, a company declared and paid a $60,000 cash dividend and a 10 percent stock dividend. How will these two items be treated on the current year's statement of cash flows?

18–15.   Would a sale of equipment for cash be considered a financing activity or an investing activity? Why?

18–16.   A merchandising company showed $250,000 in cost of goods sold on its income statement. The company's beginning inventory was $75,000, and its ending inventory was $60,000. Accounts payable for merchandise were $50,000 at the beginning of the year and $40,000 at the end of the year. Using the direct method, adjust the company's cost of goods sold to a cash basis.

18–17.   (Appendix)   Certain transactions have no effect on working capital and do not appear on a statement of working capital. Give an example of such a transaction.

18–18.   (Appendix)   Would the payment of a cash dividend that was declared in the preceding year increase, decrease, or have no effect on working capital? Explain.

EXERCISES

E18–1.   For the year ended December 31, 19x2, Hanna Company reported a net income of $35,000. Balances in the company's current asset and current liability accounts at the beginning and end of the year were:

	December 31	
	19x2	19x1
Current assets:		
Cash	$ 30,000	$ 40,000
Accounts receivable, net	125,000	106,000
Inventory.	213,000	180,000
Prepaid expenses	6,000	7,000
Current liabilities:		
Accounts payable	210,000	195,000
Accrued liabilities	4,000	6,000

The Deferred Income Taxes account on the balance sheet increased by $4,000 during the year, and $20,000 in depreciation expense was deducted on the income statement.

Required: By use of the indirect method, determine the cash provided by operations for the year.

E18–2. Refer to the data for Hanna Company in Exercise 18–1. Assume that the company's income statement for 19x2 was as follows:

Sales	$350,000
Less cost of goods sold	140,000
Gross margin	210,000
Less operating expenses	160,000
Income before taxes	50,000
Less income taxes (30%)	15,000
Net income	$ 35,000

Required: Using the direct method (and the data from Exercise 18–1), convert the company's income statement to a cash basis.

E18–3. Below are certain transactions that took place in Placid Company during the past year:

a. Equipment was purchased at a cost of $30,000.
b. An $8,000 cash dividend was declared and paid.
c. Sales for the year totaled $1,000,000.
d. Short-term investments were purchased at a cost of $10,000.
e. Equipment was sold during the year.
f. A gain was realized on the equipment sold in *(e).*
g. Preferred stock was sold to investors.
h. A $6,000 stock dividend was declared and issued.
i. Interest was paid to long-term creditors.
j. Salaries and wages were paid to employees.
k. Stock of another company was purchased.
l. Bonds were issued that will be due in 10 years.
m. Rent was received from subleasing of space.
n. Common stock was repurchased and retired.

Required: Prepare an answer sheet with the following headings:

	Activity			Not
Transaction	Operating	Investing	Financing	reported
a.				
b.				
Etc.				

Enter the transactions above on your answer sheet and indicate how the effects of each transaction would be reported on a statement of cash flows by placing an "X" in the appropriate column.

E18–4.   Comparative financial statement data for Cargill Company follow:

	December 31	
	19x7	**19x6**
Cash	$ 3	$ 6
Accounts receivable, net	22	24
Inventory	50	40
Plant and equipment	240	200
Accumulated depreciation	(65)	(50)
Total assets	$250	$220
Accounts payable	$ 40	$ 36
Common stock	150	145
Retained earnings	60	39
Total liabilities and stockholders' equity	$250	$220

For 19x7, the company reported net income as follows:

Sales	$275
Cost of goods sold	150
Gross margin	125
Operating expenses . . .	90
Net income	$ 35

Dividends of $14 were declared and paid during 19x7. Depreciation expense for the year was $15.

Required: By use of the indirect method, prepare a statement of cash flows for 19x7.

E18–5.   Refer to the data for Cargill Company in Exercise 18–4.

Required: By use of the direct method, convert the company's income statement to a cash basis.

E18–6.   Balances in various accounts of Argon Company at the beginning and end of the current year are given below:

	Account balance	
	Beginning	**End**
Accounts receivable	$210,000	$180,000
Accrued interest receivable . . .	9,000	13,000
Inventory	370,000	420,000
Prepaid expenses	8,000	5,000
Accounts payable	205,000	190,000
Accrued liabilities	30,000	40,000
Deferred income taxes	60,000	72,000

Required: For each account, state whether the change should be added to net income or deducted from net income under the indirect method in computing the cash provided by operations. Use the following column headings in preparing your answers:

Account	Change (dollar increase or decrease)	Add	Deduct

E18–7. The income statement for Wiley Company for the current year is given below:

WILEY COMPANY
Income Statement
For the Year Ended December 31, 19x5

Sales	$150,000
Cost of goods sold	90,000
Gross margin	60,000
Operating expenses	40,000*
Income before taxes	20,000
Income taxes	8,000
Net income	$ 12,000

* Includes $7,500 depreciation.

Amounts from selected balance sheet accounts follow:

	Beginning of year	End of year
Accounts receivable	$30,000	$40,000
Inventory	45,000	54,000
Prepaid expenses	6,000	8,000
Accounts payable	28,000	35,000
Accrued liabilities	8,000	5,000
Income taxes payable	2,500	2,000
Deferred income taxes	4,000	6,000

Required: Using the direct method, compute the cash provided by operations for the year by converting the company's income statement to a cash basis. Show all computations.

E18–8. (Appendix) Following are selected transactions that occurred in Erie Company during the past year:

x. Issued $30,000 in long-term debt.
a. Purchased $250,000 in inventory on account.
b. Reported net income of $90,000.
c. Purchased $20,000 in equipment for cash.
d. Collected $175,000 in accounts receivable from customers.
e. Sold 500 shares of $40 par value common stock for $85 per share.
f. Retired fully depreciated equipment that had an original cost of $65,000.
g. Purchased $35,000 in equipment on a 60-day, 15 percent note.
h. Declared a cash dividend, $12,000.
i. Deducted depreciation on the income statement, $25,000.
j. Paid the cash dividend in (h).
k. Declared and issued a 10 percent stock dividend in common on common.

l. Sold equipment for $15,000 that had an original cost of $40,000 and accumulated depreciation of $25,000.

m. $60,000 in long-term debt was retired during the year.

n. $100,000 in convertible bonds were converted into common stock.

The company is in the process of preparing a statement of working capital for the year.

Required: Prepare an answer sheet with column headings as shown below. Then show the proper classification of each of the transactions above by entering either the word "Provided" or the word "Used" in the appropriate column to show the effect on working capital. If a transaction would have no effect on working capital, enter an "X" in the "No effect" column. Item *(x)* has been completed as an example.

	Activity			
Transaction	Operating	Investing	Financing	No effect
x.			Provided	

E18–9.   (Appendix)   Comparative financial statement data for Eaton Company are presented below:

| | December 31 | |
	19x6	19x5
Current assets	$ 41	$ 39
Long-term investments	9	20
Plant and equipment	170	140
Accumulated depreciation.	(80)	(72)
Total assets	$140	$127
Current liabilities	$ 25	$ 20
Bonds payable	6	15
Common stock, no par	70	60
Retained earnings	39	32
Total liabilities and stockholders' equity . . .	$140	$127

Other data relating to 19x6 follow:

Net income for the year	$12
Cash dividends declared and paid . . .	5
Depreciation expense for the year . . .	8

Required: 1.   Prepare a schedule of changes in working capital accounts.
2.   Prepare a statement of working capital for 19x6.

PROBLEMS

P18–10.   **Indirect method; statement of cash flows without working papers.**   Comparative financial statements for Weaver Company follow:

WEAVER COMPANY
Balance Sheets
June 30, 19x4, and 19x3

	19x4	19x3
Assets		
Current assets:		
Cash	$ 6	$ 5
Accounts receivable	10	12
Inventory	18	15
Total current assets	34	32
Long-term investments	9	10
Plant and equipment	30	25
Less accumulated depreciation	13	11
Net plant and equipment	17	14
Total assets	$60	$56
Liabilities and Stockholders' Equity		
Current liabilities:		
Accounts payable	$16	$10
Accrued liabilities	4	5
Total current liabilities	20	15
Bonds payable	7	14
Stockholders' equity:		
Common stock	15	13
Retained earnings	18	14
Total stockholders' equity	33	27
Total liabilities and stockholders' equity	$60	$56

WEAVER COMPANY
Income Statements
For the Years Ended June 30, 19x4, and 19x3

	19x4	19x3
Sales	$132	$120
Cost of goods sold	102	93
Gross margin	30	27
Operating expenses*	22	21
Net income	$ 8	$ 6

* Includes $2 depreciation expense each year.

The company declared and paid $4 in dividends during 19x4.

Required: 1. By use of the indirect method, compute the cash provided by operations for 19x4.
2. Use the information obtained in (1), along with an analysis of the remaining balance sheet accounts, and prepare a statement of cash flows for 19x4.

P18–11. **Direct method; statement of cash flows without working papers.** Refer to the financial statement data for Weaver Company in Problem 18–10.

Required: 1. By use of the direct method, adjust the company's income statement for 19x4 to a cash basis.
   2. Use the information obtained in (1), along with an analysis of the remaining balance sheet accounts, and prepare a statement of cash flows for 19x4.

P18–12.   **Statement of working capital without working papers.**   (Appendix)   Refer to the financial statement data for Weaver Company in Problem 18–10.

Required: 1. Prepare a schedule of changes in working capital accounts for 19x4.
   2. Prepare a statement of working capital for 19x4, to explain the change in the working capital balance.

P18–13.   **Indirect method; statement of cash flows without working papers.**   Balance sheet accounts for Decision Data, Inc., contained the following amounts at the end of years 1 and 2:

	Year 2	Year 1
Debits		
Cash	$ 1,000	$ 7,000
Accounts receivable, net	20,500	14,000
Inventory	35,000	25,000
Prepaid expenses	2,500	4,000
Long-term investments	16,000	20,000
Plant and equipment	175,000	160,000
Total debits	$250,000	$230,000
Credits		
Accumulated depreciation	$ 36,000	$ 28,000
Accounts payable	25,000	21,500
Accrued liabilities	3,000	4,500
Bonds payable.	28,000	16,000
Common stock	100,000	110,000
Retained earnings	58,000	50,000
Total credits	$250,000	$230,000

The company's income statement for year 2 follows:

Sales	$120,000
Cost of goods sold	75,000
Gross margin.	45,000
Operating expenses	30,000
Net income	$ 15,000

There were no sales or retirements of equipment during year 2. Cash dividends totaling $7,000 were declared and paid during year 2, and depreciation expense totaled $8,000 for the year.

Required: 1. By use of the indirect method, compute the cash provided by operations for year 2.
   2. Prepare a statement of cash flows for year 2.
   3. Prepare a brief explanation as to why cash declined so sharply during the year.

P18–14.   **Direct method; statement of cash flows without working papers.**   Refer to the financial statement data for Decision Data, Inc., in Problem 18–13. Bill Fryer, president of the company, views the Cash account at the end of year 2 to be at a "crisis" level. Fryer can't understand why cash declined so sharply, particularly since net income was at a record high.

Required: 1. By use of the direct method, adjust the company's income statement to a cash basis for year 2.
2. Using the data from (1) and other data from the problem as needed, prepare a statement of cash flows for year 2.
3. Explain to Mr. Fryer why cash declined so sharply during the year.

P18–15.   Statement of working capital without working papers.   (Appendix)   Refer to the financial statements for Decision Data, Inc., in Problem 18–13. With the large decline in cash during year 2, Bill Fryer, the company's president, is certain that working capital must have declined during the year as well. This concerns Fryer, since the bonds just issued contain a covenant requiring that working capital be increased to $28,000 (an amount equal to the bonds outstanding) and maintained at that level until the bonds are retired.

Required: 1. Prepare a schedule of changes in working capital accounts for year 2.
2. Prepare a statement of working capital for year 2.

P18–16.   Classifying transactions on a statement of cash flows.   Below are a number of transactions that took place in Seneca Company during the past year.

   a.   Common stock was sold for cash.
   b.   Interest was paid on a note that will be due in two years.
   c.   Bonds were retired at a loss.
   d.   A long-term loan was made to a subsidiary.
   e.   Interest was received on the loan in *(d)*.
   f.   A 10 percent stock dividend was declared and issued on common stock.
   g.   A building was acquired by the issue of 30,000 shares of common stock.
   h.   Equipment was sold for cash.
   i.   A gain was realized on the sale of equipment in *(h)*.
   j.   Because of a need to pay obligations, short-term investments were sold.
   k.   Cash dividends were declared and paid.
   l.   Preferred stock was converted into common stock.
   m.   Deferred income taxes were paid; the taxes had been carried as a long-term liability.
   n.   Dividends were received on stock of another company held as an investment.
   o.   Equipment was purchased by giving a long-term note to the seller.

Required: Prepare an answer sheet with the following column headings:

		Activity			Reported in	Not on
Transaction	Cash provided, used, or neither	Operating	Investing	Financing	a separate schedule	the statement

Enter the letter of the transaction in the left column, and indicate whether the transaction would have provided cash, used cash, or neither. Then place an "X" in the appropriate column to show the proper classification of the transaction on the statement of cash flows, or to show if it would not appear on the statement at all.

P18–17.   **Indirect method; statement of cash flows without working papers.**   Mary Walker, president of Rusco Products, considers $14,000 to be the minimum cash balance for operating purposes. As can be seen from the statements below, only $8,000 in cash was available at the end of 19x5. Since the company reported a large net income for the year, and also issued both bonds and common stock, the sharp decline in cash is puzzling to Ms. Walker.

RUSCO PRODUCTS
Balance Sheets
July 31, 19x5, and 19x4

	19x5	19x4
Assets		
Current assets:		
Cash	$ 8,000	$ 21,000
Accounts receivable	39,000	24,000
Inventory	81,000	59,000
Prepaid expenses	2,000	6,000
Total current assets	130,000	110,000
Investments in subsidiaries	40,000	70,000
Plant and equipment	400,000	291,000
Less accumulated depreciation	70,000	50,000
Net plant and equipment	330,000	241,000
Total assets	$500,000	$421,000
Liabilities and Stockholders' Equity		
Current liabilities:		
Accounts payable	$ 42,000	$ 32,000
Accrued liabilities	8,000	17,000
Total current liabilities	50,000	49,000
Bonds payable	45,000	—
Deferred income taxes	20,000	14,000
Stockholders' equity:		
Preferred stock	80,000	96,000
Common stock	225,000	200,000
Retained earnings	80,000	62,000
Total stockholders' equity	385,000	358,000
Total liabilities and stockholders' equity	$500,000	$421,000

RUSCO PRODUCTS
Income Statement
For the Year Ended July 31, 19x5

Sales	$350,000
Less cost of goods sold	240,000
Gross margin	110,000
Less operating expenses	70,000
Net operating income	40,000
Less income taxes	10,000
Net income	$ 30,000

The following additional information is available for the year 19x5:

a. The company had no sales of property and equipment during the year.
b. Dividends totaling $12,000 were declared and paid.
c. The decrease in the Preferred Stock account is the result of a conversion of preferred stock into an equal dollar amount of common stock.

Required:
1. By use of the indirect method, compute the cash provided by operations for 19x5.
2. Using the data from (1) and other data from the problem as needed, prepare a statement of cash flows for 19x5.
3. Explain to the president the major reasons for the decline in the company's cash position.

P18–18. **Direct method; statement of cash flows without working papers.** Refer to the financial statements for Rusco Products in Problem 18–17. Since the Cash account decreased so dramatically during 19x5, the company's executive committee is anxious to see how the income statement would appear on a cash basis.

Required:
1. By use of the direct method, adjust the company's income statement for 19x5 to a cash basis.
2. Using the data obtained in (1) and other data from the problem as needed, prepare a statement of cash flows for 19x5.
3. Prepare a brief explanation for the executive committee, setting forth the major reasons for the sharp decline in cash during the year.

P18–19. **Statement of working capital without working papers.** (Appendix) Refer to the data for Rusco Products in Problem 18–17. During 19x5, the company sold bonds for the first time. The bond indenture specifies that the company must maintain working capital at least equal to the amount of bonds outstanding. Thus, management must now monitor its working capital position with care to avoid violating this agreement.

Required:
1. Prepare a schedule of changes in working capital accounts for 19x5.
2. Upon seeing the results of your analysis in (1), Mary Walker, president of Rusco Products, stated: "It seems strange that working capital would increase in a year that we had such a dramatic outflow of cash. Can you explain what happened to cause the increase?" Prepare a statement of working capital to show Ms. Walker the reasons for the increase in working capital for the year.

P18–20. **Indirect method; working papers; statement of cash flows.** In early 19x7, Roberto Martens was made president of Helio Sales Company. Mr. Martens is widely regarded as a hard-hitting sales executive, but he has little patience with financial matters.

After many years of no sales growth, sales rose 25 percent in 19x7 under Mr. Martens' leadership. One major change made by Mr. Martens was to increase the number of distribution warehouses in the company in order to more adequately service customer needs. He plans further expansion of the company's warehouse facilities in 19x8, providing adequate funding can be obtained from the company's bank or from other sources.

Comparative balance sheets for the last two years are presented below.

HELIO SALES COMPANY
Balance Sheets
May 31, 19x7, and 19x6

	19x7	19x6
Assets		
Current assets:		
Cash	$ (7,000)	$ 42,000
Accounts receivable	230,000	168,000
Inventory	490,000	380,000
Prepaid expenses	16,000	23,000
Total current assets	729,000	613,000
Plant and equipment	820,000	710,000
Less accumulated depreciation	(260,000)	(290,000)
Net plant and equipment	560,000	420,000
Goodwill	71,000	87,000
Total assets	$1,360,000	$1,120,000
Liabilities and Stockholders' Equity		
Current liabilities:		
Accounts payable	$ 290,000	$ 205,000
Accrued liabilities	80,000	93,000
Total current liabilities	370,000	298,000
Long-term debt	230,000	165,000
Deferred income taxes	47,000	39,000
Stockholders' equity:		
Common stock	410,000	400,000
Retained earnings	303,000	218,000
Total stockholders' equity	713,000	618,000
Total liabilities and stockholders' equity	$1,360,000	$1,120,000

The company's income statement for 19x7 follows:

HELIO SALES COMPANY
Income Statement
For the Year Ended May 31, 19x7

Sales	$1,000,000
Less cost of goods sold	530,000
Gross margin	470,000
Less operating expenses	280,000
Net operating income	190,000
Less income taxes	60,000
Net income	$ 130,000

The following additional information is available about operations for the year 19x7:

a. Equipment that had cost $130,000 and on which there was accumulated depreciation of $112,000 was sold for its book value of $18,000.

b. Early in the year, the company repurchased 2,000 shares of stock at $35 per

share from a dissident stockholder. The shares were resold near year-end at
$40 per share.

    c. The company's goodwill is being amortized against earnings.

    d. Cash dividends declared and paid during the year totaled $45,000.

    e. There was no retirement of long-term debt during the year.

Required: 1. Prepare T-account working papers for a statement of cash flows.

    2. Using the indirect method and the data from your working papers, prepare a statement of cash flows for 19x7.

    3. Write a brief memo to Mr. Martens explaining the reasons for the decrease in cash during the year.

P18–21.   **Direct method; adjusting the income statement to a cash basis.** Refer to the data for Helio Sales Company in Problem 18–20. The company's president, Roberto Martens, was shocked when he received the 19x7 balance sheet data showing that the company's Cash account was overdrawn. After mulling over the statements for awhile, he exclaimed: "These statements don't make any sense. We've had the most profitable year in our history, our assets have increased by nearly a quarter of a million dollars, and yet we don't have a dime in the bank. It looks like the more we make, the poorer we get."

As the company's chief financial officer, you recognize that Mr. Martens doesn't fully understand the concepts of accrual accounting. Therefore, you believe it would be helpful to him to see the company's income statement on a cash basis.

Required: By the use of the direct method, adjust the company's income statement to a cash basis.

P18–22   **Statement of working capital; working papers.** (Appendix) Refer to the data for Helio Sales Company in Problem 18–20. To support expected sales growth in future years, Robert Martens plans to acquire more distribution warehouses as soon as possible. Because of the company's precarious cash situation, further acquisitions at the moment are impossible.

To bolster the cash position and to provide funds for warehouse acquisition, a decision has been made to issue bonds. Mr. Martens has been informed by underwriters, however, that investors will look carefully at the company's working capital and require that a certain level be maintained. Accordingly, Mr. Martens wants a complete analysis of what has happened to the company's working capital over the past year.

Required: 1. Prepare a schedule of changes in working capital accounts for 19x7.

    2. Prepare T-account working papers for a statement of working capital.

    3. Using the data from your working papers, prepare a statement of working capital for the year.

P18–23.   **Indirect method; working papers: statement of cash flows.** "This doesn't seem possible," said Julie Poduska, president of Brinker Skate Company. "Last year we lost $40,500, we went on paying dividends anyway, and we doubled our investment in Streeter Company. But yet our cash position is stronger than it was at the start of the year. I think a mistake has been made somewhere. Let's do a complete analysis of cash so that we can find the mistake before our report goes out."

The company's balance sheet accounts at the beginning and end of the year follow:

	December 31	
	19x3	19x2
Debits		
Cash	$ 48,000	$ 33,000
Accounts receivable	162,000	174,000
Inventory	318,000	267,000
Prepaid expenses	12,000	6,000
Long-term investments	42,000	21,000
Plant and equipment	1,120,000	1,083,000
Goodwill	38,000	54,000
Total debits	$1,740,000	$1,638,000
Credits		
Accumulated depreciation	$ 240,000	$ 228,000
Accounts payable	270,000	180,000
Accrued liabilities	30,000	37,500
Bonds payable.	435,000	360,000
Common stock, no par	510,000	450,000
Retained earnings	255,000	382,500
Total credits	$1,740,000	$1,638,000

The income statement for 19x3 is presented below:

Sales	$1,300,000
Less cost of goods sold	810,500
Gross margin	489,500
Less operating expenses	530,000
Net operating income (loss) . . .	(40,500)
Less income taxes.	—
Net loss	$ (40,500)

The following additional information relating to 19x3 has been assembled by the company:

a.   Depreciation expense for the year totaled ____?____ .
b.   The goodwill is being amortized against earnings.
c.   In order to maintain an unbroken record of dividend payments, the company declared and paid $27,000 in cash dividends.
d.   Equipment costing $48,000, on which there was accumulated depreciation of $31,000, was sold for its book value.
e.   Equipment costing ____?____ was purchased during the year.
f.   The company declared and distributed a stock dividend during the year. It consisted of 3,000 shares of stock, declared when the market value was $20 per share.

Required: 1.   Prepare T-account working papers for a statement of cash flows.
2.   Using the indirect method, prepare a statement of cash flows for the year 19x3.
3.   Prepare a brief explanation for Ms. Poduska as to why cash increased during the year.

P18–24.   **Direct method; adjusting the income statement to a cash basis.**   Refer to the data for Brinker Skate Company in Problem 18–23. Upon receiving a copy of the company's 19x3 financial statements, a loan officer at the company's bank stated,

"There's something odd here. Brinker Skate Company lost $40,500 last year and paid out $27,000 in cash dividends. But yet the Cash account increased by $15,000. I want the company to adjust its income statement to a cash basis so that we can see what's really happening with operations."

Required: 1.   Using the direct method, adjust the company's income statement for 19x3 to a cash basis.

2.   Would it be of greater value to the bank to see the "Cash provided by operations" figure computed under the direct method or the indirect method? Explain your position.

P18–25.   **Statement of working capital; working papers.**   (Appendix)   Refer to the data for Brinker Skate Company in Problem 18–23. Steve Parks, the company's controller, has just computed the company's current ratio as follows:

	19x3	19x2
Current assets *(a)*	$540,000	$480,000
Current liabilities *(b)*	300,000	217,500
Current ratio, *(a)* ÷ *(b)*	1.8 to 1	2.2 to 1

"Our working capital situation is precarious," said Parks. "Just look at that current ratio! It's slipped to only 1.8 to 1; no wonder our creditors are starting to get uneasy. We need to make a thorough analysis of our working capital to see what happened last year."

Required: 1.   Prepare a schedule of changes in working capital accounts for 19x3.

2.   Prepare working papers for a statement of working capital.

3.   Using the data from your working papers, prepare a statement of working capital for the year.

4.   Assume that next year (19x4) the company just breaks even (no income or loss). If dividends remain unchanged, and if the company makes no further purchases of equipment or investments, would you expect working capital for the year to increase, decrease, or remain unchanged? Explain your answer.

P18–26.   **Missing data; indirect method; statement of cash flows.**   Below are listed the *changes* in Yoric Company's balance sheet accounts for the past year:

	Debits	Credits
Cash	$ 17,000	
Accounts receivable	110,000	
Inventory		$ 65,000
Prepaid expenses		8,000
Loans to subsidiaries		30,000
Long-term investments	80,000	
Plant and equipment	220,000	
Accumulated depreciation		5,000
Accounts payable		32,000
Accrued liabilities	9,000	
Bonds payable		400,000
Deferred income taxes		16,000
Common stock	170,000	
Retained earnings		50,000
	$606,000	$606,000

The following additional information is available about last year's activities:

a.   Net income for the year was $ ___?___ .
b.   The company sold equipment during the year for $15,000. The equipment had cost the company $50,000 and was sold for its book value.
c.   Cash dividends were declared and paid during the year, $20,000.
d.   Depreciation expense for the year was $ ___?___ .
e.   The opening and closing balances in the Plant and Equipment and Accumulated Depreciation accounts are given below:

	Opening	Closing
Plant and equipment	$1,580,000	$1,800,000
Accumulated depreciation . . .	675,000	680,000

f.   If data are not given explaining the change in an account, make the most logical asumption as to the cause of the change.

Required: Using the indirect method, prepare a statement of cash flows for the year.

P18–27.   **Comprehensive problem; indirect method; statement of cash flows.**   Balance sheet accounts for Lomax Industries at the beginning and end of last year are given below:

	19x8	
	December 31	January 1
Debits		
Cash	$ 43,000	$ 28,000
Marketable securities	2,000	9,000
Accounts receivable	267,000	372,000
Accrued interest receivable	11,000	8,000
Inventory	610,000	404,000
Prepaid expenses	9,000	17,000
Long-term investments	280,000	310,000
Loans to subsidiaries	170,000	160,000
Plant and equipment	1,265,000	832,000
	$2,657,000	$2,140,000
Credits		
Accumulated depreciation	$ 310,000	$ 306,000
Accounts payable	518,000	441,000
Accrued liabilities	5,000	9,000
Long-term notes	400,000	200,000
Deferred income taxes	90,000	78,000
Common stock	800,000	500,000
Retained earnings	534,000	606,000
	$2,657,000	$2,140,000

The following additional information is available about activities during the year 19x8.

a.   The company reported sales, expenses, and net income as follows:

Sales	$3,000,000
Less cost of goods sold	1,900,000
Gross margin	1,100,000
Less operating expenses	860,000
Net operating income	240,000
Less income taxes (30%)	72,000
Net income	$ 168,000

b. Equipment costing $100,000 was acquired by giving a note to the seller that will be due in two years.

c. A stock dividend totaling $160,000 was declared and issued to the common stockholders.

d. Cash dividends declared and paid to the common stockholders totaled $80,000.

e. The $200,000 in long-term notes outstanding on January 1 were repaid during the year.

f. Equipment was sold during the year for $44,000. The equipment had cost the company $130,000, and it was sold for its book value.

g. Interest totaling $35,000 was paid to the holders of the long-term notes during the year, and interest totaling $15,000 was received from subsidiaries on loans that had been made to them. The net amount of this interest ($20,000) is included among the operating expenses on the income statement.

Required:
1. Prepare T-account working papers for a statement of cash flows.
2. Using the indirect method, prepare a statement of cash flows for the year.

Index